THE OXFORD HANDBOOK OF

HISTORICAL POLITICAL ECONOMY

THE OXFORD HANDBOOK OF
HISTORICAL POLITICAL ECONOMY

Edited by
JEFFERY A. JENKINS
and
JARED RUBIN

OXFORD
UNIVERSITY PRESS

Oxford University Press is a department of the University of Oxford. It furthers
the University's objective of excellence in research, scholarship, and education
by publishing worldwide. Oxford is a registered trade mark of Oxford University
Press in the UK and certain other countries.

Published in the United States of America by Oxford University Press
198 Madison Avenue, New York, NY 10016, United States of America.

© Oxford University Press 2024

All rights reserved. No part of this publication may be reproduced, stored in
a retrieval system, or transmitted, in any form or by any means, without the
prior permission in writing of Oxford University Press, or as expressly permitted
by law, by license, or under terms agreed with the appropriate reproduction
rights organization. Inquiries concerning reproduction outside the scope of the
above should be sent to the Rights Department, Oxford University Press, at the
address above.

You must not circulate this work in any other form
and you must impose this same condition on any acquirer.

Library of Congress Cataloging-in-Publication Data
Names: Jenkins, Jeffery A., editor. | Rubin, Jared, editor.
Title: The Oxford handbook of historical political economy /
edited by Jeffery A. Jenkins and Jared Rubin.
Other titles: Handbook of historical political economy
Description: New York : Oxford University Press, [2024] |
Series: Oxford handbooks series | Includes index. |
Identifiers: LCCN 2023020447 (print) | LCCN 2023020448 (ebook) |
ISBN 9780197618608 (hardback) | ISBN 9780197618615 (epub) |
ISBN 9780197618639
Subjects: LCSH: Economics—Political aspects—History.
Classification: LCC HB74.P65 O94 2024 (print) | LCC HB74.P65 (ebook) |
DDC 338.9—dc23/eng/20230601
LC record available at https://lccn.loc.gov/2023020447
LC ebook record available at https://lccn.loc.gov/2023020448

DOI: 10.1093/oxfordhb/9780197618608.001.0001

Printed by Integrated Books International, United States of America

Contents

About the Editors   ix
List of Contributors   xi

PART I. HISTORICAL POLITICAL ECONOMY: AN OVERVIEW

1. Historical Political Economy: What Is It?   3
   JEFFERY A. JENKINS AND JARED RUBIN

2. Interdisciplinary Collaboration in Historical Political Economy   17
   TRACY DENNISON AND SCOTT GEHLBACH

3. Data in Historical Political Economy   31
   ALEXANDRA CIRONE

4. Causal Inference and Knowledge Accumulation in Historical Political Economy   55
   ANNA CALLIS, THAD DUNNING, AND GUADALUPE TUÑÓN

5. Networks in Historical Political Economy   75
   ADAM SLEZ

6. Formal Models in Historical Political Economy   95
   SEAN GAILMARD

7. Historical Persistence   117
   AVIDIT ACHARYA, MATTHEW BLACKWELL, AND MAYA SEN

PART II. HOW STATES ARE ORGANIZED

8. Democracy and Historical Political Economy   145
   DAVID STASAVAGE

9. Historical Political Economy of Autocracy   161
   ANNA GRZYMALA-BUSSE AND EUGENE FINKEL

10. Dynasties in Historical Political Economy — 185
BRENDA VAN COPPENOLLE AND DANIEL M. SMITH

11. State-Building in Historical Political Economy — 209
FRANCISCO GARFIAS AND EMILY A. SELLARS

12. The Size of Polities in Historical Political Economy — 237
CHIAKI MORIGUCHI AND TUAN-HWEE SNG

13. State Capacity in Historical Political Economy — 253
MARK DINCECCO AND YUHUA WANG

14. Legal Capacity in Historical Political Economy — 271
MARK KOYAMA

15. Political Legitimacy in Historical Political Economy — 293
AVNER GREIF AND JARED RUBIN

PART III. COMPONENTS OF THE STATE

16. Rules in Historical Political Economy — 313
JOHN JOSEPH WALLIS

17. Historical Political Economy of Legislative Power — 329
GARY W. COX

18. Courts: A Historical Political Economy Perspective — 353
TOM S. CLARK AND GEORG VANBERG

19. Bureaucracies in Historical Political Economy — 373
JAN P. VOGLER

20. The Historical Political Economy of Political Parties — 401
JEFFERY A. JENKINS AND CHRISTOPHER KAM

21. Electoral Systems in Historical Political Economy — 421
DANIELE CARAMANI

22. Property Rights in Historical Political Economy — 441
LEE J. ALSTON AND BERNARDO MUELLER

23. Suffrage in Historical Political Economy — 459
W. WALKER HANLON

24. Trade Policy in Historical Political Economy 477
    DOUGLAS A. IRWIN

25. Taxation: A Historical Political Economy Approach 493
    PABLO BERAMENDI

PART IV. LONG-RUN LEGACIES

26. Economic Development in Historical Political Economy 519
    JOSE MORALES-ARILLA, JOAN RICART-HUGUET, AND
    LEONARD WANTCHEKON

27. The Historical Political Economy of Nationalism 541
    CARLES BOIX

28. The Historical Political Economy of Colonialism 559
    JENNY GUARDADO

29. The Historical Political Economy of Globalization 581
    KEVIN HJORTSHØJ O'ROURKE

30. Civil and Ethnic Conflict in Historical Political Economy 597
    SAUMITRA JHA

31. The Historical Political Economy of Financial Crises 623
    MARC WEIDENMIER

32. The Corporation and the State in Historical Political Economy 639
    RON HARRIS

33. Electoral Malfeasance in Historical Political Economy 655
    ISABELA MARES

34. Assimilation in Historical Political Economy 669
    VASILIKI FOUKA

PART V. THE STATE AND SOCIETY

35. Race and Historical Political Economy 691
    DAVID BATEMAN, JACOB M. GRUMBACH, AND CHLOE THURSTON

36. In Search of Gender in Historical Political Economy 713
    DAWN L. TEELE AND PAULINE A. GROSJEAN

37. Identity in Historical Political Economy PAVITHRA SURYANARAYAN AND STEVEN WHITE	733
38. Historical Political Economy of Migration VOLHA CHARNYSH	747
39. The Urban-Rural Divide in Historical Political Economy JONATHAN A. RODDEN	769
40. Immigration in Historical Political Economy MARGARET E. PETERS	787
41. Market and Government Provision of Safety Nets and Social Welfare Spending in Historical Political Economy PRICE FISHBACK	807
42. The Historical Political Economy of Education AGUSTINA S. PAGLAYAN	837
43. Health in Historical Political Economy JAMES J. FEIGENBAUM	857
44. Culture in Historical Political Economy SARA LOWES	887
45. Church, State, and Historical Political Economy SASCHA O. BECKER AND STEVEN PFAFF	925
Index	945

About the Editors

Jeffery A. Jenkins is a professor of political scientist interested in American national institutions, with an emphasis on Congress and parties, and American political development. Two of his recent books include *Republican Party Politics and the American South, 1865–1968* (Cambridge University Press, 2020) with Boris Heersink—which won the 2021 V. O. Key Award (from the Southern Political Science Association) and the 2021 J. David Greenstone Prize (from the American Political Science Association)—and *Congress and the First Civil Rights Era, 1861–1918* (University of Chicago Press, 2021) with Justin Peck. He is also coauthor of *Fighting for the Speakership: The House and the Rise of Party Government* (Princeton University Press, 2013) with Charles Stewart III. He was editor in chief of the *Journal of Politics* for six years (2015–2020) and recently started two new journals: the *Journal of Political Institutions and Political Economy* (2020) and the *Journal of Historical Political Economy* (2021).

Jared Rubin is a professor of economics at Chapman University. His research focuses on historical relationships between political and religious institutions and their role in economic development. He is the author of two recent books: *How the World Became Rich: The Historical Origins of Economic Growth* (Polity Press, 2022; with Mark Koyama) and *Rulers, Religion, and Riches: Why the West Got Rich and the Middle East Did Not* (Cambridge University Press, 2017). Rubin is codirector of Chapman University's Institute for the Study of Religion, Economics and Society and president of the Association for the Study of Religion, Economics, and Culture.

Contributors

Avidit Acharya is a professor of political science at Stanford University. His research is in the fields of political economy and formal theory.

Lee J. Alston is professor of economics and affiliate professor of law at Indiana University and a research associate at the National Bureau of Economic Research (NBER). Alston is past-president of the Society for Institutional and Organizational Economics, and the Economic History Association. He is Fellow of the Cliometrics Society and the Economic History Association. Alston has received Fellowships from the University of Chicago; the Rockefeller Foundation in Bellagio, Italy; the Australian National University; and the Free Market Institute at Texas Tech. Alston is the author of eight books and over eighty scholarly articles. His areas of expertise include economic history, institutional analysis, political economy, and law and economics.

David Bateman is associate professor of government at Cornell University. His research focuses broadly on democratic institutions, including legislatures and political rights, as well as on ideas and ideologies of democracy, race, and racism. His coauthored book, *Southern Nation: Congress and White Supremacy after Reconstruction* (Princeton University Press, 2018), examines the role of southern members of Congress in shaping national policy from the end of Reconstruction until the New Deal. His second book, *Disenfranchising Democracy: Constructing the Electorate in the United States, the United Kingdom, and France* (Cambridge University Press, 2018), examines the concurrent expansion of political rights alongside mass disenfranchisement in these three countries.

Sascha O. Becker is the Xiaokai Yang Chair of Business and Economics at Monash University, Melbourne, and part-time professor at the University of Warwick, England. Becker is also affiliated with CAGE, CEH@ANU, CEPR, CESifo, CReAM, ifo, IZA, ROA, and SoDaLabs.

Pablo Beramendi is professor of political science (political economy) at Duke University. He is interested in the causes and consequences of economic inequality. His research focuses on three areas: economic geography and the politics of redistribution, the comparative study of fiscal capacity and progressivity, and the political economy of participation and representation.

Matthew Blackwell is an associate professor of government at Harvard University. His research is in political methodology, with a focus on dynamic causal inference, instrumental variables, experimental design, missing data, and panel data.

Carles Boix is the Robert Garrett Professor of Politics and Public Affairs in the Department of Politics and the School of Public and International Affairs at Princeton University. His research spans the areas of political economy, empirical democratic theory, and the emergence of institutions and identities. His most recent books are *Political Order and Inequality* (Cambridge University Press, 2015) and *Democratic Capitalism at the Crossroads* (Princeton University Press, 2019).

Anna Callis is a Postdoctoral Fellow at The Center for Inter-American Policy and Research (CIPR) at Tulane University, and a research associate at the Center on the Politics of Development. Her research focuses on comparative politics and historical political economy in Latin America.

Daniele Caramani is Ernst B. Haas Chair of European Governance and Politics at the European University Institute, Florence, currently on leave from the University of Zurich, where he holds the chair of comparative politics. He is the author of articles and books on the historical structuring of electorates and party systems, the evolution of socioeconomic cleavages since the nineteenth century, and the processes of state formation, nation-building, and democratization in Europe. He has contributed datasets and documentation on electoral systems, election results at the district level, and geographical units in Europe from 1832 to the present.

Volha Charnysh is the Ford Career Development Assistant Professor of Political Science at Massachusetts Institute of Technology.

Alexandra Cirone is an assistant professor and Himan Brown Faculty Fellow in the Department of Government at Cornell University. She holds a PhD from Columbia University in New York and an AB in political science from the University of Chicago. Her research interests center on historical political economy, democratization and party systems in new democracies, and multilevel governance in European politics. She combines quantitative methods, historical data, and natural and/or quasi-experimental research designs with extensive archival research. Her work has won multiple awards and has been published in the *American Political Science Review*, the *Journal of Politics*, *World Politics*, *Political Science Research and Methods*, the *Journal of Historical Political Economy*, and the *Annual Review of Political Science*. She is one of the editors of Broadstreet.blog, a blog on historical political economy; she is also on the editorial board of the *Journal of Historical Political Economy* and organizes the Historical Political Economy Working Group.

Tom S. Clark is the Charles Howard Candler Professor of Political Science at Emory University.

Gary W. Cox is the William Bennett Munro Professor of Political Science at Stanford University. In addition to numerous articles in the areas of legislative and electoral politics, Cox is author of *The Efficient Secret* (Cambridge University Press, 1987; winner of the 1983 Samuel H. Beer dissertation prize and the 2003 George H. Hallett Award), coauthor of *Legislative Leviathan* (Cambridge University Press, 1993; winner of the 1993

Richard F. Fenno Prize), author of *Making Votes Count* (Cambridge University Press, 1997; winner of the 1998 Woodrow Wilson Foundation Award, the 1998 Luebbert Prize, and the 2007 George H. Hallett Award), coauthor of *Setting the Agenda* (Cambridge University Press, 2005; winner of the 2006 Leon D. Epstein Book Award), and author of *Marketing Sovereign Promises* (Cambridge University Press, 2016; winner of the William Riker Prize, 2016). A former Guggenheim Fellow, Cox was elected to the American Academy of Arts and Sciences in 1996 and the National Academy of Sciences in 2005.

Tracy Dennison is professor of social science history in the Division of Humanities and Social Sciences at the California Institute of Technology. She is a historian who uses the conceptual tools of social science to study institutions and long-run development in Central and Eastern Europe. Dennison has written about serfdom, peasant communes, state capacity, and demographic behavior in premodern societies, and has collaborated with colleagues in history, economics, and political science on a variety of projects. Her current research is a comparative study of the political economy of serfdom in Prussia and Russia.

Mark Dincecco is associate professor of political science at the University of Michigan. His research analyzes the long-run historical determinants of the political and economic development patterns that we observe today, with a focus on Europe and Eurasia. He is the author of numerous peer-reviewed articles and three books, including *Political Transformations and Public Finances: Europe, 1650–1913* (Cambridge, 2011) and *State Capacity and Economic Development: Present and Past* (Cambridge, 2017). His most recent book is *From Warfare to Wealth: The Military Origins of Urban Prosperity in Europe* (Cambridge, 2017; with Massimiliano Onorato). This book won the 2018 William H. Riker Best Book Award.

Thad Dunning is Robson Professor of Political Science at the University of California, Berkeley. His research focuses on comparative politics, the political economy of development, and research methods.

James J. Feigenbaum is an assistant professor in the Department of Economics at Boston University and a Faculty Research Fellow in the Development of the American Economy program at the National Bureau of Economic Research.

Eugene Finkel is Kenneth H. Keller associate professor of international affairs at the School of Advanced International Studies (SAIS) at Johns Hopkins University.

Price Fishback is the APS Professor of Economics at the University of Arizona, a research associate at the National Bureau of Economic Research (NBER), and Honorary Professor at Stellenbosch University.

Vasiliki Fouka is an associate professor of political science at Stanford University, a Faculty Research Fellow at the National Bureau of Economic Research (NBER), and a research affiliate at the Center for Economic Policy Research (CEPR). Her research interests include political behavior, political economy, cultural economics, and economic history. She studies the conditions under which minority members identify with and are accepted by a majority, and the implications of that for the design of policies and institutions. Some applications of her research include immigrant assimilation, the determinants of prejudice against ethnic and racial minorities, and the long-run effects of history for intergroup relations. She has a PhD in economics from Pompeu Fabra University.

Sean Gailmard is a professor of political science at the University of California, Berkeley. His research analyzes the structure and operation of political institutions from a strategic perspective. It focuses particularly on problems of accountability and control in political organizations, especially bureaucracies and empires.

Francisco Garfias is an associate professor of political science at the University of California, San Diego's School of Global Policy and Strategy. He studies the political economy of development, with a focus on how states build capacity, establish institutions, and navigate civil conflict in developing countries, especially Latin America. His work is published in leading political science journals such as the *American Political Science Review*, the *American Journal of Political Science*, and the *Journal of Politics*. His research on state capacity has been recognized with, among others, the Michael Wallerstein Award for best published article in political economy from the American Political Science Association. He received his PhD in political science and MA in economics from Stanford University.

Scott Gehlbach is a professor in the Department of Political Science and the Harris School of Public Policy at the University of Chicago. A specialist in the politics of authoritarian regimes, among other topics, his research is substantially motivated by the contemporary and historical experience of Russia, Ukraine, and other postcommunist states. Gehlbach has worked with several economists and political scientists to examine reform and rebellion in late Imperial Russia. His research in this area recently culminated in the publication of a short book with Eugene Finkel, *Reform and Rebellion in Weak States* (Cambridge University Press, 2020). Gehlbach is the founder and co-organizer of the annual Summer Workshop in the Economic History and Historical Political Economy of Russia.

Avner Greif is professor of economics and Bowman Family Endowed Professor in Humanities and Sciences at Stanford (Emeritus). His research interests include European economic history: the historical development of economic institutions; their interrelations with political, social, and cultural factors; and their impact on economic growth. His publications include *Institutions and the Path to the Modern Economy: Lessons from Medieval Trade* (Cambridge University Press, 2006), "Impersonal Exchange without Impartial Law: The Community Responsibility System" (*Chicago Journal of International Law*, 2004), "How Do Self-enforcing Institutions Endogenously Change? Institutional Reinforcement and Quasi-parameters" (*American Political Science Review*, 2004; with David Laitin), and *Analytic Narratives* (Oxford University

Press, 1998). He received his PhD in economics from Northwestern University and his BA in economics and history from Tel Aviv University.

Pauline A. Grosjean is a professor in the School of Economics at the University of New South Wales.

Jacob M. Grumbach is an associate professor at the Goldman School of Public Policy at the University of California, Berkeley. He received his PhD from the Department of Political Science at the University of California, Berkeley in the spring of 2018 and was a postdoctoral fellow at the Center for the Study of Democratic Politics at Princeton. He was previously an associate professor in the Department of Political Science at the University of Washington. His book, *Laboratories against Democracy* (Princeton University Press, 2022), focuses on the nationalization of state politics and its consequences for US democracy.

Anna Grzymala-Busse is the Michelle and Kevin Douglas Professor of International Studies in the Department of Political Science and Senior Fellow at the Freeman Spogli Institute at Stanford University.

Jenny Guardado is an assistant professor at the Center of Latin American Studies, School of Foreign Service at Georgetown University. Prior to joining Georgetown, she received a PhD in politics at New York University and was a postdoctoral scholar at the Harris School of Public Policy (University of Chicago). Her research examines the political and economic mechanisms affecting armed conflict, corruption, and long-run economic development. Her work has been awarded the Pi Sigma Alpha Award for best paper presented at MPSA in 2013, the Oliver A. Williamson Prize for best paper at ISNIE in 2014, and has appeared or is forthcoming at the *American Political Science Review*, the *Journal of Politics, Journal of Development Economics, International Organization, World Development*, and *Electoral Studies*, among others.

W. Walker Hanlon is an associate professor in the Department of Economics at Northwestern University.

Ron Harris is the Kalman Lubowsky Professor of Law and History and past dean at the School of Law of Tel-Aviv University. His main research field is the history of the business corporation. He studies the business corporation in Britain and comparatively, and in the wider context of legal and economic history, the history of industrialization, capitalism, colonialism, and globalization. He has published articles on various aspects of its history in economic history, business history, general history, and legal history journals. He is the author of *Going the Distance: Eurasian Trade and the Rise of the Business Corporation, 1400–1700* (Princeton University Press, 2020), and *Industrializing English Law: Entrepreneurship and Business Organization, 1720–1844* (Cambridge University Press, 2000).

Douglas A. Irwin is the John French Professor of Economics at Dartmouth College. He is the author of *Clashing over Commerce: A History of U.S. Trade Policy* (University of Chicago Press, 2017) and many other books and articles on trade policy.

Saumitra Jha is an associate professor of political economy at the Stanford Graduate School of Business, a senior fellow at Stanford's Freeman Spogli Institute for International Affairs, and a faculty fellow at the Center for Advanced Study in the Behavioral Sciences. He convenes the Stanford Conflict and Polarization Lab.

Christopher Kam is a professor of political science at the University of British Columbia. His research examines the operation and evolution of parliamentary government, political parties, and accountability. His recent work has appeared in the *American Political Science Review* and *Comparative Political Studies*. He is the author of *Party Discipline and Parliamentary Politics* (Cambridge University Press, 2009) and *The Economic Origins of Political Parties* (Cambridge University Press, 2021; with Adlai Newson). He is a past coeditor of the *Legislative Studies Quarterly*.

Mark Koyama is an associate professor of economics at George Mason University and a Senior Scholar at the Mercatus Center.

Sara Lowes is an assistant professor of economics at the University of California, San Diego. She received her PhD from Harvard University in 2017. Her research takes place at the intersection of development economics, political economy, and economic history.

Isabela Mares is the Arnold Wolfers Professor of Political Science at Yale University. She is the author of *Protecting the Ballot: How First-Wave Democracies Ended Electoral Corruption* (Princeton University Press, 2022), *From Open Secrets to Secret Voting: Democratic Electoral Reforms and Voter Autonomy* (Cambridge University Press, 2015), and *Conditionality and Coercion: Electoral Clientelism in Eastern Europe* (Oxford University Press, 2018), coauthored with Lauren Young.

Jose Morales-Arilla is an assistant professor in the Bush School of Government and Public Service at Texas A&M University. He received his PhD in public policy (economics track) at Harvard University and was a postdoctoral research associate in the Department of Politics at Princeton Univesity and a Research Fellow at Harvard's Growth Lab. His work applies microeconomic models and quantitative empirical methods to understand the political economy of current development issues.

Chiaki Moriguchi is a professor at the Institute of Economic Research, Hitotsubashi University.

Bernardo Mueller is a lecturer in the Department of Economics at the University of Brasília, where he has been since 1995. He received his PhD at the University of Illinois at Urbana-Champaign in 1994. He was a visiting scholar at the Ostrom Workshop at Indiana University (2015–2016) and at the University of Colorado (2004–2005). He was an associate editor at *Environment and Development Economics* and the *Journal of Economic Behavior and Organization*. His research areas are political economy, economic development, institutional analysis, and complex adaptive systems. His major publications address the political economy of land reform in Brazil, property rights, political institutions in Brazil, executive-legislative relations, and the political economy of regulation.

Kevin Hjortshøj O'Rourke is professor of economics at New York University, Abu Dhabi. He was formerly the Chichele Professor of Economic History at the University of Oxford and a Fellow of All Souls College. He is a member of the Royal Irish Academy, a Fellow of the British Academy, and a former research director of CEPR. His books include the prize-winning *Globalization and History* (MIT Press, 2001; with Jeffrey Williamson), *Power and Plenty: Trade, War and the World Economy in the Second Millennium* (Princeton University Press, 2007; with Ronald Findlay), and *Une Histoire Brève du Brexit* (Odile Jacob, 2018), published in English as *A Short History of Brexit: From Brentry to Backstop* (Penguin, 2019).

Agustina S. Paglayan is an assistant professor of political science at the University of California, San Diego. She is the author of the award-winning articles "The Non-democratic Roots of Mass Education: Evidence from 200 Years," "Education or Indoctrination? The Violent Origins of Public School Systems in an Era of State-Building," and "Public-Sector Unions and the Size of Government." Dr. Paglayan studies why governments choose to expand or restrict access to education, what motivates governments to improve the quality of education, and the long-term repercussions of education policy choices.

Margaret E. Peters is a professor in the Department of Political Science and the chair of the global studies major at UCLA. Her research focuses broadly on the political economy of migration. Her award-winning book, *Trading Barriers: Immigration and the Remaking of Globalization* (Princeton University Press, 2017), argues that the increased ability of firms to produce anywhere in the world combined with growing international competition due to lowered trade barriers has led to greater limits on immigration, as businesses no longer see a need to support open immigration at home. She also works on how dictators control emigration and how refugees make their decisions of when, where, and if to move from their home countries.

Steven Pfaff is a professor in the Department of Sociology at the University of Washington.

Joan Ricart-Huguet received his PhD in politics from Princeton University. He was a postdoctoral associate and lecturer at the Program on Ethics, Politics, and Economics at Yale University and is currently an assistant professor at Loyola University Maryland. His research interests include political elites, education, colonial legacies, and culture.

Jonathan A. Rodden is a professor of political science at Stanford University and a Senior Fellow at the Hoover Institution and the Stanford Institute for Economic Policy Research. In 2021–2022 he was a John Simon Guggenheim Memorial Foundation

Fellow. His research focuses on political and economic geography, political institutions, and representation.

Emily A. Sellars is an assistant professor in political science at Yale University. Her research interests are at the intersection of comparative political economy, development economics, and economic history, with a particular focus on the historical political economy of Latin America. Her work has been published or is forthcoming in the *American Journal of Political Science*, the *Journal of Politics*, the *Journal of Development Economics*, and the *Journal of Urban Economics*, among other outlets. She also serves on the editorial board of the *Journal of Historical Political Economy* and is a coeditor of and regular contributor to Broadstreet.blog. Her work has received several honors and awards, including the APSA's Mancur Olson Award for the best dissertation in political economy defended in the previous two years. Sellars received her PhD jointly in political science and agricultural and applied economics from the University of Wisconsin–Madison.

Maya Sen is a professor of public policy at Harvard University. Her research is in the fields of law, political economy, race and ethnic politics, and statistical methods.

Adam Slez graduated from the University of Wisconsin–Madison with a PhD in sociology in 2011. He is currently an associate professor in the Department of Sociology at the University of Virginia. His recent book, *The Making of the Populist Movement: State, Market, and Party on the Western Frontier* (Oxford University Press, 2020), combines traditional forms of historical inquiry with innovations in network analysis and spatial statistics to examine the origins of electoral populism in the United States during the late nineteenth century. His other work can be found in journals including the *American Journal of Sociology*, the *American Sociological Review*, and *Sociological Methods and Research*.

Daniel M. Smith is an assistant professor in the Department of Political Science at the University of Pennsylvania.

Tuan-Hwee Sng is an associate professor of economics at the National University of Singapore.

David Stasavage is the dean for the social sciences and the Julius Silver Professor of Politics at New York University. He has published several books, including most recently *The Decline and Rise of Democracy: A Global History from Antiquity to Today* (Princeton University Press, 2020).

Pavithra Suryanarayan is an assistant professor in the Government Department at the London School of Economics and Political Science. Her research focuses on historical political economy, ethnic politics, state capacity, and voting in India and the United States.

Dawn L. Teele is the SNF Agora Institute Associate Professor in the Department of Political Science at Johns Hopkins University.

Chloe Thurston is an associate professor of political science at Northwestern University. Her research is on American political development, political economy, and public policy, with a particular interest in how politics and public policy shape market inequalities along the lines of race and gender. She is the author of *At the Boundaries of Homeownership: Credit, Discrimination and the American State* (Cambridge University Press, 2018).

Guadalupe Tuñón is an assistant professor of politics and international affairs at Princeton University. She studies comparative politics and comparative political economy with a regional focus on Latin America.

Georg Vanberg is the Ernestine Friedl Professor of Political Science at Duke University.

Brenda Van Coppenolle is a Senior Research Fellow affiliated with the Centre for European Studies and Comparative Politics (CEE) at Science Po.

Jan P. Vogler is an assistant professor of quantitative social science in the Department of Politics and Public Administration at the University of Konstanz.

John Joseph Wallis is a professor of economics at the University of Maryland and a research associate at the National Bureau of Economic Research. He is an economic historian and institutional economist whose research focuses on the dynamic interaction of political and economic institutions over time. As an American economic historian, he has collected large datasets on government finances and on state constitutions, and studied how political and economic forces changed American institutions in the 1830s and 1930s. He has published *Violence and Social Orders: A Conceptual Framework for Interpreting Recorded Human History* (Cambridge University Press, 2009; with Douglass North and Barry Weingast) and *In the Shadow of Violence: Politics, Economics, and the Problem of Development* (Cambridge University Press, 2013; edited with Douglass North, Steven Webb, and Barry Weingast). He edited *Organizations, Civil Society, and the Roots of Development* (NBER/University of Chicago Press, 2017; with Naomi Lamoreaux). He is currently working on a new book examining the emergence of impersonal rules: *Leviathan Denied: Rules, Organizations, and Governments*.

Yuhua Wang is Professor of Government at Harvard University. His research focuses on two aspects of the politics of state-building: what contributes to the emergence of effective and durable statehood, and after an effective state emerges, how can it be constrained? His first book, *Tying the Autocrat's Hands: The Rise of the Rule of Law in China* (Cambridge University Press, 2015), evaluates how an authoritarian state can be constrained. His second book, *The Rise and Fall of Imperial China: The Social Origins of State Development* (Princeton University Press, 2022), examines how effective statehood emerges and endures.

Leonard Wantchekon is a professor of politics and international affairs at Princeton University, as well as associated faculty in economics. He has made substantive and methodological contributions to the fields of political economy, economic history, and development economics, and has also contributed significantly to the literature on clientelism and state capture, resource curse, and democratization.

Marc Weidenmier is the Stone Professor of Economics and Finance at Chapman University. He graduated Phi Beta Kappa from the College of William and Mary and earned a PhD in economics from the University of Illinois at Urbana-Champaign. His research interests lie at the intersection of monetary and financial economics. He has published in top economics and finance journals, including the *American Economic Review, Quarterly Journal of Economics, Journal of Political Economy, Journal of Financial Economics,* and *Review of Financial Studies.* Professor Weidenmier has also served on the editorial board of the *Journal of Economic History* and *Explorations in Economic History.*

Steven White is an assistant professor of political science at Syracuse University. His research focuses on race and American political development.

PART I

HISTORICAL POLITICAL ECONOMY

An Overview

PART I

HISTORICAL POLITICAL ECONOMY

An Overview

CHAPTER 1

HISTORICAL POLITICAL ECONOMY

What Is It?

JEFFERY A. JENKINS AND JARED RUBIN

What Is Historical Political Economy? What Is It Not?

WHAT is historical political economy (HPE)? At its core, HPE is an interdisciplinary endeavor. It combines insights from history, economics, political science, and occasionally other social sciences, such as sociology and anthropology. In short, HPE is the study of how political and economic actors and institutions have interacted in the past or over time. It differs from much of economic history in that it focuses on the causes and consequences of politics. It departs from much of conventional political economy in that its context is strictly historical, even when it has implications for contemporary political economy. It also departs from much of history in its use of social scientific theory and methods. Thus, while HPE involves elements of the traditional fields of economics, political economy, and history, it is separate from—and integrative of—them.

We believe a work must satisfy three distinct criteria to qualify as HPE. First, all works of HPE must attempt to establish a falsifiable argument, that is, one that can be tested and proven false (or logically contradicted). There are multiple methodologies that can be employed to establish a falsifiable argument. Good works in HPE may be qualitative or quantitative, theoretical or empirical, experimental or observational. As long as the work attempts to establish some form of falsifiable argument—implicitly or explicitly—it satisfies this criterion. This includes most theoretic work, which typically aims to provide propositions that are, in theory at least, falsifiable with the right historical data or narrative.[1] This may seem natural to social scientists, whose training leads them to either theorize or empirically test falsifiable, causal arguments. But this is not always the case, especially for those in the humanities, where descriptive studies are more common. Under this criterion, works that are merely descriptive do not qualify. Historical description can be incredibly valuable, and HPE scholars often draw on descriptive works of historians. For instance, Mary Beard's histories of Rome or Albert Hourani's histories of Islam and the Middle East contain both political and economic insights and beautifully dive into the histories of the polities under study. But neither attempts to formulate testable hypotheses. Although works of this type are often invaluable to HPE scholars, the works themselves are not HPE.

Second, all works of HPE must have some interest in understanding and explaining historical context. While all works by historians satisfy this criterion, a large fraction of the work of economists and political scientists does not. In some cases, it is obvious what is historical: works on classical Greece, Song China, or the Ottoman Empire clearly qualify. But in other cases, it is less obvious. Here we stress two points. First, while there is no cutoff date for what makes something historical, the subject of the work cannot be primarily contemporary. We are writing this chapter in the early 2020s; works focusing on the 1980s or 1990s may be historical, depending on whether they are primarily trying to explain some social scientific phenomena from those decades.

More important than some arbitrary cutoff date, a work of HPE must help understand some historical context. For instance, macroeconomic studies that use time series data are not HPE—even if those data go back centuries—if the purpose of the data is merely to test some theory in which the historical context does not matter. Those kinds of studies are essentially ahistorical. Note that this criterion does not preclude works on "historical persistence"—studies seeking the historical roots of contemporary phenomena—as being classified as HPE (see ch. 7, by Acharya, Blackwell, and Sen, as well as Cirone and Pepinsky [2022]). Yet for such studies there must be some interest in understanding the historical context of the "cause" that established the persistence in question. On this point, we agree with Dennison (2021, 105), who argued that "those who employ historical arguments, especially about the role of institutions and their long-term effects, must engage more actively with the findings of historians. Failing to incorporate historical research leads to models that mischaracterize the constraint structure faced by individuals and groups in the societies they seek to explain."

Third, there must be some *political economy* element of a work for it to qualify as HPE. By political economy, we mean it in the way Weingast and Wittman (2006, 3–4) defined it in their introductory chapter to *The Oxford Handbook of Political Economy*: "political economy is the methodology of economics applied to the analysis of political behavior and institutions. As such, it is not a single, unified approach, but a family of approaches. ... This is tied together by a set of methodologies, typically associated with economics, but now part and parcel of political science itself." The same is true of HPE, albeit with the stipulation that the work also be historical in nature. Works of economic history concerned with wages, prices, capital, and so on are not necessarily HPE, unless they are concerned with the political processes driving these phenomena. Works of political history concerned with the fundamentals of legislative decision making, the origins and development of political parties, or the evolution of representative government are not necessarily HPE unless they consider the political economy of these processes. That is, works of HPE not only dive into the history of the phenomenon in question, but also consider the preferences, goals, and incentives of the political actors at the heart of the processes or institutions under study.

These three criteria dovetail nicely with the criteria proposed by Pablo Beramendi in a March 31, 2021, post on Broadstreet, a blog dedicated to HPE. His definition is worth quoting in full:

> What I think identifies historical political economy (*HPE*) as an approach relative to prior efforts is a three-fold commitment. The first one is theoretical: an explicit effort not to let the description of a process substitute for an argument (often in the form of an endless forest of arrows quickly progressing towards negative degrees of freedom) and, more constructively, to develop an abstract logic about the causal relationships of interest that, subsequently, guides empirical efforts. The second one is methodological: a pledge to both dig deep into historical sources to improve measurement as a theoretically driven exercise and pursue, as far as possible given the data context, compelling research designs. Finally, the third one is a commitment to transgression, transgression of artificial disciplinary boundaries and scholarly prejudices to embrace the diffusion of tools, approaches, models and techniques to maximize access to new data (often in vast amounts) and, critically, to analyze it rigorously.

In short, we can imagine a Venn diagram between the disciplines of history, economics, and political science (see Figure 1.1). At the intersection of the three disciplines is HPE. The chapters in this handbook cover and analyze hundreds (if not thousands) of works at this intersection. While for the purposes of this volume we are concerned with the intersection, the best works of HPE draw extensively from other parts of the Venn diagram—from economic history, political history, political economy, economics, political science, and history. Each has its own methodologies, asks its own questions, and has its own context. This is also true of HPE—which is why it is a field in need of a handbook synthesizing its recent advancements.

In some respects, HPE is among the oldest of the social sciences. Certainly, the works of Alexis de Tocqueville and Karl Marx qualify as HPE by the criteria we've laid out, albeit with a nineteenth-century twist. In the early twentieth century, giants like Max Weber, Werner Sombart, and R. H. Tawney produced several important works of HPE. All these scholars engaged with history and attempted causal explanations centered on political economy. Such works of "classic HPE" differ from modern HPE in a few ways. First, the types of data used and analyzed are different. While both classic HPE and contemporary HPE have employed archival data, larger data sets with multiple variables were typically beyond the reach of earlier scholars. This is of course no fault of their own; it is mostly due to advances in computing and digitization technologies. Second, and related, the approach to causality has changed. Advances in econometrics and computational power now permit causal inference to be achieved in a manner that was unavailable even a decade ago, let alone a century. Third, the integration of formal theory into contemporary HPE has contributed a level of mathematization that was not

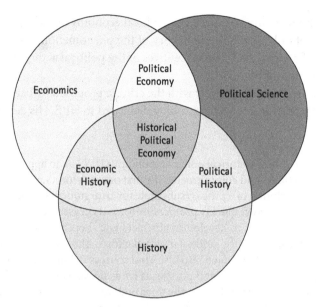

FIGURE 1.1. Venn diagram of historical political economy

present in classic HPE studies. Yet the best works of classic HPE used methods still employed by many current HPE scholars, particularly in books: they formulate (in words) some causal, falsifiable theory and substantiate it with considerable historical evidence (though not necessarily statistical evidence).

Even though classic HPE scholars have asked questions of importance for over a century, HPE is a relatively new field, at least in its current guise. Building on the work of scholars like Douglass North, William Riker, and many other economic and political historians, HPE of the twenty-first century has taken advantage of new empirical methodologies, digitized historical data, and (to a lesser extent) a deeper theoretical toolkit than what was available to their predecessors. The chapters in this handbook by and large overview this new HPE.

The very best HPE work is squarely in the mainstream of economics and political science (though not in history; for a discussion on how to bridge that gap, see chapter 2 by Dennison and Gehlbach). This can be seen from a simple scan of the references cited throughout the handbook; they regularly include the *American Economic Review*, *American Political Science Review*, *Quarterly Journal of Economics*, *American Journal of Political Science*, and most of the other top journals in the two disciplines. These include some of the most highly cited works in economics and political science of the twenty-first century. One need look no further than the works of Daron Acemoglu and James Robinson—whose joint work is clearly HPE—for evidence. Less frequently, HPE scholars publish in top history field journals within their discipline, such as the *Journal of Economic History*, *Explorations in Economic History*, and *Studies in American Political Development*.

But a field is not really a "field" without a journal of its own. Until 2021, HPE had no such journal, and thus scholars working on interdisciplinary projects did not have an obvious outlet for their work. This changed in 2021 with the introduction of the *Journal of Historical Political Economy* (*JHPE*), founded and edited by one of us (Jenkins). *JHPE* serves a latent but increasingly active and growing community in political science and economics. In recent years, more and more political scientists have been doing quantitative historical work that involves political economy. During that same time, economic historians—and applied economists more generally—have increasingly focused on political economy topics and taken seriously the "politics" in that research. Given the boundaries that typically exist across academic disciplines, these two groups of scholars rarely talk to one another or read (or cite) each other's work. *JHPE*'s goal—as well as the goal of this handbook—is to get these two groups in dialogue.

There are still hurdles the field must overcome to be viewed as established within economics and political science. First, there are no large annual conferences dedicated to HPE. This almost certainly dampens network formation—key to most academic disciplines—that often occurs at such events. This is even more the case because HPE is *interdisciplinary*, meaning that scholars working in different fields are unlikely to run into each other regularly. Second, and perhaps more important, is that academia has become increasingly siloed. Economists, political scientists, and historians are less likely to be rewarded (i.e., with tenure and promotion) by their departments for interdisciplinary work, especially when that work is not published in a known outlet within the discipline. The inherent interdisciplinarity of HPE also means that one must keep up with multiple literatures. This is time consuming, and is typically not rewarded by the profession. This of course is a bigger problem—not just for HPE—but it is one that fields like HPE can help solve. We hope that the synthesis of high-quality work provided in this handbook—and indeed, the very fact that there is an Oxford handbook on the topic—will be a step along this journey. We could think of no better outcome for the field than for this paragraph to be outdated in a decade.

Major Themes, Strengths, and Weaknesses of HPE

Several themes are central to much of the HPE literature. We have organized this handbook around what we view as five of the most general HPE themes. These themes are:

1) *Historical Political Economy: An Overview*. This set of chapters presents a broad theoretical and methodological overview of HPE as a field. Because HPE is such a new scholarly endeavor, and one that is interdisciplinary, the first section includes elements that one might find in a basic research design course.

2) *How States Are Organized*. Chapters in this section overview regime types, dynasties, and aspects of the states themselves.
3) *Components of the State*. These chapters are built around distinctly political components of the state, focusing on key political institutions, the nature of the political system itself, and functions of the state vis-à-vis its political institutions.
4) *Long-Run Legacies*. Chapters in this section focus on broad economic aspects and long-run political and economic legacies. These include macro-level phenomena as well as economic conditions or relationships in HPE that typically occur within states.
5) *The State and Society*. These chapters consider how particular aspects of a state's demography—or human population—and political economy have developed over time.

The handbook's coverage is extensive, but not in any way comprehensive. HPE is a widely encompassing field and spans important substantive areas in multiple disciplines. No single volume could ever fully capture the breadth of HPE. That said, the chapters in this volume provide a useful overview of many important subjects in HPE. They highlight the strengths of the field, while also laying out its weaknesses.

In our view, many of the best works in HPE are at the research frontier of economics and political science. The best studies contextualize history in new ways by using new tools available to social scientists, such as network theory (see Slez 2023). There are two types of studies for which HPE is at the forefront: those employing the latest techniques of causal inference, and those studying the persistence of cultural, institutional, or other societal features. The best empirical HPE studies are also able to take advantage of advances in digitization to access and analyze data in a manner that would have been impossible a mere decade ago.

In their chapter "Causal Inference and Knowledge Accumulation in Historical Political Economy," Callis, Dunning, and Tuñón (2023) argue that HPE has been greatly influenced by the so-called credibility revolution. This should not be surprising. There are many HPE questions for which rich data exist and long-run outcomes are available. Researchers can also leverage historical "natural experiments," discontinuities (e.g., political border changes), historical instruments to identify causal effects, and "shocks" or reforms that permit a difference-in-differences approach. With publication in economics and political science increasingly requiring rigorous identification, HPE seems like a natural setting to employ such techniques.

There are drawbacks, of course, to a narrow focus on causal identification. As Callis, Dunning, and Tuñón (2023) argue, external validity is not always apparent in HPE work, theory is often lacking, and the treatments that really matter for outcomes may be not random. In other words, in search of causal identification, researchers may miss out on the big picture. As Dippel and Leonard (2021, 1) recently noted, "After the credibility revolution, much of cliometrics shifted toward 'natural experiments,' especially in papers published in general-interest journals. . . . This shift comes with certain trade-offs between statistical and contextual evidence, and . . . the refereeing process currently makes these trade-offs steeper in historical settings than in other observational-data settings."

Yet Callis, Dunning, and Tuñón suggest that an emphasis on identification need not be detrimental to HPE. One reason is that while such studies themselves may lack external validity, they can also help generate cumulative learning. Certain types of historical processes build on each other. If we can gain insight into one of these steps in one study, it can help inform other studies that may seek to understand a different part of the story. Second, although mechanisms that connect a causal chain may be context specific, they help shape expectations about what one might find in a different context. This is a fundamental insight. As we argued earlier, one of the key features of HPE studies is that *historical context matters*. Indeed, we would refrain from considering a work as HPE if it used historical phenomena solely to gain identification without any regard for the historical context. Yet that does not mean that historical context is the *only* thing that matters. As long as we recognize that when A causes B in context X, it will not necessarily do so in context Y, there is much to be learned from studies that carefully identify important historical connections.

A second, related set of works for which HPE is at the research frontier include those on historical persistence. Since the publication of Acemoglu, Johnson, and Robinson's (2001) "Colonial Origins" article, a large proportion of empirical HPE studies have had some "persistence" component to them. Acharya, Blackwell, and Sen (2023) note several reasons why historical phenomena may persist, including path dependence, critical junctures, and "reproduction mechanisms." These works typically employ causal inference techniques to link some historical phenomena to later events (often to the present day). The literature on historical persistence is too large to summarize here; the interested reader should consult Acharya, Blackwell, and Sen's chapter in this handbook or comprehensive review articles by Nunn (2014), Voth (2021), and Cirone and Pepinsky (2022).

There are certainly drawbacks to the historical persistence literature. In attempting to rigorously identify historical events with future outcomes, too many studies in this literature give short shrift to historical context or are blasé regarding mechanisms of persistence. This is a common complaint regarding the persistence literature—one that both authors of this chapter have heard many times in casual conversation and one with which we both agree. Abad and Mauer (2021) likewise argue that there may have been an "overcorrection" for past oversights on historical persistence. The pitfalls they cite include "the failure to recognize institutional change ('anti-persistence'), vague mechanisms, the insufficient use (or misuse) of historical sources and narratives, the compression of history, and a failure to account for the effects of geography" (31).

Yet Callis, Dunning, and Tuñón's insights regarding causal inference apply here as well. Taken as a whole, we know much more than we used to about when and why historical phenomena persist. This is evident in Acharya, Blackwell, and Sen's chapter. Taking a broad view of the literature, they are able to address such issues as "What persists?" "What explains persistence?" "When is persistence broken?" and "proximate versus distal effects." Importantly, their insights come from our *cumulative knowledge*, attained mostly in the twenty-first century, and not on just one or two studies. In short, the very best persistence studies have greatly enhanced our knowledge of what might persist, why, and under what conditions, while paying careful attention to historical context.

A third margin on which HPE is at the cutting edge is the creative use of gathering data. As Cirone (2023) documents, advances in digitization and investment in online repositories have opened up a new world to researchers. More data are available now than ever before, and we have every reason to believe that this will only become more the case over time. Cirone (p. 31) classifies HPE data into seven broad categories: "sociodemographic and population data, government or institutional records, geographic and spatial data, political data, economic data, ethnographic data, and civil society data." Newly acquired access to such data places HPE on the research frontier for two reasons. First, we are now able to gain insight into *historical contexts* that were unavailable just a decade or so ago. While historical context requires more than just what is available with quantitative data, such data help shape the context as we understand it and (sometimes) as those who lived through the period in question understood it. This type of context is not always possible with qualitative evidence or individual case studies. Second, new questions can now be answered that were unanswerable with any type of precision until recently. As Alexandra Cirone notes (in personal correspondence), HPE scholars are "better at systematically considering and addressing challenges that come with historical data, such as missing data, archival silences, and sample selection." As more data become available and accessible, questions that previous generations would not have considered tackling—indeed, may simply not have considered at all—are becoming common fodder for PhD dissertations.

Overall, the best works in HPE are much closer to the research frontier than ever. Yet there are still some aspects of the field that could use improvement in our opinion. An obvious one, discussed earlier, is that too many studies—including many of those published in top journals—eschew historical context in favor of focusing on causal identification. This is certainly not true of the best HPE work. And, as also discussed, this does not mean that such studies add nothing to our cumulative knowledge. Yet one of our goals in editing the present volume and the creation of the *Journal of Historical Political Economy* is to encourage scholars to take historical context as central to any HPE analysis, even if its primary purpose is to show "persistence."

Second, we agree with Gailmard (2023) that HPE is now undertheorized. To be clear, this is not just an issue with HPE; the pendulum has swung in large parts of economics and political science toward data-driven empirical analysis at the expense of theory. Of course, many of the best works do both, but this is no longer required for publication in top journals. As Gailmard (p. 95) eloquently notes, "Credibly identified treatment effects of some X on some Y do not explain why an effect occurs. They simply rule out all explanations in which X is unrelated to Y . . . or in which the relationship is driven by a confounder W. . . . We use models because we want to know more than this." Gailmard (2021) went further in a post on *Broadstreet*: "While credible identification has obvious and important benefits for empirical HPE, making it the centerpiece of any research program in HPE is going to distort the kinds of historical and theoretical understanding we create. In particular, centering the demands of causal identification will slant case selection without any corresponding benefits for generalized historical knowledge."[2]

This is an important point that may help square Callis, Dunning, and Tuñón's more optimistic take that *cumulatively* the field has learned much from individual studies, even if individually those studies do not speak to general mechanisms. The missing connection is theory. The question is whether the pendulum will swing back toward HPE being "appropriately" theorized. Fouka (2022, italics ours) provides a reason to be skeptical this will happen, at least in the short run:

> HPE researchers, in their majority empiricists, do not put enough effort in engaging with existing abstract theory in designing their studies and interpreting their findings. What currently tends to happen in a lot of HPE work is either total absence of theory or the proliferation of ad-hoc "theories" generated by researchers to explain the empirical findings in the context that they study. These theories are usually narrow hypotheses with little generalizability. Often, *disciplinary incentives in some fields in which HPE scholars operate push them to generate overarching "big" theories out of very context-dependent cases, because new theorizing is valued more than empirical testing of existing theories.*

The disciplinary incentives highlighted by Fouka are difficult, though not impossible, to overcome. Fortunately, several chapters in this volume suggest that some topics in HPE have received significant theoretical treatment. These include, among others, theories of authoritarianism (Grzymala-Busse and Finkel 2023), state-building (Garfias and Sellars 2023), political legitimacy (Greif and Rubin 2023), assimilation (Fouka 2023), and identity (Suryanarayan and White 2023). There has also been much theorizing of topics in HPE with respect to particular areas of the world, like theories of parties (Jenkins and Kam 2023) and legislatures (Cox 2023) in the United States and Western Europe, but less so outside of those areas. Some topics in HPE have received very little theoretical treatment, like bureaucracy, thus making Vogler's (2023) chapter of particular interest. As empirical methods become even more developed and data become even more widely available, we believe that the relative dearth of theory will become even more obvious in HPE (and, more generally, in economics and political science).

The Future of HPE

For all the reasons given so far—and for reasons repeated again and again throughout this volume—the future of HPE is extraordinarily bright. It is at the same time one of the oldest and one of the newest fields in the social sciences. Its best work is published in the best economics and political science journals. Its practitioners are relatively junior (as evidenced by the authors of the chapters in this handbook, who are among the best current scholars of HPE). These are all signs of a growing field whose influence will only expand over time.

But where is the future of HPE headed? What are the topics and parts of the world for which there is still low-hanging fruit for the HPE scholar to pick? First and foremost, the geographical coverage of HPE studies leaves much to be desired. The United States and Western Europe receive a lion's share of attention in the field, and for good reasons: these regions have the best data and, after all, they are where the modern economy and liberal governance first emerged. There is still much to learn about the HPE of the United States and Western Europe, and we fully expect some of the best work in the field to be on these regions for decades to come. Yet, given the paucity of research on regions outside the United States and Western Europe, there is much catching up to do regarding the HPE of other parts of the world that have unique historical and cultural contexts. Sub-Saharan Africa, the Middle East, Latin America, South Asia, and Southeast Asia have all received relatively little attention in the literature, despite their large populations and historical (and contemporary) importance. Even though HPE interest in China has grown in the last decade, it too is understudied. Given its relative importance in world history (and in the present), we expect to see much more work on the HPE of China in years to come.

The biggest stumbling block to unearthing the HPE of the "non-Western" world is data constraints. But on this margin, there is ample reason for hope. Heroic efforts to uncover, clean, and analyze new data are being taken for areas around the globe. Many of the authors of chapters in this handbook are contributing to this effort: in Africa (Leonard Wantchekon and Sara Lowes), Latin America (Emily Sellars, Francisco Garfias, Jenny Guardado, and Agustina Paglayan), Imperial Russia and the Soviet Union (Tracy Dennison, Evgeny Finkel, and Scott Gehlbach), South Asia (Saumitra Jha and Pavithra Suryanarayan), and East Asia (Yuhua Wang, Chiaki Moriguchi, and Tuan-Hwee Sng). Of course, there are also many more HPE scholars whose work does not appear in this handbook who are helping to lead the effort.

As we've noted, another margin on which we hope to see more HPE work in the near future is formal theory. The relative paucity of theory is a deeper issue in economics and political science, where the "credibility revolution" has pushed young scholars into more empirical work. Much good has come of this, and the best works using modern causal identification techniques have provided new insights into key HPE topics. But there is also the distinct possibility that these fields are now undertheorized. As Sean Gailmard's (2023) chapter in this handbook notes, theory helps us place reasonable constraints on what is possible and why it is possible. In our opinion, too many papers in HPE (and economics and political science more generally) rigorously establish causal connections without applying that same level of rigor to the *mechanisms* driving those connections. This is where we need formal theory the most: it is a complement, not a substitute, of rigorous causal analysis.

The future of HPE is very bright for many reasons. First and foremost, we have just begun to scratch the surface of the available HPE data. Thanks to the efforts of historians working in archives, new digitization techniques, optical character recognition, and geographic information systems (GIS), we are able to say more about the past than ever. The digital humanities are opening up new lines of research inquiry that were unthinkable as recently as two decades ago. Scholars can now use historical text and images as data themselves. Advances in GIS allow for insights into spatial components of HPE that were difficult, if not impossible, to address quantitatively in the past. There is every reason to believe that progress on this front will grow exponentially. Data that used to take a lifetime to uncover can now be downloaded in a matter of minutes, freeing up scholars to ask—and answer—new types of questions that would have been beyond the traditional purview of HPE.

But challenges also exist. The immediate one, as Cirone and Spirling (2021) note in their *JHPE* article on working with historical data, is establishing best research practices. In particular, they underscore the need to be "transparent about the selection of qualitative evidence, how the evidence is analyzed, and how the ultimate results are framed." Another challenge is to overcome language issues in the collection of country-specific historical data. More HPE scholars from different parts of the world who speak different languages will be necessary for archival work. Alternatively, HPE scholars may find it conducive to collaborate with foreign-language scholars in the future as a way to leverage different skill sets.

In the end, we believe the future of HPE is very bright. While it is still a young field, its presence has grown considerably in recent years. Indeed, the very fact that there is an Oxford Handbook for the field is prima facie evidence of its growing importance. In their recent survey of HPE in political science, Charnysh, Finkel, and Gelbach (2023) found that the proportion of HPE articles in the discipline's top journals more than doubled over the last decade. And while HPE's ascension has included some prominent senior scholars, the emergence of young scholars has fueled the tremendous growth in the field. These young scholars are very well trained in techniques of causal inference, but they also care deeply about history and getting the story right. They are also at the forefront of spreading the gospel by teaching HPE courses at their universities.

The hope is that these talented young scholars will mold the future of the field, train PhD students, teach HPE courses at the undergraduate and graduate levels, and increase HPE's prominence in top journals and academic presses. There are still hurdles to be overcome. The field could certainly use an annual conference, and it is important for the field that journals specializing in HPE, like the *Journal of Historical Political Economy*, continue to grow in visibility and citation counts. The field is well on its way to clearing these hurdles. In the end, we feel confident that HPE will continue its march toward even greater influence in political science, economics, and allied fields.

Acknowledgments

We thank Alexandra Cirone, Sean Gailmard, and Scott Gehlbach for thoughtful comments. All errors are our own.

Notes

1. Works that are purely theoretical with no possibility of falsification are unlikely to seriously engage with the historical context, which (as we describe later) is another criterion of HPE work.
2. Sellars (2021), in a discussion of political borders in HPE, endorses this idea: "Political and institutional boundaries are multifaceted, and it is not clear how any locally estimated causal effects will generalize across even similar cases."

References

Abad, Leticia Arroyo, and Noel Mauer. 2021. "History Never Really Says Goodbye: A Critical Review of Persistence Literature." *Journal of Historical Political Economy* 1, no. 1: 31–68.

Acemoglu, Daron, Simon Johnson, and James A. Robinson. 2001. "The Colonial Origins of Comparative Development: An Empirical Investigation." *American Economic Review* 91, no. 5: 1369–401.

Acharya, Avidit, Matthew Blackwell, and Maya Sen. 2023. "Historical Persistence." In *The Oxford Handbook of Historical Political Economy*, ed. J. Jenkins and J. Rubin, 117–141. Oxford: Oxford University Press.

Beramendi, Pablo. 2021. "On the Transmission of Influence." *Broadstreet Blog*, March 31, 2021. https://broadstreet.blog/2021/03/31/on-the-transmission-of-influence/.

Callis, Anna, Thad Dunning, and Guadalupe Tuñón. 2023. "Causal Inference and Knowledge Accumulation in Historical Political Economy." In *The Oxford Handbook of Historical Political Economy*, ed. J. Jenkins and J. Rubin, 55–74. Oxford: Oxford University Press.

Charnysh, Volha, Eugene Finkel, and Scott Gehlbach. 2023. "Historical Political Economy: Past, Present, and Future." *Annual Review of Political Science* 26, no. 1: 175–191.

Cirone, Alexandra. 2023. "Historical Data." In *The Oxford Handbook of Historical Political Economy*, ed. J. Jenkins and J. Rubin, 31–54. Oxford: Oxford University Press.

Cirone, Alexandra, and Thomas B. Pepinsky. 2022. "Historical Persistence." *Annual Review of Political Science* 25: 241–59.

Cirone, Alexandra, and Arthur Spirling. 2021. "Turning History into Data: Data Collection, Measurement, and Inference in HPE." *Journal of Historical Political Economy* 1, no. 1: 127–54.

Dennison, Tracy. 2021. "Context Is Everything: The Problem of History in Quantitative Social Science." *Journal of Historical Political Economy* 1, no. 1: 105–26.

Dennison, Tracy, and Scott Gehlbach. 2023. "Interdisciplinary Collaboration in Historical Political Economy." In *The Oxford Handbook of Historical Political Economy*, ed. J. Jenkins and J. Rubin, 17–30. Oxford: Oxford University Press.

Dippel, Christian, and Bryan Leonard. 2021. "Not-So-Natural Experiments in History." *Journal of Historical Political Economy* 1, no. 1: 1–30.

Fouka, Vasiliki. 2022. "Explaining Assimilation—And Thoughts on Theory and Empirics in Historical Political Economy." *Broadstreet Blog*, April 18, 2022. https://broadstreet.blog/2022/04/18/explaining-assimilation-and-thoughts-on-theory-and-empirics-in-historical-political-economy/.

Fouka, Vasiliki. 2023. "Assimilation in Historical Political Economy." In *The Oxford Handbook of Historical Political Economy*, ed. J. Jenkins and J. Rubin, 669–687. Oxford: Oxford University Press.

Gailmard, Sean. 2021. "What Are We Doing in Historical Political Economy?" *Broadstreet Blog*, January 8, 2021. https://broadstreet.blog/2021/01/08/what-are-we-doing-in-historical-political-economy/.

Gailmard, Sean. 2023. "Formal Models in Historical Political Economy." In *The Oxford Handbook of Historical Political Economy*, ed. J. Jenkins and J. Rubin, 95–115. Oxford: Oxford University Press.

Garfias, Francisco, and Emily Sellars. 2023. "State Building in Historical Political Economy." In *The Oxford Handbook of Historical Political Economy*, ed. J. Jenkins and J. Rubin, 209–235. Oxford: Oxford University Press.

Greif, Avner, and Jared Rubin. 2023. "Political Legitimacy in Historical Political Economy." In *The Oxford Handbook of Historical Political Economy*, ed. J. Jenkins and J. Rubin, 293–310. Oxford: Oxford University Press.

Grzymala-Busse, Anna, and Eugene Finkel. 2023. "Historical Political Economy of Autocracy." In *The Oxford Handbook of Historical Political Economy*, ed. J. Jenkins and J. Rubin, 161–184. Oxford: Oxford University Press.

Nunn, Nathan. 2014. "Historical Development." *Handbook of Economic Growth* 2: 347–402.

Sellars, Emily. 2021. "Borders and Boundaries in HPE Research." *Broadstreet Blog*, March 12, 2021. https://broadstreet.blog/2021/03/12/borders-and-boundaries-in-hpe-research/.

Suryanarayan, Pavithra, and Steven White. 2023. "Identity in Historical Political Economy." In *The Oxford Handbook of Historical Political Economy*, ed. J. Jenkins and J. Rubin, 733–746. Oxford: Oxford University Press.

Slez, Adam. 2023. "Networks in Historical Political Economy." In *The Oxford Handbook of Historical Political Economy*, ed. J. Jenkins and J. Rubin, 75–94. Oxford: Oxford University Press.

Voth, Hans-Joachim. 2021. "Persistence: Myth and Mystery." In *The Handbook of Historical Economics*, ed. A. Bisin and G. Federico, 243–67. London: Elsevier.

Weingast, Barry R., and Donald Wittman. 2006. "The Reach of Political Economy." In *The Oxford Handbook of Political Economy*, ed. B. R. Weingast and D. Wittman, 3–25. New York: Oxford University Press.

CHAPTER 2

INTERDISCIPLINARY COLLABORATION IN HISTORICAL POLITICAL ECONOMY

TRACY DENNISON AND SCOTT GEHLBACH

HISTORICAL political economy (HPE) is a field of study that comprises (at least) three separate disciplines: history, politics, and economics. As with any such interdisciplinary endeavor, there are inevitable challenges in collaborating and communicating across disciplinary boundaries. Differences in method, in theory, and in motivating questions conspire to harden those boundaries and erode the commensurability necessary for a common dialogue (Kuhn 1962).

Such challenges are particularly pronounced in the relationship between history, on the one hand, and the social sciences, on the other. Even as the decades-long divergence between economics and political science has begun to reverse, the mathematicization and quantification of the social sciences, coupled with history's cultural turn, have made it more difficult for historians and social scientists to learn from each other. When scholars in one "camp" approach a topic that has traditionally been the preserve of the other, the response is not even defensiveness but rather indifference, with neither side compelled to acknowledge the work of the other. It sometimes seems that historians and social economists each practice their own HPE.

That said, it is easy to exaggerate the divide. In fact, it is too easy—it lets historians and social scientists both off the hook, when in fact engagement across the disciplines is critical to good research. In what follows, we argue that historians and social scientists have different but complementary skills: historical and social-scientific research illuminate distinct aspects of a shared experience. Interdisciplinary collaboration brings these skills together. In so doing, it forces researchers to think harder about the questions they are asking, and about how to best interpret their findings; it expands the frontiers of our knowledge and suggests new avenues of inquiry. We acknowledge the formidable obstacles to such collaboration, but we insist that they are not impossible to surmount, especially if we consider forms of cooperation beyond traditional co-authorship.

By way of example, we often point to our own field of study—the historical political economy of late Imperial Russia—though we also cite precedents from others of inquiry. Our awareness of the divide between history and the social sciences is not abstract; we have ourselves witnessed more than one conversation about "the relationship." We have, nonetheless, seen enough examples of successful collaboration to understand what is possible. Those examples point the way to a renewed and truly interdisciplinary historical political economy.

Understanding the *Methodenstreit*

The tension between history and the social sciences is not new. It goes back at least as far as the nineteenth-century central European "*Methodenstreit*" between mathematically inclined economists and their historically minded colleagues (Tribe 1995). These tensions have flared up repeatedly ever since and remain present to this day (Postan 1939; Coleman 1995; Ogilvie 2007). In the contemporary academy, this divide has been exaggerated by increasingly sharp disciplinary boundaries and the self-selection of scholars with distinct backgrounds and tastes into the various disciplines. The differences that result are as much cultural as they are methodological.

Disciplinary cultures, like other cultures, can be difficult to observe and evaluate from inside. Those who have been acculturated tend to take the rules and norms entirely for granted; we are rarely asked to articulate to ourselves why we do things *this* way and not *that* way. It's not so much that we are intolerant of other approaches, it's that we tend not to engage them in ways that force us to be explicit about why—or in what circumstances—we think one approach might be preferable to another.[1] This raises the costs of interdisciplinary engagement, both by making disciplinary research inaccessible to outsiders (since so many methodological choices are implicit and unquestioned by insiders[2]) and by making it difficult for those acculturated in one set of practices to productively question and critique others. On those occasions when historians and social scientists are forced to engage with each other's work, they often struggle to articulate their concerns. Their comments end up sounding dismissive: historians assert that "those numbers can't be used that way" and social scientists deride textual evidence as "anecdotal." Such uninformed responses only harden existing attitudes and exacerbate the divergence.

While it is true that most historians do not understand econometric technique and most social scientists do not know how to analyze texts, these aren't actually the main obstacles to interdisciplinary collaboration—they are just the most readily apparent. Many of the disagreements that motivate the *Methodenstreit* concern more fundamental questions: What can be measured, what constitutes evidence, and how we should think about causation in historical context? These disagreements give rise to stereotypes: the social scientist who wants to measure everything, thinks only numbers are "empirical," and believes her regression model captures all that is important—the historian who finds measurement morally suspect, worries about the whole concept of "evidence," and thinks searching for historical causes is pointless (because everything is inextricably related).

Such caricatures enable historians and quantitative social scientists to go on ignoring one another. But when serious discussions do happen across disciplinary lines—usually around specific projects or questions (more on this shortly)—the stereotypes quickly unravel. It turns out that historians aren't that bothered about measuring changes in population or GDP or land allotment sizes, though they are worried about attempts to measure things that they know are very tricky to define and isolate, like the effects of cultural norms or those of an institutional system. And few social scientists would argue against the idea of multiple causes—indeed, any social scientist trained in modern methods of causal inference would maintain that the whole point is to find some plausibly exogenous source of variation in a single "treatment" variable, so as to bracket the role of other factors. Historians are trained in source criticism, which makes them skeptical of social scientists' treatment of data; they view it as inattentive to the messy reality of how digitized records first entered the archives. Social scientists are trained in econometric technique that enables them to correct for measurement error and isolate the role of some variable of interest.

Behind the skepticism on both sides is a lack of understanding of what each is trying to do, of the questions that motivate research, and why these questions are considered important. At a fundamental level, these questions differ in their approach to the specific versus the general. Historians aim to understand a particular society in its historical context, whether that be seventeenth-century English Puritans, the court of Maria-Theresa, or the village of Montaillou. Their knowledge comes from immersion in a specific period, a specific region, a specific stratum of society, and often a specific language. It follows that it is far more natural for historians to think in terms of "sources" than "data." Qualitative, textual information is as important as the quantitative in helping the historian to build a picture of a historical phenomenon or locality. The historian reads sources with an eye not only to what is present but to what is missing—and how to interpret the silences. Not least, she is attentive to the language used: How do villagers in a society without formal mechanisms for assigning property rights articulate conflicts over property? Do they use possessive forms of speech, do they talk of "rights" or "trespass" or "theft," and can this language help us better understand their property regimes?

The historian's expertise is often hidden from view. It is easy to imagine that anyone who can read can do history, that it is a matter of learning "the facts" and arranging them to tell a compelling story. But which facts and how to interpret these in the larger context? Unlike many social scientists, historians tend to return to the same periods and the same places in their research. Their tools are languages, a knowledge of sources, and a deep understanding of a specific subject. Yet with this expertise comes a cost: an emphasis on depth often leads to skepticism about breadth. Historians tend to eschew more general explanatory frameworks, making it challenging to engage across different subfields of history, never mind across disciplinary lines.

In contrast to historians, social scientists are far more comfortable with the general. This takes various forms. When considering evidence that spans space or time, social scientists speak of "stylized facts," that is, broad generalizations that abstract from particular detail. Thus, for example, Paine and Lee (2022) document the divergence in revenue collection between Western and non-Western countries in the early twentieth century—a pattern that they use to motivate a model of investments in fiscal capacity. When social scientists do restrict attention to a particular time and place, they often use the historical context to explore broad theoretical conjectures. A study of local institutions of self-government in imperial Russia (the *zemstva*), which offered political representation to recently freed serfs, therefore sheds light not only on governance in Russia in the era of the "Great Reforms," but also on bigger, more general questions in political economy, such as when autocratic elites transfer power to excluded groups (Castañeda Dower, Finkel, Gehlbach, and Nafziger 2018). On occasions when existing theory provides no good explanation for some empirical phenomenon, social scientists offer new theory, thus contributing to the "library of mechanisms" (Guala 2005) used to understand the world (Gailmard 2021).

In an ideal world, these two forms of expertise would come together naturally: social scientists' comfort with theory and data as the perfect complement to historians' ease with historical context and textual sources. After all, historians and social scientists share a set of goals in historical work: to understand history for its own sake, and to use history to understand the present (Charnysh, Finkel, and Gehlbach 2023).[3] Yet here again disciplinary culture creates obstacles to intellectual exchange. Social scientists are increasingly accustomed to team production, with multiple authors on the typical paper. Historians, in contrast, tend to work alone. This, in turn, relates to the mechanics of research in the respective disciplines: data collection and analysis are more naturally shared across members of a team than is the process of reading and interpreting archival texts.

None of this would matter if historians and social scientists were able to fully exploit gains from intellectual trade, with each building on what the other has done (Gehlbach 2015). But even getting historians and social scientists to read each other's work can be a challenge. It is true that social scientists are far more likely to curl up with a good history book than a historian is to peruse the latest issue of the *American Political Science Review* or the *American Economic Review* before going to bed,[4] but this is not a reliable gauge of genuine interdisciplinary engagement. A social scientist working in the field of HPE is clearly interested in history, but is she interested enough to do a deep dive into a larger historiography or to struggle through a book filled with unfamiliar jargon and analytical categories to find the bits that are relevant to her project? This seems about as likely as that a historian will push past the mathematical notation and "sociological gobbledygook" in much of social science.

Self-selection reinforces the problem. The sort of young scholar who a generation ago might have gravitated toward comparative politics—interested in the world, good with languages, skeptical of the mathematical methods employed by her Americanist colleagues—today is more likely to choose a career as a historian. Even small differences in comparative advantage can generate large differences in preferences about the proper nature of historical work, as investment in skills and the acculturation described above mold scholars into different "types."

All of these obstacles are real. There have, nonetheless, been periodic attempts to bring together history and the social sciences—though not always historians and social scientists. In political science and economics, the *Analytic Narratives* project sought to marry historical description and rational-choice theorizing (Bates et al. 1998; see also Skarbek and Skarbek 2022). With the benefit of hindsight, this was a sort of proto-HPE that emphasized formal theory over statistical inference. It was not always well received, with the authors of *Analytic Narratives* criticized for lack of fidelity to the facts; for considering overly restrictive game forms; for failing to fully incorporate uncertainty, emotions, and other relevant factors in decision-making; and for much more (e.g., Carpenter 2000; Elster 2000). Perhaps the authors were simply ahead of their time—or perhaps true interdisciplinarity requires active collaboration across disciplinary lines.

In what follows, we present three cases of what we understand to be successful interdisciplinary collaboration—settings and research agendas in which historical and social scientific expertise were effectively brought together. We draw substantially on our own experience as members of a community of scholars working on Imperial and Soviet Russia, though we also lean on the example of others. Our examples are different in nature: the first is a kind of asynchronous collaboration, the second is interdisciplinary co-authorship, and the third is "institutional" collaboration. What these examples have in common is an overriding sense that the divide between history and the social sciences is not so large as one might imagine. Together, they demonstrate that interdisciplinary collaboration can be intellectually rewarding to those who are willing to make the investment.

Collaborating across the Divide

Intergenerational Collaboration

A first example of successful collaboration between historians and social scientists is notable for the fact that the historians and social scientists did not actually know each other. They were, in fact, representatives of different generations and political-economic systems—the historians working in the USSR during the Khrushchev Thaw, the social scientists building on their research five decades later in North America. This spatial, temporal, and ideological distance notwithstanding, the research that emerged from this collaboration is a model for what can be achieved when methodological complementarities are exploited.

Soviet historians, working in a Marxist tradition, had long been interested in the "peasant movement" that preceded the Bolshevik Revolution. Beginning in the 1950s, a team of historians drew upon various archival records to document peasant resistance from 1795 to 1917. The primary research output from this project is a multivolume publication—*Krest'ianskoe Dvizhenie v Rossii* (The Peasant Movement in Russia, with various editors)—that combines an incident-by-incident chronicle of thousands of events and transcriptions of important primary documents. Numerous subsidiary publications build on the context provided by this investigation to explore important historical events, including especially the emancipation of Russia's serfs in 1861 (e.g., Zaionchkovskii 1968).

Social scientists, of course, are also interested in political unrest. Finkel, Gehlbach, and Olsen (2015; see also Finkel and Gehlbach 2020) saw in the Soviet data and the context of Imperial Russia's so-called Great Reforms an opportunity to test key theories of the relationship between reform and rebellion in autocratic states. Drawing on four volumes of *Krest'ianskoe Dvizhenie v Rossii* that dealt with the period before and after emancipation (Okun' 1962; Okun' and Sivkov 1963; Ivanov 1964; Zaionchkovskii and Paina 1968), Finkel et al. assembled a data set of nearly four thousand events across fifty-five provinces from 1851 to 1871. Although the initial goal of the project was to understand the effect of reform (emancipation) on unrest, subsequent work (Castañeda Dower, Finkel, Gehlbach, and Nafziger 2018) examined the impact of unrest on reform (peasant representation in district *zemstvo* assemblies, created by further edict in 1864).

From a social scientist's perspective, it is nearly the ideal interdisciplinary collaboration. The archival work on which the chronicle is based is well beyond the reach of the best-funded social scientist. It takes a historian's understanding of sources to pull together even a single entry in the historical record, such as that depicted in Figure 2.1. Where does one begin to look for mentions of peasants refusing to plow their fallow fields in response to the loss of land following emancipation? What records does one investigate to corroborate such evidence? How does one understand the incentives of those who recorded such information? These are the skills of a historian—or, in this case, a five-year plan's worth of historians.

Yet it is hard to know what to make of this mountain of evidence, without some exercise in aggregation. The authors of the chronicle attempted something along these lines, with tables in the final volume that summarized events in cross-tabular form. The

---

Ранее 29 июня — 6 июля. Симбирская губ. Отказ вр.-об. крестьян деревень Каирова, Недремаловки, Протопоповки, Перетяжкиной и с. Шатрашаны Буинского у. в имениях Сабаниных, Горемыкина, Пятницкого и Чертковой запахивать свои паровые поля из-за отрезки хорошей земли; была введена военная команда.
    ЦГИА, ф. 1291, оп. 52, 1862 г., д. 117, л. 1—6, 13—16; ЦГАОР, ф. 109-И, 4 эксп., 1862 г., д. 223, л. 21—27; ЦГВИА, ф. 395, оп. 299, ОА, 1862 г., д. 362, л. 49—50, 101—101 об., 108—109 об., 117—117 об.; *Левашев*, стр. 54.

FIGURE 2.1. A typical chronicle entry

resulting counts (e.g., by region and year) are the sort of "raw data" that have been used in a few papers, including Finkel, Gehlbach, and Kofanov's (2017) separate work on rural unrest during the 1917 Russian Revolution. It is better than nothing, but it is not the same thing as being able to aggregate up from the original chronicle entries.

By way of example, consider those same accounts of nineteenth-century peasant rebellion. Some of these are quite substantial, involving multiple estates and thousands of participants. Others are more isolated acts of resistance—not quite "weapons of the weak" (Scott 1987), but the sort of thing that would have flown below the radar, if not for the idiosyncratic presence of a local observer. One wants to ensure that any statements about temporal or geospatial patterns of peasant rebellion are not sensitive to the inclusion of such "small" events. Hence the importance of the raw event data: we can check robustness to counts of "large" events only.

Aggregating up from the raw event data can also address other forms of measurement error. A particular concern in Finkel, Gehlbach, and Olsen (2015) is the relative incidence of unrest among serfs and "state peasants" (peasants who lived on state lands) before and after Tsar Alexander II's emancipation of the serfs in 1861. As part of the emancipation process, "peace arbitrators" (Leo Tolstoy was one) were tasked with negotiating settlements between landowners and former serfs. It is conceivable that acts of peasant rebellion during this period would have been better documented on estate lands than on state land, given the temporary presence of peace arbitrators on the former but not the latter. Thankfully, the Soviet historians who assembled the event data were meticulous about documenting the archives on which each chronicle entry is based (these are listed at the end of the entry depicted in Figure 2.1). As an alternative aggregation, Finkel, Gehlbach, and Olsen (2015) therefore restrict attention to events drawn from the Central State Archive of the October Revolution (TsGAOR), which are primarily disturbances recorded by the tsarist political police—that is, not peace arbitrators.

The picture of peasant rebellion that emerges from this collaboration is more complete, the conclusions more confident, than would have been possible had the project ended in the 1960s. Still, this is not full interdisciplinarity. The Soviet historians working during the Khrushchev Thaw were writing for other historians. Finkel, Gehlbach, and Olsen were writing mostly for other social scientists. The two groups are separated by theory and method as well as by generations.

Nonetheless, in this experience there is the seed of a model that could support interdisciplinary collaboration in real time. One can imagine groups of historians and social scientists teaming up to identify, digitize, and analyze archival records. Historians' sensitivity to sources would impart meaning to those documents that are collected. Social scientists' comfort with data would serve to summarize that information in useful ways. The motivating questions would be substantially distinct, but through collaboration there might be some convergence of interests.

One recent example of a collaboration along these lines involves the calculation of new estimates of GDP per capita for the Russian Empire (Broadberry and Korchmina 2022). Here the econometric expertise of the economist (Broadberry) and the historian's knowledge of archives and historical context (Korchmina) have been combined to investigate Russia's place in debates about the "little divergence" in Europe. New sources of information about population, grain yields, prices, and incomes in the two centuries before the Russian Revolution of 1917 have been identified in the archives and used to create measures of long-run economic growth. The findings raise interesting new questions about how to interpret Russian history, challenging the existing views of historians and social scientists on serfdom, tsarist-era reforms, and industrialization.

Interdisciplinary Co-Authorship

Our second example differs in various respects from the first. In this case, a historian (Dennison) and an economist (Alexander Klein) collaborated on an interdisciplinary "state of the field" project, bringing together findings from history and the social sciences to create a historical account of economic divergence in Eastern Europe over the nineteenth and twentieth centuries.

Dennison and Klein's (2021) charge was to produce a chapter for the *Cambridge Economic History of the Modern World* on the economic history of Eastern Europe since 1870. This was a complicated task for several reasons. First, the notion of "Eastern" Europe (insofar as there is any agreement on what that is) did not remain constant between 1870 and the present. The past 150 years have seen multiple changes in borders, as old empires collapsed, new ones appeared, and military conflicts repeatedly altered old territorial boundaries. Two world wars, plus the Russian Revolution and ensuing civil war, complicate the task of calculating growth indices for the twentieth century. Until very recently, data for the Soviet Union and its satellite states were not readily available, and the methods and approaches employed by Western scholars (in both history and the social sciences) were unknown to their East European counterparts, leaving large gaps in the relevant literatures. Not least, it was necessary to construct a general narrative that could accommodate a number of different societies, each with its own peculiar circumstances and specific historical contingencies.

Many of the disciplinary concerns outlined earlier in the chapter came into play. For instance, the historian first had to be convinced that there were reasonable ways of dealing with the problem of border changes and gaps in the data that could be explained and defended (to herself and to readers). Moreover, both had to agree on a historical narrative that was consistent with the data as well as the historiography of the region. As a starting point, the project used the quantitative social science literature (to which Klein had contributed with novel work on national income accounting for parts of eastern Europe), as this was the more recent economic history of the region. Both that and the historical literature emphasized institutions and historical political economy, so these emerged as key themes, helping to ensure that the survey would be accessible both to social scientists and to historians.

From the perspective of social science, it was important to incorporate as much quantitative evidence—and cite as much of that literature—as possible. The resulting chapter offers a synthesis of existing research on Central and Eastern Europe and incorporates recent studies for countries such as Bulgaria, Romania, and Serbia, where data had been less reliable or altogether left out of prior work (especially for the twentieth century). Estimates from this synthesis show no evidence of convergence in the growth trajectories of Eastern and Western Europe; in fact, they suggest that divergence had roots deeper than the twentieth century. Disaggregating long-term growth performance by sector (agriculture, industry, trade) provides a much more nuanced portrait of regional development across the period, offering new insight into such topics as the collapse of the Austro-Hungarian Empire and the rise of new political regimes, the possible effects of nationalism and protectionism, the role of state corporatism, and the political economy of coercion and corruption in the Soviet empire.

The macroeconomic approach that this synthesis required is especially challenging for a historian—it is not an obvious arena for cross-disciplinary collaboration. Nonetheless, there are parts of this project where the two forms of expertise were brought together very effectively. Perhaps the best example concerns inequality, which arises in the context of the Soviet command economy. On the quantitative side, Gini coefficients for eastern Europe are substantially lower than those for the West in the same period. On the surface, it appears that communist regimes achieved greater equality, though at much lower levels of income. But the more qualitative work of historians has revealed hidden inequalities in the Soviet system—aspects for which it has been difficult to get systematic, reliable data, because so much economic activity was illicit. These include unequal access to power and money (to better jobs and promotions), to basic goods (food, housing), and to services (decent medical care, entrance to special schools and universities, travel). Historical accounts offer evidence (often from textual sources) of corruption, the importance of social networks for obtaining goods and services that markets did not provide, and the disproportionate effects of inequality on women and other groups.

It is worth emphasizing that this collaboration also fell outside the boundaries of traditional co-authorship. The participants were charged with writing something together, but they were relieved of the pressure to agree on a research question and, more importantly, a research design. It was not necessary to find common ground on methodology or on an approach to existing sources and data. Instead the collaboration focused on ensuring that the most salient findings from each side of the disciplinary divide were used to create a coherent narrative about the history of this region. This cooperative approach helped to bring greater breadth and balance to the account of history in ways that are less likely when only one disciplinary perspective is represented.

This promise is borne out in other instances of interdisciplinary scholarship. One recent example is a study of the wool market in medieval England (Bell, Brooks, and Dryburgh 2007). In this case, new light is cast on medieval economies by taking sources with which medievalists were already well acquainted—advance contracts for wool from ecclesiastical and lay archives—and analyzing them using the theoretical tools of economics. In bringing together expertise in the archives of the late medieval English period with tools from modern financial economics, the authors offer a fresh take on an old subject. They present advance contracts for wool (by way of example) as relatively complicated financial instruments, suggesting that local economies and long-distance trading relationships were both more sophisticated than often portrayed. Interestingly, there are few econometric pyrotechnics here (medieval data do pose considerable constraints!) but a great deal of qualitative evidence from primary texts. The contribution from financial economics is more of a conceptual toolkit that enables us to see these documents in a different way, revealing new information about the society that generated them.

A similar approach can be found in Rosenthal and Wong (2011), who combine expertise in economics and history as well as knowledge of two very different historical societies and their archives. Their comparative study of the politics of economic development in Europe and China incorporates deep knowledge of local sources and historical context, some economic theory, and findings from a large secondary literature. The interdisciplinarity brings something extra to their comparison; it makes the research collaborative in terms of both methodology and regional expertise, and it allows for a more suggestive reinterpretation of existing narratives. The same can be said for Pincus and Robinson (2014), who reexamine institutional change in the context of England's Glorious Revolution—a "critical juncture" famously explored by North and Weingast (1989) but also examined by many historians, including especially Pincus (e.g., Pincus 2009). In their case, political-economic theory illuminates the relative importance of de jure and de facto institutional change following the Glorious Revolution, with the latter rather the former proving to be the mechanism through which English governance was reshaped after 1688.

Institutional Collaboration

The examples discussed so far concern implicit or explicit collaboration on particular research projects. In this section, we describe an alternative, more institutional form of collaboration that can help to realize gains from trade between historians and social scientists.

We begin by recounting the recent history of institutional collaboration in our own field. In November 2017, historians and social scientists gathered for a panel at the annual meeting of the Association for Slavic, East European, and Eurasian Studies (ASEEES) on "Number Trouble"—a response to a contentious debate on quantitative studies of history in the *Slavic Review* earlier that year. The discussion that followed illustrated the work to be done if there was to be productive conversation across the disciplinary divide. Swedish economic historian Martin Kragh was the first to suggest a mechanism to facilitate that conversation: a pair of panels at the 2018 meetings, one in which social scientists would present and historians would comment, the other with the opposite configuration. The willingness to participate was heartening, and the inaugural sessions were so successful that similar panels have been organized in subsequent years.

On the heels of this initiative, Gehlbach organized a Summer Workshop in the Economic History and Historical Political Economy of Russia in Madison, Wisconsin, in May 2019. The workshop aimed to build on the interdisciplinarity that the ASEEES sessions had so successfully harnessed, but to push it further with a "Clio-style" conference, where papers would be pre-circulated and then read and discussed by all participants. The aim was to force historians and social scientists—graduate students, postdocs, faculty—into dialogue about each other's work. This, too, has become an annual event, through which a core group of participants and a growing community of junior scholars have come to know, and learn from, each other.

What has made ASEEES panels and the workshop so successful is the combination of realistic expectations and a hospitable, collegial environment for discussion and (friendly) disagreement. There is no expectation that historians will be turned into social scientists, or vice versa. There is no explicit aim of co-authorship or joint research or even that all of one's comments and suggestions will make it into the next version of the paper or book manuscript. The meetings bring together researchers from different disciplines to share their own expertise and learn from that of others. The rapport that has been built through repeated engagement has created an atmosphere where questions can be raised, criticisms offered, and suggestions proffered in ways that are helpful and productive—making the work of historians and social scientists better. In the best cases, these discussions have helped to identify misunderstandings (related to the use of quantitative methods or textual analyses), to clarify methodological disagreements, and to think about ways to make our work more accessible to researchers in other fields.

Such institutional collaboration is, of course, not unique to the study of Imperial and Soviet Russia. In 2002, Ira Katznelson and Gregory Wawro organized a Congress and History Conference to bring together an interdisciplinary group of Congress scholars in common dialogue; twenty years later, the annual conference continues. Perhaps illustrating the sort of intellectual exchange that might follow from the Russia initiatives described earlier, Katznelson and Wawro have worked to understand the ways in which historical and quantitative methods can be bridged, a project culminating in their important monograph *Time Counts: Quantitative Analysis for Historical Social Science* (Katznelson and Wawro 2022). In similar fashion, Katznelson and Barry Weingast led a group of scholars working in historical institutionalism and rational choice institutionalism to explore "points of intersection" in the study of endogenous preferences (Katznelson and Weingast 2005).

There have also been efforts in recent years to overcome the increasing narrowness of academic journals by creating new venues for work in fields that transcend disciplinary boundaries. Two notable examples are the *Journal of Historical Political Economy* (edited by Jeffery Jenkins) and *Capitalism: A Journal of History and Economics* (edited by Marc Flandreau, Julia Ott, and Francesca Trivellato). Both consider articles from historians and from social scientists (not necessarily writing together), so long as the work relates to the journal's field (HPE) or theme (capitalism).

Not least, there is the Broadstreet Blog, organized by Jeffery Jenkins in 2020. This is an interdisciplinary space that brings together political scientists, economists, historians, and sociologists with a common interest in historical political economy. Representatives of different disciplines present the latest research in HPE, discuss the econometric challenges of working with historical data, share knowledge about sources and archives, and address the challenges of working across disciplinary divides. Behind the scenes, a smaller group of disciplinarily diverse editors makes the blog work. They share ideas and knowledge, offer comments and criticisms on each other's posts, and maintain what is effectively a running interdisciplinary conversation about historical political economy.

Conclusion

We are not naive about the increasingly divergent trajectories of history and the social sciences, nor about the challenges that genuine interdisciplinary engagement poses. But we are optimistic, because we have observed, in some important cases, a willingness to talk across interdisciplinary lines and an interest in engaging with each other's work. True, traditional forms of collaboration, especially co-authorship, are difficult: journals have become more specialized, and criteria for tenure and promotion discourage interdisciplinarity. Nonetheless, as our examples make clear, it is still possible. And there are many other ways to collaborate: large team projects that bring together historians and social scientists to identify and analyze sources for a specific society under a broad theme; articles or chapters for reference volumes that pair historians with social scientists to discuss the state of the field; and conference panels, workshops, journals, and blogs that provide historians and social scientists an opportunity to discuss recent work in their respective disciplines.

The current academic landscape rewards specialization and obscures latent demand for cooperation across disciplinary boundaries. Even so, researchers on both sides of the divide continue to see returns to investment in interdisciplinary work. By exploiting the complementary expertise and perspectives of social scientists and historians, we increase our chances of getting things right; our research projects are more thoughtfully and intentionally designed; our work is founded on the most robust findings from *all* the relevant literatures. And it is fun! For many of us, one of the best aspects of historical political economy is the opportunity to learn from scholars in other disciplines. This chapter shows the many ways that is possible.

Notes

1. Undergraduates, who tend to select into a field because they have found classes in that area especially exciting and interesting, are typically left on their own to consider the relative merits of different approaches to the study of history. Ideally, courses in economic, political, or social history would address comparative methodological approaches with a view to other disciplines, but this is hardly possible without regular, sustained engagement across disciplinary boundaries.

2. Decisions, for instance, about quantitative versus qualitative studies—not decisions internal to disciplines such as the proper identification strategy or whether to choose one set of archive documents over another.
3. As discussed earlier, a third goal—to use history as a setting to explore theoretical conjectures—seems to be more idiosyncratic to social scientists.
4. The narrative structure most historians employ to present their research findings means that historical works are, at least superficially, more accessible to other audiences than work in the social sciences.

References

Bates, Robert H., Avner Greif, Margaret Levi, Jean-Laurent Rosenthal, and Barry R. Weingast. 1998. *Analytic Narratives*. Princeton, NJ: Princeton University Press.

Bell, Adrian R., Chris Brooks, and Paul R. Dryburgh. 2007. *The English Wool Market, c. 1230-1327*. Cambridge: Cambridge University Press.

Broadberry, Stephen, and Elena Korchmina. 2022. "Catching Up and Falling Behind: Russian Economic Growth, 1690s–1880s." CEPR Discussion Paper 17458.

Carpenter, Daniel. 2000. "Commentary: What Is the Marginal Value of Analytic Narratives?" *Social Science History* 24, no. 4: 653–67.

Castañeda Dower, Paul, Evgeny Finkel, Scott Gehlbach, and Steven Nafziger. 2018. "Collective Action and Representation in Autocracies: Evidence from Russia's Great Reforms." *American Political Science Review* 112, no. 1: 125–47.

Charnysh, Volha, Eugene Finkel, and Scott Gehlbach. 2023. "Historical Political Economy: Past, Present, and Future." *Annual Review of Political Science* 26, no. 1: 175–191.

Coleman, Donald. "History, Economic History, and the Numbers Game." 1995. *Historical Journal* 38, no. 3: 635–46.

Dennison, Tracy, and Alexander Klein. 2021. "The Socialist Experiment and Beyond: The Economic History of Eastern Europe since 1870." In *The Cambridge Economic History of the Modern World: Volume 2: 1870–Present*, ed. Stephen Broadberry and Kyoji Fukao, 74–99. Cambridge: Cambridge University Press.

Elster, Jon. "Rational Choice History: A Case of Excessive Ambition." 2000. *American Political Science Review* 94, no. 3: 685–95.

Finkel, Evgeny and Scott Gehlbach. 2020. *Reform and Rebellion in Weak States*. New York: Cambridge University Press.

Finkel, Evgeny, Scott Gehlbach, and Dmitrii Kofanov. 2017. "(Good) Land and Freedom (for Former Serfs)." *Slavic Review* 76, no. 3: 710–21.

Finkel, Evgeny, Scott Gehlbach, and Tricia Olsen. 2015. "Does Reform Prevent Rebellion? Evidence from Russia's Emancipation of the Serfs." *Comparative Political Studies* 48, no. 8: 984–1019.

Gailmard, Sean. 2021. "Theory, History, and Political Economy." *Journal of Historical Political Economy* 1, no. 1: 69–104.

Gehlbach, Scott. 2015. "The Fallacy of Multiple Methods." *Comparative Politics Newsletter* 25, no. 2: 11–12.

Guala, Francesco. 2005. *The Methodology of Experimental Economics*. New York: Cambridge University Press.

Ivanov, Leonid, ed. 1964. *Kret'ianskoe Dvizhenie v Rossii v 1861–1869 gg: Sbornik Dokumentov*. Moscow: Mysl'.

Katznelson, Ira, and Gregory Wawro. 2022. *Time Counts: Quantitative Analysis for Historical Social Science*. Princeton, NJ: Princeton University Press.

Katznelson, Ira, and Barry R. Weingast. 2005. *Preferences and Situations: Points of Intersection Between Historical and Rational Choice Institutionalism*. New York: Russell Sage Foundation.

Kuhn, Thomas S. 1962. *The Structure of Scientific Revolutions*. Chicago: University of Chicago Press.

North, Douglass, and Barry R. Weingast. 1989. "Constitutions and Commitment: The Evolution of Institutions Governing Public Choice in Seventeenth-Century England." *Journal of Economic History* 49, no. 4: 803–32.

Ogilvie, Sheilagh. 2007. "'Whatever Is, Is Right'? Economic Institutions in Pre-industrial Europe." *Economic History Review* 60, no. 4: 649–84.

Okun', Semen, ed. 1962. *Kret'ianskoe Dvizhenie v Rossii v 1850–1856 gg: Sbornik Dokumentov*. Moscow: Izdatel'stvo Sotsial'no-ekonomicheskoi Literatury.

Okun', Semen, and Konstantin Sivkov, eds. 1963. *Kret'ianskoe Dvizhenie v Rossii v 1857–mae 1861 gg: Sbornik Dokumentov*. Moscow: Izdatel'stvo Sotsial'no-ekonomicheskoi Literatury.

Paine, Jack, and Alexander Lee. 2022. "The Great Revenue Divergence." *International Organization*.

Pincus, Steven C. A. 2009. *1688: The First Modern Revolution*. New Haven, CT: Yale University Press.

Pincus, Steven C. A., and James A. Robinson. 2014. "What Really Happened during the Glorious Revolution?" In *Institutions, Property Rights, and Economic Growth: The Legacy of Douglass North*, ed. Sebastian Galiani and Itai Sened, 192–222. New York: Cambridge University Press.

Postan, M. M. 1939 [1972]. "The Historical Method in Social Science: An Inaugural Lecture." Reprinted in *Fact and Relevance: Essays in Historical Method*, ed. M. M. Postan, 22–34. Cambridge: Cambridge University Press.

Rosenthal, Jean-Laurent, and R. Bin Wong. 2011. *Before and beyond Divergence: The Politics of Economic Change in China and Europe*. Cambridge, MA: Harvard University Press.

Scott, James. 1987. *Weapons of the Weak: Everyday Forms of Peasant Resistance*. New Haven, CT: Yale University Press.

Skarbek, David, and Emily Skarbek. 2022. "Analytic Narratives in Political Economy." *History of Political Economy*.

Tribe, Keith. 1995. *Strategies of Economic Order: German Economic Discourse 1750–1950*. Cambridge, UK: Cambridge University Press.

Zaionchkovskii, Petr. 1968. *Otmena Krepostnogo Prava v Rossii*. 3rd ed. Moscow: Prosveshchenie.

Zaionchkovskii, Petr, and Esfir' Paina, eds. 1968. *Kret'ianskoe Dvizhenie v Rossii v 1870–1880 gg: Sbornik Dokumentov*. Moscow: Nauka.

CHAPTER 3

DATA IN HISTORICAL POLITICAL ECONOMY

ALEXANDRA CIRONE

EMPIRICAL data are essential for studies in historical political economy (HPE). Thanks to advances in both digitization and investment in online archives and data repositories, it is increasingly possible to assemble comprehensive collections of quantitative historical data (Cirone and Spirling 2021; Bisin and Giovanni 2021; Kim 2022). As a result, the range of applications is vast: scholars have collected novel data on kinship networks using tomb epitaphs in imperial China (Wang 2022), anti-Semitism using children's stories in Germany (Braun 2022), political participation using handwritten petitions in the United States (Carpenter 2021), as well as the locations of Holy Land Crusaders (Blaydes and Paik 2016) and seventeenth-century peasant uprisings in Mexico (Garfias and Sellars 2022). Readers of this handbook will also find a wealth of historical studies with corresponding data in each themed chapter.

This chapter provides an overview of different types of quantitative historical data commonly used in historical political economy. While the chapter is by no means exhaustive, its goal is to provide an introduction to academic examples and considerations for each type. By "historical data," I refer to data from and preceding World War II. This scope condition is perhaps arbitrary, but it restricts the focus to data collected and stored by prior generations that are more challenging to work with because we have limited contact with those generations and thus limited ability to supplement or correct this data. It also allows this chapter to focus on the collection of data prior to the advent of modern survey and data collection methods.

There are many different types of historical data, but for ease of exposition, this chapter discusses a number of broad categories: sociodemographic and population data, government or institutional records, geographic and spatial data, political data, economic data, ethnographic data, and civil society data. These categories are not definitive—and aren't even mutually exclusive—but they allow for a reasonable grouping to discuss salient characteristics. Scholars of historical political economy collect quantitative information from primary and secondary sources, and the scope of data collection over time and space should be dictated by the hypotheses and design of the research study. Yet research highlighted in this chapter serves as a starting point, in that scholars interested in similar data exercises can find inspiration from such work.

Sociodemographic and Population Data

Sociodemographic and population data contain information about individuals or populations, typically consisting of 'vital records' such as age, education, marriage, family, race, religion, class, income, occupation, and location. The most common source of this type of information is census or equivalent population survey data. Sociodemographic data was inherently valuable throughout history, for economic and social control, so there were strategic incentives to collect and preserve population data; fortunately, this means historical census data are more readily available. Online access to and consolidation of historical census data are also improving. For example, IPUMs (https://www.ipums.org) is a growing central repository for survey and linked census data (including new methods of linking, see Helgertz et al. 2022). It holds US census data at the county and state level since 1790; it also has census data for over one hundred countries around the world, with some originating in the 1960s and 1970s.

The regularity and depth of census information doesvary by country, however. The United States is a notable case with extensive local and national data since its founding; scholars have used micro-level data from the US census to study the modern-day effects of slavery (Acharya, Blackwell, and Sen 2016), rugged individualism in frontier culture (Bazzi, Fiszbein, and Gebresilasse 2020), post–Civil War Reconstruction (Chacon and Jensen 2020; Suryanarayan and White 2021), and the socioeconomic backgrounds of politicians (Feigenbaum et al. 2022). Prussia and the German central state are other notable examples for high-quality census data, in that there exist regular and detailed censuses of the population over time (Becker and Pascali 2019; Hollenbach 2021). Even if a full population census is lacking, smaller surveys or population registers can still provide insight into historical populations. For example, the China Multi-Generational Panel Datasets provide the records of two million people between 1749 and 1913 (Campbell and Lee 2020). Even for historical cases that didn't have regular data collection exercises, there might exist premodern censuses or the equivalent, like the medieval census of India's Emperor Akbar (Jha 2013).

A good example of the use of historical sociodemographic data comes from the study of migrations, in particular the Age of Mass Migration (1860–1920). Scholars have compiled data tracking migration across countries from 1850 to the present day (Özden et al. 2011; Clemens 2020). Scholars have also used census data to analyze the effects of immigrants on industrialization and economic growth (Sequeira, Nunn, and Qian 2020), labor movements and strikes (Karadja and Prawitz 2019), racial inequalities (Nix and Qian 2015) or long-term social mobility (Abramitzky and Boustan 2022). Other scholars have looked at the social ties and economic fortunes of refugees in Germany (Burchardi and Hassan 2013) and Poland (Charnysh 2019) after World War II, or societal outcomes for descendants of German immigrants in the United States after World War I (Fouka 2020). The collective study of the Age of Mass Migration has also resulted in technological innovations in the methods for linking census records across individuals and time (Abramitzky and Boustan 2022; Abramitsky et al. 2021). These papers all highlight the possibilities and challenges that come with working with census data.

Government or Institutional Records

Government or institutional records are the source for key information on bureaucracy or state capacity, and records of the human and physical capital needed for state administration. Examples of this data focus on government officials, administrative structures and staffing, tax collection and extractive capacity, institutions of law enforcement, or public goods and financial institutions (railways, banks, etc.). I also include institutional data relating to health and healthcare in this category. Such information is typically found in official government archives or libraries, though records can also be located elsewhere. This type of data is also more likely to be systematically collected in recent periods, and more reliable after the advent of institutionalized record keeping.

Potential data held in state records are vast, which means the types of variables that can be collected varies quite a bit by case. Some historical cases are notable for their state capacity. France is a good example; after the French Revolution, the French Constituent Assembly began a process of state-building that involved extensive local and national administration (Chambru et al. 2022; Acemoglu et al. 2011; Cirone and van Coppenolle 2018; Kreuzer 2001), resulting in high-quality data over time. China is another fascinating case; well-documented historical records are available from Imperial China, including historical land, taxation, and population data as well as detailed data on bureaucrats (Liang 2008; Sng 2014; Campbell and Lee 2020; Jiang and Kung 2021; Dincecco and Wang 2021; Wang 2022). It's often also the case that bureaucratic data go hand in hand with census data; polities that are able to sustain one type often have good records on the other; the United States (Suryanarayan and White 2021) and Prussia (Mares and Queralt 2020; Hollenbach 2021) are cases in point.

State records can also include information not only from the collecting country but data gathered from other countries. This is especially the case for colonial archives, which can contain significant amounts of useful data. India is a notable example, thanks to the British East India Company archive (Srivastava 2022), though colonial archives are widespread. For example, Guardado (2018) uses colonial archives to assemble a dataset of the price of provincial offices sold by the Spanish Crown during times of fiscal crisis, while Xu (2018; 2023) exploits personnel records with vital statistics from 1856 onward to study colonial officers and bureaucratic representation in India. Bolt et al. (2021)

provide detailed district-level data on the existence of native authority institutions during colonial rule in British Africa, Garfias and Sellars (2020) look at the value of holding office in colonial Mexico, and Mattingly (2017) uses data on schooling, health, and bureaucratic density as a result of the Japanese colonization of northern China. Johnson-Kanu (2021) uses the composition of bureaucrats in the Nigerian Federal Civil Service spanning nearly a century to study colonial-era access to bureaucracy. Overall, colonial records provide an alternative source of information on state capacity.

Another important source of institutional data relates to healthcare, though systematic data collection is more likely to be found in the past two centuries, and could be collected or stored outside of government records (particularly if healthcare is private or not distributed by the state).[1] One good example of large-scale historical data collection involving health data comes from Ansell and Lindvall (2020). Here, they assembled cross-national data from 1800 onward, including on midwifery services and training, mental healthcare institutions, and vaccination programs; they also cross-checked this data with information on centralized versus decentralized funding and provision across countries. A number of studies have also collected data or proxies on the long-term health outcomes of populations, while studying the effects of exogenous shocks or crises—looking at how the 1918 flu epidemic (Almond 2006; Arroyo Abad and Maurer 2021), nineteenth-century phylloxera blight (Banerjee et al. 2010), nineteenth-century food shortages (Baten, Crayen and Voth 2014), yellow fever (Saavedra 2017), and the Black Death (Jedwab, Johnson, and Koyama 2022) affected human capital and health outcomes.

Geographic and Spatial Data

Geographic and spatial data exploit the geographic location of information. Many types of data can be associated with a specific location, mapped, and then analyzed, and scholars are collecting data to employ spatial econometric models to study political or economic phenomena (see Whitten et al. 2021 for a review). This might take the form of natural data, such as regarding agricultural suitability, elevation, natural resources, mountains, or rivers. It also could be data on cities, borders, or nation states; trade routes, railroads, or churches; or polling places, protests, or radio stations. All historical data could be spatial data, though our ability to precisely geocode information in time and space depends on the archival material available.

Maps and atlases are important sources of historical data in this category. One of the largest resources for historical maps and atlases is the Library of Congress's Geography and Maps collection (both physical and digital collections; see https://www.loc.gov/rr/geogmap/). Many maps are also in the public domain and can be found online via various websites created by academic or private initiatives (for example, https://www.oldmapsonline.org). While we primarily consider maps as a source of political or natural boundaries and features, other kinds of historical maps can provide quantitative information. One example is the Sanborn Fire Insurance Maps, which are atlases that provided detailed rendering of US cities and neighborhoods in the eighteenth and nineteenth centuries and that were used to help insurance companies assess risk. These maps document building materials and infrastructure, property lines and land use restrictions, public good provision data (sprinkler systems, fire hydrants, gas and water mains), other elements of the city (e.g., schools), and how urban geography has changed over time.

Maps are convenient because they are a standalone resource, but spatial data can also be reconstructed from a variety of sources. For example, Blaydes and Paik (2016) created a spatial dataset combining the geolocational origins of Crusaders and medieval cathedrals' construction across Europe, taking information from a number of primary source accounts and projecting this data onto historical maps from the time. In another example, Abramson (2017) created a new dataset on all political units in Europe between 1100 and 1790 by manually georeferencing several sets of historical maps and combining secondary and primary cartographic sources to verify the coding of units.

Geographic information systems (GIS) can also help input, analyze, and map this type of spatial data, and a number of GIS tools can be applied to historical datasets (Giuliano and Matranga 2021). The number of dedicated GIS resources are also increasing. Spatial data for the United States since 1790 can be found using the National Historical Geographic Information System (NHGIS), and similarly the International Historical Geographic Information System (IHGIS) provides shape files and boundaries for administrative and statistical units for countries around the world (though this data is more recent; see https://www.nhgis.org and https://ihgis.ipums.org, respectively). These new technologies, combined with advances in the field of digital humanities (Crompten et al. 2016), are an important frontier for historical spatial data.

Political Data

Political data relate to information on leaders, governments, and political institutions; this could be data on representative assemblies or predemocratic governing bodies, data on governance under nondemocratic monarchs or autocrats, or measures of political participation (such as voter turnout or suffrage). Political data from recent centuries have been compiled from official state records, while data further back is typically a composite of records, historical narratives, and primary sources.

Many resources document rulers and succession patterns throughout history. Data on world leaders and their successions are readily available, both cross nationally and sometimes dating back to before AD 1000 (Blaydes and Chaney 2013; Kokkonen and Sundell 2020; Kokkonen and Møller 2020; Jones and Olken 2005; Goemans, Gleditsch, and Chiozza 2009). Scholars have used historical data on leadership to study the effect of queenly rule on going to war (Dube and Harish 2020), the effect of the national leader on economic growth (Jones and Olken 2005; Acharya and Lee 2019), or regime transitions (Goemans, Gleditsch, and Chiozza 2009).

There is also a large literature on early governing bodies—their emergence, evolution, and relationship with modern political institutions today (Stasavage 2010; Van Zanden et al. 2012, Angelucci et al. 2022, among many others). For example, Abramson and Boix (2019) and Kokkonen and Møller (2020) have documented the emergence of political bodies in Europe over the centuries. These scholars help to catalog the existence of parliaments, local councils, territorial assemblies, or other early legislative or executive bodies, as well as their relationships with monarchs between 1000 and 1900. Other studies focus on the existence of various institutions of self-governance under autocratic or predemocratic regimes; for example, Dower et al. (2018) collected data on peasant representation in local assemblies called zemstvo in Imperial Russia under Tsar Alexander II, and Charnysh and Ziblatt (2022) and Mares (2015) studied citizen experience with elections in pre-democratic Imperial Germany.

Data on elections and political parties are also comprehensive, from about the eighteenth century onward. The Constituency-Level Elections Archive (CLEA) has constituency and party data for the lower and upper chambers of legislative bodies around the world, with data beginning as far back as 1788 (https://electiondataarchive.org). ParlGov, a cross-national database for parliaments and governments since 1945, is also currently expanding to include pre–World War II data (see http://www.parlgov.org). The cross-national Varieties of Democracy (V-Dem) dataset is a comprehensive set of indicators measuring democracy and aspects of democratic institutions, including elections, political parties, executive and legislative institutions, as well as civil society and the media. Historical V-Dem extends these indicators back to 1789, for eighty polities across the world. Historical election returns by country can also be found using data repositories in the social sciences, such as Inter-university Consortium for Political and Social Research (ICSPR) or the Harvard Dataverse. There's even a comprehensive dataset on the origins, tenure, and characteristics of autocratic ruling parties since 1940 (Miller 2020).

Roll call votes are another key source of data when studying legislative politics, and this field was defined in research on the US Congress by Keith T. Poole and Howard Rosenthal. They created a multidimensional scaling technique to determine legislator ideal points called NOMINATE (and iterations such as DW-NOMINATE, etc.). Subsequent work has resulted in the analysis of over thirteen million individual roll call votes in the United States (Rosenthal 2007 Poole 2005), and a comprehensive dataset and website called VoteView that contains every Congressional roll call vote in American history (see Voteview.com). Scholars have now extended spatial models of roll call voting and discussed their use in historical contexts (Clinton, Jackman, and Rivers 2004; Caughey and Schickler 2016; Bateman and Lapinski 2016; Jenkins and Sala 1998; Jenkins and Nokken 2000; Jenkins and Stewart 2013) as well as applied them to countries around the world (for example, Lupu 2015; Bräuninger, Müller, and Steckler 2016; Hix and Noury 2016, among others). Scholars have also created other ideological measures and datasets for other political bodies; for example, one can access the dataset of ideal point "Martin-Quinn" measures for every US Supreme Court justice since 1937

(Martin and Quinn 2002, or see https://mqscores.lsa.umich.edu), or a dataset of roll call votes in the UN General Assembly from 1946 to 2021 (Voeten et al. 2009).

There is also a large body of scholarship using parliamentary data from the nineteenth and twentieth centuries, digitizing the text of legislative speeches, roll call votes, committee assignments, and ministerial appointments (see Cirone 2020 for a review of the HPE of parliaments). Some examples include Victorian Britain (Cox 1987; Eggers and Spirling 2014; Kam 2014), the French Third Republic (Cirone and van Coppenolle 2018), Weimar and post–World War II Germany (Sieberer et al. 2020; Hansen and Debus 2012; Hage 2019), nineteenth-century Canada (Godbout and Hoyland 2017), and the nineteenth-century United States (Jenkins, Peck, and Weaver 2010; Bateman et al. 2017; Gordon and Simpson 2020. The databases featured in such studies are usually available for public use.

Political participation data can be collected from a number of different sources. The most common measures of participation are suffrage[2] and voter turnout, and many scholars have collected data on which individuals can vote when, over the course of democratic development. Notable research looks at suffrage expansion, turnout, and the presence of voting restrictions in Europe (Berlinski and Dewan 2011; Berlinski, Dewan, and van Coppenolle 2014; Kam 2014; Kam 2017; Aidt and Jensen 2009; Amat et al. 2020) or the United States (Miller 2008; Teele 2018; Bateman 2018; Gray and Jenkins 2022; Williams 2022). Political participation under no or limited suffrage can be measured in alternative ways, such as using data on petitions (statements of grievances with signatures, submitted to the government). Carpenter (2021) collected a comprehensive dataset on petitions in the United States from 1790 to 1870 in the United States, offering a way to measure political participation for women and men excluded from other types of democratic participation.

Finally, there are many sources for data on political culture, or the relationship between the individual and the state. This often takes the shape of event data—on protests, violence, strikes, and repression—collected from primary source accounts or newspapers. For example, the Dynamics of Collective Action dataset records demonstrations of collective action in the United States from 1960 to 1965 during the civil rights movement and Mazumder (2018) uses this data to study how historical civil rights protest activity affects modern racial attitudes. For an earlier period of the United States, García-Jimeno, Iglesias, and Yildirim (2022) used newspaper-based data on antiliquor protests by the Women's Temperance Crusade in 1873. Geloso and Kufenko (2019) created a database that matched census data with rebellious event data to explain the 1837–38 rebellion of the British colonies of Upper and Lower Canada. Aidt et al. (2022) collected social unrest events as part of the English Swing riots of 1830–31. Arnon, McAlexander, and Rubin (2023) look at civilian agency under conflict and collect data on citizen evacuation and forced displacement by combining historical accounts from archives and contemporary surveys of Arab Palestinian villages conducted during the early 1940s. The range of scholarship using event data is vast, and many future historical datasets could fall under this banner.

Economic Data

Economic data contain information relating to economic growth or economic development, and historical economic data (and corresponding proxies for missing data) are plentiful. Luckily for those looking for data, historical economics has long been a robust academic area of inquiry. The recent *Handbook of Historical Economics* (Bisin and Giovanni 2021) provides an excellent overview of the field, as well as the many sources of data; notably the chapter on economic data (Giuliano and Matranga 2021) provides a useful review. Recent books on global historical wealth and growth (Piketty 2014; Pietty and Saez 2013; Rubin and Koyama 2022; Hamilton and Hepburn 2017) also demonstrate the vast quantities of time-series, cross-sectional data available.

There are many existing datasets relating to economic history—on stock prices, global financial data, labor statistics, import and export data, public debt, bonds, and countless other variables too many to list—but fortunately they are easily found and accessible by researchers. Notable examples include the International Monetary Fund's Historical Public Debt database (see https://www.imf.org/external/datamapper/datasets/DEBT), which provides data on GDP and government debt from 1800 onward or the NBER Macrohistory database (https://www.nber.org/research/data/nber-macrohistory-database), which takes a more expansive view and provides data on all aspects of a nation's economy (adding variables like employment, trade, and government capacity to data on money, prices, and assets). The Economic History Association also provides a convenient listing of historical datasets (https://eh.net/databases/).

It's worth noting that agricultural and geographic data are also relevant to historical studies of economic outcomes. The Food and Agriculture Organization's Global Agro-Ecological Zones dataset (GAEZ) (Fischer et al. 2002) provides time series data on land and water resources, agro-climatic resources, crop suitability, and production data for a wide range of countries. Scholars have used this data to create measures of caloric viability or caloric potential, from medieval periods to today, as in the cases of Ahmed and Stasavage (2020) or Huning and Wahl (2016). However, agricultural data are going to be country-specific; many countries also have agricultural censuses or other forms of internal data. The United States is a good example in that it has collected detailed data on farms, income, expenditures, and other factors from 1840 onward in a publicly accessible archive. Rubin and Koyama (2022) engage with a variety of empirical data to discuss to what extent climate, soil, access to coasts, disease environments, and mountains have affected global economic growth. Agricultural and natural resource suitability can be measured far back in time and often provide a proxy for economic capacity.

Detailed data on global trade has been preserved throughout the centuries, and scholars have used trade data to study a broad range of economic and political development outcomes. The Bilateral Trade Historical Series 1827-2014 is a useful general resource (Fouquin and Hugot 2016), while articles on specific cases can also provide insight into the type of data available. For example, Gaikwad (2014) uses original archival data to study the effects of trading hubs built in India by the various European East India Companies in the sixteenth to eighteenth centuries, while Jia (2014) analyzes the economic development of colonial treaty ports in China, and Arteaga, Desierto, and Koyama (2020) look at Spain's monopoly of trade routes to Manila for 250 years. Pascali (2017) even exploits the invention of the steamship to study the effects of trade globalization, using a unique dataset on shipping times, trade, and development from 1850 to 1900. A number of papers also use detailed historical shipping data on the volume and prevalence of the African slave trade to study the momentous impacts it had on economic and political development (e.g., Nunn 2008; Nunn and Wantchekon 2011; Gershman 2020; Acharya, Blackwell, and Sen 2016, among others).

Ethnographic Data

Cultural and ethnographic data present information about human societies, and substantial data collection in this category focuses on identifying the types or locations of preindustrial ethnic groups. This type of data also often includes information on cultural practices and traits. Data availability varies; depending on the group and region—and the presence or absence of written record-keeping cultures—specific details of many groups' practices have been lost to history. The data we do have are often assembled by relying on the accounts of contemporary sociologists, historians, explorers, or others with knowledge of the group.

Existing work is grounded in a number of canonical datasets—namely, the Ethnographic Atlas and the Murdock ethnic group boundary map (Murdock 1959; Murdock 1967), as well as the related Standard Cross Cultural Survey (Murdock and White 1969). The original datasets provided ancestral data on the economic, cultural, political, and environmental characteristics of 1,265 ethnic groups, as well as approximate historical geographic boundaries. The range of variables collected is impressive; over one hundred variables track economic subsistence, types of dwellings, political organization and religion, language, marriage practices, and location. More recent work has critiqued or extended this data by adding several ethnicities, reducing measurement error, challenging boundary measures, or arguing for alternative coding (Wig 2016; Paine 2019; Bahrami-Rad, Becker, and Henrich 2021). A relevant and notable dataset descending from this work is the Ancestral Characteristics Database (Giuliano and Nunn 2018).

Related data sources include but are not limited to the Ethnic Power Relations Dataset family, which provides data on ethnic groups' access to state power, transitional ethnic connections, and interethnic cleavages from 1946 onward (Vogt et al. 2015); the Ethnologue, which tracks global world languages (Gordon 2005); and the Seshat Global History Databank, which focuses on the social and political organization of human societies. Other large-scale data initiatives exist to combine and extend access to ethnographic data. One example is the Linking Ethnic Data from Africa (LEDA) Project, which combines eleven prominent datasets on ethnic groups in Africa to the Ethnologue database (Müller-Crepon, Schvitz, and Cederman 2022; Müller-Crepon, Pengl, and Bormann 2021). Another is the Spatially Interpolated Data on Ethnicity (SIDE) dataset, a collection and GIS resource of 253 near-continuous maps of local ethno-linguistic, religious, and ethno-religious settlement patterns (Müller-Crepon and Hunziker 2018).

Ethnographic data are used to study a range of topics in both political science and economics (for an excellent review, see Lowes 2021). Alesina, Giuliano, and Nunn (2013) and Becker (2019) used this data to study if traditional agricultural practices can explain the historical persistence of gender norms and restrictions on women's sexuality. Wig (2016) and Paine (2019) study ethnic violence in Africa, as a function of pre- and postcolonial traditional institutions, while Baldwin and Ricard-Huguet (2022) look at the relationship between land quality and leaders. Müller-Crepon et al. (2022) use spatial data on European ethnic geography from 1887 to study modern patterns of nationalism. It's worth noting that cultural data can also provide insight into the development of premodern political institutions and political organization, as studied by Ahmed and Stasavage (2020). Scholars interested in ethnographic data should also note and respect the interdisciplinary nature of these datasets, pulling from fields like sociology and archaeology in addition to political science, history, and economics.

Civil Society Data

Civil society data contain information relating to associations or organizations that largely exist outside the state, family, or market. This typically includes a wide variety of voluntary associations, including nonprofit groups, organized religions, professional associations, cultural or ethnic organizations, or philanthropic groups, among others. In this section I also discuss educational data (though this could also be classified with state records). Historical data on these groups can range from archival records and group activities or membership lists to descriptions from contemporary accounts or newspapers. Interested scholars can consult the large literature on social capital (Putnam 1995), which is characterized by collecting unique historical data on social clubs and associations (e.g., Guiso, Sapienza, and Zingales 2016; Padró I Miquel et al. 2015; Satyanath, Voigtländer, and Voth 2017; Montolio and Tur-Prats 2018; Bozcaga and Cansunar 2021). In the interest of space, I focus here on two different types of civil society data: data on education and data on religion.

Education data provide information about educational institutions and facilities, student enrollment and attainment, and teachers and staffing, from early childhood to adult. It's worth noting that widespread formal education is a more recent phenomenon in human history. While it's possible to get centuries-old data on schooling, such as data on medieval universities (Cantoni and Yuchtman 2014), data from far back in time often instead focuses on the collection of variables like literacy or access to printed materials. Dittmar (2011) exploits the introduction of the printing press to show how access to printed materials affected European cultural and economic development, and Pengl, Roessler, and Rueda (2022) use data on the prevalence of printing technologies and publications in Africa from the 1920s.

Much of the historical data on education focuses on the expansion of mass schooling and primary school enrollments in the past two centuries (Ansell and Lindvall 2013, Go and Lindert 2010). For example, Lee and Lee (2016) assembled country-level data on primary school enrollment rates as a proportion of the school-age population for 111 countries from 1820 to 2010, as well as data on secondary and tertiary enrollment rates. Paglayan (2021) extends this data, to add school enrollment for additional countries in Europe and Latin America, as well as data on the years when central government began to regulate the provision of primary education. In terms of the transition to mass secondary schooling, Goldin and Katz (2011) use micro-data on educational attainment from US censuses to study the expansion of secondary education and the building of high schools, and Bandiera et al. (2019) similarly use enrollment rates for five- to fourteen-year-olds from 1830 through 1890 for the United States.

Data on educational spending and educational facilities is also a potential resource, as shown by Ansell's comprehensive study of education policy over country and over time (2010). Others have studied specific cases, such as Aaronson and Mazumder (2011), who analyzes the socioeconomic impact of the Rosenwald School initiative in the early twentieth century, which constructed five thousand schools for Black children in the US South. In another example, Gao (2018) used data on public primary schools and expenditure on education to chart the rise of mass schooling in China in the early twentieth century. Karger (2021) even maps library construction grants to census data to estimate the effect of proximate library access from 1900 to 1940 on children's later occupation and educational outcomes.

Organized religion is another important source of historical data (Kuran 2012; Gryzmala Busse 2020; Becker, Rubin, and Woessmann 2021). Religious institutions can provide individual-level information on church organization and staffing, attendees and members, local associations, or charitable activity; organized religions were also notable for keeping extensive economic and social records. Data on missionary activity is also a valuable resource, and sometimes religious outposts collected information for areas that might not have records otherwise. I discuss each of these in turn.

Substantial data are available on the organized religions, even for earlier periods. The Database of Religious History (https://religiondatabase.org) serves as a centralized database for group-level data on religion around the world. Scholars have also collected extensive data on religious institutions over the past millennia. Gryzmala-Busse (2023) conducts a comprehensive study of the powerful role of the Catholic Church in the medieval era (1100–1350), collecting new data on papal conflict and early state fragmentation in Europe, as well as noting that the church provided institutional templates to rulers for administration, taxation, and record keeping. Rubin (2017) compares and contrasts the role of Christianity and Islam in technological and economic advancements (loans, printing presses, and commercial policy) that later led to the rise of the West. Chaney (2013) uses data collected on religious authorities in Egypt, from the start of the Ayyubid dynasty in 1169. Cansunar and Kuran (2020) gathered detailed financial and investment data via Islamic trusts from the late Ottoman Empire.

Other notable sources of religious data come from more recent periods. There is a large literature on the Protestant Reformation and its socioeconomic consequences (e.g., Cantoni, Dittmar, and Yuchtman 2018; Dittmar and Meisenzahl 2020; Becker and Woessmann 2009; Spenkuch and Tillmann 2018; Becker, Pfaff, and Rubin 2016). Organized religion played a role in communist infiltration in World War II (Nalepa and Pop-Eleches 2022). Missionaries are also a rich source of data. For example, Dulay (2022) uses detailed data on the presence of Catholic religious missions in the 1900s in the Philippines to study how missionary activity affects state-building. Similar papers use missionary data from countries in Africa (e.g., Wantchekon, Klašnja, and Novta 2014, China (Bai and Kung 2015), and Mexico (Waldinger 2017), or comparatively (Valencia Caicedo 2019).

Since population surveys on religiosity or religious participation are not available for the premodern period, scholars also use creative historical data to measure religion. Andersen and Bentzen (2022) use given names to construct a novel proxy for average religiosity, in a sample of 450,000 European-based authors born between 1300 and 1940 and another sample of 50,000 university students born in the Holy Roman Empire from 1300 to 1550; the authors use this to study human capital formation and economic growth over time. Blaydes, Grimmer, and McQueen (2018) study the texts of advice manuals from medieval Muslim and Christian polities, documenting the rise and fall of religious discourse. Malik and Mirza (2021) study the impact of religious leaders on long-run development in Pakistan by compiling a dataset on historically significant shrines from colonial-era gazetteers in the nineteenth century. Chen et al. (2022) show that Confucian clans maintained for two millennia affected the growth of financial markets in China, using data on location of Confucian academies and banking data in the nineteenth century. Such studies good examples of creativity in collecting historical data.

Conclusion

The collection of historical data is not for the faint of heart. It goes without saying that historical data are generally more detailed, accurate, and available in recent periods, opposed to past periods. Historical data also tend to be disproportionately found in countries that were stable enough, rich enough, and capable of collecting, storing, and preserving records. Working with historical data can also present numerous other challenges—selection bias, missing data, time decay, and confirmation bias must all be considered during historical data collection (Cirone and Spirling 2021 Kim 2022), and these apply to all categories of data discussed here.

Still, sources of historical data abound, and this chapter has provided a brief survey of data types often used in historical political economy—sociodemographic and population data, government or institutional records, geographic and spatial data, political data, economic data, ethnographic data, and civil society data. Going forward, the sky is the limit. Researchers in HPE are collecting and sharing data across disciplines, and discussions about historical data on interdisciplinary blogs for HPE such as Broadstreet. Blog only serve to help in this collective endeavor. Hopefully the resources and articles listed here, and generally throughout this handbook, can not only provide interested scholars with a way to access the historical data they need, but serve as examples of comprehensive research that engages with the specific challenges that come when using this type of data.

Notes

1. Interested readers can also consult James Feigenbaum's chapter in this volume on health in historical political economy.
2. Readers should also consult W. Walker Hanlon's chapter on suffrage in this volume.

References

Aaronson, Daniel, and Bhashkar Mazumder. 2011. "The Impact of Rosenwald Schools on Black Achievement." *Journal of Political Economy* 119, no. 5: 821–88. https://doi.org/10.1086/662962.

Abramitzky, Ran, and Leah Boustan. 2022. Streets of Gold: America's Untold Story of Immigrant Success. PublicAffairs.

Abramitzky, Ran, Leah Boustan, Katherine Eriksson, James Feigenbaum, and Santiago Pérez. 2021. "Automated Linking of Historical Data." *Journal of Economic Literature* 59, no. 3: 865–918.

Abramson, Scott F. 2017. "The Economic Origins of the Territorial State." *International Organization* 71, no. 1: 97–130.https://doi.org/10.1017/S0020818316000308.

Abramson, Scott F., and Carles Boix. 2019. "Endogenous Parliaments: The Domestic and International Roots of Long-Term Economic Growth and Executive Constraints in Europe." *International Organization* 73, no. 4: 793–837. https://doi.org/10.1017/S00208 18319000286.

Acemoglu, Daron, Davide Cantoni, Simon Johnson, and James A. Robinson. 2011. "The Consequences of Radical Reform: The French Revolution." *American Economic Review* 101, no. 7 (December): 3286–307.https://doi.org/10.1257/aer.101.7.3286.

Acharya, Avidit, Matthew Blackwell, and Maya Sen. 2016. "The Political Legacy of American Slavery." *Journal of Politics* 78, no. 3 (July): 621–41. https://doi.org/10.1086/686631.

Acharya, Avidit, and Alexander Lee. 2019. "Path Dependence in European Development: Medieval Politics, Conflict, and State Building." *Comparative Political Studies* 52, no. 13–14 (November 1): 2171–206. https://doi.org/10.1177/0010414019830716.

Ahmed, Ali T., and David Stasavage. 2020. "Origins of Early Democracy." *American Political Science Review* 114, no. 2 (May): 502–18. https://doi.org/10.1017/S0003055419000741.

Aidt, Toke, Gabriel Leon-Ablan, and Max Satchell. 2022. "The Social Dynamics of Collective Action: Evidence from the Diffusion of the Swing Riots, 1830–1831." *Journal of Politics* 84, no. 1 (January): 209–25. https://doi.org/10.1086/714784.

Aidt, Toke S., and Peter S. Jensen. 2009. "Tax Structure, Size of Government, and the Extension of the Voting Franchise in Western Europe, 1860–1938." *International Tax and Public Finance* 16, no. 3 (June 1): 362–94. https://doi.org/10.1007/s10797-008-9069-9.

Alesina, Alberto, Paola Giuliano, and Nathan Nunn. 2013. "On the Origins of Gender Roles: Women and the Plough." *Quarterly Journal of Economics* 128, no. 2 (May 1): 469–530. https://doi.org/10.1093/qje/qjt005.

Almond, Douglas. 2006. "Is the 1918 Influenza Pandemic Over? Long-Term Effects of In Utero Influenza Exposure in the Post-1940 U.S. Population." *Journal of Political Economy* 114, no. 4: 672–712. https://doi.org/10.1086/507154.

Amat, Francesc, Carles Boix, Jordi Muñoz, and Toni Rodon. 2020. "From Political Mobilization to Electoral Participation: Turnout in Barcelona in the 1930s." *Journal of Politics* 82, no. 4 (October): 1559–75.https://doi.org/10.1086/708684.

Andersen, Lars Harhoff, and Jeanet Bentzen. 2022. "In the Name of God! Religiosity and the Transition to Modern Growth." SSRN Scholarly Paper. Rochester, NY: Social Science Research Network, January 1. https://papers.ssrn.com/abstract=4026842.

Angelucci, Charles, Simone Meraglia, and Nico Voigtländer. 2022. "How Merchant Towns Shaped Parliaments: From the Norman Conquest of England to the Great Reform Act." *American Economic Review* 112, no. 10: 3441–87.

Ansell, Ben W., ed. 2010. *From the Ballot to the Blackboard: The Redistributive Political Economy of Education*. Cambridge Studies in Comparative Politics. Cambridge: Cambridge University Press. https://doi.org/10.1017/CBO9780511730108.004.

Ansell, Ben, and Johannes Lindvall. 2013. "The Political Origins of Primary Education Systems: Ideology, Institutions, and Interdenominational Conflict in an Era of Nation-Building." *American Political Science Review* 107, no. 3 (August): 505–22. https://doi.org/10.1017/S0003055413000257.

Ansell, Ben W., and Johannes Lindvall. 2020. *Inward Conquest: The Political Origins of Modern Public Services*. Cambridge Studies in Comparative Politics. Cambridge: Cambridge University Press, 2020. https://doi.org/10.1017/9781108178440.

Arroyo Abad, Leticia, and Noel Maurer. 2021. "Do Pandemics Shape Elections? Retrospective Voting in the 1918 Spanish Flu Pandemic in the United States." Technical report, CEPR Discussion Paper No. DP15678.

Arnon, Daniel, Richard McAlexander, and Michael Rubin. 2023. "Social Cohesion and Community Displacement in Armed Conflict: Evidence from Palestinian Villages in the 1948 War." APSA Preprints. doi: 10.33774/apsa-2020-8cotn-v6. This content is a preprint and has not been peer-reviewed.

Arteaga, Fernando, Desiree Desierto, and Mark Koyama. 2020. "Shipwrecked by Rents." CEPR Discussion Paper No. DP15300.

Bahrami-Rad, Duman, Anke Becker, and Joseph. Henrich. 2021. "Tabulated Nonsense? Testing the Validity of the Ethnographic Atlas and the Persistence of Culture." *Economics Letters* 204.

Bai, Ying, and James Kai-sing Kung. 2015. "Diffusing Knowledge While Spreading God's Message: Protestantism and Economic Prosperity in China, 1840–1920." *Journal of the European Economic Association* 13, no. 4: 669–98. https://doi.org/10.1111/jeea.12113.

Baldwin, Kate, and Joan Ricart-Huguet. 2022. "Does Land Quality Increase the Power of Traditional Leaders in Contemporary Africa?" SSRN Scholarly Paper. Rochester, NY: Social Science Research Network, March 4. https://doi.org/10.2139/ssrn.3834837.

Bandiera, Oriana, Myra Mohnen, Imran Rasul, and Martina Viarengo. 2019. "Nation-Building through Compulsory Schooling during the Age of Mass Migration." *Economic Journal* 129, no. 617 (January 1): 62–109. https://doi.org/10.1111/ecoj.12624.

Banerjee, Abhijit, Esther Duflo, Gilles Postel-Vinay, and Tim Watts. 2010. "Long-Run Health Impacts of Income Shocks: Wine and Phylloxera in Nineteenth-Century France." *Review of Economics and Statistics* 92, no. 4 (November 1): 714–28. https://doi.org/10.1162/REST_a_00024.

Bateman, David A. 2018. *Disenfranchising Democracy*. Cambridge University Press. https://www.cambridge.org/core/books/disenfranchising-democracy/CEC53B21976CC3E3F17D2E585257320E.

Bateman, David A., Joshua D. Clinton, and John S. Lapinski. 2017. "A House Divided? Roll Calls, Polarization, and Policy Differences in the U.S. House, 1877–2011." *American Journal of Political Science* 61, no. 3: 698–714. https://doi.org/10.1111/ajps.12281.

Bateman, D., and J. Lapinski. 2016. "Ideal Points and American Political Development: Beyond DW-NOMINATE." *Studies in American Political Development* 30, no. 2: 147–71. https://doi.org/10.1017/S0898588X16000080.

Baten, Jörg, Dorothee Crayen, and Hans-Joachim Voth. 2014. "Numeracy and the Impact of High Food Prices in Industrializing Britain, 1780–1850." *Review of Economics and Statistics* 96, no. 3 (July 1): 418–30. https://doi.org/10.1162/REST_a_00403.

Bazzi, Samuel, Martin Fiszbein, and Mesay Gebresilasse. 2020. "Frontier Culture: The Roots and Persistence of 'Rugged Individualism' in the United States." *Econometrica* 88, no. 6: 2329–68. https://doi.org/10.3982/ECTA16484.

Becker, Anke. 2019. "On the Economic Origins of Restrictions on Women's Sexuality." EconStor. https://www.econstor.eu/bitstream/10419/201996/1/cesifo1_wp7770.pdf.

Becker, Sascha O., and Luigi Pascali. 2019. "Religion, Division of Labor, and Conflict: Anti-Semitism in Germany over 600 Years." *American Economic Review* 109, no. 5: 1764–804. https://doi.org/10.1257/aer.20170279.

Becker, Sasha O., Steven Pfaff, and Jared Rubin. 2016. "Causes and Consequences of the Protestant Reformation." *Explorations in Economic History* 62: 1–25.

Becker, Sascha O., Jared Rubin, and Ludger Woessmann. 2021. "Religion in Economic History: A Survey." In *Handbook of Historical Economics*, ed. Alberto Bisin and Giovanni Federico, 585–639. London: Elsevier.

Becker, Sascha O., and Ludger Woessmann. 2009. "Was Weber Wrong? A Human Capital Theory of Protestant Economic History*." *Quarterly Journal of Economics* 124, no. 2 (May 1): 531–96. https://doi.org/10.1162/qjec.2009.124.2.531.

Berlinski, Samuel, and Torun Dewan. 2011. "The Political Consequences of Franchise Extension: Evidence from the Second Reform Act." *Quarterly Journal of Political Science* 6, no. 3–4 (November 15): 329–76. https://doi.org/10.1561/100.00011013.

Berlinski, Samuel, Torun Dewan, and Brenda Van Coppenolle. 2014. "Franchise Extension." *Legislative Studies Quarterly* 39: 531–58. https://doi.org/10.1111/lsq.12057.

Bisin, Alberto, and Federico Giovanni. 2021. *The Handbook of Historical Economics*. Edited by Alberto Bisin and Giovanni Federico. London: Elsevier Press. https://www.elsevier.com/books/the-handbook-of-historical-economics/bisin/978-0-12-815874-6.

Blaydes, Lisa, and Eric Chaney. 2013. "The Feudal Revolution and Europe's Rise: Political Divergence of the Christian West and the Muslim World before 1500 CE." *American Political Science Review* 107, no. 1 (February): 16–34. https://doi.org/10.1017/S0003055412000561.

Blaydes, Lisa, Justin Grimmer, and Alison McQueen. 2018. "Mirrors for Princes and Sultans: Advice on the Art of Governance in the Medieval Christian and Islamic Worlds." *Journal of Politics* 80, no. 4 (October): 1150–67. https://doi.org/10.1086/699246.

Blaydes, Lisa, and Christopher Paik. 2016. "The Impact of Holy Land Crusades on State Formation: War Mobilization, Trade Integration, and Political Development in Medieval Europe." *International Organization* 70, no. 3: 551–86.

Bolt, Jutta, Leigh Gardner, Jennifer Kohler, James A. Robinson, and Jack Paine. 2021. "Political Constraints in British Africa: Quantitative Evidence from Native Authority Institutions." Becker_Friedman Institute Working Paper Series, Working Paper No. 2022-146. https://bfi.uchicago.edu/wp-content/uploads/2022/10/BFI_WP_2022-146.pdf.

Bozcaga, Tugba, and Asli Cansunar. 2021. "The Unintended Consequences of Nation-Making Institutions for Civil Society Development." *Journal of Historical Political Economy* 1, no. 4 (November 30): 591–613. https://doi.org/10.1561/115.00000021.

Braun, Robert. 2022. "Blood Lines." Unpublished manuscript. https://broadstreet.blog/2021/07/09/borderlands-and-antisemitism-in-weimar-germany-evidence-from-childrens-stories/.

Bräuninger, T., J. Müller, and C. Stecker. 2016. "Modeling Preferences Using Roll Call Votes in Parliamentary Systems." *Political Analysis* 24, no. 2: 189–210.

https://www.sciencegate.app/app/redirect#aHR0cHM6Ly9keC5kb2kub3JnLzEwLjEwOTMvcGFuLzIwdzAwNg==.

Burchardi, Konrad B., and Tarek A. Hassan. 2013. "The Economic Impact of Social Ties: Evidence from German Reunification*." *Quarterly Journal of Economics* 128, no. 3 (August 1): 1219–71. https://doi.org/10.1093/qje/qjt009.

Campbell, Cameron, and James Lee. 2020. "Historical Chinese Microdata. 40 Years of Dataset Construction by the Lee-Campbell Research Group." *Historical Life Course Studies* 9: 130–57. https://doi.org/10.51964/hlcs9303

Cansunar, Asli, and Timur Kuran. 2020. "Economic Harbingers of Political Modernization: Peaceful Explosion of Rights in Ottoman Istanbul." December 13. Economic Research Initiatives at Duke (ERID) Working Paper No. 288, revised December 2020. https://ssrn.com/abstract=3434656.

Cantoni, Davide, Jeremiah Dittmar, and Noam Yuchtman. 2018. "Religious Competition and Reallocation: The Political Economy of Secularization in the Protestant Reformation*." *Quarterly Journal of Economics* 133, no. 4 (November 1): 2037–96. https://doi.org/10.1093/qje/qjy011.

Cantoni, Davide, and Noam Yuchtman. 2014. "Medieval Universities, Legal Institutions, and the Commercial Revolution." *Quarterly Journal of Economics* 129, no. 2 (May 1): 823–87.https://doi.org/10.1093/qje/qju007.

Carpenter, Dan. 2021. *Democracy by Petition: Popular Politics in Transformation, 1790–1870*. Cambridge, MA: Harvard University Press.

Caughey, D., and E. Schickler. 2016. "Substance and Change in Congressional Ideology: NOMINATE and Its Alternatives." *Studies in American Political Development* 30, no. 2: 128–46. https://doi.org/10.1017/S0898588X16000092.

Chacón, Mario L., and Jeffrey L. Jensen. 2020. "Democratization, De Facto Power, and Taxation: Evidence from Military Occupation during Reconstruction." *World Politics* 72, no. 1 (January): 1–46. https://doi.org/10.1017/S0043887119000157.

Chambru, Cédric, Emeric Henry, and Benjamin Marx. 2022. "The Dynamic Consequences of State-Building: Evidence from the French Revolution." Centre for Economic Policy Research. https://cepr.org/active/publications/discussion_papers/dp.php?dpno=16815.

Chaney, Eric. 2013. "Revolt on the Nile: Economic Shocks, Religion, and Political Power." *Econometrica* 81, no. 5: 2033–53.

Charnysh, Volha. 2019. "Diversity, Institutions, and Economic Outcomes: Post-WWII Displacement in Poland." *American Political Science Review* 113, no. 2 (May): 423–41. https://doi.org/10.1017/S0003055419000042.

Charnysh, Volha and Daniel Ziblatt. 2022. Working Paper. Consequences of Competition Under Autocracy: From Imperial to Weimar Germany. http://charnysh.net/documents/Charnysh_Ziblatt_Competition.pdf.

Chen, Zhiwu, Chicheng Ma, and Andrew J. Sinclair. 2022. "Banking on the Confucian Clan: Why China Developed Financial Markets So Late." *Economic Journal* (October 7): https://doi.org/10.1093/ej/ueab082.

Cirone, Alexandra. 2020. "Historical Political Economy of Parliaments." In *Handbook of Parliamentary Studies*, ed. Cyril Benoît and Olivier Rozenberg. Edgar Elger Publishing. https://www.elgaronline.com/view/edcoll/9781789906509/9781789906509.00029.xml.

Cirone, Alexandra, and Brenda Van Coppenolle. 2018. "Cabinets, Committees, and Careers: The Causal Effect of Committee Service." *Journal of Politics* 80, no. 3 (July): 948–63. https://doi.org/10.1086/697252.

Cirone, Alexandra, and Arthur Spirling. 2021. "Turning History into Data: Data Collection, Measurement, and Inference in HPE," *Journal of Historical Political Economy* 1, no. 1: 127–54. http://dx.doi.org/10.1561/115.00000005.

Clemens, Michael A. 2020. "The Emigration Life Cycle: How Development Shapes Emigration from Poor Countries." IZA Institute of Labor Economics. Discussion Paper Series, IZA DP Bo. 13614. https://www.iza.org/publications/dp/13614/the-emigration-life-cycle-how-development-shapes-emigration-from-poor-countries.

Clinton, J., S. Jackman, and D. Rivers. 2004. "The Statistical Analysis of Roll Call Data." *American Political Science Review* 98, no. 2: 355–70. https://doi.org/10.1017/S0003055404001194.

Cox, Gary. 1987. *The Efficient Secret: The Cabinet and the Development of Political Parties in Victorian England* (Political Economy of Institutions and Decisions). Cambridge: Cambridge University Press. 10.1017/CBO9780511571473.

Crompton, Constance, Richard J. Lane, and Ray Siemens. 2016. *Doing Digital Humanities Practice, Training, Research*. Routledge.

Dincecco, Mark, and Yuhua Wang. 2021. "Internal Conflict and State Development: Evidence from Imperial China." SSRN Scholarly Paper. Rochester, NY: Social Science Research Network. August 25. https://doi.org/10.2139/ssrn.3209556.

Dittmar, Jeremiah E. 2011. "Information Technology and Economic Change: The Impact of the Printing Press*." *Quarterly Journal of Economics* 126, no. 3 (August 1): 1133–72. https://doi.org/10.1093/qje/qjr035.

Dittmar, Jeremiah E., and Ralf R. Meisenzahl. 2020. "Public Goods Institutions, Human Capital, and Growth: Evidence from German History." *The Review of Economic Studies*, 87, no. 2 (March): 959–96. https://doi.org/10.1093/restud/rdz002.

Dower, Paul Castañeda, Evgeny Finkel, Scott Gehlbach, and Steven Nafziger. 2018. "Collective Action and Representation in Autocracies: Evidence from Russia's Great Reforms." *American Political Science Review* 112, no. 1 (February): 125–47. https://doi.org/10.1017/S0003055417000454.

Dube, Oeindrila, and S. P. Harish. 2020. "Queens." *Journal of Political Economy* 128, no. 7 (July): 2579–652. https://doi.org/10.1086/707011.

Dulay, Dean. 2022. "The Search for Spices and Souls: Catholic Missions as Colonial State in the Philippines." *Comparative Political Studies* (January 24): 00104140211066222. https://doi.org/10.1177/00104140211066222.

Eggers, Andrew C., and Arthur Spirling. 2014. "Ministerial Responsiveness in Westminster Systems: Institutional Choices and House of Commons Debate, 1832–1915." *American Journal of Political Science* 58, no. 4: 873–87. https://doi.org/10.1111/ajps.12090.

Feigenbaum, James, Andrew B. Hall, Daniel M. Thompson, and Jesse Yoder. 2022. "Who Becomes a Member of Congress? Evidence From De-Anonymized Census Data (No. w26156)." National Bureau of Economic Research https://jamesfeigenbaum.github.io/research/who-runs/.

Fischer, Günther, Harrij van Velthuizen, Mahendra Shah, and Freddy Nachtergaele, 2002. Global Agro-ecological Assessment for Agriculture in the 21 Century. IIASA Research Report. International Institute for Applied Systems Analysis, Laxenburg, Austria. https://gaez.fao.org.

Helgertz, Jonas, Joseph Price, Jacob Wellington, Kelly J. Thompson, Steven Ruggles, and Catherine A. Fitch. 2022. "A New Strategy for Linking U.S. Historical Censuses: A Case Study for the IPUMS Multigenerational Longitudinal Panel." *Historical Methods: A Journal of Quantitative and Interdisciplinary History* 55, no. 1: 12–29. 10.1080/01615440.2021.1985027.

Fouka, Vasiliki. 2020. "Backlash: The Unintended Effects of Language Prohibition in U.S. Schools after World War I." *Review of Economic Studies* 87, no. 1 (January 1): 204–39. https://doi.org/10.1093/restud/rdz024.

Fouquin, M., and J. Hugot. 2016. "Two Centuries of Bilateral Trade and Gravity Data: 1827–2014." CEPII Working Paper No. 2016-14.

Gaikwad, Nikhar. 2014. "East India Companies and Long Term Economic Change in India." Paper presented at the American Political Science Association. ncgg.princeton.edu/IPES/2014/papers/F1130_rm3.pdf.

Gao, Pei. 2018. "Risen from Chaos: The Development of Modern Education in China, 1905-1948." *Australian Economic History Review* 58: 187–192. https://doi.org/10.1111/aehr.12156.

García-Jimeno, Camilo, Angel Iglesias, and Pinar Yildirim. 2022. "Information Networks and Collective Action: Evidence from the Women's Temperance Crusade." *American Economic Review* 112, no. 1 (January): 41–80. https://doi.org/10.1257/aer.20180124.

Garfias, Francisco, and Emily Sellars. 2020. "Epidemics, Rent Extraction, and the Value of Holding Office." *Journal of Political Institutions and Political Economy* 1, no. 4: 559–83.

Garfias, Francisco, and Emily A. Sellars. 2022. "When State Building Backfires: Elite Coordination and Popular Grievance in Rebellion." *American Journal of Political Science* 66, no. 4 (October): 977–92. https://doi.org/10.1111/ajps.12611.

Geloso, Vincent, and Vadim Kufenko. 2019. "Can Markets Foster Rebellion? The Case of the 1837-38 Rebellions in Lower Canada." *Journal of Economic Behavior and Organization* 166 (October 1): 263–87. https://doi.org/10.1016/j.jebo.2019.06.005.

Geloso, Vincent J., Phillip Magness, John Moore, and Philip Schlosser. 2022. "How Pronounced Is the U-Curve? Revisiting Income Inequality in the United States, 1917–1960." *Economic Journal* 132, no. 647: 2366–91. https://doi.org/10.1093/ej/ueac020.

Gershman, Boris. 2020. "Witchcraft Beliefs as a Cultural Legacy of the Atlantic Slave Trade: Evidence from Two Continents." *European Economic Review* 122 (February 1): https://doi.org/10.1016/j.euroecorev.2019.103362.

Giuliano, Paola, and Andrea Matranga. 2021. "Historical Data: Where to Find Them, How to Use Them." In *The Handbook of Historical Economics*, ed. Alberto Bisin and Giovanni Federico, 95–123. Elsevier Press.

Giuliano, Paola, and Nathan Nunn. 2018. "Ancestral Characteristics of Modern Populations." *Economic History of Developing Regions* 33, no. 1 (January 2): 1–17. https://doi.org/10.1080/20780389.2018.1435267.

Go, Sun, and Peter Lindert. 2010. "The Uneven Rise of American Public Schools to 1850." *Journal of Economic History* 70, no. 1: 1–26.

Godbout, Jean-François, and Bjørn Høyland. 2017. "Unity in Diversity? The Development of Political Parties in the Parliament of Canada, 1867–2011." *British Journal of Political Science* 47, no. 3 (July): 545–69. https://doi.org/10.1017/S0007123415000368.

Goemans, Henk E., Kristian Skrede Gleditsch, and Giacomo Chiozza. 2009. "Introducing Archigos: A Dataset of Political Leaders." *Journal of Peace Research* 46, no. 2 (March 1): 269–83. https://doi.org/10.1177/0022343308100719.

Goldin, Claudia, and Lawrence F. Katz. 2011. "Mass Secondary Schooling and the State: The Role of State Compulsion in the High School Movement." In *Understanding Long-Run Economic Growth. Understanding Long-Run Economic Growth*. Chicago: University of Chicago Press. https://doi.org/10.7208/chicago/9780226116426.003.0010.

Gordon, Raymond G., Jr. (ed.), 2005. Ethnologue: Languages of the World, Fifteenth edition. Dallas, Texas: SIL International. Online version: http://www.ethnologue.com/15.

Gordon, Sanford C., and Hannah K. Simpson. 2020. "Causes, Theories, and the Past in Political Science." *Public Choice* 185: 315–33. https://doi.org/10.1007/s11127-019-00703-6.

Gray, Thomas, and Jeff Jenkins. 2022. "Estimating Disenfranchisement in U.S. Elections, 1870-1970." https://www.dropbox.com/s/mt8oio0gbqsmgkl/Full%20Draft%20v0.3.pdf?dl=0.

Grzymala-Busse, Anna. 2020. "Beyond War and Contracts: The Medieval and Religious Roots of the European State." *Annual Review of Political Science* 23, no. 1 (May 11): 19–36. https://doi.org/10.1146/annurev-polisci-050718-032628.

Grzymala-Busse, Anna. 2023. Sacred Foundations: The Religious and Medieval Roots of the European State. Princeton University Press. https://doi.org/10.1515/9780691245133.

Guardado, Jenny. 2018. Office-Selling, Corruption, and Long-Term Development in Peru. *American Political Science Review* 112, no. 4: 971–95. https://doi.org/10.1017/S000305541800045X.

Guiso, Luigi, Paola Sapienza, and Luigi Zingales. 2016. "Long-Term Persistence." *Journal of the European Economic Association* 14, no. 6 (December 1): 1401–36. https://doi.org/10.1111/jeea.12177.

Häge, Frank M. 2019. "Political Conflict in Bismarck's Germany: An Analysis of Parliamentary Voting, 1867–1890." *Party Politics* 25, no. 2: 179–91. https://doi.org/10.1177/1354068817702058.

Hamilton, Kirk, and Cameron Hepburn, eds. 2017. *National Wealth: What Is Missing, Why It Matters*. Oxford: Oxford University Press. https://doi.org/10.1093/oso/9780198803720.001.0001.

Hansen, Martin Ejnar, and Marc Debus. 2012. "The Behaviour of Political Parties and MPs in the Parliaments of the Weimar Republic." *Party Politics* 18, no. 5: 709–26.

Hix, S., and A. Noury. 2016. "Government-Opposition or Left-Right? The Institutional Determinants of Voting in Legislatures." *Political Science Research and Methods* 4, no. 2: 249–73. https://doi.org/10.1017/psrm.2015.9.

Hollenbach, Florian M. 2021. "Elite Interests and Public Spending: Evidence from Prussian Cities." *Review of International Organizations* 16, no. 1 (January 1): 189–211. https://doi.org/10.1007/s11558-019-09347-z.

Huning, Thilo R., and Fabian Wahl. 2016. "You Reap What You Know: Observability of Soil Quality, and Political Fragmentation." Working Paper. EHES Working Papers in Economic History. https://www.econstor.eu/handle/10419/247032.

Jedwab, Remi, Noel D. Johnson, and Mark Koyama. 2022. "The Economic Impact of the Black Death." *Journal of Economic Literature* 60, no. 1 (March): 132–78. https://doi.org/10.1257/jel.20201639.

Jenkins, Jeffery A., and Timothy P. Nokken. 2000. "The Institutional Origins of the Republican Party: Spatial Voting and the House Speakership Election of 1855–56." *Legislative Studies Quarterly* 25: 101–30.

Jenkins, Jeffery A., Justin Peck, and Vesla M. Weaver. 2010. "Between Reconstructions: Congressional Action on Civil Rights, 1891–1940." *Studies in American Political Development* 24, no. 1 (April): 57–89. https://doi.org/10.1017/S0898588X10000015.

Jenkins, Jeffery A., and Brian R. Sala. 1998. "The Spatial Theory of Voting and the Presidential Election of 1824." *American Journal of Political Science* 42: 1157–79.

Jenkins, Jeffery A., and Charles Stewart III. 2013. *Fighting for the Speakership: The House and the Rise of Party Government*. Princeton, NJ: Princeton University Press.

Jha, Saumitra. 2013. "Trade, Institutions, and Ethnic Tolerance: Evidence from South Asia." *American Political Science Review* 107, no. 4: 806–32.

Jia, Ruixue. 2014. "The Legacies of Forced Freedom: China's Treaty Ports." *Review of Economics and Statistics* 96, no. 4: 596–608.

Jiang, Qin, and James Kai-sing Kung. 2021. "Social Mobility in Late Imperial China: Reconsidering the 'Ladder of Success' Hypothesis." *Modern China* 47, no. 5 (September 1): 628–61. https://doi.org/10.1177/0097700420914529.

Johnson-Kanu, A. 2021. Colonial Legacies in State Building: Bureaucratic Embeddedness, Public Goods provision, and Public Opinion in Nigeria. *UC Merced*. ProQuest ID: JohnsonKanu_ucmerced_1660D_10687. Merritt ID: ark:/13030/m5994wph. Retrieved from https://escholarship.org/uc/item/6hj8c72h.

Jones, Benjamin F., and Benjamin A. Olken. 2005. "Do Leaders Matter? National Leadership and Growth Since World War II.*" *Quarterly Journal of Economics* 120, no. 3 (August 1): 835–64. https://doi.org/10.1093/qje/120.3.835.

Kam, Christopher. 2014. "Enfranchisement, Malapportionment, and Institutional Change in Great Britain, 1832–1868." *Legislative Studies Quarterly* 39, no. 4: 503–30.

Kam, Christopher. 2017. "The Secret Ballot and the Market for Votes at 19th-Century British Elections." *Comparative Political Studies* 50, no. 5 (April 1): 594–635. https://doi.org/10.1177/0010414015626451.

Karadja, Mounir, and Erik Prawitz. 2019. "Exit, Voice, and Political Change: Evidence from Swedish Mass Migration to the United States." *Journal of Political Economy* 127, no. 4 (August): 1864–925. https://doi.org/10.1086/701682.

Karger, Ezra. 2021. "The Long-Run Effect of Public Libraries on Children: Evidence from the Early 1900s." SocArXiv, Center for Open Science.

Kim, Diana S. 2022. "Taming Abundance: Doing Digital Archival Research (as Political Scientists)." *PS: Political Science & Politics* (February 22): 1–9. https://doi.org/10.1017/S1049096521001920X.

Kokkonen, Andrej, and Jørgen Møller. 2020. "Succession, Power-Sharing and the Development of Representative Institutions in Medieval Europe." *European Journal of Political Research* 59, no. 4: 954–75.

Kokkonen, Andrej, and Anders Sundell. 2020. "Leader Succession and Civil War." *Comparative Political Studies* 53, no. 3–4 (March 1): 434–68. https://doi.org/10.1177/0010414019852712.

Kreuzer, Marcus L. 2001. *Institutions and Innovation: Voters, Parties, and Interest Groups in the Consolidation of Democracy—France and Germany, 1870–1939*. Ann Arbor: University of Michigan Press.

Kuran, Timur. 2012. *The Long Divergence: How Islamic Law Held Back the Middle East*. Princeton, N.J.: Princeton University Press.

Lee, Jong-Wha, and Lee, Hanol. 2016. "Human Capital in the Long Run." *Journal of Development Economics* 122: 147–69.

Liang, Fangzhong. 2008. *Zhongguo Lidai Hukou, Tiandi, Tianfu Tongji* [Statistics on Chinese historical demography, land, and land tax]. Zhonghua shuju.

Lowes, Sara. 2021. "Ethnographic and Field Data in Historical Economics." In *The Handbook of Historical Economics*, ed. Bisin Alberto and Federico Giovanni, 147–77. London: Elsevier.

Lupu, Noam. 2015. "Party Polarization and Mass Partisanship: A Comparative Perspective." *Political Behavior* 37: 331–56. https://doi.org/10.1007/s11109-014-9279-z.

Malik, Adeel, and Rinchan Ali Mirza. 2021. "Pre-Colonial Religious Institutions and Development: Evidence through a Military Coup." *Journal of the European Economic Association* 20, no. 2: 907–56. https://doi.org/10.1093/jeea/jvab050.

Mares, Isabela. 2015. *From Open Secrets to Secret Voting: Democratic Electoral Reforms and Voter Autonomy*. Cambridge Studies in Comparative Politics. Cambridge: Cambridge University Press. https://doi.org/10.1017/CBO9781316178539.

Mares, Isabela, and Didac Queralt. 2020. "Fiscal Innovation in Nondemocratic Regimes: Elites and the Adoption of the Prussian Income Taxes of the 1890s." *Explorations in Economic History* 77, no. C. https://econpapers.repec.org/article/eeeexehis/v_3a77_3ay_3a2020_3ai_3ac_3as0014498320300310.htm.https://ideas.repec.org/a/eee/exehis/v77y2020ics0014498320300310.html.

Martin, Andrew D., and Kevin Quinn. 2002. "Dynamic Ideal Point Estimation via Markov Chain Monte Carlo for the U.S. Supreme Court, 1953–1999." *Political Analysis* 10: 134–53.

Mattingly, Daniel C. 2017. "Colonial Legacies and State Institutions in China: Evidence from a Natural Experiment." *Comparative Political Studies* 50, no. 4 (March 1): 434–63. https://doi.org/10.1177/0010414015600465.

Mazumder, Soumyajit. 2018. "The Persistent Effect of U.S. Civil Rights Protests on Political Attitudes." *American Journal of Political Science* 62, no. 4: 922–35.

Miller, Grant. 2008. "Women's Suffrage, Political Responsiveness, and Child Survival in American History*." *Quarterly Journal of Economics* 123, no. 3 (August 1): 1287–327. https://doi.org/10.1162/qjec.2008.123.3.1287.

Miller, Michael K. 2020. "The Autocratic Ruling Parties Dataset: Origins, Durability, and Death." *Journal of Conflict Resolution* 64, no. 4: 756–82. https://doi.org/10.1177/0022002719876000.

Montolio, Daniel, and Ana Tur-Prats. 2018. "Long-Lasting Social Capital and Its Impact on Economic Development: The Legacy of the Commons." SSRN Scholarly Paper. Rochester, NY: Social Science Research Network. October 11. https://doi.org/10.2139/ssrn.3281542.

Müller-Crepon, Carl, and Philipp Hunziker. 2018. "New Spatial Data on Ethnicity: Introducing SIDE." *Journal of Peace Research* 55, no. 5 (September 1): 687–98. https://doi.org/10.1177/0022343318764254.

Müller-Crepon, Carl, Yannick Pengl, and Nils-Christian Bormann. 2021. "Linking Ethnic Data from Africa (LEDA)." *Journal of Peace Research* 59, no. 3: 00223433211016528. https://doi.org/10.1177/00223433211016528.

Müller-Crepon, Carl, Guy Schvitz, and Lars-Erik Cederman. 2022. "Shaping States into Nations: The Effects of Ethnic Geography on State Borders." Working Paper. http://www.carlmueller-crepon.org/publication/state_shape/.

Murdock, George Peter. 1959. *Africa: Its Peoples and Their Culture History*. McGraw-Hill.

Murdock, George Peter. 1967. *Ethnographic Atlas*. Pittsburgh: University of Pittsburgh Press.

Murdock, George Peter, and Douglas R. White. 1969. "Standard Cross-Cultural Sample." *Ethnology* 8, no. 4: 329–69.

Nalepa, Monika, and Grigore Pop-Eleches. 2022. "Authoritarian Infiltration of Organizations: Causes and Consequences." *Journal of Politics* 84, no. 2 https://doi.org/10.1086/715999.

Nix, Emily, and Nancy Qian. 2015. "The Fluidity of Race: 'Passing' in the United States, 1880–1940." Working Paper. National Bureau of Economic Research Working Paper Series. January. https://doi.org/10.3386/w20828.

Nunn, Nathan. 2008. "The Long-Term Effects of Africa's Slave Trades*." *Quarterly Journal of Economics* 123, no. 1 (February 1): 139–76. https://doi.org/10.1162/qjec.2008.123.1.139.

Nunn, Nathan, and Leonard Wantchekon. 2011. "The Slave Trade and the Origins of Mistrust in Africa." *American Economic Review* 101, no. 7 (December): 3221–52. https://doi.org/10.1257/aer.101.7.3221.

Özden, Çağlar, Christopher Parsons, Maurice Schiff, and Terrie Walmsley. 2011. "Where on Earth Is Everybody? The Evolution of Global Bilateral Migration 1960–2000." *World Bank Economic Review* 25, no. 1: 12–56. doi: 10.1093/wber/lhr024.

Padro i Miquel, Gerard, Nancy Qian, Yao Yiqing, and Yang Yao. 2015. Making Democracy Work: Culture, Social Capital and Elections in China. https://www.nber.org/papers/w21058

Paine, Jack. 2019. "Ethnic Violence in Africa: Destructive Legacies of Pre-Colonial States." *International Organization* 73, no. 3: 645–83. https://doi.org/10.1017/S0020818319000134.

Paglayan, Agustina. 2021. "The Non-Democratic Roots of Mass Education: Evidence from 200 Years." *American Political Science Review* 115, no. 1: 179–98. doi:10.1017/S0003055420000647.

Pascali, Luigi. 2017. "The Wind of Change: Maritime Technology, Trade, and Economic Development." *American Economic Review* 107, no. 9 (September): 2821–54. https://doi.org/10.1257/aer.20140832.

Pengl, Yannick I., Philip Roessler, and Valeria Rueda. 2022. "Cash Crops, Print Technologies, and the Politicization of Ethnicity in Africa." *American Political Science Review* 116, no. 1 (February): 181–99. https://doi.org/10.1017/S0003055421000782.

Piketty, Thomas. 2014. *Capital in the Twenty-First Century*. Cambridge, MA: Harvard University Press. https://www.hup.harvard.edu/catalog.php?isbn=9780674430006.

Piketty, Thomas, and Emmanuel Saez. 2003. "Income Inequality in the United States, 1913–1998*." *Quarterly Journal of Economics* 118, no. 1 (February 1): 1–41. https://doi.org/10.1162/00335530360535135.

Poole, K. 2005. *Spatial Models of Parliamentary Voting (Analytical Methods for Social Research)*. Cambridge University Press. https://doi.org/10.1017/CBO9780511614644

Putnam, Robert D. 1995. "Bowling Alone: America's Declining Social Capital." *Journal of Democracy* 6, no. 1: 65–78. https://doi.org/10.1353/jod.1995.0002.

Rosenthal, H. 2007. *Ideology and Congress: A Political Economic History of Roll Call Voting* (2nd ed.). Routledge. https://doi.org/10.4324/9780203789223

Rubin, Jared. 2017. *Rulers, Religion, and Riches: Why the West Got Rich and the Middle East Did Not.* Cambridge Studies in Economics, Choice, and Society. Cambridge: Cambridge University Press. https://doi.org/10.1017/9781139568272.

Rubin, Jared, and Mark Koyama. 2022. *How the World Became Rich*. Polity.

Saavedra, Martin. 2017. "Early-Life Disease Exposure and Occupational Status: The Impact of Yellow Fever during the 19th Century." *Explorations in Economic History* 64: 62–81.

Satyanath, Shanker, Nico Voigtländer, and Hans-Joachim Voth. 2017. "Bowling for Fascism: Social Capital and the Rise of the Nazi Party." *Journal of Political Economy* 125, no. 2 (April): 478–526. https://doi.org/10.1086/690949.

Sequeira, Sandra, Nathan Nunn, Nancy Qian. 2020. "Immigrants and the Making of America." *The Review of Economic Studies* 87, no. 1: 382–419. https://doi.org/10.1093/restud/rdz003.

Sieberer, Ulrich, Thomas Saalfeld, Tamaki Ohmura, Henning Bergmann, and Stefanie Bailer. 2020. "Roll-Call Votes in the German Bundestag: A New Dataset, 1949–2013." *British Journal of Political Science* 50, no. 3 (July): 1137–45. https://doi.org/10.1017/S0007123418000406.

Sng, Tuan-Hwee. 2014. "Size and Dynastic Decline: The Principal-Agent Problem in Late Imperial China, 1700–1850." *Explorations in Economic History* 54 (October 1): 107–27. https://doi.org/10.1016/j.eeh.2014.05.002.

Spenkuch, Jörg L., and Philipp Tillmann. 2018. "Elite Influence? Religion and the Electoral Success of the Nazis." *American Journal of Political Science* 62, no. 1: 19–36. https://doi.org/10.1111/ajps.12328.

Srivastava, Swati. 2022. "Corporate Sovereign Awakening and the Making of Modern State Sovereignty: New Archival Evidence from the English East India Company." *International Organization* 76, no.3: 690–712. https://doi.org/10.1017/S002081832200008X.

Stasavage, David. 2010. "When Distance Mattered: Geographic Scale and the Development of European Representative Assemblies." *American Political Science Review* 104, no. 4 (November): 625–43. https://doi.org/10.1017/S0003055410000444.

Suryanarayan, Pavithra, and Steven White. 2021. "Slavery, Reconstruction, and Bureaucratic Capacity in the American South." *American Political Science Review* 115, no. 2 (May): 568–84. https://doi.org/10.1017/S0003055420000933.

Teele, Dawn. 2018. *Forging the Franchise*. https://press.princeton.edu/books/hardcover/9780691180267/forging-the-franchise.

Valencia Caicedo, Felipe. 2019. "Missionaries in Latin America and Asia: A First Global Mass Education Wave." In *Globalization and Mass Education*, ed. G. Cappelli and D. Mitch, 61–97. London: Palgrave Macmillan.

Van Zanden, Jan Luiten, Eltjo Buringh, and Maarten Bosker. 2012. "The Rise and Decline of European Parliaments, 1188–1789." *Economic History Review* 65, no. 3: 835–61. https://doi.org/10.1111/j.1468-0289.2011.00612.x.

Voeten, Erik, Anton Strezhnev, Michael Bailey. 2009. "United Nations General Assembly Voting Data." Harvard Dataverse, V29. https://doi.org/10.7910/DVN/LEJUQZ.

Vogt, Manuel, Nils-Christian Bormann, Seraina Rüegger, Lars-Erik Cederman, Philipp Hunziker, and Luc Girardin. 2015. "Integrating Data on Ethnicity, Geography, and Conflict: The Ethnic Power Relations Data Set Family." *Journal of Conflict Resolution* 59, no. 7 (October 1): 1327–42. https://doi.org/10.1177/0022002715591215.

Waldinger, Maria. 2017. "The Long-Run Effects of Missionary Orders in Mexico." *Journal of Development Economics* 127 (July 1): 355–78. https://doi.org/10.1016/j.jdeveco.2016.12.010.

Wang, Yuhua. 2022. "Blood Is Thicker Than Water: Elite Kinship Networks and State Building in Imperial China." *American Political Science Review* 115, no. 3: 896–910. https://doi.org/10.1017/S0003055421001490.

Wantchekon, Leonard, Marko Klašnja, and Natalija Novta. 2014. "Education and Human Capital Externalities: Evidence from Colonial Benin." *Quarterly Journal of Economics* 130, no. 2. https://academic.oup.com/qje/article/130/2/703/2330445.

Whitten, Guy D., Laron K. Williams, and Cameron Wimpy. 2021. "Interpretation: The Final Spatial Frontier." *Political Science Research and Methods* 9, no. 1 (January): 140–56. https://doi.org/10.1017/psrm.2019.9.

Wig, Tore. 2016. "Peace from the Past: Pre-Colonial Political Institutions and Civil Wars in Africa." *Journal of Peace Research* 53, no. 4 (July 1): 509–24. https://doi.org/10.1177/0022343316640595.

Williams, Jhacova. 2022. "Historical Lynchings and the Contemporary Voting Behavior of Blacks." *American Economic Journal: Applied Economics* 14, no. 3: 224–53.

Xu, Guo. 2018. "The Costs of Patronage: Evidence from the British Empire." *American Economic Review* 108, no. 11: 3170–98.

Xu, Guo. 2023. "Bureaucratic Representation and State Responsiveness during Times of Crisis: The 1918 Pandemic in India." *Review of Economics and Statistics*. 1–10. https://doi.org/10.1162/rest_a_01060.

CHAPTER 4

CAUSAL INFERENCE AND KNOWLEDGE ACCUMULATION IN HISTORICAL POLITICAL ECONOMY

ANNA CALLIS, THAD DUNNING, AND
GUADALUPE TUÑÓN

EMPIRICAL research on historical political economy (HPE) has been transformed over recent decades by what is sometimes called the "design-based" turn. Historical natural experiments, instrumental variables, and regression-discontinuity designs—and especially different varieties of difference-in-differences methods—are the workhorses of much contemporary research on politics and economics in historical settings.[1] For many quantitatively oriented scholars, these methods have replaced a previous reliance on the selection-on-observables assumptions made in applications of multivariate regression and related approaches. These days, claims to valid causal inference in quantitative work often rely on some plausible as-if random assignment to a treatment variable or some means of testing key identifying assumptions, for example, through placebo tests.[2] The so-called credibility revolution appears firmly established in HPE: the revolutionaries are practically retirees.[3]

Yet many scholars voice unease—we think rightly—about what design-based empirical research can contribute to our general knowledge of historical political economy. Sometimes this discomfort is cast in terms not only of a paucity of theory but also in terms of the kinds of theory that a focus on as-if random assignment can test. Rozenas (2021), for example, suggests that prioritizing the role of as-if random for empirical assessment may give pride of place to contingent factors as key causes in quantitative HPE. Yet the treatments that may really matter for outcomes about which we care may be sticky, very nonrandom, and quite difficult to manipulate. Other times, the worry is more about the difficulty of extrapolating findings beyond the particular design features that allow for credible design-based causal inference in specific, sometimes apparently idiosyncratic, settings. Gailmard (2021a; 2021b; 2022), for instance, argues that achieving the important goal of extrapolation from empirical findings in a particular case depends, first, on theory, and second, often on "weaker" methods relying mainly on selection-on-observables assumptions. Yet, if theory and those weaker methods are sufficient for extrapolation to a new case, he argues, then they may be sufficient for inference in the original setting in which the design-based method was used—casting some doubt on the utility or inferential priority granted to the tools of the credibility revolution in the first place.

These concerns about the contributions of design-based methods are multifaceted.[4] As a whole, though, we think they often relate to the capacity of the credibility revolution to generate *cumulative learning*, also known as the accumulation of knowledge. By this, we mean valid, useful, or correct insights—for example, about the working of the social and political world—that build on or depend on one another, often (though not always) across distinct studies conducted by different researchers.[5] While internal validity is a key part of learning, two other dimensions of causal assessment seem especially critical: the *generalizability* of causal claims and findings, and evidence on the *mechanisms* that connect causes to effects. These topics are not identical, but they are certainly related. As many philosophers of science have underscored, mechanisms can be critical for generalizability. For example, knowing the mechanism that led cause X to produce effect Y in context A shapes expectations about whether we would predict a similar effect in context B, where the key mechanism may or may not be operative (Cartwright and Hardie 2012). We do not presume that cumulative learning is always the key goal of HPE; sometimes, assessing treatment effects in a particular case or historical event, by means of a single discrete study, is highly valuable. For political scientists and economists, though, the accumulation of generalizable knowledge about mechanisms does often appear critical, so we take this as a central, if sometimes implicit, goal.

To the extent that cumulative learning is the—or an—important goal for HPE, key issues seem to revolve around (a) whether or to what extent any empirical method can aid the accumulation of knowledge about generalizability and mechanism; and (b) how well design-based methods for causal inference can do this, relative to other tools. Our goal in this chapter is to engage these questions. For (a), we highlight the general difficulties of assessing generalizability and mechanism, whatever the method. The challenge of cumulative learning about generalizability or mechanism is not an obvious function of method, however. Sometimes, the seeming advantages of "selection-on-observables" types of methods is only apparent.

This takes us to (b). While there are important challenges to cumulative learning from design-based approaches, we highlight the useful, if necessarily limited, routes to generalizability and mechanism that can be—and increasingly have been—achieved using methods associated with the credibility revolution. We lay out several strategies for knowledge accumulation about generalizability and mechanism and show how they have been or can be leveraged, implicitly or explicitly, in historical political economy. However, we also argue that greater explicit attention to these goals in the design and interpretation of studies would aid cumulative learning. We consider especially research on European colonialism and the global expansion of the West, including work on the slave trade, extractive institutions of forced labor, and modes of colonial rule (e.g., indirect versus direct), as well as related questions about the impacts of missionary activity. Across these different areas, scholars have addressed questions of generalizability by using related designs to examine similar questions in different contexts. The comparison of findings from related studies with similar treatments and different outcomes, or with variation in classes of a treatment variable, can also shed light on operative mechanisms. Moreover, the credible evidence base that design-based studies can provide is critical for developing, disciplining, and validating generalizable theory and thus can provide a route to knowledge accumulation.

To clarify our earlier "we think rightly" in this chapter's second paragraph: we think that critics are correct to raise concerns. Yet we also think that the challenge of assessing generalizability and mechanism is substantial, whatever the empirical method and whatever the theoretical focus. Theory can narrow the range of plausible mechanisms consistent with an empirical finding, but we think it is critical for an empirical field such as HPE to consider and advance credible empirical routes to generalizability and mechanism. Our point is not to suggest that the modes of cumulative learning we highlight represent the only or even always best route to cumulative learning. Our goal, however, is to highlight how the apparently stark conflict between achieving internal validity in particular contexts using design-based methods and understanding of generalizability and mechanism can be overstated. Greater attention to generalizability and the ways in which different studies may replicate and build on one another can help to soften the trade-offs between internal and external validity, or between the estimation of treatment effects and the understanding of mechanisms. This can foster more useful knowledge accumulation.

The Credibility Revolution, Generalizability, and Mechanisms

Cumulative learning about generalizability and mechanism may not always be the explicit or even the implicit goal of historical political economy. Even where scholars care about generalizable lessons, assessing the validity of inferences about causal relations in a particular case or event may rightly take priority. If we are not even right about the historical consequences of the Glorious Revolution—to take just one example—then extrapolating lessons about the effects of parliamentary checks on royal authority for investment, government borrowing, or economic development in general might seem beside the point.[6]

Yet there are many reasons that HPE as a field focuses or should focus on generalizability and mechanism. Whether empirical work is seen as an avenue for developing new theoretical insights or a means for testing theory, the question of how findings apply beyond the setting at hand is often implicit, if not explicit. Substantive work in HPE is also often—though of course not always—especially concerned with empirical phenomena that extend beyond a particular case, in the sense that many cases may be shaped in similar ways by similar phenomena. Indeed, claims to generalizable knowledge may help to define HPE as a field and in some ways distinguish it from cognate work in the discipline of history. How, then, can we best make progress in this area?

The assessment of generalizability and of mechanism relies critically on theory, a point made well, for example, by Gailmard (2021a); see also, inter alia, Ashworth, Berry, and Bueno de Mesquita (2021). A mechanism itself can be seen as a theoretical construct of a social process that causes an event rather than as an intervening variable (Waldner 2016). This does not gainsay the role of observables, however. We can call a "mediating variable" a mechanism, an indicator of a mechanism, or a variable that would take on a particular value if a specific theory of mechanism were true without doing undue violence to interpretation. What seems critical is (at least) to assess whether particular theories are consistent or inconsistent with specific patterns of evidence. Not all theories can explain a particular observed set of facts, and multiplication of the relevant facts sharpens the theoretical challenges but also the potential insights. Theories can also generate new observable implications that can be tested against additional evidence from a case, a perspective echoed in diverse work on within-case process tracing (e.g., Collier, Brady, and Seawright 2010; Collier 2011) as well as other advice on theoretical development in relation to qualitative evidence (e.g., King, Keohane, and Verba 1994).

Empirical routes to the evaluation of generalizability and mechanism are thus essential in any field. They are perhaps all the more so in HPE, focusing as it does definitionally on concrete temporal processes that have unfolded in "the past." Without empirical means of validating claims to generalizability, HPE could risk getting not only the political economy but also the history wrong. Thus, we are explicitly concerned here with empirical routes to the identification of mechanisms and generalizability—what could be called an "inductive approach"—even though theory can and should play a critical potential role in identifying classes of important mechanisms. We ask how empirical methods can best work together with theory to aid the accumulation of valid knowledge about mechanisms and generalizable causal relations in HPE. In other words, we do not take the central task to be the identification of the relevance of findings in one case for likely findings in a case that has not yet been or will not be studied empirically (Gailmard 2021a). Rather, we aim to explore how empirical research can best aid—and help to validate—theory and inference about generalizability and mechanism across a variety of cases.

From this perspective, one role of strong design is to provide believable "stubborn facts" that theory can seek to reconcile—while sometimes also generating new lines of testable inquiry. The "believable" part is perhaps the key focus of the credibility revolutionaries, dating at least from Leamer (1983). However, this point has most often been made with respect to the internal validity of causal claims in a particular case or event.[7] In this context—notwithstanding debate about the virtues of particular designs in specific studies—the potential usefulness of design-based methods is by now fairly widely extolled. We largely agree with the positive view, though we also think that different inferential tools and methods are appropriate for different kinds of problems, and we recognize that there are many difficulties with natural experiments, discontinuities, and the like.

What seems more controversial is whether and to what extent such methods can contribute to the accumulation of knowledge about the generalizability of causal findings and the mechanisms that undergird them. A simple—but we think essential—point that we make here is that for purposes of assessing generalizability and mechanism, the same reciprocal relationship between credible evidence and theoretical development that we sometimes find within cases should apply across cases. Yet what are good methods for advancing this reciprocal relationship?

Challenges of Assessing Generalizability and Mechanism

It is useful to start with the recognition that assessing mechanisms and the generalizability of findings empirically can be extraordinarily hard—whatever the method. With respect to mechanisms, the difficulties are underscored by the critical literature on path models, post-treatment bias, and mediation analysis. Even in a randomized controlled experiment where researchers manipulate the treatment, controlling for post-treatment variables—also known as mediators—destroys the expected symmetry between treatment and control groups (Angrist and Pischke 2009, 64–68). Unobservables that influence a mediator are also likely to influence the outcome, leading to bias in Baron and Kenny–type analyses in a regression framework (Glynn 2012; Bullock and Green 2021); and the response schedules implied by path models often involve other untenable assumptions (Freedman 2009, 94–101). In a more flexible potential outcomes framework, even the definition of direct and indirect effects involves imagining impossibilities that are inherently unobservable (as distinct from counterfactual), such as "complex potential outcomes" (Gerber and Green 2012, 329). Identifying assumptions such as sequential ignorability may be so strong as to be untenable in applications (Imai, Keele, and Yamamoto 2010). Moreover, direct manipulation of a mediator does not necessarily identify the indirect effect of a treatment working *through* a mediator.

Against these kinds of arguments with respect to randomized experiments—where the possibility of successful mediation analysis might initially appear plausible—the empirical assessment of mechanisms in HPE applications could seem like hubris. In the domain of observational studies, neither treatments nor mediators are manipulated, and many other threats to inference arise. We agree with Gailmard (2021a) and others: empirical studies can rule out some mechanisms and provide support that a given channel is "a" mechanism, yet they are often unlikely to identify "causal uniqueness" when it comes to mechanisms or successfully to parse a treatment's direct and indirect effects.

Assessing generalizability is also highly challenging in HPE. Researchers sometimes advance the idea that we get more leverage from selection-on-observables assumptions.

It is common, for example, to contrast the "local" average treatment effect estimated in, say, an instrumental-variables or regression-discontinuity design with some presumably more general or nonlocal causal effect estimated under a selection-on-observables assumption—such as a research design using a cross-national regression. However, this advantage is often more apparent than real. One familiar but important point is that if confounding or selection effects lead to misleading estimates in the more comprehensive data set, the findings may simply distort—rather than generalize—our understanding of causal relationships. The apparent generality can also be undercut by the mechanics of modeling selection effects. A country fixed-effects analysis regression upweights units with greater within-country (over time) variation in treatment status. As Aronow and Samii (2016) nicely show, this results in an "effective sample" that can differ sharply from—and is substantially less "general" than—the full study group, undercutting the apparent virtues for generalizability of a more comprehensive data set.

Empirical Strategies for Cumulative Learning

Despite these difficulties, we think that real—if limited and modest—progress can be made toward understanding mechanisms and generalizability through a combination of mixed methods, qualitative information, theory, and research design. Our goal is to lay out empirical strategies that we think are plausible, to show how elements of those strategies are in practice today, and to propose potential modifications to current practice that may bolster learning about mechanisms and generalizability.

As we have explored elsewhere (Callis, Dunning, and Tuñón 2022), at least three strategies appear broadly important as empirical (or "inductive") routes to cumulative learning about causal relations:

(1) replicating a similar study design across different contexts or with different populations;
(2) varying a component of a bundled treatment while measuring the same outcome of interest; and
(3) maintaining the same treatments while examining different outcomes, or the same outcome at different points over time.

These strategies are relatively "design-based" in that they do—or potentially can—rely on variation akin to that which could—hypothetically—be introduced by an experimental researcher. Response schedules and modeling assumptions play a role, but to a much less constricting degree than the more "model-based" assumptions associated with path models and other modes of formal mediation analysis.[8] Of course, in the observational studies that characterize HPE, there is no experimental intervention; yet an analysis may take advantage of such potential manipulations in a way that is relatively simple and that avoids many of the inferential challenges associated with, for example, path models and formal mediation.

Here, (1) is clearly most central to the assessment of generalizability, while (depending on the aim), (2) and (3) could be used to assess either generalizability or mechanism (or both). With respect to strategy (1), it is very substantially an empirical question whether an effect found in one context replicates in another. If one finds an effect of treatment X on outcome Y in context W, one may be able to assess empirically whether such an effect also holds in context Z. In principle, one can do this without any insight into the operative mechanism that engendered the effect in context W or any theoretical understanding of whether we would expect a similar mechanism to be active in context Z. We would argue that even if potentially atheoretical, such an effort contributes to a base of evidence that is important for cumulative learning—and certainly, for a historically and empirically grounded route to the accumulation of knowledge.

However, the replication effort implied by strategy (1) may result in different conclusions. One possibility is that a treatment effect found in context W is broadly similar or goes in the same direction in context Z (and perhaps contexts N, O, P, and Q as well, if we are lucky enough to have multiple studies of a similar phenomenon in different contexts). We give examples of this kind of finding from diverse HPE literatures later. Even if such an empirical finding does not advance our theoretical understanding of how X produced Y across diverse contexts, the set of findings is valuable on its own: the results may speak directly to the external validity of a historically important treatment. A different possible conclusion, however, is that the effect of treatment X on outcome Y differs in contexts W and Z (and perhaps also in N, O, P, and Q) such that we estimate positive, negative, and null effects in distinct contexts. This especially amplifies the onus on *explanation*.

Understanding why a cause has an effect—an important aspect of explanation—is a multifaceted problem, but one facet relates to understanding the "active" element of a treatment. In natural experiments, treatments are often "bundled," complicating inferences (Dunning 2012, ch. 10). Strategy (2) can be seen as a form of "implicit mediation analysis" (Gerber and Green 2012, 333–336)—implicit because it does not seek precisely to parse direct and indirect effects but rather to take advantage of variation across versions of a treatment to assess active "channels." The strategy is also "design-based" in its reliance on variation that could be induced by a manipulation, as in an experiment (Bullock and Green 2021).[9] Such analyses sometimes shed light empirically on mechanisms in an admittedly limited and blunt—but nonetheless potentially very useful—way.

Strategy (3) can address other key questions for mechanisms. Finding an impact of a treatment on some outcomes but not others can shed light on why the effect sometimes occurs: for example, a given treatment might have an effect on behavioral but not attitudinal outcomes, possibly suggesting that it changes incentives without changing perceptions or beliefs. In addition, researchers may assess impacts on "intermediate outcomes," which are themselves conceptualized as mechanisms. To be sure, leveraging such variation is also an aspect of formal mediation analysis, but the goals here are more modest—and the inferences, if more limited, are also perhaps more credible. It is possible in principle for an intermediate outcome to be a mediator even if a treatment has no average effect on it, for instance, in a potential outcome framework in which an effect in one direction for some subjects and an effect in a different direction for others averages to zero across subjects. These are fairly knife-edged cases though. From a pragmatic perspective, knowing whether a treatment moves—or fails to move—such a variable can be substantially helpful for evaluating claims about mechanisms.

In sum, these three broad empirical strategies can provide, we think, a useful empirical route to cumulative learning about generalizability, mechanism, or both. For explanation, we highlight especially the potential utility of strategies (2) and (3). These strategies may be most effective when they leverage a wide source of qualitative and quantitative information and when they engage substantially with theoretical insights. For example, they might be used to distinguish between two theoretical explanations that are both consistent with some observed event, fact, or treatment effect.

These strategies could in principle be leveraged by the same set of authors and sometimes even within a single study. More often, however, new knowledge generated by one researcher or set of researchers may be linked to or depend on the knowledge previously obtained *by other researchers*; and the use of the three strategies emerges through such a collective endeavor. For this reason, we consider the assessment of generalizability and mechanism as a facet of knowledge accumulation (Mahoney 2003;). Moreover, empirical knowledge of mechanism often does build cumulatively. Indeed, across different areas of scientific inquiry, an impact of X on Y may be well established long before the mechanism is understood.[10] Replication in the form of strategy (1) also can have ancillary benefits, for example, as a check on routines and procedures in an original study—and sometimes more generally as a way to generate critical scholarly dialogue that can lead to further verification of the first study's findings in a given context. Such replication may not always arise, of course: cumulative learning about generalizability and mechanism may occur (or fail to occur) as a function, for example, of the nature of the professional production of knowledge in an academic discipline.

Reflecting on the three strategies, we see little tension in principle between the goal of constructing a credible evidence base against which generalizable theories can be assessed and the design-based turn in HPE. (Practice may be another question; we turn to that next.) Several caveats are useful, however. One potential price of weaker modeling assumptions is more limited conclusions. For instance, strategies (2) or (3) compromise on the ability to parse direct and indirect effects exactly, relative to the apparent precision provided by a path model. Because of the omnipresent and distorting role of unobservables in applications of those models, however, we think "apparent" is often right: the precision is illusory. Where some might see a bug, we therefore see a feature and even a virtue of these simpler methods. The aims for assessing mechanisms are more modest but, we think, more credibly achievable.

We also note that the ability to assess mechanisms and infer generalizability may vary substantially across different modes of HPE, especially studies with different goals. Much historical work emphasizes the importance of temporality and sequence, and also the ways in which historical treatments or critical junctures may generate aftermaths and long-run legacies that consolidate their impact (see Acharya, Blackwell, and Sen's 2022 chapter on historical persistence for a review). A valid natural experiment can in principle (and sometimes in practice) identify long-run impacts, for example, by using treatment-control comparisons measured across a longue durée. But a long-run effect need not imply a legacy, conceptualized as the consequence of a series of reactions and counterreactions that follow a critical juncture.[11] Some historical treatments are only found to be impactful under certain later, often contingent historical conditions; in the argument of Wilfahrt (2021) in her excellent book, for example, the legacies of precolonial kingdoms in Senegal only become effective for generating shared public goods across villages after postcolonial democratic decentralization. The ability of the tools of the credibility revolution to identify such complex modes of moderation and mediation implied by arguments that emphasize temporality, sequence, and legacies can be limited (though other kinds of methods face substantial challenges in validating such claims empirically as well). As for generalizability, although arguments involving sequence and temporality in one context may heighten our attention to the possibility of similar patterns in others, generalizable inference may be neither the goal nor a primary metric by which we should evaluate the success of such studies.

Cumulative Learning in Historical Political Economy

Research on historical political economy since the design-based turn has led to important forms of cumulative learning. In this section we address recent research in HPE that collectively leverages empirical strategies we discussed in the previous section (or that can be seen, from the perspective of a systematic review, as doing so). Our goal is to survey this progress and to highlight the attention that some scholars have brought to issues both of generalizability and mechanism, while also suggesting possible improvements that could foster stronger accumulation.

One clarifying note is important before turning to our survey. We describe work that has used natural experiments (with either randomized or as-if random assignment to treatment conditions), discontinuities, instrumental-variables methods, or a combination of the three. Our focus, however, is not on the internal validity of the causal claims in particular studies. We recognize that in some of the studies we discuss, as-if random or other key identifying assumptions—such as exclusion restrictions or noninterference— might fail. Our goal is not to judge such elements of the designs but to assess how the combination of such studies may contribute to assessment of generalizability or mechanism, using the strategies we outlined earlier.

European Expansion

A broad array of scholarship examines the long-term effect of European colonial expansion on contemporary political and economic outcomes. There is no question that many of the institutions associated with European colonialism reaped devastating consequences on colonized societies. Yet different forms of colonialism may be more or less destructive, and some may even exhibit some positive externalities on outcomes ranging from economic growth to state capacity.[12] Understanding this variation—in terms of both the presence of different types of effects across settings and the causal mechanisms that drive these effects—has been a focus of recent work in historical political economy.

Direct Versus Indirect Colonial Rule

A first set of studies explores the impact of direct versus indirect colonial rule on economic development. For colonial India, Iyer (2010) examines the effect of being governed directly by the British Crown, versus indirectly through Indian princely states, on economic development. Between 1848 and 1856, the British assumed direct control over any Indian states whose king died without a natural heir. Iyer leverages possibly as-if random variation in the absence of an heir at the time of a ruler's death—introduced by this "Doctrine of Lapse"—to instrument for the effects of direct rule. She finds that states that experienced direct rule as a result had fewer public goods and lower levels of economic development. This finding contrasts markedly with a (likely confounded) cross-sectional comparison of directly and indirectly colonized areas: the British tended to prefer direct rule in more fertile, wetter regions, creating the appearance of a direct-rule advantage for some development outcomes. Lee and Schultz (2012) report similar findings in Cameroon, where regions colonized by the British were more likely to experience indirect rule than regions under French control. Leveraging a geographic discontinuity design, they find that areas under British control have higher levels of wealth and public goods provision in the contemporary period.

In contrast to this work, studies on Namibia find a combination of null and positive effects of direct colonial rule on economic development. In the 1890s, Germany divided colonial Namibia into two regions based on the prevalence of an infectious cattle disease—one region ruled directly and the other ruled indirectly through Indigenous elites. The border is possibly exogenous, cross-cutting existing ethnic boundaries and other attributes that might affect outcomes such as development. Using a geographic discontinuity design, Lechler and McNamee (2018) leverage this colonial division to estimate the effect of direct rule on economic outcomes. They find no effect of direct rule on economic development, as measured by educational attainment, density of night lights, poverty indices, and infrastructure quality. In related work, Chlouba and He (2021) leverage this same colonial division to estimate a *positive* effect of direct versus indirect rule on a different set of development outcomes—the commercialization of agriculture, household living standards, and paved roads.[13]

The divergent findings in India and Cameroon on the one hand, and Namibia on the other, raise important questions about the causal mechanisms driving the effect of (in) direct colonial rule on economic development. One potential mechanism is the role of land tenure regimes in areas with indirect rule. Lechler and McNamee (2018) describe the importance of communal land tenure in areas of Namibia under indirect colonial rule.[14] Similarly, Chlouba and He (2021) point to the role of this land tenure arrangement in curbing economic development in areas under indirect rule.

Might different forms of land tenure help to explain the distinct effects of direct rule on economic development? For land tenure to be a compelling explanation of the variation in effects, we would want to establish both that (i) more secure land tenure systems have a positive effect on economic development, and that (ii) the link between direct rule and more secure land tenure regimes described in Namibia is not present in contexts where scholars have found a negative effect of direct rule on economic development.[15] These are not trivial inferential targets, but design-based variation in land tenure systems (as an independent variable) and assessing the impact of direct rule on security of land tenure (as a dependent variable) is useful.

Studies in India provide suggestive evidence on both these counts. First, using an instrumental-variables design, Banerjee and Iyer (2005) find that areas in which peasants' property rights were less secure experienced lower levels of economic development over the long term. Second, to explain the negative effect of direct rule on economic development, Iyer (2010) examines whether land tenure arrangements vary across regions assigned to different types of colonial rule. She finds no evidence of a difference. We can think of Banerjee and Iyer (2005) as directly "manipulating" the mediator of interest (land tenure arrangements) and Iyer (2010) as probing the impact of the treatment variable on an intermediate outcome (i.e., the mediator). Combined, these studies suggest that land tenure arrangements play an important role in shaping the economic effects of direct, versus indirect, colonial rule.

In sum, here we see a combination of strategy (1)—related study designs across India, Cameroon, and Namibia—and strategies (2) and/or (3). In Namibia, the treatment bundles the form of rule and the security of property rights, while there is no such bundling in India. Alternatively, one can think of land tenure regimes as an intermediate outcome—and a possible mechanism—and assess impacts of direct versus indirect rule on it. Implicit mediation analysis and/or variation in effects on distinct outcomes thus give useful insights that may help to explain the differences in the effects across contexts. To be sure, other mechanisms are likely consistent with the divergent effects, and the evidence is therefore perhaps only suggestive. Yet this is also an area where theory could play an important role in developing further testable implications that discriminate between rival explanations. A key point is that a body of evidence from a *set* of related studies is important for explanation and for illuminating generalizability and mechanism.

Missionary Activity

Another recent literature explores the long-term effects of missionary activity during colonialism on contemporary educational outcomes. This research builds on Woodberry (2004; 2012), who documents a positive association between the historical presence of missionaries and current per capita income and democracy across former nonsettler colonies and suggests this is due to religion's role in fomenting education. Scholars have subsequently explored the role of missionary activity during colonial rule in shaping educational attainment today.

One notable feature of this literature is its breadth; scholars have probed the effect of missionary activity on educational outcomes across vastly different geographic contexts. A first set of studies focuses on different areas of Africa, leveraging the possibly as-if random location of missions historically to study their effects on contemporary outcomes.[16] Gallego and Woodberry (2010) provide evidence that regions of Africa in which Protestant missionaries predominated in the colonial period have higher literacy rates today than those regions with predominantly Catholic missionaries. Nunn (2014) finds that Protestant and Catholic missionary activities in Africa both exerted long-term, positive impacts on education. Studying colonial Benin, Wantchekon, Klašnja, and Novta (2015) show that families who live in close proximity to historical missions assign greater value to education.

More recently, scholars have extended these findings beyond Africa. Valencia Caicedo (2019) finds that Jesuits had a positive effect on education in South America, where a key component of their missionary activities was teaching the indigenous Guaraní to read and write. He shows that educational attainment today is higher in places that had a Jesuit mission prior to the Jesuits' expulsion from the Americas in 1767. Waldinger (2017) examines the long-run effects of Catholic missionary orders in colonial Mexico on educational outcomes. She finds that mendicant orders—which were committed to reducing poverty by educating Native populations—improved educational attainment in the regions of Mexico's countryside where their historical presence was greater.[17] In China, Bai and Kung (2015) find that regions with a greater presence of Protestant missionaries in the nineteenth century had higher urbanization rates at the beginning of the twentieth century. Though the primary outcome is not education, the causal mechanism the authors identify is knowledge diffusion through the schools and hospitals that missionaries built.

Through strategy (1), these studies probe the external validity of the causal relationship between missionary activity and educational outcomes. Across a wide array of settings, they find that the presence of missionaries increased literacy, educational attainment, and related outcomes. Unlike studies that pursue strategies (2) and (3), these do not make the leap to explanation through design-based, within- and cross-case comparisons that allow us to assess effects on intermediate outcomes or use implicit mediation analysis. Yet they do help inform our understanding of the generalizability of this causal relationship.

Forced Labor

A prominent body of scholarship in HPE examines the role of institutions of forced labor in shaping contemporary economic development. Building on Acemoglu, Johnson, and Robinson (2001; 2002), who argue that extractive institutions hamper economic growth over the long run, these studies have explored such effects for a particular type of extraction: forced labor under colonialism. For example, Dell (2010) employs a geographic discontinuity design to document the negative effect of exposure to forced labor in the silver mines of Peru and Bolivia during Spanish colonization on a range of social and development outcomes today. Lowes and Montero (2021) leverage a similar empirical strategy to examine extractive rubber concessions in the Democratic Republic of the Congo, which entailed the forced cultivation of rubber. They find similarly negative effects.

Not all studies reach the same conclusion, however. Dell and Olken (2020) employ a geographic regression discontinuity design to identify the effect of forced labor in colonial Java's sugar industry. Notably, they find that this institution had a *positive* effect on economic development. They tentatively suggest that this divergent finding is due to the role of the institutions and economic industries that accompanied forced labor in Java, which facilitated economic growth over the long term, perhaps outweighing the negative effect of forced labor itself.

This literature engages in strategy (1) to explore the effects of forced labor across different contexts (Peru, the Democratic Republic of the Congo, and Java). While the differences in observed effects may be due to the complementary institutions that accompanied forced labor, as suggested by the Java study, no empirical work assesses the validity of this claim. Indeed, Gailmard (2021a) highlights Dell and Olken's (2020) research in Java as indicative of a body of empirical work that does little to inform our understanding of theory and generalizability. Yet this is partly an empirical issue that reflects the bundled "treatment" in colonial Java, which includes both an extractive institution and a set of complementary institutions that sprung up in tandem with the country's system of forced labor. Future research might pursue strategy (2) to begin to parse the effects of these distinct institutions, and thus gain purchase on important theoretical questions about the causal relationship between forced labor and economic development.

One potentially fruitful direction may also be to explore the possibly contrasting impacts of forced labor in a single context on different outcomes, per strategy (3). In recent work on Peru, for example, Carter (2021; 2022) suggests that labor conscription to rebuild the Inca Road in the 1920s triggered mobilization by indigenous elites to secure protections for their communal land and other traditional institutions. Such institutions, however, can have mixed welfare effects, and under some conditions they may limit the ability of indigenous communities to secure government benefits or broader economic development. Such a strategy may not resolve many questions related to the generalizable effects of forced labor in this context—but it can help shed important light on variation in effects across different domains, by leveraging contrasting impacts on different outcomes.

The Slave Trade

Other research studies an alternative form of extraction—the slave trade in Africa. Nunn (2008) explores the effect of slave trading on contemporary levels of economic development. Using the distance of African countries to the markets where slaves were received to instrument for the intensity of the slave trade, he identifies a significant and negative causal effect on economic development today. While few would question slavery's devastating impact on societies across Africa, Nunn's findings are important to quantify the dimensions of that harm, and may help to pinpoint the origins of underdevelopment across the region.

Subsequent scholarship has sought to shed light on the mechanism linking the slave trade with contemporary economic development. Nunn and Wantchekon (2011) argue that slave trading engendered a culture of mistrust among individuals who were most affected, which has persisted to the present day.[18] In complementary work, Whatley and Gillezeau (2011) examine the effect of the slave trade on ethnic fragmentation along Africa's western coast.[19] They find that slave trading increased the number of ethnic groups in Africa, an important source of social conflict that is often theorized to impede economic growth.[20]

These studies contribute to the cumulation of knowledge by exploring the causal mechanisms that may link the slave trade with lower levels of contemporary development. They rely on strategy (3), employing similar designs across overlapping regions of Africa to explore the effects of slave trading on distinct but related outcomes. Collectively, they suggest the slave trade's pernicious effects are driven—at least partially—by changing social dynamics, both across and within African ethnic groups. The studies provide evidence of impacts on intermediate outcomes—like trust—that may be mechanisms linking the slave trade to development outcomes. While other causal mechanisms may also be in play, this research nevertheless provides useful empirical purchase on questions of mechanism and generalizability, and uses relatively design-based empirical strategies to investigate explanations of the effect. Future work might attempt to identify complementary mechanisms by further employing strategies (2) and (3).

Conclusion

Empirical routes to the evaluation of generalizability and mechanism are essential in most areas of social science and perhaps especially in historical political economy—a field focusing definitionally on the empirical terrain of "history." Social scientists have laid out a range of strategies, ranging from qualitative process tracing to path models. We have proposed an alternative approach in this chapter, describing how design-based replication, implicit mediation analysis, and assessment of impacts on varied outcomes may help us learn cumulatively about generalizability and mechanism. A credible evidence base is critical both for testing and developing theory. For generalizable theory, it is important that the evidence spans contexts, helps to unbundle treatments, or allows assessment of varied effects on distinct outcomes.

Our partial review of work in several substantive areas of HPE suggests that some elements of the strategies we describe are at work in practice, either implicitly or explicitly. Beyond European colonial expansion, one can also see elements of these strategies at work in research on Black migration from the southern to the northern United States (Calderon, Fouka, and Tabellini forthcoming; Derenoncourt 2022), the electoral consequences of technological innovations in agriculture (Dasgupta 2018; Dasgupta and Ruiz Ramirez 2022), and other research areas. However, we found in our survey several important practical issues, with implications for the construction of the evidence base. In related work (), we have studied knowledge accumulation via natural experiments focused on "contemporary" politics. Our impression is that, in that context, examples were somewhat easier to find than in HPE. Part of the explanation might indeed be that these strategies are harder to implement in historical work, due perhaps to data constraints and the fact that relatively off-the-shelf designs—such as close race regression discontinuity designs that rely on the presence of democratic elections—are less prevalent in historical settings. However, we also believe that more systematic focus on replication and extension of previous work, with an eye to assessing generalizability and mechanism, will bear fruit in HPE as well.

Another critical issue, raised by other scholars, relates to case selection. We think it is only partially true that the idiosyncratic nature of natural experiments and other design-based methods undermines the ability to select cases theoretically (as opposed to inductively, based on where as-if random variation arises). Moreover, issues of case selection also arise in the analysis of more ostensibly comprehensive (e.g., cross-national) data sets, where it is not however always readily apparent which cases contribute most to inferences. Formal meta-analysis may not be desirable with the strategies we have outlined here; there is usually not a large enough N of cases nor enough consistency or harmonization across cases for that to be possible. However, by taking advantage of design-based variation both across and within cases and by comparing findings across studies and contexts, we can enhance the credibility of inferences about generalizability of causal relationships and the mechanisms that undergird them.

We see no necessary tension between the credibility revolution and the construction of a cross-case evidence base that can be used to discipline, advance, and validate generalizable theory. However, it seems important that the goal of assessing generalizability and mechanism be explicit. We think it would be useful if strategies for cumulative learning—such as those we have laid out here—were leveraged more purposively by different sets of scholars, using design-based variation both within and across studies.

Notes

1. See, e.g., Angrist and Krueger (2001); Diamond and Robinson (2010); Cantoni and Yuchtman (2021); or Valencia Caicedo (2021). For reviews of other important approaches employed in HPE, see Gailmard and Bateman and Teele (2020).
2. On placebo tests, see, e.g., Eggers, Tuñón, and Dafoe (2022).
3. On the revolution and the revolutionaries, see Angrist and Pischke (2010).
4. The utility of these methods is the subject of long-standing debates in both political science and economics; see, e.g.. Deaton (2010), Imbens (2010), and Angrist and Pischke (2010).
5. For discussion and definitions, see, e.g., Mahoney (2003), Dunning et al. (2019), or Callis, Dunning, and Tuñón (2022).
6. North and Weingast (1989); for critiques, see Stasavage (2002; 2007), Pincus and Robinson (2014), among others.

7. We use "internal validity" as Campbell and Stanley (1963, 5) did with respect to quasi-experiments: "the basic minimum without which any experiment is uninterpretable: Did in fact the experimental treatments make a difference in this specific experimental instance?"
8. See, e.g., Bullock and Green (2021); Gerber and Green (2012, 322–25).
9. Gerber, Green, and Larimer (2008), for example, devise varied experimental prompts to distinguish between (a) a sense of civic duty, (b) Hawthorne (or "observer") effects, and (c) social pressure as the mechanisms that explain why a mobilization message may spark voter turnout.
10. See, e.g., Freedman (2009) on how the knowledge that infected waste and water causes cholera transmission preceded the theory of germs.
11. Collier and Munck (2022) make the presence of a legacy definitional to a critical juncture: no legacy, no critical juncture. This does not gainsay the possibility of long-run effects that are not legacies, however.
12. Other studies, not discussed here, have documented divergent effects based on the national identity of colonizers. See, e.g., Feyrer and Sacerdote (2009). See also Mattingly (2017), which examines the effects of non-European colonial rule in China.
13. While relying on the same discontinuity as Lechler and McNamee (2018), Chlouba and He (2021) limit their sample to a subset of households and employ matching on either side of the colonial border.
14. In related work, McNamee (2019) finds suggestive evidence of the enduring role of communal land tenure arrangements in areas of Namibia that experienced indirect colonial rule.
15. Finding evidence in support of (i) and (ii) may be neither necessary nor sufficient to establish that variation in land tenure regimes explains the differences in the effects of direct versus indirect rule across contexts. In this sense, testing these claims is comparable to a "straw in the wind" test in process tracing (Van Evera 1997; Bennett 2010; Collier 2011).
16. Jedwab, Meier zu Selhausen, and Moradi (2022) examine missionary expansion in Ghana and find that missionaries settled in healthier, safer, and richer areas, and prioritized investments in these locations. The authors argue that these factors might explain why places with past missions are more developed today.
17. In contrast, the presence of Jesuit missionaries, who focused educational efforts on the colony's elite in the city centers, had no lasting effects.
18. They instrument for the incidence of the slave trade using the distance of a given ethnic group from the African coast, where slaves were purchased before being sent to their final destination. The geographic focus of this paper covers all of sub-Saharan Africa except Cameroon, Gabon, the Democratic Republic of the Congo, Angola, Sudan, Ethiopia, and Eritrea.
19. Their study extends from Tunisia in the north to South Africa in the south.
20. See, e.g., Easterly and Levine (1997).

References

Acemoglu, Daron, Simon Johnson, and James A. Robinson. 2001. "The Colonial Origins of Comparative Development: An Empirical Investigation." *American Economic Review* 91, no. 5: 1369–401.

Acemoglu, Daron, Simon Johnson, and James A. Robinson. 2002. "Reversal of Fortune: Geography and Institutions in the Making of the Modern World Income Distribution." *Quarterly Journal of Economics* 117, no. 4: 1231–94.

Acharya Avidit, Matthew Blackwell, and Maya Sen. 2022. "Historical Persistence." in *The Oxford Handbook of Historical Political Economy*, ed. Jeffery Jenkins and Jared Rubin, 117–41. New York: Oxford University Press.

Angrist, Joshua D., and Alan B. Krueger. 2001. "Instrumental Variables and the Search for Identification: From Supply and Demand to Natural Experiments." *Journal of Economic Perspectives* 15, no. 4: 69–85.

Angrist, Joshua D., and Jörn-Steffen Pischke. 2009. *Mostly Harmless Econometrics*. Princeton, NJ: Princeton University Press.

Angrist, Joshua D., and Jörn-Steffen Pischke. 2010. "The Credibility Revolution in Empirical Economics: How Better Research Design Is Taking the Con out of Econometrics." *Journal of Economic Perspectives* 24, no. 2: 3–30.

Aronow, Peter M., and Cyrus Samii. 2016. "Does Regression Produce Representative Estimates of Causal Effects?" *American Journal of Political Science* 60, no. 1: 250–67.

Ashworth, Scott, Christopher R. Berry, and Ethan Bueno de Mesquita. 2021. *Theory and Credibility: Integrating Theoretical and Empirical Social Science*. Princeton, NJ: Princeton University Press.

Bai, Ying, and James Kai-sing Kung. 2015. "Diffusing Knowledge While Spreading God's Message: Protestantism and Economic Prosperity in China, 1840–1920." *Journal of the European Economic Association* 13, no. 4: 669–98.

Banerjee, Abhijit, and Lakshmi Iyer. 2005. "History, Institutions, and Economic Performance: The Legacy of Colonial Land Tenure Systems in India." *American Economic Review* 95, no. 4: 1190–213.

Bateman, David A., and Dawn Langan Teele. 2020. "A Developmental Approach to Historical Causal Inference." *Public Choice* 185, no. 3: 253–79.

Bennett, Andrew. 2010. "Process Tracing and Causal Inference." In *Rethinking Social Inquiry*, ed. D. Collier and H. E. Brady, 207–20. New York: Rowman and Littlefield.

Bullock, John G., and Donald P. Green. 2021. "The Failings of Conventional Mediation Analysis and a Design-Based Alternative." *Advances in Methods and Practices in Psychological Science* 4, no. 4: 25152459211047228.

Calderon, Alvaro, Vasiliki Fouka, and Marco Tabellini. Forthcoming. "Racial Diversity and Racial Policy Preferences: The Great Migration and Civil Rights." *Review of Economic Studies*.

Callis, Anna, Thad Dunning, and Guadalupe Tuñón. 2022. "Causal Inference and Knowledge Accumulation in Historical Political Economy."

Campbell, Donald T., and Julian Stanley. 1963. *Experimental and Quasi-Experimental Designs for Research*. 1st edition. Belmont, CA: Cengage Learning.

Cantoni, Davide, and Noam Yuchtman. 2021. "Historical Natural Experiments: Bridging Economics and Economic History." In *The Handbook of Historical Economics*, ed. A. Bisin and G. Federico, 213–41. Academic Press.

Carter, Christopher L. 2021. "The Representational Effects of Communal Property: Evidence from Peru's Indigenous Groups." *Comparative Political Studies* 54, no. 12: 2191–225.

Carter, Christopher L. 2022. "Extraction, Assimilation, and Accommodation: The Historical Foundations of Indigenous-State Relations in Latin America."

Cartwright, Nancy, and Jeremy Hardie. 2012. *Evidence-Based Policy: A Practical Guide to Doing It Better.* Oxford University Press.

Chlouba, Vladimir, and Jianzi He. 2021. "Colonial Legacy, Private Property, and Rural Development: Evidence from Namibian Countryside." *Economic History of Developing Regions* 36, no. 1: 30–56.

Collier, David. 2011. "Understanding Process Tracing." *PS: Political Science & Politics* 44, no. 4: 823–30.

Collier, David, Henry E. Brady, and Jason Seawright. 2010. "Sources of Leverage in Causal Inference: Toward an Alternative View of Methodology." In *Rethinking Social Inquiry: Diverse Tools, Shared Standards*, ed. H. E. Brady and D. Collier, 229–66. Lanham, MD: Rowman and Littlefield.

Collier, David, and Gerardo L. Munck. 2022. *Critical Junctures and Historical Legacies: Insights and Methods for Comparative Social Science.* Rowman and Littlefield.

Dasgupta, Aditya. 2018. "Technological Change and Political Turnover: The Democratizing Effects of the Green Revolution in India." *American Political Science Review* 112, no. 4: 918–38.

Dasgupta, Aditya, and Elena Ruiz Ramirez. 2022. "Explaining Rural Conservatism: Political Consequences of Technological Change in the Great Plains."

Deaton, Angus. 2010. "Understanding the Mechanisms of Economic Development." *Journal of Economic Perspectives* 24, no. 3: 3–16.

Dell, Melissa. 2010. "The Persistent Effects of Peru's Mining Mita." *Econometrica* 78, no. 6: 1863–903.

Dell, Melissa, and Benjamin Olken. 2020. "The Development Effects of the Extractive Colonial Economy: The Dutch Cultivation System in Java." *Review of Economic Studies* 87, no. 1: 164–203.

Derenoncourt, Ellora. 2022. "Can You Move to Opportunity? Evidence from the Great Migration." *American Economic Review* 112, no. 2: 369–408.

Diamond, Jared, and James A. Robinson. 2010. *Natural Experiments of History.* Edited by J. Diamond. Cambridge, MA: Belknap Press of Harvard University Press.

Dunning, Thad. 2012. *Natural Experiments in the Social Sciences: A Design-Based Approach.* Cambridge University Press.

Dunning, Thad, Guy Grossman, Macartan Humphreys, Susan D. Hyde, Craig McIntosh, and Gareth Nellis. 2019. *Information, Accountability, and Cumulative Learning: Lessons from Metaketa I.* Cambridge University Press.

Easterly, William, and Ross Levine. 1997. "Africa's Growth Tragedy: Policies and Ethnic Divisions." *Quarterly Journal of Economics* 112, no. 4: 1203–50.

Eggers, Andrew C., Guadalupe Tuñón, and Alan Dafoe. 2022. "Placebo Tests for Causal Inference."

Feyrer, James, and Bruce Sacerdote. 2009. "Colonialism and Modern Income: Islands as Natural Experiments." *Review of Economics and Statistics* 91, no. 2: 245–62.

Freedman, David A. 2009. "Statistical Models and Shoe Leather." In *Statistical Models and Causal Inference: A Dialogue with the Social Sciences*, ed. D. Collier, J. S. Sekhon, and P. B. Stark, 45–62. Cambridge: Cambridge University Press.

Gailmard, Sean. 2021a. "Theory, History, and Political Economy." *Journal of Historical Political Economy* 1, no. 1: 69–104.

Gailmard, Sean. 2021b. "What Are We Doing in Historical Political Economy?" *Broadstreet.* https://broadstreet.blog/2021/01/08/what-are-we-doing-in-historical-political-economy/.

Gailmard, Sean. 2022. "Formal Models in Historical Political Economy." In *The Oxford Handbook of Historical Political Economy*, ed. Jeffery Jenkins and Jared Rubin, 95–115. New York: Oxford University Press.

Gallego, Francisco, and Robert Woodberry. 2010. "Christian Missionaries and Education in Former African Colonies: How Competition Mattered." *Journal of African Economies* 19, no. 3: 294–329.

Gerber, Alan S., and Donald P. Green. 2012. *Field Experiments: Design, Analysis, and Interpretation*. Illustrated edition. New York: W. W. Norton & Company.

Gerber, Alan S., Donald P. Green, and Christopher W. Larimer. 2008. "Social Pressure and Voter Turnout: Evidence from a Large-Scale Field Experiment." *American Political Science Review* 102, no. 1: 33–48.

Glynn, Adam N. 2012. "The Product and Difference Fallacies for Indirect Effects." *American Journal of Political Science* 56, no. 1: 257–69.

Imai, Kosuke, Luke Keele, and Teppei Yamamoto. 2010. "Identification, Inference and Sensitivity Analysis for Causal Mediation Effects." *Statistical Science* 25, no. 1: 51–71.

Imbens, Guido W. 2010. "Better LATE Than Nothing: Some Comments on Deaton (2009) and Heckman and Urzua (2009)." *Journal of Economic Literature* 48, no. 2: 399–423.

Iyer, Lakshmi. 2010. "Direct versus Indirect Colonial Rule in India: Long-Term Consequences." *Review of Economics and Statistics* 92, no. 4: 693–713.

Jedwab, Remi, Felix Meier zu Selhausen, and Alexander Moradi. 2022. "The Economics of Missionary Expansion: Evidence from Africa and Implications for Development." *Journal of Economic Growth* 27: 149–92.

King, Gary, Robert O. Keohane, and Sidney Verba. 1994. *Designing Social Inquiry: Scientific Inference in Qualitative Research*. Princeton, NJ: Princeton University Press.

Leamer, Edward. 1983. "Let's Take the Con out of Econometrics." *American Economic Review* 73, no. 1: 31–43.

Lechler, Marie, and Lachlan McNamee. 2018. "Indirect Colonial Rule Undermines Support for Democracy: Evidence from a Natural Experiment in Namibia." *Comparative Political Studies* 51, no. 14: 1858–98.

Lee, Alexander, and Kenneth A. Schultz. 2012. "Comparing British and French Colonial Legacies: A Discontinuity Analysis of Cameroon." *Quarterly Journal of Political Science* 7, no. 4: 365–410.

Lowes, Sara, and Eduardo Montero. 2021. "Concessions, Violence, and Indirect Rule: Evidence from the Congo Free State." *Quarterly Journal of Economics* 136, no. 4: 2047–91.

Mahoney, James. 2003. "Knowledge Accumulation in Comparative Historical Research: The Case of Democracy and Authoritarianism." In *Comparative Historical Analysis in the Social Sciences*, Cambridge Studies in Comparative Politics, ed. D. Rueschemeyer and J. Mahoney, 131–74. Cambridge: Cambridge University Press.

Mattingly, Daniel C. 2017. "Colonial Legacies and State Institutions in China: Evidence from a Natural Experiment." *Comparative Political Studies* 50, no. 4: 434–63.

McNamee, Lachlan. 2019. "Indirect Colonial Rule and the Salience of Ethnicity." *World Development* 122: 142–56.

North, Douglass C., and Barry R. Weingast. 1989. "Constitutions and Commitment: The Evolution of Institutions Governing Public Choice in Seventeenth-Century England." *Journal of Economic History* 49, no. 4: 803–32.

Nunn, Nathan. 2008. "The Long-Term Effects of Africa's Slave Trades." *Quarterly Journal of Economics* 123, no. 1: 139–76.

Nunn, Nathan. 2014. "Gender and Missionary Influence in Colonial Africa." In *Africa's Development in Historical Perspective*, ed. E. Akyeampong, R. H. Bates, N. Nunn, and J. A. Robinson, 489–512. New York: Cambridge University Press.

Nunn, Nathan, and Leonard Wantchekon. 2011. "The Slave Trade and the Origins of Mistrust in Africa." *American Economic Review* 101, no. 7: 3221–52.

Pincus, Steve, and James A. Robinson. 2014. *Institutions, Property Rights, and Economic Growth: The Legacy of Douglass North*. New York: Cambridge University Press.

Rozenas, Arturas. 2021. "History and Theory in Historical Political Economy." *Broadstreet*. https://broadstreet.blog/2021/11/12/history-and-theory-in-historical-political-economy/.

Stasavage, David. 2002. "Credible Commitment in Early Modern Europe: North and Weingast Revisited." *Journal of Law, Economics, and Organization* 18, no. 1: 155–86.

Stasavage, David. 2007. "Partisan Politics and Public Debt: The Importance of the 'Whig Supremacy' for Britain's Financial Revolution." *European Review of Economic History* 11, no. 1: 123–53.

Valencia Caicedo, Felipe. 2019. "The Mission: Human Capital Transmission, Economic Persistence, and Culture in South America." *Quarterly Journal of Economics* 134, no. 1: 507–56.

Valencia Caicedo, Felipe. 2021. "Historical Econometrics: Instrumental Variables and Regression Discontinuity Designs." In *The Handbook of Historical Economics*, ed. A. Bisin and G. Federico, 179–211. Academic Press.

Van Evera, Stephen. 1997. *Guide to Methods for Students of Political Science*. Ithaca, NY: Cornell University Press.

Waldinger, Maria. 2017. "The Long-Run Effects of Missionary Orders in Mexico." *Journal of Development Economics* 127: 355–78.

Waldner, David. 2016. "Invariant Causal Mechanisms." *Qualitative & Multi-Method Research* 14, no. 1: 28–34.

Wantchekon, Leonard, Marko Klašnja, and Natalija Novta. 2015. "Education and Human Capital Externalities: Evidence from Colonial Benin." *Quarterly Journal of Economics* 130, no. 2: 703–57.

Whatley, Warren, and Rob Gillezeau. 2011. "The Impact of the Transatlantic Slave Trade on Ethnic Stratification in Africa." *American Economic Review* 101, no. 3: 571–76.

Wilfahrt, Martha. 2021. *Precolonial Legacies in Postcolonial Politics: Representation and Redistribution in Decentralized West Africa*. Cambridge University Press.

Woodberry, Robert D. 2004. "The Shadow of Empire: Christian Missions, Colonial Policy, and Democracy in Postcolonial Societies." PhD dissertation, University of North Carolina, Chapel Hill.

Woodberry, Robert D. 2012. "The Missionary Roots of Liberal Democracy." *American Political Science Review* 106, no. 2: 244–74.

CHAPTER 5

NETWORKS IN HISTORICAL POLITICAL ECONOMY

ADAM SLEZ

CONTEMPORARY research in historical political economy (HPE) is characterized by, among other things, the use of quantitative methods to examine historical materials reflecting the conditions of economic and political life within a delimited spatiotemporal context. While regression remains the dominant approach to quantitative analysis in HPE, there is now a sizable interdisciplinary literature drawing on the use of network analysis. Whereas conventional approaches to quantitative data analysis tend to focus on the relationship between attributes, network analysis focuses on the connection between entities, giving rise to questions about the relational environment in which they are embedded. This environment can be viewed from the perspective of individual entities or from the perspective of the set of entities as a whole, with local relationships tending to concatenate upward to produce a larger social structure.

The use of formal network analysis in HPE can be traced back to the rise of the Harvard School under Harrison White starting in the 1960s. Coming to sociology by way of physics, White succeeded in bringing together the existing strains of network analytic thinking that had begun to emerge in cognate fields such as social psychology and anthropology (Freeman 2004; Prell 2012). More importantly, White succeeded in conveying the utility of this approach to multiple generations of colleagues and students, many of whom used network analysis to shed new light on the origins of market and state, as well as the patterns of political contention that accompanied the rise of these institutions. The ability to apply network analysis to these types of questions was, in many respects, endogenous to the object of inquiry, in the sense that the existence of historical documents capturing the vast webs of ties created through the extension of credit, the creation of business partnerships, the exchange of goods, and the provision of patronage was a byproduct of the organizational changes that came with the growth of the modern corporation and the expansion of centralized authority.

While the development of modern network analysis may have begun in sociology, the use of network analytic tools in HPE has since been taken up in fields such as economics and political science. After introducing the basic concepts behind the use of historical network data, I discuss the various ways that network data have been used to study the transition to economic and political modernity. Despite the considerable progress that has been made in establishing network analysis as a standard tool in the HPE toolkit, a number of challenges remain. With this in mind, I conclude by reflecting on the issues associated with trying to integrate network analysis with causal inference. The fundamental problem is that the very thing that makes networks interesting—the connection between observations—undermines our ability to identify and infer causal effects from observational data using standard methods. Recent work suggests that stochastic actor-oriented models and latent space approaches may provide a way forward in cases where longitudinal data are available.

Historical Network Data

In the social sciences, the notion of data is used to refer to empirical observations that allow us to speak to processes in the social world. For quantitative researchers, these observations are traditionally represented in terms of a matrix describing a set of entities or cases in terms of a set of attributes or variables. Working within this framework, techniques such as regression serve as a method for describing how the expected value of a given outcome or dependent variable varies as a function of a given treatment or independent variable. From this perspective, social phenomena are explained in terms of the relationship between variables. While it is by no means antithetical or even wholly separate from regression, network analysis is characterized by an emphasis on the relationship between entities. These relationships can be formally represented as a graph in which the various entities of interest are treated as nodes that are linked to one another by edges.

We can distinguish between different types of networks based on the number of types of nodes that they contain, as well as the nature of the relationship between the nodes in question. When first learning network analysis, it is not uncommon to start with data depicting the presence or absence of a relationship between members of a single set of entities. One of the best-known examples of this type of data comes from fifteenth-century Florence, where marriage served as a mechanism for binding elite families to one another, creating the basic structure around which early economic and political institutions were built. Drawing on information originally presented by Breiger and Pattison (1986), Figure 5.1 depicts the structure of marital ties among sixteen Florentine families, along with the entity-by-entity adjacency matrix used to store the underlying data on which this simple graph is based.

Looking at the adjacency matrix, we see that the simplicity of the graph stems not only from the fact that we are considering a single set of entities, but from the fact that the ties between them are both binary and symmetric. The ties are binary in the sense that they are either present—as denoted by a 1—or absent—as denoted by a 0. To put

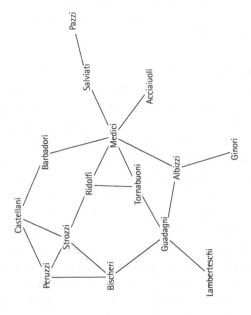

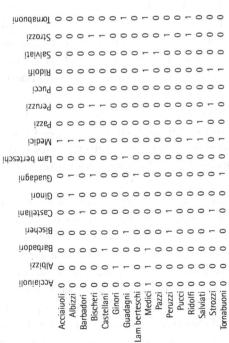

FIGURE 5.1. Graph of marriages among sixteen Florentine families, c. 1430

it another way, a pair of families is either joined by marriage or not. This relationship is symmetric in the sense that family i cannot be married to family j without family j also being married to family i. The existence of relational symmetry is reflected in the fact that the pattern of 1s and 0s below the diagonal is identical to the pattern of 1s and 0s above the diagonal.

While the use of 1s and 0s makes sense when considering relationships based on marriage, which is either present or not, there is nothing stopping us from introducing information on the strength, direction, and valence of a given relationship, where appropriate. When considering Florentine credit relations, for example, Padgett and McLean (2011) examine the amount of credit that flowed from one industry to another, giving rise to a graph in which ties are both valued and asymmetric. In the case of the credit example, the values assigned to each edge can be interpreted as a measure of the strength of the relationship between pairs of industries, with differences in strength reflected in differences in magnitude. In other cases, however, the relevant question is not how much stuff flows from one entity to another, but whether the connection between the entities in question is positive or negative. Obert (2014), for example, examines patterns of conflict and alliance among gunfighters in the American Southwest during the late nineteenth century. The resulting network can be represented as a signed graph in which the edges referring to alliances are denoted by a 1 in the underlying adjacency matrix, while the edges referring to conflicts are denoted by a –1.

When working with historical materials, it is not uncommon to find records listing connections between different types of entities. The number of types of entities in a network is commonly referred to in terms of the number of modes. A one-mode network, for example, describes the set of relationships between entities of a single type, while a two-mode network describes the set of relationships between entities of two different types. What sets a two-mode network apart from a one-mode network such as the Florentine marriage network described earlier is not simply the number of types of nodes, but the fact that there are no edges between nodes of the same type. As Breiger (1974) shows, however, every two-mode matrix can be recast as a pair of one-mode matrices representing the set of indirect relationships that exist between nodes belonging to the same mode by virtue of their common connection to nodes belonging to the other mode.

This can be seen in Figure 5.2, which depicts the relationship between individuals and organizations for the twenty-five largest railroad corporations in the United States in 1905 based on data compiled by economist David Bunting. In the case of the full two-mode network shown in panel A, an individual is said to be tied to a corporation if they sit on its board of directors. In the case of the corresponding one-mode network shown in panel B, a pair of individuals is said to be tied to one another if they share at least one board in common. By extension, a pair of corporations is said to be tied to one another if they share at least one director in common, as illustrated in panel C. So while we can view the original two-mode data from the perspective of either individuals or organizations, it is impossible to tell the story of one without implicitly telling the story of the other. This has important implications for how we think

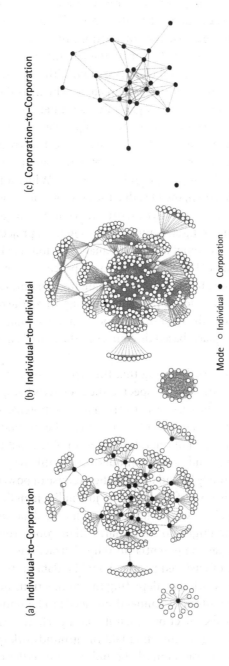

FIGURE 5.2. Graph of board interlocks among the twenty-five largest railroad corporations in the United States in 1905

about relational properties such as centrality and structural equivalence (see Everett and Borgatti 2013).

The use of network analysis in HPE is not limited to the study of social networks, by which I mean networks comprising concrete relationships among human actors or organizations. This idea is exemplified by the work of John Mohr, who used network analytic tools to examine the structure of relationships between cultural categories and relief practices in New York City during the late nineteenth and early twentieth centuries (e.g., Mohr 1994; Mohr and Duquenne 1997). The data for this analysis come from copies of the New York City Charity Directory, which, as the name suggests, included a listing of the various welfare organizations located throughout the city. More importantly, it included descriptions of the types of people served by each organization and the types of relief that it provided. Turning the connections between categories and practices into a two-mode matrix, Mohr used network analysis to reveal the symbolic logic of welfare provision during the period in question. While some were skeptical of this approach (e.g., Gould 2003), the idea that the relationship between signifiers could be formally expressed in network analytic terms was central to ongoing efforts to quantify the measurement of meaning structures (Mohr 1998)—a project that has since been reinforced by the arrival of computational text analysis (Mohr et al. 2020). Though still relatively new to the field of HPE, natural language processing and related techniques have been used to examine subjects such as the changing dynamics of treaty-making between the United States and American Indians (Spirling 2012), the material foundations of ideological polarization in the wake of the American Revolution (Hoffman 2019), and the emergence of durable, place-based discourses in the American women's movement (Nelson 2021).

Before moving on, it is worth noting that the types of data described in this section are not necessarily neutral with respect to the processes being studied. While this is by no means unique to the case of network data, the potential for endogeneity is especially pronounced in the context of HPE, where the production of quantifiable documents was part and parcel of the rationalization of the institutions that marked the transition to economic and political modernity. In this respect, the existence of such documents was routinely bound up with the exercise of power over marginalized populations. This point is powerfully made by journalist Jamelle Bouie (2022), who questions whether the public availability of quantitative data on the history of the trans-Atlantic slave trade might do more harm than good. The risk of relying on numbers alone is that it has the potential to reify abstractions borne out of the systematic dehumanization of enslaved people. So while data on the slave trade can be readily translated into network data depicting the connections between both people and places, the resulting pattern of connections needs to be understood in the context of the larger historical project of which it was a part. This is no less true when considering the array of relationships that laid the groundwork for the expansion of centralized authority, which was similarly bound up with settler colonialism and the political economy of empire more generally.

Market-Building and the Rise of the Modern Economy

Going hand in hand with the appearance of the modern state, the transition to economic modernity was marked by the emergence of the market economy, which was driven by the expansion of long-distance trade, giving rise to both global and national markets. Since the marginalist revolution of the late nineteenth century, market relationships have overwhelmingly been understood in terms of the intersection of supply and demand. This conceptualization, which is closely associated with the advent of neoclassical economics, stands in stark contrast to that of classical political economy, as well as contemporary economic sociology, both of which focus on the concrete institutions and social structures around which markets are built (Swedberg 2003). The use of network analysis proved integral to the success of the new economic sociology movement of the 1970s and 1980s. Growing out of the work of the Harvard School and its descendants at the State University of New York at Stony Brook (Convert and Heilbron 2007), the movement took aim at conventional understandings of economic behavior that tended to treat economic phenomenon as a product of disembedded interests. This influence is evident in work on HPE, where network analysis has been used to examine the relational foundations of markets in history, along with the concomitant changes in economic organization that ultimately culminated in the rise of the modern corporation.

The Geography of Market-Building

There is a long tradition of using network analysis to study the geography of historical trade patterns, going as far back as Pitts's (1965) work on urban centrality and the structure of the river network in medieval Russia. Much like the development of the medieval river network, the expansion of overseas trade played a crucial role in shaping the geographic hierarchy of the early modern period, albeit on a much larger scale. This is exemplified by the ascent of the British Empire on the back of the English East India Company (EIC), which progressively overtook its rivals in France and, perhaps more notably, the Netherlands. Drawing on data from EIC shipping logs, Erikson (2014) shows that the success of the EIC in the period between 1601 and 1835 was an unintended consequence of private trade on the part of ship captains who extended their voyages beyond what the company officially dictated. Faced with considerable uncertainty about where to go in search of trade, captains working for the EIC relied on information transmitted by their peers while sharing time in port. The diffusion of organizational knowledge helped to expand the number of ports with which the company actively engaged, directly contributing to the geographic structure of the emerging global market of which the EIC was a part.

While rivers and oceans served as a natural conduit of trade throughout history, the driving force behind the construction of national markets during the nineteenth century was the advent of the railroad. Estimating the effect of changes in market access between 1870 and 1890, economic historians find that the substantial increase in agricultural land values during this period was largely due to the expansion of the railroad network (Donaldson and Hornbeck 2016). One of the reasons why the expansion of market infrastructure was so important was that it helped bring new land into production. This led to a boom in the market for agricultural commodities such as wheat. In an effort to maximize throughput in the form of long-distance, high-volume traffic, railroad corporations partnered with the large grain buyers who owned the grain elevators used to load stored grain on to waiting railroad cars. Drawing on data collected by the South Dakota Board of Railroad Commissioners, Slez (2020) shows that the structure of the grain market in South Dakota in 1890 can be formally represented as a tripartite network depicting the connection between rail lines, towns, and elevator owners. The overwhelming tendency toward mutually exclusive partnerships between rail lines and elevator owners contributed to a world in which lines served as a venue for the creation of distinct market communities, with the degree of internal differentiation within any given system depending on the degree of overlap in the geographic reach of the elevator companies with which each line partnered.

The expansion of trade in material goods was predicated on concomitant innovations in the market for money and credit. European bills of exchange were particularly significant insofar as they included a mechanism for currency exchange, which allowed lenders to legally profit off differences in exchange rates across locales (Rubin 2010). This contributed to the institutionalization of impersonal exchange and the emergence of a global market for foreign currency, with London at its center. The effects of this process were reflected in the relationships around which individual bills of exchange were based (Accominotti, Lucena-Piquero, and Ugolini 2021), as well as in the flow of investments in foreign currency more generally. Using stochastic blockmodeling to sort countries into groups of structurally equivalent observations on the basis of historical exchange listings, Flandreau and Jobst (2005) find that the contours of the international monetary system at the turn of the twentieth century could be succinctly described in terms of a divide between what they refer to as key, intermediary, and peripheral countries. Whereas the currencies from key countries such as Great Britain, Germany, and France tended to circulate globally, the currencies from intermediate countries such as Belgium, Italy, and the Netherlands tended to circulate regionally within Europe, while the currencies for peripheral countries such as Mexico, Argentina, and Brazil tended to circulate locally, only rarely making it beyond the domestic market.

Networked Organizations and the Emergence of the Modern Firm

The construction of global and national markets was characterized by changes in the connection between places, as well as in the relationships around which economic activity was organized, eventually leading to the rise of the modern corporation, as famously described by Chandler (1977), among others. In telling this story, it is tempting to fall back on a stylized narrative in which large bureaucratic organizations progressively supplanted both atomized markets and patrimonial networks as the fundamental locus of economic activity. Yet one of the chief contributions of network analytic research to the literature on HPE has been to show that the distinction between hierarchy, market, and network is not nearly as neat as it seems. This is evident in Erikson's (2014) work on the English East India Company discussed earlier. On the one hand, the EIC was a multidivisional firm with a formal monopoly over trade in the area to the east of the Cape of Good Hope and the west of Cape Horn. On the other hand, the EIC thrived because of its tolerance for private trading on the part of ship captains bound together as part of a larger social network that served as a conduit for the diffusion of information within the firm.

The EIC was not alone in combining social networks with formal organization. As research on the Italian city states during the late Middle Ages and early Renaissance reveals, the origins of the modern economy can be attributed to organizational innovations born out of a generative blending of social and economic imperatives. In Genoa, for example, the introduction of short-term equity partnerships known as *commenda* fueled the expansion of long-distance trade, bringing together a diverse and increasingly decentralized network of actors who mixed trading with other economic activities. Once the commercial revolution began to take off, however, Genoese traders were increasingly likely to form partnerships within their own status and occupational groups, transforming the city's feudal nobility into a newly emerging merchant elite (Van Doosselaere 2009). In Florence, the international traders who made up the city's ruling elite used political mobilization and marital ties to shore up support among domestic bankers, helping to bring the guild-based logic of Florentine banking into the global economy. This led to the rise of diversified partnership systems, which were characterized by, among other things, the existence of a legal partnership between a controlling partner and a set of independently managed branches, each with its own set of books (Padgett and McLean 2006). The cultivation of marital ties among Florentine banking partners was especially important in solidifying the role of the partnership system in the modern economy insofar as it made the logic of banking inseparable from that of the family, thereby embedding the partnership system within a larger social structure, turning a discrete economic innovation into a thoroughgoing invention.

While economic ties were often used to reinforce existing social distinctions, the resulting partnership networks often took on a life of their own. Focusing on the case of Saint-Malo, France, Hillmann (2021) argues that the growth of the Malouin economy during the eighteenth century was due in large part to the network of relationships that emerged around privateering. These relationships were unique in the extent to which they generated economic cohesion in what was otherwise a highly stratified community. As Hillmann shows, however, the effect of privateering ventures on the cohesiveness of the Malouin merchant network was not readily reducible to a tendency to partner with neighbors or family members. Whether it made sense to build cross-group ties varied depending on the context in which actors were embedded. This can be seen in the case of late Imperial Russia, where reputation and brokerage emerged as alternative mechanisms for accumulating economic resources. Examining patterns of capital mobilization in the period between 1869 and 1913, Hillmann and Aven (2011) find that reputation effects tended to be significantly greater in the periphery of the Russian partnership network where local tie structures tended to be more constrained and corporate founders were more likely to partner with individuals from the same industry, region, or family. At the same time, the amount of capital raised tended to be greater in the core, where founding teams benefitted from the reach of their ties.

As the scale of economic activity grew over the late nineteenth and early twentieth centuries, the prevalence of ties between firms became a point of considerable concern (Fennema and Schijf 1978). This was especially true in the United States in 1912–1913, when the Pujo Committee launched an inquiry into, among other things, the role of interlocking directorates in the consolidation of corporate control. While corporate interlocks were a regular feature of the American economy since at least the early nineteenth century (Bunting 1983), the degree of interlocking and the nature of the underlying connections changed considerably over time. There was, for instance, a noticeable jump in the prevalence of interindustry ties in the period between 1886 and 1905, with the railroad, banking, coal, and telegraph industries becoming increasingly central (Roy 1983). The ubiquity of corporate interlocks was similarly apparent within industries, as highlighted by the case of the railroad industry, where companies could be sorted into distinct "communities of interest," each of which was dominated by a handful of leading firms (Bonacich and Roy 1986; Roy and Bonacich 1988). Though the mean number of interlocks declined significantly following the passage of the Clayton Act in 1914, this trend was short-lived. As Mizruchi (1982) shows, the density of the corporate network remained relatively stable from 1935 onward, with financial corporations maintaining a central role within this larger system for much of the twentieth century.

States, Parties, and Movements

Global and national markets were not a natural phenomenon, in the sense that the expansion and maintenance of trade over long distances depended on the emergence of centralized authority in the form of the modern nation state. According to Erikson (2021), modern conceptions of the economy were born out of the jostling over economic policy in England during the sixteenth century, when merchants actively competed with one another over the provision of corporate charters. Occupying a structurally disadvantaged position in the political network that surrounded the state, members of the merchant class turned to the publication of public tracts as a means of influencing state policy. In an effort to legitimize what might otherwise be viewed as purely self-interested claims, merchant authors began using empirical evidence to make abstract arguments about the benefits afforded to state and nation. Along the way, long-standing concerns regarding just price and husbandry were progressively replaced by questions regarding national growth, thereby linking market and state in the collective imagination.

In the context of the early modern period, appeals to the public sphere can be understood as part of an effort to transcend the unambiguous pursuit of self-interest that characterized the formation of the patron-client networks around which emerging political institutions were built. It is hard to overstate the significance of the patronage system, which embedded the practice of favor-seeking within a larger cultural repertoire (McLean 2007), while also serving as a source of structural stability, with patronage pyramids providing the foundation around which the first states and parties were built (Martin 2009). The formation of states and parties tended to go together, with parties emerging as the primary means through which political elites competed with one another for control of the nascent states with which they were tied. This was a volatile process, due in no small part to concomitant changes in the economic and religious landscape, which produced a complex array of categorical distinctions that could be readily leveraged to mobilize support for or against the state. The alignment of categories and networks was an especially powerful force, contributing to movements on the part of elites and masses alike. From this perspective, the use of network analysis in HPE provides a theoretical and methodological framework for understanding the connection between social movement organizations, the structural foundation of interests and identities, and the diffusion of mass protest.

State and Party Formation

Network analysis has been used to examine the process of state and party formation in a range of settings, including Song China (Wang 2022), Renaissance Florence (Padgett and Ansell 1993), Stuart England (Bearman 1993; Hillmann 2008b), the Polish-Lithuanian Commonwealth (McLean 2004; 2011), and the early United States (Gould 1996; Hillmann 2008a; Hoffman 2019; Parigi and Bergemann 2016). Perhaps the most well-known example from this literature is Padgett and Ansell's (1993) work on the rise of the Florentine state under Cosimo de' Medici. The ability of the Medici family to seize control of the city's political machinery was predicated on their position within a doubly disarticulated system of ties that allowed them to make claims on behalf of both patricians, as well as the upwardly mobile "new men" who were only recently admitted to the Signoria. This type of structural ambiguity is relatively unique in the context of state-building, where the provision of state resources in the form of offices tends to divide beneficiaries from their less-advantaged counterparts. Such was the case in the lead up to the English Civil War, which saw elites divide along religious lines. As Bearman (1993) demonstrates, the fact that political rivalries could be summarily expressed in terms of categorical distinctions rooted in abstract ideology was a byproduct of the expansion of patron-client networks, which progressively replaced kinship networks as the primary determinant of power and prestige at the local level. As the distribution of religious patronage became more unbalanced under James I, losing elites were forced to rally their already mobilized network of supporters against the Crown, effectively tearing the state in two before factional rivalries could be folded into a stable party system.

While we observe a similar connection between the uneven distribution of patronage and the rise of violent opposition in the Whiskey Rebellion of 1794 (Gould 1996), the key difference between seventeenth-century England and the early United States is that the introduction of a zero-sum competition for the presidency preceded the push for sustained mobilization among the electorate, allowing for a more orderly expansion of conflict that ultimately resulted in the formation of two national-level parties—the Federalists and the Democratic-Republicans (Martin 2009). Regardless of how these contests ultimately unfolded, network brokers played an important role in forging the alliances around which the conflicts in question were organized. For example, the emergence of parliamentary opposition in London before the start of the English Civil War was made possible in part because of members of a rising class of colonial merchants who helped bridge the divide between the Puritan leaders in Parliament with whom they did business and the radical Puritan citizens' movement with whom they shared political ties (Hillmann 2008b). The situation in the early United States was quite different, in the sense that local brokers worked to strengthen ties within their communities without threatening the stability of the state-building project. Using data on personal credit networks in late-eighteenth- and early-nineteenth-century Vermont, Hillmann (2008a) shows that not only were these local brokers more likely to be elected to public office, but the factional disputes that motivated local politics could be readily mapped onto the divide between Federalists and Democratic-Republicans, thus preserving local identities while simultaneously reinforcing the divides that characterized the national-level party system at the time.

Social networks continued to play an important role in American party politics throughout much of the early nineteenth century. Since the work of Young (1966), considerable attention has been paid to the informal boardinghouse networks that once organized the life of elected officials in Washington, DC (e.g., Bogue and Marlaire 1975; Parigi and Bergemann 2016). The most sophisticated treatment of this matter comes from Minozzi and Caldeira (2021), who examine the effect of co-residence on the propensity for legislators to vote together. The data indicate that in the period between 1801 and 1861, representatives who lived together in the same boardinghouse were consistently more likely to vote together in Congress. Yet the magnitude of the boardinghouse effect varied considerably across different types of dyads. New co-residents were more likely to vote together than co-residents who had lived together earlier. This was especially true of dyads where at least one of the members was new to Congress. On the whole, the propensity for new co-residents to vote together peaked during the Jacksonian period, only to fall off again as the boardinghouse culture began to decline in the years leading up to the Civil War.

Contentious Politics

Party politics was by no means the only way of making claims on the state. As Tilly (1983) describes, the transition to political modernity was marked by a transformation in the repertoire of political contention, with social movement organizations emerging as a standard vehicle for collective claim-making. To the extent that these organizations are bound together by the members they share in common, they collectively constitute what Curtis and Zurcher (1973) refer to as a "multi-organizational field." This idea is nicely illustrated by Rosenthal et al. (1985), who describe the evolving structure of ties between women's reform organizations in New York State between 1840 and 1914. Using techniques originally applied to the study of interlocking directorates, the authors show that while the reform movement in New York State was overwhelmingly dominated by women's rights organizations, the relationship between the various reform movements changed over time. Prior to the end of the Civil War, a wide-reaching push for equality and temperance contributed to the development of a women's rights movement that was primarily organized through annual conventions. The movement became increasingly focused on the question of suffrage over the course of the late nineteenth and early twentieth centuries, with organizations such as the National American Woman Suffrage Association drawing in clubwomen as well as proponents of labor reform.

When it comes to the study of contentious politics in history, network analysis has been used to not only depict the connections between the organizations tasked with mass mobilization, but to fundamentally reconceptualize the connection between interest, identity, and action. The work of the Harvard School has proven particularly influential in this regard. Drawing on ideas originally introduced in 1965 as part of Harrison White's undergraduate course on social relations, Tilly (1978) argues that the potential for collective mobilization is a function of the extent to which categories of people sharing a common characteristic are bound together in a dense network to produce what White referred to as a "catnet" (White 2008). In its most extreme form, the emphasis on the role of relationships over attributes translates into what Emirbayer and Goodwin (1994) refer to as the "anticategorical imperative." The implication is that categories have no intrinsic meaning independent of the relationships to which they are attached, with the idea that categories often emerge out of relations, providing actors with cultural and cognitive cues that allow them to quickly parse the relational structures in which they are embedded.

Perhaps the fullest expression of this line of thinking comes from Bearman (1993), who explicitly links the concepts of interest and identity to the use of blockmodels, which were first introduced by White and his collaborators in the 1970s (Breiger, Boorman, and Arabie 1975; Lorrain and White 1971; White, Boorman, and Breiger 1976). The key idea behind this approach is that network data can be meaningfully summarized in terms of the pattern of ties between groups of structurally equivalent actors. A group of actors is said to occupy a structurally equivalent position or block if the actors share a common tie profile. According to Bearman, actors occupying the same position share common interests insofar as they are similarly situated vis-à-vis the other actors in the network. Collective identities emerge in cases where the actors in question not only share a similar pattern of ties to the other actors in the network but are also tied to one another, thus giving rise to a cohesive subgroup. Within this framework, the categories attached to a given position serve as a form of relational shorthand. From this perspective, collective action is not a product of categorical attributes in and of themselves, so much as it is a product of the larger system of relations around which categorical *distinctions* are based.

While the use of blockmodels in HPE is most closely associated with work on the patterns of elite conflict that surround the formation of states and parties (e.g., Bearman 1993; Padgett and Ansell 1993), this approach has been productively applied to the study of mass contention. Barkey and Van Rossem (1997), for example, use blockmodels to examine the structural foundations of peasant mobilization in the Ottoman Empire in the period between 1650 and 1654, focusing in particular on the aggregate distribution of dyadic ties within and between villages in western Anatolia. The results suggest that the village network was characterized by a core-periphery structure organized around the town of Manisa. Villages in the periphery differed from one another in terms of their relationship to Manisa, with more distant and isolated villages tending to occupy a common position at the extreme periphery. The probability of peasant mobilization was more pronounced in the villages occupying positions in the intermediate periphery, where peasants embedded in a mixed agricultural economy came head-to-head with the market as well as the extractive apparatus of the state.

In addition to shaping the interests and identities around which social movements form, networks also play an important role in facilitating their diffusion, as evidenced most clearly by work on the spread of labor activism during the nineteenth and early twentieth centuries (e.g., Aidt, Leon-Ablan, and Satchell 2022; Hedstrom 1994; Hedstrom, Sandell, and Stern 2000). Gould's (1995) work on the Paris Commune of 1871 is particularly notable insofar as it pushes back on the claim that the Commune marked the peak of class formation in France, which began in earnest with the Revolution of 1848. While variation in the distribution of insurgency across Paris neighborhoods in 1848 was closely associated with variation in the size of the working-class population, this was not the case in 1871. According to Gould, the declining salience of working-class identity as a basis for collective action in the period between 1848 and 1871 was a byproduct of urban restructuring under Georges-Eugène Haussmann. The rebuilding of the city center pushed poorer residents into newly annexed neighborhoods along the periphery, where they formed networks that crossed class lines, while tending to adhere to neighborhood boundaries. When insurrection finally broke out in the spring of 1871, the residents of these outlying neighborhoods tended to mobilize on the basis of community as opposed to class. In the end, the diffusion of mass protest was facilitated by the formation of the Paris National Guard, which helped generate cross-neighborhood solidarity by linking informal networks of neighborhood insurgents to one another through overlapping enlistments.

Conclusion

As this chapter suggests, network analysis has been used to good effect in the study of historical political economy. The power of this approach lies in the productive coupling of theory and method, in the sense that networks serve as both a conceptual device as well as an object of measurement. From this vantage point, the emergence of modern institutions such as the market economy and the nation state can be understood as a product of concerted action on the part of individuals bound to one another through the formation of marital ties, business partnerships, patron-client relationships, and so on. In addition to contributing to the formation of large-scale institutions, the resulting networks provided the relational foundation around which categorical interests and identities were built. This implies that the ability to describe the transition to modernity as a product of, say, class struggle is a byproduct of, among other things, the tendency for workers to occupy a structurally equivalent position vis-à-vis owners, and vice versa. Whether this held in practice is an open question. Insofar as network analysis serves as both a theory and a method, the availability of quantifiable records allows these types of questions to be translated into formal claims.

While this growing body of work has undoubtedly contributed to our understanding of the relational dynamics underlying the transition to economic and political modernity, the use of network analysis in HPE is not without its difficulties. Foremost among them is the mismatch between the relational ontology of historical network analysis and the assumptions underlying traditional approaches to statistical inference, which depend on the idea that the observations in front of us are independent of one another. This assumption is hard to maintain when working with historical network data where the observations at hand refer not only to individual nodes but to the edges that connect them. In this respect, the thing that draws us to network analysis in the first place—the connection between observations—is the same thing that makes it so difficult to integrate network analytic thinking into a conventional statistical framework.

The extent to which the interdependence of observations poses a problem depends on the nature of the analysis. In many instances, the potential for interdependence is incidental to the substantive question at hand and can be reasonably addressed using standard inferential palliatives such as simulation and robust standard errors, which correct for the effect of dependence on the shape of the sampling distribution. In other cases, however, the effect of network dependence is itself an object of inquiry, thus requiring explicit parameterization. While simulation has traditionally played a role here as well (e.g., quadratic assignment procedure regression), this style of work has been fundamentally transformed by recent innovations in inferential network analysis, including exponential random graph models, stochastic actor-oriented models, and latent space models (see Cranmer, Desmarais, and Morgan 2021). With a few notable exceptions (e.g., Gondal and McLean 2013), these approaches have yet to take hold in HPE, leaving considerable room for methodological innovation.

This is easier said than done in the context of a literature that is increasingly oriented toward causal inference (see, for example, Callis, Dunning, and Tuñón's chapter in this volume). Many popular approaches to causal inference depend on the assumption that there are no spillovers, meaning that the treatment effect associated with a given case is unaffected by whether other cases receive treatment, which is unlikely to hold in the presence of network effects (see Morgan and Winship 2014, 48–52). This does not preclude the possibility of causal inference, but it does make it more difficult, particularly when working with the type of observational data we see in HPE. For a network effect to be causally identified, we need to be able to separate the extent to which observations are similar because they are tied to one another, which is consistent with the idea of contagion or influence, from the propensity for cases to form ties to one another because they are similar, which is consistent with the idea of homophily or selection. It is often believed that this problem can be solved using panel or time-series–cross-section data, which allow one to control for prior conditions. As Shalizi and Thomas (2011) describe, however, the effect of social influence is generally unidentified in the presence of unobserved homophily, even when working with longitudinal data.

When it comes to the future of network analysis in HPE, the good news for causally oriented scholars is that there are several ways of mitigating the various biases that arise from the inability to completely disentangle influence from selection. Recent reviews highlight the potential of stochastic actor-oriented models, which can be used to capture the coevolution of a network's structure and the node-level attributes that the network in question is said to affect (Frank and Xu 2020; VanderWeele and An 2013). Their considerable promise notwithstanding, coevolution models are hardly a panacea. Not only are there questions about the applicability of the behavioral assumptions on which stochastic actor-oriented models are based (Martin 2018), it is unclear whether this approach necessarily outperforms conventional alternatives (Ragan et al. 2022). A fundamental concern when using coevolution models to estimate contagion effects is that the ability to correct for the effect of homophily depends on the ability to model the selection process in terms of observable covariates. With this issue in mind, Xu (2018) suggests the use of latent space models as a possible alternative, with McFowland and Shalizi (2023) providing further support for this general approach. So while there is no guarantee that the integration of network analysis and casual inference will come to fruition in a straightforward way, the HPE community has good reason to hope for continued progress on this front.

Acknowledgments

This chapter benefitted from comments from Chad Borkenhagen and John Levi Martin, with special thanks going to editors Jeffery A. Jenkins and Jared Rubin for their constructive feedback and their considerable patience. The final draft of this chapter would not have been possible without the watchful eyes of Fiona Greenland and Simone Polillo.

References

Accominotti, Olivier, Delio Lucena-Piquero, and Stefano Ugolini. 2021. "The Origination and Distribution of Money Market Instruments: Sterling Bills of Exchange during the First Globalization." *Economic History Review* 74, no. 4: 892–921.

Aidt, Toke, Gabriel Leon-Ablan, and Max Satchell. 2022. "The Social Dynamics of Collective Action: Evidence from the Diffusion of the Swing Riots, 1830–1831." *Journal of Politics* 84, no. 1: 209–25.

Barkey, Karen, and Ronan Van Rossem. 1997. "Networks of Contention: Villages and Regional Structure in the Seventeenth-Century Ottoman Empire." *American Journal of Sociology* 102, no. 5: 1345–82.

Bearman, Peter S. 1993. *Relations into Rhetorics: Local Elite Social Structure in Norkfolk, England, 1540–1640*. New Brunswick, NJ: Rutgers University Press.

Bogue, Allan G., and Mark Paul Marlaire. 1975. "Of Mess and Men: The Boardinghouse and Congressional Voting, 1821–1842." *American Journal of Political Science* 19, no. 2: 207–30.

Bonacich, Phillip, and William G. Roy. 1986. "Centrality, Dominance, and Interorganizational Power in a Network Structure: Interlocking Directorates among American Railroads, 1886–1905." *Journal of Mathematical Sociology* 12, no. 2: 127–35.

Bouie, Jamelle. 2022. "We Still Can't See American Slavery for What It Was." *New York Times*, January 28.

Breiger, Ronald L. 1974. "The Duality of Persons and Groups." *Social Forces* 53, no. 2: 181–90.

Breiger, Ronald L., Scott A. Boorman, and Phipps Arabie. 1975. "An Algorithm for Clustering Relational Data with Applications to Social Network Analysis and Comparison with Multidimensional Scaling." *Journal of Mathematical Psychology* 12, no. 3: 328–83.

Breiger, Ronald L., and Philippa E. Pattison. 1986. "Cumulated Social Roles: The Duality of Persons and Their Algebras." *Social Networks* 8, no. 3: 215–56.

Bunting, David. 1983. "Origins of the American Corporate Network." *Social Science History* 7, no. 2: 129–42.

Chandler, Alfred D. 1977. *The Visible Hand: The Managerial Revolution in American Business*. Cambridge, MA: Belknap Press.

Convert, Bernard, and Johan Heilbron. 2007. "Where Did the New Economic Sociology Come From?" *Theory and Society* 36, no. 1: 31–54.

Cranmer, Skyler J., Bruce A. Desmarais, and Jason W. Morgan. 2021. *Inferential Network Analysis*. Cambridge: Cambridge University Press.

Curtis, Russell L., and Louis A. Zurcher. 1973. "Stable Resources of Protest Movements: The Multi-Organizational Field." *Social Forces* 52, no. 1: 53–61.

Donaldson, Dave, and Richard Hornbeck. 2016. "Railroads and American Economic Growth: A 'Market Access' Approach." *Quarterly Journal of Economics* 131, no. 2: 799–858.

Emirbayer, Mustafa, and Jeff Goodwin. 1994. "Network Analysis, Culture, and the Problem of Agency." *American Journal of Sociology* 99, no. 6: 1411–54.

Erikson, Emily. 2014. *Between Monopoly and Free Trade: The English East India Company, 1600–1757*. Princeton, NJ: Princeton University Press.

Erikson, Emily. 2021. *Trade and Nation*. New York: Columbia University Press.

Everett, Martin G., and Stephen P. Borgatti. 2013. "The Dual-Projection Approach for Two-Mode Networks." *Social Networks* 35, no. 2: 204–10.

Fennema, Meindert, and Huibert Schijf. 1978. "Analysing Interlocking Directorates: Theory and Methods." *Social Networks* 1, no. 4: 297–332.

Flandreau, Marc, and Clemens Jobst. 2005. "The Ties That Divide: A Network Analysis of the International Monetary System, 1890–1910." *Journal of Economic History* 65, no. 4: 977–1007.

Frank, Kenneth A., and Ran Xu. 2020. "Causal Inference for Social Network Analysis." In *The Oxford Handbook of Social Networks*, ed. R. Light and J. Moody, 288–310. New York: Oxford University Press.

Freeman, Linton C. 2004. *The Development of Social Network Analysis: A Study in the Sociology of Science*. Vancouver: Empirical Press.

Gondal, Neha, and Paul D. McLean. 2013. "What Makes a Network Go Round? Exploring the Structure of a Strong Component with Exponential Random Graph Models." *Social Networks* 35, no. 4: 499–513.

Gould, Roger V. 1995. *Insurgent Identities: Class, Community, and Protest in Paris from 1848 to the Commune*. Chicago: University of Chicago Press.

Gould, Roger V. 1996. "Patron-Client Ties, State Centralization, and the Whiskey Rebellion." *American Journal of Sociology* 102, no. 2: 400–429.

Gould, Roger V. 2003. "Uses of Network Tools in Comparative Historical Research." In *Comparative Historical Analysis in the Social Sciences*, ed. D. Rueschemeyer and J. Mahoney, 241–69. Cambridge: Cambridge University Press.

Hedstrom, Peter. 1994. "Contagious Collectivities: On the Spatial Diffusion of Swedish Trade Unions, 1890–1940." *American Journal of Sociology* 99, no. 5: 1157–79.

Hedstrom, Peter, Rickard Sandell, and Charlotta Stern. 2000. "Mesolevel Networks and the Diffusion of Social Movements: The Case of the Swedish Social Democratic Party." *American Journal of Sociology* 106, no. 1: 145–72.

Hillmann, Henning. 2008a. "Localism and the Limits of Political Brokerage: Evidence from Revolutionary Vermont." *American Journal of Sociology* 114, no. 2: 287–331.

Hillmann, Henning. 2008b. "Mediation in Multiple Networks: Elite Mobilization before the English Civil War." *American Sociological Review* 73: 426–54.

Hillmann, Henning. 2021. *The Corsairs of Saint-Malo: Network Organization of a Merchant Elite under the Ancien Régime*. New York: Columbia University Press.

Hillmann, Henning, and Brandy L. Aven. 2011. "Fragmented Networks and Entrepreneurship in Late Imperial Russia." *American Journal of Sociology* 117, no. 2: 484–538.

Hoffman, Mark Anthony. 2019. "The Materiality of Ideology: Cultural Consumption and Political Thought after the American Revolution." *American Journal of Sociology* 125, no. 1: 1–62.

Lorrain, Francois, and Harrison C. White. 1971. "Structural Equivalence of Individuals in Social Networks." *Journal of Mathematical Sociology* 1: 49–80.

Martin, John Levi. 2009. *Social Structures*. Princeton, NJ: Princeton University Press.

Martin, John Levi. 2018. *Thinking through Statistics*. 1st ed. Chicago: University of Chicago Press.

McFowland III, Edward and Cosma Rohilla Shalizi (2023) Estimating Causal Peer Influence in Homophilous Social Networks by Inferring Latent Locations, *Journal of the American Statistical Association*, 118, no. 541: 707–18.

McLean, Paul D. 2004. "Widening Access While Tightening Control: Office-Holding, Marriages, and Elite Consolidation in Early Modern Poland." *Theory and Society* 33, no. 2: 167–212.

McLean, Paul D. 2007. *The Art of the Network: Strategic Interaction and Patronage in Renaissance Florence*. Durham, NC: Duke University Press.

McLean, Paul D. 2011. "Patrimonialism, Elite Networks, and Reform in Late-Eighteenth-Century Poland." *ANNALS of the American Academy of Political and Social Science* 636, no. 1: 88–110.

Minozzi, William, and Gregory A. Caldeira. 2021. "Congress and Community: Coresidence and Social Influence in the US House of Representatives, 1801–1861." *American Political Science Review* 115, no. 4: 1292–307.

Mizruchi, Mark S. 1982. *The American Corporate Network, 1904–1974*. Beverly Hills, CA: SAGE.

Mohr, John W. 1994. "Soldiers, Mothers, Tramps and Others: Discourse Roles in the 1907 New York City Charity Directory." *Poetics* 22, no. 4: 327–57.

Mohr, John W. 1998. "Measuring Meaning Structures." *Annual Review of Sociology* 24, no. 1: 345–70.

Mohr, John W., Christopher A. Bail, Margaret Frye, Jennifer C. Lena, Omar Lizardo, Terence E. McDonnell, Ann Mische, Iddo Tavory, and Frederick F. Wherry. 2020. *Measuring Culture*. New York: Columbia University Press.

Mohr, John W., and Vincent Duquenne. 1997. "The Duality of Culture and Practice: Poverty Relief in New York City, 1888–1917." *Theory and Society* 26, no. 2/3: 305–56.

Morgan, Stephen L., and Christopher Winship. 2014. *Counterfactuals and Causal Inference: Methods and Principles for Social Research*. 2nd ed. New York: Cambridge University Press.

Nelson, Laura K. 2021. "Cycles of Conflict, a Century of Continuity: The Impact of Persistent Place-Based Political Logics on Social Movement Strategy." *American Journal of Sociology* 127, no. 1: 1–59.

Obert, Jonathan. 2014. "The Six-Shooter Marketplace: 19th-Century Gunfighting as Violence Expertise." *Studies in American Political Development* 28, no. 1: 49–79.

Padgett, John F., and Christopher K. Ansell. 1993. "Robust Action and the Rise of the Medici, 1400–1434." *American Journal of Sociology* 98, no. 6: 1259–319.

Padgett, John F., and Paul D. McLean. 2006. "Organizational Invention and Elite Transformation: The Birth of Partnership Systems in Renaissance Florence." *American Journal of Sociology* 111, no. 5: 1463–568.

Padgett, John F., and Paul D. McLean. 2011. "Economic Credit in Renaissance Florence." *Journal of Modern History* 83, no. 1: 1–47.

Parigi, Paolo, and Patrick Bergemann. 2016. "Strange Bedfellows: Informal Relationships and Political Preference Formation within Boardinghouses, 1825–1841." *American Journal of Sociology* 122, no. 2: 501–31.

Pitts, Forrest R. 1965. "A Graph Theoretic Approach to Historical Geography." *Professional Geographer* 17. no. 5: 15–20.

Prell, Cristina. 2012. *Social Network Analysis: History, Theory and Methodology*. Thousand Oaks, CA: SAGE.

Ragan, Daniel T., D. Wayne Osgood, Nayan G. Ramirez, James Moody, and Scott D. Gest. 2022. "A Comparison of Peer Influence Estimates from SIENA Stochastic Actor–Based Models and from Conventional Regression Approaches." *Sociological Methods and Research* 51, no. 1: 357–95.

Rosenthal, Naomi, Meryl Fingrutd, Michele Ethier, Roberta Karant, and David McDonald. 1985. "Social Movements and Network Analysis: A Case Study of Nineteenth-Century Women's Reform in New York State." *American Journal of Sociology* 90, no. 5: 1022–54.

Roy, William G. 1983. "The Unfolding of the Interlocking Directorate Structure of the United States." *American Sociological Review* 48, no. 2: 248–57.

Roy, William G., and Philip Bonacich. 1988. "Interlocking Directorates and Communities of Interest among American Railroad Companies, 1905." *American Sociological Review* 53, no. 3: 368–79.

Rubin, Jared. 2010. "Bills of Exchange, Interest Bans, and Impersonal Exchange in Islam and Christianity." *Explorations in Economic History* 47, no. 2: 213–27.

Shalizi, Cosma Rohilla, and Andrew C. Thomas. 2011. "Homophily and Contagion Are Generically Confounded in Observational Social Network Studies." *Sociological Methods & Research* 40, no. 2: 211–39.

Slez, Adam. 2020. *The Making of the Populist Movement*. New York: Oxford University Press.

Spirling, Arthur. 2012. "US Treaty Making with American Indians: Institutional Change and Relative Power, 1784–1911." *American Journal of Political Science* 56, no. 1: 84–97.

Swedberg, Richard. 2003. *Principles of Economic Sociology*. Princeton, NJ: Princeton University Press.

Tilly, Charles. 1978. *From Mobilization to Revolution*. Reading, MA: Addison-Wesley.

Tilly, Charles. 1983. "Speaking Your Mind without Elections, Surveys, or Social Movements." *Public Opinion Quarterly* 47, no. 4: 461–78.

VanderWeele, Tyler J., and Weihua An. 2013. "Social Networks and Causal Inference." In *Handbook of Causal Analysis for Social Research, Handbooks of Sociology and Social Research*, ed. S. L. Morgan, 353–74. Dordrecht: Springer Netherlands.

Van Doosselaere, Quentin. 2009. *Commercial Agreements and Social Dynamics in Medieval Genoa*. Cambridge: Cambridge University Press.

Wang, Yuhua. 2022. "Blood Is Thicker Than Water: Elite Kinship Networks and State Building in Imperial China." *American Political Science Review* 16, no. 3:896–910.

White, Harrison C. 2008. "Notes on the Constituents of Social Structure: Soc. Rel. 10 - Spring '65." *Sociologica* 1/2008: 1–14.

White, Harrison C., Scott A. Boorman, and Ronald L. Breiger. 1976. "Social Structure from Multiple Networks. I. Blockmodels of Roles and Positions." *American Journal of Sociology* 81, no. 4: 730–80.

Xu, Ran. 2018. "Alternative Estimation Methods for Identifying Contagion Effects in Dynamic Social Networks: A Latent-Space Adjusted Approach." *Social Networks* 54: 101–17.

Young, James Sterling. 1966. *The Washington Community, 1800–1828*. New York: Columbia University Press.

CHAPTER 6

FORMAL MODELS IN HISTORICAL POLITICAL ECONOMY

SEAN GAILMARD

What Do Formal Models Do in Historical Political Economy?

SCHOLARS of political economy have long applied the field's tools to analyze historical events and development. The emergence of historical political economy (HPE) as a subfield provides an opportunity to reflect on how we accomplish this, and how we can do it better. In this chapter I argue that formal models are an indispensable part of our toolkit, and I provide an incomplete survey of major formal-theoretic work in the field to date.

Consistent with broader directions in political economy, much research in HPE attempts to identify treatment effects based on randomizations or as-if randomizations throughout history. But this kind of knowledge has a limit. Credibly identified treatment effects of some X on some Y do not explain why an effect occurs. They simply rule out all explanations in which X is unrelated to Y (which garden-variety observational correlations usually also do), or in which the relationship is driven by a confounder W (which garden-variety observational correlations usually cannot do).

We use models because we want to know more than this. There are two important contributions of models in historical political economy. The first is that we usually wish to *explain why* variables are related. Models represent the social, political, and economic forces that lead to decisions and in turn historical events—that is, they embed causal mechanisms. Showing that X causes Y does not in itself identify the social forces that bring about the effect. A model, and only a model, can explain what those forces are.

A second rationale for modeling is that we usually wish to *generalize causal mechanisms* across specific contexts. Generalizing requires knowing what other scenarios are like the one in which we observed an effect. Models, especially formal models, enable this, because formal models define an *equivalence class* of scenarios in which a specific causal mechanism operates. No two social settings are exactly alike, but two settings that are both in a model's equivalence class are similar enough in relevant ways that the same mechanism operates in both. Without a model to relate distinct social settings, we have no way to know if the effect of X on Y from one setting should apply in another or not. To be sure, causal generalization by models brings us far short of the identificationist demands of the self-styled credibility revolution, but it is the best causal generalization we can get (Gailmard 2021b; cf. Pearl and Bareinboim 2014).

These arguments apply to theoretical models of any kind. The additional benefit of *formal* models is twofold (see Gailmard 2020). First, formalization and the use of deductive methods ensure *consistency* of assumptions and conclusions. With a valid deductive argument, it is not possible to state implications that are incompatible with premises. This provides necessary discipline for those of us who are tempted to see our arguments explain more than they do. Second, formalization brings *clarity* of assumptions and their connection to implications. The real downside of formalization is that it poses a barrier to engagement for scholars unfamiliar with formal techniques. But once the cost is paid to overcome that barrier, formalization requires assumptions to be clearly stated, and deductive arguments show clearly the role they play in deriving implications.

In HPE, formal models are almost always game theoretic, because game theory provides a flexible language to express an extremely wide variety of strategic decision problems, and thus identify how seemingly disparate situations are actually fundamentally alike. These models typically assume canonically rational actors, which has been sharply criticized in previous reviews of formal models of historical events (e.g., Elster 2000, 692). In my view the criticism is overstated. To impute rationality to the agents in a model is simply to model agents who had their reasons to do what they did. One way to understand decisions is to reconstruct what those reasons were, which is simply to build a rational model of them. A commitment to rationality does not eschew emotions or other-regarding preferences as motivations—avoiding embarrassment or pursuing glory can be powerful motivators. To be sure, any given historical event surely admits of nonrational explanations. There is nothing wrong with this, but a scholar interested in the event should be interested in all the explanations for it. If some of them involve strategic rationality, this per force implies an interest in rational models.

Game theoretic models in HPE "explain" historical events in the sense that their equilibria depict the operation of fundamental strategic forces that underlay major decisions in those events. These strategic forces embed some combination of the "library of mechanisms" that political economists draw upon to explain anything: commitment problems, information asymmetries, agency problems, and the like (Guala 2005; Cox 2004), and in some cases models in HPE may add to that library of mechanisms. That said, formal models in HPE cannot succeed unless they are thoroughly grounded in the historiography of the place, time, and developments they analyze. Yet successful formal models in HPE cannot simply reproduce the causal arguments already present in historiography; they must make new arguments about the historical process under consideration. In this sense, formal models in HPE are making historical as well as theoretical arguments.

With that background in mind, I next provide an (alas, incomplete) survey of formal models in HPE. I primarily consider models focused on and developed for a specific historical process or context, and exclude models that are in principle applicable to history but not built around any setting in particular (because that would include all models). Following this, I characterize predominant approaches to formal modeling in HPE, and consider the sort of understanding that different types of models offer.

An Incomplete Survey of Formal Models in Historical Political Economy

Formal HPE has considered a relatively small number of general substantive topics. On the one hand, this tends to be self-reinforcing. When there is already a body of modeling literature on a topic, it provides a foothold for building more models and a community of scholars to read them.

On the other hand, the marginal value of formal models may be particularly high on substantive topics where few or none have been written. The portability of models allows communication of major issues to substantive nonspecialists in a short space.

State Development, Capacity, and Structure

Some of the foundational questions in political economy involve why states and statelike organizations come to exist, what they do, and how they operate.[1] Models in historical political economy have provided answers based on extraction and its management, pursuit of trade, and protection of the powerful. Noticeably absent from the list of explanations HPE has offered is the state as maximizer of a broad-based social welfare function. This is probably not an oversight.

Focusing on state institutions in the earliest sedentary societies, Mayshar, Moav, and Neeman (2017) develop a foundational model of state institutions that depend on transparency of agricultural production. The model is embedded in a simple but flexible repeated principal-agent framework, and thus takes a state hierarchy as given. The agent produces high output in a period if both its effort is high and conditions are good, and produces low output otherwise. The agent observes local conditions; the principal observes output and a noisy signal of local conditions. The probability of an accurate signal represents "transparency" of the agent's production process to the principal. The agent's incentive scheme is a mix of "sticks" (threat of dismissal and replacement by an ex ante identical agent, at a cost to the principal) and "carrots" (bonuses). The key result is that if transparency is low enough, then the optimal contract is a "pure carrot" scheme, but if transparency is high, then the optimal contract is a carrots-and-sticks scheme: the agent receives a bonus when output is high, but is dismissed when output is low and the signal indicates favorable conditions. In either case the agent exerts high effort during every period, but the "stick" allows the principal to induce high effort with smaller bonuses. So as production becomes more transparent to the ruler, the ruler extracts more output and keeps agents closer to subsistence wages. Mayshar, Moav, and Neeman (2017) apply the model to growth of state power in the ancient Near East, but the results can be extended easily to colonial contexts.

Dal Bó, Hernández-Lagos, and Mazzuca (2022) also focus on state-building in the first sedentary societies. They argue that the decision to form these societies required not just material prosperity, but security from outside attackers. They posit a two-period model in which a settler society has a resource endowment it can consume, invest in future output, or devote to security. In the first period, an outsider can attack the settlement. Success in conflict is determined by a contest function, which depends on the settler's and attacker's expenditure on conflict. The winner has secure control over the settlement's output in period 2. Therefore, high investment by the settler in future output makes it a more attractive target for attackers, and thus requires increased security expenditures to secure prosperity. The settler can achieve "civilization potential"—a combination of prosperity and security—only if investment returns are sufficiently high, and security expenditure is sufficiently effective. The key point is that high potential for material growth is not in itself sufficient to bring about civilization; potential for defense is also necessary. However, there is an asymmetry in how these parameters contribute to civilization. Greater investment returns increase the settler's future prosperity, but also make the settler a more attractive target for attack, so require greater security expenditure. On the other hand, greater effectiveness of security expenditures benefits the settler with no countervailing effects.

Fast-forwarding to early modern Europe (which reveals a massive lacuna in the field), Bates and Lien (1985) present one of the first formal models in HPE that looks recognizably like the contemporary literature. They model the interaction of a ruler and a (homogeneous) mass of subjects in jointly determining taxes, other policies, and output. The ruler and subjects have different preferences over both taxes and other policies. The model makes the simple but powerful point that the ruler is constrained in policy choice by the preferences and consumption of the subjects. Therefore, the equilibrium tax rate is inversely related to other policy concessions from monarch to subjects. Insofar as legislative representation is a natural device to ensure policy concessions, the model explains rulers' grant of assembly rights in exchange for greater taxes, a now-standard argument about elite bargaining over assemblies and representation.

Gennaioli and Voth (2015) consider state centralization in early-modern Europe. They posit a model of states centralizing power over localities in their jurisdictions,[2] which is costly due to local resistance but allows the state to claim more revenue. After deciding how much to centralize, states go to war with exogenous probability. There are two key parameters: first, internal fragmentation within a state. This determines the center's cost of overcoming local resistance. Second is the financial demand of war, which allows the chance of victory to range from 1/2 irrespective of revenue differences, to sure chance of victory for the side with more revenue. When the financial demands of war are low, rulers have little incentives to centralize: it does not help much in winning wars, and so a centralizing ruler may incur the cost of local resistance only to have the gains lost from the flip of a coin. In this case, a greater chance of war reduces centralization. By contrast, when the financial demands of war are high, rulers have strong incentives to centralize: centralization brings more revenue, and thus not only a markedly greater chance of keeping it after war, but also of winning the rival's revenue. In addition, the centralization of fragmented versus cohesive states diverge. Rulers in cohesive areas centralize more—the sensitivity of war outcomes to revenue leads them to amplify their advantage—while rulers in fragmented areas centralize less.

In short, "war makes states" (see Tilly 1990), but only when the fiscal demands of war are high. Gennaioli and Voth (2015) relate this parameter to the "military revolution" in early modern Europe, which scholars have argued greatly increased the sensitivity of war outcomes to fiscal resources. The model explains why European state-building before this period was (1) generally low and (2) relatively similar for internally homogeneous versus fragmented states, and why state-building after this period was high, especially for internally cohesive states.

One of the signal attributes of governance around the world is a system of sovereignty divided among states that are more or less territorially contiguous. Acharya and Lee (2018) explore the emergence and stability of this system. They posit a "market for governance" for individuals or localities. Each individual is located on an interval and attaches a constant value to "governance." Two potential suppliers of governance—would-be states—are located at the end points. The states compete for the allegiance of each individual. Each ruler offers a "price" of governance that depends on an individual's location (all bargaining power rests with the rulers), and incurs a cost for governing any individual. A key assumption is that the cost of governance of an individual by a ruler is increasing in their distance. Prospective rulers offer their price schedules simultaneously, and individuals voluntarily decide which ruler's governance to accept.

Under natural assumptions, there is a range of locations to which only one state can profitably supply governance, and therefore have the full surplus extracted by that state. However, there may be a range of locations where both rulers can benefit from supplying governance. For these locations, Bertrand competition between the potential rulers threatens to drive down the price of governance. Acharya and Lee show that in a repeated game, the rulers can still sustain full rent extraction for locations in the overlapping market, with the static Bertrand pricing outcome as the off-equilibrium punishment. Thus, the model explains (1) the territorial contiguity of states and (2) the respect of rulers for the territorial claims of other rulers. The implication, especially of point (2), is that the territorial state system is simply a cartel in the "market" for governance, for the benefit of states at the expense of individuals in overlapping "markets" for governance.

Greif, Milgrom, and Weingast (1994), a foundational model in HPE, explores the institutional foundations of extra-national trade in the medieval world.[3] The issue is that extra-national traders were exposed to expropriation in foreign states, which could threaten valuable exchange. Traders organized in guilds could impose embargoes on hosts that failed to uphold traders' security. However, this presented a second-order problem: if all guild members observed the embargo, it would be particularly tempting for a trader to violate it and have a city's trade all to itself. Greif, Milgrom, and Weingast (1994) explain the structure and powers of medieval merchant guilds as institutional solutions to those problems. The paper is a landmark both substantively, for demonstrating the institutional foundations of economic exchange, and methodologically, for combining sophisticated, original, and generative theoretical modeling with deep investigation of economic history.

Larson (2017) analyzes the relationship between peer sanctions, cooperation, and social network structure. The model posits a population of individuals interacting over time in pairwise prisoners' dilemma games. Population members are uniformly randomly matched each period. In any period, individuals spread information about misbehavior by their counterpart through an exogenous social network. Information about an individual's past defection induces a punishment phase in which the previous defector is expected to cooperate while their counterpart defects. The key point is that individuals in a peripheral network position cannot spread information very far. Therefore their counterparts can cheat against them with little risk of entering the punishment phase. Larson applies the model to understand the breakdown of social order between white and Chinese settlers in the nineteenth-century American West. Despite the lack of formal institutions, social order among white settlers in boomtowns was often surprisingly stable, even among immigrants. On the other hand, defection against Chinese immigrants quickly shifted from initially low levels to rampant, egregious mistreatment. Larson notes that Chinese settlers held an unusually peripheral and isolated network position, even relative to other immigrant groups, and therefore were uniquely vulnerable to rampant defection.

Egorov and Sonin (2015) model the endogenous emergence of violence in political (nondemocratic) succession. The setup is a simple dynamic model: an incumbent ruler faces a challenger in a fight for power, with the result exogenously determined. The winner then decides whether to execute the loser. If the winner spares the loser, the loser challenges again in the next period. If the winner executes the loser, the winner either faces no challenger in the next period or faces a new challenger, with exogenous probabilities. This simple setup produces a crisp trade-off: if the winner executes the loser, it has some chance of uncontested rule. But when a ruler with a history of executions eventually loses, the challenger defeating them may have no choice but to execute them. An important implication of the analysis is that violence is fundamentally history-dependent. Leaders with a history of violence are deposed violently, because they pose the gravest threat to their successors if spared. But with a history of nonviolent deposition, leaders can alternate in power indefinitely without executions.

In a creative twist, Koyama, Rahman, and Sng (2021) focus not on political-economic development, but on military forces—in particular, the development of navies in a competitive environment. In their setting, competing states choose naval investments in a Stackelberg model. Naval investments determine a chance to win a fixed prize via a contest success function. Both states incur a fixed cost of investment. These aspects of the model differentiate naval power from land-based military forces and produce several stylized facts about naval power throughout history: cycles of investment, higher concentration across states than land power, and periodic arms-race-type competitions.

Institutional Persistence

Political-economic development is as much a story of institutional *stasis* as institutional *change*. To this end, an extensive subliterature focuses on why political and economic institutions persist, particularly in the substantively important and theoretically challenging case when they are inefficient.[4] A common theme in the models is that inefficient institutions persist because they protect the power of entrenched elites, whereas successors to that power under alternative institutions cannot commit to compensate them sufficiently. Markov games are a natural match for these themes and predominate in this subliterature.

Modeling institutional persistence is one of several strands of formal HPE particularly influenced by Acemoglu and Robinson. Acemoglu and Robinson (2006) first address this issue in a model positing that political and economic power are linked. Moreover, if an economic elite is replaced, the new elite cannot commit to preserve the old elite's political power. Therefore, elites fearing replacement block efficiency-enhancing economic change to preserve their hold on power. Paradoxically, strongly entrenched elites have less concern for replacement and therefore are more open to efficiency-enhancing change. The paper applies the model to interpret economic modernization in Britain, Germany, Japan, Russia, and the Habsburg Empire.

Acemoglu and Robinson (2008) elaborate on the theme by considering de jure political power, such as that conferred by formal institutions, and de facto power, which is conferred by capacity for collective organization and action. In this model, elites can offset loss of de jure power with investment in de facto power. The key implication of this logic is that changes in formal institutions, such as the end of colonialism in Latin America or slavery in the US South, may not alter economic institutions—because, facing de jure institutional change, elites alter their investment in de facto power to preserve their privileges.

Iyigun, Rubin, and Seror (2021) extend Acemoglu and Robinson (2006) to consider another channel of entrenchment of elites: culture. They model elites' capability to provide a public good as a function of the proportion of nonelites that share a cultural attribute with them. This production technology then influences cultural transmission: parents socialize children to share that cultural attribute so that they can consume larger levels of the public good. Yet this socialization perpetuates elites' hold on power, which allows them to block threatening economic changes even when they are efficient. The paper applies the model to understand "cultural revivals" in the Jim Crow South and the Gülen movement in early-twentieth-century Turkey.

Similar themes abound. Besley and Persson (2009) argue that elites may obstruct state capacity development to prevent rivals from having effective means of taxation when they take power. Acemoglu, Vindigni, and Ticchi (2010) show that state weakness can prevent the future emergence of a powerful military with which the elites would be forced to share rents. Acemoglu, Ticchi, and Vindigni (2011) argue that when elites anticipate democratization, they have an incentive to retain an inefficient public administration based on patronage politics. Patronage enhances elite control over democratic politics and thus can limit redistribution. Acemoglu, Robinson, and Torvik (2020) focus on barriers to efficient state centralization. In their model, centralization allows more efficient public goods provision and regulation, but it also allows non-elites to identify common interests, in turn confronting and making demands on the state in new ways. Decentralization, though inefficient, enables elites to pursue a sort of divide-and-conquer strategy over non-elites and thus control the political agenda. Moreover, Dippel, Greif, and Trefler (2020) argue that elites use their political power to inhibit development of a productive informal sector: this reduces workers' outside options, and thus their bargaining power over wages in the formal sector that elites control.

Robinson and Torvik (2016) analyze emergence of presidential versus parliamentary regimes. Their key assumptions are that parliamentarism grants stronger protections to minorities (in the form of some chance to claim agenda setting power), and presidentialism grants presidents stronger control over their political coalition than parliamentarism grants to prime ministers. Therefore, while political leaders generally prefer presidentialism, their supporters may not because it erodes their influence within their coalition. At the same time, when an empowered faction fears losing agenda control to another coalition, then both leaders and followers prefer presidentialism. The model is applied to interpret the emergence of presidentialism, especially transitions to it from parliamentarism, in Latin America and Africa.

Colonialism and Imperial Governance

Empires have been historically important vehicles for dispersing structures of both state organization and political coercion around the globe. Besides its substantive importance, imperial governance is strategically interesting: it requires projecting power, preserving order, and ensuring compliance at distance and with limited information at the center. For these reasons, imperial governance has been a significant focus of formal modeling in HPE.[5]

Principal-agent problems are among the most salient in imperial governance. Sng (2014) presents a model of a central government that delegates tax collecting to an agent. The central government sets the legal tax rate, but the agent can extract larger rents from peasants. The center wishes to maximize tax rates, but is constrained by the possibility of local revolt if effective tax rates are too high. The center can monitor the agent and punish peculation, but the efficacy of monitoring declines exogenously in state size. Agents extract more from peasants in larger states (because monitoring is weaker); therefore, to prevent unrest, the center sets lower official tax rates. Sng uses this model to explain high corruption and low revenue collection from distant provinces in late imperial China.

Padró i Miquel and Yared (2012) develop a dynamic moral hazard model to analyze the problem of indirect control that was ubiquitous in imperial governance. In their model a principal can either use an agent to control a disturbance in the agent's territory through unobservable effort, or intervene to control the disturbance itself. The intensity of intervention is chosen by the principal, and greater intensity is costly to both principal and agent. Further, the principal cannot commit to future intervention decisions, and the agent cannot commit to future effort after intervention subsides. Due to limited commitment, the optimal dynamic incentive scheme exhibits periods of delegation alternating with occasional costly interventions by the principal. Padró i Miquel and Yared (2012) apply this model to early imperial Rome, where indirect governance of imperial dominions through client states was occasionally punctuated by incursions from the Roman legions to preserve order.

In a series of papers, Gailmard (2017; 2019; 2021a) explored the development of New World institutions under English colonial rule. These models all turn on agency problems between the English Crown and colonial governors. The general thrust is that these agency problems determined English imperial institutions and set the stage for American institutions that borrowed from them. In particular, Gailmard (2017) argues that colonial governors had incentives to extract rents from colonists even when costly to the Crown, and the cost of replacing governors limited the Crown's discipline. In response, the Crown supported assembly rights in colonies: assemblies could restrain rent extraction when the Crown itself could not.

However, English colonial assemblies proved adept at shifting power to themselves away from the Crown's colonial agents. The Crown then faced another agency problem with colonial governors: how to induce them to stand up to assembly encroachments on the Crown's prerogative. Gailmard (2019) argues that review of colonial legislation by royal bureaucrats in England helped with this effort. While designed to mitigate inconsistencies between colonial and English law, legislative review could also reveal capitulation by governors to assembly demands, and thus cause governors to resist assemblies. Yet Gailmard (2021a) explains why these approaches were ultimately unsuccessful at restraining assembly power in the English colonies. In bargaining over colonial revenues, the Crown was typically in a weak position because it usually desired more revenue than assemblies did. At the same time, governors typically had superior information about exactly how much revenue an assembly would grant.

Ma and Rubin (2019) model another facet of the principal-agent problem in imperial administration: absolutist rulers who are well-informed of what agents take from subjects cannot commit not to expropriate their wages. This degrades the incentives of provincial agents to administer imperial taxation. Ma and Rubin contend that low investment by the ruler in administrative capacity makes the ruler ignorant of the stakes of confiscation. In turn it gives administrators incentives to implement imperial taxes. Ma and Rubin apply this model to explain the low-wage / low-revenue equilibrium of imperial China under the Qing dynasty. They further argue that limited rulers can avoid the problem of expropriating wages de jure, and thus implement a high-wage / high-tax equilibrium.

Garfias and Sellars (2021) analyze the imposition of direct rule by the Spanish Empire in colonial Mexico. The Spanish initially governed much of Mexico through indirect rule by local potentates (*encomenderos*). Garfias and Sellars argue that the potentates were generally better at preserving local order than state agents, but they extracted excessive revenues from the Crown. In their model, a region generates revenue proportional to its population, and is exogenously split between the Crown and the potentate. The Crown can attempt to impose direct rule, thereby keeping all revenue for itself. Following this, the potentate makes two choices: first, how strongly to resist direct rule; second, whether to guard his region against local unrest. Generally, resistance against the Crown and local protection are complements for the potentate. In particular, if regional population (thus income) falls below a parametric threshold, guarding against rebellion is not worth the potentate's cost, and the potentate's resistance to direct rule falls as well. In turn, the Crown's benefit from direct rule increases, both because the potentate is less useful when not guarding against unrest, and because the potentate's resistance to the Crown declines. Garfias and Sellars argue that this dynamic drove imperial centralization in Mexico. Specifically, Indigenous demographic collapse in the sixteenth century caused declines in regional incomes, weakened *encomendero* resistance, and facilitated imposition of direct rule.

Garfias and Sellars (2022) extend this analysis to consider the subtle effects of state-building on peasant rebellion. In particular, centralization can weaken both the power and the loyalty of local potentates who mediate between peasants and the state. This creates fragile authority structures in which local resource or climate shocks can result in widespread peasant unrest, which reduces the central state's ability to punish elite defectors, thus reinforcing the defection. This positive feedback loop reveals why even mild shocks that, while easy for the government to control in times of strength, can threaten the regime's survival in times of weakness. Garfias and Sellars use evidence from late colonial Mexico to argue that tax centralization interacted with resource shocks to cause greater peasant unrest.

Departing from the principal-agent approach, Arias and Girod (2014) model the origins of extractive institutions in the Spanish Empire. A colonizer encounters an Indigenous leader with a given "technology"—essentially, a social organization—for extracting output from Indigenous laborers. The colonizer can either retain the Indigenous leader to "mediate" with local laborers, and share output from the leader's technology, or replace the technology at some cost. Technologies correspond to the degree of hierarchy in Indigenous labor processes. The key assumptions are that for any technology, the leader's mediation raises output; but the difference between mediated and unmediated output is smaller for higher levels of Indigenous labor hierarchy. This means that the Indigenous leader's bargaining power is lower when there is already a strong hierarchy. In this case, the colonizer obtains a high share of the output in bargaining with the leader, and the leader and the existing labor hierarchy remain in place. By contrast, when the existing Indigenous labor hierarchy is low, the colonizer's bargaining power is lower. In this case, the colonizer's decision depends on local resource endowments. When they are small, the cost of removing the leader and remaking the labor technology is not worth the cost, so the leader remains in place and the colonizer accepts unfavorable bargains. But when local resources are very valuable and Indigenous hierarchy is low, the colonizer removes the leader altogether and builds a hierarchy at its own cost. In short, the model implies that colonizers practiced strongly hierarchical organization of Indigenous labor in regions where either Indigenous labor organization was already strongly hierarchical or Indigenous resources were very valuable.

Taking a macro perspective, Grossman and Iyigun (1997) analyze the end of European colonialism in Africa and Southeast Asia. In their model an Indigenous population allocates time between productive activities (which the colonizer exploits) and subversive activity (which hinders exploitation). The key result is that increasing population causes an increase in the return of Indigenous people to subversive action, and thus reduced the gain to European states of holding colonies. By this result the paper argues that population increase contributed to the end of colonialism in these regions.

Gartzke and Rohner (2011) focus on a related development: the decline in territorial acquisitiveness by militarily powerful states. Their model incorporates several key factors to simultaneously explain cycles of colonial acquisition and the secular decline of acquisitiveness. Technological shocks in one state allow sufficient military power to expropriate resources from another—to colonize it. But shocks decay over time, which causes recession in specific territorial claims. In addition, increasing capital abundance makes empire increasingly costly over time, such that nations use power to control terms of trade rather than to expropriate resources for production. This accounts for a general decline in territorial acquisition over time. Moreover, when the most powerful states transition away from territorial acquisition, it means that less powerful states need not hold their own colonies to keep up, thus sparking a wave of decolonization.

Democratization, Franchise, and Representation

Acemoglu and Robinson (2000) initiated a sea change in political economy with a dynamic model of economic redistribution and institutional change.[6] Their model begins with a nondemocratic state, with elites in control of redistribution. In each period, the threat of collective resistance by the masses is stochastically drawn. The elite can respond to this threat in any period either by redistributing resources within the period but retaining future power for themselves, or by changing institutions and granting the masses political power in the future. The key result is that when the masses are likely to pose a collective threat in every period, elites redistribute a lot whenever the threat materializes—but they also retain future power for themselves, and stave off revolution.

When the masses are unlikely to pose a collective threat, elites respond by granting the masses formal institutional power when the threat materializes. The reason is that when the chance of collective threat from the masses is low, elite promises of future redistribution are not credible—everyone knows the elites will not redistribute in periods when they face no threat. Thus in the rare case that the masses pose a high collective threat, they must cement it into formal political power or lose out on redistribution for a long time. In turn, the elites face a stark choice between accepting a revolution of the masses, in which the elites lose everything, or voluntarily ceding political power, in which the masses partially redistribute. In equilibrium elites expand political power to the masses and thereby commit to future redistribution. This grant of power to the masses can be accomplished through a variety of institutions; Acemoglu and Robinson focus on suffrage expansion. They compare nineteenth-century suffrage expansion in England and Germany. In Germany, mass organization through unions was strong, and elites responded with routine redistribution—but kept political power. In England, the masses were not so well organized, but when threat arose, elites responded by expanding political power.

Lizzeri and Persico (2004) construct an alternative explanation for franchise expansion, tied specifically to nineteenth-century Britain. Their model removes the revolutionary threat and focuses entirely on elite incentives. The model involves Downsian competition between two parties, which can promise either public goods or targeted redistribution. With the franchise restricted to elites, a winning platform can be constructed to redistribute from disenfranchised masses to a subset of elites; thus, the public good is underprovided. But with a broad franchise, platforms of public good spending always win. The logic is that with a restricted franchise, fewer votes are needed to win, so targeted redistribution to elites succeeds. But with a broad franchise, more voters need to be bought off, and public goods are better suited for this. When public goods are sufficiently valuable (due, e.g., to rising urbanization), even most elites prefer public goods programs to targeted redistribution. Thus, elites use expanded franchise as a tool to commit parties to broad-based public goods expenditures.[7]

Llavador and Oxoby (2005) present a third major argument for franchise extension and its connection to economic growth. In their model, the population consists of elites—exogenously divided between capitalists and landowners—and workers—endogenously divided between skilled (industrial labor) and unskilled (agricultural). Political parties associated with each elite faction choose policy and voting institutions to build a winning electoral coalition with politically unattached masses. In equilibrium, when the landowners' party is ex ante weak and there is a sufficiently large group of industrial workers, political competition results in both franchise expansion to workers (because it will cement the power of industrial elites relative to landowners) and economic growth (because elites choose productivity-enhancing policies). When these conditions are not met, the equilibrium entails either autocracy or democracy but not economic growth. Llavador and Oxoby find support for these implications from qualitative investigations on growth and franchise expansion across eleven countries in the nineteenth century.

Dower et al. (2018) build on the Acemoglu-Robinson model, focusing on nineteenth-century imperial Russia. In this case institutional liberalization consisted of local representative institutions that gave voice to the poor, rather than on suffrage in national legislative elections. Formally, they use a continuous version of the Acemoglu-Robinson model, where elites choose a degree of power for the masses rather than a binary choice: democratize or not. This both avoids some technical complications of equilibrium characterization in the Acemoglu-Robinson model, and maps more naturally into their historical setting.

Galiani and Torrens (2019) invert the Acemoglu-Robinson logic in the context of the American Revolution, to explain why British Whigs opposed solving the crisis by granting Parliamentary representation to the Americans.[8] The issue is, once again, a commitment problem. This time, it lies with the unrepresented actors: Galiani and Torrens argue that the colonists, if represented in Parliament, would have been tempted to align with the democratically inclined British opposition, which would have threatened the ruling Whigs' power in their own backyard. Thus, the optimal choice for the ruling British Whigs was to prevent Parliamentary representation for America, and risk revolution.

Looking to deeper foundations of assemblies, Leon (2020) argues that England opened the long path to democratization with the Norman Conquest. To recruit collaborators again baronial revolts, William I extended elite status and legal rights to a relatively large group. Leon models elite status as a partially rival club good. Compensation by expanding the elite was a self-reinforcing strategy for the king, because the proportional cost of admitting new members declines with the number of members. Crucially for Leon's account, elite status brought expanded legal rights and remedies, which eventually formed a core of its democratization. Thus, path dependence following the Norman conquest led to expanding rights in England.

In a creative study, Penn (2009) analyzes the effect of democratic representation on the formation of collective identity (thus taking representation as the explanatory rather than dependent variable). In Penn's model, individuals can identify with either the nation or their community (e.g., their state), and this identification depends on the well-being of each unit. In equilibrium, identity choices determine a policy, which induces the identity choices that produce the said policy. Penn shows that when state-level interests are correlated with population, then large groups can dominate small ones in policymaking under fully proportional representation. Further, members of dominant groups may be unwilling to choose identities in common with members of dominated ones, so proportional representation can inhibit formation of a common identity. Malapportionment, by providing for some representation at the group level, mitigates group-based domination in policymaking. Therefore, federated representation can better promote formation of collective identity than fully proportional representation.

Political Reform and Development in Party Systems

Models of franchise extension typically sidestep the issue of whether elections are fair or corrupt. Several scholars have addressed the institutionalization of "clean" elections, again focusing on nineteenth-century Britain. Eggers and Spirling (2014) model the decision of candidates to engage in corrupt election practices as a function of the quality of postelection monitoring. In their model, corrupt electioneering is costly for candidates but increases their chance of winning. Corruption is punished after the fact by imperfect monitors. The key result is that electoral corruption declines in the quality of monitoring. Eggers and Spirling map this model onto a change in British election monitoring in 1868: up to that time, monitoring was performed by tribunals drawn from Parliament, but subsequently was delegated to courts. Through a variety of ingenious indirect measures, Eggers and Spirling (2014) show that Parliamentary tribunals had substantially higher error rates than judicial ones and petitions declined but convictions rose after judicialization. This second result is exactly the pattern one would expect if judicialization actually deterred corruption.

Camp, Dixit, and Stokes (2014) analyze the decline of political parties' use of "agents" to recruit votes in nineteenth-century Britain—analogous to American political machines. They argue that agents were increasingly ineffective late in the century, but parties were locked in a prisoners' dilemma over campaign strategy so continued to use them. Their model implies that, given declining benefits of agents to parties, the penalties imposed by the 1883 Corrupt and Illegal Practices Act catalyzed parties' exit from this prisoners' dilemma.[9]

Kam (2017) presents a bargaining model between candidates and voters in the market for votes. The key to the model is that a market exists only if the gain to candidates from voter bribery exceeds a voter's opportunity cost of voting. This intuitive finding has the important implication that a secret ballot can collapse the market for votes, by decreasing candidates' assessment of the efficacy of vote buying. This causal mechanism explains Kam's finding that bribe prices declined sharply with the introduction of the secret ballot.

Miller and Schofield (2003) shift the focus to partisan electoral realignment, considering the case of the United States. They present a two-dimensional spatial model to argue that party realignment is effectively a slow-moving manifestation of coalitional instability in multidimensional space. The key assumptions that generate equilibrium platforms in any period, and make the instability slow moving, are that voters vary in the salience they attach to various dimensions and candidates need the support of activists. Activists endogenously cluster according to policy preferences, including dimensional salience. Therefore, in equilibrium platforms, candidates choose platforms that appeal to activists on their high salience dimension, but outflank them on low salience dimensions to appeal to disaffected voters. Miller and Schofield (2003) apply this model to explain changing party positions in the United States from 1896 to 2000, specifically how the main cleavage between parties shifted from social to economic and back to social again.[10]

Taking Stock of Formal Models in HPE

The preceding survey indicates that the formal HPE literature has made important contributions in several substantive areas. At the same time, few strands of formal work in HPE have produced a cumulative research agenda about specific historical events or processes (the chief exceptions being persistence of inefficient institutions, and franchise extension). Most formal research in this area develops a bespoke model applied to a specific process or event rather than building on other formal models in HPE.

In my view this state of the literature reflects an implicit consensus about the role of formal models in historical analysis. Scholars use formal models to depict and analyze a causal mechanism that explains how specific historical events unfolded. By definition, all formal modeling in HPE involves some attempt to connect a model to historical evidence: a pure theory paper with no historical referent is not an HPE paper. The best use of models in HPE must remain closely tied to historical evidence, and probably heavily tied to historiography written by historians. To contribute to HPE, it is not much use to study and critique the formal models in HPE as models. It is necessary to understand the historical process that previous models are trying to capture, and to adduce historical evidence that these models ignore or contradict.

Despite some apparent consensus, there are distinct approaches to connecting formal models and historical evidence. These approaches can be placed on a continuum corresponding to how systematically they engage historical evidence before constructing a model. At one pole are models developed with no particular reference to specific historical events. Typically the modeler engages with historical evidence by searching out cases consistent with the model. This is used primarily as "proof of concept" for the model, that is, a demonstration that its logic has arguably applied somewhere and at some time in recorded human history. However, engagement with historical evidence tends to be superficial.

The polar opposite approach is to start with an existing and known body of historical evidence, and produce a model to explain it. Scholars following this approach essentially "reverse engineer" a strategic environment, the equilibrium of which corresponds to the known evidence.[11] These models obtain their value from demonstrating an underlying causal logic, and thus helping us to understand how important events or institutions in the world came about. They may not even be intended to ever be applied to any other empirical setting. Clear examples of the reverse-engineering approach are Greif, Milgrom, and Weingast (1994), Lizzeri and Persico (2004), Gailmard (2017; 2019; 2021a), Koyama, Rahman, and Sng (2021), and Aldaz Peña (2021).

Most formal research in HPE falls somewhere between these poles: models are specified from some historical evidence, but other evidence is set aside (or identified after model building) to use for evaluation. A typical approach is to take a body of historical evidence and partition it into two parts. One part describes a "decision environment"—an institutional configuration, a sequence of actions, and evidence about preferences. The other part describes historical "outcomes," which the process is supposed to explain. The modeling and historical assessment work as follows. First, historical evidence on the decision environment is used to construct a formal model: specifying utilities, action sequences, and information sets that seem "reasonable" in light of historical evidence on the decision environment. Second, the model is solved. Third, the solution is assessed against historical evidence on outcomes. Clear examples are Eggers and Spirling (2014) and Garfias and Sellars (2021). The explanation consists of a model to depict a causal process, and an empirical test of the correspondence between the model and the data. When the correspondence between model and data is strong (e.g., estimated parameters take the hypothesized sign), it is held as evidence that the causal mechanism in the model is a reasonable depiction of the historical process.

Despite differences in process, in each approach, the models depict a causal mechanism, and the evidence shows the consistency of this mechanism and historical observation. This is held as a reason to believe that the mechanism depicted in the model actually operated in the case. No approach shows that its causal mechanism is the only reasonable depiction of a historical process, and no approach shows that its causal mechanism applies to any processes other than the ones around which it was designed and evaluated. Indeed, no approach can do these things (cf. Gailmard 2021b).

However, in any of these approaches, a benefit of formal models is that they allow some basis for causal generalization across social and historical settings. Roughly speaking, all models have two elements: an "analytical core" and "contextual information." The analytical core is an entrant in the "library of mechanisms" that political economists draw on to explain events—collective action problems, coordination problems, dynamic inconsistency, principal-agent problems, and the like. Contextual information makes claims about relevant actors, preferences and decision rules, information sets, and sequences of action. This element is more situation-specific and almost always based on some historical evidence; it may not generalize at all beyond a fairly circumscribed class of situations or even one particular event.

The analytical core of a model provides a bridge to show how superficially distinct social and historical events may be driven by the same causal mechanism. That is, two situations may have very different contextual factors (time period, place, actors involved, etc.), but if models explaining them have the same analytical core, they are strategically or theoretically similar. In this sense, theory provides a basis—I would argue the only available basis—for generalizing findings from a specific case to others. However, even when empirical findings in a single case are rigorously causally identified, we should resist the temptation to infer that theoretical generalization implies the same empirical credibility in other cases.

Though all approaches share these deliverable payoffs, the reverse-engineering approach seems subject to particular skepticism or criticism. This criticism overlaps with criticism of "analytic narrative" (AN; see Bates et al. 1998): reverse-engineered models are often models of a single case or small number of cases, which coincides with at least one definition of AN (Defigueiredo, Rakove, and Weingast 2006).

One type of criticism is that there is nothing to learn from such an exercise (see, e.g., Clarke and Primo 2012), because any one case can be explained perfectly by some model (usually a variety of models). In my view this reflects a misunderstanding of what we do with models, which is not simply to explain or predict outcomes, but to depict causal mechanisms. Any single case can be perfectly explained by some model(s), but not by every model. Therefore, when a model is put forward that can explain it, we learn something about both the set of candidate explanations for the case, and about the reach of whatever causal mechanism is embedded in that model. These seem like valuable types of knowledge.

Reverse engineering also runs afoul of the supposedly scientific prohibition on observing outcomes before developing theory. Again, in my view this prohibition is misguided. If one's objective is to understand the range of causal mechanisms that can produce an outcome, it makes no difference whether the outcome is observed before the mechanism is developed theoretically. All that matters is that the mechanism is consistent with the empirical observation; if it is, the mechanism is a candidate explanation.[12]

Whatever the process of interfacing models with historical evidence, the explanation in a model is only as good as its assumptions. In game theoretic models, these amount to statements about the decision environment (actors, actions, information sets) and motivations of actors. In rational models—which predominate in HPE to date—motivations come down to maximizing a consistent preference relation in light of correctly derived beliefs about uncertain variables. When a model makes far-fetched assumptions about a decision environment, it is usually easy enough for critics with subject-matter expertise to pinpoint them. Thus it is usually the behavioral postulates of rationality that are highlighted as particularly problematic or unreasonable (e.g., Elster 2000). After all, haven't we known for a long time that people are not rational?

An issue with this line of argument is that rationality is a property of decisions (more specifically, sets of decisions), not of people. Sometimes our choices are rational; sometimes they are not. If a rational model accounts for a set of decisions, it seems odd to set that explanation aside because in some other decision problems, some other people have behaved irrationally. Methodologically, a search for rational explanations for historical events is useful because rational decisions are always intelligible to a reasoning observer—possibly tragic or frustrating, but intelligible nonetheless. And making the world intelligible is a recognized goal of both scientific and humanistic inquiry.

In short, formal models are built in HPE through a variety of processes. The fundamental similarities across these processes are that (1) at least some historical evidence is used to specify the model; (2) models depict causal mechanisms that, insofar as they imply relations between variables that are observed in historical processes, are candidate explanations for those processes; and (3) models supply *reasons why* treatment effects exist that cannot be supplied by empirical identification alone. *Formal* models are particularly useful because they depict mechanisms with unusual clarity; they ensure logical consistency of arguments; and they enable causal generalization across cases that are unified by the operation of a specific theoretical mechanism.

Conclusion

Historical political economy should exist because political economy provides powerful theoretical tools to understand decisions and institutions, and therefore the reasons why the world has developed as it has in social, political, and economic terms. Formal models are important in HPE because they offer unmatched precision and clarity for formulating and communicating those causal explanations. In addition, HPE is important for formal modelers because history furnishes cases of important dilemmas in governance and political decision-making that can expand the library of mechanisms that political economists can deploy to understand the world.

Notes

1. See also Dincecco and Wang (2023) in this volume for a review of this area.
2. Thus, unlike Acharya and Lee (2018), Gennaioli and Voth (2015) assume that only one ruler can possibly centralize a given locality.
3. See also Milgrom, North, and Weingast (1990) and Greif (1993).
4. See Acharya, Blackwell, and Sen (2023) in this volume for a review of this area.
5. See also Guardado (2023), this volume, for a review of this area.
6. See also Hanlon (2023) and Stasavage (2023), this volume, for reviews of HPE literature on suffrage and democracy.
7. However, Chapman (2018) argues that when the median prereform voter is middle class rather than poor, democratization can actually reduce public goods expenditure.
8. See Defigueiredo, Rakove, and Weingast (2006) for a model of how this crisis emerged, emphasizing incompatible beliefs of the British and Americans.
9. Camp, Dixit, and Stokes (2014) argue that the act was a *catalyst* of electoral reform, in the sense that it accelerated the decline of machines, but not a *cause* in the sense of a necessary condition. However, the act is a "cause" in the sense of the potential outcomes model of causation.
10. See also Schofield and Miller (2007) and Schofield, Miller, and Martin (2003).
11. Reverse-engineered models are the same as the dreaded "just so story" (Elster 2000). Just so stories are supposed to be problematic because they may not generalize to other events. But if one's objective is to explain a specific event, it is not clear why it matters that the explanation is *sui generis*. Sometimes specific events have specific explanations.
12. It may be objected that simply proposing a candidate explanation is insufficiently ambitious, and we would like to isolate a single causal mechanism that accounts for case evidence. However, because there are essentially always multiple explanations for a finite body of evidence, this is probably impossible. Even the most rigorous causal identification does produce not a single reason why one variable causes another; it simply rules out confounding as a reasonable explanation.

REFERENCES

Acemoglu, Daron, and James A. Robinson. 2000. "Why Did the West Extend the Franchise? Democracy, Inequality, and Growth in Historical Perspective." *Quarterly Journal of Economics* 115, no. 4: 1167–99.

Acemoglu, Daron, and James A. Robinson. 2006. "Economic Backwardness in Political Perspective." *American Political Science Review* 100, no. 1: 115–31.

Acemoglu, Daron, and James A. Robinson. 2008. "Persistence of Power, Elites, and Institutions." *American Economic Review* 98, no. 1: 267–93.

Acemoglu, Daron, James A. Robinson, and Ragnar Torvik. 2020. "The Political Agenda Effect and State Centralization." *Journal of Comparative Economics* 48, no. 4: 749–78.

Acemoglu, Daron, Davide Ticchi, and Andrea Vindigni. 2011. "Emergence and Persistence of Inefficient States." *Journal of the European Economic Association* 9, no. 2: 177–208.

Acemoglu, Daron, Andrea Vindigni, and Davide Ticchi. 2010. "Persistence of Civil Wars." *Journal of the European Economic Association* 8, no. 2–3: 664–76.

Acharya, Avidit, Matthew Blackwell, and Maya Sen. 2023. "Historical Persistence." In *Oxford Handbook of Historical Political Economy*, ed. Jeffery Jenkins and Jared Rubi, 117–141. New York: Oxford University Press.

Acharya, Avidit, and Alexander Lee. 2018. "Economic Foundations of the Territorial State System." *American Journal of Political Science* 62, no. 4: 954–66.

Arias, Luz Marina, and Desha Girod. 2014. "Indigenous Origins of Colonial Institutions." *Quarterly Journal of Political Science* 9, no. 3: 371–406.

Bates, Robert H., Avner Grief, Margaret Levi, Jean-Laurent Rosenthal, and Barry Weingast. 1998. *Analytic Narratives*. Princeton, NJ: Princeton University Press.

Bates, Robert H., and Donald Da-Hsiang Lien. 1985. "A Note on Taxation, Development, and Representative Government." *Politics & Society* 14, no. 1: 53–70.

Besley, Timothy, and Torsten Persson. 2009. "The Origins of State Capacity: Property Rights, Taxation, and Politics." *American Economic Review* 99, no. 4: 1218–44.

Camp, Edwin, Avinash Dixit, and Susan Stokes. 2014. "Catalyst or Cause? Legislation and the Demise of Machine Politics in Britain and the United States." *Legislative Studies Quarterly* 39, no. 4: 559–92.

Chapman, Jonathan. 2018. "Democratic Reform and Opposition to Government Expenditure: Evidence from Nineteenth-Century Britain." *Quarterly Journal of Political Science* 13, no. 4: 363–404.

Clarke, Kevin A., and David M. Primo. 2012. *A Model Discipline: Political Science and the Logic of Representations*. New York: Oxford University Press.

Cox, Gary. 2004. "Lies, Damned Lies, and Rational Choice Analyses." In *Problems and Methods in the Study of Politics*, ed. Ian Shapiro, Rogers Smith and Tarek Masoud, 167–85. New York: Cambridge University Press.

Dal Bó, Ernesto, Pablo Hernández-Lagos, and Sebastián Mazzuca. 2022. "The Paradox of Civilization: Preinstitutional Sources of Security and Prosperity." *American Political Science Review* 116, no. 1: 213–30.

Defigueiredo, Rui, Jack Rakove, and Barry R. Weingast. 2006. "Rationality, Inaccurate Mental Models, and Self-Confirming Equilibrium: A New Understanding of the American Revolution." *Journal of Theoretical Politics* 18, no. 4: 384–415.

Dincecco, Mark, and Yuhua Wang. 2023. "State Capacity in Historical Political Economy" In *Oxford Handbook of Historical Political Economy*, ed. Jeffery Jenkins and Jared Rubin, 253–69. New York: Oxford University Press.

Dippel, Christian, Avner Greif, and Daniel Trefler. 2020. "Outside Options, Coercion, and Wages: Removing the Sugar Coating." *Economic Journal* 130, no. 630: 1678–714.

Dower, Paul Castañeda, Evgeny Finkel, Scott Gehlbach, and Steven Nafziger. 2018. "Collective Action and Representation in Autocracies: Evidence from Russia's Great Reforms." *American Political Science Review* 112, no. 1: 125–47.

Eggers, Andrew C., and Arthur Spirling. 2014. "Guarding the Guardians: Legislative Self-Policing and Electoral Corruption in Victorian Britain." *Quarterly Journal of Political Science* 9, no. 3: 337–70.

Egorov, Georgy, and Konstantin Sonin. 2015. "The Killing Game: A Theory of Non-democratic Succession." *Research in Economics* 69, no. 3: 398–411.

Elster, Jon. 2000. "Rational Choice History: A Case of Excessive Ambition." *American Political Science Review* 94, no. 3: 685–95.

Gailmard, Sean. 2017. "Building a New Imperial State: The Strategic Foundations of Separation of Powers in America." *American Political Science Review* 111, no. 4: 668–85.

Gailmard, Sean. 2019. "Imperial Politics, English Law, and the Strategic Foundations of Constitutional Review in America." *American Political Science Review* 113, no. 3: 778–95.

Gailmard, Sean. 2020. "Game Theory and the Study of American Political Development." *Public Choice* 185, no. 3: 335–57.

Gailmard, Sean. 2021a. "Imperial Governance and the Growth of Legislative Power in America." *American Journal of Political Science* 65, no. 4: 912–25.

Gailmard, Sean. 2021b. "Theory, History, and Political Economy." *Journal of Historical Political Economy* 1, no. 1: 69–104.

Galiani, Sebastian, and Gustavo Torrens. 2019. "Why Not Taxation and Representation? British Politics and the American Revolution." *Journal of Economic Behavior & Organization* 166: 28–52.

Garfias, Francisco, and Emily A. Sellars. 2021. "From Conquest to Centralization: Domestic Conflict and the Transition to Direct Rule." *Journal of Politics* 83, no. 3: 992–1009.

Garfias, Francisco, and Emily A. Sellars. 2022. "When State Building Backfires: Elite Coordination and Popular Grievance in Rebellion." *American Journal of Political Science* 66, no. 4: 977–92.

Gartzke, Erik, and Dominic Rohner. 2011. "The Political Economy of Imperialism, Decolonization and Development." *British Journal of Political Science* 41, no. 3: 525–56.

Gennaioli, Nicola, and Hans-Joachim Voth. 2015. "State Capacity and Military Conflict." *Review of Economic Studies* 82, no. 4: 1409–48.

Greif, Avner. 1993. "Contract Enforceability and Economic Institutions in Early Trade: The Maghribi Traders' Coalition." *American Economic Review* 83, no. 3: 525–48.

Greif, Avner, Paul Milgrom, and Barry R. Weingast. 1994. "Coordination, Commitment, and Enforcement: The Case of the Merchant Guild." *Journal of Political Economy* 102, no. 4: 745–76.

Grossman, Herschel, and Murat Iyigun. 1997. "Population Increase and the End of Colonialism." *Economica* 64, no. 255: 483–93.

Guala, Francesco. 2005. *The Methodology of Experimental Economics*. New York: Cambridge University Press.

Guardado, Jenny. 2023. "Long-Run Economic Legacies of Colonialism." In *Oxford Handbook of Historical Political Economy*, ed. Jeffery Jenkins and Jared Rubin, 559–80. New York: Oxford University Press.

Hanlon, W. Walker. 2023. "Suffrage in Historical Political Economy", In *Oxford Handbook of Historical Political Economy*, ed. Jeffery Jenkins and Jared Rubin, 459–75. New York: Oxford University Press.

Iyigun, Murat, Jared Rubin, and Avner Seror. 2021. "A Theory of Cultural Revivals." *European Economic Review* 135: 103734.

Kam, Christopher. 2017. "The Secret Ballot and the Market for Votes at 19th-Century British Elections." *Comparative Political Studies* 50, no. 5: 594–635.

Koyama, Mark, Ahmed Rahman, and Tuan-Hwee Sng. 2021. "Seapower." *Journal of Historical Political Economy* 1, no. 2: 155–82.

Larson, Jennifer M. 2017. "Why the West Became Wild: Informal Governance with Incomplete Networks." *World Politics* 69, no. 4: 713–49.

Leon, Gabriel. 2020. "Feudalism, Collaboration and Path Dependence in England's Political Development." *British Journal of Political Science* 50, no. 2: 511–33.

Lizzeri, Alessandro, and Nicola Persico. 2004. "Why Did the Elites Extend the Suffrage? Democracy and the Scope of Government, with an Application to Britain's 'Age of Reform.'" *Quarterly Journal of Economics* 119, no. 2: 707–65.

Llavador, Humberto, and Robert J. Oxoby. 2005. "Partisan Competition, Growth, and the Franchise." *Quarterly Journal of Economics* 120, no. 3: 1155–89.

Ma, Debin, and Jared Rubin. 2019. "The Paradox of Power: Principal-Agent Problems and Administrative Capacity in Imperial China (and Other Absolutist Regimes)." *Journal of Comparative Economics* 47, no. 2: 277–94.

Mayshar, Joram, Omer Moav, and Zvika Neeman. 2017. "Geography, Transparency, and Institutions." *American Political Science Review* 111, no. 3: 622–36.

Milgrom, Paul R., Douglass C. North, and Barry R. Weingast. 1990. "The Role of Institutions in the Revival of Trade: The Law Merchant, Private Judges, and the Champagne Fairs." *Economics & Politics* 2, no. 1: 1–23.

Miller, Gary, and Norman Schofield. 2003. "Activists and Partisan Realignment in the United States." *American Political Science Review* 97, no. 2: 245–60.

Padró i Miquel, Gerard, and Pierre Yared. 2012. "The Political Economy of Indirect Control." *Quarterly Journal of Economics* 127, no. 2: 947–1015.

Pearl, Judea, and Elias Bareinboim. 2014. "External Validity: From Do-Calculus to Transportability across Populations." *Statistical Science* 29, no. 4: 579–95.

Aldaz Peña, Raúl. 2021. "No Need for Democracy: Interelite Conflict and Independence in the Andes." *Journal of Historical Political Economy* 1, no. 3: 561–90.

Penn, Elizabeth Maggie. 2009. "From Many, One: State Representation and the Construction of an American Identity." *Journal of Theoretical Politics* 21, no. 3: 343–64.

Robinson, James A., and Ragnar Torvik. 2016. "Endogenous Presidentialism." *Journal of the European Economic Association* 14, no. 4: 907–42.

Schofield, Norman, and Gary Miller. 2007. "Elections and Activist Coalitions in the United States." *American Journal of Political Science* 51, no. 3: 518–31.

Schofield, Norman, Gary Miller, and Andrew Martin. 2003. "Critical Elections and Political Realignments in the USA: 1860–2000." *Political Studies* 51, no. 2: 217–40.

Sng, Tuan-Hwee. 2014. "Size and Dynastic Decline: The Principal-Agent Problem in Late Imperial China, 1700–1850." *Explorations in Economic History* 54: 107–27.

Stasavage, David. 2023. "Democracy and Historical Political Economy." In *Oxford Handbook of Historical Political Economy*, ed. Jeffery Jenkins and Jared Rubin, 145–60. New York: Oxford University Press.

Tilly, Charles. 1990. *Coercion, Capital, and European States, AD 990–1990*. Cambridge, MA: Basil Blackwell.

CHAPTER 7

HISTORICAL PERSISTENCE

AVIDIT ACHARYA, MATTHEW BLACKWELL,
AND MAYA SEN

> The past is never dead. It's not even past.
> —William Faulkner, *Requiem for a Nun*

INTRODUCTION: WHAT IS HISTORICAL PERSISTENCE?

HISTORICAL *persistence* refers to the idea that historical causes can have effects that persist long into the future. There is a rich tradition of research on historical persistence in political science and economics. In the field of American politics, for example, Key and Munger (1959) noted that the variation in partisan shares across counties in Indiana was stable over a period of eight decades despite the "disappearance of issues that created the pattern, and the existence of contrasting patterns in essentially similar counties" (p. 287). They attributed this to the fact that some counties were settled by southern farmers, while others were settled by farmers from the Northeast, and each group brought with them a different set of political beliefs. In the study of comparative politics, Dogan (1967), contributing to Lipset and Rokkan's (1967) seminal work on party systems in Europe, laid out the hypothesis that the radicalism of the Toulouse region in France—noticeable even in the 1960s—reflects a persistent effect of the thirteenth-century Albigensian Crusades.

In economics, and the quantitative social sciences more broadly, interest in historical persistence resurfaced with the work of Acemoglu, Johnson, and Robinson (2001), who documented a statistical link between the mortality rates faced by Europeans when they first arrived to colonize the New World, Africa, and Asia and the per capita incomes of the independent states that now govern these ex-colonies. They argued that the negative correlation between settler mortality and modern incomes in the former colonies is explained by the fact that colonial powers set up very different institutions in places that they could settle from those that they could not, and these institutions have persisted over time.

The new historical persistence literature has Ieoretical Ioots in an older historical institutionalism literature, which seeks to understand social phenomena as arising through the unfolding of historical processes. This literature builds upon two key ideas. The first is the concept of a critical juncture, which goes back to Lipset and Rokkan (1967) and Collier and Collier (1991). A *critical juncture* is a key moment in time at which a historical cause exerts its influence.

The second is the concept of a reproduction mechanism, discussed by Thelen (1999), Mahoney (2000), Pierson (2004), and others. A reproduction mechanism is an answer to the question of why a historical cause might have persistent effects. Such mechanisms explain how the effects of historical causes can propagate and reproduce themselves over long periods, even after the initial causal forces cease to exert new pressures. These ideas relate to the concept of *path dependence*, which asserts that the evolution of society follows a certain trajectory—a path that is difficult to abandon after society begins to take it (cf. Page 2006).

The early work in historical institutionalism follows its established methods of process-tracing to connect historical causes to the persistent effects they have. In the last couple decades, the new literature on historical persistence in economics and political science has complemented this earlier work by taking a quantitative statistical approach as well, studying historical causation within the framework of causality devised by econometricians and quantitative political methodologists. The focus of this chapter is to review this new work, explain the various methodological approaches it takes, and discuss some open questions.

We add to the existing set of excellent review articles on historical persistence that include Voth (2021) and Nunn (2014), who focus on the economic history literature, and Abad and Maurer (2021) and Cirone and Pepinsky (2022), who provide critiques of the literature that range from data collection to inference and publication bias. These previous reviews focus mainly on empirical methodology. We also discuss methodological issues, but focus instead on what we have learned theoretically from this literature—and what we have yet to learn.

What Persists?

Prior work points to the persistent effects of historical practices and events on institutional and economic development, social attitudes, and politics. In this section, we review some of the major findings from the persistence literature.

Development Outcomes

By *development outcomes*, we mean institutional and economic outcomes that include direct measures of development (such as income and consumption) as well as measures of institutional quality such as bureaucratic capacity and the rule of law. The literature documents the effects of a variety of factors on such development outcomes, which we review here.

Effects of Historical Institutions and Practices

Many studies document the long-lasting effects of historical institutions and practices—including governance practices—on long-run development outcomes.

Perhaps the most well-known studies are those showing the long-lasting effects of European colonization of Africa, Asia, and the Americas. In the finance literature, for example, La Porta et al. (1998) show that countries that operate under the French civil law system have the weakest legal protections for investors, while those that operate under British common law have the strongest protections. They point out that the use of different legal systems in their sample of countries is a legacy of European colonialism, and argue that the identity of the colonizer has major effects on development today. Grier (1999), Lange (2004), and Glaeser and Shleifer (2002) also provide evidence that British former colonies diverge from French former colonies on an array of other development measures.[1]

In a more micro-level study, Lee and Schultz (2012) look at the two sides of the colonial boundary between French and British Cameroon and show that villages that were on the British side have higher levels of prosperity and public goods provision than those on the French side. Similarly, Cogneau and Moradi (2014) study the legacy of colonial rule in Togoland and show that a British (vs. French) legacy is associated with persistently better educational attainment and human capital.

Looking at subnational variation in governance practices by a single colonizer, Banerjee and Iyer (2005) show that Indian regions that used a landlord-based system of tax collection under the British Raj have lower levels of productivity and investments in agriculture, health, and education than those that used a more decentralized system in which the cultivators had proprietary rights.[2] In follow-up work, Iyer (2010) elaborates on these findings, showing that places that experienced direct rule have lower public goods provision and worse economic outcomes in the long term.

Turning to South America, Dell (2010) shows that places in contemporary Peru in which the *mita*, a system of forced labor, was in operation have had persistently worse development outcomes than other places, and argues that these differences are explained by the persistent differences in land tenure systems across *mita* and non-*mita* areas. Also looking at Peru, Guardado (2018) shows that in the seventeenth and eighteenth centuries, the Spanish Crown sold provincial governorships at higher prices in regions that had greater potential for revenue extraction, and these regions have worse development outcomes today. She hypothesizes that the most corrupt governors bid more for the most lucrative regions and governed in a way that increased conflict in the population and lowered trust in the state.

A handful of other studies also document the legacies of imperial and colonial rule by non-European powers, or by European powers within Europe. For example, a study by Mattingly (2017) uses a geographic regression discontinuity design to show that the Japanese colonization of northern China led to the long-term persistence of better economic outcomes despite the coerciveness of Japanese rule. He emphasizes the strengthening of Chinese state institutions—specifically, the bureaucracy—under Japanese rule. Similarly, Vogler (2019) argues that bureaucratic efficiency in Poland today is affected by the legacy of imperial rule under Austria, Prussia, and Russia. These polities controlled different parts of Poland during the nineteenth century and into the early twentieth century and established different practices of public administration during the imperial period, which in turn has had lasting effects.[3]

Finally, while much of the literature traces the effects of colonial and imperial rule on modern development outcomes, Michalopoulos and Papaioannou (2013) also emphasize precolonial conditions (in their case, precolonial ethnic institutions—specifically, political centralization in Africa) that reaches past the colonial period in affecting long-run economic development.

Effects of War and Conquest

Another major focus of the literature has been in documenting the long-lasting effects of war and conquest on development.

In Europe, Acemoglu et al. (2011) show that the parts of present-day Germany that were ravaged and occupied by Napoleon's armies experienced more rapid economic growth after 1850, hypothesizing a mechanism by which French occupation resulted in the old extractive feudal institutions being replaced by more inclusive ones. Blaydes and Paik (2016) argue that the mobilization of crusaders during the Holy Land Crusades affected urbanization centuries later in the twelfth century and state development during the late Middle Ages. Acemoglu, Hassan, and Robinson (2011) show that oblasts in Russia that experienced the Holocaust more intensely have worse economic and political outcomes today, and Ochsner (2017) shows how the Soviet pillaging of the Austrian state of Styria led to a massive decline in population, which never recovered.

Outside of Europe, Paik and Vechbanyongratana (2019) show that areas that were centralized into the Thai state earlier have higher levels of public goods provision and economic development today. Wantchékon and García-Ponce (2013) show that countries that had rural insurgencies during the period of decolonization in Africa are more likely to have autocratic regimes today, while those in which political contention took place in urban areas are more likely to be democratic. And finally, looking globally, Dincecco and Prado (2012) show that the extent of human casualties in premodern wars predicts a state's fiscal capacity today.

Economic Activity

The concepts of historical persistence, and path dependence generally, have been central to the trade and economic geography literatures going back to work by Krugman (1991a; 1991b) on the importance of history in determining to which of multiple equilibria a society will converge. Recent empirical work by Bleakley and Lin (2012), Allen and Donaldson (2020), and Jedwab, Kerby, and Moradi (2017) documents the persistence of the historical location of economic activity through the economics of agglomeration.

Other work in the literature looks more closely at economic structure and the extent and nature of economic activity. Examples include Esposito and Abramson (2021), who document the persistence of lower levels of development in European regions that historically mined coal, showing that former coal mining regions are now poorer than comparable regions in the same country that did not mine coal; Pascali (2016), who shows the persistence of banking development in Italy from the period of the Italian Renaissance to now, and documents the long-run positive economic effects of banking development; and Gaikwad (2014), who argues that access to trade in precolonial times has had a persistent effect on economic outcomes in India, lasting all the way through the colonial period to present.

Cultural and Political Outcomes

Historical events and practices also have major effects not just on economic outcomes but also on culture and social attitudes. For example, the practices of many religious traditions have persisted geographically over long periods of time. Islam, to take one illustration of this, has been the main religion of much of the Arabian peninsula since the Muslim conquests of the seventh century.

Alongside the institutional persistence literature, past research has shown that social norms, gender bias, racism, anti-Semitism, and other forms of prejudice also persist through a cultural channel. The factors that affect such persistent outcomes overlap considerably with those that affect development paths.

Effects of Historical Institutions and Practices

In one of the most striking examples of persistent effects on cultural outcomes, Alesina, Giuliano, and Nunn (2013) show that parts of the world in which the soil was more suitable to plow agriculture as opposed to the hoe or digging stick treat women less favorably today. They argue that because the plow requires greater upper body strength to use, a division of labor norm was set in which men worked outside the home while women did domestic work, and this norm was passed down culturally across generations. They provide evidence for this cultural transmission by showing that the labor participation rate among first-generation immigrants to the United States (individuals who were born and raised in the United States) is lower for women whose parents immigrated from plow-heritage societies. Another study, by Olsson and Paik (2016), shows that individuals from Western countries that adopted agriculture early during the Neolithic period report having more collectivist values, value obedience more, and feel less in control of their lives.

There is also work that examines the effects of historical institutions on political ideology, policy preferences, and policy outcomes. Alesina and Fuchs-Schundeln (2007) document the persistence of differences in views about redistribution and the role of government between East and West Germans even fifteen years after reunification; and Lechler and McNamee (2018) examine the legacy of colonial institutions in Namibia, showing that places that were ruled directly by the German colonizers now display greater support for democracy and participation in elections than places in the north that were ruled indirectly.

Analogous to the effects of forced labor institutions on the long-run development outcomes discussed earlier, Acharya, Blackwell, and Sen (2016b) show that the parts of American South where slavery was most prevalent are those where White attitudes toward African Americans are also the most hostile today.[4] Also looking at US history, Beramendi and Jensen (2019) study the persistent effects of malapportionment in the legislatures of the original thirteen US colonies and whether states chose representation based purely on population versus an English system based on townships or parishes. They show that this early choice in how to organize political representation predicts not just political equality but also the provision of public goods in the long run.

Societal Disruptions

Just as war and conquest have had persistent effects on long-run development outcomes, numerous papers have documented the long-run consequences of various societal disruptions on culture, attitudes, and ideology. A seminal paper in this literature is Nunn and Wantchekon (2011), who show that African communities that were targeted by the slave trade four centuries ago display lower levels of social capital today.

In addition, several studies document the persistent effects of societal disruptions on intergroup animosities. Voigtländer and Voth (2012) show that German towns that persecuted and murdered their Jewish populations during the Black Death had higher levels of support for the Nazi party in the interwar period and greater levels of anti-Semitism by other measures as well. Charnysh and Finkel (2017) show the persistence of anti-Semitism from the Holocaust to now in Polish areas that are closer to the Treblinka death camp. Charnysh (2015) also finds that these animosities can have spillover effects on public policy, showing that opposition to EU membership in the 2003 Polish referendum in which right-wing Euroskeptics used anti-Semitic rhetoric to spread opposition to the EU is predicted by interethnic conflict in the interwar period and the locations of a series of pogroms that took place in 1941.

In explaining the persistence of intergroup animosities, Lupu and Peisakhin (2017) suggest that past violence influences self-perceptions and hardens group identities and cleavages. They conduct a multigenerational survey of Crimean Tatars who were displaced from their homes in 1944 and find that the descendants of those who faced greater hardship have stronger ethnic attachments and express more negative views toward Russia. Consistent with these findings, Rozenas, Schutte, and Zhukov (2017) show that Stalin's repression of Ukraine had a lasting effect on attitudes toward Russia: pro-Russian politicians fare worse in the most repressed regions a half century later. Ochsner and Roesel (2017) look at the sieges of Vienna by Turkish invaders in the sixteenth and seventeenth centuries, and find that present-day individuals living in places that were attacked display greater Islamophobia than others who live in places that were not attacked.

The effects of societal disruptions on intergroup animosities can also result in persistent conflict. Ito (2021) examines the effects of postcolonial borders on long-term armed conflict in Africa, showing that when ethnic groups are split by a border, armed conflict increases among politically excluded ethnic groups.[5] In another study that also focuses on the persistent effects of borders, Abramson and Carter (2016) argue that the political tensions that underlie interstate territorial disputes have persisted based on the fact that historical border precedents predict territorial claims. They show that historical boundaries set between the seventeenth and early nineteenth centuries predict territorial claims made after the Congress of Vienna.

In explaining attitudes toward the state, Wang (2021) shows that individuals from parts of China that experienced greater state terror during the Cultural Revolution of the 1960s are less trusting of national leaders and more critical of the Chinese regime today (with the effect being stronger among those who say that they discuss politics with their parents) but are less likely to participate in protest. Komisarchik, Sen, and Velez (2022) likewise show that Japanese Americans who were incarcerated in internment camps during World War II by the US government had persistently lower rates of political engagement in US politics. On the other hand, Lee, Qi, and Sun (2021) find that the Mao-era exile of millions of urban youth increased support for the regime, arguing that the exile isolated them from other social influences that would lead them to be more critical of the controlling power.

In general, societal disruptions can also have lasting effects on political ideology and electoral outcomes. Fontana, Nannicini, and Tabellini (2017) document a persistence in left-wing ideology in northern Italy, showing that the communist vote share has been persistently higher in places that experienced longer periods of occupation by the Nazis, and where the Italian civil war lasted longer. Homola, Pereira, and Tavits (2020b) show that support for right-wing parties and causes in present-day Germany traces back to the Nazi era: places that are closer to former concentration camps are on average more right wing, and these political attitudes are not explained by geographic sorting, the location of the camps, or the current use of these sites.

Past Politics and State Policy

Several studies have shown that historical governance regimes and state policies set in the distant past also exert long-run effects on political ideology, culture, and attitudes.

For example, Miguel (2004) shows that the effects of ethnic diversity are conditioned by the state's investments in nation-building: groups on the Tanzanian side of the Kenya-Tanzania border had more success in overcoming the challenges of collective action in public goods provision than similarly diverse groups on the Kenyan side, where the state did not invest as much in nation-building.

Other studies explain the formation of political cultures more generally. Guiso, Sapienza, and Zingales (2016) test Putnam's hypothesis that the differences in civic traditions between northern and southern Italy have persisted since the Middle Ages, with social capital being higher in cities that experienced self-government centuries ago. Bazzi, Koehler-Derrick, and Marx (2020) show greater support for Islamism today in parts of Indonesia that invested more resources in religious institutions to avoid expropriation by the state in the 1960s. Chen, Kung, and Ma (2020) show that the effects of the Chinese civil examination system known as *keju* on human capital acquisition have persisted since the Ming and Qing periods to now.

In the US context, Nall (2018) attributes some of the geographic variation in political ideology to the legacy of the federal highway program, which took off in the middle of the twentieth century. Rodden (2019) shows that cities have been persistently liberal in comparison to rural areas, attributing some of these geographic differences to the fact that cities were places where unions mobilized workers to support ideologically liberal causes. Bazzi, Fiszbein, and Gebresilasse (2020) provide evidence for a persistent political culture that favors individualism (against collectivism) in counties that were on the American frontier for longer periods.

Theories of Persistence

Now that we have provided an overview of different examples of persistence from across the literature, we turn to discussing explanations for historical persistence and how persistence may be broken.

What Explains Persistence?

Historical persisntence can take place for seemingly mechanical reasons. For example, people who are rich today are rich tomorrow and the next day, because they simply keep their wealth and are able to invest it just as well as anyone else.

In this way, many examples of persistence are quite natural. New York City has persisted as the most populous city in the United States every decade since at least 1790. Even if cities did not attract new migrants at different rates, the relative size of cities is likely to persist because more children are born in larger cities than in smaller ones; and if they are likely to continue to reside in their cities of birth because moving is costly, then there is a very natural and seemingly mechanical reason why the relative sizes of cities should be stable over time.

Of course, such persistence in relative rank need not occur, let alone be mechanical. Chicago, for example, was America's second-most-populous city every decade from

1880 to 1980 but has since been overtaken by Los Angeles. But even if persistence can be broken in this way, it is not surprising that there should be a large set of mechanical forces at play in explaining persistence in many instances. Besides these kinds of mechanical forces, a set of broad categories of explanations for historical persistence is as follows.

Increasing Returns and Switching Costs

Persistence of institutions can take place because the returns to an institution increase over time, and institutional change is inherently costly. For example, it would involve high "transaction costs" (in the terminology of North [1991]) for the United States to change from a presidential system to a parliamentary system and back every three years.

The idea of increasing returns can be used to explain why even small shocks can have large effects that amplify over time. Dell (2012), for instance, shows that the differential impact of an early-twentieth-century drought affected the level of insurgent activity in the Mexican civil war, which in turn had long-run economic effects. She concludes that "relatively modest events can have highly nonlinear and persistent influences, depending on the broader societal circumstances." Nunn and Qian (2011) leverage the differential timing of the introduction of the potato (a New World crop) in the Old World to estimate that the introduction of the potato accounts for 25 percent of the growth in Old World population between 1700 and 1900. They argue that the potato's effects work through improvements in nutrition and agricultural production. Acharya and Lee (2019) show that the likelihood of the availability of male heirs predicts contemporary GDP per capita across European regions today, and the size of the effects on development measures is increasing over time. These studies are in line with Pierson's (2000) view that "path dependent arguments based on positive feedback suggest that not only 'big' events have big consequences; little ones that happen at the right time can have major consequences as well" (263).

The fact that the effects of small shocks can amplify over time is an important basis for growth and divergence, as depicted in the left example of Figure 7.1. In this

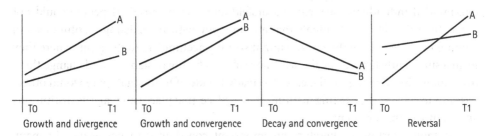

FIGURE 7.1. Growth and divergence: A starts very close to B, both units are growing, but A is growing faster so the units are diverging; Growth and convergence: A starts ahead of B, both units are growing, but B is growing faster and catching up to A, so the units are converging; Decay and convergence: A starts ahead of B, both are decaying, but A is decaying faster so the units are converging; Reversal: B starts ahead of A; in the picture, both are growing, but A grows faster and by time T_1, A is ahead of B.

example, two societies A and B are very similar at time T_0 but a small shock hits A, giving it an immediate boost over B. It then starts growing faster and diverging from B as a result of the time T_0 shock. By time T_1, it is significantly ahead of B and may possibly be increasing its lead.

Political and Social Equilibrium

Another classic explanation for persistence is that societies tend to find a stable political or social equilibrium that, by definition of its stability, is resistant to change.

A long tradition in political economy has argued that many institutions persist in part because of increasing returns to political power: those who are in power get to choose the institutions, and will choose institutions that are good for them. These institutions will in turn help them grow their power, and they will use this power to guard these institutions against change. The institutions will thus stay in place even if others would like to change them. Acemoglu, Johnson, and Robinson (2005) provide a summary and overview of this argument.

Closely related to this is the view of rational choice instituionalists such as Shepsle (1986), Calvert (1995), and Schotter (1981) that institutions themselves are a stable equilibrium: they are defined by the condition that everyone expects everyone else to behave a certain way, and chooses their own behavior optimally. Nobody has any incentive to act differently, and if the institution is a *stable* equilibrium then it is robust to small disruptions, such as, for example, a small handful of agents trying to destabilize it. This leads to institutional stability and persistence.

Geographic Sorting

When people who do not benefit from an institution that is in place cannot change it, they may still have the ability to pick up and move to places with institutions or social arrangements that they find more favorable.

This type of geographic sorting can also be an important contributor to persistence (especially cultural persistence), and can take place for a variety of other reasons as well, including *homophily*: people simply want to live around, and interact with, other like-minded individuals (see, e.g., Lazarsfeld and Merton 1954). If people could not move, then the set of individuals that are unhappy with the existing institutions and cultural practices where they reside might steadily accumulate to the point where they form a sufficiently large critical mass that is able to finally destabilize and change these institutions. By allowing for the exit of a steady trickle of individuals who would otherwise like to subvert the existing institutions of a place, that place can make its institutions and culture more persistent.

Geographic sorting is therefore an important contributor to persistence in many contexts. Most of the studies that we have reviewed document persistence by comparing outcomes across geographic units. Since these outcomes are population-specific (culture, income, etc.), it is always possible that population shifts are driving some of the results. In some studies, population movement may even be the primary driver behind persistence.

In fact, Olsson and Paik (2016) suggest that their results on the cultural divergence that took place after the Neolithic revolution is explained by migration patterns. And in the Bazzi, Fiszbein, and Gebresilasse (2020) study of the effects of the frontier on American individualism that we mentioned earlier, the authors show that that selective migration is an important channel by which the frontier effect is transmitted, though they also claim a direct causal effect of frontier exposure on individualism that does not operate through migration.

However, in some instances, the theoretical mechanism being posited for historical persistence does not admit sorting as an explanation. There are several ways that persistence studies have attempted to underemphasize the importance of sorting. Some studies, such as Lupu and Peisakhin (2017), have data on lineages (family histories) rather than geographic units, and thus can rule out sorting as the exclusive channel for persistence. When outcomes and migration status are available at the individual level, it is also possible to see if the persistence endures among migrants with different historical backgrounds but the same current environment; such tests are conducted by Alesina, Giuliano, and Nunn (2013) and Nunn and Wantchekon (2011). This approach, however, has the disadvantage of requiring researchers to condition on "post-treatment" variables like migrant status and migration destination.[6] On the other hand, studies like Dell (2010) and Acharya, Blackwell, and Sen (2016b) have attempted to show that the initial cause of the persistence does not have differential impacts on the profile of migrants into or out of the regions of interest, an approach that avoids the major concerns of post-treatment bias.

Intergenerational Socialization

In the theory of behavioral path dependence that we developed in chapter 2 of our book on American slavery (Acharya, Blackwell, and Sen 2018a) we argued that the persistence of culture can take place through both institutional channels and via intergenerational socialization.

This explanation for persistence builds on prior work by Jennings and Niemi (1968) that empirically documents the transmission of values from parents to children, as well as theoretical work by Bisin and Verdier (2000), Boyd and Richerson (1988), Acharya, Blackwell, and Sen (2018b), and others who model the intergenerational transmission of culture. The basic idea is that children are socialized into the beliefs of their parents and other members of their community when they are young. They maintain these beliefs as they age and are likely to pass them on to their own children, leading to persistence. Part of this socialization involves institutions such as churches, schools, and local formal laws and informal practices that acculturate children into local traditions and locally predominant cultural attitudes.

Of course, there are many instances in which traditions are broken and children develop independent beliefs of their own as they mature. If this is frequently the case, then links to the past are broken more rapidly. It is even possible that there is a reversal: the culture of the past is replaced by a new and very different culture, and historical persistence is broken. We turn to this possibility next.

When Is Persistence Broken?

If everything always persisted, then societies would never change. But in fact societies do change. The literature has so far focused on documenting persistence, while critics of the literature have rightly pointed out that history is not always destiny (e.g., Abad and Maurer 2021). Unfortunately, neither side has offered constructive research on explaining the conditions under which persistence takes place or under which it is broken. We have yet to develop a general theoretical understanding of the conditions under which persistence takes place, and the conditions under which it does not.

Reversals

Persistence is broken when there is a reversal. As the rightmost example in Figure 7.1 shows, a *reversal* occurs when the relative ranking of two societies A and B on some measure changes from one period in time to the next. For example, society B may be richer than A at time T_0 but then by time T_1 society A is richer because its GDP has grown faster than B's.

Reversals are well documented in the literature. Acemoglu, Johnson, and Robinson (2002) show that societies that were among the most prosperous in 1500 (e.g., India and China) were among the least prosperous in the twentieth century, while those that were not very prosperous back then were among the most prosperous five centuries later. Relative differences in prosperity do tend to persist (the United States has been richer than Ghana for a very long time), but in many cases they do not (North Korea was richer than South Korea before 1975, but is today much poorer). These examples make it important to understand where a reversal in relative prosperity like this would come from, and whether we could anticipate such reversals.

Another study that highlights an important reversal is Olsson and Paik (2020). These authors provide evidence for a reversal within the Western agricultural core: regions that made an early transition to agriculture during the Neolithic revolution are now poorer than regions that made a later transition, and this reversal started to emerge before the Age of Imperialism. In another example, Acharya and Lee (2019) look at the reversal that took place between Naples and Paris. Naples was a more prosperous city than Paris in the early Middle Ages but faced a series of destructive wars tied to royal succession disputes in a period when Paris enjoyed a tremendous run of dynastic stability. Today, Naples is significantly poorer than Paris.

Examples of reversals in politics include democratic reversals. For example, democracy had persisted in Chile for many decades until the 1973 coup deposed President Salvador Allende.[7] Another example of a political reversal is the partisan realignment of American politics in the 1960s. The Democratic Party had enjoyed widespread support among southern white voters in the early twentieth century. Their dominance persisted until the Goldwater-Johnson election of 1964, and since then the Republican Party has dominated among southern whites—a situation that has again persisted for the last fifty years.

Just as important as understanding what causes persistence is understanding what causes these kinds of reversals. Explanations so far have varied depending on the study, but some studies point to general ideas. Garfias and Sellars (2021), for example, argue that institutional persistence is broken after major shocks like the sixteenth-century demographic collapse in Mexico. They show that following this calamity, the state that had been persistently weak grew rapidly stronger, expanding the areas over which it exercised direct rule. Similarly, Sellars and Alix-Garcia (2018) look at the long-term consequences of the same collapse for modern institutions, and show that property rights are weaker today in places that experienced a greater collapse in population.[8] While these studies are suggestive of the importance of shocks in generating reversals, we still have yet to understand the mechanisms by which these major shocks operate, and when and how they exert their effects.

Decay

Besides the two examples of growth and divergence and reversals (first and last of Figure 7.1), there are also the possibilities of growth and convergence and decay and convergence. Convergence is an important concept in the macroeconomics literature, with foundational models predicting that low-income countries should catch up to high-income countries as both sets of countries grow but the low-income ones grow faster (see, e.g., Barro and Sala-i Martin 1992).

Convergence is also an important concept in the persistence literature. For example, Alesina and Fuchs-Schundeln (2007), who find persistent differences in the views of East and West Germans on redistribution following the reunification of Germany, also show that the views of these two groups have been converging. They estimate that it will take two to four decades from the time of their study for the differences to disappear.

Similarly, Jha (2013), who shows that peaceful relations between Muslim and Hindu communities in medieval port cities on the shores of the Arabian Sea in India have persisted for centuries, also finds that the social harmony of these port cities has started to unravel, potentially resulting in a convergence in outcomes between port and nonport cities. Moreover, the mechanism that he posits to explain the persistence of religious harmony in Indian port cities also offers clues as to why convergence might also occur between these two sets of cities: in the port cities, Hindus and Muslims provided complementary skills, and each group needed the other to reap the gains from trade; this complementarity, however, is less relevant today than it was historically. That the structure of economic relationships can shape intergroup animosity is also a point that also comes out of Voigtländer and Voth (2012)'s finding that the effects of the medieval pogroms are weaker in the high-trade cities of the Hanseatic League, as well as Acharya, Blackwell, and Sen (2016b)'s finding that the effects of slaveholding on long-term racist attitudes are weaker in counties that mechanized their agriculture earlier (which made them less reliant on Black labor) in response to shocks like the boll weevil and the Mississippi floods.[9] If intervening events such as these can attenuate the differences between treated and control units in a study, then their occurrence can explain convergence that takes place between these units over time.[10]

Finally, the difference between decay and convergence is important. Even if differences in anti-Semitism among Germans in pogrom regions and those elsewhere (or in racism between southern Whites in former slaveholding counties and non-slaveholding counties) are converging to each other, we do not know if anti-Semitism (and racism) overall grew over time or declined. We suspect (and would like to believe) that it has declined. But showing convergence by showing declining treatment effects (i.e., comparing outcomes across units) is not the same thing as showing decay, which requires documenting changes over time within units. Convergence is consistent with both growth and decay, as the second and third examples of Figure 7.1 show.

The point is that convergence is a property of a relative comparison, while growth and decay are absolute features of specific units. The United States was richer than China in 1980 in per capita terms, but the ratio of GDP per capita between the two countries has been moving closer to 1 even as they have both been getting richer: the two countries are converging. Growth and decay, on the other hand, are not properties of a relative comparison. If we said that GDP per capita in the United States is decaying, we would mean that it is decreasing, regardless of what is happening in China.

Absolute versus Relative Persistence

We now distinguish between *relative persistence*, where a comparison persists across time, and *absolute persistence*, in which a particular institution or feature of society persists. In the first three examples of Figure 7.1, A is persistently ahead of B (though in the second and third examples, A's lead is shrinking). New York has been persistently more populous than Chicago, Africa has been persistently poorer than Europe, and so on. These are claims of relative persistence because they are based on a comparison: New York with Chicago, Africa with Europe, and so on.

When a persistence claim does not require a comparison, it is one of absolute persistence. The English monarchy has persisted in the absolute sense: it has been around for more than a thousand years, making its persistence tangible and obvious. Another example is that the United States has persisted as a presidential democracy under the same constitution since the late eighteenth century. No comparison across units is necessary to establish these facts; no causal effects have to be estimated.

It is crucial for work in the historical persistence literature to clarify which form of persistence is being claimed. We are often in the position of seeing relative persistence between two groups over time while absolute persistence fails for both groups. For example, in 1950, real US GDP per capita was just about ten thousand dollars (measured in 2000 dollars). This figure has clearly not persisted, as GDP growth has outpaced population growth. However, the relative difference between the GDP per capita of the United States and that of Ghana has mostly persisted over this period: the United States was just about ten times richer per capita than Ghana back in 1950, and is just over ten times richer than Ghana now. Similarly, the populations of New York and Chicago increased rapidly over the twentieth century, but New York was just over twice as populous as

Chicago was in 1900, and continued to be throughout this period. In both examples, growth has taken place as in either the first or second examples of Figure 7.1, but neither divergence nor convergence has taken place since the income ratio in the US–Ghana example and the population ratio in the New York–Chicago example have remained essentially constant.

Most empirical studies nowadays tend to explain observed variation (often variation in outcomes at the level of a geographic unit) and typically make claims of relative persistence rather than absolute persistence. Claims of absolute persistence such as the persistence of institutions within a state, or the world, on the other hand, are typically made using formal and qualitative approaches. For example, a provocative paper by Gailmard (2017) looks at the system of separation of powers in the United States and argues that the system has persisted since long before American independence.[11] In another "system level" analysis, Acharya and Lee (2018) argue that the current system of international borders and norms of state sovereignty in the world have persisted since the Early Modern period because it enables states to exercise greater control over their subjects than alternative systems would.

Studies like these are close in spirit to others in the historical institutionalism literature, such as Ertman (1997), Tilly (1992), Fukuyama (2011) and North and Weingast (1989), who study the origins of various institutions that have persisted. Some of these studies use formal models and equilibrium analysis to make sense of the stability of persistent systems while others use qualitative methods such as process-tracing. But these methodological differences are less important than the common goal of many of these studies in explaining absolute persistence.[12]

Methodological Issues

We now turn to some frequently arising methodological issues that affect persistence studies. We focus on two interrelated issues that concern the fact that many persistence studies operate by documenting a statistical relationship between two variables that are measured very far apart in time. Both address how we think about and handle everything that has happened in the intervening time between events.

Proximate versus Distal Effects

One source of confusion in persistence studies comes from the difference between what we call *proximate* and *distal* causal effects. Most of the causal effects that researchers measure are relatively proximate. For example, we randomly assign survey respondents to read different vignettes and then, minutes later, measure their opinions on policy outcomes. Persistence studies work at much longer time scales and, thus, focus on more distal, or longer-term, effects. If so much has happened between the time the treatment

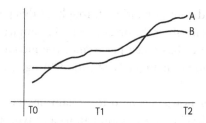

FIGURE 7.2. *A* is a treated unit and *B* is a control unit. If assignment to treatment is random, then we can measure a causal effect of the treatment at any moment in time, including time T_1 when it is negative and T_2 when it is positive.

was administered and the time the outcome was measured, how can we attribute any differences between treated and control units to the distant cause? What if several reversals took place between these two periods in time?

Figure 7.2 depicts an interesting example. There are two units *A* and *B*, and a treatment is administered to *A* at time T_0 while *B* is a control unit. The treatment has a positive effect at time T_0, a negative effect at time T_1, and a positive effect again at time T_2, when the outcome is measured on the *y*-axis. As the figure makes clear, the effect of the treatment has reversed twice between time T_0 and time T_2. Can we still say that the positive effect measured at time T_0 has persisted to time T_2? One answer is no, because the effect at time T_1 is negative. Another answer is yes, because the time T_2 effect is the same as the time T_0 effect regardless of what is true at time T_1. The difference between the answers is semantic in that it depends on the definition of "persistence" that is relevant to the research question.

One thing is clear, however: causal effects are well defined regardless of the temporal distance between treatment and outcome. What matters for establishing an overall causal effect is finding a research design that can identify a causal effect under plausible assumptions, whether it be selection-on-observables, instrumental variables, or some other design.[13] To take an example that comes from our own work, the causal effect of slavery on Republican vote share may be negative in 1900 but positive in 2000. That's because of the partisan realignment that took place in the middle of the twentieth century. Such reversals imply that the treatment effect (here, slavery's effect on partisan vote share) has not persisted. But the fact that it has not persisted does not in and of itself discredit the estimation of a precisely defined treatment effect that includes—as part of the definition of the estimand—the time at which the outcome is measured.

To see this point another way, imagine the following experiment. We take a sample of children who are treated with a new drug at age five that is supposed to generally improve health outcomes throughout life and lower their risk of suffering a heart attack after they cross seventy years of age. There is a treatment group that receives the pill, a control group that does not, and possibly another placebo group that receives a sugar pill. It is a large clinical trial where assignment to treatment is random. Suppose we wait at least sixty-five years before we start measuring the outcome. If we find that the pill works in that the treated group suffered lower rates of heart attack than the other two groups, which suffered the same rates, then it is irrelevant that sixty-five years of activity, life choices, food intake, exercise, and so on, elapsed between the time of treatment and the time that the outcome is measured.

If the pill is supposed to improve health outcomes throughout life, then we would of course like to measure these outcomes along the way, instead of waiting sixty-five years to start measuring them. Perhaps those who took the pill are less likely to suffer from obesity at age forty-five, age fifty-five, and so on. Measuring that would be ideal. But even if we did not measure those intermediate health outcomes, the effect of the pill on heart attacks after age seventy is not negated. Again, what matters is how assignment to treatment took place, and whether we have enough statistical power to make sharp inferences about the pill's effect.

Post-Treatment Bias

Where the issue of proximate versus distal causal effects matters more is not in the measurement of the overall effect of a treatment, but rather in the adjudication between different causal mechanisms. Often scholars want to "control for" a rival mechanism to isolate an estimate of their own preferred mechanism.

Unfortunately, however, the most common approach that researchers have taken to do this—conducting a mediation analysis by conditioning on post-treatment variables much in the same way we condition on pre-treatment variables—leads to post-treatment bias when there is confounding between the mediator and the outcome affected by treatment. Given the long timelines and strong treatments in the historical persistence literature, the latter situation is likely very common. We highlight this issue in Acharya, Blackwell, and Sen (2016a) and illustrate one possible way to avoid these types of biases by focusing on a quantity of interest called the *controlled direct effect*: the effect of treatment when the mediator is held to a fixed, researcher-chosen value, which can help assess if a rival mechanism is explaining all of the estimated effect. The identification of these direct effects is not free, however: we must have a research design that identifies not only the effect of treatment on the outcome but also the effect of the post-treatment variable on the outcome. This may be difficult in many settings. Despite these issues, many research studies continue to condition on post-treatment variables, which has led to debates in the literature. One illustration of this debate is Pepinsky, Goodman, and Ziller (2020), which re-estimates the model in Homola, Pereira, and Tavits (2020b) after introducing state fixed effects. Pepinsky, Goodman, and Ziller (2020) find that proximity to Nazi concentration camps no longer predicts contemporary political outcomes, as Homola, Pereira, and Tavits (2020b) show. However, Homola, Pereira, and Tavits (2020a) point out that the state fixed effects dummies in the Pepinsky-Goodman-Ziller specification are post-treatment, as the state boundaries of Germany were redrawn (often with citizen participation) and thus contaminate the estimation of the causal effect of concentration-camp proximity.

Conclusion: What Next?

What comes next in the literature on historical persistence? As we have already mentioned, we have yet to develop a general theoretical understanding of when persistence happens and when it is broken. Although it is likely that there is no general theory that covers all instances of persistence, the literature has now amassed a large enough set of findings that the time for theoretical synthesis is ripe. As theories of persistence and change are developed, new empirical studies will be necessary to test their propositions and implications.

One important issue that will arise in this process of theory-building will be to assess whether studies that find and document instances of persistence overstate the extent of persistence that takes place. After all, it is understandably harder to publish a result showing that historical persistence did not take place in a specific instance where it was not expected to, than a more surprising result that documents long-term persistence in an instance where our priors suggested that it was unlikely to occur. The issue is one of publication bias, which is a complicated problem that has no clear answers.

However, part of addressing this issue may be to change our expectations as to whether persistence is natural or surprising, and the extent to which persistence is the consequence of active versus passive choices. For if we change our priors to think that it is not historical persistence that is surprising, but rather the failure of persistence in many instances, then that could potentially encourage more studies to look into the causes of why things do not persist.

To see this, consider the familiar example of driving on the "wrong side" of the street. Why do we drive on the left in some countries but on the right in others? An important part of the answer is that left-side driving in many British ex-colonies has persisted for decades even after these places gained independence. While it is always possible for a country that uses left-side driving to switch to right-side driving, and vice versa, most societies rarely do so. These road policies are choices that most societies made long ago, and we expect them to persist even though policymakers can choose to change the policy at any time. Some institutions and behaviors are simply the result of historical causes, and occasionally these causes go back a long way. There is nothing surprising or unnatural about this.

What would be more surprising is if a British ex-colony that had adopted left-side driving for many years made the switch to right-side driving. This happened in Nigeria and Belize, which are still members of the Commonwealth. Why did these societies choose to break the pattern of historical persistence? And what explains why a handful of countries like Japan, Indonesia, and Thailand that were not British colonies adopted left-side driving? These may be the more interesting questions.

The basic point we wish to make is that historical persistence is often a very natural phenomenon, that in many cases persistence is not surprising, and that in some cases it is more interesting to ask when and why persistence is broken. Adopting this view may provide researchers with enough of an incentive to study instances in which persistence is broken and, in so doing, improve our understanding of the processes that underlie both persistence and change.

Acknowledgments

For comments and feedback we thank Alex Lee, and the editors, Jeffery A. Jenkins and Jared Rubin.

Notes

1. A counterpoint to these arguments is Musacchio and Turner (2013), which shows that differences in the effects of a British or French colonial legacy for the outcomes studied in the legal origins literature do not hold if the effects are estimated in an intermediate period of time.
2. However, Iversen, Palmer-Jones, and Sen (2013) critique these findings, arguing that they are generated by coding errors, while Lee (2019) argues that the mechanism specified by the authors is incorrect: it is differences in state capacity rather than political conflict (the mechanism highlighted by Banerjee and Iyer) that explains their findings.
3. A counterpoint to these claims comes from Backhaus (2019), who also studies the legacy of imperial rule in Poland and finds that, although there were large differences in human capital formation across the formerly Austrian, Prussian, and Russian areas in 1911, these differences disappeared completely in the next half century.
4. In recent work, Bazzi et al. (2021) supplement this evidence by showing that regions of the United States outside the South that experienced greater White migration from the South many decades ago are more politically conservative today.
5. Fearon and Laitin (2012) also show more generally that the propensity of the inhabitants of a certain location to engage in armed conflict tends to persist over long periods of time.
6. Marbach (2021) presents a formal methodological analysis of the post-treatment bias issue with migration and persistence studies using a principle stratification framework.
7. As this example shows, the occurrence of a "reversal," generally defined, does not actually require a comparison between two societies as suggested by the depiction in Figure 7.1. In this example, Chile starts as an autocracy, becomes democratic, and reverts to authoritarianism in 1973. There is no comparison country needed. This point relates to our discussion of absolute persistence (which does not require comparisons between units) versus relative persistence (which does) in the next section.
8. On the other hand, looking at the effects of the Black Death in Germany, Gingerich and Vogler (2021) show that places that were hit the hardest have more inclusive political institutions and more equitable land ownership centuries later.
9. Becker and Pascali (2019) also provide evidence that the structure of economic relationships matters. They show that after the Protestant Reformation removed the ban on usury, competition in moneylending between Christians and Jews grew in the Protestant cities of Germany, leading to increases in anti-Semitism relative to Catholic cities.
10. That being said, persistence can be quite stubborn even in the face of intervening events that one might expect would unravel the original treatment effects. For example, Wittenberg (2006) shows that right-wing political ideology persisted in Hungary

between the elections of 1948 and 1990 despite there being no elections during the period of Communist rule in which voters could express their right-wing ideology at the ballot box.

11. In fact, the paper traces its origins to the way in which the British crown mitigated the agency problem of governors. By setting up an assembly that constrains the governor from taxation (in the same way that North and Weingast [1989] argue that Parliament did in Britain), governors, he claims, were restricted from taxing much more than what was optimal for the Crown.

12. See also Katznelson and Weingast (2005) on the relationship between historical and rational choice institutionalism.

13. One such assumption, which we do not discuss in depth (because it is covered extensively in the other historical persistence review articles that we mentioned in the introduction) is the Stable Unit Treatment Variance Assumption (SUTVA). This assumption often comes into play with persistence studies because historical forces are rarely cleanly confined to a specific area. For example, Kelly (2019) shows that using geographic units of analysis but failing to account for spatial auto-correlation can create inferential challenges. In addition, selecting the right geographic unit of analysis is important. For example, Lee (2021) shows that the effects of colonial land tenure institutions in India disappear at finer units even if they are present at coarser units, providing a counterpoint to prior research findings on colonial legacies.

References

Abad, Leticia Arroyo, and Noel Maurer. 2021. "History Never Really Says Goodbye: A Critical Review of the Persistence Literature." *Journal of Historical Political Economy* 1, no. 1: 31–68.

Abramson, Scott F., and David B. Carter. 2016. "The Historical Origins of Territorial Disputes." *American Political Science Review* 110, no. 4: 675–98.

Acemoglu, Daron, Davide Cantoni, Simon Johnson, and James A. Robinson. 2011. "The Consequences of Radical Reform: The French Revolution." *American Economic Review* 101, no. 7: 3286–307.

Acemoglu, Daron, Tarek A. Hassan, and James A. Robinson. 2011. "Social Structure and Development: A Legacy of the Holocaust in Russia." *Quarterly Journal of Economics* 126, no. 2: 895–946.

Acemoglu, Daron, Simon Johnson, and James A. Robinson. 2001. "The Colonial Origins of Comparative Development: An Empirical Investigation." *American Economic Review* 91, no. 5: 1369–401.

Acemoglu, Daron, Simon Johnson, and James A. Robinson. 2002. "Reversal of Fortune: Geography and Institutions in the Making of the Modern World Income Distribution." *Quarterly Journal of Economics* 117, no. 4: 1231–94.

Acemoglu, Daron, Simon Johnson, and James A. Robinson. 2005. "Institutions as a Fundamental Cause of Long-Run Growth." *Handbook of Economic Growth* 1: 385–472.

Acharya, Avidit, Matthew Blackwell, and Maya Sen. 2016a. "Explaining Causal Findings without Bias: Detecting and Assessing Direct Effects." *American Political Science Review* 110, no. 3: 512–29.

Acharya, Avidit, Matthew Blackwell, and Maya Sen. 2016b. "The Political Legacy of American Slavery." *Journal of Politics* 78, no. 3: 621–41.

Acharya, Avidit, Matthew Blackwell, and Maya Sen. 2018a. *Deep Roots: How Slavery Still Shapes Southern Politics*. Princeton, NJ: Princeton University Press.

Acharya, Avidit, Matthew Blackwell, and Maya Sen. 2018b. "Explaining Preferences from Behavior: A Cognitive Dissonance Approach." *Journal of Politics* 80, no. 2: 400–411.

Acharya, Avidit, and Alexander Lee. 2018. "Economic Foundations of the Territorial State system." *American Journal of Political Science* 62, no. 4: 954–66.

Acharya, Avidit, and Alexander Lee. 2019. "Path Dependence in European Development: Medieval Politics, Conflict, and State Building." *Comparative Political Studies* 52, no. 13–14: 2171–206.

Alesina, Alberto, and Nicola Fuchs-Schundeln. 2007. "Goodbye Lenin (or Not?): The Effect of Communism on People." *American Economic Review* 97, no. 4: 1507–28.

Alesina, Alberto, Paola Giuliano, and Nathan Nunn. 2013. "On the Origins of Gender Roles: Women and the Plough." *Quarterly Journal of Economics* 128, no. 2: 469–530.

Allen, Treb, and Dave Donaldson. 2020. "Persistence and Path Dependence in the Spatial Economy." Technical report. National Bureau of Economic Research.

Backhaus, Andreas. 2019. "Fading Legacies: Human Capital in the Aftermath of the Partitions of Poland." Technical report.

Banerjee, Abhijit, and Lakshmi Iyer. 2005. "History, Institutions, and Economic Performance: The Legacy of Colonial Land Tenure Systems in India." *American Economic Review* 95, no. 4: 1190–213.

Barro, Robert J., and Xavier Sala-i Martin. 1992. "Convergence." *Journal of Political Economy* 100, no. 2: 223–51.

Bazzi, Samuel, Andreas Ferrara, Martin Fiszbein, Thomas Pearson, and Patrick Testa. 2021. "The Other Great Migration: White Southern Migrants and Right-Wing Politics in the U.S." Working Paper.

Bazzi, Samuel, Martin Fiszbein, and Mesay Gebresilasse. 2020. "Frontier Culture: The Roots and Persistence of 'Rugged Individualism' in the United States." *Econometrica* 88, no. 6: 2329–68.

Bazzi, Samuel, Gabriel Koehler-Derrick, and Benjamin Marx. 2020. "The Institutional Foundations of Religious Politics: Evidence from Indonesia." *Quarterly Journal of Economics* 135, no. 2: 845–911.

Becker, Sascha O., and Luigi Pascali. 2019. "Religion, Division of Labor, and Conflict: Anti-Semitism in Germany over 600 years." *American Economic Review* 109, no. 5: 1764–804.

Beramendi, Pablo, and Jeffrey Jensen. 2019. "Economic Geography, Political Inequality, and Public Goods in the Original 13 U.S. States." *Comparative Political Studies* 52, no. 13–14: 2235–82.

Bisin, Alberto, and Thierry Verdier. 2000. "A Model of Cultural Transmission, Voting and Political Ideology." *European Journal of Political Economy* 16, no. 1: 5–29.

Blaydes, Lisa, and Christopher Paik. 2016. "The Impact of Holy Land Crusades on State Formation: War Mobilization, Trade Integration, and Political Development in Medieval Europe." *International Organization* 70, no. 3: 551–86.

Bleakley, Hoyt, and Jeffrey Lin. 2012. "Portage and Path Dependence." *Quarterly Journal of Economics* 127, no. 2: 587–644.

Boyd, Robert, and Peter J. Richerson. 1988. *Culture and the Evolutionary Process*. Chicago: University of Chicago Press.

Calvert, Randall L. 1995. "Rational Actors, Equilibrium, and Social Institutions." In *Explaining Social Institutions*, ed. Jack Knight and Itai Sened, 57–93. Ann Arbor, MI: University of Michigan Press.

Charnysh, Volha. 2015. "Historical Legacies of Interethnic Competition: Anti-Semitism and the EU Referendum in Poland." *Comparative Political Studies* 48, no. 13: 1711–45.

Charnysh, Volha, and Evgeny Finkel. 2017. "The Death Camp Eldorado: Political and Economic Effects of Mass Violence." *American Political Science Review* 111, no. 4: 801–18.

Chen, Ting, James Kai-sing Kung, and Chicheng Ma. 2020. "Long Live *Keju*! The Persistent Effects of China's Civil Examination System." *Economic Journal* 130, no. 631: 2030–64.

Cirone, Alexandra E., and Thomas B. Pepinsky. 2022. "Historical Persistence." *Annual Review of Political Science* 25: 241–59.

Cogneau, Denis, and Alexander Moradi. 2014. "Borders That Divide: Education and Religion in Ghana and Togo since Colonial Times." *Journal of Economic History* 74, no. 3: 694–729.

Collier, Ruth Berins, and David Collier. 1991. *Shaping the Political Arena: Critical Junctures, the Labor Movement, and Regime Dynamics in Latin America*. Princeton, NJ: Princeton University Press.

Dell, Melissa. 2010. "The Persistent Effects of Peru's Mining *Mita*." *Econometrica* 78, no. 6: 1863–903.

Dell, Melissa. 2012. "Path Dependence in Development: Evidence from the Mexican Revolution." Harvard University. Unpublished manuscript.

Dincecco, Mark, and Mauricio Prado. 2012. "Warfare, Fiscal Capacity, and Performance." *Journal of Economic Growth* 17, no. 3: 171–203.

Dogan, Mattei. 1967. "Political Cleavage and Social Stratification in France and Italy." In *Party Systems and Voter Alignments: A Cross-National Perspective*, ed. Seymour M. Lipset and Stein Rokkan, 129–92. New York: Free Press.

Ertman, Thomas. 1997. *Birth of the Leviathan: Building States and Regimes in Medieval and Early Modern Europe*. Cambridge, UK: Cambridge University Press.

Esposito, Elena, and Scott F. Abramson. 2021. "The European Coal Curse." *Journal of Economic Growth* 26, no. 1: 77–112.

Fearon, James D., and David D. Laitin. 2012. "How persistent is armed conflict?" Working Paper.

Fontana, Nicola, Tommaso Nannicini, and Guido Tabellini. 2017. "Historical Roots of Political Extremism: The Effects of Nazi Occupation of Italy." IZA Discussion Paper No. 10551.

Fukuyama, Francis. 2011. *The Origins of Political Order: From Prehuman Times to the French Revolution*. New York: Farrar, Straus and Giroux.

Gaikwad, Nikhar. 2014. "East India Companies and Long-Term Economic Change in India." American Political Science Association. ncgg.princeton.edu/IPES/2014/papers/F1130 rm3.pdf. Working Paper

Gailmard, Sean. 2017. "Building a New Imperial State: The Strategic Foundations of Separation of Powers in America." *American Political Science Review* 111, no. 4: 668–85.

Garfias, Francisco, and Emily A. Sellars. 2021. "From Conquest to Centralization: Domestic Conflict and the Transition to Direct Rule." *Journal of Politics* 83, no. 3: 992–1009.

Gingerich, Daniel W., and Jan P. Vogler. 2021. "Pandemics and Political Development: The Electoral Legacy of the Black Death in Germany." *World Politics* 73, no. 3: 393–440.

Glaeser, Edward L., and Andrei Shleifer. 2002. "Legal Origins." *Quarterly Journal of Economics* 117, no. 4: 1193–229.

Grier, Robin M. 1999. "Colonial Legacies and Economic Growth." *Public Choice* 98, no. 3: 317–35.

Guardado, Jenny. 2018. "Office-Selling, Corruption, and Long-Term Development in Peru." *American Political Science Review* 112, no. 4: 971–95.

Guiso, Luigi, Paola Sapienza, and Luigi Zingales. 2016. "Long-Term Persistence." *Journal of the European Economic Association* 14, no. 6: 1401–36. http://dx.doi.org/10.1111/jeea.12177.

Homola, Jonathan, Miguel M. Pereira, and Margit Tavits. 2020a. "Fixed Effects and Post-Treatment Bias in Legacy Studies." Working Paper

Homola, Jonathan, Miguel M. Pereira, and Margit Tavits. 2020b. "Legacies of the Third Reich: Concentration Camps and Out-Group Intolerance." *American Political Science Review* 114, no. 2: 573–90.

Ito, Gaku. 2021. "Why Does Ethnic Partition Foster Violence? Unpacking the Deep Historical Roots of Civil Conflicts." *Journal of Peace Research* 58, no. 5: 986–1003.

Iversen, Vegard, Richard Palmer-Jones, and Kunal Sen. 2013. "On the Colonial Origins of Agricultural Development in India: A Re-examination of Banerjee and Iyer, 'History, Institutions and Economic Performance.'" *Journal of Development Studies* 49, no. 12: 1631–46.

Iyer, Lakshmi. 2010. "Direct versus Indirect Colonial Rule in India: Long-Term Consequences." *Review of Economics and Statistics* 92, no. 4: 693–713.

Jedwab, Remi, Edward Kerby, and Alexander Moradi. 2017. "History, Path Dependence and Development: Evidence from Colonial Railways, Settlers and Cities in Kenya." *Economic Journal* 127, no. 603: 1467–94.

Jennings, M. Kent, and Richard G. Niemi. 1968. "The Transmission of Political Values from Parent to Child." *American Political Science Review* 62, no. 1: 169–84.

Jha, Saumitra. 2013. "Trade, Institutions, and Ethnic Tolerance: Evidence from South Asia." *American Political Science Review* 107, no. 4: 806–32.

Katznelson, Ira, and Barry R. Weingast. 2005. *Preferences and Situations: Points of Intersection Between Historical and Rational Choice In.* New York, NY: Russell Sage Foundation.

Kelly, Morgan. 2019. "The Standard Errors of Persistence." Working Paper.

Key, V. O., and Frank Munger. 1959. "Social Determinism and Electoral Decision: The Case of Indiana." In *American Voting Behavior*, ed. Eugene Burdick and Arthur J. Brodbeck, 281–299. New York: Free Press.

Komisarchik, Mayya, Maya Sen, and Yamil Velez. 2022. "The Political Consequences of Ethnically Targeted Incarceration: Evidence from Japanese-American Internment during WWII." *Journal of Politics*. In press.

Krugman, Paul. 1991a. "History versus Expectations." *Quarterly Journal of Economics* 106, no. 2: 651–67.

Krugman, Paul. 1991b. "Increasing Returns and Economic Geography." *Journal of Political Economy* 99, no. 3: 483–99.

Lange, Matthew K. 2004. "British Colonial Legacies and Political Development." *World Development* 32, no. 6: 905–22.

La Porta, Rafael, Florencio Lopez-de Silanes, Andrei Shleifer, and Robert W. Vishny. 1998. "Law and Finance." *Journal of Political Economy* 106, no. 6: 1113–55.

Lazarsfeld, Paul F., and Robert K. Merton. 1954. "Friendship as a Social Process: A Substantive and Methodological Analysis." *Freedom and Control in Modern Society* 18, no. 1: 18–66.

Lechler, Marie, and Lachlan McNamee. 2018. "Indirect Colonial Rule Undermines Support for Democracy: Evidence from a Natural Experiment in Namibia." *Comparative Political Studies* 51, no. 14: 1858–98.

Lee, Alexander. 2019. "Land, State Capacity, and Colonialism: Evidence from India." *Comparative Political Studies* 52, no. 3: 412–44.

Lee, Alexander. 2021. "Historical Inequality at the Grassroots: Local Public Goods in an Indian District, 1905–2011." Working Paper.

Lee, Alexander, Weihong Qi, and Dehua Sun. 2021. "State Mobilization and Political Attitudes: The Legacy of Maoist Rural Resettlement in Contemporary China." Working Paper.

Lee, Alexander, and Kenneth A. Schultz. 2012. "Comparing British and French Colonial Legacies: A Discontinuity Analysis of Cameroon." *Quarterly Journal of Political Science* 7, no. 4: 365–410.

Lipset, Seymour M., and Stein Rokkan. 1967. *Party Systems and Voter Alignments: A Cross-National Perspective*. New York: Free Press.

Lupu, Noam, and Leonid Peisakhin. 2017. "The Legacy of Political Violence across Generations." *American Journal of Political Science* 61, no. 4: 836–51.

Mahoney, James. 2000. "Path Dependence in Historical Sociology." *Theory and Society* 29, no. 4: 507–48.

Marbach, Moritz. 2021. "Causal Effects, Migration and Legacy Studies." Working Paper.

Mattingly, Daniel C. 2017. "Colonial Legacies and State Institutions in China: Evidence from a Natural Experiment." *Comparative Political Studies* 50, no. 4: 434–63.

Michalopoulos, Stelios, and Elias Papaioannou. 2013. "Pre-colonial Ethnic Institutions and Contemporary African Development." *Econometrica* 81, no. 1: 113–52.

Miguel, Edward. 2004. "Tribe or Nation? Nation Building and Public Goods in Kenya versus Tanzania." *World Politics* 56, no. 3: 327–62.

Musacchio, Aldo, and John D. Turner. 2013. "Does the Law and Finance Hypothesis Pass the Test of History?" *Business History* 55, no. 4: 524–42.

Nall, Clayton. 2018. *The Road to Inequality: How the Federal Highway Program Polarized America and Undermined Cities*. New York, NY: Cambridge University Press.

North, Douglass C. 1991. "Institutions." *Journal of Economic Perspectives* 5, no. 1: 97–112.

North, Douglass C., and Barry R. Weingast. 1989. "Constitutions and Commitment: The Evolution of Institutions Governing Public Choice in Seventeenth-Century England." *Journal of Economic History* 49, no. 4: 803–32.

Nunn, Nathan. 2014. "Historical Development." In *Handbook of Economic Growth*, ed. Phillippe Aghion and Steven N. Durlauf, vol. 2, 347–402. Oxford, UK: Elsevier.

Nunn, Nathan, and Nancy Qian. 2011. "The Potato's Contribution to Population and Urbanization: Evidence from a Historical Experiment." *Quarterly Journal of Economics* 126, no. 2: 593–650.

Nunn, Nathan, and Leonard Wantchekon. 2011. "The Slave Trade and the Origins of Mistrust in Africa." *American Economic Review* 101, no. 7: 3221–52.

Ochsner, Christian. 2017. "Dismantled Once, Diverged Forever? A Quasi-Natural Experiment of Red Army Misdeeds in Post-WWII Europe." IDEAS Working Paper.

Ochsner, Christian, and Felix Roesel. 2017. "Activated History: The Case of the Turkish Sieges of Vienna." Working Paper.

Olsson, Ola, and Christopher Paik. 2016. "Long-Run Cultural Divergence: Evidence from the Neolithic Revolution." *Journal of Development Economics* 122: 197–213.

Olsson, Ola, and Christopher Paik. 2020. "A Western Reversal since the Neolithic? The Long-Run Impact of Early Agriculture." *Journal of Economic History* 80, no. 1: 100–135.

Page, Scott E. 2006. "Path Dependence." *Quarterly Journal of Political Science* 1, no. 1: 87–115.

Paik, Christopher, and Jessica Vechbanyongratana. 2019. "Path to Centralization and Development: Evidence from Siam." *World Politics* 71, no. 2: 289–331.

Pascali, Luigi. 2016. "Banks and Development: Jewish Communities in the Italian Renaissance and Current Economic Performance." *Review of Economics and Statistics* 98, no. 1: 140–58.

Pepinsky, Thomas B., Sara Wallace Goodman, and Conrad Ziller. 2020. "Does Proximity to Nazi Concentration Camps Make Germans Intolerant? Modeling Spatial Heterogeneity and Historical Persistence." SSRN.

Pierson, Paul. 2000. "Increasing Returns, Path Dependence, and the Study of Politics." *American Political Science Review* 94, no. 2: 251–67.

Pierson, Paul. 2004. *Politics in Time: History, Institutions, and Social Analysis*. Princeton, NJ: Princeton University Press.

Rodden, Jonathan A. 2019. *Why Cities Lose: The Deep Roots of the Urban-Rural Political Divide*. Hachette UK.

Rozenas, Arturas, Sebastian Schutte, and Yuri Zhukov. 2017. "The Political Legacy of Violence: The Long-Term Impact of Stalin's Repression in Ukraine." *Journal of Politics* 79, no. 4: 1147–61.

Schotter, Andrew. 1981. *The Economic Theory of Social Institutions*. Cambridge University Press.

Sellars, Emily A., and Jennifer Alix-Garcia. 2018. "Labor Scarcity, Land Tenure, and Historical Legacy: Evidence from Mexico." *Journal of Development Economics* 135: 504–16.

Shepsle, Kenneth A. 1986. "Institutional Equilibrium and Equilibrium Institutions." *Political Science: The Science of Politics* 51: 51.

Thelen, Kathleen. 1999. "Historical Institutionalism in Comparative Politics." *Annual Review of Political Science* 2, no. 1: 369–404.

Tilly, Charles. 1992. *Coercion, Capital, and European States, AD 990–1992*. Cambridge, MA: Wiley-Blackwell.

Vogler, Jan P. 2019. "Imperial Rule, the Imposition of Bureaucratic Institutions, and Their Long-Term Legacies." *World Politics* 71, no. 4: 806–63.

Voigtländer, Nico, and Hans-Joachim Voth. 2012. "Persecution Perpetuated: The Medieval Origins of Anti-Semitic Violence in Nazi Germany." *Quarterly Journal of Economics* 127, no. 3: 1339–92.

Voth, Hans-Joachim. 2021. "Persistence: Myth and Mystery." In *The Handbook of Historical Economics*, ed. Alberto Bisin and Giovanni Federico, 243–67. London: Elsevier.

Wang, Yuhua. 2021. "The Political Legacy of Violence during China's Cultural Revolution." *British Journal of Political Science* 51, no. 2: 463–87.

Wantchékon, Léonard, and Omar García-Ponce. 2013. "Critical Junctures: Independence Movements and Democracy in Africa." Department of Economics, University of Warwick.

Wittenberg, Jason. 2006. *Crucibles of Political Loyalty: Church Institutions and Electoral Continuity in Hungary*. Cambridge: Cambridge University Press.

PART II

HOW STATES ARE ORGANIZED

CHAPTER 8

DEMOCRACY AND HISTORICAL POLITICAL ECONOMY

DAVID STASAVAGE

THERE could hardly be a more central question to political science than asking how, when, and why democracy thrives and when it fails. In recent years scholars in the field of historical political economy (HPE) have made important progress in helping us answer this question. In what follows I am going to proceed in three steps, first focusing on the deep origins of modern democracy in Europe and what this can tell us about democracy today. Then I examine the history of universal suffrage as a core element of modern democracy. Finally, I ask when and why the principle that differences be settled through free and fair elections is sometimes respected and sometimes not. I survey a broad variety of contributions using different methodologies. Some of this involves empirical work focused on causal identification while other work will be more suggestive and descriptive, providing what Sean Gailmard (2021) has called "candidate explanations" for further study.

Democracy is a form of governance that has existed in a great many human societies, arguably stretching across multiple continents and far back in time.[1] For the Greeks the concept of *demokratia* meant simply that the people ruled or that the people had power. This is a definition that does not refer to a specific set of institutions, even though in Athens it had a particular manifestation with the participation of all classes—with the prominent exception of women and slaves—in the assembly, the *ekklesia*, combined with the right for all to hold office. Many societies outside the Greek world also had assemblies and councils for governance, and in these, particularly at the local level, participation could be quite broad and sometimes could involve participation by women. The key feature of these early democracies—both inside and outside the Greek world—was that participation was most commonly direct rather than being indirect through representatives.

The deep origins of modern democracy involve first the development of representative assemblies in medieval Europe, a phenomenon that many scholars in historical political economy have considered. The key questions here are how this happened, and why it happened in Europe first as opposed to other world regions. Europeans did not invent collective governance—that was practiced by many societies—but they did succeed in developing a form of political representation that could operate at scale. Asking how and why this happened is not only of historical interest; it may also help tell us something about the foundations of democracy even today and its future prospects.

Modern democracy is a system where citizens elect representatives via universal suffrage. A broad (though not yet universal) suffrage—for free white males—emerged first in the United States before spreading elsewhere. The story of this spread, and its expansion to include previously excluded groups, has been a principal area of focus for scholars in historical political economy. Recent work suggests that rather than being something that emerged because it was a commitment to redistribute, universal suffrage has advanced in many cases because elites have learned that they can find ways to live with it without fearing losing their wealth. Today universal suffrage has become such a strong norm that even those who seek to mute its effect feel compelled to suggest that they are only trying to make the suffrage more secure. Scholarship in historical political economy helps show us how the principle of universal suffrage emerged and took root.

Together with universal suffrage, modern democracy involves elections with multiple political parties, and it is sometimes described as a system where incumbents can actually lose.[2] The notion that someone would hold power and then be willing to give it up is not something to be taken for granted. The question then becomes when and where this is more likely to take place. Recent work in historical political economy calls into question the idea that there is an inevitable causal link between a country's level of per capita gross domestic product and the likelihood that electoral democracy will flourish. The survival of democracy may depend more on the presence of civil society organizations, institutionalized political parties, and also finally on efforts by the state itself to make investments such as educating the citizenry.

Representative Assemblies

The deep origins of modern democracy lie in the representative assemblies of medieval and early modern Europe. The simple fact that so many current parliaments bear the names of their medieval forebears shows this quite clearly. But why did this happen in Europe and not elsewhere? Why at this time, and how was it accomplished? We should not say here that Western Europe was unique in having representatives, because other societies, from the Wendat (Huron) in what is now Ontario to the Ashanti in what is now Ghana, also sent individuals to central assemblies. However, the sheer number of parliaments that emerged in Europe remains something to be explained, as does the ability of Europeans to construct parliaments that drew representatives from vast territories. While Europeans established assemblies that allowed for societal participation in governance—particularly for elites—this was a system that excluded women.[3] In the next section we need to ask why this changed so dramatically in the case of women with the eventual adoption of universal adult suffrage.

There is clear evidence that the threat of war and actual outbreaks of war favored the development of representative assemblies in medieval and early-modern Europe, and the literature on this topic is lengthy, dating back to the classic political science contributions of Levi (1988) and Bates and Lien (1985). Gary Cox, Mark Dincecco, and Massimiliano Onorato (2021) provide one of the most recent and complete econometric assessments of the role of warfare in leading to the rise of European parliaments.[4] In doing so they follow the standard assumption that war incidence prompted representative assemblies to emerge because of the need for revenue. However, they also make another telling point; assembly emergence was dependent on the presence of communes—cities and towns that enjoyed a substantial amount of autonomy to manage their own affairs—because it was the communes who played a major role in providing resources to monarchs. Cox, Dincecco, and Onorato argue, therefore, that the presence of communes was a necessary enabling condition for representative assemblies to emerge.

The European data appear to support the idea that autonomous cities and parliaments were the product of a process of urban agglomeration as part of the commercial revolution of the Middle Ages, a phenomenon that began in the eleventh century and which lasted until the Black Death.[5] When we look at urbanization cross-regionally, though, we need to recognize that medieval China also had a commercial revolution, yet it led to a very different political outcome. Instead of strengthening society with respect to the state, the opposite took place as the existing Chinese bureaucratic state moved to tax commerce and as merchants used their capital to invest in education that gave their offspring a better chance of passing China's civil service exam for entry into the bureaucracy.[6] Under the Song dynasty, state revenues as a share of GDP exceeded those in medieval France and England by an order of magnitude.[7] This is indicative of a very strong state.

The contrast between China and Western Europe suggests that something else was afoot apart from the simple facts of war and commercial growth. I have argued that representative assemblies flourished in medieval Europe because its rulers lacked the sort of strong state bureaucracies that would have allowed them to tax commerce without the need for agreeing to a consensual form of governance like a representative assembly (Stasavage 2020). More generally, the extreme weakness of bureaucracies in medieval Europe meant that princely rulers of territorial states had to govern collectively with members of society, albeit with a very elite version of society.

We can draw an important lesson for today based on this comparison of China and Western Europe: sequencing matters. If collective governance is your goal, then it helps to have it develop first before a powerful state bureaucracy emerges. Other authors have recently provided evidence of this phenomenon (e.g., Gjerlow et al. 2022). Jørgen Møller (2015) makes a similar point with respect to European state development over the long run. If, on the other hand, a bureaucratic state emerges prior to the establishment of collective governance, then developing democracy is more difficult. Important work by Lisa Blaydes (2017) has established this for the modern Middle East.

The emergence of European parliaments depended not only on a particular geopolitical and bureaucratic environment; it also required institutional creativity. As Anna Grzymala-Busse shows in her forthcoming book, much of the technology to make a representative assembly work—in terms of core guiding principles—was first developed within the Catholic Church.[8] Accounts of European assemblies date back to the famous account by Tacitus written around the turn of the first century of the common era.[9] But these were assemblies where people spoke for themselves. The problem medieval Europeans faced was how to organize an assembly with representatives. In the case of nobles or bishops, attending an assembly was relatively straightforward—they already, in theory, spoke for a region or diocese. But what of the inhabitants of a city who also desired some form of representation that did not depend on the whim of a bishop or knight? The solution here—echoing an innovation in the church—was to think of a city as a fictitious person; here again the inspiration for this was a prior practice from the medieval church, an idea said to have come from Augustine's notion that after Peter received the keys to the church, he signified the Holy Church (Tierney 1982).

One of the final intellectual innovations from the medieval era was an evolution that took place within the English parliament: the disappearance of mandates for representatives. One singular feature of modern democracy—something that has been agreed on since the ratification of the US Constitution as well as the French Revolution—is that, barring illegal behavior, the only way in which representatives can be sanctioned, controlled, or disciplined is at the ballot box. In most early European assemblies the situation was very different; towns that sent representatives to a meeting sought to bind these individuals by issuing strict instructions regarding what the representatives could or could not agree to or do. This was the case with the Cortes of Castile, the Estates General of the Netherlands, and numerous other assemblies. While these mandates helped provide a degree of security for constituents, they also made for unwieldy decision-making that continually frustrated monarchs. The English Parliament proved to be an exception to this rule. By the middle of the fourteenth century a norm was established that representatives in the House of Commons should debate and decide without being bound by mandates from their constituents and without the possibility of referring back to their constituents for further instructions. The reasons why this transformation took place are not entirely clear, though they may relate to the fact that, dating back to Anglo-Saxon times, English monarchs were in a relatively strong position with respect to local elites, or at least a stronger position when compared with other European monarchs.[10] With its absence of mandates the English Parliament provided an example that all modern democracies would subsequently follow.

Universal Suffrage

Unlike earlier forms of collective governance, which often had restrictive participation, modern democracy requires universal suffrage. The question of how this practice emerged has stimulated a substantial amount of work in historical political economy. While most of this research has focused on the advent of universal male suffrage, in recent years scholars have focused on the question of how the suffrage was also extended to women and racial minorities.

The most common story of the establishment of universal suffrage involves a distributional struggle where those with wealth end up conceding the vote to those without, and the policy outcome is then greater economic redistribution.[11] For scholars who follow this approach, the question then is what factors might prompt a transition from a limited suffrage of the sort that many European countries practiced in the nineteenth century toward universal access to the vote. While it is hard to deny the reality and importance of class conflict over the suffrage, particularly in the Western European cases, subsequent empirical work has raised important questions about the distributional argument. Take the canonical English case; the reform acts of 1832 and 1867 did not result in significant redistribution, at least by twentieth-century standards, nor was it apparent that the poorer members of society voted for the political parties that the distributional argument would predict, nor is it even clear that the 1832 act was principally about redistribution at all.[12]

What if, instead of conceding the suffrage as a commitment to redistribute wealth, elites gradually learned that this would not be the outcome? The flip side of the distributional argument for suffrage extensions is that elites eventually accepted universal suffrage because over time they learned that they had less to fear from it than they initially believed. Evidence from government bond markets—a very large source of elite wealth at this time—allows us to look at this learning mechanism more directly. In an important pair of articles, Aditya Dasgupta and Daniel Ziblatt (2021; 2015) have shown that initial suffrage extensions, such as that which occurred in the United Kingdom in 1832, led to large spikes in yields on government bonds—a prime asset for wealth holders at the time. Over time, with subsequent suffrage extensions these spikes grew less and less pronounced: there was less fear about extending the suffrage. This does not mean that the suffrage had no redistributive consequences—Dasgupta and Ziblatt certainly do not say this—but in my opinion their evidence suggests how elites learned that they could live with universal suffrage without suffering the drastic consequences that some had initially feared.

Outside of Western Europe we see a related phenomenon where elites learned to live with the suffrage because they were able to take the step of reducing state capacity in order to blunt the effect of this reform. In India, elites strengthened their position by reducing state tax collecting capacity in advance of suffrage reforms (Suryanarayan 2022). The recent article by Suryanarayan and White (2021) provides evidence of a similar phenomenon in the American South during Reconstruction as white elites were able to blunt the impact of suffrage granted to former slaves by hollowing out the state. The lesson would again seem to be that there were ways that elites could learn to live with the suffrage.

A further twist on the redistributive model for the origins of universal manhood suffrage brings war mobilization into the picture. The idea here is that if the masses are going to be expected to fight in a war, then they would demand redistribution in exchange (Ticchi and Vindigni 2008). The problem with this argument is that it again relies on the assumption that the extension of the suffrage represents a commitment to redistribute. In practice, the European evidence may support an alternative version of this argument that does not rely on a promise of redistribution. The idea here would be simply that if men were subject to universal conscription, then they felt that they should have the right to vote, or as the Swedish social democrats said, "One man, one gun, one vote." The European evidence shows quite a strong relationship whereby passage of a universal conscription law, irrespective of whether a war is underway, is a strong predictor of the subsequent adoption of male universal suffrage.[13]

If we step outside of the redistributive model, then there is a further alternative explanation for the expansion of the suffrage that those who do historical political economy have spent less time considering. Maybe universal suffrage was simply a very compelling idea, and therefore it diffused rapidly? As historian Jonathan Israel has recently shown, events like the establishment by the state of Pennsylvania of something akin to universal male suffrage had a clear impact on thinkers in Europe.[14] It is hard to question that universal suffrage is an appealing principle. In the end, though, it would be equally hard to believe that the idea alone carried the day, because it would be a long time before universal suffrage was established in Europe, to say nothing of the continued racial restrictions on the suffrage in the United States and the general exclusion of women from the suffrage.

While the literature on historical political economy has dwelt extensively on the question of how male universal suffrage first emerged, the achievement of female suffrage has received less attention. The same can be said for the removal of suffrage restrictions based on race. Unlike with universal male suffrage, it seems hard to make the case that the expansion of the suffrage to women was driven by the anticipation of war or wartime mobilization. A number of countries did expand the suffrage to women in the wake of the two world wars, but this was true both for war participants and for countries that had remained neutral.[15]

Two recent histories of how women gained the right to vote, one by Dawn Teele (2018) and the other by Corinne McConnaughy (2014), suggest that the forces that led to female suffrage were quite different than those that have been proposed for male suffrage. In an environment where there was already significant electoral competition, Dawn Teele shows that existing political parties were willing to advocate for female suffrage when they thought that it would benefit them electorally.[16] Relatedly, McConnaughy shows that the adoption of female suffrage in the United States depended on coalition politics and partisan maneuvering, rather than being solely the work of great crusaders like Susan B. Anthony. Beyond investigating the existence of absence of the female suffrage, one other area for historical political economy analysis would involve examining the ways in which women sought to play political roles in the absence of having the suffrage, such as participating in campaign rallies and events. Historians have considered this point for the antebellum United States.[17]

The broader question raised by the contributions of Teele (2018) and McConnaughy (2014) is that if the timing of the extension of the suffrage to women ended up depending on what might call "ordinary" electoral politics concerns, then why did this not happen until the early part of the twentieth century? One possibility is that once there was universal suffrage for men, the existence of this principle increased the ability of other groups to stake a similar claim. Still, it is interesting that in a country like the United States, the Whig Party was active in trying to enlist women to participate in rallies as early as the 1840 presidential campaign, but it would take a considerably longer time before major parties accepted female suffrage.

The story of African American suffrage in the United States has been quite different from either suffrage for white males or white women. The extent of African American suffrage has ebbed and flowed over time in response to changing political conditions. We saw earlier that after theoretically enfranchising free African Americans in 1776, the state of Pennsylvania withdrew this right some sixty-two years later. Recent HPE scholarship has provided a new view of the effects of voter suppression in the American South. Using extensive data from the state of Louisiana, Keele, Cubbison, and White (2021) chart the early rise of voter registration for African Americans after the Civil War and the dramatic decline after the imposition of poll taxes and literacy requirements after 1898. Subsequent institutional innovations such as the "understanding clause" of the 1950s served to suppress the African American vote even after poll taxes were abolished. Chacon, Jensen, and Yntiso (2021) show how during Reconstruction, African American voting was supported by the direct presence of US federal troops, which soon disappeared.[18] If for the vast majority of countries, the extension of the franchise to all adult men and then all adult women was an absorbing state, the story of African American suffrage in the United States has been anything but that.

Rather than propose such a clear violation of the principle of universal suffrage, as was done in the American South, other governments have used subterfuge. Daniel Gingerich has shown how the introduction of the Australian ballot in Brazil led to an (intended) reduction in voter turnout because this method of voting proved more difficult for those unable to read (Gingerich 2019). In short, universal adult suffrage has become an idea that is so compelling that, for the most part, the only way you can undermine it is to use various artifices and in doing so say that you are actually taking steps to support the suffrage by making it more secure.[19]

While the right to vote is critical for modern democracy to function, we should also acknowledge that some forms of political participation other than voting can prove critical to the health of a democracy. In an important recent book, Daniel Carpenter (2021) has provided extensive evidence to suggest that the health of democracy in the early republic and antebellum eras in the United States depended critically on the growth of petitions to Congress as a way for citizens to express their preference. Petitioning allowed for the expression of specific views in a frequent manner, which helped when elections occur only episodically. In practice, it was also useful for and used by those who did not yet have the right to vote: women, free African Americans, and sometimes also Indigenous groups. Future work in historical political economy might do more to ask when and where these forms of nonelectoral participation have strengthened democracy.

Elections with Alternation

Along with universal suffrage, the companion principle of modern democracy is that political differences are settled through competitive elections in which incumbents sometimes lose. Today, while the norm of universal adult suffrage is generally taken for granted, the loser respecting the outcome of a competitive election is a much less certain thing. What have we learned lately regarding how this system is actually sustained?

While there is no shortage of explanations on offer, perhaps the most prominent has been that a country's level of economic development—or sometimes its level of modernity more generally—is the best predictor of whether electoral democracy is sustainable.[20] As with many arguments about democracy, the initial impetus for this hypothesis came from European evidence: as Europe grew rich, it democratized. One of the things often overlooked in this literature—where modernization is generally proxied by GDP per capita—is that if we want to understand why a region like Western Europe is universally democratic today, then instead of looking at contemporary correlations, we ought to consider how rich or poor European countries were when they first democratized. If we do this, we see, for example, that France in 1870 at the outset of the Third Republic had the same level of per capita income that Tanzania does today.[21] Nor did 1870s France have any of the accoutrements of modernity Lipset (1959) emphasized, such as telephones, radios, or televisions. If the first great wave of democratization took place in a set of countries that were quite poor by today's standards, we may need to look elsewhere for an explanation.

Recent HPE work suggests, based on within-country evidence, several new directions for considering the link between economic modernization and democracy. It does so by going beyond investigating the correlation between democracy and levels of per capita GDP. Using evidence from the United Kingdom, Adriane Fresh (2018) shows how industrialization fostered increased competition in parliamentary elections by diversifying the portfolios of MPs. Using cross-country data, Sam van Noort (2021) has found evidence of a correlation between the size of the manufacturing sector and democracy, which he suggests is significant because this economic transformation made it easier for the working class to mobilize. This is an argument that Seymour Martin Lipset himself would have certainly recognized, but it has not been given an airing in some time. The lesson of all this work would seem to be that there may indeed be a link between economic modernization and democracy, but it may not be found where most people have been looking.

If many scholars point to potential deep determinants of democracy, such as culture and economic development, whether a democracy survives or dies may also depend upon the short-term decisions of political elites. The current political context, especially in the United States but also in Europe, has prompted some scholars to look to the interwar period. An approach most famously taken by Steven Levitsky and Daniel Ziblatt (2017) points to the importance of decisions made by political elites, particularly on the right, in a polarized environment, asking whether traditional conservatives ally themselves with extremists and their strategies. Their conclusions here rely on a deep vein of historical research.[22]

While the interwar period is most often used as an example of behavior to avoid, in an insightful recent book, Cornell, Møller, and Skanning (2020) remind us that in spite of the massive economic dislocations of the interwar period—shocks that make the Great Recession and the COVID pandemic seem small—the large majority of established democracies survived those years quite well. The authors use evidence from Europe and the Americas to make their point, suggesting that three factors were critically important in sustaining democracy during this difficult era. First, perhaps not surprisingly, was whether a country had an extensive democratic history. The second factor was the presence of strong civil society organizations, and third was the presence of institutionalized political parties. These conditions helped prevent a transition to authoritarian rule.

Another possibility is that mass education helped to sustain electoral democracy, though we need to be careful to ask how exactly this might happen. One of the fears expressed by political elites in the early republic in the United States —kindled in particular by Shays Rebellion of 1786 and the Whiskey Rebellion of 1794—was that ordinary citizens might opt out of trying to achieve their goals through the electoral process and instead resort to violent revolt.[23] These concerns may not have been unfounded given the low turnout rates that prevailed for federal elections in the republic's first years.[24]

One of the responses by elites to these two crises—apart from suppressing them by force—was to consider how providing increased basic education might mold citizens into active democratic participants. The cross-country political economy literature on democracy and education generally finds it difficult to show that education, particularly if measured in years, solidifies democracy.[25] One reason may be that children sitting in schools in different countries are learning very different things. In recent work, Agustina Paglayan (2022; 2021) has shown that historically, many autocratic governments have also promoted education with the goal of creating obedient populations. Recent within-country evidence from (Paulsen et al. 2022) points to a different effect for democracies such as the early republic in the United States. In this instance, increased provision of basic schooling—with a particular emphasis on democratic civic duty—was associated with a significant increase in voter turnout from very low initial levels.[26] This may have helped to solidify American democracy. Taking the contributions by Paglayan and Paulsen et al. together, we see support for a principle that Aristotle espoused: if you seek to maintain a particular type of political regime, then the format of education should be tailored to that type of political regime (*Politics* 8.1).

One final point regarding elections is that while they are synonymous with modern democracy, HPE scholars ought to continue to study other systems of democratic governance as they existed in the past given that our current institutions may need to evolve. Bernard Manin (1997) famously showed that the principle of elections, as opposed to choosing those who rule by lot, was not an inevitable consequence of trying to practice democracy at scale. It was instead motivated by the notion that elections led to better outcomes. Recently, political theorist Hélène Landemore (2020) has explored how older forms of political selection based on sortition might be used to construct a more open form of democracy. More historical work that would look back at systems of collective governance over the millennia could help shed light on possibilities for reform today. Alexandra Cirone (2019a) has recently produced a useful survey suggesting exactly how this work might be done for the case of lottery-based procedures for decision-making.[27] If in the nineteenth and twentieth centuries a number of democracies experimented with alternative forms before settling on the current model, perhaps in the twenty-first century we ought to be open to the idea that further experimentation is needed in order to give ordinary citizens a better sense of feeling connected to the state.

Conclusion

The emergence of modern democracy has been an extended process. While the quantitative political science work of twenty years ago often focused for reasons of data constraints on developments since World War II, more recent work in the field of historical political economy shows us what we can learn from going back in time. This has enabled us to understand more about deep determinants involving the relative balance of power between state and society, something that in Europe allowed for representative government to flourish and expand in a way that did not happen in China. Recent studies have also allowed us to understand the history of the suffrage and how the principle of universal suffrage came to be such a powerful idea. Scholars in HPE are approaching this question with a renewed emphasis, rightly focusing on the question of how previously disadvantaged groups were able to use the principle of universal suffrage to gain a voice. Finally, in an era of what many consider democratic backsliding—where some democracies previously thought stable suddenly seem threatened—looking to the past can help us better understand how real these fears should be, and also perhaps also how to avoid democratic breakdown.

Looking further to the future, if democracy of one form or another has been around for a very long time in a great number of societies, we can probably have confidence that this will continue to be a common way in which some humans govern themselves. Democracy is not like a torch that will fail in general because it is extinguished in one place. But this does not necessarily mean that any individual democracy will continue to survive. One of the principal lessons of this chapter is that sustaining collective governance periodically requires institutional creativity. This has been clear ever since the medieval era when Europeans—aided heavily by members of the church—developed a technology for political representation that could operate at scale. In our current moment, with fears of democratic backsliding, it is perhaps a time to be creative anew. This chapter's second lesson for the future is that maintaining a modern democracy also requires investments by the state, and one thinks in particular of education. The goal here is not simply to see that people are educated in some general sense. Rather their education should serve to encourage people to participate in and sustain democracy by following an agreed-upon set of norms.

Notes

1. In Stasavage (2020) I make the case for the existence of early democracy among many societies. For a different view, see Cartledge (2016). Carles Boix (2015) has written on the variety of political regimes in early states.
2. This succinct definition derives from the minimalist definition of democracy proposed by Adam Przeworski et al. (2000). A more expansive definition of democracy, proposed by Robert Dahl (1998 [2020], 38) emphasizes five criteria: (1) "effective participation," meaning that all members must have equal opportunities for influence, and presumably not only through voting; (2) "voting equality"; (3) "enlightened understanding," meaning that each member has an opportunity to learn about policies and their consequences; (4) "control of the agenda," meaning that the members have the exclusive right to decide; and (5) inclusion of all adults.
3. Europeans were not unique in this regard, but governance in a number of different non-European societies did allow for women to play a role in politics. See Stasavage (2020) on the examples of the Wendat (Huron) and Haudenosaunee (Iroquois). See Achebe (2005) on the political role of women in precolonial Igboland.
4. For other recent work see de Magalhaes and Giovannoni (2019).
5. See Abramson and Boix (2019) for a broader view of the link between urban agglomeration in Europe and the rise of parliaments.
6. See Chen and Kung (2021) on this development. See also the important recent work by Yuhua Wang (2022a; 2022b) on the links between the Chinese examination system, elite lineage ties, and the construction of the Chinese state.
7. See Stasavage (2020, 12) and Guo (2019) for more details on Chinese revenue data across several dynasties.
8. See Anna Grzymala Busse (2022). Historians, such as Brian Tierney (1982), have also placed a heavy emphasis on the Catholic Church as a sort of laboratory in which principles of representation developed. See Schwartzberg (2014) on voting procedures in assemblies and their churchly origins, in particular with regard to supramajority rules.
9. Tacitus, *Germania* (Penguin Classics edition).
10. Chris Wickham (1997) suggests that circa 1000 CE Anglo-Saxon England was arguably the sole society in Western Europe, outside of Arab-controlled Spain, that was able to maintain a system of direct taxation of agriculture. In an important recent book, Deborah

Boucoyannis (2021) has also emphasized the ability to English monarchs to compel local elites to take certain actions.

11. Following the classic work of Acemoglu and Robinson (2000) and Boix (2003) as well as Przeworski (2008) and Aidt and Franck (2015), this was conceived in terms of a distributional struggle where the key issue is who gets taxed and by how much, and who receives redistributive benefits.
12. See Berlinski and Dewan (2011) on voting patterns following the Second Reform Act as well as Berlinski, Dewan, and Van Coppenolle (2014) for the limited consequences of franchise extension for the British aristocracy. Scheve and Stasavage (2016) provide evidence on the limited effect of suffrage extensions on top rates of income and inheritance taxation. Scheve and Stasavage (2017) offer evidence on top wealth shares and the suffrage. Cox, Fresh, and Saiegh (2021) present evidence to suggest that the motivation for the Great Reform Act of 1832 on the part of the Whigs was to constrain the executive. Recent work by Erik Bengtsson (2021; 2019) suggests that beyond the suffrage, we need to consider complementary forms of mobilization involving popular meetings to understand when and where significant equalizing change took place.
13. I discuss this in more detail in Stasavage (2020, 265–68).
14. See Israel (2017, 8). The Pennsylvania constitution of 1776 stipulated that adult males who paid taxes had a right to vote irrespective of how much or how little wealth the owed. As the constitution did not state that black citizens did not benefit from this right, many availed themselves of the opportunity, although often with no small amount of personal risk. The Pennsylvania Constitutional Convention of 1838 stipulated that black citizens did not have the right to vote.
15. See the analysis in Teele (2018).
16. See also the survey by Teele and Grosjean (2022) in this volume
17. See, e.g., Arendt (2020) and Varon (1995).
18. See also David Bateman (2018) on the broader case of democratic disenfranchisement.
19. The rare exception here would be the case of a current political theorist, Jason Brennan (2016), who has advocated an "epistocracy" where the votes of those who are better informed count more.
20. The modern literature on this question began with Lipset (1959), and some of the most notable contributions have been Przeworski et al. (2000), Boix and Stokes (2003), Boix (2011), and Acemoglu et al. (2009).
21. Based on data from the Maddison Project. https://www.rug.nl/ggdc/historicaldevelopment/maddison/releases/maddison-project-database-2020.
22. See in particular Ziblatt (2017).
23. See Condon (2015) on the context for Shays Rebellion and the responses that it prompted, as well as Kaestle (1983, 5) on the idea of investing in common schooling to help prevent future actions of this type. See Rasmussen (2021) for the ideas of John Adams regarding using education to promote "virtue" among the citizenry.
24. See the evidence in Rusk (2001).
25. Acemoglu, Johnson, Robinson, and Yared (2005) were perhaps the first to show that cross-country cross-sectional correlations between education and democracy disappear once one adopts a difference in differences design.
26. This dramatic rise in turnout was emphasized in a classic piece by Burnham (1965).
27. See also Cirone (2019b).

References

Abramson, Scott, and Carles Boix. 2019. "Endogenous Parliaments." *International Organization.* 73: 793–837.

Acemoglu, Daron, Simon Johnson, James Robinson, and Pierre Yared. 2009. "Reevaluating the Modernization Hypothesis." *Journal of Monetary Economics* 56: 1043–58.

Acemoglu, Daron, Simon Johnson, James Robinson, and Pierre Yared. 2005. "From Education to Democracy?" *American Economic Review* 95: 44–49.

Acemoglu, Daron, and James A. Robinson. 2000. "Why Did the West Extend the Franchise? Democracy, Inequality, and Growth in Historical Perspective." *Quarterly Journal of Economics* 115: 1167–99.

Achebe, Nwando. 2005. *Farmers, Traders, Warriors, and Kings: Female Power and Authority in Northern Igboland, 1900–1960.* London: Heinemann.

Aidt, Toke, and Raphael Franck. 2015. "Democratization under the Threat of Revolution: Evidence from the Great Reform Act of 1832." *Econometrica* 83, no. 2: 505–47

Arendt, Emily. 2020. "'Two Dollars a Day, and Roast Beef': Whig Culinary Partisanship and the Election of 1840." *Journal of the Early Republic* 40: 83–115.

Bateman, David. 2018. *Disenfranchising Democracy.* Cambridge: Cambridge University Press.

Bates, Robert, and Donald Lien. 1985. "A Note on Taxation, Development, and Representative Government." *Politics and Society.*

Bengtsson, Erik. 2019. "The Swedish Sonderweg in Question: Democratization and Inequality in Comparative Perspective, c. 1750–1920." *Past and Present* no. 244:

Bengtsson, Erik. 2021. "The Evolution of Popular Politics in Nineteenth-Century Sweden and the Road from Oligarchy to Democracy."

Berlinski, Samuel, and Torun Dewan. 2011. "The Political Consequences of Franchise Extension: Evidence from the Second Reform Act." *Quarterly Journal of Political Science.*

Berlinski, Samuel, Torun Dewan, and Brenda Van Coppenolle. 2014. "Franchise Extension and the British Aristocracy." *Legislative Studies Quarterly* 39: 531–58.

Blaydes, Lisa. 2017. "State Building in the Middle East." *Annual Review of Political Science* 20: 487–504.

Boix, Carles. 2003. *Democracy and Redistribution.* Cambridge: Cambridge University Press.

Boix, Carles. 2011. "Democracy, Development, and the International System." *American Political Science Review.* 105: 809–28.

Boix, Carles. 2015. *Political Order and Inequality.* Cambridge: Cambridge University Press.

Boix, Carles, and Susan Stokes. 2003. "Endogenous Democratization." *World Politics* 55: 517–49.

Boucoyannis, Deborah. 2021. *Kings as Judges: Power, Justice, and the Origins of Parliaments.* Cambridge: Cambridge University Press.

Brennan, Jason. 2016. *Against Democracy.* Princeton, NJ: Princeton University Press.

Burnham, Walter Dean. 1965. "The Changing Shape of the American Political Universe." *American Political Science Review* 1: 7–28.

Carpenter, Daniel. 2021. *Democracy by Petition: Popular Politics in Transformation, 1790–1870.* Cambridge, MA: Harvard University Press.

Cartledge, Paul. 2016. *Democracy: A Life.* Oxford: Oxford University Press.

Chacon, Mario, Jeffrey Jensen, and Sidak Yntiso. 2021. "Sustaining Democracy with Force: Black Representation during Reconstruction." *Journal of Historical Political Economy* 1: 319–51.

Chen, Ting, and James Kai-sing Kung. 2021. "Commercial Revolution in Medieval China: Origins and Consequences." University of Hong Kong.

Cirone, Alexandra. 2019a. "When Democracy Is Broken: Roll the Dice: Lotteries in Political Selection." APSA Comparative Politics Section Newsletter. https://www.comparativepoliticsnewsletter.org/wp-content/uploads/2019/12/CP-Newsletter-Fall-19-CP-and-History.pdf.

Cirone, Alexandra. 2019b. "Bridging the Gap: Lottery-Based Procedures in Early Parliamentarization." *World Politics* 71: 197–235.

Condon, Sean. 2015. *Shays Rebellion: Authority and Distress in Post-Revolutionary America*. Baltimore: Johns Hopkins University Press.

Cornell, Agnes, Jørgen Møller, and Sven-Erik Skaaning. 2020. *Democratic Stability in an Age of Crisis: Reassessing the Interwar Period*. Oxford: Oxford University Press.

Cox, Gary, Mark Dincecco, and Massimiliano Onorato. 2021. "Window of Opportunity: War and the Roots of Representative Governance." Working Paper.

Cox, Gary, Adriane Fresh, and Sebastian Saiegh. 2021. "The Political Economy of Suffrage Reform: The Great Reform Act of 1832." Working Paper.

Dahl, Robert. 1998. *On Democracy*. New Haven, CT: Yale University Press.

Dasgupta, Aditya, and Daniel Ziblatt. 2015. "How Did Britain Democratize? Views from the Sovereign Bond Market." *Journal of Economic History* 75: 1–29.

Dasgupta, Aditya, and Daniel Ziblatt. 2021. "Capital Meets Democracy: The Impact of Franchise Extension on Sovereign Bond Markets." *American Journal of Political Science*.

de Magalhaes, Leandro and Francessco Giovannoni. 2019. Working Paper. University of Bristol.

Fresh, Adrienne. 2018. "Industrial Revolution and Political Change: Evidence from the British Isles."

Gailmard, Sean. 2021. "Theory, History, and Political Economy." *Journal of Historical Political Economy* 1: 69–104.

Gjerlow, Haakon, Carl Henrik Knutsen, Tore Wig, and Matthew Charles Wilson. 2022. "One Road to Riches: How State Building and Democratization Affect Economic Development." *Cambridge Elements in Political Economy*.

Gingerich, Daniel. 2019. "Ballot Reform as Suffrage Restriction: Evidence from Brazil's Second Republic." *American Journal of Political Science* 63: 920–35.

Guo, Jason Qiang. 2019. "The History of Taxation in China."

Grzymala Busse, Anna. 2022. *Sacred Foundations: The Medieval and Religious Roots of State Formation*.

Israel, Jonathan. 2017. *The Expanding Blaze: How the American Revolution Ignited the World, 1775–1848*. Princeton, NJ: Princeton University Press.

Kaestle, Carl. 1983. *Pillars of the Republic: Common Schools and American Society, 1780–1860*. New York: Hill and Wang.

Keele, Luke, William Cubbison, and Ismail White. 2021. "Suppressing Black Votes: A Historical Case Study of Voting Restrictions in Louisiana." *American Political Science Review* 115: 694–700.

Landemore, Hélène. 2020. *Open Democracy: Reinventing Popular Rule for the Twenty-First Century*. Princeton, NJ: Princeton University Press.

Levi, Margaret. 1988. *Of Rule and Revenue*. Berkeley: University of California Press.

Levitsky, Steven, and Daniel Ziblatt. 2017. *How Democracies Die*. New York: Crown.

Lipset, Seymour Martin. 1959. "Some Social Requisites of Democracy: Economic Development and Political Legitimacy." *American Political Science Review*. 53: 69–105.

Manin, Bernard. 1997. *Principles of Representative Government*. Cambridge: Cambridge University Press.

McConnaughy, Corinne. 2014. *The Woman Suffrage Movement in America: A Reassessment*. Cambridge: Cambridge University Press.

Møller, Jørgen. 2015. "The Medieval Roots of Democracy." *Journal of Democracy* 26: 110–23.

Paglayan, Agustina. 2021. "The Non-Democratic Roots of Mass Education: Evidence from 200 Years." *American Political Science Review* 115: 179–98.

Paglayan, Agustina. 2022. "From Rebellion to Indoctrination: The Violent Roots of Primary Education Systems." *American Political Science Review*, 116, no. 4: 1242–57.

Paulsen, Tine, Kenneth Scheve, and David Stasavage. 2022. "Foundations of a New Democracy: Schooling, Inequality, and Voting in the Early Republic." *American Political Science Review*, forthcoming.

Przeworski, Adam. 2008. "Conquered or Granted: A History of Suffrage Extensions." *British Journal of Political Science* 39: 291–321.

Przeworski, Adam, Michael Alvarez, José Antonio Cheibub, and Fernando Limongi. 2000. *Democracy and Development*. Cambridge: Cambridge University Press.

Rasmussen, Dennis. 2021. *Fears of a Setting Sun: The Disillusionment of America's Founding Fathers*. Princeton, NJ: Princeton University Press.

Rusk, Jerrold G. 2001. *Statistical History of the American Electorate*. Washington D.C.: CQ Press.

Scheve, Kenneth, and David Stasavage. 2016. *Taxing the Rich: A History of Fiscal Fairness in the United States and Europe*. Princeton, NJ: Princeton University Press.

Scheve, Kenneth, and David Stasavage. 2017. "Wealth Inequality and Democracy." *Annual Review of Political Science* 20: 451–68.

Schwartzberg, Melissa. 2014. *Counting the Many: The Origins and Limits of Supermajority Rule*. Cambridge: Cambridge University Press.

Stasavage, David. 2020. *The Decline and Rise of Democracy: A Global History from Antiquity to Today*. Princeton, NJ: Princeton University Press.

Suryanarayan, Pavithra. 2022. "Hollowing Out the State: Franchise Expansion and Fiscal Capacity in Colonial India." Working Paper.

Suryanarayan, Pavithra, and Steven White. 2021. "Slavery, Reconstruction, and Bureaucratic Capacity in the American South." *American Political Science Review* 115: 56–584.

Teele, Dawn. 2018. *Forging the Franchise: The Political Origins of the Women's Vote*. Princeton, NJ: Princeton University Press.

Teele, Dawn, and Pauline Grosjean. 2022. "In Search of Gender in Historical Political Economy." *Handbook of Historical Political Economy*.

Ticchi, Davide, and Andrea Vindigni. 2008. "War and Endogenous Democracy." Working Paper.

Tierney, Brian. 1982. *Religion, Law, and the Growth of Constitutional Thought, 1150–1600*. Cambridge: Cambridge University Press.

Van Noort, Sam. 2021. "Industrialization and Democracy." Working Paper.

Varon, Elizabeth. 1995. "Tippecanoe and the Ladies, Too: White Women and Party Politics in Antebellum Virginia." *Journal of American History* 82: 494–521.

Wang, Yuhua. 2022a. *The Rise and Fall of Imperial China: The Social Origins of State Development*. Princeton, NJ: Princeton University Press.

Wang, Yuhua. 2022b. "Blood Is Thicker Than Water: Elite Kinship Networks and State Building in Imperial China." *American Political Science Review*, 116, no. 3: 896–910.

Wickham, Chris. 1997. "Lineages of Western European Taxation, 1000-200. In *Actes: Colloqui corona, municipi I fiscalitat a la baixa edat mitiana*, ed. M. Sanchez and A. Furió. Lleida: Institut d'Estudio Ilerdenes.

Ziblatt, Daniel. 2017. *Conservative Parties and the Birth of Democracy*. Cambridge: Cambridge University Press.

CHAPTER 9

HISTORICAL POLITICAL ECONOMY OF AUTOCRACY

ANNA GRZYMALA-BUSSE AND EUGENE FINKEL

AUTOCRACY is the most widespread and durable type of political regime since the emergence of early states. This regime type has also proven to be remarkably dynamic and able to adapt to changing political and economic realities over the past millennia. From absolutist early monarchies to the emergence of early representative assemblies to the interwar period, autocracy reformed, changed its shape, retreated but never disappeared as an organizing principle of political life and governance. Even when the decisive triumph of democracy seemed all but inevitable (Fukuyama 1992), autocracy persevered and is making a spectacular comeback around the globe, from Central Europe to Southeast Asia to, as many fear, the United States.

Historical political economy (HPE) approaches, we argue, are especially well positioned to make important contributions to the better understanding of nondemocratic regimes. Because it resists the temptation to narrowly focus on the present, the HPE scholarship can help uncover the origins of authoritarian institutions and practices. Broadening the temporal perspective also allows scholars to analyze how these institutions and practices evolved and changed over time. A mixed-method approach utilized by many HPE studies brings us closer to identifying the causal pathways to and from autocracy.

In this chapter we focus on several key questions that dominate the scholarship on autocratic regimes: how autocracies emerge, how they are sustained, how autocracies die, and the legacies autocratic regimes leave behind. In the final section, we suggest directions for future research and discuss how HPE scholarship can move forward.

How Autocracies Emerge

How do autocracies arise in the first place? Scholars have identified three broad categories of explanations for the historical rise of autocracy. First, there are efficiency gains: autocracies are more likely to survive. Second, when state capacity expands, the lack of executive constraints produces autocracies. Third, societal characteristics, whether preferences or heterogeneity, may lead people to *choose* autocratic governments.

When would an autocracy be more efficient? Earlier theorists such as Jean Bodin or Thomas Hobbes proposed autocracy as an effective way to provide security and order and defeat internal factions. Robert Michels and Joseph Schumpeter also argued that oligarchy could be a feasible and functional government that avoided the costs of democratic factionalism (see Frantz 2016).

Mancur Olson's famous distinction between roving and stationary bandits summarizes the answer: tyranny is more Pareto-efficient than anarchy. Both society and potential rulers can realize greater gains under autocracy. Stationary bandits have longer time horizons and are more willing to promote economic growth in order to keep revenues and rents flowing (Olson 1993). Gambetta (1993) offers a similar account, arguing that the Mafia arose as a state substitute, and its longer time horizons constrained its predation. If these stationary bandits achieve a monopoly (i.e., an autocracy), their rate of predation is lower, since they bear the entire loss of community income. This very act of self-restraint transforms a monopolistic stationary bandit into an autocratic state ruler (Olson 2000, 5, 10–11). If the state is a protection racket, offering security from the very threat it poses (Tilly 1985, 169; Tilly 1994), an autocracy is a virtuous monopolist, limiting the very exploitation it practices.

In a similar vein, Gerring et al. (2021) argue that monarchies offer an efficient solution to the problem of order where the societies are large and citizens isolated, by resolving coordination difficulties. Monarchy elongates the tenure of a ruler and institutionalizes power in the hands of a ruling house. Once the costs of communication drop, however, citizens can coordinate more easily and cheaply, and the advantages of monarchy begin to disappear (Gerring et al. 2021, 589, 593). The converse of this argument is that democracy flourished more readily in small-scale settings (Stasavage 2020).

Other important conditions for autocracy are state capacity and state institutions. Autocracy and state capacity are two distinct dimensions: many early states were largely autocratic; borne of war, coercion, and elite self-interest. They were often rudimentary, and struggled to expand and to develop their capacity (Bean 1973; Centeno 2002; Dincecco and Wang 2018; Downing 1992; Hui 2005; Thies 2005; Wang 2022; but see Stasavage 2020).[1]

All rulers need state capacity: the ability to ensure security and enforce laws, peace, and order can build national identities and provide rulers with extraction and redistribution. As state capacity expands, so do the durability and effectiveness of all regimes. For its part, state capacity is a double-edged sword: powerful institutions with a broad reach into society can serve the cause of responsiveness and accountability as well as they can enable surveillance and control (Scott 1998).

Two kinds of institutions are especially important to the rise and maintenance of autocracy: executive constraint and bureaucracies. The former constrains autocratic discretion: the ability to choose policies autonomously. The latter makes it possible to enact these decisions: to surveil society, extract resources, and maintain autocratic rule, at a lower cost than simply relying on coercion or terror (Wintrobe 1998; see also Mann 1986).

First, several kinds of institutions can limit the ruler's discretion, whether representative assemblies, autonomous judiciaries, or a strong civil society (Johnson and Koyama 2017). This is in keeping with a storied tradition in historical political economy that sees the balance of power between nobles and kings as critical to either executive constraint or absolutism (Barzel and Kiser 1997; Kiser and Barzel 1991; Levi 1988; North, Wallis, and Weingast 2009; North and Weingast 1989). Weaker rulers, in this account, need and tolerate stronger parliaments (Stasavage 2020). Van Zanden, Buringh, and Bosker (2012) similarly argue that the absolutist turn in Europe around 1500 was the result of greater bureaucratic and state capacity: parliaments could fight back in some places but not others. Such arguments follow Montesquieu, who argued that despots succeed when they do away with intermediary bodies that could provide oversight and constraint, such as the judiciary (see *Spirit of the Laws* 8; *Persian Letters* 92) or the counterweight of the nobility.[2] Where rulers controlled the nobility or were under severe geopolitical pressure, they could rule as absolutists, extracting resources and changing policy with little pushback (Downing 1992; Ertman 1997; Wang 2022).

Second, a state bureaucracy with coercive force behind it wields the technologies of surveillance, extraction, and record keeping that make societal control relatively easier, and weaken the bargaining position of the society (Scott 1998; Stasavage 2020; Wang 2022; Xi 2019). Many despots inherit, rather than build, strong bureaucracies, as in the Middle East or China (Stasavage 2020, 10). As a result, the ruler can govern by exercising control over the bureaucracy rather than seeking popular consent to govern. Thus, an institutionalized bureaucratic system made it possible to manage the trade-off between loyalty and performance in Qing China (1644–1911), according to Xi (2019). State strength more broadly also appears to promote autocracy in the colonial setting. Where states already existed, colonizing powers were less likely to colonize: but if they did, they tended to rely on existing powerbrokers and institutions (indirect rule), with little direct rule, colonial settlement, or export of institutions. That in turn led to the survival of traditional governance, and in turn autocracy (Hariri 2012).

Although state strength and regime type are clearly distinct, it is all too easy to both explain and to define successful autocracies with state capacity. To avoid this sort of tautology, Wang (2022) offers a useful corrective, by examining how state strength in China transformed over time, despite the same regime type. Similarly, the modal early state in Europe was a constrained autocrat rather than a powerful tyrant. Territorial authority was fragmented, and nascent royal administrations relied on the expertise and institutional templates of the church, rather than their own innovations (Grzymala-Busse 2020). Rather than summoning standing armies or powerful machineries of state, autocratic kings cajoled and negotiated with their nobles to obtain resources and support. We similarly need to avoid conflating the lack of executive constraint as an enabling condition—and as a hallmark of autocracy. Stasavage (2020) provides a helpful distinction by showing how the initial lack of constraining institutions can then enable an autocrat to further weaken and preclude constraining institutions. Another analytical issue here is causation: Does autocratic ruler weakness promote greater constraint? Or vice versa? While several authors argue that weak rulers allow for stronger parliaments, others disagree. In a pathbreaking analysis, Deborah Boucoyannis (2021) argues that parliaments, emblematic of executive constraint, only arise and gain power under a ruler strong enough to *compel* attendance.

A third enabling condition for autocracies is the societies in which these regimes are nestled. Here, societal structures and choices can both aid in the rise of autocracy. First, heterogeneous populations make it easier to establish autocratic rule. Population diversity shaped the character of political institutions, which in turn has a persistent effect on subsequent political institutions (Galor and Klemp 2017). Population diversity means lower social cohesiveness and higher potential for inequality, both of which permit domination and thus autocracy. This same heterogeneous population, however, may make state capacity more difficult to establish (Johnson and Koyama 2017; Voth 2011). The result is greater susceptibility to autocracy, but lower likelihood of its success.

Conversely, self-selection may also make some societies more susceptible to autocracy: in their examination of the Neolithic revolution, Olsson and Paik (2016) argue that the strong collectivism of agrarian societies (characterized by a collective nature of production, prevalence of pathogens, and threat of predation) leads some individualists to escape. These more individually minded emigrants in turn colonize other lands, with lower pressures for collectivism—and more and more outflow of the most determined individualists. As a result, the greater the distance from the agrarian core first established around 10,500 BCE, the greater the individualism of societal members, and thus the lower their susceptibility to autocratic rule.[3]

In perhaps the best-examined episode of voters *choosing* autocracy, scholars have examined the 1932 election in Weimar Germany that brought Hitler and the National Socialists (NSDAP) to power. Here, one clear pattern is that Catholics voted against the Nazis, while Protestant voters were more likely to support them. Religious denomination thus explains 58 percent of the variation in voting (Spenkuch and Tillmann 2018). This correlation is a function of institutional influence, not theology: the Catholic Church clerical hierarchy opposed the rise of the Nazis and instructed their parishioners accordingly. In areas with "Brown" priests or where the bishops gave up, Catholic resistance crumbled. Moreover, Catholics and Protestants were equally likely to support another autocratic alternative, the Communists (KDP). When it comes to economic voting, no one constituency was responsible: voters most hurt by the Depression were a heterogeneous lot and had diverse interests. Disproportionate support for the Nazis were found among those not as badly hurt by the Depression: shopkeepers, professionals, and domestic workers (King et al. 2008). Peasants and domestic workers were loyal to the main center-right Catholic party, the Zentrum, in Catholic areas, but elsewhere formed a key constituency for the Nazis.

Societal choices aided the rise of the Nazis in other ways. Weimar's rich associational life was borne of frustration with the failures of the national government and served as a critical training ground for NSDAP cadres (Berman 1997). Access to radio under

Weimar slowed down the growth of Nazi support—until the last competitive campaign, when Nazi propaganda took over the airwaves and led to increases in party membership, increased denunciations of citizens, and anti-Semitic incidents (Adena et al. 2015). Yet as Nancy Bermeo (2003), reminds us in her study of interwar democratic breakdown and autocratic rise in Europe, ordinary people often do not support authoritarianism, even as they allow illiberal elites to arise and take over power. Myerson (2004) argues the same regarding Weimar: given the Allied reparations policy, German elites had the incentive to sabotage their own economy, aiding the rise of extremist right-wing politicians. Societal characteristics may aid the rise of authoritarianism, but autocracy is fundamentally an elite choice.

How Autocracies Are Sustained

If efficiency gains, inherited bureaucracies, and societal choices all offer routes to autocracy, how do autocratic regimes operate and survive? What are their strategies of maintaining rule and how effective are they? To retain power, autocrats need to neutralize potential rivals and maintain control over society.

First, if obtaining power means overcoming the obstacles to monopoly over authority, maintaining autocratic rule necessitates *sharing* power while guarding its autocratic concentration. The same elites who help to sustain autocratic rule can undermine it—and this is a fundamental problem of autocratic governance. Thus, of the 303 dictators Svolik (2012) examines, 205 (66.2 percent) were removed by regime insiders, and only 32 (10.6 percent) by a popular uprising, a phenomenon we discuss in greater detail later. Managing these potential rivals, then, is a critical aim. Unlike democratic rulers, who can resolve conflict among rival elites through elections and the courts, there is no independent conflict-resolution authority that is autonomous of the ruler. While violence is an option, it is costly, and a coercive apparatus that is strong enough to keep the autocrat in power is also strong enough to overthrow the leader.

So how do rulers achieve these goals? Institutions and endowments are both important. A variety of institutions can help to reassure rival elites and lower the threat they pose. Executive constraint creates a trade-off between discretion and durability: rulers willing to forgo the former can extend the latter. Autocratic rule is shorter and more volatile than that of more constrained rulers (Blaydes and Chaney 2013). Yet in China, as state capacity declined, autocratic rulers stayed in power longer, largely because elite networks had fragmented, and dividing and conquering potential rivals was easier (Wang 2022). Similarly, Xi (2019) finds a trade-off between loyalty and performance in Qing China, and shows that threatened autocrats will plump for loyal bureaucrats to survive in the short term.

Political parties are a critical way to share power and to ensure succession. Ruling autocratic parties are institutionalized organizations that mobilize and encapsulate society, coopt elites and potential opponents, fuse the party with the state apparatus, and offer clear rules for the resolution of elite conflict (Grzymala-Busse 2002; Miller 2015; Svolik 2012). Accordingly, autocratic regimes led by ruling parties are the most durable of modern autocracies (Geddes 1999; Geddes et al. 2018; Reuter 2017). Geddes (1999) finds that dictators who created parties survived over fourteen years on average, while those who allied with existing parties survived for an average of eleven. Those without a political party fared considerably worse, surviving less than seven years on average. She concludes that parties are expensive but worth the investment because they deter rival military factions from attempting coups. This is a relatively recent option for would-be autocrats: political parties are very much the creation of modern political entrepreneurs, arising first in the late nineteenth century (Kalyvas 1996; Przeworski and Sprague 1986).

Similarly, autocratic elections allow political parties to identify rivals and recruit new elites, signal strength to society, and redistribute goods (Blaydes 2010; Geddes 1999; Lust-Okar 2005; Magaloni 2006). Autocratic elections were common for centuries, but historically they involved high contestation and low participation prior to 1940, as in Britain and Sweden. In contrast, modern electoral authoritarians mobilize high participation but effectively limit contestation (Miller 2015). This bodes ill for democracy—and well for authoritarian durability—since, historically, contestation has a positive relationship to democratization and participation generally negative.

Earlier autocrats had to rely on other institutions to manage elite conflict and societal expectations. The first of these are monarchies, which were more stable than other forms of government (Gerring et al. 2021; Menaldo 2012). A critical mechanism of ensuring succession, preventing the familiar problem of elite challenges to the incumbent and lengthening monarchical durability, was the primogeniture (Acharya and Lee 2019; Kokkonen and Sundell 2014). There were holdouts to primogeniture, otherwise widespread in Europe by the twelfth century (Blaydes and Chaney 2013); the Holy Roman Empire, Poland, Hungary, and others did not adopt hereditary succession, much less primogeniture, and instead relied on royal elections by nobles. Royal elections also sought to fend off elite challenges, this time by ensuring that the incumbent was acceptable to a majority of elites, but elections did not produce as durable a rule as hereditary monarchies (Kokkonen and Sundell 2014). Large families also protected European monarchs from deposition (Kokkonen et al. 2021; see also Wang 2018). Royal marriage offered opportunities for territorial acquisition, and monarchies led by queens were more likely to engage in war than king-led polities: but married queens attacked more, while single queens were more likely to be attacked (Dube and Harish 2020). More broadly, Sharma (2015) argues that dynastic unions led to territorial expansion.

Many kings made use of parliaments: national assemblies that grew out of councils of advisers surrounding the king. Starting in the thirteenth century, kings summoned parlement, cortes, or parliaments, often with the explicit representation of different classes (clergy, nobles), cities, and rural areas. These representatives were not democratically elected, nor was there any notion of suffrage: nonetheless, they offered both representation and binding consent to taxation, military ventures, and so on. They were autocratic institutions that also served an important role as courts, adjudicating elite and societal conflict (Boucoyannis 2021; Ertman 1997). Not all leaders could summon parliaments; communications and transport were both costly, so such assemblies could meet more frequently in smaller polities (Stasavage 2020). In another vein of research linking durability with regime types, Leon (2020) links the emergence of political rights in medieval England to the expansion of the elite. To fend off challenges from powerful barons, the king had to rely on nonnoble allies, who were subsequently promoted. Each such expansion of the nobility generated positive feedback and reduced the costs of future expansions, thus establishing a path-dependent channel of granting political rights to ever-growing segments of society.

The impact of parliaments went beyond executive constraint and its ability to extend ruler survival (Blaydes and Chaney 2013). Dincecco (2009) argues that nineteenth-century fiscal gains in Europe were driven by parliamentary control over spending and centralization of tax administration. Karaman and Pamuk (2013) show that such control was exerted even earlier, in the sixteenth century, and was conditioned on the power and cooperation of urban (Dutch Republic, Venice, 1640s England) or rural (Poland) elites. In turn, more representative regimes with urban elites extracted more taxes during wartime. Authoritarian regimes in more urban and representative settings and representative regimes in rural settings underperformed. In short, economic structure and political regime both mattered, as did the "match" between them that determines whether the state could respond to pressures of war (Karaman and Pamuk 2013, 619). Closer to our own time, Gandhi and Przeworski (2007) argue that parliaments allowed autocrats to control negotiations and select groups with influence, exerting considerably more control over elites than their monarchical counterparts in previous centuries. An autocrat can buy off rival elites and groups (de Mesquita et al 2005; Magaloni 2008, or he can give them influence over the policy process (Gandhi and Przeworski 2007). In both cases, these would-be rivals would now share a common fate with the dictator: their stream of payments is conditioned on support of the autocrat and his survival.

Finally, autocrats build their own institutions. As Geddes (1999) noted, since institutions are largely endogenous to autocrats, we may assume they serve the rulers' interests. Constitutions can consolidate new configurations of power and rights. Autocrats who adopt and follow constitutions thus tend to stay in power longer (Albertus and Menaldo 2012). Turning to extraction and redistribution, Mares and Queralt (2015) show how systems with low suffrage and high income inequality tended to adopt an income tax, shifting the burden to the nonenfranchised. Politicians representing fixed assets supported the introduction of income taxes, because landed elites would not pay it. They then conditioned voting rights on direct tax payments, as a way to exclude low-income voters from parliamentary representation. Thus, in contrast to Acemoglu and Robinson (2006), who argue that elites fear potential redistribution under suffrage, Mares and Queralt (2015) demonstrate how immediate political and economic advantages drove institution-building.

A second critical goal for autocrats in maintaining power is managing society, of effectively exercising authoritarian control over the masses (Svolik 2012). This is a critical, if less well-examined, aspect of autocratic rule. Here, Wintrobe (1998) sees two main strategies of control: coercion and cooptation. He conceptualizes them as substitutes, with a relatively steep tradeoff: coercion is effective in the short run but costly, while cooptation requires longer time horizons, if fewer resources. Svolik (2012) argues that they can be complements, and it may be cheaper for some regimes to suppress the opposition rather than to assuage it. Magaloni (2008), in contrast, argues that part of the reason for the oversized coalitions in autocratic Mexico was to coopt potential opposition, as a cost-effective way of managing it.

Society-state relationships vary considerably across and within autocracies. Wang (2022) explores a millennium of Chinese history to examine the state-society relationship. He shows how elite networks can vary in their shape, geographic dispersion, and strength of ties. As a result, these networks can (1) promote centralized state rule, (2) lead elites to try and hollow out the state to provide order and public goods locally (the most durable equilibrium, and one that kept highly fragmented polities such as the Holy Roman Empire stable for centuries), or (3) lead to weak central rule where the state depends on society to carry out functions, but loses control over these strata. Beyond coercion and cooptation, educational systems can serve the goals of autocrats (Paglayan 2021), as part of projects of redistribution, fostering loyalty, industrialization, and nation-building (see also Darden and Grzymala-Busse 2006). Democratization itself has little impact on education—primarily because the spread of education took place mostly under earlier, autocratic regimes. Consistent with this explanation, some scholars have argued that cultural factors also help to explain monarchical survival (Karawan 1992; see also Gerring et al. 2021).

If institutions influence power sharing and societal control, endowments may offer constraints and opportunities in these efforts. A long tradition dating back to Moore (1966) and Domar (1970) argues that land ownership is associated with repression and support for autocracy.[4] Perry Anderson argued that the path to absolutism was paved with state protection for landowning elites from capitalist competition (Anderson 1974). Similarly, Acemoglu and Robinson (2006) argue that the very existence of powerful landowners is enough to block autocracy: with no mobile assets, these elites have nowhere to run.

Other scholars have explored the factors that condition the relationship between landowning and autocracy. Stasavage (2020) follows Scott (1998) in arguing that intensive agriculture may make state surveillance easier—and thus pave the way for autocratic extraction and rule. Rueschemeyer, Stephens, and Stephens (1992) argue that the power of landowners explain regime patterns in interwar Europe, with cheap agricultural labor blocking democratization. Similarly, Boix shows that concentrated landownership blocked democracy: the dominance of landholders is a sufficient condition for autocracy, and its absence a necessary condition for democracy (Boix 2003, 40). Others argue that, under some conditions, conservative landowners could nonetheless support democratization in Britain (Skocpol 1973; Ziblatt 2017). Ziblatt (2008) shows that landowners in Prussia lobbied against suffrage and access to election in late nineteenth century. Mares and Zhu (2015) refine this argument by showing that the impact of landownership was conditioned on labor availability: where large landowners faced labor abundance, they preferred electoral intimidation. Mahoney (2001) argues that labor-dependent rather than labor-repressive elites were responsible. Ansell and Samuels (2010; 2014), using a similar specification to Boix's (share of farms held in family-sized plots as a proxy for land concentration), argue that egalitarian smallholders preferred democracy as a way to protect their property rights. Albertus (2017, 236) argues that the negative influence of labor-dependent agriculture on democracy started to turn positive in the 1970s, as neighboring land reform and civil conflict led to support for democracy as a way to defend stability.

How Autocracies Die

Why, when, and under which conditions do autocracies collapse? Mass mobilization by aggrieved citizens raising up against their oppressors is the most visible and memorable channel of regime change. Yet scholars of historical and contemporary contentious politics have long recognized that grievances, even very strong ones, are necessary but not sufficient conditions for mass mobilization (see, e.g., Fearon and Laitin 2003; Goldstone 1980; 1982; Skocpol 1979). Furthermore, mobilization from below does not necessarily lead to regime collapse; some autocrats are swept away by revolutions, whereas others successfully weather popular challenges to their rule.

What explains contentious politics in nondemocracies? Several studies have linked popular unrest and protest to a regime's attempts to introduce major reforms. As early as 1856, Alexis de Tocqueville recognized that "the most dangerous time for a bad government is usually when it begins to reform." Finkel and Gehlbach (2020) apply Tocqueville's insight to the study of peasant unrest in settings ranging from ancient Rome to the twentieth-century Latin America. The authors argue that reforms lead to mass unrest when the reforming state's capacity is low and the implementation of reforms is outsourced to local actors with a vested interest in the prereform status quo. These local actors were thus able to manipulate the implementation of the reform to their favor. Under-implementation, coupled with increased expectations and government weakness, leads to mass unrest. This argument is in line with several other studies of mass mobilization in nondemocratic regimes that emphasize the importance of opportunity structure (i.e., Goldstone and Tilly 2001; Tarrow 1998; Tilly and Tarrow 2015), expectations (Garfias and Sellars, 2022), and implementation of reforms as drivers of popular mobilization (Albertus 2020; Albertus and Kaplan 2013).

An important feature of autocracy is that its repressive apparatus forces people to hide their true preferences, acting as if they support the regime (Wedeen 1998; but see Hager and Krakowski 2022). When true preferences are revealed and citizens realize the extent of popular opposition (Kuran 1991), mobilization spreads. The presence of a revolutionary vanguard and organizers committed to protests also facilitates mobilization (Bueno de Mesquita 2010). Aidt, Leon-Alban, and Satchell (2020) zoom in on the 1830–1831 Swing Riots in England to demonstrate how networks, information flows, and organizers explain the diffusion of mass protest. Scaling up the level of analysis, several studies show that revolutions and autocratic reactions both tend to come in waves, underscoring the need to unpack the processes of both spatial and temporal diffusion (Finkel and Brudny 2012; Huntington 1993; Weyland 2009; 2014).

Why then, when confronted by mass mobilization, do some autocrats lose powers while others emerge unscathed? The literature on the autocratic ability to withstand revolutionary challenges highlights the importance of a regime's internal cohesion and consistency in using (or refraining from) violent repression. Autocratic regimes that are internally united are less likely to collapse than those in which the elites are split and factions within the government are thus more likely to switch over to the opposition's side to gain advantage in an intraelite struggle (Goldstone 2001; Hale 2014; Svolik 2012). The ruler's indecisiveness and oscillation between violent repression and accommodation of protesters' demands signals weakness, thus emboldening the revolutionaries (Goldstone and Useem 1999; Rasler 1996).

The demise of autocracy does not always require actual mass mobilization and street violence. Peaceful regime collapse might be less prominent in the popular imagination, yet the puzzle of dictators (more or less) voluntarily relinquishing power has produced a number of influential models of regime change. A widespread line of argument posits that a credible threat of mass violence might suffice. This view is most explicitly articulated by Adam Przeworski, who claims that "extensions of rights are a response of the incumbent holders of rights to revolutionary threats by the excluded" (Przeworski 2009, 292; see also Boix 2003; Svolik 2012).

Acemoglu and Robinson (2006) put forward a related theory of democratization. When threatened with frequent unrest, they argue, autocratic elites opt for redistribution and expansion of material benefits. However, when the threat of unrest is severe, but rare, rulers cannot credibly commit to redistribution and, in order to stave off revolution, choose to grant citizens political rights. The observable implications of this argument have been examined in settings ranging from Latin America to the Russian Empire (Albertus 2015; Albertus and Menaldo 2014; Dower et al. 2018; Elis 2011) and provide mixed empirical support for the theory. Dower et al. (2018) studied the establishment of local self-governance institutions in 1860s Russia and found that the allocation of seats to recently emancipated serf peasants was in line with the Acemoglu and Robinson model and inconsistent with arguments such as those of Boix (2003) and Przeworski (2009). At the same time, the Dower et al. (2018) findings did not support the central mechanism of Acemoglu and Robinson's theory. Further theoretical and empirical work needs to be done to determine the relationship between mass mobilization and representation.

Another set of explanations focuses not on the masses but the intraelite dynamics and conflicts in the downfall of autocrats. As we noted earlier, autocrats need to retain the support of key elite factions to survive, and institutions such as parliaments or succession mechanisms exist to lock in their support. Primogeniture and the appointment of successors capable of uniting the elites partially reduce uncertainty and might help ensure peaceful transition from one autocrat to another (Brownlee 2007; Hale 2005; Kokkonen and Sundell 2014). The existence of these institutions suggests that elite support can be fickle. Periods of instability and ruler transition might change the elites' calculus and usher in a different government. Economic elites uncertain about the identity of the next autocrat and how repressive her policies might be can instead opt for democratization as a less threatening outcome (Albertus and Gay 2017). Contingency also plays a key role in the demise of autocracy. Thus, according to Treisman (2020), the emergence of democracy is more often a result of rulers' costly mistakes and miscalculations rather than the elite's deliberate choice to extend political rights.

Transitions to democracy are also impacted by preexisting institutions and conditions. Past experience helps: holding elections under autocracy increases the likelihood of successful, durable subsequent democracy (Miller 2015). Federalism may aid the survival of islands of autocracy: in the nineteenth- and early-twentieth-century US South, Mickey (2015) shows, state-level elite responses to the national Democratic Party and federal institutions shaped the dismantling of the White-dominated southern autocracy. More broadly, autocratic islands can persist despite democratization at the national level by maintaining control over local conflict, as a considerable literature on subnational authoritarianism has shown (Gibson 2013; Gel'man 2010). Elite calculations regarding democracy are also influenced by urbanization (Abramson and Boix 2019), technological innovations that transform the nature of production and economic relations (Samuels and Thomson 2021), or reforms in neighboring countries (Albertus 2017).

When autocracies fail, democracy is not the only possible—or even likely—outcome. Hadenius and Teorell (2007) argue that collapsed autocratic regimes have historically been replaced by a different form of autocracy rather than a democracy. Geddes, Wright, and Frantz (2014) show that about half of regime transitions were those from one autocratic government to another. In a recent contribution, Edgell, Wilson, and Maerz (2021) contend that regime transformation—a gradual change within a certain regime type—is a more common occurrence than regime change. Many autocracies do become more liberal over time, but not all of them end up being democracies. And even if the transition to democracy does occur, backsliding and return to authoritarian rule is always a possibility, as shown by the history of democratization in Latin America in the nineteenth and twentieth centuries, or in Europe in the twentieth and twenty-first.

These and similar broadly historical analyses (e.g., Djuve, Knutsen, and Wig 2020) have improved our understanding of the multifaceted patterns of regime transitions and potential ways out of (or across) autocracies. The next major task for the scholarship of autocracy is identifying the specific mechanisms of not only democratization or autocratic survival but also of autocratic adaptation to change. The HPE literature has already identify several such mechanisms. Thus, Dower et al. (2018) show that the nineteenth-century Russian Empire granted newly emancipated peasants less representation in self-governance bodies in areas that experienced higher levels of rural unrest prior to the reform. Focusing on Imperial Germany, Ziblatt (2009) discusses how practices and procedures of elections—in this case, electoral disputes—can subvert the de jure representative nature of institutions. The governments' social engineering and development programs can create a large middle class that opposes democratization, thus shoring up the autocrats' survival chances (Lankina and Libman 2021; for contemporary cases, see also Rosenfeld 2020).

THE LEGACIES AUTOCRACIES LEAVE BEHIND

A still relatively small but fast-growing body of research focuses on the longer-term legacies of nondemocratic regimes. The existing scholarship has already identified durable and meaningful long-term effects of autocracy both as a form of government and a set of institutions. Scholars have also analyzed the impact of specific policies pursued by nondemocratic regimes, most notably state repression and mass violence. Autocratic legacies, we now know, shape institutions, perceptions, and political behavior.

Yet this line of research also suffers from several limitations, most notably the lack of a generally accepted definition of "legacies," problems with identifying causal mechanisms, and a divergent treatment of legacies of different types of autocratic regimes. Simpser, Slater, and Wittenberg (2018) provide a comprehensive overview of the existing approaches and argue for a better convergence among studies that focus on the legacies of different types of nondemocracies, most notably colonial regimes, autocracies, and communist systems.[5] Other studies offer a more limited focus, such as LaPorte and Lussier (2011; 2022), who center on the legacies of communism in Eastern Europe. Recent research on legacies (e.g., Beissinger and Kotkin 2014; Wittenberg 2015) is conscious of the need to better conceptualize the term, rather than viewing "legacy" as a shorthand for the past or history. In the most basic sense, argues Wittenberg (2015), legacy is an observed outcome of factors that are no longer present.

Scholars have identified lasting consequences of autocracies at three levels: institutions, attitudes, and behavior. Mattingly (2017) shows that, in northern China, exposure to Japanese colonial institutions influenced contemporary outcomes such as the density and extent of bureaucratic bodies, public services provisions, schooling, and health. Dell, Lane, and Querubin (2018) extend the analysis even further back in time and demonstrate how precolonial statehood affects local governance in parts of contemporary Vietnam. These and other recent studies (e.g., Foa 2017; Lee 2017; Verghese and Teitelbaum 2019) bridge the gap between the (predominantly) earlier, macrohistorical, and qualitative studies such as Collier and Collier (1991), Boone (2003), or Mahoney (2010), and the political economy approaches, most notably Acemoglu, Johnson, and Robinson (2001). These recent studies all identify causal factors and mechanisms across time and often combine quantitative and qualitative methods. The legacies of autocracies also extend to physical infrastructure, such as railroad networks (Grosfeld and Zhuravskaya 2015), and the share of the state sector in the economy and welfare provision (Orenstein 2008; Pop-Eleches 2015). Autocratic legacies also help explain the ethnic composition of bureaucracies (Johnson-Kanu 2021) and the ability of some autocratic parties to thrive after transitioning to democracy (Grzymala-Busse 2002), as well as broader patterns of voting and party systems (Kitschelt et al. 1999; Wittenberg 2006).

On the individual level, the legacies of autocratic systems of government impact political and social attitudes and behavior for decades, possibly even centuries, later. Alesina and Fuchs-Schündeln (2007) demonstrate how the experience of communism made former residents of East Germany more likely to support higher levels of state intervention, welfare, and wealth redistribution compared to West Germans. One of the most profound legacies of autocracy is its impact on trust, though the exact direction of this impact is less clear and likely depends on context. Thus, Grosfeld, Rodnyansky, and Zhuravskaya (2011) show that the area of the Russian Empire's Pale of Settlement exhibits higher contemporary levels of in-group trust among ethnic majority populations. Becker et al. (2016) posit that the legacy of the Habsburg Empire explains higher levels of trust in regions that were previously a part of Austro-Hungary. Conversely, Pop-Eleches and Tucker (2011; 2017) argue that lack of trust, especially trust in political institutions is a legacy of communist regimes.

Whether communist or imperial, nondemocracies also leave a legacy of increased intolerance and xenophobia (Grosfeld, Rodnyansky, and Zhuravskaya 2011; Homola, Pereira, and Tavits 2020; Pop-Eleches and Tucker 2017). In the American South, Whites still exhibits higher levels of racial resentment and opposition to affirmative action in areas where slavery was more prevalent (Acharya, Blackwell, and Sen 2016).

Areas that were governed by autocratic regimes experienced a long-term impact not only on attitudes but behavior. Many of the effects uncovered by legacy studies are detrimental to successful economic and social development. Thus, the experience of the Pale of Settlement created a persistent antimarket culture and made people living in the area less entrepreneurial (Grosfeld, Rodnyansky, and Zhuravskaya 2011). Bernhard and Karakoç (2007) observe that the experience of living in an autocracy makes people less likely to partake in protests and join social society groups. This finding is in line with Howard (2003), who focuses more narrowly on postcommunist Eastern Europe and echoes Jowitt's (1992) broader argument that limited participation in politics is one of communism's main legacies.

Yet not all legacies of autocracies are negative. The effects vary depending on the regimes' specific policies and institutional makeup. An important legacy of the Habsburg Empire is a lower rate of corruption in former Austro-Hungarian areas compared to neighboring regions, which were governed by other autocracies (Becker et al. 2016). In some parts of Vietnam, higher levels of participation in public work projects is a legacy of the precolonial (and autocratic) Dai Viet state; localities subject to the rule of a different, less centralized autocracy, the Khmer Empire, do not exhibit these characteristics (Dell, Lane, and Querubin 2018).

These findings exemplify the importance of further unpacking the concept of autocratic legacies and shedding light on the long-term impacts of authoritarian governments' specific institutions and policies. In this area, the most progress has occurred in the study of legacies of authoritarian repression and state violence. The bulk of this research on legacies of state violence focuses on Europe, more specifically the legacies of communist and Nazi violence.

The legacies of violence affect attitudes and behavior. In Spain, the brutal civil war and the subsequent Franco dictatorship hardened cleavages and perpetuated individual attitudes along the lines of wartime political divisions, yet predominantly for those whose families experienced the most extreme violations (Balcells 2012). Living in proximity to the former Nazi camps and being exposed daily to the memory of the Nazi oppression leads to cognitive dissonance among contemporary Germans and increases xenophobic attitudes (Homola, Pereira, and Tavits 2020). Among the Crimean Tatars, families who suffered higher levels of Soviet violence in 1944 still exhibit more negative attitudes toward Russia and identify more closely with their group (Lupu and Peisakhin 2017).

Importantly, attitudes also translate to political and social behavior. Crimean Tatars from families that experienced higher levels of Soviet repression not only exhibit more anti-Russian attitudes but are also more actively involved in politics in this Russian-occupied territory. In western Ukrainian localities subject to Stalinist state violence and deportations, pro-Russian parties received fewer votes; in Russia, localities subject to Stalinist purges still have lower levels of political participation (Rozenas, Schutte, and Zhukov 2017; Zhukov and Talibova 2018). Ukraine's districts that suffered higher casualties during the Holodomor, the Soviet man-made famine of 1932–1933, exhibit different behavioral and voting patterns than those that were less affected (Rozenas and Zhukov 2019; Toews and Vezina 2020).

The legacies of Nazi violence are no less pronounced. Thus, those living close to the former Nazi camps not only hold more xenophobic views but are also more likely to vote for far-right parties (Homola, Pereira, and Tavits 2020). In Poland, villages closest to the Treblinka death camp benefited from the property of the murdered Jews. These places also had a substantially higher vote share for the far-right, anti-Semitic League of Polish Families in the 2001 election compared to villages that were more distant from the camp and thus did not benefit from Jewish property (Charnysh and Finkel 2017). Conversely, areas of the Russian Federation that experienced higher levels of anti-Jewish violence during the Holocaust were more likely to vote for the Communist Party well into the 1990s (Acemoglu, Hassan, and Robinson 2011). In northern Italy, higher vote share for the communists well into the 1980s is a legacy of Nazi violence and the longer duration of German occupation compared to other parts of the country (Fontana, Nannicini, and Tabellini 2018).

Research on autocratic legacies faces important challenges. That autocratic regimes and the violence they perpetrate leave a long-term legacy is well established. Less clear is which mechanism or set of mechanisms are responsible for the observed effects and how durable these legacies are.

The mechanisms that account for the impact of autocracies on contemporary outcomes range from individual lived experiences (e.g., Pop-Eleches and Tucker 2017) to social structure (Acemoglu, Hassan, and Robinson 2011) to psychology (Homola, Pereira, and Tavits 2020) to resources (Rozenas and Zhukov 2019) to education (Lupu and Peisakhin 2017). Some, especially earlier studies do not or cannot provide a clear explanation for the persistence they observe (e.g., Kitschelt 2003). Thus, it is important not only to unpack the broad concept of "autocratic legacy" and tease out the effects of specific policies and institutions but also to establish more general categories of mechanisms and explanations present across cases (Grzymala-Busse 2002).

The effects of autocracy might be persistent, but lie dormant. Autocratic legacies may become activated only when relevant political issues become salient (Charnysh and Finkel 2017). The impact and the direction of a legacy can also change depending on context. Thus, the Holodomor made Ukrainians more obedient toward the Kremlin when the government was strong, and more likely to act against it during times of state weakness (Rozenas and Zhukov 2019).

Finally, more work needs to be done to establish the half-life of autocratic legacies. The legacies discussed by the exisssting scholarship span from several years (LaPorte and Lussier 2011) to several decades or generations (e.g., Alesina and Fuchs-Schündeln 2007; Charnysh and Finkel 2017; Lupu and Peisakhin 2017) to centuries (Acemoglu, Johnson, and Robinson 2001; Dell, Lane, and Querubin 2018; Voigtländer and Voth 2012). The next key task for legacy scholarship is to establish if and how legacies weaken over time, and how quickly. Autocratic legacies always have a starting point, but we not yet know when they end, if at all.

Concluding Remarks: The Way Forward

The HPE literature on autocracy has made a substantial contribution to better understanding of this type of regime. The key strength of the HPE scholarship is in incorporating the insights and methods of several disciplines: political science, history, sociology, and economics—yet this might only be just the beginning. Autocracy is an ancient phenomenon, and thus to better understand its origins, development, and functioning, we can include the findings of archaeologists, physical anthropologists, or scholars of cultural evolution. HPE research on autocracy needs to be as interdisciplinary as possible and not stop at the cross-disciplinary dialogue that already exists.

Current research is also heavily dominated by scholarship on Europe, East Asia, and the Middle East and North Africa (MENA) regions. Yet autocracy is a global phenomenon, and a better focus on the development of autocratic policies and institutions in regions such as precolonial Africa, the Americas, and Oceania will undoubtedly provide scholars with new theories and insights. The existing scholarship is also too heavily centered on formal institutions and political and economic elites; expanding the list of actors and institutions on which HPE scholars focus, such as religious bodies (Cansunar and Kuran 2019; Grzymala-Busse 2020), might provide new insights. Scholars also need to better examine how interactions between various institutions and social groups shape authoritarian politics and governance, both now and in the past.

Finally, by combining qualitative and quantitative research methods, the HPE scholarship is especially well positioned to identify causal mechanisms and processes of longue durée transformations. This would augment the advances in the identification of causal factors through plausible research design. Better understanding the longevity of historical legacies and the mechanisms of transition and persistence help the field not only to analyze the present but also to offer insights about the future of autocratic regimes.

Notes

1. That said, war is neither a necessary nor sufficient condition for the rise of the state. States develop and arise independently of conflict: see Strayer (1970); Wang (2022); Grzymala-Busse (2020).
2. In contrast, Anderson (1974) saw the roots of absolutism in royal protection of the nobles from the vicissitudes of economic change and market pressures.
3. Other scholars have found the roots of individualism in the medieval church's marriage and family law changes, which broke apart European kinships ties (and benefited the church financially). See Goody 1983; Henrich 2020.
4. The Domar hypothesis examined the divergent outcomes in western and eastern Europe after the fourteenth century: while western European peasants freed themselves, eastern European peasants became serfs. Domar argues that under conditions of abundant free land, abundant free peasants, and large-scale agriculture with nonworking landowners, serfdom results, as it did in Russia. If only two out of the three conditions are present, peasants can retain their freedom.
5. Cirone and Pepinsky (2021) delve further into the methodological and epistemological issues in studying historical persistence.

References

Abramson, Scott F., and Carles Boix. 2019. "Endogenous Parliaments: The Domestic and International Roots of Long-Term Economic Growth and Executive Constraints in Europe." *International Organization* 73, no. 4: 793–837.

Acemoglu, Daron, Tarek A. Hassan, and James A. Robinson. 2011. "Social Structure and Development: A Legacy of the Holocaust in Russia." *Quarterly Journal of Economics* 126, no. 2: 895–946.

Acemoglu, Daron, Simon Johnson, and James A. Robinson. 2001. "The Colonial Origins of Comparative Development: An Empirical Investigation." *American Economic Review* 91, no. 5: 1369–1401.

Acemoglu, Daron, and James A. Robinson. 2006. *Economic Origins of Dictatorship and Democracy*. New York: Cambridge University Press.

Acharya, Avidit, Matthew Blackwell, and Maya Sen. 2016. "The Political Legacy of American Slavery." *Journal of Politics* 78, no. 3: 621–41.

Acharya, Avidit, and Alexander Lee. 2019. "The Cartel System of States." Unpublished manuscript.

Adena, Maja, Ruben Enikolopov, Maria Petrova, Veronica Santarosa, and Ekaterina Zhuravskaya. 2015. "Radio and the Rise of the Nazis in Prewar Germany." *Quarterly Journal of Economics* 130, no. 4: 1885–939.

Aidt, Toke, Gabriel Leon-Ablan, and Max Satchell. 2020. "The Social Dynamics of Collective Action: Evidence from the Diffusion of the Swing Riots, 1830–1831." *Journal of Politics* 84, no. 1: 209–225.

Albertus, Michael. 2015. *Autocracy and Redistribution*. New York: Cambridge University Press.

Albertus, Michael. 2017. "Landowners and Democracy: The Social Origins of Democracy Reconsidered." *World Politics* 69, no. 2: 233–76.

Albertus, Michael. 2020. "Land Reform and Civil Conflict: Theory and Evidence from Peru." *American Journal of Political Science* 64, no. 2: 256–74.

Albertus, Michael, and Victor Gay. 2017. "Unlikely Democrats: Economic Elite Uncertainty under Dictatorship and Support for Democratization." *American Journal of Political Science* 61, no. 3: 624–41.

Albertus, Michael, and Oliver Kaplan. 2013. "Land Reform as a Counterinsurgency Policy: Evidence from Colombia." *Journal of Conflict Resolution* 57, no. 2: 198–231.

Albertus, Michael, and Victor Menaldo. 2012. "Dictators as Founding Fathers? The Role of Constitutions under Autocracy." *Economics & Politics* 24, no. 3: 279–306.

Albertus, Michael, and Victor Menaldo. 2014. "Gaming Democracy: Elite Dominance during Transition and the Prospects for Redistribution." *British Journal of Political Science* 44, no. 3: 575–603.

Alesina, Alberto, and Nicola Fuchs-Schündeln. 2007. "Good-Bye Lenin (or Not?): The Effect of Communism on People's Preferences." *American Economic Review* 97, no. 4: 1507–28.

Anderson, Perry. 1974. *Lineages of the Absolutist State*. Princeton, NJ: Princeton University Press.

Ansell, Ben, and David Samuels. 2010. "Inequality and Democratization: A Contractarian Approach." *Comparative Political Studies* 43, no. 12: 1543–74.

Ansell, Ben, and David Samuels. 2014. *Inequality and Democratization*. New York: Cambridge University Press.

Balcells, Laia. 2012. "The Consequences of Victimization on Political Identities Evidence from Spain." *Politics & Society* 40, no. 3: 311–47.

Barzel, Yoram, and Edgar Kiser. 1997. "The Development and Decline of Medieval Voting Institutions: A Comparison of England and France." *Economic Inquiry* 35, no. 2: 244–60.

Bean, Richard. 1973. "War and the Birth of the Nation State." *Journal of Economic History* 33, no. 1: 203–21.

Becker, Sascha O., Katrin Boeckh, Christa Hainz, and Ludger Woessmann. 2016. "The Empire Is Dead, Long Live the Empire! Long-Run Persistence of Trust and Corruption in the Bureaucracy." *Economic Journal* 126, no. 590: 40–74.

Beissinger, Mark, and Stephen Kotkin. 2014. *Historical Legacies of Communism in Russia and Eastern Europe*. New York: Cambridge University Press.

Berman, Sheri. 1997. "Civil Society and the Collapse of the Weimar Republic." *World Politics* 49, no. 3: 401–29.

Bermeo, Nancy Gina. 2003. *Ordinary People in Extraordinary Times: The Citizenry and the Breakdown of Democracy*. Princeton, NJ: Princeton University Press.

Bernhard, Michael, and Ekrem Karakoç. 2007. "Civil Society and the Legacies of Dictatorship." *World Politics* 59, no. 4: 539–67.

Blaydes, Lisa. 2010. *Elections and Distributive Politics in Mubarak's Egypt.* New York: Cambridge University Press.

Blaydes, Lisa, and Eric Chaney. 2013. "The Feudal Revolution and Europe's Rise: Political Divergence of the Christian West and the Muslim World before 1500 CE." *American Political Science Review* 107, no. 1: 16–34.

Boix, Carles. 2003. *Democracy and Redistribution.* New York: Cambridge University Press.

Boone, Catherine. 2003. *Political Topographies of the African State: Territorial Authority and Institutional Choice.* New York: Cambridge University Press.

Boucoyannis, Deborah. 2021. *Kings as Judges: Power, Justice, and the Origins of Parliaments.* New York: Cambridge University Press.

Brownlee, Jason. 2007. "Hereditary Succession in Modern Autocracies." *World Politics* 59, no. 4: 595–628.

Bueno de Mesquita, Ethan. 2010. "Regime Change and Revolutionary Entrepreneurs." *American Political Science Review* 104, no. 3: 446–66.

Cansunar, Asli, and Timur Kuran. 2019. "Economic Harbingers of Political Modernization: Peaceful Explosion of Rights in Ottoman Istanbul." Economic Research Initiatives at Duke (ERID) Working Paper 288.

Centeno, Miguel Angel. 2002. *Blood and Debt: War and the Nation-State in Latin America.* University Park: Penn State Press.

Charnysh, Volha, and Evgeny Finkel. 2017. "The Death Camp Eldorado: Political and Economic Effects of Mass Violence." *American Political Science Review* 111, no. 4: 801–18.

Cirone, Alexandra, and Thomas B. Pepinsky. 2021. "Historical Persistence." *Annual Review of Political Science* 25, no. 1: 241–59.

Collier, Ruth Berins, and David Collier. 1991. *Shaping the Political Arena: Critical Junctures, the Labor Movement, and Regime Dynamics in Latin America.* Princeton, NJ: Princeton University Press.

Darden, Keith, and Anna Maria Grzymala-Busse. 2006. "The Great Divide: Literacy, Nationalism, and the Communist Collapse." *World Politics* 59, no. 1: 83–115.

Dell, Melissa, Nathan Lane, and Pablo Querubin. 2018. "The Historical State, Local Collective Action, and Economic Development in Vietnam." *Econometrica* 86, no. 6: 2083–121.

De Mesquita, Bruce Bueno, Alastair Smith, Randolph M. Siverson, and James D. Morrow. 2005. *The logic of political survival.* Cambridge, MA: MIT Press.

Dincecco, Mark. 2009. "Fiscal Centralization, Limited Government, and Public Revenues in Europe, 1650–1913." *Journal of Economic History* 69, no. 1: 48–103.

Dincecco, Mark, and Yuhua Wang. 2018. "Violent Conflict and Political Development over the Long Run: China versus Europe." *Annual Review of Political Science* 21: 341–58.

Djuve, Vilde Lunnan, Carl Henrik Knutsen, and Tore Wig. 2020. "Patterns of Regime Breakdown since the French Revolution." *Comparative Political Studies* 53, no. 6: 923–58.

Domar, Evsey D. 1970. "The Causes of Slavery and Serfdom." *Economic History Review* 30, no. 1: 18–32.

Dower, Paul Castañeda, Evgeny Finkel, Scott Gehlbach, and Steven Nafziger. 2018. "Collective Action and Representation in Autocracies: Evidence from Russia's Great Reforms." *American Political Science Review* 112, no. 1: 125–47.

Downing, Brian. 1992. *The Military Revolution and Political Change: Origins of Democracy and Autocracy in Early Modern Europe.* Princeton, NJ: Princeton University Press.

Dube, Oeindrila, and S. P. Harish. 2020. "Queens." *Journal of Political Economy* 128, no. 7: 2579–652.

Edgell, Amanda, Matthew Wilson, and Seraphine Maerz. 2021. "Episodes of Regime Transformation." *APSA Comparative Politics Newsletter* 31, no. 1: 5–14.

Elis, Roy. 2011. "The Logic of Redistributive Non-Democracies." PhD dissertation, Stanford University.

Ertman, Thomas. 1997. *Birth of the Leviathan: Building States and Regimes in Medieval and Early Modern Europe*. New York: Cambridge University Press.

Fearon, James, and David Laitin. 2003. "Ethnicity, Insurgency, and Civil War." *American Political Science Review* 97, no. 1: 75–90.

Finkel, Evgeny, and Yitzhak M. Brudny. 2012. "No More Colour! Authoritarian Regimes and Colour Revolutions in Eurasia." *Democratization* 19, no. 1: 1–14.

Finkel, Evgeny, and Scott Gehlbach. 2020. *Reform and Rebellion in Weak States*. New York: Cambridge University Press.

Foa, Roberto Stefan. 2017. "Persistence or Reversal of Fortune? Early State Inheritance and the Legacies of Colonial Rule." *Politics & Society* 45, no. 2: 301–24.

Fontana, Nicola, Tommaso Nannicini, and Guido Tabellini. 2018. "Historical Roots of Political Extremism: The Effects of Nazi Occupation of Italy." CESifo Working Paper Series No. 6838.

Frantz, Erica. 2016. "Autocracy." In *Oxford Research Encyclopedia of Politics*. https://doi.org/10.1093/acrefore/9780190228637.013.3.

Fukuyama, Francis. 1992. *The End of History and the Last Man*. New York: Simon and Schuster.

Galor, Oded, and Marc Klemp. 2017. *Roots of Autocracy*. Cambridge, MA: National Bureau of Economic Research.

Gambetta, Diego. 1993. *The Sicilian Mafia: The Business of Private Protection*. Cambridge, MA: Harvard University Press.

Gandhi, Jennifer, and Adam Przeworski. 2007. "Authoritarian Institutions and the Survival of Autocrats." *Comparative Political Studies* 40, no. 11: 1279–301.

Garfias, Francisco, and Emily A. Sellars. 2022. "When State Building Backfires: Elite Coordination and Popular Grievance in Rebellion." *American Journal of Political Science*, 66, no. 4: 977–92.

Geddes, Barbara. 1999. "What Do We Know about Democratization after Twenty Years?" *Annual Review of Political Science* 2, no. 1: 115–44.

Geddes, Barbara, Joseph Wright, and Erica Frantz. 2014. "Autocratic Breakdown and Regime Transitions: A New Data Set." *Perspectives on Politics* 12, no. 2: 313–31.

Geddes, Barbara, Joseph George Wright, Joseph Wright, and Erica Frantz. 2018. *How Dictatorships Work: Power, Personalization, and Collapse*. New York: Cambridge University Press.

Gel'man, Vladimir, and Cameron Ross. 2010. *The Politics of Sub-National Authoritarianism in Russia*. Farnham: Ashgate Publishing.

Gerring, John, Tore Wig, Wouter Veenendaal, Daniel Weitzel, Jan Teorell, and Kyosuke Kikuta. 2021. "Why Monarchy? The Rise and Demise of a Regime Type." *Comparative Political Studies* 54, no. 3–4: 585–622.

Gibson, Edward L. 2013. *Boundary Control: Subnational Authoritarianism in Federal Democracies*. New York: Cambridge University Press.

Goldstone, Jack. 1980. "Theories of Revolution: The Third Generation." *World Politics* 32, no. 3: 425–53.

Goldstone, Jack. 1982. "The Comparative and Historical Study of Revolutions." *Annual Review of Sociology* 8, no. 1: 187–207.

Goldstone, Jack. 2001. "Toward a Fourth Generation of Revolutionary Theory." *Annual Review of Political Science* 4, no. 1: 139–87.

Goldstone, Jack, and Charles Tilly. 2001. "Threat (and Opportunity): Popular Action and State Response in the Dynamics of Contentious Action." In *Silence and Voice in the Study of Contentious Politics*, ed. Ronald Aminzade, Jack A. Goldstone, Doug McAdam, Elizabeth J. Perry, William H. Sewell, Sidney Tarrow, and Charles Tilly, 179–94. Cambridge: Cambridge University Press.

Goldstone, Jack, and Bert Useem. 1999. "Prison Riots as Microrevolutions." *American Journal of Sociology* 104, no. 4: 985–1029.

Goody, Jack. 1983. *The Development of the Family and Marriage in Europe*. New York: Cambridge University Press.

Grosfeld, Irena, Alexander Rodnyansky, and Ekaterina Zhuravskaya. 2011. "Persistent Anti-Market Culture: A Legacy of the Pale of Settlement and of the Holocaust." Centre for Economic Policy Research Discussion Paper 8316.

Grosfeld, Irena, and Ekaterina Zhuravskaya. 2015. "Cultural vs. Economic Legacies of Empires: Evidence from the Partition of Poland." *Journal of Comparative Economics* 43, no. 1: 55–75.

Grzymala-Busse, Anna. 2002. *Redeeming the Communist Past: The Regeneration of Communist Parties in East Central Europe*. New York: Cambridge University Press.

Grzymala-Busse, Anna. 2020. "Beyond War and Contracts: The Medieval and Religious Roots of the European State." *Annual Review of Political Science* 23: 19–36.

Hadenius, Axel, and Jan Teorell. 2007. "Pathways from Authoritarianism." *Journal of Democracy* 18, no. 1: 143–57.

Hager, Anselm, and Krzysztof Krakowski. 2022. "Does State Repression Spark Protests? Evidence from Secret Police Surveillance in Communist Poland." *American Political Science Review* 116, no. 2: 564–79.

Hale, Henry E. 2005. "Regime Cycles: Democracy, Autocracy, and Revolution in Post-Soviet Eurasia." *World Politics* 58, no. 1: 133–65.

Hale, Henry E. 2014. *Patronal Politics: Eurasian Regime Dynamics in Comparative Perspective*. New York: Cambridge University Press.

Hariri, Jacob Gerner. 2012. "The Autocratic Legacy of Early Statehood." *American Political Science Review* 106, no. 3: 471–94.

Henrich, Joseph. 2020. *The WEIRDest People in the World: How the West Became Psychologically Peculiar and Particularly Prosperous*. New York: Farrar, Straus and Giroux.

Homola, Jonathan, Miguel M. Pereira, and Margit Tavits. 2020. "Legacies of the Third Reich: Concentration Camps and Out-Group Intolerance." *American Political Science Review* 114, no. 2: 573–90.

Howard, Marc Morjé. 2003. *The Weakness of Civil Society in Post-Communist Europe*. New York: Cambridge University Press.

Hui, Victoria Tin-bor. 2005. *War and State Formation in Ancient China and Early Modern Europe*. New York: Cambridge University Press.

Huntington, Samuel P. 1993. *The Third Wave: Democratization in the Late Twentieth Century*. Norman: University of Oklahoma Press.

Johnson, Noel D., and Mark Koyama. 2017. "States and Economic Growth: Capacity and Constraints." *Explorations in Economic History* 64: 1–20.

Johnson-Kanu, Ada. 2021. "The Origins and Consequences of Descriptive Representation in the Nigerian Federal Civil Service." *APSA Comparative Politics Newsletter* 31, no. 2: 13–23.

Jowitt, Ken. 1992. *The Leninist Extinction*. Berkeley: University of California Press.

Kalyvas, Stathis N. 1996. *The Rise of Christian Democracy in Europe*. Ithaca, NY: Cornell University Press.

Karaman, K. Kivanc, and Şevket Pamuk. 2013. "Different Paths to the Modern State in Europe: The Interaction between Warfare, Economic Structure, and Political Regime." *American Political Science Review* 107, no. 3: 603–26.

Karawan, Ibrahim A. 1992. "Monarchs, Mullas, and Marshals: Islamic Regimes?" *Annals of the American Academy of Political and Social Science* 524, no. 1: 103–19.

King, Gary, Ori Rosen, Martin Tanner, and Alexander Wagner. 2008. "Ordinary Economic Voting Behavior in the Extraordinary Election of Adolf Hitler." *Journal of Economic History* 68, no. 4: 951–96.

Kiser, Edgar, and Yoram Barzel. 1991. "The Origins of Democracy in England." *Rationality and Society* 3, no. 4: 396–422.

Kitschelt, Herbert. 2003. "Accounting for Post-Communist Regime Diversity: What Counts as a Good Cause." In *Capitalism and Democracy in Central and Eastern Europe: Assessing the Legacy of Communist Rule*, ed. Grzegorz Ekiert and Stephen Hanson, 49–88. New York: Cambridge University Press.

Kitschelt, Herbert, Zdenka Mansfeldova, Radoslaw Markowski, and Gabor Toka. 1999. *Post-Communist Party Systems: Competition, Representation, and Inter-Party Cooperation*. New York: Cambridge University Press.

Kokkonen, Andrej, Suthan Krishnarajan, Jørgen Møller, and Anders Sundell. 2021. "Blood Is Thicker Than Water: Family Size and Leader Deposition in Medieval and Early Modern Europe." *Journal of Politics* 83, no. 4: 1246–59.

Kokkonen, Andrej, and Anders Sundell. 2014. "Delivering Stability—Primogeniture and Autocratic Survival in European Monarchies, 1000–1800." *American Political Science Review* 108, no. 2: 438–53.

Kuran, Timur. 1991. "Now Out of Never." *World Politics* 44, no. 1: 7–48.

Lankina, Tomila V., and Alexander Libman. 2021. "The Two-Pronged Middle Class: The Old Bourgeoisie, New State-Engineered Middle Class, and Democratic Development." *American Political Science Review* 115, no. 3: 948–66.

LaPorte, Jody, and Danielle N. Lussier. 2011. "What Is the Leninist Legacy? Assessing Twenty Years of Scholarship." *Slavic Review* 70, no. 3: 637–54.

LaPorte, Jody, and Danielle N Lussier. 2022. "Leninist Extinction? Critical Junctures, Legacies, and the Study of Post-Communism." In *Critical Junctures and Historical Legacies: Insights and Tools for Comparative Social Science*, ed. David Collier and Gerardo Munk, 289–314. Lanham, MD: Rowman & Littlefield.

Lee, Alexander. 2017. "Redistributive Colonialism: The Long-Term Legacy of International Conflict in India." *Politics & Society* 45, no. 2: 173–224.

Leon, Gabriel. 2020. "Feudalism, Collaboration and Path Dependence in England's Political Development." *British Journal of Political Science* 50, no. 2: 511–33.

Levi, Margaret. 1988. *Of Rule and Revenue*. Berkeley: University of California Press.

Lupu, Noam, and Leonid Peisakhin. 2017. "The Legacy of Political Violence across Generations." *American Journal of Political Science* 61, no. 4: 836–51.

Lust-Okar, Ellen. 2005. *Structuring Conflict in the Arab World: Incumbents, Opponents, and Institutions*. New York: Cambridge University Press.

Magaloni, Beatriz. 2006. *Voting for Autocracy: Hegemonic Party Survival and Its Demise in Mexico*. New York: Cambridge University Press.

Magaloni, Beatriz. 2008. "Credible Power-Sharing and the Longevity of Authoritarian Rule." *Comparative Political Studies* 41, no. 4–5: 715–41.

Mahoney, James. 2001. *The Legacies of Liberalism: Path Dependence and Political Regimes in Central America*. Baltimore: Johns Hopkins University Press.

Mahoney, James. 2010. *Colonialism and Postcolonial Development: Spanish America in Comparative Perspective*. New York: Cambridge University Press.

Mann, Michael. 1986. *The Sources of Social Power*. Cambridge: Cambridge University Press.

Mares, Isabela, and Didac Queralt. 2015. "The Non-Democratic Origins of Income Taxation." *Comparative Political Studies* 48, no. 14: 1974–2009.

Mares, Isabela, and Boliang Zhu. 2015. "The Production of Electoral Intimidation: Economic and Political Incentives." *Comparative Politics* 48, no. 1: 23–43.

Mattingly, Daniel C. 2017. "Colonial Legacies and State Institutions in China: Evidence from a Natural Experiment." *Comparative Political Studies* 50, no. 4: 434–63.

Menaldo, Victor. 2012. "The Middle East and North Africa's Resilient Monarchs." *Journal of Politics* 74, no. 3: 707–22.

Mickey, Robert. 2015. *Paths out of Dixie: The Democratization of Authoritarian Enclaves in America's Deep South, 1944–1972*. Princeton, NJ: Princeton University Press.

Miller, Michael K. 2015. "Democratic Pieces: Autocratic Elections and Democratic Development since 1815." *British Journal of Political Science* 45, no. 3: 501–30.

Moore, Barrington. 1966. *Social Origins of Dictatorship and Democracy: Lord and Peasant in the Making of the Modern World*. Boston: Beacon Press.

Myerson, Roger B. 2004. "Political Economics and the Weimar Disaster." *Journal of Institutional and Theoretical Economics (JITE) / Zeitschrift für die gesamte Staatswissenschaft* 160, no. 2: 187–209.

North, Douglass C., John Joseph Wallis, and Barry R. Weingast. 2009. *Violence and Social Orders: A Conceptual Framework for Interpreting Recorded Human History*. New York: Cambridge University Press.

North, Douglass C., and Barry R. Weingast. 1989. "Constitutions and Commitment: The Evolution of Institutions Governing Public Choice in Seventeenth-Century England." *Journal of Economic History* 49, no. 4: 803–32.

Olson, Mancur. 1993. "Dictatorship, Democracy, and Development." *American Political Science Review* 87, no. 3: 567–76.

Olson, Mancur. 2000. *Power and Prosperity: Outgrowing Communist and Capitalist Dictatorships*. New York: Basic Books.

Olsson, Ola, and Christopher Paik. 2016. "Long-Run Cultural Divergence: Evidence from the Neolithic Revolution." *Journal of Development Economics* 122: 197–213.

Orenstein, Mitchell A. 2008. *Privatizing Pensions*. Princeton, NJ: Princeton University Press.

Paglayan, Agustina S. 2021. "The Non-Democratic Roots of Mass Education: Evidence from 200 Years." *American Political Science Review* 115, no. 1: 179–198.

Pop-Eleches, Grigore. 2015. "Pre-Communist and Communist Developmental Legacies." *East European Politics and Societies* 29, no. 2: 391–408.

Pop-Eleches, Grigore, and Joshua A. Tucker. 2011. "Communism's Shadow: Postcommunist Legacies, Values, and Behavior." *Comparative Politics* 43, no. 4: 379–408.

Pop-Eleches, Grigore, and Joshua A. Tucker. 2017. *Communism's Shadow*. Princeton, NJ: Princeton University Press.

Przeworski, Adam. 2009. "Conquered or Granted? A History of Suffrage Extensions." *British Journal of Political Science* 39, no. 2: 291–321.

Przeworski, Adam, and John Sprague. 1986. *Paper Stones: A History of Electoral Socialism*. Chicago: University of Chicago Press.

Rasler, Karen. 1996. "Concessions, Repression, and Political Protest in the Iranian Revolution." *American Sociological Review* 61, no. 1: 132–52.

Reuter, Ora John. 2017. *The Origins of Dominant Parties: Building Authoritarian Institutions in Post-Soviet Russia*. New York: Cambridge University Press.

Rosenfeld, Bryn. 2020. *The Autocratic Middle Class: How State Dependency Reduces the Demand for Democracy*. Princeton, NJ: Princeton University Press.

Rozenas, Arturas, Sebastian Schutte, and Yuri Zhukov. 2017. "The Political Legacy of Violence: The Long-Term Impact of Stalin's Repression in Ukraine." *Journal of Politics* 79, no. 4: 1147–61.

Rozenas, Arturas, and Yuri M. Zhukov. 2019. "Mass Repression and Political Loyalty: Evidence from Stalin's 'Terror by Hunger.' " *American Political Science Review* 113, no. 2: 569–83.

Rueschemeyer, Dietrich, Evelyne Huber Stephens, and John D. Stephens. 1992. *Capitalist Development and Democracy*. Cambridge: Polity.

Samuels, David J., and Henry Thomson. 2021. "Lord, Peasant . . . and Tractor? Agricultural Mechanization, Moore's Thesis, and the Emergence of Democracy." *Perspectives on Politics* 19, no. 3: 739–53.

Scott, James C. 1998. *Seeing Like a State: How Certain Schemes to Improve the Human Condition Have Failed*. New Haven, CT: Yale University Press.

Sharma, Vivek Swaroop. 2015. "Kinship, Property, and Authority: European Territorial Consolidation Reconsidered." *Politics & Society* 43, no. 2: 151–80.

Simpser, Alberto, Dan Slater, and Jason Wittenberg. 2018. "Dead but Not Gone: Contemporary Legacies of Communism, Imperialism, and Authoritarianism." *Annual Review of Political Science* 21: 419–39.

Skocpol, Theda. 1973. "A Critical Review of Barrington Moore's Social Origins of Dictatorship and Democracy." *Politics & Society* 4, no. 1: 1–34.

Skocpol, Theda. 1979. *Social Revolutions in the Modern World*. New York: Cambridge University Press.

Spenkuch, Jörg L., and Philipp Tillmann. 2018. "Elite Influence? Religion and the Electoral Success of the Nazis." *American Journal of Political Science* 62, no. 1: 19–36.

Stasavage, David. 2020. *The Decline and Rise of Democracy*. Princeton, NJ: Princeton University Press.

Strayer, Joseph. 1970. *On the Medieval Origins of the Modern State*. Princeton, NJ: Princeton University Press.

Svolik, Milan W. 2012. *The Politics of Authoritarian Rule*. New York: Cambridge University Press.

Tarrow, Sidney. 1998. *Power in Movement*. New York: Cambridge University Press.

Thies, Cameron G. 2005. "War, Rivalry, and State Building in Latin America." *American Journal of Political Science* 49, no. 3: 451–65.

Tilly, Charles. 1985. "War Making and State Making as Organized Crime." In *Bringing the State Back In*, ed. Peter Evans, Dietrich Rueschemeyer, and Theda Skocpol, 160–91. New York: Cambridge University Press.

Tilly, Charles. 1994. "The Time of States." *Social Research* 61, no. 2: 269–95.

Tilly, Charles, and Sidney G. Tarrow. 2015. *Contentious Politics*. New York: Oxford University Press.

Toews, Gerhard, and Pierre-Louis Vezina. 2020. "Enemies of the People." King's College London Quantitative Political Economy Working Paper.

Treisman, Daniel. 2020. "Democracy by Mistake: How the Errors of Autocrats Trigger Transitions to Freer Government." *American Political Science Review* 114, no. 3: 792–810.

Van Zanden, Jan Luiten, Eltjo Buringh, and Maarten Bosker. 2012. "The Rise and Decline of European Parliaments, 1188–1789." *Economic History Review* 65, no. 3: 835–61.

Verghese, Ajay, and Emmanuel Teitelbaum. 2019. "Conquest and Conflict: The Colonial Roots of Maoist Violence in India." *Politics & Society* 47, no. 1: 55–86.

Voigtländer, Nico, and Hans-Joachim Voth. 2012. "Persecution Perpetuated: The Medieval Origins of Anti-Semitic Violence in Nazi Germany." *Quarterly Journal of Economics* 127, no. 3: 1339–92.

Voth, Hans Joachim. 2011. "Debt, Default and Empire: State Capacity and Economic Development in England and Spain in the Early Modern Period." R.H. Tawney Memorial Lecture, Economic History Society Annual Conference.

Wang, Yuhua. 2018, "Sons and Lovers: Political Stability in China and Europe before the Great Divergence." Available at SSRN 3058065.

Wang, Yuhua. 2022. *The Rise and Fall of Imperial China: The Social Origins of State Development*. Princeton, NJ: Princeton University Press.

Wedeen, Lisa. 1998. "Acting 'as If': Symbolic Politics and Social Control in Syria." *Comparative Studies in Society and History* 40, no. 3: 503–23.

Weyland, Kurt. 2009. "The Diffusion of Revolution: '1848' in Europe and Latin America." *International Organization* 63, no. 3: 391–423.

Weyland, Kurt. 2014. *Making Waves: Democratic Contention in Europe and Latin America since the Revolutions of 1848*. New York: Cambridge University Press.

Wintrobe, Ronald. 1998. *The Political Economy of Dictatorship*. New York: Cambridge University Press.

Wittenberg, Jason. 2006. *Crucibles of Political Loyalty: Church Institutions and Electoral Continuity in Hungary*. New York: Cambridge University Press.

Wittenberg, Jason. 2015. "Conceptualizing Historical Legacies." *East European Politics and Societies* 29, no. 2: 366–78.

Xi, Tianyang. 2019. "All the Emperor's Men? Conflicts and Power-Sharing in Imperial China." *Comparative Political Studies* 52, no. 8: 1099–130.

Zhukov, Yuri M., and Roya Talibova. 2018. "Stalin's Terror and the Long-Term Political Effects of Mass Repression." *Journal of Peace Research* 55, no. 2: 267–83.

Ziblatt, Daniel. 2008. "Does Landholding Inequality Block Democratization?: A Test of the 'Bread and Democracy' Thesis and the Case of Prussia." *World Politics* 60, no. 4: 610–41.

Ziblatt, Daniel. 2009. "Shaping Democratic Practice and the Causes of Electoral Fraud: The Case of Nineteenth-Century Germany." *American Political Science Review* 103, no. 1: 1–21.

Ziblatt, Daniel. 2017. *Conservative Political Parties and the Birth of Modern Democracy in Europe*. New York: Cambridge University Press.

CHAPTER 10

DYNASTIES IN HISTORICAL POLITICAL ECONOMY

BRENDA VAN COPPENOLLE AND DANIEL M. SMITH

Dynasties and Political Power

POLITICAL dynasties are as old as politics. Whenever societies organize people into those with the power to rule and those who are ruled, a mechanism for selecting the former must exist. Throughout most of human history, family ties through blood or marriage to the outgoing ruler have served as an important (but not singular) organizing principle in that selection decision. Indeed, the history of the world is often organized around the reigns of monarchs—and the conflicts that arise in replacing them. The modern development of representative democracy, whereby rulers are selected via elections by a broadly enfranchised citizenry, might be expected to shift power away from dynasties. But even within democracies, members of established political families often continue to enjoy an advantage over newcomers in gaining and holding onto power.

A growing literature in political science, history, and economics considers not only the puzzle of why dynastic selection into power occurs—in both autocracies and democracies—but also whether dynastic rule produces any meaningful consequences for the quality of governance and other outcomes. When and why do dynasties emerge or fade from political life? Does hereditary succession into power produce stability or conflict? Do dynastic leaders bring long-term economic growth or stagnation? Are dynastic leaders of higher or lower quality than nondynastic leaders? And what is the relationship between the persistence of dynasties and features of the political and economic environment, such as the institutions of elections and political parties, or the relative value of political office compared to private enterprise? These kinds of questions place the puzzle of dynasties at the intersection of the various disciplines that have inspired the development of historical political economy (HPE) as a distinct field of research.

This chapter reviews the historical and contemporary roles that family ties play in political selection. Broadly, the evolution of dynastic politics over time can be characterized by three patterns of decline. First, in terms of regime type across states, there has been a long-term decline in monarchies and family-based dictatorships, in favor of representative democracy with directly or indirectly elected executives. Second, within democracies there has been a long-term decline in the presence of elected members of dynasties serving in national legislatures, as political parties have institutionalized the processes of recruitment, campaigning, and elections. Exceptions to this pattern among advanced industrialized democracies are found where parties are weak and elections are highly personalized. Third, a decline can be observed in the gendered nature of dynastic selection into politics; while women have historically been more likely to enter politics through a dynastic channel, this pattern has declined over time as gender representation has increased.

Despite these general tendencies for hereditary selection into politics to decline over time, members of dynasties continue to enjoy significant advantages in democracies—not only in getting recruited and elected, but also in reaching the highest positions of power in the executive. Although democracies select rulers through elections, and parties provide a vehicle for ambitious newcomers to enter into politics, dynasties remain relevant to understanding power in democracies around the world. The impact of these modern-day democratic dynasties on political outcomes, and how the evolution of dynastic power coincides with broader patterns in the historical development of states, are important frontiers for research in historical political economy.

The First Decline: Absolute Monarchies and Personalist Autocracies

There are numerous theories of the early origins of the state and its consolidation (see Diamond 1997; Spruyt 2002; Scott 2017; Grzymala-Busse 2020). A stylized view of the conventional wisdom begins with small kinship-based groups of nomadic peoples led by elders or chiefs. The development of agriculture and domestication of animals around 8000 BCE allowed for sedentary settlement and the accumulation of surplus food. This in turn led to technological innovation, the development of societal hierarchies, conquest and expansion, and the accumulation of greater wealth and power. While early forms of democracy (or oligarchy) existed throughout the premodern world (see Stasavage 2020), in most premodern states hereditary rule emerged as a logical extension of kinship to manage societies as they enlarged (Duindam 2016).[1]

If a society is ruled by a king, there must be some mechanism—a succession rule—for replacing him when he dies or vacates office peacefully (i.e., is not overthrown by a rival who becomes the new king). Open competition by would-be successors inevitably invites conflict and disorder, and appointing a successor in advance may create incentives for that successor to depose the king to take power for himself (Herz 1952). An expectation of hereditary succession, in contrast, reduces the pool of would-be successors to family relatives, but might still invite intrafamilial conflict over which relative will take power. In most early forms of kingship in Europe (and elsewhere), succession decisions involved some combination of hereditary right, the strength or suitability of would-be rulers, and some form of election by peers (Duindam 2016, 145).

Primogeniture emerged later and appeared throughout the world, most notably in Europe. Succession by the eldest son brings some risk of a weak ruler coming into power, but is thought to have aided political stability by constraining elite expectations about which of the many potential successors could be deemed legitimate, and by reducing the risk of early coups (Tullock 1987; Kurrild-Klitgaard 2000). As Kokkonen and Sundell (2014) summarize, primogeniture as a succession rule provides an autocrat with "an heir, who because of his young age, can afford to wait to inherit power peacefully, and it provides the elite with assurance that the regime will continue to live on and reward their loyalty."

The expectation of hereditary succession may have also created incentives for good governance by incumbent rulers, who would have viewed their rule with a longer time horizon and would have wanted to bequeath a well-functioning state to their progeny (Olson 1993). In Olson's terms, monarchs can be characterized as "stationary bandits," with incentives to respect private property and promote growth, in contrast to "roving bandits," who simply take what they can extract and move on. If an incumbent monarch expects to bequeath his realm to a son or other relative, he has greater incentives to ensure its security and economic well-being. Considering economic growth and leaders between 1874 and 2004, dynastic leaders were indeed found to improve growth, but only when executive constraints were weak (Besley and Reynal-Querol 2017).

Conflict can still arise under hereditary succession rules, whether due to a lack of male relatives or because the monarch dies before an heir is old enough to command the allegiance of the broader elite. For example, Abramson and Velasco Rivera (2016) find that (male) leaders from 505 BCE to 1900 CE with longer tenures were more often succeeded by their sons, and that these successors were less likely to be deposed or face parliamentary constraints. Kokkonen et al. (2021) similarly find that European monarchs from 1000 to 1799 CE with larger families were less frequently deposed, since the pool of potential successors was deeper. Broader kinship networks between rulers are also thought to have reduced interstate conflict in historical Europe (Benzell and Cooke 2021). When women took power in the absence of a male heir, the uncertainty that followed their succession also encouraged conflict. Exploiting gender and birth order, Dube and Harish (2020) find that single queens were more often attacked, and married queens more often went on the attack, compared to kings.

In a study of European rulers between 1000 and 1500 CE, Acharya and Lee (2019) argue that conflict over succession led to weaker state institutions and long-term negative effects on economic development, measured in contemporary GDP per capita.

Blaydes and Chaney (2013) similarly connect economic stagnation in the Islamic world to shorter tenures of Muslim sultans compared to Europe's Christian monarchs. These kinds of arguments find parallels in contemporary HPE debates over the long-run effects of war and other forms of conflict on economic and social development (e.g., Miguel and Roland 2011; Davis and Weinstein 2002; Cassar, Grosjean, and Whitt 2013; Charnysh and Finkel 2017).

In short, dynastic rule is believed to have contributed to the development of state capacity and long-term economic growth, and it arguably provided stability when no alternative (parliamentary) institutions were present to provide this role. However, hereditary succession is an imperfect solution to maintaining political stability. As noted, if a family in power lacked a sufficient number of qualified heirs, conflict often ensued in violent wars of succession. Over time, most societies have either reduced the political power of monarchs, making them subservient to elected legislatures, or rejected them entirely in favor of a republican form of government.

Figure 10.1 illustrates this pattern using comparative data from Gerring et al. (2021), who define a "monarchy" as a state in which executive office is (1) held by a single person, (2) endowed with life tenure, (3) hereditary, and (4) of nontrivial importance. From the 1700s to the early 1800s, the share of all states headed by a monarch was relatively stable—roughly 60 percent of states in Europe, and three-quarters of all states around the world. This pattern gave way to a period of decline in the 1800s. By the 1980s, fewer than 10 percent of states were ruled by a monarch. Today, only a handful

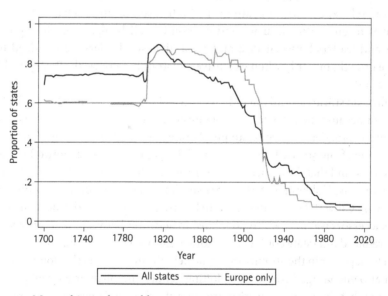

FIGURE 10.1. Monarchies in the world, 1700–present

Note: Figure created by the authors using data from Gerring et al. (2021). Each line indicates the share of monarchies among all states (and those in Europe only) over time. Monarchies are defined as states in which executive power is (1) held by a single person, (2) endowed with life tenure, (3) hereditary, and (4) of nontrivial importance.

of monarchs retain their title and powers—in Bahrain, Bhutan, Brunei, Jordan, Kuwait, Liechtenstein, Monaco, Morocco, Oman, Qatar, Saudi Arabia, Swaziland, Tonga, and the United Arab Emirates. Many of the remaining monarchies are concentrated in the Middle East, where they have proven more stable than other forms of government in the region (Herb 1999; Kostiner 2000; Menaldo 2012; McMillan 2013).

Beyond the remaining formal monarchies, a small number of personal dictatorships feature rulers with nearly absolute executive power, even if the title of king is absent. Hereditary succession in modern autocracies of this kind might persist so long as the party system or leadership selection mechanisms are weak, and power distributions and access to rents among the broader elite class are sustained (e.g., Bueno de Mesquita et al. 2003; Brownlee 2007; Svolik 2012; Meng 2021). Examples of contemporary autocratic dynasties include the Kim dynasty in North Korea and the Assad dynasty in Syria (Monday 2011; Yates 2021).

The question of when and why rulers relinquish dynastic control of power, and how representative democracy emerges, forms a broad research agenda within HPE and related disciplines (e.g., Acemoglu and Robinson 2005; Boix 2010; Capoccia and Ziblatt 2010; Albertus and Menaldo 2017; Grzymala-Busse and Finkel 2023). We leave aside the question of why these processes occurred in some countries at a certain point in time and focus in the next section on the patterns of dynastic representation following democratization.

The Second Decline: Democratization and "Democratic Dynasties"

Democracy is ostensibly the antithesis to monarchy, offering an alternative mechanism for political selection that replaces hereditary claims to legitimacy with popular election by enfranchised citizens. The development and diffusion of democratic institutions proceeded in tandem with industrialization and modernization, which might also be expected to facilitate a decline in the power of the dominant elite families (e.g., Huntington 1966; Adams 2005). In the words of Fukuyama (2011, 51), modernization entails "a transition from kinship-based forms of organization to state-level organization."

Scholars have long noticed, however, that even after the introduction of democracy, elite families tended to maintain their dominant positions of power (Michels 1915 [1911]; Pareto 1916; Mosca 1939; Manin 1997; Offerlé 1993). In many European democracies, for example, members of the predemocratic aristocracy or nobility simply entered into the practice of democratic politics, whether in fully elected bodies such as the British House of Commons, or in upper chambers with restricted membership, such as the House of Lords (Best and Cotta 2000; Berlinski, Dewan, and Van Coppenolle 2014; Rush 2000; Wasson 1991). Even in the United States, where the Constitution establishes that "no title of nobility shall be granted," several families have sent multiple members to Congress and the presidency. Many of America's early dynasties, such as the Adams family, shared an elite background, often with direct connections to the American Revolution (Hess 1966). However, as the United States grew and developed, new dynasties continued to form, in all levels of government and with various backgrounds (e.g., Clubok, Wilensky, and Berghorn 1969; Dal Bó, Dal Bó, and Snyder 2009; Gronnerud and Spitzer 2018).

Philosophers from Aristotle to Rousseau viewed any form of election as intrinsically aristocratic compared to selection by lot. Elaborating on these arguments, Manin (1997) attributes the persistent "aristocratic character" of elections to four factors: (1) the unequal evaluation of candidates by voters (voters' intrinsic preferences for certain kinds of representatives), (2) the way in which choice necessitates distinction (to be successful, a candidate must stand out above others by possessing positively valued aspects of quality), (3) the advantage of salience (name recognition or network centrality), and (4) the cost of disseminating information (wealth and other resource advantages in campaigns). Each of these factors gives members of an established elite—whether incumbent politicians or their offspring—an advantage over newcomers in winning elections.

The various advantages enjoyed by members of dynasties (voter preferences, name recognition, network connections, campaign finance resources, etc.), and how these contribute to their continued grip on power within democracies, have been the subject of several empirical studies in political science and economics, focused not only on the United States (e.g., Dal Bó, Dal Bó, and Snyder 2009; Feinstein 2010) but also other democracies around the world (e.g., Chhibber 2013; Asako et al. 2015; Querubín 2012; 2016; Chandra 2016; Rossi 2017; Smith and Martin 2017; Cruz, Labonne, and Querubín 2017; Van Coppenolle 2017; Fiva and Smith 2018; Smith 2018).

Several of the factors behind the persistence of democratic dynasties can be categorized as operating on the "supply side" of political selection (Norris 1997), because they explain why would-be dynastic candidates might desire to enter politics. These include informational advantages, political socialization, and even personality traits (Oskarsson, Dawes, and Lindgren 2018; Lawless 2012). Others are better thought of as "demand-side" factors, that is, reasons for why party elites and voters might want to select dynastic candidates. These include name recognition in candidate-centered elections, campaign finance resources, and network centrality (Feinstein 2010; Chhibber 2013; Cruz, Labonne, and Querubín 2017; Chandra 2016; Smith 2018). Dynastic ties might generally function as an important signal of quality for new candidates, as party elites or voters can infer the quality of the (unknown) junior member from the (known) quality of the senior member (e.g., Folke, Rickne, and Smith 2021).

A key empirical finding across several contexts is that longer tenures in office increase the probability of hereditary succession (e.g., Smith 2018). However, disentangling the supply and demand effects of length in office is tricky—more time in power increases the potential socialization of a politician's offspring and their desire to continue the family business, but it also increases the value of the family brand to voters and parties. Moreover, longer tenures are usually associated with higher-quality politicians, who might in turn have higher-quality offspring. A causal effect of (re)election on dynasty

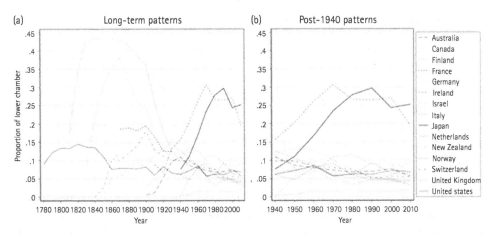

FIGURE 10.2. Dynasties in democracies over time
Note: Data are from Smith (2018), with the exception of the United Kingdom (Van Coppenolle 2017), France (Cirone and Van Coppenolle 2018; 2019), and the Netherlands (Van Coppenolle 2022). Each line indicates the share of junior dynastic politicians among members of the lower chamber of each country over time (aggregated to decades). Panel (a) provides a long-term view of the data; panel (b) focuses only on the post-1940s period.

formation for marginal candidates (who might otherwise be considered equivalent in terms of quality to marginal losers) has been found in the United States and the Philippines (Dal Bó, Dal Bó, and Snyder 2009; Querubín 2016), but not in Norway or the United Kingdom (Fiva and Smith 2018; Van Coppenolle 2017).

Despite the advantages that members of dynasties enjoy in elections, if we look at historical data on legislative backgrounds, we see again that the general tendency is for dynastic legislators in democracies to decline in prevalence over time. Figure 10.2 illustrates this pattern, using comparative data from Smith (2018), Cirone and Van Coppenolle (2018; 2019), and Van Coppenolle (2017; 2022) on national legislators in fifteen advanced industrialized democracies.[2] Panel (a) on the left provides a full view of the long-term patterns in dynasties in the lower chamber of each country. Panel (b) on the right zooms in on the post-1940 data to more clearly show variation across countries in recent decades. The data for each country are aggregated to decades.

In most democracies, the pattern that emerges is an initial increase in dynastic legislators, followed by a steady decline.[3] In the early decades of American democracy, for example, about 15 percent of the House of Representatives were dynastic, but this figure declined in the mid-1800s and has stayed in the range of 6 to 8 percent. The Senate once featured more dynasties—over 20 percent of members in the late 1800s and early 1990s—but has since come to resemble the House. Van Coppenolle (2017) similarly documents that the share of dynastic members in the British House of Commons declined from more than 30 percent in the late 1800s to less than 10 percent in recent years. The exceptions to this general pattern are Ireland and Japan, where a relatively high proportion of dynastic legislators has been attributed to highly personalistic elections and decentralized party organizations (Smith 2018; Smith and Martin 2017; Gallagher 2003).

What explains the general decline in democratic dynasties over time? Clubok, Wilensky, and Berghorn (1969) suggest that it can be attributed to political modernization rather than population growth or social change. Other theories developed to explain patterns in India and Japan would point to institutional changes, such as the development of strong parties or the introduction of primaries for candidate selection, as contributing factors in the diversification of the political elite (Chandra 2016; Smith 2018).

Yet not all institutional changes were equally effective at tipping the equilibrium away from hereditary succession in politics. Take the nineteenth-century franchise extension in the United Kingdom, whereby a broader share of the male population was given the vote conditional on meeting certain property thresholds. Berlinski, Dewan, and Van Coppenolle (2014) find no evidence that the identities of representatives in constituencies where a larger share of the population was enfranchised changed, including whether representatives came from existing dynasties. In other contexts, the mere introduction of direct accountability through elections appears to have been effective at reducing dynasties. For example, direct elections in the bicameral Netherlands, whereby the upper chamber remained indirectly elected, reduced the share of dynasties by increasing competition between incumbents (Van Coppenolle 2022).

Electoral-system reforms that strengthen parties can also reduce the power of dynasties. In Japan, dynasties became far less likely to form after an electoral reform that eliminated intraparty competition and thereby shifted the focus of electoral competition toward parties rather than candidates (Smith 2018). Redistricting can have similar effects. Van Coppenolle (2021) documents how nineteenth-century redistricting in the United Kingdom, conditional on this redistribution not having been biased toward any party, reduced the chances of politicians' relatives entering into politics. Finally, Querubin (2012) finds that the introduction of term limits in the Philippines worked counterproductively: it encouraged dynastic candidates to run when a relative was term-limited. These findings suggest that caution is warranted in taking at face value the idea that institutional reforms will automatically reduce dynasties. Precisely which institutional conditions will decrease the prevalence of dynasties may be context-specific, and untangling the causal mechanisms requires careful attention.

A small but growing set of studies examines the consequences of dynastic legislators for the quality of governance and economic outcomes (e.g., Geys and Smith 2017). In this regard, the existing evidence paints a mixed picture. For example, Asako et al. (2015) find that dynastic legislators in Japan bring more distributive benefits to their districts, but do not improve the economic performance (growth) of those districts.[4] Similarly, Dulay and Go (2021) find that mayors in the Philippines who serve concurrently with relatives spend more but do not produce higher economic growth or lower poverty. Dynastic legislators in the Philippine Congress also tend to represent districts with lower indicators of human development and higher levels of inequality (Mendoza et al. 2012), and appear to be less engaged in legislative activities (Panao 2016). In contrast, Bragança, Ferraz, and Rios (2015) find no evidence for public goods provision differences between dynastic and nondynastic legislators in Brazil. Labonne, Parsa, and Querubin (2021) also find no such differences among male and female dynastic mayors in the Philippines. There may be important differences in the effects of dynastic representation on economic performance in developed versus developing countries, or across institutional environments, which will only become clear with further empirical investigation.[5]

The Third Decline: Dynastic Pathways to Gender Representation

A third important pattern of decline in the historical evolution of dynastic politics relates to gender. Across many democracies, women in politics have been more likely to have family ties to a current or former politician than their male counterparts. This tendency has been observed both at the level of legislatures (Folke, Rickne, and Smith 2021; Schwindt-Bayer, Valleja, and Cantú 2020; Basu 2016; Hinojosa 2012) and in executive offices (Derichs and Thompson 2013; Jalalzai 2013; Jalalzai and Rincker 2018; Baturo and Gray 2018).

The first woman elected to the US House of Representatives, Jeannette Rankin, hailed from a local political family in Montana. For other early women in American politics, the dynastic pathway took the form of the so-called widow's succession, following the death of an incumbent male relative (Kincaid 1978; Gertzog 1980). Early congresswomen Rebecca Latimer Felton, Winifred S. Huck, Mae Ella Nolan, Florence Kahn, Edith Nourse Rogers, Pearl Peden Oldfield, and Ruth Bryan Owen all followed deceased husbands or fathers into office. The husband of another, Kathleen Langley, was only *politically* dead—"Pork Barrel John" Langley resigned his seat after being convicted of violating Prohibition laws by trying to sell fourteen hundred bottles of whiskey. His wife ran for his seat as a "vindication campaign."[6] Such female legislators, in the United States and elsewhere, have sometimes been characterized as proxies for their male relatives or placeholders until a male politician (sometimes from the same family) becomes available (Jalalzai 2013; Hinojosa 2012; Derichs and Thompson 2013). But as the breakers of glass ceilings, they played an important role in expanding subsequent opportunities for nondynastic women.

Folke, Rickne, and Smith (2021) explain the prevalence of dynastic women in politics on the basis of informational asymmetries in political selection decisions. As noted earlier, dynastic ties can function as a signal of quality to the party selectorate or voters, with the (unknown) quality of a would-be junior member of a dynasty being inferred from the (known) quality of the senior member. However, this signal should be more important for women due to their informational disadvantages in a male-dominated political marketplace. As a result, we may observe what Folke, Rickne, and Smith (2021) call a dynastic bias in women's representation, measured as the difference in the proportion of dynasties among female legislators and the proportion of dynasties among male legislators in a given legislature. As more women enter politics, we should expect this dynastic bias to decline.

The empirical evidence from the United States and other democracies confirms that dynastic ties become less important to women's representation as more women enter into politics. In the most recent US Congresses, for example, the dynastic bias in women's representation has been almost entirely erased. There has also been a qualitative shift, in the United States and elsewhere, in the types of dynastic women who run: from mostly widows or wives in earlier decades to daughters, nieces, and other second-generation relatives in more recent times (Folke, Rickne, and Smith 2021). For example, the most powerful woman in the 117th US Congress (2021–2023), House Speaker Nancy Pelosi, is the daughter of former representative Thomas D'Alesandro Jr., and she did not directly succeed him in the same district.

Figure 10.3 illustrates the general tendency for the dynastic bias in women's representation to decline, using pooled data from twelve advanced industrialized democracies. As panel (a) illustrates, as the overall share of women in legislatures increased over time, the share of these elected women who came from dynasties decreased. Panel (b) shows the relationship between the dynastic bias in women's representation and the share of women in the legislature. This bias is larger when there are fewer women overall. No

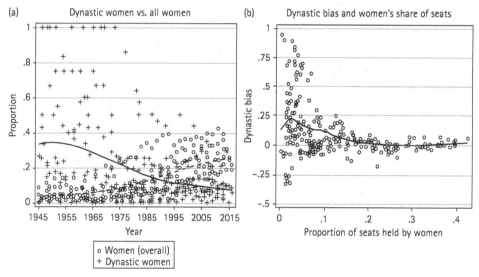

FIGURE 10.3. Dynastic paths for women into politics over time
Note: Panel (a) pools the data and plots the share of women in the legislature (gray circles; dashed lowess curve) and the share of dynasties among the women (black pluses; solid lowess curve). Panel (b) plots, for each legislature, the dynastic bias in women's representation (share of dynastic MPs among women minus the share of dynastic MPs among men) and the share of women in the legislature.

Adapted from Folke, Rickne, and Smith (2021). Data from 1945 for twelve democracies as in Smith (2018).

significant relationship exists between the share of men (or women) in office and dynastic patterns among the men.

Do male and female dynastic legislators behave differently in office? We know that electing women to political office affects policy outcomes and even wider gender attitudes in society (see, e.g., Bratton and Ray 2002; Pande 2003; Chattopadhyay and Duflo 2004; Beaman et al. 2009). Analyzing the behavioral differences between dynastic women and men forms a rich area for further study. In a study comparing male and female dynastic mayors, for example, no evidence was found that women acted differently, in terms of public goods provision, from their male dynastic colleagues (Labonne, Parsa, and Querubin 2021).[7] Future work could investigate such effects not only for women but also for other traditionally underrepresented groups, such as racial and ethnic minorities and young people, among dynastic candidates.

Finally, informational asymmetries in elections can exist not only between dynastic candidates and voters, but also on the part of the party organization tasked with candidate selection. One possibility is that dynastic women may be temporarily easier to recruit than nondynastic women after sudden changes, such as the expansion of suffrage to women or the introduction of gender quotas. Gender quotas impose a sudden shock, which has been shown in some cases to reduce the number of lower-quality men on party lists in favor of a larger slate of women (Besley, Folke, and Rickne 2017). When parties must increase the share of nominations going to women because of the introduction of a quota, dynastic women will have an informational advantage over their nondynastic competitors. Yet this equilibrium should also change once parties learn more about female candidates and the informational asymmetries abate (Folke, Rickne, and Smith 2021; Schwindt-Bayer, Vallejo, and Cantú 2020).

PERSISTENT DYNASTIC ADVANTAGE AT THE TOP

We have so far documented the general decline in the power of dynasties within democracies, despite persistent advantages in winning elections. A final advantage of dynastic family ties relates to career progression. Across many democracies, members of dynasties appear to be able to climb the ranks of power into executive offices more quickly than their nondynastic peers, particularly if they had relatives who served in previous cabinets (Smith and Martin 2017; Van Coppenolle 2017; Smith 2018). As a result, dynastic politicians can often be found at the apex of power in democracies, even where the share of dynasties among all legislators in general is low.

A possible straightforward explanation for their early and repeated electoral success is that talent or motivation for politics simply runs in families. Yet if this were the only relevant explanation, we should not observe such large interpersonal incumbency advantages, particularly among winners of narrow elections. Nor are differences in political quality—for example, talent, motivation, or skills—likely to completely explain differences in career progression between dynastic and nondynastic legislators.

Instead, an informative signal about what they will bring to politics, inferred from their relatives' reputations, is likely what makes junior members of dynasties more successful at different career stages, such as (re)selection, (re)election, and promotion to ministerial positions. In these selection processes with informational asymmetries, dynastic status can signal a politician's quality and motivation, and this signal is not as readily available to nondynastic competitors. A familiar surname, perhaps in combination with an elite education, can provide a positive informative signal directly; but dynastic legislators may also signal more indirectly, if they enter parliament at an earlier age and tend to stay longer, building up more experience along the way. In addition to advantages in signaling, dynastic candidates may also have improved access to information because of their networks and connections (Smith and Martin 2017). Nepotism cannot be ruled out, but it is unlikely to be the primary driver of the dynastic bias in executive appointments, as parliaments hold executives to account in democracies.

Of course, while executives and their dynastic members may be dependent on parliaments, they are not necessarily directly elected by these parliaments. Differences in parliamentarism and presidentialism may help explain some variation in dynastic membership of executives. Moreover, not all parliamentary democracies require ministers to be selected from parliament. Yet where they are, the composition of parliament will matter. Therefore, the proportion of dynastic members of the executive will certainly be associated with the proportion of dynastic members in parliament.

Within parties, we know that seniority matters for selection into higher office (Cirone, Cox, and Fiva 2021), and this likely extends to the top offices of the cabinet. Therefore, if dynastic members have longer tenures, this could explain part of their higher selection chances. It is difficult to think of a good counterfactual to selection by parties—that is, an alternative, or baseline, political selection rule. One such rule could be the random draw. For obvious reasons, executives are not drawn randomly from the legislature. However, some past work has exploited random draws from the legislature to study election to committees and subsequent cabinet appointment (Cirone and Van Coppenolle 2018). Under this alternative of lottery-based selection rule, dynasties were not particularly advantaged (Cirone and Van Coppenolle 2019). Smith (2018) shows that dynastic legislators in Japan enjoyed no significant advantage in promotion when seniority norms were in place, but that they gained an advantage when those norms were relaxed.

To illustrate some of these patterns of dynastic cabinet selection, Table 10.1 presents the results of several simple regression models on a combined comparative sample of parliaments over time (see Cirone and Van Coppenolle 2018; 2019; Smith 2018; Van Coppenolle 2017; 2022). We investigate the career outcomes (promotion to cabinet at any point) for legislators based on their characteristics at the time of their first entry into parliament, and consider as explanatory variables their junior dynastic status, whether their relative had previously served as a cabinet minister, their age at entry,

Table 10.1. Dynastic advantage in reaching the executive (cabinet)

DV: Ever appointed to cabinet?	(1)	(2)	(3)	(4)	(5)	Before 1940 (6)	After 1940 (7)
Junior	0.061***	0.044***	0.040***	0.058***	0.045***	0.012*	0.084***
	[0.005]	[0.006]	[0.006]	[0.005]	[0.007]	[0.006]	[0.012]
Cabinet junior		0.083***	0.089***		0.077***	0.065***	0.079***
		[0.012]	[0.013]		[0.013]	[0.014]	[0.019]
Age			-0.001***	-0.001***	-0.001***		
			[0.000]	[0.000]	[0.000]		
Junior *Age			<0.001				
			[0.001]				
Cabinet junior *Age			0.002**				
			[0.001]				
Female				-0.002	-0.001		
				[0.006]	[0.006]		
Junior *Female				-0.034	-0.049*		
				[0.022]	[0.025]		
Cabinet junior *Female					0.013		
					[0.051]		
Observations	45,526	37,827	37,573	44,186	37,027	15,093	22,734
R-squared	0.075	0.075	0.076	0.078	0.075	0.063	0.074

Note: Dependent variable is a dummy indicating MPs who are ever appointed to a cabinet position from the lower chamber Data are from Smith (2018), with the exception of the United Kingdom (Van Coppenolle 2017), France (Cirone and Van Coppenolle 2019), and the Netherlands (Van Coppenolle 2022), excluding the United States and Italy, for which cabinet information is unavailable. Sample includes legislators at first entry to the lower chamber, for the following countries and years: Australia (1901–2013), Canada (1867–2015), Finland (1907–2011), France (1877–1932), Germany (1949–2013), Ireland (1918–2016), Israel (1949–2015), Japan (1947–2014), the Netherlands (1815–1940), New Zealand (1853–2014), Norway (1945–2013), Switzerland (1848–2011), and the UK (1832–2010). Models 2, 3, 5, 6, and 7 exclude Switzerland and France (for which cabinet legacy information is unavailable). Columns 4 and 5 exclude the Netherlands (for which gender information is unavailable). Columns 6 and 7 split the sample from column 2 into two time periods. Age is demeaned by sample; average age is about 46. All regressions include country and year fixed effects.

* p-value < 0.10; ** p-value < 0.05; *** p-value < 0.001.

and their gender. Each of the models includes year and country fixed effects, and robust standard errors.

In the full sample, dynastic legislators are about 6 percentage points more likely than nondynastic legislators to be appointed to a cabinet position at some point in their careers (Model 1). Yet once we split up that group into those with and without ties to a former cabinet minister, we find that junior members are only 4 percentage points more likely to enter the cabinet than others. In contrast, cabinet legacies are an additional 8 percentage points more likely to enter the cabinet than those without any family connections (Model 2).

One reason dynastic legislators enjoy an advantage could be their age; they tend to be younger than nondynastic legislators when they enter parliament, and a lower age at entry should be particularly important in legislatures or parties operating under a seniority system. Controlling for age at first entry does not substantively change the estimated dynastic advantage in entering the cabinet (Model 3). Age at entry itself seems unimportant—except for the cabinet legacies (Model 3). Junior relatives of former cabinet ministers are more likely to be appointed the older they are at first entry. In general, the effect size for the dynastic advantage in promotion is largely unchanged by controlling for age at entry and its interaction with dynastic status.

The next pair of models considers whether women, and dynastic women in particular, are more often appointed to the cabinet. The results suggest that dynastic women are not more likely to enter the cabinet (Models 4 and 5). If anything, female dynastic legislators are less likely than their male dynastic colleagues to have entered the cabinet over time—and any differences among male and female relatives of past cabinet ministers are insignificant (Model 5). The coefficients on junior and cabinet junior also remain virtually unchanged after controlling for gender. These findings suggest a need for more research on the gendered dynastic paths to executive power, and how cabinet composition differs from that of presidents and prime ministers (see, e.g., Jalalzai 2013; Jalalzai and Rincker 2018; Baturo and Gray 2018).

Notably, regardless of country and year fixed effects, the R-squared of these regressions remains low. That means a lot of variation in cabinet appointments cannot be explained by these simple individual-level characteristics alone. Yet the junior dynastic advantage in entering a cabinet remains quite stable between 4 and 6 percentage points across our models. Moreover, the advantage appears to have become larger over time. The estimated cabinet selection advantage for dynastic legislators is smaller when restricting the sample to legislators who first entered parliament prior to 1940 (Model 6) than for those who entered after 1940 (Model 7). Viewed in the context of the historical patterns we document in this chapter, this implies that the dynastic advantage in reaching the top echelons of power has increased even as the relative share of dynasties in politics has declined. This could be because the average quality of dynastic legislators increases as the overall prevalence of dynasties declines (i.e., suggesting better selection from among would-be dynastic candidates), though we lack the kind of observable data on legislators' quality that would be needed to test this hypothesis.

Moving Forward

We see several opportunities and challenges for future historical political economy research on dynasties.

First, a more complete understanding of the historical role of dynasties in democratic transitions and development will require more data and within-case identification from different countries. Much of the existing data collection efforts have focused on advanced developed democracies, where historical biographical records have often been digitized (e.g., Smith 2018; Van Coppenolle 2017), or developing democracies where dynasties are especially prevalent, such as the Philippines (e.g., Querubin 2016; Cruz, Labonne, and Querubín 2017), or India (Chandra 2016). This raises the possibility of selection bias in comparative analyses and limits the number of explanatory variables related to institutions and economic development that can be tested. Several recent efforts to collect data on dynasties in other countries will help push the boundaries of research on contemporary dynastic politics (e.g., Batto 2018; Patrikios and Chatzikonstantinou 2015; Amundsen 2016; Purdey 2016; Thananithichot and Satidporn 2016; Nishizaki 2018). More data from bicameral legislatures and local assemblies will also be helpful, as will data on family ties beyond executive leaders in authoritarian regimes (e.g., Shih, Adolph and Liu 2012).

Collecting and coding historical information on family ties also presents challenges (Cirone and Spirling 2021), but such data could contribute to understanding causes of dynasties or their decline by exploiting quasi-natural experiments within specific countries. A clear opportunity for HPE scholars in particular is to focus on particular historical episodes—democratization, expansion of the franchise, electoral system reforms, introduction of primaries, term limits, quotas, redistricting, direct elections, and so on—and how these episodes broadened opportunities for nondynastic politicians. Is the general decline in democratic dynasties an inevitable part of democratic modernization, or can it be sped up through specific institutional reforms? How dynastic politics interact with party development is a broad, open research agenda.

Second, there is also a need to better connect the largely separate literatures on monarchies, kinship networks, and democratic dynasties. The literature reviewed in this chapter is a first effort to connect some of these literatures' themes, but few studies have directly considered the evolution of family ties in politics over time and across regime types. Further opportunities may lie in considering how the historical patterns of hereditary succession in politics we review here connect to patterns of occupational inheritance outside of politics, and social mobility and inequality in general (e.g., Blau and Duncan 1967; Laband and Lentz 1983; Clark 2014). The political behavior of family-run firms (e.g., Balan, Dodyk and Puente 2022), the politics of business connections to dynastic politicians (e.g., Fisman 2001; Wang 2017), and the cross-pollination of dynasties with political and economic power—what Mills (1956) famously termed the "power elite"—are additional areas that are ripe for comparative and historical reinvestigation.

Conclusion

As democracies mature, a common assumption is that the decline of dynasties—or families in politics—follows in tandem. In fact, this idea is so natural that it forms part of how we think about democracy. The absence of dynasties is a presumed characteristic of any meaningfully democratic regime. A pluralistic definition of democracy requires that power is shared by competing interests (see, e.g., Dahl 1989), and therefore cannot be dominated by a limited group of families.

The prevalence and power of dynasties has evolved over time, but they remain a common feature of many democracies. In an optimistic view of democratic development, any dynastic relations that remain among powerful individuals today are nothing more than curiosities. And in any case—this line of reasoning goes—these days we should no longer worry about families' undue influence on democracies as traditional family structures become less and less relevant; instead, we should worry about other vested interests, such as networks of professionals from large multinational corporations. What matters most are the institutions that have meaningfully enabled pluralistic power-sharing throughout history—such as the right to vote, the development of parties and civil society organizations, and the rise of social movements.

Rather than viewing dynasties as a curiosity or a temporary phenomenon that has been made largely obsolete by modern democratic institutions, we believe that scholars should link such institutions more explicitly to dynasties, and investigate the broader causes and consequences of increasing or declining dynastic proportions in parliament and executives. Dynasties are not only able to persist within legislative and executive offices, but often find ways to enrich and entrench themselves beyond politics. Our presumed perspective of steady dynastic decline along with democratic development may be biased by our specific position in time, which more systematic information about dynasties across space and time can address.

The problem is that without more research on dynasties in democracies, and the causes of their rise and decline, we do not know whether they are in fact harmless curiosities. Dynastic monopolization of power goes directly against the idea of broad representation in democracies and reflects political inequality across space and time—similar to how top incomes can function as an indicator of economic inequality (Van Coppenolle 2020). Whenever a small group of individuals dominates the exercise of political power, others inevitably lack representation and feel excluded by the elite. In a world of increasing economic inequality, the question of how we can expect political inequality to develop—and what, if anything, can be done about that—is ever more important.

Recent research has made considerable progress in testing the causal factors we typically attribute to dynasty formation, as well as those attributed to dynastic decline—such as the growth of elections, incumbency, or changes in gender inclusion. But the puzzles of why dynasties persist in democracies and what consequences they might bring in terms of political and economic outcomes remain important topics for future study.

Notes

1. Queens and other female rulers have been less common, although women frequently exercised influence as advisers to their male relatives (Duindam 2016); see also Dube and Harish (2020). Broader kinship networks remained an important component in the organization of power and a tool for expanding the control of the king or central leader over larger territories (e.g., Wang 2022). On oligarchy, see Winters (2011) and Ramseyer and Rosenbluth (1995). On political legitimacy more broadly, see Greif and Rubin (2023)
2. "Dynasties" are defined here as any family with two or more individuals who have served in national political office, and we only count the junior relatives who had at least one relative in parliament before their first entry (e.g., Van Coppenolle 2017; Smith 2018). This basic definition could be relaxed or constrained to include or exclude different types of relationships and different types of political offices (e.g., local versus national offices, elected or appointed). Another distinction is whether family members serve in the same office over time (vertical dynasties) or simultaneously across different offices (horizontal dynasties) (see, e.g., Dulay and Go 2021).
3. The initial increases are not especially substantively interesting, since the limited number of previous legislators in early periods means fewer potential family connections to observe.
4. Muraoka (2018) also finds that dynastic legislators in Japan tend to adopt particularistic appeals in campaign materials (candidate manifestos), and Smith (2018) finds that dynastic legislators whose relatives previously served in the cabinet are more active in legislative debates.
5. Other effects of democratic dynasties are also only beginning to be investigated. For example, members of dynasties may be more inclined to try to protect democracy when it comes under threat (Lacroix, Méon, and Oosterlinck 2019).
6. See "Katherine Gudger Langley," in *Women in Congress, 1917–2006*, prepared under the direction of the Committee on House Administration by the Office of History and Preservation, US House of Representatives (Washington, DC: Government Printing Office, 2006), https://history.house.gov/Exhibition-and-Publications/WIC/Women-in-Congress.
7. In this context, many of the dynastic female majors serve only a single term, which indicates that they are placeholders for their temporarily term-limited relatives.

References

Abramson, Scott, and Carlos Velasco Rivera. 2016. "Time Is Power: The Non-institutional Sources of Stability in Autocracies." *Journal of Politics* 78, no. 4: 1279–95.

Acemoglu, Daron, and James A. Robinson. 2005. *Economic Origins of Dictatorship and Democracy*. Cambridge: Cambridge University Press.

Acharya, Avidit, and Alexander Lee. 2019. "Path Dependence in European Development: Medieval Politics, Conflict, and State Building." *Comparative Political Studies* 52, no. 13–14: 2171–206.

Adams, Julia. 2005. *The Familial State: Ruling Families and Merchant Capitalism in Early Modern Europe*. Ithaca: NY: Cornell University Press.
Albertus, Michael, and Victor Menaldo. 2017. *Authoritarianism and the Elite Origins of Democracy*. Cambridge: Cambridge University Press.
Amundsen, Inge. 2016. "Democratic Dynasties? Internal Party Democracy in Bangladesh." *Party Politics* 22, no. 1: 49–58.
Asako, Yasushi, Takeshi Iida, Tetsuya Matsubayashi, and Michiko Ueda. 2015. "Dynastic Politicians: Theory and Evidence from Japan." *Japanese Journal of Political Science* 16, no. 1: 5–32.
Balan, Pablo, Juan Dodyk, and Ignacio Puente. 2022. "The Political Behavior of Family Firms: Evidence from Brazil." *World Development* 151: 105747.
Basu, Amrita. 2016. "Women, Dynasties, and Democracy in India." In *Democratic Dynasties: State, Party, and Family in Contemporary Indian Politics*, ed. Kanchan Chandra, 127–60. Cambridge: Cambridge University Press.
Batto, Nathan F. 2018. "Legacy Candidates in Taiwan Elections, 2001–2016: Just a Bunch of Bullies." *Asian Survey* 58, no. 3: 486–510.
Baturo, Alexander, and Julia Gray. 2018. "When Do Family Ties Matter? The Duration of Female Suffrage and Women's Path to High Political Office." *Political Research Quarterly* 71, no. 3: 695–709.
Beaman, Lori, Raghabendra Chattopadhyay, Esther Duflo, Rohini Pande, and Petia Topalova. 2009. "Powerful Women: Does Exposure Reduce Bias?" *Quarterly Journal of Economics* 124, no. 4: 1497–540.
Benzell, Seth G., and Kevin Cooke. 2021. "A Network of Thrones: Kinship and Conflict in Europe, 1495–1918." *American Economic Journal: Applied Economics* 13, no. 3: 102–33.
Berlinski, Samuel, Torun Dewan, and Brenda Van Coppenolle. 2014. "Franchise Extension and the British Aristocracy." *Legislative Studies Quarterly* 39, no. 4: 531–58.
Besley, Timothy, Olle Folke, and Johanna Rickne. 2017. "Gender Quotas and the Crisis of the Mediocre Man: Theory and Evidence from Sweden." *American Economic Review* 107, no. 8: 2204–42.
Besley, Timothy, and Marta Reynal-Querol. 2017. "The Logic of Hereditary Rule: Theory and Evidence." *Journal of Economic Growth* 22, no. 2: 123–44.
Best, Heinrich, and Maurizio Cotta, eds. 2000. *Parliamentary Representatives in Europe 1848–2000*. Oxford: Oxford University Press.
Blau, Peter M., and Otis Dudley Duncan. 1967. *The American Occupational Structure*. New York: John Wiley and Sons.
Blaydes, Lisa, and Eric Chaney. 2013. "The Feudal Revolution and Europe's Rise: Political Divergence of the Christian West and the Muslim World before 1500 CE." *American Political Science Review* 107, no. 1: 16–34.
Boix, Carles. 2010. "Origins and Persistence of Economic Inequality." *Annual Review of Political Science* 13: 489–516.
Bragança, Arthur, Claudio Ferraz, and Juan Rios. 2015. "Political Dynasties and the Quality of Government." Unpublished paper, Universidade Federal de Minas Gerais, Pontifícia Universidade Católica do Rio de Janeiro (PUC-Rio), BREAD, and Stanford University.
Bratton, Kathleen A., and Leonard P. Ray. 2002. "Descriptive Representation, Policy Outcomes, and Municipal Day-Care Coverage in Norway." *American Journal of Political Science* 46, no. 2: 428–37.

Brownlee, Jason. 2007. "Hereditary Succession in Modern Autocracies." *World Politics* 59, no. 4: 595–628.

Bueno de Mesquita, Bruce, Alastair Smith, Randolph Siverson, and James Morrow. 2003. *The Logic of Political Survival*. Boston: MIT Press.

Capoccia, Giovanni, and Daniel Ziblatt. 2010. "The Historical Turn in Democratization Studies: A New Research Agenda for Europe and Beyond." *Comparative Political Studies* 43, no. 8–9: 931–68.

Cassar, Alessandra, Pauline Grosjean, and Sam Whitt. 2013. "Legacies of Violence: Trust and Market Development." *Journal of Economic Growth* 18: 285–318.

Chandra, Kanchan. 2016. "Democratic Dynasties: State, Party, and Family in Contemporary Indian Politics." In *Democratic Dynasties: State, Party, and Family in Contemporary Indian Politics*, ed. Kanchan Chandra, 10–50. Cambridge: Cambridge University Press.

Charnysh, Volha, and Evgeny Finkel. 2017. "The Death Camp Eldorado: Political and Economic Effects of Mass Violence." *American Political Science Review* 111, no. 4: 801–18.

Chattopadhyay, Raghabendra, and Esther Duflo. 2004. "Women as Policy Makers: Evidence from a Randomized Policy Experiment in India." *Econometrica* 72, no. 5: 1409–43.

Chhibber, Pradeep. 2013. "Dynastic Parties: Organization, Finance and Impact." *Party Politics* 19, no. 2: 277–95.

Cirone, Alexandra, and Brenda Van Coppenolle. 2018. "Cabinets, Committees and Careers: The Causal Effect of Committee Service." *Journal of Politics* 80, no. 3: 948–63.

Cirone, Alexandra, and Brenda Van Coppenolle. 2019. "Bridging the Gap: Lottery-Based Procedures in Early Parliamentarization." *World Politics* 71, no. 2: 197–235.

Cirone, Alexandra, Gary W. Cox, and Jon H. Fiva. 2021. "Seniority-Based Nominations and Political Careers." *American Political Science Review* 115, no. 1: 234–51.

Cirone, Alexandra, and Arthur Spirling. 2021. "Turning History into Data: Data Collection, Measurement, and Inference in HPE." *Journal of Historical Political Economy* 1, no. 1: 127–54.

Clark, Gregory. 2014. *The Son Also Rises: Surnames and the History of Social Mobility*. Princeton, NJ: Princeton University Press.

Clubok, Alfred B., Norman M. Wilensky, and Forrest J. Berghorn. 1969. "Family Relationships, Congressional Recruitment, and Political Modernization." *Journal of Politics* 31, no. 4: 1035–62.

Cruz, Cesi, Julien Labonne, and Pablo Querubín. 2017. "Politician Family Networks and Electoral Outcomes: Evidence from the Philippines." *American Economic Review* 107, no. 10: 3006–37.

Dahl, Robert A. 1989. *Democracy and Its Critics*. New Haven, CT: Yale University Press.

Dal Bó, Ernesto, Pedro Dal Bó, and Jason Snyder. 2009. "Political Dynasties." *Review of Economic Studies* 76, no. 1: 115–42.

Davis, Donald R., and David E. Weinstein. 2002. "Bones, Bombs, and Break Points: The Geography of Economic Activity." *American Economic Review* 92, no. 5: 1269–89.

Derichs, Claudia, and Mark R. Thompson, eds. 2013. *Dynasties and Female Political Leaders in Asia*. Lit Verlag Gmbh.

Diamond, Jared. 1997. *Guns, Germs, and Steel*. W. W. Norton.

Dube, Oeindrila, and S. P. Harish. 2020. "Queens." *Journal of Political Economy* 128, no. 7: 2579–652.

Duindam, Jeroen. 2016. *Dynasties: A Global History of Power, 1300–1800*. Cambridge: Cambridge University Press.

Dulay, Dean, and Laurence Go. 2021. "When Running for Office Runs in the Family: Horizontal Dynasties, Policy, and Development in the Philippines." *Comparative Political Studies* 0, no. 0: 1–40.

Feinstein, Brian D. 2010. "The Dynasty Advantage: Family Ties in Congressional Elections." *Legislative Studies Quarterly* 25, no. 4: 571–98.

Fisman, Raymond. 2001. "Estimating the Value of Political Connections." *American Economic Review* 91, no. 4: 1095–102.

Fiva, Jon H., and Daniel M. Smith. 2018. "Political Dynasties and the Incumbency Advantage in Party-Centered Environments." *American Political Science Review* 112, no. 3: 706–12.

Folke, Olle, Johanna Rickne, and Daniel M. Smith. 2021. "Gender and Dynastic Political Selection." *Comparative Political Studies* 54, no. 2: 339–71.

Fukuyama, Francis. 2011. *The Origins of Political Order*. Farrar, Straus and Giroux.

Gallagher, Michael. 2003. "Ireland: Party Loyalists with a Personal Base." In *The Political Class in Advanced Democracies*, ed. Jens Borchert and Jürgen Zeiss, 187–202. Oxford: Oxford University Press.

Gerring, John, Tore Wig, Wouter Veenendaal, Daniel Weitzel, Jan Teorell, and Kyosuke Kikuta. 2021. "Why Monarchy? The Rise and Demise of a Regime Type." *Comparative Political Studies* 54, no. 3: 585–622.

Gertzog, Irwin N. 1980. "The Matrimonial Connection: The Nomination of Congressmen's Widows for the House of Representatives." *Journal of Politics* 42, no. 3: 820–33.

Geys, Benny, and Daniel M. Smith. 2017. "Political Dynasties in Democracies: Causes, Consequences, and Remaining Puzzles." *Economic Journal* 127, no. 605: F446–F454.

Greif, Avner, and Jared Rubin. 2023. "Political Legitimacy in Historical Political Economy." In *The Oxford Handbook of Historical Political Economy*, ed. Jeffery A. Jenkins and Jared Rubin, 293–310. Oxford University Press.

Gronnerud, Kathleen, and Scott J. Spitzer, eds. 2018. *Modern American Political Dynasties: A Study of Power, Family, and Political Influence*. Praeger.

Grzymala-Busse, Anna. 2020. "Beyond War and Contracts: The Medieval and Religious Roots of the European State." *Annual Review of Political Science* 23: 19–36.

Grzymala-Busse, Anna, and Evgeny Finkel. 2022. "Historical Political Economy of Autocracy." In *The Oxford Handbook of Historical Political Economy*, ed. Jeffery A. Jenkins and Jared Rubin, 161–84. Oxford University Press.

Herb, Michael. 1999. *All in the Family: Absolutism, Revolution, and Democracy in the Middle Eastern Monarchies*. Albanny, NY: SUNY Press.

Herz, John H. 1952. "The Problem of Successorship in Dictatorial Regimes: A Study in Comparative Law and Institutions." *Journal of Politics* 14, no. 1: 19–40.

Hess, Stephen. 1966. *America's Political Dynasties: From Adams to Kennedy*. Doubleday.

Hinojosa, Magda. 2012. *Selecting Women, Electing Women: Political Representation and Candidate Selection in Latin America*. Philadelphia: Temple University Press.

Huntington, Samuel P. 1966. "The Political Modernization of Traditional Monarchies." *Daedalus* 95, no. 3: 763–88.

Jalalzai, Farida. 2013. *Shattered, Cracked, or Firmly Intact? Women and the Executive Glass Ceiling Worldwide*. New York: Oxford University Press.

Jalalzai, Farida, and Meg Rincker. 2018. "Blood Is Thicker Than Water: Family Ties to Political Power Worldwide." *Historical Social Research* 43, no. 4: 54–72.

Kincaid, Diane D. 1978. "Over His Dead Body: A Positive Perspective on Widows in the U.S. Congress." *Western Political Quarterly* 31, no. 1: 96–104.

Kokkonen, Andrej, Suthan Krishnarajan, Jørgen Møller, and Anders Sundell. 2021. "Blood Is Thicker Than Water: Family Size and Leader Deposition in Medieval and Early Modern Europe." *Journal of Politics* 83, no. 4: 1246–59.

Kokkonen, Andrej, and Anders Sundell. 2014. "Delivering Stability: Primogeniture and Autocratic Survival in European Monarchies 1000–1800." *American Political Science Review* 108, no. 2: 438–53.

Kostiner, Joseph, ed. 2000. *Middle East Monarchies: The Challenge of Modernity*. Boulder, Colorado: Lynne Rienner.

Kurrild-Klitgaard, Peter. 2000. "The Constitutional Economics of Autocratic Succession." *Public Choice* 103: 63–84.

Laband, David N., and Bernard F. Lentz. 1983. "Like Father, Like Son: Toward an Economic Theory of Occupational Following." *Southern Economic Journal* 50, no. 2: 474–93.

Labonne, Julien, Sahara Parsa, and Pablo Querubín. 2021. "Political Dynasties, Term Limits and Female Political Representation: Evidence from the Philippines." *Journal of Economic Behavior and Organization* 182: 212–28.

Lacroix, Jean, Pierre-Guillaume Méon, and Kim Oosterlinck. 2019. "A Positive Effect of Political Dynasties: The Case of France's 1940 Enabling Act." CEPR Discussion Paper No. DP13871.

Lawless, Jennifer L. 2012. *Becoming a Candidate: Political Ambition and the Decision to Run for Office*. Cambridge: Cambridge University Press.

Manin, Bernard. 1997. *The Principles of Representative Government*. Cambridge: Cambridge University Press.

McMillan, M. E. 2013. *Fathers and Sons: The Rise and Fall of Political Dynasty in the Middle East*. New York: Palgrave Macmillan.

Menaldo, Victor. 2012. "The Middle East and North Africa's Resilient Monarchs." *Journal of Politics* 74, no. 3: 707–22.

Mendoza, Ronald U., Edsel L. Beja Jr., Victor S. Venida, and David B. Yap. 2012. "Inequality in Democracy: Insights from an Empirical Analysis of Political Dynasties in the 15th Philippine Congress." *Philippine Political Science Journal* 33, no. 2: 132–45.

Meng, Anne. 2021. "Winning the Game of Thrones: Leadership Succession in Modern Autocracies." *Journal of Conflict Resolution* 65, no. 5: 950–81.

Michels, Robert. 1915 [1911]. *Political Parties: A Sociological Study of the Oligarchical Tendencies of Modern Democracy*. New York: Hearst's International Library Co.

Miguel, Edward, and Gérard Roland. 2011. "The Long-Run Impact of Bombing Vietnam." *Journal of Development Economics* 96, no. 1: 1–15.

Mills, C. Wright. 1956. *The Power Elite*. New York: Oxford University Press.

Monday, Chris. 2011. "Family Rule as the Highest Stage of Communism." *Asian Survey* 51, no. 5: 812–43.

Mosca, Gaetano. 1939. *The Ruling Class (Elementi di Scienza Politica)*. New York: McGraw-Hill.

Muraoka, Taishi. 2018. "Political Dynasties and Particularistic Campaigns." *Political Research Quarterly* 71, no. 2: 453–66.

Nishizaki, Yoshinori. 2018. "New Wine in an Old Bottle: Female Politicians, Family Rule, and Democratization in Thailand." *Journal of Asian Studies* 77, no. 2: 375–403.

Norris, Pippa. 1997. "Introduction: Theories of Recruitment." In *Passages to Power: Legislative Recruitment in Advanced Democracies*, ed. Pippa Norris, 1–14. Cambridge: Cambridge University Press.

Offerlé, Michel. 1993. "Usages et Usure de l'Hérédité en Politique." *Revue Française de Science Politique* 43, no. 5: 850–56.

Olson, Mancur. 1993. "Dictatorship, Democracy, and Development." *American Political Science Review* 87, no. 3: 567–76.

Oskarsson, Sven, Christopher T. Dawes, and Karl-Oskar Lindgren. 2018. "It Runs in the Family: A Study of Political Candidacy among Swedish Adoptees." *Political Behavior* 40, no. 4: 883–908.

Panao, Rogelio Alicor L. 2016. "Tried and Tested? Dynastic Persistence and Legislative Productivity at the Philippine House of Representatives." *Asian Politics & Policy* 8, no. 3: 394–417.

Pande, R. 2003. "Can Mandated Political Representation Provide Disadvantaged Minorities Policy Influence? Theory and Evidence from India." *American Economic Review* 93, no. 4: 1132–51.

Pareto, Vilfredo. 1916. *Trattato di Sociologia Generale*. Firenze: G. Barbéra.

Patrikios, Stratos, and Michalis Chatzikonstantinou. 2015. "Dynastic Politics: Family Ties in the Greek Parliament, 2000–12." *South European Society and Politics* 20, no. 1: 93–111.

Purdey, Jemma. 2016. "Political Families in Southeast Asia." *South East Asia Research* 24, no. 3: 319–27.

Querubín, Pablo. 2012. "Political Reform and Elite Persistence: Term Limits and Political Dynasties in the Philippines." Unpublished manuscript.

Querubín, Pablo. 2016. "Family and Politics: Dynastic Persistence in the Philippines." *Quarterly Journal of Political Science* 11, no. 2: 151–81.

Ramseyer, J. Mark, and Frances M. Rosenbluth. 1995. *The Politics of Oligarchy: Institutional Choice in Imperial Japan*. Cambridge: Cambridge University Press.

Rossi, Martín A. 2017. "Self-Perpetuation of Political Power." *Economic Journal* 127, no. 605: F455–F473.

Rush, Michael. 2000. "The Decline of the Nobility." In *Democratic Representation in Europe: Diversity, Change, and Convergence*, ed. Maurizio Cotta and Heinrich Best, 29–50. Oxford: Oxford University Press.

Schwindt-Bayer, Leslie A., Agustín Vallejo, and Francisco Cantú. 2020. "Gender and Family Ties in Latin American Legislatures." *Politics & Gender*, online first.

Scott, James C. 2017. *Against the Grain: A Deep History of the Earliest States*. New Haven, CT: Yale University Press.

Shih, Victor, Christopher Adolph, and Mingxing Liu. 2012. "Getting Ahead in the Communist Party: Explaining the Advancement of Central Committee Members in China." *American Political Science Review* 106, no. 1: 166–87.

Smith, Daniel M. 2018. *Dynasties and Democracy: The Inherited Incumbency Advantage in Japan*. Stanford: Stanford University Press.

Smith, Daniel M., and Shane Martin. 2017. "Political Dynasties and the Selection of Cabinet Ministers." *Legislative Studies Quarterly* 42, no. 1: 131–65.

Spruyt, Hendrik. 2002. "The Origins, Development, and Possible Decline of the Modern State." *Annual Review of Political Science* 5: 127–49.

Stasavage, David. 2020. *The Decline and Rise of Democracy: A Global History from Antiquity to Today*. Princeton, NJ: Princeton University Press.

Svolik, Milan. 2012. *The Politics of Authoritarian Rule*. Cambridge: Cambridge University Press.

Thananithichot, Stithorn, and Wichuda Satidporn. 2016. "Political Dynasties in Thailand: The Recent Picture after the 2011 General Election." *Asian Studies Review* 40, no. 3: 340–59.

Tullock, Gordon. 1987. *Autocracy*. Boston: Kluwer Academic.

Van Coppenolle, Brenda. 2017. "Political Dynasties in the UK House of Commons: The Null Effect of Narrow Electoral Selection." *Legislative Studies Quarterly* 42, no. 3: 449–75.

Van Coppenolle, Brenda. 2020. "How Do Political Elites Persist? Political Selection, Political Inequality, and Empirical Historical Research." *French Politics* 18: 175–88.

Van Coppenolle, Brenda. 2021. "Unbreakable Legacies? Redistricting, Political Capital and the Personal Vote." Unpublished.

Van Coppenolle, Brenda. 2022. "Political Dynasties and Bicameralism: Direct Elections and Democratisation in the Netherlands." *Electoral Studies* 76: 102454.

Wang, Yuhua. 2017. "Betting on a Princeling." *Studies in Comparative International Development* 52: 395–415.

Wang, Yuhua. 2022. "Blood Is Thicker Than Water: Elite Kinship Networks and State Building in Imperial China." *American Political Science Review*, first view.

Wasson, Ellis Archer. 1991. "The House of Commons, 1660–1945: Parliamentary Families and the Political Elite." *English Historical Review* 106, no. 420: 635–51.

Winters, Jeffrey A. 2011. *Oligarchy*. Cambridge: Cambridge University Press.

Yates, Douglas A. 2021. "Dynastic Rule in Syria and North Korea: Nepotism, Succession, and Sibling Rivalry." *International Political Science Review*, online first.

CHAPTER 11

STATE-BUILDING IN HISTORICAL POLITICAL ECONOMY

FRANCISCO GARFIAS AND EMILY A. SELLARS

The consolidation of power under a strong central authority has important long-term economic and political consequences (see, e.g., Boone 1994; Mamdani 1996; Lange 2004; Gennaioli and Rainer 2007; Iyer 2010; Michalopoulos and Papaioannou 2013; Osafo-Kwaako and Robinson 2013; Dell, Lane, and Querubin 2018; Lee 2019; Paik and Vechbanyongratana 2019; Ahmed and Stasavage 2020; Stasavage 2020).* However, strong states and centralized forms of political authority have historically been the exception rather than the rule. When, why, and how does state-building occur?

In this chapter, we provide a framework for thinking about these questions, drawing on recent research in historical political economy (HPE). This work has accumulated important theoretical insights about state-building and a growing number of empirical findings from diverse contexts. This chapter synthesizes some of these disparate sets of mechanisms and empirical results in a common framework. In doing so, we highlight important themes that have emerged in this work, illustrate the connections between some of the subliteratures that have developed in parallel with one another, and suggest new directions for future research.[1]

Our framework focuses on the choice of a central authority—for example, a monarch, dictator, or unified ruling coalition—to extract resources from society to bolster the strength of the central government, potentially at the expense of others in the polity. We conceive of this central authority as a coherent, rational, and self-interested actor who is motivated primarily by the desire to remain in power. This conceptualization builds on Levi's (1988) insight that the interests and actions of a central ruler—and not

---

*We are grateful to Alex Debs, Jeffery A. Jenkins, Didac Queralt, Jared Rubin, Jan Vogler, Austin Wright, and seminar participants at Yale for their comments and suggestions.

of state institutions in general—represent a useful starting place for a theory of state policy; "rulers rule," as she famously argues (p. 2). All rulers, however, are constrained in their ability to wield power and often face threats from external sources and from within. Revenue can be used to defend against these threats, but increased extraction comes with its own political and economic costs.

We build our theory from a decision-theoretic model in which a ruler or central authority weighs the costs and benefits of taxing the population to defend against a threat. This simple model captures important arguments in the state-building literature related to the technology of taxation, the availability of nontax revenues, and wealth in society. Most directly, the model highlights the importance of external conflict, the central factor in the bellicist theory of state emergence.

We then introduce local elites—the subjects of state taxation and an important political constituency—as strategic actors who can either back the state or work to undermine it from within. This second model illustrates a potential tension between the central authority's need for revenue and the risk of alienating elites through excessive extraction, especially in situations where elite and ruler preferences are not aligned and where elites hold significant independent power. This second model also highlights some of the competing pressures facing elites, who may want to limit state extraction but who also rely on tax-funded public goods, such as military defense against external enemies.

Our final model introduces non-elite citizens who can pressure elites and the central authority from below through the threat of rebellion. These non-elite actors may have little direct stake in national political battles between elites and the ruler, but their actions influence elite behavior and thus the incentives of the government to centralize power through extraction. This formulation illustrates several additional complexities in the relationship between domestic political conflict and state-building, highlighting in particular how divisions between different domestic actors can influence state-building, how even highly localized political conflicts can take on national significance in the process of state centralization, and how seemingly unrelated political shocks can cause state-building efforts to backfire.

As we develop this framework, we incorporate insights from different strands of the HPE literature on state-building and discuss how these insights interact. Though we adopt a formal-theoretic approach, we provide intuition for the main arguments qualitatively in each section. We conclude the chapter with some reflections on potential future directions for research in this field, building on our analysis.

The State and State-Building

We begin by outlining the conceptual definitions that underlie the framework in this chapter. Following Hoffman (2015), we adopt a broad definition of the "state" as a community that can use force and has the capacity to impose and collect taxes on a substantial and permanent basis. This definition omits or abstracts away from some factors that contribute to state structure or that differentiate ancient from modern states, such as well-defined territorial boundaries, the rule of law, political legitimacy, or national identity. It is also considerably less restrictive than Weber's requirement that a state can claim a monopoly over the legitimate use of violence within a territory (Weber 1999). We use this expansive yet parsimonious definition to highlight the roles of coercion and taxation in state-building, both of which are central to the HPE literature on this topic.

We further clarify our definition of "state-building." Our focus is on the consolidation of power and revenue under the control of a central authority in an existing state, as opposed to the emergence of new states (see, e.g., Olson 1993; Boix 2015; Scott 2017; Allen, Bertazzini, and Heldring 2020; Dal Bo, Hernandez, and Mazzuca 2022; Mayshar, Moav, and Pascali 2022) or the political incorporation of new regions (see, e.g., Spruyt 1996; Pierskalla, De Juan, and Montgomery 2017; Acharya and Lee 2018). As Mazzuca (2021) argues, the processes of state *formation* and state *building* are conceptually distinct, may be motivated by different factors, and may not work in tandem. State-building under our definition encompasses political centralization and an increase in the resources and strength of the central government.

A Simple Theory of State-Building

The classic account of the formation of modern territorial states centers on early-modern Europe. This was a period of intense warfare during which the nature of military conflict was changing. The introduction of gunpowder, the increasing use of siege warfare and artillery weapons, and an increasing reliance on a trained and disciplined infantry in combat, among other factors, substantially raised the monetary costs of war. To finance expensive conflicts, states began to increase resource extraction from the citizenry and underwent important organizational transformations in the process. France is an illustrative example. One of the first states to establish a standing army, the French state began to fund its military through domestic debt secured against future tax revenue, encouraging a steady increase in taxation starting in the sixteenth century. This shift was enabled by a rising tax base and the presence of domestic creditors in wealthy cities like Paris, Toulouse, and Montpellier (Tilly 1990, 47–49, 74). Over time, this process led to important changes in the structure of the French state, including a transition from tax farming to direct taxation and investment in fiscal legibility (Tilly 1990, 107–10; Johnson and Koyama 2014). By the end of the eighteenth century, France had not only survived as a political entity after centuries of external threat, it had also developed a strong state with a centralized bureaucracy and high levels of taxation.

Inspired by the Western European example, we begin our theoretical discussion of state-building by focusing on the decision of a central authority to extract revenue from society to strengthen the state against a threat. We develop a simple decision-theoretic model in which a ruler, who cares only about surviving in power, weighs the cost of taxation against the benefit that tax revenue provides in bolstering state strength against this threat. Because taxation is costly, the ruler's choice of how much to extract depends on the extent of expected threat, the technologies of taxation and defense, and the size of the resource base. As we discuss, this model both captures several well-known theories about how each of these factors shapes state-building in isolation and illustrates some interesting connections between them. We develop the model in the following subsection and then qualitatively discuss its implications for understanding the HPE literature on this topic.

A Basic State-Building Model

A central authority A rules over a society of wealth $\omega > 0$. The authority chooses to extract some amount T of this wealth to invest in bolstering state strength. The cost of extracting revenue is given by cT, where $c > 0$. This cost (c) might capture the immediate cost of extracting wealth from private holders, the cost of tax enforcement or processing, or an investment in fiscal capacity or pacification that is required to enable taxation.

The strength of the state (S) depends on tax revenue (T) and any exogenous nontax revenue (ρ). Nontax revenue might include resource rents, external financing, or other endowments that the authority can appropriate without taxation. Specifically, let $S = f(T + \rho)$ represent state strength, where the function $f(\cdot)$ captures how easy or hard it is for the authority to convert revenue into strength. We assume that f is increasing and concave in total revenue, so that revenue improves defensive capability but with decreasing marginal benefits.

The state faces an exogenous threat—for example, a foreign invasion or domestic challenge—the severity of which is stochastic, given by $\underline{S} \sim Unif[\sigma - \delta, \sigma + \delta]$. The parameter σ can be interpreted as the expected level of threat, which might capture factors like the proximity of foreign rivals or any natural defensive advantages of the state's geographic position. The parameter δ captures uncertainty about the severity of threat, which might depend on unknown factors like the intentions of political rivals or the risk of natural disasters. The realized severity of the threat ($\underline{S}$) is revealed after the ruler has made his extraction choice. We assume that the state survives only if strength $S > \underline{S}$. If the state survives, the central authority receives $u_A = \alpha > 0$ as the value of maintaining power. If the state falls, the authority loses power and receives a payoff of 0 (α can thus be thought of as the relative utility of maintaining to losing power).

Discussion

What determines how much a ruler decides to (and is able to) extract? As we show in the Appendix to this chapter, the authority's preferred level of taxation in the model depends on the extent of external conflict, the availability of nontax revenue, the amount

Table 11.1. Baseline ruler model: Summary of predictions

Theme in literature	Parameter in model	Predicted change in centralization/taxation
External conflict	Expected threat severity (σ)	Increases taxation window, unless threat is overwhelming
	Uncertainty about threat (δ)	Ambiguous (see conclusion)
Military technology	Importance of revenue in military power ($f'(\cdot)$)	Increases
Nontax revenue	Nontax revenue (ρ)	Decreases
Societal wealth/capital	Total wealth (ω)	Increases taxation window
Taxation technology and legibility	Cost of taxation (c)	Decreases

of appropriable wealth, and features about the technologies of extraction and defense (Appendix Section A.1). The central tension of this first model surrounds a direct cost-benefit analysis of taxation for the ruler. Because taxation is costly, the ruler does not always benefit from increasing extraction, even when doing so increases his probability of survival. Whether the costs of taxation are worth paying depends on how high these costs are, whether alternative sources of revenue are available, and the degree to which any increased revenue pays off in raising the likelihood that the state will survive.

We summarize the key predictions in Table 11.1. We provide some intuition for these results and discuss our analysis in light of several key literatures in HPE in the next section.

External Conflict

We begin by revisiting the classic relationship between state-building and external conflict, most famously associated with the works of Otto Hintze and Charles Tilly. These theories, initially formulated in the context of early-modern Europe, propose that interstate war gave rise to the territorial state. One of the mechanisms proposed for this relationship is that the presence of external threats push states to develop capacity to mobilize resources for the war effort. As in the bellicist framework, an exogenous threat, such as that posed by external conflict, is what drives extraction in our model. Because taxation is costly and revenue is exclusively used for defense (an assumption we revisit below in a model extension), there is no incentive to tax without a threat, and the maximum level of extraction is increasing in the expected level of this threat.

The relationship between external conflict and state-building is one of the most well-documented empirical findings in this literature, beginning with the case studies and small-n comparisons of early-modern Europe that inspired the bellicist conjecture (Schumpeter 1954; Ardant 1975; Hintze 1975; Tilly 1975; 1990; Levi 1988; Brewer 1990; Ertman 1997). More recently, cross-national associations between historic warfare and present-day fiscal outcomes (Besley and Persson 2009; 2014; Dincecco, Fenske, and

Onorato 2019) and panel evidence on Europe in the early-modern period (Dincecco 2009; 2011; Dincecco, Federico, and Vindigni 2011; Karaman and Pamuk 2013), the early twentieth century (Scheve and Stasavage 2010), and even the late Middle Ages (Blaydes and Paik 2016) have provided additional empirical support for this argument. Related work has examined how the emergence of a new military threat, such as the rise of the Ottoman Empire in early-modern Europe (Cantoni, Mohr, and Weigand 2021), can encourage investment in fiscal capacity. Regional differences in state development are also generally consistent with the bellicist argument. Strong centralized states arose in Western Europe, an area of intense territorial conflict, and not in regions like Latin America or sub-Saharan Africa, which had distinctive political histories (see, e.g., Herbst 2000; Centeno 1997; 2002).

Military Technology

Our model highlights an important mediating factor in the relationship between external conflict and state-building: military/defense technology. When a slight increase in revenue has little impact on the defensive capability of the state (i.e., $f'(\cdot)$ is small), the ruler has little reason to extract wealth. As military technology becomes more efficient, the benefit of raising taxes to defend against external threat increases.

This result is consistent with existing scholarly work in HPE. Gennaioli and Voth (2015), for instance, focus on how the relationship between external warfare and state emergence shifted with the military revolution in Europe that began with the introduction of gunpowder. Revenue, they argue, only affected coercive power following the dramatic increase in the monetary costs of war following this military revolution. This explains the timing of the rise of the European territorial state specifically during the early-modern period (see also Hoffman [2012]). The puzzling absence of a connection between warfare and state-building in other contexts—such as Latin America (see, e.g., Soifer 2015) or during the nineteenth century (see, e.g., Goenaga, Sabate, and Teorell 2018)—may similarly be explained by the weak connection between revenue and military power in those settings.

Nontax Revenue

Nontax revenue (ρ) is a perfect substitute in our model for revenue extracted through taxation. A ruler who can count on a large resource windfall may not need to incur the costs of taxation to ensure state survival. As nontax revenue increases, the window where taxation is attractive for the ruler therefore shrinks.

This is consistent with a prominent literature on how the availability of nontax revenue, such as natural-resource rents, shapes state-building. Nontax revenue is often modeled as an attractive substitute to costly taxation (see, e.g., Besley and Persson 2009; 2014). Several empirical studies have found a negative relationship between the availability of nontax resources and measures of fiscal capacity. For example, Cassidy (2019) shows that present-day tax revenue is lower in areas that are geologically conducive to oil extraction (see also Dunning 2008). A complementary literature on the availability of international finance has similarly found that states' ability to borrow from abroad weakened the relationship between war and domestic extraction in nineteenth-century Latin America (Centeno 1997; 2002; Soifer 2015). Though international finance is distinctive from resource rents in that it typically entails a promise of future payment, Queralt (2019; 2022) shows that debt-financed war during the nineteenth century did not lead to a long- or even short-term increases in extractive capacity, given the continual possibility of debt relief and refinancing.

Societal Wealth

Extraction in our model is bounded above by the amount of available wealth (ω). A ruler cannot tax beyond ω, even if he faces strong incentives to do so. In a society with a very small resource base, there may simply not be enough wealth for the state to survive a major threat.

This simple argument has roots in classic literature. For example, Tilly describes how the accumulation of capital in European cities during the early-modern period allowed rulers to better fund war efforts through increased access to domestic loans, revenue-producing state enterprises, and a larger tax base (Tilly 1990). More recently, Abramson (2017) presents evidence consistent with the idea that an increase in wealth enabled the survival of small urban states against encroachment by larger (but more rural) neighbors during this period. A related set of arguments highlights the role of economic productivity in state formation and state-building alongside defensive concerns due to resource constraints and other factors (see, e.g., Acharya and Lee 2018; Fernandez-Villaverdé et al. 2020; Dal Bo, Hernandez, and Mazzuca 2022).

Taxation Technology and Legibility

When the cost of taxation (c) is very high, the authority has little incentive or ability to extract resources to bolster state strength. Conversely, if the cost is low, taxation remains attractive even when the marginal defensive benefit of additional revenue is small.

The cost of taxation may be determined by many factors, including geography. It may be costly, for example, to extend political control over a large territory relative to a smaller one, especially when threats emerge from multiple directions (Stasavage 2011; Ko, Koyama, and Sng 2018; Koyama, Moriguchi, and Sng 2018; Mazzuca 2021). Terrain ruggedness can inhibit a state's ability to tax by increasing transportation costs or providing citizens with an opportunity to escape the reach of the state in mountains or jungles (see, e.g., Fearon and Laitin 2003; Scott 2009; Fernandez-Villaverdé et al. 2020). Population density can shape both the ability and the incentive of central rulers to tax the population, as the literature on sub-Saharan Africa in particular has emphasized (Herbst 2000; Boone 2003).

The cost of taxation is also determined by fiscal legibility, a ruler's ability to monitor the economy or population (Scott 1998; Brambor et al. 2020). Features of agricultural production, such as crop characteristics or irrigation methods, can make it easier or more difficult for the central authority to observe economic activity, which in turn shapes incentives for state-building (Mayshar, Moav, and Neeman 2017; Scott 2017). Technology also plays a role. Stasavage (2020), drawing on evidence from ancient states, describes how innovations like writing, geometry, and land surveying techniques facilitated the emergence of early bureaucracies. Garfias and Sellars (2022a) show how a technological innovation in silver mining facilitated state centralization in colonial Mexico by making it easier for officials to monitor production and tax the population. Rulers can also invest in improving legibility through the creation of tax offices, censuses, and land registers to lower the future costs of taxation. The positive feedback between political centralization and fiscal capacity can lead to divergent paths of state development, as Garfias and Sellars (2022a) show in colonial Mexico and Johnson and Koyama (2014) in early-modern France and England.[2]

Because taxation entails the extraction of resources from the citizenry, there are also political costs to consider. Next we consider these costs in greater detail, expanding our framework to examine the strategic interaction between the central ruler and economic elites who hold wealth and may stand to lose from state-building projects.

STATE-BUILDING AND ELITES

Societal wealth is typically held by domestic actors—elites and other taxpayers—whose interests may not align with those of the central authority. For this reason, the internal politics of state building are often contentious rather than cooperative. There are countless historical and contemporary examples of powerful elites deterring or sabotaging state-building efforts when threatened by centralization. This is why political centralization often, but not always, occurs during times of elite weakness. In ancient China, for example, the Qin state that emerged from a period of intense interstate conflict—the Warring States era (475–221 BCE)—was able to centralize power in an unprecedented way because it faced a severely weakened aristocracy (Kiser and Cai 2003). Key reforms, such as the abolition of feudal titles and the establishment of a centrally controlled bureaucracy, would have been difficult to implement had the aristocracy been strong enough to mount an effective resistance to these policies, which they perceived as threatening (Hui 2015).

Though domestic political conflict is often thought to inhibit state-building, there are also conditions under which it may encourage rather than discourage taxation. The spectacular expansion of the British state following the Glorious Revolution, for example, was made possible because the Crown faced a powerful taxpaying elite that was able to force its policy preferences on the government (North and Weingast 1989; Stasavage 2003). To develop these and other related ideas, we extend our model to consider the strategic interaction between the central authority and domestic elites.

State-Building Model with Elites

We model the central authority's (A) choice of how much tax revenue (T) to extract from domestic elites (E), modeled as a unified strategic actor. Elites are endowed with wealth

(ω), which they either own or control indirectly. The central authority is again assumed to be office-motivated, receiving α if the state survives and 0 if the state falls. Rather than assuming that taxation carries a fixed cost, we directly model the political cost of alienating elite wealth holders through overzealous taxation.

After the authority determines how much wealth to extract, elites decide whether to back the central ruler in a crisis ($e = 1$) or to defect ($e = 0$). Elite defection weakens the central government by, for example, overtly supporting an internal or external political rival against the ruler, shirking on internal defense by depriving the ruler of logistical assistance during war, or refusing to cooperate with state officials. Compliance with the central authority is assumed to be costly for elites, with the compliance cost given by μ.

The strength of the central government (S) is now modeled as a function of both state revenue and elite backing or defection. As earlier, the base strength of the government is $S = f(T)$, where the function f is increasing and concave.[3] If elites defect, state strength is lowered by ζ, which represents elite coercive power (i.e., their influence in state strength). Also as earlier, the state survives a threat only if strength $S > \underline{S}$, where $\underline{S} \sim \text{Unif}\,[\sigma - \delta, \sigma + \delta]$. To highlight the role of elite politics, we focus on interior cases where the state cannot fully ensure its survival against external threat and where elite actions meaningfully influence but do not fully determine the probability of survival (i.e., where $f(\omega) < \sigma + \delta$ and $f(0) - \zeta > \sigma - \delta$).

We normalize the payoffs of state collapse to 0 for both the central authority and the elite. If the state survives, the ruler receives rents from office $\alpha > 0$ and elites receive their posttax wealth ($\omega - T$) and λ, which represents the utility of state survival relative to a postcollapse alternative. If elites fear state breakdown or have an affinity for the central ruler, λ would be very high. If elites would prefer to see the state fall—for example, if they have an acrimonious relationship with the central authority, support internal political rivals, or have attractive outside options—λ might be negative.

If the state survives despite elite defection, defecting elites pay a punishment cost of $\pi > 0$. The severity of this cost could vary from a small fine to violent retribution depending on the context and form of elite defection.

Discussion

The extended model illustrates how domestic political bargaining structures state-building. A central authority's ability and willingness to strengthen the state is driven not only by perceived threat but also by the anticipated resistance from elites. As we discuss in this section and show in Appendix Section A.2, the model highlights two paths of state-building, one cooperative and one coercive. In the cooperative path, the ruler limits his extraction to a level acceptable to elites in exchange for their support. In the coercive path, the ruler extracts all of the elite's wealth to counter their anticipated defection.

The optimal path for the ruler depends on elites' willingness to accept taxation (T), which is determined by the parameters summarized in Table 11.2. An increase in

Table 11.2. Elite model: Summary of additional predictions

Theme in literature	Parameter in model	Predicted change in elite's willingness to accept taxation
Preference alignment	Survival payoff (λ)	Increases
Economic benefits	Residual wealth ($\omega - T$)	Increases
Center coercive threat	Punishment cost (π)	Increases
Elite coercive power	Elite power (ζ)	Depends on balance between benefits of state survival (λ) and cost of punishment (π)

taxation affects elite preferences through two mechanisms. Higher taxation reduces the benefit of state survival for elites, but it also increases state strength and thus the likelihood that elite defection will be punished. As elites are more aligned with the center for material (ω) or political/social (λ) reasons and as the threat of punishment (π) increases, elites become more willing to back the government at high tax levels, and the cooperative approach becomes less costly for the ruler.

The model illustrates a nonlinear relationship between the elites' willingness to back the government and the optimal tax level the ruler chooses (Figure 11.1). When elites are highly aligned with the center, the ruler can increase taxation at little political cost. As elites' willingness to pay taxes decreases—perhaps because they possess better outside

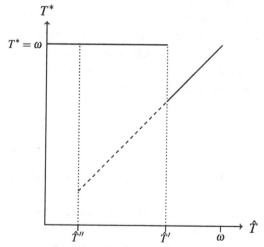

FIGURE 11.1. Central authority extraction as a function of elite willingness to pay

The figure presents the optimal tax level for the central ruler (T^*) over the maximum tax that the elite is willing to pay without defecting ($\hat{T}$). If elite power $\zeta = \zeta'$, the ruler will set $T^* = \hat{T}$ for $\hat{T} > \hat{T}'$, where $f(\hat{T}' = f(\omega) - \zeta')$, and $T^* = \omega$ otherwise. If elite power increases to $\zeta'' > \zeta'$ this expands the range of values where the ruler will set $T^* = \hat{T}$ to $\hat{T} > \hat{T}''$, as represented in the dashed line. See Appendix Section A.2 for the analysis.

options or fear punishment less—they can successfully demand that the ruler limit extraction. However, once the maximum tax that elites are willing to pay falls below a certain threshold, the ruler will revert to a coercive strategy to maximize the probability of state survival. As shown in Figure 11.1, this threshold depends on the domestic political power of elites, ζ. A stronger domestic elite has a greater ability to demand reduced taxation.

The degree of political conflict or consensus between elites and the state has been central to the HPE literature on state-building. In the remainder of this section, we discuss this literature in light of our theoretical framework.

Preference Alignment

The preference alignment between elites and the ruler plays an important role in this framework. Elites are more willing to accept higher taxation when they benefit more from state survival for material, social, or political reasons. Conversely, elites who have less to lose from state collapse become less willing to tolerate state extraction.

One factor that contributes to preference alignment between elites and the center is elites' reliance on state-provided public goods, such as military defense. Besley and Persson (2009; 2014), for example, describe why incumbent and opposition political actors should be more willing to invest in fiscal capacity if revenue will be spent on common-interest goods like defense (see Arias 2013 for a related argument on colonial Mexico). As Slater's (2010) work on state development in Southeast Asia illustrates, elites and central authorities may also find common ground against shared domestic threats.

Central authorities may take steps to increase elite preference alignment to encourage support for the state under higher levels of taxation. For example, they might allow rising elites to have greater influence in state policy and public goods provision (Kurtz 2013; Saylor 2014; Beramendi, Dincecco, and Rogers 2019) or attempt to incorporate rival elites into the state (Chen, Wang, and Zhang 2021). Elite homogeneity—such as through concentration in a single urban core—can make it easier for the state to tailor its activities to align with elite preferences, encouraging state-building (Soifer 2015; Mazzuca 2021). Greater geographic dispersion among already linked elites might shift their preferences toward state-building so that public goods like defense can be spread across a larger territory, as Wang (2022) shows in Imperial China. A common interest in state-building may emerge among rival elites if greater taxation is tied to political restrictions for the masses (Mares and Queralt 2015; 2020).

Conversely, threatened, nonaligned elites may be able to exploit the political environment to sabotage state-building (see, e.g., Migdal 1988). Suryanarayan (2021) and Suryanarayan and White (2021), for example, describe how elites can exploit social-status cleavages to create broad coalitions in support of weakening the central government. Sanchez-Talanquer (2020) further shows how elites can co-opt state-building efforts to reshape their influence and undermine their effectiveness.

Elite Political Power

A more powerful elite that can damage the government through defection can more effectively demand lower taxation. This can deter state-building when elites and the central authority have opposing interests. In contexts where elites control considerable coercive power—such as in what North, Wallis, and Weingast (2009) characterize as "natural states" or Besley and Persson (2014) describe as "weak states"—central rulers may be outgunned by rivals in the periphery, limiting any potential for significant state-building. At the other extreme, when elites are too weak to threaten the government through defection, the ruler has little reason to limit extraction to cater to their preferences.

Shifts in the coercive power of elites can therefore precipitate changes in state-building trajectories. Because the potential for political centralization is limited where rival elites remain strong, a sharp decline in elite power may enable state-building. Garfias (2018), for example, shows how an economic shock that temporarily weakened local elites in postrevolutionary Mexico provided a window for local political authorities to consolidate their advantage and invest in state capacity. A shock that bolsters the coercive power of nonaligned elites, by contrast, can curb state extraction by raising the costs and reducing the benefits of taxation for the ruler.

Limited Government

This model illustrates that elites' bargaining power, their ability to secure a lower level of taxation than would be favored by the ruler, depends both on their political power (ζ) and preference alignment with the central authority (λ). Elites must be sufficiently powerful to pose a threat to the ruler through defection, and they must have a moderate (but not perfect) degree of preference alignment so that the central authority has an incentive to appease them through lower taxation. This illustrates a connection to the literatures on fiscal contracts and institutions of limited government. Institutions that bolster elite political power or improve the quality of elites' outside options can place effective limits on state extraction and can promote state-building.

This connection is clearer if one considers an extension of the model where the ruler is able to divert tax revenue for personal rents at the expense of state strength. In the baseline model with elites, an increase in taxation represents a double-edged sword. Greater taxation lowers elites' benefit of backing the ruler, but it also bolsters state strength and thus increases the chance that elite defection is punished. If the ruler were to spend this extra revenue on rents, the increase in taxation would reduce elites' utility without the corresponding increase in the threat of punishment, unequivocally reducing elites' willingness to back the state. Thus, when elite power (ζ) is high enough (provided outside option λ is moderate), the threat of defection places a natural limit on rent-seeking. "Limited government" in our model thus arises endogenously from specific domestic political coalitions, which must be sustained for credibility to endure (Stasavage 2003; 2007), rather than as exogenous features of the institutional environment (see, e.g., Besley and Persson 2009; 2014).[4]

The prospects for state-building are therefore greater when rulers are constrained to spend in ways that align with the preferences of taxpaying or debt-granting elites (Bates and Lien 1985; Levi 1988; North and Weingast 1989; Hoffman and Rosenthal 1997; Gehlbach 2008; Cox 2016) or where institutions limit a ruler's ability to increase extraction (Garfias 2019). These ideas have found empirical support in studies that examine institutional changes along these lines cross-nationally (Dincecco 2009; 2011; Cox 2016) and subnationally (Garfias 2019).[5]

Elites and Commoners in State-Building

The model of the previous section illustrates how a particular form of domestic political conflict, that between elites and the central authority, can shape the trajectory of state-building. We now expand our discussion of domestic politics to consider the actions and interests of another social group. Ordinary citizens or commoners—such as peasants, workers, or the urban poor—can also alter the political costs and benefits of centralization, both directly and indirectly via their relationship with local elites. As the literatures on state collapse and revolution illustrate, the complex interplay between commoner, elite, and ruler incentives during an unforeseen crisis can lead even a seemingly stable political system to unravel (see, e.g., Skocpol 1979).

The outbreak of Mexico's War of Independence provides one example. Spanish colonial authorities depended on local elites to control the threat of commoner rebellion in the periphery. During the eighteenth century, the colonial state implemented a series of centralizing reforms at the expense of these intermediaries, aimed at increasing tax revenue. Though largely effective, the true political costs of these reforms only became apparent years later when a large-scale drought affected the peasant economy during a period of state weakness. Faced with an upsurge of commoner rebellion, the disaffected elites became unwilling to bear the costs of maintaining order, allowing the localized peasant crisis to grow out of control and eventually threaten the survival of the central government (Garfias and Sellars 2022b).

We extend our framework to incorporate commoners, focusing in particular on the role of elites as intermediaries between commoners and the central authority. We model commoners as a separate political class that is not directly taxed (an assumption we revisit later) and whose primary motivations are unrelated to national politics, elite conflict, or the exogenous threat. As our model illustrates, even when commoners have no direct stake in state-building, their political actions may have important consequences for centralization, both directly and via shifting incentives for elite intermediaries to back the central authority during times of crisis.

State-Building Model with Elites and Commoners

The central authority (A) again chooses how much tax revenue (T) to extract from the economic elite (E), who control wealth (ω), some of which may originate from the broader population. As earlier, tax revenue bolsters state strength, and the level of taxation may influence the willingness of elites to back the state, now by restoring local political order ($e = 1$) or by defecting ($e = 0$) when faced with local rebellion by commoners (C).

The commoners' choice to rebel depends on local conditions (η), the benefits of rebellion (β), and the perceived threat of repression by elites. We model η —which might capture commoners' economic opportunities or the current quality of their social or political situation—as stochastic and unrelated to political centralization or taxation (however, see the Discussion section for a relaxation of this assumption). Specifically, $\eta \sim Unif[\,\bar{\eta} - v,\ \bar{\eta} + v\,]$. If commoners rebel, they forgo η and instead receive the material and social benefits of rebellion (β), which could encompass both social components (e.g., feelings of collective belonging) and material components (e.g., goods seized during rioting). If the elite represses the rebellion, commoners suffer a cost ψ from repression. We assume that $\beta - \psi < \bar{\eta} - v < \beta < \bar{\eta} + v$, so that the possibility of repression remains a meaningful deterrent to mobilization even when conditions are poor. We further assume that commoner payoffs do not directly depend on whether the state survives.

If commoners do not rebel, elites take no action. If they do rebel, elites choose whether to back the authority and repress the uprising or to defect. The cost of repression is $\mu > 0$. Because commoner uprisings might affect elites, this parameter can be alternatively interpreted as the immediate cost of backing the government relative to inaction (i.e., μ would be low if elites directly absorbed the costs of allowing a rebellion to continue). As earlier, we assume that elite defection lowers the strength of the central government by ζ, which might capture the need to divert resources to reestablish order or a decrease in defensive capability against the exogenous threat due to ongoing political upheaval. If the government survives despite commoner rebellion and elite defection, elites pay a punishment cost of $\pi > \mu$, which implies that elites are better off complying if they expect the state to survive.

The model otherwise proceeds as in the prior section. The strength of the government is given by $S = f(T)$, or $S = f(T) - \zeta$ if elites defect. A stochastic shock, $\underline{S} \sim Unif[\sigma - \delta, \sigma + \delta]$, determines the extent of the threat after the elites' decision. The state survives if $S \geq \underline{S}$ and falls otherwise. We provide a summary and analysis of this model in Appendix Section A.3.

Discussion

Incorporating the threat of rebellion from below allows us to draw connections to other prominent arguments about state-building and state collapse, as summarized in Table 11.3. This formulation draws attention to an alternative view of elite bargaining

Table 11.3. Commoner model: Summary of additional predictions

Theme in literature	Parameter in model	Predicted change in the central authority's dependence on elites
Elite cost of compliance	Repression cost (μ)	Increases
Commoner conditions	Average material/social benefits of status quo ($\bar{\eta}$)	Decreases
Attractiveness of rebellion	Material/social benefits of rebellion (β)	Increases

power, the role of elite-mass relations, and the connection between local and national political conflict in state-building.

Elite Bargaining Power Revisited

As in the previous section, elite bargaining power in this extended model depends jointly on elites' political strength and their preference alignment with the center. Now, however, elite coercive power is linked to the threat of rebellion from below. When the threat of rebellion is high (when commoner conditions are poor or the attractiveness of rebellion is high), rulers are more dependent on elite cooperation for state survival, which increases elites' ability to demand lower taxation. When there is little risk of rebellion, by contrast, the ruler has less to lose from alienating elites through increased extraction.

Factors that decrease the willingness and ability of commoners to rebel should therefore also decrease the bargaining power of elites to demand lower taxation. HPE research has found some empirical support for this assertion. Garfias and Sellars (2021) show that a sudden decline in the potential for commoner rebellion facilitated state centralization in early colonial Mexico. Bai and Jia (2016) conversely illustrate how alienating elites was especially dangerous for central authorities facing a high risk of commoner rebellion in late Imperial China, in part because the center relied on local elites for backing when rebellions broke out (Bai, Jia, and Yang 2021).

As in the previous model, preference alignment is an important mediator in the relationship between elites' coercive and bargaining power. As elites themselves stand to lose more from allowing commoner rebellion to grow out of control (i.e., when μ is lower), they become more willing to back the state even when taxation is high. As Dincecco and Wang (2018a) document, elites threatened by rebellion in Imperial China benefited from bolstering the state as a way of enhancing their own security and therefore accepted increased taxation. However, when the state became weaker following China's defeat in the Opium War, elites turned to the private substitute of family clans for security, contributing to eventual state collapse. This example illustrates the importance of state stability in encouraging elite compliance. There is little reason for elites to invest in bolstering a state that cannot survive, as our model demonstrates.

Local and National Interdependence

Commoners' behavior in this framework influences the path of state-building, even though commoner preferences do not directly depend on elite taxation or state survival. Because the political negotiation between elites and the central authority differs based on the threat of rebellion from below (which determines elite bargaining power), local conditions affecting commoners influence decisions about political centralization and taxation made at the national level. Similarly, while commoners in the model are assumed to care only about local conditions, their choice to rebel depends on elite taxation because this influences elites' willingness to repress revolt. This illustrates an interdependence between local and national political concerns, a central feature of the classic literature on rebellion (Moore 1966; Wolf 1969; Tilly 1978).

A natural extension of this model might allow commoners' local conditions to differ based on the level of elite taxation. For example, elites may be able to shift the burden of taxation to commoners through, for example, extracting wealth from local individuals or villages. This would lower commoner welfare, increasing their willingness to rebel. Slantchev and Kravitz (2019) build on this idea to examine how tax revolts can provide information to rulers about the burdens of taxation that are being passed on to the poor in areas where the government lacks monitoring capacity. In our model, a shift in the burden of taxation from elites to commoners would have an ambiguous effect on state-building. It would increase the relative benefits of rebellion for commoners, increasing the bargaining power of elites to demand lower taxation from the central authority. However, the ability to pass on the burden of taxation to commoners would also insulate elites from the consequences of increased extraction, which would raise their willingness to remain loyal to the government even under high tax levels. Elites would therefore bear lower direct but higher indirect costs of increased taxation.

How State-Building Backfires

This extended model once again illustrates how the strength of the central government depends on both the size of the state (i.e., tax revenue) and the political support that the state enjoys from taxpayers. By incorporating commoners, this model provides a more complex view of how political stability or instability can shape state-building. In the model, as commoners become less willing to rebel, either because their status quo conditions are better or because rebellion becomes less attractive, central authorities become more willing to risk elite defection through high taxation. In other words, state-building should accelerate where political control over commoners is most secure.

However, when authorities decide to tax beyond a level that elite intermediaries will accept, they are implicitly gambling that commoner local conditions will be favorable. If η is realized much lower than expected—for example, if there is adverse weather like a severe drought or other shock affecting the commoner economy—authorities will not be able to count on elite support to contain rebellion. This illustrates how efforts to strengthen the government through high taxation can backfire, reducing the strength of the state during crisis and facilitating state collapse. This idea is developed further in Garfias and Sellars (2022b), who show how unrelated political shocks converged to bring about the collapse of colonial rule in Mexico through a similar mechanism. Skocpol (1979) develops a related argument on how peasant rebellion and higher-level pressures often coalesced to bring about revolutionary political change.

CONCLUSIONS AND FUTURE DIRECTIONS

We conclude with some general observations about the literature on state-building in HPE and some potential directions for future work. As our chapter illustrates, this literature has grown considerably beyond the classic works of Tilly, Hintze, and others on Western Europe to examine the scope conditions of the bellicist argument, the interplay between internal and external conflict, the role of nontax revenue, and the shifting influence of military technology and fiscal legibility, among other factors. In the process, HPE scholars have broadened the substantive focus of this research area beyond early-modern Europe to examine contexts as diverse as twentieth-century Southeast Asia, colonial Latin America, eleventh-century China, and the United States following Reconstruction. This work has produced a large and growing "library of mechanisms" (Gailmard 2021) to explain when and why political centralization takes place, the process through which state-building and state collapse occur, and the contextual factors that may enable or foreclose specific paths of state consolidation.

An important next step in moving this research area forward is to move toward summarizing and synthesizing the insights that have been generated through this work. The framework we develop here begins this effort and provides an organizational structure for thinking about some of the different ways in which HPE scholars have expanded this literature, some general lessons that might be drawn from their work, some interesting connections between subliteratures that are often discussed in isolation from one another, and some of the unanswered questions that remain. Scholarship has approached this topic from a variety of angles, both in terms of substantive focus and methodological approach. There are, however, important commonalities in how HPE scholars have thought about state-building across time and space that might be missed when taking a narrower view of the specific contexts or causal processes highlighted by any given contribution. The variables that capture external security considerations, the balance of power between the center and the periphery, the structure of the international political or economic system, and preexisting technological and environmental conditions differ considerably by context, but many of the lessons for how these factors structure state-building are plausibly general.

Our theoretical framework also suggests several avenues for future research. One approach might be to explore some of the new or less examined predictions of the framework developed here. For example, the model suggests that the *variance*—not just the level—of external threat may shape rulers' incentives to strengthen the state. When there is substantial uncertainty about the severity of a threat, this simultaneously expands the range of situations where state-building could occur while also reducing the expected benefit of marginally increasing state strength. This hypothesis has not, to our knowledge, been explored empirically.

Another path forward might be to expand on some of the connections between different strands of the literature. For example, elite bargaining power in state-building—the extent to which elites are willing and able to demand a lower extraction from the center—should depend not just on elites' political strength but also on their preference alignment with the ruler and the elasticity of state coercive power with respect to revenue. This prediction could be investigated empirically or further analyzed theoretically.

Finally, the stylized setting that we examine in this chapter could be complicated in several ways to generate new insights. Some black boxes that might be worth opening include thinking about different ways that central authorities might use tax revenue to shore up political strength or further unpacking the coarse set of social actors that we examine here—a unified center, a unified elite, and a unified set of commoners—to think about how divisions within these categories or identity cleavages (e.g., class, nationality, or ethnicity) might alter the path of state-building.

Notes

1. Our framework is intended to complement more exhaustive reviews of the study of the state in HPE and across the social sciences, such as Dincecco and Wang (2023), Koyama (2023), Moriguchi and Sng (2023), and Vogler (2023) in this volume. Other examples include Levi (2002), Spruyt (2002), Brautigam (2008), Besley and Persson (2014), Hoffman (2015), Bardhan (2016), Blaydes (2017), Johnson and Koyama (2017), Berwick and Christia (2018), and Dincecco and Wang (2018b).
2. Related but distinct literatures examine how prior institutional development (Gerring et al. 2011) and the diffusion of technologies of legibility, taxation, and administration (e.g., Grzymala-Busse 2020; Huang and Kang 2022) can facilitate state development.
3. We omit nontax revenue in this model extension, though predictions are unchanged if it is included.
4. Though distinctive, this argument is also somewhat reminiscent of Acemoglu and Robinson's (2017; 2020) path to an "inclusive state."
5. See also Cox (2023) in this volume.

References

Abramson, Scott F. 2017. "The Economic Origins of the Territorial State." *International Organization* 71, no. 1: 97–130.

Acemoglu, Daron, and James A. Robinson. 2017. "The Emergence of Weak, Despotic and Inclusive States." NBER Working Paper.

Acemoglu, Daron, and James A. Robinson. 2020. *The Narrow Corridor: States, Societies, and the Fate of Liberty*. New York: Penguin Random House.

Acharya, Avidit, and Alexander Lee. 2018. "Economic Foundations of the Territorial State System." *American Journal of Political Science* 62, no. 4: 954–66.

Ahmed, Ali T., and David Stasavage. 2020. "Origins of Early Democracy." *American Political Science Review* 114, no. 2: 502–18.

Allen, Robert C., Mattia C. Bertazzini, and Leander Heldring. 2020. "The Economic Origins of Government." Working Paper. Oxford University/NYU-Abu Dhabi.

Ardant, Gabriel. 1975. "Financial Policy and Economic Infrastructure of Modern States and Nations." In *The Formation of National States in Western Europe*, ed. Charles Tilly, 164–242. Princeton, NJ: Princeton University Press.

Arias, Luz Marina. 2013. "Building Fiscal Capacity in Colonial Mexico: From Fragmentation to Centralization." *Journal of Economic History* 73, no. 3: 662–93.

Bai, Ying, and Ruixue Jia. 2016. "Elite Recruitment and Political Stability: The Impact of the Abolition of China's Civil Service Exam." *Econometrica* 84, no. 2: 677–733.

Bai, Ying, Ruixue Jia, and Jiaojiao Yang. 2021. "The Nexus of Elites and War Mobilization." Working Paper.l University of California, San Diego.

Bardhan, Pranab. 2016. "State and Development: The Need for a Reappraisal of the Current Literature." *Journal of Economic Literature* 54, no. 3: 862–92.

Bates, Robert, and Da-Hsiang Lien. 1985. "A Note on Taxation, Development, and Representative Government." *Politics & Society* 14, no. 1: 53–70.

Beramendi, Pablo, Mark Dincecco, and Melissa Rogers. 2019. "Intra-Elite Competition and Long-Run Fiscal Development." *Journal of Politics* 81, no. 1: 49–65.

Berwick, Elissa, and Fotini Christia. 2018. "State Capacity Redux: Integrating Classical and Experimental Contributions to an Enduring Debate." *Annual Review of Political Science* 21, no. 1: 71–91.

Besley, Timothy, and Torsten Persson. 2009. "The Origins of State Capacity: Property Rights, Taxation, and Politics." *American Economic Review* 99, no. 4: 1218–44.

Besley, Timothy, and Torsten Persson. 2014. "Why Do Developing Countries Tax So Little?" *Journal of Economic Perspectives* 28, no. 4: 99–120.

Blaydes, Lisa. 2017. "State Building in the Middle East." *Annual Review of Political Science* 20, no. 1: 487–504.

Blaydes, Lisa, and Christopher Paik. 2016. "The Impact of Holy Land Crusades on State Formation: War Mobilization, Trade Integration, and Political Development in Medieval Europe." *International Organization* 70, no. 3: 551–86.

Boix, Carles. 2015. *Political Order and Inequality*. Cambridge University Press.

Boone, Catherine. 1994. "States and Ruling Classes in Postcolonial Africa: The Enduring Contradictions of Power." In *State Power and Social Forces: Domination and Transformation in the Third World*, ed. Joel Migdal, Atul Kohli, and Vivienne Shue, 108–39. Cambridge University Press.

Boone, Catherine. 2003. *Political Topographies of the African State*. Cambridge University Press.

Brambor, Thomas, Agustín Goenaga, Johannes Lindvall, and Jan Teorell. 2020. "The Lay of the Land: Information Capacity and the Modern State." *Comparative Political Studies* 53, no. 2: 175–213.

Brautigam, Deborah. 2008. "Introduction: Taxation and State-Building in Developing Countries." In *Taxation and State-Building in Developing Countries: Capacity and Consent*, ed. Deborah Brautigam, Odd-Helge Fjeldstad, and Mick Moore, 1–33. Cambridge University Press.

Brewer, John. 1990. *The Sinews of Power*. Cambridge, MA: Harvard University Press.

Cantoni, Davide, Cathrin Mohr, and Matthias Weigand. 2021. "The Rise of Fiscal Capacity." Working Paper. Ludwig-Maximilians-Universität München.

Cassidy, Traviss. 2019. "The Long-Run Effects of Oil Wealth on Development: Evidence from Petroleum Geology." *Economic Journal* 129, no. 623: 2745–78.

Centeno, Miguel Angel. 1997. "Blood and Debt: War and Taxation in Nineteenth-Century Latin America." *American Journal of Sociology* 102, no. 6: 1565–605.

Centeno, Miguel Angel. 2002. *Blood and Debt: War and the Nation-State in Latin America*. Penn State University Press.

Chen, Joy, Eric H. Wang, and Xiaoming Zhang. 2021. "Leviathan's Offer: State-Building with Elite Compensation in Early Medieval China." Working Paper. Cheung Kong Graduate School of Business.

Cox, Gary. 2016. *Marketing Sovereign Promises: Monopoly Brokerage and the Growth of the English State*. Cambridge University Press.

Cox, Gary. 2023. "Historical Political Economy of Legislative Power." In *The Oxford Handbook of Historical Political Economy*, ed. Jeffery A. Jenkins and Jared Rubin, 329–51. Oxford University Press.

Dal Bo, Ernesto, Pablo Hernandez, and Sebastián Mazzuca. 2022. "The Paradox of Civilization. Pre-Institutional Sources of Security and Prosperity." *American Political Science Review*. 116, no. 1: 213–30.

Dell, Melissa, Nathaniel Lane, and Pablo Querubin. 2018. "The Historical State, Local Collective Action, and Economic Development in Vietnam." *Econometrica* 86, no. 6: 2083–121.

Dincecco, Mark. 2009. "Fiscal Centralization, Limited Government, and Public Revenues in Europe, 1650–1913." *Journal of Economic History* 69, no. 1: 48–103.

Dincecco, Mark. 2011. *Political Transformations and Public Finances: Europe, 1650–1913*. Cambridge University Press.

Dincecco, Mark, Giovanni Federico, and Andrea Vindigni. 2011. "Warfare, Taxation, and Political Change: Evidence from the Italian Risorgimiento." *Journal of Economic History* 71, no. 4: 887–914.

Dincecco, Mark, James Fenske, and Massimiliano Onorato. 2019. "Is Africa Different? Historical Conflict and State Development." *Economic History of Developing Regions* 34, no. 2: 209–50.

Dincecco, Mark, and Yuhua Wang. 2018a. "Internal Conflict, Elite Action, and State Failure: Evidence from China, 1000–1911." Working Paper. University of Michigan and Harvard University.

Dincecco, Mark, and Yuhua Wang. 2018b. "Violent Conflict and Political Development over the Long Run: China versus Europe." *Annual Review of Political Science* 21. 341–58

Dincecco, Mark and Yuhua Wang. 2023. "State Capacity in Historical Political Economy." In *The Oxford Handbook of Historical Political Economy*, ed. Jeffery A. Jenkins and Jared Rubin, 253–69. Oxford University Press.

Dunning, Thad. 2008. *Crude Democracy: Natural Resource Wealth and Political Regimes*. Cambridge University Press.

Ertman, Thomas. 1997. *Birth of the Leviathan: Building States and Regimes in Medieval and Early Modern Europe*. Cambridge University Press.

Fearon, James D., and David D. Laitin. 2003. "Ethnicity, Insurgency, and Civil War." *American Political Science Review* 97, no. 1: 75–90.

Fernandez-Villaverde, Jesús, Mark Koyama, Youhong Lin, and Tuan-Hwee Sng. 2020. "The Fractured-Land Hypothesis." NBER Working Paper.

Gailmard, Sean. 2021. "Theory, History, and Political Economy." *Journal of Historical Political Economy* 1, no. 1: 69–104.

Garfias, Francisco. 2018. "Elite Competition and State Capacity Development: Theory and Evidence from Post-Revolutionary Mexico." *American Political Science Review* 112, no. 2: 339–57.

Garfias, Francisco. 2019. "Elite Coalitions, Limited Government, and Fiscal Capacity Development: Evidence from Bourbon Mexico." *Journal of Politics* 81, no. 1: 94–111.

Garfias, Francisco, and Emily A. Sellars. 2021. "From Conquest to Centralization: Domestic Conflict and the Transition to Direct Rule." *Journal of Politics* 83, no. 3: 992–1009.

Garfias, Francisco, and Emily A. Sellars. 2022a. "Fiscal Legibility and State Development: Theory and Evidence from Colonial Mexico." Working Paper. University of California, San Diego and Yale University.

Garfias, Francisco, and Emily A. Sellars. 2022b. "When State Building Backfires: Elite Coordination and Popular Grievance in Rebellion." *American Journal of Political Science* 66, no. 4: 977–92.

Gehlbach, Scott. 2008. *Representation through Taxation: Revenue, Politics, and Development in Postcommunist States*. Cambridge University Press.

Gennaioli, Nicola, and Ilia Rainer. 2007. "The Modern Impact of Pre-Colonial Centralization in Africa." *Journal of Economic Growth* 12, no. 3: 185–234.

Gennaioli, Nicola, and Joachim Voth. 2015. "State Capacity and Military Conflict." *Review of Economic Studies* 82, no. 4: 1409–48.

Gerring, John, Daniel Ziblatt, Johan Van Gorp, and Julian Arévalo. 2011. "An Institutional Theory of Direct and Indirect Rule." *World Politics* 63, no. 3: 377–433.

Goenaga, Agustín, Oriol Sabate, and Jan Teorell. 2018. "The State Does Not Live by Warfare Alone: War and Public Revenue in the Long Nineteenth Century." STANCE Working Paper.

Grzymala-Busse, Anna. 2020. "Beyond War and Contracts: The Medieval and Religious Roots of the European State." *Annual Review of Political Science* 23: 19–36.

Herbst, Jeffrey. 2000. *States and Power in Africa: Comparative Lessons in Authority and Control*. Princeton, NJ: Princeton University Press.

Hintze, Otto. 1975. *Historical Essays*. Oxford University Press.

Hoffman, Philip T. 2012. "Why Was It Europeans Who Conquered the World?" *Journal of Economic History* 72, no. 3: 601–33.

Hoffman, Philip T. 2015. "What Do States Do? Politics and Economic History." *Journal of Economic History* 75, no. 2: 303–32.

Hoffman, Philip, and Jean-Laurent Rosenthal. 1997. "Divided We Fall: The Political Economy of Warfare and Taxation." Working Paper. California Institute of Technology.

Huang, Chin-Hao, and David C. Kang. 2022. "State Formation in Korea and Japan, 400–800 CE: Emulation and Learning, Not Bellicist Competition." *International Organization* 76, no. 1: 1–31

Hui, Victoria. 2015. *War and State Formation in Ancient China and Early Modern Europe*. Cambridge University Press.

Iyer, Lakshmi. 2010. "Direct versus Indirect Colonial Rule in India: Long-Term Consequences." *Review of Economics and Statistics* 92, no. 4: 693–713.

Johnson, Noel D., and Mark Koyama. 2014. "Tax Farming and the Origins of State Capacity in England and France." *Explorations in Economic History* 51, no. 1, 1–20.

Johnson, Noel D., and Mark Koyama. 2017. "States and Economic Growth: Capacity and Constraints." *Explorations in Economic History* 64: 1–20.

Karaman, K. Kivanc, and Şevket Pamuk. 2013. "Different Paths to the Modern State in Europe: The Interaction between Warfare, Economic Structure, and Political Regime." *American Political Science Review* 107, no. 3: 603–26.

Kiser, Edgar, and Yong Cai. 2003. "War and Bureaucratization in Qin China: Exploring an Anomalous Case." *American Sociological Review* 68, no. 4: 511–39.

Ko, Chi Yu, Mark Koyama, and Tuan-Hwee Sng. 2018. "Unified China and Divided Europe." *International Economic Review* 59, no. 1: 285–327.

Koyama, Mark, Chiaki Moriguchi, and Tuan-Hwee Sng. 2018. "Geopolitics and Asia's Little Divergence: State-Building in China and Japan after 1850." *Journal of Economic Behavior & Organization* 155: 178–204.

Koyama, Mark. 2023. "Legal Capacity in Historical Political Economy." In *The Oxford Handbook of Historical Political Economy*, ed. Jeffery A. Jenkins and Jared Rubin, 271–92. Oxford University Press.

Kurtz, Marcus. 2013. *Latin American State-Building in Comparative Perspective: Social Foundations of Institutional Order*. Cambridge University Press.

Lange, Matthew K. 2004. "British Colonial Legacies and Political Development." *World Development* 32, no. 6: 905–22.

Lee, Alexander. 2019. "Land, State Capacity, and Colonialism: Evidence from India." *Comparative Political Studies* 52, no. 3: 412–44.

Levi, Margaret. 1988. *Of Rule and Revenue*. University of California Press.

Levi, Margaret. 2002. "The State of the Study of the State." In *Political Science: The State of the Discipline*, ed. Ira Katznelson and Helen V. Milner, 33–55. W. W. Norton & Company.

Mamdani, Mahmood. 1996. *Citizen and Subject: Contemporary Africa and the Legacy of Late Colonialism*. Princeton, NJ: Princeton University Press.

Mares, Isabela, and Didac Queralt. 2015. "The Non-Democratic Origins of Income Taxation." *Comparative Political Studies* 48, no. 14: 1974–2009.

Mares, Isabela, and Didac Queralt. 2020. "Fiscal Innovation in Non-Democratic Regimes: Elites and the Adoption of the Prussian Income Tax of the 1890s." *Explorations in Economic History* 57, no. 1: 62–76.

Mayshar, Joram, Omer Moav, and Luigi Pascali. 2022. "The Origin of the State: Land Productivity or Appropriability?" *Journal of Political Economy* 130, no. 4: 1091–144.

Mayshar, Joram, Omer Moav, and Zvika Neeman. 2017. "Geography, Transparency, and Institutions." *American Political Science Review* 111, no. 3: 622–36.

Mazzuca, Sebastian. 2021. *Latecomer State Formation: Political Geography and Capacity Failure in Latin America*. New Haven, CT: Yale University Press.

Michalopoulos, Stelios, and Elias Papaioannou. 2013. "Pre-colonial Ethnic Institutions and Contemporary African Development." *Econometrica* 81, no. 1: 113–52.

Migdal, Joel. 1988. *Strong Societies and Weak States: State-Society Relations and State Capabilities in the Third World*. Princeton, NJ: Princeton University Press.

Moore, Barrington. 1966. *Social Origins of Dictatorship and Democracy: Lord and Peasant in the Making of the Modern World*. Boston: Beacon.

Moriguchi, Chiaki, and Tuan-Hwee Sng. 2023. "The Size of Polities in Historical Political Economy." In *Oxford Handbook of Historical Political Economy*, ed. Jeffery Jenkins and Jared Rubin, 237–51. Oxford University Press.

North, Douglass, and Barry R. Weingast. 1989. "Constitutions and Commitment: The Evolution of Institutions Governing Public Choice in Seventeenth-Century England." *Journal of Economic History* 49, no. 4: 803–32.

North, Douglass, John Joseph Wallis, and Barry R. Weingast. 2009. *Violence and Social Orders*. Cambridge University Press.

Olson, Mancur. 1993. "Dictatorship, Democracy, and Development." *American Political Science Review* 87, no. 3: 567–76.

Osafo-Kwaako, Philip, and James Robinson. 2013. "Political Centralization in Pre-Colonial Africa." *Journal of Comparative Economics* 41, no. 1: 534–64.

Paik, Christopher, and Jessica Vechbanyongratana. 2019. "Path to Centralization and Development: Evidence from Siam." *World Politics* 71, no. 2: 289–331.

Pierskalla, Jan, Alexander De Juan, and Max Montgomery. 2017. "The Territorial Expansion of the Colonial State: Evidence from German East Africa 1890–1909." *British Journal Political Science* 49, no. 2: 711–37.

Queralt, Didac. 2019. "War, International Finance, and Fiscal Capacity in the Long Run." *International Organization* 73, no. 4: 713–53.

Queralt, Didac. 2022. *Pawned States: State-Building in the Era of International Finance*. Princeton, NJ: Princeton University Press.

Sánchez-Talanquer, Mariano. 2020. "One-Eyed State: The Politics of Legibility and Property Taxation." *Latin American Politics and Society* 63, no. 3: 65–93.

Saylor, Ryan. 2014. *State-Building in Boom Times: Commodities and Coalitions in Latin America and Africa*. Oxford University Press.

Scheve, Kenneth, and David Stasavage. 2010. "Democracy, War, and Wealth: Lessons from Two Centuries of Inheritance Taxation." *American Political Science Review* 106, no. 1: 81–102.

Schumpeter, Joseph. 1954. "The Crisis of the Tax State." *International Economics Papers*, no. 4: 5–38.

Scott, James C. 1998. *Seeing Like a State: How Certain Schemes to Improve the Human Condition Have Failed*. New Haven, CT: Yale University Press.

Scott, James C. 2009. *The Art of Not Being Governed*. New Haven, CT: Yale University Press.

Scott, James C. 2017. *Against the Grain: a Deep History of the Earliest States*. New Haven, CT: Yale University Press.

Skocpol, Theda. 1979. *States and Social Revolutions: A Comparative Analysis of France, Russia and China*. Cambridge University Press.

Slantchev, Branislav L., and Tory A. Kravitz. 2019. "No Taxation without Administration: Wealth Assessment in the Formation of the Fiscal State." Working Paper, 1–70. University of California, San Diego.

Slater, Dan. 2010. *Ordering Power: Contentious Politics and Authoritarian Leviathans in Southeast Asia*. New York: Cambridge University Press.

Soifer, Hillel. 2015. *State-Building in Latin America*. Cambridge University Press.

Spruyt, Hendrik. 1996. *The Sovereign State and Its Competitors*. Princeton, NJ: Princeton University Press.

Spruyt, Hendrik. 2002. "The Origins, Development, and Possible Decline of the Modern State." *Annual Review of Political Science* 5, no. 1: 127–49.

Stasavage, David. 2003. *Public Debt and the Birth of the Democratic State: France and Great Britain 1688–1789*. Cambridge University Press.

Stasavage, David. 2007. "Partisan Politics and Public Debt: The Importance of the 'Whig Supremacy' for Britain's Financial Revolution." *European Journal of Economic History* 11, no. 1: 123–53.

Stasavage, David. 2011. *States of Credit: Size, Power, and the Development of European Polities*. Princeton, NJ: Princeton University Press,

Stasavage, David. 2020. *The Decline and Rise of Democracy: A Global History from Antiquity to Today*. Cambridge University Press.
Suryanarayan, Pavithra. 2021. "Status Politics Hollows Out the State: Evidence from Colonial India." Working Paper. London School of Economics and Political Science.
Suryanarayan, Pavithra, and Steven White. 2021. "Slavery, Reconstruction, and Bureaucratic Capacity in the American South." *American Political Science Review* 115, no. 2: 568–84.
Tilly, Charles. 1975. "Reflections on the History of European State-Making." In *The Formation of National States in Western Europe*, ed. Charles Tilly, 3–83. Princeton, NJ: Princeton University Press.
Tilly, Charles. 1978. *From Mobilization to Revolution*. Addison-Wesley.
Tilly, Charles. 1990. *Coercion, Capital, and European States, A.D. 990–1990*. Cambridge, MA: Blackwell.
Vogler, Jan. 2023. "Bureaucracies in Historical Political Economy." In *The Oxford Handbook of Historical Political Economy*, ed. Jeffery A. Jenkins and Jared Rubin, 373–99. Oxford University Press.
Wang, Yuhua. 2022. "Blood Is Thicker Than Water: Elite Kinship Networks and State Building in Imperial China." *American Political Science Review* 1–15.
Weber, Max. 1999. *Gesammelte politische Schriften von Max Weber*. Potsdamer Internet-Ausgabe.
Wolf, Eric. 1969. *Peasant Wars of the Twentieth Century*. New York: Harper and Row.

Appendix

STATE-BUILDING IN HISTORICAL POLITICAL ECONOMY

A.1 Analysis of Ruler Model

We solve for the ruler's optimal level of taxation as a function of the parameters of the model. Using the distribution of $\underline{S}$, his maximization problem is:

$$\max_{T} \left(\frac{f(T+\rho) - (\sigma - \delta)}{2\delta} \right) \alpha - cT \tag{A1}$$

subject to $0 \leq T \leq \omega$. The first order conditions are given by:

$$\frac{f'(T+\rho)\alpha}{2\delta} = c \tag{A2}$$

Note that $f'(T+\rho)$ is positive and decreasing in T by the concavity assumption. When this expression holds, optimal tax revenue is increasing in the rents from office (a) and decreasing in non-tax revenue (ρ), in the uncertainty about the threat (δ), and in the cost of taxation (c).

We additionally consider potential corner solutions. If $f'(\rho) < \frac{2\delta c}{\alpha}$, the ruler's optimal choice will be to collect no taxes. This is more likely to hold when the expected threat (σ) is very low, non-tax revenue (ρ) is very high, the technology $f(\cdot)$ is very inefficient (i.e., $f'(T)$ is very small), the cost of taxation (c) is very high, and the benefits of maintaining power (a) are very small. Because taxation is costly, the ruler will also never tax beyond what is necessary to ensure state survival (i.e., $f(T+\rho) = \sigma + \delta$). At the opposite extreme, there are no benefits to taxation when state failure is inevitable (if $f(\omega + \rho) < \sigma - \delta$).

If $f'(\omega+\rho) > \dfrac{2\delta c}{\alpha}$, the ruler will extract all wealth. This is more likely when societal wealth (ω) and non-tax revenue (ρ) are small, when the benefits of maintaining power (a) are very high, and when the technologies of defense ($f(\cdot)$) and taxation (c) are highly efficient.

A.2 Analysis of Elite Model

To summarize, the game timing and payoffs are:

1. The authority chooses tax revenue (T) to extract from the elite.
2. Elite chooses whether to side with the government ($e = 1$) or to defect ($e = 0$).
3. A stochastic shock drawn by Nature ($\underline{S}$) determines the extent of the threat and the survival of the government.

- **State survives:** The authority receives $u_A = \alpha$. If elites back the authority, they receive $u_E = \omega - T + \lambda - \mu$. If they defect, they receive $u_E = \omega - T + \lambda - \pi$.
- **State collapses:** The authority receives $u_A = 0$. If elites back the authority, they receive $u_E = -\mu$. If they defect, they receive $u_E = 0$

We solve for the subgame-perfect Nash equilibrium (SPNE) of this game by backwards induction, beginning with the elite's choice to back the government or defect after observing the tax level. Elites back the government if the expected benefit of doing so exceeds the expected cost, or if:

$$\left(\frac{f(T)-(\sigma-\delta)}{2\delta}\right)(\omega-T+\lambda)-\mu \geq \left(\frac{f(T)-\zeta-(\sigma-\delta)}{2\delta}\right)(\omega-T+\lambda-\pi) \quad (A3)$$

or if $\zeta T - \pi f(T) \leq \zeta(\omega + \lambda) + \pi(\delta - \sigma - \zeta) - 2\delta\mu$. Elites are more likely to back the government when their utility under state survival (wealth ω and benefit λ) and the cost of punishment (π) are higher and when the cost of compliance (μ) and expected level of external threat (σ) are lower. If $\omega - T + \lambda > \pi$, elites are more likely to back the government as elite power (ζ) increases. Otherwise, an increase in ζ will encourage defection (see the chapter for a discussion).

We are interested in how an increase in taxation influences the willingness of elites to back the government. For some parameter values, elites' best response does not depend on the level of taxation. We concentrate on cases where the elite backs the government under some tax levels but not others. Taking the derivative of expression A3 with respect to T, we see that whether compliance is increasing or decreasing in T depends on the sign of the expression $\zeta - \pi f'(T)$.

We turn to the rulers' problem. Let $\hat{T}$ represent the maximum feasible (i.e., between 0 and ω) level of taxation under which the elite would back the government. When the elite's best response does not depend on the tax level or when $\hat{T} = \omega$, the ruler sets $T = \omega$ to maximize the probability of remaining in power, with or without elite support. When $\hat{T} < \omega$, the authority's optimal choice is to either maximize extraction subject to retaining elite support ($T = \hat{T}$) to maximize extraction in general $T = \omega$. The authority chooses the lower tax level $T^* = \hat{T} < \omega$ when:

$$\zeta > f(\omega) - f(\hat{T}) \tag{A4}$$

See Figure 11.1 and the chapter discussion.

A.3 Analysis of Commoners Model

The timing of the game is:

1. The authority chooses amount T of tax revenue to extract from the elite's wealth (ω).
2. A stochastic shock drawn by Nature reveals the local conditions for the commoners (η) and commoners decide to rebel ($c = 1$) or not ($c = 0$)
3. If commoners rebel, the elites choose whether to restore order ($e = 1$) or to defect ($e = 0$). They otherwise take no action.
4. A stochastic shock drawn by Nature (S) determines the magnitude of the threat to the state; it survives if $S \geq \underline{S}$ and falls otherwise.

Payoffs are given by:

- Central authorities: They receive $u_A = \alpha$ if the state survives, $u_A = 0$ if it collapses.
- Elites: If commoners do not rebel, they receive $u_E = \omega - T + \lambda$ if the state survives and $u_E = 0$ if it falls. If the elite represses rebellion, they receive $u_E = \omega - T + \lambda - \mu$ if the state survives and $u_E = -\mu$ if it falls. If elites defect when facing rebellion, they receive $u_E = \omega - T + \lambda - \pi$ if the state survives and $u_E = 0$ if it falls.
- Commoners: They receive $u_C = \eta$ if they do not rebel, $u_C = \beta$ if they rebel and the elite does not repress, and $u_C = \beta - \psi$ if they rebel and the elite represses.

We solve for the SPNE by backwards induction, beginning with the elite's decision to repress if rebellion occurs. Note that if elites are faced with this choice, their problem is identical to the one in the previous model (see equation A3). We focus our discussion on situations where the elite backs the authority under some but not all levels of taxation (i.e., when $\hat{T} < \omega$, where $\hat{T}$ is the maximum taxation that the elite is willing to accept without defecting, as above).

Turning to the commoners stage, note that commoners face no relevant uncertainty because opportunity cost (η) and taxation (T, which determines elite compliance) have been set at the time of their action and because their payoffs do not depend on state survival. By the assumption that $\bar{\eta} + \nu < \beta - \psi$, commoners will only rebel when two conditions are met: local conditions are sufficiently poor ($\eta < \beta$) and elites who face rebellion defect ($T > \hat{T}$).

The ruler's problem is analogous to the above: he decides whether to set $T = \hat{T}$ (to count on elite backing) or $T = \omega$ (to maximize the state's ability to withstand elite defection). Using the distribution of local conditions (η) and the assumption that $\bar{\eta} - v < \beta < \bar{\eta} + v$, the probability of commoner rebellion if $T > \hat{T}$ is $\frac{\beta - \bar{\eta} + v}{2v}$. Using this expression and rearranging, the authority sets the lower tax level $\check{T}$ when:

$$\zeta \left(\frac{\beta - \bar{\eta} + v}{2v} \right) > f(\omega) - f(\hat{T}) \tag{A5}$$

As commoners become more likely to rebel (as β increases or η declines) or as uncontrolled rebellion becomes more dangerous (as ζ rises), authorities face more pressure to appease domestic elites with lower taxation to maintain control.

CHAPTER 12

THE SIZE OF POLITIES IN HISTORICAL POLITICAL ECONOMY

CHIAKI MORIGUCHI AND TUAN-HWEE SNG

INTRODUCTION

A very populous city can rarely, if ever, be well governed.
—Aristotle

Confucius said, "There are not two suns in the sky, nor two sovereigns over the people."
—Mencius

Polities vary widely in size, in terms of geography as well as population, both today and over the course of history. Russia, the largest country in the world, has a land area almost forty million times that of Vatican City, the smallest country. In the late nineteenth century, Queen Victoria's British Empire—the largest polity in world history—comprised more than one-fifth of the world's land area and population. Less than fourteen hundred kilometers from Buckingham Palace, Charles Bertoleoni, a self-proclaimed king, ruled over a population of around fifty-five inhabitants on the island of Tavolara, off the northeast coast of Sardinia (Maddison 2001; New York Times 1896; 1928).

The size of polities has varied not only across space at any given time but also over time in any given space. Ancient Chinese texts claimed that there were tens of thousands of states or statelets in China during the time of King Yu (c. 2200 BCE). As polities grew in size, the number of polities shrank. By the time of King Tang six hundred years later (Sellmann 2002), there were three thousand polities. In 221 BCE, the state of Qin became the sole polity when it annexed its neighbors and expanded its borders to complete the first unification of China.

Occasionally such changes may occur within a short span of time. In classical Greece, several hundred poleis or city states traditionally occupied the small plains and narrow valleys that were surrounded by rugged mountains. Each polis was so small that Plato spoke of a population of 5,040 citizens (household heads) as the ideal size of a polis. Yet less than four decades after Plato's death, Alexander the Great—taught by Plato's student and colleague, Aristotle—created an empire that extended from Greece and Egypt to India, ruling as many as twenty million people (McEvedy and Jones 1978, 125). For a more recent example, we only need to look back to the last century. In 1950, there were sixty member states in the United Nations. But the collapse of colonial empires and the Soviet Union in the second half of the twentieth century more than tripled the number of UN member states within fifty years.

Historically, the size and number of polities have captivated scholars from various parts of the world. Most would agree that a polity's size has a salient impact on the welfare of its citizens. Yet scholars from different cultural traditions have held very different views on the impacts of polity size and the optimal size of a polity. In this short chapter, we first review how philosophers in Europe and China traditionally viewed the subject. Then we present the findings from modern historical research on the consequences of polity size. We then shift our attention to the causes of polity size before drawing some conclusions.

It is neither our goal, nor is it possible, to provide a comprehensive discussion on a topic as important as this. Our modest objective is to highlight a few salient aspects of the size of polities and to make some suggestions for the way forward. We recommend that readers refer to other chapters of the handbook, especially Mark Dincecco and Yuhua Wang's chapter on state capacity (Chapter 13) and Mark Koyama's chapter (Chapter 14) on legal capacity, both of which share a number of overlapping and complementary themes with our chapter.

Historical Thinkers on the Consequences of Size

A long tradition in Western philosophy, traceable to the classical Greeks, views size as detrimental to good governance. Plato extolled the virtue of smallness in enabling citizens to know and care for each other. Aristotle stressed that while a polity must be large enough to be self-sufficient, there should be a limit to its size; otherwise, its citizens will not have sufficient knowledge of each other's characters to elect the right governors and judges. As a rule of thumb, he proposed that a state should not be so large that its citizens could not gather in an open space to hold a public conversation (Dahl and Tufte 1973; Aristotle 2016).

The thinkers of the Enlightenment, especially Montesquieu and Rousseau, continued to equate smallness with citizen participation and cohesiveness. Rousseau put forth a particularly lucid analysis arguing that extending the social bond weakens it. As the state enlarges, he claimed, individuals will care more about their personal interests and less about their collective well-being, for "the people have less affection for their leaders whom they never see, for their country, which is in their eyes like the world, and for their fellow-citizens, most of whom are strangers to them" (Rousseau 2002, 186). Meanwhile, administrative costs will increase due to the need to set up multiple layers of government to administer a large territory. Eventually, the "many additional burdens perpetually exhaust the subjects; and far from being better governed by all these different orders, they are less well governed than if they had but a single order above them" (185).

As the epigraphs for this chapter suggest, the perspectives of mainstream philosophers in China could not have been more different from their Western counterparts. Mencius, a contemporary of Aristotle, saw political disunity as a root cause of instability. He was not alone in this belief. With few exceptions, Chinese thinkers in history promoted the virtues of maintaining a large and unified state to avoid the misery of war. This consensus was not simply a product of China's recurring unifications in history, for those who lived before the first unification by Qin Shi Huang in 221 BCE already repeatedly echoed it. Pines (2000; 2012) observes that each of the major philosophies that emerged in the pre-Qin period of political fragmentation contended that the division of "All under Heaven" into competing warring states was the cause of the endless conflicts and sufferings that China witnessed during the Axial Age. Leading thinkers, including Confucius, Mozi, Laozi, and Shangyang—who represented different schools of thoughts and argued fiercely over a wide range of sociopolitical and philosophical issues—concurred on the desirability of political unification, which they believed would bring order and an enormous peace dividend in terms of lives and resources saved. *Lü shi chunqiu*, a collection of political essays compiled around 239 BCE that fused the ideas of the major Chinese philosophies, puts it as follows: "There is no turmoil greater than the absence of the Son of Heaven; without the Son of Heaven, the strong overcome the weak, the many lord it over the few, they incessantly use arms to harm each other" (Pines 2000, 316).

Modern Studies on the Consequences of Polity Size

Studies in political science and economics largely endorse the classical Western perspective that polity size has a negative impact on governance quality. In a study of pre-industrial Europe, Stasavage (2011) finds that representative assemblies in large states were less likely to convene regularly and therefore functioned less effectively due to high communication and travel costs.[1] Other researchers argue that the size and number of polities affect long-run economic development. In fact, a long list of scholars attribute the rise of Europe to its political fragmentation, which, according to them, gave Europe a decisive developmental edge. Baechler (1975) considers Europe's political anarchy as the driving force behind its willingness to engage in political, economic, and scientific experimentations. Cowen (1990) traces the development of capital markets and pro-market policies in Europe to its vibrant interstate competition. Tilly (1990) attributes the emergence of nation states in early-modern Europe to the capital-intensive city states of the Middle Ages. Mokyr (2007, 24) notes that "many of the most influential and innovative intellectuals took advantage of . . . the competitive 'states system.'" Diamond (1997, 414) argues that in contrast to China, where "a decision by one despot could and repeatedly did halt innovation," "Europe's geographic balkanization resulted in dozens or hundreds of independent, competing statelets and centers of innovation."

According to Stasavage (2016), the collapse of the Roman Empire—which led to the breakdown of western Europe into a set of small, fragmented states—kept the transaction costs of maintaining assemblies low. This, in turn, set Europe on a different political trajectory that culminated in its economic rise. Scheidel (2019), too, views the failure of empire building in Europe after the fall of Rome as the enabler of the rise of the West. He argues that Europe's enduring polycentrism after the sixth century ensured that there was no empire to suppress competition and innovation. To reinforce his notion that there would have been no modernity without polycentrism, he even quotes an unlikely source, Chairman Mao, who commented that "one good thing about Europe is that all its countries are independent. Each of them does its own thing, which makes it possible for the economy of Europe to develop at a fast pace. Ever since China became an empire after the Qin dynasty, our country has been for the most part unified. One of its defects has been bureaucratization, and excessively tight control. The localities could not develop independently" (Scheidel 2019, 338).

As Mao's quote suggests, if polity size is indeed detrimental to good governance, the evidence should have been most salient in China, given the long history of the Chinese Empire. As Figure 12.1A illustrates, for more than half of the past two millennia, the country was ruled by a unified state with the emperor as a figure of political and moral authority at the top of the administrative pyramid (Ko and Sng 2013). The opening line of the novel *Romance of the Three Kingdoms* succinctly captures the expectation among the Chinese that every episode of political fragmentation must be followed by a new cycle of unification: "The empire, long divided, must unite; long united, must divide" (Luo 2014). No other region in the world has produced and sustained large empires with such regularity.

History suggests that unified Chinese regimes may have experienced considerable administrative diseconomies of scale. As William Skinner (1977) highlights, the number of Chinese counties had a tendency to shrink during times of political unification. For instance, during the mid-sixth century when China was ruled by three competing regimes, there were about 2,300 counties in total. Several decades later, only 1,255 counties were left after the Sui dynasty reunified China and reorganized its territorial administration.

Furthermore, as Figure 12.1B illustrates, in the early-modern period, counties—the lowest level of formal administration in imperial China—were densely distributed in the vicinity of the capital city, Beijing, in the north, and grew progressively sparser

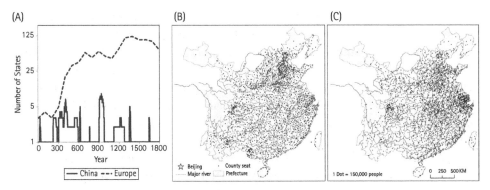

FIGURE 12.1. (A) Number of regimes in China between 0 CE and 1800.

Adapted from Ko, Koyama, and Sng (2018)

(B) There were fewer than 1,400 counties in China in 1820. Counties were more sparsely distributed in the south than in the north, where the capital city was located.

Adapted from Sng (2014)

(C) In 1820, the most densely populated region in China was the Yangtze River Delta. There were more people residing in the south than in the north.

Adapted from Sng (2014)

farther to the south despite the fact that more people lived in the south than in the north (Figure 12.1C). The patterns suggest that despite the popular perception of the early-modern Chinese state as an autocratic regime with virtually unchecked powers, in reality it was hamstrung by a limited capacity to extend its reach (Sng 2014), especially to areas far away from the capital city.

Indeed, the early-modern Chinese state apparatus was unusually small even by pre-industrial standards. In 1800, only around twenty thousand ranked officials governed a population that may have exceeded three hundred million. This translates to a ratio of one official per fifteen thousand people.[2] To give a loose comparison, Pintner (1980, 192) estimates that tsarist Russia had one official per ten thousand people. The direct tax system of Louis XIV's France hired three thousand officers, or one tax officer for every seventy-seven hundred people (Collins 2009, 208, 245). England, traditionally viewed as a state of small government, in the sixteenth century had one royal official for every four thousand people (Sacks 1994, 36). The imperial Chinese state also taxed lightly. It captured a mere 2.4 percent of the national income in the early twentieth century (Wang 1973). When measured in silver, per capita tax revenue in China was only 11 percent England's in 1750 (Ko, Koyama, and Sng 2018, Table 5).[3]

Sng and Moriguchi (2014) posit that in the age of premodern communication technologies, a large and centralized state like China faced a severe principal-agent problem that imposed acute limitations on the exercise of state power, which in turn led to low state capacity. To test their conjecture, they build a dynamic model and use the Tokugawa shogunate in Japan as a counterfactual to pre-1850 China, utilizing the shared cultural, institutional, and technological heritages of the two countries as a basis to investigate the impact of territorial size on administrative performance. The authors show theoretically and empirically that Japan's geographical compactness allowed the Tokugawa shogunate to tax more and provide more public goods (coins, roads, urban management, forest management, and famine relief) on a per capita basis, while Qing China faced stiffer administrative challenges in managing a sprawling empire from its capital city. Despite producing a host of institutional innovations to improve administrative efficiency, many of which Tokugawa Japan subsequently adopted, Qing China suffered from more severe corruption and exhibited a lower degree of fiscal resilience over time (Figure 12.2).

An example of a Chinese invention that turned out to function more effectively in Japan than in China is the petition system. First instituted in the seventh century, the petition system was designed to offer a channel for commoners to complain directly to the emperor about officials' abuse of power and other malfeasance. However, the sheer size of the Chinese population made it impossible for the emperor to verify the authenticity of every accusation (Ocko 1988; Fang 2009). During the Qing dynasty (1644–1912), two emperors, Qianlong (r. 1736–1795) and Jiaqing (r. 1796–1820), actively encouraged petitions from their subjects when they came to the throne. But in each instance, the emperor swiftly reversed his stance after discovering that he could not possibly handle the resulting flood of complaints (Fang 2009). By contrast, the petition system functioned reasonably well when it was implemented in Tokugawa Japan in the eighteenth century (Ohira 2003). Historical evidence suggests that while irrelevant requests and false accusations were a constant nuisance, the volume of complaints was manageable and the petitions were duly processed. Punishments were regularly meted out to corrupt officials as well as to petitioners who were found to have made misstatements. In addition to exposing corruption, individual petitions also led to the creation of fire brigades and the establishment of a hospital for the poor in the shogun's capital city, Edo (Roberts 1994).

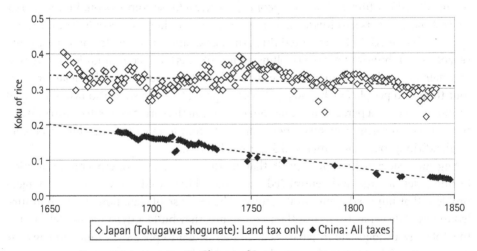

FIGURE 12.2. Per capita tax revenue in China and Japan, 1650–1850

Adapted from Sng and Moriguchi (2014)

The Determinants of Polity Size

The studies we have discussed thus far suggest that small is beautiful. However, these studies, by design, focus primarily on the costs of polity size while largely overlooking the benefits. The consequences of polity size cannot be singularly negative; otherwise, our world would be one of extreme political fragmentation. As the ancient Chinese philosophers pointed out, interstate military competition could cause severe resource wastage and the neglect of considerable economic externalities. Western philosophers were also concerned that states that are too small may be incapable of preserving their autonomy. Rousseau stressed that while large states risk being crushed under their own weight, small states are in danger of being easily overrun by their neighbors; it is therefore "not the least of a statesman's talents to find the proportion between the two which is most advantageous for the preservation of the State" (2002, 186). Clearly, we need a holistic approach that looks at both the costs and benefits of polity size to evaluate its causes and consequences.

Friedman (1977) and Alesina and Spolaore (1997; 2003) have made pioneering efforts in using formal models to study the determinants of polity size. Friedman (1977) conjectures that a territory ought to be assigned—voluntarily or by coercion—to a polity that places the highest value on its revenue. He then investigates changes in Europe's political map from Roman to modern times and finds reasonable explanatory power to his conjecture. In a paper written after the disintegration of the former Soviet bloc, Alesina and Spolaore (1997) build a theoretical framework that explains the number and size of polities based on the trade-off between the benefits of maintaining a large polity (i.e., a large domestic market and lower per capita cost in the provision of public goods) and the costs of managing a large population with heterogeneous preferences. Robert Barro summarized this trade-off in an earlier *Wall Street Journal* article published in 1991:

> We can think of a country's optimal size as emerging from a tradeoff: A large country can spread the cost of public goods, such as defining a legal and monetary system and maintaining national security, over many taxpayers, but a large country is also likely to have a diverse population that is difficult for the central government to satisfy.[4]

Alesina and Spolaore's (1997) framework produces several testable predictions, including (i) nonautocratic or democratic states will be smaller than autocratic ones, (ii) majority voting is likely to produce too many small states, and (iii) economic integration will likely increase the number of polities while reducing the size. Alesina, Spolaore, and Wacziarg (2000) provide empirical support of some of these predictions.

Despite these efforts, much remains to be done. One particular area that needs attention, as Gerring and Veenendaal (2020) highlight, is the phenomenon that the size of polities vary by a substantially greater margin than the size of other institutions. For instance, China's population of 1.3 billion is 130,000 times that of Tuvalu. By contrast, Indira Gandhi National Open University in India, possibly the largest university in the world by enrollment, has a student population of four million, which is *only* 2,600 times larger than École normale supérieure, which has about fifteen hundred students. Alesina and Spolaore (1997) focus on the symmetric equilibrium: that is, the model "predicts" that all states have equal size. While this feature is necessary to keep their model mathematically tractable, it also means that the framework has limited explanatory power on why very large states and very small ones coexist; if all states face more or less the same trade-off in size, why the immense variation in real-world outcomes at any single point in time?

We do not have a panacea, but we argue that maintaining a historical perspective is critical in the quest to explain the size of polities. History helps us to look beyond the present and the immediate past, and to consider the sources of stability and variation over time. We highlight three insights that history brings to the table. First, historians as well as social scientists studying the past generally agree that the particularities of individual regions and societies matter. Factors including geography, institutions, and culture, which vary widely across space and over time, have played influential roles in driving state formation. For instance, Montesquieu and David Hume, among others, argued that Europe's geography discouraged the emergence of empires, as its large mountain ranges and long and indented coastlines cut the continent into several geographical cores that fostered a plurality of independent political centers (Hume 1987; Montesquieu 1989).[5] Diamond (1998, 433-34) claims that, by contrast, China, with "a much less indented coastline, no islands large enough to achieve autonomy, and less formidable internal mountain barriers," has been subjected to fewer geographical constraints to political unification. And "once a unified Chinese state was founded, geography prevented any other state from gaining lasting autonomy in any part of China."[6]

Others have drawn attention to further characteristics of geography, culture, and institutions to explain observed patterns of political consolidation (Qian and Sng 2021). Wittfogel's (1957) theory of Oriental despotism contends that climatic conditions drove many societies, mostly in Asia, to organize large-scale irrigation projects, which in turn led to the birth of a strong state capable of projecting its power far and wide.[7] Lattimore (1940) and others have highlighted the influence of nomadic tribes of the Eurasian steppe—who enjoyed a distinctive advantage in war due to their expertise on horseback—on empire formation in Eurasia (see, in particular, Grousset 1970; Barfield 1989; Turchin 2009). Yet others emphasize cultural and institutional factors. Pines (2000; 2012), whom we discussed earlier, sees the shared conviction among major Chinese philosophies in the desirability of a unitary state as a key driver of China's recurring unification. Miyazaki (1983) and Bodde (1986) highlight the role in keeping China unified of the iconographic Chinese script, which allowed local elites from different parts of the country to communicate with one another. Ma and Rubin (2019) argue that the absolutist nature of the Chinese state drove it to expand into hostile territories. A small yet influential literature studying the legacy of imperialism in the form of artificial boundaries in the Middle East and Africa finds that polities whose size and shape disregard ethnic and cultural patterns are more likely to be exposed to civil conflict and economic instability (Alesina, Easterly, and Matuszeski 2011; Michalopoulos and Papaioannou 2016). None of these arguments are uncontested, yet all highlight the perils of thinking about the number and size of polities in a region without considering the region's unique traits and circumstances. Do geography, climate, a common language, militarism, colonialism, and other factors influence the size of polities in different parts of the world in similar ways? If not, why? These interesting and important questions cannot be answered adequately without an understanding of history.

Acknowledging that the particularities of individual regions matter does not imply that we should give up on the goal of building theoretical frameworks to explain the size of polities. Instead, incorporating the insights gained from studying different historical societies can enrich our models and improve their explanatory powers. For instance, Alesina and Spolaore (2003) use cultural diversity as a determinant of the cost of polity size in their model. Historical studies could help shed light on the extent to which such costs exist. Building on the steppe theory of Lattimore (1940) and others, Ko, Koyama, and Sng (2018) use historical analyses of violent conflicts between nomads in the Eurasian steppe and their agrarian neighbors to construct a Hotelling-style comparative model that examines the causes and consequences of political unification and fragmentation at the two ends of Eurasia. They hypothesize that China faced a severe, recurring nomadic threat on its northern frontier due to its proximity to the Eurasian steppe but was otherwise relatively isolated, while western Europe was exposed to periodic invasions from the rest of Eurasia on various fronts, but was protected by distance from the steppe threat. The hypothesis generates predictions on the size of polities, the locations of capital cities, and variations in population growth, which are in turn used to explain patterns in historical China and Europe. As these examples illustrate, much more can be done in marrying history and political economy analyses to investigate the size of polities in general or comparative contexts.

Second, besides variations across space, a historical approach offers a rich set of examples to help identify the forces that shape polity size over time. For instance, Bean (1973) provides an insightful analysis on how military technological change influenced the size of states in late medieval Europe. He argues that the rise of the professional infantry, which proved to be effective in battles against the heavy cavalry, as well as the improved siege cannon undermined the military importance of the knights and rocked the very foundation of the feudal society. These changes in the art of war led to a dramatic increase in the size of armies and military expenditures. Polities that were unable to centralize power and resources were eliminated. Those remaining became larger and more centralized. By 1600, the number of autonomous and semiautonomous domains had fallen compared with just two centuries before, and the first generation of European nation states had emerged. Bean's study highlights technology as a powerful force instigating episodes of synchronized drifts toward either political centralization or political fragmentation throughout history.

Last but not least, we argue that investigating regional systems in history may shed light on the wide variation in state size. Take the Pax Tokugawa for instance. A remarkably long period of peace was maintained in Japan between 1615, after the Tokugawa shogunate annihilated the Toyotomi clan in the Siege of Osaka, and 1853, when the Black Ships arrived from the United States to coerce Japan into opening its ports to American trade. Under Pax Tokugawa, Japan, with a land area smaller than present-day Italy, was a collection of more than 260 domains, each led by a daimyo or lord. The shogun, the largest daimyo, controlled four million koku of land.[8] Fewer than ten other daimyos each controlled more than half a million koku of land. Many domains were no more than ten thousand koku. The shogun's relation with the other daimyo was one of first among equals. The daimyo swore allegiance to the shogun and were constrained by a system of regulations and norms designed to prevent dissent. But otherwise the daimyo retained virtually complete autonomy over their individual domains. This "international" system showed remarkable resilience, prevailing for more than two centuries before its collapse fifteen years after the Black Ships Incident of 1853. When the shogunate proved incapable of holding on its own against the Western imperialist powers, the domains entered into civil war, which ultimately ended with Japan's political unification (see Koyama, Moriguchi, and Sng 2018, for a formal analysis).

Likewise, under the traditional East Asian tributary system, China's tributary states acknowledged the superior position of the Chinese emperor in exchange for peace and trading opportunities, as well as occasional military protection. When the Toyotomi clan of Japan invaded the Korean Peninsula in the 1590s, China intervened militarily to preserve Joseon Korea's political autonomy. Once the power of the Chinese state declined in the nineteenth century, Korea lost its de facto independence. The Ryukyu kingdom shared a similar fate. A tributary state of China for more than four centuries, Japan annexed Ryukyu in 1872.

We can also draw a parallel to the world system today. If we think of the United States as the anchor of an international system, small states proliferated in the 1990s not only because of an increase in economic integration as Alesina and Spolaore (1997) have argued, but also because the United States expanded its sphere of influence—and the boundary of the American-led system—after the demise of the Soviet Union. By the same reasoning, a weakened Britain and France and the refusal of the United States to interfere with European affairs contributed to Germany's and Russia's annexations of Austria, Czechoslovakia, and a few other small European states preceding World War II. Put differently, very small states survive and thrive often not in spite of but because of the presence of a large and dominant state, which helps to maintain regional or international order by playing hegemon.

Conclusion

In *Federalist No. 10*, James Madison robustly rebutted the classical view that size presents a challenge to good governance. He contended that in an indirect democracy, there exists the risk that unworthy candidates be elected into office "by intrigue, by corruption or by other means ... and then betray the interests of the people" (Hamilton, Madison, and Jay 2003, 44). Considering this potential risk, size is an advantage: "As each representative will be chosen by a greater number of citizens in the large than in the small republic, it will be more difficult for unworthy candidates to practise with success the vicious arts" (45).

Although Madison, in later writings, also warned about the drawbacks of a distant state,[9] his name has been regularly invoked to refute doubters who see large territorial states as either ill-suited for democracy or destined to suffer poor governance altogether. In recent years, confidence in the optimism of *Federalist No. 10* may have been undermined by growing political polarization in mature democracies, especially the United States. While the timeline is still too short to draw any conclusion, it is a timely reminder of the potential implications of polity size.

In this short chapter, we first highlighted an intriguing distinction in the traditional views of the ideal polity size in Europe and China: Western philosophers since Plato have extolled the virtues of a small state, which is believed to bring about good governance, while Chinese thinkers see a plethora of small states as a recipe for disaster, in the form of endless wars. It is tempting to speculate why this difference in perception exists in the first place. Perhaps geography played a role. The lack of natural obstacles to deter invaders in the agriculturally rich North China plain, and hence a high frequency of destructive wars, led the ancient Chinese thinkers to favor the arrival of a Son of Heaven to end the bloodbath. Meanwhile, the rugged terrain of Greece promoted a system of city states, and in the process shaped the worldview of the classical Greek philosophers. Equally fascinating is how these ideas, once they had taken root, may have subsequently influenced the choices of decision-makers and hence the political maps of China and Europe. These are fertile areas of research.

Next we discussed modern studies in political science and economics on the consequences of polity size. While much of the literature emphasizes the cost of size in democratic or republican regimes, some studies show that size harms autocracies too. Meanwhile, there appears to be a dearth of empirical work on the benefits of size. Hopefully, future work will address the gap.

Finally, the causes and consequences of size are interconnected. Therefore, there are merits to taking a unified approach that considers both causes and consequences in a single theoretical framework. Alesina and Spolaore (1997; 2003) offer a useful template that uses the costs and benefits of size to determine optimal polity size. We argue that historical insights have much to enrich such frameworks and contribute to our understanding of the drivers and implications of polity size.

Acknowledgments

We thank the editors for comments on an earlier draft of this chapter and Yidan Han for research support.

Notes

1. Contemporary studies corroborate the finding. An investigation of capital cities of US states finds that isolated capital cities are more likely to encounter issues of accountability, corruption, and inefficient public goods provision (Campante and Do 2014). Olsson and Hansson (2011) suggest that the burden of size affects democracies and nondemocracies alike. The authors empirically investigate 127 contemporary countries varying across regime types and detect a negative relationship between territorial size and the rule of law.
2. By conventional measures, early-modern China had a very small government. In 1820, there were fewer than fourteen hundred counties governing a population that had reached 380 million (Skinner 1977; Cao 2000). The difficulties faced by understaffed county yamen and overworked magistrates in collecting taxes, arresting criminals, hearing court cases, and enforcing judgments, and the consequent neglect of many government tasks are recurring themes in many historical studies (see, e.g., Ch'u 1962; Watt 1977; Macauley 1998; Buoye 2004).
3. Rosenthal and Wong (2011) argue that the Chinese state taxed lightly because it was under no pressing need to collect more due to a relatively peaceful external environment. However, in instances when such a need arose, efforts to raise revenue often escalated political instability to the point of threatening regime survival. For example, the Ming dynasty's (1368–1644) attempt to raise taxes to meet a rising military threat from Manchuria sparked a wave of rebellion in North China that led to its downfall.
4. See also Robinson (1960), the conference proceeding of a workshop organized in 1957 by the International Economic Association on the "Economic Consequences of the Size of Nations." While dated, the volume provides scores of case studies investigating the costs and benefits of polity size. Simon Kuznets's paper on the viability of small states, in particular, offered perceptive insights that remain relevant today.
5. Scheidel (2019) holds that the rise of Roman Empire was sui generis, enabled by a fortuitous coincidence of conditions, including the possession of an unusually bellicose military culture that helped maintain exceptionally high military participation rates. Reale and Dirmeyer (2000) provide evidence of favorable climatic conditions around the Mediterranean Sea during the classical period, which might have contributed to the emergence and endurance of the Roman Empire.
6. Hoffman (2015), Hui (2005), and others have challenged this argument. See Fernández-Villaverde et al. (2020) for a recent take and a formal test of the hypothesis.
7. While the theory has been widely criticized for some perceived empirical inconsistencies, a recent paper finds evidence that societies historically dependent on irrigation are generally less equal and more autocratic today (Bentzen, Kaarsen, and Wingender 2017).
8. Koku is a measure of volume, equivalent to 180.4 liters. One koku of rice has been historically regarded in Japan as the annual rice consumption of an adult man.
9. In 1791, Madison wrote that "the larger a country, the less easy for its real opinion to be ascertained . . . the more insignificant is each individual in his own eyes. This may be unfavorable to liberty" (Madison 1983, 170). See Stasavage (2020, ch. 12) for a recent discussion.

References

Alesina, Alberto, William Easterly, and Janina Matuszeski. 2011. "Artificial States." *Journal of the European Economic Association* 9, no. 2: 246–77.

Alesina, Alberto, and Enrico Spolaore. 1997. "On the Number and Size of Nations." *Quarterly Journal of Economics* 112, no. 4: 1027–56.

Alesina, Alberto, and Enrico Spolaore. 2003. *The Size of Nations*. Cambridge, MA: MIT Press.

Alesina, Alberto, Enrico Spolaore, and Romain Wacziarg. 2000. "Economic Integration and Political Disintegration." *American Economic Review* 90, no. 5: 1276–96.

Aristotle. 2016. *Aristotle's Politics: Writings from the Complete Works*. Princeton, NJ: Princeton University Press.

Baechler, Jean. 1975. *The Origins of Capitalism*. Oxford: Basil Blackwell.

Barfield, Thomas. 1989. *The Perilous Frontier: Nomadic Empires and China*. Oxford: Basil Blackwell.

Barro, Robert. 1991. "Small Is Beautiful." *Wall Street Journal*, October 11.

Bean, Richard. 1973. "War and the Birth of the Nation State." *Journal of Economic History* 33, no. 1: 203–21.

Bentzen, Jeanet Sinding, Nicolai Kaarsen, and Asger Moll Wingender. 2017. "Irrigation and Autocracy." *Journal of the European Economic Association* 15, no. 1: 1–53.

Bodde, Derk. 1986. "The State and Empire of Ch'in." In *Cambridge History of China*, Volume 1: *The Ch'in and Han Empires, 221 BC–AD 220*, ed. D. C. Twitchett and J. Fairbank, 20–102. Cambridge: Cambridge University Press.

Buoye, Thomas. 2004. "Litigation, Legitimacy, and Lethal Violence: Why County Courts Failed to Prevent Violent Disputes over Property in Eighteenth-Century China." In *Contract and Property in Early Modern China*, ed. Madeleine Zelin, Jonathan K. Ocko, and Robert Gardella, 94–119. Stanford: Stanford University Press.

Campante, Filipe R., and Quoc-Anh Do. 2014. "Isolated Capital Cities, Accountability, and Corruption: Evidence from US States." *American Economic Review* 104, no. 8: 2456–81.

Cao, Shuji. 2000. *Zhongguo Ren Kou Shi [The Demographic History of China]*. Shanghai: Fudan Press.

Ch'u, Tung-Tsu. 1962. *Local Government in China Under the Ch'ing*. Cambridge, MA: Harvard University Press.

Collins, James. 2009. *The State in Early Modern France*. Cambridge: Cambridge University Press.

Cowen, Tyler. 1990. "Economic Effects of a Conflict-Prone World Order." *Public Choice* 64: 121–34.

Dahl, Robert A., and Edward R. Tufte. 1973. *Size and Democracy*. Stanford, CA: Stanford University Press.

Diamond, Jared. 1997. *Guns, Germs, and Steel: The Fate of Human Societies*. New York: W. W. Norton & Company.

Diamond, Jared. 1998. "Peeling the Chinese Onion." *Nature* 391: 433–34.

Fang, Qiang. 2009. "Hot Potatoes: Chinese Complaint Systems from Early Times to the Late Qing (1898)." *Journal of Asian Studies* 68, no. 4: 1105–35.

Fernández-Villaverde, Jesus, Mark Koyama, Youhong Lin, and Tuan-Hwee Sng. 2020. "The Fractured-Land Hypothesis." NBER WP 27774.

Friedman, David. 1977. "A Theory of the Size and Shape of Nations." *Journal of Political Economy* 85, no. 1: 59–77.

Gerring, John, and Wouter Veenendaal. 2020. *Population and Politics: The Impact of Scale*. Cambridge: Cambridge University Press.

Grousset, René. 1970. *The Empire of the Steppes: A History of Central Asia*. Translated by Naomi Walford. New Brunswick, NJ: Rutgers University Press.

Hamilton, Alexander, James Madison, and James Jay. 2003. *The Federalist.* Cambridge: Cambridge University Press.

Hoffman, Philip. 2015. *Why Did Europe Conquer the World?* Princeton, NJ: Princeton University Press.

Hui, Victoria Tin-bor. 2005. *War and State Formation in Ancient China and Early Modern Europe.* Cambridge: Cambridge University Press.

Hume, David. 1987. *Essays: Moral, Political, and Literary.* Indianapolis: Liberty Fund.

Ko, Chiu Yu, Mark Koyama, and Tuan-Hwee Sng. 2018. "Unified China and Divided Europe." *International Economic Review* 59, no. 1: 285–327.

Ko, Chiu Yu, and Tuan-Hwee Sng. 2013. "Regional Dependence and Political Centralization in Imperial China." *Eurasian Geography and Economics* 54, no. 5–6: 470–83.

Koyama, Mark, Chiaki Moriguchi, and Tuan-Hwee Sng. 2018. "Geopolitics and Asia's Little Divergence: State Building in China and Japan after 1850." *Journal of Economic Behavior and Organization* 155: 178–204.

Lattimore, Owen. 1940. *Inner Asian Frontiers of China.* New York: American Geographical Society.

Luo, Guanzhong. 2014. *Three Kingdoms: A Historical Novel.* Translated by Moss Roberts. Berkeley: University of California Press.

Ma, Debin, and Jared Rubin. 2019. "The Paradox of Power: Principal-Agent Problems and Administrative Capacity in Imperial China (and Other Absolutist Regimes)." *Journal of Comparative Economics* 74: 277–94.

Macauley, Melissa Ann. 1998. *Social Power and Legal Culture: Litigation Masters in Late Imperial China.* Stanford, CA: Stanford University Press.

Maddison, Angus. 2001. *The World Economy: A Millennial Perspective.* Paris: OECD.

Madison, James. 1983. *The Papers of James Madison.* Volume 14: *6 April 1791–16 March 1793.* Edited by Robert A. Rutland and Thomas A. Mason. Charlottesville: University Press of Virginia.

McEvedy, Colin, and Richard Jones. 1978. *Atlas of World Population History.* Harmondsworth, UK: Penguin.

Michalopoulos, Stelios, and Elias Papaioannou. 2016. "The Long-Run Effects of the Scramble for Africa." *American Economic Review* 106, no. 7: 1802–48.

Miyazaki, Ichisada. 1983. *Chūgoku [A history of China].* Tokyo: Iwanami Shoten.

Montesquieu. 1989. *The Spirit of the Laws.* Cambridge: Cambridge University Press.

Mokyr, Joel. 2007. "The Market for Ideas and the Origins of Economic Growth in Eighteenth-Century Europe." *Tijdshrift voor Sociale en Economische Geschidenis* 4, no. 1: 3–38.

New York Times. 1896. "Smallest State in the World," June 19.

New York Times. 1928. "Tavolara's King Dies; Ruled Tiniest Realm." February 1.

Ocko, Jonathan. 1988. "I'll Take It All the Way to Beijing: Capital Appeals in the Qing." *Journal of Asian Studies* 47, no. 2: 291–315.

Ohira, Yuichi. 2003. *Meyasubako no Kenkyu [A study of the petition box].* Tokyo: Sobunsha.

Olsson, Ola, and Gustav Hansson. 2011. "Country Size and the Rule of Law: Resuscitating Montesquieu." *European Economic Review* 55, no. 5: 613–29.

Pines, Yuri. 2000. "'The One That Pervades the All' in Ancient Chinese Political Thought: The Origins of 'the Great Unity'" Paradigm." *T'oung Pao* 86, no. 4/5: 280–324.

Pines, Yuri. 2012. *The Everlasting Empire: The Political Culture of Ancient China and Its Imperial Legacy.* Princeton, NJ: Princeton University Press.

Pintner, Walter. 1980. "The Evolution of Civil Officialdom, 1755–1855." In *Russian Officialdom: The Bureaucratization of Russian Society from the Seventeenth to the Twentieth Century,* ed. W. M. Pintner and D. K. Rowney, 190–226. Chapel Hill: University of North Carolina Press.

Qian, Jiwei, and Tuan-Hwee Sng. 2021. "The State in Chinese Economic History." *Australian Economic History Review* 61, no. 3: 359–95.

Reale, Oreste, and Paul Dirmeyer. 2000. "Modeling the Effects of Vegetation on Mediterranean Climate during the Roman Classical Period: Part I. Climate History and Model Sensitivity." *Global and Planetary Change* 25, no. 3: 163–84.

Roberts, Luke. 1994. "The Petition Box in Eighteenth-Century Tosa." *Journal of Japanese Studies* 20, no. 2: 423–58.

Robinson, Austin, ed. 1960. *Economic Consequences of the Size of Nations*. London: Palgrave Macmillan.

Rosenthal, Jean-Laurent, and R. Bin Wong. 2011. *Before and beyond Divergence: The Politics of Economic Change in China and Europe*. Cambridge, MA: Harvard University Press.

Rousseau, Jean-Jacques. 2002. *The Social Contract and The First and Second Discourses*. New Haven, CT: Yale University Press.

Sacks, David Harris. 1994. "The Paradox of Taxation: Fiscal Crises, Parliament, and Liberty in England, 1450–1640." In *Fiscal Crises, Liberty, and Representative Government, 1450–1789*, ed. P. T. Hoffman and K. Norberg, 7–66. Stanford, CA: Stanford University Press.

Scheidel, Walter. 2019. *Escape from Rome: The Failure of Empire and the Road to Prosperity*. Princeton, NJ: Princeton University Press.

Sellmann, James. 2002. *Timing and Rulership in Master Lü's Spring and Autumn Annals*. Albany: State University of New York Press.

Skinner, G. William, ed. 1977. *The City in Late Imperial China*. Stanford, CA: Stanford University Press.

Sng, Tuan-Hwee. 2014. "Size and Dynastic Decline: The Principal-Agent Problem in Late Imperial China, 1700–1850." *Explorations in Economic History* 54: 107–27.

Sng, Tuan-Hwee, and Chiaki Moriguchi. 2014. "Asia's Little Divergence: State Capacity in China and Japan before 1850." *Journal of Economic Growth* 19, no. 4: 439–70.

Stasavage, David. 2011. *States of Credit: Size, Power, and the Development of European Polities*. Princeton, NJ: Princeton University Press.

Stasavage, David. 2016. "Representation and Consent: Why They Arose in Europe and Not Elsewhere." *Annual Review of Political Science* 19, no. 1: 145–62.

Stasavage, David. 2020. *Decline and Rise of Democracy: A Global History from Antiquity to Today*. Princeton, NJ: Princeton University Press.

Tilly, Charles. 1990. *Coercion, Capital, and European States, AD 990–1990*. Oxford: Blackwell.

Turchin, Peter. 2009. "A Theory for Formation of Large Empires." *Journal of Global History* 4: 191–217.

Wang, Yeh-Chien. 1973. *Land Taxation in Imperial China, 1750–1911*. Harvard East Asian series 73. Cambridge, MA: Harvard University Press.

Watt, John. 1977. "The Yamen and Urban Administration." In *The City in Late Imperial China*, ed. G. William Skinner, 353–90. Stanford: Stanford University Press.

Wittfogel, Karl August. 1957. *Oriental Despotism: A Comparative Study of Total Power*. New Haven, CT: Yale University Press.

CHAPTER 13

STATE CAPACITY IN HISTORICAL POLITICAL ECONOMY

MARK DINCECCO AND YUHUA WANG

The study of the state is both central to the social sciences and of great practical importance. From Afghanistan to the Democratic Republic of the Congo to the Northern Triangle (El Salvador, Guatemala, and Honduras), states across many parts of the world today struggle to carry out core governance tasks. Historically, the establishment of modern states in western Europe was an arduous and protracted process. We cannot take well-functioning states for granted.

This chapter examines state capacity from a long-run historical perspective. We first discuss how to define and measure state capacity. We then consider how society can create order even in the absence of a state, along with the economic and social costs that these types of arrangements can bring. We explain how the establishment of a high-capacity state can overcome such costs and enhance domestic peace, raise material prosperity, and promote more pluralistic norms. —We show stylized evidence in support of the view that greater state capacity improves development outcomes. If having a capable state is beneficial, then why don't all societies establish one? We address this question next. Further, we describe how a high-capacity state can also act despotically. We characterize different ways in which society can harness the various public goods that a capable state can provide, while mitigating its potential for despotism. The chapter concludes by reflecting on lessons from history.

DEFINITIONS AND MEASUREMENTS

To define state capacity, we must first clarify what we mean by the state. Weber's (1946, 78) classic definition is, "[A] state is a human community that (successfully) claims the monopoly of the legitimate use of physical force within a given territory." The historical process of state development was challenging and drawn out (Dincecco 2011; O'Brien 2011; Hoffman 2015). Further, a lack of adequate state capacity continues to stymie developing nations today (Besley and Persson 2011; 2013). Thus, Weber's classic definition is best viewed as a (somewhat idealized) endpoint of the state development process, rather than a starting point for historical analysis.

Our preferred definition of the state instead draws on Bates (2020), due to its historical relevance and tractability. We conceive of "the state" as a political hierarchy that contains tax collectors to gather revenue, a police force and military to help provide security, and a judiciary to administer legal justice. A chief executive (i.e., "the ruler") presides over this political entity, in conjunction with a noble or parliamentary council.

With this definition of the state in hand, we can now characterize what we mean by state capacity. Following Mann (1986), we define "state capacity" as the state's ability to attain its intended policy goals, whether they be economic, fiscal, or otherwise. A state with high capacity is thus more likely to produce the policy outcomes that the government wants than one with low capacity (Brambor, Goenaga, Lindvall, and Teorell 2020). The basic reason is that a high-capacity state has access to greater fiscal and informational resources that it can exploit to achieve its policy aims.[1]

A state does not always exploit its full capacity for action. In this respect, state capacity is a latent feature that we do not directly observe (Hanson and Sigman 2021). Scholars can nevertheless employ a range of visible indicators from which historical levels of state capacity can be inferred. These include measures of the state's ability to extract fiscal resources and information from society, as well as the extent of the state's administrative infrastructure. We now discuss each of these types of indicators.

Fiscal strength is integral to state capacity. As Levi (1988, 2) writes, "One major limitation on rule is revenue, the income of the government. The greater the revenue of the state, the more possible it is to extend rule." Further, data on historical budgets are often more widely available than alternative types of data. For example, Dincecco (2011) constructs annual fiscal data on revenue, expenditure, and sovereign credit risk for major states in western Europe from the early-modern era to the start of World War I, while Karaman and Pamuk (2013) produce complementary revenue data that extend back to the year 1500. Wang (2022a) gathers fiscal data for imperial China from the dawn of the first millennium (1 CE) to the fall of the Qing dynasty in 1911. Beramendi, Dincecco, and Rogers (2019) compile annual fiscal capacity data for more than thirty nations globally since 1870, while Lee and Paine (2022) amass revenue data that include at least one yearly observation from the nineteenth century for more than forty non-Western states. Albers, Jerven, and Suesse (2020) put together annual tax data for Africa that spans forty-six states since 1900.

There is a modern policy debate over the government's ability versus its willingness to engage in revenue extraction (Alesina, Glaeser, and Sacerdote 2001). This debate implicitly assumes adequate fiscal capacity. This assumption, however, does not make much sense for historical analysis, as most governments lacked such capacity (see, e.g., Dincecco 2011).[2]

Revenue collection, military conscription, and the prevention of popular rebellion all require accurate information about a polity's population and territory. Lee and Zhang (2017), for example, produce annual data on the "legibility" (Scott 1998) of society by state administrators that measure the accuracy of age data in national censuses for a global sample since 1960, while Brambor, Goenaga, Lindvall, and Teorell (2020) construct an annual cross-national index of the "information capacity" of states from 1789 onward. This index makes use of five practices that state administrators employ to gather and process information about society: introduction of a census, introduction of civil registers, introduction of population registers, establishment of a statistical agency, and publication of statistical yearbooks.

In addition to fiscal and information capacity, scholars have measured historical state capacity in terms of the extent of the state's administrative infrastructure across space. To evaluate the local reach of the federal government in the nineteenth-century United States, for example, Acemoglu, Moscona, and Robinson (2016) construct data on the number of post offices in each county. Similarly, Rogowski, Gerring, Maguire, and Cojocaru (2021) produce annual data on the global spread of postal services since 1875. Acemoglu, Garcia-Jimeno, and Robinson (2015) assess the local presence of the colonial state in Colombia in terms of the number of royal employees and agencies and the distance to the nearest royal road, while Lee (2019) collects data on the local presence of village officials in colonial India. Lu, Luan, and Sng (2020) measure differences in state capacity across mid-twentieth-century Sichuan (China) in terms of the number of members of the communist party.

To gain an accurate picture of a state's overall capacity, it might be ideal to incorporate capacity measures across major government agencies (Fukuyama 2013). This can be difficult in practice, however, particularly when attempting to measure state capacity historically. Fortunately, the fiscal, informational, and administrative indicators described earlier should be highly correlated (Hanson and Sigman 2021, 1503). Thus, exploiting any one of them will likely provide a meaningful proxy of state capacity overall.[3]

Why Society May Want a Capable State

The classic thinker Thomas Hobbes (1651) argued that chaos and destruction were the only outcomes in a society in which the state was absent. Recently, scholars including Bates, Greif, and Singh (2002), Greif (2006a), Bates (2010; 2020), Boix (2015), and Acemoglu and Robinson (2019) have explained how society can create order even without a state.

Threats of retaliation are the first factor that helps society avoid outbreaks of violence in the absence of third-party enforcement by the state (Bates 2010; 2020). To deter criminal activity from taking hold, individuals must starkly convey their willingness to fight—for example, by publicly bearing weapons. Gluckman (1955) labels this phenomenon "peace in the feud."

Beliefs facilitate order in the no-state context (Axelrod 1986; Ellickson 1991). Individuals may adhere to a code of honor that requires them to take revenge for any criminal offenses. Further, individuals may believe in witchcraft, whereby ill health and bad luck befall those who do not seek revenge. The purpose of both types of beliefs is to raise the cost of potential criminal activity and thus prevent its outbreak in the first place.

Cross-cutting ties including marriage outside of clans and dispersed residence are the second factor that helps society maintain order in the state's absence (Gluckman 1955; Henrich 2020; Wang 2022a). For example, if female members of clan 1 are the wives of members of clan 2, then they can lobby to prevent a cycle of violence from taking hold, even after an initial outbreak of violence between the two clans. Similarly, if members of clan 1 live in different villages, then that can reduce the chance of collective retaliation (or predation) by them. Further, if they live among members of clan 2 in the same village, then that can promote quick settlements, as lasting disputes will impede village life.

While such arrangements can help society avoid outbreaks of violence in the state's absence, they carry high costs (Bates 2010; 2020). The logic of revenge promotes a hair-trigger society. To provide order, individuals must publicly bear arms and imply their willingness to use them. Given the importance of honor codes, any initial violence can deteriorate into a never-ending cycle. Grosjean (2014), for example, shows that a traditional culture of honor helps explain the high historical homicide rates of Whites in the US South.[4] More generally, Pinker (2011, 51–53) finds that the average annual death rate in societies that lacked states was more than 500 per 100,000 individuals. For comparison, the average annual homicide rate in the United States during the turbulent 1970s and 1980s was approximately 10 per 100,000 (i.e., more than fifty times lower).

Poverty is one negative outcome that derives from the hair-trigger logic of society in the absence of a state (Bates 2010; 2020; Boix 2015). To reduce the incentive of individuals to engage in criminal activity, which can devolve into a cycle of violence, members of society may opt to limit material consumption and production. Further, technological innovations that do not lend themselves to widespread replication may falter in an attempt to prevent resourceful individuals from achieving material success—which can make others envious and thus threaten the fragile peace (Boix 2015).

Another negative outcome is what Acemoglu and Robinson (2019) term the "cage of norms." "Norms" refer to the standards of proper and expected behavior in society, which help create a common understanding of morality and justice. In the state's absence, society must rely wholly on norms both for preventing and resolving conflicts. While norms are key to order and stability in the state's absence, they can create an illiberal "cage" that restricts personal freedoms and perpetuates unequal power relations, often subjugating women (Acemoglu and Robinson 2019).

State Capacity and Development

The preceding discussion indicates that, contra Hobbes's classic argument, order can in fact be achieved in a society in which the state is absent. However, it comes at a high cost in terms of the lack of incentives to make investments in physical and human capital, as well as illiberal norms. Thus, society might want to establish a state in an attempt to better ensure domestic peace, improve material prosperity, and promote more pluralistic norms.[5] Further, society will likely want this state to have a high-enough capacity to reach its intended development goals.

The most basic way in which a capable state can enhance development outcomes is by providing what North (1981) calls the "rules of the game": law and order, private property rights, and external defense. The state's provision of these sorts of public goods speaks directly to the fundamental problems of criminal activity and violence in society as described in the previous section. By reducing the chance of expropriation by rival individuals or kin groups, the state's establishment and enforcement of the rules of the game can incentivize individuals to make investments in physical capital, education, and technological innovations that promote development.

A high-capacity state may support development in several ways besides the rules of the game (Dincecco 2017). One way is to provide a competitive market for the exchange of goods and services. For example, the elimination of internal customs borders within a polity can promote market exchange by reducing time holdups at border frontiers (Epstein 2000). Providing transportation infrastructure (e.g., roads, bridges, railways, and airports) and communications networks (e.g., postal service and internet connectivity) is another way to support development. This infrastructure can reduce the costs of products as well as commuting costs, and can facilitate the spread of new ideas that spark technological innovations and change belief systems. A further way is through mass education. Greater human capital can improve productivity, make technological innovations more likely, and expose individuals to new ways of thinking. Selective incentives for individuals (Olson 1965) and monitoring of society (Scott 1998), both of which can help social groups overcome collective action problems, are two additional approaches to encouraging development.

The stylized evidence is consistent with the view that a capable state may improve development outcomes. Taking a historical perspective, Figure 13.1 shows evidence for a strong positive correlation between the state's ability to extract revenue—a basic measure of fiscal capacity for which historical data are available—and economic performance in western Europe from the early-modern era to the start of World War I. Figure 13.2 depicts a similar pattern in the modern data. To measure the fiscal capacity of the modern state, we use the share of income tax revenue in total tax revenue, as the collection of an income tax calls for high administrative capacity to ensure compliance (Besley and Persson 2013). The modern state's information capacity is another way to gauge state capacity (Lee and Zhang 2017; Brambor, Goenaga, Lindvall, and Teorell 2020). Figure 13.3 plots an index of information capacity averaged between 1789 and 2000 against economic performance today. We observe a strong positive correlation between the two variables.

While the stylized evidence supports the view that high state capacity enhances development outcomes, we do not want to mistake correlation with causation, as the correct causal logic may run in the opposite direction. Fortunately, a growing body of literature spanning multiple geographical and temporal contexts provides causal (or causal-like)

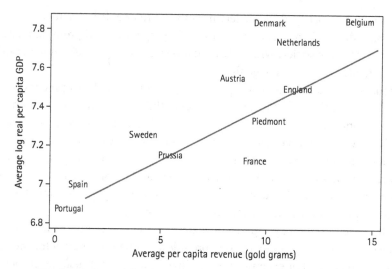

FIGURE 13.1. Fiscal capacity and development in Western Europe, 1650–1913
Note: Average log real per capita GDP is in 1990 international Geary-Khamis dollars. All data are averaged over 1650–1913. For sources, see Dincecco (2017, 54).

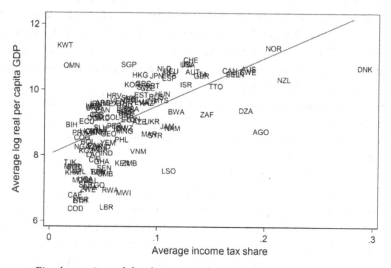

FIGURE 13.2. Fiscal capacity and development today
Note: Log real per capita GDP is in constant 2011 national prices (in millions of 2011 US dollars). Income tax share is the ratio of income tax revenue to total tax revenue. All data are averaged over 2000–2009. Nations with populations of less than one million in 2000 are excluded. For sources, see Dincecco (2017, 5).

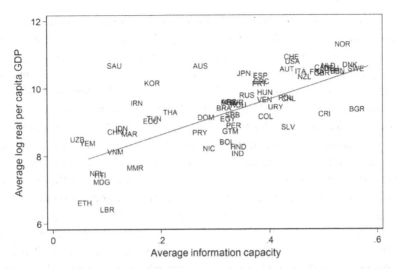

FIGURE 13.3. Information capacity and development today
Note: Log real per capita GDP is in constant 2011 national prices (in millions of 2011 US dollars). The GDP data are averaged over 2000–2009. Information capacity is an aggregate index of information capacity computed via a hybrid two-parameter and graded-item response model according to five component indicators: an index of the state's census ability, an index of the state's statistical yearbook ability, whether there was a civil register in place, whether there was a population register in place, and whether there was a statistical agency in place. The information capacity data are averaged over 1789–2000. Nations with populations of less than one million in 2000 are excluded. For sources, see Brambor, Goenaga, Lindvall, and Teorell (2020) for the information capacity data and Feenstra, Inklaar, and Timmer (2015) for the GDP data.

evidence for a significant positive relationship running from higher state capacity to greater development.[6]

Why State Capacity Might Fall Short

The preceding discussion suggests that having a high-capacity state is beneficial, as it has the potential to enhance domestic peace, improve material prosperity, and promote more pluralistic norms. Why, then, don't all societies establish capable states?

Western Europe is the birthplace of the modern state. However, the historical record indicates that the state development process there was arduous and drawn out over several hundred years (Dincecco 2011; O'Brien 2011; Hoffman 2015). There are arguably several reasons for this, including problems of geographic scale in governance (Stasavage 2011), resistance by traditional elites to centralizing reforms (Dincecco 2011), and economic underdevelopment (Abramson 2017).

A variety of factors have obstructed the historical development of high-capacity states in the non-European parts of the world. In imperial China, the localization of social networks turned elites away from the central state, producing a powerful opposition interest group (Wang 2022a). In early-twentieth-century India, high-caste elites preemptively weakened the state's ability to tax, since they feared that the extension of voting rights to the lower castes would increase the demand for public goods and thus place a higher tax burden on them (Suryanarayan 2021). The sultan in the Ottoman Empire exploited a divide-and-rule strategy that pitted different elite groups against one another, hindering the ability of elites to act collectively (Barkey 1994). In sub-Saharan Africa, central governments have long faced the challenge of extending authority over broad swaths of territory, due both to difficult geography and low population density (Herbst 2000). Vested elites in Latin America thwarted reform efforts by central governments to project greater power (Soifer 2015; Garfias 2018). Rulers themselves have often had weak incentives to increase state capacity, due both to the historical availability of international finance and an emphasis on trade exports of raw materials (Centeno 2002; Queralt 2019; Mazzuca 2021).

Further, European colonization has played a significant role in impeding the development of high-capacity states. In Africa, the Middle East, and elsewhere, European colonizers established artificial borders that did not match well with group identifications at the ground level (Alesina, Easterly, and Matuszeski 2011; Michalopoulos and Papaioannou 2016). This action limited the radius of identification to fellow kin members or home villages (or regions), making it more difficult to reach consensus on providing national public goods. Arbitrary ethnic partitioning by European colonizers across different nations, moreover, has significantly increased political violence (Michalopoulos and Papaioannou 2016).

A related factor was patronage appointments by colonial governments, which reduced the incentives of bureaucrats to practice good governance. Xu (2018) shows that patronage governors in the British colonial administration were associated with significantly lower fiscal investments and greater political turmoil. Nations that experienced patronage governance during the colonial era, moreover, continue to have significantly lower fiscal capacity today (Xu 2019).

Beyond patronage, European colonization has influenced the bureaucratic capacity of modern states in other ways. For example, the French retained and enhanced the existing state bureaucracy in Tunisia by incorporating local elites (Anderson 2014). This helped promote a relatively strong postindependence Tunisian state. By contrast, the Italians replaced the existing state bureaucracy in Libya with one that excluded locals (Anderson 2014). Following independence, traditional kin groups captured key government roles, weakening the Libyan state's efficacy.

Finally, it appears difficult to establish a high-capacity state through brute force only. Even with the support of the US military, the Afghan state was generally unable to fulfill key governance functions outside the capital of Kabul during the first two decades of the 2000s (Berman 2010). Henn, Mugaruka, Ortiz, Sanchez de la Sierra, and Wu (2021) provide evidence that a major military attempt by the state to establish a monopoly over violence in an area of the Democratic Republic of the Congo that was under the control of armed nonstate actors not only exacerbated violence against citizens but also created a power vacuum in another nearby area.

The Dark Side of a Capable State

Thus far, we have focused on the benefits that derive from a capable state (so long as one can be established), including the potential for greater order and stability, material progress, and support for more pluralistic belief systems. By virtue of the same authority from which such benefits can flow, however, a high-capacity state can also act despotically (Acemoglu and Robinson 2019). It can ignore, repress, or predate on society, or at least on certain parts of it. Obviously, states themselves can propagate illiberal belief systems. Further, states—and nondemocratic regimes in particular—can use mass education to instill norms of obedience and respect for authority that help sustain the status quo structure of society (Paglayan 2022).

Scott (2009) argues that states have historically been unfree. To meet state-organized (or state-sanctioned) agricultural goals, "civilization" has meant subordination, drudgery, and immobility for many (e.g., the *mita* in colonial Latin America; slavery in the antebellum US South). Bentzen, Kaarsen, and Wingender (2017) show that societies in which states organized large-scale irrigation were more economically unequal in history and remain more autocratic today.

Scott (2009) heralds what he terms "barbarians by design": individuals who developed specific political, cultural, and economic organizations to ward off incorporation by the state. Such individuals live in remote areas (e.g., hills, deserts, and swamps) over which it is difficult for the state to establish authority. Nunn and Puga (2012), for example, show that, while rugged terrain is generally an economic disadvantage (e.g., because of high transportation costs), in Africa ruggedness is associated with significantly better economic outcomes, which they argue is because rugged terrain enabled individuals to escape the devastating effects of the (state-sanctioned) historical slave trades.

Davenport (2007) focuses on the ways in which state actors (e.g., the executive, the police, the military) can repress individuals in society, including violations of one's personal security; rights to free speech, travel, assembly, and boycott; and due process of the law. Davenport (2007) identifies an empirical "law of coercive responsiveness" by which states generally respond to challenges to the status quo with repressive actions.

How to Constrain the State

On one hand, a high-capacity state can enhance domestic peace, improve material prosperity, and promote more pluralistic norms. On the other hand, such a state can act despotically. How, then, to harness the various public goods that a capable state can provide, while mitigating its potential to act despotically?

First, any state led by a ruler with a long-enough time horizon—what Olson (1993) calls a "stationary bandit"—should have an incentive to provide (at least a modicum of) order and limit the overall taxation of and violence against subjects, and to enjoy continual revenue flows (e.g., from agricultural production). For their part, subjects may appreciate the order that the ruler imposes as it precludes theft by other "roving" bandits. Haber (2008), however, casts doubt on the historical and theoretical relevance of stationary bandits.

Beyond this basic level of constraint that stationary banditry might provide to society, scholars including North and Weingast (1989) and Cox (2016) have emphasized the importance of parliamentary supremacy over the ruler, in particular with respect to budgetary matters. According to this view, parliament must have a governance role that is both permanent and independent of the executive. Further, parliament must possess the de jure and de facto abilities to oversee the state's budget. This includes authority over taxation and the right to veto new spending and audit previous expenditures.[7] By improving the state's ability to productively use public funds, parliamentary supremacy should enhance revenue collection (Bates and Lien 1985; Levi 1988; Besley and Persson 2011).

Acemoglu and Robinson (2019; 2022) conceive of a dynamic process—what they term the "red queen effect"—in which society's ability to organize collectively and make its demands heard must strengthen in response to increases in the state's ability to enforce the rules of the game, manage the economy, and make war. In addition to political innovations such as parliamentary supremacy as described earlier, Acemoglu and Robinson highlight the importance of specific cultural arrangements that support popular sovereignty—namely, the cultural notion that society delegates power to the ruler on the understanding that the ruler's actions must align with their policy preferences.

Is parliamentary supremacy necessary to constrain the executive in a high-capacity state? Besley and Kudamatsu (2008) argue that, in the absence of parliamentary authority, government accountability depends on the ability of political insiders—what Bueno de Mesquita, Smith, Siverson, and Morrow (2003) call the "selectorate"—to remove executives that perform poorly. In Besley and Kudamatsu's view, government accountability can take place so long as the selectorate's political power does not derive wholly from the current executive's power while in office. Besley and Kudamatsu claim that the Politburo in China (i.e., the group of twenty-five that oversees the communist party), for example, has been relatively effective at replacing poor leaders with competent ones over the last several decades.

Apart from voice, societal actors can threaten what Hirschman (1970) terms "exit" in order to constrain rulers. Wang (2015) argues that authoritarian leaders limit predatory actions when they need cooperation from organized business groups that, while not politically connected, remain in control of valuable mobile assets. Foreign business investors in China, for example, have leveraged exit threats to pressure the government to (partially) commit to the rule of law, thereby providing a more level economic playing field.

Conclusion

In the *Federalist Papers*, James Madison portrayed the basic challenge of governance as follows: "In framing a government which is to be administered by men over men, the great difficulty lies in this: you must first enable the government to control the governed; and in the next place oblige it to control itself" (Hamilton, Madison, and Jay 1788 [2008], 257).

Like Madison, we view high state capacity and meaningful constraints on rulers as integral—and intertwined—components of a well-functioning state. A historical perspective reveals that Madison's governance challenge will only be met if the ruler, elites, and ordinary citizens all find it in their best interests to support a capable state that simultaneously adheres to rules (de jure, de facto, or both) that limit the government's predatory might. To be achieved, therefore, a strong yet constrained state must constitute an equilibrium for all the main political actors.

Our traditional understanding of how the state increases its capacity draws from the historical experience of western Europe. Yet a growing literature investigates the development of state capacity beyond this traditional case.[8] This newer literature analyzes alternative patterns of state development on their own terms. Many developing nations have not established rule based on society's consent and are still governed by authoritarian leaders. The odds may be against the emergence of European-style nation-states in such places. We view the study of alternative paths of the development of state capacity as a promising avenue for additional research.

Acknowledgments

We thank Jeffery Jenkins, Jared Rubin, and Jan Vogler for helpful comments.

Notes

1. The conceptualization and measurement of state capacity is the main topic of the recent review by Berwick and Christia (2018). For this reason, we limit our discussion of this topic here. Berwick and Christia organize their framework around three types of state capacity: extraction, coordination, and compliance. For complementary discussions of conceptualizations and measurements, see Soifer (2008), Johnson and Koyama (2017), and Hanson and Sigman (2021), as well as the chapters in this handbook by Garfias and Sellars (2023) on state-building, Koyama (2023) on legal capacity, and Vogler (2023) on bureaucracy. Wang (2021) traces the evolution of the scholarly study of the state, ranging from the

society-centered perspective (e.g., Dahl 1961) to the state-centered perspective (e.g., Evans, Rueschemeyer, and Skocpol 1985) to the state-in-society perspective (e.g., Migdal 1988).
2. Levi (1988) and Berwick and Christia (2018) discuss the enduring revenue imperatives of rulers.
3. Obviously, this is not always true. In their study of the different economic interventions undertaken by the US government in the 1930s, for example, Skocpol and Finegold (1982) show that a state that has high capacity in one policy realm need not have an equivalent level in another. Scholars should therefore remain cognizant of this challenge when evaluating evidence about historical levels of state capacity.
4. Nisbett and Cohen (1996) trace this violent culture of honor to the eighteenth-century arrival of settlers from the Scottish Highlands and Ulster, two historically pastoral and lawless zones in North Britain.
5. Scholars have identified several factors that help explain why and how states form, including geography (Carneiro 1970; Stasavage 2010; Sng and Moriguchi 2014; Mayshar, Moav, and Neeman 2017), interstate war (Tilly 1992; Hui 2005; Scheve and Stasavage 2012; Blaydes and Paik 2016; Dincecco and Onorato 2017; Queralt 2019; Becker, Ferrara, Melander, and Pascali 2020), elite competition (Mares and Queralt 2015; Garfias 2018; Beramendi, Dincecco, and Rogers 2019), information (Lee and Zhang 2017; Sanchez de la Sierra 2020), economic development (Abramson 2017; Acharya and Lee 2018), religion (Grzymala-Busse 2020); kin and social structures (Greif 2006b; Wang 2022b), and cultural diversity (Charnysh 2019). Since state-building is the main topic of the chapter by Franciso Garfias and Emily Sellars in this handbook, we do not discuss it at length here.
6. For European history, see Acemoglu, Cantoni, Johnson, and Robinson (2011); Dincecco and Katz (2016); Charnysh (2019); and Dittmar and Meisenzahl (2020). For the United States, see Acemoglu, Moscona, and Robinson (2016) and Rogowski, Gerring, Maguire, and Cojocaru (2021). For Latin America, see Acemoglu, Garcia-Jimeno, and Robinson (2015). For Africa, see Michalopoulos and Papaioannou (2013). For China, see Lu, Luan, and Sng (2020). For India, see Lee (2019) and Dincecco, Fenske, Mukherjee, and Menon (2022). For Southeast Asia, see Dell, Lane, and Querubin (2018).
7. Stasavage (2003) makes the point that exerting (de jure) constraints over the executive must actually be in the political interest of influential groups in parliament.
8. We have cited several such works in previous sections of this chapter.

References

Abramson, S. 2017. "The Economic Origins of the Territorial State." *International Organization* 71: 97–130.

Acemoglu, D., D. Cantoni, S. Johnson, and J. Robinson. 2011. "The Consequences of Radical Reform: The French Revolution." *American Economic Review* 101: 3286–307.

Acemoglu, D., C. García-Jimeno, and J. Robinson. 2015. "State Capacity and Economic Development: A Network Approach." *American Economic Review* 105: 2364–409.

Acemoglu, D., J. Moscona, and J. Robinson. 2016. "State Capacity and American Technology: Evidence from the Nineteenth Century." *American Economic Review: Papers and Proceedings* 106: 61–67.

Acemoglu, D., and J. Robinson. 2019. *The Narrow Corridor*. New York: Penguin.

Acemoglu, D., and J. Robinson. 2022. "Non-Modernization: Power-Culture Trajectories and the Dynamics of Political Institutions." *Annual Review of Political Science* 25: 323–39.

Acharya, A., and A. Lee. 2018. "Economic Foundations of the Territorial State System." *American Journal of Political Science* 62: 954–66.

Albers, T., M. Jerven, and M. Suesse. 2020. "The Fiscal State in Africa: Evidence from a Century of Growth." African Economic History Working Paper Series 55.

Alesina, A., E. Glaeser, and B. Sacerdote. 2001. "Why Doesn't the United States Have a European-Style Welfare State?" Brookings Paper on Economics Activity: 187–278.

Alesina, A., W. Easterly, and J. Matuszeski. 2011. "Artificial States." *Journal of the European Economic Association* 9: 246–77.

Anderson, L. 2014. *The State and Social Transformation in Tunisia and Libya, 1830–1980*. Princeton, NJ: Princeton University Press.

Axelrod, R. 1986. "An Evolutionary Approach to Norms." *American Political Science Review* 80: 1095–111.

Barkey, K. 1994. *Bandits and Bureaucrats*. Ithaca, NY: Cornell University Press.

Bates, R. 2010. *Prosperity and Violence*. New York: Norton.

Bates, R. 2020. *The Political Economy of Development*. Cambridge: Cambridge University Press.

Bates, R., A. Greif, and S. Singh. 2002. "Organizing Violence." *Journal of Conflict Resolution* 46: 599–628.

Bates, R., and D. H. Lien. 1985. "A Note on Taxation, Development, and Representative Government." *Politics & Society* 14: 53–70.

Becker, S., A. Ferrara, E. Melander, and L. Pascali. 2020. "Wars, Taxation and Representation: Evidence from Five Centuries of German History." CEPR Discussion Paper 15601.

Bentzen, J., N. Kaarsen, and A. Wingender. 2017. "Irrigation and Autocracy." *Journal of the European Economic Association* 15: 1–53.

Beramendi, P., M. Dincecco, and M. Rogers. 2019. "Intra-Elite Competition and Long-Run Fiscal Development." *Journal of Politics* 81: 49–65.

Berman, S. 2010. "From the Sun King to Karzai Lessons for State Building in Afghanistan." *Foreign Affairs*, March 1.

Berwick, E., and F. Christia. 2018. "State Capacity Redux: Integrating Classical and Experimental Contributions to an Enduring Debate." *Annual Review of Political Science* 21: 71–91.

Besley, T., and M. Kudamatsu. 2008. "Making Autocracy Work." In *Institutions and Economic Performance*, ed. E. Helpman, 452–510. Cambridge, MA: Harvard University Press.

Besley, T., and T. Persson. 2011. *The Pillars of Prosperity*. Princeton, NJ: Princeton University Press.

Besley, T., and T. Persson. 2013. "Taxation and Development." In *Handbook of Public Economics*, ed. A. Auerbach, R. Chetty, M. Feldstein, and E. Saez, 51–110. Amsterdam: Elsevier.

Blaydes, L., and C. Paik. 2016. "The Impact of Holy Land Crusades on State Formation: War Mobilization, Trade Integration, and Political Development in Medieval Europe." *International Organization* 70: 551–86.

Boix, C. 2015. *Political Order and Inequality*. Cambridge: Cambridge University Press.

Brambor, T., A. Goenaga, J. Lindvall, and J. Teorell. 2020. "The Lay of the Land: Information Capacity and the Modern State." *Comparative Political Studies* 53: 175–213.

Bueno de Mesquita, M., A. Smith, R. Siverson, and J. Morrow. 2003. *The Logic of Political Survival*. Cambridge, MA: MIT Press.

Carneiro, R. 1970. "A Theory of the Origin of the State." *Science* 169, no. 3947: 733–38.

Centeno, M. 2002. *Blood and Debt*. University Park: Pennsylvania State University Press.

Charnysh, V. 2019. "Diversity, Institutions, and Economic Outcomes: Post-WWII Displacement in Poland." *American Political Science Review* 113: 423–41.

Cox, G. 2016. *Marketing Sovereign Promises*. Cambridge, UK: Cambridge University Press.

Dahl, R. 1961. *Who Governs?* New Haven, CT: Yale University Press.

Davenport, C. 2007. "State Repression and Political Order." *Annual Review of Political Science* 10: 1–23.

Dell, M., N. Lane, and P. Querubin. 2018. "The Historical State, Local Collective Action, and Economic Development in Vietnam." *Econometrica* 86: 2083–121.

Dincecco, M. 2011. *Political Transformations and Public Finances*. Cambridge: Cambridge University Press.

Dincecco, M. 2017. *State Capacity and Economic Development*. Cambridge: Cambridge University Press.

Dincecco, M., and G. Katz. 2016. "State Capacity and Long-Run Economic Performance." *Economic Journal* 126: 189–218.

Dincecco M., and M. Onorato. 2017. *From Warfare to Wealth*. Cambridge: Cambridge University Press.

Dincecco, M., J. Fenske, S. Mukherjee, and A. Menon. 2022. "Pre-Colonial Warfare and Long-Run Development in India." *Economic Journal* 132: 981–1010.

Dittmar, J., and R. Meisenzahl. 2020. "Public Goods Institutions, Human Capital, and Growth: Evidence from German History." *Review of Economic Studies* 87: 959–96.

Ellickson, R. 1991. *Order without Law*. Cambridge, MA: Harvard University Press.

Epstein, S. 2000. *Freedom and Growth*. London: Routledge.

Evans, P., D. Rueschemeyer, and T. Skocpol. 1985. *Bringing the State Back In*. Cambridge: Cambridge University Press.

Feenstra, R., R. Inklaar, and M. Timmer. 2015. "The Next Generation of the Penn World Table." *American Economic Review* 105: 3150–82.

Fukuyama, F. 2013. "What Is Governance?" *Governance* 26: 347–68.

Garfias, F. 2018. "Elite Competition and State Capacity Development: Theory and Evidence from Post-Revolutionary Mexico." *American Political Science Review* 112: 339–57.

Garfias, F., and E. Sellars. 2023. "State Building in Historical Political Economy." In *Oxford Handbook of Historical Political Economy*, ed. J. Jenkins and J. Rubin, 209–35. Oxford: Oxford University Press.

Gluckman, M. 1955. "The Peace in the Feud." *Past & Present* 8: 1–14.

Greif, A. 2006a. *Institutions and the Path to the Modern Economy*. Cambridge: Cambridge University Press.

Greif, A. 2006b. "Family Structure, Institutions, and Growth: The Origins and Implications of Western Corporations." *American Economic Review: Papers and Proceedings* 96: 308–12.

Grosjean, P. 2014. "A History of Violence: The Culture of Honor and Homicide in the US South." *Journal of the European Economic Association* 12: 1285–316.

Grzymala-Busse, A. 2020. "Beyond War and Contracts: The Medieval and Religious Roots of the European State." *Annual Review of Political Science* 23: 19–36.

Haber, S. 2008. "Authoritarian Government." In *Oxford Handbook of Political Economy*, ed. D. Wittman and B. Weingast, 693–707. Oxford: Oxford University Press.

Hamilton, A., J. Madison, and J. Jay. 1788 [2008]. *Federalist Papers*. Oxford: Oxford University Press.

Hanson, J., and R. Sigman. 2021. "Leviathan's Latent Dimensions: Measuring State Capacity for Comparative Political Research." *Journal of Politics* 83: 1495–510.

Henn, S., C. Mugaruka, M. Ortiz, R. Sanchez de la Sierra, and D. Wu. 2021. "The Perils of Building States by Force: How Attempts to Assert the State's Monopoly of Violence Create Lasting Incentives for Violent Banditry." NBER Working Paper 28631.

Henrich, J. 2020. *The WEIRDest People in the World*. New York: Farrar, Straus and Giroux.

Herbst, J. 2000. *States and Power in Africa*. Princeton, NJ: Princeton University Press.

Hirschman, A. 1970. *Exit, Voice, and Loyalty*. Cambridge, MA: Harvard University Press.

Hobbes, T. 1651. *Leviathan*. Project Gutenberg. https://www.gutenberg.org/files/3207/3207-h/3207-h.htm.

Hoffman, P. 2015. "What Do States Do? Politics and Economic History." *Journal of Economic History* 75: 303–32.

Hui, V. T. B. 2005. *War and State Formation in Ancient China and Early Modern Europe*. Cambridge: Cambridge University Press.

Johnson, N., and M. Koyama. 2017. "States and Economic Growth: Capacity and Constraints." *Explorations in Economic History* 64: 1–20.

Karaman, K., and Ş. Pamuk. 2013. "Different Paths to the Modern State in Europe: The Interaction between Domestic Political Economy and Interstate Competition." *American Political Science Review* 107: 603–26.

Koyama, M. 2023. "Legal Capacity in Historical Political Economy." In *Oxford Handbook of Historical Political Economy*, ed. J. Jenkins and J. Rubin, 271–92. Oxford: Oxford University Press.

Lee, A. 2019. "Land, State Capacity, and Colonialism: Evidence from India." *Comparative Political Studies* 52: 41–44.

Lee, A., and J. Paine. 2022. "The Great Revenue Divergence." *International Organization*, forthcoming.

Lee, M., and N. Zhang. 2017. "Legibility and the Informational Foundations of State Capacity." *Journal of Politics* 79: 118–32.

Levi, M. 1988. *Of Rule and Revenue*. Berkeley: University of California Press.

Lu, Y., M. Luan, and T. H. Sng. 2020. "Did the Communists Contribute to China's Rural Growth?" *Explorations in Economic History* 75: 101–35.

Mann, M. 1986. "The Autonomous Power of the State: Its Origins, Mechanisms, and Results." In *States in History*, ed. J. Hall, 109–36. Oxford: Oxford University Press.

Mares, I., and D. Queralt. 2015. "The Non-Democratic Origins of Income Taxation." *Comparative Political Studies* 48: 1974–2009.

Mayshar, J., O. Moav, and Z. Neeman. 2017. "Geography, Transparency, and Institutions." *American Political Science Review* 111: 622–36.

Mazzuca, S. 2021. *Latecomer State Formation*. New Haven, CT: Yale University Press.

Michalopoulos, S., and E. Papaioannou. 2013. "Pre-Colonial Ethnic Institutions and Contemporary African Development." *Econometrica* 81: 113–52.

Michalopoulos, S., and E. Papaioannou. 2016. "The Long-Run Effects of the Scramble for Africa." *American Economic Review* 106: 1802–48.

Migdal, J. 1988. *Strong Societies and Weak States*. Princeton, NJ: Princeton University Press.

Nisbett, R., and D. Cohen. 1996. *Culture of Honor*. Boulder, CO: Westview Press.

North, D. 1981. *Structure and Change in Economic History*. New York: Norton.

North, D., and B. Weingast. 1989. "Constitutions and Commitment: The Evolution of Institutions Governing Public Choice in Seventeenth-Century England." *Journal of Economic History* 49: 803–32.

Nunn, N., and D. Puga. 2012. "Ruggedness: The Blessing of Bad Geography in Africa." *Review of Economics and Statistics* 94: 20–36.

O'Brien, P. 2011. "The Nature and Historical Evolution of an Exceptional Fiscal State and Its Possible Significance for the Precocious Commercialization and Industrialization of the British Economy from Cromwell to Nelson." *Economic History Review* 64: 408–46.

Olson, M. 1965. *The Logic of Collective Action*. Cambridge, MA: Harvard University Press.

Olson, M. 1993. "Dictatorship, Democracy, and Development." *American Political Science Review* 87: 567–76.

Paglayan, A. 2023. "Education or Indoctrination? The Violent Origins of Public School Systems in an Era of State-Building." *American Political Science Review* 116, no. 4: 1242–57.

Pinker, S. 2011. *The Better Angels of Our Nature*. New York: Penguin.

Queralt, D. 2019. "War, International Finance, and Fiscal Capacity in the Long Run." *International Organization* 73: 713–53.

Rogowski, J., J. Gerring, M. Maguire, and L. Cojocaru. 2021. "Public Infrastructure and Economic Development: Evidence from Postal Systems." *American Journal of Political Science*, forthcoming.

Sanchez de la Sierra, R. 2020. "On the Origins of the State: Stationary Bandits and Taxation in Eastern Congo." *Journal of Political Economy* 128: 32–74.

Scheve, K., and D. Stasavage. 2012. "Democracy, War, and Wealth: Lessons from Two Centuries of Inheritance Taxation." *American Political Science Review* 107: 81–102.

Scott, J. 1998. *Seeing Like a State*. New Haven, CT: Yale University Press.

Scott, J. 2009. *The Art of Not Being Governed*. New Haven, CT: Yale University Press.

Skocpol, T., and K. Finegold. 1982. "State Capacity and Economic Intervention in the Early New Deal." *Political Science Quarterly* 97: 255–78.

Sng, T. H., and C. Moriguchi. 2014. "Asia's Little Divergence: State Capacity in China and Japan before 1850." *Journal of Economic Growth* 19: 439–70.

Soifer, H. 2008. "State Infrastructural Power: Approaches to Conceptualization and Measurement." *Studies in Comparative International Development* 43: 231–51.

Soifer, H. 2015. *State Building in Latin America*. Cambridge: Cambridge University Press.

Stasavage, D. 2003. *Public Debt and the Birth of the Democratic State*. Cambridge: Cambridge University Press.

Stasavage, D. 2010. "When Distance Mattered: Geographic Scale and the Development of European Representative Assemblies." *American Political Science Review* 104: 625–43.

Stasavage, D. 2011. *States of Credit*. Princeton, NJ: Princeton University Press.

Suryanarayan, P. 2021. "Status Politics Hollows Out the State: Evidence from Colonial India." Working Paper. Johns Hopkins University.

Tilly, C. 1992. *Coercion, Capital, and European States, 1990–1992*. Malden, MA: Blackwell.

Vogler, J. 2023. "Bureaucracies in Historical Political Economy." In *Oxford Handbook of Historical Political Economy*, ed. J. Jenkins and J. Rubin, 373–99. Oxford: Oxford University Press.

Wang, Y. 2015. *Tying the Autocrat's Hands*. Cambridge: Cambridge University Press.

Wang, Y. 2021. "State-in-Society 2.0: Toward Fourth-Generation Theories of the State." *Comparative Politics* 54: 175–98.

Wang, Y. 2022a. *The Rise and Fall of Imperial China*. Princeton, NJ: Princeton University Press.

Wang, Y. 2022b. "Blood Is Thicker Than Water: Elite Kinship Networks and State Building in Imperial China." *American Political Science Review* 116, no. 3: 896–910.

Weber, M. 1946. *Essays in Sociology*. Oxford: Oxford University Press.

Xu, G. 2018. "The Costs of Patronage: Evidence from the British Empire." *American Economic Review* 108: 3170–98.

Xu, G. 2019. "The Colonial Origins of Fiscal Capacity: Evidence from Patronage Governors." *Journal of Comparative Economics* 47: 263–76.

CHAPTER 14

LEGAL CAPACITY IN HISTORICAL POLITICAL ECONOMY

MARK KOYAMA

THE legal system is a meta-institution. It spells out the formal rules of the game and how they are enforced. Social scientists are interested in the question "How well does it function?" That is, to what degree does it support overall human flourishing (where this can be interpreted either narrowly, as in higher levels of per capita GDP, or more broadly)?

Economists and political scientists increasingly use the term "legal capacity" to assess the legal institutions of a society. The concept is not always precisely defined, but we can think of it as referring to the overall capabilities of the courts, the judiciary, the police, and the legal system. Societies with greater legal capacity are widely held to better support trade and market through the enforcement of property rights.

The concept of legal capacity was introduced to the literature in political science and economics by Besley and Persson (2009; 2010; 2011). They employed the term to describe the dimension of state capacity associated with rules that support markets, and specifically with the protection of property rights. Besley and Persson were motivated by dissatisfaction with traditional approaches in economics that presume the existence of a government that costlessly enforces contracts. In their argument, in contrast, the policy choices of a state are constrained by existing institutions or "legal" capacity.[1]

The concept of legal capacity is thus closely related to the broader concept of state capacity as developed by scholars in historical sociology (Hintze 1975 [1906]); Mann 1986; Tilly 1985; 1990; Ertman 1997). Johnson and Koyama (2017) provide a detailed survey of the state capacity literature, particularly how it pertains to our understanding of economic history and comparative economic development, and Dincecco and Wang (2022) (in this volume) provide a complementary discussion of these issues.[2] While attention to state capacity has grown rapidly in recent years both in economics and political science, the majority of scholars have focused on fiscal capacity—that is, a state's ability to raise revenue—with less attention being paid to other aspects of state capacity, such as legal capacity.[3]

Legal capacity is also related to the concept of transaction costs, an important idea in the New Institutional Economics. North and Thomas (1973) and North (1981; 1990) built on Ronald Coase's (1937; 1960) insight that there are costs to using the market system and that these costs determine the extent and scope of the division of labor. Transaction costs were thus central to North's understanding of how institutions functioned. North viewed the legal system as among the most important of such institutions, writing, "In the Western world, the evolution of courts, legal systems, and a relatively impartial system of judicial enforcement has played a major role in permitting the development of a complex system of contracting that can extend over time and space, an essential requirement for economic specialization" (North 1992, 8). However, he did not investigate in detail the evolution of legal systems themselves. Subsequent work by North, Wallis, and Weingast (2009) paid greater attention to the importance of the law. Specifically, North, Wallis, and Weingast focused on the evolution of land law in medieval England (described later in this chapter). For more on the relationship between specific elements of the legal system and political economy, I refer readers to the chapter in this volume on the courts system by Clark and Vanberg (2023).

This chapter evaluates the concept of legal capacity. First, I discuss the relationship between legal capacity and the more widely used concept of the rule of law. I suggest that one benefit of legal capacity as a concept is that it is more straightforward to measure and hence employ in empirical research. Second, I discuss various measures of legal capacity and explore its relationship with income. Third, I go on to consider its relationship to the research on legal origins and to the wider literature on state capacity and political economy. The penultimate section examines how the concept of legal capacity has been used in recent research in historical political economy (HPE) by exploring two historical case studies: medieval England and early-modern France. Finally, I discuss some provisional conclusions and avenues for future research.

Legal Capacity and the Rule of Law

The concept of legal capacity is closely related to a more widely used term: the "rule of law." Indeed, a large literature relates some measure of the rule of law to positive development outcomes. For example, scholars have examined the link between contracting institutions and economic development (e.g., Knack and Keefer 1995; Acemoglu, Johnson, and Robinson 2001; 2005). However, major challenges exist to using the rule of law as an explanatory concept in HPE (see Haggard and Tiede 2011).

The first challenge is that the definition is contested. Legal scholarship in the late twentieth century emphasized a "thin" definition of the rule of law—one that stressed adherence to procedural norms without specifying anything about the content of the laws themselves.[4] Consider, for instance, Fuller's (1969) popular definition of the rule of law: that laws prospective, clear, and stable over time; that the judiciary be independent; and that rules are uniform and applicable to all. This definition contains nothing specific about the *content* of the law. Taking this thin view to its logical extreme, Raz (2009 [1979]) argued that in principle even a totalitarian regime can satisfy these requirements.

Legal scholars have therefore sought to empty the concept of the rule of law of substance and to treat it as a matter of procedure.[5] In contrast, in social scientific research, rule of law is typically associated with the content of specific laws, such as the extent to which private property rights are protected.

Indeed, as Rodriguez, McCubbins, and Weingast (2009–2010, 1458) note, "Rule of law is an attractive ideal, but its attractiveness may stem mainly from its imprecision, which allows each of us to project our own sense of the ideal government onto the phrase 'rule of law.'" Legal scholars distrust the expansion of the concept of the rule of law. Waldron (2020) writes,

> Once we open up the possibility of the Rule of Laws having a substantive dimension, we inaugurate a sort of competition in which everyone clamors to have their favorite political ideal incorporated as a substantive dimension of the Rule of Law. Those who favor property rights and market economy will scramble to privilege their favorite values in this regard. But so will those who favor human rights, or those who favor democratic participation, or those who favor civil liberties or social justice. The result is likely to be a general decline in political articulacy, as people struggle to use the same term to express disparate ideals.

Here, I am not necessarily taking a stance on whether the rule of law should have substantive content. But whatever one's position on the content of the rule of law, there is likely a benefit from employing less loaded and contested terminology.

Moreover, measurement of the rule of law is problematic. Empirical papers tend to use proxies such as the *World Bank Doing Business Report*. Recent scandals, however, have exposed the politicization of this measure. Even absent these problems, the *World Bank Doing Business Report* captured only one aspect of the rule of law. The implicit assumption that researchers made was that different aspects of the rule of law are positively correlated. However, as Rodriguez, McCubbins, and Weingast (2009–2010) emphasize, there are often conflicts between different aspects of the rule of law and hence no reason to expect that its dimensionality can be reduced to a single linear scale. Haggard and Tiede (2011) find that different measures of the rule of law are correlated across developed economies but are not tightly linked in developing economies.

One advantage of "legal capacity" is that it is a more neutral term than "rule of law." To describe a state as having more or less legal capacity does not presume whether that capacity is used for good or ill.

Another way to conceptualize the relationship between legal capacity and the rule of law is to distinguish between different types of rules. Adherence to general rules is one important component of how, as we have seen, all scholars define the rule of law.

General rules can be contrasted with rules that are either personal or based on the social identity of the individuals in question (see Johnson and Koyama 2019). Personal rules—that is, rules that are specific to each individual—can support cooperation in small-scale societies. Families are governed by personal rules, and as long as humans lived as hunter-gatherers, there was no incentive or need to develop more complex systems of governance. Interactions would have been repeated indefinitely, and the promise of repeated play sustains cooperation (see the discussion in Koyama and Carvalho 2010). Such personal rules, however, are seriously limited when it comes to dealing with strangers.

To enable cooperation with strangers, numerous societies leveraged rules that exploited salient aspects of social identity. Such identity rules treated individuals differently based on aspects of their identity, such as ethnicity, gender, or religion. Identity rules can be effective in scaling up cooperation; the Maghribi traders that Greif (2006) studied offer a famous example. But such rules require markers of identity. Different individuals receive different treatment based on these markers, which limited the scale of the trade that could be sustained. In contrast to both personal and identity rules, general rules are applicable equally to all individuals in a society. General rules require a high degree of legal capacity if they are to be enforced.

A key element of general rules is legal uniformity. Legal uniformity reduces transactions and facilitates market integration. For example, studying early-modern Poland, Malinowski (2019) finds that during periods when the state was able to invest in legal capacity, there was greater price integration in grain markets. Specifically, he argues that during the sixteenth century, when the Polish parliament (Seym) was functioning as a coherent body, it was able to push policies that lowered transaction costs in the grain market and facilitated the growth of export markets. When these institutions broke down in the seventeenth century, however, the result was both political weakness and market fragmentation. Similarly, research shows that the decline in the state capacity of late Qing China was associated with a decrease in market integration (Bernhofen et al. 2020).

A range of different institutions can support markets, but the high degree of legal capacity characteristic of modern states may be necessary for the emergence of more sophisticated organizational forms such as the business corporation. Large-scale economic activity such as the business corporation appears to require legal institutions capable of enforcing general rules and a degree of legal uniformity. Specifically, Zhang and Morley (2022) note that corporations have to treat shareholders uniformly to function effectively and that this matters more for larger commercial organizations. The promise of uniform treatment is often a precondition for a large number of unrelated individuals to be willing to invest in a business venture. It is also a precondition for centralized management, as inconsistent enforcement of laws could allow some owners to arbitrarily make commitments against the wishes of the central managers. Uniformity is also important for both entity-shielding—the protection of a firm's assets from nonfirm creditors—and for the tradability of shares, both crucial elements in the modern corporation.

General rules also provide protection for minorities, which is the thesis of Johnson and Koyama (2019), who argue that robust protection of religious minorities was only possible in states with high capacity that were capable of enforcing general rules. Fragmented societies such as the Holy Roman Empire were unable to offer such protection (Anderson, Johnson, and Koyama 2017; Finley and Koyama 2018).

Measuring Legal Capacity

Besley and Perrson (2009; 2010; 2011) use the level of private property protection as their measure of legal capacity. Specifically, they use the International Country Risk Guide published in 1997, which economists employed widely in the 1990s and early 2000s as a proxy for institutional quality. Besley and Perrson demonstrated that fiscal capacity and legal capacity are positively correlated and that both are associated with higher levels of per capita GDP. However, while this measure of private property protection does correspond closely to the relevant variable in the theoretical model of Besley and Persson (2011), the measure does not fully capture what most social scientists would mean by the term "legal capacity."[6]

Reassuringly, Besley and Persson (2011, 156–65) show that these empirical patterns also hold when they use other variables. These measures include the annual measure of government antidiversion from the International Country Risk Guide, a country's rank on the Doing Business Survey, the ease of registering property, access to credit, and the degree to which contracts are enforced. Nonetheless, even these measures miss some important aspects of the legal system and are only a partial measure of legal capacity.

A more complete measure of legal capacity is available from the Economic Freedom of the World Report (Gwartney et al. 2021b). This report categorizes economic freedom along five dimensions or areas—one of which, Area 2, is the legal system and property rights. Area 2 assesses each country on the following criteria: (i) judicial independence; (ii) impartial courts; (iii) protection of property rights; (iv) military interference in the rule of law and politics; (iv) integrity of the legal system; (v) legal enforcement of contracts; (vi) regulatory restrictions on sale of real property; and (vii) reliability of the police. Due to its greater breadth, I prefer it as a measure of legal capacity.

Figure 14.1 depicts the positive correlation between per capita GDP (2021) and this measure of legal capacity (2019). This figure confirms the basic patterns uncovered by Besley and Persson (2011). This relationship is robust to the inclusion of numerous covariates, as shown in Figure 14.2, which depicts the results of a simple regression analysis. The controls include a country's political system, its colonial origins, its legal origins, oil as a percentage of GDP, settler mortality, malaria ecology, soil suitability, and world region fixed effects. Needless to say, these relationships are descriptive. More research is required to investigate the extent to which legal capacity has a causal impact on other aspects of state capacity or on GDP per capita.

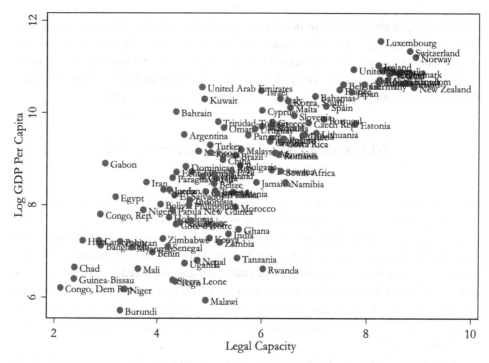

FIGURE 14.1. Legal capacity and GDP per capita today

Per capita GDP is from the World Bank national accounts data. The measure of legal capacity used here is Area 2 from Gwartney et al. (2021a). I used the data without the Gender Legal Rights Adjustment.

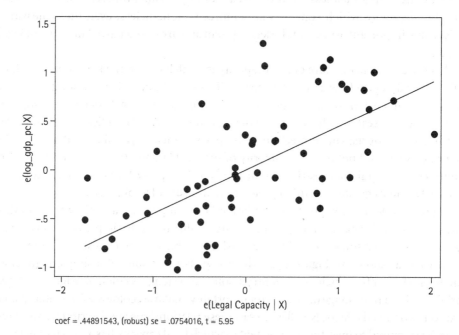

coef = .44891543, (robust) se = .0754016, t = 5.95

FIGURE 14.2. Legal capacity and GDP per capita today conditional on baseline controls

Standard errors are clustered at the country level. Legal capacity data is from Gwartney et al. (2021a). The controls include a country's political system, its colonial origins, its legal origins, oil as a percentage of GDP, settler mortality, malaria ecology, soil suitability, and world region fixed effects. These variables are from Grier, Young, and Grier (2021).

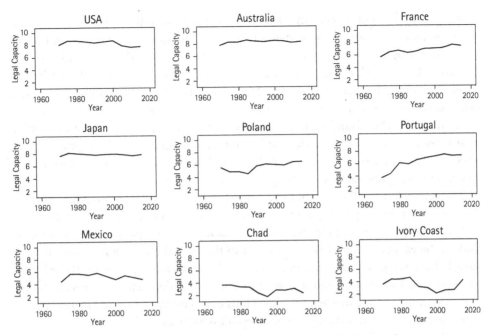

FIGURE 14.3. The evolution of legal capacity in selected countries (1960–2019)

Legal capacity is taken from Area 2 of the Economic Freedom Index, Gwartney et al. (2021a).

Examining the relationship between legal capacity, fiscal capacity, and GDP across countries and over time is fraught with empirical challenges. Figure 14.3 depicts the evolution of legal capacity over time in selected countries (the United States, Australia, France, Japan, Poland, Portugal, Mexico, Chad, and the Ivory Coast). The main takeaways are as follows: as expected, measures of legal capacity are consistently higher in developed countries than in developing countries. Political transitions such as democratization in Portugal and Poland are associated with improvements in legal capacity. There is little within-country variation, however, and a high amount of serial autocorrelation, which suggests that standard empirical methods may be ill-suited for estimating causal relationships between legal capacity and other variables of interest such as fiscal capacity and GDP.[7] One attempt to overcome these limitations comes from Grier, Young, and Grier (2021). The authors focus on discrete "jumps" in legal capacity. They find little support that such jumps are associated with marked increases in fiscal capacity. One way forward, is to focus on historical studies that permit the use of more desegregated and fine-grained data.

LEGAL CAPACITY AND LEGAL ORIGINS

Legal capacity is one way of evaluating a society's legal system. The recent attention paid to legal capacity builds on an earlier literature that focused on the type of legal system that a society has, and specifically whether its origins were in the English common law or the Roman law tradition. This literature draws inspiration from writings on English common law by Dicey (1908) and Hayek (1960). It blossomed in the 1990s with the seminal contributions of La Porta et al. (1998), who took to the data the hypothesis that the English common law tradition is associated with better protection of property rights, less regulations, and a more favorable environment for markets than legal systems based on Roman law. They found support for these findings, and particularly for the finding that investors, that is, shareholders and creditors, obtained better legal protection in common law countries. Subsequent studies found that common law origins were associated with less government ownership and less legal formalism.[8]

This research was influential but also contested, particularly by economic historians. One problem for the legal origins hypothesis is the fact that financial development varies greatly over time. For example, in 1913 France's stock market capitalization, as a proportion of the economy, was almost twice that of the United States (Rajan and Zingales, 2003). This, along with the fact that some of the empirical findings on the relationship between legal origins and investor protection were dependent on specific coding decisions, cautions one that legal origins is only one of many factors that matter for how effective a legal system is at supporting economic development.

Looking at the nineteenth century, Sgard (2006) found no evidence that English common law was substantively more protective of creditor rights. Indeed French, German, and English laws in this period all granted substantial protections to creditors. Within France, which had both civil and common law traditions prior to the revolution, there is little evidence that civil law was associated with worse economic outcomes (Bris 2019).[9]

Charron, Dahlström, and Lapuente (2012) note that, for many societies, the choice of legal system was political. For example, when designing the Napoleonic Code, Napoleon chose a particularly autocratic interpretation of Roman law—the so-called Justinian deviation (Charron, Dahlström, and Lapuente 2012, 178). At the time, other choices could have been made. Similarly, Russian and Japanese policymakers, respectively, made the choice of French and German legal codes on voluntary political grounds. Legal origins are only plausibly exogenous for colonies that were obliged to adopt a specific legal system. Even then, over time legal origins may matter less as countries borrow legal rules and decisions from neighbors or from supranational bodies like the European Union rather than from countries with similar legal codes. Many countries have reformed their legal systems over time. Indeed, Malmendier (2009) documents how the Roman legal system evolved during the Republican period to facilitate larger and more complex organizational forms. She notes that "the adaptability mechanism to which the growth-friendliness of common-law systems is attributed was at work also 'at the origin' of civil law" (Malmendier 2009, 1097). The decline in these large-scale organizations was likely driven by political factors (i.e., the autocratic power of the emperors or the general political instability of the third century) rather than reflecting any intrinsic limitations of the Roman legal system. At a more general level, Guerriero (2016) explores the hypothesis that the evolution of the legal

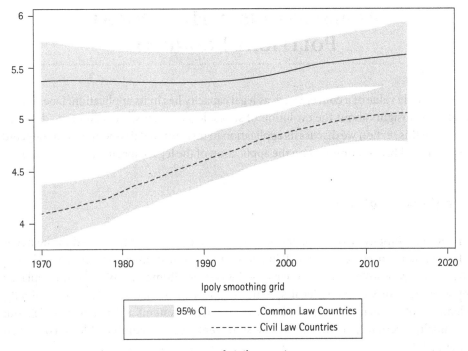

FIGURE 14.4. Legal capacity in common and civil countries

Legal capacity is taken from Area 2 of the Economic Freedom Index, Gwartney et al. (2021a).

systems, in common and civil law countries, depends on how heterogeneous a population is and on the quality of political institutions. Bradford et al. (2021) find that legal origins does predict the substantive content of the law in long-standing fields such as property law. But the authors find little relationship between legal origins and how legal systems react to more recent areas of law, such as antitrust. These results further qualify the weight that earlier literature placed on the importance of legal origins.

In the cross-section, legal capacity is higher on average in countries with a common law legal tradition than a French civil law legal tradition. Over time, however, this difference has diminished significantly (see Figure 14.4). This finding is related to the argument of Charron, Dahlström, and Lapuente (2012) that the differences between civil law and common law countries when it comes to the extent of financial regulation, contract enforcement, tenure of judges, and legal formalism are largely driven by countries that had low levels of state capacity.

Rather than legal origins being irrelevant or unimportant, the lesson of this research is that legal origins is far from the only determinant of the effectiveness of a legal system. The capacity of a legal system also matters—that is to say, the number and training of the judiciary, the presence of a court system that can hear and process cases in a timely matter, the existence of a professional and noncorrupt police force, and lawyers able to deal with complex cases.

Applications in Historical Political Economy

The scholarly value of a concept such as legal capacity lies in its application. Does it generate new insights about the evolution of states, legal systems, and economic development? In this section we discuss its application to institutional developments in England and France. I briefly comment on the application of the legal capacity in other settings.

Medieval England

The Roman Empire had a sophisticated legal system, one highly attuned to the needs of a commercialized economy (Malmendier 2009). But Roman law was largely lost in Western Europe following the collapse of the Western Roman Empire.[10] It was replaced by a mixture of Germanic legal systems—known as the *leges barbarorum*. Initially, elements of Roman law survived as the two legal systems existed in parallel. But eventually—certainly by the end of the sixth century CE—combined legal codes had emerged.

These legal codes, however, were simple compared to the system of Roman law that had existed. They reflected the decline in economic complexity that occurred in Western Europe between 400 and 600 CE. These post-Roman legal codes shared common features: the criminal code was based on the notion of compensation—in old English, *werguild*—which reflects the personal nature of the legal system; there was no means of public enforcement; laws were identity rules with different levels of compensation and punishment depending on the social status of the victim and perpetrator; and the legal system was focused on questions of inheritance and limiting the damage that could arise from blood feuds. There was little in the way of a law of contracts.

The absence of legal capacity is reflected in the fact that monarchies of this period lacked legislative capacity. The closest analogy to central government was the person of the king, but the king could neither levy taxes nor make new laws. They were constrained "not only in theory but in practice, by the *Lex Terrae* (the customs of the country), which was thought of as a thing immutable" (Jouvenel 1948).

The nadir of political and economic complexity occurred in the tenth century. From the eleventh century onward, economic recovery spurred institutional and legal developments.

Private or Public Order Institutions?

Before proceeding further, we should note that much trade and commercial relations in the medieval period depended heavily on informal and private order institutions.

Indeed, a voluminous literature has arisen analyzing these institutions (see, e.g., Benson 1989; North 1990; Greif 1989; 2006; Greif, Milgrom, and Weingast 1994). One might conclude that this literature's one lesson is that public institutions and indeed legal capacity are less important than we would otherwise consider for supporting trade and markets. The latest scholarly research, however, does not support this conclusion.

Private order institutions did flourish in medieval Europe and they played a role in the rise in legal capacity. However, they tended to be complementary to public order institutions rather than a direct substitute for them. This is the case for the Champagne fairs, for instance, which emerged as centers for international trade in the fourteenth century. The counts of Champagne played a crucial role in safeguarding merchants and enforcing property rights through their own law courts (Ogilvie 2011; Ogilvie and Carus 2014). Private order arrangements thus often existed in the shadow of formal, public order institutions.

The literature on the law merchant tells a similar story. Economists interested in private ordering picked up on the research by legal scholars on merchant law in the Middle Ages and specifically on the concept of the law merchant. This referred to a body of customary law that supported trade during the commercial revolution in Europe. In particular, Benson (1989) claimed that privately produced and privately adjudicated customary law were responsible for the rise of trade in medieval Europe. The problem is the weak historical and empirical basis for these claims (Kadens 2011–2012; 2015). Rather, long-distance merchants typically relied on local legal systems either at organized fairs, such as the Champagne fair, or in entrepôt cities. In the major towns, commerce was highly regulated by local councils and guilds. There was competition between legal systems and plenty of private ordering, but it did not take place within a world in which there was no state to enforce contracts or protect property rights. Nor did it result in a standardized set of laws for governing commerce.

Transaction costs were high in the medieval economy. Long-distance trade was risky, with that risk reflected in high interest rates. Trade disputes, boycotts, and sometimes violence were commonplace. Medieval merchants innovated in order to reduce these transaction costs through bills of exchange, insurance contracts, and partnerships. Legal systems also became more complex, integrating concepts from Roman law in order to better support trade (see, e.g., Berman 1983). But the fractured and fragmented nature of local legal systems remained a problem for merchants throughout the entire Middle Ages and into the early-modern period.

Common Law: Constraining or Empowering

Across Europe, however, the Roman legal tradition had been largely lost. In particular, Roman commercial and contractual law had disappeared along with the market economy of the Roman period. These concepts had to be rediscovered in the Middle Ages.

To proceed, I focus on medieval England as that country played a central role in the emergence of the rule of law.[11] Anglo-Saxon England had a more extensive and better-functioning legal system than existed in Continental Europe by 1000 CE.[12] Nonetheless, the Anglo-Saxon legal system was based on identity rules. It focused on mediating interpersonal conflict rather than supporting trade or cooperation between strangers.

Following the Norman Conquest, onto this Anglo-Saxon system of law were superimposed legal traditions from Normandy that included trial by battle and trial by ordeal. Compared to the rest of Europe, the Norman monarchy was stronger and more centralized. The reign of Henry II (r. 1154–1189) saw a series of reforms associated with the establishment of English common law. Through this process of centralization, a new basis for monarchic power was established. This systematization and codification was also the precondition for the rise of a class of legal experts or lawyers. Thus, there was a marked increase in both royal power (relative to the barons) and legal capacity. Indeed, the late twelfth century saw numerous complaints about the arbitrary rule of royal offices, particularly sheriffs. Another common complaint was a lack of certainty concerning the content or enforcement of the laws. The many different levels of authority within feudal society meant that legal authority was routinely contested.[13]

These developments have attracted the attention of economists as well as legal scholars. Glaeser and Shleifer (2002) developed an analytical narrative to account for the divergence that took place between English and French law in this period. Specifically, they argued that greater political stability in medieval England permitted English kings to allow a for a decentralized legal system (in contrast to France, which they see as having a centralized legal system). However, as Klerman and Mahoney (2007) demonstrate, Glaeser and Shlefier substantially misread certain key facts of English and French history. The establishment of common law involved the creation of a small cadre of professional judges and insulated the provision of justice from local lords. In contrast, the French king was unable to do this and law remained controlled by local elites. Contrary to the claims of Shleifer and Glaeser, customary law prevailed in much of France until the sixteenth and seventeenth centuries.

According to Berman (1983), Henry II's reliance on legal and royal writs and summons was vital because it ensured that law became the basis of royal government. Henry II had centralized power in such a manner so as to also set the limits of that power: he "extended his jurisdiction as against that of both feudal and ecclesiastical courts; but the conditions of his assertion of royal jurisdiction were expressly stated and they would therefore serve as limitations" (Berman 1983, 458).

North, Wallis, and Weingast (2009) examine the development of property law in the context of the broader framework of institutional development. In agrarian economies such as medieval England, land is the primary asset and source of wealth and power. Control of the land, and how tight that control is, determines how the dominant coalition governs and structures itself. If the king had the discretion to reallocate land, this weakened potential challengers. William the Conqueror in 1066 had made himself the feudal lord of all land in the country, which was held in fief from him. In the early years of the occupation huge swathes of land were taken from Anglo-Saxon nobles and redistributed to William's followers. But the corresponding insecurity of property rights in land reduced efficiency and increased uncertainty. In particular, the rights of inheritance were poorly defined, with heirs having to pay the Crown a fine for the right to inherit. Over time, therefore, the nobles demanded greater security of tenure.

These issues were closely intertwined with Magna Carta and the rise of Parliament. The legal reforms inaugurated by Henry II gave the king much greater power of adjudication. These powers were used and abused by Henry and especially by his son John (r. 1199–1217), and these abuses provoked a reaction from barons. This baronial opposition succeeded in forcing John to accede to Magna Carta. Magna Carta established several important principles, including the right to a trial before one's peers and the right to swift justice. Though John soon renegaded on the treaty, and though many of its more binding initial provisions were rapidly jettisoned, Magna Carta did successfully introduce the idea that law could be a check on a ruler's power.

The crisis that produced Magna Carta was at root fiscal. John was embroiled in an ongoing conflict with the French king over the extensive domains he inherited from Henry II (the so-called Angevin Empire). However, as he lost lands, John lacked the means to finance this war. There was little in the way of tax capacity, and the revenues that English kings had traditionally relied upon—the customary feudal revenues, consisting of the proceeds of royal farms, profits of justice, feudal incidents, tolls, and fines—were all in decline. And it was the king's abuse of his feudal rights for fiscal purposes that was one of the main provocations that brought John to Runnymede. For John's successor Henry III (r. 1217–1274), the alternative path—one that would avoid conflict with the nobility—was for the king to obtain revenue by ruling in consent with the nobility.

This lesson had to be reinforced through violence on several occasions during the thirteenth century: most notably in the Second Barons' War (1264–1267), which saw the leading barons rebelled against what they saw as arbitrary royal behavior. Nonetheless, prior to the Second Barons' War, Henry III had already begun the practice of calling together the leading nobles of the realm in what would become known as Parliaments.[14] This did not prevent conflict between the king and his barons, but following the Second Barons' War, Henry and then his son Edward I (r. 1274–1307) did seek to govern through the consent of the barons and of the wider political nation. In the words of one historian, "Edward, far more than any previous king, reached out and won the favour of the knights and those below them in local society, precisely the group who had, through their representatives in parliament, to consent to the new taxation" (Carpenter 2003, 478).

Legal reforms such as Quia Emptores (1290) provided more stable property rights. From the perspective of North, Wallis, and Weingast (2009), these reforms reflected the interests of elites in both the option of creating alienable landownership and imposing complex restrictions on ownership. They established a measure of rule of law for elites, at least when it came to property law.

The rise of legal capacity in medieval England thus laid the foundations both for a stronger state and limitations to be placed on that state. Legal capacity strengthened the power of the king vis-à-vis this barons. But it also made it possible for the king to be constrained and pointed the way towards constitutional government. As North, Wallis, and Weingast (2009) argue, rule of law was first attained by elites before being expanded to non-elites. They provide a detailed discussion of how landholdings in England became increasingly secure over the course of the Middle Ages as institutions emerged that governed the inheritance, sale, and reallocation of property rights. These developments would prove crucial in the seventeenth century, when Parliament eventually succeeded in constraining royal power.

Notably, much of our evidence pertains to the rise in legislative capacity in this period. We know less about enforcement capacity. Contemporary accounts suggest that during periods of royal weakness—for example, the 1320s and the 1450s—lords and local officials such as sheriffs abused their powers. More systematic and uniform enforcement of legal rules occurred only in the sixteenth and seventeenth centuries, and only in the nineteenth century did England see the establishment of a police force capable of enforcing criminal law (see Koyama 2014).

Early Modern France

France, as we have seen, was dominated by customary law in the Middle Ages. Klerman and Mahoney (2007) discuss how the process of legal centralization in France began later than in England and took longer.[15]

As late as 1600, the French legal system and fiscal system remained fragmented. This fragmentation reflected the gradual manner in which territory had been added to the French Crown during the Middle Ages (Goubert 1969). Legal and fiscal fragmentation was part of the political equilibrium of medieval France: the ruler protected local privileges, and in return local elites were loyal to the Crown. As new lands were acquired, the king conceded privileges to those new regions to retain their allegiance. J. Russell Major observed that medieval monarchs made concessions to local interests in order to survive: "They had encouraged the codification of local customs instead of trying to create a common law. They had accepted the growth of provincial loyalties. ... In short, at the very time when they appeared to be creating a unified kingdom by driving the English out, they were permitting the formation of centrifugal forces that threatened to keep the nation forever divided" (Major 1994, 58).

The result was that the king's legal authority was weak. French judges were independent of the king, and the provincial nobility retained many privileges. Even where the king's authority was substantial, local families dominated the regional parlements.[16] The end result was the absence of "a coherent and common set of laws" (Moote 1971, 8). Within a locality, laws varied tremendously, and the courts, meanwhile, were controlled by provincial elites who ran them for their own benefit. Nepotism and venality were commonplace: positions were often hereditary and a source of patronage (Beik 1985). Indeed this venality increased with the fiscal demands placed upon the state, as selling offices was always a lucrative source of revenue for the Crown (for a model of this dynamic, see Crettez et al. 2023).

The costs of legal fragmentation manifested themselves in the administration of justice. France possessed no single criminal code, and the concept of equality before the law was "unknown" (Heckscher 1955, 168). In principle, a decentralized legal system could have provided greater legal capacity at the local level. Similarly, reliance on customary law could have allowed legal rules to be tailored to local circumstances. The historical record, however, suggests that whatever benefits could have accrued from legal decentralization in theory, the practice saw widespread rent-seeking and elite capture. "Because there was no uniform criminal code in France, judges in conjunction with procureurs generaux had great latitude in deciding what constituted a crime and its appropriate punishment. Many individuals withered in prison for months before their cases were heard, and upon the decision of the presiding magistrate prisoners were denied counsel and subjected to torture" (Hamscher 1976, 161–62). Simply put, there was an absence of general rules. The lack of a common criminal code gave discretion to local elites who staffed the courts and who used this power to extract rents. There were "perennial jurisdictional conflicts among the courts and in great expense to litigants who faced a vast judicial hierarchy if they were entitled to appeal a decision from a lower court" (Hamscher 1976, 160). In comparison to England, legal capacity was low.

While allowances must be made for the state-centric biases of contemporary writers and historians, some of the concrete costs of this legal fragmentation are evident in the witchcraft trials of this era. Decades after the Parlement of Paris had all but ceased to execute individuals for witchcraft because of the difficulty of obtaining credible witnesses or the required "legal proofs" needed to subject individuals to torture, witchcraft trials continued in those parts of France where the judiciary remained under local control (Johnson and Koyama 2014; 2019).

As the French monarchy embarked on a series of expansionary wars from the third decade of the seventeenth century onward, new pressures were placed on the fiscal system. This process of fiscal consolidation, however, both necessitated and enabled reform of the legal system. As Hamscher (1976, 157) notes, financial reforms and judicial reforms "dovetailed perfectly" for "if justice could be dispensed swiftly and inexpensively, all segments of the population would have more funds at their disposal to develop the economy and to place in the service of the monarchy."

Therefore, on paper at least, a dramatic increase took place in the state's ability to enforce its laws. The number of government officials grew from 4,041 in 1515 to over 46,047 by 1665 (Kwass 2000, 29). The *intendants*, first sent out into the countryside in the 1630s, and then on a more systematic basis from the 1660s onward, had the power to overrule local elites. The intendants were part of a new elite, the "nobility of the robe," who were distinct from the old "nobility of the sword." Unlike other venal officials, the intendants had not purchased their positions. They were commissioned employees of the king who could be dismissed at will (Collins 1988, 54). Consequentially, their interests were aligned with the central government. Indeed, they can be seen as a "quasi-bureaucracy" that was connected into a central, Paris-based system of clientelism and patronage, and independent of the local nobility (Kettering 1986).

This program of centralization was, of course, only partially successful. As one historian has observed, the "modern characteristics of Louis XIV's government should not be exaggerated—it was an early modern state that was only quasi-bureaucratic and, although formally centralized and hierarchical, it was also cumbersome, incoherent, and fragmented by special interest groups. But it provided a stronger, more stable government than its predecessors had" (Kettering 1986, 224).

Nonetheless, on the eve of the French Revolution, approximately 80 general customs and 380 local customs were applied across France (Bris 2019). Competing and overlapping jurisdictions resulted in impediments to market integration, such as numerous internal tariff barriers and different systems of weights and measures across regions (Heckscher 1955, 55–56).[17] Local public goods (such as irrigation projects) were underprovided, as high transaction costs created holdup problems (Rosenthal 1992). Disputes over contested property rights could go on for years, and litigants ran up high legal bills (Collins 1995).

Only following the French Revolution was this legal fragmentation fully reversed. As part of this process, judges were prohibited from making law and the status of judges was diminished to that of civil servants. Indeed the high degree of centralization associated with the Napoleonic Code can be viewed as a reaction to the previous fragmentation (see Klerman and Mahoney 2007, 287–89). Alternatively, Crettez, Deffains, and Musy (2018) view it as a product of the Enlightenment. Whereas under the Old Regime, legal inequality had been tolerated by political elites, the new political elite who emerged following the revolution saw these inequalities as odious.

As discussed in the context of the legal origins literature, the creation of a centralized legal system by Napoleon had costs and benefits. On the benefits side of the ledger, creating a uniform legal system facilitated market integration and interregional trade. On the costs side, it also elevated the state above the legal system. The ability of judges to make law as circumstances evolve and change by interpreting among different statues was severely curtained (see Beck, Demirgüç-Kunt, and Levine 2003). The result was a highly centralized but also relatively inflexible legal system.

Concluding Comments

This chapter has only touched on the literature on the historical evolution of legal capacity. Many topics deserve attention in future research. For example, there has been recent work on feuding in Germany (see Broman and Vanberg 2022) and on fiscal and legal capacity in twentieth-century Haiti (Palsson 2023).

A final few matters are worthy of mention. First, the importance of state capacity has come under critical scruntiny. For example, Geloso and Salter (2020) have argued that the correlation we observe in the data between state capacity and economic development is not a causal one. That is, as states develop they have to invest in state capacity in order to defend themselves, but it is not necessarily the case that state capacity directly leads to beneficial development outcomes. This argument has merit when it comes to investment in fiscal capacity; as noted in Johnson and Koyama (2017), the increases in tax revenues raised by early-modern states were predominately spent on warfare and are unlikely to have directly benefited taxpayers. French peasants did not benefit from the greater fiscal extractions of Louis XIV's state. But Geloso and Salter (2020) are on weaker grounds when it comes to investment in legal capacity.[18] As I have documented, there are prima facie reasons and some provisional empirical evidence for believing that investments in legal capacity had direct economic benefits.

Second, the concept of legal capacity seems well suited to explain the evolution of legal and political institutions in western Europe. It is less clear how this concept applies in either the Islamic Middle East or in East Asia. China has been autocratic for almost its entire history. The influence of legalism ensured that the law was subordinated to the ruler. China possessed the first "modern state," according to Fukuyama (2011). Certainly, it had tremendous bureaucratic power relative to any of its historical peers, possessing a meritocratic and disciplined civil service—but it lacked legal capacity. This basic fact continues to shape political and economic development in China.

Third, this survey has necessarily focused on the development of legal capacity at the national level. Less is known about the effectiveness of more decentralized legal systems, in part because it is hard to evaluate the "output" of historical legal systems. From medieval England we know that manorial courts were capable of supporting credit markets (Briggs 2009; Briggs and Koyama 2013). Future work can explore the extent to which it is sufficient to focus on the rise of legal capacity at the national level, at the expense of local developments.

Finally, there has been less research on legal capacity in developing countries. One benefit of high state capacity is that it enables rules to be simplified. But, as Rajagopalan and Tabarrok (2021) show, poorer countries often have a combination of weak state capacity and highly complex rules. These overly complex rules offer opportunities for corruption and rent-seeking, which, in turn, help keep poor countries poor. Future research should be directed toward examining example where states successfully overcame such challenges.

Acknowledgments

I thank the editors Jeffery A. Jenkins and Jared Rubin as well as Noel Johnson, Daniel Klerman, Ryan Murphy, and Jan Vogler for suggestions and comments. I am grateful to Kevin Grier, Robin Grier, and Andrew Young for sharing the data on legal capacity and fiscal capacity and to Alexander Taylor for research assistance. I thank Kashiff Thompson for proofreading.

Notes

1. Besley, Dann, and Persson (2021) update their analysis, introducing a third dimension that they call "collective capacity."
2. Also see Dincecco (2015; 2017).

3. O'Reilly and Murphy (2022) provide a broader measure of state capacity for an unbalanced panel of countries extending as far back as 1789.
4. Fernández-Villaverde (2016) documents the rise of this modern interpretation and how it differs from early legal theorists' conception for the rule of law.
5. See Bingham (2007, 67–68) for a summary of these critiques.
6. More recently, O'Reilly and Murphy (2022) use data from the V-Dem project to construct estimates of state capacity that extend back to 1789.
7. For example, in simple two-way fixed effects model improvements in past legal capacity are strongly associated with improvements in both fiscal capacity and per capita GDP. But the inclusion of the lag of the dependent variable tends to significantly weaken the relationship. The results of dynamic panel models are also highly sensitive to the choice of specification.
8. Many of these arguments were restated by Shleifer, Lopez de Silanes, and La Porta (2008).
9. For a discussion of these points, see also Koyama and Rubin (2022, 43–47).
10. In the words of legal historian John Maxcy Zane, "All that part of the law which is concerned with business, trade, and commerce was fully developed. Contacts, of sale, of mortgage, of pledge and all the legal implements of credit and banking and for the transfer of funds, contracts of various kinds pertaining to trading and business ventures, including insurance, the law of partnership and corporations of almost every condition, all the law of what were called bailments and the law of loan and surety-ship and warranty, were fully developed, but were to pass away as soon as commerce was destroyed" (1927, 180).
11. This discussion draws on Koyama (2016).
12. In Continental Europe, written laws ceased to be passed after the collapse of the Carolingian Empire in the second half of the ninth century. Laws were oral and customary, and varied tremendously from place to place.
13. One example are the laws of the forest. The scope of the royal forest was a matter of serious contention between the king and his subjects throughout this period.
14. Parliament emerged from the *curia regis* or royal council that comprised the king's relatives and magnates. The parliaments of the first part of Henry's reign had been informal gatherings of the major barons; in the aftermath of the civil war, Edward elevated the importance of parliament. Parliament was "a royal innovation begun by John, frequently used by Henry III, and developed by Edward I into an integral par of the constitutions, and all three kings had used the practice for their own purposes, financial, administrative or political, as and when they saw fit" (Treharne 1986, 26). This is also consistent with the account of Congleton (2010).
15. This section draws on Johnson and Koyama (2014); Johnson, Koyama, and Nye (2015); and Johnson and Koyama (2019).
16. The parlements were judicial bodies, akin to courts of appeal, but with an added legislative component.
17. The north and south of France had different systems of regulation and administration. To transport goods between Rouen and Nantes, one paid thirty different tolls and each provided an opportunity for a local official to overcharge by as much as 300 or 400 percent (Heckscher 1955, 85–85).
18. Moreover, as Hendrickson, Salter, and Albrecht (2018) discuss, even if state capacity—specifically military capacity—does not directly affect production, if it is essential for defense in world where conflict is possible, then it may nonetheless be critical for long-run economic development.

REFERENCES

Acemoglu, Daron, Simotin Johnson, and James A. Robinson. 2001. "The Colonial Origins of Comparative Development: An Empirical Investigation." *American Economic Review* 91, no. 5: 1369–401.

Acemoglu, Daron, Simon Johnson, and James A. Robinson. 2005. "Institutions as a Fundamental Cause of Long-Run Growth." In *Handbook of Economic Growth*, ed. Philippe Aghion and Steven Durlauf, 385–472. Elsevier.

Anderson, R. Warren, Noel D. Johnson, and Mark Koyama. 2017. "Jewish Persecutions and Weather Shocks, 1100–1800." *Economic Journal* 127, no. 602: 924–58.

Beck, Thorsten, Asli Demirgüç-Kunt, and Ross Levine. 2003. "Law and Finance: Why Does Legal Origin Matter?" *Journal of Comparative Economics* 31, no. 4: 653–75.

Beik, William. 1985. *Absolutism and Society in Seventeenth-Century France*. Cambridge: Cambridge University Press.

Benson, B. L. 1989. "The Spontaneous Evolution of Commercial Law." *Southern Economic Journal*: 644–61.

Berman, Harold J. 1983. *Law and Revolution, the Formation of the Western Legal Tradition*. Cambridge, MA: Harvard University Press.

Bernhofen, Daniel, Markus Eberhardt, Jianan Li, and Stephen Morgan. 2020. "The Secular Decline of Market Integration during Qing China's Golden Age." Unpublished manuscript.

Besley, Timothy, and Torsten Persson. 2009. "The Origins of State Capacity: Property Rights, Taxation, and Politics." *American Economic Review* 99, no. 4: 1218–44.

Besley, Timothy, and Torsten Persson. 2010. "State Capacity, Conflict, and Development." *Econometrica* 78, no. 1: 1–34.

Besley, Timothy, and Torsten Persson. 2011. *Pillars of Prosperity*. Princeton, NJ: Princeton University Press.

Besley, Timothy J., Chris Dann, and Torsten Persson. 2021. *Pillars of Prosperity: A Ten-Year Update*. CEPR Discussion Papers 16256.

Bingham, Tom. 2007. "The Rule of Law." *Cambridge Law Journal* 66, no. 1: 67–85.

Bradford, Anu, Yun-chien Chang, Adam Chilton, and Nuno Garoupa. 2021. "Do Legal Origins Predict Legal Substance?" *Journal of Law and Economics* 64, no. 2: 207–31.

Briggs, Chris. 2009. *Credit and Village Society in Fourteenth-Century England*. Oxford: Oxford University Press.

Briggs, Chris, and Mark Koyama. 2013. "Medieval Microcredit." Manuscript.

Bris, David le. 2019. "Testing Legal Origins Theory within France: Customary Laws versus Roman Code." *Journal of Comparative Economics* 47, no. 1: 1–30.

Broman, Benjamin, and Georg Vanberg. 2022. "Feuding, Arbitration, and the Emergence of an Independent Judiciary." *Constitutional Political Economy* 33: 162–99.

Carpenter, David. 2003. *The Struggle for Mastery*. London: Penguin.

Charron, Nicholas, Carl Dahlström, and Victor Lapuente. 2012. "No Law without a State." *Journal of Comparative Economics* 40, no. 2: 176–93.

Clark, Tom S., and Georg Vanberg. 2023. "Courts: A Political Economy Perspective." In *Oxford Handbook of Historical Political Economy*, ed. Jeffery A. Jenkins and Jared Rubin, 353–72. Oxford: Oxford University Press.

Coase, R. H. 1937. "The Nature of the Firm." *Economica* 4, no. 16: 386–405.

Coase, R. H. 1960. "The Problem of Social Cost." *Journal of Law and Economics* 3, no. 1: 1.

Collins, James B. 1988. *Fiscal Limits of Absolutism*. Berkeley: University of California Press.

Collins, James B. 1995. *The State in Early Modern France*. Cambridge: Cambridge University Press.

Congleton, Roger D. 2010. *Perfecting Parliament*. Cambridge: Cambridge University Press.
Crettez, Bertrand, Bruno Deffains, and Olivier Musy. 2018. "Legal Centralization: A Tocquevillian View." *Journal of Legal Studies* 47, no. 2: 295–323.
Crettez, Bertrand, Bruni Deffains, Olivier Musy, and Ronan Tallec. 2023. "State Capacity, Legal Design and the Sale of Judicial Offices in Old Regime France." Available at SSRN: https://ssrn.com/abstract=3552920.
Dicey, A. V. 1908. *Introduction to the Study of the Law of the Constitution*. London: Macmillan and Co.
Dincecco, Mark. 2015. "The Rise of Effective States in Europe." *Journal of Economic History* 75, no. 03: 901–18.
Dincecco, Mark. 2017. *State Capacity and Economic Development: Present and Past*. Elements in Political Economy. Cambridge University Press.
Dincecco, Mark, and Yuhua Wang. 2023. "State Capacity in Historical Political Economy." In *Oxford Handbook of Historical Political Economy*, ed. Jeffery A. Jenkins and Jared Rubin, 253–69. Oxford: Oxford University Press.
Ertman, Thomas. 1997. *Birth of Leviathan*. Cambridge: Cambridge University Press.
Fernández-Villaverde, Jesús. 2016. "Magna Carta, a Commentary on the Great Charter of King John, the Rule of Law, and the Limits on Government." *International Review of Law and Economics* 47: 22–28.
Finley, Theresa, and Mark Koyama. 2018. "Plague, Politics, and Pogroms: The Black Death, the Rule of Law, and the Persecution of Jews in the Holy Roman Empire." *Journal of Law and Economics* 61, no. 2: 253–77.
Fukuyama, Francis. 2011. *The Origins of Political Order*. London: Profile.
Fuller, Lon L. 1969. *The Morality of Law*. New Haven, CT: Yale University Press.
Geloso, Vincent J., and Alexander W. Salter. 2020. "State Capacity and Economic Development: Causal Mechanism or Correlative Filter?" *Journal of Economic Behavior & Organization* 170: 372–85.
Glaeser, Edward L., and Andrei Shleifer. 2002. "Legal Origins." *Quarterly Journal of Economics* 117, no. 4: 1193–229.
Goubert, Pierre. 1969. *L'Ancien Régime*. Paris.
Greif, Avner. 1989. "Reputation and Coalitions in Medieval Trade: Evidence on the Maghribi Traders." *Journal of Economic History* 49, no. 4: 857–82.
Greif, Avner. 2006. *Institutions and the Path to the Modern Economy*. Cambridge: Cambridge University Press.
Greif, Avner, Paul Milgrom, and Barry R. Weingast. 1994. "Coordination, Commitment, and Enforcement: The Case of the Merchant Guild." *Journal of Political Economy* 102, no. 4: 745–76.
Grier, Robin, Andrew T. Young, and Kevin Grier. 2021. "The Causal Effects of Rule of Law and Property Rights on Fiscal Capacity." *European Journal of Political Economy*: 102169.
Guerriero, Carmine. 2016. "Endogenous Legal Traditions and Economic Outcomes." *Journal of Comparative Economics* 44, no. 2: 416–33.
Gwartney, James, Robert A. Lawson, Ryan Murphy, Matanda Abubaker, Andrea Celico, Alexander C.R. Hammond, Fred McMahon, and Martin Rode. 2021a. "Economic Freedom Dataset," published in *Economic Freedom of the World: 2021 Annual Report*. Fraser Institute.
Gwartney, James, Robert A. Lawson, Ryan Murphy, Matanda Abubaker, Andrea Celico, Alexander C.R. Hammond, Fred McMahon, and Martin Rode. 2021b. *Economic Freedom of the World: 2021 Annual Report*. Technical report. Fraser Institute.
Haggard, Stephan, and Lydia Tiede. 2011. "The Rule of Law and Economic Growth: Where Are We?" *World Development* 39, no. 5: 673–85.

Hamscher, Albert N. 1976. *The Parlement of Paris after the Fronde, 1653–1673*. Pittsburgh: University of Pittsburgh Press.

Hayek, F. A. 1960. *The Constitution of Liberty*. London: Routledge.

Heckscher, Eli F. 1955. *Mercantilism*. Volume 1. Translated by E. F. Soderlund. London: George Allen & Unwin.

Hendrickson, Joshua R., Alexander William Salter, and Brian C. Albrecht. 2018. "Preventing Plunder: Military Technology, Capital Accumulation, and Economic Growth." *Journal of Macroeconomics* 58: 154–73.

Hintze, Otto. 1975 [1906]. "Military Organization and the Organization of the State." In *The Historical Essays of Otto Hintze*, ed. Felix Gilbert, 178–215. Oxford: Oxford University Press.

Johnson, Noel D., and Mark Koyama. 2014. "Taxes, Lawyers, and the Decline of Witch Trials in France." *Journal of Law and Economics* 57.

Johnson, Noel D., and Mark Koyama. 2017. "States and Economic Growth: Capacity and Constraints." *Explorations in Economic History* 64: 1–20.

Johnson, Noel D., and Mark Koyama. 2019. *Persecution and Toleration: The Long Road to Religious Freedom*. Cambridge: Cambridge University Press.

Johnson, Noel D., Mark Koyama, and John V. C. Nye. 2015. "Establishing a New Order: The Growth of the State and the Decline of Witch Trials in France." In *Institutions, Innovation, and Industrialization Essays in Economic History and Development*, ed. Avner Greif, Lynne Kiesling, and John V. C. Nye, 149–77. Princeton, NJ: Princeton University Press.

Jouvenel, Betrand de. 1948. *On Power, the Natural History of Its Growth*. Translated by J. F. Huntington. Indianapolis: Liberty Fund.

Kadens, Emily. 2011–2012. "Myth of the Customary Law Merchant." *Texas Law Review* 90, no. 5: 1153–206.

Kadens, Emily. 2015. "The Medieval Law Merchant: The Tyranny of a Construct." *Journal of Legal Analysis* 7, no. 2: 251–89.

Kettering, Sharon. 1986. *Patrons, Brokers, and Clients in Seventeenth-Century France*. Oxford: Oxford University Press.

Klerman, Daniel, and Paul G. Mahoney. 2007. "Legal Origin?" *Journal of Comparative Economics* 35, no. 2: 278–93.

Knack, Stephen, and Philip Keefer. 1995. "Institutions and Economic Performance: Cross-Country Tests Using Alternative Institutional Measures." *Economics and Politics* 7, no. 3: 207–27.

Koyama, Mark. 2014. "The Law & Economics of Private Prosecutions in Industrial Revolution England." *Public Choice* 159, no. 1: 277–98.

Koyama, Mark. 2016. "The Long Transition from a Natural State to a Liberal Economic Order." *International Review of Law and Economics* 47: 29–39.

Koyama, Mark, and Jean-Paul Carvalho. 2010. "Instincts and Institutions: The Rise of the Market." In *Advances in Austrian Economics*, Vol. 13, ed. William N. Butos. 285–309.

Koyama, Mark, and Jared Rubin. 2022. *How the World Became Rich*. Cambridge: Polity.

Kwass, Michael. 2000. *Privilege and the Politics of Taxation in Eighteenth-Century France: liberté, égalité, é égalité, fiscalité*. Cambridge: Cambridge University Press.

La Porta, Rafael, Florencio Lopez-de-Silanes, Andrei Shleifer, and Robert W. Vishny. 1998. "Law and Finance." *Journal of Political Economy* 106, no. 6: 1113–55.

Major, J. Russell. 1994. *From Renaissance Monarchy to Absolute Monarchy: French Kings, Nobles & Estates*. Baltimore: Johns Hopkins University Press.

Malinowski, Mikolaj. 2019. "Economic Consequences of State Failure—Legal Capacity, Regulatory Activity, and Market Integration in Poland, 1505–1772." *Journal of Economic History* 79. no. 3: 862–96.

Malmendier, Ulrike. 2009. "Law and Finance 'at the Origin.'" *Journal of Economic Literature* 47, no. 4: 1076–108.
Mann, Michael. 1986. *The Sources of Social Power*. Vol. 1. Cambridge: Cambridge University Press.
Moote, A. Lloyd. 1971. *The Revolt of the Judges*. Princeton, NJ: Princeton University Press.
North, Douglass C. 1981. *Structure and Change in Economic History*. New York: Norton.
North, Douglass C. 1990. *Institutions, Institutional Change, and Economic Performance*. Cambridge: Cambridge University Press.
North, Douglass C. 1992. *Transaction Costs, Institutions, and Economic Performance*. Technical report. San Francisco: International Center for Economic Growth.
North, Douglass C., and Robert Paul Thomas. 1973. *The Rise of the Western World*. Cambridge: Cambridge University Press.
North, Douglass C., John Joseph Wallis, and Barry R. Weingast. 2009. *Violence and Social Orders: A Conceptual Framework for Interpreting Recorded Human History*. Cambridge: Cambridge University Press.
Ogilvie, Sheilagh. 2011. *Institutions and European Trade: Merchant Guilds, 1000–1800*. Cambridge: Cambridge University Press.
Ogilvie, Sheilagh, and André W. Carus. 2014. "Institutions and Economic Growth in Historical Perspective." In *Handbook of Economic Growth*, Vol. 2, ed. Philippe Aghion and Steven Durlauf, 403–513. Elsevier.
O'Reilly, Colin, and Ryan H. Murphy. 2022. "An Index Measuring State Capacity, 1789–2018." *Economica* 89, no. 355: 713–45.
Palsson, Craig. 2023. "State Capacity, Property Rights, and External Revenues: Haiti, 1932–1949." *Journal of Economic History* 83, no. 3: 709–46.
Rajagopalan, Shruti, and Alex Tabarrok. 2021. "Simple Rules for the Developing World." *European Journal of Law and Economics* 52, no. 2: 341–62.
Rajan, Raghuram G., and Luigi Zingales. 2003. "The Great Reversals: The Politics of Financial Development in the Twentieth Century." *Journal of Financial Economics* 69, no. 1: 5–50.
Raz, Joseph. 2009 [1979]. *The Authority of Law: Essays on Law and Morality*. Oxford: Oxford University Press.
Rodriguez, Daniel B., Matthew D. McCubbins, and Barry R. Weingast. 2009–2010. "The Rule of Law Unplugged." *Emory Law Journal* 59, no. 6: 1455–94.
Rosenthal, Jean-Laurent. 1992. *The Fruits of Revolution*. Cambridge: Cambridge University Press.
Sgard, Jerome. 2006. "Do Legal Origins Matter? The Case of Bankruptcy Laws in Europe 1808–1914." *European Review of Economic History* 10, no. 3: 389–419.
Shleifer, Andrei, Florencio Lopez de Silanes, and Rafael La Porta. 2008. "'The Economic Consequences of Legal Origins." *Journal of Economic Literature* 46, no. 2: 285–332.
Tilly, Charles. 1985. "Warmaking and Statemaking as Organized Crime." In *Bringing the State Back In.*, ed. Peter Evans, Dietrich Rueschemeyer, and Theda Skocpol, 169–92. Cambridge: Cambridge University Press.
Tilly, Charles. 1990. *Coercion, Capital, and European States, AD 990–1990*. Oxford: Blackwell.
Treharne, R. F. 1986. *Simon de Montfort and Baronial Reform*. London: Hambeldon.
Waldron, Jeremy. 2020. "The Rule of Law." In *The Stanford Encyclopedia of Philosophy*, ed. Edward N. Zalta. Summer 2020. Metaphysics Research Lab, Stanford University.
Zane, John Maxcy. 1927. *The Story of Law*. Second edition. Indianapolis: Liberty Fund.
Zhang, Taisu, and John Morley. 2022. "The Modern State and the Rise of the Business Corporation." *Yale Law Journal* 132, no. 7: 1970–2047.

CHAPTER 15

POLITICAL LEGITIMACY IN HISTORICAL POLITICAL ECONOMY

AVNER GREIF AND JARED RUBIN

What Is Political Legitimacy?

Why do people follow political authorities? Access to coercive power is one answer. As Mao Zedong famously noted, "Power grows out of the barrel of a gun." But rule by force is expensive, and authorities who rule by force alone constantly fear revolt and disobedience. However, force is not the only reason why people follow political authorities. They are also followed when they are viewed as *legitimate*. How do political authorities become viewed as having legitimacy? What exactly is political legitimacy?

The study of political legitimacy dates to at least Thomas Hobbes (2002 [1651]), who famously argued in the *Leviathan* that any ruler who could provide the basics of safety and security is legitimate and should be followed. In this conception, coercive power begets legitimacy; so long as the coercive power of the state provides safety to its people, the government is legitimate. Yet, while providing safety may be the bare minimum an authority needs to gain legitimacy, subsequent literature has largely viewed it as not being sufficient. David Hume (1985 [1777]) proposed a more general view of legitimate governance, suggesting that legitimacy is founded on "opinion only." It follows that anything that people in power do to shift opinion in their favor—form political parties, provide targeted public goods, appeal to nationalism or religion—affects their legitimacy (Razi 1990; Landis 2018).

Some of the giants of the twentieth century built on the definitions laid out by Hobbes and Hume, focusing on how *beliefs* shape legitimacy. Famously, Max Weber (1964 [1920], 382) proposed that political authority derives in part from beliefs in the political system itself: "the basis of every system of authority, and correspondingly of every kind of willingness to obey, is a belief, a belief by virtue of which persons exercising authority are lent prestige." Similarly, Seymour Martin Lipset (1959, 86) wrote that legitimacy "involves the capacity of a political system to engender and maintain the belief that existing political institutions are the most appropriate or proper ones for the society."

For the sake of the discussion in this chapter, we build on the belief-based approach to political legitimacy, defining *legitimacy* as the internalized belief that a political authority has the right to govern and have its demands obeyed. That is, the more an authority is perceived as legitimate, the more that its subjects believe that the authority has the right to rule and to be obeyed (Hurd 1999; Tyler 2006; Hechter 2009; Levi, Sacks, and Tyler 2009).[1] Defined this way, political legitimacy falls on a continuum—some authorities are more legitimate than others.

Political legitimacy is therefore one of the tools that authorities have at their disposal to encourage compliance. Such a tool is necessary when authorities wish for their subjects to comply with rules they would otherwise not follow (Hart 2012 [1961], chs. 1 and 4). While extrinsic, coercive incentives often play a role in encouraging compliance, legitimacy is typically the least expensive tool that authorities have at their disposal, since it incentivizes compliance even in the absence of monitoring or coercion (Tyler 2006; Levi and Sacks 2009; Levi, Sacks, and Tyler 2009). Legitimacy therefore helps keep authorities in power when coercive power is ineffective. Even when coercive power is effective, some degree of legitimacy is needed to rule effectively: "no government exclusively based upon the means of violence has ever existed. Even the totalitarian ruler, whose chief instrument of rule is torture, needs a power basis. . . . Single men without others to support them never have enough power to use violence" (Arendt 1969, 17–18).

Within political science, the "traditional approach" to analyzing political legitimacy is performance-based, not belief-based. It focuses on the *effectiveness* of the political system. In the performance-based conception, beliefs are shaped by how effective the government is on certain metrics. Such theories, which are mostly applied to democratic legitimacy (e.g., Dahl 1956; Lipset 1959), focus on four attributes: accountability, efficiency, procedural fairness, and distributive fairness (Weatherford 1992). It follows that a population will view as more legitimate an authority that shows it can provide good governance (e.g., protect property rights, deliver public goods) (Gilley 2006a; Levi and Sacks 2009). According to Levi, Sacks, and Tyler (2009), trustworthiness of government and procedural justice are necessary antecedents of legitimacy. In the long run, legitimacy based on good governance can augment a society's normative basis of legitimate rule; whatever worked in the past is legitimate in the present (Lipset 1959).

Yet, these traditional, performance-based conceptions of political legitimacy have limitations. For one, works focusing on the effectiveness of governance have difficulty accounting for the actions taken by *ineffective* governments to maintain legitimacy, especially those that are undemocratic and cannot appeal to democratic norms for legitimacy. Under such theories, nearly every ineffective government in world history (e.g., prior to the democratic reforms that swept many parts of the world in the nineteenth and twentieth centuries) was not legitimate (Mittiga 2022). While this is possibly the case (though we do not believe it to be so), such a framework limits our capacity to understand actions by political authorities to bolster their legitimacy in such settings.

Second, such studies view legitimate rule as a historically *constant* and *exogenous* variable. In the social sciences, any theory in which the main explanatory variable is exogenous and unobservable has limited explanatory power. Therefore, under this paradigm, the importance of legitimacy for economic and political outcomes remains a black box (Marquez 2016). It has little to say about how authorities can enhance their legitimacy (beyond ruling more effectively), how their actions affect political and economic outcomes, and the observable implications therein.

This chapter builds on Greif and Rubin (2022) to address these issues and layout a framework for conceptualizing history-dependent, endogenous political legitimacy. It begins with the straightforward supposition that a political authority is more effective in achieving her objectives the higher her legitimacy and thus the more her subjects comply with her policies (e.g., regarding taxation, economic regulations, or military service). Compliance is never perfect because political authorities' policies generally demand from their agents actions that some of them would prefer to avoid (particularly if others comply). Thus, authorities invest in the capacity to punish noncompliance. For such investment to be effective and influence compliance, it must render the punishment credible. In other words, it must be common knowledge that inflicting a sufficiently large penalty is the authority's ex-post best response to noncompliance. However, motivating compliance by punishment is costly because the capacity to punish and the credibility of the threat both require expenditures (e.g., police forces, prisons, inspectors, property registrars). Punishment is thus costly even if it is off the equilibrium path. For this reason, an authority's power is often identified in the political economy literature with wealth: resources are key to political power and thus authority (North and Weingast 1989; Tilly 1990; Acemoglu, Johnson, and Robinson 2005; Stasavage 2011; Acemoglu and Robinson 2012).

Political legitimacy reduces such governance costs. In fact, legitimacy motivates compliance exactly when coercive power is least effective: when the authority faces an existential threat (e.g., an invasion) that reduces the motivation effect of expected future punishments. Legitimacy motivates compliance based on intrinsic motivation and does not depend on future extrinsic rewards or punishment. Thus, although legitimacy is not the sole basis for political authority, it can be crucial for a regime's effectiveness and longevity. In general, punishment and legitimacy coexist and they can be substitutes in motivating compliance.

The framework proposed in this chapter reveals the implications of legitimating arrangements on political and economic outcomes. The basic building block in the framework is that there are two (interrelated) foundations of legitimacy: cultural and institutional. The cultural foundation is the historically derived, shared cultural beliefs specifying the conditions necessary for political legitimacy. Being historically derived, such beliefs can differ across cultures and over time. Unlike studies seeking principles that form the basis of legitimate governance across many societies (Gilley 2006a; 2006b; Levi and Sacks 2009), the framework proposed here implies that such principles are historically unique across societies, even if there are many cross-cultural commonalities (e.g., principles related to hereditary monarchy or democratic governance). In turn, it follows that social scientific studies of the determinants or consequences of political legitimacy should be context-specific.

In this framework, the bases of the shared beliefs regarding who is a rightful political authority are called the society's *legitimacy principles*. Legitimacy principles are fixed in the short run and specify the conditions required for a particular individual or organization to have legitimate authority or the legitimate capacity to enact certain policies. Legitimacy principles provide a basis of legitimacy, or as Scott (1995, 59–60) notes, legitimacy is "a condition reflecting perceived consonance with relevant rules and laws, normative support, or alignment with cultural-cognitive frameworks." For instance, in many monarchies, the eldest son of the previous king or queen has the most legitimate claim to the throne. This is a key reason why monarchs with longer tenure and larger families have fewer dynastic disputes upon their death; longer-lasting rulers with larger families are more likely to have sons, and they are more likely to establish succession procedures if they have no legitimate heir (Abramson and Rivera 2018; Acharya and Lee 2019; Kokkonen et al. 2021).[2] Meanwhile, in a democracy, the winner of a fair and free election has the right to rule.[3] These are legitimacy principles that shape shared beliefs about who has a right to rule and whether one should comply with such rules.[4]

The institutional foundations of legitimacy are the means fostering the shared beliefs that the authority satisfies these conditions. They are endogenous and can be fostered by agents the society has deemed capable of conferring legitimacy (Scott 1995, 60; Deephouse 1996, 1025; Coşgel, Miceli, and Rubin 2012a; 2012b; Rubin 2017). Such a *legitimating agent* must be relatively independent from the political authority; agents under the authority's thumb provide no new information about whether the authority satisfies the conditions necessary to rule, and they thus do little to affect shared beliefs in the authority's legitimacy. On the other hand, such agents have *delegitimating power*; their actions do not do much to support beliefs in the authority's right to rule, but their condemnation of the authority is a strong signal that the authority is illegitimate exactly because these agents have much to lose by declaring the authority illegitimate. Statements by a sidekick in support of an authority are cheap talk, but their statements opposing an authority are costly signals.

While the power of these agents to legitimate depends on exogenous features such as their identity and the legitimacy principles, it also evolves over time. Legitimating power thus has endogenous elements. The authority's act of publicly consenting that an agent is the one to legitimate her increases the agent's future legitimating power by coordinating beliefs. It follows that the historical actions of the relevant actors shape the society's institutional foundation of legitimacy as well as its legitimacy principles, meaning that these principles will have unique elements that differ by society. In the words of Arendt (1969, 19), "Legitimacy, when challenged, is claimed by an appeal to the past."

As in much of the literature (Hurd 1999; Tyler 2006; Levi and Sacks 2009; Levi, Sacks, and Tyler 2009), the framework proposed in this chapter is guided by the idea that coercion and legitimacy both can be used to rule—that is, to foster compliance—and they are substitutes in this process. The framework considers the various agents that authorities can employ to strengthen their legitimacy or coercive power—and the policy concessions these agents receive in return. These interactions between authorities and their agents in turn highlight the connection between endogenously generated political legitimacy and a society's institutions, policies, and even the players involved in policymaking. It also highlights the dynamic interaction between exogenous parameters and endogenous variables, as in Greif (2006) and Greif and Laitin (2004). The selection of legitimating agents and legitimacy principles is constrained by the society's historical heritage at any given point in time, but the choices made under these constraints affect the strength of the legitimacy principle and the legitimating power of particular agents in the future.

In short, this chapter proposes a path forward for studying political legitimacy in historical and contemporary societies. Any such study—historical or not—must understand the various historically determined cultural and institutional attributes that yield legitimacy effective in that society. Such forces are endogenously and historically determined, and they are at the heart of numerous phenomena in historical political economy (HPE).

A Framework for Analyzing Political Legitimacy in HPE

Greif and Rubin (2022) propose a framework for considering the interactions between a political authority and her many potential legitimating agents. Authorities have a set of policy objectives, but how do they convince people to comply with actions consistent with those objectives? As noted earlier, the literature views political authorities as having two, non–mutually exclusive mechanisms: coercion and legitimacy. That is, for people to be willing to comply with the authority's objectives, they must either believe they have a moral obligation to follow the policy or fear punishment from failing to comply.

Political authorities are endowed with some degree of legitimacy and resources. Their legitimacy endowment depends on whether their personal characteristics and actions align with the society's legitimacy principle. For instance, in a traditional European-style monarchy, being the oldest legitimate son (i.e., born within wedlock) of the previous monarch typically gave one more legitimacy than otherwise. Such characteristics are meaningless in a democracy. An authority's own legitimacy and resource endowments are exogenous to the authority.

Legitimacy can be an effective tool of governance even if many in the population do not believe they have a moral obligation to comply. All that is needed are widespread *beliefs* that others believe there is a moral obligation to comply. Coordination of beliefs can therefore increase compliance with the demands implied by the authority's policies. How can authorities coordinate such beliefs? Can authorities take certain actions to enhance both their legitimacy and resources?

People and organizations in every society have the capacity to enhance the legitimacy of the political authority. Greif and Rubin (2022) call these people and organizations *legitimating agents*. Depending on the society's legitimacy principle, effective legitimating agents may be, among others, religious authorities (Gill 1998; Coşgel and Miceli 2009; Rubin 2011; Bentzen and Gokmen 2023), economic elites (Rubin 2017), bureaucrats (Ma and Rubin 2022), or military elites (Blaydes and Chaney 2013). Agents can coordinate beliefs about the authority's right to rule by participating in public legitimating events such as coronation ceremonies, inaugurations, public executions, observable legislation, tribute payments, and military parades. During such events, subjects are exposed to information relevant to the belief-formation process.[5] The public nature of such events makes one aware that everyone else has been exposed to the same information as well (Kuran 1995; Chwe 2001). This, in turn, may convince them to publicly express the morality of the authority's rule even if they personally hold a different view of what type of rule is moral (Greif and Tadelis 2010).[6]

One's capacity to serve as a legitimating agent depends in part on the society's legitimacy principles. But what is the source of legitimacy principles? At any given point in time, they are exogenous to the authorities and agents in question—they derive from previous interactions between authorities and their agents, especially how often an independent agent was used in the past. Hence, while the legitimacy principle is exogenous at any given point in time, it is endogenous over time.[7] Authorities often have multiple legitimacy principles they can promote, but the strength of each principle depends on past interactions between authorities and agents. Authorities can also strengthen a legitimacy principle over time via use: the act of requesting legitimation from an agent increases the power of that agent to legitimate in the future. Authorities therefore face a trade-off when seeking legitimacy: legitimation from an agent increases compliance in the present but also increases that agent's bargaining power in the future.

Using these basic building blocks, it is possible to first consider how political bargains between authorities and their legitimating agents are affected by each actor's endowed legitimacy. First, it is possible that the authority may not enter the bargain at all. When their endowed legitimacy or access to resources—or both—is sufficiently high, political authorities may be able to secure compliance without the support of an agent. In this case, the authority would prefer to not enter the political bargain and hence not yield policy concessions in return. Not using the agent also reduces the agent's future legitimating power, which may be in the interest of the authority, since it entails a less powerful agent with which to bargain (Pant 2018). Such an outcome is noncooperative, and it results in few constraints on the authority's power. An authority in this position may be able to pay off coercive agents and rule as a (legitimate or illegitimate) autocrat.

Consider instead the case where the authority's endowed legitimacy and resources are not enough to secure sufficient compliance. In this case, she will seek legitimation or resources (or both) from her legitimating agent(s). Greif and Rubin (2022) envision a bargaining game, in the spirit of a Nash bargain, in which the authority first chooses if and which of many potential agents to bargain with, taking into account the agent's preference, legitimating power, and resources. There is a drawback for the authority from relying on an agent since doing so increases the agent's future legitimating power, and thus the authority increases the agent's future bargaining power by bringing it into the bargain in the present. This weakens the authority's relative bargaining power in the future. The authority must weigh this cost against the potential benefits of bargaining with the agent.

If the authority chooses to rely on an agent, she can offer the agent a say in current or future policy, and in return may request resources, legitimation, or both for the policy in question. Compliance with the policy therefore depends on how much legitimacy and resources the authority and agent contribute. While the authority makes concessions regarding the content of the policy, it increases compliance by increasing its legitimacy, resources, or both required to make punishment for noncompliance credible.

After a policy bargain is agreed upon, the authority faces a commitment problem, namely, the authority can implement any policy she wants. This is where legitimacy being reversible has bite: if the authority attempts to enact a policy besides the one agreed to in the bargain, the policy loses any legitimacy bestowed on it by the agent(s). Reneging on the agreement may be attractive for the authority because resources, unlike legitimacy, are not reversible. The authority can therefore enact her desired policy with the resources transferred from the agent(s).

This framework yields two predictions. The first regards the *qualities* of the agent an authority will choose to legitimate her rule. There are numerous factors to consider. First, all else being equal, the authority will want to bargain with an agent whose optimal policies are more closely aligned with her own. In this case, the authority does not have to cede much in the bargain, and the authority would thus desire an agent who has significant legitimating power, since this would increase compliance with the policy. Second, an authority with low legitimacy will desire an agent with high legitimating power, all else being equal. While the authority cedes future bargaining power to the agent(s) by choosing to negotiate with it, this may be beneficial to a low-legitimacy authority, who gains significantly from the legitimacy the agent(s) bestows. This is not the case for a high-legitimacy authority. For such an authority, the probability of compliance with the policy is high in the absence of legitimation from the agent(s). Hence, if a high-legitimacy authority is to bargain with agent(s) for additional legitimacy or resources, she would prefer to bargain with one with little legitimating power. A powerful agent is unattractive to a highly legitimate authority because the authority must cede more in the bargain and, by entering into the bargain, makes an already powerful agent all the more powerful in the future. Finally, the greater the authority's access to resources, the lower is the optimal legitimacy of the legitimating agent(s). Since resources and legitimacy are substitutes, a rich authority gains less on the margin from having a highly legitimate agent. Meanwhile, it stands to lose more on the margin by giving the agent more future bargaining power. These insights can be summarized as follows:

Prediction 1: All else being equal, the level of legitimating power for the authority's optimal legitimating agent(s) is weakly decreasing in the authority's endowed legitimacy, its access to resources, and the difference in the authority's and agent's preferences.

The second prediction regards when authorities will cooperate or conflict with their agents. Cooperation can be considered as occurring when the authority enters the bargaining game with the appropriate legitimating agent(s) (as dictated by the legitimacy principle) and the agent(s) accepts the proposal. On the other hand, conflict occurs either when the authority rules without an agent or the agent declines the proposed bargain. For instance, in the United States, an Act of Congress that is signed by the president indicates cooperation between the two, whereas in early-modern England, cooperation was signified by an Act of Parliament, which must be agreed upon by Parliament and the Crown. On the other hand, the English Civil Wars are an extreme example of conflict. King Charles I attempted to rule without Parliament for over a decade (the period of Personal Rule, 1629–1640); we classify this as nonviolent conflict between an authority and his legitimating agents. When Parliament was finally called in 1640, conflict of a much more violent nature ensued between the parties.

Several factors contribute to cooperation (or conflict) occurring between authorities and their agents. The first is the degree to which the preferences of the authority and her agents are aligned and are expected to remain aligned. When their preferences are closely aligned, the agents benefit from the authority implementing her own ideal policy, and the agents therefore benefit from accepting the authority's proposal to cooperate. Similarly, the authority is motivated to approach the agents because cooperation provides it with legitimation and resources without ceding much with respect to the content of the policy. At some sufficiently large divergence in preferences, no bargain will be available that satisfies both the authority and her agents. Knowing this, the authority will not approach the agents in the first place and the players will not cooperate.

A second set of factors comprises the authority's endowed legitimacy and access to resources. A highly legitimate authority or one with access to significant resources will find it difficult to commit to implementing the agreed-upon policy if it is not sufficiently close to one she desires, since compliance with the policy will be high even without legitimation from the agents. If such a commitment is impossible, the agents will not accept the authority's proposal. Knowing this, the authority will not approach the agents in the first place. In other words, conflict between the authority and her agents is more likely when the authority's endowed legitimacy and access to resources are greater.

A final factor is the agent's capacity to legitimate rule. A low-legitimacy or resource-poor authority gains more on the margin the more legitimate the agents are, since the authority cannot ensure compliance on her own. Using the agents comes with the drawback of bargaining in the future with more powerful agents. This means that the bargain will tend to increasingly favor the agents over time. This drawback is not worth it for a high-legitimacy or resource-rich authority. Such an authority benefits less from bargaining with agents the more legitimate those agents are. These insights can be summarized as follows:

Prediction 2: All else being equal, the likelihood that the authority and her agents cooperate is increasing in the agents' legitimating power for low-legitimacy and resource-poor authorities, while it is decreasing in the agents' legitimacy for high-legitimacy and resource-rich authorities. Cooperation is decreasing in the difference between their preferences, the authority's endowed legitimacy, and the authority's access to resources.

Before proceeding, it is worth pointing out one key difference between the Greif and Rubin (2022) framework and other frameworks proposed in the literature. Numerous works in the literature, dating back to Hobbes, view *effectiveness* as the path to legitimacy; the more effective an authority is at doing their job, the more legitimate they will be viewed in the eyes of their subjects (Lipset 1959; Levi and Sacks 2009; Mittiga 2022). In the Greif and Rubin (2022) framework, the focus is on shared beliefs. Effectiveness is only a qualification for legitimate rule if this is designated as such in the society's legitimacy principle. It does not necessarily need to be the case that effectiveness confers legitimacy rather than popularity. An authority can be viewed as legitimate even if she is ineffective, so long as she satisfies the conditions for legitimacy under the society's legitimacy principle and is supported by the appropriate legitimating agents. On the other hand, an effective ruler may also be viewed as illegitimate. The key distinction between the two concepts is that legitimacy entails a moral obligation to obey, whereas effectiveness may encourage obedience because it is in the subject's material interest. To illustrate the difference between legitimacy and effectiveness, consider that numerous US presidents have had approval ratings well below 40 percent even though few citizens considered them to be anything but the rightful president. For instance, one of the least effective presidents in US history, James Buchanan, was considered legitimate by most of the population. However, his successor, Abraham Lincoln, was one of the most effective presidents in US history but was also considered illegitimate by many Southern Democrats.

Implications of Legitimating Arrangements in HPE

What is the potential of the above framework to advance our comprehension of fundamental issues in historical political economy? In this section, we present some of the questions it has the promise of tackling and the related scholarship. In particular, the discussion here focuses on issues inspired by the comparative HPE of China, the Muslim Middle East, and northwestern Europe.

With respect to economic development, China and the Middle East surpassed Western Europe around the beginning of the second millennium if not earlier. Western Europe, however, was well ahead at the end of the millennium. Even prior to industrialization, Europeans explored the world and gradually established intercontinental empires. By the early twentieth century, the European states and some former European colonies became the most economically advanced countries in the world. China, in contrast, industrialized only in the late twentieth century and although it is now the world's second-largest economy, it is far beyond Europe in terms of GDP per capita. The Middle East is still to industrialize and is among the world's poorest regions (excluding the oil-rich nations).

These three regions' political histories are also distinct. Over the last millennium, Europe experienced multiple political revolutions that reshaped its political system. Political power shifted from popes to monarchs to elected representatives. In contrast, large landed empires characterized the political histories of the Middle East and China. In these empires, revolts were similarly common but revolutions were rare. In China, the empire survived until 1911 although several dynasties crumbled following revolts and invasions. Each time, however, a new dynasty eventually came to power, and during most of the last millennium the emperors were not Han Chinese but either Mongol or Manchu. In the Middle East, the Ottoman Empire survived from the thirteenth century to 1922 when it faced a republican revolution. During this time, successful revolts and coups led to the succession of some regions or replacement of one member of the ruling dynasty by another. Yet the empire and the ruling dynasty survived past World War I.

What are the relationships between these economic and political outcomes? The proposed framework that links society and state (Greif 2016) sheds light on the role that political legitimacy played in these reversals of fortunes. We begin with the relative reversal between the Muslim Middle East and Christian Western Europe. A recent literature has emerged suggesting that the degree to which religious legitimacy was employed by political authorities in both regions had important consequences for economic and political development.

A key initial condition that led to these two separate paths is the political circumstances under which the religions were born. Islam formed conterminously with empire, and hence the doctrine of early Islam supports its use as a tool of political legitimation. Meanwhile, Christianity formed as a minority cult in the Roman Empire, which was hardly in need of legitimation. Early Christian doctrine stressed a separation between the spiritual and the worldly. In the terminology of the framework, religious legitimacy played a more important role in the *legitimacy principle* of Middle Eastern states than it did in Western Europe.

The first prediction of the framework therefore indicates that medieval Muslim rulers should have been more likely than Christian rulers to employ religious legitimacy. This was the case to an even greater extent as new forms of tax revenue became available to Christian rulers during the Commercial Revolution (tenth to thirteenth centuries). A growing literature confirms this insight. Rubin (2017) argues that Muslim religious agents maintained their important position as legitimating agents as part of an equilibrium in which religious legitimacy was effective, religious agents held political power, rulers tended to not publicly transgress religious dictates, and other types of agents were kept away from the political bargaining table. This equilibrium became entrenched in different places at different times, but mostly arose in the tenth to twelfth centuries as the religious classes consolidated and the madrasa movement institutionalized their power (Rubin 2017; Kuru 2019). Moreover, Bisin et al. (2023) propose that Muslim rulers refrained from bringing such elites to the political bargain table not because they were afraid of giving them too much power, but because by doing so they would have weakened the efficacy of religious legitimacy.

Meanwhile, Western European rulers turned away from religious legitimacy, instead seeking legitimacy and revenue from their parliaments, where the increasingly powerful urban and landed interests came together (along with men of the church) to collectively bargain with the Crown. As the framework predicts, the relatively weaker European rulers ultimately benefited from negotiating with more powerful agents, even though those agents (i.e., the economic elite) often wanted policy concessions such as property rights and public good investment that conflicted with the interests of the authorities. This can be seen in the type of advice given to medieval rulers. Blaydes, Grimmer, and McQueen (2018) find, in an analysis of medieval political advice texts, that advice cloaked in religious overtones dropped significantly after 1200 in Europe but remained high in the Muslim world. Instead, European rulers were advised to focus on the art of good rulership and being virtuous in their private lives.

The framework also indicates that political authorities should lean more heavily on legitimating agents when they do not have the resources to deal with crises. These are precisely the times when legitimacy may be most effective at keeping an authority in power. A study by Eric Chaney (2013) on Egypt in the twelfth to fourteenth centuries provides evidence in support of this insight. He finds that religious authorities were much less likely to be replaced when the water levels in the Nile River were either much higher or lower than normal (meaning flooding or drought, respectively). Such weather conditions placed Egyptian rulers in peril, as the population was sent to the brink of subsistence and there were not enough resources for relief. This is precisely when religious authorities are most effective at providing legitimacy and thus should have been given the greatest voice in the laws and policies of the state. This is consistent with Prediction 2; when Egyptian rulers lacked resources, they were much more likely to cooperate with their key legitimating agents. Chaney (2013, 2038) notes that during Nile failures, "the sultan would bow to ... pressure [from the head judge] and enforce decrees against ... prostitution, hashish eating, beer drinking, the wearing of immodest or over-luxurious dress [or] Christian and Jewish functionaries lording it over Muslims."

Can the framework account for how Europe, in particular *northwestern* Europe, pulled ahead? There were key political changes that preceded industrialization. Chief among these was England's transition to limited, constitutional governance. Greif and Rubin (2022) apply the framework laid out above to explain this transition. Conventional accounts in the social sciences of England's transition to a limited, constitutional monarchy focus on the Civil Wars (1642–1651) and Glorious Revolution (1688) as key events that enabled property holders in Parliament to constrain the predatory Stuart monarchs (North and Weingast 1989; Acemoglu and Robinson 2012). However, these accounts typically ignore the role that (endogenously generated) legitimacy played in England's transition. Greif and Rubin's framework leads them to focus on the key events of the sixteenth century, when the low-legitimacy Tudors came to power. Their low legitimacy was a result of their weak claim to inherited monarchy; Henry VII won the crown on the battlefield, his claim was through his maternal line and by illegitimate descent, and his parental line was Welsh, not English. Consistent with Prediction 1, Greif and Rubin argue that the Tudors should have sought legitimating agents with high legitimating power, and they should have done what they could to increase the legitimating power of those agents. In lieu of the great lords (many of whom were rivals of the Tudors following the Wars of the Roses) and the Catholic Church (which was a legitimating agent under Henry VII but lost its legitimating power in the wake of the English Reformation), the Tudors turned to Parliament to legitimate its rule. By the end of Elizabeth I's reign in 1603, the legitimacy principle guiding English governance was the "Crown in Parliament," whereby the Crown ruled by following the law as established by the consent of both the Crown and Parliament.

The Stuarts inherited the "Crown in Parliament" legitimacy principle when they came to power in 1603. Having greater legitimacy than the Tudors according to the legitimacy principle of inherited monarchy (which prevailed alongside the "Crown in Parliament" legitimacy principle), Prediction 2 indicates that the Stuarts should have sought legitimating agents with less legitimating power than Parliament. In fact, the Stuarts sought to promote the legitimacy principle of the divine right of kings and sought uniformity within the Church of England along Episcopalian/Arminian lines, which would have placed the Crown and bishops at the top of the ruling hierarchy, with no place for Parliament. Greif and Rubin contend, therefore, that the conflicts of the seventeenth century were over legitimacy principles, not transgression of property rights by the Stuarts. The Stuarts desired a legitimacy principle that left Parliament out of the ruling coalition. Their transgressions were manifestations of this legitimacy conflict.

Political legitimacy played a role in several other important economic and political outcomes in European history. Johnson and Koyama (2019) argue that medieval European authorities sought to foster their religious legitimacy by scapegoating religious minorities when facing threats to stability. Persecutions of Jews, witches, and other "heretics" were thus related to political economy considerations, at least until religious legitimacy became less important in the early-modern period. Cantoni, Dittmar, and Yuchtman (2018) argue that one consequence of the Reformation was that it reduced the legitimating role of the religious authorities. This resulted in a shift away from investment in religious pursuits (e.g., church building) and toward secular ones in Protestant regions. This, in turn, incentivized university students in Protestant regions to study law rather than theology, which set the stage for the growing bureaucracies of early-modern Protestant states.

Finally, the framework sheds light on Chinese political and economic development. Several legitimacy principles have historically justified Chinese rule. These include the Mandate of Heaven (the belief that heaven grants the ruler's right to rule), the Confucian belief of "rule by virtue" (only a virtuous ruler has the right to rule), popular consent, and legality (Guo 2003). Twentieth-century Chinese rulers have appealed to the principles that best suited their rule. Mao had "revolutionary legitimacy," imbued with popular consent, while "communist ideology was carefully used to replace the traditional idea of 'mandate of Heaven'" (Guo 2003, 8). With such strong personal legitimacy, Mao did not need to negotiate with strong legitimating agents, as Prediction 1 of the framework indicates, and the result was a repressive autocracy. The Communist government merely perpetuated the long-standing tradition, dating back many dynasties, of strong central control over law and order (Brandt, Ma, and Rawski 2014).

This changed in the 1980s and 1990s, when the Chinese Communist Party could no longer claim Mao's "charismatic" legitimacy. Deng Xiaoping, who served as China's leader from 1978 to 1989, began a process of economic decentralization. This ultimately resulted in some degree of political decentralization, with townships having more say in local leadership, even if national politics remain highly centralized (Gilley 2008). These changes had precedent in the Qing period, where economic decentralization and local experimentation were predominant (Brandt, Ma, and Rawski 2014). As Prediction 2 of the framework suggests, Chinese rulers following Mao, who did not have his charismatic legitimacy, had to cooperate with traditional legitimating agents to support their regimes. Although the traditional bureaucracy no longer existed (it had long been a primary legitimating agent of imperial China; see Ma and Rubin 2022), individuals who were highly educated and held local power took their place in China's legitimating regime.

Concluding Thoughts and the Path Forward

This chapter provides a framework for understanding the causes and consequences of *endogenously generated political legitimacy*. This framework, which builds on a large literature that considers legitimacy as an exogenous variable, has numerous implications for studies of historical political economy. First, it provides insight into the type of agents with whom political authorities choose to bargain. This has important implications for the makeup of ruling coalitions and the type of policies they enact (North, Wallis, and Weingast 2009). Second, it spells out the conditions under which rulers can stay in power *despite* having little access to coercive power. In doing so, it highlights how outcomes of the political process differ in such settings and how the bases of legitimacy (what we call the "legitimacy principles") may change over time as a result. Third, it provides insight into why domestic conflict between powerful groups occurs, and why the side with greater access to coercive power does not always prevail. The latter two insights do not make sense in a world where political power derives primarily from coercive power.

There is much work to be done to gain greater insights into how endogenous political legitimacy has affected political economy outcomes in history. Work in this field would be greatly enhanced with more precisely defined empirical measures of legitimacy, legitimacy principles, and bargaining power between various agents. Although there has been some work in political science attempting to measure state legitimacy (Weatherford 1992; Gilley 2006a; 2006b), this has been done largely in a Weberian framework, seeking commonalities across cultures. The conception of the legitimacy principle espoused in this chapter suggests that the appropriate metrics of state legitimacy will change endogenously over time and place. Hence, context-specific data and analyses are needed. Second, the framework points to history as being essential for understanding legitimating frameworks in the present. Careful studies of how and why legitimacy principles changed in various societies would reveal commonalities and distinctions across different times and places. Finally, there are many parts of the world for which very little work has been done regarding principles of legitimate governance. Tribal societies offer glimpses into how smaller-scale societies legitimate rule, and there is significant variation across such societies. Understanding where this variation comes from will almost certainly shed light on the political economy of larger-scale societies. Likewise, linking precolonial legitimacy principles to postcolonial legitimacy principles can provide insight into the role that colonialism has played in the continuing economic and political problems of the formerly colonized world. This is just the tip of the iceberg. We suspect that studies of political legitimacy—how it is generated and its economic and political implications—will yield many new insights in the HPE literature for years to come.

Acknowledgments

We thank Jeffery Jenkins and Steven Pfaff for comments on early drafts of this chapter. All errors are our own.

Notes

1. Gilley (2006a; 2006b) uses a similar definition to measure legitimacy across countries. Weatherford (1992) proposes a metric for measuring legitimacy that marries structural approaches based on a society's institutional features with survey data based on subjective views of government, no. i.e., their "legitimacy orientations"). Similarly, Suchman (1995) defines *organizational legitimacy* as "a generalized perception or assumption that the actions of an entity are desirable, proper, or appropriate within some socially constructed system of norms, values, beliefs, and definitions."
2. For much more on the role of dynasties in both monarchical and democratic settings, see van Coppenolle and Smith [oxfordhb-9780197618608-e-10], no. 2023).
3. Patty and Penn (2014) argue that, in the democratic setting, unique principles of legitimate governance can help resolve conflicts inherent in collective decisions based on the aggregation of preferences.
4. This insight extends well beyond formal political governance. For instance, Pfaff and Hechter (2020) show that it was important that seaman in the British Royal Navy during the Age of Sail believe in the legitimacy of their officers. What made officers legitimate was based on how the officers treated their subordinates in accordance with the unique customs and conventions (i.e., the legitimacy principle) of the ship.

5. In a similar vein, Lipset (1959, 89) argues that "a major test of legitimacy is the extent to which given nations have developed a common 'secular political culture,' national rituals and holidays which serve to maintain the legitimacy of various democratic practices." For more on nationalism in historical political economy, see Boix [oxfordhb-9780197618608-e-28], no. 2023).
6. For more on why people follow rules in general in historical settings, see Wallis 2022; [oxfordhb-9780197618608-e-16]; 2023).
7. In the terminology of Greif and Laitin (2004) and Greif (2006), the legitimacy principle is a quasi-parameter.

References

Abramson, Scott, and Carlos Velasco Rivera. 2018. "Time Is Power: The Non-Institutional Sources of Stability in Autocracies." *Journal of Politics* 78, no. 4: 1279–1295.

Acemoglu, Daron, and James A. Robinson. 2012. *Why Nations Fail: The Origins of Power, Prosperity, and Poverty*. New York: Crown.

Acemoglu, Daron, Simon Johnson, and James A. Robinson. 2005. "The Rise of Europe: Atlantic Trade, Institutional Change, and Economic Growth." *American Economic Review* 95, no. 3: 546–79.

Acharya, Avidit, and Alexander Lee. 2019. "Path Dependence in European Development: Medieval Politics, Conflict, and State Building." *Comparative Political Studies* 52, no. 13–14: 2171–2206.

Arendt, Hannah. 1969. "Reflections on Violence." *Journal of International Affairs* 23, no. 1: 1–35.

Bentzen, Jeanet, and Gunes Gokmen. 2023. "The Power of Religion." *Journal of Economic Growth* 28, no. 1: 45–78.

Bisin, Alberto, Jared Rubin, Avner Seror, and Thierry Verdier. 2023. "Culture, Institutions, and the Long Divergence." *Journal of Economic Growth*, forthcoming.

Blaydes, Lisa, and Eric Chaney. 2013. "The Feudal Revolution and Europe's Rise: Political Divergence of the Christian West and the Muslim World before 1500 CE." *American Political Science Review* 107, no. 1: 16–34.

Blaydes, Lisa, Justin Grimmer, and Alison McQueen. 2018. "Mirrors for Princes and Sultans: Advice on the Art of Governance in the Medieval Christian and Islamic Worlds." *Journal of Politics* 80, no. 4: 1150–67.

Boix, Carles. 2023. "The Historical Political Economy of Nationalism." In *Oxford Handbook of Historical Political Economy*, ed. J. Jenkins and J. Rubin, 541–57. Oxford: Oxford University Press.

Brandt, Loren, Debin Ma, and Thomas G. Rawski. 2014. "From Divergence to Convergence: Reevaluating the History behind China's Economic Boom." *Journal of Economic Literature* 52, no. 1: 45–123.

Cantoni, Davide, Jeremiah Dittmar, and Noam Yuchtman. 2018. "Religious Competition and Reallocation: The Political Economy of Secularization in the Protestant Reformation." *Quarterly Journal of Economics* 133, no. 4: 2037–2096.

Chaney, Eric. 2013. "Revolt on the Nile: Economic Shocks, Religion, and Political Power." *Econometrica* 81, no. 5: 2033–2053.

Chwe, Michael Suk-Young. 2001. *Rational Ritual: Culture, Coordination, and Common Knowledge*. Princeton, NJ: Princeton University Press.

Coşgel, Metin M., and Thomas J. Miceli. 2009. "State and Religion." *Journal of Comparative Economics* 37, no. 3: 402–16.

Coşgel, Metin M., Thomas J. Miceli, and Jared Rubin. 2012a. "The Political Economy of Mass Printing: Legitimacy and Technological Change in the Ottoman Empire." *Journal of Comparative Economics* 40, no. 3: 357–31.

Coşgel, Metin M., Thomas J. Miceli, and Jared Rubin. 2012b. "Political Legitimacy and Technology Adoption." *Journal of Institutional and Theoretical Economics* 168, no. 3: 339–61.

Dahl, Robert A. 1956. *A Preface to Democratic Theory*. Chicago: University of Chicago Press.

Deephouse, David L. 1996. "Does Isomorphism Legitimate?" *Academy of Management Journal* 39, no. 4: 1024–1039.

Gill, Anthony. 1998. *Rendering unto Caesar: The Catholic Church and the State in Latin America*. Chicago: University of Chicago Press.

Gilley, Bruce. 2006a. "The Determinants of State Legitimacy: Results for 72 Countries." *International Political Science Review* 27, no. 1: 47–71.

Gilley, Bruce. 2006b. "The Meaning and Measure of State Legitimacy: Results for 72 Countries." *European Journal of Political Research* 45, no. 3: 499–525.

Gilley, Bruce. 2008. "Legitimacy and Institutional Change: The Case of China." *Comparative Political Studies* 41, no. 3: 259–84.

Greif, Avner. 2006. *Institutions and the Path to the Modern Economy: Lessons from Medieval Trade*. New York: Cambridge University Press.

Greif, Avner. 2016. "Society and State in Determining Economic Outcomes." In *Involving Approaches to the Economics of Public Policy: Views of Award-Winning Economists*, ed. Jean Kimmel, 57–92. Kalamazoo, MI: Upjohn Institute for Employment Research.

Greif, Avner, and David Laitin. 2004. "A Theory of Endogenous Institutional Change." *American Political Science Review* 98, no. 4: 14–48.

Greif, Avner, and Jared Rubin. 2022. "Political Legitimacy and the Institutional Foundations of Constitutional Government: The Case of England." Working Paper, Chapman University.

Greif, Avner, and Steven Tadelis. 2010. "A Theory of Moral Persistence: Crypto-Morality and Political Legitimacy." *Journal of Comparative Economics* 38, no. 3: 229–44.

Guo, Baogang. 2003. "Political Legitimacy and China's Transition." *Journal of Chinese Political Science* 8, no. 1/2: 1–25.

Hart, H. L. A. 2012 [1961]. *The Concept of Law*. 3rd ed. Oxford: Oxford University Press.

Hechter, Michael. 2009. "Legitimacy in the Modern World." *American Behavioral Scientist* 53, no. 3: 279–88.

Hobbes, Thomas. 2002 [1651]. *Leviathan*. Project Gutenberg eBook. https://www.gutenberg.org/files/3207/3207-h/3207-h.htm.

Hume, David. 1985 [1777]. *Essays: Moral, Political, and Literary*. Edited by Eugene F. Miller. Indianapolis: Liberty Fund. https://oll-resources.s3.us-east-2.amazonaws.com/oll3/store/titles/704/0059_Bk.pdf.

Hurd, Ian. 1999. "Legitimacy and Authority in International Politics." *International Organization* 53, no. 2: 379–408.

Johnson, Noel D., and Koyama, Mark. 2019. *Persecution & Toleration: The Long Road to Religious Freedom*. New York: Cambridge University Press.

Kokkonen, Andrej, Suthan Krishnarajan, Jørgen Møller, and Anders Sundell. 2021. "Blood Is Thicker Than Water: Family Size and Leader Deposition in Medieval and Early Modern Europe." *Journal of Politics* 83, no. 4: 1246–1259.

Kuran, Timur. 1995. *Private Truths, Public Lies: The Social Consequences of Preference Falsification.* Cambridge, MA: Harvard University Press.

Kuru, Ahmet T. 2019. *Islam, Authoritarianism, and Underdevelopment: A Global and Historical Comparison.* Cambridge: Cambridge University Press.

Landis, Joel E. 2018. "Whither Parties? Hume on Partisanship and Political Legitimacy." *American Political Science Review* 112, no. 2: 219–30.

Levi, Margaret, and Audrey Sacks. 2009. "Legitimating Beliefs: Sources and Indicators." *Regulation & Governance* 3, no. 4: 311–33.

Levi, Margaret, Audrey Sacks, and Tom Tyler. 2009. "Conceptualizing Legitimacy, Measuring Legitimating Beliefs." *American Behavioral Scientist* 53, no. 3: 354–75.

Lipset, Seymour Martin. 1959. "Some Social Requisites of Democracy: Economic Development and Political Legitimacy." *American Political Science Review* 53, no. 1: 69–105.

Ma, Debin, and Jared Rubin. 2022. "Ideology and Economic Change: The Path to the Modern Economy in China and Japan." Working Paper, Chapman University. Mimeo.

Marquez, Xavier. 2016. "The Irrelevance of Legitimacy." *Political Studies* 64, no. 1: 19–34.

Mittiga, Ross. 2022. "Political Legitimacy, Authoritarianism, and Climate Change." *American Political Science Review*, 116, no. 3: 998–1011.

North, Douglass C., John Joseph Wallis, and Barry R. Weingast. 2009. *Violence and Social Orders: A Conceptual Framework for Interpreting Recorded Human History.* New York: Cambridge University Press.

North, Douglass C., and Barry R. Weingast. 1989. "Constitutions and Commitment: The Evolution of Institutions Governing Public Choice in Seventeenth-Century England." *Journal of Economic History* 49, no. 4: 803–32.

Pant, S. 2018. "Power-Sharing 'Discontinuities': Legitimacy, Rivalry, and Credibility." *Journal of Theoretical Politics* 30, no. 1: 147–77.

Patty, John W., and Elizabeth Maggie Penn. 2014. *Social Choice and Legitimacy: The Possibilities of Impossibility.* New York: Cambridge University Press.

Pfaff, Steven, and Michael Hechter. 2020. *The Genesis of Rebellion: Governance, Grievance, and Mutiny in the Age of Sail.* New York: Cambridge University Press.

Razi, G. Hossein. 1990. "Legitimacy, Religion, and Nationalism in the Middle East." *American Political Science Review* 84, no. 1: 69–91.

Rubin, Jared. 2011. "Institutions, the Rise of Commerce and the Persistence of Laws: Interest Restrictions in Islam and Christianity." *Economic Journal* 121, no. 557: 1310–1339.

Rubin, Jared. 2017. *Rulers, Religion, and Riches: Why the West Got Rich and the Middle East Did Not.* New York: Cambridge University Press.

Scott, W. Richard. 1995. *Institutions and Organizations: Ideas and Interests.* Los Angeles: SAGE.

Stasavage, David. 2011. *States of Credit: Size, Power, and the Development of Modern European Polities.* Princeton, NJ: Princeton University Press.

Suchman, Mark C. 1995. "Managing Legitimacy: Strategic and Institutional Approaches." *Academy of Management Review* 20, no. 3: 571–610.

Tilly, Charles. 1990. *Coercion, Capital, and European States, A.D. 990–1990.* Berkeley: University of California Press.

Tyler, Tom R. 2006. "Psychological Perspectives on Legitimacy and Legitimation." *Annual Review of Psychology* 57: 375–400.

Van Coppenolle, Brenda, and Daniel M. Smith. 2023. "Dynasties in Historical Political Economy." In *Oxford Handbook of Historical Political Economy*, ed. J. Jenkins and J. Rubin, 185–207. Oxford: Oxford University Press.

Wallis, John Joseph. 2022. "An Alternative Institutional Approach to Rules, Organizations, and Development." *Journal of Economic History* 82, no. 2: 335–67.

Wallis, John Joseph. 2023. "Rules in Historical Political Economy." In *Oxford Handbook of Historical Political Economy*, ed. J. Jenkins and J. Rubin, 313–28. Oxford: Oxford University Press.

Weatherford, M. Stephen. 1992. "Measuring Political Legitimacy." *American Political Science Review* 86, no. 1: 149–66.

Weber, Max. 1964 [1920]. *The Theory of Social and Economic Organization*. Edited by Talcott Parsons. New York: Free Press.

PART III
COMPONENTS OF THE STATE

CHAPTER 16

RULES IN HISTORICAL POLITICAL ECONOMY

JOHN JOSEPH WALLIS

CREATING and enforcing rules are essential features of governments and core elements of political economy. Access to rules to order relationships, to write and enforce contracts, and to delineate property both real and intangible is an essential part of the institutional structure of economies. Governments and economies interface through rules, and understanding what rules are and how they work is central to understanding a society's historical political economy (HPE). This chapter provides a lexicon of rules, a collection of the different dimensions of rules, and some brief thoughts about how the dimensions interact, have developed historically, and their implications for HPE.

Like any central concept, there are many definitions of rules and institutions. The most well-known and widely used definition of "institutions" in HPE is North's (1990, 3) formulation that "institutions are the rules of the game." North segregates rules into formal rules and informal rules, as well as into rules that are "devised" and rules that "evolve." While these characteristics of rules are heuristically useful, they are not very clear. Are the rules that parents articulate within a family formal or informal? North himself says that the common law evolves, implying that the common law was not devised (deliberately created), but the common law is the cumulative result of thousands of intentional decisions by judges. In his John Commons speech, North gave examples of informal rules: "informal constraints (conventions, norms of behavior, and self-imposed rules of behavior)" (North 1992, 4). You may wonder, as have I, how a self-imposed rule of behavior that applies internally to only one person could be considered an institution, and even more puzzling, why is it a rule?

This is not simply to criticize North. *Institutions, Institutional Change, and Economic Performance* (1990) is a justifiable classic and a big step forward in how we think out the political economy of institutions and governments. Yet North reflected the existing confusion about what rules really are. We need to rethink our ideas about rules. In the institutional literature, a "rule" is any aspect of the external world that constrains and shapes individual behavior. Durkheim (1982) called these "social facts." Social facts easily become social rules: laws are rules, norms of behavior are rules, conventions are rules, and customs are rules (just to name a few). In short, there are too many types of rules in the institutional lexicon. If we shift our focus onto agreed upon rules, we can begin to see different aspects of rules obscured by the traditional approach. A glossary of agreed upon rules follows in an appendix to this chapter.

AGREED UPON RULES AND NOT AGREED UPON RULES

A more useful concept of rules for HPE is to separate rules that are *agreed to* by some collective action process from rules that are *not agreed to*. Behavioral rules like norms, conventions, customs, and culture are not agreed to. In the logic of David Lewis's *Conventions* (2002 [1969]), the lack of agreement about a convention is what enables him to argue that a convention is a self-enforcing aspect of human behavior, a pattern of behavior that repeats even though no one agreed to the pattern or intended to produce the pattern. Conventions are behavioral norms. Conventions are not agreed upon rules.

An agreed upon rule results from a collective action process within an organization—a family, firm, or government. What does "agreed upon" imply? We can define an "organization" as a group of people who agree to some rules to govern their interactions. Organizations are distinguished from groups by the adoption of rules. Within organizations there *must be* an agreement about how rules are formed and changed. "Primary rules" are the rules that govern relationships between people. H. L. A. Hart (2012 [1961; 1994]) identified "secondary rules" as the rules an organization adopts for forming new rules or amending existing rules. Agreed upon rules are always created by organizations, and how the rules are agreed to depends on the secondary rules. Secondary rules specify who can make the rules, which could be a specific individual or individuals or an office, following what procedures for reaching agreements, as well as prescriptions about what rules can and cannot be about. Agreed upon rules, therefore, apply to many people who were not part of the process of reaching an agreement about the rule. "Agreed upon" does not imply "consent."

The division of rules into agreed upon and not agreed upon is more tractable than a formal-informal division. Norms, conventions, customs, and culture all belong in the not agreed upon category. "Not agreed to" does not mean "not important." Human behavior and human coordination are just as affected by norms, convention, and culture as by agreed upon rules. But the proper subject of HPE is agreed upon rules. HPE is understanding the collective choice processes that give rise to agreed upon rules and their enforcement. In fact, I would venture to say it is historical political economy's primary concern.

Primary and Secondary Rules

Many legal approaches to rules conceptualize legal rules as codifying the coercive power of the sovereign. Hart develops the idea of primary and secondary rules in the context of an autocratic ruler, Rex, whose word is law. Hart explains why even an arbitrary autocrat would need to develop secondary rules to build a legal system. If Rex can wake up each morning and create new rules, then there is no way for the legal system to know what the rules are at any point in time. Only if there are secondary rules about how rules are created will the legal system be able to recognize when the rules have changed. Hart, therefore, calls secondary rules "rules of recognition."

If organizations adopt agreed upon rules to govern and enhance the relationships within the organizations, then the Hobbesian approach to rule making in *Leviathan* seems clearly inappropriate. Hobbes offers no "collective choice" process for making rules. In fact, the power to make laws must be the jealously guarded sole prerogative of the sovereign Leviathan. The Hobbesian approach to governments and rule making, a very common approach in political economy, is inherently limiting. In Hobbes, there is only one secondary rule: a rule is anything Leviathan says is a rule. Focusing on the state as a single actor ignores many of the important dynamics that affect how and why governments make and enforce rules. It also leads us to focus on laws, rather than on the institutional structure of agreed upon rules in a society of which laws are only a part.

Internal and External Rules

Organizations create rules throughout the entire society. Those rules are linked together in ways that I talk about shortly, and understanding the links are critical to understanding how and why governments make and enforce rules. The heuristic idea that rules are adopted to increase the value of relationships is powerful, but complicated. For example, the value of whose relationships? Organizations deal with some of these complication by agreeing to the secondary rules for creating and amending rules. Families are organizations. Mothers and fathers make rules, and their secondary rules vary from family to family. Agreed upon rules apply to children, even if the children do not consent to the rule. "Agreed upon" does not imply consent. Many rules within organizations are applied to people who do not like the rules but prefer to stay in the organization because of the value of relationships they find within it. Because agreement does not imply consent, however, a tension within organizations is always present between rules and relationships.

The rules that an organization adopts to govern relationships between its members are *internal rules*. A second tension between rules and relationships within organizations often make it difficult to predictably enforce internal rules. If rules exist to increase the value of relationships, then the organization will not follow or enforce a rule that decreases the value of relationships. A rule that enhances the value of relationships in most circumstances may reduce the value of relationship in some circumstances, and in those circumstances the rule may not be enforced. Relationships always change through time; they cannot be fixed. Rules that cannot be predictably enforced, however, are less valuable coordinating devices. How can organizations deal with this tension between rules and relationships?

Organizations also form relationships with other organizations. These "organizations of organizations" reach agreements to adopt rules that increase the value of their relationships. The logic of an organization of organizations is the same as the logic of an organization of individuals. An organization exists when its members adopt rules to govern relationships between the members. Within the agreements that form organizations of organizations, it sometimes happens that rules created and enforced by one organization are used by another organization to increase the value of relationships within the organization using the rule. These rules are *external rules* to the using organization. External rules are rules that an organization can use internally, but are rules created and enforced by another, external organization.

Since the tension between rules and relationships within organizations often make it difficult to predictably enforce internal rules, organizations would like to access external rules whose enforcement is lodged in another organization, particularly if the organizations enforcing the external rule are insulated from relationships within the organization using the rule. In large societies, groups of organizations often reach agreements with each other to create a *coordinating organization* to enforce external rules for the organizations within the group. Sometimes the coordinating organizations are private organizations, like trade associations, but often they are public organizations.

Governments are prime examples of a coordinating organization. Governments are organizations that provide a venue for reaching agreements about rules through a collective choice process and then enforcing those rules in the agreed upon ways. The venues vary from the court of a sovereign, which brings together local leaders, a republic with some form of monarchy and an elite representative body, to a democracy with elected officials, formal secondary rules, and executive and legislative organizations. In most societies, powerful organizations reach agreements between themselves to form a government or governments to create and enforce external agreed upon rules that the members to the agreement can access.

You can easily see how the availability of an external rule can make an organization more productive by enabling the organization to coordinate better through more predictable rules, if enforcement of the external rules is not eroded by relationships within the organization itself. In order to be effective, the external rule has to be insulated from the relationships with the organizations to which it is applied. Insulating rule enforcement is an important aspect of external rules and an essential feature of "rule of law." For now, however, the key point to grasp is that by providing external rules, governments and private coordinating organizations can enhance the ability of organizations to coordinate relationships between their members, and between organizations that are members of an organization of organizations.

An essential feature of governments is that they publicly signify agreements about rules—what the rules are, how they will be enforced, and to whom the rules will apply. Governments are not the only source of rules in a society, however. How the governments in a society create and structure the external rules they provide to the rest of society have a significant impact on how the rules in other organizations work. To understand those interactions, we need to probe deeper into the nature and operation of different types of rules.

Prescriptive and Default Rules

When we think about rules or laws, we typically think of them as the result of an agreement within an organization that prescribes how people should behave in certain situations, provides for consequential punishments for not following the rules, and specifies how the rule is to be enforced. "Prescriptive rules" are designed to be followed. Even if the rules are not followed, individuals understand that consequences may ensue if the failure to follow the rule is discovered by the right people in the right circumstance. This is very much what North (1990) had in mind when he said that institutions are the rules of the game and the means of enforcement.

Rule following is a central pillar of scholars who believe that good institutions improve political and economic systems. If rules are known and people expect other people to follow the rules, then we can all better predict how we are going to behave. Rule following behavior enables more accurate expectations and thereby supports higher levels of coordination. No doubt these ideas are present in all of the institutional literatures, not just political economy, but the ideas are particularly important to HPE because governments often do not follow the rules that they establish. Since governments are responsible for enforcing laws, laws that are not reliably enforced do a worse job of supporting coordination between people.

While prescriptive rule following is certainly important to how institutions work, it is also true that not all rules are followed, or are indeed meant to be followed. "Default rules" are rules that can be enforced but do not have to be followed. For the most part, the institutional literatures in the social sciences, law, philosophy, and history have focused on prescriptive rules and ignored default rules. As a result, we have not built up intuitions about how default rules work in a society, nor do examples of default rules immediately spring to mind. Later I show that many rules that we think are prescriptive rules are really default rules in practice.

An example of a default rule can help. Many American states have adopted no fault or unilateral divorce laws. Under these laws either spouse can ask the courts to grant a divorce. The court has a set of agreed upon rules governing aspects of divorce, like child support and alimony, that will be applied to the parties if the divorcing couple cannot come to an agreement themselves. The divorce rules will be enforced by the courts if needed, but the parties do not have to follow them when they reach their agreement. Divorcing spouses have wide latitude to shape their own agreements (although there are constraints about child care and support, for example). The couple reaches their agreement in the "shadow of the rule." If they cannot come to their own agreement and go to the court, the court will apply the predictable rules governing divorce agreements. So the default rules are enforced. Yet, if the parties can find an agreement that makes both of them better off than the court enforced agreed upon default rules, then the court will grant the divorce under the terms of the parties' agreement. The divorce default rules are clear, predictable, and will be enforced, but the divorcing spouses do not have to follow the rules. Mnookin and Kornhauser (1979) suggest that 90 percent of divorces in no fault states reach their own agreement.

Rather than rules that *prescribe* behavior, default rules provide *outside options* that are only invoked if the parties who use the rules cannot agree on how to use the rules, that is, if they cannot coordinate. This gives individuals much more freedom to structure their relationships within the shadow of the rule.

Default rules can be internal rules or external rules. Families all adopt their own internal rules and, in most societies, families also operate in an environment of external rules. Some of those external rules are prescriptive rules and others are default rules. Many of the rules that governments in societies create to govern relationships within families are prescriptive in form, but default rules in practice. For example, the use of physical violence against a spouse is often prescribed behavior. But many societies devote little or no resources to actively enforcing the prescription. As a result, the rules prescribing spousal violence *are only enforced if one party brings a charge against the other to the police or a court*. In other words, those laws are prescriptive rules in form, but default rules in practice.[1] They are rules that are enforced, but not always followed. As should be clear, the rules against spousal violence are external to individual families: they are rules created and enforced by an external organization. Understanding the close relationships between external rules and default rules is very important.

Let me give one more example that builds from my own experience. In my twenties I worked construction jobs and was a member of the Laborer and Hod Carriers Union, the lowest rung of the construction unions. I often worked with carpenters as a helper, and the union rules were clear that "carpenters drive nails, laborers don't." Nonetheless, despite the clear and well-understood rules, I often drove nails. The union nail rules were default rules: whether a laborer drove nails or not depended on his relationship with the carpenter, and those relationships varied widely across laborer/carpenter pairs (heterogeneous relationships). If there was a dispute between a laborer and a carpenter, or with the firm they worked for, the dispute went to the union to resolve. The unions, in principle just like the courts, always apply the rule impersonally; they always rule in favor of the carpenter.

Default rules specify how relationships will be ordered potentially, but the rules do not have to be followed unless there is a dispute between the parties affected by the rule. In order to invoke the rule the parties have to "go to court." Going to court is the act of going to another organization and asking that a rule be applied, a judgment reached, and if appropriate, consequences imposed. What makes a default rule a default rule is not how it is enforced once the parties approach the court, it is a default rule because the court (or the organization to which the court belongs) makes no effort to ensure that the rule is followed in practice.

It is extremely important to realize that external rules are often default rules in practice because the enforcing organization will only enforce the rule if a dispute is brought before it. How and whether a government will enforce external rules that it creates for other organizations to use has two important but poorly understood aspects. The first aspect concerns who has access to the rule. Which citizens can go to the government and ask for a rule to be enforced? The second aspect concerns the form of the rules themselves: how do the rules apply to different individuals within the society? We return to the first aspect in a bit; the second aspect is the last dimension of rules we need to consider.

Identity and Impersonal Rules

A basic presumption in many legal theories is that rules, once created, will apply to everyone, or at least to every citizen (however defined). While that presumption is not too far off base in twenty-first-century Western democracies, in most societies in the contemporary world and in human history before 1850, rules did not apply to every citizen in the same way. "Identity rules" are rules whose form or enforcement depend on the social identities of the individuals to whom the rule is applied.[2] In contrast, an "impersonal rule" treats everyone the same, applies in the same way to all the individuals to whom the rule affects. Identity and impersonal rules differ in both the form of the rules and the enforcement of the rules. A simple impersonal rule—for example, theft is not allowed—can be impersonal in form (no one can steal) and identity in enforcement (powerful people are not convicted of theft). In the sixteenth-century Ottoman courts, Christians and Jews could bring cases against Muslims in the Muslim courts, but Christians and Jews could not give testimony against Muslims (Kuran and Rubin 2018). The rules about testifying were identity rules in form as well as in enforcement. The Fourteenth Amendment to the US Constitution prohibits laws that apply differently to different races (i.e., no identity rules by race), but in fact enforcement rule in the United States is racially biased (identity enforcement).

In the modern, developed West the idea that all rules should apply equally to all people has become a norm, even if not a reality. Historically, the evidence seems clear that most laws created by governments before 1850 were identity rules in form, as well as in enforcement. In both the British Parliament and the American states before 1850, roughly three quarters of all legislation applied to specific individuals, specific organizations, or specific localities (see Hoppit 2017 or Parliament, and Lamoreaux and Wallis 2021 for states in the United States).

In historical terms, the first societies to adopt impersonal rules on a broad scale started in the mid- to late nineteenth century. "Broad scale" means that the impersonal rules the government creates and enforces for a wide range of functions apply equally to all citizens. Indiana was the first government to require that its legislature only pass "general laws" for seventeen purposes in its 1851 constitution (see Lamoreaux and Wallis 2021). In no society are all the rules impersonal. By 1910 there were roughly twelve countries that had adopted some form of impersonal rule provisions. There are, unfortunately, no general histories of impersonal rule adoptions, not even for the United States where constitutional changes like Indiana's make it easy to date when the rules changed. We do know that, by 1910, twelve countries had made it possible to create a corporation through an administrative procedure: an impersonal rule for forming corporations, which we can infer from the number of corporations in those societies. I list them later.

The Economic Effects of Impersonal Rules

The transition from identity to rules to impersonal rules has both economic and political effects. The most important economic effect comes through how impersonal rules affect relationships within and between organizations. Go back to the union nail example. Laborers and carpenters work together in construction firms, and their productivity as pairs of workers determines the productivity of the firm as an organization. When a laborer and carpenter form a pair, there is no doubt about who has the "power" to determine who will drive nails, as the carpenter has been allocated the authority to determine who drives nails. But laborers and carpenters are endlessly variable in their personal attributes and professional skills. The firm would like to find out which pairs are most productive, and given that a pair exists, find the most productive arrangement for that pair. The union nail rule helps solve the coordination problem by giving the carpenter the authority to drive nails, but then allowing the firm and each of the laborer/carpenter pairs to find the arrangement that works best for them. No two laborer/carpenter pairs are alike, and the default nature of the nail rule allows each pair to adopt their own relationship. Because the nail rule is enforced, but not followed, both the pairs and the firm are more productive. Rather than a prescriptive rule designed to produce *homogeneous behavior*, the default rule supports *heterogeneous behavior* across the laborer/carpenter pairs. As Adam Smith taught economists long ago, heterogeneity in a population is a first order source of economic growth, as long as people can trade with one another.

We can do a simple thought experiment. Suppose the union did not enforce the nail rule impersonally, that is, always ruling in favor of the carpenter. Suppose, as unions do, they value seniority and were more likely to rule in favor of a laborer who was more senior than the carpenter. Now the costs of the laborer/carpenter pair negotiating an agreement between themselves would rise, as they would have to determine who had the authority to drive nails should a disagreement go to the union. The cost to the firm of matching laborers and carpenters increases, because different pairs will operate under different rules. The ability of an identity based nail rule to coordinate laborer/carpenter pairs will be considerably weaker than the ability of an impersonal nail rule to coordinate.

Effects like these exist in organizations throughout the economy. Most government rules are external rules, and even though they take a prescriptive form, governments usually devote resources to enforcing only part of the rules prescriptively. If the rest of the rules are *only enforced when the government is called on to enforce them: they are effectively default rules*.[3] If the rules in an identity rule regime are suddenly enforced as impersonal rules, the result is to increase coordination throughout all the organizations with access to the rules.

In an identity rule system, many people do not have access to the external rules. When a society decides to adopt impersonal rule provisions, like Indiana's in 1851, several things happen simultaneously. First, impersonal rules are more effective coordinating tools than identity rules, so the existing rules work better, ceteris paribus. Second, people who previously did not have access to the external rules enforced by the government now obtain access. In principle, impersonal rules apply to all citizens dramatically expanding the number of potential relationships in which the now impersonal rules can be used as outside options.[4] Third, the number and heterogeneity of relationships that can be supported increases.

These are all effects that operate at the level of organizations. The changing patterns of behavior induced by a transition to impersonal rules will not be reflected in the form of the rules themselves. That is, individuals and organizations will not become more noticeably "rule following" in their behavior. Most of the effect of a government adopting impersonal rules will be on the operation of government rules as external default rules, even if the forms of the government rule are prescriptive. Because impersonal external default rules support more heterogeneous behavior, the induced behavior will not be directly attributable to the rules, since the supported behavior will not follow the rules. When Indiana adopted impersonal rule provisions in its 1851 constitution, all of the external rules that became impersonal rules supported more effective coordination. The institutional rules in Indiana became more effective, even though the security of property rights did not change before and after 1851.

The adoption of impersonal rule provisions often include impersonal rules for forming organizations. These are known as general incorporation laws in the United States and registration laws in Britain and France. Adopting these impersonal rules leads to a dramatic increase in the number of organizations, as the political system is no longer manipulating economic entry for political purposes (North, Wallis, and Weingast 2009). More organizations, more productive organizations, and more heterogeneous organizations are all a consequence of adopting impersonal rule provisions. As societies in Western Europe and a few former British colonies began adopting impersonal rule provisions after 1850, their economies began to change, grow, and develop along these lines.

The Political Effects of Impersonal Rules

A central function of all governments is to create and enforce agreed upon rules, agreed upon through some process determined by the organization of the government and its secondary rules. How does the transition from identity rules to impersonal rules affect the operation of a government? In very general terms, how are impersonal rules sustained by the political system when all political systems before 1850 were identity rule regimes? Which organizations in either the government or the political system, or both, acquired interests in maintaining impersonal rules?

I can only sketch the answers to these questions here, but the answers themselves involve rules. Between 1800 and 1900 the character of political organizations fundamentally changed in the countries that adopted impersonal rules,—at least as measured by the number of corporations, which result from impersonal rules for forming corporations. In Leslie Hannah's 1910 global census, when measured by corporations per million people, the impersonal rule societies were the United States, Norway, Canada, New Zealand, Australia, the United Kingdom, the Netherlands, Switzerland, Sweden, Denmark, and Finland. The United States had 2,913 corporations per million people and Finland 850. Belgium with 551, Germany with 403, and France with 306 came next.

The twelve countries with the most corporations—as well as France and Belgium, but not Germany—had adopted impersonal rules for forming organizations, as well as other functions that we cannot identify precisely in the historical record (with the exception of places like Indiana). The character of political organizations had also changed fundamentally. Mature, durable, professional political parties had appeared in the democracies of all twelve countries. Political organizations had changed from factions to political parties. The terms "faction" and "party" were used interchangeably in the early nineteenth century. By 1900, *long-lived, durable, well-organized* political parties came to dominate the political systems of the twelve impersonal rule societies. Their *party systems* were no longer factional. The recognition that a new type of modern political party and party systems had appeared by 1900 was articulated by Schattschneider (2004 [1942]) and Sartori (2005 [1976]) as well as by the pluralists, as in the case studies in Dahl (1966). Recent research into the organization of parties in Britain (Cox 1987), comparing the development of conservative parties in Britain and Germany (Ziblatt 2017) and surveys of democratic development in the nineteenth and twentieth centuries (Berman 2019) affirms the change in the structure and organization of political parties in the impersonal rule societies. In the European societies with nascent democracies that did not adopt impersonal rules—Germany, Spain, Portugal, Italy, and Austria—modern political parties did not appear before 1920.

That political parties became longer lived and better organized, and that parties stopped using violence to influence voters or each other, is not in dispute. The question is how did they become longer lived. In an identity rule regime, as both the United States and Britain were before the 1850s, most of the legislation that is passed through the legislative process is identity legislation that affects specific individuals, organizations, or localities. In those political systems, the political organizations that vie for control of or influence over governments focus on narrow benefits: they are *factions*. Factions are narrow groups with narrow interests that interact with one another in a fluid and changeable political environment. Political organizations could not reasonably enter into agreements with each other that required long periods to come to fruition because the expected lifetime of factions and coalitions is limited.

Identity rules keep the legislative machine running. They are the lubrication that makes it possible for coalitions of political factions to form and pursue narrow short-term goals, but the agreements produced by such a system are always fragile and subject to change. The political system depends on the rent creating power of identity rules to build and hold together agreements between powerful organizations, including government organizations. In classic political economy/public choice language, we can think of the rule making process as one gigantic and ongoing logroll, in which the outcome of the rule making process is identity rules that create specific benefits or impose specific costs on narrowly defined interests.

Imposing an impersonal rule provision on such a system strikes at the very nature of the rule making process, by making it impossible to craft a legislative coalition package out of a bundle of identity rules. A major tool for creating rents is taken away. Coalition building now requires more complicated deals that stretch over longer periods of time and across legislation that necessarily affects larger numbers of legislators and constituents directly, as every piece of legislation now applies to everyone. Short-term agreements built around rules that apply to specific groups no longer suffice to assemble coalitions. *When impersonal rule provisions are implemented, the organizational structure of the political system has to change.* How could politicians and legislators, living in a world where no one could expect that a particular coalition would last for more than a legislative session or two, come to believe that a political party could have a durable life of decades or longer?

Sustaining a political system where parties have more durable lives requires that politicians themselves develop expectations that parties would be around longer in the future. Politicians and political organizations collectively control the rule creation process. We can ask what set of agreed upon rules could be enacted to guarantee parties would have longer lives? The agreements involve three elements, three sets of agreed upon rules, all within the control of the political organizations that make up the legislative and political process. The three elements are competitive elections, constitutional changes in government administration, and impersonal rules. Together these three sets of institutional rules create a *party system* capable of sustaining durable long-lived political parties, the parties identified by Schattschneider (2004 [1942]) and Sartori (2005 [1976]).

Competitive elections. Durable parties have to believe when they lose an election that they will be able to return and compete in an open and fair election in the future. Ultimately, free, fair, and open elections require rules under which voters are allowed to cast their ballots without undue outside influence. Sustaining competitive elections also involved parties forswearing the use of violence as an electoral technique, either against other parties or directly threatening voters. In a party system where elections are competitive and open, major parties know they will lose elections in the future, but they also believe they will have a chance to compete in future elections even if they lose.

Constitutional arrangements for government administration. All parties must agree to changes in constitutional structures so that the leaders of government organizations, such as cabinet ministers, are either directly subject to election or are appointed and easily removed by elected officials. Elections must matter to governments, and elections matter much less if control of the government lies outside of the electoral system, say with a king. By placing control of government administration with elected officials, political party leaders became both government officials when their parties are in power and party officials when their parties are out of power. Robert Dahl described this as a system of "reciprocal control." The parties put themselves under the discipline of elections and ensure that the parties that win elections have access to positions of control within the government. How then was the winning party to be prevented from using its control of the government and legislature to change the rules in order to suppress or eliminate the losing parties?

Impersonal rule provisions. Since the party that wins an election has disproportionate influence over the legislative process and the formation of new rules, all parties have to agree that whatever rules they pass when in power apply equally to everyone. The party in control cannot pass identity rules that discriminate against or suppress the parties out of power. A firm commitment to impersonal rules ensures that when a party loses an election, it is capable of competing again in the next election. Support for impersonal rule provisions must be baked into the institutional agreed upon rules that structure the party system. All the organizations with a legitimate chance to control the legislative process and the government must have clear incentives to support and sustain impersonal rules.

The three elements of the agreement are sets of rules that the political parties can create through the legislative or constitutional process. The agreement can be institutionalized in agreed upon rules. Together, the three elements make up the institutional framework for a mature *party system*: the rules and patterns of interaction within which parties competed for reciprocal control of the government. In the process, the new party system virtually eliminated the kind of political breakdowns that lead to civil wars and coups. Within the new party system, political parties controlled governments and the rule making process, and the parties all had a strong interest in sustaining impersonal rules as a way to ensure that a party that lost in this election could compete in the next one.

Some Implications

This chapter has tried to show how thinking of rules in a more detailed way—primary and secondary rules, internal and external rules, prescriptive and default rules, and identity and impersonal rules—can give us richer concepts about institutions as rules. Rules in one organization affect other organizations. This is obviously the case with laws created and enforced by governments, but we have not systematically investigated how external rules function across organizations. The three elements of the party system all affect how political parties behave, even though none of the component rules in the three elements apply directly to parties (except that electoral rules constrain how parties compete in elections).

The focus on rule following in the institutional literature has led us to overlook these aspects of rules and organizations. The narrow focus on prescriptive rules affects both what we see and what we do not see in political history. Two examples. I have placed emphasis on the difference between identity rules and impersonal rules. In the early twenty-first century the difference is hardly noted, except in the development literature where identity rules are an example of "corruption." In other words, identity rules are just impersonal rules gone bad. As late as the 1840s, however, 75 percent of all Parliamentary legislation was explicitly identity based (Hoppit's "specific rules"). What was widely recognized in the early nineteenth century but has been almost forgotten now is that Parliament had a highly developed set of institutional rules for dealing with identity rules, what they called "private bills." Private parties could approach Parliament, usually through an individual member, who would then start the private bill process. This involved a multistep process involving clerks who were paid fees to move the bill along. It was an elaborate system, deliberately cultivated, and deeply embedded in the institutions of Parliament that had essentially disappeared by 1900.[5] Rather than a historical anomaly, identity rules were essentially how legislatures operated in Britain and the United States before 1850 and are still essentially how they operate in most societies outside the developed core today. But we do not see identity rules as the "before" condition in the process of development and so we miss a critical element of historical political economy that needs to be understood.

The second example is the development of stable, durable, competitive political parties. The new party systems that appeared in the late nineteenth century do not include many rules about the formation and operation of political parties themselves. Instead of rules about parties, the party system elements create rules about elections, government administration, and impersonal rule provisions that are external to the parties themselves. As E. E. Schattschneider put it about parties in the United States, "The extralegal character of political parties is one of their most notable qualities. In a highly legalistic system of government such as the United States, therefore, the parties seem to be a foreign substance. It is profoundly characteristic that the fundamental party arrangements are unknown to the law" (2004 [1942], 11). If governments created rules that directly governed parties, then any party that could change those rules when in power had the potential to cripple its opponents. Instead, a party system of stable, durable, and competitive parties was supported institutionally by external rules and default rules: rules that enabled free and open elections, political control of governments to the parties that won elections, and continued support and expansion of impersonal rules. There is no institutional political history about the development of parties that relies on prescriptive rules about parties, because that history never happened.

The core questions that HPE seeks to address are about how societies become arrangements that allow for the creation and enforcement of agreed upon rules, agreed to through some collective choice process. That is the central element of what governments are and do. In order to have a more complete historical political economy, we need to develop a richer conceptual repertoire of rules.

Glossary

The following definitions address ideal types of rules and organizations. The definitions of rules are paired along dimensions, where the ideal definitions refer to either end of a continuum. In practice, rules lie along these continuous dimensions. I usually refer to the types of rules in the paper as discrete entities without the "continuous" qualification.

Agreed Upon Rules: All agreed upon rules are deliberately created within organizations. These rules include:

Primary and secondary rules: Primary rules apply to the behavior and relationships of individuals (or subunits) within an organization. Secondary rules are the rules for forming new rules or amending existing rules within the organization. All organizations have secondary rules.

Internal and external rules: Internal rules are created by organizations and apply within the organization that created them. External rules are created and enforced by one organization and used by other organizations. Governments are a key example of an organization that specializes in the creation and enforcement of external rules that other organizations and individuals use.

Identity and impersonal rules: The form and/or the enforcement of identity rules depends upon the social identity of the individuals or organizations to whom the rule applies. Impersonal rules apply the same to everyone. Impersonal rules can also apply to categories of people. For example, all citizens, all subjects, all men, all women, all children, all cities over one hundred thousand population, and the like. As a result, a rule's form may be impersonal, but its application may be so specific that it in practice is an identity rule.

Prescriptive and default rules: The form of prescriptive rules defines some behavior that is mandated or proscribed, and defines consequences for behavior that does not follow the rule. Organizations devote resources to enforcing prescriptive rules and applying sanctions to rulebreakers. Default rules are enforced, but not followed. Default rules are enforced in case of a dispute between individuals or organizations brought to the appropriate third party, but actual behavior is not required to follow the form of the rule.

There is no category of "Not Agreed to Rules." Within many definitions of institutions, however, there are norms, beliefs, values, conventions, customs, and cultures that are often referred to as "rules." They are not referred to as "rules" in this chapter; the term "rules" applies only to "agreed upon rules."*Coordinating organizations* are organizations whose primary purpose is to enforce rules for other organizations. Coordinating organizations are often created by groups of organizations in order to provide external rules that members of the group can use.

Notes

1. The rules governing spousal abuse were intended to be prescriptive. But if invoking the rule requires that an abused spouse bring a case before the court and an abused spouse either worries that the court cannot protect her or the abused spouse values the ongoing relationship, then often the victim of abuse will not proceed with the case. My state, Maryland, has recently changed the laws to allow police or social workers who observe or suspect abuse to bring cases directly to the courts. That shifts the enforcement of the rule from default to prescriptive.
2. A more accurate definition may be that the form or enforcement of an identity rule differs according to the identity of the people to whom the rule applies, and the identity has nothing to do with the substance of the rule. There are, for example, rules that apply differently to men and women because the substance of the rule deals with differences between men and women. The boundary of identity rules is often difficult to draw in a hard and fast way. Impersonal rules often apply to categories of people, organizations, or places. Manipulating the categories can make what seems to be an impersonal rule into an identity rule.
3. If the government enforces the rules arbitrarily, then the organizations will be worse off as well.
4. Whether the rules are identity rules applying to just one person or impersonal rules that apply equally to everyone or rules somewhere in the middle is an important distinction, but too complicated to go into here.
5. For the history of private bills see Williams, 1948.

References

Berman, Sheri. 2019. *Democracy and Dictatorship in Europe: From the Ancien Régime to the Present Day*. New York: Oxford University Press.

Cox, Gary. 1987. *The Efficient Secret: The Cabinet and the Development of Political Parties in Victorian England*. New York: Cambridge University Press.

Dahl, Robert, ed. 1966. *Political Oppositions in Western Democracies*. New Haven: Y*ale University Press.

Durkheim, Emile. 1982. *The Rules of Sociological Method*. Edited with an introduction by Steven Lukes. Translated by W. D. Halle. New York: Free Press.

Hart, H. L. A. 2012 [1961/1994]. *The Concept of Law*. 3rd edition. Oxford: Oxford University Press.

Hobbes, Thomas. 2012 [1651]. *Leviathan*. Oxford: Oxford University Press.

Hoppit, Julian. 2017. *Britain's Political Economies: Parliament and Economic Life, 1660–1800*. New York: Cambridge University Press.

Kuran, Timur, and Jared Rubin. 2018. "The Financial Power of the Powerless: Socio-Economic Status and Interest Rates under Weak Rule of Law." *Economic Journal* 128, no. 609: 758–96.

Lamoreaux, Naomi R., and John Joseph Wallis. 2021. "Economic Crisis, General Laws, and the Mid-Nineteenth-Century Transformation of American Political Economy." *Journal of the Early Republic* 41, no. 3: 403–33.

Lewis, David. 2002 [1969]. *Convention: A Philosophical Study*. Cambridge. MA: Harvard University Press.

Mnookin, Robert H., and Lewis Kornhauser. 1979. "Bargaining in the Shadow of the Rules: The Case of Divorce." *Yale Law Journal* 88, no. 5: 950–97.

North, Douglass C. 1990. *Institutions, Institutional Change, and Economic Performance.* New York: Cambridge University Press.

North, Douglass C. 1992. "Institutions and Economic Theory." *American Economist* 36, no. 1 (Spring): 3–6.

North, Douglass C., John Joseph Wallis, and Barry R. Weingast. 2009. *Violence and Social Orders: A Conceptual Framework for Interpreting Recorded Human History.* New York: Cambridge University Press.

Sartori, Giovanni. 2005 [1976]. *Parties and Party Systems: A Framework for Analysis.* Colchester, UK: ECPR Press.

Schattschneider, E. E. 2004 [1992]. *Party Government.* New Brunswick, NJ: Transaction Publishers.

Williams, O. Cyprian. 1948. *The Historical Development of Private Bill Procedure and Standing Orders in the House of Commons, Vol. 1.* London: His Majesty's Stationary Office.

Ziblatt, Daniel. 2017. *Conservative Parties and the Birth of Democracy.* New York: Cambridge University Press.

CHAPTER 17

HISTORICAL POLITICAL ECONOMY OF LEGISLATIVE POWER

GARY W. COX

The allocation of lawmaking power within a polity is a central aspect of its constitutional structure. Some polities concentrate all legislative power in a single ruler's hands. Others share legislative power horizontally (between rulers and assemblies at the central-state level) or vertically (across levels of government). In this essay, I review the historical political economy (HPE) of how legislative power has been allocated in European polities.

One question concerns how central executives have been constrained via the separation of power (SOP) within the central state and the delegation of power (DOP) to other levels of government. A handful of premodern European polities—the constitutional monarchies and republics—constrained executive power mainly by imposing SOP within the central state. Absolutist monarchies, meanwhile, constrained the executive mainly via DOP. These differing methods of constraint had several important consequences.

Another question this essay addresses concerns the extent to which legislative processes at different levels of government have influenced one another. To what extent should we expect congruence across levels of government—for example, separations of power at all levels (or none)? What combinations of SOP and DOP are "in equilibrium"? To set the stage, I begin by describing the mechanics of SOP and DOP, and how they each contribute to executive constraint.

SOP AND DOP

The process of central-state lawmaking can take many forms. At one extreme, the executive might legislate by decree (facing no legislative veto), as in historical empires and contemporary dictatorships. At another extreme, the legislature might legislate by statute (facing no executive veto), as in some medieval republics and contemporary city councils. In between are various separation-of-power regimes—for example, when the legislature proposes bills, the executive can veto them, and the legislature can then override the executive's veto.[1]

In addition to regulating which actors play a role in making the central state's laws, polities can also delegate legislative (and administrative) power to subordinate governmental units. Here I focus on delegations of power to spatially dispersed units such as provinces and cities.

The factor most often cited to explain the emergence of European DOP is the collapse of central authority in post-Roman Europe. Local nobles filled the resulting power vacuum, creating de facto delegations of power that were subsequently legalized in the form of banal lordships (Mitterauer 2009). A nobility that owned propertylike rights of lawmaking, administration, and justice spread widely, creating a durable form of local government.[2]

It was not just nobles who acquired local governance rights. Especially after the invention of a new form of corporation during the medieval legal revolution (Huff 1993, ch. 4), merchant elites in many areas formed town corporations—aka communes—to purchase governance rights (Lopez 1966), and many villagers formed rural communes (Blickle 1998). This delegation of legislative, administrative, and judicial power to corporate bodies created another durable form of local government. Indeed, some European cities are still governed in part under medieval charters.

Those wielding delegated power were subject to varying levels of oversight. Some became fully sovereign. Others, such as units in the Holy Roman Empire or the Polish-Lithuanian Commonwealth, were subject to very few legislative directives from above. Still other units, such as towns in England, continued to be subject to royal decrees and parliamentary statutes that, while not violating their local "liberties," regulated important aspects of local life.

Corporate recipients of delegated power also varied in their internal governance practices. Town corporations invented an array of procedures—including various forms of election, sortition, and cooptation—to choose councilors and other officials (Manin 1997; Wahl 2016; Uckelman and Uckelman 2020). Relatedly, town corporations promulgated many different rules to define and confer citizenship (Prak 2018).

Towns also invented myriad varieties of legislative procedures. Among other things, this meant that SOP could arise at the local level, independently of whether it existed at the level of the central state. I am not aware of a survey of town legislative procedures from an HPE perspective but detailed studies of particular cases, such as Puga and Trefler's (2014) analysis of Venice, shed light on this matter.

In general, autonomous European towns became laboratories experimenting with new constitutional structures. One consequence was that constitutional innovations spread via horizontal diffusion, as opposed to vertical imposition. The communal movement was an early and characteristic example in which formulaic rights diffused from a few points of origin—the *fueros* in the Iberian Peninsula, the Lübeck Law in the Baltic region, the Frankfurt Law in central Germany, and so on. The "church ordinances" of the German Protestant towns diffused from a single area (Dittmar and Meisenzahl 2020). Many other examples of diffusion could be cited.

Another consequence of many towns autonomously trying new methods of governance was that western communes provided a large array of services. For example, western towns stood out in comparison to Islamic towns in terms of (1) producing written documents and the infrastructure, such as town halls and archives, to store them (Rothstein and Broms 2013; Buringh and van Zanden 2009); (2) investing in cranes, mills, public clocks, and other largely immovable capital goods (van Bavel, Buringh, and Dijkman 2018; Boerner and Severgnini 2019; Boerner, Rubin and Severgnini 2021); and (iii) competing to attract top professorial talent to local universities (De la Croix, Docquier, Fabre, and Stelter 2020). Kuran (2018, 1322–1325) attributes the relative inactivity of Islamic cities to their being governed by frequently rotated appointees, their lack of legal personhood, and the provision of many local public services by waqfs (endowments established to provide specific social services in perpetuity).

All told, we can say that a distinctive European tradition of DOP began in the medieval era with the creation of banal lordships and rural and urban communes (Mitterauer 2009; Blickle 1998), and that many governance forms innovated in the medieval era survived into, or influenced, modern forms. In the next two subsections, I consider how SOP and DOP relate to executive constraints. In principle, central-state executives can be constrained by either separating powers within the central state or delegating legislative and administrative powers to local units of governance. European polities experimented with both kinds of constraint.[3]

Constraint via Co-Legislation (SOP)

One method of executive constraint that Europeans explored involved requiring monarchs to secure parliamentary approval of laws (Montesquieu 1989 [1748]). Most of the political economy literature has focused on this kind of constraint, following North and Weingast's (1989) seminal article.

However, only a few European nations established strong and durable parliaments in the premodern era. Ignoring the smaller states, the list includes only England and the Netherlands.[4] Elsewhere, although central parliaments of various types emerged, their legislative powers were later suppressed (Cox, Dincecco, and Onorato 2021)—on which more appears later.

When nineteenth-century Europeans again experimented with legislative institutions, it became conventional to distinguish parliamentary polities, whose legislatures could remove cabinet ministers via votes of no confidence, from presidential polities, whose legislatures lacked such power. In both types of regime, assemblies controlled the budget, which resulted in substantial revenue increases (North and Weingast 1989; Dincecco 2011; Cox 2016; Cox and Dincecco 2020).[5] However, the purer separation of powers entailed in presidential systems opened the possibility for legislative gridlock (Cox 2016), and a large literature explores the consequences. For example, separation-of-powers models analyze the discretion that gridlock affords to bureaucrats (e.g., Huber and Shipan 2002; Gailmard and Patty 2012) and judges (e.g., Hasen 2019). While these models focus on modern times, the insight that agents subject to less effective monitoring will be able to consume more rents is very relevant in the premodern era, as the next section discusses.

Constraint via Co-Administration (DOP)

An older method of executive constraint in Europe involved delegating some of the central state's legislative and administrative authority to dispersed actors who were not subject to effective oversight by the Crown.[6] When the ruler could implement state policies only with the cooperation of these holders of delegated authority, they could delay the implementation of state policies simply by refusing to cooperate (Greif 2008). Consider three examples.

First, Spanish town officials followed the precept "Obedecer y No Cumplir," accepting the legality of the Crown's orders while refusing to implement them in practice (Fernández Hevia 2001). As it was costly to overcome such passive resistance, towns could significantly delay new policies while bargaining for improvements. A similar situation held in England: "Although towns were required to follow specified policy directives of English kings, the actual implementation was left to the burghers themselves who would carry them through or drag their feet as they saw fit" (Downing 1989, 223).

Second, some French courts of law (*parlements*) could refuse to register royal decrees in their jurisdictions, publishing their objections (*remonstrances*). The king could then summon the relevant justices to meet with him (in a *lit de justice*), override their *remonstrance*, and order registration of the law. In effect, France had a decentralized system of constitutional review in which justices exploited an administrative power (of registering new laws) in order to wield a suspensory veto.

Third, in England all domestic policing duties were exercised by unpaid magistrates and private associations (Koyama 2014). English elites viewed unpaid magistracy and private policing as the prices they needed to pay to avoid centrally controlled police forces, which they equated with continental absolutism (Cox 2018). Charles James Fox, leader of the Whig opposition, expressed the traditional view during a parliamentary debate:

> The police of this country was well administered ... by gentlemen who undertook to discharge the duty without deriving any emolument from it, and in the safest way to the freedom of the subject, because those gentlemen being under no particular obligation to the executive power, could have no particular interest in perverting the law to oppression.
>
> (Debrett, *The Parliamentary Register* 1792, 53)

In other words, decentralized and unpaid police would prevent abuse of the police system by the monarch.

It was not just Spanish and English town officials, French justices, and English magistrates who could exercise "suspensory administrative vetoes" over royal policies. Many "venal" officeholders had the right to charge fees for certain services, and this right was protected as a form of private property by the courts (Blackstone 1979). Relative to salaried bureaucrats, venal officeholders could delay implementing royal policies with greater impunity—because they faced lower income risks even if monitored. From this perspective, the armies of venal officeholders in the patrimonial states of southern Europe significantly constrained royal power (Swart 1949; Figueroa 2021b).

THE GLOBAL CORRELATION BETWEEN LOCAL AND CENTRAL-STATE GOVERNANCE

One theme of this essay, to which I turn in this section, concerns the correlation between local and central-state governance structures. Today's countries are more likely to be democratic if, prior to the emergence of modern states, ethnic groups contained within their borders chose their leaders by election or consensus (Giuliano and Nunn 2013; Bentzen, Hariri, and Robinson 2017). One interpretation of this striking correlation is that when ethnic proto-states combined via conquest or negotiation to form modern states, the proto-states' institutional structures were replicated in the larger polity. Assuming that proto-states with elective-consensual leaders also had some degree of SOP, then the correlation can be interpreted as evidence that aggregating proto-states into states tended to preserve both leadership succession and SOP institutions.

A concrete example of institution-preserving aggregation is Downing's (1988) study of how village governance structures gave rise to the *Riksdag* in Sweden. Other examples include the Old Swiss Confederacy, the Dutch Republic, and the American Confederation. In all these cases of *bottom-up* state formation, explicit negotiations between dispersed units, each already constraining local executive power, resulted in the implementation of similar practices at the confederal level.

What if states formed top-down when a large ethnic group conquered its neighbors? To the extent that warlike ethnic groups had autocratic leadership-selection and lawmaking processes, the successor states they established would have been scaled-up versions of their autocratic proto-states.

Given some combination of bottom-up aggregation and top-down conquest, one expects the correlation between proto-state and successor state designs to be positive but with larger ethnic groups having larger weights. This is consistent with the argument and findings of Bentzen, Hariri, and Robinson (2017).

In the next several sections, I explore the correlation between local and polity-wide governance institutions more systematically in the case of Europe—where a rich HPE literature touching on this issue exists. I begin by describing the types of DOP in Europe.

The European Correlation between Local and Central-State Governance

A long tradition of European scholarship has pointed toward a correlation between local and central forms of governance. I review these ideas next, dividing them into (nonexclusive) bottom-up and top-down processes of state formation.

Bottom-Up Origins of Representative Institutions

Alexis de Tocqueville (2000 [1835], i, 3) argued that "the establishment of communes carried democratic freedom right into the heart of the feudal monarchy." In his view, municipal institutions served as training grounds for liberty, with town-level democratic practices inspiring national-level corollaries. Downing's "Medieval Origins of Constitutional Government in the West" (1989) provides a more detailed account along the same lines. Squire's (2017) analysis of the American colonies has some of the same flavor. Kuran (2018) and Rothstein and Broms (2013), meanwhile, argue that the *absence* of participative local governance in the areas brought under Islamic rule during the Arab conquests underpin the lack of national-level democracy in that area today.

The thesis that local governance practices aggregated to influence central-state practices is similar to the idea that ethnic proto-states' practices aggregated to influence their successor states' structures. In Europe, local participative practices could sometimes aggregate to form bottom-up assemblies. Even a quick survey reveals dozens of durable and important city confederations (Spruyt 1994), and all of them re-created legislative and leadership processes at the confederal level mirroring those in place among the participants. Combinations of rural and urban communes could also form, giving rise to parliaments such as the Old Swiss Confederacy's *Tagsatzung*.

Parliaments comprising representatives of local units of government were also convened by monarchs in the peripheral kingdoms—England, Scotland, Scandinavia, Poland, and Hungary—where the requirements of attracting settlers to frontier regions had produced more participatory forms of local governance (Ertman 1997, 19–25). In other cases, communal influence was more contingent. Only if towns could defend their liberties against revocation and prevent royal infiltration—on which more appears later—could they seek to transport their local legislative and leadership selection practices into the central state. It should be noted, however, that sufficiently strong towns preferred simply to secede, establishing their own city-states. Thus, only when towns were strong enough to remain autonomous, but not so strong as to become sovereign, did they seek to exercise their voice rather than exit options (Hirschman 1970).

A bottom-up perspective may also help understand the diverse structures of early parliaments. Building on Hintze (1975 [1931]), Ertman (1997) claims that experience with participatory local institutions led local elites to demand territorially based rather than estate-based parliaments. Coordination among representatives was easier in the former, facilitating constraint on the executive. Estate-based chambers, in contrast, "were often more than willing to give up rights of co-legislation or even taxation as long as the social and economic privileges of their respective status groups were guaranteed" (Ertman 1997, 21; see also Møller 2017b).

The Top-Down Administrative Origin of Representative Institutions

A long line of scholars argues that town corporations became key players in collecting royal taxes, especially the "extraordinary" taxes that financed warfare. Thus, where monarchs had previously consulted only with their great feudatories—whose assistance in collecting extraordinary taxes was already essential—they now expanded their councils by adding representatives of the towns, giving rise to what are generally called "parliaments" (Pirenne 1946, 180; Mitterauer 2009, 135).

The background to this story is that, after the collapse of the Carolingian Empire, no European monarch possessed a central bureaucracy capable of collecting taxes, and none had the wherewithal to create one (Stasavage 2020, ch. 5). Such monarchs accordingly were forced to farm out tax-collecting rights and responsibilities, packaged with other rights and responsibilities of lordship. The first recipients were banal lords, who attended their monarch's councils (Mitterauer 2009, ch. 4). Once town corporations acquired similar rights and responsibilities, monarchs began to call "the burghers into the councils of prelates and nobles with whom they conferred upon their affairs" (Pirenne 1946, 220). Thus, urban "self-government [was] a *precondition* for [towns'] representation in territorial and imperial Estates" (Mitterauer 2009, 135; italics added). As van Zanden, Buringh, and Bosker (2012, 847) put it, the "key event . . . that lead to the formation of parliaments was the communal movement."

Recent scholarship in HPE has developed these ideas. In particular, Greif (2008, 31) stresses that "political assemblies were composed of individuals and corporate bodies with independent administrative capacity," explaining that "administrative power leads to political representation because constitutional and other rules specifying rights are inherently incomplete contracts" (Greif 2008, 30). In other words, once the monarch had delegated tax-collecting responsibilities to urban corporations, many details of the extraordinary taxes that fueled the medieval war machine remained to be arranged—and parliaments were an efficient way of doing so (Pasquet 1964, 225; Bates and Lien 1985: 56; Van Zanden, Buringh, and Bosker 2012, 847). Similarly, Angelucci, Meraglia, and Voigtlander (2020, 6) invoke "a literature in both economic history and organizational economics that connects administrative autonomy to [the need for] centralized coordination" to explain the formation of parliaments.

Following a similar logic, Cox, Dincecco, and Onorato (2021) stress that European rulers needed to secure the *active cooperation* of their tax administrators, since the latter could cause substantial delays or shortfalls in revenue collection simply by dragging their feet—and monarchs lacked the bureaucratic capacity to detect and punish such foot-dragging. To secure active cooperation, monarchs could offer compensation up front, promise to share the spoils of victory, or both. Either way, the expected profit of the proposed war(s) effectively constituted the surplus over which the ruler and his tax farmers might bargain, and parliaments were the fora in which the necessary negotiations were conducted (Barzel and Kiser 2002).[7]

The accounts just given argue that DOP prompted the rise of central-state SOP: the act of delegating power created an incomplete contract (Greif 2008; Angelucci, Meraglia, and Voigtlande 2020) or a surplus (Barzel and Kiser 2002; Cox, Dincecco, and Onorato (2021), thereby necessitating regular consultation. This raises the question: when will delegations of power to towns survive? Abstractly, such DOPs must survive two threats: royal efforts to retract delegated powers or to undermine the independence of those wielding them, and town efforts to leverage their delegated powers into sovereignty. When royal and town powers were balanced, so that neither could renege on the original terms of the delegation of power, DOP survived.

The survival of DOP in balanced polities had important developmental consequences. In the economic realm, systems of autonomous towns chasing mobile factors could give rise to Tieboutian competition (Tiebout 1956), market-preserving federalism (Weingast 1995), and urban stratification (Cox and Figueroa 2021). In the political realm, towns had strong incentives to exercise voice (about how the central state operated) to preserve their delegated powers. This narrow path of political development, which required a balance of power between towns and Crowns, is illustrated in the next section.

The Suppression of Parliaments

Monarchs had two main options to overcome "the common . . . paralyzing conflicts" between themselves and their parliaments (Glete 2002, 193). One was to remove their powers (ending SOP). Another was to attack the communes (reengineering DOP).

Ending SOP

Pure transfers of legislative power from parliament to the Crown were rare. One example was Denmark's Lex Regia (1665). Another was England's short-lived Dominion of New England (1688–1689).

The more common pattern was for central parliaments to stop meeting, with key powers transferring to local units. In Spain, the Castilian Cortes ceased to meet after 1632, but the towns continued to exercise a collective tax veto until the onset of Bourbon absolutism (Jago 1981). In France, the Estates General ceased to meet for 175 years after 1614, but provincial parliaments in the *pays d'etat* continued to exercise local tax vetoes.[8]

Reengineering DOP

Under the category of reengineering DOP, one option was to end the communes' role in collecting taxes and replace them with royal bureaucrats. Once communes were no longer crucial in tax *collection*, securing their parliamentary representatives' consent to new tax *legislation* was no longer as crucial. Consistent with this observation, parliaments with the right to approve taxes tended to survive just as long as tax administration remained out of the hands of royal bureaucrats (and in the hands of urban elites, landowning gentry, and lords). For example, when a French province was converted into a *pays d'election*—an area in which royal bureaucrats collected taxes—its parliament typically ceased meeting (Barbiche 2012, 99–100). More generally, Ertman (1997, 19–25) argues that parliaments were more likely to survive where their members were representatives of local units of government.

Recognizing this point, several scholars have stressed that the delegation of power from monarchs to town corporations enabled urban elites to coordinate against later princely decisions to revoke or revise their liberties (Ertman 1997, 22; Blickle 1998, 10; Bentzen, Hariri, and Robinson 2017, 683). Coordination—which took the form of planning in local assemblies, raising local taxes and militias, innovating new forms of public debt (Stasavage 2011), and building town walls—enabled towns to defend both their local (communal) and collective (parliamentary) rights.

Another option was to pack town councils with royal supporters (George 1940; Clark and Slack 2007; Angelucci, Meraglia, and Voigtlander 2020). If enough towns could be flipped into the royalist camp, the Crown could reliably win majorities in parliament, thereby ending gridlock. In other words, undermining DOP was a route to undermining SOP. Contemporaries clearly recognized this threat. For example, in 1572 Emperor Maximillian II granted the noble Estates in Lower Austria the exclusive right to regulate admission to their ranks, in order to allay fears that he would otherwise use his powers to destroy the Estate's independence (Godsey 2018, ch. 1). In America's colonial assemblies, the cleavage between Crown loyalists and "patriots" was clearly visible in the roll-call voting record (Napolito and Peterson 2021).

When monarchs succeeded in removing towns' administrative power or ending their independence, they created absolutist central states facing weakened or nonindependent local units of governance (although often at the price of more venal officeholders). When royal efforts failed, more constitutionalized central states emerged which faced stronger and more autonomous local units. Thus, the correlation between central-state and local units tended to persist.

Consequences of Co-Administration

In this section, I first consider how co-administrative mechanisms constraining royal power could enhance the ruler's ability to commit at the cost of enabling administrators' rent extraction. I then discuss some path dependencies affecting polities with extensive co-administration.

Co-Administration and Ruler Survival

At the heart of Europe's feudal system was co-administration of military forces. Blaydes and Chaney (2013) argue that the emergence of this military system should have lowered the stakes of who the monarch was. In contrast, rulers in the Islamic world retained unitary command of all military forces, raising the stakes of who the sultan was. Consistent with their argument, Blaydes and Chaney show that, prior to the emergence of feudalism, Christian monarchs and Islamic sultans reigned (and lived) for similar periods of time. Afterward, however, the reigns and lives of European rulers perceptibly lengthened relative to their Middle Eastern counterparts.

Co-Administration and Commitment: Sovereign Debt

Medieval monarchs' inability to commit to repay borrowed money meant they had more difficulty in procuring loans and paid higher interest rates than city republics (Stasavage 2011). It is surprising, then, that the early modern monarchs who built absolutist states—thereby worsening any co-legislative basis for credible commitment—were nonetheless able to borrow more than their predecessors at lower interest rates. They accomplished this feat by borrowing on the security of future taxes, while delegating various administrative rights over tax collection to their lenders.

To elaborate, consider Emperor Charles V's agreement with the provincial parliaments of the Low Countries in 1542. Charles levied a new excise tax and authorized the parliaments to collect it and to sell annuities secured on their future tax collections. Most of the sale revenues went to Charles, while provincial officials earned management fees (Gelderblom and Jonker 2013, 177). This "indirect royal borrowing"—royals selling the joint right to farm taxes and sell annuities, tax farmers then borrowing on the security of their future collections—was imitated widely, becoming "the model for public debt in Europe up to the end of the nineteenth century" (Stasavage 2011, 10).

The popularity of indirect royal borrowing stemmed from the fact that, if the monarch's own bureaucrats collected the taxes earmarked to repay a particular loan, the monarch might use the money for something else. When monarchs never got their hands on the money, repayment was much more secure—since tax farmers, unlike monarchs, could be bound by legal contracts (Álavarez-Nogal and Chamley 2013; Cox, Dincecco, and Onorato 2021). A similar system was instituted in Spanish colonial America, where *consulados* (merchant guilds) and *cabildos* (corporate bodies of local government) secured rights of tax collection and in return performed fiscal transfer and credit operations for the Crown (Grafe and Irigoin 2012).

Co-Administration and Rent Extraction

Constraining royal power mainly by co-administration had important consequences. Insulating officeholders from royal oversight enabled them not only to deter royal tyranny but also to extract greater rents. Indeed, the rapacity of undersupervised Crown agents was legendary throughout Latin Christendom (personified by the sheriff of Nottingham in the legend of Robin Hood).

Recent HPE work exploiting colonial data have illuminated how much undersupervised agents warped the provision of public services (Xu 2018; Arteaga, Desierto, and Koyama 2020), the reaction to natural disasters (Garfias and Sellars 2020), and long-term development (Guardado 2018). When both supervisory and supervised positions were sold in the colonies, rent extraction by the latter worsened—suggesting either vertical integration in corruption or systematic kickbacks (Guardado 2020).

Monarchs understood that their agents' rent extractions could reduce their own revenues. When agents were near enough, monarchs might launch supervisory campaigns—such as the English king Henry II's famous Inquest of Sheriffs. When agents were far away, monarchs might impose separations of power upon their governors in order to empower settlers to curb rent extractions that harmed them both (Gailmard 2017), or create institutions outside the main colonial governance structures (Garfias 2019; Franco-Vivanco 2021).

Those monarchs who opted to mitigate their agency losses by imposing local separations of power upon their agents put their polities on a developmental path that was hard to leave. In England's American colonies, assemblies imposed detailed appropriations (statutory specifications of how public revenues should be spent) on their governors (Gailmard 2021) a century before comparably detailed appropriations became common in the mother country (Daunton 2001, ch. 3).

Co-Administration and State-Building

Polities that relied on co-administration to constrain their monarchs found it difficult to build royal bureaucracies. The basic problem was that existing office- and rights-holders stoutly opposed the construction of royal bureaucracies (Cox 2018; Figueroa 2021b). While they could sometimes be bought out or muscled aside, both options were costly.

Monarchs who adopted Protestantism and confiscated the Catholic monasteries' wealth gained a massive windfall with which they could finance their wars and state-building projects. In contrast, their Catholic counterparts had to resort to selling more state offices in order to raise money for the wars of religion. Thus, the stock of hereditary officeholders, previously similar across Latin Christendom, became relatively larger in Catholic lands. As Figueroa (2021b) explains, the Reformation shock put Catholic and Protestant Europe on different state-building trajectories—with premodern bureaucracies appearing only in the latter.

The Towns' Interest in Executive Constraint

I have discussed two secular mechanisms of executive constraint: co-legislation and co-administration. It is also worth analyzing the incentives that towns, which played a role in both mechanisms, had to constrain the central executive. These incentives differed from those of the landed nobility, given the differing sources of their income.

In particular, towns wished to protect themselves against arbitrary or predatory trade policies. The agent of a lord or monarch who governed a town might tax merchants' inputs, tax their finished goods as they exited town, or collect tolls at booths erected along nearby roads. Once their goods reached the next principality, merchants might face further tariffs and fees. This process could continue until their goods reached their final market(s).

When merchant elites purchased town charters—creating a town council and town courts that they would dominate—they protected themselves against "in town" predation by their own monarch and nobility (see Gelderblom 2013; Cox 2017). When a town gained representation in parliament, its merchants could lobby against "out of town" (but still in-polity) predation, such as currency debasement (Blockmans 1997, 60; van Zanden, Buringh, and Bosker, 846) and arbitrary transport fees (Blockmans 1997, 40–41; Lopez 1966, 265). Finally, merchants typically negotiated "safe passage" rights with the rulers of other domains through which their merchandise passed (for example, *Geleitrecht* in the Holy Roman Empire) and sought rights to ensure themselves against predation (Greif, Milgrom, and Weingast 1994).

Merchants' exposure to many kinds of taxation at different locations (and by different authorities) meant that all mechanisms protecting their goods against predation—including rights of self-government and representation in parliament—were complements to their productive assets. For example, Pirenne (1946, 202) stresses that merchants greatly valued (the right to build) town walls, since such walls protected their human and physical capital. In contrast, most rural lords had smaller shares of their assets in town and were thus less concerned with (the right to make) decisions about town defense. As another example, merchants would suffer more, if a town developed a reputation for predating on visiting merchants, merchants would suffer more would local lords. Thus, *merchants should have valued urban governance rights more than lords because (1) they could combine such rights with a wider array of complementary assets (e.g., trading networks, machinery) than the nobility, and (2) neither monarchs nor lords could easily confiscate these complementary assets.* The complementarity between urban governance rights and merchant elites' other productive nonconfiscable assets led to several connections between trade potential, on the one hand, and communal birth, persistence, and behavior, on the other.

Trade Potential Predicted Which Towns Acquired Rights of Self-Government

If governance rights were complements to merchants' other (nonconfiscable) assets, then towns with better prospects for trade should have been more likely to obtain communal rights. Consistent with this expectation, the communal movement began in the two most important trading regions of eleventh- and twelfth-century Europe: Northern Italy and the Low Countries (Lopez 1966). Moreover, recent HPE work has shown that English towns with geographic characteristics conducive to trade (Angelucci, Meraglia, and Nico Voigtlander 2020), Italian towns with greater urban potential (Cox, Dincecco, and Onorato 2021), and Spanish towns with greater exposure to Atlantic trade (Figueroa 2021a) were all more likely to acquire communal rights than otherwise similar towns in their respective polities.

Trade potential likely affected not just merchants' incentives to acquire governance rights, but also their ability to do so. In part, this was a simple income effect—richer merchants could afford to bid for rights—as Pirenne (1946) suggests. But Belloc, Drago, and Galbiati (2017) show that the western corporation, the invention of which helped merchants pool their capital (Berman 1983), was quickly used to help them bid for governance rights.

Other recent HPE works have examined how the opposition of bishops (Belloc, Drago, and Galbiati 2016), the support of Cluniac reformers (Doucette and Møller 2021), the early church's prohibitions on cousin marriage (Schulz 2019), and the papal church's geopolitical strategy (Grzymala-Busse 2021) affected communal births. The correlation between trade potential and communal birth remains robust when controlling for these important factors (Cox, Dincecco, and Onorato 2021).

Notably, a similar logic operated outside of Europe but was mediated by ethnic groups rather than formal institutions of governance. In particular, Jha (2013, 806) shows that when "Hindus and Muslims could provide complementary, non-replicable services" in the trade between India and the Middle East, they were more likely to devise "a mechanism to share the gains from exchange." Similar intracity cooperation between nongovernmental actors seeking trade profits was presumably widespread throughout Eurasia. The west stood out in that the lure of trade profits engendered cooperation between governmental units: horizontal cooperation between self-governing cities (via city leagues) and vertical cooperation between towns and monarchs (via parliaments).

Trade Potential Predicted Which Towns Kept Their Rights of Self-Government

Consistent with the idea that local self-government acted as a complementary input in merchants' trading activities, Blaydes and Paik (2016, 575–578) find that communal rights survived for longer periods in towns that acquired trading connections to the Middle East during the Crusades. Similarly, Angelucci, Meraglia, and Voigtlander (2020) show that English towns with better trade endowments were more able to resist royal efforts to undermine communal independence, while Becker, Ferrara, Melander, and Pascali (2018) show that medieval trading cities in the German lands were more likely to have elected and independent town councils.

Shocks to Trade Potential Predicted More Innovative Local Government

If governance rights were complements to merchants' other assets, then autonomous towns that experienced positive shocks to their trade potential should have responded with changes in governance designed to capture their new trading opportunities. In particular, a city whose location afforded it access to a large new potential flow of trade would benefit more by creating efficient and honest markets and judicial processes than an otherwise similar city located farther from trade routes. Competition between autonomous cities located nearest least-cost trade routes should thus have promoted innovation in governmental transparency and efficiency.

The literature on the two biggest positive trade shocks experienced by premodern Europe—the eleventh-century commercial revolution (sparked by the resurgence of trade with the Middle East; Lopez 1971) and the Gutenberg-Atlantic shock of the fifteenth century (sparked by the discovery of movable-type printing and of Atlantic sea routes)—provides evidence consistent with this conjecture. Each shock was associated with significant governmental innovation at the local level led by trading communes.

Consider first the region that led the eleventh-century commercial revolution: Northern Italy. On the one hand, this area introduced the most important innovations in trade-related legal processes, including new methods of incorporation (Huff 1993, ch. 4), the bill of exchange (Hunt and Murray 1999, 65), partnership (*commenda*) contracts (Pryor 1974; Greif 2006), and deposit banking (Hunt and Murray 1999, 64–65). On the other hand, this area also innovated in public finance—including public debt, public accounts, and transparent procedures (Stasavage 2011; Rothstein and Broms 2013). Investigating a wider swathe of European regions, Blaydes and Paik (2016, 551) show that "areas with large numbers of Holy Land crusaders"—who could learn of new trade opportunities while on crusade—"witnessed increased ... institutional development as well as greater urbanization associated with rising trade and capital accumulation."

When the Atlantic trade routes opened, self-governing cities with good Atlantic ports should have led the pack in governmental innovations useful in capturing the new trade opportunities. In the context of a sudden surge of global trade with many participating cities, the ability to contract efficiently outside of family and kin networks ("impersonal exchange") would have become very valuable. Consistent with this conjecture, a series of studies has shown that cities like Amsterdam, Antwerp, and London were at the forefront of constructing impersonal markets and supporting them with appropriate contractual infrastructure (Ogilvie 2011; Gelderblom 2013; Puttevils 2015). To examine this pattern more systematically, Raj (2020) constructs a panel data set documenting the extent to which Europe's largest cities supported impersonal exchange in the fourteenth to sixteenth centuries. He finds that the most innovative cities were Atlantic communes heavily exposed to Gutenberg's new printing technology.

Complementarities and the Debate over the Direction of Causality

Students of both premodern and modern polities often debate whether good political institutions promote economic growth or economic growth promotes good political institutions. For example, did town self-government promote growth, or did growing towns acquire governance rights?

If governance rights complemented merchants' other productive assets, then causal mechanisms should have operated in both directions. First, when merchants purchased governance rights, the value of their other assets should have increased, shifting their demand curve for labor upward and increasing the amount they invested in confiscable assets. Consistent with this expectation, several studies find that towns acquiring communal status grew faster (De Long and Shleifer 1993; Bosker, Buringh, and van Zanden 2013; Cox 2017). This growth could later peter out, if urban elites decided that local rent extraction was the most profitable use of their governance powers (Stasavage 2014).

Second, when trade was expanding, merchants should have valued governance rights more and had more resources to purchase them. Evidence I reviewed earlier shows that communes were indeed more likely to emerge where trade was more vibrant.

OUTSIDE EUROPE

Although beyond the scope of this article, some summary remarks about legislative power in other parts of Eurasia are in order. First, there was no secular SOP. While noble councils were common (Ahmed and Stasavage 2020), they lacked the de jure right to block imperial decrees.

Second, when legislative power was delegated, it often took the simple form of viceroyalty. In other cases, power was delegated to appointed agents who had to act in concert. For example, the market official and the *kadi* jointly set market prices in the Ottoman Empire (Boyar 2013, 282). One might speculate that the purpose of joint delegation was to restrain rent extraction.

Third, the delegation of legislative power to corporate bodies was extremely rare outside Europe. Weber's (1958 [1921]) claim that self-governing towns emerged only in Europe has stood up. Japanese towns (Inaba 2010) and Vietnamese villages (Dell, Lane, and Querubin 2018) had some elements similar to European town governance—collective responsibility for taxes, along with some capacity for local rule-making and collective action. However, they lacked rights that crucially underpinned European towns' bargaining position—most notably the rights to raise militias, build walls, and exclude royal officials from entering town on official business.

Fourth, the delegation of administrative powers outside Europe sometimes looked similar to delegations in the patrimonial states of Europe. For example, during the Abbasid Caliphate, merchant elites in the trading cities of central Asia secured hereditary holds on certain offices (Grinberg 2013, 901), an arrangement reminiscent of venal office-holding.

Fifth, many forms of de facto urban autonomy emerged throughout Eurasia: "Heaven is high and the emperor is far away," as the Chinese maxim put it. But merchants could not invest on the security of de facto autonomy in the same way that their European counterparts could invest on the security of de facto autonomy that had been legalized and could be defended militarily (van Bavel, Buringh, and Dijkman 2018). There were important differences between episodic de facto and entrenched de jure autonomy.

Conclusion

In this essay, I have reviewed the HPE of separating and delegating legislative power in Europe. The separation of power has been a familiar theme at least since Montesquieu's (1989 [1748]) *Spirit of the Laws*. However, the delegation of legislative power predated the sharing of legislative power between executives and legislatures and created durable local governmental units whose successors still exist throughout Europe.

One theme of my essay has concerned the interrelations between levels of government. In particular, to what extent should we expect congruence across levels of government, with separations of power at all levels (or none)?

Another theme has concerned executive constraint. In particular, I have reviewed the two main secular institutional constraints on executive power devised in premodern Europe. The first and older method was co-administration—a system in which, however they were made, laws' implementation was left up to a wide array of officeholders who did not serve at the pleasure of the Crown and exercised considerable discretion in performing their official duties. Such officeholders were present within the central state itself and at various lower levels of government. The second method of executive constraint was co-legislation—anchored by the requirement that certain types of law had to receive the prior approval of an assembly of nobles, clerics, and eventually commoners. While the co-administrative constraint operated ex post and was something like a suspensory veto, co-legislative constraints operated ex ante and eventually became legally recognized veto rights.

Co-administration and co-legislation both created opportunities for gridlock. In the first case, the high cost of monitoring dispersed agents across vast spaces enabled foot-dragging in the implementation of royal laws—which I have analogized to ex post suspensory vetoes. In the second case, the Crown and parliament might not be able to agree on new laws—blocking each other's ambition with ex ante vetoes.

Acknowledgments

I thank Valentín Figueroa, Jacob Gerner Hariri, Jeffery Jenkins, and Jared Rubin for their helpful comments.

Notes

1. In another form of SOP, the executive issues decrees that are then subject to some form of veto by the legislature (Carey and Shugart 1998).
2. Some may prefer to reserve the word "delegation" for situations in which a monarch willingly alienates some power they possess. Here I view a monarch who had lost control over a territory as also "delegating" power, when he converted the de facto situation into a de jure right.
3. There is also a growing literature on religious constraints on executive power (e.g., Chaney 2013; Rubin 2017; Grzymala-Busse 2021).
4. I do not count the Polish *sejm* as a strong assembly since it could make decisions only by consensus.
5. In contrast, polities in which constraint was achieved by decentralizing legislative power suffered significant collective action problems and ended up with highly inegalitarian tax systems (Spain, France) or chronic inabilities to raise sufficient funds (Poland-Lithuania).
6. As several have noted, co-administration would have been essential to motivate effort where rulers lacked the capacity to monitor salaried bureaucrats (e.g., Kiser and Kane 2001; Coşgel and Miceli 2009).
7. I have focused on tax-based reasons to establish parliaments. However, early parliaments were also involved in royal successions (Møller 2017a; Kokkonen and Møller 2020).
8. In Poland-Lithuania, the provincial parliaments (*sejmiks*) exercised local tax vetoes that the central parliament (*sejm*) could not override, since it operated by consensus (eventually formalized via the *liberum veto*).

References

Ahmed, Ali, and David Stasavage. 2020. "Origins of Early Democracy." *American Political Science Review* 114, no. 2: 502–518.

Álavarez-Nogal, Carlos, and Christophe Chamley. 2013. "Debt Policy Under Constraints: Philip II, the Cortes, and Genoese Bankers." *Economic History Review* 67, no. 1: 192–213.

Angelucci, Charles, Simone Meraglia, and Nico Voigtlander. 2020. "How Merchant Towns Shaped Parliaments: From the Norman Conquest of England to the Great Reform Act." Working Paper, Columbia University.

Arteaga, Fernando, Desiree Desierto, and Mark Koyama. 2020. "Shipwrecked by Rents." Centre for Economic Policy Research Discussion Paper DP15300.

Barbiche, Bernard. 2012. *Les institutions de la monarchie française à l'époque modern XVIe-XVIIIe siècle*. Paris: Presses Universitaires de France.

Barzel, Yoram, and Edgar Kiser. 2002. "Taxation and Voting Rights in Medieval England and France." *Rationality and Society* 14, no. 4: 473–507.

Bates, Robert, and Da-Hsiang Donald Lien. 1985. "A Note on Taxation, Development, and Representative Government." *Politics and Society* 14, no. 1: 53–70.

Becker, Sascha, Andreas Ferrara, Eric Melander, and Luigi Pascali. 2018. "Wars, Local Political Institutions, and Fiscal Capacity: Evidence from Six Centuries of German History." Warwick Economics Research Paper 1182.

Belloc, Marianna, Francesco Drago, and Roberto Galbiati. 2016. "Earthquakes, Religion, and Transition to Self-Government in Italian Cities." *Quarterly Journal of Economics* 131, no. 4: 1875–1926.

Belloc, Marianna, Francesco Drago, and Roberto Galbiati. 2017. "Law, Human Capital, and the Emergence of Free City-States in Medieval Italy." CESifo Working Paper 6719.

Bentzen, Jeanet Sinding, Jacob Gerner Hariri, and James A. Robinson. 2017. "Power and Persistence: The Indigenous Roots of Representative Democracy." *Economic Journal* 129 (February): 678–714. https://doi.org/10.1111/ecoj.12568.

Berman, Howard. 1983. *Law and Revolution*. Cambridge, MA: Harvard University Press.

Blackstone, William. 1979. *Commentaries on the Laws of England: A Facsimile of the First Edition of 1765–1769*. Chicago: University of Chicago Press.

Blaydes, Lisa, and Eric Chaney. 2013. "The Feudal Revolution and Europe's Rise: Political Divergence of the Christian West and the Muslim World before 1500 CE." *American Political Science Review* 107, no. 1: 16–34.

Blaydes, Lisa, and Christopher Paik. 2016. "The Impact of Holy Land Crusades on State Formation: War Mobilization, Trade Integration, and Political Development in Medieval Europe." *International Organization* 70, no. 3: 551–586.

Blickle, Peter. 1998. *From the Communal Reformation to the Revolution of the Common Man*. Leiden: Brill.

Blockmans, Wim. 1997. "Representation (since the Thirteenth Century)." In *The New Cambridge Medieval History*, ed. Christopher Allmand, 29–64. Cambridge: Cambridge University Press.

Boerner, Lars, Jared Rubin, and Battista Severgnini. 2021. "A Time to Print, a Time to Reform." *European Economic Review* 138: 103826.

Boerner, Lars, and Battista Severgnini. 2019. "Time for Growth." King's Business School Working Paper No. 2019/4.

Bosker, Maarten, Eltjo Buringh, and Jan Luiten van Zanden. 2013. "From Baghdad to London: Unraveling Urban Development in Europe, the Middle East, and North Africa, 800–1800." *Review of Economics and Statistics* 95, no. 4: 1418–1437.

Boyar, Ebru. 2013. "The Ottoman City, 1500–1800." In *The Oxford Handbook of Cities in World History*, ed. Peter Clark, 275–291. Oxford: Oxford University Press.

Buringh, Eltjo, and Jan Luiten van Zanden. 2009. "Charting the 'Rise of the West': Manuscripts and Printed Books in Europe, a Long-Term Perspective from the Sixth through Eighteenth Centuries." *Journal of Economic History* 69, no. 2: 409–445.

Carey, John, and Matthew S. Shugart, eds. 1998. *Executive Decree Authority*. Cambridge: Cambridge University Press.

Chaney, Eric. 2013. "Revolt on the Nile: Economic Shocks, Religion, and Political Power." *Econometrica* 81, no. 5: 2033–2053.

Clark, Peter, and Paul Slack. 2007. "Introduction." In *Crisis and Order in English Towns, 1500-1700: Essays in Urban History, Volume 2*, 1–56. London: Routledge.

Coşgel, Metin M., and Thomas J. Miceli. 2009. "Tax Collection in History." *Public Finance Review* 37, no. 4: 399–420.

Cox, Gary W. 2016. *Marketing Sovereign Promises*. Cambridge: Cambridge University Press.

Cox, Gary W. 2017. "Political Institutions, Economic Liberty and the Great Divergence." *Journal of Economic History* 77, no. 3: 724–755.

Cox, Gary W. 2018. "British State Development after the Glorious Revolution." *European Review of Economic History* 24, no. 1: 24–45.

Cox, Gary W., and Mark Dincecco. 2020. "The Budgetary Origins of Fiscal-Military Prowess." *Journal of Politics* 83, no. 3: 851–866.

Cox, Gary W., Mark Dincecco, and Massimiliano Onorato. 2021. "War and the Roots of Representative Governance." Unpublished typescript, Stanford University.

Cox, Gary W., and Valentín Figueroa. 2021. "The Communal Revolution, Assortative Matching and the Great Divergence." Unpublished typescript, Stanford University.

Daunton, Martin. 2001. *Trusting Leviathan: The Politics of Taxation in Britain*. Cambridge: Cambridge University Press.

De la Croix, David, Frederic Docquier, Alice Fabre, and Robert Stelter. 2020. "The Academic Market and the Rise of Universities in Medieval and Early Modern Europe (1000–1800)." Unpublished typescript.

Debrett, J. 1792. *The Parliamentary Register: Or, History of the Proceedings and Debates of the House of Commons*. London: John Stockdale.

Dell, Melissa, Nathan Lane, and Pablo Querubin. 2018. "The Historical State, Local Collective Action, and Economic Development in Vietnam." *Econometrica* 86, no. 6: 2083–2121.

De Long, J. Bradford, and Andrei Shleifer. 1993. "Princes and Merchants: European City Growth before the Industrial Revolution." *Journal of Law and Economics* 36, no. 2: 671–702.

Dincecco, Mark. 2011. *Political Transformations and Public Finances Europe, 1650–1913*. Cambridge: Cambridge University Press.

Dittmar, Jeremiah, and Ralf Meisenzahl. 2020. "Public Goods Institutions, Human Capital, and Growth: Evidence from German History." *Review of Economic Studies* 87, no. 2: 959–996.

Doucette, Jonathan, and Jørgen Møller. 2021. "The Collapse of State Power, the Cluniac Reform Movement, and the Origins of Urban Self-Government in Medieval Europe." *International Organization* 75, no. 1: 204–223.

Downing, Brian. 1988. "Constitutionalism, Warfare, and Political Change in Early Modern Europe." *Theory and Society* 17, no. 1: 7–56.

Downing, Brian. 1989. "Medieval Origins of Constitutional Government in the West." *Theory and Society* 18, no. 2: 213–247.

Ertman, Thomas. 1997. *Birth of the Leviathan: Building States and Regimes in Medieval and Early Modern Europe*. Cambridge: Cambridge University Press.

Fernández Hevia, José María. 2001. "El Ejercicio de la Fórmula 'Obedecer y No Cumplir' por Parte de la Junta General del Principado durante el Siglo XVI." *Boletín del Real Instituto de Estudios Asturianos* 157: 123–50.

Figueroa, Valentín. 2021a. "The Consolidation of Royal Control: Evidence from Northern Castile, 1352–1787." *European Review of Economic History* 25, no. 3: 447–66.

Figueroa, Valentín. 2021b. "The Protestant Road to State Bureaucracy." Unpublished PhD dissertation, Stanford University.

Franco-Vivanco, Edgar. 2021. "Justice as Checks and Balances: Indigenous Claims in the Courts of Colonial Mexico." Unpublished typescript, University of Michigan.

Gailmard, Sean. 2017. "Building a New Imperial State: The Strategic Foundations of Separation of Powers in America." *American Political Science Review* 111, no. 4: 668–85.

Gailmard, Sean. 2021. "Imperial Governance and the Growth of Legislative Power in America." *American Political Science Review* 65, no. 4: 912–25.

Gailmard, Sean, and John W. Patty. 2012. "Formal Models of Bureaucracy." *Annual Review of Political Science* 15: 353–77.

Garfias, Francisco. 2019. "Elite Coalitions, Limited Government, and Fiscal Capacity Development: Evidence from Bourbon Mexico." *Journal of Politics* 81, no. 1: 94–111.

Garfias, Francisco, and Emily Sellars. 2020. "Epidemics, Rent Extraction, and the Value of Holding Office." *Journal of Political Institutions and Political Economy* 1, no. 4: 559–83.

Gelderblom, Oscar. 2013. *Cities of Commerce*. Princeton, NJ: Princeton University Press.

Gelderblom, Oscar, and Jonker Joost. 2013. "Low Countries Finance, 1348–1700." In *Handbook of Key Global Financial Markets, Institutions, and Infrastructure*, ed. Douglas W. Arner, Thorsten Beck, Charles W. Calomiris, Larry Neal, and Nicolas Veron, 175–83 Amsterdam: Elsevier.

George, Robert H. 1940. "The Charters Granted to English Parliamentary Corporations in 1688." *English Historical Review* 55, no. 217: 15–46.

Giuliano, P., and N. Nunn. 2013. "The Transmission of Democracy: From the Village to the Nation-State." *American Economic Review, Papers and Proceedings* 103, no. 3: 86–92.

Glete, Jan. 2002. *War and the State in Early Modern Europe*. London: Routledge.

Godsey, William. 2018. *The Sinews of Habsburg Power*. Oxford: Oxford University Press.

Grafe, Regina, and Alejandra Irigoin. 2012. "A Stakeholder Empire: The Political Economy of Spanish Imperial Rule in America." *Economic History Review* 65, no. 2: 609–51.

Greif, Avner. 2006. *Institutions and the Path to the Modern Economy*. Cambridge: Cambridge University Press.

Greif, A. 2008. "The Impact of Administrative Power on Political Economic Development: Toward a Political Economy of Implementation." In *Institutions and Economic Performance*, ed. E. Helpman, 17–63. Cambridge, MA: Harvard University Press.

Greif, Avner, Paul Milgrom, and Barry Weingast. 1994. "Coordination, Commitment and Enforcement: The Case of the Merchant Guild." *Journal of Political Economy* 102, no. 4: 745–76.

Grinberg, Lyuba. 2013. "'Is This City Yours or Mine?' Political Sovereignty and Eurasian Urban Centers in the Ninth to Twelfth Centuries." *Comparative Studies in Society and History* 55, no. 4: 895–921.

Grzymala-Busse, Anna. 2021. *Sacred Foundations: The Medieval and Religious Roots of European State Formation*. Unpublished typescript, Stanford University.

Guardado, Jenny. 2018. "Office-Selling, Corruption, and Long-Term Development in Peru." *American Political Science Review* 112, no. 4: 971–95.

Guardado, Jenny. 2020. "Hierarchical Oversight and the Value of Public Office: Evidence from Colonial Peru." Unpublished typescript, Georgetown University.

Hasen, Richard. 2019. "Polarization and the Judiciary." *Annual Review of Political Science* 22: 261–76.

Hintze, Otto. 1975 [1931]. "The Preconditions of Representative Government in the Context of World History." In *The Historical Essays of Otto Hintze*, ed. Felix Gilbert, 171–96. New York: Oxford University Press.

Hirschman, Albert. 1970. *The Passions and the Interests.* Princeton, NJ: Princeton University Press.

Huber, John D., and Charles Shipan. 2002. *Deliberate Discretion? The Institutional Foundations of Bureaucratic Autonomy.* New York: Cambridge University Press.

Huff, Toby. 1993. *The Rise of Early Modern Science.* Cambridge: Cambridge University Press.

Hunt, Edwin S., and James M. Murray. 1999. *A History of Business in Medieval Europe, 1200–1550.* Cambridge: Cambridge University Press.

Inaba, Tsuguharu. 2010. "Community Vitality in Medieval Japan." In *War and State Building in Medieval Japan*, edited by John A. Ferejohn and Frances McCall Rosenbluth, 71–90. Stanford, CA: Stanford University Press.

Jago, Charles. 1981. "Habsburg Absolutism and the Cortes of Castile." *American Historical Review* 86, no. 2: 307–26.

Jha, Saumitra. 2013. "Trade, Institutions and Ethnic Tolerance: Evidence from South Asia." *American Political Science Review* 107, no. 4: 806–32.

Kiser, Edgar, and Joshua Kane. 2001. "Revolution and State Structure: The Bureaucratization of Tax Administration in Early Modern England and France." *American Journal of Sociology* 107, no. 1: 183–223.

Kokkonen, Andrej, and Jørgen Møller. 2020. "Succession, Power-Sharing and the Development of Representative Institutions in Medieval Europe." *European Journal of Political Research* 59, no. 4: 954–75.

Koyama, Mark. 2014. "The Law and Economics of Private Prosecutions in Industrial Revolution England." *Public Choice* 159: 277–98.

Kuran, Timur. 2018. "Islam and Economic Performance." *Journal of Economic Literature* 56, no. 4: 1292–359.

Lopez, Robert. 1966. *The Birth of Europe.* New York: M. Evans and Co.

Lopez, Robert. 1971. *The Commercial Revolution of the Middle Ages, 950–1350.* New York: Prentice-Hall.

Manin, Bernard. 1997. *The Principles of Representative Government.* Cambridge: Cambridge University Press.

Mitterauer, Michael. 2009. *Why Europe?* Chicago: University of Chicago Press.

Møller, Jørgen. 2017a. "The Birth of Representative Institutions: The Case of the Crown of Aragon." *Social Science History* 41, no. 2: 175–200.

Møller, Jørgen. 2017b. *State Formation, Regime Change and Economic Development.* London: Routledge.

Montesquieu, Charles de Secondat. 1989 [1748]. *Spirit of the Laws.* Cambridge: Cambridge University Press.

Napolito, Nicholas, and Jordan Carr Peterson. 2021. "Institutional Foundations of the American Revolution: Legislative Politics in Colonial North America." *Journal of Historical Political Economy* 1: 235–57.

North, Douglass C., and Barry R. Weingast. 1989. "Constitutions and Commitment: The Evolution of Institutions Governing Public Choice in Seventeenth-Century England." *Journal of Economic History* 49, no. 4: 803–32.

Ogilvie, S. 2011. *Institutions and European Trade: Merchant Guilds, 1000–1800.* Cambridge: Cambridge University Press.

Pasquet, D. 1964. *An Essay on the Origins of the House of Commons.* 2nd ed. London: Merlin Press.

Pirenne, Henri. 1946. *Medieval Cities: Their Origins and the Revival of Trade.* Oxford: Oxford University Press.

Prak, Maarten. 2018. *Citizens without Nations.* Cambridge: Cambridge University Press.

Pryor, John. 1974. "The Origins of the Commenda Contract." *Speculum* 52, no. 1: 5–37.

Puga, Diego, and Daniel Trefler. 2014. "International Trade and Institutional Change: Medieval Venice's Response to Globalization." *Quarterly Journal of Economics* 129, no. 2: 753–821.

Puttevils, J. 2015. *Merchants and Trading in the Sixteenth Century: The Golden Age of Antwerp.* London: Routledge.

Raj, Prateek. 2020. "Trade and Information Shocks, and Market Development: Evidence from Early Modern Europe." Working Paper, George J. Stigler Center for the Study of the Economy and the State, University of Chicago.

Rothstein, Bo, and Rasmus Broms. 2013. "Governing Religion: The Long-Term Effects of Sacred Financing." *Journal of Institutional Economics* 9, no. 4: 469–90.

Rubin, Jared. 2017. *Rulers, Religion, and Values: Why the West Got Rich and the Middle East Did Not.* Cambridge: Cambridge University Press.

Schulz, Jonathan. 2019. "Kin Networks and Institutional Development." Working Paper, Harvard University.

Spruyt, Hendrik. 1994. *The Sovereign State and Its Competitors.* Princeton, NJ: Princeton University Press.

Squire, Peverill. 2017. *The Rise of the Representative: Lawmakers and Constituents in Colonial America.* Ann Arbor: University of Michigan Press.

Stasavage, David. 2011. *States of Credit: Size, Power, and the Development of European Polities.* Princeton, NJ: Princeton University Press.

Stasavage, David. 2014. "Was Weber Right? The Role of Urban Autonomy in Europe's Rise." *American Political Science Review* 108, no. 2: 337–54.

Stasavage, David. 2020. *The Decline and Rise of Democracy: A Global History from Antiquity to Today.* Princeton, NJ: Princeton University Press.

Swart, Koenraad Wolter. 1949. *Sale of Offices in the Seventeenth Century.* 'S-Gravenhage: Martinus Nijhoff.

Tiebout, Charles. 1956. "A Pure Theory of Local Expenditures." *Journal of Political Economy* 64, no. 5: 416–24.

Tocqueville, Alexis de. 2000 [1835]. *Democracy in America.* Chicago: University of Chicago Press.

Uckelman, Sara, and Joel Uckelman. 2020. "Strategy and Manipulation in Medieval Elections." Brewminate. July 20. https://brewminate.com/strategy-and-manipulation-in-medieval-elections/.

van Bavel, Bas, Eltjo Buringh, and Jessica Dijkman. 2018. "Mills, Cranes, and the Great Divergence: The Use of Immovable Capital Goods in Western Europe and the Middle East, Ninth to Sixteenth Centuries." *Economic History Review* 71, no. 1: 31–54.

Van Zanden, Jan Luiten, Eltjo Buringh, and Maarten Bosker. 2012. "The Rise and Decline of European Parliaments, 1188–1789." *Economic History Review* 65, no. 3: 835–61.

Wahl, Fabian. 2016. "Participative Political Institutions in Pre-Modern Europe: Introducing a New Database." *Historical Methods* 49: 67–79.

Weber, Max. 1958 [1921]. *The City*. New York: Free Press.

Weingast, Barry R. 1995. "The Economic Role of Political Institutions: Market-Preserving Federalism and Economic Development." *Journal of Law, Economics, and Organization* 20, no. 1: 1–31.

Xu, Guo. 2018. "The Costs of Patronage: Evidence from the British Empire." *American Economic Review* 108, no. 11: 3170–98.

CHAPTER 18

COURTS

A Historical Political Economy Perspective

TOM S. CLARK AND GEORG VANBERG

INTRODUCTION

JUDICIAL institutions are ubiquitous and fundamental to social life—even in "stateless" societies, which typically feature (quasi-)judicial institutions for dispute resolution. Of course, there are significant differences between such early "mediation" institutions and the complex judicial institutions found in contemporary advanced industrial societies. The history, development, and functioning of judicial systems have been the subject of a voluminous scholarly literature, and it would be impossible to treat all but a small slice in the confines of a chapter. Here we focus on the conceptual contributions to our understanding of the role and development of judicial institutions that have emerged from the historical political economy (HPE) literature.

We organize the chapter around three main themes.[1] The first deals with the origins and impetus for the creation of courts as dispute resolution mechanisms in private interactions. We describe research that documents the development of informal, quasi-judicial institutions into more formal judicial structures. A second major theme concerns the expansion of courts into institutions that constrain the exercise of political power. We describe analytic and historical studies that trace the integration of courts from stand-alone mechanisms of dispute resolution to essential and ubiquitous components of most modern forms of government. Finally, we consider judicial influence and independence. Courts can only serve as impartial conflict resolution mechanisms and constrain power if relevant actors comply with their decisions, and if courts are reasonably insulated against inappropriate interference and pressure.

Courts as Private Dispute Resolution Mechanisms

Informal and formal institutions that govern dispute resolution are among the earliest features of human societies. This is, of course, not surprising. Social life inevitably gives rise to two types of disputes: conflicts among individuals that arise out of involuntary interactions (such as assault or theft, but also unintentional harms such as those covered by modern tort law) and disputes that emerge among individuals engaged in voluntary, cooperative ventures (e.g., disagreements over the performance of contractual obligations). One way to resolve such conflicts, and to deter the behavior that gives rise to them, lies in recourse to violence among the disputants and their allies. The institution of the feud—common in many "anarchic" societies—represents the institutionalized form of this dispute resolution mechanism (Bates 1983; Volckart 2004).

Scholars have long recognized that despite its violent character, the institution of the feud can be an important source of social order. The threat of violence can deter behavior that is likely to provoke a dispute, and it encourages individuals to settle their differences before a confrontation occurs. Thus, there can be a kind of "justice" or "peace in the feud" (Bates 1983; Gluckman 1955; Wormald 1980). Nevertheless, as scholars have also argued, the threat of private violence has significant drawbacks as a general mechanism for resolving disagreements. Most obviously, when deterrence fails and violence breaks out, it undermines social order and may lead to spirals of retaliation. Second, violence is destructive for the disputants as well as for third parties who may suffer the spillover effects of conflict, as ex post both parties (and outside observers) would prefer to have agreed to that settlement immediately without engaging in a fight. Institutions providing adjudication offer significant benefits for society at large.

Appeal to a (neutral) third party that mediates between the disputants and suggests a settlement offers an obvious solution—and one that is virtually universal in recorded human history. Thus, "feuding societies" are typically characterized by strong social norms that require disputants to seek third-party adjudication before resorting to violence. The "leopard-skin chief" among the Nuer tribe provides an example: a prominent religious leader, the chief also had the role of mediating and resolving disputes, although he had little authority to impose a solution. Nevertheless, as Evans-Pritchard (1940, 164) reports, such mediation could often avert violence because a man "can give way to the chief ... where he would not have given way to his opponent." Similarly, scholars have emphasized the role of "peacemakers" and arbitrators (often religious elites) in mediating disputes in feud-ridden medieval Europe (e.g., see Koziol 1987; Miller 1990; White 1986) and in settling myriad conflicts in societies that have otherwise few or no formal rules of governance (e.g., Malinowski 1926). Perhaps more important than the resolution of actual disputes are the anticipatory effects of these institutions. Knowing that disputes can be resolved peacefully can transform behavior as individuals become willing to engage in ventures they would not pursue in the absence of effective adjudication.

The significance of these anticipatory effects is evident with respect to the economic consequences of effective (quasi-)judicial institutions. As North (1993) stresses, economic growth depends on institutional developments that reduce transactions costs. Institutions that lower these costs make exchanges worthwhile that would not be profitable in the presence of higher transactions costs, thus leading to economic growth. Milgrom, North, and Weingast (1990) and Greif (2006) apply this general insight to the development of medieval legal institutions that governed commercial transactions.

The expansion of trade and financial transactions in medieval Europe created significant opportunities for opportunistic behavior. Trades were often not simultaneous, and they typically extended across political jurisdictions; for example, cloth merchants from northern Italy might offer samples at the Champagne fairs outside Paris, take orders and partial payment, and promise to return in a few months' time with their wares to complete the exchange. Clearly, such transactions raise the specter that a trader might cheat a partner and disappear, or attempt to renege on a contract at a later date. Successful expansion of trade thus required mechanisms that could deter cheating and provide reliable enforcement of contractual obligations. The development of the "law merchant," a set of "legal codes governing commercial transactions and administered by private judges drawn from the commercial ranks" (Milgrom, North, and Weingast 1990, 4) provided one solution. The merchant legal code clarified and stabilized expectations, and merchant courts provided swift adjudication of disputes. Records were available to other merchants for inspection, providing information about the past behavior of potential trading partners, including compliance with adverse rulings. Similarly, Greif (2006) studies "community responsibility systems" that were widely used across medieval Europe; in such systems, traders were held jointly responsible for the behavior of all members of their community. For example, if a Florentine trader was cheated in London, Florentine officials might seize goods from English traders in Florence to compensate the victim. This system created significant incentives for local communities to ensure the fair treatment of outsiders within their jurisdiction. That is, in order to protect the reputation and equitable treatment of their own members when abroad, trading communities faced strong incentives to ensure that local courts would "protect alien merchants' property rights and to dispense impartial justice" (Greif 2006, 232). As scholars continue to demonstrate, the presence of efficient and (reasonably) impartial judiciaries continues to be a significant ingredient for economic development and growth (see, e.g., Voigt, Gutmann, and Feld 2015; Feld and Voigt 2003).

As these examples suggest, "quasi-judicial" institutions (such as mediators in feuding societies) emerged prior to the development of organized states, as well as separately and independently of existing states (such as medieval merchant courts). Indeed, as David Hume suggested in his essay "On the Origin of Government," contrary to the common perception that governments develop (in part) in order to provide institutions of justice, the historical development may be precisely the other way around: organized political power evolves endogenously out of "anarchic" arbitration institutions.

Hume offers a conjectural but plausible account: The first origins of "authority" in social groups emerge during times of intertribal conflict and war, when leadership is critical to military success. The social status ("salience") achieved by a war chief, Hume (1985, 40) conjectures, makes him a natural candidate as third-party arbitrator of disputes even in times of peace—a position that can, over time, grow into "government":

> If the chieftain possessed as much equity as prudence and valour, he became even during peace, the arbiter of all differences, and could gradually, by a mixture of force and consent, establish his authority ... and if his son enjoyed the same good qualities, government advanced the sooner to maturity and perfection; but was still in a feeble state, till the farther progress of improvement procured the magistrate a revenue, and enabled him to bestow rewards on the several instruments of his administration, and to inflict punishments on the refractory and disobedient.... Submission was no longer a matter of choice in the bulk of the community, but was rigorously exacted by the authority of the supreme magistrate.

The discussion so far suggests a number of claims about the role and impact of third-party dispute resolution:

Claim 1. *Even in the absence of formal government, third-party mediation is a nearly ubiquitous institution of dispute resolution in human societies.*

Claim 2. *Effective third-party mediation of disputes is central to expanding opportunities for cooperation and trade.*

Quasi-judicial Institutions versus Courts

Hume's conjectural history points to a crucial distinction between quasi-judicial mediation institutions and full-fledged, state-backed judicial systems. As Hume stresses, the initial emergence of effective third-party adjudication is contingent on the parties' consent. There are two elements to this: Ex ante, disputing parties must agree to seek mediation by the arbiter; ex post, the parties must voluntarily abide by the arbiter's proposed solution. More generally, unlike full-scale judicial systems backed by the coercive force of the state, quasi-judicial institutions (such as informal arbiters in feuding societies or the courts of the medieval law merchant) typically cannot compel attendance or compliance by the parties. They must rely on the willingness of disputants to seek out their services and their voluntary compliance with their (suggested) resolution of a dispute. These features impose significant constraints.

Most obviously, third-party arbitration can only be effective if it is incentive-compatible for the parties. What does this entail? The potential benefit of third-party resolution lies in the avoidance of (destructive) violence. The fact that violence is costly for both parties creates a bargaining range: A skilled arbitrator can identify a settlement that—given that accepting it avoids the costs of violence—is preferable for both parties to an armed conflict. If such a settlement is proposed, both parties are willing to abide by its terms. Moreover, an arbiter known for reliably suggesting such settlements can attract "business" since both parties can benefit from her services. In contrast, an arbiter whose suggested resolution falls outside of the bargaining range of one of the parties will be ignored.

In other words, quasi-judicial institutions must be sensitive to the distributional outcomes that are expected to prevail if the disputants choose to forgo arbitration or to ignore an arbiter's decision. These outcomes define the reversion point for the parties, and only decisions that respect these floors can find acceptance. In this limited sense, the need to ensure voluntary compliance generates powerful incentives for arbiters to be "impartial" (or, as Hume puts it, to possess "equity").

Of course, such "impartiality" need not (indeed, often will not) conform to particular normative visions of what it means to be impartial or what a "just" settlement entails. Instead, it merely reflects the de facto distribution of power between the parties if they forgo arbitration. Because quasi-judicial institutions cannot compel obedience and must secure voluntary compliance, their decisions will typically split the difference between the parties; a solution that is too one-sided is likely to fall outside the bargaining range and meet with defiance. However, what this difference is, and which kinds of settlements are too one-sided, depends critically on the outside option. Parties who are left in a strong position by the outside option must be treated more favorably by the arbiter's decision.

Claim 3. *When third-party dispute resolutions are voluntary, the extent to which a party finds it beneficial will often be related to his or her underlying power in the absence of the judicial institution.*

Broman and Vanberg (2022) illustrate that, paradoxically, the advantages bestowed on stronger parties are not all good news. Recognizing that they are not likely to "get justice" in arbitration because the arbiter is constrained by the need to satisfy a strong opponent, individuals will avoid interactions with those whose actions arbitration cannot effectively regulate. Critically, "such avoidance ... is costly for weak *and* strong players: Ironically, reliance on a dispute resolution mechanism that seemingly favors those who are (militarily) strong limits the ability of these players to engage in mutually advantageous exchange" (Broman and Vanberg 2022, 19). These dynamics undercut judicial institutions' ability to lower transaction costs and enlarge the scope for cooperation.

A paper by Kuran and Rubin (2018) provides intriguing evidence of this dynamic in the context of financial markets in the Ottoman Empire. Ottoman courts were systematically biased in favor of individuals from certain social groups: men, Muslims, and elites with close connections to the sultan. As a result, anyone engaging in financial transactions with such individuals had to fear that contractual disputes would be adjudicated in a venue sympathetic to the other party. This implied that privileged individuals constituted more significant risks, suggesting a higher risk premium compared to those who were *not* members of the privileged classes. This is precisely what

Kuran and Rubin (2018) find: interest rates charged to privileged individuals typically exceeded the interest rates paid by the "powerless," including women and non-Muslims.

Moving toward Compulsory Adjudication

The fact that quasi-judicial institutions rely on voluntary cooperation by the parties is thus potentially problematic in two senses. First, the resolution of conflicts must be consistent with the underlying power of the parties, and therefore may not correspond to prevailing normative visions of what justice requires. Second, the fact that such institutions do not allow "strong" parties credibly to commit to being constrained undercuts the (economic) benefits of third-party dispute resolution (see Claim 2). A solution to these problems is to move to dispute resolution backed by the ability to compel compliance. This, of course, is precisely one of the key characteristics of formal, state-backed judicial systems. As state capacity grows, societies typically establish formal judicial institutions that are able to impose resolutions (see, e.g., Messick 2002). The sweeping description of the evolution of judicial institutions in England following the Norman Conquest offered more than one hundred years ago by Pollock (1898, 229) captures more general trends:

> Here then was the beginning of a new system of jurisdiction. It grew and prevailed in a manner thoroughly typical of English reforms, not by any exclusive establishment, but by superior merit. The King had to do justice for some particular purposes. His justice was much stronger than any other; if costly, it was well worth the cost; and its extension was as welcome to suitors as unwelcome to those who made their profit of small folk's weakness or timidity. Not that the King's justice was offered to the people at large in the first instance; it was eagerly sought after as a privilege. Even when it became general, there was no word of abolishing the old popular courts and their procedure. They were merely superseded by the greater convenience of the royal courts, or of private lords' courts which imitated the royal methods as closely as they could; at last, and very gradually, they perished by disuse, leaving but a few traces to be swept away by systematic modern legislation.

Origins of Courts as Institutions of Governance

In most states, the peaceful, efficient, and equitable mediation of conflict is critical to the maintenance of social order and is the judiciary's primary task. However, in many political systems, the role of state-sponsored courts goes beyond the resolution of conflicts between private parties. Courts also offer a mechanism for resolving grievances by citizens against rulers, and for enforcing the political rules of the game, including limits on the power of the state. Although there are some historical precursors, this political function of courts is a phenomenon that has come into its own only over the past few hundred years. Moreover, in what some scholars have characterized as a "global expansion of judicial power," the political role of courts has expanded dramatically since World War II, particularly in democratic states (Tate and Vallinder 1995). What explains such an extension of the judicial role to include constraining those who hold political power?

The most important factor that explains this expansion is the desire by powerful interests outside of the formal machinery of government—most obviously, citizens at large—to subject the political process to rules and constraints. Courts are an important tool for doing so. The institutional reforms initiated in England during the Glorious Revolution provide a clear illustration. North and Weingast (1989) analyze these reforms through a political economy lens. Throughout the seventeenth century, the English Crown responded to significant financial pressures it was facing by adopting a series of predatory fiscal practices, including forcing loans or reneging on their terms, as well as outright confiscation. Elites felt their (property) rights were under threat and lost trust in the Crown. North and Weingast (1989) argue that existing political institutions had little ability to limit the king's excesses, as the monarch controlled judges and could dismiss or ignore Parliament. The resulting civil war ended with the deposition of James II, and his replacement—at the hands of parliament—by William of Orange and his wife, Mary, conditional on their acceptance of a number of institutional reforms that would rein in royal power. These included giving Parliament control over major fiscal matters, subordinating royal prerogatives to the common law, and beginning a process of judicial reforms (including abolition of the Star Chamber) that had the effect of making judges independent of the Crown and—so ran the expectation—capable of resisting royal encroachments. While the story is more complex, a key takeaway for our purposes is the fact that, fueled by a desire to constrain royal power, powerful interests opposed to the Crown pushed for reforms that constrained royal power and elevated the role of courts in enforcing these limits.

The desire to limit power, including using courts to do so, has been a consistent theme in the emergence of constitutionally constrained democratic governance over the past few centuries. Hayek (1960) famously argues it was the political thought surrounding the creation of the 1787 US constitution that developed the first thorough conception of judicial review and the role of judges in maintaining constitutional limits. Gordon (1999, 320) concludes,

> Indeed, no clearer statement of the doctrine of judicial review can be found in the literature before [*The Federalist Papers*], and Hamilton's exposition of it is at least the equal of Chief Justice John Marshall's in the Supreme Court's decision in *Marbury v. Madison* (1803), which is commonly referred to by constitutional historians as its locus classicus.

While the institution of judicial review developed in a robust manner in American federal and state courts over the course of the nineteenth century, it did not take hold in

European parliamentary systems, based largely on the civil law tradition, until the twentieth century. In proposing the explicit introduction of constitutional review in his draft of the 1920 Austrian Constitution, Hans Kelsen drew directly on the American experience (see Cappelletti 1989; Vanberg 2005). Significantly, Kelsen's model of constitutional review departs in key ways from the decentralized form of judicial review exercised by US courts. Skeptical of the ability of ordinary courts to handle the politically sensitive task of evaluating executive and legislative action against constitutional norms, Kelsen advocated the creation of a separate tribunal—a constitutional court—outside of the ordinary judicial hierarchy, in which constitutional review was to be concentrated. Such "Kelsen courts" have become a standard feature of most parliamentary democracies and play a central—and often powerful—role in shaping politics. The creation of such courts since the end of the Cold War demonstrates the present presumption among constitution-writers that good governance requires oversight of political actors by independent courts (e.g., see Schwartz 2000). More recently, even international courts have become increasingly important in constraining national governments. For example, the European Court of Justice's emergence as a powerful constraint on EU governments is largely attributable to the court adjusting its jurisprudence to align with citizen preferences in member states (see, e.g., Carrubba 2009; Carrubba and Gabel 2014).

Claim 4. *A desire among constitution-makers to impose constitutional limits on political power leads to an empowerment of courts and an expanded political role for the judiciary.*

However, that constitution-writers have looked to judges to enforce constitutional limits on executives and legislatures does not directly explain how and why judges are willing and able to exercise these newfound powers. What has led judges to exercise the power of judicial review more expansively, and what explains their power to do so? We begin with the first question, and treat the second in the chapter's final section.

The "Activation" of Courts

A key feature that distinguishes courts from other governance institutions—most notably legislatures and executives—is that they are reactive; unlike other branches, which can take policy initiatives on issues of their choosing, courts are largely constrained to act on the cases that outside actors bring to them.[2] They may have some ability to "signal" their willingness to hear certain cases and thereby encourage litigants. But they remain constrained to act within the set of issues brought before them.

Thus, to understand the expansion of courts' reach—especially judicial review—into wider areas of political life (Tate and Vallinder 1995), we must examine the role private actors play in bringing issues to courts that allow for such growth. Scholars refer to this process as "activation from below." Epp (1998) examines the "rights revolution," arguing that the central factor is the presence of well-organized interests that have the resources to sustain systematic litigation campaigns in the courts. If such groups turn to courts to advance their claims, "judges who are sympathetic to expanding the role of courts have more opportunities to do so—and judges who are reluctant will often have no choice but to wade into waters that might ordinarily have been left as the exclusive domain of elected policymakers" (Vanberg 2020, 11). It is not difficult to see why the *organized* groups are so central to this process: effective legal action to achieve systemic policy change requires long-term litigation that builds on incremental victories, provides an ability to monitor compliance, and renews litigation when policymakers resist. Individual litigants, whose interests are primarily tied to the specific dispute in which they are involved, are typically not in a position—legally or with respect to resources—to wage such a campaign. In contrast, organized interests can take on such a task, backing individual litigants in specific cases as part of a broader strategic initiative.

Naturally, the ability as well as the incentive for organized groups to pursue their claims through the courts depends on a number of other factors. One concerns the relevant legal framework. Judges are expected to provide a legal basis for their decisions—they are, at least in theory, constrained by law (e.g., see Friedman 2006). As a result, where constitutional language or relevant precedents provide more immediate grounding for particular claims, such as expanded rights protections, the prospects for "judicialization" increase. A second aspect focuses on groups' prospects for success from legal action compared to advancing their claims in other venues. Specifically, where political fragmentation is high (for example, under a strict separation of powers compared to a parliamentary system), achieving policy change through the regular political process may be difficult. This increases the incentives for organized groups to turn to courts, especially if the legal environment is favorable. As Ferejohn (2002, 55) observes, "When the political branches cannot act, people seeking resolution to conflicts will tend to gravitate to institutions from which they can get solutions; courts (and associated legal processes) often offer such venues." The expansion of marriage equality provides a useful example. In the United States, a highly fragmented (and polarized) political system offered little prospect of legislative enactment of same-sex marriage. Instead, supportive groups focused on a long-term legal campaign in the courts, culminating ultimately in the Supreme Court's decision in *Obergefell v. Hodges* (576 U.S. 644). In contrast, in Europe, where parliamentary systems ensure that executives are backed by a cohesive legislative majority, the push for same-sex marriage focused primarily on legislative action.

Whence Judicial Power?

Of course, this political role for courts gives rise to the potential for high-stakes conflict between courts and other branches of government. That conflict has ranged from relatively low-level arguments, such as modern-day American politicians criticizing the US Supreme Court (see, e.g., Nagel 1964; Rosenberg 1992; Clark 2011) to much more serious forms of conflict, such as Latin American experience with violent and force-based pressure against judges (see, e.g., Brinks, Helmke, and Ríos-Figueroa 2011; Helmke 2017; Ríos-Figueroa 2007). Significantly, courts are typically in a relatively weak institutional position relative to the other branches of government when such conflicts occur. As compared with legislatures and executives, which command purse strings and military, police, and executive force, courts rely on the force of their words and little more—a point Alexander Hamilton famously made in *Federalist 78*. What, then, puts courts in a position to exercise these powers effectively?

Judicial Power and Independence

Under what conditions can courts be powerful and influential? This involves two aspects. First, other political actors must comply with (or enforce) judicial decisions. Second, other actors must respect judges' ability to make decisions free of inappropriate interference and pressure.

Both of these components are central to the ideal of judicial independence—a feature of judicial systems that is typically regarded as central to constitutionally constrained democratic systems. Independent courts are able to reach decisions that will be respected and that are grounded in considerations that are regarded as normatively and legally relevant. It is not difficult to see why judicial independence is valuable—at least from the perspective of citizens as ultimate political sovereigns, when resolving private disputes, judicial impartiality toward the parties before them is key. By preventing inappropriate interference in the judicial process on behalf of a particular disputant, judicial independence enhances impartiality (Burbank 2002, 336). The value of judicial independence is even more self-evident with respect to the *political* role of courts: judges are unlikely to be able to police constitutional boundaries effectively unless they enjoy protections against inappropriate pressure by the other branches.

Historically, some of the earliest attempts to secure judicial independence arose precisely out of these twin concerns. For example, consider the creation of the Imperial Chamber Court—the Supreme Court of the Holy Roman Empire. Feuding, particularly among the nobility, had become increasingly disruptive, despite a number of attempts at judicial reform to secure peaceful resolution of disputes. By 1495, pressure became so powerful that King (later Emperor) Maximilian I consented to the creation of the Imperial Chamber Court. In exchange, the king secured continued funding for his military campaigns in Hungary and Italy (Wilson 2016).

This court was unique for its time but anticipates many of the formal features commonly associated with judicial independence. The judges were appointed for fixed terms in a complex system that blended selection powers for the king as well as feudal and ecclesiastical elites in a way that made it impossible for any estate or actor to dominate the court. Moreover, the court was located in a free imperial city and given an independent financial basis through a new tax designated for its budget. The court was also given the power to impose the imperial ban, a punishment traditionally reserved to the emperor (Broman and Vanberg 2022). In short, the Imperial Chamber Court enjoyed remarkable institutional independence for its day (see, e.g., Hartung 1972). Importantly, however, this institutional insulation of the court against political manipulation was not motivated by a desire to enable the court to oversee or constrain the *king's* actions—indeed, the court's jurisdiction did not include such powers. Instead, the goal of the "reform party" was to ensure that the court could act as an effective impartial arbiter in private disputes, thus replacing feuding with an "eternal public peace" (Hartung 1972, 94). This brief history illustrates that a concern for "for peace and order can underpin demand for judicial independence—not because courts regulate political power, but because the effectiveness of judicial dispute resolution hinges on protecting the impartiality of courts" (Vanberg, Broman, and Ritter, 2023, 10).

In contrast, consider the emergence of judicial independence in England. Following the Norman Conquest, the English legal system featured a patchwork of competing common law, ecclesiastical, and royal courts (Pollock 1898). Over time, the king's control over judges' tenure and compensation emerged as powerful tools that could be wielded to persecute political opponents and to expropriate wealth (North and Weingast 1989). The Glorious Revolution, mentioned earlier, led to institutional protections for judicial independence that were enshrined in law. The 1701 Act of Settlement provided for judicial tenure during good behavior, and prescribed that judges could only be removed with the approval of both houses of Parliament or the king's death. Over the next few decades, these protections were expanded. By 1760 the tenure of judges was extended beyond the king's death, and judges were provided with fixed pensions by 1799 (Stevens 2001; Shetreet and Turenne 2013). Unlike with the establishment of the Imperial Chamber Court, the primary goal of all of these reforms was not to ensure the impartiality of courts in resolving private disputes. Instead, the aim was to insulate the courts from royal interference and enable them to police effectively newly established boundaries on the monarchy (Vanberg, Broman, and Ritter 2023, 13).[3]

These examples stress the institutional aspects of judicial independence: the presence of particular formal structures—such as secure tenure in office or protection of judicial salaries—that are thought to enhance the ability of judges to resist pressure by outside actors.[4] Scholars refer to these features as "de jure" judicial independence, and distinguish it from "de facto" judicial independence, that is, the extent to which judges are, in practice, able to act independently (Hayo and Voigt 2019; Melton and Ginsburg 2002). Significantly, empirical work suggests that the connection between de facto and de jure independence is tenuous at best. In many countries, formal protections for the courts appear to go hand in hand with significant political interference in the judicial process, bringing to mind James Madison's famous observation that formal rules may simply be "parchment barriers" unless a mechanism exists to give them life.

Claim 5. *Formal institutions of judicial independence commonly include insulation for individual judges, such as tenure and salary protection. However, these rules do not ensure judges will have independence in practice.*

What, then, explains the emergence and maintenance of judiciaries that enjoy de facto independence? Put differently, under what circumstances are political actors in the executive and legislative branches either unable or unwilling to undermine judicial independence and to resist judicial decisions? This question is not trivial: To the extent that one of the critical roles of the judiciary is to enforce constitutional limits on the other branches, political actors in those branches may regularly find themselves in situations in which the courts pose unwelcome constraints.

Roughly speaking, scholars have identified three aspects, which we treat in turn:

- Conditions that constrain the ability of the other branches to threaten judicial independence.
- Conditions that generate prohibitive costs for the other branches to threaten judicial independence.
- Conditions that make judicial independence of direct value to the other branches.

The Political Capacity to Constrain Judicial Independence

The broader institutional environment within which courts are situated constitutes one critical factor. If power is fragmented across institutions, and undermining judicial independence or resisting judicial decisions requires coordination across separate political actors whose agreement is needed to make policy, courts are in a more powerful position. Thus, features such as presidentialism (in contrast to parliamentary systems), bicameralism, or federalism place greater obstacles in the way of formal attacks on judicial independence (Friedman 2004; Ríos-Figueroa 2007; Whittington 2003).[5] However, as scholars have pointed out more generally with respect to the impact of formal separation of powers, the presence of reasonably disciplined political parties in most advanced industrial democracies implies that the effect of formal institutional structures is contingent. Parties can coordinate policy initiatives across branches, and formal separation may have little practical impact when the same party controls the relevant institutions. For example, Clark (2011) demonstrates in the US context that when one party becomes dominant, attempts to engage in court-curbing increase, and judicial independence declines (see also Whittington 2003). Ramseyer (1994) shows that the dominant position of the Japanese Liberal Democratic Party (LDP) resulted in severe limits on judicial independence despite formal protections. In short, while formal structures can—under some conditions—inhibit attacks on judicial independence, de facto independence requires that actors who have opportunities to undermine the independence of the courts do not find it in their interest to do so. One reason may be that the political costs to be paid for threatening judicial independence are prohibitively high. A second—and more interesting—reason is that an independent judiciary can provide positive benefits to other political actors that outweigh any negatives.

The Political Costs of Undermining Independence

While political actors may have opportunities to undermine judicial independence, there may be costs for doing so. In all political systems, those who exercise authority are subject to pressure from other actors. Democratically accountable leaders, for example, must take into account the reactions of (sufficiently large groups of) citizens and organized interests to their political choices. A broad line of scholarship has argued that such outside actors may often have an interest in the presence of an independent judiciary, and therefore react negatively to perceived attempts to threaten it. Thus, as we described earlier, powerful forces—including citizens—likely have an interest in imposing constitutional constraints on the political process—which creates a strong (secondary) interest in maintaining an independent judiciary that can police these limits. Faced by clear outside support for the judiciary, political actors may conclude that even if courts pose unwelcome obstacles to their ambitions, it is politically too costly to move against them.

The two historical episodes of early attempts to establish independent courts clearly reflect this logic. Recall that the Imperial Chamber Court was created as a direct result of the pressure placed on King Maximilian I at the Diet of Worms. Why did this institution emerge, despite royal opposition? One reason was that the estates perceived an urgent need for an effective, independent court in order to establish peace in a society plagued by feuding nobles. Maximilian, in turn, depended on their cooperation in raising the funds necessary for his military campaigns. Similarly, the movement to secure the institutional independence of English courts from the Crown emerged in response to the perception that effective constraints on the monarchy required oversight by an independent judiciary—a demand that could be enforced by well-organized reform movements within Parliament.

In contemporary democratic settings, scholars point primarily to public support for the judiciary as a critical factor in maintaining judicial independence, focusing on a number of aspects. For example, employing archival work as well as elite interviews, Vanberg (2005) demonstrates that the deference of political elites to the German Bundesverfassungsgericht—widely regarded as one of the most powerful constitutional courts in the world—derives to a significant degree from the perception that political attempts to limit the court's power or its decisions would result in a significant public backlash. Building on these insights, Staton (2010) argues that judges—recognizing the importance of public support for their institutional standing—act strategically to heighten public awareness of the court and its decisions. A detailed study of the Mexican Supreme Court's public outreach efforts provides support for this argument. Finally, Clark (2011), focusing on the US Supreme Court, demonstrates that the importance of public support for judicial independence also affects judicial decision-making: if judges are aware that their power and independence derive primarily from public support for the court as an institution, they should pull back when public support for the court and its decisions falls—a phenomenon Clark is able to demonstrate through a combination of quantitative analysis of the court's willingness to strike down legislation as well as interviews with justices and Court insiders.

> **Claim 6.** *Public support for an independent judiciary is an important constraint on democratic leaders' ability to constrain judicial independence. Judges and politicians alike respond to public perceptions of the value of independent courts.*

Melton and Ginsburg (2002) argue that the central role of public support for judicial independence also suggests a connection between de jure and de facto judicial independence. Recall that the correlation between these two dimensions of judicial independence is empirically not particularly high. Courts in many places that feature formal guarantees of judicial independence enjoy little of it de facto. Conversely, many courts have a high degree of de facto independence despite the absence of formal guarantees. What, then, is the connection between the two? Melton and Ginsburg argue that de facto independence is primarily a function of external pressure on political actors—such as public support. Suppose that such support is present. To be effective in deterring attacks on judicial independence, political actors must be convinced that moving against the judiciary will be recognized as an illegitimate move by the public, and that doing so will be met with a backlash. Formal (de jure) provisions for judicial independence, including protections of judicial tenure and salaries, as well as carefully specified procedures for the removal of judges, can "make it easier to identify, and react to, attempts to threaten the independence of courts" (Vanberg, Broman, and Ritter 2023, 12). As Melton and Ginsburg (2002, 192) conclude, de jure independence increases "the cost of interfering with judges, in part because it informs other actors (e.g., the public, governmental institutions, and other interested audiences) about potential threats to the judiciary. This increases the likelihood that other actors will coordinate to defend the judiciary's independence when it is threatened."

The Value of Judicial Independence to Political Actors

The previous argument suggests that external actors force respect for judicial independence upon political actors. In that sense, it represents an unwelcome constraint. Another important line of scholarship challenges this supposition and argues that establishing and maintaining independent courts can provide actors in the other branches with significant direct benefits. For example, the presence of independent courts may allow political actors to shift blame for unpopular decisions to the courts—a move that will not be credible unless these courts enjoy a reasonable measure of independence (Graber 1993; Salzberger 1993; Whittington 2005).

Related research has pointed to the fact that independent courts can be valuable to other political actors as vehicles that allow them to make "credible commitments," particularly to respecting property rights (North and Weingast 1989; Cho 2020; Moustafa 2007). If citizens (and other relevant actors) anticipate that they are subject to predation by the state, and that the state can easily renege on its commitments, they are likely to adjust their behavior in anticipation. For example, individual incentives to invest in long-term projects will be sharply reduced—with negative economic consequences that also affect the ruler. In contrast, a ruler who can *credibly* commit to honoring its agreements and to respecting property rights is likely to benefit from investments that spur economic growth. Paradoxically, accepting limits on their power—including oversight by independent courts—can thus be beneficial for rulers. North and Weingast (1989) provide intriguing evidence: the fiscal situation of the British monarchy, including its ability to borrow funds, improved dramatically following the restrictions that were placed on the Crown's fiscal powers. While suggestive, these arguments raise a critical question, particularly in the context of nondemocratic politics: Rulers may have incentives to commit to the existence of effective, independent courts in order to reap the economic benefits of such a commitment. But what makes the commitment to respecting judicial independence itself credible? As Tushnet (2015, 422–3) puts it, autocratic "rulers might want to make credible commitments, but they cannot do so, precisely because they can alter the constitution whenever they want—and the target audiences know that the rulers can do so." It is precisely for this reason that Olson (1993) suggests that democratic governments—in which power is constrained both institutionally and by public opinion—are in a stronger position to make such commitments credible, and—therefore—that democratic governments will typically be economically more successful.

Claim 7. *Effective judicial control of government shifts incentives from short-term predation in favor of long-term growth and development.*

A final argument regarding the direct benefits that independent courts can provide to officeholders focuses on the impact of political competition on the institutional preferences of political parties and politicians. Consider a competitive political environment—such as a well-functioning democracy with parties that regularly alternate in power. In such a setting, parties and politicians confront independent courts in two different roles. When holding office, courts may represent unwelcome constraints on their power. But when in opposition, independent courts—by limiting the power of the incumbents—may be valuable in protecting the rights of the opposition, and providing a potential source of influence. That is, judicial independence functions as "insurance" for political actors who may find themselves out of power (Ginsburg 2003; Ramseyer 1994; Whittington 2003). In particular, when judges have long tenure, for example, long after a politician has left office, she may rely on the judges to uphold her policies against attacks from future elected majorities. That possibility paradoxically increases the incentive to politicize judicial selection so that current majorities can maximize the temporal reach of their ideological objectives (see also Landes and Posner 1975). Gillman (2002) documents one such example from the United States, when Republicans sought to expand the federal judiciary to enshrine Reconstruction-era policies.

Stephenson (2003) formalizes the insurance theory in a model highlighting a number of important, and subtle, conditions. First, the mere threat that the incumbent will lose power is not sufficient to maintain an independent judiciary. If a "declining hegemon" is replaced by a newly dominant coalition, the exiting incumbent may favor an independent judiciary—but the new hegemon has little reason to respect it. Instead, the insurance logic requires a continually competitive environment. Empirical evidence—quantitative (Stephenson 2003; Ginsburg and Versteeg 2014) as well as qualitative (Magalhaes 2003; Ginsburg 2003)—provides strong support for this claim.

Claim 8. *Independent judiciaries are important mechanisms for inducing credible commitment. By limiting political actors' ability to back out of agreements, independent judiciaries facilitate intertemporal cooperation.*

A second implication of the insurance theory—also consistent with the general argument that respect for judicial independence represents a political choice by actors who could threaten it—is that there are "limits to judicial independence" (Clark 2011). In preserving an independent judiciary, current officeholders are engaging in an intertemporal trade-off, weighing the costs imposed by respecting judicial constraints against the potential benefits of judicial protection when out of power. This trade-off depends both on the likelihood that an incumbent will find herself out of power, and the costs that current judicial decisions impose. Stephenson (2003) argues these factors produces in conjunction a region of judicial decisions within which current officeholders are willing to observe norms of judicial independence. But when judicial decisions fall outside of this interval and become too costly for current officeholders, such norms will break down.[6]

Conclusion

Modern courts are ubiquitous institutions in modern government and have deep historical roots, tracing their lineage to and through preinstitutionalized society. Part of the long and deep history of judicial and quasi-judicial institutions is the centrality of dispute resolution to human society. Courts ultimately emerged as central components of governance with the rise of limited forms of government. Over the centuries, courts have played a key role in facilitating limits on sovereign power and enforcing a balance of power among separated branches of government. At the same time, courts have become increasingly independent of political pressure, though their institutional position often remains precarious. Courts are most effective when they help politicians realize their long-term objectives, but conditions can emerge under which courts can be reduced, as Madison feared, to mere parchment barriers.

Notes

1. Space constraints force us to focus on Western courts. However, an important literature explores the development and role of courts in non-Western societies. For example, see Ginsburg (2003) and Moustafa (2007).
2. Of course, judges can choose how to allocate their effort among the cases brought to them (see, e.g., Clark and Strauss 2010).
3. As North and Weingast (1989) and Hayek (1960, 262) observe, in seventeenth-century England, the problem of judicial independence was primarily seen as one of constraining the Crown's ability to interfere with the judicial process. Over the next centuries, the problem of protecting the judiciary against legislative interference became increasingly clear.
4. Notably, even modern governments in otherwise highly developed systems do not always fully embrace the ideal notion of a truly independent, Kelsen-style court exercising an autonomous role in the separation of powers. For example, not until the twenty-first century did the British establish a completely independent Supreme Court. Similarly, the French Conseil Constitutionnel did not gain the authority to declare enacted law unconstitutional until early in the twenty-first century, and then only in response to pressure from the European Court of Human Rights.
5. Tushnet (2015) argues that fragmentation of power depends not only on formal structures but also on the nature of political parties. Thus, internal divisions within a dominant party may also offer protections against attacks on judicial independence.
6. Some work argues that political competition is contingent. Specifically, Aydin (2013) contends that in developing democracies, with more fluid party systems, political competition may undermine judicial independence because securing office is paramount.

References

Aydin, Aylin. 2013. "Judicial Independence across Democratic Regimes: Understanding the Varying Impact of Political Competition." *Law and Society Review* 47: 105–34.

Bates, Robert H. 1983. "The Preservation of Order in Stateless Societies: A Reinterpretation of EvansPritchard's The Nuer." *Frontiers of Economics* 4: 7–20.

Brinks, Daniel, Gretchen Helmke, and Julio Ríos-Figueroa. 2011. "Faithful Servants of the Regime." In Courts in Latin America, ed. Gretchen Helmke and Julio Ríos-Figueroa, 128–53. Cambridge: Cambridge University Press.

Broman, Benjamin, and Georg Vanberg. 2022. "Feuding, Arbitration, and the Emergence of an Independent Judiciary." *Constitutional Political Economy* 33: 162–99.

Burbank, Stephen. 2002. "What Do We Mean by Judicial Independence?" *Ohio State Law Journal* 64: 323–39.

Cappelletti, Maurizio. 1989. *The Judicial Process in Comparative Perspective*. Oxford: Oxford University Press.

Carrubba, Cliff. 2009. "A Model of Endogenous Development of Judicial Institutions in Federal and International Systems." *Journal of Politics* 71: 55–69.

Carrubba, Clifford, and Matthew Gabel. 2014. *International Courts and the Performance of International Agreements*. Cambridge: Cambridge University Press.

Cho, Moohyung. 2020. *Rethinking Judicial Independence in Democracy and Autocracy.* PhD thesis, Duke University.

Clark, Tom S. 2011. *The Limits of Judicial Independence.* Cambridge: Cambridge University Press.

Clark, Tom S., and Aaron B. Strauss. 2010. "The Implications of High Court Docket Control for Resource Allocation and Legal Efficiency." *Journal of Theoretical Politics* 22, no. 2: 247–68.

Epp, Charles. 1998. *The Rights Revolution: Lawyers, Activists, and Supreme Courts in Comparative Perspective.* Chicago: University of Chicago Press.

Evans-Pritchard, Edward Evan. 1940. *The Nuer: A Description of the Modes of Livelihood and Political Institutions of a Nilotic People.* Oxford: Clarendon.

Feld, Lars P., and Stefan Voigt. 2003. "Economic Growth and Judicial Independence: Cross-Country Evidence Using a New Set of Indicators." *European Journal of Political Economy* 19: 497–527.

Ferejohn, John. 2002. "Judicializing Politics, Politicizing Law." *Law and Contemporary Problems* 65 no. 3: 41–68.

Friedman, Barry. 2004. "History, Politics, and Judicial Independence." In *Judicial Integrity*, edited by A. Sajo, 99–123. Amsterdam: Koninklijke Brill NV.

Friedman, Barry. 2006. "Taking Law Seriously." *Perspectives on Politics* 4: 261–76.

Gillman, Howard. 2002. "How Political Parties Can Use the Courts to Advance Their Agendas: Federal Courts in the United States, 1875–1891." *American Political Science Review* 96, no. 3: 511–24.

Ginsburg, Tom. 2003. *Judicial Review in New Democracies: Constitutional Courts in Asian Cases.* Cambridge: Cambridge University Press.

Ginsburg, Tom, and Mila Versteeg. 2014. "Why Do Countries Adopt Constitutional Review?" *Journal of Law, Economics, and Organization* 30, no. 3: 587–622.

Gluckman, Max. 1955. "The Peace in the Feud." *Past and Present* 8: 1–14.

Gordon, Scott. 1999. *Controlling the State: Constitutionalism from Ancient Athens to Today.* Cambridge, MA: Harvard University Press.

Graber, Mark. 1993. "The Nonmajoritarian Difficulty: Legislative Deference to the Judiciary." *Studies in American Political Development* 7: 35–73.

Greif, Avner. 2006. "History Lessons. The Birth of Impersonal Exchange: The Community Responsibility System and Impartial Justice." *Journal of Economic Perspectives* 20: 221–36.

Hartung, Fritz. 1972. "Imperial Reform, 1485–1495: Its Course and Characteristics." In *PreReformation Germany*, ed. Gerald Strauss, 73–135. New York: Harper & Row.

Hayek, Friedrich. 1960. *The Constitution of Liberty.* Chicago: University of Chicago Press.

Hayo, Bernd, and Stefan Voigt. 2019. "The Long-Term Relationship between De Jure and De Facto Judicial Independence." *Economic Letters* 183: 1–5.

Helmke, Gretchen. 2017. *Institutions on the Edge: The Origins and Consequences of Inter-branch Crises in Latin America.* Cambridge: Cambridge University Press.

Hume, David. 1740/1985. "Of the Origin of Government." In *Essays Moral, Political, and Literary*, ed. Eugene F. Miller, 37–42. Indianapolis: Liberty Fund.

Koziol, Geoffrey G. 1987. "Monks, Feuds, and the Making of Peace in Eleventh-Century Flanders." *Historical Reflections / Réflexions Historiques* 14: 531–49.

Kuran, Timur, and Jared Rubin. 2018. "The Financial Power of the Powerless: Socio-Economic Status and Interest Rates under Partial Rule of Law." *Economic Journal* 128: 758–96.

Landes, William M., and Richard A. Posner. 1975. "The Independent Judiciary in an Interest-Group Perspective." *Journal of Law and Economics* 18, no. 3: 875–901.

Magalhaes, Pedro. 2003. *The Limits of Judicialization: Legislative Politics and Constitutional Review in Iberian Democracies*. PhD thesis, Ohio State University.

Malinowski, B. 1926. *Crime and Custom in Savage Society*. New York: International Library of Psychology.

Melton, James, and Tom Ginsburg. 2002. "Does De Jure Judicial Independence Really Matter? A Reevaluation of Explanations for Judicial Independence." *Journal of Law and Courts* 187–217.

Messick, Richard. 2002. "The Origins and Development of Courts." *Judicature* 85, no. 4: 175–81.

Milgrom, Paul R., Douglass C. North, and Barry R. Weingast. 1990. "The Role of Institutions in the Revival of Trade: The Law Merchant, Private Judges, and the Champagne Fairs." *Economics and Politics* 2: 1–23.

Miller, William Ian. 1990. *Bloodtaking and Peacemaking: Feud, Law, and Society in Saga Iceland*. Chicago: University of Chicago Press.

Moustafa, Tamir. 2007. *The Struggle for Constitutional Power: Law, Politics, and Economic Development in Egypt*. Cambridge: Cambridge University Press.

Nagel, Stuart S. 1964. "Court-Curbing Periods in American History." *Vanderbilt Law Review* 18: 925–44.

North, Douglass C. 1993. "Institutions and Credible Commitment." *Journal of Institutional and Theoretical Economics* 149, no. 1: 11–23.

North, Douglass C., and Barry R. Weingast. 1989. "Constitutions and Commitment: The Evolution of Institutions Governing Public Choice in Seventeenth-Century England." *Journal of Economic History* 49, no. 4: 803–32.

Olson, Mancur. 1993. "Dictatorship, Democracy, and Development." *American Political Science Review* 87, no. 3: 567–76.

Pollock, Frederick. 1898. "The King's Justice in the Early Middle Ages." *Harvard Law Review* 12, no. 4: 227–42.

Ramseyer, Mark. 1994. "The Puzzling (In)dependence of Courts: A Comparative Approach." *Journal of Legal Studies* 23: 721–47.

Ríos-Figueroa, Julio. 2007. "Fragmentation of Power and the Emergence of an Effective Judiciary in Mexico, 1994–2002." *Latin American Politics and Society* 49, no. 1: 31–57.

Rosenberg, Gerald N. 1992. "Judicial Independence and the Reality of Political Power." *Review of Politics* 54, no. 3: 369–98.

Salzberger, Eli. 1993. "A Positive Analysis of the Doctrine of Separation of Powers, or: Why Do We Have an Independent Judiciary?" *International Review of Law and Economics* 13: 349–79.

Schwartz, Herman. 2000. *The Struggle for Constitutional Justice in Post-communist Europe*. Oxford: Oxford University Press.

Shetreet, Shimon, and Sophie Turenne. 2013. *Judges on Trial: The Independence and Accountability of the English Judiciary*. Cambridge: Cambridge University Press.

Staton, Jeffrey. 2010. *Judicial Power and Strategic Communication in Mexico*. Cambridge: Cambridge University Press.

Stephenson, Matthew C. 2003. "'When the Devil Turns . . .': The Political Foundations of Independent Judicial Review." *Journal of Legal Studies* 32, no. 1: 59–89.

Stevens, Robert. 2001. "The Act of Settlement and the Questionable History of Judicial Independence." *Oxford University Commonwealth Law Journal* 29: 253–67.

Tate, C. Neil, and Torbjorn Vallinder. 1995. *The Global Expansion of Judicial Power*. New York: New York University Press.

Tushnet, Mark. 2015. "Authoritarian Constitutionalism." *Cornell Law Review* 100: 391–461.

Vanberg, Georg. 2005. *The Politics of Constitutional Review in Germany*. Cambridge: Cambridge University Press.

Vanberg, Georg. 2020. "Judicialization and the Political Executive." In *The Oxford Handbook of Political Executives*, ed. Rudy Andeweg, Robert Elgie, Ludger Helms, Juliet Kaarbo, and Ferdinand Mueller-Rommel, 566–87. Oxford: Oxford University Press.

Vanberg, Georg, Benjamin Broman, and Christopher Ritter. 2023. In *Elgar Handbook of Constitutional Law*, ed. Mark Tushnet and Dimitry Kochenov, 246–61. New York: Edward Elgar.

Voigt, Stefan, Jerg Gutmann, and Lars Feld. 2015. "Economic Growth and Judicial Independence, a Dozen Years On: Cross-Country Evidence Using an Updated Set of Indicators." *European Journal of Political Economy* 38: 197–211.

Volckart, Oliver. 2004. "The Economics of Feuding in Late Medieval Germany." *Explorations in Economic History* 41: 282–99.

White, Stephen D. 1986. "Feuding and Peace-Making in the Touraine around the Year 1100." *Traditio* 42: 195–263.

Whittington, Keith. 2003. "Legislative Sanctions and the Strategic Environment of Judicial Review." *International Journal of Constitutional Law* 1: 446–76.

Whittington, Keith. 2005. "'Interpose Your Friendly Hand': Political Supports for the Exercise of Judicial Review by the United States Supreme Court." *American Political Science Review* 99, no. 4: 583–96.

Wilson, Peter H. 2016. *Heart of Europe*. Cambridge, MA: Harvard University Press.

Wormald, Jenny. 1980. "Bloodfeud, Kindred and Government in Early Modern Scotland." *Past and Present* 87: 54–97.

CHAPTER 19

BUREAUCRACIES IN HISTORICAL POLITICAL ECONOMY

JAN P. VOGLER

The Relevance of Modern Bureaucracies

Since the emergence of modern public bureaucracies in the late eighteenth century, these administrative organizations have become indispensable to most polities. They are responsible for essential governmental tasks that help maintain (or achieve) social order and material prosperity, including policy implementation and the supply of public goods. The extent and properties of the latter not only affect states' prospects for economic growth (Evans and Rauch 1999; Pierskalla et al. 2017) and development (Evans 1995; Johnson 1982; Vries 2019), but also citizens' quality of life (Vogler 2019a).

While executives and legislatures are the primary decision-making centers regarding countries' *broad* trajectories, no policy can take effect without implementation by the state apparatus (Geddes 1994, 138; Ingraham 1995, xxii). Furthermore, bureaucracies often have leeway regarding the concrete design of laws (Huber and Shipan 2002), and variation in administrative performance affects societies every day (Vogler 2019b).

Therefore, scholars of historical political economy (HPE) have examined the causes of bureaucratization and bureaucracies' impacts throughout history. Both historically and in the present, significant variation in bureaucratic institutions is observed (Dahlström and Lapuente 2017; Painter and Peters 2010; Peters 2021; Vogler 2019c). The starkest differences in the performance of public administration existed between states that developed modern bureaucracies and those that retained traditional administrations.[1] Bureaucracies were also critical to major historical processes: (1) they shaped and were shaped by industrialization (Skowronek 1982; Vogler 2022b); (2) empires frequently implemented administrative systems in colonies (Eisenstadt 1993; Mattingly 2017); (3) states' military capacities often partly depended on efficient bureaucratic organization (Tilly 1990);[2] and (4) governments' ability to promote economic growth has been closely tied to public services (cf. Baum and Lake 2003; Besley and Persson 2009).

The emergence of modern bureaucracies, which primarily took place in the late eighteenth and nineteenth centuries, was only one step in the overall development of modern states—a centuries-long process that began in the medieval period. "Modern states" are political entities led by a central government with an effective monopoly on violence within a defined territory. Their development began in Europe in the twelfth and thirteenth centuries when England and France established central fiscal and judicial institutions (Strayer 1970).[3] In the early-modern period, states also created standing armies (Kennedy 1988; Parrott 2010; Tilly 1990) and provided internal security and economic standards that reduced transaction costs (Olson 1993; Spruyt 1996).[4] The creation of additional ministries and mutual international recognition were further key developments (Raadschelders and Rutgers 1996, 72–73). Yet the emergence of modern bureaucracies only began in the late eighteenth century, initially only affected a few countries, and was most visible in the military domain (Fischer and Lundgreen 1975; Hintze 1975; Kennedy 1988, 75–76; Mann 1993, chs. 11–13; Vries 2002, 106–7).[5]

What Is a "Bureaucracy"?

Definition of Modern Public Bureaucracy

A "modern public bureaucracy" is an (internally hierarchical) administrative organization that is subordinated to the government[6] and has the following features:

(1) a strict separation of offices and officeholders (implying no private possession of offices);
(2) recruitment procedures that emphasize relevant skills and ensure that officeholders have at least minimal competence (applicable to the vast majority of positions);
(3) a written set of rules and regulations that establish standards for official conduct;
(4) stable salaries (and salary progression) that are primarily—though not exclusively— determined by rank within the organization; and
(5) administrators have only limited discretion in their work routines, and bureaucratic operations primarily follow political goals[7] or legal principles rather than goals of economic efficiency or service orientation.[8]

We may think of administrations that only partly meet criteria 1 to 4 as "protomodern bureaucracies."[9]

While the aforementioned features primarily refer to *internal* bureaucratic organization, an auxiliary *output* criterion[10] may be that "modern" bureaucracies must be capable of addressing the fundamental service needs of industrialized (or postindustrial) societies or economies (including the provision of infrastructure, education, and healthcare) and of managing complex militaries and police forces.[11]

Modern public bureaucracies gradually became the dominant form of administrative organization beginning in the 1850s, and this superiority lasted at least until the 1980s (Raadschelders and Rutgers 1996; Silberman 1993; Skowronek 1982; Vogler 2019c). Prior to 1850, only a few countries had adopted them (Mann 1993, ch. 13; Vries 2002, 106–7), and in the 1980s, bureaucracy was challenged by "new public management."

Distinction from Other Forms of Public Administrative Organization

The first three characteristics just mentioned are key to distinguishing modern bureaucracies from previous forms of administration. Premodern administrations typically did not have a clear separation of office and officeholder. Instead, positions often were private property, inherited within families, given to powerful ecclesiastical representatives, or awarded based on personal or political loyalty (Ertman 1997; Fischer and Lundgreen 1975; Raadschelders and Rutgers 1996).[12] These practices allowed for the abuse of offices and implied the absence of procedures that ensure officials' competence. Although recruitment in many modern bureaucracies was and is influenced by applicants' socioeconomic status, gender, or ethnicity, most of their hiring procedures do require a certain level of competence. Finally, in premodern administrations, standards of conduct were loose, often based on local custom, and violations were not systematically punished.

Moreover, the last two features discussed in the previous section distinguish bureaucracies from recent forms of public administration. Although bureaucracies still remain predominant, there has been a partial reorientation toward incentive-based payment schemes and the goal of economic efficiency (Dunleavy et al. 2006; Hood 1991; Hood 1995; Osborne and Gaebler 1992).[13]

Comparison to Max Weber's Perspective

In some respects, my definition deviates from Max Weber's prominent characterization of bureaucracies. To Weber (1978, 220–221, ch. 11), several additional features distinguished the ideal type of modern bureaucracies from "patrimonial administration," including (1) recruitment that is (primarily/exclusively) based on individuals' qualification, (2) strict career paths for all bureaucrats, (3) a complete separation from politics, and (4) clearly delineated and exclusive spheres of competence for officials and agencies.[14]

The problem with using a definition derived from Weber's work is that the vast majority of historical and contemporary administrations would not satisfy these criteria.[15] To Weber, too, "ideal types" were abstractions of reality that cannot be fully observed in practice (Fry and Raadschelders 2022, ch. 1; Sager and Rosser 2021), which underscores the desirability of a definition that is applicable to (historical) real-world bureaucracies, such as the one developed in this chapter.

East Asian Administrations and Modern Bureaucracy

It is possible to argue that several historical East Asian administrative systems (such as the Chinese, Korean, and Vietnamese administrations) represented the first modern bureaucracies (Drechsler 2013; Drechsler 2018; Fukuyama 2011, 19–21, 113–14). Indeed, they partly resembled modern bureaucracies. However, some aspects of their organization make this classification difficult. First, while modern bureaucracies emphasize practical skills, these systems often asked applicants to master more abstract cultural or philosophical contents, which could require more than a decade of preparation (Ebrey 2016, 42; Hong, Paik, and Yun 2021; Jiang and Kung 2020; Painter and Peters 2010, 27; Wang 2022, ch. 7).[16] Additionally, Bell (2016, 223–24) points out that Chinese administrators were generalists with broad political power, whereas modern bureaucrats are specialists with more limited discretion.

Moreover, recruitment and advancement within these administrations often strongly depended on candidates' social networks or family background (Hong, Paik, and Yun 2021; Jiang and Kung 2020; Paik 2014; Wang 2022), and consideration for the Chinese civil service examination necessitated a recommendation from local elites, which introduced patronage into the system (Wang 2022, ch. 3). The result was widespread corruption and abuses of power, and that the administration was "far less meritocratic than it appeared to be" (Vries 2002, 107). Also, with respect to the discussed output criteria, the Chinese state may not qualify, as its reach was limited (Ebrey 2016, 47; Finer 1997, 73–74; Vries 2002, 109; Vries 2015).[17]

In line with these observations, Raadschelders and Rutgers (1996) suggest that the first modern bureaucracies emerged in Europe, not China.[18] However, because East Asian administrations already mostly satisfied the criteria of (1) formal separation of office and officeholder, (2) comprehensive and consistent regulations for conduct, and (3) stable salaries (see, e.g., Ebrey 2016, 37–42, 46), we may categorize them as "protomodern bureaucracies."

TYPES OF BUREAUCRACIES

Beyond the five discussed core features, bureaucracies exhibit substantial organizational variation. This has historically led to fundamental differences in (1) policy implementation effectiveness, (2) public service quality, and (3) state-citizen interactions. Thus, understanding these differences allows us to better evaluate the impact of bureaucracies on societies.

Organizational versus Professional Bureaucracies

Silberman (1993) primarily differentiates between two types: (1) *organizational* and (2) *professional* bureaucracies. The former place emphasis on coherent internal career paths and administrative hierarchies. Moreover, the training of civil servants takes place in the organization itself, which results in strong administrative cultures with a shared feeling of loyalty toward the organization. Examples are "Japan, France, Germany, Spain, Italy, and the Soviet Union" (Silberman 1993, 12).

The main alternative is professional bureaucracies, which have looser recruitment and promotion systems. Training of bureaucrats often takes place outside of the organization, and bureaucrats can introduce external skills through lateral entry. Consequently, these systems' organizational cultures are less coherent, hierarchies are less pronounced, and career tracks are less stable. Examples include the "United States, Great Britain, Canada, and Switzerland" (Silberman 1993, 14).

Bureaucracies with Integrated versus Separated Career Tracks

Dahlström and Lapuente (2017) develop four categories of bureaucracies along two dimensions. The first dimension of *open* versus *closed* bureaucracies is similar to Silberman's categorization. Open systems have hiring practices similar to the private sector (including job interviews). Closed systems require applicants to take specialized examinations and provide special employment protections.

Importantly, Dahlström and Lapuente (2017) place greater emphasis on the second dimension: *integrated* versus *separated* career tracks for politicians and bureaucrats. In integrated systems, there is significant overlap in the careers of these groups. In separated systems, they have much sharper distinctions, which incentivizes them to monitor each other. Such mutual elite monitoring has multiple beneficial consequences for governance, which includes fewer opportunities for corruption.

Four categories of bureaucracies emerge (Dahlström and Lapuente 2017, 38) (see Table 19.1). The first type—open and integrated—is the "patronage bureaucratic system" (historical party machines in the United States, Western European public administrations prior to the nineteenth century, developing countries in the present day). The second type—closed and integrated—is labeled the "corporatist bureaucratic system" (France, Spain, Italy, and Japan). The third type of system—open and separated—is a "managerial bureaucratic system" (Australia, Canada, New Zealand,

Table 19.1. Typology by Dahlströhm and Lapuente

	Open bureaucratic systems	Closed bureaucratic systems
Integrated Career Tracks	Patronage system	Corporatist system
Separated Career Tracks	Managerial system	Autonomous system

and Sweden). Finally, the fourth type—closed and separated—is labeled an "autonomous bureaucratic system" (Germany and South Korea).

Political Control and Meritocracy

Vogler (2019c, ch. 2) provides a typology focused on Europe and North America. He differentiates between two continuous dimensions: (1) the level of political control (through appointments and dismissals of upper-level bureaucrats[19]) and (2) the level of meritocracy in recruitment (the extent to which applicants' qualifications matter[20]). There is a complex interplay between these dimensions. While they are substantively different, they are not fully orthogonal.

Based on this typology, three kinds of systems are observed: Some systems, such as Italy's, combine high levels of political control with low-meritocracy recruitment. On the other extreme, some systems, such as the Netherlands', combine few political appointments with high levels of meritocracy in recruitment. Finally, a third type of (hybrid) bureaucratic system, such as in the United States, combines high degrees of control at the upper levels with relatively high meritocratic recruitment standards.

Families of Administrative Traditions

Painter and Peters (2010) differentiate between nine administrative traditions that entail both organizational features and bureaucratic culture: (1) Anglo-American, (2) Napoleonic, (3) Germanic, (4) Scandinavian, (5) Latin American, (6) Postcolonial South Asian and African, (7) East Asian, (8) Soviet, and (9) Islamic. Since this chapter has already covered Western systems extensively, I provide brief illustrations of three non-Western traditions.[21]

Latin American administrations, especially in former Spanish colonies, were historically characterized by strict hierarchies and inflexibility. Therefore, once these states gained independence, they engaged in comprehensive administrative reforms. Yet the newly emerging formalism on the surface merely hid deeply entrenched patronage recruitment, corruption, and the imperfect implementation of regulations (Painter and Peters 2010, 23–24).

In East Asia, many countries had administrations that reflected some of the principles of modern bureaucracies long before the arrival of European colonial powers, with Confucianism being an essential influence. Colonial powers then shaped these systems through imposed institutions, which led to a combination of traditional and imported principles (Painter and Peters 2010, 25–27).

Finally, in Soviet systems, communist parties played a key role. Bureaucracies were either subordinated in hierarchical relationships or could even practically fuse with them. As a result, adherence to official ideology and uncritical deference to superiors were often key to bureaucrats' career success. Nevertheless, Soviet systems, like other modern bureaucracies, generally required at least minimal competence (Painter and Peters 2010, 27–28).

Additional Dimensions of Organizational Differentiation

Four further organizational distinctions of bureaucracies are noteworthy. First, Bustikova and Corduneanu-Huci (2017) differentiate between low- and high-capacity bureaucracies.[22] Low-capacity systems are organizationally unable to comprehensively deliver public services, which spurs demand for clientelistic exchange between voters and politicians. Also, Huber and Shipan (2002) show that administrative systems vary widely in the extent to which they allow for bureaucratic discretion in the implementation of laws, with some allowing for significant leeway, while others severely restrict bureaucrats.[23]

Moreover, Gingerich (2013) and Bersch, Praça, and Taylor (2017) highlight substantial interagency variation in organization and capacity, which underscores the utility of disaggregated analysis. Finally, the existence of another type of "hybrid" (proto-)bureaucratic system is discussed by Brierley (2021), who identifies a distinct combination of meritocratic recruitment for leading positions with patronage recruitment for lower positions.

The Historical Emergence of Bureaucracies

In the late eighteenth and early nineteenth centuries, Prussia and Austria created the first modern bureaucracies. Military defeats and unsustainable war-related expenditures were the main reason for the introduction of wide-ranging changes to these countries' administrations, including (1) the separation of office and officeholder, (2) the introduction of salaries, (3) comprehensive rules, (4) protections from arbitrary dismissal, and (5) more rigorous recruitment procedures that ensured officeholders' (minimal) competence (Deak 2015, esp. 9–17; Fischer and Lundgreen 1975, esp. 516; Hochedlinger 2003;

Judson 2016; Kann 1974; Kiser and Schneider 1994; Mann 1993, chs. 12–13; Raphael 2000, 53–61; Unruh 1977, 26–28; Wunder 1986, 21–22; Vogler 2019b; 2022a).[24]

While many European states had already developed (proto-)bureaucratic structures in the military domain before 1800 (Hintze 1975; Mann 1993, chs. 11–12; Kennedy 1988, 75–76), the nineteenth and early twentieth centuries were crucial for the emergence of modern bureaucracies for four reasons (Carpenter 2001; Fischer and Lundgreen 1975; Raadschelders and Rutgers 1996; Silberman 1993; Vogler 2019c). First, bureaucracies (with all five institutional features discussed previously) became the dominant form of administrative organization among the great powers (Buzan and Lawson 2015; Vogler 2019c).[25] Second, bureaucracies massively increased the degree of intervention in society and the supply of public services.(Ansell and Lindvall 2020; Mann 1993, chs. 13–14). Third (and partly as a consequence), their size and public spending on their activities grew significantly (Fischer and Lundgreen 1975, esp. 462–63; Mitchell 2022). Fourth, they became indispensable to imperialism (Buzan and Lawson 2015; Vogler 2019b; 2022c).

In this period, three trends caused the emergence of bureaucracies:

- **External military pressures.** Even before modern bureaucracies emerged, warfare was typically associated with a growth in the state's (military) administrative apparatus and significant fiscal burdens (Besley and Persson 2009; Hintze 1975, esp. 201; Kennedy 1988, esp. 70–72, 75–86; Mann 1993, chs. 11–12; Tilly 1990; Vogler 2022c). As observed in Prussia and Austria, such massive expenditures created pressure to reform the state apparatus with the goal of increasing its efficiency and competence ("rationalization").
- **Increasing socioeconomic complexity.** Industrialization made economies and societies much more complex and increased the demand for public services, especially security, education, social insurance, and infrastructure (Ansell and Lindvall 2020; Mann 1993, chs. 11–14; Potter and Vogler 2021; Raadschelders and Rutgers 1996, 86; Saylor 2014; Skowronek 1982; Vogler 2022b).[26] Thus, governments created more competent administrations capable of delivering these services. Furthermore, effective taxation of increasingly complex socioeconomic structures often also required additional bureaucratic capacity, with more substantial capacity increases in early industrializing states (see Beramendi, Dincecco, and Rogers 2019).[27] (Importantly, the process described here—that is, bureaucratization due to increases in socioeconomic complexity—is not merely a historical phenomenon. As societies keep growing more complex, we also witness further growth of the administrative state.)
- **Imperialism (and threat of imperial occupation).** Already before industrialization, large colonial administrations were created by imperial centers (see, e.g., McClellan and Regourd 2011). When imperial expansion intensified in the nineteenth century (Vogler 2022c), major powers introduced a variety of administrative institutions to colonies (Buzan and Lawson 2015, esp. 130–38).[28] In this process, imperial centers also improved the capacities of domestic bureaucracies

to manage extensive overseas territories. (In this respect, however, Cornell and Svensson [2022] find only very limited evidence for the traditional claim that domestic British civil service reforms were inspired by the Indian Civil Service.) Additionally, similar to military competition, pressure resulting from a credible threat of imperial domination could result in administrative reforms in targeted polities, such as Japan or Siam (Paik and Vechbanyongratana 2019). Japan later became an imperial power itself and imposed state-building on others (Kohli 2004, ch. 1; Matsuzaki 2019; Mattingly 2017).

Although these three factors explain the broader emergence of modern bureaucracies, they generally do not suffice to explain variation in bureaucratic organization, which is the subject of the next section.

Factors That Shaped Bureaucratic Institutions

While Weber's (1978) classical perspective—that economic development and social progress automatically lead to the establishment of modern bureaucracies—does not leave sufficient space to explain the significant institutional variation we observe across (historical) bureaucracies (Mann 1993, 359; Vogler 2019a, 100–101), a multitude of theories aim to explain this divergence.

First, with respect to politically autonomous countries, there are intense debates regarding *which* domestic factor shaped early bureaucracies. Candidates include (1) differences in socioeconomic development, (2) macro-political and macro-legal circumstances, (3) interest groups and parties,[29] and (4) sociocultural determinants. Second, with respect to countries under foreign rule, external factors had a decisive influence on bureaucratic organization.

Domestic Factors

In terms of socioeconomic developments, Skowronek (1982) suggests that industrialization and urbanization in nineteenth-century America necessitated a strong and centralized administrative state. As new social groups emerged and conflicts between them arose, the state needed the capacity to intervene. Such intervention was initially difficult because the United States did not yet have a modern bureaucracy. Instead, America's patronage-ridden state was considered to be a (premodern) "spoils system" (Ingraham 1995, 20–25; Shefter 1994, ch. 3; Silberman 1993, 243–49; Van Riper 1958, ch. 3).[30]

Moreover, Johnson and Libecap (1994) argue that significant growth of this administrative state contributed to the infeasibility of maintaining an inefficient patronage recruitment system. In 1883, Congress passed the Pendleton Act that brought America significantly closer to a modern bureaucracy by introducing merit recruitment for some bureaucrats (Hoogenboom 1968; Theriault 2003; Van Riper 1958, ch. 5; Vogler 2019c, 61–65). Protection from dismissal allowed those bureaucrats to develop domain-specific expertise, increasing the bureaucracy's overall effectiveness (Gailmard and Patty 2012b).[31]

Another contribution that considers the impact of socioeconomic development on the state is from Kurtz (2013), who suggests that the mobility of workers in Latin America was a key factor that influenced local elites' ability to resist centralized state-building processes. Similarly, Garfias and Sellars (2021) argue that the weakening of elites as intermediaries following demographic collapse allowed for the strengthening of central bureaucratic institutions in colonial Mexico.[32]

In terms of macro-political factors, Silberman (1993) posits that "uncertainty about leadership succession" in the nineteenth century was essential to bureaucratic development: In high-uncertainty settings, organizational bureaucracies reduced risks associated with governing and provided more stability. However, in low-uncertainty settings, political elites were not as dependent on administrations' organizational coherence, which led to professional bureaucracies.

With respect to the American states, Ting et al. (2013) argue that incumbent governments that anticipated electoral defeat had incentives to insulate bureaucracies from political pressure (to protect their own appointees). Similarly, Ruhil and Camões (2003) find that political competitiveness and the secret ballot influenced the adoption of merit recruitment. Alternatively, Theriault (2003) argues that general political pressure from constituents caused administrative reform.

Another macro-political argument comes from Waldner (1999), who emphasizes elite conflict and the inclusion of popular classes in determining bureaucratic structures in late-developing countries. In cases with significant intraelite conflicts, political leaders needed to build broader (cross-class) coalitions to achieve a stable administration. Thus, they created bureaucratic capacity for channeling resources into welfare measures, which resulted in more politicized administrations, designed to maintain economic interventionism.[33]

An example of an interest-group perspective is Vogler (2019c, ch. 2), who suggests that three social groups were crucial for the institutional design of early bureaucracies. First, traditional elites sought to maintain a bureaucracy under the control of nondemocratic institutions and with socially selective recruitment. Second, the entrepreneurial and professional middle classes preferred a competent bureaucracy capable of delivering high-quality public services, which required meritocratic recruitment. Additionally, they sought to minimize political influence to shield the bureaucracy from landed-elite or working-class manipulation. Finally, the urban working class preferred broad access to public sector jobs, but its members lacked higher education, so they were against academic recruitment standards. With respect to political control, workers' representatives sought maximum control through democratic institutions. Given these diverging preferences, Vogler argues that these groups' relative political power was crucial to bureaucracies' institutional design.

Carpenter (2001) also embraces an interest-group perspective and finds that the early structures of American bureaucracy were heavily influenced by mid-level bureaucrats. Through substantial expertise, the construction of political networks, and an achievement-oriented administrative culture, those mid-level bureaucrats were sometimes able to establish their agencies as "autonomous" actors with the power to set political agendas.

In the postbellum American South, too, interest groups shaped bureaucracies. Suryanarayan and White (2021) find that coalitions of (White) elites weakened administrative capacity to prevent economic redistribution to former slaves. Further elite-centered arguments regarding the development of bureaucratic capacity (that emphasize conflicts among elites, however) have been made by Beramendi, Dincecco, and Rogers (2019) and Garfias (2018).

In political economy, there are only a few sociocultural explanations for variation in bureaucracies. For example, in a literature survey, Johnson and Koyama (2017) find that existing human capital and ethnolinguistic fractionalization likely influence the development of state capacity.[34] Importantly, however, Pardelli and Kustov (2022) highlight the possibility of endogeneity in the relationship of ethnic demography and public goods provision through bureaucracies.

In addition to perspectives that rely on the analysis of a single factor, several "hybrid" frameworks combine multiple types of explanations. For instance, with a focus on US states, Potter and Vogler (2021) argue that, as socioeconomic systems became more complex, more diverse economic elites pushed for the creation of competent, professional, and independent bureaucracies. Bureaucratic independence meant an insurance mechanism against the possibility of other elites fundamentally changing administrative intervention in society.

Another hybrid theory is developed by Saylor (2014), who posits that historical commodity booms sometimes led to the expansion of bureaucratic capacity through increased demand for public goods provision. However, this effect depended on interest-group coalitions as some (political) actors found it in their interest to block state expansion.

Finally, Soifer (2015) provides a framework that combines several of the aforementioned factors, contending that the discrete choices of political leaders/elites (interest groups) matter most. But he also suggests that those choices are based on elites' material circumstances—especially urbanization (socioeconomic development)—as well as ideology (a sociocultural determinant).

External Factors

As detailed earlier, military competition in Europe spurred administrative reforms, even prior to the emergence of modern bureaucracies (Tilly 1990). Connecting to this perspective, Centeno (2002) argues that the relative absence of war in South America meant that states did not have strong incentives for centralization and bureaucratization.[35]

Similarly, Herbst (2014) suggests that Africa's geography combined with low population densities made the formation of territorial states unlikely; Queralt (2019) finds that participation in wars only strengthened states' fiscal capacity if it was financed through taxation, not loans. Thus, the self-reinforcing dynamics of war-making and administrative development were not realized in all world regions.

However, Schenoni (2021) argues that Latin American wars sometimes did shape state-building because defeat enabled peripheral elites (with the goal of replacing incumbents) to weaken the state apparatus, including the bureaucracy. Conversely, military victories allowed incumbent elites to strengthen their dominant position by consolidating the state.

Yet even persistent presence of external military pressure tells us little about historical divergence in bureaucratic institutions. An external factor that was more decisive in determining bureaucracies' specific institutional design was imperialism. The two most important imperial powers that sought to implement aspects of their administrative and legal systems in their colonies were France and Britain (La Porta et al. 1997). The French bureaucracy was highly regulated, with strict internal career paths and standardized examinations (Silberman 1993, chs. 4–5). The British civil service also introduced competitive examinations in the nineteenth century, but access remained socially selective, and political control decreased over time (Vogler 2019c, 65–68).

Additionally, empires such as Austria, Prussia, and Russia occupied large parts of Central and (South)Eastern Europe, often implementing their own administrative institutions (Becker et al. 2016). Poland serves as a good example: Prussia and Austria imposed institutions that were close to modern bureaucracies. Russia, however, imposed a corrupt and inefficient administration. These stark differences in bureaucratic organization created fundamentally different equilibria of state-citizen interactions, which affected administrative performance and recruitment in the long run (Vogler 2019b).

Moreover, Romania is a good case to illustrate the consequences of information asymmetries between imperial centers and local populations. When unable or unwilling to delegate tasks to local elites, empires often experienced difficulties with bureaucratic control. Combined with the underfinancing of administrations, local populations frequently found ways to resist against external bureaucratic institutions, which thwarted their effectiveness and simultaneously reduced the potential for long-term legacies (Vogler 2022a).

Additionally, Mattingly (2017) finds that the historical state-building attempts by the Japanese occupiers of Northeastern China still have long-term effects on the capacity of bureaucracies in terms of public goods provision. He suggests that, although Japan ruled through brutal and extractive methods, the effectiveness of their administrative institutions generated a variety of positive legacies in bureaucratic organization.

Mazzuca (2021) argues that the external factors that influenced state capacity-building varied over time and across world regions. While European states were historically formed due to war, state formation in Latin America took place as a result of international trade, which generally resulted in lower state capacity and authority.[36] Mazzuca then lays out three paths ("port-driven," "lord-driven," and "party-driven") to different state types. Similarly, Buzan and Lawson (2015) suggest that creation of modern bureaucracies (as a key aspect of rational state-building processes) was part of a complex web of global developments in the long nineteenth century.

Finally, external cultural explanations for the character of bureaucratization remain underexplored. But there are noteworthy contributions: Gorski (2003) focuses on the emergence of modern states and attributes importance to Calvinism as a transnational cultural force. Also, Sager et al. (2018) suggest that the transnational dissemination of ideas regarding administrative reform historically affected bureaucracies.

Path Dependence in Bureaucratic Organization

An analytical perspective of path dependence is useful when analyzing bureaucracies because administrative organizations are known for exhibiting extremely high levels of organizational persistence (Carpenter 2001; Gimpel'son 2003; Richards 2003; Silberman 1993; Wunder 1986). "Path dependence" refers to the disproportionate and lasting influence of institutional design at the moment of an organization's creation, which we may consider a "critical juncture" (Capoccia and Kelemen 2007).[37]

What are the theoretical reasons behind bureaucratic path dependence? Vogler (2019c, 43–46) identifies four factors:[38]

(1) Bureaucrats often form strong and coherent interest groups. In part because their skills are usually nontransferable to other professions and because they profit from organizational autonomy (low transparency), they often reject administrative reform (see Asatryan, Heinemann, and Pitlik 2017; Vogler 2019c).
(2) Governments fundamentally depend on bureaucracies to implement policies, which incentivizes even revolutionary governments to leave the state apparatus intact to exercise political power.
(3) Administrative culture is often highly persistent over time.
(4) There can be self-reinforcing equilibria in state-citizen interactions, in which citizens' expectations toward and views of bureaucracy are reinforced by the actual behavior of bureaucrats (see Bustikova and Corduneanu-Huci 2017; Vogler 2019b). For example, in contexts where corruption is common, the behavior of public officials and the expectations of citizens are typically aligned in a way that perpetuates corrupt practices (Corbacho et al. 2016).

Usually, at least one of these factors constitutes bureaucratic path dependence in any specific context. However, while fundamental structures rarely change, through multifaceted interactions with their environment, bureaucracies still change on the margins (Vogler 2019a).

How Bureaucracies Historically Influenced Economies, Societies, and Politics

The effect of bureaucracies on economies and societies is manifold. On one hand, governments can use bureaucracies to provide public goods and implement growth-enhancing policies (cf. Besley and Persson 2009; Hanson 2014; Kohli 2004). On the other hand, if elites pursue economically harmful policies, "effective" bureaucracies could be detrimental to growth (Cornell, Knutsen, and Teorell 2020; Johnson and Koyama 2017, 11). Bureaucracies also represent potential tools of repression, used by authoritarian governments to harm or even murder groups in society (cf. Aaskoven and Nyrup 2021; Hilberg, Browning, and Hayes 2019).

Scholars of political economy have investigated in detail the historical effects of bureaucracies on development. For instance, Johnson (1982) examined the role of the Japanese central bureaucracy in coordinating the country's economic policy and found that it was successful at implementing an aggressive export-oriented growth strategy. Furthermore, Vries (2015; 2019) details how historical administrative capacity was essential to British and Japanese development, respectively. Also, Pierskalla et al. (2017) and Hough and Grier (2015) suggest that exposure to centralized and effective state authority (which is directly linked to administrative capacity) has positive effects on economic development.

Moreover, Evans (1995) suggests that public administrations historically achieved maximum economic growth when they were embedded in society (representing broad interests), but also autonomous (not captured by special interests). Similarly, Evans and Rauch (1999) find a positive effect on growth of meritocratic recruitment and bureaucratic career paths. They suggest that such "Weberian" institutions make bureaucrats less susceptible to corruption and promote an esprit de corps that improves bureaucratic performance and thus the quality of public goods.[39] However, the perspective that bureaucracies were key contributors to economic growth throughout history is challenged by Cornell, Knutsen, and Teorell (2020), who find a positive but mostly insignificant effect.[40]

With respect to the effects of imperial bureaucracies, Lee and Schultz (2012) compare indirect British rule with the imposition of French administrative institutions in Cameroon and find that the latter had negative effects on the quality of public goods. Moreover, while the Spanish colonial administration in the Americas did not meet all the criteria of modern bureaucracy, it did have multifaceted economic effects on colonies: Irigoin and Grafe (2008) argue that it had an important redistributive function. Based on a complex fiscal bargaining process between the Crown, local officials, and elites, a system of fiscal redistribution emerged.

Although modern public bureaucracies are technically "subordinated" to the government, their performance can also have substantial effects on politics (Yazaki 2018).

Specifically, from the perspective of Bustikova and Corduneanu-Huci (2017), a complex interactive equilibrium exists between political strategies and state capacity. Low-capacity bureaucratic systems amplify clientelistic political exchange as public services remain in poor condition.

Moreover, Stasavage (2020) argues that the capacity of premodern central administrations was essential to the prospects for democracy. Where central administrations were powerful, such as in China, rulers did not need the consent of the governed to collect taxes. This allowed authoritarian political structures to persist. Only in systems that had weak central administrative capacity did rulers need to govern with the consent of other societal actors, which laid the foundations for more collaborative forms of government.

The institutions of public bureaucracy may also have significant influence on other aspects of state-building. For instance, Charron, Dahlström, and Lapuente (2012) suggest that preexisting administrative structures shaped the development of legal systems, arguing that administrations with more standardized forms of recruitment were historically more likely to represent a strong check on the ruler, which benefited the emergence of robust legal systems. Additionally, the bureaucratic (infrastructural) capacity of central versus regional political entities may have influenced whether countries adopted federalism (Ziblatt 2008).

Furthermore, scholars have investigated the effects of public goods on the ability of citizens to engage with the state. For instance, Zhang and Lee (2020) find that increases in literacy (which are typically the result of more extensive public education) lead to improvements in state-society interactions. Specifically, Zhang and Lee (2020) observe that a decrease in transaction costs through easier access to state services improves the ability of citizens to interact with the bureaucracy and make use of existing laws and regulations.

On the flip side, authoritarian governments may use public administration to manipulate society through education (see Paglayan 2022), propaganda, or repression. Even when they are unable to fundamentally alter citizens' beliefs, exposure to the state apparatus can "inform" citizens about authoritarian elite preferences and shape their behavior (see de Juan, Haass, and Pierskalla 2021).

Historical public administrations outside Europe, which generally did not qualify as modern bureaucracies, typically had a very uneven impact on societies due to the widespread delegation of tasks to agents (such as tax farmers) and the low state capacity in rural areas. For instance, both in the Ottoman Empire and in India, the state delegated tax collection to privately owned offices, which then constituted at most an indirect influence on society (Vries 2002, 104–9). Similarly, the practice of selling offices may have enabled unqualified or predatory individuals to take on high-level positions in the Spanish Empire, which led to dramatic cross-regional variation in socioeconomic outcomes (Guardado 2018).

Yet the historical civil service exam of China's proto-modern bureaucracy might still have a positive long-term effect on society because it instilled a "deep respect for learning" among local elites (Chen, Kung, and Ma 2020, 2030–31). Through cultural transmission, social capital, and educational institutions, this respect was handed down through several generations and manifests itself in contemporary educational outcomes across China (Chen, Kung, and Ma 2020).[41]

Conclusion

Modern public bureaucracies are central to both the task of governing and to major historical processes like imperialism, industrialization, and interstate warfare. Since the eighteenth century they have gradually become an indispensable part of most polities.

While existing studies have delivered crucial insights, enormous room for further contributions remains. Most importantly, we still have much to learn about historical administrations and (proto-)bureaucracies in Africa, the Middle East, and the Asia-Pacific region, which differ from Western ones in important respects (cf. Pepinsky, Pierskalla, and Sacks 2017; Slater 2008; Thies 2007). Also, in these regions, precolonial structures likely had a lasting effect, even if modern bureaucracies were introduced later (cf. Wilfahrt 2018).

Furthermore, we know a great deal about the dynamics of principal-agent relationships between governments and bureaucracies (Bertelli 2012, ch. 2; Gailmard and Patty 2012a; Lewis 2003; McCubbins, Noll, and Weingast 1987; Toral 2022), but we still need to explore them more extensively from a historical perspective. For instance, Workman (2015) and Potter (2019) highlight the rule-making power of bureaucrats, which could be extended to the period prior to the twentieth century. Similarly, Lee's (2020) insights regarding how foreign states can weaken domestic administrative structures and Ding's (2020) theory about "performative governance" could be applied to historical contexts. Finally, the relationship of bureaucracies and the territorial dimension of state-building and state effectiveness has recently found increased attention (McDonnell 2020; Vogler 2019b), but this issue could be explored further, especially from a historical perspective (see Braun and Kienitz 2022).

All in all, historical political economy has gained critical insights into bureaucracies. Yet this field is just at its inception. Many future studies will help us more comprehensively understand the origins, character, and impacts of bureaucracies throughout history.

Acknowledgments

Helpful comments were provided by Agnes Cornell, Claudiu Craciun, Carl Dahlström, John Deak, Anne Degrave, Iza Ding, Wolfgang Drechsler, Niklas Hänze, Friedrich Heinemann, Jeffery A. Jenkins, Edgar Kiser, Mark Koyama, Joe Kratz, Victor Lapuente, Melissa Lee, Reo Matsuzaki, Dan Mattingly, Christopher Paik, Daniel Podratsky, Jos Raadschelders, Jared Rubin, Steffi Rueß, Fritz Sager, Yu Sasaki, Ryan Saylor, Luis Schenoni, Matthias Scheu, Charles Shipan, Peer Vries, David Waldner, Yuhua Wang, and Bernd Wunder. I also thank participants of virtual presentations at the University of Konstanz (which was a part of the public lecture series "The Historical Political Economy of Bureaucracy and State Building") and MPSA's annual conference.

Notes

1. I use the term "bureaucracy" to refer to *modern public bureaucracies*. Other kinds of systems are labeled "(public) administrations." As elaborated upon later, some administrative systems may be classified as "proto-bureaucratic" if they partly meet the criteria of modern bureaucratic organization. Finally, the term "administrative state" is more commonly applied to *fully modern* bureaucracies and less commonly used when describing premodern forms of public administration.
2. On the related topic of military (state) capacity, see also Hendrix (2010).
3. On the importance of fiscal institutions, see Fischer and Lundgreen (1975, 458). Moreover, on the influence of the medieval church on state development, see Grzymala-Busse (2020).
4. On the relevance of transaction costs, see also North (1990).
5. For comparisons of early public administrations, see Vries (2002, 104–9); Fischer and Lundgreen (1975); Lapuente Gine (2006); and Finer (1997) (including subsequent volumes).
6. This term mainly refers to executives, but legislatures often also have influence on bureaucratic operations and personnel.
7. For instance, such goals could be comprehensive public service access or the maintenance of an authoritarian regime.
8. Several of these characteristics have similarities with Weber's (1978) characterization of modern bureaucracies (220–21, ch. 11). Nevertheless, as elaborated upon later, there are important differences between these two definitions. Furthermore, Painter and Peters (2010, 8) also make a similar distinction between political/legal goals and efficiency/effectiveness principles.
9. Ertman also uses this term (e.g., 1997, 5–9). Moreover, for a minimalist definition of bureaucracy with broader historical applicability, see Crooks and Parsons (2016, 17–18).
10. These criteria are not part of the "core definition" of modern bureaucracy because we may want to treat *outputs* both conceptually and empirically separately.
11. These forces are critical, respectively, to defending a state's *external* sovereignty and maintaining its *internal* monopoly on violence.
12. Weber (1978) differentiates between "patrimonial" and "bureaucratic-legal" administration. Moreover, for a detailed analysis of the historical example of France, see Sasaki (2021).
13. Political and efficiency goals are often contradictory. For instance, a political (equity) goal may be to supply public services even to remote villages and towns, but this practice could be considered too costly ("equity versus efficiency").
14. This is not an exhaustive list of the essential characteristics of modern bureaucracies according to Weber, but these are the criteria most clearly violated by numerous empirical cases. On Weber's perspective, see also Kiser and Schneider (1994, 188), Mann (1993, 444), and Sager and Rosser (2021).
15. On this subject, see also Ang (2017).
16. Importantly, there were also other, more practically oriented examinations. For details on Korean examinations, see Paik (2014, 439–41).

17. This becomes evident in comparison with Japan (Vries 2019).
18. This also corresponds with Weber's perspective (Drechsler 2020; Ebrey 2016, 47; Schluchter 2014; Weber 1946; Weber and Gerth 1951).
19. Although administrative law and procedures are essential for the political control of bureaucracies (McCubbins, Noll, and Weingast 1987), personnel appointments are possibly even more critical because they allow politicians to fill leading positions with loyalists (Lewis 2010; Wood and Waterman 1991), which has major implications for political outcomes and bureaucratic effectiveness (see Wood and Lewis 2017), among others.
20. The effects of meritocratic recruitment on the efficiency and corruptibility of bureaucracies have been well documented (Dahlström, Lapuente, and Teorell 2012; Evans and Rauch 1999; Nistotskaya and Cingolani 2016). Crucially, political appointments are only *one* way to undermine meritocracy (that applies mainly to bureaucrats in leading positions). In addition, many bureaucracies have socially selective recruitment, which also undermines meritocracy.
21. For a critical perspective on this categorization of administrative traditions, see Raadschelders and Vigoda-Gadot (2015, 432–35). Also, for an updated perspective on administrative traditions, see Peters (2021).
22. This distinction is more closely related to the quality of bureaucratic outputs than other classifications.
23. The character of delegation is also directly related to the important topic of "information asymmetries" between political principals and bureaucratic agents (Bertelli 2012; Gailmard and Patty 2012a; Lewis 2003; McCubbins, Noll, and Weingast 1987). On the related topic of independent regulatory agencies, see also Gilardi (2009).
24. Importantly, the argument that Prussia previously already had a "bureaucratic" form of tax apparatus is rejected by Kiser and Schneider (1994), who provide a comprehensive overview of Prussian tax collection prior to 1794/1806. Furthermore, Sasaki (2021) provides an analysis of proto-bureaucratic institutions (in the form of "Intendancy") in France prior to 1800.
25. This also included Britain, an imperial state that not only imposed administrative systems on many colonies, but which has been an essential political-administrative model for numerous countries (Irigoin and Grafe 2008, 173; Patapan, Wanna, and Weller 2005).
26. For a similar argument that is applied to preindustrial Prussia, see Kiser and Schneider (1994, 200–201). Furthermore, for a critical perspective on this theory, see Higgs (1987, ch. 1).
27. On the general relevance of standardized or uniform tax systems for the rise of effective states in Europe, see Dincecco (2015).
28. As the example of Poland shows, this also applied to Europe (Vogler 2019b).
29. For an overview of how political parties shaped post-communist states, see Grzymala-Busse (2007).
30. High politicization through patronage appointments is generally considered to weaken bureaucratic competence (Gallo and Lewis 2012; Gilmour and Lewis 2006; Hollibaugh, Horton, and Lewis 2014; Lewis 2009; 2010; Wood and Lewis 2017).
31. However, initially only a *minority* of bureaucrats were recruited through the merit system. It took several more presidencies for merit recruitment to cover a majority of bureaucrats (Ingraham 1995, ch. 3).
32. See also Garfias and Sellars (2023) in this volume.

33. Soifer (2015) makes a related argument about institutional capture, arguing that the involvement of local elites in Latin American bureaucracies often prevented effective state-building.
34. See also Koyama (2022) in this volume.
35. See also Kurtz (2013) and Saylor (2014).
36. On the impact of trade (especially in terms of import substitution policies) on regime type and bureaucratic organization, see also O'Donnell (1973).
37. On path dependence, see also Cirone and Pepinsky (2022), Mahoney (2000), and Raadschelders (1998).
38. From Mahoney's (2000) perspective, we may categorize the first factor as a "power" explanation and the second one as a "functional" or "utilitarian" explanation. Moreover, the fourth factor may be viewed as the equilibrium of a coordination game (cf. David 1994).
39. See also Rauch (1995).
40. Similarly, Gjerløw et al. (2021) challenge the argument that the sequence of building state capacity and democratization matters for development.
41. Yet China's experience with the civil service exam did not lead to an appreciation of "bureaucratism." Instead, the Communist Party has rejected this concept (Ding and Thompson-Brusstar 2021).

References

Aaskoven, L., and J. Nyrup. 2021. "Performance and Promotions in an Autocracy: Evidence from Nazi Germany." *Comparative Politics* 54, no. 1: 51–85.

Ang, Y. Y. 2017. "Beyond Weber: Conceptualizing an Alternative Ideal Type of Bureaucracy in Developing Contexts." *Regulation & Governance* 11, no. 3: 282–98.

Ansell, B. W., and J. Lindvall. 2020. *Inward Conquest: The Political Origins of Modern Public Services*. Cambridge, UK: Cambridge University Press.

Asatryan, Z., F. Heinemann, and H. Pitlik. 2017. "Reforming the Public Administration: The Role of Crisis and the Power of Bureaucracy." *European Journal of Political Economy* 48: 128–43.

Baum, M. A., and D. A. Lake. 2003. "The Political Economy of Growth: Democracy and Human Capital." *American Journal of Political Science* 47, no. 2: 333–47.

Becker, S. O., K. Boeckh, C. Hainz, and L. Woessmann. 2016. "The Empire Is Dead, Long Live the Empire! Long-Run Persistence of Trust and Corruption in the Bureaucracy." *Economic Journal* 126, no. 590: 40–74.

Bell, D. A. 2016. *The China Model: Political Meritocracy and the Limits of Democracy*. Princeton, NJ: Princeton University Press.

Beramendi, P., M. Dincecco, and M. Rogers. 2019. "Intra-elite Competition and Long-Run Fiscal Development." *Journal of Politics* 81, no. 1: 49–65.

Bersch, K., S. Praça, and M. M. Taylor. 2017. "State Capacity, Bureaucratic Politicization, and Corruption in the Brazilian State." *Governance* 30, no. 1: 105–24.

Bertelli, A. M. 2012. *The Political Economy of Public Sector Governance*. Cambridge, UK: Cambridge University Press.

Besley, T., and T. Persson. 2009. "The Origins of State Capacity: Property Rights, Taxation, and Politics." *American Economic Review* 99, no. 4: 1218–44.

Braun, R., and O. Kienitz. 2022. "Comparative Politics in Borderlands: Actors, Identities, and Strategies." *Annual Review of Political Science* 25: 303–21.

Brierley, S. 2021. "Combining Patronage and Merit in Public Sector Recruitment." *Journal of Politics* 83, no. 1: 182–97.

Bustikova, L., and C. Corduneanu-Huci. 2017. "Patronage, Trust, and State Capacity: The Historical Trajectories of Clientelism." *World Politics* 69, no. 2: 277–326.

Buzan, B., and G. Lawson. 2015. *The Global Transformation: History, Modernity and the Making of International Relations*. Cambridge, UK: Cambridge University Press.

Capoccia, G., and R. D. Kelemen. 2007. "The Study of Critical Junctures: Theory, Narrative, and Counterfactuals in Historical Institutionalism." *World Politics* 59, no. 3: 341–69.

Carpenter, D. P. 2001. *The Forging of Bureaucratic Autonomy: Reputations, Networks, and Policy Innovation in Executive Agencies, 1862–1928*. Princeton, NJ: Princeton University Press.

Centeno, M. A. 2002. *Blood and Debt: War and the Nation-State in Latin America*. University Park, PA: Penn State University Press.

Charron, N., C. Dahlström, and V. Lapuente. 2012. "No Law without a State." *Journal of Comparative Economics* 40, no. 2: 176–93.

Chen, T., J. K.-s. Kung, and C. Ma. 2020. "Long Live Keju! The Persistent Effects of China's Civil Examination System." *Economic Journal* 130, no. 631: 2030–64.

Cirone, A., and T. B. Pepinsky. 2022. "Historical Persistence." *Annual Review of Political Science* 25: 241–59.

Corbacho, A., D. W. Gingerich, V. Oliveros, and M. Ruiz-Vega. 2016. "Corruption as a Self-Fulfilling Prophecy: Evidence from a Survey Experiment in Costa Rica." *American Journal of Political Science* 60, no. 4: 1077–92.

Cornell, A., C. H. Knutsen, and J. Teorell. 2020. "Bureaucracy and Growth." *Comparative Political Studies* 53, no. 14: 2246–82.

Cornell, A., and T. Svensson. 2022. "Colonial Origins of Modern Bureaucracy? India and the Professionalization of the British Civil Service." *Governance*: 1–21.

Crooks, P., and T. H. Parsons. 2016. *Empires and Bureaucracy in World History: From Late Antiquity to the Twentieth Century*. Cambridge, UK: Cambridge University Press.

Dahlström, C., and V. Lapuente. 2017. *Organizing Leviathan: Politicians, Bureaucrats, and the Making of Good Government*. Cambridge, UK: Cambridge University Press.

Dahlström, C., V. Lapuente, and J. Teorell. 2012. "The Merit of Meritocratization: Politics, Bureaucracy, and the Institutional Deterrents of Corruption." *Political Research Quarterly* 65, no. 3: 656–68.

David, P. A. 1994. "Why Are Institutions the 'Carriers of History'? Path Dependence and the Evolution of Conventions, Organizations and Institutions." *Structural Change and Economic Dynamics* 5, no. 2: 205–20.

Deak, J. 2015. *Forging a Multinational State: State Making in Imperial Austria from the Enlightenment to the First World War*. Stanford, CA: Stanford University Press.

de Juan, A., F. Haass, and J. Pierskalla. 2021. "The Partial Effectiveness of Indoctrination in Autocracies: Evidence from the German Democratic Republic." *World Politics* 73, no. 4: 593–628.

Dincecco, M. 2015. "The Rise of Effective States in Europe." *Journal of Economic History* 75, no. 3: 901–18.

Ding, I. 2020. "Performative Governance." *World Politics* 72, no. 4: 525–56.

Ding, I., and M. Thompson-Brusstar. 2021. "The Anti-bureaucratic Ghost in China's Bureaucratic Machine." *China Quarterly* 248: 116–40.

Drechsler, W. 2013. "Wang Anshi and the Origins of Modern Public Management in Song Dynasty China." *Public Money & Management* 33, no. 5: 353–60.

Drechsler, W. 2018. "Beyond the Western Paradigm: Confucian Public Administration." In *Public Policy in the "Asian Century": Concepts, Cases and Futures*, ed. S. Bice, A. Poole, and H. Sullivan, 19–40. London, UK: Palgrave Macmillan.

Drechsler, W. 2020. "Max Weber and the Mandate of Heaven." *Max Weber Studies* 20, no. 1: 25–56.

Dunleavy, P., H. Margetts, S. Bastow, and J. Tinkler. 2006. "New Public Management Is Dead—Long Live Digital-Era Governance." *Journal of Public Administration Research and Theory* 16, no. 3: 467–94.

Ebrey, P. 2016. "China as a Contrasting Case: Bureaucracy and Empire in Song China." In *Empires and Bureaucracy in World History: From Late Antiquity to the Twentieth Century*, ed. P. Crooks and T. H. Parsons, 31–53. Cambridge, UK: Cambridge University Press.

Eisenstadt, S. N. 1993. *The Political Systems of Empires*. Transaction.

Ertman, T. 1997. *Birth of the Leviathan: Building States and Regimes in Medieval and Early Modern Europe*. Cambridge, UK: Cambridge University Press.

Evans, P. B. 1995. *Embedded Autonomy: States and Industrial Transformation*. Princeton, NJ: Princeton University Press.

Evans, P. B., and J. E. Rauch. 1999. "Bureaucracy and Growth: A Cross-National Analysis of the Effects of 'Weberian' State Structures on Economic Growth." *American Sociological Review* 64, no. 5: 748–65.

Finer, S. E. 1997. *The History of Government from the Earliest Times*, Volume 1: *Ancient Monarchies and Empires*. Oxford, UK: Oxford University Press.

Fischer, W., and P. Lundgreen. 1975. "The Recruitment and Training of Administrative and Technical Personnel." In *The Formation of National States in Western Europe*, ed. C. Tilly, 456–561. Princeton, NJ: Princeton University Press.

Fry, B. R., and J. C. N. Raadschelders. 2022. *Mastering Public Administration: From Max Weber to Dwight Waldo*. Washington, DC: CQ Press.

Fukuyama, F. 2011. *The Origins of Political Order: From Prehuman Times to the French Revolution*. New York, NY: Farrar, Straus and Giroux.

Gailmard, S., and J. W. Patty. 2012a. "Formal Models of Bureaucracy." *Annual Review of Political Science* 15: 353–77.

Gailmard, S., and J. W. Patty. 2012b. *Learning While Governing: Expertise and Accountability in the Executive Branch*. Chicago, IL: University of Chicago Press.

Gallo, N., and D. E. Lewis. 2012. "The Consequences of Presidential Patronage for Federal Agency Performance." *Journal of Public Administration Research and Theory* 22, no. 2: 219–43.

Garfias, F. 2018. "Elite Competition and State Capacity Development: Theory and Evidence from Post-revolutionary Mexico." *American Political Science Review* 112, no. 2: 339–57.

Garfias, F., and E. A. Sellars. 2021. "From Conquest to Centralization: Domestic Conflict and the Transition to Direct Rule." *Journal of Politics* 83, no. 3: 1399–416.

Garfias, F., and E. A. Sellars. 2023. "State-Building in Historical Political Economy." In *The Oxford Handbook of Historical Political Economy*, ed. J. A. Jenkins and J. Rubin, 209–35. Oxford, UK: Oxford University Press.

Geddes, B. 1994. *Politician's Dilemma: Building State Capacity in Latin America.* Berkeley and Los Angeles, CA: University of California Press.

Gilardi, F. 2009. *Delegation in the Regulatory State: Independent Regulatory Agencies in Western Europe.* Cheltenham, UK: Edward Elgar Publishing.

Gilmour, J. B., and D. E. Lewis. 2006. "Political Appointees and the Competence of Federal Program Management." *American Politics Research* 34, no. 1: 22–50.

Gimpel'son, V. 2003. "The Size and Composition of the Russian Bureaucracy." *Problems of Economic Transition* 46, no. 5: 52–78.

Gingerich, D. W. 2013. "Governance Indicators and the Level of Analysis Problem: Empirical Findings from South America." *British Journal of Political Science* 43, no. 3: 505–40.

Gjerløw, H., C. H. Knutsen, T. Wig, and M. C. Wilson. 2021. *One Road to Riches? How State Building and Democratization Affect Economic Development.* Cambridge, UK: Cambridge University Press.

Gorski, P. S. 2003. *The Disciplinary Revolution: Calvinism and the Rise of the State in Early Modern Europe.* Chicago, IL: University of Chicago Press.

Grzymala-Busse, A. 2007. *Rebuilding Leviathan: Party Competition and State Exploitation in Post-communist Democracies.* Cambridge, UK: Cambridge University Press.

Grzymala-Busse, A. 2020. "Beyond War and Contracts: The Medieval and Religious Roots of the European State." *Annual Review of Political Science* 23: 19–36.

Guardado, J. 2018. "Office-Selling, Corruption, and Long-Term Development in Peru." *American Political Science Review* 112, no. 4: 971–95.

Hanson, J. K. 2014. "Forging Then Taming Leviathan: State Capacity, Constraints on Rulers, and Development." *International Studies Quarterly* 58, no. 2: 380–92.

Hendrix, C. S. 2010. "Measuring State Capacity: Theoretical and Empirical Implications for the Study of Civil Conflict." *Journal of Peace Research* 47, no. 3: 273–85.

Herbst, J. 2014. *States and Power in Africa: Comparative Lessons in Authority and Control.* Princeton, NJ: Princeton University Press.

Higgs, R. 1987. *Crisis and Leviathan.* New York: Oxford University Press.

Hilberg, R., C. Browning, and P. Hayes. 2019. *German Railroads, Jewish Souls: The Reichsbahn, Bureaucracy, and the Final Solution.* Oxford, UK: Berghahn Books.

Hintze, O. 1975. "Military Organization and the Organization of the State." In *The Historical Essays of Otto Hintze,* ed. F. Gilbert, 178–215. Oxford, UK: Oxford University Press.

Hochedlinger, M. 2003. *Austria's Wars of Emergence, 1683–1797: War, State, and Society in the Habsburg Monarchy.* London, UK: Longman/Pearson Education.

Hollibaugh, G. E., G. Horton, and D. E. Lewis. 2014. "Presidents and Patronage." *American Journal of Political Science* 58, no. 4: 1024–42.

Hong, S. C., C. Paik, and Y. Yun. 2021. "The Road to Ascension: Exams, Lineages and Civil Servants of the Joseon Dynasty." Working Paper, Available at SSRN: https://dx.doi.org/10.2139/ssrn.4011834.

Hood, C. 1991. "A Public Management for All Seasons?" *Public Administration* 69, no. 1: 3–19.

Hood, C. 1995. "The 'New Public Management' in the 1980s: Variations on a Theme." *Accounting, Organizations and Society* 20, no. 2–3: 93–109.

Hoogenboom, A. A. 1968. *Outlawing the Spoils: A History of the Civil Service Reform Movement, 1865–1883.* Urbana, IL: University of Illinois Press.

Hough, J. F., and R. Grier. 2015. *The Long Process of Development: Building Markets and States in Pre-industrial England, Spain and Their Colonies.* Cambridge, UK: Cambridge University Press.

Huber, J. D., and C. R. Shipan. 2002. *Deliberate Discretion? The Institutional Foundations of Bureaucratic Autonomy.* Cambridge, UK: Cambridge University Press.

Ingraham, P. W. 1995. *The Foundation of Merit: Public Service in American Democracy.* Baltimore, MD: Johns Hopkins University Press.

Irigoin, A., and R. Grafe. 2008. "Bargaining for Absolutism: A Spanish Path to Nation-State and Empire Building." *Hispanic American Historical Review* 88, no. 2: 173–209.

Jiang, Q., and J. K.-s. Kung. 2020. "Social Mobility in Late Imperial China: Reconsidering the 'Ladder of Success' hypothesis." *Modern China* 47, no. 5: 628–61.

Johnson, C. 1982. *MITI and the Japanese miracle: The Growth of Industrial Policy, 1925–1975.* Stanford, CA: Stanford University Press.

Johnson, N. D., and M. Koyama. 2017. "States and Economic Growth: Capacity and Constraints." *Explorations in Economic History* 64: 1–20.

Johnson, R. N., and G. D. Libecap. 1994. *The Federal Civil Service System and the Problem of Bureaucracy.* Chicago, IL: University of Chicago Press.

Judson, P. M. 2016. *The Habsburg Empire: A New History.* Cambridge, MA: The Belknap Press of Harvard University Press.

Kann, R. A. 1974. *A History of the Habsburg Empire, 1526–1918.* Berkeley and Los Angeles, CA: University of California Press.

Kennedy, P. 1988. *The Rise and Fall of the Great Powers: Economic Change and Military Conflict from 1500 to 2000.* London, UK: Unwin Hyman.

Kiser, E., and J. Schneider. 1994. "Bureaucracy and Efficiency: An Analysis of Taxation in Early Modern Prussia." *American Sociological Review* 59, no. 2: 187–204.

Kohli, A. 2004. *State-Directed Development: Political Power and Industrialization in the Global Periphery.* Cambridge, UK: Cambridge University Press.

Koyama, M. 2023. "Legal Capacity in Historical Political Economy." In *The Oxford Handbook of Historical Political Economy*, ed. J. A. Jenkins and J. Rubin, 271–92. Oxford, UK: Oxford University Press.

Kurtz, M. J. 2013. *Latin American State Building in Comparative Perspective: Social Foundations of Institutional Order.* Cambridge, UK: Cambridge University Press.

La Porta, R., F. Lopez-de Silanes, A. Shleifer, and R. W. Vishny. 1997. "Legal Determinants of External Finance." *Journal of Finance* 52, no. 3: 1131–50.

Lapuente Gine, V. 2006. *A Political Economy Approach to Bureaucracies.* Dissertation (DPhil), Oxford, UK: University of Oxford.

Lee, A., and K. A. Schultz. 2012. "Comparing British and French Colonial Legacies: A Discontinuity Analysis of Cameroon." *Quarterly Journal of Political Science* 7, no. 4: 365–410.

Lee, M. M. 2020. *Crippling Leviathan: How Foreign Subversion Weakens the State.* Ithaca, NY: Cornell University Press.

Lewis, D. E. 2003. *Presidents and the Politics of Agency Design: Political Insulation in the United States Government Bureaucracy, 1946–1997.* Stanford, CA: Stanford University Press.

Lewis, D. E. 2009. "Revisiting the Administrative Presidency: Policy, Patronage, and Agency Competence." *Presidential Studies Quarterly* 39, no. 1: 60–73.

Lewis, D. E. 2010. *The Politics of Presidential Appointments: Political Control and Bureaucratic Performance.* Princeton, NJ: Princeton University Press.

Mahoney, J. 2000. "Path Dependence in Historical Sociology." *Theory and Society* 29, no. 4: 507–48.

Mann, M. 1993. *The Sources of Social Power, Volume 2: The Rise of Classes and Nation-States 1760–1914.* Cambridge, UK: Cambridge University Press.

Matsuzaki, R. 2019. *Statebuilding by Imposition: Resistance and Control in Colonial Taiwan and the Philippines*. Ithaca, UK: Cornell University Press.

Mattingly, D. C. 2017. "Colonial Legacies and State Institutions in China: Evidence from a Natural Experiment." *Comparative Political Studies* 50, no. 4: 434–63.

Mazzuca, S. 2021. *Latecomer State Formation: Political Geography and Capacity Failure in Latin America*. New Haven, CT: Yale University Press.

McClellan, J. E., and F. Regourd. 2011. *The Colonial Machine: French Science and Overseas Expansion in the Old Regime*. Turnhout, Belgium: Brepols.

McCubbins, M. D., R. G. Noll, and B. R. Weingast. 1987. "Administrative Procedures as Instruments of Political Control." *Journal of Law, Economics, & Organization* 3, no. 2: 243–77.

McDonnell, E. M. 2020. *Patchwork Leviathan: Pockets of Bureaucratic Effectiveness in Developing States*. Princeton, NJ: Princeton University Press.

Mitchell, A. M. 2022. "Structured Stability Spending in Late Modern Empires: Japan, Germany, Ottoman State, and Brazil." *Journal of Historical Political Economy* 2, no. 2: 363–89.

Nistotskaya, M., and L. Cingolani. 2016. "Bureaucratic Structure, Regulatory Quality, and Entrepreneurship in a Comparative Perspective: Cross-Sectional and Panel Data Evidence." *Journal of Public Administration Research and Theory* 26, no. 3: 519–34.

North, D. C. 1990. "A Transaction Cost Theory of Politics." *Journal of Theoretical Politics* 2, no. 4: 355–67.

O'Donnell, G. 1973. *Modernization and Bureaucratic-Authoritarianism: Studies in South American Politics*. Berkeley, CA: Institute of International Studies, University of California.

Olson, M. 1993. "Dictatorship, Democracy, and Development." *American Political Science Review* 87, no. 3: 567–76.

Osborne, D., and T. Gaebler. 1992. *Reinventing Government: How the Entrepreneurial Spirit Is Transforming the Public Sector*. New York, NY: Penguin Press.

Paglayan, A. S. 2022. "Education or Indoctrination? The Violent Origins of Public School Systems in an Era of State-Building." *American Political Science Review*.

Paik, C. 2014. "Does Lineage Matter? A Study of Ancestral Influence on Educational Attainment in Korea." *European Review of Economic History* 18, no. 4: 433–51.

Paik, C., and J. Vechbanyongratana. 2019. "Path to Centralization and Development: Evidence from Siam." *World Politics* 71, no. 2: 289–331.

Painter, M., and B. G. Peters. 2010. *Tradition and Public Administration*. New York, NY: Palgrave Macmillan.

Pardelli, G., and A. Kustov. 2022. "When Coethnicity Fails." *World Politics* 74, no. 2: 249–84.

Parrott, D. 2010. "From Military Enterprise to Standing Armies: War, State, and Society in Western Europe, 1600–1700." In *European Warfare, 1350–1750*, ed. F. Tallett and D. J. B. Trim, 74–95. Cambridge, UK: Cambridge University Press.

Patapan, H., J. Wanna, and P. M. Weller. 2005. *Westminster Legacies: Democracy and Responsible Government in Asia and the Pacific*. UNSW Press.

Pepinsky, T. B., J. H. Pierskalla, and A. Sacks. 2017. "Bureaucracy and Service Delivery." *Annual Review of Political Science* 20: 249–68.

Peters, B. G. 2021. *Administrative Traditions: Understanding the Roots of Contemporary Administrative Behavior*. Oxford, UK: Oxford University Press.

Pierskalla, J., A. Schultz, E. Wibbels. 2017. "Order, Distance, and Local Development over the Long Run." *Quarterly Journal of Political Science* 12, no. 4: 375–404.

Potter, R. A. 2019. *Bending the Rules: Procedural Politicking in the Bureaucracy*. Chicago, IL: University of Chicago Press.

Potter, R. A., and Vogler, J. P. 2021. "Building Better Bureaucracy: The Historical Origins of the American Administrative State." Working Paper Presented at the Annual Meeting of the American Political Science Association.

Queralt, D. 2019. "War, International Finance, and Fiscal Capacity in the Long Run." *International Organization* 73, no. 4: 713–53.

Raadschelders, J. 1998. "Evolution, Institutional Analysis and Path Dependency: An Administrative History Perspective on Fashionable Approaches and Concepts." *International Review of Administrative Sciences* 64, no. 4: 565–82.

Raadschelders, J., and M. R. Rutgers. 1996. "The Evolution of Civil Service Systems." In *Civil Service Systems in Comparative Perspective*, ed. H. A. G. M. Bekke, J. L. Perry, and T. A. Toonen, 67–99. Bloomington, IN: Indiana University Press.

Raadschelders, J., and E. Vigoda-Gadot. 2015. *Global Dimensions of Public Administration and Governance: A Comparative Voyage*. Hoboken, NJ: John Wiley & Sons.

Raphael, L. 2000. *Recht und Ordnung: Herrschaft durch Verwaltung im 19. Jahrhundert [Law and order: Rule through administration in the nineteenth century]*. Frankfurt am Main, Germany: Fischer Taschenbuch Verlag.

Rauch, J. E. 1995. "Bureaucracy, Infrastructure, and Economic Growth: Evidence from U.S. Cities during the Progressive Era." *American Economic Review* 85, no. 4: 968–79.

Richards, D. 2003. "The Civil Service in Britain: A Case Study in Path Dependency." In *Civil Service Systems in Anglo-American Countries*, ed. J. Halligan, 27–69. Cheltenham, UK: Edward Elgar Publishing.

Ruhil, A. V., and P. J. Camões. 2003. "What Lies Beneath: The Political Roots of State Merit Systems." *Journal of Public Administration Research and Theory* 13, no. 1: 27–42.

Sager, F., and C. Rosser. 2021. "Weberian Bureaucracy." In *Oxford Research Encyclopedia of Politics*. https://doi.org/10.1093/acrefore/9780190228637.013.166. Oxford, UK: Oxford University Press.

Sager, F., C. Rosser, C. Mavrot, and P. Y. Hurni. 2018. *A Transatlantic History of Public Administration: Analyzing the USA, Germany and France*. Cheltenham, UK: Edward Elgar Publishing.

Sasaki, Y. 2021. "The Royal Consultants: The Intendants of France and the Bureaucratic Transition in Pre-modern Europe." *Journal of Historical Political Economy* 1, no. 2: 259–82.

Saylor, R. 2014. *State Building in Boom Times: Commodities and Coalitions in Latin America and Africa*. Oxford, UK: Oxford University Press.

Schenoni, L. L. 2021. "Bringing War Back In: Victory and State Formation in Latin America." *American Journal of Political Science* 65, no. 2: 405–21.

Schluchter, W. 2014. "'How Ideas Become Effective in History'—Max Weber on Confucianism and Beyond." *Max Weber Studies* 14, no. 1: 11–31.

Shefter, M. 1994. *Political Parties and the State: The American Historical Experience*. Cambridge, UK: Cambridge University Press.

Silberman, B. S. 1993. *Cages of Reason: The Rise of the Rational State in France, Japan, the United States, and Great Britain*. Chicago, IL: University of Chicago Press.

Skowronek, S. 1982. *Building a New American State: The Expansion of National Administrative Capacities, 1877–1920*. Cambridge, UK: Cambridge University Press.

Slater, D. 2008. "Can Leviathan Be Democratic? Competitive Elections, Robust Mass Politics, and State Infrastructural Power." *Studies in Comparative International Development* 43, no. 3: 252–72.

Soifer, H. D. 2015. *State Building in Latin America*. Cambridge, UK: Cambridge University Press.

Spruyt, H. 1996. *The Sovereign State and Its Competitors: An Analysis of Systems Change.* Princeton, NJ: Princeton University Press.

Stasavage, D. 2020. *The Decline and Rise of Democracy: A Global History from Antiquity to Today.* Princeton, NJ: Princeton University Press.

Strayer, J. R. 1970. *On the Medieval Origins of the Modern State.* Princeton, NJ: Princeton University Press.

Suryanarayan, P., and S. White. 2021. "Slavery, Reconstruction, and Bureaucratic Capacity in the American South." *American Political Science Review* 115, no. 2: 568–84.

Theriault, S. M. 2003. "Patronage, the Pendleton Act, and the Power of the People." *Journal of Politics* 65, no. 1: 50–68.

Thies, C. G. 2007. "The Political Economy of State Building in Sub-Saharan Africa." *Journal of Politics* 69, no. 3: 716–31.

Tilly, C. 1990. *Coercion, Capital, and European States, AD 990–1992.* Cambridge, MA: Basil Blackwell.

Ting, M. M., J. M. Snyder Jr., S. Hirano, and O. Folke. 2013. "Elections and Reform: The Adoption of Civil Service Systems in the US States." *Journal of Theoretical Politics* 25, no. 3: 363–87.

Toral, G. 2022. "How Patronage Delivers: Political Appointments, Bureaucratic Accountability, and Service Delivery in Brazil." *American Journal of Political Science.*

Unruh, G.-C. v. 1977. "Verwaltungsreformen—Vorhaben und Ergebnisse seit dem Ausgang des 19. Jahrhunderts [Administrative reforms—plans and results since the end of the nineteenth century]." In *Verwaltungsgeschichte—Aufgaben, Zielsetzungen, Beispiele [Administrative history—Tasks, goals, examples]*, ed. R. Morsey, 23–60. Berlin, Germany: Duncker & Humblot.

Van Riper, P. P. 1958. *History of the United States Civil Service.* Evanston, IL: Row, Peterson and Company.

Vogler, J. P. 2019a. "The Entanglement of Public Bureaucratic Institutions: Their Interactions with Society, Culture, Politics, and the Economy." In *Interdisciplinary Studies of the Political Order: New Applications of Public Choice Theory*, ed. D. J. Boudreaux, C. J. Coyne, and B. Herzberg, 99–129. Lanham, MD: Rowman & Littlefield International.

Vogler, J. P. 2019b. "Imperial Rule, the Imposition of Bureaucratic Institutions, and Their Long-Term Legacies." *World Politics* 71, no. 4: 806–63.

Vogler, J. P. 2019c. *The Political Economy of Public Bureaucracy: The Emergence of Modern Administrative Organizations.* PhD dissertation, Duke University. https://hdl.handle.net/10161/19818.

Vogler, J. P. 2022a. "The Complex Imprint of Foreign Rule: Tracking Differential Legacies along the Administrative Hierarchy." *Studies in Comparative International Development.*

Vogler, J. P. 2022b. "Managing Social and Economic Externalities: Industrialization and the Rise of the Bureaucratic State." Working Paper Presented at the Annual Conference of the European Political Science Association, http://janvogler.net/Managing_Externalities.pdf.

Vogler, J. P. 2022c. "Rivalry and Empire: How Competition among European States Shaped Imperialism." *Journal of Historical Political Economy* 2, no. 2: 189–234.

Vries, P. H. H. 2002. "Governing Growth: A Comparative Analysis of the Role of the State in the Rise of the West." *Journal of World History* 13: 67–138.

Vries, P. H. H. 2015. *State, Economy and the Great Divergence: Great Britain and China, 1680s–1850s.* New York, NY: Bloomsbury Publishing.

Vries, P. H. H. 2019. *Averting a Great Divergence: State and Economy in Japan, 1868–1937*. New York, NY: Bloomsbury Publishing.

Waldner, D. 1999. *State Building and Late Development*. Ithaca, NY: Cornell University Press.

Wang, Y. 2022. *The Rise and Fall of Imperial China: The Social Origins of State Development*. Princeton, NJ: Princeton University Press.

Weber, M. 1946. "The Chinese Literati." In *From Max Weber: Essays in Sociology*, ed. H. H. Gerth and C. W. Mills, 416–67. Oxford, UK: Oxford University Press.

Weber, M. 1978. *Economy and Society: An Outline of Interpretive Sociology*. Berkeley and Los Angeles, CA: University of California Press.

Weber, M., and H. H. Gerth. 1951. *The Religion of China: Confucianism and Taoism*. Glencoe, IL: The Free Press.

Wilfahrt, M. 2018. "Precolonial Legacies and Institutional Congruence in Public Goods Delivery: Evidence from Decentralized West Africa." *World Politics* 70, no. 2: 239–74.

Wood, A. K., and D. E. Lewis. 2017. "Agency Performance Challenges and Agency Politicization." *Journal of Public Administration Research and Theory* 27, no. 4: 581–95.

Wood, B. D., and R. W. Waterman. 1991. "The Dynamics of Political Control of the Bureaucracy." *American Political Science Review* 85, no. 3: 801–28.

Workman, S. 2015. *The Dynamics of Bureaucracy in the US Government: How Congress and Federal Agencies Process Information and Solve Problems*. Cambridge, UK: Cambridge University Press.

Wunder, B. 1986. *Geschichte der Bürokratie in Deutschland [The history of bureaucracy in Germany]*. Frankfurt am Main, Germany: Suhrkamp Verlag.

Yazaki, Y. 2018. "The Effects of Bureaucracy on Political Accountability and Electoral Selection." *European Journal of Political Economy* 51: 57–68.

Zhang, N., and M. M. Lee. 2020. "Literacy and State-Society Interactions in Nineteenth-Century France." *American Journal of Political Science* 64, no. 4: 1001–16.

Ziblatt, D. 2008. *Structuring the State: The Formation of Italy and Germany and the Puzzle of Federalism*. Princeton, NJ: Princeton University Press.

CHAPTER 20

THE HISTORICAL POLITICAL ECONOMY OF POLITICAL PARTIES

JEFFERY A. JENKINS AND CHRISTOPHER KAM

WE discuss the historical transformation of political parties in terms of three "revolutionary" phases: an intellectual revolution of limited government that permitted the conceptual development of a constitutional opposition; a legislative revolution that was driven by the need to secure predictability in the face of the vagaries of majority rule and to address the socioeconomic demands of the Industrial Revolution; and an electoral revolution that was occasioned by the advent of mass suffrage.

While our narrative touches on elements of both sociological and rational choice accounts of political parties, it does not evaluate their relative merits; that has been done elsewhere (see Boix 2008). Rather, our aim is to highlight two themes. The first is legislative in nature and centers on the interaction between the (1) pathologies of majority rule, (2) legislative rules, and the (3) incentives for leaders to organize political parties inside the legislature. The second is electoral in nature and centers on the resource demands that a mass electorate made of political parties, the organizational strategies that parties adopted to meet these demands, and the implications of these organizational strategies for parties' autonomy and the stability of the party system.

We develop these themes discursively, using examples drawn mainly from American and British history but also from Germany and France. We conclude that the legislative research agenda on parties' needs to pay closer attention to the symbiotic relationship between parties and legislative rules; correspondingly, the electoral research agenda should focus on the changing nature of candidate nominations and campaign financing.

The Intellectual Revolution

Classical writers, like Montesquieu and Madison, used "party" and "faction" interchangeably to signal their disapproval of political parties, but over the course of the eighteenth century a distinction began to be drawn between the two terms. Bolingbroke, for example, defined *party* as "a national Division of Opinions, concerning the Form and Methods of Government, for the benefit of the whole Community," whereas *faction* was "a Set of Men arm'd with Power, and acting upon no one Principle of Party, or any Notion of Publick Good, but to preserve and share the Spoils amongst Themselves, as their only Cement" (quoted from Skjönsberg 2016). Bolingbroke thus distinguished party and faction along three dimensions: scope, disposition, and motivation. A party was national in scope, ethical in disposition, and public spirited in motivation; a faction, by contrast, was cliquish, venal, and selfish.

Burke provided the next evolution in thinking on parties. It is useful to quote fully the passage in which Burke defined parties because the first sentence is often used in isolation to imply that Burke understood parties as mere agglomerations of like-minded individuals; the full quote dispels this misconception:

> Party is a body of men united, for promoting by their joint endeavours the national interest, upon some particular principle in which they are all agreed. For my part, I find it impossible to conceive, that any one believes in his own politicks, or thinks them to be of any weight, who refuses to adopt the means of having them reduced into practice. It is the business of the speculative philosopher to mark the proper ends of Government. It is the business of the politician, who is the philosopher in action, to find out proper means towards those ends, and to employ them with effect. Therefore every honourable connexion *will avow it as their first purpose, to pursue every just method to put the men who hold their opinions into such a condition as may enable them to carry their common plans into execution, with all the power and authority of the State.*
>
> (Burke 1878 [1770], p. 86, emphasis added).

Burke's last sentence makes clear that a party's principal objective is to (legally) obtain power in order to enact its favored policies. Burke's definition is thus much closer to Schumpeter's (i.e., "a group whose members propose to act in concert in the competitive struggle for political power" [1942, 283]) than is commonly held. The key difference is whether parties are (and ought to be) animated by sincerely held principles (Burke) or whether such principles are instrumental (hence malleable) to the pursuit of power (Schumpeter). The overriding similarity, however, is that parties pursue power.

Burke's definition was revolutionary because it explicitly rejected the traditional presumption that the organized pursuit of power was inherently discreditable or dangerous. This was a watershed in that such a definition admits the possibility of pluralism and constitutional opposition (Sartori 1976). Such a notion is itself contingent on a theory of limited government in that it is only when government is limited that the existence of an opposition party no longer threatens the regime. In this respect, parties are fundamentally liberal institutions (Caramani 2017). Once these ideas—of limited government, pluralism, and constitutional opposition—were in place, the extension of the suffrage created incentives for parties to argue that their claims were validated by the support of a disinterested electorate and, consequently, to ensure that their claims attracted electoral support. In this manner, *responsible* government became *responsive* government (Sartori 1976).

This intellectual and institutional revolution took place at different speeds in different countries. In England, limited government arrived with the Glorious Revolution of 1689 in the form of a constitutional monarchy (North and Weingast 1989; Pincus 2009). Parties, albeit in the limited sense of groups of like-minded individuals, were active in Parliament in advance of 1689, of course. Their normative and constitutional status remained contentious, however, and these issues were argued out over the course of the eighteenth century by theorists and politicians alike. Hence, the argument over the place of parties in the constitution was itself part of the evolution of responsible government. The confidence convention was the most important aspect of this institutional evolution because it created powerful incentives for the cabinet to organize its parliamentary supporters via a whipping system (Cox 1992). We discuss later the legislative and electoral consequences of the British intellectual acceptance of political parties.

Other countries do not fit Sartori's model of party development so neatly. The United States secured limited government in 1776 and manhood suffrage by 1820. Yet the political elite scorned parties. When the Founding Fathers organized a convention in 1787 to dispense with the Articles of Confederation, "they framed a Constitution, which, among its other ends, was meant to control and counteract parties" (Hofstadter 1969, viii). They soon found parties necessary to effective governance, however. By the mid-1790s, the Federalists, led by Alexander Hamilton and John Adams, were the party in power, while the Republicans, led by Thomas Jefferson and James Madison, positioned themselves as the "legitimate opposition." This legitimacy—and the larger legitimacy of a "party system"—was solidified in 1800 when Jefferson defeated Adams for the presidency and "gave the world its first example of the peaceful transit of a government from the control of one popular party to another" (Hofstadter 1969, ix).

Continental Europe accepted liberal ideals of limited government and religious toleration only fitfully. In many countries, liberal constitutionalism had to contend with an overbearing Catholic Church, on one hand, and reactionary monarchs, on the other hand—all while questions of national integration were still being fought out. Thus, we see flashes of democracy in 1848, with constituent assemblies elected at Frankfurt and Paris. The speed with which deputies in these assemblies grouped themselves into parties, and the extent to which parties structured the outcomes of these assemblies is a matter of current research (e.g., Sieberer and Herrmann 2019).

The French Second Empire that followed the abortive constitutional experiment of 1848 shows how an electoral regime based on universal suffrage can function without vibrant parties.[1] This was accomplished by a variety of means. First, the regime regularly employed plebiscites rather than elections to legitimate its measures. Citizens were thus habituated to vote for proposals, not parties. Second, when elections did occur, they were tightly managed by the government. Political meetings were limited, newspapers were censored, and civil servants oversaw the electoral machinery. These constraints deprived parties of the means to mobilize voters and imbued elections with a technocratic rather than a popular character. Finally, the regime's assembly was consultative in nature; the assembly could not initiate legislation, and ministers were responsible to the emperor. These arrangements undercut the incentives to organize parliamentary parties. Thus, a weak legislature generated weak incentives to organize parties. It presumably follows that strong legislatures—ones capable of checking executives and shaping legislation—generated strong incentives to organize parties.

The Legislative Revolution

The American Case, Part I: Instability and the Early Constitutional System

Aldrich (1995) argues that American political parties arose in response to the collective choice problems that hampered decision-making in the early Congresses. The "Great Principle" of the day was how strong and active the federal government was to be, with "federalists" favoring a strong federal government and "anti-federalists" preferring a limited federal government. The federalists had a majority in the First Federal Congress (1789–91) but were unable to translate that support into legislative victories. This was because the anti-federalists succeeded in injecting into debates and votes secondary issues on which the federalists were internally divided. In this way, the anti-federalist minority stymied the federal majority.

The anti-federalist strategy made the choice space multidimensional so that policy questions involved *more* than just how strong the federal government was to be. In doing so, the anti-federalists exploited how majority-rule operates in multidimensional policy spaces. As social choice theorists would later show, majority rule outcomes in one dimension are stable, with the median voter's ideal point as the equilibrium (Black 1958; Downs 1957). In two or more dimensions, however, majority rule outcomes are generally unstable (Plott 1967) and potentially "chaotic" in that there exists an agenda that can lead via some series of majority votes to any outcome in the policy space (McKelvey 1976). The real-world implication of these theoretical results is that losers from a prior round of voting can always raise secondary issues or manipulate the agenda to disrupt an erstwhile majority and overturn prior decisions.

Hamilton recognized the problem and set about creating informal institutions (caucuses, floor leaders, and whip systems) to encourage federalists to focus *exclusively* on the Great Principle and ignore any secondary issues raised by anti-federalists. The federalists quickly began to win more often. Those informal institutions would combine with the underlying policy preferences of the federalists to form the core of an institutional political party—the Federalists. (Here, Aldrich adopts Schwartz's [1989; 2021] definition of parties as "long coalitions" or "ones organized and elected to stick together on all or most legislative votes.") The anti-federalists copied those informal institutions to form an opposition political party—the Republicans.[2] By the Third Federal Congress (1793–95), Congressional voting was visibly partisan (Aldrich 1995; Hoadley 1980; 1986).[3]

The American Case, Part II: Building the Cartel

By the early twentieth century, Congressional parties had transformed from "long coalitions" into *legislative cartels* (Cox and McCubbins 1993). A legislative cartel had an organizational part and a procedural part. Specifically, the majority party first had to reliably secure the key leadership positions in the House (and become an *organizational cartel*) before it could later tamp down on minority obstruction of legislative business (and become a *procedural cartel*).

This transformation began in the 1830s, when Martin Van Buren, the Democratic leader, recognized that House officer positions—principally the Speaker, but also the Printer and Clerk—controlled resources that could provide substantial benefits for the majority party (Jenkins and Stewart 2013). The problem was that officer elections exhibited the same type of instability that plagued voting in the early Congresses; dissident majority-party members sometimes undermined their party's efforts to win the officer elections by voting with the minority for ideological reasons. Van Buren consequently pushed for House officer elections to be held by a public ballot rather than a secret ballot (as had been the case) and for the creation of a legislative party caucus. With the public ballot in place, the party caucus would be the venue for intraparty coordination on officer elections. Decisions made in caucus would be honored by all party members on the floor and enforced by a system of carrots and sticks: "losers" were compensated with various benefits (policy, committee assignments); dissidents were threatened with expulsion. By the late 1860s, the "binding party caucus on organizational matters" had fully developed into an equilibrium institution (Jenkins and Stewart 2013, 242). The majority party thus became an organizational cartel capable of controlling the selection of the Speaker and other key House officers.

Thomas B. Reed's (R-ME) innovative Speakership during the 51st Congress (1889–91) was critical to completing the transformation of the majority party into a legislative cartel. Prior to Reed's ascension, the House majority used mechanisms like special orders to manage business, but they did little to stifle minority obstruction (Binder 1997; Dion 1997). Accordingly, Cox and McCubbins (2005) argue that House politics during this era was governed by a "dual veto," wherein dilatory threats (and often behavior) by the minority and antiquated procedural rules meant that the two major parties effectively shared agenda power. Reed sought to eliminate minority obstruction by changing the rules by which quorums were counted, reducing the quorum requirement in the Committee of the Whole, and granting the Speaker the discretion to rule dilatory motions out of order (Schickler 2001). He also transformed special orders into special rules, which further enhanced the authority of the Rules Committee (chaired by the Speaker) and increased the majority party's control over the legislative agenda. Thanks to these changes, the House majority party was able to govern more effectively and efficiently. Specifically, the majority party's ability to control the agenda in a *negative* way, by preventing legislative change that would harm a majority of its members, spiked with Reed's innovations and has remained strong ever since (Cox and McCubbins 2005). Reed's actions thus transformed the House majority party into a procedural cartel.[4]

The British Case: The Industrial Revolution and the Plenary Bottleneck

Cox (2006) explains the partisan character of democratic legislatures by asking us to conceive of a "legislative state of nature" in which all legislators enjoy unfettered access to the plenary agenda. In this institutional environment, legislators who are pressured to advance legislation that delivers particularistic benefits to their supporters invariably overproduce legislation and overconsume plenary time. The result of this collective action problem is a plenary bottleneck: legislation grinds to a halt because there is simply not enough time to process it.

Cox (1987) argues that this was the situation in which British MPs found themselves at the beginning of the nineteenth century. The cabinet was under pressure to pass legislation to deal with the wide-ranging consequences of the Industrial Revolution. The rules of the House, however, treated all MPs' bills equally, imposed few constraints on how many bills an MP might introduce, and did not limit how long an MP could speak on them. The result was a legislative backlog for which the cabinet was held responsible. The cabinet reacted by revising the House's procedural rules to prioritize government business and limit the legislative time available to private MPs. The knock-on effects of this procedural revolution were twofold. First, MPs came to realize that their legislative aims could only be achieved through their active support of either the cabinet of the day or of a shadow cabinet that acted as a government-in-waiting (Eggers and Spirling 2018). Second, as MPs increasingly aligned themselves for or against the cabinet of the day, voters came to vote for MPs on that same basis. The long-run and perhaps unintended consequence of the Commons' plenary bottleneck was thus a party-based form of responsible government and a party-oriented electorate.

Considering the Commons' plenary bottleneck in greater detail shows the full impact of the Industrial Revolution on the internal organization of the House of Commons and the development of British parties. Fraser (1960) records that the House considered 2,348 items of business in 1760, increasing to 8,270 items by 1806. Private bills constituted a significant fraction of this increase (Harris 2000, 134). A private bill related to a private locality or entity, and it typically granted the entity a charter to enclose land, engage in trade, incorporate, and so on; they were, in short, vital to economic activity. In the eighteenth century, the practice was for economic actors to engage a Member of Parliament (MP) to guide their private bill through the House (Cox 1987, 15–18). Take, as an example, the parliamentary and commercial activities of Francis Egerton, the 3rd Duke of Bridgewater. In 1759, Egerton secured the passage of a private bill to establish a canal to transport coal from his Lancashire mines to the Manchester market (Harris 2000, 95–97). Egerton was not an MP (he sat in the House of Lords) and appears to have relied on Marshe Dickinson—a longstanding friend for whom Egerton had secured election at Brackley, a borough that Egerton's family controlled[5]—to guide his bill through the Commons. Egerton was thus able to achieve his aims without relying on parties to organize elections or to pass legislation; he simply worked through his own intermediaries.

Whether the main business of the eighteenth-century House was conducted on such an independent (as opposed to a partisan) basis is contentious, however, with suggestions that independence and cross-party cooperation was confined to local affairs (Holmes 1987). Bogart's (2018) analysis of 107 private bills relating to river navigation speaks to this controversy. Bogart states that it was routine for towns downstream on a river to protect their privileged position by opposing private bills that sought to extend the river's navigability upstream. His analysis shows that a river navigation bill was more likely to fail as the share of majority-party MPs downstream of the sponsoring town increased (Bogart 2018, Table 8). The inference is that party connections mattered. How they mattered is less obvious, however. Prior to 1832, many towns were unrepresented in Parliament, crowded out by dozens of pocket boroughs where MPs (often dominant businessmen or landowners in the locality) bought their seats. Hence, it is not clear whether Bogart's results indicate that by the mid-1700s "party" was an institution that independently adjudicated the contending claims of organized interests, or whether "party" was merely a vehicle for and captured by those same interests.

Political scientists describe such matters in terms of the "institutionalization" and "autonomy" of political parties (Polsby 1968). A party is institutionalized and autonomous when it can operate and sustain itself independently of wider social and economic interests. The question, then, is when and how could British parties prevent their MPs from acting independently or as proxies for outside interests in ways that threatened the party's organizational effectiveness or continuity. As we've noted, the House undertook a variety of reforms between 1790 and 1850 that dramatically reduced MPs' scope for acting independently: MPs who held government contracts were made to give up their seats in 1792; government business was given priority on certain days in 1811; the right of MPs to petition the House was curtailed in 1835; and committees were reformed in 1855 so that MPs could not influence legislation on matters in which they had vested interests. That party cohesion in divisions rose only in advance of the First Reform Act (1832) suggests that these reforms did not immediately increase the leverage of cabinet ministers over backbenchers.[6] By the late 1850s, however, party cohesion had recovered from the Conservatives' 1847 split over the Corn Laws to the fairly high levels of the 1830s. Moreover, recent research indicates that the increased party cohesion of the latter half of the nineteenth century was due more to efficacious whipping than to MPs sorting themselves into two homogeneous groups (Eggers and Spirling 2016; Cox and Nowacki 2023; Cox 2022).

Thus by the 1860s the two main British parties were highly cohesive and fully capable of effecting well-defined policy programs. As the parties became more cohesive, they also became more internally differentiated and hierarchical (Cox 1987; Eggers and Spirling 2014; 2018; Goet 2021). That is, government parties dominated opposition parties in terms of agenda control and legislative production, and within all parties, front-benchers overshadowed back-benchers in terms of speaking time and legislative activity.

The Electoral Revolution

The arrival of universal (manhood) suffrage marked the third revolution in the development of political parties. Parties required more resources—money, candidates, and activists—to contest elections in an expansive electorate rather than a limited one, and as we relate further, they used a number of strategies to acquire these resources. A long-standing argument in the literature is that the strategies by which parties acquired the resources to contest elections shaped their capacity to respond to the diverse demands of a mass electorate (Duverger 1959 [1951]; Panebianco 1988). This dynamic interacted with electoral rules to incentivize new parties to enter the party system (see Caramani 2023), with significant implications for the stability of the party system and, sometimes, of the regime itself.

While scholarly attention has focused on the role of the electoral formula in generating multiparty competition, variations in the historical timing and legal basis of enfranchisement are also theorized to shape electoral competition. Where mass suffrage occurred after the integration of the nation state, the class cleavage dominated and the social demand for new parties was attenuated (Duverger 1959 [1951]; Lipset and Rokkan 1967). By contrast, in countries where the suffrage was extended before church-state, urban-rural, or center-periphery questions had been settled, opportunities arose for confessional, agrarian, or ethnic parties to enter the party system. In theory, the abolition of censitary voting in favor of manhood suffrage imparted an economic gradient to these entry opportunities because the poorer the district, the greater the proportion of new and receptive voters in the district electorate (on which see Hanlon 2023 and Stasavage 2023). In practice, however, local notables frequently exploited their authority as mayors or justices of the peace to subvert voter registration or manipulate the ballot (Capoccia and Ziblatt 2010; Mares 2015; Stokes et al. 2013). The suppression of political contestation was thus a viable electoral response to enfranchisement; it explains why elections in many rural areas and company towns went uncontested even after the franchise was extended (Caramani 2003), and further why inducing candidates to contest hostile districts was one of party leaders' major challenges.

The American Precedent: Van Buren's Spoils System and the Progressive Reaction

American politicians confronted the organizational challenge of a mass electorate in the 1820s, when most states dropped their property qualifications for voting (Engerman and Sokoloff 2005). The challenge was twofold: first, leaders had to mobilize large numbers of voters who were scattered across diverse districts; second, leaders had to find candidates to contest (and fund) elections in all these districts. The initial solution to this challenge was the *spoils system*. Developed in New York by Aaron Burr and scaled up to national politics by his protege, Martin Van Buren, the spoils system was a distributive bargain: legislators provided legislative support in exchange for control of government patronage in their respective districts. This patronage—which consisted of local government appointments, post office jobs, and the like—was in turn distributed to local activists in exchange for their assistance in organizing elections. This system met two objectives: first, it provided a disciplined block of legislative support; second, it exploited the resources and the geographic reach of the state to meet the challenges of conducting campaigns in the context of a mass electorate.

Van Buren's most important innovation was to link the spoils system to the convention system for nominating candidates. The chief product of the convention was the party (or "slip") ticket, which listed the party's nominees for every level of elective office. The party ticket served to unite the local, state, and national elements of the Democratic coalition, but it can also be understood as a contractual expression of the distributive bargain on which the Democratic Party was based.

Van Buren was the first politician to organize the distribution of patronage so that it generated a mutually reinforcing relationship between the party's legislative and electoral coalitions. Government patronage was used to secure party discipline in the legislative chamber; that legislative power was then used to direct more patronage to legislators' districts; recipients of that patronage then mobilized voters and fought elections on the legislator's behalf. The system allowed American parties to contest mass elections without the need to develop and adhere to detailed policy platforms. Over time, the spoils system evolved into machine politics, with spoils distributed based on electoral performance: those who delivered more votes received more lucrative sinecures (James 2006). The political efficacy of this organizational model is evidenced by the fact that it was widely copied and remains in effect in many countries (Piattoni 2001; Kitschelt and Wilkinson 2007; Robinson and Verdier 2013).

American political machines were strongest in the large cities of the Northeast where they could exploit dense social networks to monitor and mobilize voters. By contrast, they were much weaker in the western states. This was so for two reasons. First (and consistent with Lipset and Rokkan's argument), voters in the West were integrated into the national electorate in piecemeal fashion, as Western territories acquired statehood over the latter half of the nineteenth century. Second, the entry of the Republican and Democratic political machines into the Western states was retarded by the railway companies, which had little interest in voter mobilization (Shefter 1983); they used their economic position and communications networks to stage-manage the elections of pliant state assemblies. The large pools of unmobilized voters in these later-integrated Western states served as the electoral cores of a series of third-party efforts, including the Greenbacks, Populists, and Progressives. (A similar story could be told about Canada, with agrarian and populist third parties emerging from a later-integrated west).[7]

These third parties enjoyed significant electoral success at the local and state levels, but not at the national level. Nonetheless—and despite significant differences in their economic policies and social bases—the activists embodying these third parties sought a series of institutional reforms that eventually overturned the caucus and convention systems at the heart of machine politics. These reforms had their biggest "bite" during the Progressive Era (1870–1920). Two of them, the introduction of direct primaries and the direct election of US senators, are worth further discussion.

Direct primaries, which were adopted by a majority of states in the first two decades of the twentieth century, allowed voters to choose party nominees directly. This was especially important in states that were one-party-dominated and citizens were little more than spectators. Hirano and Snyder (2019) find that direct primaries were almost always adopted when one party had a distinct electoral advantage; indeed, they find that in forty of forty-five cases, primaries were adopted when one party had unified control of state government. Yet Ware (2002) cautions us to avoid claiming that progressive reformers *forced* change (via primaries) onto the parties. He argues that the parties themselves had incentives to move beyond the convention system, as intraparty conflict over convention decisions (at different levels) had been increasing for some time. Party leaders needed nominations to be viewed as legitimate—that is, free of fraud and corruption—by co-partisans, so that nomination "losers" and their factions would continue mobilizing voters (and working generally) for the party. Direct primaries were seen as an institutional reform that provided that intraparty legitimacy. Thus, direct primaries generated benefits both externally (to antiparty reformers) and internally (to party leaders).

The direct election of US senators—instead of indirect election by state legislatures (where party caucuses controlled the nominations)—was a reform effort pushed at the same time as party primaries. In addition to making the Senate more reflective of the popular will, progressive reformers sought direct election to limit corruption in the electoral process by making influence costlier, since it had to be spread over many more people, and to avoid the increasingly common seat vacancies that resulted from deadlocked state legislatures (Schiller and Stewart 2015). And there is reason to believe that direct election (following the adoption of the Seventeenth Amendment to the Constitution in 1913) was successful: seat vacancies became less common and the ostensible "buying" of senators became harder. Over time, Senate elections more closely mirrored House and presidential elections (Engstrom and Kernell 2014), and senators shifted their voting behavior toward the median voter in their state electorate (Gailmard and Jenkins 2009). But, like the story of direct primaries, the direct election of senators should not be seen as something that was forced on the parties. As Schiller and Stewart (2015, 11) note, the major parties came to realize that direct elections would "enable them to knock out minor parties more easily in the contest for Senate seats." This gave them a strong incentive to support the change to direct elections.

Organic Innovation and Mass Parties in Britain

In Britain, organizational innovation to address the challenge of a mass electorate quickly followed the passage of the 1832 Reform Act. Recognizing the importance of registering voters under the new franchise, party leaders encouraged the establishment of local registration societies (Salmon 2002). The Carleton and Reform Clubs were also founded shortly after the passage of the 1832 Reform Act. The two clubs were less headquarters than clearinghouses where prospective candidates could be matched to parliamentary constituencies (Gash 1983; Thévoz 2018). These initial developments were not centrally directed, however; the rise of voter registration societies was organic, the nomination of candidates remained the preserve of local notables, and funding remained largely the preserve (and burden) of individual candidates (Gash 1953; Gash 1983; Newbould 1985). Thus, up until 1867 British parties operated as networks in which central party figures coordinated with provincial notables rather than as centralized and hierarchical bureaucracies.

The further extension of the suffrage in 1867 provoked the invention of the Birmingham Caucus. The caucus was a grassroots organization that mobilized and coordinated Liberal voters, and which over time came to exert influence over the nomination of Liberal candidates. The caucus model was transplanted in other localities, and its influence on nominations was eventually placed in the hands of the Liberal whip. The Conservative Party developed the Primrose League as a counterpart to the Birmingham Caucus (Ostrogorski 1964 [1902]), and by the late nineteenth century Conservative whips were also able to influence the odds of favored candidates being adopted in safe seats (Cox and Nowaki 2023).

The passage of the 1883 Corrupt and Illegal Practices Act pushed the British Liberal and Conservative Parties to expand and diversify their resource base. The act limited the amounts that individual candidates could spend on their own elections, and thus made the central parties principally responsible for campaign finances. The National Liberal Federation (the descendant of the Birmingham Caucus) and the Primrose League provided the Liberals and Conservatives, respectively, with volunteers and subscriptions. These resources were supplemented by contributions from business, industry, and labor, which increasingly pushed the parties to develop programmatic policies (Kuo 2018). Consequently, by the 1890s, the Liberals and Conservatives were well-funded mass organizations that fought elections on a programmatic basis.[8] A substantial fraction of this funding was nonetheless obtained via a species of patronage: the sale of aristocratic titles (Hanham 1960). These lucrative transactions were handled by the party whips, with the funds directed to the central parties' coffers (Jenkins 1990).

The organizational changes generated by extension of the franchise in Britain were important for three reasons. First, the shift in financial capacity and responsibility from candidates to central parties gave leaders greater control over candidate nominations. The standard view is that British party leaders' increased control over nominations reinforced party discipline, but just as importantly such control enabled leaders to recruit candidates to contest hard-to-win districts. This was critical to the nationalization of British electoral politics. Second, the development of extra-parliamentary parties provided British party leaders with the labor if not the capital to contest elections. Third, these changes allowed the parties to build broad coalitions with civil society and interest groups, without making them overreliant on any one element of their support coalitions. In short, these organizational changes enhanced party autonomy.

Organizational Stagnation: Germany's Conservative and Liberal Parties

The importance of a party's organization to its autonomy is demonstrated by the experience of the German Conservative and Liberal parties. The German Conservative Party (Deutschkonservative Partei [DKP]) was, by dint of its opposition to democratic reform and its agricultural protectionism, increasingly confined to rural East Elbia. In this region, the DKP could rely on its candidates' positions as major landowners and local government officials (*Landräte*) to stifle and subvert electoral competition. However, when Bismarck was removed from power in 1890, the antisocialist laws were allowed to expire and Prussian municipal government was reformed. The DKP was simultaneously deprived of a powerful government ally, exposed to the full force of the **Sozialdemokratische Partei Deutschlands** [SPD], and left with weakened control over local government. Without a popular base, the DKP was wholly reliant on the Agrarian League (Bunde der Landwirte [BdL]) for resources. The BdL hamstrung the DKP's ability to moderate its economic policies to widen its electoral appeal. This made the party even more reliant on the restricted Prussian franchise and electoral intimidation to win elections. The result was a vicious cycle: reliance on state-assisted electoral fraud led the DKP to ignore the construction of a mass base, leaving it more vulnerable to the demands of the BdL, which further limited the DKP's capacity to broaden its electoral appeal and made it even more reliant on electoral subversion. In this fashion, Ziblatt (2017) argues, the DKP became an implacable opponent of electoral democracy.

Kreuzer (2001) offers a similar analysis of the German Liberal parties (the Deutsche Demokratische Partei [DDP] and the Deutsche Volkspartei [DVP]) in the Weimar era. The Liberals were caught between the deflationary demands of their urban middle-class electorate and the inflationary demands of their industrial and business backers. The large size of Weimar's electoral districts under proportional representation, and its frequent elections and referenda, resulted in massive electioneering costs that the DDP's and DVP's small membership could not cover. This left the two Liberal parties reliant on the financial backing of the *Kuratoriam*, a business lobby, which demanded both strict adherence to its preferred policies and also safe positions on the party list for its own members—to ensure that the DDP and DVP pursued those policies in the legislature. The result, as with the DKP, was that the two parties were wholly captured by an interest group that was indifferent to the concerns of liberal voters. The DDP and DVP slid into electoral irrelevance.

The corollary of the German Conservatives' and Liberals' incapacity to retain their electoral support is that their electorates were available for the Nazis to capture. In this fashion, the organizational strategies that parties adopted to mobilize voters in the context of a mass electorate shaped their autonomy vis-à-vis socioeconomic interests. Where these strategies see parties cede their autonomy to interest groups, they lose their capacity to retain electoral support, which opens the door to new parties.

Conclusion

The Legislative Research Agenda

We have argued that parties originated in "strong" legislatures, that is, legislatures that were capable of checking their executive counterparts, and without which the executive could not govern effectively. The first legislatures to enjoy this kind of strength were the British House of Commons and the US Congress—and this is where we first see parties emerge. By the late 1700s, American and British legislators appreciated that their assemblies were susceptible to a set of pathologies, notably, the unpredictability of majority rule and the inefficiency of egalitarian and open-ended agenda rules. There is a broad consensus that the groups of like-minded politicians who came together to control access to the parliamentary agenda were the general solution to these problems. These procedural coalitions—that is, parties—operated by altering legislative rules to obtain disproportionate influence over both the distribution of perks and access to the legislative agenda. Leaders then selectively distributed perks and legislative access to maintain members' loyalty to the procedural coalition. This relationship explains the historical correlation and interplay between legislative rules, on one hand, and the existence and strength of legislative parties, on the other.

While this interpretation of the development and raison d'être of political parties enjoys a broad scholarly consensus, it is worth emphasizing that it remains in many places a post-hoc induction based on two canonical cases. Thus, one of the area's most pressing needs is simply for data on the evolution of parties outside the United States and Britain, because our continued reliance on just a few canonical cases leaves us poorly positioned to discern whether we are eliding idiosyncratic historical outcomes with the evolution of a set of common institutional responses to the generic problems of majority rule.

This straightforward research agenda of digitizing and analyzing roll calls of a more diverse set of national cases is proceeding (e.g., Hansen and Debus 2012; Godbout and Høyland 2013; Høyland and Søyland 2019). Ideally, the development of these efforts will be as comprehensive as the renewed research agenda on British political development (Spirling 2014). Students of British political development are now able to draw on a variety of electronic resources to link together MPs' voting records, biographies, speeches, and statistical portraits of their constituencies and constituents. These resources have facilitated increasingly sophisticated descriptions of the evolution of British political parties in the House of Commons (e.g., Eggers and Spirling 2016; Cox 2022).

In future work, we need to think harder about—or simply describe in a more systematic and detailed way—the interplay between legislative rules and party organization (e.g., Goet 2021). The current thinking is that defective or incomplete rules generate incentives to construct alternative institutions like parties. But once parties are formed, they often make further changes. Party leaders alter existing rules to strengthen their hold over their followers, and established parties do the same to limit the power of minor parties or to foreclose the entry of new parties. Of course, as in the American case, minor parties also seek to change the rules of the game to enhance their own electoral prospects.

The Electoral Research Agenda

Party theorists have long argued not just that "parties matter" but that how a party is organized matters. Our take on this idea is that the strategy by which a party acquires the resources necessary to contest elections in the context of a mass electorate affects the party's ability to attract, turn out at the polls, and retain the loyalty of voters. These resources included money, increasingly derived from interest groups rather than wealthy individuals; workers, preferably voluntary in nature; and candidates.

Parties responded to the demands of a mass electorate in several ways: some rejected electoral democracy and fell back on electoral subversion, others transformed themselves into political machines that exploited state patronage, others developed into programmatic mass parties, and yet others forged close links with economic interest groups. Our comparison of American, British, and German parties suggests that two aspects of these organizational strategies were critical to party autonomy: election funding and candidate nominations.

A dominant strand of the historical democratization literature focuses on the decline of clientelism and the concomitant rise of programmatic electoral competition. Politics in the first-wave democracies was undoubtedly "cleaner" by the end of the nineteenth century than it was at the beginning. The arrival of the mass electorate nonetheless ensured that money remained critical to elections—and that parties required much more of it. This begs the questions: Who provided these funds? Who controlled them? How candidates were nominated and who controlled those nominations are similarly important questions. Contemporary scholars tend to view the control of candidate nominations as a bulwark of party discipline: it is stronger where leaders exercise central control over nominations, and weaker where they do not. Such a perspective assumes an oversupply of candidates. By contrast, one of the historical party leader's major challenges was finding enough candidates to contest elections, especially in hard-to-win districts. The capacity of existing parties to field candidates was critical to electoral mobilization and to preventing new competitors from emerging. Together, these observations suggest a research agenda focused on intraparty battles over candidate nominations and the changing relationship of interest groups with parties.

Notes

1. This section draws heavily on Price (2001).
2. The Republican Party of Jefferson and Madison would later be known as the Democratic-Republicans and then simply the Democrats.
3. Parties were the "structure" that kept vote decisions one-dimensional and prevented voting cycles from emerging. In other eras, other institutions—like standing committees—provided similar structure (Gamm and Shepsle 1989; Jenkins 1998). Poole and Rosenthal (1997) find that instability has not impacted congressional voting much over time; aside from a few short periods—the Era of Good Feelings, the early 1850s, and the 1960s—a one-dimensional spatial model explains Congressional vote choices extremely well. This implies that structure (parties, committees, and rules) has done its job.
4. In the Senate, the lack of a Speaker-like presiding officer made it more difficult for party leadership to emerge. Instead of a single individual, a group of four powerful Republican senators coordinated party activities in the early 1890s. Key to their success was the expanding power of the Republican caucus (Gamm and Smith 2002).
5. See John Brooke, "Brackley," History of Parliament Online, November 10, 2022. https://www.historyofparliamentonline.org/volume/1754-1790/constituencies/brackley/, and also Sir Lewis Namier, "DICKINSON, Marshe (?1703-65), of Cheapside, London and Dunstable, Beds.," History of Parliament Online, November 10, 2022. https://www.historyofparliamentonline.org/volume/1754-1790/member/dickinson-marshe-1703-65.
6. The rate and magnitude of the increase in party cohesion is hard to pin down because division lists were systematically recorded only after 1835. Popa (2015) provides a concise description of the condition and availability of recorded divisions from the eighteenth century.
7. There is an extensive literature on these agrarian populist movements, for example, Lipset (1950), Leithner (1993), Lewis-Beck (1977), Mayhew (1972), and McGuire (1981).
8. Various scholars find that the central parties' financial capacities increased tenfold between the 1840s and 1910s (Gash 1953; Hanham 1960; Jenkins 1990; Rix 2016; Kam and Newson 2021).

References

Aldrich, John H. 1995. *Why Parties?: The Origin and Transformation of Political Parties in America*. Chicago: University of Chicago Press.

Binder, Sarah A. 1997. *Minority Rights, Majority Rule: Partisanship and the Development of Congress.* Cambridge: Cambridge University Press.

Black, Duncan. 1958. *The Theory of Committees and Elections.* Cambridge: Cambridge University Press.

Boix, Carles. 2008. "The Emergence of Parties and Party Systems." In *The Oxford Handbook of Comparative Politics*, ed. Carles Boix and Susan C. Stokes, 499–521. Oxford: Oxford University Press.

Bogart, Dan. 2018. "Party Connections, Interest Groups and the Slow Diffusion of Infrastructure: Evidence from Britain's First Transport Revolution." *Economic Journal* 128, no. 609: 541–75.

Brooke, John. "Brackley." History of Parliament Online. November 10, 2022. https://www.historyofparliamentonline.org/volume/1754-1790/constituencies/brackley/

Burke, Edmund. 1878 [1770]. "Thoughts on the Cause of the Present Discontents and the Two Speeches on America." In *Select Works of Edmund Burke*. Vol. 1, ed. E. J. Payne. Oxford: Clarendon Press, 1878.

Capoccia, Giovanni, and Daniel Ziblatt. 2010. "The Historical Turn in Democratization Studies: A New Research Agenda for Europe and Beyond." *Comparative Political Studies* 43, no. 8–9: 931–68.

Caramani, Daniele. 2003. "The End of Silent Elections: The Birth of Electoral Competition, 1832–1915." *Party Politics* 9, no. 4: 411–43.

Caramani, Daniele. 2017. "Will vs. Reason: The Populist and Technocratic Forms of Political Representation and Their Critique to Party Government." *American Political Science Review* 111, no. 1: 54–67.

Caramani, Daniele. 2023. "Electoral Systems in Historical Political Economy. "In *The Oxford Handbook of Historical Political Economy*, ed. J. A. Jenkins and J. Rubin, 421–39. Oxford, UK: Oxford University Press.

Cox, Gary W. 1987. *The Efficient Secret: The Cabinet and the Development of Political Parties in Victorian England.* Cambridge: Cambridge University Press.

Cox, Gary W. 1992. "The Origins of Whip Votes in the House of Commons." *Parliamentary History* 11, no. 2: 278–85.

Cox, Gary W. 2006. "The Organization of Democratic Legislatures." In *The Oxford handbook of Political Economy.* ed. Barry R. Weingast and Donald A. Wittman, 141–61. New York: Oxford University Press.

Cox, Gary W. 2022. "Comparing 'Responsible Party Government' in the US and the UK." Stanford University. Unpublished manuscript. https://cape.ucmerced.edu/sites/cape.ucmerced.edu/files/page/documents/minority_rolls_v05.pdf.

Cox, Gary W., and Mathew D. McCubbins. 1993. *Legislative Leviathan: Party Government in the House.* Berkeley: University of California Press.

Cox, Gary W., and Mathew D. McCubbins. 2005. *Setting the Agenda: Responsible Party Government in the House.* Cambridge: Cambridge University Press.

Cox, Gary W., and Tobias Nowacki. 2023. "The Emergence of Party-Based Political Careers in the UK, 1801–1918." *Journal of Politics* 85, no. 1: 178–91.

Dion, Douglas. 1997. *Turning the Legislative Thumbscrew: Minority Rights and Procedural Change in Legislative Politics.* Ann Arbor: University of Michigan Press.

Downs, Anthony. 1957. *An Economic Theory of Democracy.* New York: Harper and Row.

Duverger, Maurice. 1959 [1951]. *Political Parties, Their Organization and Activity in the Modern State.* Translated by Barbara and Robert North. London: Metheun.

Eggers, Andrew C., and Arthur Spirling. 2014. "Ministerial Responsiveness in Westminster Systems: Institutional Choices and House of Commons Debate, 1832–1915." *American Journal of Political Science* 58, no. 4: 873–87.

Eggers, Andrew C., and Arthur Spirling. 2016. "Party Cohesion in Westminster Systems: Inducements, Replacement and Discipline in the House of Commons, 1836–1910." *British Journal of Political Science* 46, no. 3: 567–89.

Eggers, Andrew C., and Arthur Spirling. 2018. "The Shadow Cabinet in Westminster Systems: Modeling Opposition Agenda Setting in the House of Commons, 1832–1915." *British Journal of Political Science* 48, no. 2: 343–67.

Engerman, Stanley L., and Kenneth L. Sokoloff. 2005. "The Evolution of Suffrage Institutions in the New World." *Journal of Economic History* 65, no. 4: 891–921.

Engstrom, Erik J., and Samuel Kernell. 2014. *Party Ballots, Reform, and the Transformation of America's Electoral System*. Cambridge: Cambridge University Press.

Fraser, Peter. 1960. "The Growth of Ministerial Control in the Nineteenth-Century House of Commons." *English Historical Review* 75, no. 296: 444–63.

Gailmard, Sean., and Jeffery A. Jenkins. 2009. "Agency Problems, the 17th Amendment, and Representation in the Senate." *American Journal of Political Science* 53, no. 2: 324–42.

Gamm, Gerald, and Kenneth Shepsle. 1989. "Emergence of Legislative Institutions: Standing Committees in the House and Senate, 1810–1825." *Legislative Studies Quarterly* 14, no. 1: 39–66.

Gamm, Gerald, and Steven S. Smith. 2002. "Emergence of Senate Party Leadership." In *U.S. Senate Exceptionalism*, ed. B. I. Oppenheimer, 212–40. Columbus: Ohio State University Press.

Gash, Norman. 1953. *Politics in the Age of Peel: A Study in the Technique of Parliamentary Representation*. Atlantic Highlands, NJ: Harvester Press.

Gash, Norman. 1983. "The Organization of the Conservative Party 1832–1846: Part II: The Electoral Organization." *Parliamentary History* 2, no. 1: 131–52.

Godbout, Jean-François, and Bjørn Høyland. 2013. "The Emergence of Parties in the Canadian House of Commons (1867–1908)." *Canadian Journal of Political Science* 46, no. 4: 773–97.

Goet, Niels D. 2021. "The Politics of Procedural Choice: Regulating Legislative Debate in the UK House of Commons, 1811–2015." *British Journal of Political Science* 51, no. 2: 788–806.

Hanham, H. J. 1960. "The Sale of Honours in Late Victorian England." *Victorian Studies* 3, no. 3: 277–89.

Hanlon, W. Walker. 2023. "Suffrage in Historical Political Economy." In *The Oxford Handbook of Historical Political Economy*, ed. J. A. Jenkins and J. Rubin, 459–75. Oxford, UK: Oxford University Press.

Hansen, Martin E., and Marc Debus. 2012. "The Behaviour of Political Parties and MPs in the Parliaments of the Weimar Republic." *Party Politics* 18, no. 5: 709–26.

Harris, Ron. 2000. *Industrializing English Law: Entrepreneurship and Business Organization, 1720–1844*. Cambridge: Cambridge University Press.

Hirano, Shigeo, and James M. Snyder Jr. 2019. *Primary Elections in the United States*. Cambridge: Cambridge University Press.

Hoadley, John F. 1980. "The Emergence of Political Parties in Congress: 1789–1803." *American Political Science Review* 74, no. 3: 757–79.

Hoadley, John F. 1986. *Origins of American Political Parties, 1789–1803*. Lexington: University Press of Kentucky.

Hofstadter, Richard. 1969. *The Idea of a Party System: The Rise of Legitimate Opposition in the United States, 1780–1840*. Berkeley: University of California Press.

Holmes, Geoffrey. 1987. *British Politics in the Age of Anne*. London: Bloomsbury.
Høyland, Bjørn, and Martin G. Søyland. 2019. "Electoral Reform and Parliamentary Debates." *Legislative Studies Quarterly* 44, no. 4: 593–615.
James, Scott C. 2006. "Patronage Regimes and American Party Development from 'The Age of Jackson' to the Progressive Era." *British Journal of Political Science* 36, no. 1: 39–60.
Jenkins, Jeffery A. 1998. "Property Rights and Standing Committee Dominance in the Nineteenth-Century House." *Legislative Studies Quarterly* 23, no. 4: 493–519.
Jenkins, Jeffery A., and Charles Stewart III. 2013. *Fighting for the Speakership: The House and the Rise of Party Government*. Princeton: Princeton University Press.
Jenkins, T. A. 1990. "The Funding of the Liberal Unionist Party and the Honours System." *English Historical Review* 105, no. 417: 920–38.
Kam, Christopher, and Adlai Newson. 2021. *The Economic Origin of Political Parties*. New York: Cambridge University Press.
Kitschelt, Herbert., and Steven I. Wilkinson, eds. 2007. *Patrons, Clients and Policies: Patterns of Democratic Accountability and Political Competition*. New York: Cambridge University Press.
Kreuzer, Marcus. 2001. *Institutions and Innovation: Voters, Parties, and Interest Groups in the Consolidation of Democracy—France and Germany, 1870–1939*. Ann Arbor: University of Michigan Press.
Kuo, Didi. 2018. *Clientelism, Capitalism, and Democracy: The Rise of Programmatic Politics in the United States and Britain*. Cambridge: Cambridge University Press.
Leithner, Christian. 1993. "The National Progressive Party of Canada, 1921–1930: Agricultural Economic Conditions and Electoral Support." *Canadian Journal of Political Science* 26, no. 3: 435–53.
Lewis-Beck, Michael S. 1977. "Agrarian Political Behavior in the United States" *American Journal of Political Science* 21, no. 3: 543–65.
Lipset, Seymour M. 1950. *Agrarian Socialism: The Co-operative Commonwealth Federation in Saskatchewan*. Berkeley: University of California Press.
Lipset, Seymour M. and Stein Rokkan. 1967. "Cleavage Structures, Party Systems, and Voter Alignments: An Introduction." In *Party Systems and Voter Alignments: Cross-National Perspectives*, ed. Seymour Martin Lipset and Stein Rokkan, 1–64. New York: Free Press.
Mares, Isabela. 2015. *From Open Secrets to Secret Voting: Democratic Electoral Reforms and Voter Autonomy*. Cambridge: Cambridge University Press.
Mayhew, Anne. 1972. "A Reappraisal of the Causes of Farm Protest in the United States, 1870–1900." *Journal of Economic History* 32, no. 2: 464–75.
McGuire, Robert A. 1981. "Economic Causes of Late Nineteenth-Century Unrest: New Evidence." *Journal of Economic History* 41, no. 4: 835–49.
McKelvey, Richard E. 1976. "Intransitivities in Multidimensional Voting Models and Some Implications for Agenda Control." *Journal of Economic Theory* 12, no. 3: 472–82.
Namier, Sir Lewis. "DICKINSON, Marshe (?1703-65), of Cheapside, London and Dunstable, Beds." History of Parliament Online. November 10, 2022. https://www.historyofparliamentonline.org/volume/1754-1790/member/dickinson-marshe-1703-65.
Newbould, Ian. 1985. "Whiggery and the Growth of Party 1830–41: Organization and the Challenge of Reform." *Political History* 4, no. 1: 137–56.
North, Douglass C., and Barry R. Weingast. 1989. "Constitutions and Commitment: The Evolution of Institutions Governing Public Choice in Seventeenth-Century England." *Journal of Economic History* 49, no. 4: 803–32.

Ostrogorski, M. 1964 [1902]. *Democracy and the Organization of Political Parties.* Vol. 1. Edited and abridged by Seymour Martin Lipset. Garden City, NY: Anchor Books.

Panebianco, Angelo. 1988. *Political Parties: Organization and Power.* Cambridge: Cambridge University Press.

Piattoni, Simona, ed. 2001. *Clientelism, Interests, and Democratic Representation: The European Experience in Historical and Comparative Perspective.* Cambridge: Cambridge University Press.

Pincus, Steven. 2009. *1688: The First Modern Revolution.* New Haven, CT: Yale University Press.

Plott, Charles 1967. "A Notion of Equilibrium and Its Possibility under Majority Rule." *American Economic Review* 57, no. 4: 146–60.

Polsby, Nelson W. 1968. "The Institutionalization of the U.S. House of Representatives." *American Political Science Review* 62, no. 1: 144–68.

Poole, Keith T., and Howard Rosenthal. 1997. *Congress: A Political-Economic History of Roll Call Voting.* Oxford: Oxford University Press.

Popa, Mircea. 2015. "Elites and Corruption: A Theory of Endogenous Reform and a Test Using British Data." *World Politics* 67, no. 2: 313–52.

Price, Roger. 2001. *The French Second Empire: An Anatomy of Political Power.* Cambridge: Cambridge University Press.

Rix, Kathryn. 2016. *Parties, Agents, and Electoral Culture in England, 1880–1910.* Rochester, NY: Boydell Press.

Robinson, James A., and Thierry Verdier. 2013. "The Political Economy of Clientelism." *Scandinavian Journal of Economics* 115, no. 2: 260–91.

Salmon, Philip. 2002. *Electoral Reform at Work: Local Politics and National Parties, 1832–1841.* Woodbridge: Boydell Press for the Royal Historical Society.

Sartori, Giovanni. 1976. *Parties and Party Systems: A Framework for Analysis.* Cambridge: Cambridge University Press.

Schickler, Eric. 2001. *Disjointed Pluralism: Institutional Innovation and the Development of the U.S. Congress.* Princeton, NJ: Princeton University Press.

Schiller, Wendy J., and Charles Stewart III. 2015. *Electing the Senate: Indirect Democracy before the Seventeenth Amendment.* Princeton, NJ: Princeton University Press.

Schumpeter, Joseph A. 1942. *Capitalism, Socialism and Democracy.* New York: Harper & Brothers.

Schwartz, Thomas. 1989. "Why Parties?" Unpublished manuscript. University of California, Los Angeles.

Schwartz, Thomas. 2021. "Parties." *Constitutional Political Economy* 32, no. 4: 462–75.

Shefter, Martin. 1983. "Regional Receptivity to Reform: The Legacy of the Progressive Era." *Political Science Quarterly* 98, no. 3: 459–83.

Sieberer, Ulrich, and Michael Herrmann. 2019. "Bonding in Pursuit of Policy Goals: How MPs Choose Political Parties in the Legislative State of Nature." *Legislative Studies Quarterly* 44, no. 3: 455–86.

Skjönsberg, Max. 2016. "Lord Bolingbroke's Theory of Party and Opposition." *Historical Journal* 59, no. 4: 947–73.

Spirling, Arthur. 2014. "British Political Development: A Research Agenda." *Legislative Studies Quarterly* 39, no. 4: 435–37.

Stasavage, David. 2023. "Democracy and Historical Political Economy." In *The Oxford Handbook of Historical Political Economy*, ed. J. A. Jenkins and J. Rubin, 145–60. Oxford, UK: Oxford University Press.

Stokes, Susan, C., Thad Dunning, Marcelo Nazareno, and Valeria Brusco. 2013. *Brokers, Voters, and Clientelism: The Puzzle of Distributive Politics*. Cambridge: Cambridge University Press.

Thévoz, Seth A. 2018. *Club Government: How the Early Victorian World Was Ruled from London Clubs*. London: I. B. Tauris.

Ware, Anthony. 2002. *The American Direct Primary: Party Institutionalization and Transformation in the North*. Cambridge: Cambridge University Press.

Ziblatt, Daniel. 2017. *Conservative Political Parties and the Birth of Modern Democracy in Europe*. Cambridge: Cambridge University Press.

CHAPTER 21

ELECTORAL SYSTEMS IN HISTORICAL POLITICAL ECONOMY

DANIELE CARAMANI

The Politics of Electoral Systems

Electoral systems are rules for translating citizens' preferences into votes and, in turn, votes into parliamentary or congressional seats.[1] They are instruments to authorize and mandate representatives to legislate on behalf of voters. The choice of an electoral system also matters for accountability—it makes changing majorities and, by extension, executives in parliamentary systems more or less difficult—and for the degree to which legislative bodies mirror the composition of society, with a more or less distorted descriptive representation of classes (occupation, education, and status), religions, genders, and ethnic groups.[2] Together with franchise, electoral systems thus constitute the core component in the distribution of power between groups.

Far from being neutral rules of the game, electoral systems are highly political because of their redistributive function in representative democracies. Different groups represented by parties have different preferences for the type of system to allocate parliamentary seats. While some may favor the exclusion of minorities by means of high thresholds (most typically, only the "first," that is, the candidate with the most votes, "past the post" in single-member districts), and by doing so may entrench the power of society's majoritarian groups, others favor systems that facilitate their representation (typically, through large-magnitude districts that allocate seats in proportion to votes).[3] Normative motives certainly exist: majoritarian systems favor accountability by making it easier to replace single-party cabinets or minimal-winning coalitions with swings of a few votes, whereas proportional systems increase representation. However, rather than discussing ideal systems that optimize representation and governability through electoral engineering, political economy perspectives focus on the interaction between societal groups that compete to maximize their influence by controlling larger shares of seats. These perspectives are especially relevant during the democratization process, when confrontation between the entrenched elites of the past regime and the classes newly mobilized by economic transformation (Industrial Revolution) and nationalism and liberalism (National Revolution) was more acute.[4]

This chapter deals precisely with electoral systems as a matter of contentious politics. It adopts a political economy perspective that bridges the dual understanding of this label: structural and agent-oriented. It discusses how competitive interactions between societal groups, as actors organized through parties and candidates, lead to the choice of electoral system.[5] This approach also makes it possible to overcome the somewhat artificial separation that the study of electoral systems has established between their causes and effects on party systems. A political economy perspective interprets the origins of electoral systems, that is, the institutional choices that political systems have made historically, through the lens of actors' anticipation of how they would (re)distribute power. This anticipation of the consequences that electoral systems will have on the distribution of seats pushes actors toward diverging preferences about the rules of the electoral game.

The empirical concern of the historical political economy (HPE) perspective is twofold: temporal and cross-sectional variation. Why did democratizing parliaments in the nineteenth century adopt majoritarian systems, and why did a divergence between countries that almost simultaneously shifted toward proportional representation (mainly but not exclusively in continental Europe) and Anglo-Saxon countries that kept their majoritarian institutions take place at the beginning of the twentieth century? The chapter starts with the theoretical argument. It then presents the historical context of the shift to proportional systems. The main section provides the HPE account of the origins of electoral systems following two main approaches: electoral-political and socioeconomic. The conclusion offers an assessment of the literature.

The Political Economy Argument

The political economy argument about the origins of electoral systems is one of choice: rational players decide the rules of the game with the aim of maximizing power and minimizing risk. From a macro-sociological and historical perspective, these players are political parties not simply conceptualized as "Downsian" campaign organizations, but as complex, deeply rooted expressions of broad social groups and economic cleavages that is, a combination of structure and agency (Rokkan 1970; Rogowski 1989; Boix 1999; Cusack, Iversen, and Soskice 2007).[6] There is a mutual relationship between electoral systems and parties. It is parties that chose an electoral system in anticipation of the consequences that it would have on their payoffs.[7]

Payoffs are primarily considered through a seat-maximizing model of electoral reform (Benoit 2004). Competition takes place between parties, but also between existing parties and potential competitors, between local branches and parliamentary parties, as well as between intraparty factions. These anticipations are largely based on the electoral effects spelled out by Duverger (1951), namely that—through mechanical and psychological effects—majoritarian systems tend to reduce the number of parties in parliament, in a way that systems based on a principle of seat allocation that is proportional to vote share do not. "Strong" systems with high thresholds for election (generally, those allocating few seats in low-magnitude districts) create incentives for parties to merge, and for voters to strategically converge on parties with a chance of winning a majority and to drop their first preference if it does not stand a chance of getting elected. In contrast, "weakly" distorting proportional systems set incentives for parties to maintain autonomy and distinctive identities, and do not penalize votes for small parties.[8]

A number of nondistributive payoffs can be derived from the seat-maximizing perspective. First, denying representation to minorities by means of high thresholds increases the pressure on nonelectoral channels in the form of more or less violent protest and therefore increases the risk of instability.[9] Second, by overrepresenting large parties, majoritarian systems make it easier to form stable single-party cabinets or minimum-winning coalitions that do not need to share power. Rather than stability through representation, historical examples like the Weimar Republic, France's Fourth Republic, and Italy since World War II point to the need of stability through governability. In both scenarios, the payoff is systemic stability—through either inclusion or exclusion.[10]

Assuming that actors have the ability to broadly anticipate such effects, the issue for a political economy approach becomes the identification of the conditions under which large and small parties, those with geographically diffuse or concentrated support, and those anticipating either future gains or losses (including the emergence of new competitors)—converge on reforms that deviate from the simple logic whereby large parties at the national level prefer a majoritarian system, whereas small parties prefer a proportional one,[11] and switch to non-zero-sum cooperative interaction through inclusive electoral systems. Two broad conditions foster the convergence of parties' preference for proportional representation:

- *Electoral costs*: Parties' uncertainty about their future electoral strength and their consequent wish to minimize risk induce them to prefer systems that guarantee survival in cases of electoral decline and increased competition from new challengers (such as in periods of franchise extension).
- *Nonelectoral costs*: Parties' interest in avoiding nonparliamentary, possibly violent consequences induces them to prefer inclusive systems, especially in consensus-seeking societies that need coordination, and when nonrepresentative institutions allow minorities to act as veto players and block parliamentary majorities.[12]

Both conditions contribute to the likelihood of parties' interests converging on an electoral system that diffuses the risk of a single winner-takes-all outcome. To analyze these mechanisms empirically, the historical political economy literature has logically focused on older democracies, and therefore on the industrialized West (and to a lesser extent on Latin America), and more particularly on the divergence caused by the shift to proportional systems in most Western European countries in the first two decades of the twentieth century.

Electoral Reform and Democratization: The Historical Context

Representative government in the nineteenth century reconciled demands for inclusion, resulting from the unprecedented mass mobilization produced by industrialization and nationalism, with elites' efforts to retain their power and privilege coupled with the need to foster state capacity and socioeconomic modernization in a context of international competition. The intention to retain elite autonomy was quite explicit and manifested itself institutionally in the rejection of direct democracy, the refusal to bind representatives through the imperative mandate, and the dismissal of lot systems used to select legislators. Instead, representation triumphed, and elections (indirect in a number of countries) were adopted. Several of the parliaments reintroduced after the absolutist interruption of medieval representation were divided into "estates" that variously represented the aristocracy, the clergy, cities, peasants and universities. Only progressively did general representation and universal suffrage make gains, with voting rights long remaining restricted and unequal (plural voting) by means of wealth and education requirements.[13]

Most importantly given the focus of this chapter, electoral systems everywhere were majoritarian, either in single- or multimember districts, based either on plurality or absolute majority, and with either one, two, or sometimes three ballots. One reason is that these systems maintained the medieval principle of territorial representation. Parliaments represent territorial units, rather than functional groups. Another reason is that territory still trumped ideology in a phase in which production was localized, elites were not yet organized in parties, the working class was still largely excluded from the franchise, and cross-district linkages between candidates were very limited.[14] The main reason, however, is that majoritarian systems allowed elites to be shielded from competition arising from mass mobilization. As analyses of the "birth of electoral competition" show (Caramani 2003), local candidates remained unopposed and districts were uncontested (*stille Wahlen* in the German-speaking world, and *élections tacites* in the French, which have been translated as "silent elections") between the 1830s and the 1910s. Seats were "safe" due to districting and the high thresholds imposed by majoritarian systems, and local notables were able to get reelected over and over again—long, sometimes decades, after the introduction of elected parliaments and even after universal male suffrage. Majoritarian systems were thus part and parcel of an institutional strategy of controlled political liberalization throughout the second half of the nineteenth century and well into the first decades of the twentieth century.

Not surprisingly, the pressure to lower the threshold for representation was strong. It mainly came from social democratic and agrarian parties that organized the rising working masses and the peasantry (in the processes of industrialization and urbanization), and from parties representing ethnolinguistic and religious minorities opposed to a centralizing administration (in the process of state formation) and a homogeneous, secular political culture (in the process of nation-building).[15] Indeed, starting in Belgium in 1899 and continuing in Finland (1907), Sweden (1909), and Denmark (1915), a wave of national-level electoral system reforms swept through Western Europe and Japan after World War I, following pilot experiments at the local level.[16] In many cases, the introduction of proportional representation at the national level was gradual: it started in one or two districts (as in Denmark and Portugal) or was embedded in mixed systems (as in Iceland). Reversals back to majoritarian systems after an initial introduction of proportional representation also took place (for example, in France).

This was a major, and arguably unique, shift in the history of electoral systems only partially paralleled by developments in Latin America (Negretto and Visconti 2018). It caused a major divergence with Anglo-Saxon countries. Quite naturally, this shift has attracted the attention of scholars trying to explain the origins of electoral systems in various countries. Explaining this shift and the divergent historical outcomes in the origins of electoral systems is a main topic in the HPE approach to electoral systems.

The Historical Political Economy of Electoral Systems' Choice

Contemporary thinkers and later scholars have both seen proportional representation in democratic terms. Arguments in Europe, the United States, and Latin America in the last decades of the nineteenth century and the first half of the twentieth century revolve around the representation of ethnolinguistic, religious, and racial minorities (Lublin 2014). During those early debates, mathematicians in various countries, from Belgium to Ireland, Switzerland, and Britain, devised formulas for allocating seats in parliaments in proportion to the distribution of votes across party lists in multimember districts.[17]

The political economy approach focuses instead on the aggregation of interests and cost calculations on the part of actors in anticipation of the electoral and nonelectoral consequences of different systems. Actors are mainly parties (we see later that internal factions also play a role) that represent different socioeconomic groups. Under the restricted franchise in the nineteenth century, these were mainly liberal and conservative elites (in some countries, Catholics), who were increasingly challenged by parties of the socially and politically mobilized masses: social democrats (everywhere), agrarians (particularly in the Nordic countries but also in Switzerland and Eastern Europe), and ethnoregionalists.[18] There are two types of explanation of actors' alignment around proportional representation in some countries and the maintenance of majoritarian systems in others. One is political-electoral; the other is socioeconomic. The two are closely related.

The Competitive-Electoral Explanation

This explanation starts with the process of enfranchisement, which increases electoral competition and the number of parties. Inspired by Braunias's (1932) classic work, Rokkan (1970) formulates two hypotheses about the support of right-wing parties (liberals, conservatives, and Catholics) for electoral reforms that would lower the threshold for representation.

The first hypothesis, directly concerned with competition, states that the threat presented by the rise of mass-mobilizing socialist parties was magnified by majoritarian rules that would overrepresent the latter at the expense of incumbent elitist parties. Reform is therefore presented as a defensive mechanism in a context of uncertainty about elitist parties' future electoral success endangered by male enfranchisement. In a milder version of this threat hypothesis, support for proportional representation is a step in a controlled political liberalization process, which had begun with the introduction of parliaments and enfranchisement.[19] This hypothesis fits a number of cases of adoption of proportional representation—Germany, Norway, and Sweden in particular, but also Austria, Italy, and the Netherlands—as noted in studies conducted in the wake of this hypothesis, most notably by Boix (1999; 2010). Support for reform exists under the condition that right-wing parties (liberals on the one hand and either conservatives or Catholics on the other) are equally balanced and that they do not "coordinate" their strategies (i.e., they do not enter electoral pacts and do not merge) to counter socialist candidates in the various districts. On the contrary, if one of the two right-wing parties dominates, the incentives to adopt proportional representation diminish.

These analyses have weaknesses due to their aggregate nature: they operate nationally, and coordination is poorly operationalized through the effective number of parties, which fails to capture the constellation of competition at the district level. Most importantly, these analyses do not take into account the opportunities offered by majoritarian systems to fend off threats by working-class challengers. On the one hand, socialist representation in majoritarian systems could be packed in a few urban districts, keeping working-class challengers at bay, while established right-wing parties benefit from widely spread support in rural districts throughout the country. On the other hand, the approach mixes together various types of majoritarian systems. For example, runoff systems eliminating parties in the first round (and also plurality in multimember districts) did indeed offer coordination opportunities that plurality systems with a single round and single-member districts did not.[20]

The second hypothesis that Rokkan formulates follows his observation that established parties also agreed to depart from majoritarian rules in the absence of a major socialist threat, namely in Belgium, Denmark, and Switzerland. While quite vague with a rather unconvincing lack of self-interested cultural minority protection motivation, this alternative hypothesis did, however, spur efforts to generalize the competitive challenges argument beyond the socialist threat. The argument in this alternative account of support for proportional representation is also based on the notion that enfranchisement increases competition. However, rather than just mobilizing workers, enfranchisement results in competitive multiparty systems more generally.

The mechanism driving reform in this more general electoral-competitive account is that majoritarian electoral rules are ill suited to multiparty competition. The distortions inherent in such systems (disproportionality between votes and seats) and the huge effects of districting—which leave nationwide competition between two large parties unaffected—are exacerbated in competitions between more than two parties, especially when some are homogenously spread across districts, while others are territorially concentrated. Majoritarian systems favor parties that can optimize the geographical distribution of their electoral support, namely territorially concentrated distributions that allow them to reach the high threshold of representation in many districts, as opposed to more homogenous, even large, but nowhere near majoritarian support dispersed across the country. These differences create tensions between parties.

The socialist threat factor is not so central or, rather, forms part of a larger picture of electoral competition in this "second road" to proportional representation (Calvo 2009). The core argument is about competition more generally: territorially concentrated newcomers are at an advantage over established "nationalized" parties, which naturally support proportional representation in a bid to restore a more favorable seats/votes ratio.[21] Enfranchisement led to an increase in the number of parties, and territorially concentrated newcomers crowded out nationally dispersed liberals and conservatives through biases inherent in majoritarian systems in multiparty competitive settings. Evidence shows that in countries with a revolutionary threat from socialism at the end of the nineteenth century, electoral reform did indeed grant socialists more representation.[22] This strategy did not necessarily prevent losses for established right-wing parties and can, therefore, not be considered a seat-maximizing strategy on the part of established parties in countries with a socialist threat. In contrast, seat-maximizing protection of established right-wing parties can be observed in countries where they were challenged electorally by newcomers advantaged by territorial biases.[23]

A possible limitation of these analyses is the assumption that more competition is uniquely the result of enfranchisement. In fact, the increase in competition—more plausibly—stems from parties' own strategies, that is, seat maximization through them penetrating in districts from which they had previously been absent or where they had not been competitive (Caramani 2003; 2004). The "birth" of electoral competition is a consequence of parties' appetite for support in new areas. An increase in competition is a natural result of parties' struggle to conquer new territories.[24] Evidence from these analyses very clearly shows an increase in competition, not only in terms of "contestability" as mentioned earlier through a reduction in the number of uncontested districts, but also of "decidability" (the number of competitors) and "vulnerability" (incumbents' safety of tenure in the margin between first and second candidates).[25] In Denmark, for example, the number of uncontested constituencies decreased from around eighty in the 1850s to zero in the first decade of the twentieth century. Similar figures apply to the United Kingdom. In two-ballot systems, the number of constituencies in which seats were allocated already in the first ballot decrease steadily in Belgium, Germany, the Netherlands, and Norway. This indicates increasing competition across territories. Proportional representation was used as an instrument to facilitate this territorial spread of parties, overcome territory-based cleavages (particularly in culturally heterogeneous countries), and harvest seats in districts where votes were few because of a geographically uneven distribution of social groups. Proportional representation was therefore not only a defensive instrument against these encroachments but, first and foremost, an offensive strategy to make such encroachments in the first place.

An extension of this electoral-competitive account of the introduction of proportional representation is provided by analysis of intraparty competition and, in particular, of competition between the local and the national party levels. As discussed, district-level alliances between bourgeois members of parliament at the local level allowed them to counter the socialist threat before the introduction of proportional representation.[26] However, cross-party coordination at the local level created trade-offs in terms of party cohesion since compromises with other parties were necessary (Cusack, Iversen, and Soskice 2010). Cross-party coordination at the local level reduces cohesion at the legislative level (in the parliamentary group). Proportional representation is then an alternative to avoid such trade-offs. Using again the case of Germany, Schröder and Manow (2020) show that proportional representation provides a solution to problems of intraparty cohesion, especially in large countries where district magnitudes vary across the national territory. The preservation of cohesion, rather than proportionality, leads parties to adopt proportional representation. Such analyses of intraparty dynamics have also been carried out on Latin America. Negretto and Visconti (2018) analyse the switch from majoritarian systems to proportional representation in the absence of a socialist threat in the region between 1910 and 1950 and highlight the role of incumbent party dissident factions (that oppose the party's official leadership) as one road to electoral reform.

While there is a structural element in this political economy logic of actors and interests, namely the rise of class politics resulting from industrialization, this explanation remains a partisan electoral story about competition. For a social and economic explanation of proportional representation, the next section turns to the structural and systemic factors underpinning actors' preferences.

The Socioeconomic Explanation

The focus of the socioeconomic approach, which is indebted to the seminal work published in two pathbreaking contributions (Cusack, Iversen, and Soskice 2007; 2010), is not diametrically opposed to the competitive account, and to a large extent, the two share a similar starting point: that an increase in national competition brings majoritarian systems under pressure, changing parties' electoral incentives and eventually leading to reform. There are, however, three main differences with the partisan-electoral approach. First, the focus is more clearly cross-national: why did some countries adopt proportional representation, while others retained majoritarian systems in single-member districts?[27] Second, the increase in competition is conceptualized differently: not so much as an increase in competition within specific districts (through the horizontal spread of parties across districts) but rather as a vertical displacement of competition from the local to the national level. Third, and most crucially, the competitive logic is embedded in the macro-political-economic structures of the countries under analysis.

According to this explanation, the historical choice that led a number of countries to abandon majoritarian electoral systems and adopt proportional representation in the first quarter of the twentieth century must be traced back to their economic structure. Proportional representation was adopted in countries that Cusack, Iversen, and Soskice (2007; 2010) identify as "protocorporatist"—that is, economies based on the traditions of cooperation and negotiated decision-making. These are consociational systems in which decision-making takes place through consensus-seeking bargaining, leading to agreements in a densely populated institutional context of diverse sectoral and local interests.[28] These countries are characterized by a high degree of economic coordination, which relies on the *Ständestaat* tradition, in which guilds and tightly knit professional networks, rural cooperatives, employer coordination, and centralized unions play key roles in policymaking. The core feature of such cooperative systems is reliance on co-specific assets (in particular, skills in the export sector) between employers and workers, which require cooperation between them.

When consensus is required as a fundamental principle, it brings about an inclusionary form of representation insofar as various stakeholders share an interest in long-term investment in co-specific assets. This investment should therefore not be subject to government or majority fluctuations and should be assured of a certain policy continuity. Such patterns of asset ownership tie together interests that would otherwise be in competition (Cusack, Iversen, and Soskice 2010). The pressure to reach agreement is particularly strong in small states under pressure in international markets (Katzenstein 1985).

Reform toward proportional representation was directly linked to the problems that majoritarian systems in single-member districts created for this type of representation. A coordinated economy that invests in co-specific assets relies on a punctuated interest-based representation rather than a broad, encompassing type. Diverse but specific interests could be effectively and fairly represented under majoritarian systems as long as they coincided with local and regional interests. However, when specific interests were no longer tied to localities, they could no longer be represented through an electoral system that underrepresented them at the national level. They were factually cut out from representation, which created an incongruity between the electoral system and coordinated decision-making. Actors in interest-based types of representation, which are typical of protocorporatist economies, therefore favored proportional representation to allow their inclusion in a coordinated type of decision-making.[29]

Displacement of policy from the local to the national level is therefore a core element in this argument. Coordination among economic sectors took place in the parliamentary arena, rather than locally. Their common interest was in a regulatory and social-insurance system that called for legislative institutions facilitating coordination at the national level. As the literature on the "nationalization of politics" mentioned earlier shows, nineteenth-century macro-processes of transformation increasingly detached such interests from locality. It was through state formation (centralization, administrative standardization, strengthening of central government), nation-building (army and education), and the need for national policies in the process of modernization and international competition that economic networks and legislation became national.[30] Regulatory issues, collective bargaining, confessional and linguistic agreements were all transferred to the national level.

Workers' organizations turned into national movements and mass parties developed, which increased the role of national-level policymaking. In this sense, nationalization is not just a horizontal spread of parties creating district competition, but rather a vertical shift of coordination from the local to the national level. Representation of localities lost meaning and was replaced with nationwide representation. With the transformation of cleavages from territorial to functional cutting across localities (Caramani 2004), proportional representation became instrumental to facilitating links across districts of interests that were nationwide, not territorially segmented. The cross-district linkage among candidates representing the same social groups and interests brought about nationwide representation.

Parliaments based on territorial, rather than functional, representation of groups could no longer be representative of nationwide social and economic interests that cut across localities. Insofar as in protocorporatist countries the representation of diverse interests could not work through the territorial channel, majoritarian systems created a collective action problem. They became inadequate as they could not support a negotiation-based political system at the national level—first because of local representation, and second because it underrepresented minorities who were not territorially concentrated. It was to re-establish the conditions for negotiation between all relevant interests that parties supported proportional representation in protocorporatist countries.[31]

In liberal market economies the pressure to include and represent various interests, to put negotiating institutions in place, and to reach consensus for the sake of investment in co-specific assets was absent. Anglo-Saxon countries do not have guild and *Ständestaat* traditions. France, which relied on a strong statist tradition whereby the *corps intermédiaires* were weak, also belongs to this group (although its elections after World War I used a system that can be considered proportional). Early industrialization in Britain had imposed class on a nationwide basis before crucial franchise extensions. The overwhelming weight of the class dimension, the flexible labor market, and the reduced role of the state in the economy left little room for negotiations between social partners. Rather than cooperative, the system is competitive as the aforementioned literature on "varieties of capitalism" shows. Organized interests are weak, investment is made in general assets (in particular, general education), and a broad middle-class is dominant.

Parties mostly represent broad class interests on roughly equal terms across the country. In Britain, most of the distortive districting effects that worked against the left were corrected through redistricting and a progressive homogenization of apportionment in various rounds of reform acts in the nineteenth century.[32] Arguably, in the United States it is possible to observe today a territorial distortion in favor of nonurban electorates due to districting and seat-vote disproportionality. Historically, in the United States the crucial phases of nationalization took place during the New Deal, which replaced the "solid South" political geography with the issue of race (Schattschneider 1960).

One of the central features of the types of market economies that adopted proportional representation is specialization in a large skill-based export sector and reliance on trade. Economic incentives from export specialization account for the proportionality of electoral systems in Western Europe at the beginning of the twentieth century. Katzenstein's (1985) classical analysis of small states portrays proportional representation as a core "enabling condition" for corporatism. More directly related to the link with trade, Rogowski (1987) has highlighted the "natural affinity" and positive empirical association between trade and proportional representation. The higher a country's dependence on external trade, the more likely it will be drawn to adopt proportional representation. His analysis attributes stability in such countries to proportional representation, especially in later periods, namely after World War II. Proportional representation with large district magnitudes follows the convergence of pressures from free trade groups that unite to face insulation. Analyses in this stream of literature and on larger samples have shown that pressure for proportional systems increases with the cost of maintaining a closed economy, because proportional systems are more credible in their commitment to compensate losers from globalization (Martin and Steiner 2016).[33] These analyses find an association between the global integration level and the likelihood of electoral reforms toward more proportional systems. Liberalization uncertainty is lower under proportional representation.

To reiterate and conclude, this approach is not incompatible with the competitive one. Interest-based parties in protocorporatist economies face the trilemma of what to do when competition increases (Cusack, Iversen, and Soskice 2010): ally or even merge with other parties to overcome the high thresholds, water down their platforms to appeal to a larger electoral base, or opt for proportional representation. The latter option has proven the least costly given the socioeconomic context and nationalization.

Conclusion: An Assessment of the Literature

The literature on the origins of electoral systems is impressive in its theoretical sophistication, historical scholarship, and cumulative knowledge creation. It combines structural and actor-oriented maximization approaches together with historical explanation, and it bridges the origins and consequences of electoral institutions. It considers an array of actors—from aggregate groups (classes, economic sectors, and social groups more generally) to organizations such as parties, intraparty factions, and local candidates—and employs rigorous methods to empirically test theoretical hypotheses. Not least, contributions are published in the top outlets of the discipline.

Given its very nature, a historical political economy approach aims at broad cross-country associations. Critiques have consequently focused on the role of specific contexts and called for more within-case analysis, more precise historical data, and more attention to dynamics within collective actors such as parties and risks of endogeneity between electoral systems and economic structures. Methodologically, historical approaches have been proposed as actors, and processes are too complex for methods based on cross-national variation. The number of factors, and their interactions, that account for collective decisions can only be dealt with appropriately if quantitative methods are complemented with historical, qualitative ones.[34] Indeed, while early formulations about the adoption of proportional representation were general with a comparative aim, more recent contributions have focused on fewer cases for which data are available at the district level.

In a different way, the strong elements in the field also harbor the seeds of its weaknesses. The cumulative aim that characterizes each contribution has funneled analyses in a specific direction that may reduce the space for alternative explanations. While contemporary debates seemed to point to the role of cross-national influences, diffusion mechanisms have hardly been investigated quantitatively. Some analyses address the issue (see, in particular, Bol, Pilet, and Riera 2015), but for periods after 1945 and not for the crucial period of the first decades of the twentieth century. The role of ideas and their spread has been analyzed by Blais, Dobryznyska, and Indridason (2005), whereas Blais and Massicotte (1997) have addressed the impact of colonial legacies. Birch et al. (2002) have addressed the role of external experts in the adoption of electoral systems in Eastern Europe after the democratic transition. The challenge would be to incorporate such analyses of cross-country influences in an HPE framework and to apply them to the beginning of the twentieth century. In addition, too little attention is given to the institutions in place with which actors choose electoral systems, the number of veto players, and the veto instruments they have at their disposal.

Connected to this is the vast question of enfranchisement. First, it is reductive to see enfranchisement in broad terms as increasing the number of players and therefore competition. In fact, enfranchisement has often been accompanied by compensating restrictions, like plural voting (an example is the Belgian case). Second, analyses do not allow for the variation in the way in which enfranchisement played out. In some cases, it has been a progressive reduction of restrictions on the right to vote, in others a sudden introduction of universal suffrage. Third, the competitive logic is not applied to the enfranchisement of women. While it has been done for enfranchisement itself (Teele 2018), the effect of women's voting rights on electoral competition, and indirectly on electoral systems, remains understudied.

All this obviously matters and should be integrated in the historical political economy approach, as long as it does not undermine its important distinctive contribution. This contribution is comparative and based on cross-country variation. Contributions specific to single cases can be made to inform, rather than replace, comparisons that test general hypotheses. The way in which the field is set up is able to incorporate diffusion mechanisms, qualitative country-specific analyses, and local/intraparty factors, thus maintaining the cumulative spirit that characterizes the HPE approach to electoral systems.

Notes

1. The chapter covers the election of legislatures in parliamentary systems in Europe and presidential systems in the Americas (usually referred to as parliaments and congresses).
2. These are the dimensions of representation (Pitkin 1967). The notion that electoral systems are "instruments" that maximize particular dimensions of representation is taken from Powell (2000). The political nature of electoral systems is best conveyed by Sartori (1968) as the institutions that can be most easily manipulated.
3. The term "district" (rather than "constituency") is used here to designate the territorial unit within which votes are translated into seats in parliaments and congresses.
4. The concept of two revolutions as broad historical critical junctures is taken from Rokkan (1970). They constitute "twin" (Bendix 1964), highly related processes.
5. "Macro-historical sociology" is a broader label than "historical political economy," which is mostly limited to economic structures and overlooks ethnolinguistic and religious groups. On contentious politics, see Tilly (1990).
6. This combination of agency and structure is intrinsic to the definition of a cleavage in terms of a social base (say, class), the membership of which is reinforced by identity and solidarity ties, and is mobilized by a political organization (Bartolini and Mair 1990).
7. As reviewed in Benoit (2007), "endogeneity" is an old argument (Grumm 1958; Lipson 1964; Rokkan 1970) that has recently been revived (Colomer 2004; 2005). The role of partisan interests in the design of electoral systems is clearest in the new democracies of Eastern Europe after the fall of communism (Birch et al. 2002), and in the electoral reforms in Italy, Japan, and New Zealand (Renwick, Hanretty, and Hine 2009; Rudd and Taichi 1994). Debates during reforms show that actors possess sufficient knowledge to anticipate broad consequences.
8. Since Duverger's seminal work, a vast number of studies have analyzed the consequences of electoral systems (e.g., Rae 1971; Sartori 1986; Shugart and Carey 1992; Lijphart 1994) on the "effective" number of parties (Laakso and Taagepera 1979).
9. This is generally true for cooperation between language and religious groups, and also race and castes. A prime example is interethnic cooperation in Sri Lanka (Horowitz 1985).
10. It is difficult to separate distributive from nondistributive consequences. A case in point is policy consequences: proportional representation is associated with higher spending on broad public goods (for example, education), while majoritarian systems usually go hand in hand with targeted goods, such as tariffs, lower public deficits, and lower inflation (Persson and Tabellini 1999; Persson, Roland, and Tabellini 2007).
11. This is known as the "micro-mega rule" (Colomer 2004).

12. This refers to both direct democracy instruments, such as referenda and popular initiatives, and territorial representation (in upper houses) and federalism.
13. At this level of generality, all electoral devices can be seen as attempts to contain the enfranchised working class (Ahmed 2010; 2013a). Comparative developments are presented in Meyer (1901); Seymour and Frary (1918); Braunias (1932); Rokkan and Meyriat (1969); Sternberger and Vogel (1969); Caramani (2000); Nohlen (2005); Nohlen and Stöver (2010); and Nohlen et al. (1999, 2001). On the election's "triumph" and the oxymoron of "democratic aristocracy" echoing Schumpeter's definition of an "elitist democracy," see the historical reconstruction in Manin (1997).
14. Burke is the first to point to "virtual representation," namely, that representatives of a specific group in a district represent the interest of similar groups in other districts. This is one of the themes in the nationalization of politics literature (Caramani 2004), describing the process of deterritorialization by means of the ideological left–right dimension overwhelming pre-industrial territorial cleavages. On cross-district coordination see Cox (1997).
15. These macro transformations in the nineteenth century led to the cleavage-based party families that form part of Rokkan's (1970) model of political development in Western Europe.
16. Between 1854 and 1864, a transferable-vote proportional system was used in the Danish *Rigsdåg* (the common assembly with Schleswig) for the election of fifty-five out of eighty members. In Switzerland, proportional representation was introduced in eight cantons before the federal level. In the Austrian Empire, Moravia introduced it in 1905, and in the German Empire, Württemberg in 1906. For details, see Caramani (2000, 58–63).
17. Rokkan's democratization sequence (1970) makes this quite explicit with the third threshold consisting of lowering the entry barriers for minorities. The normative debate was widespread from the 1760s among philosophers and mathematicians (de Borda, Condorcet, Hill, Hare, Droop, D'Hondt, and Hagenbach-Bischoff, among many others) and gave rise to associations for reform. The normative goals were to avoid tyranny by the majority, gerrymandering, malapportionment, and clientelism, to allow faithful representation of society (Considérant's *vote représentatif*), to make each vote count and to solve "paradoxes" of cyclical majorities. See Caramani (2000, 58–63) for details. Such debates are the basis of the "public choice" approach, but not the focus of the HPE approach.
18. For an encompassing picture of the development of the European party landscape since the early nineteenth century, see Caramani (2015).
19. A pattern of controlled political liberalization is what Negretto and Visconti (2018) also observe in Latin America. The threat posed by other mass mobilization parties—such as fascist parties after World War I—is not considered in these analyses.
20. See Cusack, Iversen, and Soskice (2007); Blais, Dobryznyska, and Indridason (2005); and Leemann and Mares (2014). On coordination opportunities that attenuate the winner-takes-all effect under majoritarian systems in Germany from 1890 to 1920, see Schröder and Manow (2020) and Walter (2021). Based on a recalculation of Boix's data that includes electoral system choices in Eastern Europe in the 1990s, Andrews and Jackman (2005) argue that it is an implausible assumption that established parties possessed enough information to make self-interested choices and that this led to serious miscalculations regarding the success of parties under certain electoral systems.
21. This approach owes much to investigations of party and electoral systems at the district level. See Cox (1997), Caramani (2000, 2004), and Chhibber and Kollman (2004), among others.

22. Rather than defending themselves from electoral losses following the rise of socialism, this strategy alleviated the revolutionary pressure inherent in the exclusion of working masses from representation. Ahmed (2013b) makes the argument that the level of threat, in particular the one stemming from workers' movement radicalism in its opposition to liberalism and capitalism, plays a role in focusing the strategies of liberal-conservative elites. For Alesina and Glaeser (2004), too, the left forced reform through its radicalism.
23. Leemann and Mares's (2014) analysis of the German case shows precisely this competition at the district level and offers support to the thesis that proportional representation was introduced following local-level vulnerabilities due to inroads by social democratic candidates under general conditions of vote-seat disproportionality.
24. In this sense, before competing in the ideological space, parties competed in the physical space, acting as catch-all over parties across spatial units before acting as catch-all parties across social groups, since they could not become majoritarian using a purely class strategy (Przeworski and Sprague 1986).
25. These are dimensions of competition identified by Bartolini (1999; 2000).
26. In yet another iteration on coordination between established parties in the wake of the entry of social democrats in Germany between 1890 and 1920, Walter (2021) finds that they were able to overcome their coordination problems within the institutional setting of a majoritarian electoral system.
27. This focus also leads to analysis of a different time period: no longer the main phases of democratization (enfranchisement, abolition of the plural vote, introduction of cabinet responsibility, etc.) but rather the period after World War I, when one main democratic issue—namely, district distortion—remained outstanding (Cusack, Iversen, and Soskice 2010).
28. These are countries variously labeled consociational, consensus, or plural, and that Lijphart (1984) has systematized as consociational (as opposed to Westminster) democracies (see also Powell 2000). The classification of countries largely overlaps with the distinction between coordinated (or social) and liberal market economies (CME vs. LME) in the varieties of capitalism literature (Hall and Soskice 2001).
29. Cusack, Iversen, and Soskice (2007) report a strong association between the "coordination index" (built additively with various components, in which the skilled export sector weighs heavily; see Martin and Steiner 2016) and the effective electoral threshold.
30. On the role of the international system in the process of state formation and nationalism, see Tilly (1990).
31. The inclusion of veto players who are potentially able to block legislation was sometimes enhanced by the availability of direct democracy, as in Switzerland.
32. The Arab Spring and the prospect of a fourth wave of democratization has revived questions about the choice of electoral rules in transitional nations. Clement (2016), in an analysis of sixty-five countries, supports the hypothesis that coordinated market economies are associated with proportional representation, with similar arguments relating to this type of economy's investment in education and reliance on co-specific assets.
33. These authors find a strong association between the effective electoral threshold (i.e., the proportionality of electoral systems) and the skill-based export sector (rather than "coordination" more generally, of which the export sector is only one component, as in Cusack, Iversen, and Soskice 2007).
34. These are the points made by Kreuzer (2010) in a polemic directed against the quantitative analysis proposed by Cusack, Iversen, and Soskice (2007).

References

Ahmed, Amel. 2010. "Reading History Forward: The Origins of Electoral Systems in European Democracies." *Comparative Political Studies* 43, no. 8/9: 1059–88.

Ahmed, Amel. 2013a. *Democracy and the Politics of Electoral System Choice*. Cambridge: Cambridge University Press.

Ahmed, Amel. 2013b. "The Existential Threat: Varieties of Socialism and the Origins of Electoral Systems in Early Democracies." *Studies in Comparative International Development* 48: 141–71.

Alesina, Alberto, and Edward L. Glaeser. 2004. *Fighting Poverty in the US and Europe: A World of Difference*. Oxford: Oxford University Press.

Andrews, Josephine T., and Robert W. Jackman. 2005. "Strategic Fools: Electoral Rule Choice under Extreme Uncertainty." *Electoral Studies* 24, no. 1: 65–84.

Bartolini, Stefano. 1999. "Collusion, Competition and Democracy: Part I." *Journal of Theoretical Politics* 11, no. 4: 435–70.

Bartolini, Stefano. 2000. "Collusion, Competition and Democracy: Part II." *Journal of Theoretical Politics* 12, no. 1: 33–65.

Bartolini, Stefano, and Peter Mair. 1990. *Identity, Competition and Electoral Availability: The Stabilization of European Electorates, 1885–1985*. Cambridge: Cambridge University Press.

Bendix, Reinhard. 1964. *Nation-Building and Citizenship: Studies of Our Changing Social Order*. New York: Wiley.

Benoit, Kenneth. 2004. "Models of Electoral System Change." *Electoral Studies* 23, no. 3: 363–89.

Benoit, Kenneth. 2007. "Electoral Laws as Political Consequences: Explaining the Origins and Change of Electoral Institutions." *Annual Review of Political Science* 10: 363–90.

Birch, Sarah, Frances Millard, Marina Popescu, and Kieran Williams. 2002. *Embodying Democracy: Electoral System Design in Post-Communist Europe*. Basingstoke: Palgrave Macmillan.

Blais, André, Agnieska Dobrzynska, and Indridi H. Indridason. 2005. "To Adopt or Not to Adopt Proportional Representation." *British Journal of Political Science* 35, no. 1: 182–90.

Blais, André, and Louis Massicotte. 1997. "Electoral Formulas: A Macroscopic Perspective." *European Journal of Political Research* 32, no. 1: 107–29.

Boix, Carles. 1999. "Setting the Rules of the Game: The Choice of Electoral Systems in Advanced Democracies." *American Political Science Review* 93, no. 3: 609–24.

Boix, Carles. 2010. "Electoral Markets, Party Strategies, and Proportional Representation." *American Political Science Review* 104, no. 2: 404–13.

Bol, Damien, Jean-Benoît Pilet, and Pedro Riera. 2015. "The International Diffusion of Electoral Systems: The Spread of Mechanisms Tempering Proportional Representation Across Europe." *European Journal of Political Research* 54: 384–401.

Braunias, Karl. 1932. *Das parlamentarische Wahlrecht: Ein Handbuch über die Bildung der gesetzgebenden Körperschaften in Europa*. 2 vols. Berlin-Leipzig: Walter de Gruyter.

Calvo, Ernesto. 2009. "The Competitive Road to Proportional Representation: Partisan Biases and Electoral Regime Change under Increasing Party Competition." *World Politics* 61, no. 2: 254–95.

Caramani, Daniele. 2000. *Elections in Western Europe since 1815: Electoral Results by Constituencies*. London: Palgrave Macmillan.

Caramani, Daniele. 2003. "The End of Silent Elections: The Birth of Electoral Competition, 1832–1915." *Party Politics* 9, no. 4: 411–43.

Caramani, Daniele. 2004. *The Nationalization of Politics: The Formation of National Electorates and Party Systems in Western Europe*. Cambridge: Cambridge University Press.

Caramani, Daniele. 2015. *The Europeanization of Politics: The Formation of a European Electorate and Party System in Historical Perspective*. Cambridge: Cambridge University Press.

Chhibber, Pradeep K., and Ken Kollman. 2004. *The Formation of National Party Systems: Federalism and Party Competition in Canada, Great Britain, India, and the United States*. Princeton, NJ: Princeton University Press.

Clement, Jessica. 2016. "Electoral Rule Choice in Transitional Economies." *Journal of Institutional Economics* 12, no. 4: 895–919.

Colomer, Josep M.. 2004. "The Strategy and History of Electoral System Choice." In *Handbook of Electoral System Choice*, ed. Josep M. Colomer, 3–78. London: Palgrave Macmillan.

Colomer, Josep M.. 2005. "It's Parties That Choose Electoral Systems, or, Duverger's Laws Upside Down." *Political Studies* 53, no. 1: 1–21.

Cox, Gary, W. 1997. *Making Votes Count: Strategic Coordination in the World's Electoral Systems*. Cambridge: Cambridge University Press.

Cusack, Thomas, Torben Iversen, and David Soskice. 2007. "Economic Interests and the Origins of Electoral Systems." *American Political Science Review* 101, no. 3: 337–91.

Cusack, Thomas, Torben Iversen, and David Soskice. 2010. "Coevolution of Capitalism and Political Representation: The Choice of Electoral Systems." *American Political Science Review* 104, no. 2: 393–403.

Duverger, Maurice. 1951. *Political Parties: Their Organization and Activity in the Modern State*. New York: Wiley.

Grumm, John G. 1958. "Theories of Electoral Systems." *Midwest Journal of Political Science* 2, no. 4: 357–76.

Hall, Peter A., and David Soskice, eds. 2001. *Varieties of Capitalism: The Institutional Foundations of Comparative Advantage*. Oxford: Oxford University Press.

Horowitz, Donald L. 1985. *Ethnic Groups in Conflict*. Berkeley: University of California Press.

Katzenstein, Peter J. 1985. *Small States in World Markets*. Ithaca, NY: Cornell University Press.

Kreuzer, Marcus. 2010. "Historical Knowledge and Quantitative Analysis: The Case of the Origins of Proportional Representation." *American Political Science Review* 104, no. 2: 369–92.

Laakso, Markku, and Rein Taagepera. 1979. "'Effective' Number of Parties: A Measure with Application to West Europe." *Comparative Political Studies* 12, no. 1: 3–27.

Leemann, Lucas, and Isabela Mares. 2014. "The Adoption of Proportional Representation." *Journal of Politics* 76, no. 2: 461–78.

Lijphart, Arend. 1984. *Democracies: Patterns of Majoritarian and Consensus Government in Twenty-One Countries*. New Haven, CT: Yale University Press.

Lijphart, Arend. 1994. *Electoral Systems and Party Systems: A Study of Twenty-Seven Democracies, 1945–1990*. Oxford: Oxford University Press.

Lipson, Leslie. 1964. *The Democratic Civilization*. Oxford: Oxford University Press.

Lublin, David. 2014. *Minority Rules: Electoral Systems, Decentralization, and Ethnoregional Party Success*. Oxford: Oxford University Press.

Manin, Bernard. 1997. *The Principles of Representative Government*. Cambridge: Cambridge University Press.

Martin, Christian W., and Nils D. Steiner. 2016. "Economic Globalization and the Change of Electoral Rules." *Constitutional Political Economy* 27, no. 4: 355–76.

Meyer, Georg. 1901. *Das parlamentarische Wahlrecht*. Berlin: Verlag O. Haring.

Negretto, Gabriel L., and Giancarlo Visconti. 2018. "Electoral Reform under Limited Party Competition: The Adoption of Proportional Representation in Latin America." *Latin American Politics and Society* 60, no. 1: 27–51.

Nohlen, Dieter, ed. 2005. *Elections in the Americas: A Data Handbook*. Oxford: Oxford University Press.

Nohlen, Dieter, Florian Grotz, and Christof Hartmann, eds. 2001. *Elections in Asia and the Pacific: A Data Handbook*. Oxford: Oxford University Press.

Nohlen, Dieter, Michael Krennerich, and Bernhard Thibaut, eds. 1999. *Elections in Africa: A Data Handbook*. Oxford: Oxford University Press.

Nohlen, Dieter, and Philip Stöver, eds. 2010. *Elections in Europe: A Data Handbook*. Baden-Baden: Nomos.

Persson, Torsten, Gerard Roland, and Guido Tabellini. 2007. "Electoral Rules and Government Spending in Parliamentary Democracies." *Quarterly Journal of Political Science* 2, no. 2: 155–88.

Persson, Torsten, and Guido Tabellini. 1999. "The Size and Scope of Government: Comparative Politics with Rational Politicians." *European Economic Review* 43, no. 4–6: 699–735.

Pitkin, Hanna F. 1967. *The Concept of Representation*. Berkeley: University of California Press.

Powell, Bingham G. 2000. *Elections as Instruments of Democracy: Majoritarian and Proportional Visions*. New Haven, CT: Yale University Press.

Przeworski, Adam, and John D. Sprague. 1986. *Paper Stones: A History of Electoral Socialism*. Chicago: University of Chicago Press.

Rae, Douglas. 1971. *The Political Consequences of Electoral Laws*. 2nd ed. New Haven, CT: Yale University Press.

Renwick, Aland, Christopher Hanretty, and David Hine. 2009. "Partisan Self-Interest and Electoral Reform: The New Italian Electoral Law of 2005." *Electoral Studies* 28, no. 3: 437–47.

Rogowski, Ronald. 1987. "Trade and the Variety of Democratic Institutions." *International Organization* 41, no. 2: 203–23.

Rogowski, Ronald. 1989. *Commerce and Coalitions: How Trade Affects Domestic Political Alignments*. Princeton, NJ: Princeton University Press.

Rokkan, Stein. 1970. *Citizens, Elections, Parties: Approaches to the Comparative Study of the Processes of Development*. Oslo: Universitetsforlaget.

Rokkan, Stein, and Jean Meyriat, eds. 1969. *International Guide to Electoral Statistics*. Vol. 1. *National Elections in Western Europe*. The Hague: Mouton.

Rudd, Chris, and Ichikawa Taichi. 1994. *Electoral Reform in New Zealand and Japan: A Shared Experience?* Palmerston North: Massey University Press.

Sartori, Giovanni. 1968. "Political Development and Political Engineering." In *Public Policy*, ed. John D. Montgomery and Albert O. Hirschman, 261–98. Cambridge, MA: Harvard University Press.

Sartori, Giovanni. 1986. "The Influence of Electoral Systems: Faulty Laws or Faulty Method?" In *Electoral Laws and Their Political Consequences*, ed. Bernard Grofman and Arendt Lijphart, 43–68. New York: Agathon Press.

Schattschneider, Elmer E.. 1960. *The Semisovereign People: A Realist's View of Democracy in America*. New York: Holt, Rinehart and Winston.

Schröder, Valentin, and Philip Manow. 2020. "An Intra-Party Account of Electoral System Choice." *Political Science Research and Methods* 8, no. 2: 251–67.

Seymour, Charles, and Donald P. Frary. 1918. *How the World Votes: The Story of Democratic Development in Elections*. 2 vols. Springfield, MA: Nichols.

Shugart, Matthew S., and John Carey. 1992. *Presidents and Assemblies: Constitutional Design and Electoral Dynamics*. Cambridge: Cambridge University Press.

Sternberger, Dolf, and Bernhard Vogel, eds. 1969. *Die Wahl der Parlamente und anderer Staatsorgane: Ein Handbuch*. Vol. 1. *Europa*. Berlin: Walter de Gruyter.

Teele, Dawn L. 2018. *Forging the Franchise: The Political Origins of the Women's Vote*. Princeton, NJ: Princeton University Press.

Tilly, Charles. 1990. *Coercion, Capital, and European States, AD 990–1990*. Oxford: Blackwell.

Walter, André. 2021. "Letter: Socialist Threat? Radical Party Entry, Electoral Alliances, and the Introduction of Proportional Representation." *American Political Science Review* 115, no. 2: 701–708.

CHAPTER 22

PROPERTY RIGHTS IN HISTORICAL POLITICAL ECONOMY

LEE J. ALSTON AND BERNARDO MUELLER

In this chapter we are most interested in the economic property rights that individuals or groups have in political markets. By "economic property rights." we mean the de facto rights that actors hold after expending transaction costs to capture and hold onto rights. Because of transaction costs, de facto rights differ from de jure rights. Inclusive sets of property rights in terms of open entry—for example, rights to set up a corporation or vote, have led to better outcomes in terms of economic growth and prosperity than limited or extractive property rights (Sokoloff and Engerman 2000; North, Wallis, and Weingast 2009; Acemoglu and Robinson 2012; 2019). There is sufficient consensus around this proposition that we take it as a given in this chapter and focus instead on the corollary question to which it gives rise. If open and inclusive property rights are the path to greater welfare and prosperity, why have most countries and societies throughout history and today not pursued this path? In the early 1800s the richest countries were approximately four times wealthier than the poorest countries in gross domestic product (GDP) per capita. Today the difference is more than a hundredfold. The pattern of growth trajectories over this period is that of a small group of fast-growth rich economies, a large group of slow-growth poor economies, and an increasingly large gap between both groups, with few historical cases of nations transitioning from one group to the other (exceptions are mostly Asian tigers, such as South Korea, Taiwan, and Singapore).

Poor countries do not reform their property rights to tap into the wealth-enhancing power of inclusion and political open access because changes to property rights are always redistributive. Individuals, groups, and organizations that would be harmed by changes in property rights resist change and maintain the status quo set of property rights because they hold rights to wealth and political power, enabling them to block change. Much work in historical political economy (HPE) chronicles successes and failures to promote inclusion.

Successful adaptation of property rights rest on bargains and side payments that improve the positions of all parties. Can these bargains be achieved, or are there impediments of any kind that drive an insurmountable wedge between the current property rights and those that would enhance prosperity? The wedge results from transaction costs being positive. If transaction costs are zero, then wedges would not exist. The goal of our paper is to specify the transaction costs that prevent or allow changes. Transaction costs of maintaining the status quo can change with demographic, technological, political, or other shocks that in turn affect the rents of those who specify the property rights.

Transaction Costs of Changing Property Rights: Why We Are Not in a First- or Second-Best World

Prominent work in economics presumes that existing forces eliminate these wedges and ensure efficient outcomes or second-best approximations. The model of perfect competition, for example, does just that. It models situations where nothing stops all mutually beneficial trades from being realized, thus automatically eliminating the wedges that could prevent the optimal outcome (Arrow and Debreu 1954). Though Arrow and Debreu's work pertained to economic markets, exchanges are even more difficult in political markets where rights are less secure and less easily tradeable.

In a cross-country perspective, convergence theory expects the forces of mobile capital, labor, and ideas to raise the output and welfare of lagging countries, leading to a world where all nations are as equally prosperous as their initial endowments allow (Barro and Sala-i-Martin 1992). In a similar manner, Rostow's (1960) model of stages of economic growth postulates that countries follow a path through five well-determined stages en route to becoming developed. Modernization theory asserts that once countries become rich, they automatically become democratic, which is in essence a process that rearranges political property rights (Lipset 1959). All of these authors model a world of zero transaction costs, though none explicitly believed that the world works this way.

The Coase "theorem" has been much misunderstood (Barzel and Allen 2023). The Coase theorem states that if property rights are secure and if transaction costs are zero, then an efficient allocation of resources ensues (Coase 1960). Resources will end up in the hands of those who value them the most, regardless of who initially held the rights. Coase's purpose in modeling a zero-transaction-cost world was to establish a benchmark that does not exist, precisely to bring our attention to bear on the importance of assigning property rights to those who would have the highest-valued use, given that transaction costs would prevent exchanges from lower- to higher-valued uses.

North (1990) coined the term "adaptive efficiency" to describe societies that adapt to shocks by changing institutions that promote prosperity. North does not suggest that institutions are generally adaptively efficient. Quite to the contrary, he stresses the "uncertain success of institutional adaptation, and the limits of adaptive efficiencies" in most countries (North 2005, 169).

Finally, there is Harold Demsetz's (1967) influential paper "Towards a Theory of Property Rights," which we use in this review as a guide to classify the literature on property rights in HPE. This is the quintessential approach to postulating corrective forces for property rights. It has given rise to much debate on the extent to which such forces exist and the circumstances in which they fail to emerge. Demsetz argued that if the extant property rights were no longer capable of assuring the highest-value use of a resource, then economic forces would induce a change in property rights to better exploit the resource and reduce rent dissipation.

Demsetz did not make explicit the mechanism through which a society transitioned from one set of property rights to another. Rather he assumed that the existence of greater net benefits from the new arrangements would be enough to induce the change. This presumption of a march toward efficiency-inducing property rights was applauded by some scholars and contested by others (see Merrill 2002 for an overview of a special issue of the *Journal of Legal Studies* dedicated to discussing Demsetz's approach). Critics provided examples and mechanisms through which new inefficiency-correcting property rights could fail to materialize even when the losses due to current arrangements were large and obvious and the alternative well known and viable. In the example that Demsetz used, property rights among some Indian tribes in Canada transitioned from open access to private property in response to the increase in the price of beaver pelts that was induced by the opening of trade with European settlers. Some scholars found other examples consistent with the Demsetz case—for example, bison (Lueck 1995); rhinoceros horns (Allen 2002); federal land in the United States (Libecap 1993); land in Hawaii (La Croix and Roumasset 1990; La Croix 2019); and US mining rights (Libecap 1978). However, various other examples explored cases where property rights failed to adjust, such as land (Alston, Libecap, and Mueller 1999; Anderson and Hill 1975; Besley 1995; among many others), oil fields (Wiggins and Libecap 1985), and timber (Libecap 1993), among many others. In some situations, the changes in property rights can take a situation from bad to worse. Higgs illustrated such a case with salmon fisheries (Higgs 1996).

Given that there are examples of successful adjustment of property rights in response to shocks that alter relative prices, as well as examples where these adjustments fail to materialize, much of the literature has turned to determining the conditions that lead to one path instead of the other. For example, to what extent and how does it matter if the efforts to block or change the property rights come from elites and interest groups rather than bottom up from community-based norms? Also, do property rights always move toward private rights, as Demsetz supposed, or can they also revert when price shocks go the other way (Merrill 2002)?

In the literature cited here, the examples were mostly of property rights over economic goods, such as land, minerals, water, and animals. Yet the same issues of self-correcting versus sticky property rights are also valid when what is at play are property rights in political markets. The property rights in political markets and in particular the bundle of rights under the umbrella of open access, open entry, and inclusion are our focus in this chapter, given their centrality to historical political economy. We thus organize our review by sorting between cases where the rights in political markets did and did not change to promote overall prosperity.[1]

To give this organizing principle more clarity, we define the notion of a Demsetz wedge.[2] The *Demsetz wedge* is the difference in the returns to owning an asset under first best efficient property rights with zero transaction costs and the return from de facto property rights, where de facto property rights include the return on the asset after accounting for the transaction costs of capturing the property right.[3] This measures the rents that accrue to changing the property rights and therefore the demand for the new rights (Alston and Mueller 2008; 2014). It also measures the level of compensation that would need to be paid to those who hold the property right to change the extant distribution of rights.

Figure 22.1 provides a graphic representation of the Demsetz wedge.[4] The horizontal axis measures scarcity decreasing from left to right. You could think of this as the return from having a secure title to land versus a squatted claim (Alston, Libecap, and Schneider 1996). The vertical axis measures the net present value (NPV) from having the good or asset. The upper line in the graph is the NPV in a zero-transaction-cost world. The lower line is the NPV under de facto economic property rights. In the case of

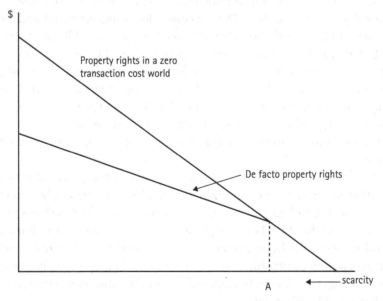

FIGURE 22.1. The Demsetz wedge in the evolution of property rights

land, this could include the costs of enforcing one's claim on a squatted piece of land as well as any differences in crop choices. At low levels of scarcity, property rights are not consequential for resource use. But as scarcity increases and changes relative prices, a wedge emerges between what can be achieved if transaction costs were zero versus the extant de facto property rights. The wedge is larger when the security is greater. A large wedge means greater losses from sticking with the status quo property rights, and thus a greater pressure for change. One could think of the wedge as measuring the benefits from having a secure legal title versus a squatted claim and a payment that would need to be made in a political market. Alston, Libecap, and Mueller (1999) found that the states titled land more quickly than the federal government in Brazil. State politicians titled land prior to elections anticipating voter support from those who received titles.[5] The HPE literature is full of cases where large wedges existed and persisted. The central theme in this review is to discern which contexts and mechanisms throughout history induced changes in property rights in political markets and which led to their persistence.

THE INITIAL EMERGENCE OF PROPERTY RIGHTS

A common account of the origins of property rights is that the grand shock initiating the progression from shared property to private property on a global scale was the transition from the Pleistocene to the Holocene twelve thousand years ago, ushered in by milder and less variable weather conditions that enabled farming. According to this view, once farming became viable it was readily "invented" and quickly diffused, given its superior productivity. To become viable, however, it required secure property rights, given the time-deferred nature of agricultural output and the uncertainties of storage. Also, in enabling sedentary, larger, and more complex societies, new property rights had to be developed to mediate a whole new and different set of conflicts.

Bowles and Choi (2013; 2019) dispute this standard account. They note that initially, and for a long time in most places, farming was not a superior technology to foraging, requiring more labor than hunting and gathering, and leading in many places to smaller stature and poorer health. Bales and Choi highlight the chicken-and-egg problem by noting that farming required private property rights to emerge but that private property rights could not exist in the mobile environments and with the fugitive perishable goods of hunter-gatherers. The solution Bowles and Choi (2013; 2019) propose is that private property rights and farming must have coevolved, in ways where advances along one margin enabled advance along the other in autocatalytic fashion. The rise of property right conventions and norms over dwellings and some crops and animals may have occurred in places where environmental conditions were right, possibly through evolutionary dynamics like those discussed earlier. If a sufficient subset of the population adhered to such norms, they could then enable the introduction of some types of farming, which even though less productive would have the evolutionary advantage for the group of reducing within-group conflict and lowering the cost of rearing children in sedentary rather than nomadic living. Technological change would eventually improve the productivity of agriculture, leading to higher demographic growth and further spread of the new property rights. This was a protracted process that did not come in clear stages. As the authors note,

> Enduring transitions occurred no more than 12,000 years ago and they were rare; in most ethnolinguistic units, the farming-cum-private property package did not independently emerge. Transitions were slow and sometimes witnessed reversals. The passage from initial domestication of one or two species accounting for a modest portion of the diet to a primary commitment to food production in some cases extended over as many as six millennia. As a result, mixed societies with substantial portions of the diet coming from both farming and hunting-gathering persisted over long periods.
>
> (Bowles and Choi 2013, 8832)

Though not a direct contradiction, this is a very different picture of the time frame to adapting property rights in response to a shock that one imagines Demsetz had in mind.

Other papers have examined the origins of property rights by looking at how settlers in previously unoccupied frontiers established their initial claims and how these changed over time. One of the most influential papers in this area is the analysis by Engerman and Sokoloff (2002) of how local factor endowments in labor, soil quality, minerals, climate, and so forth determined the early property rights chosen by colonizing nations for their New World possessions. The initial choices led to persistent outcomes in terms of inequality in wealth, human capital, and political power, and ultimately in long-term growth. Engerman and Sokoloff's interpretation contradicts Demsetz's approach as early property right choices persisted over centuries, even when they clearly hindered growth. Countries whose endowments favored slavery, extraction, and narrow elite domination followed development paths that maintained those characteristics over centuries, even though the opposite path of greater equality proved to be superior in the long run in most cases. Of course, these condition were not superior from the point of view of the elites who had the property rights over politics to change the extant property rights hindering growth. Acemoglu and Robinson (2012) bring together a series of historical cases that extend the Engerman and Sokoloff path dependence/persistence approach to other contexts. The persistence literature has mushroomed, offering many examples of the early distribution of property rights, institutions, and cultural traits having long-lasting effects on modern outcomes (e.g., see Dell [2010] and Nunn and Wantchekon [2011]).

In a more nuanced analysis of the origins of property rights on frontiers in Australia, Brazil, and the United States, Alston, Harris, and Mueller (2012) show that whether the initial rights of settlers get codified into de jure property rights in a smooth/peaceful or a convoluted/conflict-ridden manner depends crucially on context and political realities. The authors show that the state opted not to enforce extant de jure property rights, leaving the economic property rights in the hands of those with low cost of enforcement of de facto property rights. In early frontiers, settlers both specified and enforced property rights in a de facto manner. Regardless of who had the de facto rights, conflict was low because at first the original settlers had a much greater violence potential than the newcomers seeking to establish property rights. As such, the land remained under control of the original settlers. Over time, political pressure prompted the state to enforce de jure property rights of the newcomers, and the state had a greater violence potential than the original settlers. This was case with cattlemen's associations in the US West, squatters in Australia, and coffee growers in Brazil.[6]

WHEN PROPERTY RIGHTS DO NOT ADJUST: PERSISTING WEDGES

When property rights do not adapt to a new reality, something must be preventing the forces that should work to reduce the wedge. In very broad terms we could just say that transaction costs alter, hinder, or prevent the agreements, contracts, trades, negotiations, and other interactions necessary to realize the change to more "optimal" property rights. Among others, the property rights literature has covered cases where the nature of the adjustment-hindering transaction cost is related to politics, commitment problems, the cost of collective action, culture, identity, religion, ergodicity, rent-seeking, free riding, social and public choice problems, disorder, informational asymmetries, poverty, inequality, and leadership. In this section we discuss just a few examples related to politics, commitment, and culture.

Acemoglu, Johnson, and Robinson (2005a, 413) note that the existence of inefficient institutions raises the question: why not a political Coase theorem? This is like asking why the Demsetz wedge doesn't wither. Society could simply choose the most wealth-enhancing property rights and then establish compensating payments that make the deal acceptable to all. Those with the power to block the change would rationally chose not to do so, and the society would thrive.

The authors dismiss some explanation for why such adjustments do not happen, and then submit a social-conflict view that puts commitment issues as the key change-impeding transaction cost. They reject (1) a first best efficient institutions view that assumes efficiency considerations can be separated from their effect on distribution; (2) an ideology-based explanation where leaders or societies choose property rights based on their beliefs; and (3) an incidental institutions view where property rights are not explicitly chosen, but rather result from historical contingencies at critical junctures and their effects persist through time.[7] Instead, they favor a social conflict view that focuses on political power—that is, those who are in a position to change property rights do so with their own rents in mind, and the result generally will not coincide with what is best for society as a whole.

The key to the social conflict view is specifying the impediments to making the intertemporal political transactions that are necessary to adjust property rights. These transactions require commitment to future action, which is hard to do in the absence of impartial third-party enforcement. For one, there are hold-up problems: once property rights have changed, who assures that the compensating payments will be made and maintained? More importantly, fearing that the new property rights will undermine their future political power, political elites may opt instead to keep things as they are rather than risk an uncertain bargain:

> Thus poor economic institutions, here lack of property rights and hold-up, persist in equilibrium because to solve the problem, holders of political power have to voluntarily constrain their power or give it away. They may increase the security of property in society and increase incentives to invest, but it also undermines the ability of rulers to extract rents. They may be better off with a large slice of a small pie.
> (Acemoglu, Johnson, and Robinson 2005a, 437)

According to this view, North Korean leaders don't adhere to institutions, property rights, and policies that promote economic growth because of ideology or because there are no viable alternatives, but rather because their own rents in other viable scenarios are dramatically worse than what they currently enjoy.

Another example of politics and social conflict hindering the adjustment of property rights is the comparative performance of the Atlantic traders in the rise of Europe after 1500. Acemoglu, Johnson, and Robinson (2005b) argue that it was not the direct inflows of resources from colonial trade that caused England and the Netherlands to achieve faster economic growth in the subsequent centuries while Portugal and Spain lagged. Rather, trade was dominated by merchants and companies that were independent of the Crown, while in the Iberian nations the trading activities were a monopoly of the Crown. Thus, colonial trade enriched and empowered groups in England and the Netherlands that opposed and checked the monarch, leading to more inclusive institutions that in turn led to greater economic growth. In Spain and Portugal, on the contrary, colonial riches strengthened the monarchy and entrenched extractive institutions that would be a drag on growth in the following centuries.

It would be hard to imagine any compensating scheme through which the Portuguese and Spanish Crowns could be convinced to relinquish their hold on the colonial enterprise. Besides its effect on the political equilibrium, a further impediment to adjusting property rights can come in the form of the coevolution of institutions and culture. Mueller and Leite (2020) show how the medieval Portuguese culture of state-centric patrimonialism and honor through war and violence was well suited for promoting the conquest of a sea route to Asia, which they dominated for nearly one hundred years before any other nation could follow. Yet those very same cultural traits favored a violence-based enterprise in Asia in which principal-agent problems between the Crown and its agents dissipated a large share of the potential profits. In contrast, when the British and Dutch managed to reach Asia, their much more commerce-friendly cultural beliefs led them to quickly take over trade. Mueller and Leite explain how the Portuguese Crown eventually realized the nature of the losses inherent in the centralized and violence-ridden nature of the organization of their enterprise in Asia and tried to reform and even emulate the English and Dutch, for example, by creating a Portuguese East India Company in 1628. Yet the impact of mismatched culture ultimately undermined the attempt to truly alter the nature of those new institutions and property rights. The Portuguese Company never managed to attract private subscription and failed within a few years.

In many cases, the clearly "inefficient" property rights are not mistakes, unintended effects, or afterthoughts, but rather they are "constrained efficient" and purposefully designed to create rents that keep natural states from descending into violence (North, Wallis, and Weingast 2009). These rents are monopolies, exemptions, favors, special access, and other privileges that are distributed to social groups and organizations that have the capacity for violence. The distribution of these rents forms a grand deal in which each party voluntarily refrains from violence, thus enabling an environment of peace in which economic activity can thrive, while the coalition lasts. Viewed narrowly, the property rights that enable these rents are inefficient. But in the context of natural states, they are the crucial wedges that sustain greater—yet still limited—prosperity by warding off the threat and use of violence that destroys resources.

When Property Rights Adjust: Wedges That Wither

In the North, Wallis, and Weingast (2009) framework, it is possible for countries to eliminate the rents and not fall back into violence, yet this must be done by expanding access to the creation and functioning of organizations to more members of society. That is, the rents cannot just be removed; rather they must be dissipated by competition in economic and political markets. This transition from limited-access to open-access societies is a difficult process that only a small subset of twenty-five to thirty countries have managed to achieve.[8] It is, therefore, harder to find examples of property rights that successfully adjust than cases where they persist despite their negative impact on overall prosperity.

Perhaps the most notable case of virtuous property rights adjustment in history is the evolution of constitutional arrangements in England following the Glorious Revolution in 1688. The classic treatment is by North and Weingast (1989), who interpret the rise of representative government and institutions constraining arbitrary government behavior (i.e., Parliament) as the key change in property rights that enabled greater access of the Crown to debt and enabled Britain to defeat the French. Parliament's constraining of the Crown ultimately paved the way for the Industrial Revolution. This followed centuries of opportunistic and coercive Crown behavior that stifled wealth creation and innovation, as happened in all other absolutist regimes at the time. The new institutions that followed the Glorious Revolution worked by creating a credible commitment that the Crown would no longer violate property rights, unleashing the productive and creative potential that initiated the Great Divergence. This interpretation of the Glorious Revolution renders it as a dramatic example of property rights adjusting in an efficient direction. Despite (or maybe because of) the prominence of this interpretation, subsequent authors have forcefully questioned it. (see. e.g., Allen 2011; Cox 2012; Hodgson 2017; McCloskey 2010; Pincus and Robinson 2011; Stasavage 2002; Sussman and Yafeh 2004). We highlight it because of its use of the concept of credible commitment to ensure bargains.

One of the criticisms some of these papers make is that the Glorious Revolution was not so revolutionary, as property rights in medieval England were already reasonably secure. So, if we are willing to accept for this section examples where property rights adjusted in the right direction, yet did so only gradually, several other examples are better suited. Acemoglu and Robinson (2000) argue that the gradual march in many Western societies during the nineteenth century toward extended voting rights, greater inclusion, and democracy was not so much an ideological choice as a series of reactions by elites to unrest and the threat of revolution.[9] Incrementally extending rights and the franchise is a credible way to dissuade conflict and violence, because instead of simply ceding goods and resources that can later be reclaimed, they change the political equilibrium by giving voice in future decisions. Thus, in countries where the masses were more politically organized, political property rights adapted slowly through a centuries-long sequence of crises and defusing responses by extending the franchise. We have chosen to put this example in the section for adapting property rights, but one might just as well hold it up as an example of how property rights are slow to respond to change.

So far, we have laid out forces that can wither wedges, but our analysis has been silent about individual leaders who can play a role in changing the beliefs about the extant set of property rights and make the necessary side payments to move to a new set of property rights. The move in the United States from the Articles of Confederation to the US Constitution represents changing beliefs about weaknesses of the Articles of Confederation and the ability of the Constitution to address those weaknesses (Alston et al. 2018; Alston 2017). The Second Continental Congress passed the Articles of Confederation in 1777, and they stayed in place until nine states ratified the Constitution in 1788. The colonies won the war with Great Britain despite weaknesses in funding stemming from being a confederation. Nevertheless, there were not major forces pushing for change immediately following the war. The weaknesses included an unanimity rule to change provisions in the Constitution, disputes across states on who should pay the state debts from the war, an inability to engage in foreign treaties at the national level, an inability to raise taxes at the federal level, and a fear that the United States could not continue to defend its borders in the future.

Despite the weaknesses, there were many proponents of the status quo, including most of the governors of states who perceived that they would lose power. George Washington felt the lack of funding for the war was an early motivation for a larger role for the federal government. Alexander Hamilton was the most vocal proponent and in 1786 called for a Constitutional Convention to be held in May 1787. In late 1786 Congress agreed to send delegates. Before the convention, Washington, Hamilton, John Jay, and James Madison all played major roles in promoting a new constitution. Washington, once convinced to attend, brought moral authority; Hamilton brought incredible imagination in getting the convention to materialize; Jay brought his experience as diplomat at the peace conference following the Revolutionary War; and Madison was an amazing strategist who drafted a new constitution prior to the convention, and this quickly became the focal point.

The convention ultimately passed the Constitution, but it needed to be ratified by two-thirds of the states. The major architects of the Constitution went on a media blitz and produced the Federalist Papers, eighty-five essays published in New York newspapers. The governor of NY was an opponent of the Constitution. There were competing essays arguing against the Constitution, but they were for naught. The arguments that won the day changed the beliefs about moving property rights over some matters from the states to the federal government, but it took leadership to make it happen. Side payments had to be arranged to convince some states to go along. Abolishing slavery was off the table as the South would have resisted any changes. States voted to ratify, but many wanted amendments in the form of guaranteeing their personal liberties. Jay convinced others that to increase the acceptance of the Constitution the United States needed a bill of rights. Madison heeded the advice and drafted a bill, which became the starting point for bargaining in the first session of Congress following the ratification of the Constitution.

The Constitution and the Bill of Rights codified a new belief in federalism over supreme states' rights. The belief was not held by all but over time became more dominant with institutional deepening on other margins, which entailed subsequent actions in legislation or deeds that strengthened the original set of rights. For example, early on, the central government paid for the war debt, established a national bank, and put down the Whiskey Rebellion, which showed the ability of the federal government to tax. The Supreme Court, under John Marshall, voted for judicial review of legislation of the states. Institutional deepening continued reaching its peak with the Civil War to prevent secession (and end slavery). The lessons from this episode show the importance of leadership seizing a window of opportunity—the perceived weaknesses of the Articles of Confederation—to change beliefs about the extent of property rights held by the states versus the federal government. Windows of opportunity generally emerge following a diminution in the rents that actors receive because of a shock. Alternatively, some leaders can frame an issue such that those who win from a change in property rights outnumber those who currently benefit from the status quo.[10]

Another prominent set of examples of property rights that adjust to induce more efficient resource use comes from the work of Elinor Ostrom (1990) for understanding common property resources. These are group-level property rights where members can exclude outsiders from accessing the resources, but within the group there is the problem of open access. Before Ostrom a consensus prevailed that only private property rights or direct state control could avoid the tragedy of the commons (Hardin 1968; Scott 1955). Ostrom showed that common property rights have often emerged in a wide variety of contexts in a bottom-up way that successfully dealt with problems of collective action, free riding, and opportunistic behavior. In many cases these collective arrangements can be superior to private property rights by tapping into traditional knowledge and community values. Ostrom's research trawled through large numbers of cases where these arrangements worked and where they didn't to come up with a list of design principles that can guide the crafting and adaptation of property rights to shocks (McGinnis and Ostrom 1996). This approach can be understood as an effort to find the conditions under which property rights adapt to changing circumstances, especially in cases where resorting to private or state property is not desirable or possible, as in the looming crises related to the global commons that humanity is currently facing.

Comparative Cases of Changes in Property Rights

Most of the examples examined so far have focused on a single unit or country and analyzed whether a shock led to an adjustment of property rights. A different approach is to analyze how two different yet comparable societies react to a similar shock. This allows a means to identify whether a treated society was differently impacted by the shock in its subsequent development compared to the control society, where property rights did not adjust. In this final section we review a small sample of research that followed this strategy.

Greif (2006) compares how two different societies involved in premodern Mediterranean trade, the Maghrib traders of the eleventh century and the Genoese traders of the twelfth century, avoided what he calls the fundamental problem of exchange, that is, how to realize the gains from trade that is sequential in time, spread out in space, and often done with strangers. His focus is on how the culture of these two groups managed to deal with these problems first in the context of local impersonal trade, and subsequently as the commercial revolution expanded trade to a larger set of markets, partners, and opportunities.

Maghribs were characterized by a collectivist culture that rested on strong kinship ties and personal relations, relying on reputation, and with an ingrained suspicion and distrust of strangers. This cultural package led to institutions, norms, and property rights that promoted within-group trade to overcome the fundamental problem of exchange. Individuals who cheated or violated contracts were punished by all members of the group, not just the individual directly harmed. If a given agent chose to employ an agent who had cheated another, other agents were free to cheat him without punishment. These property rights arrangements were well suited for local and short-distance trade and enabled a modicum of prosperity. But due to their reliance on personal relations and restrictions to engage only with in-group members, they precluded the Maghrib from more fully taking advantage of the reemergence of long-distance Mediterranean and European trade and the much greater long-term prosperity it enabled.

The Genoese, on the other hand, had developed in the previous centuries an individualistic cultural set of norms, based on the smaller nuclear rather than the extended family. In an individualistic society an individual is not beholden to become involved and to punish others who have cheated third parties in their dealings. Rather than rely on a network of personal connections, these societies had to create a system of institutions and property rights to overcome the fundamental problem of exchange, including laws, codes, courts, police, and property rights innovations such as merchant guilds and family firms based on permanent partnership. These institutions and property rights formed the springboard that enabled the takeoff of considerable trade across some regions in Europe.

The distinction between the collectivist culture package, which has prevailed throughout most of humanity, historically and today, and the more recent individualistic package often associated with WEIRD societies (Western, educated, individualistic, rich, and developed) refers to norms, beliefs, psychology, and other cultural attributes, but they also come with distinct property right components (Henrich 2020). These cultural characteristics of societies have been found to have first-order effects on economic growth and prosperity, innovation, and effectiveness of institutions (Gorodnichenko and Roland 2011; Mokyr 2016). So how did individualism arise in only some societies and not in others?

Schulz et al. (2019) and Henrich (2020) have argued that it was the undermining by the Western church of intensive kin-based institutions in the Middle Ages that set the change in motion. The church's marriage and family program banned cousin marriages and polygynous marriage that were standard in collectivist cultures; reformed inheritance rights, dowries, and bride prices; pressured for independent residence after marriage; and favored individual ownership of land instead of collective forms of ownership. By 1500 this agenda had profound effects on the culture, beliefs, attitudes, and psychology of the societies exposed to it, which became "more individualistic and independent, less conforming and obedient, and more inclined towards trust and cooperation with strangers" (Schulz et al. 2019, 707).

A thriving literature attempts to measure cultural distance or divergence across societies using a wide variety of data and proxies, from surveys to genetic markers, languages to geographic location of population, blood donations to lost wallets returned, among others. This literature has given rise to numerous classifications besides collective-individual cultures, such as tight-loose cultures, cultural value orientation, personality classifications, among many others. In the end they all correlate closely to WEIRD and non-WEIRD cultures (Muthukrishna et al. 2020). WEIRD cultures have distinctively higher levels of GDP per capita and innovation, and are more democratic.

The property right component of WEIRD cultures appears to be more individualistic and better suited to modern market economies.

To the extent that many of these outcomes are desirable, one may wonder whether individualistic or WEIRD institutions will eventually disseminate to most other countries and dominate the globe. Mueller (2021) found that, even in non-WEIRD countries, younger cohorts have systematically more individualistic beliefs and attitudes than older cohorts, indicating a global shift in that direction over time. One is tempted to interpret such a change as an erosion of the Demsetz wedge that held maladapted beliefs and property rights in place.

A final example of a comparative analysis of the effects of different property rights arrangements is Rubin (2017), who investigates why the West got rich and the Middle East did not, despite the Middle East being further ahead economically, technologically, and scientifically before the year 1200. Rubin finds that the reversal of fortune that ensued as Western Europe eventually overtook and left behind the Middle East is not due to culture or religion directly. Rubin's analysis focuses on which legitimizing agents were key in each region historically. Legitimizing agents are groups that can bolster the beliefs of subjects in the ruler's right to rule. They are often crucial elements of a political equilibrium. It was not Islam as a set of beliefs that obstructed the continued progress of the Middle East, but the political role that Islamic religious authorities played as legitimizing agents. The reason, according to Rubin, is that—in general and not only in the Middle East—religious authorities as legitimizing agents make governments less able to adapt to change. Religious beliefs are often burdened by doctrine that makes them less flexible, impeding adjustments to property rights and institutions when shocks or opportunities hit a country, for example, technological change.

Although the church also served as a legitimizing agent in Western Europe initially, over time that role was undermined by a combination of factors, such as the Reformation and the emergence of national kingdoms, leading instead to economic elites increasingly playing a role in politics. Economic elites, contrary to political authorities, are better able to adapt to changing opportunities, as doing so is often in their own interest. In the long run, even small differences in this ability to adjust institutions and property rights leads to a great difference in prosperity.

Conclusion

In genetic evolution, maladapted design is quickly outcompeted. In cultural evolution, suboptimal design can persist for extended periods even when better ways of organization are known and available. We called this dislocation from optimal design a Demsetz wedge, as an illustration of the expectation that extant property rights that do not induce the highest-value use of resources will change with relative prices or other shocks, for example, demographic or technological. In this brief review of property rights in historical political economy, we showed that the experience with property rights covers the full set of outcomes. While many forces are typically pushing for property rights to change to internalize externalities and induce the most productive and valued use of resources, all sorts of transaction costs are also preventing those changes. Especially when it comes to political property rights, the intertemporal, collective transactions that are involved in achieving new property rights arrangements are often overwhelmed by transaction costs, so Demsetz wedges can endure indefinitely. The status quo, with respect to political property rights, has a heavy hand.

Acknowledgments

We thank Douglas Allen, Eric Alston, Jeffery A. Jenkins, Gary Libecap, Thomas Nonnemacher and Jared Rubin for comments.

Notes

1. We use the term "property rights" in political markets to apply to rights such as voting, having a voice in collective affairs, congregating, forming organizations, accessing credit, etc. The distinction between economic and political property rights is not always clear—for example, the right to open a business. We recognize that the term "rights" connotes different notions to different scholars, and some prefer property rules. We stick with property rights because this term is used in the literature that we survey.
2. Demsetz did not use the term "wedge," but we use it to illustrate the gains if transaction costs were zero.
3. For a discussion of legal rights (de jure property rights), economic rights (de facto property rights), and natural rights, see Barzel and Allen (2023).
4. The figure was first used in Alston, Libecap, and Schneider (1996) and again in Alston, Libecap, and Mueller (1999).
5. See Albertus (2020) for a discussion of the failure of land reform projects in Latin America and the rents that politicians received in crafting "reforms" without secure property rights.
6. Allen and Leonard (2021) find that land use in 2012 on land that was homesteaded from 1862 to 1940 was less developed than land purchased. The reason for the difference is that homesteaded land had to be worked, whereas land purchased could be used for subsequent commercial uses, e.g., stores, railroad depots, inter alia. In short, a wedge persisted for a long period of time.
7. In later work, Acemoglu and Robinson (2012) argue for the importance of critical junctures.
8. Rather than "open access," we prefer the term "open entry." "Open access" in natural resource economics typically connotes dissipation of a resource.
9. Allen (2011) credits reductions in measurement costs to leading to many of the changes in the nineteenth century that brought prosperity to Great Britain.
10. In the case of the US Constitution, state governors who held powerful rights stood to lose from a document that shifted rights to the federal level. Expected winners included citizens at large and members of Congress.

References

Acemoglu, Daron, Simon Johnson, and James A. Robinson. 2005a. "Institutions as a Fundamental Cause of Long-Run Growth. *Handbook of Economic Growth* 1: 385–472.

Acemoglu, Daron, Simon Johnson, and James A. Robinson. 2005b. "The Rise of Europe: Atlantic Trade, Institutional Change, and Economic Growth." *American Economic Review* 95, no. 3: 546–79.

Acemoglu, Daron, and James A. Robinson. 2000. "Why Did the West Extend the Franchise? Democracy, Inequality, and Growth in Historical Perspective." *Quarterly Journal of Economics* 115, no. 4: 1167–99.

Acemoglu, Daron, and James A. Robinson. 2012. *Why Nations Fail: The Origins of Power, Prosperity, and Poverty*. New York: Crown Business.

Acemoglu, Daron, James Robinson. 2019. *The Narrow Corridor. States, Societies, and the Fate of Liberty*. New York. Penguin Publishers.

Albertus, Michael. 2020. *Property Without Rights: Origins and Consequences of the Property Rights Gap*. Cambridge: Cambridge University Press.

Allen, Doug. 2002. "The Rhino's Horn: Incomplete Property Rights and the Optimal Value of an Asset." *Journal of Legal Studies* 31 (June): 339–58.

Allen, Doug. 2011. *The Institutional Revolution: Measurement and The Economic Emergence of the Modern World*. Chicago: University of Chicago Press.

Allen, Doug, and Brian Leonard. 2021. "Property Rights Acquisition and Path Dependence: Nineteenth-Century Land Policy and Modern Economic Outcomes." *Economic Journal* 131 (November): 3073–102.

Alston, Eric, Lee J. Alston, Bernardo Mueller, and Thomas Nonnenmacher. 2018. *Institutional and Organizational Analysis: Concepts and Applications*. Cambridge: Cambridge University Press.

Alston, Lee J. 2017. "Beyond Institutions: Beliefs and Leadership." *Journal of Economic History* 77, no. 2 (June): 353–72.

Alston, Lee J., Edwyna Harris, and Bernardo Mueller. 2012. "The Development of Property Rights on Frontiers: Endowments, Norms, and Politics." *Journal of Economic History* 72, no. 3: 741–70.

Alston, Lee J., Gary D. Libecap, and Bernardo Mueller. 1999. *Titles, Conflict, and Land Use: The Development of Property Rights and Land Reform on the Brazilian Amazon Frontier*. Ann Arbor: University of Michigan Press.

Alston, Lee J., Gary Libecap, and Robert Schneider. 1996. "The Determinants and Impact of Property Rights: Land Titles on the Brazilian Frontier." *Journal of Law, Economics, and Organization* 12, no. 1: 25–61.

Alston, Lee J., and Bernardo Mueller. 2008. "Property Rights and the State." In *Handbook of New Institutional Economics*, ed. C. Ménard and M.M. Shirley, 573–90. Berlin: Springer.

Alston, Lee J., and Bernardo Mueller. 2014. "Towards a More Evolutionary Theory of Property Rights." *Iowa Law Review* 100, no. 6: 2255–74.

Anderson, Terry L., and Peter J. Hill. 1975. "The Evolution of Property Rights: A Study of the American West." *Journal of Law and Economics* 18, no. 1: 163–79.

Arrow, Kenneth J., and Gerard Debreu. 1954. "Existence of an Equilibrium for a Competitive Economy." *Econometrica: Journal of the Econometric Society* 22, no. 3: 265–90.

Barro, Robert J., and Xavier Sala-i-Martin. 1992. "Convergence." *Journal of Political Economy* 100, no. 2: 223–51.

Barzel, Yoram, and Douglas W. Allen. 2023. *Economic Analysis of Property Rights*, 3rd Edition. New York: Cambridge University Press.

Besley, Timothy. 1995. "Property Rights and Investment Incentives: Theory and Evidence from Ghana." *Journal of Political Economy* 103, no. 5: 903–37.

Bowles, Samuel, and Jung K. Choi. 2013. "Coevolution of Farming and Private Property during the Early Holocene." *Proceedings of the National Academy of Sciences* 110, no. 22: 8830–35.

Bowles, Samuel, and Jung K. Choi. 2019. "The Neolithic Agricultural Revolution and the Origins of Private Property." *Journal of Political Economy* 127, no. 5: 2186–228.

Coase, Ronald. 1960. "The Problem of Social Cost." *Journal of Law and Economics* 3 (October): 1–44.

Cox, Gary W. 2012. "Was the Glorious Revolution a Constitutional Watershed?" *Journal of Economic History* 72, no. 3: 567–600.

Dell, Melissa. 2010. "The Persistent Effects of Peru's Mining Mita." *Econometrica* 78, no. 6: 1863–903.

Demsetz, Harold 1967. "Towards a Theory of Property Rights." *American Economic Review* 57, no. 2: 347–59.

Engerman, Stanley L., and Kenneth L. Sokoloff. 2002. "Factor Endowments, Inequality, and Paths of Development among New World Economies." NBER Working Paper Series, Working Paper 9259.

Gorodnichenko, Yuri, and Gerard Roland. 2011. "Individualism, Innovation, and Long-Run Growth." *Proceedings of the National Academy of Sciences* 108 (Supplement 4): 21316–319.

Greif, Avner. 2006. *Institutions and the Path to the Modern Economy: Lessons from Medieval Trade*. Cambridge: Cambridge University Press.

Hardin, Garrett. 1968. "The Tragedy of the Commons: The Population Problem Has No Technical Solution; It Requires a Fundamental Extension in Morality." *Science* 162, no. 3859: 1243–48.

Henrich, Joseph. 2020. *The WEIRDest People in the World: How the West Became Psychologically Peculiar and Particularly Prosperous*. New York: Farrar, Straus and Giroux.

Higgs, Robert 1996. "Legally Induced Technological Regress in the Washington Salmon Fishery." In *Empirical Studies in Institutional Change*, ed. Lee J. Alston, Thrainn Eggertsson, and Douglass North, 247–51. New York: Cambridge University Press.

Hodgson, Geoffrey M. 2017. "1688 and All That: Property Rights, the Glorious Revolution and the Rise of British Capitalism." *Journal of Institutional Economics* 13, no. 1: 79–107.

La Croix, Sumner J. 2019. *Hawai'i: Eight Hundred Years of Political and Economic Change*. Chicago: University of Chicago Press.

La Croix, Sumner J., and J. Roumasset. 1990. "The Evolution of Private Property in Nineteenth-Century Hawaii." *Journal of Economic History* 50, no. 4: 829–52.

Libecap, Gary D. 1978. "Economic Variables and the Development of the Law: The Case of Western Mineral Rights." *Journal of Economic History* 38, no. 2: 338–62.

Libecap, Gary D. 1993. *Contracting for Property Rights*. New York: Cambridge University Press.

Lipset, Seymour Martin. 1959. "Some Social Requisites of Democracy: Economic Development and Political Legitimacy." *American Political Science Review* 53 (March): 69–105.

Lueck, Dean. 1995. "The Rule of First Possession and the Design of the Law." *Journal of Law and Economics* 38: 393–436.

McCloskey, Diedre N. 2010. *Bourgeois Dignity: Why Economics Can't Explain the Modern World*. University of Chicago Press.

McGinnis, Michael, and Elinor Ostrom. 1996. "Design Principles for Local and Global Commons." In *The International Political Economy and International Institutions, Volume 2*, ed. O. R. Young, 465–93. Brookfield, VT: Edward Elgar.

Merrill, Thomas W. 2002. "Introduction: The Demsetz Thesis and the Evolution of Property Rights." *Journal of Legal Studies* 31(S2): S331–S338.

Mokyr, Joel. 2016. *A Culture of Growth: The Origins of the Modern Economy.* Princeton, NJ: Princeton University Press.

Mueller, Bernardo. 2021. "How Culture Evolves: Measuring Cultural Distance and Variation." Available at SSRN 3819833. https://papers.ssrn.com/sol3/papers.cfm?abstract_id=3819833.

Mueller, Bernardo, and João G. Leite. 2020. "How the East was Lost: Coevolution of Institutions and Culture in the 16th-Century Portuguese Empire." Available at SSRN: https://ssrn.com/abstract=3548654.

Muthukrishna, Michael, Adrian V. Bell, Joseph Henrich, Cameron M. Curtin, Alexander Gedranovich, Jason McInerney, and Branden Thue. 2020. "Beyond Western, Educated, Industrial, Rich, and Democratic (WEIRD) Psychology: Measuring and Mapping Scales of Cultural and Psychological Distance." *Psychological Science* 31, no. 6: 678–701.

North, Douglass C. 1990. *Institutions, Institutional Change, and Economic Performance.* New York: Cambridge University Press.

North, Douglass C. 2005. *Understanding the Process of Economic Change.* Princeton, NJ: Princeton University Press.

North, Douglass C., and Barry R. Weingast. 1989. "Constitutions and Commitment: The Evolution of Institutions Governing Public Choice in Seventeenth-Century England." *The Journal of Economic History* 49, no. 4: 803–32.

North, Douglass C, John J. Wallis, and Barry R. Weingast. 2009. *Violence and Social Orders: A Conceptual Framework for Interpreting Recorded Human History.* Cambridge: Cambridge University Press.

Nunn, Nathan, and Wantchekon, Leonard. 2011. "The Slave Trade and the Origins of Mistrust in Africa." *American Economic Review* 101, no. 7: 3221–52.

Ostrom, Elinor 1990. *Governing the Commons: The Evolution of Institutions for Collective Action.* Cambridge: Cambridge University Press.

Pincus, Steven C., and James A. Robinson. 2011. "What Really Happened during the Glorious Revolution?" National Bureau of Economic Research, NBER Working Paper Series No. w17206.

Rostow, Walt W. 1960. "The Five Stages of Growth—A Summary." In *The Stages of Economic Growth: A Non-Communist Manifesto*, 4–16. Cambridge: Cambridge University Press.

Rubin, Jared. 2017. *Rulers, Religion, and Riches: Why the West got Rich and the Middle East Did Not.* New York: Cambridge University Press.

Schulz, Jonathan F., Duman Bahrami-Rad, Jonathan P. Beauchamp, and Joseph Henrich. 2019. "The Church, Intensive Kinship, and Global Psychological Variation." *Science* 366, no. 6466: eaau5141.

Scott, Anthony. 1955. "The Fishery: The Objectives of Sole Ownership." *Journal of Political Economy* 63, no. 2: 116–24.

Sokoloff, Kenneth L., and Stanley L. Engerman. 2000. "Institutions, Factor Endowments, and Paths of Development in the New World." *Journal of Economic Perspectives* 14, no. 3: 217–32.

Stasavage, David. 2002. "Credible Commitment in Early Modern Europe: North and Weingast Revisited." *Journal of Law, Economics, and Organization* 18, no. 1: 155–86.

Sussman, Nathan, and Yishay Yafeh. 2004. "Constitutions and Commitment: Evidence on the Relation between Institutions and the Cost of Capital." Available at SSRN 558641.

Wiggins, Steven N., and Gary D. Libecap. 1985. "Oil Field Unitization: Contractual Failure in the Presence of Imperfect Information." *American Economic Review* 75, no. 3: 368–85.

CHAPTER 23

SUFFRAGE IN HISTORICAL POLITICAL ECONOMY

W. WALKER HANLON

WHY have enfranchised groups within partially democratic systems chosen voluntarily to expand suffrage to include previously excluded groups? This is a seminal question for understanding of how political systems operate, one that has drawn the attention of some of the very best political scientists, economists, historians, and others, and one that remains as hotly debated today as at any point in history. When approaching this question, whether from a theoretical or empirical perspective, most researchers have turned to history as a source of motivation or a setting for examination. In fact, this topic can almost be said to be dominated by studies focused on or motivated by historical experiences.

This chapter aims to provide a guide to, and evaluation of, the extensive literature on suffrage reforms. Before setting out, it is useful to lay out the parameters of the discussion. My focus in this essay is on the extension or retraction of voting rights to previously disenfranchised groups within systems in which at least some political power is exercised through voting. Of course, there are many interesting and closely related topics that, for space reasons, I cannot examine in detail. Examples include rules governing who can stand for office, regulations such as the secret ballot, and so on. I also abstract from other paths toward democratization, such as suffrage obtained by the gaining of nationhood or suffrage imposed by foreign powers. It is also necessary to place strict limits on the set of literature considered. I focus specifically on studies where the primary aim is understanding suffrage, and particularly in developing or testing general theories of suffrage. Beyond these, a much larger set of work focuses on other related issues, where suffrage reforms may play an important role but are not the main focus; I do not have the space to discuss these in detail.

My discussion proceeds in three steps. First I discuss the various types of suffrage extensions and their characteristics. Keeping these various types in mind is important when I move to reviewing the leading theories of the causes of suffrage reforms, as well as empirical studies that can be used to evaluate these theories. The next section of the chapter examines the largely empirical literature on the consequences of suffrage reforms, ranging from economic consequences, such as taxes and redistribution, to political consequences, such as changes in the form of party competition or the background of representatives. Some brief concluding thoughts finish my discussion.

A Taxonomy

It is useful to begin by offering a rough taxonomy of the primary types of suffrage extensions that we observe. This is useful partly because different types of suffrage extensions are likely to be amenable to different causal explanations and effects. The typology here focuses on the margins between enfranchised and disenfranchised groups, rather than the specific mechanisms used to limit the franchise. Keep in mind that many of the tools used to limit the franchise in the past, such as poll taxes or literacy tests, operated across more than one of these margins.

Historically, one of the most important criteria along which suffrage was extended or denied is income levels within a group. For example, in Britain, a central feature of the nineteenth-century reform acts was to extend franchise rights to lower-income groups within the set of adult males. A key feature of this "income-based suffrage extension" is that political power is highly correlated with economic power, as political power is extended downward to groups with limited economic power.

A second type of suffrage reform involves extending the vote across gender lines. "Gender-based suffrage reforms" differ from income-based reforms in several important dimensions. First, if we consider socioeconomic background or household wealth, then women are distributed similarly to, though not the same as, men across these dimensions. Thus, when suffrage is extended across gender boundaries, the expansion of political power may be largely orthogonal to the distribution of (household-level) economic resources. Second, extending the franchise across gender boundaries interacts in potentially important ways with intrahousehold bargaining and societal and cultural gender norms. Thus, while extending the suffrage to women may not dramatically change the income or wealth distribution of voters, it may have a substantial impact on the types of cultural or societal barriers faced by the voting population. Finally, reforms that extend suffrage to women are also, in some cases, dependent on marital status. These differences raise potentially important issues that should be considered when seeking to explain the causes or consequences of enfranchising women.

A third group of reforms involves extending franchise rights across other group boundaries. Prominent examples of this variety include extending suffrage across racial or religious boundaries, but suffrage reforms may also operate across other groupings, such as decisions about whether to disenfranchise convicted felons who have completed their sentence. A prominent example of this type of "group-based suffrage reform" is the extension of voting rights to African Americans in the United States as a result of the civil rights movement. In that case, the group that gained political power was also economically disadvantaged. However, that is not always the case. In some settings, group-based suffrage reforms have extended political power to economically successful minority groups. The progressive expansion of Jewish political rights in Europe from the eighteenth to the twentieth centuries provides one such example.

A fourth type of suffrage reform involves extending voting rights to voters of different ages. Many of the reforms of the mid- to late twentieth century fall into this "age-based suffrage reform" category. In India, for example, the world's most populous democracy, the voting age was reduced from twenty-one to eighteen in 1988. Similar reforms appear in a number of other countries. This type of reform differs from other types in that younger cohorts clearly have different concerns and incentives than older groups. Also, young cohorts, while they may have low income themselves, are also drawn from a broad cross-section of socioeconomic groups, so age-based suffrage reforms may have only a weak effect on the correlation between economic and political power.

A final major dimension along which franchise extensions can occur is geography. "Geography-based suffrage reforms" are typically associated with the elevation of a territory or protectorate within a country, with limited or no voting rights in national elections, to a status that allows full voting rights. The extension of statehood to new regions within the United States provides one example. Another comes from French colonies, which sent deputies to the French Parliament for various periods before independence. While geography-based reforms often come together with a basket of other rights and responsibilities, the fact that voting rights are being extended to new groups of people, with new concerns, and in some cases different cultures or languages, should not be overlooked. In fact, it seems probable that some of the most contentious debates over franchise reform in the near future—over extending statehood to Washington, DC, or Puerto Rico, for example—or over expanding the voting rights of residents of the Palestinian Territories, may occur along the geographic dimension.

Beyond these five main typologies of suffrage extensions, others are less prominent. Still, this list provides a useful grouping of the most important.

Explaining Suffrage Reforms: Theory and Evidence

This section reviews theoretical work from across economics and political science that seeks to explain suffrage reforms and empirical work relevant for evaluating these theories. An early attempt to explain democratization in general, and suffrage reforms in particular, is the "modernization hypothesis" that emerged in the middle of the twentieth century. While the particular ideas that fall under this broad umbrella are up for debate, important contributions were made by authors including Lipset (1960) and Almond and Coleman (1960), who emphasized the correspondence between economic development and democratization. Purely deterministic modernization theories have proven difficult to reconcile with the complex patterns of democratization and suffrage reforms observed in the real world (Moore 1966; Przeworski and Limongi 1997), but there has been a wealth of interesting work that has parsed how particular development paths may or may not have led to broad democratic systems. Moore (1966), for example, emphasized the "bourgeois revolution" path taken in England, France, and the United States. For Rueschemeyer, Stephens, and Stephens (1992), the core argument is that capitalist development led to democratization because it strengthened the urban/industrial working class, the group most supportive of democracy, while weakening aristocratic landowners, the staunchest opponents.[1]

In more recent work, a number of competing explanations for suffrage reforms have emerged. One prominent strand emphasizes the role that the threat of violence can play in convincing an enfranchised elite to extend voting rights. Put simply, this theory posits that a currently enfranchised elite may choose to share political power as an optimal strategy aimed at avoiding violence or revolution, while an initially disenfranchised "proletariat" will choose to forgo a damaging revolution if they are compensated through the sharing of political power and commensurate economic redistribution.

Acemoglu and Robinson (2000) provided a seminal exposition of this idea in a paper that draws motivation from Britain's nineteenth-century franchise reforms.[2] Their model is focused primarily on explaining the extension of the franchise downward from the elite to lower socioeconomic groups, though the mechanisms may also apply to other types of suffrage reforms. Within this context, they highlight a key question: why does the elite need to extend the franchise in order to avoid a revolution, instead of simply compensating the disenfranchised group through economic redistribution? Their answer is related to their theoretical assumption that opportunities for revolution are rare. Because of this, when revolution is possible, the disenfranchised majority wants to ensure that promises of economic redistribution are durable and credible. The point made by Acemoglu and Robinson (2000) is that extending the franchise allows the elite to make a credible commitment to future redistribution.

Aidt and Franck (2015) provide a test of the relationship between the threat of violence and suffrage reform in one setting, the British election of 1831 that set the stage for the First Reform Act. They find that voters more exposed to the "Swing riots" were more likely to support the Whigs, the party of reform. This provides evidence in favor of the idea that the threat of violence may play an important role in inducing elites to extend suffrage, which has also found support in some papers examining more recent settings.[3] However, the specifics of the empirical setting examined by Aidt and Franck are more complicated than that reflected in Acemoglu and Robinson's simple model. In particular, the population enfranchised as part of the First Reform Act was middle class, very different from the groups that participated in the Swing riots. Thus, while violence does appear to have played a role, it likely did so through a more complicated model of coalition formation in the face of the threat of revolution. Cox, Fresh, and Saiegh (2020) make this point in a recent paper that argues that the First Reform Act suffrage extension was part of a package of reforms aimed at co-opting the middle class in order to strengthen government and its ability to deal with internal and external threats. This strengthening involved, among other things, large expansions in expenditure on policing in order to repress lower-class unrest. Thus, while the threat of violence plays a role, the mechanisms emphasized by Cox, Fresh, and Saiegh (2020) are substantially different than those envisioned by Acemoglu and Robinson (2000).

Carles Boix (2003) takes an alternative approach that emphasizes factors that lead the elite to resist reform. Specifically, Boix argues that the level of inequality in a society and the extent to which productive assets are immobile determine the resistance of the elite to democratic reforms. In societies that are more equal, elites stand to lose less from the redistributive effects of granting suffrage to the lower classes. The same is true when assets are more mobile and therefore more difficult to redistribute. Interestingly, Boix's theory makes exactly the opposite prediction about the relationship between inequality and democratic reforms as Acemoglu and Robinson (2000).

Using a combination of historical and more recent cross-country data, Boix (2003) provides evidence that inequality was negatively related to the probability of a democratic transition. He also draws on case study evidence. In Switzerland, for example, Boix describes how alpine cantons, where most residents were farmers and equality was high, adopted a more democratic approach to government than those cantons dominated by cities, but city cantons where many of the assets were mobile (e.g., wealth in business rather than land) were more democratic than those dominated by land-based wealth.

There are striking parallels between Boix's discussion of variation in the level of democracy across Swiss cantons and recent work by Puga and Trefler (2014) on the expansion, and then contraction, of the franchise in medieval Venice. In particular, Puga and Trefler describe how the expansion of long-distance trade after 800 CE led to the emergence of a wealthy merchant class. This expanded bourgeoisie was incorporated into the political system through the end of the hereditary Doge (1032) and the establishment of a parliament (1172), a pattern that seems consistent with Boix's argument that an enfranchised elite will be less resistant to extending political power to the middle class when the two groups are more equal in terms of their economic resources and when assets are more mobile. However, after 1297, this process reversed, as a small group of wealthy Venetian merchant families consolidated their hold on political and economic power.

One feature that Acemoglu and Robinson (2000) and Boix (2003) have in common is that they both focus on franchise extensions along income lines. However, as discussed earlier, this is only one of the dimensions along which suffrage reforms have operated, albeit an important one. For other types of suffrage reforms, alternative explanations may be more compelling. One of these alternatives is political expediency—the idea that conflict between enfranchised (often elite) groups prompts a subset of the enfranchised group to adopt suffrage reforms in order to gain political advantage. This idea appears in a number of different guises.

Llavador and Oxoby (2005) provide a theoretical exposition of this view, motivated by the first wave of franchise reforms in nineteenth-century Europe. The authors set out to explain what may initially appear to be somewhat surprising patterns in this first wave, such as the early adoption of universal manhood suffrage within the otherwise conservative German political system. At the heart of Llavador and Oxoby's argument is that elite groups favor extending the franchise when they believe that doing so will benefit them in their conflict with other elite groups over economic policy choices. So, conservatives might have supported extending the franchise to rural peasants when they thought they were likely to side politically with agrarian landowners, while liberals might enfranchise urban workers if they believed that they would side with them on issues such as tariff reform. As Bismarck explained, referring to the adoption of universal manhood suffrage in Germany, a system that he largely designed,[4]

> *At the moment of decision the masses will stand on the side of kingship regardless of whether the latter happens to follow a liberal or a conservative tendency. . . . General suffrage, by eliminating the influences of the liberal bourgeois classes, will also lead to monarchical elections.*

Gertrude Himmelfarb (1966) makes essentially the same point with respect to the far-reaching Second Reform Act in Britain, passed by the Conservatives in 1867, writing that, "the Tories were democratic, one might say, because they assumed that the demos was Tory."

This argument also emerges in a recent examination of women's suffrage by Dawn Langan Teele (Teele 2018a). Teele contends that "winning the vote depends on the alignment of interests between elected politicians and suffragists" (6). As a result, she argues, the impression that suffragists gave politicians about the likely voting preferences of women played an important role in determining when suffrage reform occurred. In France, for example, she describes how women's suffrage was defeated in 1919 because of a perception that women were more likely to oppose the governing Radical Party. A contrasting view is offered by McConnaughy (2013), who argues that the suffragists' ability to convince existing voting blocs to support suffrage, rather than the prospects of future electoral support, was key to the success of women's suffrage in the United States.

The idea that the timing of franchise extensions is likely to depend on how the newly enfranchised groups will affect the political balance offers a potential rationalization for the rich variation in historical patterns that we observe. Moreover, this explanation appears to be particularly helpful when considering expansions of the franchise beyond the extension of rights downward from an economically and politically powerful elite to middle-class or working-class groups. However, while explanations of this type have the potential to explain a wide variety of franchise reforms, improved models providing sharper predictions that can be tested quantitatively are needed if we want to move beyond the existing case-study approach.

Another theory emphasizes the potential economic efficiency gains of extending the franchise. A leading example is Lizzeri and Persico (2004). Their model "is inspired by the observation that [in England] since the eighteenth century, the contemporaries felt a growing need to address the failure of political institutions. . . . Politicians viewed reform as essential to reduce the pervasiveness of patronage and to coax the machinery of government to serve the public purpose" (p. 709). In their model, expanding the franchise can help improve efficiency because it forces politicians to move away from patronage politics and toward providing benefits to a broader constituency through the provision of public goods. In support of their theory, Lizzeri and Persico argue that their explanation is more consistent with the patterns of taxation and redistribution observed in nineteenth-century Britain (a topic discussed in more detail in the next section).

Perhaps surprisingly, few empirical studies have sought to evaluate simultaneously the relative explanatory power of multiple theories of suffrage reform. One that does is Aidt and Franck (2019), which focuses on voting patterns for the Great Reform Act of 1832 in the British Parliament. In this context, they are able to construct rough measures of exposure to the threat of violence (riots), peaceful mass mobilization (public meetings), lobbying (petitions for reform), as well as the direct impact of reforms on the political situation of individual MPs as a result of seat reallocation and other changes in election rules. While they find that all of these factors mattered, peaceful agitation appears to have been the most important factor in passing the reform bill.[5] Przeworski (2009) takes an alternative approach, using cross-country data on different varieties of suffrage extensions and comparing them to variables meant to reflect different motivations for extending the franchise. While the available explanatory variables are far from perfect, Przeworski finds suggestive evidence that the threat of violence is a promising explanation for extensions of the franchise to lower income classes, but that different dynamics are at work for female suffrage.

One area where research has been quite active in recent years, though much remains to be done, is understanding the causes of woman's suffrage. Bertocchi (2011), for example, builds and tests a political economy model that explicitly recognizes the interaction between woman's suffrage, intrahousehold bargaining, and variation in policy preferences across genders. The key theoretical result is that a reduction in gender wage inequality will lead to woman's suffrage in order to avoid an (unspecified) societal cost of excluding women from the vote. She finds that this prediction is consistent with patterns observed in data for twenty-two countries covering the 1870–1930 period. By grappling with the specifics of woman's suffrage, Bertocchi's model represents an important advance over previous work in this area.

Other studies provide empirical examinations of factors that influence the acceptance of woman's suffrage. Braun and Kvasnicka (2013), for example, offer evidence that a scarcity of women in western US states was associated with earlier female suffrage. This pattern, which is also consistent with the early adoption of woman's suffrage in places like New Zealand and Australia, can be rationalized in a number of ways. For example, fewer women may reduce the political shifts generated by expanding suffrage, or suffrage extensions may act as a means for attracting more women to an area. Teele (2018b), however, argues that it was the fluid and competitive political environment that caused political parties in western states, in search of political advantage, to embrace female suffrage.[6] Moehling and Thomasson (2020) provide a valuable review of the US case and an evaluation of available theories.

While recent empirical work has focused on testing models of income-based suffrage extensions, or improving our understanding of woman's suffrage, other aspects of suffrage have remained relatively unexplored. This includes the extension of suffrage across group boundaries (religious, racial), age groups, or geographies. While a small number of studies have looked at the causes and consequences of these types of franchise extensions (see, for example, Koukal, Schafer, and Eichenberger [2020] and Koukal and Portmann [2020] on the causes and consequences of enfranchising migrants in Switzerland, or Eubank and Fresh [2022] on the consequences of enfranchising African Americans in the United States). this area still remains largely unexplored, theoretically and empirically.

Another area where empirical evidence is currently thin is the influence on suffrage of public opinion, cultural factors, or changing social norms. While theories of suffrage reform reliant on these factors have not been as widely examined as the alternative explanations already described, casual observation suggests that in some examples of suffrage extension, such factors were likely important. Among these are the reduction in the voting age from twenty-one to eighteen in the United States in the wake of the Vietnam War, as well as the extension of suffrage to all men over age twenty-one in the United Kingdom at the end of World War I (1918). The scarcity of studies in this area is surprising, given the growing recognition of the influence of culture and norms on economic and political outcomes. However, one recent exception is Koukal (2020), which shows the impact of the Second Vatican Council (1962–1965) on acceptance of female enfranchisement in Switzerland. As interest in the influence of culture on other economic and political outcomes expands, empirical work on the impact of cultural change on suffrage reform seems primed to be a growth area.

While the vast majority of work on suffrage focuses on the extension of rights, voting rights may also be removed. In Europe, Ziblatt (2006, p. 313) notes, "Democratization . . . often entailed and—perhaps required—combining democratic reforms with microlevel formal and informal *undemocratic* elite safeguards, including undemocratic upper chambers, gerrymandered electoral districts, clientelism, and corrupt voting rules." At the extreme, some previously enfranchised voting groups may be completely disenfranchised. The most prominent example of this is the suppression of African American voting rights in the period between Reconstruction and the civil rights movement. This setting is the focus of two important books as well as a number of other studies. Valelly (2004) focuses on the United States only and analyzes two separate waves of African American enfranchisement, during Reconstruction and through the civil rights movement of the 1960s. Bateman (2018) broadens the focus to consider, in addition to the US case, episodes of disenfranchisement in the United Kingdom and France. Studying disenfranchisement offers a different and valuable perspective from which to analyze suffrage reforms.

The Policy Consequences of Suffrage Extension

The most active area for empirical work related to suffrage reforms focuses on the consequences of the reforms. Motivated by the theories of franchise extensions discussed earlier, much of the work in this area looks at the impact of suffrage extensions on redistribution. Other work is interested in the political effects of suffrage extensions, such as whether the types of candidates elected or their behavior changed. This section reviews the largely empirical literature examining the effects of suffrage extensions.

Historical studies offer some distinct advantages in examining the relationship between franchise reforms and public goods expenditures, relative to more modern settings. In particular, modern studies looking at the relationship between democratization and public goods provision often focus on developing countries, in places like Africa (Stasavage 2005; Harding and Stasavage 2014) or Latin America (Brown and Hunter 2004). In these settings, a potential concern is that international pressure—from organizations such as the World Bank or the United Nations, or operating through bilateral foreign aid relationships—may interact with democratization and simultaneously affect levels of public good provision. These sorts of concerns are absent in most historical settings, which is a potentially important and underappreciated advantage of historical work in this area.

A number of the theories of suffrage reform predict that suffrage expansions will lead to increased redistribution toward poorer and previously disenfranchised voters. This feature, which builds on earlier theoretical work by Meltzer and Richard (1981), has led to a great deal of interest in establishing empirically the relationship between franchise extensions and redistribution. However, several factors present difficulties for straightforward tests of this relationship. Most importantly, redistribution can come in a variety of forms. While direct fiscal transfers to poorer citizens, such as through welfare support, are the most obvious example of redistributive policies, other policies may be even more important. In nineteenth-century Britain, for example, much of the debate over redistributive policies was focused on regulation, such as the Ten Hours Bill, rather than fiscal expenditure. Unfortunately, the complexity and variety of regulation makes systematically identifying those acts with a particularly redistributive nature, beyond a few prominent examples, extremely difficult. As a result, most attention has instead focused on other outcomes. However, because different avenues for redistribution may be substitutes, it is difficult to clearly establish whether franchise extensions led to increased redistribution by examining only one redistributive mechanism. This remains a key challenge for empirical work in this area.

A second challenge is due to the fact that the provision of public goods, ranging from public parks and schools to clean air and water, may be an important means for redistribution. While it is often easier to establish what group ended up paying for public goods, for some public goods it may be very difficult to reasonably identify the primary beneficiaries. Nevertheless, a reasonable assumption is that public goods funded largely by taxes on wealthier groups, and open to all residents, are likely to be redistributive in nature. Given this, a number of recent studies look at how the level of public goods provision changes when suffrage is expanded beyond the wealthy elite.

One prominent study in this vein, Aidt, Daunton, and Dutta (2010), proposes and tests what they label the retrenchment hypothesis: that the relationship between spending on local public goods and the share of the adult population with the vote is

U-shaped. This hypothesis emerges from a model in which the urban upper and lower classes prefer higher levels of public goods spending than the middle class. As a result, extensions of the franchise into the middle class lowers public goods spending and taxes, while further extensions raise public goods spending. They provide evidence in support of this hypothesis using panel data from English and Welsh boroughs.

Chapman (2018) examines the same issue but pushes identification further. In particular, he grapples with the possibility that franchise restrictions may be endogenously related to other factors that influence public goods expenditures. To obtain plausibly exogenous variation in franchise restrictions, he takes advantage of a national reform that eliminated existing variation in franchise rules across town councils in 1894. He finds that expanding the franchise led to lower government expenditure. In follow-up work using a similar approach, Chapman (2020) finds evidence of an *inverted* U-shaped relationship between the enfranchised share of the (male) population and local government expenditures. This suggests that extending the vote to the middle class appears to have increased local expenditures, while there is evidence that poorer citizens resisted expenditure increases.

Alternative methods have also been tried. Aidt and Jensen (2013) use cross-country data from Europe for the 1820–1913 period. Consistent with their previous work, they find a U-shaped relationship between franchise extensions and revenue per capita, and a positive association with expenditures per capita. Also using cross-country evidence, Aidt and Jensen (2009) document a non-monotonic relationship between franchise extensions and the imposition of the income tax. While more generalizable than within-country studies, these cross-country analyses are typically not as well identified.

Looking over the existing evidence on the relationship between extensions of the franchise to lower-income groups and either redistribution, overall government expenditures, or public goods prediction, the only conclusion to emerge is that results are mixed. No simple and clear relationship, of the type that leading theories would lead us to expect, appears to emerge. Instead, we observe complex, often non-monotonic relationships that tend to depend on context. Interestingly, as I discuss next, this variation contrasts with the much more consistent results that emerge in studies looking at other types of suffrage reforms.

A distinct set of work examines the impact of woman's suffrage on government activities such as public goods. As discussed earlier, woman's suffrage differs from other types of suffrage reforms in fundamental ways. Miller (2008), for example, cites a number of studies, many from modern developing countries, showing that women's choices with respect to child welfare and public goods spending differ systematically from men's. Motivated by these findings, Miller documents a systematic relationship between female suffrage in the United States and local public health expenditures, leading to substantial declines in child mortality. A number of other papers looking at the impact of women's suffrage provide evidence that this was associated with increases in welfare spending.[7] Examples include Abrams and Settle (1999), which studied Switzerland; Lott and Kenny (1999), using data for US states from 1870 to 1940; and Aidt and Dallal (2008), which use data for six Western European countries from 1869 to 1960. All of these find that expanding woman's voting rights led to increases in government expenditures and public goods provision. The consistent positive effect documented across this wide range of different settings is striking, particularly when compared to papers examining the impact of expanding voting rights to poorer males in the absence of female suffrage, described earlier. That these two types of suffrage appear to have systematically different impacts on levels of government expenditure and public goods provision suggest that not only do we need to be careful about conflating these different types of empirical findings, but also that we are likely to need different theoretical tools to analyze these different types of suffrage reform.

A third strand of work focuses on franchise reforms that primarily affected minority groups. A seminal paper in this literature is Husted and Kenny (1997), which examines data on government expenditures from US states covering the 1950–1988 period. To obtain variation in the franchise, they focus on the effects of the US Voting Rights Acts in the 1960s, which eliminated poll taxes and literacy tests that limited voting access for poorer, and particularly minority, voters in some (mainly southern) states. For example, the reform increased the share of voting-age Blacks registered to vote in the South from 24.9 percent to 62 percent from 1956 to 1968. This group was substantially poorer than the average pre-reform voter, so this franchise expansion represents an extension of voting rights down the income ladder. However, it also simultaneously expanded voting rights across group boundaries, since it brought many Black voters into the system. The primary finding of the paper is that the reform led to meaningful increases in welfare spending, but not other types of spending, in states where the relative income level of voters dropped more as a result of the reform. A more recent study focusing on the same set of events, Cascio and Washington (2014), finds a similar pattern: locations where the 1965 Voting Rights Act led to a greater increase in voter turnout also saw a relative increase in state transfers.

When interpreting their results, Husted and Kenny argue, "We ... provide direct evidence on the effects on spending caused by changes in the income of a state's voters relative to that of its population" (1997, p. 57). While this statement is technically correct, the fact that the poor who gained access to the vote were disproportionately from a minority group means that we should be careful in interpreting the results purely through the lens of models written with income-based suffrage reforms in mind. In particular, if African Americans had a different demand for government services than Whites, perhaps due to a history of discrimination, then these results may be due to expanding the franchise across group boundaries rather than down the income ladder.

In assessing the relationship between suffrage reforms and redistribution, care is needed to avoid the trap of interpreting historical patterns through a modern lens. The case of education provides a clear example of this risk. While today we may think of public education as a public good that particularly benefits poorer segments of the population, mass primary education was historically often used by elites as a tool for exerting control over the lower classes. An example from the introduction of mass public education in Britain through the 1870 Education Act illustrates this point. The 1870 act closely followed the Second Reform Act (1867), which expanded the franchise to urban workers. For the Members of Parliament who pushed for educational reform in 1870, a strong motivation was the perceived need to civilize groups of voters who had gained voting power. As Robert Lowe argued in Parliament, "The moment that you intrust the masses with absolute power their education becomes an absolute necessity." This point is made more broadly in a recent paper by Agustina Paglayan (2022), which highlights the historical role of education as a state-building tool used by elites to reduce violent unrest.[8]

Beyond the policy consequences of suffrage reforms, it is also natural to expect that they affect the identity and behavior of political representatives. In recent years, this topic has been the focus of a lively empirical literature. These studies have examined topics including the impact of suffrage on turnout and voting patterns, electoral competition, candidate selection, party development, Parliamentary rhetoric, and the topics that occupied the time and attention of government. This area has been dominated by studies focusing on nineteenth-century Britain and the twentieth-century United States, leaving ample room for additional work looking at other settings.

Naturally, one would expect newly enfranchised voters to vote: but how often, and for whom? An active line of research now aims to answer these sorts of questions, with women's suffrage as a primary focus. Corder and Wolbrecht (2016) provide a key contribution; focusing on the US case, they present new data that shed light on the experience of newly enfranchised women voters. Their work has been followed by several others. Morgan-Collins (2021), for example, examines how the strength of the social movement leading to suffrage affects the mobilization of newly enfranchised voters. Kim (2019) and Teele (2021a) both examine how the structure of elections influences the participation of newly enfranchised groups. Teele (2021b) examines the heterogeneity of women's response to enfranchisement in Sweden.

Studies of the impact of franchise reforms on political parties and representatives include Stephens and Brady (1976) on the electoral reforms of 1884–1885 in Britain, Berlinski and Dewan (2011) on the Second Reform Act, and De Bromhead, Fernihough, and Hargaden (2020) on the election following the Fourth Reform Act. Berlinski, Dewan, and Van Coppenolle (2014) focus specifically on the impact of suffrage extensions on the presence of the British aristocracy in Parliament and government. Perhaps surprisingly, though in line with earlier work by Laski (1928), Berlinski, Dewan, and Van Coppenolle (2014) find no evidence that expanding the franchise to the working class led to reductions in the share of aristocrats in Parliament, at least in the near term.

In a particularly creative study, Spirling (2016) uses data from British parliamentary speeches to examine how the linguistic complexity of MPs evolved as suffrage expanded across the nineteenth century. He finds a notable reduction in the linguistic complexity of MPs following the Second Reform Act, consistent with MPs trying to appeal to newly enfranchised working-class voters. Hanlon (2022) takes a different approach that focuses on changes in the topics considered by the British Parliament using data covering almost two centuries (1810–2005). Specifically, that study looks at whether substantial changes occurred in the types of issues under consideration in the wake of major suffrage extensions. Of the four major reform acts passed in Britain between 1832 and 1918, only the First Reform Act (1832) and possibly the Fourth Reform Act (1918) were associated with substantial changes in the agenda of Parliament. Surprisingly, while the Second and Third Reform Acts extended voting rights to the working class, they seem to have had little impact on the parliamentary agenda.

Finally, a small set of studies has compared the passage of suffrage reforms to financial variables, in order to assess how the market viewed the reforms or how suffrage influenced financial development. Examples include Turner and Zhan (2012), Dasgupta and Ziblatt (2015), and Degryse, Lambert, and Schwienbacher (2018).

Conclusion

The two previous sections reveal a rich literature, theoretical and empirical, examining the causes and consequences of suffrage reforms. Historical experience plays a key role in this work, providing the motivation for theoretical studies and the setting for much of the empirical work.

Yet despite the extensive interest in this topic from economists and political scientists, in some sense it feels as if our understanding of suffrage is only in its infancy. Most of the available work on this topic is (1) aimed primarily at understanding suffrage expansions from high- to low-income groups; (2) motivated and tested mainly in a small set of empirical contexts, principally Europe, particularly Britain, in the nineteenth-century and the United States in the twentieth; and (3) mainly focused on theories emphasizing the threat of violence. This leaves enormous opportunities for expanding our understanding by considering different types of suffrage expansions, doing so in a wider variety of empirical contexts, and examining a wider range of motivations.

Recently, a few scholars have been pushing to broaden examinations of suffrage beyond the traditional focus. Examples include empirical work on enfranchising migrants in Switzerland (Koukal, Schafer, and Eichenberger 2020; Koukal and Portmann 2020) and on African American suffrage in the United States (Eubank and Fresh 2022), as well as theoretical work taking more seriously the specifics of different types of suffrage reforms (e.g., Bertocchi [2011] on woman's suffrage). Others have been pushing to improve identification (Cascio and Washington 2014; Chapman 2018) or offering novel approaches to measurement (Spirling 2016; Hanlon 2022). These are all promising signs for the future of historical work aimed at understanding suffrage reform.

Acknowledgments

I thank Alan de Bromhead, Adriane Fresh, Jeffery A. Jenkins, Jared Rubin, and Dawn Langan Teele for their many helpful comments.

Notes

1. Another example in this vein is Collier (1999).
2. This theory is updated and expanded in Acemoglu and Robinson (2006). Another closely related paper is Conley and Temimi (2001).
3. See Burke and Leigh (2010), Brückner and Ciccone (2011), and Aidt and Leon (2016). Taking a different view, Lacroix (2020) looks at how suffrage affects political violence.
4. From *Die gesammelten Werke* (1st ed., 15 vols. [Berlin, 1924], vv. 429, 457), cited from Craig (1978).
5. A related paper, Dasgupta and Ziblatt (2015), offers a creative approach to measuring political risk, by using data on the UK bond market. They find that bond market yields increased before the passage of the First and Second Reform Acts (1832 and 1867) but not preceding the Third Reform Act (1884), as well as during the failed Chartist agitation for reform in the 1840s. After all of these episodes, bond yields rapidly declined, suggesting that the period of political risk was brief. In a similar vein, Turner and Zhan (2012) look at the response of the stock market to the Second Reform Act. They find that the market reacted negatively to the passage of that act.
6. Another interesting paper on the causes of woman's suffrage is Koukal and Eichenberger (2020), which examines how the presence of direct democracy influences acceptance of woman's suffrage.
7. In addition, De Bromhead (2018) looks at how women's suffrage influenced trade policies.
8. Eubank and Fresh (2022) provides another example of how suffrage extension may lead to corresponding investments in systems of elite control.

References

Abrams, Burton A, and Russell F. Settle. 1999. "Women's Suffrage and the Growth of the Welfare State." *Public Choice* 100, no. 3: 289–300.

Acemoglu, Daron, and James A. Robinson. 2000. "Why Did the West Extend the Franchise? Democracy, Inequality, and Growth in Historical Perspective." *Quarterly Journal of Economics* 115, no. 4: 1167–99.

Acemoglu, Daron, and James A. Robinson. 2006. *The Economic Origins of Dictatorship and Democracy.* Cambridge: Cambridge University Press.

Aidt, Toke S., and Bianca Dallal. 2008. "Female Voting Power: The Contribution of Women's Suffrage to the Growth of Social Spending in Western Europe (1869-1960)." *Public Choice* 134, no. 3: 391–417.

Aidt, Toke S., and Raphaël Franck. 2015. "Democratization under the Threat of Revolution: Evidence from the Great Reform Act of 1832." *Econometrica* 83, no. 2: 505–47.

Aidt, Toke S., and Raphaël Franck. 2019. "What Motivates an Oligarchic Elite to Democratize? Evidence from the Roll Call Vote on the Great Reform Act of 1832." *Journal of Economic History* 79, no. 3: 773–825.

Aidt, Toke S., and Peter S. Jensen. 2009. "The Taxman Tools Up: An Event History Study of the Introduction of the Personal Income Tax." *Journal of Public Economics* 93, no. 1-2: 160–75.

Aidt, Toke S., and Peter S. Jensen. 2013. "Democratization and the Size of Government: Evidence from the Long 19th Century." *Public Choice* 157, no. 3-4: 511–42.

Aidt, Toke S., and Gabriel Leon. 2016. "The Democratic Window of Opportunity: Evidence from Riots in Sub-Saharan Africa." *Journal of Conflict Resolution* 60, no. 4: 694–717.

Aidt, Toke S., Martin Daunton, and Jayasri Dutta. 2010. "The Retrenchment Hypothesis and the Extension of the Franchise in England and Wales." *Economic Journal* 120, no. 547: 990–1020.

Almond, Gabriel, and James S. Coleman. 1960. *The Politics of Developing Areas*. Princeton, NJ: Princeton University Press.

Bateman, David A. 2018. *Disenfranchising Democracy*. Cambridge: Cambridge University Press.

Berlinski, Samuel, and Torun Dewan. 2011. "The Political Consequences of Franchise Extension: Evidence from the Second Reform Act." *Quarterly Journal of Political Science* 6, no. 34: 329–76.

Berlinski, Samuel, Torun Dewan, and Brenda Van Coppenolle. 2014. "Franchise Extension and the British Aristocracy." *Legislative Studies Quarterly* 39, no. 4: 531–58.

Bertocchi, Graziella. 2011. "The Enfranchisement of Women and the Welfare State." *European Economic Review* 55, no. 4: 535–53.

Boix, Carles. 2003. *Democracy and Redistribution*. Cambridge: Cambridge University Press.

Braun, Sebastian, and Michael Kvasnicka. 2013. "Men, Women, and the Ballot: Gender Imbalances and Suffrage Extensions in the United States." *Explorations in Economic History* 50, no. 3: 405–26.

Brown, David S., and Wendy Hunter. 2004. "Democracy and Human Capital Formation: Education Spending in Latin America, 1980 to 1997." *Comparative Political Studies* 37, no. 7: 842–64.

Brückner, Markus, and Antonio Ciccone. 2011. "Rain and the Democratic Window of Opportunity." *Econometrica* 79, no. 3: 923–47.

Burke, Paul J., and Andrew Leigh. 2010. "Do Output Contractions Trigger Democratic Change?" *American Economic Journal: Macroeconomics* 2, no. 4: 124–57.

Cascio, Elizabeth U., and Ebonya Washington. 2014. "Valuing the Vote: The Redistribution of Voting Rights and State Funds Following the Voting Rights Act of 1965." *Quarterly Journal of Economics* 129, no. 1: 379–433.

Chapman, Jonathan. 2018. "Democratic Reform and Opposition to Government Expenditure: Evidence from Nineteenth-Century Britain." *Quarterly Journal of Political Science* 13, no. 4: 363–404.

Chapman, Jonathan. 2020. "The Extent of the Franchise and Government Spending: A Non-Monotonic Relationship in Nineteenth-Century England." September. Working Paper.

Collier, Ruth Berins. 1999. *Paths toward Democracy*. Cambridge: Cambridge University Press.

Conley, John P., and Akram Temimi. 2001. "Endogenous Enfranchisement When Groups Preferences Conflict." *Journal of Political Economy* 109, no. 1: 79–102.

Corder, J. Kevin, and Christina Wolbrecht. 2016. *Counting Women's Votes*. Cambridge: Cambridge University Press.

Cox, Gary, Adriane Fresh, and Sebastian Saiegh. 2020. "Political Economy of Suffrage Reform: The Great Reform Act of 1832." August. Working Paper.

Craig, Gordon A. 1978. *Germany 1866–1945*. Oxford: Oxford University Press.

Dasgupta, Aditya, and Daniel Ziblatt. 2015. "How Did Britain Democratize? Views from the Sovereign Bond Market." *Journal of Economic History* 75, no. 1: 1–29.

De Bromhead, Alan. 2018. "Women Voters and Trade Protectionism in the Interwar Years." *Oxford Economic Papers* 70, no. 1: 22–46.

De Bromhead, Alan, Alan Fernihough, and Enda Hargaden. 2020. "Representation of the People: Franchise Extension and the Sinn Féin Election in Ireland, 1918." *Journal of Economic History* 80, no. 3: 886–925.

Degryse, Hans, Thomas Lambert, and Armin Schwienbacher. 2018. "The Political Economy of Financial Systems: Evidence from Suffrage Reforms in the Last Two Centuries." *Economic Journal* 128, no. 611: 1433–75.

Eubank, Nick, and Adriane Fresh. 2022. "Enfranchisement and Incarceration after the 1965 Voting Rights Act" American Political Science Review, First Look, p. 1–16.

Hanlon, W. Walker. 2022. "Analyzing the Agenda of Parliament over the Long Run." November. National Bureau of Economic Research Working Paper No. 30021.

Harding, Robin, and David Stasavage. 2014. "What Democracy Does (and Doesn't Do) for Basic Services: School Fees, School Inputs, and African Elections." *Journal of Politics* 76, no. 1: 229–45.

Himmelfarb, Gertrude. 1966. "The Politics of Democracy: The English Reform Act of 1867." *Journal of British Studies* 6, no. 1: 97–138.

Husted, Thomas A., and Lawrence W. Kenny. 1997. "The Effect of the Expansion of the Voting Franchise on the Size of Government." *Journal of Political Economy* 105, no. 1: 54–82.

Kim, Jeong Hyun. 2019. "Direct Democracy and Women's Political Engagement." *American Journal of Political Science* 63, no. 3: 594–610.

Koukal, Anna Maria. 2020. "Leader-Induced Cultural Change: How Vatican II Triggered Female Enfranchisement." July. Working Paper.

Koukal, Anna Maria, and Reiner Eichenberger. 2020. "Direct Democracy and Discrimination: Lessons from Swiss Female Enfranchisement." May. Working Paper.

Koukal, Anna Maria, and Marco Portmann. 2020. "Political Integration of Foreigners: How Does Foreigner's Suffrage Impact Native's Attitudes?" April. CREMA Working Paper No. 2020-05.

Koukal, Anna Maria, Patricia Schafer, and Reiner Eichenberger. 2020. "Enfranchising Non-Citizens: What Drives Natives' Willingness to Share Power." May. CREMA Working Paper No. 2019-10.

Lacroix, Jean. 2020. "Ballots Instead of Bullets? The Effect of the Voting Rights Act on Political Violence." Universite Libre de Bruxelles Working Paper CEB 20-007.

Laski, Harold J. 1928. "The Personnel of the English Cabinet, 1801–1924" *American Political Science Review* 22, no. 1: 12–31.

Lipset, S. M. 1960. *Political Man*. Garden City, NY: Doubleday.

Lizzeri, Alessandro, and Nicola Persico. 2004. "Why Did the Elites Extend the Suffrage? Democracy and the Scope of Government, with an Application to Britain's Age of Reform." *Quarterly Journal of Economics* 119, no. 2: 707–65.

Llavador, Humberto, and Robert J. Oxoby. 2005. "Partisan Competition, Growth, and the Franchise." *Quarterly Journal of Economics* 120, no. 3: 1155–89.

Lott, John R. Jr., and Lawrence W. Kenny. 1999. "Did Women's Suffrage Change the Size and Scope of Government?" *Journal of Political Economy* 107, no. 6: 1163–98.

McConnaughy, Corrine M. 2013. *The Woman Suffrage Movement in America*. Cambridge: Cambridge University Press.

Meltzer, Allan H., and Scott F. Richard. 1981. "A Rational Theory of the Size of Government." *Journal of Political Economy* 89, no. 5: 914–27.

Miller, Grant. 2008. "Women's Suffrage, Political Responsiveness, and Child Survival in American History." *Quarterly Journal of Economics* 123, no. 3: 1287–327.

Moehling, Carolyn M., and Melissa A. Thomasson. 2020. "Votes for Women: An Economic Perspective on Women's Enfranchisement." *Journal of Economic Perspectives* 34, no. 2: 3–23.

Moore, Barrington, Jr.. 1966. *Social Origins of Dictatorship and Democracy*. Boston: Beacon.

Morgan-Collins, Mona. 2021. "The Electoral Impact of Newly Enfranchised Groups: The Case of Women's Suffrage in the United States." *Journal of Politics* 83, no. 1: 150–65.

Paglayan, Agustina S. 2022. "Education or Indoctrination: The Voilent Origins of Publis School Systems in an Era of State-Building." *American Political Science Review*, First View, 1–16.

Przeworski, Adam. 2009. "Conquered or Granted? A History of Suffrage Extensions." *British Journal of Political Science* 39, no. 2: 291–321.

Przeworski, Adam, and Fernando Limongi. 1997. "Modernization: Theories and Facts." *World Politics* 49, no. 2: 155–83.

Puga, Diego, and Daniel Trefler. 2014. "International Trade and Institutional Change: Medieval Venice's Response to Globalization." *Quarterly Journal of Economics* 129, no. 2: 753–821.

Rueschemeyer, Dietrich, Evelyne H. Stephens, and John D Stephens. 1992. *Capitalist Development and Democracy*. Chicago: University of Chicago Press.

Spirling, Arthur. 2016. "Democratization and Linguistic Complexity: The Effect of Franchise Extension on Parliamentary Discourse, 1832–1915." *Journal of Politics* 78, no. 1: 120–36.

Stasavage, David. 2005. "Democracy and Education Spending in Africa." *American Journal of Political Science* 49, no. 2: 343–58.

Stephens, Hugh W., and David W. Brady. 1976. "The Parliamentary Parties and the Electoral Reforms of 1884–85 in Britain." *Legislative Studies Quarterly, vol. 1. no. 4*: 491–510.

Teele, Dawn L. 2018a. *Forging the Franchise*. Princeton, NJ: Princeton University Press.

Teele, Dawn Langan. 2018b. "How the West Was Won: Competition, Mobilization, and Women's Enfranchisement in the United States." *Journal of Politics* 80, no. 2: 442–61.

Teele, Dawn Langan. 2021a. "Gender and the Impact of Proportional Representation: A Comment on the Peripheral Voting Thesis." October. Working Paper.

Teele, Dawn Langan. 2021b. "Geography, Gender and Education: Evidence from Post Suffrage Sweden." February. Working Paper.

Turner, John D., and Wenwen Zhan. 2012. "Property Rights and Competing for the Affections of Demos: The Impact of the 1867 Reform Act on Stock Prices." *Public Choice* 150, no. 3-4: 609–31.

Valelly, Richard M. 2004. *The Two Reconstructions*. Chicago: University of Chicago Press.

Ziblatt, Daniel. 2006. "How Did Europe Democratize?" *World Politics* 58, no. 2: 311–38.

CHAPTER 24

TRADE POLICY IN HISTORICAL POLITICAL ECONOMY

DOUGLAS A. IRWIN

Every sovereign state has some decision-making process to determine its policy regarding international trade. This process could range from a popular referendum to legislative voting to a simple executive decision. Regardless of which procedure is used, decisions about trade policy are inherently political. Opposing domestic interest groups—some having an economic stake in the policy outcome, others motivated by an idealistic conception of what they believe policy ought to be—will seek to influence decision-makers and push for a policy outcome that is close to their preferences. In the case of trade, the policy outcome is the degree to which a country is open to foreign commerce. That policy can range from autarky, in which a country is self-sufficient and does not engage in trade at all, to free trade, in which it is completely open to exchange with the rest of the world.

Historical political economy (HPE) studies the interaction between the structure of a country's political system and the conflicting political and economic forces that shape the policy outcome within that system. The academic literature on the HPE of trade policy is large and rich in the timespan covered and the regions of the world considered. However, there has been a tendency to focus on the United States, where HPE is an outgrowth of the field of American political development. As a large, economically diverse, representative democracy, the United States has a multitude of interest groups and other factions that operate more openly than in restrictive political systems (such as autocracies) where ruling groups are closed to public participation and interest group politics is not transparent.

This chapter discusses some of the main themes in the HPE of trade policy. It does not provide a systemic review of the literature in economics and political science, which is simply too enormous to be covered in one short chapter.[1] Regrettably, the focus is largely on the United States, for the reasons just mentioned, but there are many opportunities to apply the logic developed here to other countries and historical time periods.

Conceptual Framework

Economists since Adam Smith have generally emphasized the economic gains to a country from international trade. This is not to say that economists have always endorsed a policy of completely free trade, which has long been a controversial proposition. Rather, it is simply to say that most economists would agree with the proposition that a country will enjoy a higher real national income with trade than without.[2]

If everyone in a country benefited from the higher income that came with trade, there would be no reason for domestic political conflict over trade policy. No one would be economically worse off with trade, shifting the debate to one about relative gains for different groups or about the cultural, political, and national security effects of trade. However, economists have long recognized that not all groups within a country benefit from trade. Specifically, some imports can harm domestic industries (and their workers) that compete directly with the foreign goods—just as exports benefit the producers and workers of the goods that get sold abroad. This insight was formalized as the famous Stolper-Samuelson (1941) theorem that highlighted the distributional consequences of trade: some factors of production (workers, owners of capital, owners of land) will benefit from trade while other factors will be harmed.

The recognition that some groups will be better off and others worse off because of trade is the starting point for work on the political economy of trade policy. Because trade has consequences for the distribution of income, there will be a political fight over what a country's trade policy should be. Put another way, a country's trade policy affects the prices that prevail in its domestic market and therefore the relative rewards to different economic activities. It should come as no surprise that trade policy is politically contentious because dollars and jobs are at stake whenever prices change as a result of trade or changes in trade policy.

Decisions about trade policy are inherently political (conflictual) and have to be mediated by a country's political institutions. The decision will be decided differently depending on how society's underlying economic interests interact with the structure of the political system. Historical political economy examines the determinants of trade policy, mainly by taking a positive political (or rational choice) approach in studying how political actors pursue their interests while being constrained by the formal and informal institutional arrangements of the political system. Of course, different countries have different configurations of interests and different political institutions, giving researchers a wide variety of observed policy outcomes. These outcomes are rarely at the extremes of the policy spectrum—either complete free trade or complete autarky—although those outcomes are sometimes observed. For example, Japan and Korea were closed to trade in the mid-nineteenth century.[3] At the other extreme, Britain pursued a policy of almost complete free trade in the late nineteenth century.[4]

Before considering the HPE of trade policy in the case of the United States, let us set out some general principles that have guided the historical analysis of trade policy.

The Types of Trade Policies: Tariffs and Subsidies

International trade consists of exchanging exports of domestic goods and services for imports of foreign goods and services. Governments can either encourage this trade with subsidies or discourage it with taxes. This gives us four possible trade policies to consider: export taxes, export subsidies, import taxes, and import subsidies.

Import subsidies are almost never seen because governments rarely pay firms to bring foreign-made products into the country. Export subsidies also tend to be limited if only because they are a financial burden on governments. Export taxes are sometimes employed by producers of natural resources. For example, the Organization of Petroleum Exporting Countries (OPEC) restricts oil production, something akin to an export tax, with the goal of raising the world price and redistributing income to itself from the rest of the world. Argentina taxes agricultural exports (soybeans and meat) as a way of raising revenue and redistributing income away from the few (wealthy) landowners to more numerous (and politically influential) urban workers.

The main instrument of trade policy is the import tariff, which is a tax on foreign goods as they enter a country. Such a tax increases the price of foreign goods in the domestic market and reduces the quantity that will be imported. The economic impact of a tariff can be studied in two different ways. The first considers the impact of a tariff on a particular product in one market (partial equilibrium) and its effect on domestic producers, domestic consumers, and the government. Domestic producers of goods that compete with the imports benefit from the higher price and increase their production; domestic consumers lose from the higher prices of these goods and reduce their consumption; the government collects tax revenue on the smaller volume of imports entering the country. The second considers a tariff from an economy-wide view (general equilibrium). In this perspective, a tariff shifts resources away from export producers in the economy and toward import-competing producers, generating income gains and losses for different factors of production associated with those sectors. This approach also reveals that import tariffs implicitly act as an export tax as well. In other words, if a country systematically reduces the value of foreign goods that it purchases from other countries, the value of domestic goods that it sells to other countries will also fall.

A major theme in research on the historical political economy of trade policy is explaining how tariff rates get set and who benefits and loses from those tariffs.

The Goals of Trade Policy: Revenue, Restriction, and Reciprocity

What objectives are political authorities trying to achieve in levying taxes on imports? Three stand out: to raise revenue for the government, to restrict imports and protect domestic producers from foreign competition, and to achieve reciprocity through agreements that reduce trade barriers. These have been called the "three R's" of trade policy: revenue, restriction, and reciprocity (Irwin 2017).

All governments require revenue to function. Throughout history, one of the easiest ways for a government to raise revenue, aside from taxing landowners, is to collect taxes on foreign goods entering the country. This usually happens at seaports because ports are one of the few bottleneck points in which foreign goods enter a country, which limits evasion and eases collection.

Governments also impose tariffs on imported goods to restrict their entry into the market and protect domestic producers from foreign competition. The purpose of such "protective" tariffs is to raise the domestic price and help domestic producers, at the expense of consumers. Such a policy may serve the interests of some domestic producers, while harming others and likely reducing real income, but it is sometimes argued that such tariffs are necessary to promote industrialization or help industries related to national security.

The third purpose of trade policy is reciprocity in which countries can reach agreements with each other to reduce their tariffs on each other's products. A country could always reduce its tariffs unilaterally (acting alone), but sometimes there are economic and political advantages to doing so in a trade agreement. Some examples of bilateral and regional trade agreements include the European Economic Community (now the European Union) and the North American Free Trade Agreement (now the US-Mexico-Canada Agreement [USMCA]). And then there are multilateral arrangements, such as the General Agreement on Tariffs and Trade (GATT) and the World Trade Organization (WTO). The goal of these agreements is to promote trade and the economic benefits derived therefrom as well as deepen political ties between countries.

A negative form of reciprocity is when one country increases its tariff in response to others doing the same. That is known as "retaliation" and reduces rather than expands trade. There have been many "trade wars" in history, such as the US Smoot-Hawley tariff of 1930 or the US-China trade war under the Trump administration.

The Drivers of Trade Policy: Interests, Institutions, and Ideology

The factors influencing the political economy of trade policy are sometimes categorized as the three I's: interests, institutions, and ideology (or ideas).

HPE largely focuses on how different economic interest groups strive to shape government policy. Economic interests have the strongest stake in policy questions and are highly motivated to influence policy through the political system. Those interests can take the form of producers or consumers, or different factors of production (landowners, labor, and capital owners). In the United States, the government has long enacted restrictions on imports of goods such as sugar and steel. Such policies help the few domestic producers of those goods (firm owners and their workers) but harm the many consumers of those goods. Some key insights from Mancur Olson (1965) help explain why producer interests are often more politically influential than consumer interests in shaping policy. The benefits of protection are concentrated on a few producers, giving them a strong motive to organize in favor of such a policy. Meanwhile, the costs of such a policy are spread across many consumers, giving them a weak motive to organize any opposition to the policy because of the free rider problem. This imbalance in economic incentives gives rise to an imbalance in the forces facing politicians and pushes policy in a protectionist direction.

Institutions are another feature of the policy process. These institutions include not just the rules of the political game but which entities are authorized to make policy decisions. The political system could be a representative democracy (presidential or parliamentary system), an oligarchy or authoritarian system (in which just a few interests are key to support for a regime), or a dictatorship. In the case of a representative democracy, regardless of whether the legislature or the executive is able to make decisions, not all economic interests are necessarily represented equally. This may be because some are excluded by voting rules or because they are not organized. Partisan factors may also filter the interests that get heard in the political system.

The final element to policymaking is the role of ideas or ideology. This is perhaps the most elusive and difficult factor to pin down because its impact is difficult to measure. Political scientists seem more open to the role of ideas than economists, who tend to emphasize material economic interests as the most important factor driving policy (Goldstein 1993). While the identification of these interests helps locate the winners and losers from a particular policy, that does not necessarily help explain how or why policies change. As Rodrik (2014, 205) argues, "Because of their neglect of ideas, political economy models often do a poor job of accounting for policy change."

For example, interest groups cannot explain one of the biggest shifts in US trade policy, discussed further later, the delegation of trade policymaking authority from Congress to the president in the Reciprocal Trade Agreements Act of 1934. This act elicited almost no interest among various economic interests that usually cared deeply about tariff policy, but it marked a key transition in American trade politics. In addition, sometimes trade policy is employed not to serve domestic interest groups but to achieve foreign policy goals, such as furthering peace through cooperative agreements to expand trade, or national security goals, such as punishing or weakening enemies through trade sanctions, or domestic political objectives, such as preventing foreign corruption and influence at home. All of these factors point to a role for ideas in shaping policy.

All three of these factors—interests, institutions, and ideology—contribute in different ways to shaping policy. The nineteenth-century British debate over the Corn Laws, which instituted restrictive duties on imported wheat, provides a classic illustration of how all three can influence trade policy. The main beneficiary of the import restraints were British landowners, the small but wealthy aristocratic elite who earned their income from land rents. The benefits of the Corn Laws were highly concentrated on this small group: by restricting imports of grain, the Corn Laws raised the domestic price of grain and hence increased the value of arable land. The institution that determined trade policy was the British Parliament. Because voting rights were restricted to wealthy property owners, the members of Parliament came largely from the landed aristocracy. This political power was used to keep cheap, imported grain out of the country.

Meanwhile, the large majority of the population—the wage-earning working-class laborers who spend a large share of their earnings on food—had a strong interest in cheap and abundant food and were therefore harmed by the policy but were disenfranchised and not well represented in Parliament. The Anti–Corn Law League, a lobbying group formed by Richard Cobden, provided the intellectual (or ideological) basis for opposing the import restrictions. All of these factors contributed to the debate over whether the Corn Laws should be repealed, which occurred in 1846 (Schonhardt-Bailey 2006; Irwin and Chepeliev 2021).

Application to US Trade Policy

With its long history, fairly open and competitive system of government, and unique political institutions, the United States provides a good testing ground for examining the HPE of trade policy.

Under Article I, Section 8 of the Constitution, Congress has the power "To regulate Commerce with foreign Nations." Therefore, Congress has been the institutional locus of US trade policymaking since 1789. (The president had a secondary role in trade policy until the 1930s.) A standard assumption among political scientists is that members of Congress seek to be reelected and therefore vote on legislation in a way that satisfies the interests of their constituents. These constituent interests tend to be producers, not consumers, because producers are better organized for political action and employ many workers who are voters.

The economic interests of a member's district or senator's state differ depending on whether the local producers make goods for export or face foreign competition. The nineteenth-century US economy was primarily agricultural, with cotton and wheat being the major exports. Imports consisted of manufactured goods, such as textiles and iron and steel. The nation's producer interests were not uniformly distributed across the country because different regions specialize in different economic activities. For example, for about two centuries, cotton has been produced in Mississippi and Alabama, corn in Iowa and Illinois, wheat in Kansas and Nebraska, tobacco in Kentucky and North Carolina, sugar in Louisiana and Florida, coal in Pennsylvania and West Virginia, iron and steel in Pennsylvania and Ohio, and farm equipment in Illinois and Indiana. In the twentieth century, automobiles have been produced in Michigan, aircraft in Washington, and high-technology and intellectual-property-intensive products in California, and so forth.

This regional specialization can persist for many decades.[5] The persistence of this regional specialization is consistent with region-specific resource endowments (such as arable land suitable for certain crops) or locational advantages that imply significant adjustment costs in moving capital and labor between regions. These factors lock in a state's production pattern for many decades. This framework implies that trade-related interests are divided along industry lines, depending on whether they produce goods for export or goods facing competition from imports: workers in exporting industries have an interest in low tariffs, and workers in industries competing against imports have an interest in high tariffs.[6]

Just as the geography of production tends to be stable over time, the pattern of trade—the types of goods a country exports and imports—also tends to be stable over time. This is because the deep determinants of trade—technology and factor endowments—evolve slowly. As a resource-rich nation, the United States has tended to export land-intensive agricultural products and resource-intensive manufactured goods. For most of the nineteenth century, the United States exported cotton, wheat, and other agricultural produce and imported manufactured goods and consumer products (coffee) or raw materials (tin). Due to its high ratio of land to labor, the United States has always been a high-wage country and therefore a net importer of unskilled labor-intensive manufactured goods, such as textiles and apparel.[7]

This framework suggests that the economic interests of different regions combined with the pattern of foreign trade gives rise to regional interests with respect to trade. Because the different states have different economic interests with respect to trade, it is difficult to reach a consensus on the "right" policy with respect to how easily imports should be allowed into the economy. Still, these regional factors get represented in Congress and must bargain and compromise to produce the ultimate policy outcome. Figure 24.1 provides a diagram of this framework.

The stable geographic location of domestic production and the stable composition of foreign trade means that regional economic interests are stable over time. Because political representation is based on geography, regional economic interests should translate into a stable political geography of voting patterns in Congress. In fact, this is something that we see. For most of the nation's history, the most important political divide over trade policy has been a geographic one on a North-South axis. This reflected a stark division in the location of trade-affected production. In the early nineteenth century, a manufacturing belt developed that stretched across the Northeast, including cotton textiles in New England and iron in Pennsylvania and Ohio—industries that usually faced competition from imports. Meanwhile, the South produced agricultural crops such as cotton and tobacco that were exported. Consequently, from the time of the 1787 Constitutional Convention until the Smoot-Hawley tariff in 1930, Congressional voting on trade measures has shown a distinctive North-South split.

To illustrate this persistence divide, Figure 24.2 depicts voting in the House of Representatives on two tariff bills more than a century apart, one in 1828 and another in 1929, the last House vote ever on the tariff schedule. Despite the vast changes in the US economy over that century—including large-scale industrialization, mass immigration, westward movement in population, and enormous technological change—the Congressional vote is remarkably similar. Even today, representatives from the Rust Belt of old manufacturing industries that stretches from upstate New York into the industrial Midwest are largely opposed to trade agreements and other measures that would

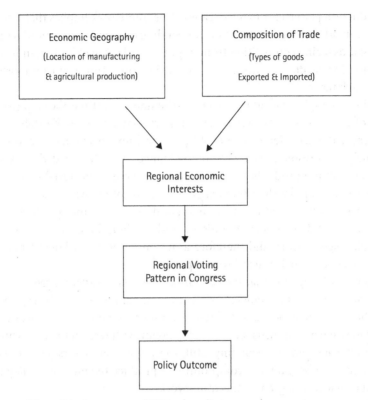

FIGURE 24.1. The political economy of US trade policy

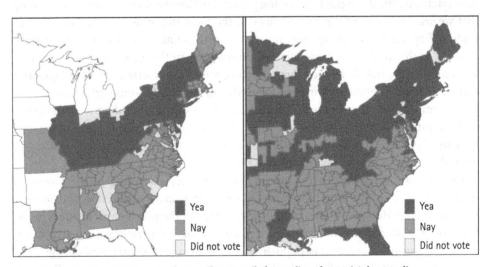

FIGURE 24.2. House voting on the tariff in 1828 (left panel) and 1929 (right panel)

Source: Irwin (2017, 16).

increase trade, while representatives from the South and West tend to be more favorable to such agreements and the expansion of trade.

Given this underlying stability, what could possibly change trade policy? There could be changes in economic interests, changes in trade patterns that affect those interests, changes in the political power of different regions, or changes in the institutional way in which trade policy is made. One example of an industry changing its geographic location is the gradual migration of the cotton textile industry from New England, where it originally arose in the early nineteenth century, to the South in the early twentieth century. In another case, owing to improvements in internal transportation (canals and railroads) in the antebellum period, the previously isolated Midwest became open to foreign trade and began exporting large amounts of wheat and flour. Congressional voting from the Midwest shifted from high tariffs to low tariffs as the Midwest shifted alliance from South to North, providing the marginal votes to reduce tariffs (Irwin 2008).

An important example of a changing trade pattern is America's shift from being a net importer to a net exporter of manufactured goods in the late nineteenth century due to the exploitation of mineral resources.[8] This change in the pattern of trade gave more producers an interest in opening up foreign markets to US exports than in protecting the domestic market from foreign competition. In the late twentieth century, the United States became a large net importer of manufactured goods once again. Imports from Japan in the 1980s and then from China in the 2000s forced changes in output and employment among US industries and led to political pressure for protectionist policies.

One implication of different regions having different trade-related economic interests is that political parties will take opposing positions on trade policy issues if they draw on different regions for their political support. Political parties emerged to help facilitate the reaching of policy bargains. These parties had a strongly regional basis: Whigs (and later Republicans) in the North, and Democrats in the South. Thus, trade policy became a partisan issue very early in US history primarily because the parties were highly regional in terms of their support.

Despite the similarity in the pattern of Congressional voting on the tariff across long periods of time, US trade policy has shifted in important ways over the past two centuries. These shifts have to do with the goal of trade policy (revenue, restriction, and reciprocity), the region that exerts power over American politics (North versus South), and the political party that dominates American politics (Democrats or Whigs/Republicans). Table 24.1 summarizes four different eras in which one region and political party was politically dominant and could implement its preferred policy of either revenue, restriction, or reciprocity.

From 1837 to 1860, from the start of the second party system until the outbreak of the Civil War, the Democratic Party dominated American politics. Democrats drew their political strength from the export-oriented South, which was opposed to protective tariffs. Prior to 1860, revenue considerations were paramount in the setting of tariffs for the period because import duties raised about 90 percent of receipts for the federal government.

Table 24.1. Three eras of US trade policy

Period	Trade policy objective	Congressional voting	Dominant political party	Region represented
1837–1860	Revenue	Tariff schedule	Democrats	South
1861–1933	Restriction	Tariff schedule	Republicans	North
1934–1993	Reciprocity	Negotiating authority and trade agreements	Democrats	Mixed

From 1861 to 1932, Republicans dominated American politics and drew their political support from the North, where manufacturing interests were concentrated. They wanted high duties to restrict imports, which is why tariffs jumped to 40 to 50 percent during the Civil War and remained at that level for several decades.

From 1933 to 1993, Democrats again dominated American politics and ensured that reciprocity through trade agreements would reduce tariffs and keep them low. During this period, the primary goal of trade policy was to reach trade agreements with other countries, either multilaterally through the General Agreement on Tariffs and Trade (GATT) and the World Trade Organization (WTO), regionally in agreements such as the North American Free Trade Agreement (NAFTA) or the Central American Free Trade Agreement (CAFTA), or bilaterally in agreements with countries such as Israel, Singapore, Australia, Korea, and others.

In each of these eras, the opposition party heatedly disputed the existing trade policy. The status quo never went unchallenged, with one side or the other complaining that the country would be ruined if tariffs were not raised higher or lowered further. And yet, despite all the debate and controversy, it proved very difficult to dislodge existing policies once they were established. Partisan dominance and political rules enforced a status quo bias that kept trade policy relatively stable within the two eras. A key political rule that helped lock in the policy preferences of the dominant party and prevent major policy changes was the requirement that the passage of legislation have the approval of the House of Representatives, the Senate, and the president. This usually can happen only when one party has unified control of government, that is, when one party controls all three entities. If there is divided government, partisan differences make significant policy change unlikely and the status quo remains secure.[9] Since 1993, divided government has been more frequent, but the president has usually been in favor of maintaining the status quo or furthering the reduction in trade barriers. Donald Trump was the first president since 1930 who was intent on raising import tariffs and import restrictions, not lowering them in trade agreements.

How have all of these factors played out over time in determining the course of US trade policy? Figure 24.3 shows the average tariff on total and dutiable imports from 1790 to 2020. The average tariff on total imports includes imports of all goods (dutiable and duty-free), whereas the average tariff on dutiable imports includes goods that are

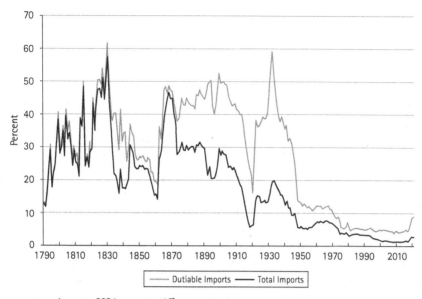

FIGURE 24.3. Average US import tariff, 1790–2020

Source: US Bureau of the Census 1975, series U-211-12 for 1790–1970; US International Trade Commission, "U.S. Imports for Consumption, Duties Collected, and Ratio of Duties to Value, 1891–2020," March 2021, for 1970–2020.

subject to import duties.[10] Many of the fluctuations seen in Figure 24.3 do not reflect deliberate policy actions by the government, but movements in import prices interacting with specific duties, which are a tax of a particular dollar amount per imported quantity rather than a percentage of the import value.[11]

This figure allows one to see a rough delineation of the three eras just discussed. In the revenue period from 1790 to 1860, average tariffs rose from about 20 percent to 60 percent and then fell back down to 20 percent. In the restriction period from 1861 to 1933, the average tariff on dutiable imports jumped to 50 percent and remained at about that level for several decades. In the reciprocity period from 1934 to the present, the average tariff fell sharply, and then leveled off at about 5 percent.

The delineation of US tariff history into three periods and three regimes—the revenue, restriction, and reciprocity eras—suggests that there have been only two major disruptions to American trade politics that have brought about a shift from one objective to another. The shifts resulted from exogenous shocks that realigned political power between regions of the country and the political parties representing them. These shocks were the Civil War (1861–1865) and the Great Depression (1929–1933).

The Civil War redistributed political power away from the South and toward the North and led to a political realignment in favor of the Republican Party and against the Democratic Party. Because Republicans from the North favored protective tariffs, the primary goal of trade policy shifted from revenue to restriction and the average tariff rose accordingly. There was no change in the institutional way in which tariff rates were determined, in that Congress still voted on the tariff schedule in bills that required floor votes, but political power shifted in a way that strengthened import-competing industries located in the North.

The Great Depression led to a political realignment with the Democratic sweep in the 1932 election. This election ended Republican dominance of American politics and ushered in more than five decades of Democratic political control of government. This realignment shifted power to the political party that put greater emphasis on export-oriented interests in the South. As a result, the primary goal of trade policy changed from restriction to reciprocity, and average tariffs fell considerably.

This transition was also marked by an important institutional change in policymaking: the delegation of trade-negotiating authority to the president by Congress. In 1934, the Democrats enacted the Reciprocal Trade Agreements Act (RTAA), a landmark piece of legislation that authorized the president to negotiate agreements to reduce tariffs with other countries. Congress no longer set import duties in long and complicated tariff bills. Rather, the president was authorized to change import duties in trade agreements with other countries. All Congress voted on was the negotiating authority (which included permission to reduce tariffs) or, starting in 1979, the trade agreements themselves. This shifted the locus of trade policy decision-making from the legislative branch, which seemed susceptible to special-interest politics and therefore biased in favor of higher tariffs, to the executive branch, which tended to link trade policy to foreign policy and view trade policy in terms of the national interest. The RTAA also altered the political balance of power toward export interests at the expense of import-competing interests. By directly tying lower foreign tariffs to lower domestic tariffs, the RTAA encouraged exporters to organize in opposition to high tariffs and in support of trade agreements (Haggard 1988; Schnietz 2000; Bailey, Goldstein, and Weingast 1997).

Another important shift occurred in the 1980s and 1990s when the political parties switched their long-standing positions on trade policy. Figure 24.4 illustrates the partisan division on trade by showing the percentage of each party in the House voting for lower tariffs (or trade authority or trade agreements) or against higher tariffs. From the 1830s until the 1970s, Democrats were uniformly in favor of lower tariffs. Republicans mainly voted in favor of protective tariffs, although after the Civil War they supported reducing some duties on noncompeting imports for consumers, such as tea and coffee. After World War II, however, they began to support trade liberalization. From the early 1950s until the early 1990s, there was a historically anomalous period of bipartisan consensus when the two parties voted in sync with one another. This was during the Cold War when foreign policy concerns were salient and partisan divisions were suppressed (Bailey 2003). Since the NAFTA vote in 1993, just after the end of the Cold War, Democratic support for lower tariffs or trade agreements has diminished considerably. By this time, the political parties had clearly switched positions on trade policy (Karol 2009).

This partisan repositioning largely reflects the fact that the parties switched which region of the country they represented: the South flipped from being a region controlled by Democrats to being dominated by Republicans (Kuziemko and Washington 2018), while the Northeast became a stronghold of Democrats. Thus, the regions of the country

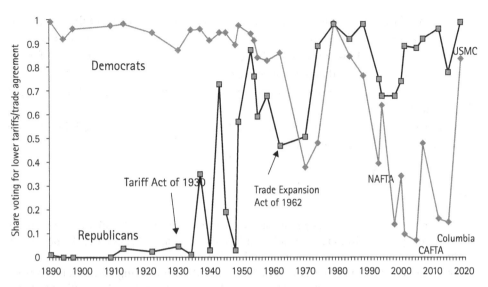

FIGURE 24.4. Share of party voting (House) for lower trade barriers, 1890–2015

Source: Irwin (2017, 658).

did not change their trade policy views, but the parties changed which regions of the country they represented.

Conclusion

Historical political economy examines how economic interests and the political system interact to generate policy outcomes. The distributional consequences of trade policy have made it a ripe area for research, particularly in the case of the United States. Being a large country with vastly different economic structures across regions, the country is an almost ideal laboratory to investigate how political and economic forces give rise to policy outcomes. One factor that has been emphasized here is that the United States has a political system in which policy change is difficult. This means that the stability of economic interests across regions gives an underlying stability to trade policy and ensures the persistence of the status quo. While political conflict is ever present, two major events—the Civil War and the Great Depression—led to a political realignment that altered the balance of power between contending parties and regions and led to a change in the main objective of trade policy.

Of course, the United States is not the only country that has had a robust political debate about trade policy in which different economic interests and political factions play a role. Mention has already been made of Britain's trade policy in the nineteenth century. One can go back further in history, such as to early-modern Venice, and find fascinating episodes in which the merchant class that had prospered as a result of foreign trade changed the political system to reduce competition and social mobility (Puga and Trefler 2014). One can also go to other regions of the world and explore, through the lens of political economy, how trade policy has evolved over time. In Latin America, for example, highly concentrated natural resource ownership in exported products (whether minerals or agricultural produce) has led governments to seek to redistribute the rents that accrued to those few by trade.[12]

All this points to the nearly endless opportunities for research on the HPE of trade policy in countries around the world.

Notes

1. For surveys of work (generally nonhistorical) by economists on the political economy of trade policy, see Rodrik 1995; Gwande and Krishna 2003; and McClaren 2016. For surveys by political scientists, see Milner (1999) and Oatley (2017).
2. There has long been a debate about whether free trade or protecting some industries from foreign competition will best serve the national interest. Adam Smith's *Wealth of Nations*, published in 1776, made the classic case for free trade. In 1841, Friedrich List published *The National System of Political Economy*, which argued that a country could use trade barriers to build up its productive capabilities and become a manufacturing power. On this debate, see Irwin (1996). On the economics of trade policy, see Corden (1974).
3. Because autarky is economically costly, there must be domestic political reasons for such a policy, the most obvious of which is that it helps leaders maintain power. For example, Lee and Temin (2010) suggest that Korea chose economic isolation in the nineteenth century because the political elite believed engagement with the rest of the world through trade would threaten the country's political stability. Bernhofen and Brown (2005) find that the static gains from trade for Japan were around 8 to 9 percent of GDP during this time.
4. The government did not levy any discriminatory taxes or quantitative restrictions on imports or exports (although it did tax some imports in lieu of collecting them domestically as excise duties or to match taxes imposed on domestic producers). See Howe (1997).
5. As Holmes and Stevens (2004) note, "For industries producing nontradable goods or services like retail, there is little [geographic] specialization, while for tradable goods like manufactures, mining output, and agricultural products, there is a substantial amount of specialization across regions."
6. Other models focus on mobile factors of production and have political divisions based on different interests of those factors (landowners, capital owners, different types of labor, etc.) rather than industry; see Rogowski (1990) and Hiscox (2002) for historical evidence on the question of specific versus mobile factors.
7. Of course, cotton exports were based on the mass use of unskilled (slave) labor before the Civil War.
8. In the mid-1890s, the United States became a net exporter of natural-resource-intensive manufactured goods, which slowly began to crowd out exports of cotton and other products. Wright (1990) examined the factor content of US trade in manufactures from 1879 to 1940 and showed that exports were intensive in nonreproducible natural resources.

9. For example, during the 1861–1932 period, there were thirty-five Congresses, twenty-one with unified governments (seventeen Republican, four Democratic), and fourteen divided governments. Over these seventy-two years, Democrats only had two opportunities to reduce tariffs, which they did in 1894 and 1913. In each case, these reductions were immediately reversed when Republicans came back into office. During the 1933–1993 period, there were thirty Congresses, sixteen unified governments (fifteen Democratic, one Republican), and fourteen divided governments. During this sixty-year period, very few changes were made to the overriding goal of seeking reciprocal trade agreements, even during the two years (1953–1955) in which the Republicans had unified control of government.
10. A large gap between these two series appeared after the Civil War when some products (such as coffee and tea, bananas, and tin) were put on the duty-free list. These items were generally not produced in the United States so that no domestic producer would be harmed by giving the goods free entry. Setting aside such imports, the average tariff on dutiable imports can be interpreted, somewhat simplistically but still usefully, as the average degree of protection given to domestic producers facing foreign competition.
11. For most of US history, specific duties comprised about two-thirds of the rates in the tariff schedule. The ad valorem equivalent of specific duties is inversely related to the price of imports. For example, if the specific duty on an imported shirt is ten dollars, the ad valorem tariff is 10 percent on a hundred-dollar shirt but 20 percent on a fifty-dollar shirt. As a result, exogenous fluctuations in import prices have sometimes produced large changes in average tariffs, even when there was no change in the actual rates of duty set by policymakers and applied to imports. See Irwin (1998).
12. For example, in Argentina, there has been a century-long fight that has pitted rural landowners who export staples such as soybeans and meat and want open markets against the more numerous urban working class that benefits from import restrictions (Brambilla, Galiani, and Porto 2018).

References

Bailey, Michael A., Judith Goldstein, and Barry R. Weingast. 1997. "The Institutional Roots of American Trade Policy: The Origin and Effects of the Reciprocal Trade Agreements Act." *World Politics* 49: 309–38.

Bailey, Michael A. 2003. "The Politics of the Difficult: The Role of Public Opinion in Early Cold War Aid and Trade Policies." *Legislative Studies Quarterly* 28:147–78.

Bernhofen, Daniel M., and John C. Brown. 2005. "An Empirical Assessment of the Comparative Advantage Gains from Trade: Evidence from Japan." *American Economic Review* 95: 208–25.

Brambilla, Irene, Sebastian Galiani, and Guido Porto. 2018. "Argentine Trade Policies in the XX Century: 60 Years of Solitude." *Latin American Economic Review* 27: 1–30.

Corden, W. M. 1974. *Trade Policy and Economic Welfare*. Oxford: Clarendon Press.

Goldstein, Judith. 1993. *Ideas, Interests, and American Trade Policy*. Ithaca, NY: Cornell University Press.

Gwande, Kishore, and Pravin Krishna. 2003. "The Political Economy of Trade Policy: Empirical Approaches." In *Handbook of International Trade*, ed. E. Kwan Choi and James Harrigan, 212–50. Oxford: Basil Blackwell.

Haggard, Stephan. 1988. "The Institutional Foundations of Hegemony: Explaining the Reciprocal Trade Agreements Act of 1934." *International Organization* 42: 91–119.

Hiscox, Michael J. 2002. *International Trade and Political Conflict: Commerce, Coalitions, and Mobility*. Princeton, NJ: Princeton University Press.

Holmes, Thomas J., and John J. Stevens. 2004. "Spatial Distribution of Economic Activities in North America." In *Handbook on Urban and Regional Economics*, Vol. 4, ed. J. V. Henderson and J. F. Thisse, 2797–2843. Amsterdam: North Holland.

Howe, Anthony. 1997. *Free Trade and Liberal England, 1846-1946*. Oxford: Clarendon Press.

Irwin, Douglas A. 1996. *Against the Tide: An Intellectual History of Free Trade*. Princeton, NJ: Princeton University Press.

Irwin, Douglas A. 1998. "Changes in U.S. Tariffs: The Role of Import Prices and Commercial Policies." *American Economic Review* 88, no. 4 (1998): 1015–26.

Irwin, Douglas A. 2008. "Antebellum Tariff Politics: Regional Coalitions and Shifting Economic Interests." Journal of Law and Economics 51:715–42.

Irwin, Douglas A. 2017. *Clashing over Commerce: A History of U.S. Trade Policy*. Chicago: University of Chicago Press.

Irwin, Douglas A., and Maksym Chepeliev. 2021. "The Economic Consequences of Sir Robert Peel: The Repeal of the Corn Laws Revisited." *Economic Journal* 131: 3322–37.

Karol, David. 2009. *Party Position Change in American Politics*. New York: Cambridge University Press.

Kuziemko, Ilyana, and Ebonya Washington. 2018. "Why Did the Democrats Lose the South? Bringing New Data to an Old Debate." *American Economic Review* 108: 2830–67.

Lee, Hun-Chang, and Peter Temin. 2010. "The Political Economy of Preindustrial Korean Trade." *Journal of Institutional and Theoretical Economics* 166: 548–71.

McLaren, John. 2016. "The Political Economy of Commercial Policy." In *Handbook of Commercial Policy*, Vol. 1A, ed. Kyle Bagwell and Robert W. Staiger, 109–59. Amsterdam: North Holland.

Milner, Helen V. 1999. "The Political Economy of International Trade." *Annual Review of Political Science* 2, no. 1: 91–114.

Oatley, Thomas. 2017. "Open Economy Politics and Trade Policy." *Review of International Political Economy* 24: 699–717.

Olson, Mancur. 1965. *The Logic of Collective Action*. Cambridge: Harvard University Press.

Puga, Diego, and Daniel Trefler. 2014. "International Trade and Institutional Change: Medieval Venice's Response to Globalization." *Quarterly Journal of Economics* 129: 753–821.

Rodrik, Dani. 1995. "Political Economy of Trade Policy." In *Handbook of International Economics*, Vol. 3, ed. Gene M. Grossman and Kenneth Rogoff, 1457–94. Amsterdam: North Holland.

Rodrik, Dani. 2014. "When Ideas Trump Interests: Preferences, Worldviews, and Policy Innovations." *Journal of Economic Perspectives* 28, no. 1: 189–208.

Rogowski, Ronald. 1990. *Commerce and Coalitions: How Trade Affects Domestic Political Alignments*. Princeton, NJ: Princeton University Press.

Schnietz, Karen. 2000. "The Institutional Foundations of U.S. Trade Policy: Revisiting Explanations for the 1934 Reciprocal Trade Agreements Act." *Journal of Policy History* 12: 417–44.

Schonhardt-Bailey, Cheryl. 2006. *From the Corn Laws to Free Trade: Interests, Ideas, and Institutions in Historical Perspective*. Cambridge, MA: MIT Press.

Stolper, Wolfgang, and Paul A. Samuelson. 1941. "Protection and Real Wages." *Review of Economic Studies* 41: 58–73.

Wright, Gavin. 1990. "The Origins of American Industrial Success, 1879–1940." *American Economic Review* 80:651–68.

CHAPTER 25

TAXATION

A Historical Political Economy Approach

PABLO BERAMENDI

TAXATION is the process by which the state secures sufficient revenue to perform its many functions. In Joseph Schumpeter's words, "Taxes not only helped to create the state. They helped to form it. The tax system was the organ the development of which entailed the other organs" (Schumpeter 1991 [1918], 106). The modern fiscal state—that is, an institutionalized organization capable of collecting and reallocating revenues according to democratically adopted legal provisions—plays an essential role as a *pillar of prosperity* (Besley and Persson 2011). Regardless of the specific indicator of development at use (from GDP per capita to infant mortality rate or the human development index), polities with large, effective, and democratic fiscal states fare better. Well-organized markets and well-designed states reinforce each other over time. Historically, however, this combination is rather exceptional. Securing such a virtuous relationship is relatively rare, the outcome of a very specific combination of factors that set a "narrow corridor" in historical terms (Acemoglu and Robinson 2019; Stasavage 2020).

The purpose of a historical political economy (HPE) of taxation is to understand the roots of different institutionalized forms of taxation across space and time and their legacy on redistributive politics today. To this end, and to analytically distinguish between the multiple forces behind the dynamics of tax development in different countries, I conceptualize tax development as a collective action process in which rational elites engage in repeated interactions, subject to domestic and international constraints, and in which there is room for significant institutional inertia.

In reviewing the comparative evolution of tax systems, this chapter makes three points:

1. The historical evolution of taxation is nonlinear. There are significant anchoring effects. In some cases, early investment in tax development sets the path towards larger and more effective fiscal states in providing redistribution. Others are

consistent laggards (Islamic countries) or late developers (Latin America, or to a lesser extent the United States or Spain). But among the fiscally capable states today, there are cases that began very early on in the process of economic and political modernization (England, Prussia-Germany) and cases that began their institutional modernization rather late—well after World War II—such as South Korea. Moreover, some places are early tax developers that subsequently fell behind (China).

2. All cases show significant breaks in their taxation trends. Sometimes these changes happen at different moments, pointing to the impact of "local" processes. Other times, several polities seem to respond at the same time to common external processes, such as wars.

   This variation derives from the interdependency between domestic and international factors. The domestic bargain over tax development results from a mix of preferences and constraints that reflects different combinations of geography, institutions, and international pressures. Neither of these factors dominates the HPE of taxation. At the same time, no systematic account can do without them.

3. Historical legacies have significant consequences in the medium to long run in two realms: the ability to redistribute—that is, to reshape the allocation of economic resources in society—and the capacity to cope with external shocks and crises. As a result, historical legacies are consequential for current distributional outcomes.

To provide context for the discussion in the rest of the chapter, I begin by reviewing a few established facts in the comparative historical analysis of taxation.[1]

A Few Facts

The left panel in Figure 25.1 displays a well-known pattern for political economists: taxation and economic development go together, yet at high levels of development there is significant variation in the state's tax reach. Part of the story behind this variation speaks to the tax mix: a high reliance on direct (income) taxes is essential for overall taxation to grow, but in several of the largest states, supplementing income taxes with growing indirect taxation is required. Hence, the relationship between overall and direct taxation is nonlinear, because there are limits in the extent to which wage and income earners are willing to contribute the lion's share of public revenues.

These choices condition the state's ability to provide redistribution and reduce inequality, as Figure 25.2 illustrates. The close connection between the size of the fiscal budget and the ability of the state to limit market inequalities through taxes and transfers should come as no surprise. The size of the public purse is a central element of the gap between the two forms of inequality used to define the level of redistribution (see, for instance, the cases of Mexico or Brazil). Some interesting deviations, however, occur

TAXATION 495

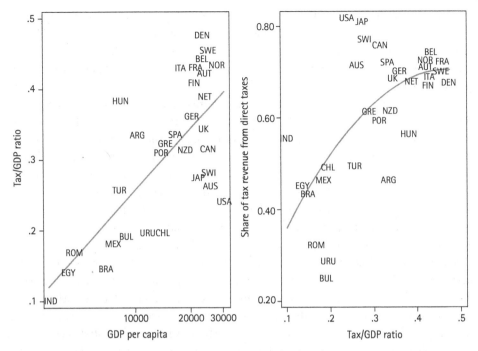

FIGURE 25.1. Development, tax size, and tax composition (2010)

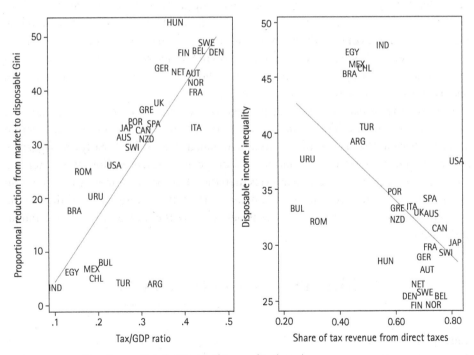

FIGURE 25.2. Taxation, redistribution, and inequality (2010)

at both ends of the relationships: the size of the tax budget in Turkey and Argentina is significantly higher than one would expect from the level of redistribution actually provided. A similar phenomenon occurs in Italy. By contrast, places like Germany, or more markedly Hungary, redistribute more than one would anticipate from the size of their public purses.

Regarding the incidence of inequality, the tax mix is important. Despite a relatively higher reliance on direct, more progressive taxation, the United States features, consistently and over time, much higher levels of inequality than many of its Continental counterparts, particularly Scandinavia, where the tax mix allows for a relatively higher share of consumption taxes that render the overall fiscal system marginally more regressive. At the other end of the spectrum, the most unequal nations on earth are both weak and relatively regressive fiscal states. Whether countries are able to combine high levels of direct and indirect taxation, as opposed to relying relatively more on either, depends, as I elaborate here, on historical legacies and political coalitions.

When considering the structure of taxation and its effectiveness in curbing inequalities, historical trajectories matter. Figure 25.3 maps out the fiscal history of democracies with different economic and political development trajectories.[2] Early fiscal state developers (such as the United Kingdom and to a lesser extent Sweden) feature large fiscal bureaucracies taking off in the early decades of the twentieth century and a relatively progressive structure. At the other of the spectrum, late fiscal developers—such as Brazil or Argentina—are both smaller and more regressive, that is, they rely less on direct taxes on labor and capital income and more on tax tools, such as consumption taxes, that draw primarily on transactions involving goods and services among the low- and middle-income strata. Between these two ends, the United States and Spain reveal intermediate trajectories, with relatively late starts and an effort to catch up, which account for a relatively smaller size in comparison to Sweden or the United Kingdom, yet at the same time relatively recent efforts to consolidate direct taxation (from the 1980s in Spain and the 1940s–1950s in the United States).

The diversity of experiences widens when one broadens the scope to include the experiences in the Middle East and Asia. China was an early riser in the introduction of relatively centralized taxation, but its system failed to consolidate early on, triggering a reversal of fortune relative to continental European experiences. Both the center and local elites extracted taxes at higher levels than their European counterparts, a situation that reversed after industrialization (Hui 2005). The Ottoman Empire, and the Islamic world more broadly, has remained a fiscal laggard since the early modern era (Karaman and Pamuk 2013).

Making Sense of Taxes

The expansion of taxation reflects the choice by elites to incur costly public investments. Across space and time, these fall under three broad categories: protection against

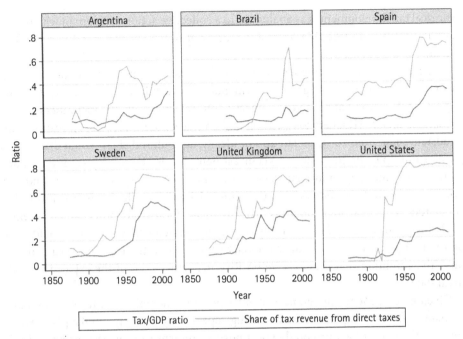

FIGURE 25.3. Tax size and composition over time

"enemies" both foreign (armies) and domestic (law and order), integration of national markets through large-scale infrastructures that reduce transportation costs, and the provision of public services, from public social insurance to education and healthcare. The relative importance of each category in the composition of public spending varies across space and time (Lindert 2004).

The returns to any investment are driven by the economic implications of the policies funded by public revenues and the share that each group expects to obtain. Thus, political choices about taxation are multidimensional. They concern the size of the fiscal state—what share of the economy is to be reallocated or consumed by the state—and its design—who pays into the public purse and benefits from it. Elites make their calculus on these two dimensions and aspire to maximize their net returns based on the expected distributional incidence of the overall fiscal system. As a result, the analysis of any particular tax tool must consider other sources of revenue and who benefits from the way these resources are spent.

The goal of maximizing net returns implies that any group only supports taxes if it expects to benefit from public spending. For any given group, the best scenario is one in which they stand to benefit from public allocation of revenues without contributing to them (and vice versa). Accordingly, there is a direct link between the nature of the multiplier effect of income among the different sectors and the organization of taxation: unless the (expected) income effects associated with increases in public investments and spending are sufficiently high, elites will support neither investments nor an increase in capacity to raise revenue to finance them. From this perspective, a useful way to think of historical tax development is as analogous to a collective action problem in which elites have an incentive to free ride on costly efforts out of which they stand to potentially benefit.

Preferences are heterogeneous by both factor (land, capital, labor) and sector. In theory, the nature of public good investments may work in favor of any type of elite. Before the development of the tax state, agricultural elites were the incumbent powerholders in society (Kuznets 1955; Ansell and Samuels 2014; Moore 1993; Justman and Gradstein 1999; Boix 2003; Ziblatt 2008). Ideally, agricultural elites would like to see a positive multiplier on their income via investments funded by consumers and the commercial and emerging industrial classes.[3] In some areas, as a result of trade and economic modernization, industrial and commercial elites challenge their status (Allen 2009; Kaldor 1963; Congleton 2010; Rostow 1959). Industrial and commercial elites, while happy to share in the cost of supporting investments they stand to benefit from, on the margins will seek to reduce the relative burden on their income basis, so as to meet the condition that they receive positive net returns out of the expansion of the fiscal state.

Given heterogeneous preferences, if elites perceive the politics of taxation as a one-off game, efforts to expand revenue-raising capacity are unlikely to take place even if some of the relevant actors could expect positive returns from it. The incentive in the short run is to shift the political and economic costs of the investment onto other groups through the reduction of the specific tax tools affecting them more directly. In a one-off exchange, uncertainty about the realization of the multiplier effect associated with the investment and concerns about marginal costs lead elites to be uncooperative. The politics of tax investments is about preserving relative advantage.

If, however, competing elites perceive the politics of taxation as a repeated interaction over public investments, the possibility emerges of coordination over investments potentially generating positive returns to several groups. The ultimate results of these interactions depends on the combination of the balance of power between groups, external factors (primarily war and major economic shocks) shaping elites' incentives and constraints, and the presence of institutional mechanisms to govern the inherent commitment problems associated with any agreement among elites sharing costs in the short run in the expectation of medium- to long-run benefits. The different paths to taxation in HPE reflect the combination of these three factors.

Varieties of Taxation

In the early stages of fiscal development, preferences concern three issues: first, whether to invest in a higher amount of public goods that may improve economic productivity; second, how to fund these public goods; and third, where in the nation to make those investments—throughout the nation, or in one or a small number of locations with comparative advantage in economic geography. When the distance in preference over investments among groups is not too large or institutions facilitate logrolls between groups with competing preferences, coordination of who bears the burden becomes more feasible politically and time horizons expand. By contrast, when preferences are multidimensional and divergent, the scope for agreement narrows down.

The demand to invest in public goods to enhance productivity reflects the incentives to adopt labor-saving technologies in the economy's most advanced sectors. Such incentives were a major engine behind the Industrial Revolution, which took place in areas where labor costs are high, energy is cheap, scientific progress is sufficiently developed, and last but not least, institutions protect property rights and allow for public investments to encourage the integration and consolidation of national and international markets. A rich literature debates the marginal contribution of each of these factors. Allen's critical insight (2009) was to show that the first two conditions—namely, high labor costs and cheap energy—are always necessary for the demand for technology investments to emerge. And with that comes a major source of structural pressures for tax expansion (Lizzeri and Persico 2004; Aidt and Jensen 2009).

Two channels link the Industrial Revolution to tax development. The first one is social. It concerns the change in the composition and balance of power among economic elites (Fresh 2022; Seligman 1914; Perkin 2003; Thompson 1963). The second one is spatial. The historical evolution of taxation is deeply intertwined with political conflicts over centralization (Herbst 2014; Dincecco 2017; Garfias 2018). The economic and political geography (Beramendi and Rogers 2022; Rodden 2019) of modernization have significant political implications. Nearly all countries of the world exhibit an enormous spatial skew in prosperity, as certain regions and cities within a nation pull far ahead of the rest. Such a skew reflects the combined effect of geographic endowments and industrialization processes. Concentration of economic advantage, in turn, translates into political influence.

The Early Path to Taxation: Conflict, Commitment, and the Rise of the Tax State

The first and second waves of the Industrial Revolution triggered the removal of barriers to the internal movement of factors, primarily thorough the construction of dense railway networks. The integration of national markets in early industrializers balances the influence between different types of elites. It also increases administrative capacity and implementation of provisions for raising revenue collection. Relatively lower levels of spatial skew and a more balanced pattern of political influence open the possibility for elites to compete over the scope of public services and their funding and, eventually, facilitate advances in tax development. At the same time, there are significant differences in speed, scope, and the shape of fiscal structures among countries with similarly comparable levels of industrialization and spatial dynamics (as implicitly illustrated in Figure 25.1). A key factor for understanding this variation is the design, functioning, and feedback effects of political and economic institutions.

The calculus by elites has a temporal element: political conflicts are not just about allocating resources in the short run but also about the institutions that govern extraction and distribution over sustained periods of time. What, then, is the nature of the interaction between the state and social groups that allows for the rise of modern taxation?

A large body of HPE work has identified several factors leading to the expansion and modernization of tax collection. With the rise of industrial and financial elites, both the tax base and the balance of power changed significantly. As a result, incumbent power holders, mostly the rural aristocracy, had to adapt. Mares and Queralt (2015; 2020) map the nature of the early responses by elites nicely: an initial transfer of the income tax to the new tax bases and, more importantly, the explicit strategic use of a taxation-for-representation link. Higher contributions to the public purse were the right of entry into the electoral body and legislative body. This cooptation of the rising groups separated them from the lower ranks, but more importantly facilitated a political dynamics in which (1) the new groups could advocate for their policy interests and (2) positive complementarities between the interests of different groups became feasible.[4] As a result, taxation is no longer a zero-sum game. It is a repeated, multidimensional bargain to be adjusted regularly through organized political conflict Besley and Persson (2011). This process illustrates well how, over time, there can emerge a substantial difference between the scope and incidence of tax tools intended by the introducers of taxation and its evolution in the medium run.

However, a *positive complementarity between taxation and representation* is not a given. How this conflict unfolds depends on the nature of political and administrative institutions. A prominent mechanism in the literature is the existence of effective parliamentary rule—that is, the existence of parliaments capable of controlling the executive, monitoring the budget, and ensuring that agreements are enforced (Congleton 2010). Such parliaments presuppose elections that are not determined "from above" and at least a partial level of enfranchisement. Once parliamentary politics becomes institutionalized, a second channel bearing on the elite's ability to think long term emerges. Parties grow stronger as organization and local, factionalized interests give way to programmatic platforms. As national organizations gain prominence, logrolls undertaken at the country level, often implying the partial sacrifice of local actors' first preferences, become enforceable as local notables also factor into their actions their own career concerns (Caramani 2004). By contrast, weak parliaments and weak parties magnify the constraints that a heterogeneous distribution of preferences imposes on the politics of fiscal development. Strong parties and regular control over revenues and spending limit the risks associated with defection for all parties and facilitate the rise of the tax state (Cox 2016; Pincus and Robinson 2014). The case of England, again, points to legislative representation as a key factor, the main features of which result from the institutional overhaul caused by the Glorious Revolution in 1688.

As this dynamic consolidates, taxation levels transcend initial adaptation strategies, and societies themselves change. Schumpeter 1991 [1918]) captures well this dynamic institutional aspect of taxation: "Tax bill in hand, the state penetrated the private economies and won increasing dominion over them. The tax brings money and calculating spirit into corners in which they do not dwell as yet, and thus becomes a formative factor in the very organism which has developed it. The kind and level of taxes are determined by the social structure, but once taxes exist they become a handle, as it were, which social powers can grip in order to change this structure" (108). Part of the change concerns elites themselves: through marriage across classes and sectors, the very composition of who governs changes as the tax capacity of the state grows (Rubinstein 1977). From the perspective of the old aristocracy, adaptation may be seen as "decline under another name" (Cannadine 1990). For the historian of political economy, it reflects a combination of international and domestic forces, leading to a new social and fiscal equilibrium.

Among the former, war occupies a prominent role. A long tradition of research has highlighted the tight link between interstate conflicts and state formation, including tax development, at various times in history. Tilly (1975) famously tied the balance of coercion and capital to the internal power balance and the specific form that modern European states took. In a recent engagement with this line of work, Dincecco and Onorato (2018) point to urbanization as the linking mechanism between war and state formation in Europe. More focused on revenue capacity, Karaman and Pamuk (2013) show how capital (cities) and coercion (agrarian autocracies) are alternative paths to revenue collection when experiencing war (at times with one another).

When it comes to the consolidation of the fiscal state, the two world wars facilitated the expansion of the state as a provider of insurance, regulator of markets, and, critical to our argument, collector of revenues. Scheve and Stasavage (2010; 2012), for example, show evidence that class conflict over progressive direct taxation did not typically emerge until World War I and World War II. By the time World War I war arrived, domestic politics had shifted from a conflict between rural landholders and liberal industrialists to a conflict between the latter (joined by financial industry and the remains of the old aristocracy) and a complex web of organizations (socialist, communist, social-Catholic) demanding higher levels of economic and political equality. By then, the transition from a baron-led, faction-based, largely clientelistic power politics to a more institutionalized programmatic contest was underway, though far from completed. Wars facilitated a rewriting of the social contract and changed the bargaining space among domestic actors. Universalization of the franchise and the associated expansion of public goods created additional revenue demands. The consolidation of tax-to-spend agreements on a regular basis and the acceptance by elites of the introduction and, more often, an expanded implementation of both assets and progressive income taxation helped meet these demands. Partisan politics ultimately became the way of structuring a recurrent contention with deep historical roots (Andersson 2021).

To summarize, the rise of the fiscal state reflects the joint effect of three forces: economic modernization and the change in composition and preferences of economic and political elites, a set of political institutions that expanded elites' time horizons and allowed them to organize political conflicts over revenue and spending allocation, and the impact of war as a major source of pressure to expand taxation and accelerate changes in existing politico-economic equilibria.[5] This account speaks to the rise of taxation in England, western Continental Europe, and with some caveats the case of the United States (Mehrotra 2013). It is an exceptional combination of factors not to be found outside the small subset of early industrializers.

Limits to Taxation and Alternative Paths

We turn now to the conditions under which the modern tax state fails to develop in full. Speaking in broad terms, comparative historical research points to logics that push polities away from the path toward levels of taxation comparable to those in the rich old world. The first condition features what can be referred to as a persistent pattern of multidimensional dependency, and it speaks well to areas suffering from long periods of colonial domination by the Iberian, British, and European empires. The second condition centers around the implications of early success and the persistence of institutions for service provision and revenue generation that become constraints on the adoption of modern fiscal institutions. It captures better the dynamics in cases such as China or the Spanish and the Ottoman Empires.

A Trifecta of Dependency

Latin American states emerged relatively early after their independence primarily from Spain and Portugal. Garfias (2018) shows how elites within these states seized the available opportunity to consolidate influence and reduce the risks inherent to expansions of state capacity (territorial control, order, access to information). Yet despite these efforts and countless external interventions by international organizations, most Latin American states lag behind in both fiscal capacity and bureaucratic reach and efficiency. Mazzuca (2021) captures this contrast by distinguishing between state formation (monopoly of violence, territorial control) and state-building (modern administration with capacity to effectively implement policy within the polity), pointing out, "By the time state formation was completed, Latin American states were endowed with strong antibodies against capacity building" (6). In understanding these "antibodies," which operated even more forcefully in Africa, HPE scholars have focused on three sets of factors: colonial legacies, directly linked to a polarized political and economic geography, and a different, much weaker position in the international political economy. Ultimately, the combination of colonial legacies with smaller-scale wars and the rise of civil wars in late developers led to a different logic of political development, one that reinforces the constraining role of geography and severely limits the scope of positive complementarities between taxation and representation.

As a matter of fact, the interests of early fiscal developers play an important role in understanding the fiscal underdevelopment of the periphery. The consolidation of the fiscal state among early industrializers had strong implications for the rest of the world. The expansion of the welfare state among early industrializers coincided with a decline in their ability to hold direct control over former colonies and a significant redrawing of international influence with the onset of Cold War. As colonies became independent and the relative balance of power between empires changed, influence shifted from direct military control to indirect external economic and political influence. Yet one thing remained constant: external powers had little interest in the institutional modernization of colonies. The absence of an external push for state development in the former colonies of Latin America or Africa implied that the inherited domestic political and institutional dynamics remained in place and conditioned outcomes in the long run (Centeno 2002; Kohli 2019).

In comparing Europe to Latin America, Mazzuca (2021) draws a contrast between war-led and market-led state formation. The latter consists in organizing the state for the large-scale export of commodities. Such a strategy also implies a stronger reliance on tariffs and a late introduction and consolidation of direct income taxation. This strategy is largely the result of a polarized geography in economies with good natural conditions for the production of commodities that require large amounts of low-skilled labor and a few strategic distribution ports (already developed during colonial times). As a result of the reliance on low-skilled labor, elites lacked incentives to invest in technological innovations. Industrialization and infrastructural investments were largely subsidiary to the production and distribution of commodities to the rest of the world, further enhancing existing spatial inequalities. A few critical cities, through agglomeration and innovation, become drivers of development (Glaeser 2011), but the incorporation of the periphery in late developers was in all cases incomplete. Peripheral areas were left behind as the central cities grew more affluent and diversified.

This legacy matters for two reasons. First, elites drawing rents from this economic organization have no incentives to empower the revenue collection capacity of the state nor to coordinate investments in capacity so as to integrate the periphery or provide large-scale public goods. To be sure, elites do engage in investments to secure control of the territory, to consolidate their relative position (Garfias 2018), or to instill allegiance to the state (Paglayan 2021), but remain wary of empowering institutions that may jeopardize their relative economic advantage.[6] When this fear is real, incumbent elites use their political advantage to weaken fiscal capacity out of fear of excess extraction in the medium run (Suryanarayan 2017; Suryanarayan and White 2021). Their preference is much closer to a "paper Leviathan" (Acemoglu and Robinson 2019): a smaller state, with limited ability to enforce laws and regulations, a lower extractive capacity, and a much weaker grasp over special interests and territories.

Second, higher levels of sectoral and spatial heterogeneity tend to exacerbate the collective action problem around capacity investments. Political risks grow, as does the need to control political representation. The strategic calculus of elites changes over time. Elites not only weaken capacity directly, but they seek to organize political representation such that they can prevent undesired policy outcomes. The commitment they desire is not about the ability to allocate a growing pool of revenues, but rather the ability to prevent the very extraction of revenue in the first place. Status quo winners prior to industrialization seek as much political influence as possible. In some cases, this involves removing democracy altogether; in others, organizing representation so as to maximize their ability to veto undesired policy outcomes (Boix 2003; Albertus and

Menaldo 2018).[7] To the extent that the outcomes vetoed are those requiring large-scale capacity investments, high levels of political inequality and polarized geography become barriers to the fiscal state (Beramendi and Rogers 2022; Mazzuca 2021).

Critically, the incentives to undermine capacity associated with the politico-economic geography of colonial legacies combine with the incidence and nature of wars in ways that further constrain fiscal development. Wars were of a different kind in the postcolonial world: smaller in scale and, more importantly, often with a severed connection to fiscal development.[8] Queralt (2019; 2022) shows that the external financing of interstate wars weakened bureaucracies and undermined state-building in late developers. Borrowing to pay for war implies both a disincentive to raise revenue on your own and the need, compounding as defaults accumulate, to offer domestic sources of wealth as collateral. The outcome is enhanced dependency and persistent institutional weakness—as illustrated, for instance, by the fiscal history of Spain until the transition to democracy or that of its former colonies. The long-run effects remains to this day, as we show here in detail.

Old Empires, Fiscal Laggards

While colonialism carries a legacy of dependency and fiscal backwardness in large parts of the world, colonial status hardly determines fiscal underdevelopment. Some former colonies, like the United States and Canada, did develop modern fiscal systems, and some former dominant powers, like Spain, China, and the Ottoman Empire, carry institutional legacies that to this day keep them anchored, in relative terms, in a lower tax equilibrium.

Speaking in broad terms, the mechanisms governing the experiences in these cases are partially different from those anchoring colonial dependency. The first one consists of a sort of negative feedback loop from early successes in imperial expansion. For some global powers, colonialism came back with a vengeance in the long run. Unlike the case of England, where the empire was a necessary pillar for industrialization and institutional modernization (Hobsbawm 1968), the case of Spain illustrates a very different dynamic (Grafe 2011). Imperial revenues (out of mineral extraction and the circulation of low-skill-based commodities) were of significant size but their effect is more complex than that of a resource course: they were consumed in sustaining the very imperial organization that yielded them, leaving relatively small margins for the imperial administration. Paradoxically, this increased the need to continue to rely on consumption and local trade taxes, which prevented the formation of national markets allowing for the free circulation of goods and labor and the very formation of a modern tax system. This legacy carried well over into the nineteenth century when weak nationalization and the influence capacity of regionally concentrated elites (in particular, landed interests in the south) consistently vetoed attempts at tax modernization.

The second channel relates to what Ma and Rubin (2019) refer to as a "low-wage, low-revenue equilibrium" in the case of China. Absolutist empires rely on the successful production and distribution of large amounts of agricultural commodities. The availability of a large pool of unskilled labor empowers early on a core of rural and commercial elites. These incumbent elites are the core of the ruler's coalition and fear extraction, yielding a commitment problem of a very different nature from the one the English Parliament solved. Coordination is required to alleviate concerns about extraction rather than about how the money is spent. For the ruler, the best way to show such commitment is to underinvest in capacity, thus constraining the scope of revenue collection in the long run.[9] Indeed, the demand for underinvestment in capacity by the elite seems to depend on how close they are to the ruler. Wang (2022) shows, for instance, that dispersed kinship across an empire facilitates capacity investments as similar agents expect to benefit from economies of scale associated with expanded imperial powers; concentrated kinship, by contrast, like concentrated wealth, works to undermine a powerful center. The central administration's composition and network structure play a central role in this regard. How imperial bureaucrats are selected and the structure of their network throughout the empire became central elements in the management of fears of excessive extraction and the fiscal history of the empire (Peng 2022). The combination of this system of coordination across elites and limited extraction persisted for a very long time and carried over as a legacy into the modern era.

The experience of the Ottoman Empire illustrates the third mechanism driving imperial fiscal backwardness: the early success and persistence of institutions that were, ultimately, at odds with market integration, the development of civil society, and administrative modernization. The failure of the *zakat*, one of Islam's five canonical pillars, to seed modern taxation in the Islamic world (Kuran 2020) paved the way to a decentralized provision of public services via pious endowments by the rick (waqfs). These institutions, together with commercial and inheritance laws that prevented long-run capital and financial investments and thwarted accumulation and commercial expansion (Kuran 2012), anchored down fiscal development. Fiscal centralization in the Ottoman Empire lagged behind that of Europe in the seventeenth and eighteenth centuries largely as a result of the territorial and social fragmentation of fiscal institutions, which allowed for a large number of intermediaries (Karaman and Pamuk 2010).

Fiscal Trajectories and Belated Tax Development

By the end of World War II, the historical legacy of fiscal divergence yields a large gap between democracies with different developmental trajectories. The stock of capacity conditions the dominant style of political competition. The latter, in turn, conditions the dynamics of capacity over time. This suggests that the sequencing between capacity and democracy emerges as a critical factor in the political economy of taxation (Stasavage 2020). Among countries that industrialized early and took part in major interstate wars, complex party organizations compete over the redistributive scope of regulation, public services, and direct income taxation.[10] A sufficient level of capacity is necessary for this dynamic to consolidate. A minimum threshold of capacity becomes self-sustaining.

By contrast, among late industrializers, political competition features a combination of broad programmatic proposals with the regular mobilization of voters via targeted club goods and clientelistic exchanges (Magaloni, Diaz-Cayeros, and Estévez 2007; Diaz-Cayeros, Estévez, and Magaloni 2016).[11] This combination of mobilization strategies is both a reflection of lower levels of state capacity and a mechanism that ensures that capacity's perpetuation over time (Kasara and Suryanarayan 2020). Mobilizing poor voters via targeted exchanges is cheaper and more effective than setting out to win support from them via a large-scale expansion of public goods with uncertain future returns (Amat and Beramendi 2020). At the same time, the pervasiveness of such a strategy renders state institutions much more prone to capture by elites. As international financial integration increases, the dominant fiscal architecture in these cases transitions from tariffs to indirect taxes, with a relatively weaker role for direct income taxes relative to the fiscal structures of early industrializers (Wibbels and Arce 2003). With increasing capital mobility, latecomers to taxation find it hard to alter the fundamental aspects of the tax administration (Genschel and Seelkopf 2022; Cai and Treisman 2005). The scope of fiscal divergence widens even further when one includes fiscally underdeveloped autocracies in the mix.

It would be a mistake, however, to think of these two scenarios as fate. Advanced countries have seen their tax mixes include more and more indirect taxes as a supplement to direct sources of revenues increasingly suffocated by growing pressures and constrained by market integration. And fiscal laggards around the world have featured in many cases a significant amount of catching up in revenue collection. Part of that is a relative convergence in the size of the tax base. But it also reflects political choices, in autocracies as well as democracies. Interestingly, some of the same factors that drove up taxes in early risers remain at play, but they do so in very different contexts and facing significant anchoring effects in terms of tax development.

The Cold War brought the connection between geopolitics and state development back to center stage. The Soviet Union fast-tracked industrialization from above (Gerschenkron 1962; Wheatcroft, Davies, and Cooper 1986; Kornai 1992) to preserve economic autonomy and security. Later, East Asian countries developed various forms of state-led development in which opposition to expansions of capacity was removed by fiat if necessary (Wade 2004). Over time, revenue collection capacity begins to grow, though from a low intercept. War did not lead to rewriting the social contract in most of these cases. Rather, the need to prepare for it sped up a process of economic modernization directed from above that led to an expansion of the state.

The second driver behind observable catch-up processes is the effect over time of political competition. In young, growing democracies, the balance between programmatic and clientelistic competition keeps changing over time, with the state expanding its reach to major infrastructural investments. As this process unfolds, revenue collection and monitoring capacity over spending are bound to grow over time, even if, again, from a relatively lower starting point. The process is not easy, as the recent experience in Brazil shows, but it is observable across middle-income democracies. At the upper end of this dynamic, Spain's experience of partial convergence with the EEC/

EU since the early 1980s provides a good illustration (Torregrosa 2021). Interestingly, political competition also operates as a mechanism pushing for more revenue collection in some autocracies. Lu and Landry (2014), for instance, show that for China from 1999 to 2006, a robust, nonlinear connection between competition at the local level and revenue extraction (taken in this case as a proxy for performance in eventual promotions).

In sum, the different historical trajectories depicted so far account for the heterogeneity on the overall level of tax capacity and the differential composition of the tax mix. Early fiscal states tend to be larger and have more progressive fiscal structures (i.e., a higher reliance on direct taxes). Late fiscal states tend to be either weak and regressive or marginally stronger but still more regressive than their Western European counterparts, despite the latter's increasing reliance on indirect forms of taxation.[12] These different trajectories and the resulting tax mixes actually make a difference for a variety of outcomes.

ON THE HISTORICAL ROOTS OF FISCAL PERFORMANCE: COMPLIANCE, PROGRESSIVITY, AND REDISTRIBUTION

In this final section, I discuss the ways in which historical legacies matter for the current functioning of fiscal states. I focus on three areas: redistributive incidence; the problem of compliance, which is directly linked to the way states tax and spend; and their ability to cope with crises.

Fiscal backwardness limits considerably the feasibility of large-scale public interventions to correct market outcomes via social expenditures. With no resources, rulers' hands are tied, and no economic policy strategy is feasible beyond the satisfaction of basic consumption needs. In this situation, incumbents have very little room to maneuver, and policy features low levels of both consumption and investment in human capital to increase future productivity. Democracy forces politicians in weak fiscal states to discount the future more. Families and the informal sector emerge, or indeed remain, as functional equivalents, further undermining the state's fiscal capacity. Born under a rather adverse international and ideological environment, these state structures constrain the scope and success of egalitarian interventions. Under these conditions, the redistributive power of the fiscal apparatus remains limited.

Redistribution, as defined by standard incidence indicators such as the Kakwani index, is a function of the size of revenue collected and the progressivity of tax instruments as well as benefits. The legacy of fiscal underdevelopment constrains redistributive incidence even if the specific tools being implemented feature progressive designs. Spain's experience—the closest historically to the path followed by late industrializers in terms of tax development—helps illustrate this point.

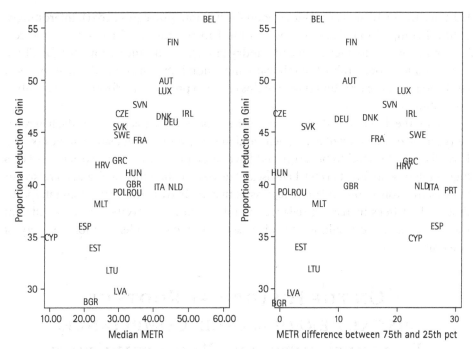

FIGURE 25.4. Size (median), progressivity (75/25 ratio), and effective redistribution, 2015–2018 (avg)

Going back to Figure 25.2 we can see how the main reason Spain is relatively weaker than others in the reallocation of income and wealth has more to do with the size of its fiscal budget than the design of its instruments. Spain has similar shares of direct taxation but higher levels of inequality than other EU members. Figure 25.4 reports EUROMOD estimates (averages for the 2015–2020 period) of the marginal effective increase in taxes given a 3 percent in income in different percentiles of the market income distribution (reported in the x-axes are the median [left panel] and the ratio between p75 and p25's marginal effective tax rates as a proxy for progressivity). The y-axis displays a standard indicator of relative redistribution, namely the proportional reduction from the Gini coefficient calculated for market income to the Gini coefficient calculated once taxes and transfers are taken into consideration.[13] A familiar pattern appears.

Spain's overall fiscal effort through taxes, as captured by the median, is below the average of the distribution, and accordingly so is its redistributive impact. This situation is present despite the fact that the actual tax design is relatively more progressive (and efficient in targeting) than many other EU countries. The weak redistributive impact of Spain's fiscal state is primarily a function of the long-run legacy of fiscal underdevelopment associated with late industrialization and late democratization.

This issue is only reinforced when less progressive policy designs combine with inherited limited capacity. Policy outcomes bear major consequences for the persistence of different taxation equilibria as they shape individual attitudes toward the state, which in turn feed back into its own weaknesses and strengths. Historical legacies condition citizens' attitudes and the latter, in turn, constrain the choices available to accountable politicians with short time horizons. This channel operates through two links: compliance and support for redistribution.

The modern fiscal state rests on citizens' quasi-voluntary compliance (Levi 1988). The willingness to pay taxes rests on punitive measures and on the perception of fairness of their contributions to the common pool. Fairness has a horizontal dimension, defined by relative comparisons with respect to other members of society, and a vertical one, defined by the perception of the goods and services that the state provides. The balance between coercion and perceived fairness in exchanges varies across political regimes, though both mechanisms operate across the board.

Under autocracy, particularly in state-led late developers that achieved high levels of monitoring and fiscal capacity, the marginal importance of coercion is likely to be higher. However, accountability links between levels of government open the door for policy evaluations to enter the political calculus as well. Under democracy, if citizens perceive the fiscal state as incapable or irrelevant from the perspective of effective redistribution, they will support neither expansions of redistribution or progressivity (Beramendi and Rehm 2016; Holland 2018), nor be willing to comply with their tax obligations. On the contrary, citizens are more willing to support the state when they perceive the net exchange of services and transfers for fiscal contributions as worthy and fair (Timmons 2005). To the extent that a distributive logic exists behind the patterns of compliance, citizens' attitudes, preferences, and behavior become channels through which different equilibria become self-sustaining.

Finally, this heterogeneity in legacies and internal political dynamics translates into the management of external shocks. Interestingly, weak fiscal democracies feature a particularly pernicious combination. During economic booms, they seem unable to take advantage of positive shocks to invest in stronger capacity in the medium run. Fully enfranchised democracies at medium to low levels of capacity face a bit of trap: because of the political pressures built in by recurrent elections, excess resources—such as the ones derived from commodity booms—are devoted to address short-term consumption needs rather than prioritizing medium- to long-run investments. At the same time, quite intuitively, such regimes suffer from negative shocks, such as COVID, more than the rest of the world. They lack the financial resources and the bureaucratic capacity to face them. Accordingly, during bad times, weak fiscal states discount the future even more. Exploring how much this trap varies across late developers and possible paths to exit it is an active area of scholarly work.[14]

The experience of crises is different in fiscally strong regimes. For democracies, the fundamental challenge is one of coordination, especially as crises transcend borders and heterogeneous domestic conditions imply an uneven allocation of costs. The higher the heterogeneity in the historical legacies of capacity across nations, the harder the coordination process will prove to be. Experiences such as the financial crisis in 2007–2008 and more recently the COVID pandemic illustrate the importance of such legacies.

For autocracies, the politics of capacity in times of crisis has its own peculiarities. Poor autocracies face similar resource constraints as fiscally weak democracies and also have major issues of regime stability. Fiscally strong autocracies are able to mobilize resources fast and use the state apparatus and new technologies to enhance repression. For them, crises are less a source of instability and more an opportunity to expand their reach. Regardless of the peculiarities of each set of cases, the shadow of the country's fiscal history looms large. Today's dilemmas largely reflect past fiscal legacies, pointing to the need for systematically increasing scholarly effort in the HPE of taxation.

Finally, different sequences between democracy and capacity (Stasavage 2020) matter both for the level of fiscal development and the internal composition of tax systems. Consolidating fiscal capacity after the full arrival of democracy seems to be a higher-order task than the reverse, given the short time horizons imposed by recurrent elections and the growing demands of fully enfranchised populations. Historically, though, democracy has generated increasing returns to capacity in early fiscal states. Understanding these differential dynamics is a major area of interest for future HPE research.

Acknowledgments

Thanks to Sjur Hamre, Fernando Martín, Didac Queralt, and Melissa Rogers for their help, comments, and suggestions on an earlier draft.

Notes

1. This is necessarily a concise review. For a recent and much more detailed overview of the introduction and evolution of different tax tools as well as the historical specificity of the different regions of the world, see Hakelberg and Seelkopf (2021) and Genschel and Seelkopf (2022).
2. See Beramendi, Dincecco, and Rogers (2019) for details on sources.
3. This is by no means the only possible outcome. Greater industrial production could "crowd out" agricultural production; see Rostow (1959). In such a case, agricultural elites stand to lose (or at least benefit less) from new public good investments, which will increase the pace at which the economy shifts from agriculture to industry.
4. For instance, Rubinstein (1977) shows how large landowners in England benefited a great deal from rents so that the railway could cross through their territories.
5. On the heterogeneity of mechanisms governing the link between war and tax development, see Emmenegger and Walter (2021).
6. Most elites in late industrializing nations were considering these investments in the middle years of the twentieth century. By this time, the expansion of the fiscal state among early industrializers would have been apparent to them. Therefore, they would not assume that fiscal capacity would remain the exclusive purview of elites—it would imply large-scale redistribution moving forward (Hollenbach and Nascimiento de Silva 2019; Gottlieb 2019).

7. These efforts are multidimensional and include, among others, constraints on programmatic political competition via high levels of internal party fractionalization with local candidates relying on dense clientelistic networks, legislative malapportionment in both chambers, and highly asymmetric forms of federalism.
8. Civil wars did push investment in national allegiance through primary education in the early stages of political modernization (Paglayan 2021), but these efforts did not translate into an overhaul of the scale and organization of the fiscal state.
9. The logic travels well to cases outside of China, across agrarian empires (Wong 1997), as absolutist states are weak and by and large rely on the tolerance of taxation from the landed elites and urban interests.
10. To be sure, remnants of prior forms of politics remain alive and well in specific areas within these nations.
11. This is the case in urban and rural areas, albeit with variations in the specific policy portfolios at work (Kitschelt 2000; Stokes et al. 2013; Gans-Morse, Mazzuca, and Nichter 2014; Ichino and Nathan 2013).
12. Autocracies living off natural resources constitute a subset of cases on their own, particularly prominent in the Middle East and northern Africa. Excessive natural resource wealth constrains taxation and helps autocracies endure through a complex set of political and economic mechanisms. For a comprehensive review of the relevant literature, see Ross (2015; 2012) and Morrison (2015).
13. Source: Author's elaboration on the basis of Solt (2020) and EUROMOD version I1.0, https://euromod-web.jrc.ec.europa.e
14. There is room for institutional innovation in medium-capacity environments, like designing programs and interventions that turn citizens and consumers themselves into auditors (Naritomi 2019).

REFERENCES

Acemoglu, Daron, and James A. Robinson. 2019. *The Narrow Corridor: States, Societies, and the Fate of Liberty*. London: Penguin.

Aidt, Toke S., and Peter S. Jensen. 2009. "The Taxman Tools Up: An Event History Study of the Introduction of the Personal Income Tax." *Journal of Public Economics* 93, no. 1: 160–75.

Albertus, Michael, and Victor Menaldo. 2018. *Authoritarianism and the Elite Origins of Democracy*. New York: Cambridge University Press.

Allen, Robert C. 2009. *The British Industrial Revolution in Global Perspective*. Cambridge: Cambridge University Press.

Amat, Francesc, and Pablo Beramendi. 2020. "Democracy under High Inequality: Capacity, Spending, and Participation." *Journal of Politics* 82, no. 3: 859–878.

Andersson, Per F. 2021. "Political Institutions and Taxation, 1800–1945." In *Handbook on the Politics of Taxation*. Hakelberg, Lukas, and Laura Seelkopf. Cheltenham: Edward Elgar. 47–63.

Ansell, Ben W., and David J. Samuels. 2014. *Inequality and Democratization: An Elite-Competition Approach*. New York: Cambridge University Press.

Beramendi, Pablo, Mark Dincecco, and Melissa Rogers. 2019. "Intra-Elite Competition and Long-Run Fiscal Development." *Journal of Politics* 81, no. 1: 49–65.

Beramendi, Pablo, and Philipp Rehm. 2016. "Who Gives, Who Gains? Progressivity and Preferences." *Comparative Political Studies* 49, no. 4: 529–63.

Beramendi, Pablo, and Melissa Rogers. 2022. *Geography, Capacity, and Inequality: Spatial Inequality*. New York: Cambridge University Press.

Besley, Timothy, and Torsten Persson. 2011. *Pillars of Prosperity*. Princeton, NJ: Princeton University Press.

Boix, Carles. 2003. *Democracy and Redistribution*. New York: Cambridge University Press.

Cai, Hongbin, and Daniel Treisman. 2005. "Does Competition for Capital Discipline Governments? Decentralization, Globalization, and Public Policy." *American Economic Review* 95, no. 3: 817–30.

Cannadine, David. 1990. *The Decline and Fall of the British Aristocracy*. New Haven, CT: Yale University Press.

Caramani, Daniele. 2004. *The Nationalization of Politics: The Formation of National Electorates and Party Systems in Western Europe*. New York: Cambridge University Press.

Centeno, Miguel Angel. 2002. *Blood and Debt: War and the Nation-State in Latin America*. University Park: Pennsylvania State University Press.

Congleton, Roger D. 2010. *Perfecting Parliament: Constitutional Reform, Liberalism, and the Rise of Western Democracy*. Cambridge: Cambridge University Press.

Cox, Gary W. 2016. *Marketing Sovereign Promises: Monopoly Brokerage and the Growth of the English State*. New York: Cambridge University Press.

Diaz-Cayeros, Alberto, Federico Estévez, and Beatriz Magaloni. 2016. *The Political Logic of Poverty Relief: Electoral Strategies and Social Policy in Mexico*. Cambridge: Cambridge University Press.

Dincecco, Mark. 2017. *State Capacity and Economic Development: Present and Past*. Cambridge: Cambridge University Press.

Dincecco, Mark, and Massimiliano Gaetano Onorato. 2018. *From Warfare to Wealth*. Cambridge: Cambridge University Press.

Emmenegger, Patrick, and André Walter. 2021. "War and Taxation: The Father of All Things or Rather an Obsession?" *Handbook on the Politics of Taxation*: 32–46, Vol 1. Hakelberg, Lukas, and Laura Seelkopf. Cheltenham, UK: Edward Elgar.

Fresh, Adriane. 2022. "Population and Political Change in Industrial Britain." Mimeo, Department of Political Science, Duke University.

Gans-Morse, Jordan, Sebastian Mazzuca, and Simeon Nichter. 2014. "Varieties of Clientelism: Machine Politics during Elections." *American Journal of Political Science* 58, no. 2: 415–32.

Garfias, Francisco. 2018. "Elite Competition and State Capacity Development: Theory and Evidence from Post-revolutionary Mexico." *American Political Science Review* 112, no. 2: 339–57.

Genschel, Philipp, and Laura Seelkopf, eds. 2022. *Global Taxation*. Oxford: Oxford University Press.

Gerschenkron, Alexander. 1962. "Economic Backwardness in Historical Perspective." *The Political Economy Reader: Markets as Institutions*, 211–28. Vogel, Steven. London: Routledge.

Glaeser, Edward. 2011. *Triumph of the City*. New York: Penguin Press.

Gottlieb, Jessica. 2019. "Keeping the State Weak to Prevent Collective Claim-Making in Young Democracies." Working Paper, The Bush School, Texas A&M.

Grafe, Regina. 2011. *Distant Tyranny: Markets, Power, and Backwardness in Spain, 1650–1800*. Princeton, NJ: Princeton University Press.

Hakelberg, Lukas, and Laura Seelkopf, eds. 2021. *Handbook on the Politics of Taxation*. Cheltenham, UK: Edward Elgar.

Herbst, Jeffrey. 2014. *States and Power in Africa: Comparative Lessons in Authority and Control.* Princeton, NJ: Princeton University Press.

Hobsbawm, Eric J. 1968. *Industry and Empire: An Economic History of Britain since 1750.* London: Weidenfeld and Nicolson.

Holland, Alisha C. 2018. "Diminished Expectations: Redistributive Preferences in Truncated Welfare States." *World Politics* 70, no. 4: 555–94.

Hollenbach, Florian M., and Thiago Nascimiento de Silva. 2019. "Fiscal Capacity and Inequality: Evidence from Brazilian Municipalities." *Journal of Politics* 81. no. 4: 1434–1445.

Hui, Victoria Tin-bor. 2005. *War and State Formation in Ancient China and Early Modern Europe.* New York: Cambridge University Press.

Ichino, Nahomi, and Noah L. Nathan. 2013. "Do Primaries Improve Electoral Performance? Clientelism and Intra-Party Conflict in Ghana." *American Journal of Political Science* 57, no. 2: 428–41.

Justman, Moshe, and Mark Gradstein. 1999. "The Industrial Revolution, Political Transition, and the Subsequent Decline in Inequality in 19th-Century Britain." *Explorations in Economic History* 36, no. 2: 109–27.

Kaldor, Nicholas. 1963. "Taxation for Economic Development." *Journal of Modern African Studies* 1, no. 1: 7–23.

Karaman, K. Kıvanç, and Şevket Pamuk. 2010. "Ottoman State Finances in European Perspective, 1500–1914." *Journal of Economic History* 70, no. 3: 593–629.

Karaman, K. Kıvanç and Şevket Pamuk. 2013. "Different Paths to the Modern State in Europe: The Interaction between Warfare, Economic Structure, and Political Regime." *American Political Science Review* 107, no. 3: 603–26.

Kasara, Kimuli, and Pavithra Suryanarayan. 2020. "Bureaucratic Capacity and Class Voting: Evidence from across the world and the United States." *Journal of Politics* 82, no. 3: 1097–112.

Kitschelt, Herbert. 2000. "Linkages between Citizens and Politicians in Democratic Politics." *Comparative Political Studies* 33, no. 6–7: 845–79.

Kohli, Atul. 2019. *Imperialism and the Developing World: How Britain and the United States Shaped the Global Periphery.* New York: Oxford University Press.

Kornai, Janos. 1992. *The Socialist System: The Political Economy of Communism.* Princeton, N.J.: PrincetonUniversity Press.

Kuran, Timur. 2012. "The Long Divergence." In *The Long Divergence*. Princeton, NJ: Princeton University Press.

Kuran, Timur. 2020. "Zakat: Islam's Missed Opportunity to Limit Predatory Taxation." *Public Choice* 182, no. 3: 395–416.

Kuznets, Simon. 1955. "Economic Growth and Income Inequality." *American Economic Review* 45, no. 1: 1–28.

Levi, Margaret. 1988. *Of Rule and Revenue.* Berkeley: University of California Press.

Lindert, Peter H. 2004. *Growing Public: Social Spending and Economic Growth since the Eighteenth Century.* Vol. 1. New York: Cambridge University Press.

Lizzeri, Alessandro, and Nicola Persico. 2004. "Why Did the Elites Extend the Suffrage? Democracy and the Scope of Government, with an Application to Britain's Age of Reform." *Quarterly Journal of Economics* 119: 707–65.

Lu, Xiaobo, and Pierre F. Landry. 2014. "Show Me the Money: Interjurisdiction Political Competition and Fiscal Extraction in China." *American Political Science Review* 108, no. 3: 706–22.

Ma, Debin, and Jared Rubin. 2019. "The Paradox of Power: Principal-Agent Problems and Administrative Capacity in Imperial China (and Other Absolutist Regimes)." *Journal of Comparative Economics* 47, no. 2: 277–94.

Magaloni, Beatriz, Alberto Diaz-Cayeros, and Federico Estévez. 2007. "Clientelism and Portfolio Diversification: A Model of Electoral Investment with Applications to Mexico." In *Patrons, Clients, and Policies: Patterns of Democratic Accountability and Political Competition*. 182–205. Kitschelt,Herbert and Wilkinson, Steven. Cambridge: Cambridge University Press.

Mares, Isabela, and Didac Queralt. 2015. "The Non-democratic Origins of Income Taxation." *Comparative Political Studies* 48, no. 14: 1974–2009.

Mares, Isabela, and Didac Queralt. 2020. "Fiscal Innovation in Nondemocratic Regimes: Elites and the Adoption of the Prussian Income Taxes of the 1890s." *Explorations in Economic History* 77: 101340.

Mazzuca, Sebastian. 2021. *Latecomer State Formation*. New Haven, CT: Yale University Press.

Mehrotra, Ajay K. 2013. *Making the Modern American Fiscal State: Law, Politics, and the Rise of Progressive Taxation, 1877–1929*. New York: Cambridge University Press.

Moore, Barrington. 1993. *Social Origins of Dictatorship and Democracy: Lord and Peasant in the Making of the Modern World*. Beacon Paperback 268, Boston: Beacon Press.

Morrison, Kevin M. 2015. *Nontaxation and Representation*. New York: Cambridge University Press.

Naritomi, Joana. 2019. "Consumers as Tax Auditors." *American Economic Review* 109, no. 9: 3031–72.

Paglayan, Agustina S. 2021. "The Non-democratic Roots of Mass Education: Evidence from 200 Years." *American Political Science Review* 115, no. 1: 179–98.

Peng, Peng. 2022. *Pen and Sword: Meritocracy, War, and State Building in Imperial China*. PhD dissertation. Duke University.

Perkin, Harold. 2003. *The Origins of Modern English Society*. London: Routledge.

Pincus, Steven C. A., and James A. Robinson. 2014. "What Really Happened during the Glorious Revolution?" In *Institutions, Property Rights, and Economic Growth: The Legacy of Douglass North*. Galiani, Sebastian, and Itai Sened. Cambridge University Press, 192–222.

Queralt, Didac. 2019. "War, International Finance, and Fiscal Capacity in the Long Run." *International Organization* 73, no. 4: 713–53.

Queralt, Didac. 2022. *Pawned States: State Building in the Era of International Finance*. Princeton, NJ: Princeton University Press.

Rodden, Jonathan A. 2019. *Why Cities Lose: The Deep Roots of the Urban-Rural Political Divide*. New York: Basic Books.

Ross, Michael L. 2012. *The Oil Curse*. Princeton, NJ: Princeton University Press.

Ross, Michael L. 2015. "What Have We Learned about the Resource Curse?" *Annual Review of Political Science* 18: 239–59.

Rostow, Walt W. 1959. "The Stages of Economic Growth." *Economic History Review* 12. no. 1: 1–16.

Rubinstein, William D. 1977. "Wealth, Elites and the Class Structure of Modern Britain." *Past & Present* 76, no. 1: 99–126.

Scheve, Kenneth, and David Stasavage. 2010. "The Conscription of Wealth: Mass Warfare and the Demand for Progressive Taxation." *International Organization* 64, no. 4: 529–61.

Scheve, Kenneth, and David Stasavage. 2012. "Democracy, War, and Wealth: Lessons from Two Centuries of Inheritance Taxation." *American Political Science Review* 106, no. 1: 81–102.

Schumpeter, Joseph A. 1991 [1918]. "The Crisis of the Tax State." In *The Economics and Sociology of Capitalism*, ed. Richard Swedwerg, 99–141. Princeton, NJ: Princeton University Press.

Seligman, Edwin Robert Anderson. 1914. *The Income Tax: A Study of the History, Theory, and Practice of Income Taxation at Home and Abroad*. Union, NJ: Lawbook Exchange.

Solt, Frederick. 2020. "Measuring Income Inequality across Countries and over Time: The Standardized World Income Inequality Database." *Social Science Quarterly* 101, no. 3: 1183–99.

Stasavage, David. 2020. *The Decline and Rise of Democracy: A Global History from Antiquity to Today*. Princeton, NJ: Princeton University Press.

Stokes, Susan C., Thad Dunning, Marcelo Nazareno, and Valeria Brusco. 2013. *Brokers, Voters, and Clientelism: The Puzzle of Distributive Politics*. Cambridge: Cambridge University Press.

Suryanarayan, Pavithra. 2017. "Hollowing Out the State: Franchise Expansion and Fiscal Capacity in Colonial India." Available at SSRN: https://papers.ssrn.com/sol3/papers.cfm?abstract_id=2951947.

Suryanarayan, Pavithra, and Steven White. 2021. "Slavery, Reconstruction, and Bureaucratic Capacity in the American South.": *American Political Science Review*, no.2: 1–17.

Thompson, Francis Michael Longstreth. 1963. *English Landed Society in the 19th Century*. London: Routledge & K. Paul.

Tilly, Charles. 1975. "Reflections on the History of European State-Making." In *The Formation of National States in Western Europe*. Charles Tilly, ed. 3–83. Princeton, NJ: Princeton University Press.

Timmons, Jeffrey F. 2005. "The Fiscal Contract: States, Taxes, and Public Services." *World Politics* 57, no. 4: 530–67.

Torregrosa, Sara. 2021. *The Spanish Fiscal Transition: Tax Reform and Inequality in the Late Twentieth Century*. Cham, Switzerland: Springer.

Wade, Robert. 2004. *Governing the Market: Economic Theory and the Role of Government in East Asian Industrialization*. Princeton, NJ: Princeton University Press.

Wang, Yuhua. 2022. "Blood Is Thicker Than Water: Elite Kinship Networks and State Building in Imperial China." *American Political Science Review*, no. 3: 1–15.

Wheatcroft, S. G., R. W. Davies, and J. M. Cooper. 1986. "Soviet Industrialization Reconsidered: Some Preliminary Conclusions about Economic Development between 1926 and 1941." *Economic History Review*, no. 2: 264–94.

Wibbels, Erik, and Moisés Arce. 2003. "Globalization, Taxation, and Burden-Shifting in Latin America." *International Organization* 57, no. 1: 111–36.

Wong, Roy Bin. 1997. *China Transformed: Historical Change and the Limits of European Experience*. Ithaca, NY: Cornell University Press.

Ziblatt, Daniel. 2008. "Does Landholding Inequality Block Democratization? A Test of the "Bread and Democracy" Thesis and the Case of Prussia." *World Politics* 60, no. 4: 610–42.

PART IV
LONG-RUN LEGACIES

CHAPTER 26

ECONOMIC DEVELOPMENT IN HISTORICAL POLITICAL ECONOMY

JOSE MORALES-ARILLA, JOAN RICART-HUGUET,
AND LEONARD WANTCHEKON

Introduction

CURRENT debates on the origins of economic development and welfare across societies take a somewhat bipolar approach, whereby development is often the result of either political institutions or human capital. On the one hand, a dense body of literature emphasizes that "getting the right political institutions" is critical for development. In economics in particular, some have emphasized that institutional constraints on executive power are a sine qua non for development. Under this paradigm, limits on rulers' capacity to govern dictatorially are very important because they improve policy and reduce arbitrary extraction that citizens may otherwise suffer, and political stability and the legal protection of property rights encourages investment, thus fostering development.

On the other hand, some scholars place human capital and technological innovation front and center. In this view, the education level of a society and its capacity to deploy cutting-edge productive knowledge and technologies are the key sources of economic growth. The Solow (1956) model of (long-run) economic growth provides an important theoretical foundation to this literature. An educated labor force and innovation through ideas are fundamental to increase productivity (the output per unit of input) and thus growth (Barro 2001). Since Solow, many political economists have realized that education and ideas do not occur in a vacuum but in a political context, hence the need to adopt a political economy approach to understand diverging patterns of human capital accumulation over time and space (Franck and Rainer 2012).

While these paradigms are part of the answer in many contexts, simple stylized facts about the world also illustrate their limits. For one, substantial variation in economic well-being exists between localities within the same country. Institutions that constrain executive power, provide political stability, and protect property rights are typically established at the national level, so the institutionalist view cannot fully account for within-country differences. Second, institutional constraints on the state cannot explain the string of national economic successes in East Asian countries in the last sixty years, or in Western countries earlier on, because these states were empowered rather than constrained. Indeed, some have argued that interventionist states fostered economic development, first in Europe and North America and later in East Asia. At the same time, many developing countries have dramatically improved access to education and health services, but only some have converged to high levels of prosperity. Similarly, knowledge-based and ideas-based explanations for development cannot fully explain cross-country differences in development in today's globalized world. Indeed, while cutting-edge growth (growth at the technological frontier) is difficult and depends on innovation, catching-up growth (the sort of growth that can be achieved by "adopting and adapting" ideas and practices from developed countries) has remained limited in many underdeveloped countries in spite of today's increased access to information and codified technologies.

The purpose of this chapter is to take stock of the historical political economy (HPE) literature on economic development and to suggest paths for future research in the field. For the remainder of the chapter, we first describe how the Industrial Revolution not only allowed for the "Great Acceleration" away from subsistence income levels, but also led to the "Great Divergence" in living standards between "Western" countries and the rest of the world. We then introduce the main arguments and key contributions behind the geographic, institutional, and human capital paradigms in HPE. Finally, we present a cross-disciplinary body of work that discusses why some regimes with largely unconstrained executives and low initial levels of human capital may nonetheless pursue effective policies that induce economic development. We conclude the chapter by arguing for increased academic attention to instances of policy and institutional experimentation as potential means for societies to discover locally effective paths to prosperity (Canen and Wantchekon 2022).

Historical Explanations of Current Differences in Economic Development

Key Facts to Be Explained: The Great Acceleration and the Great Divergence

Galor (2005) and Clark (2007) argue that the history of economic growth can be segmented around the Industrial Revolution into Malthusian and post-Malthusian periods. For most of human history, standards of living remained largely stagnant. Technological progress before the nineteenth century was meager, and so were gains in productivity. Negative population shocks brought about by war and disease, such as the Black Death, could induce discrete improvements in average standards of living, but these were largely offset over time by population growth. Similarly, population growth suppressed the potential benefits derived from better access to land, resources, and technologies in some areas of the world. So while better-endowed societies had larger populations, they were not much richer. Events until the turn of the nineteenth century were largely in line with the predictions from Malthus (1798), who argued that geometric population growth combined with linear growth in food production lead to an equilibrium characterized by high mortality rates that limit the total population to a size consistent with subsistence income levels. Yet, inadvertently, these "dismal" patterns began to change at the time of Malthus's writings.

The Industrial Revolution, which started in England at the beginning of the nineteenth century and quickly spread through Western Europe, radically altered patterns of production and induced workers to transition from agricultural work in the countryside to manufacturing activities in cities. These parallel processes of structural transformation and urbanization underpinned an economic takeoff that allowed for a Great Acceleration of living standards, initially attenuated by the concomitant increase in population growth. However, toward the end of the nineteenth century, fertility rates fell drastically as continued technological progress and productivity gains incentivized female labor participation and investments in the human capital of children. Following this *demographic transition*, productivity gains mapped directly to improvements in the average incomes enjoyed by the population, breaking from the prior Malthusian equilibrium (Clark 2007).

Western Europe and the "Western offshoots" (the United States, Canada, Australia, and New Zealand) experienced sustained growth in gross domestic product (GDP) per capita since the beginning of the nineteenth century. By contrast, total output growth rates in Latin America, Asia, and Africa only started ascending at the turn of the twentieth century, and their population growth rates did not abate until its end. The later and overall slower takeoff in these regions explains the stark differences in standards of living around the world today. Pritchett (1997) provides a number of measures that help illustrate this Great Divergence (Pomeranz 2000). While the richest country in the world was only 8.7 times richer than the poorest country in the world in 1870, this ratio grew to 38.5 in 1960 and to 45.2 in 1990. According to data from the World Bank in 2020, the ratio between the GDP per capita of the richest and poorest countries in the world, Luxembourg and Burundi, at comparable prices was 152.8.[1]

One of the main objectives of historical political economists is to explain how history and politics help account for these differences in economic development. The remainder of this section overviews the dominant long-run explanations for current differences in development across countries.

Geography Can Underpin Differences in Economic Development between Countries

Can geographic differences explain why some countries are rich and others are poor? Collier (2007) argues that there exist largely geographic "development traps," such as being landlocked with bad neighbors. Landlocked and equatorial countries as well as hinterland regions tend to be poorer. These fixed characteristics can determine the development potential of a society by imposing higher trade costs, lower agricultural productivity, and a worse disease burden (Gallup, Sachs, and Mellinger 1999). For example, malaria-ridden countries tend to be poorer because they suffer from higher mortality rates and lower levels of productivity, which in turn deter investments in physical and human capital as well as political centralization (Gallup and Sachs 2001). Additionally, Alsan (2015) finds that the tsetse fly has also long hindered the development of agricultural surplus in African regions where the parasite is prevalent.

The most popular account to highlight the impact of geography on both political and economic development is provided by Jared Diamond (1997). In *Guns, Germs, and Steel*, he argues that geography explains why Europe conquered the Global South and not the other way around. His "continental axis hypothesis" argues that the longitudinal (east-west) orientation of the Eurasian continent allowed for large territories to share similar ecological conditions that eased the spread of crops, domesticated animals, and human populations. This in turn enabled trade, the diffusion of technologies, and the creation of centralized states. By contrast, the latitudinal (north-south) orientation of the Americas and of Africa constrained the flow of goods and people. Scholars have since shown rigorously that "tall" territorial units are more linguistically diverse than "wide" ones (Laitin, Moortgat, and Robinson 2012) and that technologies flow more easily over an east-west axis than over a north-south axis (Pavlik and Young 2019).

Diamond provides a plausible macro explanation for the relative strength of Eurasia over other continents. However, it cannot explain why certain countries in Europe took off while others did not, the *timing* of the Great Acceleration, or even "reversals of fortune"—the fact that richer colonies around 1500 became poorer by the 1900s (Engerman and Sokoloff 2011; Acemoglu, Johnson, and Robinson 2002).

Similar to Koyama and Rubin (2022), we argue that the role of geography on long-term development is contingent on geography's interaction with changing political, economic, and technological environments. This point is most obvious in regard to the role of natural resources in development. For example, oil was unimportant before the internal combustion engine, and guano ceased to be valuable with the advent of industrially manufactured fertilizers. Economic geographers often refer to "locational fundamentals" to describe characteristics of a place that, while fixed, change in economic importance over time (Davis and Weinstein 2002).

Vast amounts of coal and internally navigable waterways are two locational fundamentals that might have allowed Britain to lead the Industrial Revolution. Koyama and Rubin (2022), however, argue against this view. Coal abundance was not unique to Britain and could have been easily imported by countries lacking it. Moreover, the start of the Industrial Revolution was powered through water mills. Similarly, the intensity of investments on connectivity infrastructure in Britain during this time is evidence that the country was not naturally endowed with adequate means of transportation ex ante. Nonetheless, while geography alone cannot explain the advent of the Industrial Revolution in Britain, geographic proximity to Britain does account for the faster technological adoption and earlier growth acceleration in Continental Europe (Gerschenkron 1962).

Institutions and the Incentives for Growth-Inducing Activities

As discussed earlier, geography is at best a partial explanation of differences in growth since 1800. Many HPE scholars have turned their attention toward how different societies shape the incentives of economic agents and governments to engage in activities that are conducive to economic growth. For instance, early growth in Western Europe emerged in cities and regions that had long protected property rights, which allowed individuals to invest and innovate while deterring arbitrary expropriation and rent-seeking (North and Thomas 1973). North (1990; 1993) refers to the "rules of the game" that shape economic incentives as institutions, and defines them as "humanly devised constraints that structure human interaction." Whether formal (constitutions, laws) or informal (norms, conventions), these rules and their enforcement condition people's behavior by forming generalized expectations about the consequences of pursuing different activities. While some institutional arrangements invite individuals to invest and trade, others may induce individuals to avoid entrepreneurial endeavors and invest in rent-seeking. A visible example of how national institutions shape economic development is the discrete change in the level of emitted nighttime lights at the border between North Korea and South Korea, whereby South Korea is lit and North Korea dark (see Figure 26.1).

What, then, are the institutional foundations of long-term economic growth? On the economic front, scholars focus on institutions such as property rights that protect one's land and capital and that foster competitive environments and labor mobility. On the political front, authors pay special attention to institutional constraints on executive authorities (i.e., the president or prime minister). These constraints may stem from civil society and from other political authorities like a parliament). The adoption of these institutions is often the result of sufficiently economically or ethnically homogeneous societies (Engerman and Sokoloff 2011) or high degrees of social equality that force regimes to build broader "winning coalitions" (de Mesquita et al. 2003).

The institutional paradigm identifies the existence of institutional constraints on expropriation and taxation as the key cause for the Great Divergence, in particular the divergence between parts of Western Europe and the rest of the world. In a seminal contribution, North and Weingast (1989) find that England's economy took off after civil conflicts in the seventeenth century concluded in parliamentary controls on the Crown, yielding credible commitments over the protection of property rights. While the absolutist regimes in Europe, such as Spain and France, levied high taxes to maximize their revenues into the eighteenth century, English and Dutch political elites faced checks and balances from the merchant class that prevented confiscatory taxation and

FIGURE 26.1. Nighttime lights in South and North Korea
Source: NASA Earth Observatory: Earth at Night: Flat Maps: Global Map Downloads—2016 Color.

allowed for economic growth. This is consistent with quantitative evidence that absolutist regimes in Europe tended to underperform economically in the period between 1050 and 1800 (DeLong and Shleifer 1993). Beyond Europe, Acemoglu, Johnson, and Robinson (2001) argue that higher settler mortality rates at the time of colonization induced the establishment of "extractive" institutions that allowed for only a few settlers to dominate over much larger Indigenous populations to extract local resources. As a consequence, these authors argue, colonies with higher settler mortality rates are poorer today because they continue to offer worse institutional environments compared to colonies with constrained and inclusive institutions inherited from larger colonial settlements. Finally, some scholars emphasize the role of colonies' legal origins in determining the establishment of growth-inducing institutions. La Porta et al. (1998) argue that common-law countries experienced stronger financial development because the system offered stronger protections of property rights, especially for smaller investors (see also Widner 1994).

For all their appeal, institutional explanations leave a number of questions unanswered. While executive constraints in some European cities and regions such as England preceded the advent of the Industrial Revolution, there also existed economic differences between regions with and without these institutional constraints. Such constraints resulted from slow processes of urban agglomeration and pre-industrial technological development (Galor 2005; Abramson and Boix 2019). Institutional constraints in Europe, then, likely evolved jointly along limited preindustrial economic growth rather than being a root cause (Abramson and Boix 2019).

Furthermore, as we have mentioned, institutions tend to be largely fixed at the country level, and yet there are lots of within-country differences in living standards. For example, Acemoglu and Dell (2010) document that within-country income differences are greater than between-country income differences for Latin American countries. In a short empirical exercise for this chapter, we assessed the share of the subnational variation in economic development (as proxied by the logarithm of nighttime lights per person) that can be accounted for by national borders. We find that between-country differences explain between 50 and 75 percent of the total variation. While national institutions are part of these country-fixed differences, the exercise suggests that up to half of the variation in development cannot be explained by national institutions or other country-fixed characteristics.

These results highlight how cross-national approaches to the study of development leave a lot of unexplained variation in development and rarely offer causally identified evidence. Some scholars have turned to more "micro" empirical approaches that leverage natural experiments, often at the cost of studying only one country or continent. In the case of Africa, Michalopoulos and Papaioannou (2014) compare ethnic groups that were partitioned by colonial borders. Under the assumption that such split groups are comparable on either side of the border, they find surprisingly limited effects of national political institutions on local development outcomes. This suggests that institutions may matter little in contexts of weak state capacity, a variable that we examine in the next section. Similarly, a number of studies by Melissa Dell and her coauthors challenge the assumption that inequality and extractive activities are inherently negative for economic development. For instance, Dell (2010) studies long-term differences in development outcomes between areas differently affected by colonial forced-labor policies in Peru and finds that slave labor eroded economic development by preventing the establishment of large plantations (*haciendas*), which in turn allowed for development-enhancing local public goods. Similarly, Dell and Olken (2019) find that colonial sugar cane extraction and refining activities in Indonesia led to stronger economic development in the long term.

Overall, institutions provide an endogenous and, at any rate, incomplete account for the Great Acceleration and the Great Divergence.

The Development of—and Access to—Ideas: Human Capital and Technological Innovation

The Great Acceleration and the Great Divergence are, at their core, stories of technological progress. The Industrial Revolution led to sustained increases in productivity and consequently in wealth that allowed Western countries to overcome the Malthusian Trap. Current differences in income cannot be adequately explained by differences in the relative access to productive capital inputs, but by the relative productivity in the use of those inputs (Jones and Romer 2010). That is why some scholars focus on technological innovation and its main enabler, human capital, as the root causes of the subsequent political and economic divergence between Western and non-Western countries. The importance of ideas and technological innovation in the Solow growth model is a foundational contribution in that vein. So is modernization theory, which argues that development—education, industrialization, and urbanization—is a prerequisite for inclusive institutional changes (Lipset 1959). From both of these perspectives, human capital is a key determinant of economic and political development.

A recent body of quantitative literature supports the view that human capital, and the innovation associated with it, can account for modern economic growth. For example, Cantoni and Yuchtman (2014) find that the advent of the commercial revolution in Germany was determined by the proximity to medieval universities that provided the necessary human capital for development of trade-enhancing legal institutions. Mokyr (2002) also points to the appearance of new technologies in England near the turn of the nineteenth century, made possible by the uniquely dense and interconnected network of knowledge-enhancing organizations, such as universities and professional societies. But the importance of human capital is not limited to the university-educated. The high quality of the British labor force in the second half of the eighteenth century, matched by relatively higher wages, allowed for faster technological innovation and adoption than elsewhere in continental Europe (Kelly, Mokyr, and O'Grada 2014). Continental Europe eventually caught up, as is well known. What is less well-known is that technological adoption and innovation were not the result of adopting British institutions but largely Continental efforts to acquire the necessary British technological know-how through patents and engineers (Milward and Saul 1973; Milward, Alan. S., Samuel. Berrick. Saul,. 1977). This is also true of Prussia, where technological catch-up was driven by regions with higher levels of education (Becker, Hornung, and Woessmann 2011). In the case of France, the local presence of knowledge elites led to faster growth during the country's industrialization through the improved access to technologies enshrined in British patents (Squicciarini and Voigtländer 2015).

Collectively, these results strongly suggest that the capacity to tap into and deploy British know-how drove the diffusion of the Industrial Revolution throughout Western Europe. Recent evidence suggests that migration helped these very processes of human capital diffusion at the start of the Great Acceleration. For example, Prussian areas benefiting from the arrival of relatively skilled French Huguenots in the early eighteenth century displayed stronger capacities for textile manufacturing a century later (Hornung 2014). Similarly, US patenting increased disproportionately in the fields of Jewish German scientists who migrated to America after the Nazi regime purged them from German universities (Moser, Voena, and Waldinger 2014).

Human capital, rather than institutions or geographic factor endowments, may also be critical to understanding why some colonies were rich and others poor. Settler mortality rates may have led to colonial underdevelopment, not by inducing extractive institutions that allowed for unconstrained executives, but by limiting the diffusion of human capital embedded in settlers themselves into the colonies (Glaeser et al. 2004).

This is precisely the headline finding of a robust literature on the persistent positive economic effects of historical educational interventions, and of European missionaries in particular. Wantchekon, Klašnja, and Novta (2015) leverage the fact that missionaries had little knowledge of local conditions and decided arbitrarily to settle on the left bank on the Ouémé River of present-day Benin. People in villages on the left bank, especially educated ones, enjoyed higher standards of living during colonial rule, and so did their descendants in those same villages. Similarly, Valencia Caicedo (2019) studies the location of Jesuit missions in the Guaraní area of Paraguay, Brazil, and Argentina. These "Misiones" instructed Indigenous inhabitants in reading, writing, and different crafts. Despite being abandoned when the Jesuit order was banned in 1773, treated areas remain much richer than originally similar locations even today, most likely because of their capacity to adapt high-productivity technologies in agriculture and to transition toward manufacturing activities. These results highlight the relative importance of education for local development and are consistent with the finding that 50 percent of subnational differences in well-being in Latin American countries can be accounted for by differences in human capital (Acemoglu and Dell 2010).

Discussion

We have seen the rich evidence to support the view that geographic endowments, institutions, and human capital help us account for between and within-country differences in growth. Institutions have been particularly emphasized in the political economy literature as perhaps the most important factor, so it is worth noting that elites choose institutions, which can change rapidly. This means that they can often be *endogenous* to a society's education, technological characteristics, geography, ethnic composition, and demography, among other slow-moving variables (exceptionally, sudden revolutions or shocks induced by war or colonization may sometimes lead to swift and exogenous institutional change). Thus, institutions can be epiphenomenal insofar as they are the result of these factors. Moreover, the recent microeconomic evidence discussed earlier has tended to erode a number of basic tenets of the institutional paradigm, while also establishing a strong and independent causal connection between historical investments in education and current living standards in Europe (Cantoni and Yuchtman 2014), South America (Valencia Caicedo 2019), Africa (Wantchekon, Klašnja, and Novta 2015; Ricart-Huguet 2021), and elsewhere. After all, human capital and innovation often underpin institutional choices and can have an independent and direct effect on economic development. We conclude with a third takeaway: explanations *integrating* factor endowments, human capital, and institutions to explain growth—while ambitious—may hold the most promise (Koyama and Rubin 2022).[2]

Beyond the Institutions versus Human Capital Debate: Development-Enhancing Public Policies?

There is little doubt that factor endowments, institutions, and human capital are determinants of growth, and examining their interactions seems promising if we are to understand the persistent disparities between high-growth and low-growth countries. However, these determinants are better at explaining long-run and persistent differences in growth than takeoffs. The role of the state and of policymaking is conspicuously absent in all three of these paradigms. The mainstream institutionalist explanation for development is consistent with neoclassical economics in that it takes a strikingly limited view of public policy, arguing that the main responsibility of the government is to *not* infringe on property rights and to *constrain* itself. Growth resides entirely in the hands of the private sector, and the government's role is only to create an adequate legal framework for market competition. Government, however, is not defined by its negative actions alone. Politicians under various regime types may try to *actively* foster growth, whether that is in order to gain reelection in democracies or to gain legitimacy through economic performance in autocracies. These incentives mean that governments have long been active in setting and steering economic policy *for the better and for the worse*.

Some governments have used "nonstandard" trade and industrial policies to foster early-stage development and achieve comparative advantages in certain sectors (e.g., South Korea and Taiwan) while others have failed (e.g., Senegal and Brazil). One key variable that seems to separate most successes from failures since World War II is state capacity (Wade 2004; Evans 1995; Kohli 2004). We put these successful and failed cases of "engineering development" in historical perspective to argue that state interventions were important at the advent of the Industrial Revolution. Active industrial and trade policy to develop a country's technology and improve its terms of trade are anything but new; they were used by most early industrializers, including the United Kingdom in the eighteenth century, the United States, and many Continental European powers in the nineteenth century. We discuss examples of state-led policies that have led to growth historically, and we conclude by suggesting that political economists should pay more attention to how different societies experiment with alternative policy and institutional arrangements in finding locally sustainable paths to economic growth.

State-Led Development Policies: Contemporary and Historical Examples

The view that economic policy can help stimulate development is not new. Monetary policy is perhaps the most famous example and dates back to the seventeenth and eighteenth centuries in Sweden, Britain, and other Western countries. However, other types of economic policies have long been used in attempts to foster development. Many of these policies were justified under the view that development is "path-dependent," so that in the absence of decisive government intervention, poorer countries would be at a persistent disadvantage.[3] Development economists in the mid-twentieth century argued that a "big push" was necessary to achieve large-scale production and industrialization in developing countries, and that states were primarily responsible in that endeavor (Rosenstein-Rodan 1943). Relatedly, some argued that subsidies and protection were necessary to allow for "infant industries" to grow prior to competing with those of advanced economies. These ideas date back at least to the Tudor period in England (1500s) and to the *Report on Manufactures* in the United States by Alexander Hamilton (1791), who coined the term "infant industry." We discuss the recent examples of high growth in East Asia but also draw on historical evidence from Britain, Western Europe, and the United States.

For the many failures of import-substitution strategies in Latin America and Africa, the East Asian miracle (Page 1994) remains a relevant and contested puzzle for the field. East Asian countries other than Japan were mostly lagging in wealth and education in the 1950s, many with GDP per capita similar to other underdeveloped regions. Nonetheless, they took off with unparalleled speed. This degree of success occurred both under democratic regimes, such as Japan, and dictatorial ones, such as in Taiwan and South Korea. Furthermore, South Korea's and Taiwan's democratization experiences seem consistent with modernization theory, as they only democratized after becoming rich and educated. The more recent Chinese growth miracle (Lin, Cai, and Li 2003), however, challenges both the institutional and the modernization notions of economic development. Its unparalleled experience of fast economic growth has blended liberalization with active state regulation and intervention in the absence of initially high endowments of human capital, and without conceding democratic liberties or constraining the executive. This is not to say that state-led development was the only way to grow in East Asia. Under British rule, Hong Kong strategically adopted a laissez-faire approach, more so than Singapore's developmental state, to become the financial hub of East Asia.

There has been substantive attention to the developmental state success experiences of East Asia. Focusing on the case of Taiwan, Wade (1990) argues that the regime's legacy capacities to manage economic dynamics during wartime allowed it to be a "contrapuntal partner of the market," mobilizing resources toward upstream industries relevant for military defense and economic growth. Woo (1992) discusses the political economy of South Korea's industrialization, arguing that General Park deployed state capacities first acquired under Japanese colonial rule to pursue "big push" industrialization efforts in the face of North Korean invasion threats (see also Mattingly 2017). The capacity of East Asian states to redistribute agrarian and financial resources in favor of industrialization might have been key for the region's economic takeoff (Studwell 2014), especially compared to similar attempts in low-capacity African and Latin American states, such as Ghana and Brazil. According to Wade (2004), who analyzes the Taiwanese, Japanese, and Korean experiences, building an "industrial policy bureaucracy... that is motivated to achieve its intended objectives" is the main challenge for countries hoping to replicate these successes. Of course, a bureaucracy needs to be supported and financed by a capable state, and Queralt (2022) investigates the origins of state capacity. He shows that states that developed a tax base in the nineteenth century, such as Japan and Chile, are developed today. By contrast, countries like Argentina that borrowed heavily from international finance—often to pay off debts or pay for wars—became "pawned states" and, after a short period of growth, tend to be poorer today.

Recent quantitative work complements these arguments. South Korea's developmental efforts led to persistent comparative advantages in protected sectors and downstream industries (Lane 2022). Further, government subsidies of upstream sectors, those producing the material inputs for industries in downstream sectors and commerce, likely fostered aggregate growth in 1970s South Korea and in contemporary China (Liu 2022). These cases and literature emphasize the merits of industrial policy, and thus challenge the neoliberal assumption that the only productive role of the state in the economy is to establish market-enhancing institutions and provide public goods. Taken together with the disappointing record of "Washington Consensus" types of reforms (Rodrik 2006), and exceptions such as Chile notwithstanding, the historical record suggests that the neoliberal approach is not necessary and is rarely sufficient for relatively underdeveloped economies to accelerate their growth.

An HPE approach is useful to realize that economic policies that enhance long-run growth are anything but new. Gerschenkron (1962) made this point when analyzing how industrialization occurred under different institutional and policy regimes in Continental Europe. He argued that, after England's early takeoff under relatively few interventions, the process of catch-up in other countries depended on fast and large-scale efforts in multiple sectors. Follower countries needed to pursue activist policies to overcome large disadvantages in access to human and physical capital and to develop the necessary scale to become competitive. Countries such as Germany, France, and Russia pursued different combinations of state activism, protectionism, and central banking policies to catch up with Britain.

It is less well known that successive governments in Britain and the United States also engaged in state-led development; and it is contentious to argue that such engagement is a primary cause of the long-term growth of Britain and the United States. Nonetheless, that is precisely what Chang (2002; 2007) persuasively argues: the wide range of policy interventions (tariffs, subsidies, import bans, etc.) pursued by Britain and the United States in the nineteenth century diverge dramatically from the set of market-enhancing institutions that developed countries often recommend to developing ones (see also Bairoch 1995). In the United States, Hamilton was in favor of developing "infant industries" in manufacturing, while Jefferson and other southerners favored free-trade agricultural exports. Lincoln increased tariffs once in office, and so did his successors in the second half of the nineteenth century. In Britain, these interventions began at least as early as the Tudor monarchs. According to Chang (2007, 24), "Especially Henry VII and Elizabeth I used protectionism, subsidies, distribution of monopoly rights, government-sponsored industrial espionage and other means of government intervention to develop

England's woolen manufacturing industry—Europe's high-tech industry at the time." These policies did not end after the Glorious Revolution, as a mainstream institutionalist account would suggest. Prime Minister Robert Walpole passed the Calico Acts in 1721, legislation that sought to protect British manufacturers from foreign competition. He subsidized them and encouraged their exports, much like Korea, Japan, and Taiwan did more than two hundred years later. The ban on Indian cotton products to allow Britain to develop its own infant industry is perhaps the best-known example. Only by the late 1700s, when Britain's industries were the most efficient and Adam Smith was espousing free-market policies, were these protections rolled back to allow British manufacturers to conquer much of the world market.

Reasons for Pursuing—and for Success in Pursuing—Developmental Policies

From a political economy perspective, a key question is why unconstrained executives would ever be interested in pursuing developmental policies and not simply in maximizing extraction. Olson (1993) offers a very simple logic: "stationary bandits" may realize it is in their interest to moderate their extraction and induce economic growth in order to maximize their total rents. At the heart of Gerschenkron's (1962) analysis is the idea that backwardness creates domestic expectations for achieving the levels of economic development attained elsewhere, and that this tension leads to political action and institutional innovation. This idea is connected to the principle of "performance-based legitimacy" of autocratic yet partly meritocratic regimes in East Asia, including China's (Bell 2015). Indeed, centralized decisions on the political turnover of Chinese provincial leaders seem determined by the economic performance of their provinces during their tenure (Chen, Li and Zhou 2005).

Another motive for unconstrained regimes to pursue developmental policies concerns the presence of external and even existential threats to national security. This was apparent in the cases of South Korea and Taiwan, threatened by North Korea and China, respectively, and which did not democratize until the late 1980s. Singapore faced similar existential threats from neighboring Malaysia and Indonesia (Lee 1998) as it transformed into an important entrepot without democratizing. In Finland, Soviet demands for war reparations in the mid-1940s induced the government to engage in temporary industrialization efforts that inadvertently favored the structural transformation of the Finnish economy (Mitrunen 2021). Israel's fast pace of economic growth since its foundation can also be traced to state-led developmental efforts in response to external and existential security threats (Halevi 2008). The presence of external threats and competition has long been identified as a potential motive for development-inducing policies. Tilly (1992) argued that warfare and competition between European powers led to the creation of early modern states with high military, bureaucratic, and tax capacities. Consistent with Tilly, recent contributions argue that external wars are conducive to the accumulation of state capacity (Besley and Persson 2009; Scheve and Stasavage 2010). Overall, foreign threats, competition, and pressure may induce authorities to engage in developmental activities that yield broad economic benefits.

That even nondemocratic governments may have clear incentives to perform and to facilitate growth does not mean that they always succeed. As discussed earlier, the legacy capacities and bureaucracies of South Korea and Taiwan were important for the success of their industrialization experiences (Wade 2004).[4] These two factors were largely missing in developmental efforts pursued in Latin America and Africa, although African states with more historical legitimacy grew more in the second half of the twentieth century (Englebert 2002).

Finally, some have argued that the "Asian values" of collectivism and social harmony (de Bary 2000) may have been fundamental for the independence and credibility of authorities providing temporary subsidies to industrial production. Greif and Tabellini (2010) and Nisbett (2004) have advanced economic and psychological arguments to explain the cultural bifurcation between the East and the West. Critics of culture-centric explanations rightly emphasize that cultural values alone cannot explain rapid economic growth because they are largely constant in the short run. However, the collectivist norms in East Asia may have interacted with the prevalence of state developmental ideas in the aftermath of World War II to facilitate growth. Such a cultural emphasis is in fact compatible with state-centric explanations because the success of developmental efforts may depend on cultural norms such as generalized trust and cooperation.

We conclude this section with a note of nuance. While some countries like South Korea embarked on rapid infant industry creation, that need not be the only path for state-led development. The Chinese government learned from its mistakes during the Great Leap Forward and the Cultural Revolution, and that may very well be why its transformation into a mixed economy proceeded gradually. The transformation of China into a mixed economy began in the 1980s, including gradual liberalization through Special Economic Zones, and highlights the importance of policy and institutional experimentation as means for societies to identify nuanced, locally sustainable paths for successful economic reforms (Romer 2010).

Likewise, the recent economic catch-up experienced in some African countries like Ghana and Kenya, and some Latin American countries like the Dominican Republic and Peru, might be explained by their earlier pursuit of economic liberalization and of democratization. Moreover, small countries as diverse as Singapore, Rwanda, Panama, and the Baltic states grew quickly after adopting nimble policies that favored foreign direct investment and that situated them as regional or even worldwide entrepots. Legitimacy through economic performance can again explain why leaders like Lee Kuan Yew or Paul Kagame adopted policies that opened up the country to international capital flows as a way to grow, rather than instituting capital controls, subsidies, and other interventionist policies to develop comparative advantage first and deliver export-led growth next. Collectively, the historical record suggests that no size fits all. The right institutional and policy mix for different societies to accelerate growth is determined by their specific histories, strengths, and sizes. From this view, there is ample room for studying how societies engage in policy and institutional experimentation as they discover their own paths to prosperity.

Conclusion

We finish by outlining three main messages. The first is that theories and empirical approaches that combine geography, institutions, and human capital seem most promising to understand paths to prosperity. We do not mean simply *additive* approaches—there is little argument that particular institutions and innovation can foster growth—but actually *integrative* approaches. Of course, such theoretically ambitious approaches may best explain development on one continent, such as in Latin America (Engerman and Sokoloff 2011) or Europe (Abramson and Boix 2019), as opposed to globally. That is a worthy tradeoff. After all, many historically inclined political economists as ourselves would argue that explanations for levels of development around the world may be more continent-specific than some political economists would like to believe.

Second, we noted that mainstream institutionalist explanations for development, especially in economics, take a strikingly limited view of public policy, asserting that the main responsibility of the government is to not infringe on property rights and to constrain itself. The state is at best a passive and indirect enabler of growth when it creates the right legal framework for market competition. In reality, history shows us that political leaders have often engaged in active economic and industrial policy—sometimes successfully and other times not—to gain political legitimacy and reelection through economic growth (e.g., from democracies like Norway to dictatorships like China), and to reduce national security threats thanks to a more developed industry (e.g., South Korea, Israel).

That most developed countries today used industrial policy tools such as tariffs and subsidies is beyond dispute, even if many most scholars have overlooked it.[5] The difficult questions to answer are the extent to which these tools fostered or hindered growth in general and why these efforts fostered growth in some cases and hindered it in others. We emphasize that state-led efforts to develop infant industries and gain comparative advantage in high-value-added industries seem to have often succeeded in high-capacity states but not in low-capacity states. Some have argued that this may account for the failures of most Latin American and African governments at actively engineering development (Kohli 2004).

Future research should try to understand the processes through which different types of countries have attempted to find locally effective means to grow. This agenda could include a large body of comparative case studies and analytic narratives that consider instances of policy and institutional experimentation and change. The ultimate goal is to understand how domestic politics and foreign pressures condition the collective design, iteration, and adaptation of policies and institutions as societies meander in their pursuit of economic prosperity.

A promising and related agenda for future research would consider the policy mix pursued in "positive-deviance" countries that overcame persistence and converged to higher living standards. Leveraging microeconomic empirical tools to assess within-country causal effects would help to adequately identify the merits of different policy interventions (Mitrunen 2021; Lane 2022; Liu 2022) and avoid extrapolating biased lessons. For HPE scholars in particular, a similarly rigorous agenda would estimate the effects of developmental policies of Western countries in their pre-industrial phase to understand whether it induced their economic takeoff.

The body of causally identified "micro" contributions, historical and contemporary, must continue to grow to support or challenge existing narratives that incorporate the state (e.g., Gerschenkron 1962; Wade 2004). HPE scholars should evaluate how different policies and institutional arrangements interact with largely structural societal characteristics in delivering economic growth. As we continue to learn from an expanding set of empirical findings, the need to revise "standard" theories of development into updated unified frameworks will become increasingly obvious. If one-size-fits-all policies cannot induce long-run growth everywhere, then the more promising task is to understand what size fits where.

Acknowledgments

We thank Saran Touré for providing valuable research assistance.

Notes

1. Grier and Grier (2007) find that economic divergence in the second half of the twentieth century occurred despite policy and institutional convergence. Yet recent contributions point to a possible reversion in these trends starting at the turn of the twenty-first century (Kremer, Willis, and You 2022).
2. For examples of such comprehensive explanations of long-run development, see Sokoloff and Engerman (2000) and Engerman and Sokoloff (2011) concerning the Americas, Abramson and Boix (2019) concerning Europe, and López Jerez (2014) concerning Southeast Asia.
3. Path dependence may lead to persistent multiple equilibria in economic development in the absence of policy intervention (Prebisch 1962; Singer 1950; Krugman 1991; Pierson 2000). Initial economic differences may persist in time for reasons other than their historical motives if economic activity shows increasing returns to scale, allowing early winners to converge to high-productivity equilibria that remain unavailable to others. For example, historic portage sites in the United States remain economically advantaged despite the obsolescence of portage activities (Bleakley and Lin 2012). Such divergences may be robust to sizable shocks. For instance, the relative sizes of Japanese cities, determined by historic "locational fundamentals," were robust to their leveling by Allied aerial bombardments during World War II (Davis and Weinstein 2002). Azariadis and Stachurski (2005) offer a thorough literature review on the related concept of "poverty traps"—the idea that poor countries are stuck in vicious circles that keep them from converging to higher income levels.

4. Specifically, Evans (1995) argues that the success of the developmental state in East Asia was due to its "embedded autonomy"—the independence, capacity, and interconnectedness of the bureaucrat class in charge of promoting industrialization to lead a dialogue with society about its economic goals and the policies to achieve them.
5. Chang (2007, xxiv) notes that "not all countries have succeeded through protection and subsidies, but few have done so without them."

References

Abramson, Scott. and Carles Boix. 2019. "Endogenous Parliaments: The Domestic and International Roots of Long-Term Economic Growth and Executive Constraints in Europe." *International Organization* 73, no. 4: 793–837.

Acemoglu, Daron, and Melissa Dell. 2010. "Productivity Differences between and within Countries." *American Economic Journal: Macroeconomics* 2, no. 1: 169–88.

Acemoglu, Daron, Simon Johnson, and James A. Robinson. 2001. "The Colonial Origins of Comparative Development: An Empirical Investigation." *American Economic Review* 91, no. 5: 1369–401.

Acemoglu, Daron, Simon Johnson, and James A. Robinson. 2002. "Reversal of Fortune: Geography and Institutions in the Making of the Modern World Income Distribution." *Quarterly Journal of Economics* 117, no. 4: 1231–94.

Alsan, Marcella. 2015. "The Effect of the Tsetse Fly on African Development." *American Economic Review* 105, no. 1: 382–410.

Azariadis, Costas, and John Stachurski. 2005. "Poverty Traps." *Handbook of Economic Growth*, 1, 295–384.

Bairoch, Paul. 1995. *Economics and World History: Myths and Paradoxes*. Chicago: University of Chicago Press.

Barro, Robert J. 2001. "Human Capital and Growth." *American Economic Review* 912: 12–17.

Becker, Sascha O., Erik Hornung, and Ludger Woessmann. 2011. "Education and Catch-Up in the Industrial Revolution." *American Economic Journal: Macroeconomics* 3, no. 3: 92–126.

Bell, Daniel A. 2015. *The China Model: Political Meritocracy and the Limits of Democracy*. Princeton: Princeton University Press.

Besley, Timothy, and Torsten Persson. 2009. "The Origins of State Capacity: Property Rights, Taxation, and Politics." *American Economic Review* 99, no. 4: 1218–44.

Bleakley, Hoyt, and Jeffrey Lin. 2012. "Portage and Path Dependence." *Quarterly Journal of Economics* 127, no. 2: 587–644.

Canen, Nathan, and Leonard Wantchekon, 2022. "Political Distortions, State Capture, and Economic Development in Africa." *Journal of Economic Perspectives* 36, no. 1 (Winter 2022): 101–24.

Cantoni, Davide, and Noah Yuchtman. 2014. "Medieval Universities, Legal Institutions, and the Commercial Revolution." *Quarterly Journal of Economics* 129, no. 2: 823–87.

Chang, Ha-Joon. 2002. *Kicking Away the Ladder: Development Strategy in Historical Perspective*. London: Anthem Press.

Chang, Ha-Joon. 2007. *Bad Samaritans: Rich Nations, Poor Policies, and the Threat to the Developing World*. London: Random House Business.

Chen, Ye, Hongbin Li, and Li-An Zhou. 2005. "Relative Performance Evaluation and the Turnover of Provincial Leaders in China." *Economics Letters* 88, no. 3: 421–25.

Clark, Gregory. 2007. *A Farewell to Alms: A Brief Economic History of the World*. Princeton, NJ: Princeton University Press.

Collier, Paul. 2007. *The Bottom Billion: Why the Poorest Countries Are Failing and What Can Be Done about It*. New York: Oxford University Press.

Davis, Donald R., and David E. Weinstein. 2002. "Bones, Bombs, and Break Points: The Geography of Economic Activity." *American Economic Review* 92, no. 5: 1269–89.

De Bary, William Theodore. 2000. *Asian Values and Human Rights: A Confucian Communitarian Perspective*. Cambridge, MA: Harvard Univ. Press.

Dell, Melissa. 2010. "The Persistent Effects of Peru's Mining Mita." Econometrica 78, no. 6: 1863–903.

Dell, Melissa, and Benjamin A. Olken. 2019. "The Development Effects of the Extractive Colonial Economy: The Dutch Cultivation System in Java." *Review of Economic Studies* 87, no. 1: 164–203.

De Long, J. Bradford, and Andrei Shleifer. 1993. "Princes and Merchants: European City Growth before the Industrial Revolution." *Journal of Law and Economics* 36, no. 2: 671–702.

De Mesquita, Bruce Bueno, Alastair Smith, Randolph M. Siverson, and James D. Morrow. 2003. *The Logic of Political Survival*. Cambridge, MA: MIT Press.

Diamond, Jared M. 1997. *Guns, Germs, and Steel: The Fates of Human Societies*. New York: W. W. Norton.

Engerman, Stanley L., and Kenneth L. Sokoloff. 2011. *Economic Development in the Americas since 1500: Englebert Institutions*. Cambridge University Press.

Englebert, Pierre. 2002. *State Legitimacy and Development in Africa*. Lynne Rienner Publishers.

Evans, Peter. B. 1995. *Embedded Autonomy: States and Industrial Transformation*. Princeton, NJ: Princeton University Press.

Franck, Raphael, and Ilia Rainer. 2012. "Does the Leader's Ethnicity Matter? Ethnic Favoritism, Education, and Health in Sub-Saharan Africa." *American Political Science Review* 106, no. 2: 294–325.

Gallup, John Luke, and J. D. Sachs. 2001. "The Economic Burden of Malaria." CID Working Paper Series.

Gallup, J. L., Jeffrey D. Sachs, and Andrew D. Mellinger. 1999. "Geography and Economic Development." *International Regional Science Review* 22, no. 2: 179–232.

Galor, Oded. 2005. "From Stagnation to Growth: Unified Growth Theory". *Handbook of Economic Growth*, 1, 171–293.

Gerschenkron, Alexander. 1962. *Economic Backwardness in Historical Perspective: A Book of Essays*. Cambridge, MA: Belknap Press of Harvard University Press.

Glaeser, Edward L., Rafael La Porta, Florencio Lopez-de-Silanes, and Andrei Shleifer. 2004. "Do Institutions Cause Growth?" *Journal of Economic Growth* 9, no. 3: 271–303.

Greif, Avner, and Guido Tabellini 2010. "Cultural and Institutional Bifurcation: China and Europe Compared. *American Economic Review* 100, no. 2: 135–40.

Grier, Kevin, and Robin Grier. 2007. "Only Income Diverges: A Neoclassical Anomaly." *Journal of Development Economics* 84, no. 1: 25–45.

Halevi, Nadav. 2008. "A Brief Economic History of Modern Israel." EH. Net Encyclopedia. URL: https://eh.net/encyclopedia/a-brief-economic-history-of-modern-israel/.

Hamilton, Alexander. 1791. *Report on the Subject of Manufactures*. Syrett HC et al. 1966: *The Papers of Alexander Hamilton*, 10: 230–340.

Hornung, Erik. 2014. "Immigration and the Diffusion of Technology: The Huguenot Diaspora in Prussia." *American Economic Review* 104, no. 1: 84–122.

Jones, Charles I., and Paul M. Romer. 2010. "The New Kaldor Facts: Ideas, Institutions, Population, and Human Capital." *American Economic Journal: Macroeconomics* 2, no. 1: 224–45.

Kelly, Morgan, Joel Mokyr, and Cormac O'Grada. 2014. "Precocious Albion: A New Interpretation of the British Industrial Revolution." Available at SSRN 2319855.

Kohli, Atul. 2004. *State-Directed Development: Political Power and Industrialization in the Global Periphery*. Cambridge: Cambridge University Press.

Koyama, Mark, and Jared Rubin. 2022. *How the World Became Rich: The Historical Origins of Economic Growth*, Cambridge, UK: Polity Press.

Kremer, Michael, Jack Willis, and Yang You. 2022. "Converging to Convergence." NBER Macroeconomics Annual 36, no. 1: 337–412.

Krugman, Paul. 1991. "Increasing Returns and Economic Geography." *Journal of Political Economy* 99, no. 3: 483–99.

Laitin, David D., Joachim Moortgat, and Amanda L. Robinson. 2012. "Geographic Axes and the Persistence of Cultural Diversity." *Proceedings of the National Academy of Sciences* 109, no. 26: 10263–68.

Lane, Nathan. 2022. "Manufacturing Revolutions: Industrial Policy and Industrialization in South Korea." Available at SSRN 3890311.

La Porta, Rafael, Florencio Lopez-de-Silanes, Andrei Shleifer, and Robert W. Vishny. 1998. "Law and Finance." *Journal of Political Economy* 106, no. 6: 1113–55.

Lee, Kuan Yew. 1998. *The Singapore Story: Memoirs of Lee Kuan Yew*. Prentice Hall.

Lin, Justin Y., Fang Cai, and Zhou Li. 2003. *The China Miracle: Development Strategy and Economic Reform*. Revised ed. Hong Kong: Chinese University of Hong Kong Press.

Lipset, Seymour Martin. 1959 "Some Social Requisites of Democracy: Economic Development and Political Legitimacy." *American Political Science Review* 53, no. 1: 69–105.

Liu, Ernest. 2022. "Industrial Policies in Production Networks." *Quarterly Journal of Economics* 134, no. 4: 1883–948.

López Jerez, Montserrat. 2014. "Deltas Apart-Factor Endowments, Colonial Extraction and Pathways of Agricultural Development in Vietnam." Doctoral thesis, Lund University.

Malthus, Thomas. 1798. *An Essay on the Principle of Population*. London: J. Johnson.

Mattingly, Daniel. 2017. "Colonial Legacies and State Institutions in China: Evidence from a Natural Experiment." *Comparative Political Studies* 50, no. 4: 434–63.

Michalopoulos, Stelios, and Elias Papaioannou. 2014. "National Institutions and Subnational Development in Africa." *Quarterly Journal of Economics* 129, no. 1: 151–213.

Milward, Alan, and Samuel Berrick. Saul. 1973. *The Economic Development of Continental Europe, 1780–1870*. Rowman and Littlefield.

Milward, Alan S. (Alan Steele), Saul, S. B. (Samuel Berrick). 1977. *The Development of the Economies of Continental Europe, 1850–1914*. London: Allen & Unwin.

Mitrunen, Matti. 2021. "Structural Change and Intergenerational Mobility: Evidence from the Finnish War Reparations." Unpublished. IIES Stockholm.

Mokyr, Joel. 2002. *The Gifts of Athena: Historical Origins of the Knowledge Economy*. Princeton, NJ: Princeton University Press.

Moser, Petra, Alessandra Voena, and Fabian Waldinger. 2014. "German Jewish Émigrés and US Invention." *American Economic Review* 104, no. 10: 3222–55.

Nisbett, Richard. 2004. *The Geography of Thought: How Asians and Westerners Think Differently . . . and Why*. New York: Simon and Schuster.

North, Douglass C. 1990. *Institutions, Institutional Change and Economic Performance*. New York: Cambridge University Press.

North, Douglass C. 1993. "Douglass C. North Prize Lecture: Economic Performance through Time." Nobel Prize Lecture, December, 9.

North, Douglass C., and Robert Paul Thomas 1973. *The Rise of the Western World: A New Economic History*. New York: Cambridge University Press.

North, Douglass C., and Barry R. Weingast 1989. "Constitutions and Commitment: The Evolution of Institutions Governing Public Choice in Seventeenth-Century England." *Journal of Economic History* 49, no. 4: 803–32.

Olson, Mancur. 1993. "Dictatorship, Democracy, and Development." *American Political Science Review* 87, no. 3: 567–76.

Page, John. 1994. "The East Asian Miracle: Four Lessons for Development Policy." *NBER Macroeconomics Annual* 9: 219–69.

Pavlik, Jamie Bologna, and Andrew T. Young. 2019. "Did Technology Transfer More Rapidly East–West Than North–South?" *European Economic Review* 119: 216–35.

Pierson, Paul. 2000. "Increasing Returns, Path Dependence, and the Study of Politics." *American Political Science Review* 94, no. 2: 251–67.

Pomeranz, Kenneth. 2000. *The Great Divergence. China, Europe, and the Making of the Modern World Economy*. Princeton, NJ: Princeton University Press.

Prebisch, Raul. 1962. "The Economic Development of Latin America and Its Principal Problems." *Economic Bulletin for Latin America*. Vol. VII, No. 1:1-22.

Pritchett, Lant. 1997. "Divergence, Big Time." *Journal of Economic Perspectives* 11, no. 3: 3–17.

Queralt, Didac. 2022. *Pawned States: State Building in the Era of International Finance*. Princeton, NJ: Princeton University Press.

Ricart-Huguet, Joan. 2021. "Colonial Education, Political Elites, and Regional Political Inequality in Africa." *Comparative Political Studies* 54, no. 14: 2546–80.

Rodrik, Dani. 2006. "Goodbye Washington Consensus, Hello Washington Confusion? A Review of the World Bank's Economic Growth in the 1990s: Learning from a Decade of Reform." *Journal of Economic Literature* 44, no. 4: 973–87.

Romer, Paul. 2010. "Technologies, Rules, and Progress: The Case for Charter Cities." (No. id: 2471). Washington, DC: Center for Global Development Essay

Rosenstein-Rodan, Paul. N. 1943. "Problems of Industrialisation of Eastern and South-Eastern Europe." *Economic Journal* 53, no. 210/211: 202–11.

Scheve, Kenneth, and David Stasavage. 2010. "The Conscription of Wealth: Mass Warfare and the Demand for Progressive Taxation." *International Organization* 64, no. 4: 529–61.

Singer, Hans. W. 1950. "The Distribution of Gains between Borrowing and Investing Countries." *American Economic Review* 40, no. 2: 473–85.

Sokoloff, Kenneth L., and Stanley L. Engerman. 2000. "Institutions, Factor Endowments, and Paths of Development in the New World." *Journal of Economic Perspectives* 14, no. 3: 217–32.

Solow, Robert M. 1956. "A Contribution to the Theory of Economic Growth." *Quarterly Journal of Economics* 70, no. 1: 65–94.

Squicciarini, Mara P., and Nico Voigtländer. 2015. "Human Capital and Industrialization: Evidence from the Age of Enlightenment." *Quarterly Journal of Economics* 130, no. 4: 1825–83.

Studwell, Joe. 2014. *How Asia Works: Success and Failure in the World's Most Dynamic Region*. New York: Grove Press.

Tilly, Charles. 1992. *Coercion, Capital, and European States, AD 990–1992*. Revised paperback ed. Malden, MA: Blackwell Publishing.

Valencia Caicedo, Felipe. 2019. "The Mission: Human Capital Transmission, Economic Persistence, and Culture in South America." *Quarterly Journal of Economics* 134, no. 1: 507–56.

Wade, Robert. 1990. "Bringing the State Back In: Lessons from East Asia's Development Experience." *Internationale Politik und Gesellschaft* 8, no. 2: 98–115.

Wade, Robert. 2004. *Governing the Market: Economic Theory and the Role of Government in East Asian Industrialization*. Princeton, NJ: Princeton University Press.

Wantchekon, Leonard, Marko Klašnja, and Natalija Novta. 2015. "Education and Human Capital Externalities: Evidence from Colonial Benin." *Quarterly Journal of Economics* 130, no. 2: 703–57.

Widner, Jennifer A. 1994. "Political Reform in Anglophone and Francophone African Countries." In *Economic and Political Liberalization in Sub-Saharan Africa*, ed. Jennifer A. Widner, 49–79. Baltimore: The Johns Hopkins University Press.

Woo, Jung-En. 1992. *Race to the Swift: State and Finance in Korean Industrialization*. New York: Columbia University Press.

World Bank. 2020. GDP per capita, ppp (Current international $) | data. (n.d.). Retrieved July 6, 2022, from https://data.worldbank.org/indicator/NY.GDP.PCAP.PP.CD?most_recent_value_desc=tru.

CHAPTER 27

THE HISTORICAL POLITICAL ECONOMY OF NATIONALISM

CARLES BOIX

WRITING thirty years ago, Benedict Anderson lamented that "in contrast to the immense influence that nationalism has exerted on the modern world, plausible theory about it is conspicuously meagre" (Anderson 1983, 3). Paradoxically, Anderson's complaint coincided with a flurry of works on the question of nationalism and national identity—from Breuilly's *Nationalism and the State* (1982), Ernest Gellner's *Nations and Nationalism* (1983), the English translation of Hroch's *Social Preconditions of National Revival in Europe* (1985), and E. J. Hobsbawn's *Nations and Nationalism since 1780* (1990) to Liah Greenfeld's *Nationalism* (1992).

That generation of scholars coincided in developing what has become the canonical answer on the birth of national identities and nationalism along three main theoretical propositions. First, questioning a commonly accepted view of nations as long-standing, natural phenomena, rooted in fixed characteristics (from language to ethnicity), they defined nations as cultural *constructs*. Second, they understood them as *modern* inventions or constructs. Before modernity, individuals had no national identity as we understand it today. Gellner, for example, insisted "on the dormant nature of this allegedly powerful monster [nationalism] during the pre-industrial age" (1983, 43). Or, as Anderson put it, "the very possibility of imagining the nation only arose historically when, and where, three fundamental cultural conceptions [a sacral society; the pre-eminence of monarchy; a certain conception of time], all of great antiquity, lost their axiomatic grip on men's minds" (1983, 36). Third, modern nations *were constructed by* "nationalist" agents. Nations were inventions of nationalism. A noted by Gellner (1983), "the 'age of nationalism' is [not] a mere summation of the awakening and political self-assertion of this, that, or the other nation" (55); rather, nationalism "engenders nations," imposing on a community a certain conception of itself.

In this chapter, I revisit that canonical account, pointing out its shortcomings, and then suggest a number of changes to build a more plausible theory of nationalism. Accordingly, the first section reviews "hard" constructivist theories that see nationalism as the result of deliberate or semideliberate actions of (nationalist) elites to meet some set of instrumental or functional needs. The next section turns to discuss "soft" constructivist explanations that stress the way in which modernity drew people into sharing a sense of belonging into a particular "imagined community" and, as a result, a national identity. In the following sections, I offer an explanation that better fits with the historical record. Nationhood was, at least initially, embedded within the emancipatory political project of the Atlantic revolutions of the late eighteenth century that implied both the destruction of the corporatist model of ancien régime societies and its substitution by a "liberal" order, that is, an abstract society of politically equal individuals. When that "liberal" project succeeded, political borders became congruent with national identity, leading to a unified nation state. By contrast, the failure of that liberal project, normally at the hands of its nemesis, a conservative national project, resulted in the rise of separate nationalist claims in the country's peripheries. I conclude by stressing the proposition that there have been several variations of modern nationalisms with different ideational contents—ranging from liberal patriotism to revanchism and chauvinism—due to the particular political (domestic and international) circumstances that engendered them.

Hard Constructivism: Economic Modernization and Strategic "Nationalist" Elites

The canonical literature on nationalism is adamant about the constructed nature of nations. "Neither nations nor states," Gellner writes, "exist at all times and in all circumstances." They are not "an inherent attribute of humanity," even though they "now come to appear as such," but are "contingent" phenomena (Gellner 1983, 6). For Anderson (1983) too, nations are "cultural artifacts" rather than fixed, immutable entities. As discussed in Greenfeld (1992), the meaning itself of the world "nation" changed over time. Used first as a derogatory term applied to foreigners in classical Rome, then employed to design communities of university students of different geographical origins living in medieval Paris, it was later applied to representatives in church councils, only taking its current meaning with the advent of political modernity (Greenfeld 1992, 3–5).

Nations were, in addition, modern constructs, impossible to imagine in premodern societies. In Gellner's account, pre-industrial economies were fundamentally divided between a ruling class and a mass of laborers toiling the land within the logic of a subsistence economy. Organized in "laterally separated petty communities," those peasants lived "inward-turned lives," "tied to the locality by economic need if not by political prescription." Marked by "dialectal and other differences," they could not have had any consciousness of belonging to a broader political community and even less so of having a particular "national" identity (Gellner 1983, 10). The ruling class was, by contrast, in possession of its own "high" unified culture. Yet it had neither the economic incentives nor the bureaucratic resources to impose "on all levels of society a universalized clerisy and a homogeneity with centralized norms, fortified by writing" (17). Although stressing the role of ideational factors, Anderson reaches similar conclusions. Before the Enlightenment, societal discourse, structured around "a particular script-language [offering] privileged access to ontological truth" (Anderson 1983, 36), emphasized the universality of norms and adscriptions, forestalling the possibility of separate territories legitimized by different laws. Politics, organized around a sacred ruler, could not have a secular basis, rendering nationalism as something unimaginable.

These different canonical authors parted ways, however, in their timing of the invention of the modern idea of the nation. For Gellner (1983), national identities and nationalism emerged within a broad time span defined by the effects and needs of the Scientific Revolution and industrialization. In Benedict Anderson's account, nations were "created toward the end of the eighteenth century" (1983, 4). For Greenfeld (1992), the modern nation was born earlier, in sixteenth-century England, then spreading, through a process of imitation and emulation, to other regions of the world.

They also (and relatedly) differed in identifying the nature and agency of the "nationalist elites" that created or at least midwifed national identities. For a broad range of authors whom Motyl (2002) labels as "hard" constructivists, nations appeared as a product of the instrumental or strategic actions of elites. In Hobsbawn, states cultivated (and inculcated) nationalist sentiments to prop up their legitimacy (Hobsbawn 1990, 80ff.).[1] In Gellner, political elites were key agents in the construction of nations even though they might "know not what they do" (Gellner 1983, 49). Nationalism, in his account, fulfilled a key functional requirement of an industrial society that had brought about a crucial transformation of human behavior. With industrialization, the old, premodern individual gave way to a rational individual, interested in developing scientific explanations about the world, and, above all, moved by the principle of profit maximization (21–23). That new industrial order required a system of universal education in which everyone received a standardized set of skills for the purposes of manipulating meanings instead of things. "Most jobs," Gellner writes, "if not actually involving work 'with people', involve the control of buttons or switches or levers which need to be *understood*, and are explicable, once again, in some standard idiom intelligible to all comers" (33). Communication became central to the life and efficient performance of industrial society. In turn, that standardized system of communication shared by everyone could "only be provided by something resembling a modern 'national' education system" (34), established by the state, and imposing "a school-mediated, academy-supervised idiom" for the purposes of "reasonably precise bureaucratic and technological communication" (57). That, in turn, led to a level of cultural homogeneity that "eventually appears on the surface in the form of nationalism" (39).

These explanations face, however, several shortcomings. Here I discuss four of them:[2]

1. They do not match our historical record for three reasons.

    First, industrialization played no crucial role in the emergence of the first modern national identities. The United States in the 1770s, France in the 1780s, and Latin America in the early nineteenth century were agrarian societies. It is true that Gellner already claimed in his 1964 book Thought and Change that the concept of industrialization referred to technological change and to the fact that our contemporary era is defined "not [by] industry but science" (Szporluk 1998, 25). Industrialization and modernization "are to be distinguished," according to Gellner, "as the narrower and wider aspects of the same phenomenon. Industrialisation proper may be preceded—in certain odd cases followed—by the trappings, terminology, expectations, slogans of industrial society. A complex of such anticipatory borrowings may have almost as much impact on a society as the thing itself."[3] Nonetheless, even if we were to embrace the rather broad concept of modernization as technical and scientific change, we still could not make sense of the modern nationalist sentiments (as constructed by their agents) that arose on the Atlantic seaboard more than two centuries ago. If anything, they were sparked by the promise of political emancipation, which had little to do with fulfilling the functional needs of an industrial economy.

Second, the thesis of nationalism as the impulse (or the culmination) of modernization sits uneasily with one important facet of modern nationalism: the rise of reactionary national ideologies, such as those espoused by nineteenth-century Russian slavophiles (Greenfeld 1992, 250ff.), Spanish conservatives (Krauel 2013), or recent Islamic fundamentalism (Lynch 2007).

Finally, a number of scholars have challenged the notion that the ideas of nation and national identity are strictly modern or contemporaneous—see Smith (1989) and the authors referenced in Mylonas and Tudor (2021, 113). Pericles's "Funeral Oration" in Thucydides's *War of the Peloponnesus* appealed to the political self-consciousness of the Athenian citizenry. Italian republican thinkers, even those preceding Machiavelli, talked about political communities in a way closer to the modern concept of nationhood (Skinner 1978). The Polish nobility imagined itself as a nation before Poland's partitions (Walicki 1997). Now, the purpose of these examples is not to deny that nationalism, understood as a claim to establish a sovereign political community in a well-defined territory or, to use Gellner's terms, as the "principle which holds that the political and the national unit should be congruent," (1) was a modern idea. However, the full examination of modern nationalism requires understanding how (and with what effects) it interacted with existing conceptions of what hard constructivists refer to as, at most, protonational communities.

2. Cultural and linguistic standardization does not seem essential to industrialization and growth. Contra Gellner, national markets have ended up being of different sizes, making it impossible to maintain that governments and industrialists invested in the construction of an "optimal" economic area. In addition, some of them, like Switzerland, maintained several languages and communication spaces.
3. Perhaps more importantly, hard constructivists rely on debatable behavioral assumptions, modeling elites as rational and strategic while denying any ideational abilities and political agency to non-elites. According to most canonical accounts, "premodern" individuals were blank slates or, to use Marx's terms, "the

simple addition of homonymous magnitudes, much as potatoes in a sack form a sack of potatoes," to the point that "their interests form[ed] no community, no national bond" (Marx 1994 [1852], 124).[4] Governments then instilled a national identity, through mass education, military conscription, and the standardization of linguistic and bureaucratic practices across the territory under their control. Now, if all that it takes to create a national identity is for state actors to ingrain it in the empty minds of illiterate peasants, then all state-sponsored national conceptions should have succeeded. Yet, historically, that is not how things played out across Europe and the world. In some instances, state elites succeeded. Eugene Weber's account of the transformation of France's peasants "into Frenchmen" is a case in point (Weber 1976). In many other instances, however, they failed to build a unified nation state in spite of having a well-defined national project.[5] That failure implies that Gellner's masses (or, for that matter, Marx's potatoes) intentionally chose not to assimilate to the ruling elites' "high culture."

4. The (varying) justifications developed by hard constructivists to explain the failure of state-led nationalism are not persuasive. Initially, Gellner (1964) attributed the emergence of "peripheral" nationalisms to the "uneven diffusion" of modernization and industrialization across nations. Yet such an explanation cannot account for the emergence of national claims of Greeks, Polish, or South Americans: their economies (agrarian with a smallish commercial class) were almost identical to those of their Turkish, Russian, and Spanish masters. Two decades later, in *Nations and Nationalism*, Gellner turned to stress the role of exclusion and the lack of social mobility in the rise of nationalism. Peripheral elites agitated for political independence, imbuing the peasants of their region with the sense of a separate national identity "where 'ethnic' (cultural or other diacritical marks) [were] visible and accentuate[d] the differences in educational access and power" and inhibited the "free flow of personnel across the loose lines of social stratification" (1983, 96). This explanation, however, stands in opposition to Gellner's assertion that modern nation-builders could "invent" their nations and nation states or even the more modest claim that the functional needs of modernization gave them an incentive to nationalize everyone (something akin to not excluding anyone).[6]

Soft Constructivism: Cultural Modernization and the Rise of National Communities

As in the literature reviewed so far, Benedict Anderson understood modernization as a necessary condition for nationalism to happen. Yet his book *Imagined Communities* (1983) departs from "hard" constructivism in two ways. In the first place, it predicates a "soft" version of constructivism that does not require the deliberate, strategic action of elites to elicit a national identity. The latter emerges, instead, endogenously, "almost as an unintended consequence of the actions of human beings rooted in concrete social and historical situations" (Motyl 2002, 60).[7] In the second place, *Imagined Communities* replaces technological and economic modernization with cultural and ideational modernization defined by the secularization of religious and political authority, the conceptual transformation of time, and the "vernacularization" of languages. It was in that new context that the printing technology spurred the formation of horizontal community of readers. "The newspaper of Caracas [or any other provincial capital]," Anderson writes while discussing the stirrings of Creole nationalism, "quite naturally, and even apolitically, created an imagined community among a specific assemblage of fellow-readers, to whom *these* ships, brides, bishops and princes belonged" (1983, 62). Then, in due time, "it was only to be expected that political elements would enter in" (62) giving birth to "an imagined political community—and imagined as both inherently limited and sovereign" (6).[8]

As acknowledged by Anderson, print capitalism acted as a necessary but not sufficient condition to trigger the emergence of a specific national consciousness. In the Americas, the formation of several nations derived from preexisting administrative provinces within which their respective creole elites developed a sense of "shared interests": controlling the colonial bureaucracy and tearing down the barriers to social and political ascent imposed by the metropolis. The revolutionary impulses of both San Martín and Bolívar were rooted in the disdain and sense of superiority with which Spanish high society treated them while they lived in Madrid (Anderson 1983, 57n34). Likewise, Washington became a supporter of independence once he was prevented from becoming a British officer and his London providers charged him for overpriced dresses and furniture (Chernow 2010).

To explain the rise of nineteenth-century European nationalisms, Anderson shifts track, however, substituting European linguistic discontinuities for American administrative borders. Once "the old sacred languages—Latin, Greek, and Hebrew—gave way to a motley plebeian crowd of vernacular rivals" (Anderson 1983, 70), the outcome of a plurality of nation states was only a matter of time. Internal nationalist conflicts became rampant, and if they did not happen in Britain and France, it was because "for quite extraneous reasons, there happened to be, by mid-[eighteenth] century, a relatively high coincidence of language-of-state and language of population" (78). Otherwise, and "Austro-Hungary is probably the polar example, the consequences were inevitably explosive" (78). The vernacular chosen as official language "promised enormous advantages to those of its subjects who *already* used that print-language" but "appeared correspondingly menacing to those who did not" (78).

Linguistic differences (or barriers) could not have been, however, the reason behind Europe's national fragmentation (across and within existing states). First, France was not unified linguistically as late as the 1880s or even later. Basque, Bretton, Catalan, and Provençal were spoken by the majority of the population in wide parts of the Hexagon (Weber 1976). Writing in a different language did not create any differentiated national consciousness necessarily. The Félibriges that cultivated poetry in Oc were content with belonging to the Republic (Rafanell 2006). Second, multilingual states seem to become fairly stable once they provide their minorities with reasonable cultural guarantees. Third, the costs of a language switch are not as high as constructivist theories seem to claim. Finally, linguistic practice is often endogenous to national identity—as attested by the experiences of France and the decision of the Zionist movement to revive Hebrew—and not the other way around.

Perhaps aware of the fact that linguistic discontinuity theories lead him into an empirical cul-de-sac, Anderson introduced, mostly as a passing thought, the idea of discrimination and barriers to explain the presence (or absence) of nationalism. In the eighteenth and nineteenth centuries there was no Scottish nationalism because, he writes, "in complete contrast to the Thirteen Colonies, *there were no barricades* on all those pilgrims' [i.e., Scots] paths toward the centre [i.e. sharing in imperial ruling]" (Anderson 1983, 90). By contrast, Slovaks, Indians, and Koreans developed nationalist demands because "they would not be permitted to join pilgrimages which would allow them to administer Magyars, Englishmen or Japanese" (110).

Nonetheless, if "exclusion" was the trigger of nationalism, this does not explain the nationalism of the included, that is, of the "national majorities." Moreover, as in the case of Gellner, it does not offer a plausible theory about why barriers were present in some places and not in others. At the end of the day, what underlays all these shortcomings in the current canon is its relative lack of attention to the inherently political nature of national identities and nationalism—in other words, to the political processes through which nationalism emerged.[9]

The Problem of Political Emancipation and (National) Self-Determination

Two main features define modern politics. First, the construction of sovereign states with an absolute claim over a particular human community, that is, with the capacity to legislate over the rights and obligations of the latter—in opposition to (or to the exclusion of) other states and communities. Second, the development of a legitimation principle (appealing to either the consent or the welfare of the ruled) to justify the claims of that sovereign state. Those two traits imply, almost mechanically, the definition and configuration of a modern "national" community.

A useful starting point to understand the political roots of modern nationalism is the dynamics of the French Revolution and, more specifically, its culminating ideological movement, Jacobinism. Jacobinism, which would also become the seed of all the revolutionary ideals and political tempests of the twentieth century, was, according to François Furet, "the fully developed form of a type of political and social organization that had become widespread in France" (1981, 173) from the 1750s: the "philosophical society."

The philosophical society, manifested in the form of "literary circles and societies, masonic lodges, academies, and patriotic and cultural clubs," was "a form of social life based on the principle that its members, in order to participate in it, must divest themselves of all concrete distinctions and of their real social existence" (174). As such, it "was the opposite of what the Ancien Régime called a corporate entity (*corps*), defined by a community of occupational and social interests" (174).

Even though by 1789 feudalism had been dead for a long time, the prerevolutionary social and political order was an amalgamation of corporate bodies: estates, guilds, cities, religious bodies, and administrative and political districts that retained some jurisdictional autonomy, with their own laws and regulations, rights and duties, and authorities to adjudicate in-house disputes. Internally, all these social groups and organizations were stratified—with masters and apprentices, high and low clergy, different types of nobility, a pyramid of bureaucrats and military officers. Externally, they partly overlapped and at the same time were integrated in some hierarchy of power and influence—derived from tradition, a history of violence, and secular bargaining—topped by a monarchical structure. Traditional society was, in short, "broken up into interest groups and founded on inequality (both as a social reality and as collective mental representation)" (Furet 1981, 179).

By contrast, the philosophical society was a "prefiguration of the functioning of democracy" (Furet 1981, 174)—"an abstract society made up of equal individuals, in other words, a people of voters" (175)—or as Furet writes later, "the philosophical society, being the locus of the general will, was thereby the enunciator of truth" (176). Its self-understanding and internal logic as a body based on the "abstract equality among individuals" (174) provided the impetus to reshape the whole political community, the nation, along the same principle, as a body politic made up of equal individuals.

The members of both philosophical societies and political clubs (mainly those with Jacobin allegiances) reshaped France after their image, pushing for an idea of the nation as a community of equals, through two critical moments. During the first wave of the revolution, from the fall of 1788 to the spring of 1789, the emerging political class destroyed the old model of corporatist representation—doubling of representation of the Third Estate, introducing the principle of one vote per person (rather than one per estate), and forcing the integration of all orders into a single national assembly. That transformation culminated during the second revolutionary wave, in 1793, under "the Jacobin dictatorship, the final avatar of pure democracy" (Furet 1981, 182): the *levée en masse* decreed on August 23, 1793, "implemented the social fiction by which a single collective will was substituted not just in law but in actual fact for each individual will."[10]

After its leaders were arrested and guillotined in the Thermidorian Reaction, Jacobinism collapsed as a concrete partisan project. Yet it succeeded as a constitutional blueprint, as a source of political legitimacy. At least ideationally, it swept away the fragmentary structure of the ancien régime, instead treating everyone as a co-equal—even though the precise definition of equality (formal, substantive) is still being contested today. The state could then bulldoze the interpersonal and institutional differences of the past. Even when it involved violence, that act of destruction became widely acceptable (although certainly not to the old ruling strata) because it involved a political pact that treated everyone in identical terms. According to this (national) pact (or foundational moment), individuals were to be given equal access to their common institutions—in exchange for them renouncing all loyalty to any past (corporate) allegiances. In other words, the Jacobin project entailed and underpinned the emergence of a modern conception of nation.[11]

Two points are in order here. First, the claim made here is not that national identity and nationalism were born in France in 1789. The American Revolution and the forging of a modern American identity preceded the French Revolution. Likewise, one may plausibly argue that the first signs of a modern national self-consciousness appeared during the Dutch war of independence in the late sixteenth century (Gorski 2000; Appelbaum 2013) and the English Civil War (Greenfeld 1992). However, the French Revolution, as seen through the eyes of Cochin and Furet, provides a sharp example of the political principles invented under the Enlightenment and then progressively played out around the globe—mostly through bourgeois revolutions (in the West and its offshoots) in the nineteenth century, then through socialist revolutions during the twentieth century.

Second, a broader literature on identity has insisted that individuals and human groups have (and can be) organized according to a wide range of overlapping identities such as race, tribe, or ethnicity that are both highly contingent in their foundations and varying in their political salience. Applying that literature to nationalism, some conclude that "nations and nationalism were not inevitable" (Mylonas and Tudor 2021: 114). Indeed, the features around which national claims were constructed could have been different from what they ended up being at the time those claims originated: the organizing principles of each national identity varied as a function of each country's pre-liberal institutions and culture, the strength of the liberal push, and so on. However, the breakdown of the old political order made nationalism as a political category inevitable: the idea of nation was consubstantial to the construction of—or even simply the aspirations engendered by—a modern political order.

MAKING THE NATIONAL AND THE POLITICAL CONGRUENT, PART 1: NATION STATES

At the time of the diffusion of the liberal blueprint, the Westphalian international order was fully entrenched. Even though states were still organized internally as a composite of occupational and social corporations, they controlled well-defined territories with recognized borders. From a philosophical point of view, liberal agents did not question directly the international status quo. French revolutionaries debated the limits of France's "grande nation," eventually settling for the natural borders of the Pyrenees, the Alps, and the Rhine. Yet they had no serious cosmopolitan plan or discussion about imagining Europe as the political community of reference, sharing in equal rights and a constitution. Some politicians, mostly Girondins, called for the creation of a network of sister republics in the periphery of France, a defensive glacis against absolutist powers (Godechot 1956, chapter 3). Nevertheless, this was as far as they went in using the new concept of a modern national compact to "reimagine" political borders and the international order. Liberal revolutions had to happen endogenously in each sovereign state.[12]

With borders essentially frozen (or driven by realpolitik, i.e., war), the fortunes of the liberal project within each country defined the nature of the emerging national community—in other words, of the number of competing national claims within the existing sovereign unit. The full success of the liberal project made possible the construction of an undivided nation: it involved, as emphasized earlier, the substitution of a community of equals for the old social order of inequalities. The American War of Independence, the French Revolution, the Swiss Civil War of 1848, and maybe England's 1640 Revolution (see Greenfeld 1992, 70ff.) are examples of successful liberal transformations and unified national identities. Among them, France stands out as the most successful story of national construction—precisely because it need not have ended up the way it is today. On the eve of the French Revolution, France was extremely fragmented institutionally—with powerful regional parliéments and a diverse assortment of territorial structures and bodies. Its level of linguistic diversity was close to the average African country today. Its economic and social integration was low (Weber 1976). Then the revolutionary shock of 1789–1793 broke down the old social order. The construction of a unified nation certainly took time, but, over the course of the nineteenth century, the liberal credo and its insistence on civil equality and mobility within the bureaucracy eventually became hegemonic.

The liberal revolutionary project did not entail any particular respect to cultural, ethnic, or linguistic minorities. Thinking otherwise comes from projecting into the past our understanding of contemporary liberalism as a "multicultural" project. French revolutionaries had as their goal to emancipate individuals by obliterating any political tie between them and any other community besides the nation. In the discussion on whether to grant full citizenship to French Jews, Clermont-Tonnerre, one the leading advocates of Jewish emancipation, stated before the National Assembly that the former "could be considered as a nation or as individuals." As a nation with their own laws and institutions, he added, "we should . . . deny everything to Jews" because they would be negating the very precondition of their freedom: the French nation. As individuals, however, the National Assembly "should . . . grant everything to Jews," that is, the same rights as non-Jews.[13] Likewise, the state would deliberately coerce non-French-speaking populations to learn and use French to make them, so the justification went, free and equal. Children caught using non-French languages were sent to clean out the school latrine, put on aeat diet of dry bread and water, or forced to hold out a wooden plank or a brick at arm's length until they denounced another child for not speaking French (Weber 1976, 313). In 1854, Marseillais historian François Mazuy wrote, "French is for us a language imposed by right of conquest."[14] Yet resistance was low: the promise of equality must have persuaded provincial elites, who in other countries organized periphery nationalisms, to become French.

Making the National and the Political Congruent, Part 2: The Path to Political Fragmentation

The liberal project—or to use Barrington Moore's term, the "bourgeois revolution," intent on the creation of a constitutional order establishing "an objective system of law that at least in theory confers no special privileges on account of birth or inherited status" (Moore 1966, 429)—was met with immediate resistance by key players in ancien régime societies. After all, political modernization implied the loss of all their privileges, the disappearance of all the principles that legitimized their status, and, in a word, their dissolution into the abstract society of the Enlightenment philosophers.

That political resistance often involved the construction of an alternative vision of nationhood.[15] Conservatives (here understood as those opposed to the liberal blueprint) developed a national discourse that understood the mores and institutions challenged by "Jacobinism" as rooted in a preexisting "national" community defined by a set of fixed or natural characteristics: either a religious faith, a common ethnic origin, a specific language, or a particular set of laws upheld by the traditional (monarchical) order. The conservative response to liberalism was possible because, as Motyl (2002) insists, the advent of a modern national identity did not happen in an ideational tabula rasa in which political agents at the center or outside could deliberately (Hobsbawn, Gellner) or unconsciously (Anderson) impose an identity. Ancien Régime societies may have lacked any national self-consciousness as we understand it today. Nonetheless, they housed some kind of proto-national belief system—"a special kind of set of intersubjectively held propositions" in the sense of being "a coherent package of propositions relating to origins and boundaries" (Motyl 2002, 67) or, in Anthony Smith's terms, "durable cultural communities" (1989, 344)—from which conservatives drew to challenge liberal nationalism.[16]

The efficacy of "conservative" nationalists varied across country and time. In those places where Moore's "bourgeois revolution" triumphed, they played at times an important political role without overturning, however, the liberal tide. France's nineteenth-century right—which pushed hard for the restoration of the monarchy, exploited the Dreyfus affair to convey an illiberal definition of Frenchness, and rallied around Pétain in 1940—lost all steam after World War II. Nineteenth-century Tories, defining the nation around Anglicanism (and, later in the century, Protestantism), resisted but could not avoid the final disestablishment of the Church of England.

By contrast, when the defenders of ancien régime institutions succeeded in blocking the construction of a truly liberal order (or at least denied its extension to a territorially defined population), they hindered the construction of a unified nation congruent with the political borders of the existing state. Constructing a unified political community required treating individuals as equals, even if only formally. Without that quid pro quo, a unified nation was hard to achieve.[17] Instead, the (spatially) fragmented nature of the ancien régime—which, as emphasized earlier, was a conglomerate of regions and territories with different degrees of autonomy, each linked unilaterally to a monarch—spilled over into the modern world.[18]

Those citizens and strata located in the periphery, unable to have equal access to the state or to become part of the ruling elite, were likely to develop their own national claims, that is, their own demands to become a sovereign (abstract) body of equal citizens. In doing so, they often mobilized the cultural and institutional repertoires that defined them before the liberal breakthrough, in a way similar to what conservative nationalists had done. However, periphery nationalists did so under the modern banner of emancipation.[19]

North and South American colonists insurrected against the barriers imposed by their metropolis. Ireland's separation followed directly from Tories' conception of nationhood. In Austria-Hungary, the resistance to a liberal arrangement made it impossible for Vienna and Budapest to construct the kind of political consent that had developed in France or Switzerland, making the Habsburg Empire, as Anderson fittingly put it, "an assembly of Irelands" (1983, 86). Russia could not absorb or quiet the Finnish, Balts, and Polish. The Ottoman Empire lost the Balkans to its peripheral populations over the nineteenth century and its Middle East territories after World War I.[20]

A similar process leading to the formation of separate national claims as part and parcel of a struggle for emancipation took place around the world among colonial territories in the twentieth century—initially led by liberal nationalist elites, intent on replicating the representative institutions of their masters into their own territories, later sustained by socialist revolutionaries in search of both legal and material equality.[21]

Conclusion

This chapter makes two central claims. First, to understand the emergence and substantial ideational variation of nationalism (as well as the territorial distribution of national identities it has bred), we need to focus on its *political* origins and dynamics rather than the broad processes of economic and cultural modernization that today's canonical accounts emphasize. Second, the study of nationalism implies the study of *nationalisms*, characterized by different ideational commitments, which are related to their origin and the nature of their claims.

The emergence of a modern conception of nation was coterminous with the construction of an emancipatory (and universally attractive) political project: a "liberal" order that presupposed and emphasized citizen equality under a common sovereign and therefore a unified political community and that, when successful, made the existing political borders congruent with national identity. Nonetheless, the challenge of liberal nationalism engendered its own nemesis: a conservative nationalism that, rejecting the disruptive political and cultural consequences of the former, insisted on the weight of the past as the source of legitimation of the political community.

Because the past implied a society of hierarchies and inequalities, the conservative counterproposal was often unappealing to those who were either outsiders to or had an inferior status in the old order. Their lack of recognition (understood as the demand of individuals to be approved by others as equals or as worthy of their relation) stirred the formation of emancipatory nationalisms against the center and, as a result, the multiplication of (competing) national identities.

The problem of recognition played a broad role (with different tones and consequences, though) in the evolution of nationalism over time.[22] The demand for equal treatment, both in material terms and as a principle of dignity, was behind most of the national liberation movements in the colonial world. In a twisted manner, it was also a key driver behind the evolution of conservative nationalism throughout the nineteenth century—and particularly the twentieth century. The refusal of some cultural minorities to recognize what the national majority saw as the inherent value of its national project (and therefore to assimilate to it) exacerbated conservatives' attachment to illiberal notions of nation building and fostered their resentment toward those minorities. When that rejection at home was compounded by imperial decline (the cases of Spain and Russia, for example) or full defeat at war (the French right after 1870, Germany after 1918), conservative nationalism took a reactionary turn that often evolved into chauvinism and revanchism. In its most extreme cases, that transformation resulted in a commitment to the destruction of internal minorities whose refusal to assimilate was construed as a direct cause of the decline and defeat of the majority's nation.[23]

Acknowledgments

I acknowledge the financial support of the European Research Council (ERC) under the European Union's Programme of H2020—the Framework programme for Research and Innovation (2014–2020), Project "The Birth of Party Democracy," Grant Agreement no. 694318.

Notes

1. For an application to the idea of an instrumental use of nationalism in elections, see Linz and Stepan (1992).
2. For a more extended debate on Gellner's work, see Hall, ed. (1998).
3. Gellner (1964, 171n), quoted in Szporluk (1998, 27).
4. For a recent argument in the same direction, see Darden (n.d.).

5. Constructivist scholars who acknowledge any agency among non-elites in the construction of national identities tend to attribute it to strictly utilitarian reasons. Individuals transit to a new identity when they take it to be useful to advance socially. Such a switch generally happens in the context of linguistic coordination games (Laitin 1998). This explanation, which wrongly conflates language use with national identity, still begs the question of what determines the usefulness of specific languages.
6. For a particularly enlightened critique of Gellner's theory, see O'Leary (1998).
7. Deflating the role of elites comes, however, with a price. If, as Motyl points out, "constructivism does not argue that elites create national identity consciously, if the nationalists of whom Ernest Gellner writes as 'historic agents' of nationalism 'know not what they do,' then we are, at best, left with the trivial conclusion that, since 'men make their own history,' as they obviously must for history to be more than the recording of natural events, everything in history is in some sense 'made'—constructed—by men and women" (Motyl 2002, 60).
8. Examining the conditions that lead to the successful consolidation of nation states, Wimmer (2018) sees the latter also as a by-product of economic and social modernization. Nation states fully matured in countries that had strong interethnic civil society organizations, a state capable of providing public goods evenly across a territory, a shared medium of communication.
9. A partial exception is Greenfeld (1992).
10. Augustin Cochin, quoted in Furet (1981, 190).
11. It is true that nineteenth-century liberals favored restrictive, discriminatory norms in things such as the right to vote. However, as shown by Kahan (2003), they were justified not on the principle of inequality but on the idea of lack of (rational) capacity.
12. The same occurred after the Soviet revolution. Despite calls to internationalize the revolution and unite all the world proletarians under one state, the existence of separate national communities was taken for granted and finally embraced.
13. Quoted in Boix (2022), where I show how the distinct national paths of Jews resulted from the presence or absence of a liberal emancipatory "treatment" across European countries.
14. Quoted in Weber 1976 (73).
15. The optimal outcome for old regime elites consisted in blocking all modernizing impulses, i.e., maintaining the ancient order of perfectly self-contained groups only connected to a monarch. Nonetheless, that possibility eventually crumbled everywhere after those old composite monarchies were exposed to the twin challenges of foreign modernizing competitors (European powers) and to the demands of emerging liberal actors at home. The Ottoman Empire provides a good example of that trajectory. It survived as long as its "millet" system persisted but ended up collapsing under the weight of external and internal modernizing forces.
16. The conservative challenge took place in part for instrumental reasons, such as the defense of ancient privileges or the preservation of the preeminent position of the church. But it also went beyond any material or strategic considerations in that it was triggered by the cultivation of an imagined community defined by particular norms and cultural practices rooted in the past and evoked through the power of personal and collective memories.
17. The exception was the case in which they could fully assimilate initially heterogeneous populations, that is, when they could transplant to the latter their cultural, linguistic, and institutional characteristics (meaning the power structures and relations). That was most likely to happen when there were no regional elites or when those regional elites were tied to the center through strong patronage links.

18. Most but not all periphery nationalisms followed from the success of a conservative national project at the center. Because it was also predicated on the obliteration of past cultural identities or linguistic differences, the liberal project sometimes triggered strong popular reactions that, first taking a religious character, evolved, in a few cases, into a distinct national project.
19. The justificatory basis of liberal or "Jacobin" nationalism differed from the Herderian conception of nation. The former saw the nation as an abstract body of equal individuals—reaffirmed by will and a "daily plebiscite." The latter emphasized a shared history or common ethnic—"the most natural state is also," Herder would write, "one people, with one national character" (*Ideas on the Philosophy of History of Mankind*, quoted in Patten 2010). Still, it would be wrong to equate the former with national emancipation and the latter with reactionary nationalism. A substantial number of liberal movements (among either national minorities or national communities split into different countries) saw and employed Herderian ideas while striving for political emancipation.
20. See Hroch (1985) for a mostly descriptive approximation to the mobilizational dynamics of the elites of periphery nationalism.
21. At times, the claim for full separation developed through a two-step process. As discussed by Lawrence (2013), the native elites of French African colonies first lobbied Paris for citizenship and equal voting rights after World War II. Africa' anticolonial activists embraced the cause of independence only after the French government, concerned about the fact that "representatives from the colonies would have swamped delegates from the 'hexagon' as the population of the colonies outstripped the population living in France" (105), rejected their initial demands.
22. For a discussion of the principle of recognition and its relationship to nationalism, see Taylor (1998). For a broader psychological approach, see Scheff (1990).
23. See Krauel (2013) on Spain. See Greenfeld (1992) on Germany and Russia, with one caveat: the book reifies German nationalism dating it back to the turn of the nineteenth century. Instead, German nationalism housed, as in other cases, several ideational variants. Its programmatically reactionary version became hegemonic mostly as a result of the military defeat of 1918 and the Great Depression.

References

Anderson, Benedict. 1983. *Imagined Communities: Reflections on the Origin and Spread of Nationalism*. New York: Verso.

Appelbaum, Diana Muir. 2013. "Biblical Nationalism and the Sixteenth-Century States." *National Identities* 15, no. 4: 317–32.

Breuilly, John. 1982. *Nationalism and the State*. New York: St. Martin's.

Boix, Carles. 2022. "The Struggle for Emancipation and the Formation of Modern National Identities." Princeton University. Working Paper.

Chernow, Ron. 2010. *Washington: A Life*. New York: Penguin Press.

Darden, Keith. N.d. *Resisting Occupation: Mass Literacy and the Creation of Durable National Loyalties*. Unpublished manuscript: American University.

Furet, François. 1981. *Interpreting the French Revolution*. New York: Cambridge University Press.

Gellner, Ernest. 1964. *Thought and Change*. Chicago: University of Chicago Press.

Gellner, Ernest. 1983. *Nations and Nationalism*. Ithaca, NY: Cornell University Press.

Godechot, Jacques Léon 1956. *La grande nation: l'expansion révolutionnaire de la France dans le monde de 1789 à 1799*. Paris: Aubier Montaigne.

Gorski, Philip S. 2000. "The Mosaic Moment: An Early Modernist Critique of the Modernist Theory of Nationalism." *American Journal of Sociology* 105, no. 5: 1428–68.

Greenfeld, Liah. 1992. *Nationalism: Five Roads to Modernity*. Cambridge, MA: Harvard University Press, 1992.

Hall, John A., ed. 1998. *The State of the Nation: Ernest Gellner and the Theory of Nationalism*. New York: Cambridge University Press.

Hobsbawm, Eric J. 1990. *Nations and Nationalism since 1780: Programme, Myth, Reality*. New York: Cambridge University Press.

Hroch, Miroslav. 1985. *Social Preconditions of National Revival in Europe*. New York: Cambridge University Press.

Kahan, Alan S. 2003. *Liberalism in Nineteenth-Century Europe: The Political Culture of Limited Suffrage*. New York: Palgrave Macmillan.

Krauel, Javier. 2013. *Imperial Emotions: Cultural Responses to Myths of Empire in Fin-de-Siècle Spain*. Liverpool: Liverpool University Press.

Laitin, David D. 1998. *Identity in Formation: The Russian-speaking Populations in the Near Abroad*. Ithaca, NY: Cornell University Press.

Lawrence, Adria. 2013. *Imperial Rule and the Politics of Nationalism: Anti-colonial Protest in the French Empire*. New York: Cambridge University Press.

Linz, J. J., and A. Stepan. 1992. "Political Identities and Electoral Sequences: Spain, the Soviet Union, and Yugoslavia." *Daedalus* CXXI, no. 2, 510–22.

Lynch, Marc. 2007. "Anti-Americanisms in the Arab World." In *Anti-Americanisms in World Politics*, ed. Peter J. Katzenstein and Robert O. Keohane, 196–224. Ithaca, NY: Cornell University Press.

Marx, Karl. 1994 [1852]. *The Eighteenth Brumaire of Louis Napoleon*. New York: International Publishers.

Moore, Barrington. 1966. *Social Origins of Dictatorship and Democracy: Lord and Peasant in the Making of the Modern World*. Boston: Beacon Press.

Motyl, Alexander. 2002. "Inventing Invention: The Limits of National Identity Formation." In *Intellectuals and the Articulation of the Nation*, ed. Ronald Grigor Suny and Michael D. Kennedy, 57–75. Ann Arbor: University of Michigan Press.

Mylonas, Harris, and Maya Tudor. 2021. "Nationalism: What We Know and What We Still Need to Know." *Annual Review of Political Science* 24: 109–32.

O'Leary, Brendan. 1998. "Ernest Gellner's Diagnoses of Nationalism: A Critical Overview, or, What Is Living and What Is Dead in Ernest Gellner's Philosophy of Nationalism?" In *The State of the Nation: Ernest Gellner and the Theory of Nationalism*, ed. John A. Hall, 40–88. New York: Cambridge University Press.

Patten, Alan. 2010. "The Most Natural State: Herder and Nationalism." *History of Political Thought* 31, no. 4: 657–89.

Rafanell, August. 2006. *La il·lusió occitana : la llengua dels catalans, entre Espanya i França*. Barcelona: Quaderns Crema.

Scheff, Thomas. 1990. *Microsociology*. Chicago: University of Chicago Press.

Skinner, Quentin. 1978. *The Foundations of Modern Political Thought: Volume 1, The Renaissance*. Cambridge: Cambridge University Press.

Smith, Anthony D. 1989. "The Origins of Nations." *Ethnic and Racial Studies* 12 (July): 340–67.

Szporluk, Roman. 1998. "Thoughts about change: Ernest Gellner and the history of nationalism." In ed. John Hall, *The State of the Nation: Ernest Gellner and the Theory of Nationalism*, 23–39. New York: Cambridge University Press.

Taylor, Charles. 1998. "Nationalism and Modernity." In *The State of the Nation: Ernest Gellner and the Theory of Nationalism*, ed. John A. Hall, 191–218. New York: Cambridge University Press.

Walicki, Andrzej. 1997. "Intellectual Elites and the Vicissitudes of 'Imagined Nation' in Poland,." *East European Politics and Society* 11, no. 3: 227–53.

Weber, Eugen. 1976. *Peasants into Frenchmen: The Modernization of Rural France, 1870–1914*. Stanford, CA: Stanford University Press.

Wimmer, Andreas. 2018. *Nation Building*. Princeton, NJ: Princeton University Press.

CHAPTER 28

THE HISTORICAL POLITICAL ECONOMY OF COLONIALISM

JENNY GUARDADO

THE Portuguese annexation of the port of Ceuta on the North African coast in 1415 commonly marks the start of the European[1] colonization process. From that date onward, different European powers traversed the world claiming the right to rule faraway territories. In this chapter, I focus on "formal" colonies: territories that had their domestic and international affairs dominated by a European nation state but whose populations lack the same rights as the inhabitants of the colonizer country (Becker 2019).[2] Following this definition, Figure 28.1 portrays the global distribution of current countries ever colonized.[3]

This chapter centers on the historical political economy of colonialism. Namely, *whether* and *how* did the colonization experience shape the economic trajectory of formerly subjected countries? While these questions have a longstanding pedigree, at least dating to Adam Smith (1998 [1776]), in what follows I survey more "recent" (generally post-2000) works on the topic from the fields of economics, economic history, and political science.[4] A key difference between these works and an older generation of studies is that this newer literature has greatly benefited from technological advances in data collection (OCR, GIS)[5] and places greater attention on issues of causal inference. As such, this literature fits, topically and methodologically, within the subject of this volume: the field of historical political economy.

The chapter revolves around two overarching goals. The first one is to survey the evidence on *which* and *how* different aspects of colonization influenced economic development in the long run. From these works, I find a rich body of research documenting diverse colonization experiences (positive and negative) across and within countries. The broad takeaway is that the long-run economic legacies of colonialism are largely driven by the conditions encountered by colonizers, the latter's identity, or the length of colonization, to name a few.

In light of this diversity, the second theme of the chapter is examining whether these legacies can be attributed to colonization and not to other causes. This involves engaging with two types of questions. The first and fundamental one is the what-if question of

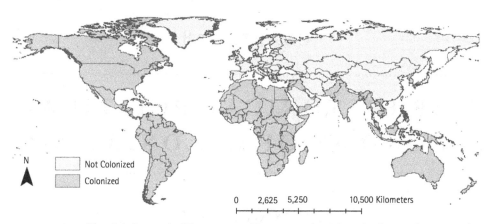

FIGURE 28.1. The global spread of European and Japanese colonialism (16th to 20th centuries)
Source: Constructed based on data from Kaniyathu (2007) and COLDAT (Becker 2019).

colonization: Are these economic outcomes (positive or negative) actually due to colonialism? How do we know they would not have happened regardless? Because the literature rarely (if at all) compares the colonization experience with a counterfactual scenario where colonization did not happen, particularly when looking across countries, we do not (yet) have a definitive answer. The few attempts to address this question discussed here pose more questions than answers,[6] thus constituting a fruitful avenue for future research.

In addition to what-if scenarios, the literature can also engage with a second set of questions centered on the *net* economic effects of different colonial policies. Thanks to a growing body of work across different fields, today we know much more about the long-run impact of specific aspects of colonialism, such as investments in human capital (e.g., education) and physical capital (e.g., railroads and irrigation), or the pernicious effects of distortionary policies, for example.[7] The question is how to weigh the economic positives and negatives, namely, how the net effect of colonization explains current development gaps across countries. Relying on findings from development accounting (Caselli 2005; Hsieh and Klenow 2010; Jones 2016), I argue that it is unlikely that the positive economic impacts from colonial investments outweigh its negatives. This is because the bulk of documented positive legacies are generally[8] confined to factors of production (human and physical capital) that contribute less to today's income gaps across countries than others, such as productivity. Therefore, future work on how colonial policies shape factor allocation and productivity and how these perform vis-à-vis other investments to determine current GDP levels is a promising area of study.

Colonialism and Development: Key Cross-Country Findings

The seminal works of Engerman and Sokoloff (1997), La Porta et al. (1997), La Porta, Lopez-de-Silanes, and Shleifer (2008), and Acemoglu, Johnson, and Robinson (2001) gave rise to a large body of work interested in the long-term political and economic consequences of colonialism. This extensive literature—partially surveyed here—has more or less convincingly linked contemporary economic outcomes to the type and intensiveness of the colonial experience across a variety of settings and time periods, and through a number of different mechanisms.

Varieties of Colonialism: European Settlement and Local Conditions

In its first iteration, the key explanatory variables for current economic performance centered on either the identity of the colonizer (La Porta et al. [1997]; La Porta, Lopez-de-Silanes, and Shleifer [2008]), the conditions that colonizers encountered upon their arrival (Acemoglu, Johnson, and Robinson [2001]; Engerman and Sokoloff [1997]), or a combination of both (Mahoney 2010). In their seminal paper, Acemoglu, Johnson, and Robinson (2001); contended that economic performance today crucially depends on the quality of institutions brought about by European settlement in colonial times. In territories with widespread European presence—due to low settler mortality, for example—institutions would be of higher quality, leading to better long-run performance. Figure 28.2a reproduces their finding: the share of European presence in early colonization phases strongly predicts gross domestic product (GDP) per capita today.

Conversely, since a major determinant of European settlement during colonization was the size of the preexisting Indigenous population, places where the latter was higher end up being economically worse off today. This is the finding of Acemoglu, Johnson, and Robinson's (2002) follow-up paper and presented in Figure 28.2b: territories with higher (Indigenous) population density around 1500 have lower GDP per capita today.

The purported reason behind the findings in Figure 28.2b is that European settlers could exploit this population as a source of labor and taxes, thus undermining institutional quality. Indeed, a common finding in the literature is the negative relationship between colonial slavery and/or forced labor and economic development.[9] In the United States and Latin America, regions with slavery are associated with some of the most nefarious economic consequences in terms of public good provision, inequality, and general underdevelopment today (Acemoglu, Garcia-Jimeno, and Robinson 2012; Engerman and Sokoloff 1997; Bruhn and Gallego 2012). Negative economic effects are also visible when considering other forms of coerced labor, such as the *mita* in Peru and Bolivia, whereby Indigenous towns had to provide workers for mining activities (Dell 2010) or for rubber extraction, as in the Democratic Republic of Congo (Lowes and Montero 2021). Even cases of debt peonage, such as the *concertaje* in Ecuador (Rivadeneira Acosta 2019)—whereby Indigenous groups in Ecuador were forced to provide labor to property owners to pay off past debts throughout generations—are today associated with worse long-run outcomes. However, the negative effects of slavery are not limited to the areas where it was practiced, since countries where people were most intensely drawn from are also worse off economically today (Nunn 2008), likely due to the culture of distrust slavery engendered in society (Nunn and Wantchekon 2011).

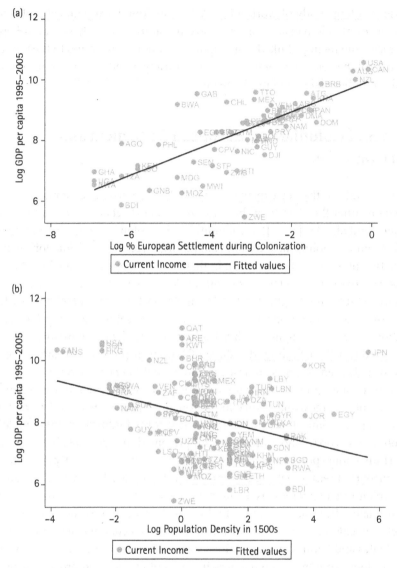

FIGURE 28.2. Early European settlement, precolonial population, and current GDP per capita

Sources: For figure 2a, Easterly and Levine (2016); for figure 2b, the dependent variable is from Easterly and Levine (2016) while population density is from Chanda et al. (2014) from Acemoglu, Johnson, and Robinson (2001).

These cross-country and within-country studies put the role of colonialism front and center of the development debate—as a major cause behind a country's economic fortune—and also (expectedly) spurred a vivid debate, mostly centered on alternative interpretations of these patterns. For example, viewing the share of European presence in a territory through the lens of institutional quality is not the only possible interpretation. European presence could also likely correlate with higher human capital, as argued in Glaeser et al. (2004) either because European colonizers were themselves bearers of higher human capital—a claim disputed in Acemoglu, Gallego, and Robinson (2014)—or due to the later influx of high-human-capital populations (Chanda, Cook, and Putterman 2014; Putterman and Weil 2010). In the latter's view, Mexico's lower GDP per capita vis-à-vis Argentina's today is due to the fact that most of Mexico's population ancestry does not come from countries that were "developed" around 1500. In contrast, Argentina's higher GDP per capita can be at least partly attributed to the higher share of descendants from developed countries around 1500, mostly European, who settled there in large numbers in the nineteenth century. While this would support the idea of human capital persistence among populations vis-à-vis that of territories, it still allows the choice of migration destination of Europeans to be driven by differences in institutional quality, for example.

Length of Colonization

A different dimension of the colonial experience is its duration. Some countries remained under colonial rule longer than others, which in turn could be associated with better or worse long-run outcomes. Moreover, it is plausible that the effect of colonization varied in its intensive and extensive margin: while the effect of colonization might be negative vis-à-vis never being colonized, once in place, longer experiences might be more conducive to economic growth than short-lived ones. This is exactly what Feyrer and Sacerdote (2009) find for the case of islands and Grier (1999) shows for a subsample of countries. Figure 28.3 replicates these results in a global sample using the latest available data. As shown, the cumulative number of years under colonial rule is associated with higher GDP per capita today.

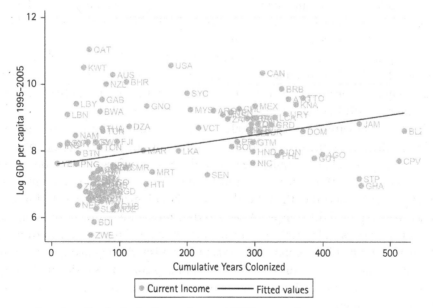

FIGURE 28.3. Length of colonization and current GDP per capita

Sources: GDP from Easterly and Levine (2016); colonization length from COLDAT (Becker 2019).

Although the effect is small (B = 0.003), it would still support the idea of longer colonization experiences positively impacting development today. Nonetheless, one should be cautious as the pattern could be driven by the subset of islands, as in Feyrer and Sacerdote (2009), or heavily influenced by the short length of colonization in Africa, which is also the poorest region in the sample, to name a few possible confounders. Nonetheless, these works are the first to consider the intensity of colonization as a factor shaping its economic impact.

Colonizer Identity

A different approach has been to examine the legacies of particular countries by linking traits of the colonizers to the observable differences among those colonized (see La Porta et al. 1997; La Porta Lopez-de-Silanes, and Shleifer 2008). For Spanish America, Lange, Mahoney and Vom Hau (2006) relate differences in outcomes across countries to the economic models of colonizers themselves. For sub-Saharan Africa, Frankema and Van Waijenburg (2014) similarly argue that the identity of colonizers—in this case, that of Britain and France—are key to understanding the disparate trajectories of countries under their rule. A more integrated approach is that of Mahoney (2010) and Müller-Crepon (2020), who combine the identity of the colonizer with key local conditions to predict current levels of economic development in Spanish America and sub-Saharan Africa, respectively.

A quick look at the data does reveal differences based on the colonizer's identity. For example, if we disaggregate the data from Figure 28.2a based on the four largest European colonizers (Britain, Spain, France, and Portugal), the relationship between current GDP per capita and European presence clearly differs depending on who the colonizer was (Figure 28.4). While in British and French colonies the average effect of more European presence during colonization on current GDP is similar[10] (blue and red lines), the effect is more muted in Spanish and Portuguese former colonies (yellow and green lines, respectively). Nonetheless, in all cases the slope is positive, with more Europeans generally leading to better outcomes.

A key problem with this type of analysis is that variation in economic outcomes within countries from the same colonizer can be larger than the variation observed in the whole sample. For example, the standard deviation of log GDP among former British colonies is 1.28 whereas it is 1.16 in the whole sample, for example—thus suggesting that factors other than the identity of the colonizer must be playing a role, such as cross-regional differences. A second difficulty is the bundled or compound nature of colonizers' "identity," which varies in so many dimensions and over time that it makes it difficult to pinpoint the exact mechanism driving divergence in GDP today. For instance, some of the key differences among colonizers reside in their legal origins, fiscal and trade regimes, reliance on direct versus indirect rule, and use of coerced labor, to name a few.

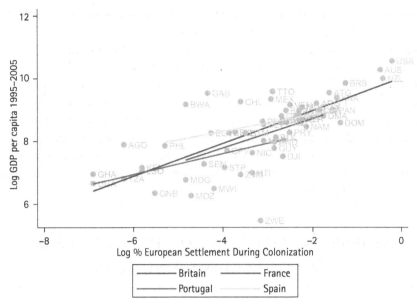

FIGURE 28.4. Colonizer identity and current GDP per capita
Sources: GDP from Easterly and Levine (2016); colonizer identity from COLDAT (Becker 2019).

Two types of research designs seek to address these concerns and clarify the role of colonizer identity vis-à-vis that of initial conditions. The first approach is to hold constant initial conditions prior to colonization and see how the effects vary by different identities. Examples of this type of research include comparisons of countries arbitrarily divided by colonizer powers and compare their outcomes today, as shown in Cameroon for Britain and France (Lee and Schultz 2012; Dupraz 2019)—with better economic and educational outcomes for British Cameroon. A second example is that of Mattingly (2017), who compares areas in northern China under Japanese rule with nearby ones spared. The evidence reveals that areas under Japanese rule performed better in the long run likely due to investments in state capacity. These findings support the idea of particular identities leading to different legacies yet still face the challenge of showing which aspect of the colonizing identity is driving the results.

The second approach has been to hold constant the identity of the colonizer and see how the effects vary by differences in initial conditions. Naritomi, Soares, and Assumção (2012) shows that different suitability for crops or mining activities translate today into different institutional and economic arrangements despite originating from the same colonizer in Brazil. Using a broader sample of countries, Bruhn and Gallego (2012) build on Engerman and Sokoloff's (1997) argument to show how the same colonizer[11] relied on different institutional arrangements, such as large-scale plantations or small-farm production, depending on the local geography and the size of the Indigenous population, thus supporting the idea that many of the differences observed are driven by these initial conditions and not necessarily the colonizer's identity. Given the support for both—colonizer identity and initial conditions—future studies could assess their relative contribution to explain GDP differences today.

In all, the first wave of studies on the economic effects of colonization showed how this varied along key dimensions: size of European settlements, initial conditions, particular identities, or the duration of colonization. While some colonies clearly thrived—say, those with a large European presence (Figure 28.2a)—those with low shares of European presence (or high levels of precolonial population) are associated with lower GDP (Figure 28.2b), likely due to the intervening factors of forced labor and slavery. Even within a country, some areas have seen their fortunes diminish if they happened to be under French as opposed to British rule (Cameroon), or if not colonized by Japan (northern China), for example.

Assessing the Economic Effects of Colonialism: A Survey

The problem is that these varied economic legacies of colonialism—sometimes positive, often negative—are not based on a comparison to a scenario of never being colonized in the first place. In other words, they do not compare these colonies' performance to a noncolonized control. Are these outcomes due to colonialism, or would have they happened regardless? Is colonialism the economic watershed event as argued earlier? To advance these questions, the literature has adopted different empirical strategies to parse out what can be attributed to colonialism and what cannot.

Leveraging the Timing of Independence

The first approach has been to leverage the timing of independence movements in Spanish America and Africa to estimate the impact of de-colonization on a country's economic and political development. In the case of Spanish America, the Napoleonic Wars of 1808 and the imprisonment of the Spanish heir exogenously "sparked" the movements for independence. In Africa and Southeast Asia, the end of World War II left many countries suddenly in charge of their own fortunes.[12] The timing, driven by events in Europe, lets researchers compare the conditions in the country just prior to independence with the immediate aftermath. If one saw, for example, a very large increase in economic productivity or fiscal revenues after independence, one could argue that colonialism was detrimental for growth and state finances, for example.

Two studies illustrate this approach. For Latin America, economic historians Coatsworth (1993; 1978) and Prados de la Escosura (2008 [1984]) show that, in the short run—the period where the immediate effects of colonialism can be "cleanly" estimated[13]—the benefits of decolonization, in fiscal terms, for example, were small and did not outweigh the costs these new countries had to assume to finance civil and international wars. In the long run these benefits might have been larger, but because many other factors have also changed, the analysis cannot pinpoint decolonization as the sole cause. In sub-Saharan Africa, Lee and Paine (2019) find little difference in economic performance, measured as GDP or revenue growth, among recently decolonized countries vis-à-vis the years immediately prior to independence.[14] However, decolonized countries in sub-Saharan Africa did see a substantial increase in democracy levels following decolonization—as measured by freedom of association and expression, clean elections, elected officials, and suffrage.

Although these studies do not strictly answer the question of how these countries would perform were they never a colony, as explicitly recognized in the text (Lee and Paine 2019, 406), they can point to some of the immediate consequences of removing colonial rule. For example, many economic complaints of colonialism centered on fiscal matters and the inability to self-govern. However, as shown in both studies, the immediate *economic* effects of decolonization are small (or even net negative in Latin America). This could be because the costs imposed by colonization did not outweigh its benefits—or, more likely, that the most growth-detrimental aspects of colonialism are difficult to change in the short run leading to no visible differences immediately after independence.

Colonialism vis-à-vis Precolonial Trends

A second approach to assess the impacts of colonialism is to engage this question: how much of a "break" did colonialism entail vis-à-vis precolonial economic trends? If colonialism had visible economic consequences for development, then we should observe different degrees of "breaks" (or even a complete reversal, e.g., Acemoglu, Johnson, and Robison [2002]) with trends observed *prior* to the arrival of colonizers.[15] The main difficulty with this strategy is that it relies heavily on data collected before the arrival of Europeans, which is often difficult to obtain. Nonetheless, a number of studies have painstakingly collected or compiled this information to paint a clearer picture of certain regions prior to European arrival, greatly contributing to the field.

Starting with the Americas, Maloney and Valencia Caicedo (2016) show that, unlike the reversal in GDP per capita noted at the country level (see Figure 28.2b), there is actually much more persistence in economic outcomes when looking at the subnational level across former colonies in the Americas. In particular, major centers of precolonial population around 1500—a measure of economic development at the time—continue to exhibit higher populations and somewhat higher GDP per capita today. The authors attribute the result to the strength of agglomeration mechanisms vis-à-vis the sometimes violent changes induced by colonization. The implication is that subnationally we do not see the kind of dramatic departures (reversals) from precolonial patterns documented earlier.[16]

In a similar vein, but different context, Gaikwad (2014) points to the numerous economic (commercial) changes taking place in India prior to colonial rule that were more critical in determining the local economic trajectories along the Indian coast vis-à-vis the changes induced by colonization itself. Precolonial trade determined the spatial allocation of commercial and economic activity driving successive waves of migration from the hinterland, adoption of new manufacturing skills (e.g., spinning), and promoting greater intercaste economic mobility, for example. In this sense, the paper de-emphasizes the importance of the formal colonial ruling period per se and pays more attention to other forms of economic influence exerted by Europeans, such as trading companies, in shaping India's trajectory.

Finally, in the case of sub-Saharan Africa, some scholars have long sustained that the duration and spatial impact of colonization were very limited (Herbst 2000), albeit others credit it with major departures in the economic trajectory of the region (see Nunn 2007). More recently, Michalopoulos and Papaioannou (2014) document the limited impact of colonial-era national institutions established by Europeans on current regional (within ethnic homeland) economic development, likely due to the limited ability of the colonial and postcolonial state to project their power through vast territories (Michalopopulos and Papaioannou 2013). These findings are in line with earlier work, most notably by Austin (2010), who made the case that colonialism did not significantly alter the trajectory of African countries, as these paths were already set in place prior to colonization and driven by the continent's global comparative advantages, for example.

The common theme of these studies is that colonization matters less for current economic outcomes—particularly at the subnational level—than what the cross-country evidence shows (e.g., Figure 28.2a). This could be because, as conjectured in Maloney and Valencia Caicedo (2016), the persistence forces of agglomeration are stronger subnationally than nationally, or as hypothesized in Herbst (2000), the colonial state was often unable to project its strength, weakening any potential legacy of colonialism (whether economically beneficial or not). One limitation with this approach is that finding continuity with precolonial trends greatly minimizes but does not fully rule out that colonization did or did not shift the economic trajectories of certain regions or countries. After all, it is possible that certain regions could have performed even better or worse than their precolonial average had colonialism not occurred. What is needed, then, is to think about what that trajectory would look like absent the arrival of Europeans.

Counterfactual Analyses

Two works exemplify the attempt to make these counterfactuals explicit—in other words, to try to answer what Zambia would look like had it not been colonized. The first study is the one by Kaniyathu (2007), who takes a global look at the effect of colonialism and compares the economic performance of countries never colonized (and did not become colonizers themselves) with similar ones that were. Using different matching techniques, the author compares GDP levels and growth rates among "second wave" colonized territories in Asia and Africa in the 1950–1959 period vis-à-vis comparable ones that have always remained independent. For example, one key variable they match on is that of precolonial centralization, a critical variable highlighted in the literature (Bockstette, Chanda, and Putterman 2002). The estimates show that colonialism had a generally negative impact on these indicators, but that the effect is too small to be economically important (Kaniyathu 2007).

In a more negative light for colonialism, Heldring and Robinson's (2012) argues that colonization likely delayed development for sub-Saharan African states that had higher levels of precolonial centralization and those with "white-settler" colonies, although the effect is less clear for other cases. For instance, Botswana, Rwanda, and Ghana clearly would have performed better were they not colonized, but the outcome is more ambiguous for places lacking political centralization in the first place (e.g., Somaliland). Under the assumption that many of the benefits of colonization (education, technology, connection to international markets, among others) would have taken place regardless, but the negative legacies in the form of "inequality and racial and ethnic conflicts [...]" distorted African political and economic institutions in the long run, the negatives are likely to outweigh the benefits (Heldring and Robinson 2012, 300).

Due to differences in the sample and type of analysis, the results between the two papers are not directly comparable. Therefore, it is possible that colonialism had clearly negative effects in sub-Saharan Africa (Heldring and Robinson 2012), but once other colonies are included, the effect is smaller (Kaniyathu 2007). The most important takeaway that emerges from these exercises is that the answer to the "colonialism question" strongly depends on the counterfactual one chooses, a key point made by Kaniyathu (2007). For example, looking at twentieth-century GDP growth between always-independent Liberia with nearby Ghana would shine a positive light on British colonialism. Yet, in other comparisons, the economic performance of always-independent Thailand is not so different from other Asian colonies, suggesting colonialism may matter less than initially thought (Kaniyathu 2007, 105–6).

Moreover, these types of analytical exercises on the effects of colonialism rest on two key assumptions: the first one is that colonized countries would have naturally coalesced into the territories that we observe today, which in many cases is not tenable due to the arbitrariness of colonial borders, yet is needed for these kinds of exercises to work (Kaniyathu 2007). The second assumption is about the economic performance after independence. Given the changes induced by colonization itself, how do we expect former colonized countries to perform after independence vis-à-vis a counterfactual scenario in which they were never colonized (Heldring and Robinson 2012)? Possibly in recognition of these difficulties, Michalopoulos and Papaioannou's (2020) review of historical development in Africa refrains from posing a specific counterfactual to this question. Yet the advent of better data, better research designs, or both can make inroads on the matter.

Given the impasse in the literature, in the rest of the chapter I instead take a different approach in assessing the economic legacies of colonialism. Relying on key findings from development accounting, I decompose and rank the contribution of different colonial policies to current income gaps across countries. How does the positive contribution of colonialism to economic growth compare to its negatives? Although this approach does not answer what would have happened absent colonization, it can help us understand and weight its most influential legacies for economic development today. The what-if question remains open (for now).

Colonial Legacies and Key Determinants of Economic Growth

A large literature, primarily but not exclusively coming from the sub-Saharan African colonization experience, highlights the persistent effect of colonial-era investments in physical and human capital. Although the studies sidestep the question of whether colonization was good as a whole, findings from these studies highlight the positive legacies of certain types of colonial policies.

Physical Capital

Starting with Huillery (2009), this literature shows that colonial investments in human and physical capital in the early twentieth century are strongly related to cross-district performance in education, health, and infrastructure across French West African countries today. A key mechanism to explain this effect is one of continuity: areas receiving early investments continued receiving more in the postcolonial era. Expanding the sample to also include British colonies in Africa, Ricart-Huguet (2022; 2021) further documents the role of colonial-era investments on current education and health outcomes and how these areas are consequently more developed.

In terms of a specific type of physical capital, Jedwab, Kerby, and Moradi (2017) and Jedwab and Moradi (2016) report in a series of papers how colonial railroad construction had important developmental consequences in sub-Saharan Africa by coordinating settlements, rural-urban migration, increasing market access, and eventually leading to greater economic development, albeit with some heterogeneity in some settings (Okoye, Pongou, and Yokossi 2019). These effects seem to have remained despite the demise of railroads in the post-independence period and the expansion of roads. This mirrors the well-documented effects of colonial railroads in British India (Bogart and Chaudhary 2013; Donaldson 2018), effects that could plausibly have persisted until today. The same pattern emerges from Italian colonial railroads constructed in the Horn of Africa in the early twentieth century that continue to facilitate current economic activity (Bertazzini 2022).

Other "bundled" investments involve infrastructure and transfers of technology and know-how that could have benefited these territories even after the colonizers' left. For example, colonial investments in sugar factories in Java in the mid-nineteenth century still exhibit higher industrialization and infrastructure levels than similar areas where the Dutch did not invest (Dell and Olken 2020). In sub-Saharan Africa, European colonialism promoted enclaves of cash-crop production for their own gain, yet these areas are still wealthier and more likely to have roads and emit nighttime light than similar ones not devoted to cash-crop production (Roessler et al. 2020). Conversely, a lack of colonial investment in infrastructure and human capital is cited as a reason behind the lasting negative effects of rubber production in the Democratic Republic of Congo under Belgian (and private) rule (Lowes and Montero 2021, 2049).

It should be noted, though, that these studies are not endorsements of the colonization experience per se. Many, if not all, of these investments were for self-serving purposes. For instance, the presence of extractive resources (Wantchekon and Stanig 2015) or the possibilities for trade (Ricart-Huguet 2022) were major determinants of where and whether these investments were located. European settlers also lobbied for more investments (Huillery 2009; Gardner 2012), presumably at the expense of areas without Europeans.[17] Yet this does not mean investments did not have a positive economic impact in the short and long run. In fact, a common criticism in these studies is that these investments were often insufficient and colonial powers could have done more to promote development (Booth 2007; Roessler et al. 2020).

Human Capital

In addition to physical capital, colonial investments in human capital are also singled out as exerting a positive influence on current levels of education and subsequent development among those colonized. Generally carried out by religious missionaries, and therefore considered "private" enterprises, the religious groups nonetheless needed the permission of and often acted in sync with the objectives of the colonial state. The 1767 expulsion of the Jesuits from the Spanish colonies is an example of the preeminence of the royal will above that of the Catholic Church, at least in this context. In other settings, Protestant missionaries were often subsidized by the British colonial state (Lugard 1922, cited by Ricart-Huguet 2021, 485), even though they often competed with and served as its counterweight (Woodberry 2004; 2011).

Some of the earliest records of missionary activity influencing current educational and development outcomes date back to the sixteenth- to eighteenth-century Mendicant and Jesuit missions in colonial Mexico (Waldinger 2017) as well as the current territory of Paraguay (Valencia Caicedo 2019). Although using different empirical approaches and identification strategies, in both cases the educational activity of these missions have led to higher educational and development levels today vis-à-vis those either farther away or lacking these missions altogether. The same pattern arises in British India (Lankina and Getachew 2013), where missionary activity is linked to higher human capital levels across Indian states today. Yet this effect is not only visible among missionaries, as there is also evidence that colonial expenditures on literacy in British India had a lasting positive effect on literacy today (Chaudhary 2010).

In Africa, the onset of colonialism in the late nineteenth and early twentieth centuries facilitated the activities of religious missionaries such that "the provision of education soon became the main reward used by missionaries to lure Africans into the Christian sphere" (Nunn 2010, 147). Micro-level evidence from colonial Benin (Wantchekon, Klasnja, and Novta 2015) shows that the impacts of colonial education persisted through generations with positive externalities even among those who did not attend school. Findings from Nigeria (Okoye and Pongou 2014) and Ghana and Togo (Cogneau and Moradi 2014) further strengthen the idea of their persistence, even if those benefits are unequally distributed.

Throughout these studies, past investments in human capital and infrastructure positively correlate with current ones, thus influencing current levels of development where present. The question is how to reconcile and weight these positive legacies with findings from other studies showing that colonization has led to worse economic outcomes overall.

THE LONG-RUN LEGACIES OF COLONIALISM IN A DEVELOPMENT ACCOUNTING FRAMEWORK

Development accounting allows researchers to quantify how different factors of production contribute to the income gap between countries. For example, using data from the Penn World Tables V.8 (PWT8) and a production function[18] based on levels of human capital (H_t), capital output ratios $\left(\dfrac{K_t}{Y_t}\right)$, and total factor productivity (TFP) $\left((A_t M_t)^{\frac{1}{1-\alpha}}\right)$[19], it is possible to calculate the contribution of each of these factors of production to the gap between rich and poor countries for the 1950–2010 period, as in Jones (2016).

The decomposition of income gaps shows that, first, most of the gap between rich and poor countries is due to TFP differences and not necessarily due to differences in human or physical capital (Caselli 2005; Hsieh and Klenow 2010). For example, in 1960, on average 63 percent of the income gap of poor countries[20] with the frontier economy (US) was due to TFP differences. In 2010, the average share due to TFP differences in poor countries is 79 percent.[21] The reasons are twofold: first, differences in human capital play a limited role in explaining income differences across countries in this formulation,[22] and second, the capital-output ratio across countries does not vary enough to explain the large differences observed in output.[23]

The limited role of human and physical capital investments means that the positive effects from colonial investments contributed less to cross-country income differences than other aspects of colonial rule, such as the distortions induced by certain economic and political systems affecting productivity (Canen and Wantchekon 2022). This is not to say that human or physical capital investments did not have a positive impact at the time or continue to have one today. Rather, even at their best, these positive investments may not be enough to offset other negative legacies from colonialism, especially those influencing TFP.

The second pattern in development accounting is that the share of the gap due to TFP differences has only increased over time, driven by the exponential growth of the United States in the second half of the twentieth century. This means that countries would become independent with an already large share of the gap with the frontier economy driven by differences in TFP,[24] which has only increased over time. While it is beyond the scope of this chapter to list all the colonial legacies due to productivity differences, below I briefly list three out of many potential sources, seeing their study within this framework as a fruitful avenue of future research.

Talent. One of the starkest examples of misallocation is that of talent, whereby individuals are unable to put their talents to their fullest use. Colonialism created a society where the place of birth or race determined which individuals were to perform which task (at farms, plantations, and mines), often through coercion and violence, and this distribution was not only ethically wrong but also economically suboptimal. The inefficiency associated with this inequality of opportunity is likely enormous and might not have been easily offset by positive investments in human capital or infrastructure in colonial times. For example, even within rich countries today (e.g., the United States), areas characterized by their reliance on slavery in the past are today, on average, relatively poorer than those that were not (Bruhn and Gallego 2012).

The distortions associated with forced labor and slavery move beyond that of talent. For example, in settings where colonization brought about demographic collapse of the Indigenous population (particularly in Spanish America), labor became scarcer vis-à-vis land, which should have translated, via a market mechanism, into higher wages for the remaining Indigenous population. The use of forced labor, however, erased any of these potential gains for the Indigenous population (Salvucci 2010). The fact that colonizers often did not have to pay for much of the labor also meant that much of it was inefficiently used—for example, in vanity projects, at suboptimal levels (oversupply), or under terrible working conditions.

Space. A second example of misallocation comes from the spatial distribution of economic activity. Although many colonial investments certainly facilitated economic activity at the time, the overall purpose was generally self-serving, such that it is possible that these are not optimally allocated. For example, a common observation of railroad construction in sub-Saharan Africa is that all the railroads lead to the sea, as they were meant to connect the interior with ports.

Other types of spatial misallocation come from colonial policies destined to limit market competition. For example, for around two centuries international trade in colonial Mexico was severely restricted. Only pre-specified quantities and types of goods ought to be exchanged in three authorized ports (Hough and Grier 2015; Baskes 2005). Although trade was later liberalized, new ports were not able to fully catch up despite sharing similar geographic and economic fundamentals (Alvarez-Villa and Guardado 2020). The differences are visible today in terms of poverty rates and provision of public goods, with the "winner" ports chosen by the Spanish Crown significantly better off.

Culture. Finally, a lack of trust among citizens or between citizens and their governments induces large transaction costs for businesses and customers alike (see Keefer and Scarstascini 2022), which in many cases can be traced to colonial policies. For example, the reliance on slavery warped the interpersonal trust among current African citizens (Nunn and Wantchekon 2011). In Peru, citizens from provinces where offices were put for sale in colonial times are today less trusting in state institutions and a fertile ground violent uprisings today (Guardado 2018) and at the time (Guardado 2022). In India, the use of indirect colonial rule generated distrust in the population toward the ruling class, which has prevented districts from taking advantage of development opportunities after independence (Banerjee and Iyer 2005).

Reinterpreting these and other legacies within the development accounting framework can help balance competing evidence and point to the most economically damaging aspects of colonialism in the long run.

Conclusion

The chapter provides a short survey of the existing literature on the historical political economy of European colonization. While the diversity of development experiences across and even within formerly colonized countries is notable, most of these studies are based on comparisons among different types of colonization experiences and not vis-à-vis a scenario of no colonization. More work needs to be done in comparing the development experiences of colonized places to a noncolonized control. In the meanwhile, researchers could move forward in thinking how the factors of production most important to explain income disparities across countries today—such as productivity—were shaped (or not) by colonialism. Insights from development accounting can thus help us reconcile the documented "positive" findings of colonialism on physical and human capital with the fact that many of these former colonies are generally poor today.

Acknowledgments

I thank Jack Paine and Steven Pennings for helpful comments and Bryan Ricciardi for his excellent research assistance on this project.

Notes

1. Although colonization is not originally or exclusively European, in this chapter I focus on colonization undertaken by current European countries and Japan.

2. Similar definition to Kaniyathu (2007): whether the government and head of state of a territory are determined by a different nation state, yet its inhabitants are not citizens of the latter.
3. Regions of always-independent countries would sometimes come under colonial rule. European countries would also subjugate one another; see Vogler (2019).
4. Due to space constraints, this is not an exhaustive review but centered on key works and findings.
5. Optical character recognition and geographic information systems, respectively.
6. See Heldring and Robinson (2018) and Kaniyathu (2007).
7. See Canen and Wantchekon (2022).
8. Some legacies bundle together physical and human capital investments and productivity gains.
9. Recent work in progress provide a more nuanced view (see Arroyo Abad and Maurer 2022; Summerhill 2010).
10. The results change little if I remove Canada from the sample (as it counts as both a British and French colony).
11. Bruhn and Gallego's (2012) results include country fixed effects, effectively controlling for the identity of the colonizer.
12. According to Abernethy (2000, 13, cited by Lee and Paine 2019, 406), around 40 percent of the world's population in 2000 lived in countries gaining independence between 1940 and 1980.
13. This approach is similar in spirit to the event study design, thus helping clarify the immediate costs imposed by the colonizer and how these change with self-government.
14. Bertocchi and Canova (2002) do find a clearer "break" with pre-independence economic performance but only in some sub-Saharan African countries.
15. This literature is distinct from others, emphasizing how different precolonial traits shape the type of colonial arrangements established (e.g., Arias and Girod 2011; Lee 2019; Gennaioli and Rainier 2007).
16. Two exceptions stand out: Chile and Argentina, which exhibited very little precolonial population and where large-scale migration took place and there is indeed a "reversal" in their initial fortunes.
17. In addition, given that many of these analyses are based on cross-sectional analysis, it is difficult to assess whether these investments increased economic activity or simply reallocated it across space. I thank Steven Pennings for this observation.
18. Solow's (1957) aggregate production function and a Cobb-Douglas specification used by Jones (2016, 43): $\frac{Y_t}{L_t} = \left(\frac{K_t}{Y_t}\right)^{\frac{\alpha}{1-\alpha}} \frac{H_t}{L_t} \cdot Z_t$, where $Z_t \equiv (A_t M_t)^{\frac{1}{1-\alpha}}$ is a measure of total factor productivity measure (TFP) in labor-augmenting units; A_t, is an economy's stock of knowledge; M_t, "other" factors behind productivity; Y_t is final output; K_t is physical capital; H_t is human capital; and α, the capital share of income, is between 0 and 1. The exercise assumes α = 1/3.
19. Which accounts for the role of technology A_t and factor allocation.
20. Defined as below the median of GDP per worker in 1960.
21. This outsized role of productivity is not limited to poor countries but even in "rich" countries (above the median), the average share of the gap due to TFP is 0.56 in 2010 and 0.46 in 1960.
22. Yet, this is an ongoing debate, as other studies claim a larger role for human capital.

23. See Jones (2016), Caselli (2005), or Hsieh and Klenow (2010) for a more detailed explanation.
24. For estimates of TFP differences for key Latin American economies at independence, see Hofman and Valderrama (2021). Former colonized countries in Africa had, on average, a share due to TFP in 1960 of 0.59.

References

Abernethy, David B. 2000. *The Dynamics of Global Dominance: European Overseas Empires, 1415-1980*. New Haven, CT: Yale University Press.

Acemoglu, Daron, Simon Johnson, and James A. Robinson. 2001. "The Colonial Origins of Comparative Development: An Empirical Investigation." *American Economic Review* 91, no. 5: 1369-1401.

Acemoglu, Daron, Simon Johnson, and James A. Robinson. 2002. "Reversal of Fortune: Geography and Institutions in the Making of the Modern World Income Distribution. *Quarterly Journal of Economics* 117, no. 4: 1231-1294.

Acemoglu, Daron, Francisco A. Gallego, and James A. Robinson. 2014. "Institutions, Human Capital, and Development." *Annual Review of Economics* 6, no. 1: 875-912.

Acemoglu, Daron, Camilo García-Jimeno, and James A. Robinson. 2012. "Finding Eldorado: Slavery and Long-Run Development in Colombia." *Journal of Comparative Economics* 40, no. 4: 534-64.

Alvarez-Villa, Daphne, and Jenny Guardado. 2020. "The Long-Run Influence of Institutions Governing Trade: Evidence from Smuggling Ports in Colonial Mexico." *Journal of Development Economics* 144: 102453.

Arias, Luz Marina, and Desha Girod. 2011. "Indigenous Origins of Colonial Institutions." *Quarterly Journal of Political Science* 9: 371-406.

Arroyo Abad, Leticia, and Noel Maurer. 2022. "The Long Shadow of History? The Impact of Colonial Labor Institutions on Economic Development in Peru." Unpublished manuscript. URL: https://assets.researchsquare.com/files/rs-1766286/v1_covered.pdf?c=1656684908.

Austin, Gareth. 2010. *African Economic Development and Colonial Legacies*. No. 1. Institut de hautes études internationales et du développement.

Banerjee, Abhijit, and Lakshmi Iyer. 2005. "History, Institutions, and Economic Performance: The Legacy of Colonial Land Tenure Systems in India." *American Economic Review* 95, no. 4: 1190-213.

Baskes, Jeremy. 2005. "Risky Ventures: Reconsidering Mexico's Colonial Trade System." *Colonial Latin American Review* 14, no. 1: 27-54.

Becker, Bastian. 2019. "Colonial Dates Dataset (COLDAT)." *Harvard Dataverse* version 2. https://doi.org/10.7910/DVN/T9SDEW.

Bertazzini, M. C. 2022. "The Long-Term Impact of Italian Colonial Roads in the Horn of Africa, 1935-2015." *Journal of Economic Geography* 22, no. 1: 181-214.

Bertocchi, Graciela, and Fabio Canova. 2002. "Did Colonization Matter for Growth? An Empirical Exploration into the Historical Causes of Africa's Underdevelopment." *European Economic Review* 46, no. 10: 1851-71.

Bockstette, Valerie, Areendam Chanda, and Louis Putterman. 2002. "States and Markets: The Advantages of an Early Start." *Journal of Economic Growth* 7: 347-69.

Bogart, Dan, and Latika Chaudhary. 2013. "Engines of Growth: The Productivity Advance of Indian Railways, 1874–1912." *Journal of Economic History* 73, no. 2: 339–70.

Booth, Anne. 2007. "Night Watchman, Extractive, or Developmental States? Some Evidence from Late Colonial South-East Asia 1. *Economic History Review* 60, no. 2: 241–66.

Bruhn, Miriam, and Francisco A. Gallego. 2012. "Good, Bad, and Ugly Colonial Activities: Do They Matter for Economic Development?" *Review of Economics and Statistics* 94, no. 2: 433–61.

Canen, Nathan, and Leonard Wantchekon. 2022. "Political Distortions, State Capture, and Economic Development in Africa." *Journal of Economic Perspectives* 36, no. 1: 101–24.

Caselli, Francesco. 2005. "Accounting for Cross-Country Income Differences." *Handbook of Economic Growth* 1: 679–741.

Chanda, Areendam, C. Justin Cook, and Louis Putterman. 2014. "Persistence of Fortune: Accounting for Population Movements, There Was No Post-Columbian Reversal." *American Economic Journal: Macroeconomics* 6, no. 3: 1–28.

Chaudhary, Latika. 2010. "Taxation and Educational Development: Evidence from British India." *Explorations in Economic History* 47, no. 3: 279–93.

Coatsworth, John H. 1978. "Obstacles to Economic Growth in Nineteenth-Century Mexico." *American Historical Review* 83, no. 1: 80–100.

Coatsworth, John H. 1993. "La independencia latinoamericana: Hipótesis sobre sus costes y beneficios." In *La independencia americana: consecuencias económicas*, eds. Prados De La Escosura, Leandro, and Samuel Amaral, 17–30. Madrid: Alianza: Editorial.

Cogneau, Denis, and Alexander Moradi. 2014. "Borders That Divide: Education and Religion in Ghana and Togo since Colonial Times." *Journal of Economic History* 74, no. 3: 694–729.

Dell, Melissa. 2010. "The Persistent Effects of Peru's Mining Mita." *Econometrica* 78, no. 6: 1863–903.

Dell, Melissa, and Benjamin A. Olken. 2020. "The Development Effects of the Extractive Colonial Economy: The Dutch Cultivation System in Java." *Review of Economic Studies* 87, no. 1: 164–203. https://doi.org/10.1093/restud/rdz017.

Donaldson, Dave. 2018. "Railroads of the Raj: Estimating the Impact of Transportation Infrastructure." *American Economic Review* 108, no. 4–5: 899–934.

Dupraz, Yannick. 2019. "French and British Colonial Legacies in Education: Evidence from the Partition of Cameroon." *Journal of Economic History* 79, no. 3: 628–68.

Easterly, William, and Ross Levine. 2016. "The European Origins of Economic Development." *Journal of Economic Growth* 21, no. 3: 225–57.

Engerman, Stanley L., and Kenneth L. Sokoloff. 1997. "Factor Endowments, Institutions, and Differential Paths of Growth among New World Economies: A View from Economic Historians of the United States." In *How Latin America Fell Behind: Essays on the Economic Histories of Brazil and Mexico, 1800-1914*, ed. Stephen H. Haber, 261–304. Stanford Unviversity Press.

Feyrer, James, and Bruce Sacerdote. 2009. "Colonialism and Modern Income: Islands as Natural Experiments." *Review of Economics and Statistics* 91, no. 2: 245–62.

Frankema, Ewout, and Marlous Van Waijenburg. 2014. "Metropolitan Blueprints of Colonial Taxation? Lessons from Fiscal Capacity Building in British and French Africa, c. 1880–1940." *Journal of African History* 55, no. 3: 371–400.

Gaikwad, Nikhar. 2014. "East India Companies and Long-Term Economic Change in India." Unpublished manuscript. URL: https://www.nikhargaikwad.com/resources/Gaikwad_EICs_2014.pdf.

Gennaioli, Nicola, and Ilia Rainer. 2007. "The Modern Impact of Precolonial Centralization in Africa." *Journal of Economic Growth* 12, no. 3: 185–234.

Glaeser, Edward L., Rafael La Porta, Florencio Lopez-de-Silanes, and Andrei Shleifer. 2004. "Do Institutions Cause Growth?" *Journal of Economic Growth* 9, no. 3: 271–303.

Grier, Robin M. 1999. "Colonial Legacies and Economic Growth." *Public Choice* 98: 317–35. https://doi.org/10.1023/A:1018322908007.

Gardner, Leigh. 2012. *Taxing Colonial Africa: The Political Economy of British Imperialism*. Oxford: Oxford University Press.

Guardado, Jenny. 2018. "Office-Selling, Corruption, and Long-Term Development in Peru." *American Political Science Review* 112, no. 4: 971–95.

Guardado, Jenny. 2022. "Hierarchical Oversight and the Value of Public Office: Evidence from Colonial Peru." *Journal of Politics* 84, no. 3: 1353–69.

Heldring, Leander, and James A. Robinson. 2012. "Colonialism and Development in Africa." In *The Oxford Handbook of Politics of Development*, eds. Carol Lancaster and Nicolas Van de Walle, 295–328. Oxford: Oxford University Press.

Herbst, Jeffrey. 2000. *States and Power in Africa: Comparative Lessons in Authority and Control*. Princeton, NJ: Princeton University Press.

Hofman, Andre A., and Patricio Valderrama. 2021. "Long-Run Economic Growth Performance in Latin America–1820–2016." *Journal of Economic Surveys* 35, no. 3: 833–69.

Hough, Jerry F., and Robin Grier. 2015. *The Long Process of Development*. Cambridge, MA: Cambridge University Press.

Hsieh, Chang-Tai, and Peter J. Klenow. 2010. "Development Accounting." *American Economic Journal: Macroeconomics* 2, no. 1: 207–23.

Huillery, Elise. 2009. "History Matters: The Long-Term Impact of Colonial Public Investments in French West Africa. *American Economic Journal: Applied Economics* 1, no. 2: 176–215.

Jones, Charles I. 2016. "The Facts of Economic Growth." In *Handbook of Macroeconomics*, eds. John B. Taylor and Harald Uhlig, Vol. 2, First Edition, 3–69. Elsevier.

Kaniyathu, Sunny John. "The Balance Sheet of Colonialism: Economic Development in the Colonial Period." PhD diss., New York University, 2007.

Keefer, Phil, and Carlos Scartascini. 2022. *Trust, Social Cohesion, and Growth in Latin America and the Caribbean*, 1–26. IDB Publications (Book Chapters). https://ideas.repec.org/h/idb/idbchp/11778-c1.html.

Jedwab, Remi, Edward Kerby, and Alexander Moradi. 2017. "History, Path Dependence and Development: Evidence from Colonial Railways, Settlers and Cities in Kenya. *Economic Journal* 127, no. 603: 1467–94.

Jedwab, Remi, and Alexander Moradi. 2016. The permanent effects of transportation revolutions in poor countries: evidence from Africa. *Review of Economics and Statistics* 98, no. 2: 268–84.

La Porta, Rafael, Florencio Lopez-de-Silanes, and Andrei Shleifer. 2008. "The Economic Consequences of Legal Origins." *Journal of Economic Literature* 46, no. 2: 285–332.

La Porta, Rafael, Florencio Lopez-de-Silanes, Andrei Shleifer, and Robert W. Vishny. 1997. "Legal Determinants of External Finance." *Journal of Finance* 52, no. 3: 1131–50.

Lange, Matthew, James Mahoney, and Matthias Vom Hau. 2006. "Colonialism and Development: A Comparative Analysis of Spanish and British Colonies." *American Journal of Sociology* 111, no. 5: 1412–62.

Lankina, Tomila, and Lullit Getachew. 2013. "Competitive Religious Entrepreneurs: Christian Missionaries and Female Education in Colonial and Post-Colonial India." *British Journal of Political Science* 43, no. 1: 103–31.

Lee, Alexander. 2019. "Land, State Capacity, and Colonialism: Evidence from India." *Comparative Political Studies* 52, no. 3: 412–44.

Lee, Alexander, and Kenneth Schultz. 2012. "Comparing British and French Colonial Legacies: A Discontinuity Analysis of Cameroon." *Quarterly Journal of Political Science* 7: 1–46.

Lee, Alexander, and Jack Paine. 2019. "What were the Consequences of Decolonization?" *International Studies Quarterly* 63, no. 2: 406–16.

Lowes, Sara, and Eduardo Montero. 2021. "Concessions, Violence, and Indirect Rule: Evidence from the Congo Free State." *Quarterly Journal of Economics* 136, no. 4: 2047–91.

Lugard, Frederick. 1922. *The Dual Mandate in British Tropical Africa*. Edinburgh: William Blackwood and Sons.

Mahoney, James. 2010. *Colonialism and Postcolonial Development: Spanish America in Comparative Perspective*. Cambridge, MA: Cambridge University Press.

Lange, Matthew, James Mahoney, and Matthias Vom Hau. 2006. "Colonialism and Development: A Comparative Analysis of Spanish and British Colonies." *American Journal of Sociology* 111, no. 5: 1412–62.

Maloney, William F., and Felipe Valencia Caicedo. 2016. "The Persistence of (Subnational) Fortune." *Economic Journal* 126, no. 598: 2363–401.

Mattingly, Daniel C. 2017. "Colonial Legacies and State Institutions in China: Evidence from a Natural Experiment." *Comparative Political Studies* 50, no. 4: 434–63.

Michalopoulos, Stelios, and Elias Papaioannou. 2013. "Pre-colonial Ethnic Institutions and Contemporary African Development." *Econometrica* 81, no. 1: 113–52.

Michalopoulos, Stelios, and Elias Papaioannou. 2014. "National Institutions and Subnational Development in Africa." *Quarterly Journal of Economics* 129, no. 1: 151–213.

Michalopoulos, Stelios, and Elias Papaioannou. 2020. "Historical Legacies and African Development." *Journal of Economic Literature* 58, no. 1: 53–128.

Müller-Crepon, C. 2020. "Continuity or Change? (In) Direct Rule in British and French Colonial Africa." *International Organization* 74, no. 4: 707–41.

Naritomi, Joana, Rodrigo R. Soares, and Juliano J. Assunção. 2012. "Institutional Development and Colonial Heritage within Brazil." *Journal of Economic History* 72, no. 2: 393–422.

Nunn, Nathan. 2007. "Historical Legacies: A Model Linking Africa's Past to Its Current Underdevelopment." *Journal of Development Economics* 83, no. 1: 157–75.

Nunn, Nathan. 2008. "The Long-Term Effects of Africa's Slave Trades." *Quarterly Journal of Economics* 123, no. 1: 139–76.

Nunn, Nathan. 2010. "Religious Conversion in Colonial Africa." *American Economic Review* 100, no. 2: 147–52.

Nunn, Nathan, and Leonard Wantchekon. 2011. "The Slave Trade and the Origins of Mistrust in Africa." *American Economic Review* 101, no. 7: 3221–52.

Okoye, Dozie, and Roland Pongou. 2014. "Historical Missionary Activity, Schooling, and the Reversal of Fortunes: Evidence from Nigeria." Unpublished manuscript. Available at: https://papers.ssrn.com/sol3/papers.cfm?abstract_id=2484020.

Okoye, Dozie, Roland Pongou, and Tite Yokossi. 2019. "New Technology, Better Economy? The Heterogeneous Impact of Colonial Railroads in Nigeria." *Journal of Development Economics* 140: 320–54.

Prados de la Escosura, Leandro. 2008 [1984]. "The Economic Consequences of Independence in Latin America." In *The Cambridge History of Latin America*, Vol. 2, ed. Leslie Bethell, 463–504. Cambridge, MA: Cambridge University Press.

Putterman, Louis, and David N. Weil. 2010. "Post-1500 Population Flows and the Long-Run Determinants of Economic Growth and Inequality." *Quarterly Journal of Economics* 125, no. 4: 1627–82.

Ricart-Huguet, Joan-Ricart. 2022. "The Origins of Colonial Investments in Former British and French Africa." *British Journal of Political Science* 52, no. 2 736–57. https://doi.org/10.1017/S0007123420000678.

Ricart-Huguet, Joan-Ricart. 2021. "Why Do Colonial Investments Persist Less in Anglophone Than in Francophone Africa?" *Journal of Historical Political Economy* 1, no. 4: 477–98.

Rivadeneira Acosta, Alex. 2019. *Essays in Economic Development*. Doctoral dissertation, Arizona State University.

Roessler, Phillip, Yannick Pengl, Robert Marty, Kyle Titlow, and Nicolas van de Walle. 2020. "The Cash Crop Revolution, Colonialism and Legacies of Spatial Inequality: Evidence from Africa." CSAE Working Paper WPS/2020-12.

Salvucci, Richard. 2010. "Some Thoughts on the Economic History of Early Colonial Mexico." *History Compass* 8, no. 7: 626–35.

Smith, Adam. 1998 [1776]. *An Inquiry into the Nature and Causes of the Wealth of Nations*. Washington, DC: Regnery Publishing.

Solow, Robert M. 1957. "Technical Change and the Aggregate Production Function." *Review of Economics and Statistics*, Vol. 39, 312–20.

Summerhill, W. 2010. "Colonial Institutions, Slavery, Inequality, and Development: Evidence from Sao Paulo, Brazil." Social Science Research Network.

Valencia Caicedo, Felipe. 2019. "The Mission: Human Capital Transmission, Economic Persistence, and Culture in South America." *Quarterly Journal of Economics* 134, no. 1: 507–56.

Vogler, Jan P. 2019. "Imperial Rule, the Imposition of Bureaucratic Institutions, and Their Long-Term Legacies." *World Politics* 71, no. 4: 806–63.

Waldinger, Maria. 2017. "The Long-Run Effects of Missionary Orders in Mexico." *Journal of Development Economics* 127: 355–78.

Wantchekon, Leonard, and Piero Stanig. 2015. "The Curse of Good Soil? Land Fertility, Roads and Rural Poverty in Africa." Unpublished manuscript. Princeton University.

Wantchekon, Leonard, Marko Klašnja, and Natalija Novta. 2015. "Education and Human Capital Externalities: Evidence from Colonial Benin." *Quarterly Journal of Economics* 130, no. 2: 703–57.

Woodberry, Robert D. 2004. *The Shadow of Empire: Christian Missions, Colonial Policy, and Democracy in Postcolonial Societies*. Chapel Hill: University of North Carolina Press.

Woodberry, Robert D. 2011. "Religion and the Spread of Human Capital and Political Institutions: Christian Missions as a Quasi-Natural Experiment" In The Oxford Handbook of the Economics of Religion *Oxford Handbooks*, ed. Rachel M. McCleary (online edn, Oxford Academic, 18 Sept. 2012). https://doi.org/10.1093/oxfordhb/9780195390049.013.0006. Accessed November 9, 2022.

CHAPTER 29

THE HISTORICAL POLITICAL ECONOMY OF GLOBALIZATION

KEVIN HJORTSHØJ O'ROURKE

Introduction

It is easy to understand the motivation for a chapter on globalization written for a Handbook of Historical Political Economy. In the first place, globalization—the economic integration of different regions of the world—has a long history.[1] That history teaches us that globalization is not irreversible: that it ebbs and flows over time, and that it would be foolish to assume that today's hyper-globalization is necessarily here to stay. And if that is the case, this is because globalization is not only a technological phenomenon, but a political one. Whether international interactions multiply to the extent permitted by the technology of the day depends on politics—domestic political economy forces in some cases, geopolitical forces in others. So globalization is shaped by political economy forces. In the second place, and just as importantly, globalization compels us to reconsider how we understand long run processes of economic development. Regions and countries have not evolved in isolation, running along parallel but separate tracks. Rather, they have continuously interacted with each other over the course of the centuries, and no credible account of why some have done better than others in particular periods can omit a detailed consideration of these interactions. Globalization compels us to take geography seriously and to think more like historians.

I begin with a review of how globalization is shaped by—and shapes—domestic and international politics, before going on to consider how our understanding of comparative historical development needs to be better informed by the history of how regions have interacted with each other across the centuries.

The Political Economy of Globalization

When Did Globalization Begin?

How old globalization is depend on how you define and measure it. The archaeological record shows conclusively that goods have been traded over surprisingly long distances for millennia. A classic example is obsidian, a volcanic glass that was used to make a variety of tools as long ago as 30,000 years ago or more. Since it only occurs in certain volcanic areas its presence elsewhere required trade, and in the Near East there is evidence of such trade almost 10,000 years ago. That trade declined with distance, as predicted by the classic gravity model, but even so some obsidian travelled more than 600 miles (Dixon et al. 1968, 44). By the sixth millennium BC obsidian was being traded between Ethiopia and Yemen; by 1000 BC it was being distributed over a range of more than 6,000 km in the Western Pacific and Southeast Asia (Rowlands and Fuller, 2018, p. 183; Spriggs, 2018, 425).

During the fifth and fourth millennia BC, during the so-called Ubaid period, a "complex web of inter-regional exchange" developed in a region encompassing present-day Iraq, Syria, parts of Turkey and Iran, as well as the western shores of the Gulf. Not only prestige goods such as various coloured stones, including lapis lazuli from present-day Afghanistan, but more "utilitarian" goods, were involved (Stein 2010, 29). By the end of the Ubaid period clay seals start to provide further evidence of long-distance trade, perhaps also indicating that merchants now needed to develop systems promoting trust when dealing with strangers (Caldwell 1976; Wilkinson 2018, 29–30).

By 3200 BC Afghan lapis lazuli was being used in Egyptian ornamentation, and during the centuries that followed the stone was increasingly used in Egyptian and Mesopotamian statuary (Wengrow 2010, 32–8). More generally, the Bronze Age saw a great expansion of long-distance trade, due at least in part to the simple fact that copper and tin were only available in a few sources but were demanded everywhere. Tin was particularly scarce, in Europe being obtained from either the western fringes of the continent or Asia. Regions across Europe thus exported goods that were in demand elsewhere so that they could import copper and tin: the Baltic supplied amber, northern Scandinavia fur, present-day Hungary wool, the Carpathians silver and salt, and so on (Earle et al. 2015, 635–6; Kristiansen 2018, 9). According to Kristiansen (ibid.) the forces of comparative advantage not only led to the Nordic region exporting amber, but to "more or less" ceasing to consume it, a remarkable early illustration of simple trade theory in action. Other regions would eventually export horses, warriors, and slaves (p. 10). Inter-regional trade not only involved raw materials unobtainable elsewhere, but manufactured goods, since woollen textiles were a key component of long-distance trade flows. Trade during the period was facilitated by better boat designs and the increasing use of horses, but the Bronze Age also saw the development of several institutions underpinning long-distance trade between strangers: the use of sealing in long-distance trade became widespread, systems of weights emerged which were standardized across regions, weights of silver were increasingly used to express prices, and attempts were made by rulers to make other polities responsible for the safety of merchants operating in their jurisdictions (Kristiansen 2018, 5, 12–3; Warburton 2018).

Another turning point, or rather turning period, came in the final two centuries of the first millennium BC, when according to Philip Curtin (1984, 90) regular overland trade spanning the vast expanses between China and Europe came into being. The causes were largely geopolitical, with the formations of the Chinese, Parthian and Roman empires making such long-distance routes safer for merchants. Excavations in Begram, in present-day Afghanistan, have found substantial quantities of luxury products from China, India, and the Roman Empire, indicating substantial inter-regional interconnections that were not only material, but cultural and religious (Mairs, 2017). The flows involved were large: Pliny the Elder famously claimed that "India, China and the Arabian Peninsula take one hundred million sesterces from our empire per annum at a conservative estimate" (cited in Gurukkal 2016, 67). While Pliny's estimate might be regarded as an exaggeration, on the basis that he was opposed to extravagant aristocratic spending on foreign luxuries, more recent documentary evidence suggests that if anything his figure may have been an under-estimate. A papyrus from the mid-second century AD values the cargo of a ship that had sailed from India to Berenice, on the western shores of the Red Sea, at over 9 million sesterces, implying customs duties (which were taken in kind) of some 2.3 million sesterces (Rathbone 2007, 318, n. 15; Wilson 2009, p 217). A century earlier, Strabo had estimated that 120 ships a year left Myos Hormos, a nearby port, for India: Andrew Wilson thus calculates that if just 100 similar ships arrived from India in a year, the resultant import duties could have paid for as much as a quarter to one third of the empire's military budget (Wilson 2012, 290). If mid-second century Roman Empire GDP amounted to some 20 million sesterces, as estimated by Scheidel and Friesen (2009), then as much as 5% of total income, or roughly 20–25% of elite income, could have been spent on Asian goods imported via the Red Sea alone. Perhaps such figures are implausibly high, but the conclusion that imports from outside the Empire—itself a vast region within which goods circulated widely—were substantial seems a safe one. There is no reason to suppose that the Chinese and Sassanian empires, as well as other major Eurasian regions, did not also experience large inflows and outflows of goods at this time.

By this period, at the very latest, it also becomes safe to use the word "trade," which I have deployed, perhaps incautiously, to describe the inter-regional exchange of goods in previous millennia. Many anthropologists and archaeologists have argued that in the past such activities often did not constitute trade, but rather gift-giving, redistribution, and a wide variety of other non-market activities (for a stimulating recent restatement of the view, see Graeber and Wengrow 2021). By the classical period, however, the case for long-distance trade in at least some parts of the world seems clear. As Wilson (2012, 287) puts it:

> Interstate treaties in Classical Greece normally specified reciprocal trading rights; Latin citizenship was defined partly in terms of trading privileges, and the Punic

Wars were fought over the control of trading zones in the central Mediterranean. The persistent reluctance of many historians in the later twentieth century to admit the extent and importance of long-distance trade in the ancient world is therefore difficult to understand, and indeed utterly incomprehensible when one considers the archaeological evidence in addition to the written record.

Trade across Eurasia became even more integrated in the late thirteenth and early fourteenth centuries, when much of the region became politically unified under the Mongols. The "world system" that emerged encompassed all of Eurasia, from Ireland to China, and from Bergen to present-day Indonesia (Abu-Lughod 1989). Northern and Eastern Africa were also—as in previous centuries—involved in economic exchanges with India and the Muslim world, and interregional contacts during the period were even broader than this, encompassing the North Atlantic as far as Greenland, which occasionally exported walrus tusks or animal skins to Iceland or Norway, and on at least one occasion received agents from Italy seeking the payment of papal tithes. Italians were at the same time travelling regularly to China, from whence not only Chinese luxury goods but Southeast Asian spices were transported back to Europe via the overland route (Findlay and O'Rourke 2007, 106–7).

From the beginnings of the Bronze Age therefore, roughly 5000 years ago, there was a series of milestones representing ever-increasing integration. I have spent some time on these since the history may be less familiar to some readers than subsequent developments. Kristiansen (2018, 2) argues that they represented a continuous process of evolution, with the basic institutional features of long-distance trade as it emerged from 3000 BC onwards—"international commodity trade, the rule of public law, the rise of urban life, city-states, and sometimes empires"—developing throughout. But if globalization is defined as a global phenomenon, then 1500 deserves to be regarded as a discontinuous turning point. Key dates include not only 1492 and 1498, but 1571, when ships from Latin America arrived in Manila, thus instituting a direct trans-Pacific trade route between China and Latin America (Flynn and Giráldez 1995). From then on, or more precisely from the late eighteenth century when trade with Australia also began, all of the inhabited continents of the world were in continuous and direct contact with each other. But the full economic implications of this would only make themselves felt once transport costs had fallen sufficiently to permit the mass trans-oceanic transportation of bulky and cheap foodstuffs, raw materials, and manufactured goods. That would only happen in the nineteenth century (although the early modern period saw the emergence of large-scale trade in such goods between the Baltic and Western Europe).

From the previous discussion it seems clear that there is a decent case to be made that some form of globalization began at the latest with the onset of the Bronze Age (Frank and Gills 1993). There is also a self-evident case to be made for 1500 as the key date, an argument advanced by no less an authority than Adam Smith himself, who famously regarded 1492 and 1498 as "the two greatest and most important events recorded in the history of mankind" (Smith 1976 [1776], volume 2, 626). But there is also a case to be made that the mid-nineteenth century saw the development of a new and more modern kind of globalization that was qualitatively as well as quantitatively different from what had gone before.

"All history is contemporary history," as Benedetto Croce once said, and the same is perhaps true of economic history. In the 1990s, as China's rise to its current superpower economic status gathered momentum, and some American economists started to worry about whether Western wages were "set in Beijing" (Freeman 1995), it seemed natural to ask whether previous globalizations had led to inter-continental factor price convergence in line with the predictions of the famous Stolper-Samuelson Theorem. It also seemed natural to look to the nineteenth century for such impacts of inter-continental trade on income distribution, since the transatlantic trade of that period between the "old" and "new" worlds was what had motivated Heckscher and Ohlin to develop their factor proportions theory of trade in the first place. O'Rourke and Williamson (1994, 1999) investigated the issue and concluded to their satisfaction that Heckscher and Ohlin had been right: the globalization of the late nineteenth century, involving the exchange of labour-intensive European manufactured goods for land-intensive New World agricultural commodities, had led *ceteris paribus* to falling European land rents, rising European real wages, rising New World land rents, and falling New World real wages. Commodity price gaps collapsed, trade flows soared, and factor prices converged internationally.

That having been established, the next question was whether this kind of rather modern globalization could be found in earlier periods. In order for inter-continental trade to change domestic factor prices, there had to be inter-continental commodity price convergence, since that was the first vital step in the Heckscher-Ohlin chain of causation. And the prices involved had to be for commodities produced in both continents, since only then would price convergence lead to the shifts in domestic production structures that constituted the second vital step in that logic. On both grounds the nineteenth century seemed different to those that had gone before (O'Rourke and Williamson 2002). True, 1500 did seem to have produced a step increase in intercontinental integration (O'Rourke and Williamson 2009), but inter-continental price gaps seemed remarkably stable during the seventeenth and eighteenth centuries, in sharp contrast to the virtually ubiquitous declines experienced in the nineteenth. When defined in terms of this kind of market integration, therefore, globalization—or if you prefer, Heckscher-Ohlin globalization—was a modern phenomenon, beginning some time in the nineteenth century. Among its causes were the new steam transportation technologies of the period, the end of the old mercantilist trading monopolies, imperialism, and the relatively peaceful state of intra-European affairs. There are certainly good grounds to prefer alternative definitions of globalization, or to argue (as do Findlay and O'Rourke 2007) that international interactions had major economic implications prior to the nineteenth century (Flynn and Giráldez 2004), and subsequent work has found some evidence of inter-continental commodity market integration prior to 1800 (e.g. Sharp and Weisdorf 2013). But the basic argument that the globalization of the nineteenth century and subsequently was not only quantitatively, but qualitatively different from what had gone before still seems to me a reasonable one. The question of when globalization began is thus largely a definitional one (which may make it a rather unsatisfactory question); and as will be seen shortly, so is the question of when it goes into reverse.

Globalization Is Not Irreversible

The previous subsection might make it seem that the history of globalization—no matter how defined—has been one of constant progress over time, whether continuous or marked by step changes in the level of international integration. Nothing could be further from the truth. On the contrary, history is replete with instances in which formerly integrated regions disintegrated, sometimes for long periods of time. In earlier periods the causes were often geopolitical. Long-distance trade required security for merchants, and thus benefited from the establishment of large empires enjoying a monopoly of violence within their territories, and willing to commit resources to promoting long-distance trade. Bryan Ward-Perkins (2005) convincingly details how long-distance trade within Western Europe collapsed along with the Roman Empire, with dramatic and negative consequences for economic specialization and living standards—a classic example of the unravelling of Smithian growth. When the Mongol Empire entered into decline in the middle of the fourteenth century, long-distance Eurasian trade declined as well. European merchants were no longer able to travel across Asia, or directly access Asian markets, and that remained the case until the European Voyages of Discovery. While intra-Asian trade continued to flourish, geopolitical turmoil, including the collapse of the Timurid Empire, eventually led to the decline of the Asian caravan trade in the late sixteenth and early seventeenth centuries also (Rossabi 1990). The French and Napoleonic Wars of the late eighteenth and early nineteenth centuries, which lasted for a quarter of a century, led to the worldwide disintegration of markets (O'Rourke 2006), while World War I ushered in a period of deglobalization which only started to unwind in Western countries in the 1950s, and lasted much longer in many other parts of the world. Indeed, thanks to communism it lasted in the former Soviet bloc until the 1990s (Findlay and O'Rourke 2007, Chapters 8, 9).

That last judgement also depends on matters of definition. Tooze and Fertik (2014, 220) argue that World War I, which was by definition global, led not to the destruction of the international economy of the late nineteenth century, but to its "repurposing and reorganization." As its name suggests, this was a global war, fought with raw materials transported across the world by the British shipping industry—"the anchor of the entire Entente war effort" (221)—and paid for in large part by American loans. "Never before had global independence been made so manifest." The point is well taken, but 1914 still emerges as a de-globalizing turning point if globalization is defined in terms of the international extension of the market and market forces, a definition which comes naturally to economists. But other definitions are of course possible.

Geopolitical disruptions have therefore caused the disintegration of international markets, but domestic political economy forces have also done so in less spectacular fashion.[2] The gradual move towards ever-freer trade in Western Europe from 1815 onwards, which accelerated after 1846 when Britain repealed the Corn Laws, and 1860, when it signed a trade agreement with France, was brought to a halt from the late 1870s onwards as France, Germany, Italy, and other countries raised tariffs in response to falling agricultural prices (Kindleberger 1951; Rogowski 1989; O'Rourke 1997). (In many if not most cases tariffs on manufactured goods were raised also.) Since agricultural prices were declining in Western Europe as a result of the globalization of the time, with steamships and railroads bringing New World prairies, outbacks, and pampas into ever more direct competition with European farmers, this was an example of globalization undermining itself. The gradual tightening of immigration restrictions in the New World was another (Hatton and Williamson 1998). Globalization really does produce winners and losers, and no-one should be surprised if the losers mobilize politically to protect their economic interests. There is an obvious analogy to be made with early twenty-first-century anti-globalization discontent in affluent countries such as the United Kingdom and United States, as documented by such authors as Autor et al. (2013), Autor et al. (2020), Colantone and Stanig (2018), and others (see O'Rourke 2019 for a comparative historical discussion).

More speculatively, globalization may also undermine itself through geopolitical as well as domestic political economy channels. The earlier discussion framed the various geopolitical shocks leading to international economic disintegration as essentially exogenous. However, as Findlay and O'Rourke (2007, p. xxv) put it, "It is natural to suspect that the accumulating economic and geopolitical tensions unleashed in the course of each period of peace, prosperity, and trade culminate in successive rounds of conflict, so that wars, rather than being exogenous or external shocks to the world system, have been inherent in its very nature." Tooze and Fertik (2014) and others argue that World War I represented an endogenous response to late nineteenth century globalization: one obvious mechanism they appeal to is economic convergence. If globalization helped nineteenth-century Russia to grow economically, then it also helped to increase tensions between that country and Germany, in the same way that Chinese growth today, also fueled by globalization, is raising tensions with the United States (217–8). According to a well-known argument, such convergence can give established powers an incentive to strike first, before it is too late. Alternatively, globalization also leads to increasing dependence on international markets for goods, including strategically vital commodities. Where established powers control international shipping lanes, this can give rising powers the incentive to attack either the leaders or resource-rich regions in an attempt to make themselves more strategically self-sufficient (Bonfatti and O'Rourke 2018). Offer (1989) makes the case that such forces help to explain the Anglo-German naval rivalry of the early twentieth century, while Tooze (2006) and Barnhart (1987) argue that concerns about raw materials supplies were important factors in the run-up to World War II.

Globalization and Historical Development

A voluminous literature in the 1990s studied the correlates of economic growth across countries. Cross-section regressions inspired by the Solow growth model explored the relationship between economic growth and initial income, savings rates, population growth, and human capital. One obvious problem was that many of the right-hand side variables were potentially endogenous. Eventually researchers added institutional and cultural variables to the explanatory mix, with endogeneity remaining a concern. It was perhaps inevitable in the circumstances that researchers would turn to the distant past in search of instruments for contemporary institutions (Acemoglu et al. 2001), and that this would in turn eventually lead to a vast literature uncovering correlations between very old variables and more recent ones, and arguing that these correlations were causal. In this manner was the so-called "persistence literature" born.

There are many well-flagged problems with the literature. Aside from obvious issues such as the potential for p-hacking, and the fact that many (but not all) papers are based on cross-section regressions, there are in some cases serious issues with the data used (Albouy 2012). Indeed, a basic data issue concerns the use of present-day boundaries, which makes less and less sense the further back you go in time, and which poses a particular problem when the supposed mechanisms rely on transmission of some sort within historically mobile populations. As Voth (2021, 246) puts it, "Since not many descendants of the people living in Germany at the time of Tacitus are still living there today, it is difficult to see how technology adoption by the ancient tribe called the Cimbri could influence technology use in modern-day Denmark, where they originated. The same is true of large parts of Greece, France, Eastern Europe, to name but a few areas." Several well-known results are vulnerable to the inclusion of such obvious control variables as malarial prevalence, or the replacement of continent dummies with World Bank economic region dummies (Kelly 2021). Just as problematically, both the left-hand and right-hand side variables typically considered exhibit a high degree of spatial correlation, and once this has been taken into account the regressions often lose statistical significance (Kelly 2019). It does not appear to be the case that this problem goes away if you consider, not the first regression in papers' key regression tables, but later regressions incorporating a greater array of control variables (Voth 2021). Kelly (2021) shows that the same problem emerges when you study the regression using the largest set of controls available.

Voth (2021) and many other economic historians have highlighted the lack of plausible mechanisms underlying some—but not all—papers in the literature, but this is not the only problem that economic historians have with the notion that the deep past in some sense pre-determines present outcomes, even if only probabilistically. The enormous income gaps motivating the econometric literature on cross-country growth and convergence emerged in the aftermath of the Industrial Revolution, which originated in Britain and gradually spread around the world, first to north-west Europe and North America, and then to the rest of Europe and further afield. It follows that variables that were high in the West before the Industrial Revolution, and low elsewhere, or low in the West and high elsewhere, are the ones that have the best chance of being correlated with living standards today. In running cross-country regressions therefore, economists can come perilously close to advocating a "Whig theory of economic history," in which (in the words of David Landes 1990, 1) the answer to the question "why are we so rich and they so poor" turns out to be "because we are so good and they so bad; that is, we are hardworking, knowledgable, educated, well-governed, efficacious, and productive, and they are the reverse." Indeed, the conclusion that Europe pulled ahead of the rest of the world because of advantages which it enjoyed and other regions did not—be those advantages cultural, institutional, or geographical—seems to be to a large extent hard-baked into the methodology. The finding that geographical variables were correlated with European development does not necessarily imply a Whiggish view of the world, but similar correlations involving political or cultural variables probably do. And all such correlations suggest a narrative in which pre-existing factors "caused" the Great Divergence, perhaps even inevitably so.

This is doubly problematic. First, historians of all stripes tend to reject overly-deterministic accounts of historical change. Very few events, still less major economic, political, and social upheavals, are "inevitable" before they occur. Second, simplistic Whiggish accounts in which British institutional or cultural advantages explain why the Industrial Revolution occurred there and not elsewhere are increasingly being questioned, at least among historians of the British Industrial Revolution. Instead, economic historians are more and more emphasizing the many interrelationships between Britain and the rest of the world which existed in the seventeenth and eighteenth centuries as well as subsequently. A striking symbol of this shift can be found in successive volumes of the standard undergraduate textbook on British economic history. In the first edition (Floud and McCloskey 1981) the chapter on trade and empire dismissed the possibility that such connections might have been necessary for growth during the Industrial Revolution. A counterfactual Britain deprived of foreign markets would have produced fewer cotton textiles, but the consequence would merely have been an alternative Industrial Revolution fueled by brewing, housebuilding and other non-traded activities (100). Welfare would have declined, but not by much, since Harberger triangles are small. The discussion is notable for its dependence on *a priori* logic and rather abstract nature. This is in total contrast to the corresponding chapter in the most recent edition of the textbook, which is far more detailed and historical in nature, engages seriously with the famous Williams (1944) thesis that Caribbean slavery was intimately linked with the birth of the Industrial Revolution, correctly rejects the use of static models to calculate the impact of trade on growth, a simple point that should be self-evident, and stresses the impact of trade on technological development and the accumulation of human capital (Zahedieh 2014).

A second symbol of the shift in the historiography is Gavin Wright's recent Tawney Lecture (Wright 2020) which argues strongly for the role of slavery in explaining the

British eighteenth century take-off. As he correctly says (356), "historical interpretation over the past 30 years strongly supports the view that distant markets were critical for the emergent technologies of eighteenth-century Britain." He notes the relationship between slavery, long-distance trade, and innovation, as well as other links such as the role of trade-related bills of exchange in creating a British capital market (Hudson, 2014). Wright's lecture is a particularly striking example of the shift in the historiography of the British Industrial Revolution, since as he makes clear later in the article the author does *not* agree with the claim that slavery was essential for nineteenth century American economic development.

Take for example the cotton textile industry, traditionally regarded as one of the key industries of the Industrial Revolution, and restored to that position by the work of Nick Crafts and Knick Harley (Crafts and Harley 1992; Harley and Crafts 2000). 0.34 percentage points of the 0.42% growth per annum in British TFP achieved between 1780 and 1860 was concentrated in just a few modernizing sectors: cottons, woolens, iron, canals, ships, and railways (Crafts and O'Rourke 2014 266). What happened in the textile sector thus had macroeconomic significance: by the mid-1830s cotton textiles accounted for 48.5% of British exports (Davis 1979 15). To state the obvious: the British taste for textiles arose in the first place as a result of exposure to Indian textiles, which stimulated new consumer markets in Britain, as well as—crucially—the search for how to supply those markets (as well as others further afield, including in Africa) with locally produced textiles using British, rather than Indian, technology (Berg 2004). The cotton industry was first established in Britain by refugees from Antwerp; its major input, raw cotton, was produced in the New World by slaves who had been shipped there from Africa; a very large share of the sector's output was exported overseas. An account of the Industrial Revolution that takes no notice of these and other international linkages makes no sense. It mattered that Britain was a major trading nation with overseas colonies and access to raw materials and markets around the world, and that fortunate state of affairs, in turn, was produced by a host of geographical, political, military, and other factors, both structural and random in nature. Economists no longer think of technological change as dropping exogenously from the skies, like manna from heaven; it is now, and was then, a profit-motivated activity. Overseas markets and resources stimulated innovation, and not only in textiles: Zahedieh (2013) shows that Caribbean sugar plantations produced a demand for copper that can be directly linked to key technological breakthroughs in both metallurgy and mining. And trade itself directly stimulated innovation: navigation spurred the development of accurate instruments, which in turn produced the skills required to produce the machinery of the Industrial Revolution (Kelly and Ó Gráda 2022).

The argument in Wright, as well as Findlay (1990), Findlay and O'Rourke (2007) and others, is not that slavery, or any other single factor, "caused" the Industrial Revolution, but that slavery, trade, warfare, imperialism, migration, scientific cooperation, and a host of other factors both domestic and international combined to produce the take-off. These factors potentially include science, education, mechanical skills, the relative prices of labour, capital, and energy, and many others that have been prominent in the literature: it is not a question of denying the importance of these, but of stressing both their endogeneity, and the fact that they operated within a global context that determined their impact. Cross-country regressions, while informative, suggest a world in which different regions grew at different rates depending, predictably, on their underlying conditions, as if they were runners in a 400 m track race each with their own advantages and disadvantages, and remaining within their separate lanes. Historical reality was much more akin to a football cup tie, with the first goal winning, in which the multiple interactions between teams, match day officials, coaching staffs, and supporters (as well as within teams themselves) produced an environment in which almost anything could happen on the day, and in which random events could therefore have a major impact on the final outcome.[3] And it was even more complicated than that, because there were many teams involved at once, and each team's efforts could increase, as well as reduce, the chances of the other teams scoring. History mattered, not just in the by-now-cliched sense that random events within a country could have long run implications, but in the sense that those implications could themselves be either reinforced or undone by chance events at a later date, and that both the shocks and their consequences could be produced by, or make themselves felt through, international interactions of various kinds.

Some regional characteristics were of course enduring, notably geography, and the history of globalization requires us to take geography seriously. Western Europe had traditionally been peripheral, for example, but after Columbus it found itself far more centrally located within an expanding Atlantic economy. Its location, which had once been a handicap, now became a major asset. But those voyages were themselves the outcome of a centuries-long process in which the Muslim conquests, Genghis Kahn, the Black Death, the end of the *pax Mongolica*, inter-European rivalry, and many other factors, all had their part to play. The world which history has bequeathed to us was produced by an almost unthinkably complex dynamic general (dis)equilibrium process, and globalization in all its dimensions is an important reason why that process was so complex. If globalization forces us to think more seriously about geography, it should also make us think about the Great Divergence, and the many consequences that flowed from it, in a far more historical fashion—that is to say, as a unique and historically contingent event that was conditioned by an elaborate web of global forces.

Acknowledgments

I am grateful to the editors and Morgan Kelly for helpful suggestions; the usual disclaimer apples.

Notes

1. Globalization thus includes, at a minimum, trade, migration, capital flows, and technology transfers, and there are of course many other dimensions of globalization, including non-economic ones. Space constraints imply that I will mostly be focusing on trade in this chapter.

2. For an overview of the domestic political economy of trade policy, see Douglas Irwin's chapter in this volume.
3. Which is why soccer is so much more interesting than track and field.

References

Abu-Lughod, Janet L. 1989. *Before European Hegemony: The World System A.D. 1250-1350*. Oxford: Oxford University Press.

Acemoglu, Daron, Simon Johnson, and James A. Robinson. 2001. "The Colonial Origins of Comparative Development: An Empirical Investigation." *American Economic Review* 91, no. 5: 1369-401.

Albouy, David Y. 2012. "The Colonial Origins of Comparative Development: An Empirical Investigation: Comment." *American Economic Review* 102, no. 6: 3059-76.

Autor, David, David Dorn, Gordon Hanson, and Kaveh Majlesi. 2020. "Importing Political Polarization? The Electoral Consequences of Rising Trade Exposure." *American Economic Review* 110, no. 10: 3139-83.

Autor, David H., David Dorn, and Gordon H. Hanson. 2013. "The China Syndrome: Local Labor Market Effects of Import Competition in the United States." *American Economic Review* 103, no. 6: 2121-68.

Barnhart, Michael A. 1987. *Japan Prepares for Total War: The Search for Economic Security, 1919-1941*. Ithaca, NY: Cornell University Press.

Berg, Maxine. 2004. "In Pursuit of Luxury: Global History and British Consumer Goods in the Eighteenth Century." *Past & Present*, no. 182: 85-142.

Bonfatti, Roberto, and Kevin Hjortshøj O'Rourke. 2018. "Growth, Import Dependence, and War." *Economic Journal* 128, no. 614: 2222-57.

Caldwell, David H. 1976. "The Early Glyptic of Gawra, Giyan and Susa, and the Development of Long Distance Trade." *Orientalia* 45: 227-50.

Colantone, Italo, and Piero Stanig. 2018. "Global Competition and Brexit." *American Political Science Review* 112, no. 2: 201-18.

Crafts, N. F. R., and C. K. Harley. 1992. "Output Growth and the British Industrial Revolution: A Restatement of the Crafts-Harley View." *Economic History Review* 45, no. 4: 703-30.

Crafts, Nicholas, and Kevin Hjortshøj O'Rourke. 2014. "Twentieth Century Growth." Chap. 6 In *Handbook of Economic Growth*, ed. Philippe Aghion and Steven N. Durlauf, 263-346. Amsterdam: Elsevier.

Curtin, Philip D. 1984. *Cross-Cultural Trade in World History*. Cambridge: Cambridge University Press.

Davis, Ralph. 1979. *The Industrial Revolution and British Overseas Trade*. Leicester: Leicester University Press.

Dixon, J. E., J. R. Cann, and Colin Renfrew. 1968. "Obsidian and the Origins of Trade." *Scientific American* 218, no. 3: 38-47.

Earle, Timothy, Johan Ling, Claes Uhnér, Zofia Stos-Gale, and Lene Melheim. 2015. "The Political Economy and Metal Trade in Bronze Age Europe: Understanding Regional Variability in Terms of Comparative Advantages and Articulations." *European Journal of Archaeology* 18, no. 4: 633-57.

Findlay, Ronald. 1990. *The" Triangular Trade" and the Atlantic Economy of the Eighteenth Century: A Simple General-Equilibrium Model*. Essays in International Finance. Vol. 177: International Finance Section, Department of Economics, Princeton University.

Findlay, Ronald, and Kevin H. O'Rourke. 2007. *Power and Plenty: Trade, War, and the World Economy in the Second Millennium*. The Princeton Economic History of the Western World. Princeton, NJ: Princeton University Press.

Floud, Roderick, and Deirdre N. McCloskey, eds. 1981. *The Economic History of Britain since 1700*. 2 vols. Cambridge: Cambridge University Press.

Flynn, Dennis O., and Arturo Giráldez. 1995. "Born with a "Silver Spoon": The Origin of World Trade in 1571." *Journal of World History* 6, no. 2: 201–21.

Flynn, Dennis O., and Arturo Giráldez. 2004. "Path Dependence, Time Lags and the Birth of Globalisation: A Critique of O'Rourke and Williamson." *European Review of Economic History* 8, no. 01: 81–108.

Frank, Andre Gunder, and Barry K. Gills. 1993. *The World System: Five Hundred Years or Five Thousand?* London: Routledge.

Freeman, Richard B. 1995. "Are Your Wages Set in Beijing?" *Journal of Economic Perspectives* 9, no. 3: 15–32.

Graeber, David, and D. Wengrow. 2021. *The Dawn of Everything: A New History of Humanity*. London: Allen Lane.

Gurukkal, Rajan. 2016. *Rethinking Classical Indo-Roman Trade: Political Economy of Eastern Mediterranean Exchange Relations*. New Delhi: Oxford University Press.

Harley, C. Knick, and N. F. R. Crafts. 2000. "Simulating the Two Views of the British Industrial Revolution." *Journal of Economic History* 60, no. 3: 819–41.

Hatton, T. J., and Jeffrey G. Williamson. 1998. *The Age of Mass Migration: Causes and Economic Impact*. New York; Oxford: Oxford University Press.

Hudson, Pat. 2014. "Slavery, the Slave Trade and Economic Growth: A Contribution to the Debate." In *Emancipation and the Remaking of the British Imperial World*, ed. Catherine Hall, Nicholas Draper and Keith McClelland, 36–59. Manchester, UK: Manchester University Press.

Kelly, Morgan. 2021. "Persistence, Randomization, and Spatial Noise." *Centre for Economic Policy Research Discussion Paper* 16609.

Kelly, Morgan. 2019. "The Standard Errors of Persistence." *Centre for Economic Policy Research Discussion Paper* 13783.

Kelly, Morgan, and Cormac Ó Gráda. 2022. "Connecting the Scientific and Industrial Revolutions: The Role of Practical Mathematics." *Journal of Economic History* 82, no. 3: 841–73.

Kindleberger, C. P. 1951. "Group Behavior and International Trade." *Journal of Political Economy* 59, no. 1: 30–46.

Kristiansen, Kristian. 2018. "Theorizing Trade and Civilization." In *Trade and Civilisation: Economic Networks and Cultural Ties, from Prehistory to the Early Modern Era*, ed. Janken Myrdal, Kristian Kristiansen and Thomas Lindkvist, 1–24. Cambridge: Cambridge University Press.

Landes, David S. 1990. "Why Are We So Rich and They So Poor." *American Economic Review* 80, no. 2 (May): 1–13.

Mairs, Rachel. 2017. "Lapis Lazuli, Homer and the Buddha: Material and Ideological Exchange in West Asia (C. 250 Bce–200 Ce)." In *The Routledge Handbook of Archaeology and Globalization*, ed. Tamar Hodos, 885–98. Abingdon, Oxfordshire: Routledge.

O'Rourke, Kevin H. 1997. "The European Grain Invasion, 1870–1913." *Journal of Economic History* 57, no. 4: 775–801.

O'Rourke, Kevin H., and Jeffrey G. Williamson. 2009. "Did Vasco Da Gama Matter for European Markets?" *Economic History Review* 62, no. 3 (August): 655–84.

O'Rourke, Kevin H., and Jeffrey G. Williamson. 1999. *Globalization and History: The Evolution of a Nineteenth-Century Atlantic Economy*. Cambridge, MA.: MIT Press.

O'Rourke, Kevin H., and Jeffrey G. Williamson. 1994. "Late Nineteenth-Century Anglo-American Factor-Price Convergence: Were Heckscher and Ohlin Right?" *Journal of Economic History* 54, no. 4: 892–916.

O'Rourke, Kevin H., and Jeffrey G. Williamson. 2002. "When Did Globalisation Begin?" *European Review of Economic History* 6, no. 1: 23–50.

O'Rourke, Kevin H. 2006. "The Worldwide Economic Impact of the French Revolutionary and Napoleonic Wars, 1793–1815." *Journal of Global History* 1, no. 01: 123–49.

O'Rourke, Kevin Hjortshøj. 2019. "Economic History and Contemporary Challenges to Globalization." *Journal of Economic History* 79, no. 2: 356–82.

Offer, Avner. *The First World War: An Agrarian Interpretation*. Oxford: Clarendon Press, 1989.

Rathbone, Dominic. 2007. "Merchant Networks in the Greek World: The Impact of Rome." *Mediterranean Historical Review* 22, no. 2: 309–20.

Rogowski, Ronald. 1989. *Commerce and Coalitions: How Trade Affects Domestic Political Alignments*. Princeton, NJ: Princeton University Press.

Rossabi, Morris. 1990. "The "Decline" of the Central Asian Caravan Trade." In *The Rise of Merchant Empires: Long Distance Trade in the Early Modern World 1350–1750*, ed. James D. Tracy. Studies in Comparative Early Modern History, 351–70. Cambridge: Cambridge University Press.

Rowlands, Michael, and Dorian Q. Fuller. 2018. "Deconstructing Civilisation: A 'Neolithic' Alternative." In *Trade and Civilisation: Economic Networks and Cultural Ties, from Prehistory to the Early Modern Era*, ed. Janken Myrdal, Kristian Kristiansen and Thomas Lindkvist, 172–94. Cambridge: Cambridge University Press.

Scheidel, Walter, and Steven J. Friesen. 2009. "The Size of the Economy and the Distribution of Income in the Roman Empire." *Journal of Roman Studies* 99: 61–91.

Sharp, Paul, and Jacob Weisdorf. 2013. "Globalization Revisited: Market Integration and the Wheat Trade between North America and Britain from the Eighteenth Century." *Explorations in Economic History* 50, no. 1: 88–98.

Smith, Adam, R. H. Campbell, and Andrew S. Skinner. 1976. *An Inquiry into the Nature and Causes of the Wealth of Nations*. Glasgow Edition of the Works and Correspondence of Adam Smith. 2 vols. Oxford: Clarendon Press.

Spriggs, Matthew. 2018. "Elliot Smith Reborn? A View of Prehistoric Globalization from the Island Southeast Asian and Pacific Margins." In *Trade and Civilisation: Economic Networks and Cultural Ties, from Prehistory to the Early Modern Era*, ed. Janken Myrdal, Kristian Kristiansen and Thomas Lindkvist, 410–40. Cambridge: Cambridge University Press.

Stein, Gil. 2010. "Local Identities and Interaction Spheres: Modeling Regional Variation in the Ubaid Horizon." In *Beyond the Ubaid: Transformation and Integration in the Late Prehistoric Societies of the Middle East*, ed. Robert A. Carter and Graham Philip, 23–44. Chicago: The Oriental Institute of the University of Chicago.

Tooze, Adam. 2006. *The Wages of Destruction: The Making and Breaking of the Nazi Economy*. London: Allen Lane.

Tooze, Adam, and Ted Fertik. 2014. "The World Economy and the Great War." *Geschichte und Gesellschaft* 40, no. 2: 214–38.

Voth, Hans-Joachim. 2021. "Persistence—Myth and Mystery." In *The Handbook of Historical Economics*, ed. Alberto Bisin and Giovanni Federico, 243–67. London, UK: Academic Press.

Warburton, David A. 2018. "Prices and Values: Origins and Early History in the near East." In *Trade and Civilisation: Economic Networks and Cultural Ties, from Prehistory to the Early Modern Era*, ed. Janken Myrdal, Kristian Kristiansen and Thomas Lindkvist, 56–86. Cambridge: Cambridge University Press.

Ward-Perkins, Bryan. 2005. *The Fall of Rome and the End of Civilization*. Oxford: Oxford University Press.

Wengrow, D. 2010. *What Makes Civilization?: The Ancient near East and the Future of the West*. Oxford: Oxford University Press.

Wilkinson, Toby C. 2018. "Cloth and Currency: On the Ritual-Economics of Eurasian Textile Circulation and the Origins of Trade, Fifth to Second Millennia BC." In *Trade and Civilisation: Economic Networks and Cultural Ties, from Prehistory to the Early Modern Era*, ed. Janken Myrdal, Kristian Kristiansen and Thomas Lindkvist, 25–55. Cambridge: Cambridge University Press.

Williams, Eric Eustace. 1944. *Capitalism & Slavery*. Chapel Hill: University of North Carolina Press.

Wilson, Andrew. 2009. "Approaches to Quantifying Roman Trade." In *Quantifying the Roman Economy: Methods and Problems*, ed. Alan K. Bowman and Andrew Wilson. Oxford Studies on the Roman Economy, 213–49. Oxford: Oxford University Press.

Wilson, Andrew. 2012. "A Forum on Trade." In *The Cambridge Companion to the Roman Economy*, ed. Walter Scheidel. Cambridge Companions to the Ancient World, 287–91. Cambridge: Cambridge University Press.

Wright, Gavin. 2020. "Slavery and Anglo-American Capitalism Revisited." *Economic History Review* 73, no. 2: 353–83.

Zahedieh, Nuala. 2013. "Colonies, Copper, and the Market for Inventive Activity in England and Wales, 1680–1730." *Economic History Review* 66, no. 3: 805–25.

Zahedieh, Nuala. 2014. "Overseas Trade and Empire." Chap. 14 In *The Economic History of Britain since 1700*, ed. Roderick Floud, Jane Humphries and Paul Johnson, 392–420. Cambridge: Cambridge University Press.

CHAPTER 30

CIVIL AND ETHNIC CONFLICT IN HISTORICAL POLITICAL ECONOMY

SAUMITRA JHA

DESPITE great falls in poverty over the past century, we continue to live in a world with tragically high levels of conflict. Since World War II, two-fifths of countries have experienced at least one civil war that took a thousand lives (Fearon and Laitin 2014). Six million died in civil conflict, ten million in all wars (Pettersson 2021). By the end of 2020, 82.1 million had been forcibly displaced.[1] With ongoing wars in Ethiopia, Syria, and Ukraine, these numbers continue to rise.

In this chapter, I examine the patterns of civil conflict around the world through a historic political economy (HPE) lens. I describe the persistence and change in conflict in space and time, and discuss the role of ethnic differences in these patterns. I compare two important approaches for measuring the impact of ethnic differences on conflict-including ethno-linguistic fractionalization and polarization. I highlight two areas that I believe are crucial but are still relatively understudied in this literature—the role of organizational capacity within groups—and complementarities between groups, that can help explain some of the historical patterns. I illustrate these relationships by focusing on the history of Hindu-Muslim relations in South Asia, as well as drawing on broader contexts. Finally, I highlight some common pitfalls that arise from neglecting history when studying these phenomena, and promising directions for future research.

PATTERNS OF CONFLICT

As Figure 30.1 shows, the nature and intensity of conflict have changed since the end of World War II. Large-scale conflicts between states, such as the Korean War, were replaced by civil conflict and proxy wars during the Cold War. The end of the Cold War

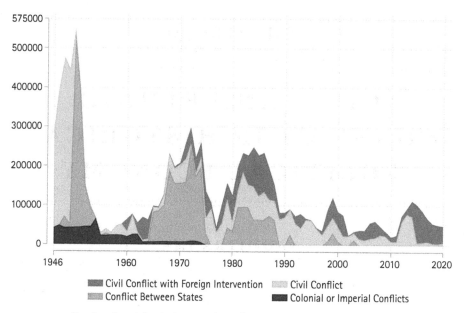

FIGURE 30.1. Battle-related deaths in armed conflicts, 1946–2020
Source: PRIO Battle Dataset (1946–2008); UCDP Battle-Related Deaths Dataset (2009–2020).

and a period of US hegemony brought a dramatic reduction in conflicts with foreign interventions, though civil conflicts continued. The decline of US hegemony and the reemergence of Great Power competition since 2010 has been accompanied by a resurgence of foreign intervention supporting civil conflict within states.

Beyond the loss of life, the economic costs of conflict have been severe as well. De Groot et al. (2022) estimate that global GDP in 2014 would have been, on average, 12 percent higher if there had been no violent conflict after 1970, corresponding to gross costs of conflict of $12 trillion and forgone gross benefits of $2.3 trillion. Again, they estimate that the lion's share of the loss ($9.1 trillion) comes from civil conflict rather than wars between states.[2]

Regionally, too, the costs of conflict have not been evenly shared. Countries in Asia experienced the greatest losses in both relative and absolute terms in the last fifty years, followed by countries in Africa and Latin America. While Europe has been relatively unaffected, North America may have even benefited from the conflicts elsewhere, to the tune of $900 billion (de Groot et al. 2022).

To what extent do these patterns of conflict demonstrate historical persistence? Figure 30.2 shows the locations of major battles around the world from the end of the Napoleonic Wars (1815) to the end of World War II (top panel), overlaid on contemporary national boundaries. The bottom panel shows major battles from 1945 to 2020, as well as a snapshot (in pink) of all battles from 2018 to 2020 in the Armed Conflict Location and Event Data (ACLED) project. As Figure 30.2 suggests, and consistent with the cost estimates just presented, there has been a dramatic shift in the locations

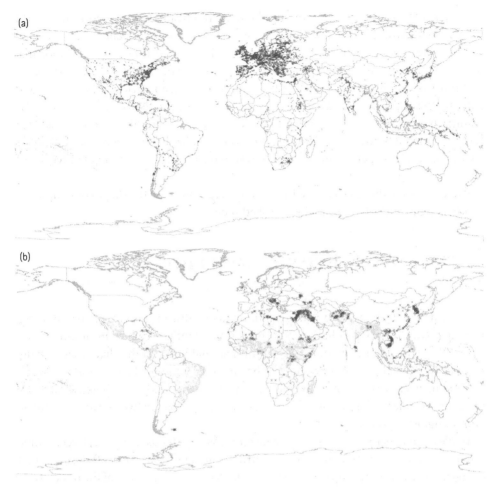

FIGURE 30.2. Battles since Napoleon and since World War II

1815–1945; 1945–2020: In dark red: contains major land battles with a definite location, combining global data from Brecke 1999; Jaques 2007 and Kitamura 2021, augmented by Dincecco et al. 2021—for India and Fenske and Kala 2017—for Africa. 2018–2020: all battles in the Armed Conflict Location and Event Data (ACLED) project (in pink).

of wars, both within and between continents and countries. The waves of battles experienced in the traditional battlefields in Europe prior to World War II largely subsided in the postwar era (with notable exceptions in the former Yugoslavia and, more recently, Ukraine). North America was the site of extensive violence as the United States expanded and then turned on itself in the nineteenth century. However, major battles have been rare since 1945. In Latin America, too, major battles have been relatively uncommon, replaced instead by extensive Cold War proxy insurgencies and later by drug-related violence (see, e.g., Dube and Vargas 2013; Castillo and Kronick 2020; Dell 2015).

Asia and Africa, in contrast, have continued to witness battles both big and small erupting in historically peaceful locations, even while others reignite in well-trodden battlefields.[3] States like Japan—among the most politically fragmented in the world in 1868, with strong caste and clan identities—ceased to experience waves of civil conflict, even while their caste divisions diminished over time (Jansen 2000; Jha, Mitchener, and Takashima, in progress). But ethnically diverse states like Indonesia, and those of South Asia, the Middle East, and sub-Saharan Africa, experience them still. In these places, the clustering of violence-prone regions obscures postwar country boundaries, suggesting that forces that drive civil conflict do not necessarily respect national borders.[4] In contrast, relatively ethnically homogeneous states, like Vietnam, despite experiencing extensive war, have not faced a subsequent legacy of low-level violence.

Under what conditions, then, do historically determined factors shape contemporary conflict? We begin by looking at the role of ethnicity.

Ethnic Conflict

As Blattman and Miguel (2010) note, "Ethnic nationalism is popularly viewed as *the* leading source of group cohesion and inter-group conflict" (italics in original). Yet, given all potential pairs of ethnicities within national borders, the share that actually engages in conflict with others tends to be small. Fearon and Laitin (1996) estimate that in thirty-six African countries between independence and 1979, there were twenty incidents of violence (or 0.03 incidents per country per year) between two subordinate ethno-linguistic groups.

While conflict between two subordinate ethnic groups tends to be rare, larger ethnic groups are more likely to try to contest control of the state. Fearon (2008) observes that of 709 minority ethnic groups around the world that exceed 1 percent of the population, at least 14.1 percent had engaged in "significant rebellion against the state on behalf of the group" between 1945 and 1998. These shares are higher in Asia (30 percent) and the Middle East and North Africa (27.1 percent) than in sub-Saharan Africa (11.8 percent) or Latin America and the Caribbean (6.1 percent) (Fearon 2008). Again, these patterns mirror the estimated costs of conflict above.

In a classic paper, Fearon and Laitin (2003) examine the determinants of the onset of civil wars between 1945 and 1999. They find that civil wars are most common in poor, large, newly independent states with rugged terrain and access to natural resources. These patterns, they argue, are factors that likely proxy for low state capacity and also allow for easier insurgency. Strikingly, and in contrast, they find that the extent to which countries are riven by ethnic divisions, as measured by their ethno-linguistic fractionalization (ELF)indices, is not related to the probability of civil war, once one controls for income.[5]

The method of measuring the extent of ethnic divisions does appear to matter, however, both theoretically and empirically. The ELF index can be interpreted as the probability that two randomly selected individuals are from different ethnic groups. In a series of papers, Esteban and Ray (1994), Montalvo and Reynal-Querol (2005), Esteban and Ray (2011), and Esteban, Mayoral, and Ray (2012) take an alternative axiomatic approach. They develop alternative sets of measures of polarization based upon all potential antagonisms that individuals in a society might have with one another. These polarization measures incorporate a set of three features. First they argue that polarization should be higher the greater the distance or dissimilarity between groups, which they call *alienation*. Second, groups should be more cohesive and *identify* more with one another when they are more similar to one another. Third is that *size* should matter: individuals or small groups should not matter for conflict as much as larger, significantly sized groups. Thus, countries with many small ethnic groups, such as Tanzania, which score highly on the ELF measure, do not score as highly according to these polarization measures. Indeed, Montalvo and Reynal-Querol (2005) find that their measure of ethnic polarization, which is maximized at two similar-sized groups, does correlate with ethnic conflict, even though ELF does not.[6]

Esteban and Ray (2011) further consider the incentives for individuals from different groups to "invest" in conflict. They suggest that winning a battle to control the state gives the dominant ethnic group two types of benefits: control over public goods and pure redistribution of resources. Public goods may have different benefits for different groups, but no group can be completely excluded. This contrasts with other resources that can simply be stolen by and shared within the ethnic group in charge.

They show that when a country's population is large, rather than income inequality (as measured by the Gini coefficient) mattering, the level of conflict will be determined by a convex combination of ethnic polarization and ethnic fractionalization, provided that groups have some sense of cohesion. Further, ethnic polarization should matter more when the state is mostly responsible for dealing out public goods, while ethnic fractionalization should matter more the more expropriable the resources of the state, and thus the more it can be privately seized and shared (Esteban and Ray 2011). Esteban, Mayoral, and Ray (2012) seek to operationalize a version of this model. They find that the coefficient on the Gini measure is (somewhat) negative: all else equal, more equal societies actually have *more* conflict. This suggests that ethnic group cohesion is important. Further the coefficient on polarization is significant and stronger than that on fractionalization. Thus, broadly speaking, ethnic conflict may be more about fighting for control over the public policies and the public goods that states provide, rather than purely over redistributive politics.[7]

These approaches have been very useful and informative in providing clues into the proximate causes of ethnic conflict, and civil conflict more generally. However, they also raise some key questions. Under what conditions can ethnic divisions actually mitigate conflict instead of only yielding potential antagonisms? Which ethnic groups are better able to organize themselves and why? When and why do individuals choose to contribute to and fight for a nation or their ethnicity and caste instead of their class? These are all processes where ignoring the relevant historical contexts, as is unfortunately still fairly common in papers published in modern economics, can lead to very skewed answers about the reasons for and implications of ethnic conflict.

Elements from History: Complementarities and Organization

The British and Americans, as George Bernard Shaw observed, are two peoples separated by a common language. Languages, common or otherwise, can be learned and forgotten, or imparted to the next generation. Ethnic distinctions can be reified through segregation or mitigated through interaction (see, e.g., Bisin and Verdier 2001). Thus, treating ethno-linguistic distinctions between groups at any particular point of time as a given, while perhaps being sensible when understanding short-term, proximate phenomena, arguably makes much less sense when taking a longer historical perspective.

In fact, arguably, a key element of understanding the role of ethnicity from a historical perspective is that ethnicity is not just a label or category that leads to antagonism, but for different groups across history, one's ethnicity has often been associated with particular economic and social endowments and opportunities. Historically, economic specialization by ethnic groups has been common in many societies, with some forming endogamous units within which to transmit skills or endowments. This is often true of immigrant groups that bring economic and cultural links with their home regions and countries that can complement local communities (see, e.g., Ottaviano and Peri 2005). However, even in societies where immigration is limited, vocational opportunities and choices often shape and are shaped by group identities.

These traditional links between ethnic identity and economic endowments create the possibility for complementarity—the possibility of gains from exchange between ethnic groups—that can weaken the incentives for violence. However, it also generates another possible reason for ethnic conflict beyond the political ones already mentioned: economic competition.

Between nations, comparative advantages are often assumed (see, e.g., Polachek and Seiglie 2006), and the extent to which trade mitigates the incentives for war between two countries is shaped by how easily the bilateral trading relationship between the two can be substituted for by others (Martin, Mayer, and Thoenig 2008). However, within countries, when individuals are geographically proximate and thus share many endowments, sustaining intergroup trade is often even more fragile. Particularly over long time horizons, individuals may face incentives to violently seize or replicate one another's production processes. This fragility of the gains from trade is accentuated when members of one group are more *vulnerable*: less capable of organizing violence. Under what conditions, then, can market exchange support peaceful coexistence and prosperity for vulnerable groups over time?

Jha (2018) considers a setting where individuals from two groups occupy a specific location.[8] Members of these groups differ along two dimensions: their *vulnerability* (their capacity to organize violence) and their *mobility* (the quality of their outside options if they choose to leave). For example, indigenous groups, with their knowledge, skills, and networks concentrated locally, may find leaving a location more costly than for immigrant groups who may have retained endowments and ties elsewhere. Every period, individuals from these groups can choose to leave. If they stay, they produce a good and can choose to target another with violence to seize their profits.

In the case of vulnerable immigrant groups, Jha (2018) shows that over long time horizons, a *peaceful coexistence equilibrium*—a subgame perfect equilibrium with mixed populations, no agent having an incentive to leave, full production, and no violence—*exists if and only if* locals and nonlocals engage in economic activities that are weak complements, and for small populations if and only if they are strong complements. If not, and instead the groups are in economic competition with one another, then, over long time horizons, the strong will have an incentive to engage in violence against the vulnerable, not just to expropriate them, but also to induce them to leave, thereby reducing the future economic competition they face. In fact, for a strong local person, for whom violence is cheap, a member of an immigrant group who competes economically will be a preferred target of violence relative to similarly weak individuals who compete from one's own ethnic group, precisely because the better outside options make it easier to induce immigrants to leave. Thus there is likely to be not just expropriative violence but *ethnic* violence.[9]

Over long horizons, in particular, the source of complementarity for vulnerable group members has to be robust in the sense of being costly to expropriate or replicate; otherwise, others will have incentives to do just that. Such robust complementarities often exist for middlemen minorities, whose complementarity stems from access to external trading networks. Trading networks are intangible and thus impossible to expropriate, and when the trading networks are large, they become difficult to replicate. Further, not only may there be incentives for reduced violence, there will also be incentives to invest in further complementary institutions that may reduce these incentives even more. These institutions may involve business, religious, and philanthropic organizations that facilitate coordination and transfers within and between groups, or cultural norms and beliefs supporting trust, trustworthiness, and continued complementarity in new areas. These can survive even if the initial complementary interethnic relationships have been undermined over time.[10]

But beyond this, over long time horizons, vulnerable group members need to be able to credibly threaten to withhold their complementary production in order to deter coercion of production or expropriative violence. For less mobile vulnerable indigenous groups occupying valuable economic niches, this has often proved difficult. And too often in Latin America, the Caribbean, and sub-Saharan Africa, new access to trade has led to violence and forced labor instead (see Nunn 2008; Dell 2010; Bobonis and Morrow 2014, Diaz-Cayeros et al. 2022). In contrast, vulnerable outsider groups, such as trading minorities, tend to be relatively mobile. As such, they can also often credibly threaten to leave.[11]

The choice to remain or relocate is also a key question for networks of individuals over longer periods of time. Given the many ways that individuals, groups, and societies can adjust to the threat of violence over time, the patterns of conflict we see today reflect the culmination of centuries of exogenous factors, including environmental, economic, and political shocks, but also individual and group decisions and their legacies. To understand contemporary civil and ethnic conflict, therefore, it helps to understand the logic of how environments prone to conflict are selected by historical factors. I now illustrate this, drawing from the history of South Asia. This setting not only covers close to one-quarter of the world's population but is also home to a rich history of immense cultural diversity. At times, while some of these South Asian towns have been punctuated at times with horrific violence, other communities nearby have exhibited remarkably resilient degrees of tolerance.

An Illustration: Hindus and Muslims in India

Fourteen centuries of interactions—many peaceful, yet too many violently conflictual as well—between Hindus and Muslims in South Asia can provide a valuable illustration of the historical forces that drive contemporary civil and ethnic conflict. Figure 30.3 provides a graphic overview of these relationships over four epochs.

Figure 30.3a depicts the deciles of the length of time a South Asian region was under Muslim rule from the beginnings of Islam to the death of the last great Mughal emperor, Aurangzeb, in 1707, along with the incidence of major battles prior to the formal establishment of the British Empire in India in 1858. Figure 30.3b shows the Muslim population share in a district in the last colonial census (in 1942) and the incidence of Hindu-Muslim riots between 1850 and the beginning of India's first mass movement for independence—the Khilafat or Non-Cooperation Movement in 1919. Figure 30.3c shows the pattern of riots from when the movement ended in 1922 to 1950. Finally, Figure 30.3d shows the post-Partition (1950) Muslim share and incidence of riots in independent India from 1950 to 2019. Comparing these different epochs makes clear that there are a number of key patterns of both striking continuity and important changes over time.

Complementarities and Competition as Drivers of Conflict

Incentives for tolerance and, unfortunately, for conflict have shaped Hindu-Muslim interactions for many centuries: Muslims came to South Asia both as traders and as conquerors. Muslim rule—and with it, Muslim patronage and faith—spread from major Muslim cities (see squares for the locations of mint towns in Figure 30.3a). A great raid in 1026, by the Sultan Mahmud of Ghazni, led to the destruction of the temple port-city of Somnath and a perception, including of contemporaries (see Alberuni 2005 [1030]) of lasting interethnic hatreds.[12] And Somnath is not alone. As Figure 30.3a also shows, multiple invasions from Afghanistan led to great battles being fought along the old trade routes that linked India to the great markets and silk routes of central Asia.[13]

Yet the first and most enduring interactions between adherents of the new religion of Islam and the existing peoples of the subcontinent were through peaceful trading relationships. Arab Muslim traders came to South Asian ports in the seventh century, providing access to Middle Eastern markets for South Asian spices and artisanal

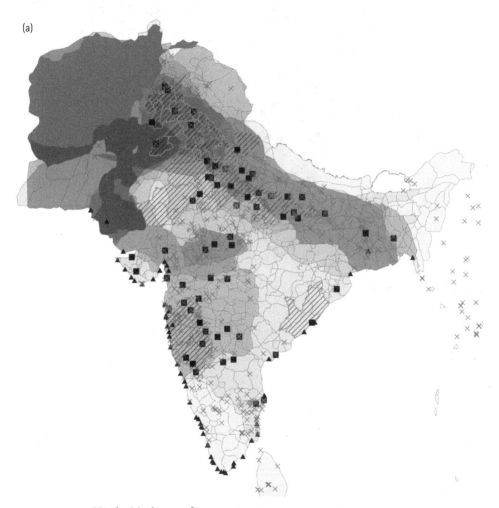

FIGURE 30.3. Hindu-Muslim conflict over time
Sources: Varshney and Wilkinson 2004; Jha and Wilkinson 2012; Jha 2013; Bhavnani and Jha 2022; Kitamura 2021; Ahmed et al. 2022.

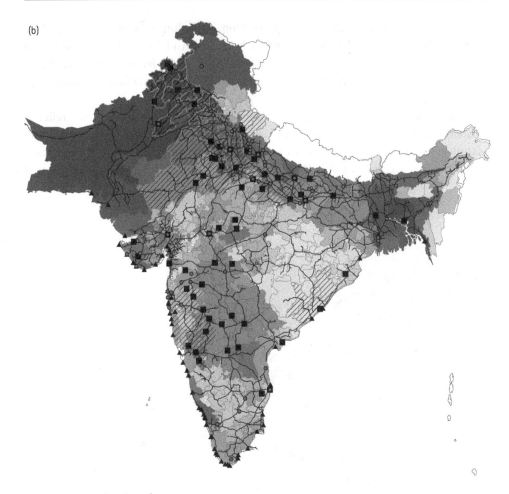

FIGURE 30.3. Continued

CIVIL AND ETHNIC CONFLICT IN HISTORICAL POLITICAL ECONOMY 607

(c)
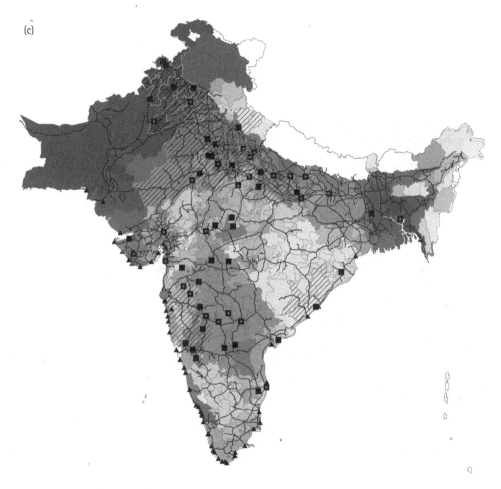

FIGURE 30.3. Continued

(d)

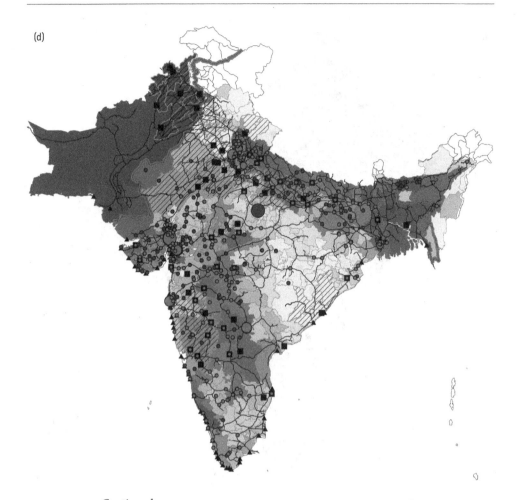

FIGURE 30.3. Continued

products. Though a vulnerable minority group, these traders provided access to markets across the Middle East, northern Africa, and Southeast Asia to local Hindus in the natural harborages that would become the ports of medieval South Asia (see triangles in Figure 30.3a). They could also credibly threaten to leave any specific port for others, cutting off its trade, should they be targeted with violence (Jha 2013; 2018). Even the authorities of the rebuilt Somnath temple would invite traders from Hormuz to settle on the temple lands and build a mosque, aware of the gains that would result from commerce (Thapar 2004).

Locals and traders both faced incentives to develop organizations and norms that would reinforce trust and trade between groups. These have persisted into the modern period, despite the attenuation of Muslim overseas trade advantages with increased European intervention. Jha (2013) shows (consistent with Figure 30.3b) that former medieval trading ports that emerged at natural harbors experienced five times fewer

Hindu-Muslim riots between 1850 and 1950. They were also less likely to experience ethnic cleansing of their Muslim populations during the Partition (Jha and Wilkinson 2012) (Figure 30.3c), and continued to show less violence after Indian independence as well, including during the Gujarat riots in 2002 (Jha 2013; 2014) (Figure 30.3d).

These erstwhile medieval ports—despite being somewhat poorer, having lost their trade—continued to enjoy greater Muslim populations into the modern period. Further, the effects of a medieval trading legacy on reducing violence were *stronger* in places where Muslims and Hindus were closer in population share to one another. As described earlier, these are areas where one might expect greater polarization and violence, not less. However, such effects are again consistent with the logic of complementarity: in environments with ethnic specialization in economic spheres, members of larger minorities are more likely to compete with each other, increasing the gains across ethnic lines. Indeed, household-level evidence from 2003 shows that Muslims in these communities remained specialized in complementary economic activities. Further, they closed the wealth gap with Hindus relative to other urban Muslims, and were as likely as Hindus to vaccinate their sons against polio, an important indicator of contemporary interethnic trust (Jha 2013). These patterns were not accompanied by increased assimilation or secularization of identity, but rather greater participation in religious organizations. Religious and other civic organizations instead played an important role in preventing events that might have triggered violence from escalating into broader religious rioting (Varshney 2002).

In contrast, other towns, particularly those where Hindus and Muslims had no incentives for interethnic trade and instead had historically competed for patronage, developed "institutionalized riot systems": organizations, often led by local political leaders, that sought to gain from such religious mobilization (Brass 2003). These towns not only witnessed regular ethnic violence but were particularly prone to it when the incumbent state governments, who controlled the police, faced lower competition and thus less need to accommodate and protect Muslim voting blocs (Wilkinson 2004).[14]

Capacities for Organizing Violence

Historical conflict also entrenched itself in specific ways in colonial policy, which would have lasting consequences for different groups in South Asia and their organizational capacity along ethnic lines.

The British East India Company often faced fierce resistance as it expanded. However, one of its gravest challenges came from within its own ranks. Led by veterans of the East India Company's wars, the Uprising of 1857 would see regiments of Hindu and Muslim soldiers revolt and unite instead under the banner of the last Mughal emperor, Bahadur Shah Zafar. The British would cease to recruit from the traditional areas of that rebellious army. Instead, they adopted a pseudoscientific theory of "martial races" for military recruitment (Streets 2004). Based on phrenology and vegetarianism, among other factors, the British classified different caste and religious groups as martial groups worthy of recruitment (see blue dashed areas in Figure 30.3). These differential recruiting policies would create important differences both within and between regions in the ability of members of different ethnic groups to organize themselves and threaten violence that would have dramatic effects on interethnic relations in the aftermath of the two world wars (Jha and Wilkinson 2012).

Counter to a narrative of primordial hatreds, while Hindu-Muslim riots did occur, they were relatively uncommon prior to World War I. As noted, this was particularly true in erstwhile medieval ports, but riots were relatively rare more generally as well (Figure 30.2b). However, this changed with a dramatic surge and spread in Hindu-Muslim riots between the world wars (Figure 30.3c). The ability to organize was crucial. British promises of autonomy for its Indian provinces in exchange for support during World War I were replaced instead by extensive crackdowns on public assembly and press freedom after the war. This was particularly the case in the heavily recruited Punjab province, which witnessed a massacre of unarmed civilians at Jallianwalla Bagh in 1919. The period that followed saw the first major mass mobilizations in South Asian politics, of Muslims, Hindus, and others.[15] Planned in part to show interreligious solidarity, these protest movements seeded local organizations that instead contributed to the first major wave of Hindu-Muslim riots in Indian history (Bhavnani and Jha 2022).

Another shock to the capacity of different groups to organize in South Asia came with World War II. Undivided India mobilized 2.5 million troops, the largest volunteer army in world history. Its 268 infantry battalions would serve in fronts as diverse as the jungles of Burma, the deserts of north Africa, and the mountains of Italy. Indian veterans would return home to a subcontinent on the brink of independence and the prospect of Partition. Partitioning the subcontinent into a Muslim-majority and a Hindu-majority state had been seen as a viable potential political compromise to ward off ethnic conflict. Instead, the Partition deteriorated into a humanitarian tragedy. One of the greatest forced migrations in world history, 14.5 million people were forcibly displaced, and another 3.4 million were unaccounted for by 1951 (Bharadwaj, Khwaja, and Mian 2008). Contemporary leaders did not anticipate either the scale nor the location of the violence that ensued (Talbot and Singh 2009; see also Figure 30.3c,d).

In this crisis environment, the war had an important impact in shaping the ability of different groups to mobilize along ethnic lines. Jha and Wilkinson (2012) exploit a shock to the organizational capacity of different groups due to World War II. Though recruited from specific caste groups in different districts, the battalions of India's line infantry were, by design, trained and equipped to be interchangeable when assigned to combat. Jha and Wilkinson (2012) show that the ethnic cleansing during the Partition was worse when organized majorities encountered large but unorganized minorities. Large minorities pose a greater political threat and offer greater potential spoils from violence. Further, disorganized minorities are less able to deter violence or move in its anticipation.

Importantly, the organizational capacity derived from war also had different effects in districts with a history of interethnic complementarity. Districts with medieval ports not only witnessed significantly less ethnic cleansing during the Partition, those that received a positive shock to organizational capacity from the war were even more likely to retain their vulnerable minority populations. Despite the great bloodlettings experienced by mixed populations in many districts of South Asia during the Partition, these medieval port towns—the focus of institutions of tolerance born from centuries of interethnic complementarities—remained oases of peace.

Complementarities and Organizations Elsewhere

Interethnic complementarities, competition, and shocks to the organizational capacity of different groups have played important roles in shaping the propensity for ethnic conflict, assimilation, and peace in places other than South Asia as well.

In Europe, an important literature has examined the determinants of anti-Semitic violence and pogroms over time. Johnson, Koyama, and Jedwab (2017) find that Jewish communities in Germany that provided complementary services to locals were also less likely to experience pogroms in the wake of the Black Death (1348–1353). Becker and Pascali (2019) show that in German Protestant jurisdictions where usury laws were relaxed during the Reformation in the sixteenth century (and thus Protestants could compete with Jews in finance), Jews faced increases in ethnic violence following these reforms. In contrast, in Catholic areas, usury proscriptions were maintained, Jews retained complementarity in financial services, and they also faced less subsequent ethnic violence. Grosfeld, Sakalli, and Zhuravskaya (2019) look at ethnic violence against Jews in the Pale of Settlement between 1800 and 1927. They find that political instability there raised ethnic violence against Jews, where they provided complementary services, while crop failures and other short-term economic shocks that were not accompanied by political instability did not have these effects. Voigtländer and Voth (2012) find that in Hanseatic towns, where Jews arguably enjoyed complementary trading relationships, anti-Semitism did not persist through to the Nazi period, particularly when compared to other towns that experienced anti-Jewish pogroms during the First Crusade. Benbassa and Rodrigue (2000) point to the complementarity between the Sephardic Jewish migrants to Ottoman Salonica as a reason that it remained the most tolerant place for Jews for centuries.

Africa has been a focus of much of the literature on ethnic conflict. But here, too, there appears to be evidence that interethnic complementarities and their legacies may play a role in mitigating local violence. Montalvo and Reynal-Querol (2021) examine the relationship between economic growth (as measured by changes in nightlight luminosity) and ethnic fractionalization when one varies the size of the grid-cells at which these are calculated. They find a remarkably robust positive relationship between growth in nightlight intensity and fractionalization for grid cells that extend up to 1.5 degrees, which also appears to correlate strongly with the presence of markets for trade at the intersection of ethnic homeland boundaries. However, the beneficial effects of fractionalization diminish and disappear as the cell sizes grow. Montalvo and Reynal-Querol (2021) argue that these patterns reflect the presence of the enhanced growth potential generated by local ethnic specialization and interethnic complementary exchange at interfaces between ethnic groups. This potential upside of diversity becomes less pronounced over large geographical spaces, where other factors may have offsetting effects.

McGuirk and Nunn (2021) find that previous interethnic complementarities can break down with climate change. Pastoral groups in sub-Saharan Africa would previously arrive on agricultural lands after harvest, providing valuable services by feeding on stubble and providing manure. However, climate shocks have led them to arrive prior to harvest, breaking these complementarities and leading to increased conflict.

In Latin America, Diaz-Cayeros, Espinosa-Balbuena, and Jha (2022) use a rich set of primary sources, including Aztec tribute rolls and early-sixteenth-century censuses, to reconstruct the fate of indigenous settlements in Mexico. The authors show that the extent of the complementarity and nonreplicability of goods produced by indigenous communities at the time of the Spanish Conquest of the Americas can explain which communities were more likely to survive the subsequent coercive violence and pandemics that led the average population to fall by 95 percent between 1548 and 1646.

As in the medieval ports of South Asia and the markets of Africa, complementarities also appear to lead to organizational legacies in the Andes of Peru. Artiles (2022) examines the role of altitude differences in generating complementary relationships within ethnic groups as well as across them, once the Spanish forced the groups to cohabit with one another. Artiles finds that ethnic groups that spanned more climatic zones historically developed more inclusive organizations—unions—and better modern development outcomes. She finds that the intersections between ethnic groups are also interfaces that lead to the development of markets.[16]

Organizational legacies can stem not just from complementarities in producing physical products but from broader environments where there are complementarities in joint effort. Cooperation within and between groups can emerge when they would benefit from managing situations where different individuals can hold up one another, such as upstream and downstream economic activities (Williamson 1985). They can also appear to help manage actual streams, watersheds, and other common pool resources (Ostrom 1990), as well as to organize and deal collectively with shared risks (Wade 1988).

Organizational legacies may also be sustained over long periods of history. For example, Moscona, Nunn, and Robinson (2020) compare sub-Saharan African ethnic groups that are organized around segmentary lineages to nearby groups that are not. The authors find that groups with such long-standing segmentary organization experience more extensive civil conflict today. Intriguing questions raised by this work are where these types of clanlike organizations emerge from, and to what extent they are shaped by past conflicts.[17]

As we have seen in South Asia, organizational capacities can emerge from more recent exogenous shocks, including war deployments and colonial practice as well. Fearon and Laitin (2014) examine whether "contemporary armed conflict has deep historical roots." They compare the incidence of conflicts in countries after World War II to the nature of conflicts in the nineteenth and early twentieth centuries. Fearon and Laitin note that within regions—specifically Asia, the Middle East, and Africa—groups that were mobilized to fight the colonial powers were more likely to fight against other groups after independence. Given that the British transplanted their martial race theories of recruitment to their African colonies as well, the organizational legacies of war visible in South Asia may also have played an important role in shaping patterns of violence among Africa's independent states.[18]

More recently, the United States' disbanding of the highly experienced Sunni-majority Iraqi military, without providing alternative paths to employment or carefully considering how such groups might find insurgency attractive in a fledgling majority-Shia democracy, is likely to go down in history as an avoidable error that proved to have tragic human and material costs.

Implications for Studying the Effects of Conflict and Identity

Thus, around the world, patterns of complementarity, competition, and differential organizational capacity are arguably commonplace in shaping the propensity for civil conflict both in specific locations and in interaction with changing political incentives at specific moments of time. However, much of the literature that studies the effects of conflict and identity remains largely ahistorical.

Regarding South Asia, for example, a number of intriguing papers find that the incidence of religious riots in a district in early childhood correlates with the likelihood that bank managers engage in religious discrimination in the provision of loans (Fisman et al. 2020) and judges similarly discriminate in bail decisions (Bharti and Roy 2022). Meanwhile, contemporaneous religious riots change the consumption of taboo foods for Hindus and Muslims such as beef and pork (Atkin, Colson-Sihra, and Shayo 2021).

These studies present informative conditional correlations on important sets of issues. However, taking the historical political economy perspective suggests some fruitful directions for this type of research going forward. As we have seen in South Asia, for example, districts prone to ethnic riots are not randomly assigned. Instead they are the result of centuries of historical processes that shape the continued presence (or absence) of ethnically mixed communities, social norms (or a lack thereof) of interethnic trust and tolerance, and underlying market conditions that make certain ethnic groups more able to integrate economically and shape local supply chains. The timing of violence also tends to reflect local political polarization and electoral incentives to protect minorities. Thus, rather than being an exogenous shock, riots, together with discrimination and identity salience, all arguably reflect differences in longer-term institutions that manifest themselves at specific times due to local political and economic incentives.[19]

A potentially valuable path forward for papers that study conflict, and others that seek to examine the effects of race riots in the United States, conflict in Africa, and so on, is to take history seriously, gathering data on the underlying interethnic economic and organizational arrangements that might drive conflict propensities particularly in interaction with changing political contexts over time, and assess how these might also bias, explain, or generate heterogeneous patterns in the measured effects.

Another increasingly popular approach in the study of contemporary conflict is to take a conflict zone and generate a *synthetic control* by weighting the trends in different unaffected areas in order to match specific trends in the conflict zone prior to the onset of the conflict (Abadie and Gardeazabal 2003). As usual, a key question is whether the weighted sum of the different nonconflict regions that is used as the synthetic control really does evolve along a similar path as the conflict zone would have done. Again this might be more plausible if the candidate regions shared similar features in the relevant historical dimensions mentioned earlier that might also affect performance. Choosing weights on candidate regions to create a synthetic control that matches the conflict zone over a broader set of relevant historical, cultural and political factors, including those described above, may increase the synthetic control's plausibility. Similarly, checking that the vector of weights of the control does not load heavily on only a few control regions that are far in terms of relevant historical and cultural characteristics from the conflict zone would improve the estimate's plausibility and robustness as well.

A third common approach is to use regression discontinuity designs, including geographical ones across old borders, to study the effects of institutional and cultural differences. In a number of important cases, these borders were shaped by repeated and constant conflict and raiding between empires, kingdoms, and ethnic groups. Such persistent conflicts may themselves be the effect of factors inducing economic or political competition, or may have direct effects separate from broader institutional and cultural differences that induce a lack of development and trust locally. Comparing regression discontinuity estimates measured right at a historically contested border with estimates that leave out different buffers along the border can help assess sensitivity to these issues.

A related regression discontinuity approach is that of using close political elections to identify the effects of having winners versus losers from a particular identity. Based as they are upon such local comparisons, these studies also have naturally been ahistorical for the most part.[20] Yet when individuals tend to vote along ethnic lines, close electoral races may accentuate the incentives for ethnic cleansing in places with historical interethnic competition and organizational differences, even while they may lower them in areas with interethnic complementarity. Thus, rather than winners being as good as random, their identities can be highly predictable by the nature of these historical factors, particularly in close races where the incentives for ethnic cleansing and intimidation may be the highest (Jha 2014).[21] Checking for balance in close races relating to historical factors that shape incentives for conflict as well as the more conventional incumbency measures can again help add confidence around political regression discontinuity designs.

Conclusion

Though we continue to live in a world with tragically high levels of conflict, taking a historical perspective offers both hope and directions to pursue, for research and for policy. Conflicts do not seem to be as primordial as they are sometimes portrayed. Instead, many places that once encountered a lot of civil and ethnic conflict have enjoyed lasting peace. Even in countries and regions where conflict remains common, studying the historical roots of the conflict suggests that they can be mitigated through economic approaches and shaped by novel organizational structures. Rather than fostering a world of mutual antagonisms formed by ethnic and cultural identities, historical cultural factors may also provide positive avenues to mitigate contemporary conflict.

Acknowledgments

The list of those to thank for sharing their wisdom on this topic with me is long, but I am particularly grateful for discussions with Alberto Diaz-Cayeros, Alessandro Saia, Avner Greif, David Laitin, Dominic Rohner, Jared Rubin, Jessica Leino, Jim Fearon, Katia Zhuravskaya, Mark Koyama, Mohamed Saleh, Nathan Nunn, Rikhil Bhavnani, Resuf Ahmed, Moses Shayo, Steven Wilkinson, Susan Athey, and Timur Kuran. I am also grateful to generations of students in my Political Development Economics class at Stanford. Thanks to Shuhei Kitamura for generously sharing his World Historical Battle Database V.11, and Sam Asher for excellent research assistance.

Notes

1. See the UNHCR. In contrast, extreme poverty fell from 74 percent to 10 percent between 1910 and 2015 (Roser and Ortiz-Ospina 2013).
2. De Groot et al. (2022) use panel fixed effects regressions, estimating both direct effects on countries involved in conflict and spillovers to others as well.
3. See Fearon and Laitin (2014), Besley and Reynal-Querol (2014), and Dincecco, Fenske, and Onorato (2019).
4. See Sambanis (2000) and Sambanis and Schulhofer-Wohl (2009) on how partitioning of groups across national borders often leads to interstate conflict. Michalopoulos and Papaioannou (2016) further find more contemporary conflict in ethnic homelands in Africa divided by straight lines during the Congress of Berlin in 1885. Such boundaries can allow co-ethnics a safe haven or hinterland for regrouping and organization that facilitate insurgency (Schram 2019).

5. The ethno-linguistic fractionalization index is $1-\sum_{i=1}^{N} S_{ij}^2$, where S_{ij} is the share of ethnic group i in country j.
6. Their measure, which puts a strong weight on group identification, is $RQ = \sum_{i=1}^{m} n_i^2(1-n_i)$, where n_i is the share in group i.
7. On how ethnic divisions lead to greater distance between the preferences of individuals and the median voter, undermining support for public goods, see Alesina and La Ferrara (2000), Alesina, Baqir, and Hoxby (2004), and Alesina and La Ferrara (2005). Desmet, Ortuño-Ortín, and Wacziarg (2017) use survey evidence to point out that there tends to be large variation in preferences and cultural differences even within ethnic groups. Power-sharing arrangements, with representatives of different ethnic groups controlling particular ministries, have become a common approach in Africa and elsewhere (Francois, Rainer, and Trebbi 2015; Mueller and Rohner 2018).
8. See also Jha (2007; 2013) and Diaz-Cayeros, Espinosa-Balbuena, and Jha (2022).
9. In the United States, for example, patterns of economic competition by different ethnic groups have been linked to race riots (see Olzak 1992; Christian 2017). Esteban and Ray (2008) provide an alternative but potentially complementary argument for why ethnic conflict is often salient over class conflict: there is complementarity between wealth and numbers in organizing violence. Rich members of an ethnic majority then prefer to invest resources to mobilize poor members of their community against minority members than face the alternative of redistributive class conflict. Relatedly, Glaeser (2005) suggests that pro-redistribution politicians have incentives to send messages inciting hatred against ethnic minorities when the minorities are relatively rich, while anti-redistribution politicians do the same when the minorities are poor. Given these incentives, the media have proven effective at coordinating violence and ethnic hatreds (see Adena et al. 2015; Wang 2021; Yanagizawa-Drott 2014; Müller and Schwarz 2020).
10. On the relationship between complementarities and robust comparative statics, see Milgrom and Roberts (1990). On how complementary investments can generate momentum and persistence, see Milgrom, Qian, and Roberts (1991) and Jha (2013). On institutions as sets of beliefs, norms, and organizations that induce regularities of behavior and evolve over time, see Greif (2005) and Greif and Laitin (2004).
11. Jha (2018) describes how, when their outside options are good—such as occurs with reduced barriers to immigration elsewhere—vulnerable outsiders who enjoyed robust complementarities, such as trading minorities in Indian Ocean ports, Europe, and elsewhere, have been able to deter acquisitive dictators and others by threatening to leave and deny future trade. However, when the costs of leaving were high, these communities were more likely to see waves of pogroms instead. See also Diaz-Cayeros, Espinosa-Balbuena, and Jha (2022).
12. Somnath remains a touchstone for modern religious mobilization, with L. K. Advani, then leader of the Bharatiya Janata Party (BJP), beginning his *Rath Yatra* from Somnath (Blakeslee 2018).
13. Dincecco et al. (2021) find that districts that experienced more conflict due to their proximity to the Khyber Pass tend also to be more developed today.
14. Elsewhere too, ethnic identification, to some extent at least, is affected by political incentives and considerations. Groups that are political complements are more likely to be tolerant, while those that compete politically are less likely to support intermarriage (Posner 2004). Ethnic identification also appears to be heightened prior to elections

(Eifert, Miguel, and Posner 2010), and may respond to status considerations as well (see, e.g. Greif and Laitin 2004; Shayo 2020). However, Jha (2013) finds that the local protective effects of historic interethnic complementarities on reducing Hindu-Muslim riots in the towns of democratic India are particularly pronounced in the run-up to elections, and in states with fewer effective parties and thus lessened political incentives to protect minorities.

15. The Khilafat movement mobilized Sunni Muslims to pressure the British government to protect the Ottoman Sultan, the Caliph of Sunni Islam, who had chosen the losing side in World War I. The Indian National Congress, under Mohandas Gandhi's leadership, mobilized in coordination with the Khilafat movement, but also to pursue greater freedoms at home.

16. In contrast, Dippel (2011) finds that when distinct Native American bands were forced into the same reservation, this had a major negative impact on income more than one hundred years later. The contrast between Dippel's findings and those of Artiles may be due to a lack of economic complementarity and enhanced political competition among bands joined into Native American reservations.

17. Indeed, Dincecco and Wang (2018) examine one thousand years of clan books in China. The writing of these books, which served to identify and record clan members, tends to coincide with times and places experiencing the most conflict. The authors argue that this is because the value of the clan was accentuated in times of conflict, causing greater investment in clan administration.

18. Similarly, Besley and Reynal-Querol (2014) find that conflicts in Africa between 1400 and 1700 predict postindependence conflict. See also Dincecco, Fenske, and Onorato (2019) and Jha and Wilkinson (in progress).

19. The common practice of adding fixed effects to control for these historical factors does not account for differing trajectories over time and different propensities to respond to economic or political factors in specific periods.

20. Interestingly, there is a measurable incumbency advantage appearing in very close US Congressional elections as well (Caughey and Sekhon 2011; Grimmer 2013).

21. For example, Jha (2014) finds that in the Gujarat elections that followed the 2002 religious riots, there appears to have been no strong incumbency effect for candidates for the incumbent BJP that many saw as complicit in the violence. Yet even in these close races, the probability that the winner of the 2002 election was from the BJP was heavily influenced by the nature of historical incentives. Relative to other close races, the BJP was less likely to win in former medieval ports following the riots, and significantly more likely in former medieval patronage cities where there was a history of interethnic competition.

REFERENCES

Abadie, Alberto, and Javier Gardeazabal. 2003. "The Economic Costs of Conflict: A Case Study of the Basque Country." *American Economic Review* 93, no. 1 (March): 113–32.

Adena, Maja, Ruben Enikolopov, Maria Petrova, Veronica Santarosa, and Ekaterina Zhuravskaya. 2015. "Radio and the Rise of Nazis in Prewar Germany." *Quarterly Journal of Economics* 130, no. 4 (July): 1885–939.

Ahmed, Resuf, Saumitra Jha, Dominic Rohner, Alessandro Saia, and Ekaterina Zhuravskaya. 2022. "A New Dataset on Hindu-Muslim Violence, 1950 to 2019." Mimeo, Stanford.

Alberuni, Abu-Raihan Muhammad Ibn Ahmad. 2005 [1030]. *Indica*. Edited by Edward C. Sachau. Delhi: Munshiram Manoharlal.

Alesina, Alberto, Reza Baqir, and Caroline Hoxby. 2004. "Political Jurisdictions in Heterogeneous Communities." *Journal of Political Economy* 112, no. 2: 348–95.

Alesina, Alberto, and Eliana La Ferrara. 2000. "Participation in Heterogeneous Communities." *Quarterly Journal of Economics* 115, no. 3 (August): 847–904.

Alesina, Alberto, and Eliana La Ferrara. 2005. "Ethnic Diversity and Economic Performance." *Journal of Economic Literature* 43, no. 3: 762–800.

Artiles, Miriam. 2022. "Within-Group Heterogeneity in a Multi-Ethnic Society." April. Mimeo, PUC.

Atkin, David, Eve Colson-Sihra, and Moses Shayo. 2021. "How Do We Choose Our Identity? A Revealed Preference Approach Using Food Consumption." *Journal of Political Economy* 129, no. 4 (April): 1193–51.

Becker, Sascha O., and Luigi Pascali. 2019. "Religion, Division of Labor, and Conflict: Anti-Semitism in Germany over 600 Years." *American Economic Review* 109, no. 5 (May): 1764–804.

Benbassa, Esther, and Aron Rodrigue. 2000. *Sephardi Jewry: A History of the Judeo-Spanish Community, 14th–20th Centuries*. Berkeley: University of California Press.

Besley, Timothy, and Marta Reynal-Querol. 2014. "The Legacy of Historical Conflict: Evidence from Africa." *American Political Science Review* 108, no. 2: 319–36.

Bharadwaj, Prashant, Asim Khwaja, and Atif Mian. 2008. "The Big March: Migratory Flows after the Partition of India." *Economic and Political Weekly* 43, no. 35 (August): 39–49.

Bharti, Nitin Kumar, and Sutanuka Roy. 2022. "The Early Origins of Judicial Stringency in Bail Decisions: Evidence from Early-Childhood Exposure to Hindu-Muslim Riots in India." Mimeo.

Bhavnani, Rikhil and Saumitra Jha. 2022. "Broken Bridges: The Effects of India's First Nonviolent Struggle on Mass Ethnic Violence." Mimeo, Stanford.

Bisin, Alberto, and Thierry Verdier. 2001. "The Economics of Cultural Transmission and the Dynamics of Preferences." *Journal of Economic Theory* 97, no. 2 (April): 298–319.

Blakeslee, David. 2018. "The *Rath Yatra* Effect: Hindu Nationalist Propaganda and the Rise of the BJP." June. NYU Working Paper.

Blattman, Christopher, and Edward Miguel. 2010. "Civil War." *Journal of Economic Literature* 48, no. 1: 3–57.

Bobonis, Gustavo J., and Peter M. Morrow. 2014. "Labor Coercion and the Accumulation of Human Capital." *Journal of Development Economics* 108: 32–53.

Brass, Paul R. 2003. *The Production of Hindu-Muslim Violence in Contemporary India*. Seattle: University of Washington Press.

Brecke, Peter. 1999. "Violent Conflicts 1400 A.D. to the Present in Different Regions of the World." Paper prepared for the Meeting of the Peace Science Society (International) on October 8–10, 1999 in Ann Arbor, Michigan.

Castillo, Juan Camilo, and Dorothy Kronick. 2020. "The Logic of Violence in Drug War." *American Political Science Review* 114, no. 3: 874–87.

Caughey, Devin, and Jasjeet S. Sekhon. 2011. "Elections and the Regression Discontinuity Design: Lessons from Close U.S. House Races, 1942–2008." *Political Analysis* 19: 385–408.

Christian, Cornelius. 2017. "Lynchings, Labour, and Cotton in the US South: A Reappraisal of Tolnay and Beck." *Explorations in Economic History* 66: 106–16.

de Groot, Olaf J., Carlos Bozzoli, Anousheh Alamir, and Tilman Brück. 2022. "The Global Economic Burden of Violent Conflict." *Journal of Peace Research* (March): 59, no. 2: 259–76.

Dell, Melissa. 2010. "The Persistent Effects of Peru's Mining Mita." *Econometrica* 78, no. 6: 1863–903.

Dell, Melissa. 2015. "Trafficking Networks and the Mexican Drug War." *American Economic Review* 105, no. 6 (June): 1738–79.

Desmet, Klaus, Ignacio Ortuño-Ortín, and Romain Wacziarg. 2017. "Culture, Ethnicity, and Diversity." *American Economic Review* 107, no. 9 (September): 2479–513.

Diaz-Cayeros, Alberto, Juan Espinosa-Balbuena, and Saumitra Jha. 2022. "Pandemic Spikes and Broken Spears: Indigenous Resilience after the Conquest of Mexico." *Journal of Historical Political Economy* 2, no. 1: 89–133.

Dincecco, Mark, James Fenske, Anil Menon, and Shivaji Mukherjee. 2021. "Pre-colonial Warfare and Long-Run Development in India." *Economic Journal* 132, no. 643 (April): 981–1010.

Dincecco, Mark, James Fenske, and Massimiliano Onorato. 2019. "Is Africa Different? Historical Conflict and State Development." *Economic History of Developing Regions* 34, no. 2: 209–50.

Dincecco, Mark, and Yuhua Wang. 2018. "Violent Conflict and Political Development over the Long Run: China versus Europe." *Annual Review of Political Science* 21, no. 1: 341–58.

Dippel, Christian. 2011. "Forced Coexistence and Economic Development: Evidence from Native American Reservations." January. Mimeo, UCLA.

Dube, Oeindrila, and Juan F. Vargas. 2013. "Commodity Price Shocks and Civil Conflict: Evidence from Colombia." *Review of Economic Studies* 80, no. 4 (March): 1384–421.

Eifert, Benn, Edward Miguel, and Daniel N. Posner. 2010. "Political Competition and Ethnic Identification in Africa." *American Journal of Political Science* 54, no. 2 (April): 494–510.

Esteban, Joan, and Debraj Ray. 1994. "On the Measurement of Polarization." *Econometrica* 62: 819–52.

Esteban, Joan, and Debraj Ray. 2008. "On the Salience of Ethnic Conflict." *American Economic Review* 98, no. 5: 2185–202.

Esteban, Joan, and Debraj Ray. 2011. "Linking Conflict to Inequality and Polarization." *American Economic Review* 101, no. 4 (June): 1345–74.

Esteban, Joan, Laura Mayoral, and Debraj Ray. 2012. "Ethnicity and Conflict: An Empirical Study." *American Economic Review* 102, no. 4 (June): 1310–42.

Fearon, James D. 2008. "Ethnic Mobilization and Ethnic Violence." In *The Oxford Handbook of Political Economy*, ed. Donald A. Wittman and Barry R. Weingast, 852–68. Oxford: Oxford University Press.

Fearon, James D., and David D. Laitin. 1996. "Explaining Interethnic Cooperation." *American Political Science Review* 90, no. 4: 715–35.

Fearon, James D., and David D. Laitin. 2003. "Ethnicity, Insurgency and Civil War." *American Political Science Review* 97, no. 1: 75–90.

Fearon, James D., and David D. Laitin. 2014. "Does Contemporary Armed Conflict Have 'Deep Historical Roots'?" August. SSRN Scholarly Paper ID 1922249, Social Science Research Network.

Fenske, James, and Namrata Kala. 2017. "1807: Economic Shocks, Conflict and the Slave Trade." *Journal of Development Economics* 126: 66–76.

Fisman, Raymond, Arkodipta Sarkar, Janis Skrastins, and Vikrant Vig. 2020. "Experience of Communal Conflicts and Intergroup Lending." *Journal of Political Economy* 128, no. 9: 3346–75.

Francois, Patrick, Ilia Rainer, and Francesco Trebbi. 2015. "How Is Power Shared in Africa?" *Econometrica* 83, no. 2: 465–503.

Glaeser, Edward L. 2005. "The Political Economy of Hatred." *Quarterly Journal of Economics* 120, no. 1 (January): 45–86.

Greif, Avner. 2005. *Institutions and the Path to the Modern Economy: Lessons from Medieval Trade*. Cambridge: Cambridge University Press.

Greif, Avner, and David D. Laitin. 2004. "A Theory of Endogenous Institutional Change." *American Political Science Review* 98, no. 4: 633–52.

Grimmer, Justin. 2013. "Appropriators Not Statesmen: The Distorting Effects of Electoral Incentives on Congressional Representation." *American Journal of Political Science* 57, no. 3 (July): 624–42.

Grosfeld, Irena, Seyhun Orcan Sakalli, and Ekaterina Zhuravskaya. 2019. "Middleman Minorities and Ethnic Violence: Anti-Jewish Pogroms in the Russian Empire." *Review of Economic Studies* 87, no. 1 (January): 289–342.

Jansen, Marius B. 2000. *The Making of Modern Japan*. Cambridge, MA: Belknap Press of Harvard University Press.

Jaques, Tony. 2007. *Dictionary of Battles and Sieges*. Westport and London: Greenwood Press.

Jha, Saumitra. 2007. "Maintaining Peace across Ethnic Lines: New Lessons from the Past." *Economics of Peace and Security Journal* 2, no. 2 (July): 89–93.

Jha, Saumitra. 2013. "Trade, Institutions and Ethnic Tolerance: Evidence from South Asia." *American Political Science Review* 107, no. 4 (November): 806–32.

Jha, Saumitra. 2014. "'Unfinished Business': Historic Complementarities, Political Competition and Ethnic Violence in Gujarat." *Journal of Economic Behaviour and Organisation* 104 (August): 18–36.

Jha, Saumitra. 2018. "Trading for Peace." *Economic Policy* (July): 485–526.

Jha, Saumitra, and Steven Wilkinson. 2012. "Does Combat Experience Foster Organizational Skill? Evidence from Ethnic Cleansing during the Partition of South Asia." *American Political Science Review* 106, no. 4: 883–907.

Jha, Saumitra, and Steven Wilkinson. In progress. *The Wars after the Wars*.

Jha, Saumitra, Kris Mitchener, and Masanori Takashima. In progress. "Swords into Bank Shares: Finance, Conflict and Political Reform in Meiji Japan."

Johnson, Noel, Mark Koyama, and Remi Jedwab. 2017. "Economic Shocks, Inter-ethnic Complementarities and the Persecution of Minorities: Evidence from the Black Death." April. Economic History Society Working Paper 17012.

Kitamura, Shuhei. 2021. "World Historical Battles Database." https://osf.io/mdjzu/. Accessed October 2021.

Martin, Philippe, Thierry Mayer, and Mathias Thoenig. 2008. "Make Trade Not War?" *Review of Economic Studies* 75, no. 3 (2008): 865–900.

McGuirk, Eoin, and Nathan Nunn. 2021. "Transhumant Pastoralism, Climate Change and Conflict in Africa." May. NBER Working Paper 28243.

Michalopoulos, Stelios, and Elias Papaioannou. 2016. "The Long-Run Effects of the Scramble for Africa." *American Economic Review* 106, no. 7 (July): 1802–48.

Milgrom, Paul, and John Roberts. 1990. "The Economics of Modern Manufacturing: Technology, Strategy and Organization." *American Economic Review* 80, no. 3: 511–28.

Milgrom, Paul, Yingyi Qian, and John Roberts. 1991. "Complementarities, Momentum and the Evolution of Modern Manufacturing." *American Economic Review: Papers and Proceedings* 81, no. 2 (May): 84–88.

Montalvo, José G., and Marta Reynal-Querol. 2005. "Ethnic Polarization, Potential Conflict and Civil Wars." *American Economic Review* 95, no. 3 (June): 796–816.

Montalvo, José, and Marta Reynal-Querol. 2021. "Ethnic Diversity and Growth: Revisiting the Evidence." *Review of Economics and Statistics* 103, no. 3 (July): 521–32.

Moscona, Jacob, Nathan Nunn, and James A. Robinson. 2020. "Segmentary Lineage Organization and Conflict in Sub-Saharan Africa." *Econometrica* 88, no. 5: 1999–2036.

Mueller, Hannes, and Dominic Rohner. 2018. "Can Power-Sharing Foster Peace? Evidence from Northern Ireland." *Economic Policy* 33, no. 95 (July): 447–84.

Müller, Karsten, and Carlo Schwarz. 2020. "Fanning the Flames of Hate: Social Media and Hate Crime." *Journal of the European Economic Association* 19, no. 4 (October): 2131–67.

Nunn, Nathan. 2008. "The Long-Term Effects of Africa's Slave Trades." *Quarterly Journal of Economics* 123, no. 1 (February): 139–76.

Olzak, Susan. 1992. *The Dynamics of Ethnic Competition and Conflict*. Stanford, CA: Stanford University Press.

Ostrom, Elinor. 1990. *Governing the Commons: The Evolution of Institutions for Collective Action*. Cambridge: Cambridge University Press.

Ottaviano, Gianmarco I. P., and Giovanni Peri. 2005. "The Economic Value of Cultural Diversity: Evidence from US Cities." *Journal of Economic Geography* 6, no. 1 (June): 9–44.

Pettersson, Therese. 2021. "UCDP Battle-Related Deaths Dataset Codebook Version 21.1." Uppsala Conflict Data Program Technical Report.

Polachek, Solomon, and Carlos Seiglie. 2006. "Trade, Peace and Democracy: An Analysis of Dyadic Dispute." In *Handbook of Defense Economics*, vol 2, eds. Keith Hartley and Todd Sandler, 1017–1073. North-Holland, Amsterdam: Elsevier.

Posner, Daniel. 2004. "The Political Salience of Cultural Difference: Why Chewas and Tumbukas Are Allies in Zambia and Adversaries in Malawi." *American Political Science Review* 98, no. 4: 529–45.

Roser, Max, and Esteban Ortiz-Ospina. 2013. "Global Extreme Poverty." *Our World in Data*. https://ourworldindata.org/poverty. Accessed May 2022.

Sambanis, Nicholas. 2000. "Partition as a Solution to Ethnic War: An Empirical test of the Theoretical Literature." *World Politics* 52, no. 4 (July): 437–83.

Sambanis, Nicholas, and Jonah Schulhofer-Wohl. 2009. "What's in a Line? Is Partition a Solution to Civil War?" *International Security* 34, no. 2 (Fall): 82–118.

Schram, Peter. 2019. "Managing Insurgency." *Journal of Conflict Resolution* 63, no. 10: 2319–53.

Shayo, Moses. 2020. "Social Identity and Economic Policy." *Annual Review of Economics* 12: 355–89.

Streets, Heather. 2004. *Martial Races: The Military, Race and Masculinity in British Imperial Culture*. Manchester: Manchester University Press.

Talbot, Ian, and Gurharpal Singh. 2009. *The Partition of India*. Cambridge: Cambridge University Press.

Thapar, Romila. 2004. *Somanatha: The Many Voices of a History*. New Delhi: Penguin.

UNHCR. https://www.unhcr.org/en-us/figures-at-a-glance.html. Accessed February 22, 2022.

Varshney, Ashutosh. 2002. *Ethnic Conflict and Civic Life: Hindus and Muslims in India*. New Haven, CT: Yale University Press.

Varshney, Ashutosh, and Steven I. Wilkinson. 2004. "Varshney Wilkinson Dataset on Hindu-Muslim Violence in India, Version 2." October. https://www.icpsr.umich.edu/web/ICPSR/studies/4342.

Voigtländer, Nico, and Joachim Voth. 2012. "Persecution Perpetuated: The Medieval Origins of Anti-Semitic Violence in Nazi Germany." *Quarterly Journal of Economics* 127, no. 3: 1339–92.

Wade, Robert. 1988. *Village Republics: Economic Conditions for Collective Action in South India*. Oakland, CA: ICS Press.

Wang, Tianyi. 2021. "Media, Pulpit, and Populist Persuasion: Evidence from Father Coughlin." *American Economic Review* 111, no. 9 (September): 3064–92.

Wilkinson, Steven I. 2004. *Votes and Violence: Electoral Competition and Ethnic Riots in India.* Cambridge Studies in Comparative Politics. Cambridge: Cambridge University Press.

Williamson, Oliver E. 1985. *The Economic Institutions of Capitalism.* New York: Free Press.

Yanagizawa-Drott, David. 2014. "Propaganda and Conflict: Theory and Evidence from the Rwandan Genocide." *Quarterly Journal of Economics* 129, no. 4 (November): 1947–1994.

CHAPTER 31

THE HISTORICAL POLITICAL ECONOMY OF FINANCIAL CRISES

MARC WEIDENMIER

THE historical political economy (HPE) of finance and financial crises is a relatively new area of research. I focus in this chapter on three areas of the historical political economy of financial markets and crises: (1) sovereign debt default, (2) central banks and financial crises, (3) and government regulation. Sovereign debt defaults have been going on for hundreds of years. Countries default on their sovereign debts for many reasons, including war, poor economic conditions, and political factors. With the publication of a new large database on sovereign debt by Meyer, Reinhart, and Trebesch (2022), there are many new opportunities to conduct historical research in this area. For example, some countries engage in selective default, servicing one debt issue while defaulting on another. Selective default is often a political issue where the country may service one debt obligation because they want to maintain a good relationship with the underwriter or a group of bondholders. In this type of case, the country will default on the more junior debt obligation given that fewer potential benefits result from servicing the junior debt (Mitchener and Weidenmier 2010).

Another important topic in the historical political economy of financial crises is central banking. Sweden established the first central bank in 1668, followed by the United Kingdom in 1694. Central banks manage the money supply and keep inflation in check. They often serve as a lender of last resort by providing liquidity to banks during financial crises to help financial institutions avoid bank runs. Many central banks are also charged with the task of maintaining financial stability by regulating the banking system and even setting margin requirements for equity markets.

Since the founding of the Swedish Riksbank in 1668, there are now more than two hundred central banks around the world. This provides a great opportunity for scholars to study the nature and evolution of central banks and their role in causing and mitigating financial crises over hundreds of years. For example, the United States did not have a central bank until the Federal Reserve Act was passed in 1913. Canada, another wealthy Western country, lacked a central bank until the 1930s.

An important long-run historical trend is that the role of central banks has dramatically expanded over the last two hundred years or so. Central banks used to focus on keeping prices stable, discounting loans, and providing check clearing services. As a result of the Great Depression, Fed policy was centralized in Washington, DC, and the regional Federal Reserve Banks lost much of their say about monetary policy. In the 1970s, the Fed adopted a dual mandate where it is charged with keeping both stable prices and maximum employment. During the financial crisis of 2008, the Fed began purchasing toxic mortgage-backed securities and offered unparalleled assistance to the financial sector. More recently, the Fed became involved in the corporate bond market, purchasing large amounts of private sector debt to prevent a potential financial panic. The historical trend of ever increasing powers by central banks around the world raises many political economy questions. History should have much to say about this.

The analysis begins with a study of why the Southern Confederacy serviced its cotton bonds in gold as late as March 1865 even though the Confederate capital of Richmond was surrounded by Union forces and the South had hyperinflation. Second, I examine the Panic of 1907 that led to the creation of the Federal Reserve System, one of the most important institutional changes in world history. Next I look at the fallout from the Great Depression, which reshaped the landscape of how banks operate as well as the centralization of monetary policy in Washington. Finally, the conclusion discusses some lessons to be learned from this historical political economy of financial crises.

The Political Economy of Confederate Cotton Bonds

The Southern Confederacy's poor capital market reputation can be traced to the US states' defaults of the 1840s as well as being a new country at war and without formal diplomatic recognition by the major powers. Several Southern states, including Arkansas, Florida, Mississippi, and Louisiana, issued debt on the New York, Philadelphia, and London exchanges during the 1830s to raise capital to establish banks (Weidenmier 2004). The Panic of 1837 and the ensuing depression forced many banks to close or suspend interest payments, or both, in the early 1840s. Mississippi's experience on the London exchange is especially noteworthy as foreigners held a large percentage of the bonds and Jefferson Davis was a US senator from the state at the time of default. Mississippi floated $2 million of state bonds in the early 1830s to establish the Planters' Bank. A few years later, the state authorized $5 million in bonds for the Union bank. The banks suspended interest payments in 1841 following the 1837 panic and economic downturn (McGrane 1935). The state officially repudiated the Union Bank bonds in 1842 and voted by plebiscite to default on the Planter's Bank bonds in 1852 (English 1996).

Mississippi senator Jefferson Davis, future president of the Southern Confederacy, championed repudiation of state debts throughout this period. US officials published pamphlets in Europe detailing the Confederate president's support of states' defaults (Walker 1864). The US government obviously did not want foreign investors to forget about Davis's position on debt repudiation. Otherwise, investors in Europe would be more inclined to purchase securities issued by the Confederacy (Weidenmier 2004).

Domestic economic policy also contributed to the fledgling nation's poor capital market reputation. The Confederacy was established on the basis of a weak central government that refused to pass tax legislation as well as collect levies that could be used to fund the war effort. Taxes accounted for only 8 percent of revenues during the war (Ball 1991). They also tried to raise war finance through domestic capital markets. The government floated two major loans during the first two years of the war, the $15 million loan of 1861 and the $100 million loan of 1862. The Confederacy originally pledged to service the issues in specie but ultimately reneged, making interest payments in depreciated government Treasury notes. Subsequent bond issues proved less fruitful as investors sought to unload their money balances by purchasing commodities rather than government obligations. Ball (1991) estimated that debt accounted for approximately 33 percent of revenues during the war. The inability to levy taxes and float bonds forced the rebel government to rely on the printing press as its principal means of war finance. Between January 1861 and February 1864, the Confederate money supply increased 1,200 percent, rising from 100 million graybacks to more than 3,500 million (Lerner 1955). Commodity prices, as measured by the Lerner Price Index, rose from an index value of 100 in early 1861 to 5,300 by March 1865. Inflation averaged more than 10 percent per month during the war. Money financing accounted for approximately 59 percent of revenues (Schwab 1901; Todd 1954; Ball 1991). The Confederacy's dependence on the inflation tax further diminished its poor capital market reputation (Weidenmier 2004).

During the first two years of the war, the South did not attempt to float debt in international capital markets. They believed that cotton was "King" and that a self-imposed cotton embargo would draw England and France into the war. They thought that European powers, especially England, were dependent on cotton to operate their textile mills. Although the Confederacy enjoyed considerable power in the world cotton market, many British textile mills were overstocked with cotton early in the war because of a bumper crop in 1860 (Irwin 2003). Southern planters shipped large quantities of cotton to England shortly after South Carolina seceded from the Union in the fall of 1860. Moreover, planters were unwilling to pass legislation that would curtail cotton production or grant the Confederate government power to confiscate the staple (Lebergott 1983).

By the end of 1862, revenues from money, debt, and taxes began to fall with rising inflation. A European loan could raise specie to buy guns and ships abroad as well as replenish gold reserves and bills of exchange depleted by the purchase of arms in England. Raising funds in Europe was a difficult prospect for the Confederacy, however, as their poor capital market reputation and unclear military prospects made it difficult to find financiers that would underwrite a foreign loan. Leading investment houses, such as the Rothschilds and Barings, refused to market war debt for a pro-slavery government with such a poor capital market reputation (Sexton 2001; Weidenmier 2004). The South discussed the possibility of floating a foreign loan with several second-tier firms during the latter part of 1862. They agreed in October to issue a twenty-year, £3 million bond obligation with Emile Erlanger and Company, a French investment house. The sterling raised from the float could buy thousands of guns as a battle rifle cost about £3.5 and gunships between £60,000 and £90,000, depending on their quality (Fenner 1969).

The twenty-year security contained several provisions to minimize the risk for investors and Erlanger and Company. The sterling-denominated issue paid 3.5 percent interest semiannually (in sterling) to minimize currency risk. The issue contained a sinking-fund provision that retired one-fortieth of the principal semiannually through a lottery drawing. The underwriting firm agreed to sell the bonds at 90 percent face value (£90) and collect an 18 percent brokerage fee. As a result, the South received only £2,160,000 (72 percent) of the £3 million issue (*The Economist* March 21, 1863). Investors paid into the subscription over a period of months. Bondholders also had the option to convert the war debt into cotton. Investors could buy New Orleans middling-class cotton for 6 pence a pound from the Confederate government and return to England and sell the fiber at the market price. At the time of issue, cotton sold for approximately 24 pence a pound on the Liverpool exchange. To undertake the transaction, the bondholder first had to exchange the debt issue for cotton certificates with the Confederate representative in Europe. The investor then ran the blockade, took possession of the cotton in the South, and returned to Europe, running the blockade a second time. To facilitate the exchange, the Confederate government agreed to transport the cotton to within ten miles of a navigable river or port (*The Economist* March 21, 1863). The rebels serviced the cotton bonds for the duration of the war, making interest payments in sterling and exchanging the war debt for cotton in accordance with the terms of the contract (Weidenmier 2004).

The reluctance of the Barings and Rothschilds to underwrite debt for the rebel nation shows that the country's poor credit reputation played a role in limiting the amount of capital it could raise in international markets. The Confederacy received approximately £1.519 million pounds sterling after accounting for the net loss from secret debt buybacks and resales, debts settled using repurchased cotton bonds, brokerage and commission costs paid to the French underwriting firm, and a loan secured using the cotton bonds as collateral. The net resource transfer amounted to less than 2 percent of Confederate war expenditures using either estimate of the net proceeds.

Although the cotton loan was quite small, there is considerable evidence that the threat of trade and trade credit sanctions enforced the war loan and debt repayment. The Confederacy secretly repurchased nearly half of the cotton bonds in April and May 1863 to buoy war debt prices after the bonds fell below their original offer price of £90. The buyback program worked, and subscribers made their scheduled payments. The South used some of the remaining repurchased bonds to settle outstanding debts. For example, the Confederacy owed the British firm Saul Isaac, Campbell and Company (hereafter SICC) £565,000. The company was one of the most important suppliers to the

Confederacy of guns and military stores such as canteens, cartridges, knapsacks, and uniforms. The firm even extended trade credit to the rebel nation during the first two years of the war. By the fall of 1862, however, the Confederacy had fallen into arrears on its gun contracts. SICC restricted trade credit and asked for debt repayment. The move reduced gun shipments to the Confederacy. The Confederacy ultimately repaid its debt to SICC by giving the firm £135,000 (market value) in cotton bonds and gold from the proceeds of the Erlanger loan in September 1863 (Fenner 1969; Weidenmier 2004).

Another reason the Confederacy may have serviced the cotton bonds is that important rebel shipbuilders purchased shares in the war debt. The *New York Times* reported on December 9, 1865, that John Laird owned two hundred cotton bonds. The Liverpool engineer designed and built the Laird Rams, two of the largest ironclads built during the Civil War (Dekay 2002). The ships were more powerful than any vessel in the Union Navy and could have inflicted substantial damage on the US Navy. The United States Foreign Service in London pressured the British government to prevent these ships from leaving harbor. The United States argued that England would violate its neutrality if it permitted these ships to sail. England ultimately forced the Confederacy to sell the warships on the open market in the fall of 1863 (Wise 1988).

The prospect of foreign intervention, especially by England, was another factor that may have promoted debt repayment. The Confederacy apparently believed that there might be political gain from floating war debt in Europe. Many high-ranking Confederate officials thought that England might recognize the rebel nation or intervene in the conflict and negotiate an armistice. The possibility of recognition or intervention was unlikely, however, after the Confederate defeat at Antietam in September 1862 and the announcement of the Emancipation Proclamation that freed the slaves in January 1863 (Owsley 1951). Many Britons were unwilling to back a rebel government that supported slavery. The British cabinet ceased discussions of recognizing the Confederacy as a sovereign country in the fall of 1862. Nevertheless, Judah Benjamin, the Confederate secretary of war, believed that with a major military victory, the Confederacy might be able to sway British opinion in favor of the South. Perhaps the Confederacy was aware that many important British politicians and businessmen planned to purchase shares in the cotton bonds (Weidenmier 2004). The *New York Times* also reported that William Gladstone, chancellor of the Exchequer and future prime minister of England, along with several Members of British Parliament (MP), apparently purchased shares in cotton bonds. William Lindsay, an MP and fervent supporter of the Confederacy, for example, apparently held more than £15,000—valued at par—of Confederate cotton bonds. Shortly after the war bonds came to market in March 1863, he tried to secure recognition of the fledgling nation.

The Confederate military situation gradually deteriorated following defeats at Gettysburg and Vicksburg. Union troops pushed Confederate forces farther south in 1864, capturing Atlanta and Nashville. Richmond, the Confederate capital, was almost completely surrounded by a Union army more than twice the size of the defending Southern forces. By early 1865, the South experienced hyperinflation as monthly commodity inflation rose above 50 percent. Confederate Treasury notes traded for less than two cents on the gold dollar, and interest rates on government debt in Richmond climbed to more than 150 percent in January 1865 (Burdekin and Weidenmier 2003). Despite the desperate military and financial situation, the Confederacy serviced the cotton bonds in September 1864 and March 1865 (Gentry 1970). The cotton bonds traded for about £50 pounds sterling (one-half par) in January 1865, a large premium to rebel money. The high price of the cotton bonds at this late stage of the war suggests that financial markets believed the South intended to service the war bonds as long as there was some hope for the "cause."

The threat of trade and trade credit sanctions by gun manufacturers promoted debt repayment by the Confederacy as late as March 1865 despite the onset of hyperinflation and Northern forces at the gates of the rebel capital (Bulow and Rogoff 1989a; 1989b; Eaton and Gersovitz 1981). The South had virtually no capital market reputation at this point of the war as rebel money was essentially worthless and interest rates on government bonds exceeded 150 percent.

The Confederate cotton bonds were a political and economic tool. The debt issue was an attempt by the Southern Confederacy to build financial ties with England that they hoped might result in military aid or support. From a military standpoint, the bonds were used to purchase guns and ships for the Southern Confederacy.

The Panic of 1907 and the Founding of the Federal Reserve

By the time the transcontinental railroad was completed in 1869, San Francisco had already established itself as the center for export trade from the Pacific Coast region. Endowed with an excellent natural harbor and easy coastal and river access to the agricultural and natural resource riches of the West, San Francisco had developed strong economic ties to other countries, particularly to Britain. Most of the wheat exported from the West Coast and bound for England was financed through San Francisco, and a sizeable number of London banks had offices in that city (Odell and Weidenmier 2004). At the same time, other British financial institutions sought to expand their business in the area. Prominent among these were the British fire insurance companies. In 1852, the Liverpool & London & Globe fire insurance company placed an agent in San Francisco: this was the first such insurance firm—foreign or domestic—in the city. Two years later, three more British firms were writing business in San Francisco, and the first American insurance firm set up an office in the city. Not until 1858, however, was a San Francisco–based company established (Kirschner 1922). By 1890 in California, there were 127 American fire insurance firms, each underwriting an average of $13.5 million in risks. On the other hand, there were 52 foreign firms (more than half of which were British), each of which underwrote $23.5 million in risks; nearly 27 percent of California term fire insurance policies were carried by British companies. In fact, the fire insurance company writing the most policies in California was Liverpool & London & Globe, with total risks of $173 million. In comparison, 28 percent of all fire insurance policy risks in New York were underwritten by foreign firms, while in Illinois foreign companies insured less than 20 percent of the value of all risks (United States 7th Census 1891). Fifteen years later, these patterns persisted. At the end of 1905, slightly more than half of insured risks were underwritten by American firms, with almost 40 percent of business still carried by foreign firms, most of which were based in Britain. On the other hand, California-based firms were writing only 7 percent of fire insurance business in the state (Kirschner 1922). The city of San Francisco was even more dependent on foreign fire insurers than the state as a whole. By the turn of the century, it was estimated that at least half of all fire insurance policies in San Francisco were issued by British companies (Cockerell and Green 1976).

One explanation for the dominance of British firms is the long history of trade relations between the city and Britain. Another is simple economics: as agents from the London and Lancashire insurance firm noted, the profit on San Francisco business equaled 30 percent—"three times greater than that yielded by its business generally" (Kirschner 1922). Evidently, adjusters failed to consider earthquake risk.

On Wednesday, April 18, 1906, an earthquake of Richter magnitude 8.3 hit San Francisco. Most of the damage was not done by the tremor itself (which was especially severe in areas of landfill where liquefaction occurred) but by the fires that followed. The majority of the city's buildings had been made of wood; this material was far more plentiful and inexpensive than brick as a result of the city's central place in the coastal lumber trade. The combination of close quarters, highly flammable building materials, and earthquake-damaged water mains hampered the efforts of firefighters. Ultimately more than four square miles—about half of the city—were destroyed. Fewer than 1,500 of the city's 375,000 residents were killed; damage was estimated at between $350 million and $500 million (*The Commercial and Financial Chronicle* October 19, 1907). Word of the disaster in San Francisco spread throughout the United States within hours, and the impact was felt almost immediately in financial markets. In particular, news of the earthquake led to a sell-off and a significant drop in the price of shares on the New York and London Stock Exchanges. The *New York Times* of April 26, 1906, reported that the San Francisco disaster led directly or indirectly to about a $1 billion (or nearly 12.5 percent) decline in the market value of NYSE stocks; railway stocks alone fell more than 15 percent (*The Economist* May 12, 1906). In London, share prices for leading insurance companies plummeted following news of the San Francisco disaster, with stock prices for most insurance companies involved in the quake suffering losses of 15 to 30 percent in the two weeks following the disaster. Equity prices for London and Lancashire, the largest British insurer in San Francisco, posted a 30 percent decline. At the same time, shares of London Assurance fell more than one-third, from 75 to 51.5. Funds for relief and rebuilding flowed into the city quite quickly. Given the preference of Californians for specie over banknotes, these funds came largely in the form of gold; in fact, San Francisco's bankers formed a clearinghouse to coordinate the distribution of gold money to their depositors shortly after the earthquake (Phillips 2002).

In late April and May 1906, nearly $50 million of gold poured into the United States from Germany, France, the Netherlands, and England (whose contribution alone amounted to $30 million). The *New York Times* (May 7, 1906) and the records of the National Monetary Commission indicated that 80 percent of these funds were transferred to San Francisco. These flows were apparently also aided by the US Treasury's policy of subsidizing gold imports by offering to place government deposits in banks while gold was in transit.

Because San Francisco was a major market for British fire insurance companies, however, much of the brunt of financing San Francisco's recovery was borne abroad. *The Economist* reported at length on the consequences of the disaster for British insurance firms, pointing out that they had more than $87 million in policies in San Francisco, with an estimated $46 million in losses (August 11, 1906). Of course, the amount of policies underwritten could not precisely predict the size of insurance payments to be made; some properties survived the earthquake undamaged. At the same time, the insurers—in a particularly bad public relations move—indicated early on that no payments would be made on damage that resulted from the earthquake itself. There were no clear means of allocating damage to the earthquake or to the fire, although some insurers proposed a 60-40 split: 40 percent of each policy claim would be denied "on the ground that the destroyed buildings were first damaged in that proportion by the temblor" (*Los Angeles Times* May 8, 1906).

In contrast to relief payments, most insurance claims took months to settle as some companies equivocated while others waited for guidance from a report of the Insurance Department of New York State on how American firms should settle claims. This four-point plan was not finalized until the end of July. At that time, most British fire insurance houses signed on and agreed to settle their claims in accordance with the New York State Insurance Department. By October, it was estimated that more than $100 million in insurance checks had been received in San Francisco (Douty 1977). Ultimately, British insurers paid out £10 million ($48 million) for earthquake damage (Cockerell and Green 1976). What made these British liabilities even more significant for international financial markets was the fact that most foreign insurers decided to pay claims out of "home funds" rather than reserves in the United States. At the same time, however, the British companies were hesitant to liquidate the home securities in which they held reserves. Given the size of losses involved, such sales would undoubtedly depress stock prices. As a consequence, a number of firms negotiated term loans with their banks and so postponed securities sales for a few months (see *Financial Times* July 6, 1906).

While the summer of 1906 saw British insurance firms shipping gold to San Francisco, New York financial institutions also faced low gold reserves resulting from their own specie transfers to San Francisco in the immediate aftermath of the earthquake (*Financial Times* July 6, 1906). New York firms were also putting pressure on Secretary of the Treasury Leslie M. Shaw to resume his policy of subsidizing gold imports by placing deposits in banks while gold was in transit. In total, quake-related payments to the United States represented 40 percent of seasonally adjusted British gold exports for all of 1906 and over 80 percent of seasonally adjusted gold imports into the United States that year.

Faced with its largest two-month net gold outflow in the 1900–1913 period and the lowest ratio of reserves to deposits since the 1893 crisis, the Bank of England began raising its discount rate. On September 12, the rate was raised from 3.5 to 4 percent. By October 19, the bank had raised the discount rate to 6 percent. Although rates had not been at this level since 1899, market watchers anticipated even more drastic measures to stem the outflow of gold. The Bank of England had stopped discounting US bills altogether, but not the bills of other countries. The Bank of England adhered to this policy until the Panic of 1907 (Sprague 1910. These actions stopped the flow of gold to the United States and put the squeeze on American financial markets.

As finance bills came due, there was a scramble for liquidity and a sell-off of railroad securities by American firms in early 1907. The decline in stock values led to a short but sharp "rich man's panic" in March, helping to push the United States into a recession. The US gold money stock contracted nearly 10 percent between May and August of 1907, and American industrial production fell 30 percent in the second half of the year. The New York money market entered the fall of 1907 low on gold reserves and vulnerable to shocks that might otherwise have been temporary in nature. Some scholars attribute the proximate cause of the panic to the failed attempt by Auguste Heinz and his associates to corner the copper market (Bruner and Carr 2009). Others blame the collapse of New York's second-largest trust company, Knickerbocker. Both events probably contributed to the panic that erupted in late October 1907, leading to a series of bank runs in New York (Frydman, Hilt, and Zhou 2015). Within a few weeks, the crisis spread to other regions of the United States.

Several measures were taken to contain the crisis. The New York Clearinghouse Association issued loan certificates, a money substitute used to clear accounts between banks. Clearinghouse loan certificates artificially increased the money supply and freed up currency for depositors who demanded cash. Federal aid came in the form of public funds deposited by the US Treasury at key New York City banks, and J. P. Morgan formed a money pool with bankers to provide liquidity assistance to trust companies and the stock market (Ramirez 1995). These measures eased conditions in the money market, but failed to prevent the suspension of specie payments. As short-term interest rates rose to over 10 percent, gold poured into the United States. The United States imported over $100 million in gold during November and December. Specie exports drained European money centers helping to transmit the "localized" New York panic to international financial markets (Goodhart 1969).

To summarize, the historical narrative provides evidence that the San Francisco earthquake caused a liquidity crisis in the New York and European money markets through its effect on gold flows. The Bank of England, in conjunction with other European central banks, responded by raising its discount rates and discriminating against US bills for the next year. These actions set off a chain of events—the interest rate increases that led to a recession and stock market decline—that ultimately ended in the Panic of 1907.

From a public opinion and political economy perspective, many Americans were not happy that Morgan and his banking associates wrote a check to shore up the New York money market during the financial crisis. Rather, there was growing public support, especially among the elite, for the United States to have its own central bank to deal with the liquidity problems in the fall created by the harvest season. Congress subsequently passed the Aldrich-Vreeland Act (1908) in response to the panic; this legislation created the National Monetary Commission and authorized banks to issue emergency currency backed by commercial paper in times of crisis (Sprague 1910). The National Monetary Commission's recommendations eventually formed the basis of the Federal Reserve Act that passed in 1913. After many years of debate over the function and form of a central bank in the United States, politics dictated that the act create regional Federal Reserve Banks that had oversight from the Federal Reserve Board. The new central bank had the power to provide for an elastic currency during periods of financial crisis. Furthermore, the Fed system was designed to improve the flow of money and credit across the United States.

In summary, the Panic of 1907 is a classic example of how a severe financial crisis led to one of the most important institutional changes in world history: the founding of the Federal Reserve System.

The Great Depression

The 1920s saw a transformation in the activities of banks in the United States. The Federal Reserve was established in 1913 to provide for a more elastic currency and play the role of lender of last resort. The stimulus to increase funding for the government during World War I, electrification, and the development of large-scale industries created new profit opportunities for industry (White 1990). Indeed, the US economy grew at an annual rate of 3.7 percent between 1920 and 1929. Banks, trusts, and related financial intermediaries dramatically increased their profits and stock prices during the 1920s as they found new ways to finance investment projects (White 1990). National banks faced competition from trusts after World War I, which offered a broader range of financial services to their customers and enabled them to combine banking services with fiduciary powers. The expansion of fiduciary powers to national banks in 1918 allowed them to compete directly with trusts and expand their services.

New government regulations for financial intermediaries accompanied the expansion of banking across the United States. The McFadden Act of 1927, for example, dealt with three crucial banking issues. First, the legislation granted the twelve Federal Reserve Banks and national banks perpetual charters, replacing their twenty-year charters. The action was taken, in part, because the US government failed to renew the twenty-year charter of the Second Bank of the United States. The McFadden Act also expanded branch banking. It permitted national banks to have branches to the extent allowed by state law. This permission meant that national banks did not have to operate in just one building as they did in many states (Rajan and Ramcharan 2015). The coastal states of the East and West generally allowed branching, while interior states were more likely to have unit banking. The legislation encouraged banks to acquire other banks and expand their services to a larger geographic area.

The economic expansion ended in August 1929, which marked a turning point in economic activity as the United States entered what appeared to be a "garden variety recession" (Friedman and Schwartz 1963). Three months later, stock prices on the New York Stock Exchange (NYSE) fell more than 20 percent over two days. The New York Fed quickly responded to the crash by adding liquidity to financial markets through open market operations. Friedman and Schwartz (1963) referred to the New York Fed's action as a textbook case of a successful lender-of-last-resort policy. They argue that the New York Fed's policy limited the effects of the financial shock from the Great Depression on real economic activity (Cortes, Taylor, and Weidenmier 2021).

The early stages of the Great Depression were relatively mild. Many government leaders and members of the business community were looking for a quick rebound in economic conditions in the fall of 1930. The economic decline accelerated over the next couple of years with four banking crises. Wicker (1996) studied the geographic incidence of the banking crises of the Depression. The first major crisis occurred in the St. Louis Federal Reserve District when Caldwell and Company collapsed in November 1930 (Wicker 1980). The bank was a rapidly growing firm that was also the largest financial holding company in the South (Richardson 2013). The firm's large stock portfolio took a big hit with the crash of 1929 and began to have financial difficulties with the meltdown in real estate and equity prices. The Bank of Tennessee, a subsidiary of Caldwell, closed its doors on November 7. Several days later, other financial intermediaries associated with Caldwell suspended operations (Richardson 2013). A financial crisis ensued as depositors rushed to take their funds out of insolvent banks. The crisis was mostly regional and did not impact the New York money market (Wicker 1996). The financial crisis deepened as the Bank of the United States closed its doors on December 11, 1930, following a failed attempt to merge with another New York bank. Again, fearful depositors withdrew their funds from the troubled financial institution and other banks with financial difficulties (Richardson 2013). As Wicker (1996) points out, the Bank of the United States collapse did not significantly impact the New York money market.

The second banking crisis of the Great Depression, from April to August of 1931, was centered in the Chicago and Cleveland Federal Reserve Districts (Wicker 1996). Chicago experienced numerous bank failures, especially in unit banks that financed the Chicago suburbs' rapid growth in the 1920s. With the onset of the Great Depression, many unit banks failed as real estate prices plummeted. The third banking crisis of the Great Depression began on September 21, 1931, when the Bank of England announced that it would leave the gold standard (Cortes, Taylor, and Weidenmier 2021). The action led investors to sell dollar assets for gold in anticipation that the United States might also abandon the gold standard. The gold drain reduced the US gold supply, and depositors withdrew funds from their banks. The internal and external drain reduced the money supply, which created deflation and exacerbated the downturn (Engemann 2013).

The fourth banking panic of the Great Depression started at the end of 1932 and lasted until March 1933. In early 1933, some states declared bank holidays, meaning that banks did not have to redeem demand deposits. Over 5,190 banks closed their doors during 1933 (Grossman 2008). People rushed to withdraw their deposits before state regulators closed their banks. National banks accounted for 1,475 of the financial intermediaries that suspended operations. President Roosevelt declared a national bank holiday a day after his inauguration on March 4, 1933. Secretary of the Treasury Henry Morgenthau began granting licenses to banks to reopen beginning on March 13, 1933 (Bernanke 1983; Grossman 2008).

Lessons

The political economy of financial markets and crises can be broadly divided into three areas: sovereign debt, central banking and financial crises, and governance regulation of central banking. The three examples studied show that political economy issues and financial crises can take very different forms. With respect to the Confederacy, the fledgling nation issued the cotton bonds to buy guns from British firms and to curry favor with the British government in hopes that the United Kingdom would provide economic or military support to the rebels. As for the Panic of 1907, the case study demonstrates how the San Francisco earthquake, a real shock, can produce a liquidity crisis in global financial markets, even in the early 1900s. J. P. Morgan played an important role in the Panic of 1907 by supplying much-needed liquidity to the market to prevent an even deeper financial crisis. His actions created a public outcry to some extent, as people would rather have a government institution provide liquidity as opposed to a private individual. Ultimately, the Panic of 1907 led to the creation of the Federal Reserve System, one of the most important institutional changes in world history.

The Great Depression's banking crises and the failure of the Federal Reserve System to respond to the severe economic downturn led to some of the most important and well-known banking legislation in American history (Flannery 1985). The severity of the Great Depression, which saw a 33 percent decrease in US economic activity, led to a sea change in the organization and functions of the Federal Reserve System. The crisis also created bipartisan support for new banking regulations. The Glass-Steagall Act of 1933, for example, created the Federal Deposit Insurance Corporation (FDIC), which insured demand deposits starting January 1, 1934. The legislation was widely supported by unit banks, which had less diversified portfolios that made them more vulnerable to a banking panic.

The Glass-Steagall Act also called for the separation of commercial and investment banking. Proponents of this policy argue that there are conflicts of interest when financial intermediaries conduct business in both commercial and investment banking. On the other hand, some policymakers believe that there are economies of scale in banking and that universal banking is a better model. The debate over the separation of commercial and investment continues to this day and will likely continue in the future.

The Banking Act of 1935 made the FDIC a permanent institution. All Federal Reserve member banks were required to join the FDIC. By mid-1934, federal deposit insurance covered over fifteen thousand banks, representing 97 percent of bank deposits. The Banking Act also reorganized the structure of the Federal Reserve (Richardson et al. 2013). The Board of Governors of the Federal Reserve System—which replaced the Federal Reserve Board—became more independent from the executive branch of government. The secretary of the treasury and the comptroller of the currency were no longer members of the Federal Reserve Board. The regional Federal Reserve Banks lost much of their control over monetary policy. The heads of the regional Federal Reserve Banks were no longer called "governors." Instead, they were given the new title of "president," which symbolized a reduction in the power of the regional banks to implement their own monetary policy. The regional Federal Reserve Banks could no longer conduct open market operations in their respective districts. Rather, the newly created Federal Open Market Committee (FOMC) determined the size and scope of open market operations, with monetary policy decision-making centralized in the nation's capital. Overall, the Great Depression demonstrates how a large financial crisis can lead to a dramatic increase in the power of a central bank to regulate a country's banking and financial system.

References

Ball, D. B. 1991. *Financial Failure and Confederate Defeat*. Urbana: University of Illinois Press.

Bernanke, B. S. 1983. "Nonmonetary Effects of the Financial Crisis in the Propagation of the Great Depression." *American Economic Review* 73: 257–76.

Bruner, R. F., and S. D. Carr. 2009. *The Panic of 1907: Lessons Learned from the Market's Perfect Storm*. New York: Wiley.

Bulow, J., and K. S. Rogoff. 1989a. "Sovereign Debt: Is to Forgive to Forget?" *American Economic Review* 79: 43–50.

Bulow, J., and K. S. Rogoff. 1989b. "A Constant Recontracting Model of Sovereign Debt." *Journal of Political Economy* 97: 155–78.

Burdekin, R. C. K., and Marc D. Weidenmier. 2003. "Suppressing Asset Price Inflation: The Confederate Experience, 1861–1865." *Economic Inquiry* 41: 420–32.

Cockerell, H. A. L., and Edwin Green. 1976. *The British Insurance Business 1547–1970*. London: Heinemann Educational Books.

Cortes, Gustavo, Bryan Taylor, and Marc Weidenmier. 2021. "Financial Factors and the Propagation of the Great Depression." *Journal of Financial Economics* 145: 577–94.

Dekay, J. T. 2002. *The Rebel Raiders: The Astonishing History of the Confederacy's Secret Navy*. New York: Ballantine Books.

Douty, C. M. 1977. *The Economics of Localized Disasters: The 1906 San Francisco Catastrophe*. New York: Arno Press.

Eaton, J., and M. Gersovitz. 1981. "Debt with Potential Repudiation: Theoretical and Empirical Analysis." *Review of Economic Studies* 48: 289–309.

Engemann, K. 2013. "Banking Panics of 1931–33." *Federal Reserve History*. https://www.federalreservehistory.org/essays/banking_panics_1931_33.

English, W. B. 1996. "Understanding the Costs of Sovereign Default: American State Debts in the 1840s." *American Economic Review* 86: 259–75.

Fenner, J. A. 1969. *Confederate Finances Abroad*. Unpublished PhD dissertation, Rice University.

Flannery, M. J. 1985. "An Economic Evaluation of Bank Securities Activities before 1933." In *Deregulating Investment Banking*, ed. I. Walter, 67–87. New York: John Wiley & Sons.

Friedman, M., and A. J. Schwartz. 1963. *A Monetary History of the United States*. Princeton, NJ: Princeton University Press.

Frydman, C. Eric Hilt, and L. Zhou. 2015. "Economic Effects of Early Runs on Shadow Banks: Trust Companies and the Impact of the Panic of 1907." *Journal of Political Economy* 123: 902–40.

Gentry, J. F. 1970. "A Confederate Success in Europe, the Erlanger Loan." *Journal of Southern History* 36: 157–88.

Goodhart, Charles E. 1969. *The New York Money Market and the Finance of Trade*. Cambridge, MA: Harvard University Press.

Grossman, R. S. 2008. "U.S. Banking History, Civil War to World War II." In *The Economic History Association's EH.Net Encyclopedia*, ed. R. Whaples. http://eh.net/encyclopedia/us-banking-history-civil-war-to-world-war-ii.

Irwin, D. A. 2003. "The Optimal Tax on Antebellum Cotton Exports." *Journal of International Economics* 60: 271–91.

Josefin Meyer, Carmen Reinhart, and Christoph Trebesch. 2022. "Sovereign Bonds Since Waterloo." Quarterly Journal of Economics 137, no. 3: 1615–80.

Kirschner, Herbert A. 1922. *Fire Insurance Development on the Pacific Coast*. San Francisco: Underwriters' Report.

Lebergott, S. 1983. "Through the Blockade: The Profitability and Extent of Cotton Smuggling, 1861–1865." *Journal of Economic History* 70: 867–88.

Lerner, E. M. 1955. "Money, Prices, and Wages in the Confederacy, 1861–65." *Journal of Political Economy* 62: 506–22.

McGrane, R. C. 1935. *Foreign Bondholders and American State Debts*. New York: Macmillan and Company.

Mitchener, K., and Marc Weidenmier. 2010. "Supersanctions and Sovereign Debt Repayment." *Journal of International Money and Finance* 29: 19–36.

Odell, Kerry, and Marc D. Weidenmier. 2004. "The San Francisco Earthquake and the Panic of 1907." *Journal of Economic History* 64: 1002–27.

Owsley, F. L. 1951. *King Cotton Diplomacy: Foreign Relations of the Confederate States of America*. Chicago: University of Chicago Press.

Phillips, Ronnie J. 2002. "Coping with Financial Catastrophe: The San Francisco Clearinghouse during the Earthquake of 1906." Manuscript.

Rajan, R. G., and R. Ramcharan. 2015. "Constituencies and Legislation: The Fight over the McFadden Act of 1927." *Management Science* 62: 1843–59.

Ramirez, Carlos. 1995. "Did J. P. Morgan's Men Add Value? Corporate Investment, Cash Flow, and Financial Structure at the Turn of the Century." *Journal of Finance* 50: 661–78.

Richardson, Gary. 2013. "Banking Panics, 1930–31." *Federal Reserve History*. https://www.federalreservehistory.org/essays/banking-panics-1930-31.

Richardson, G., A. Komai, and M. Gou. 2013. "Banking Act of 1935." *Federal Reserve History*. www.federalreservehistory.org/essays/banking-act-of-1935.

Schwab, J. C. 1901. *The Confederate States of America*. New York: Charles Scribner's Sons.

Sexton, J. 2001. "Transatlantic Financiers and the Civil War." *American Nineteenth-Century History* 2: 29–46.

Sprague, O. M. 1910. *History of Crises under the National Banking System*. Washington, DC: National Monetary Commission.

Todd, R. C. 1954. *Confederate Finance*. Athens: University of Georgia Press.

Walker, R. J. 1864. *American Slavery and Finances*. London: William Ridgeway.

Weidenmier, Marc D. 2004. "Gunboats, Reputation, and Sovereign Repayment: Lessons from the Southern Confederacy." *Journal of International Economics* 66: 407–22.

White, E. 1990. "The Stock Market Boom and the Crash of 1929 Revisited." *Journal of Economic Perspectives* 4: 67–83.

Wicker, E. 1980. "A Reconsideration of the Causes of the Banking Panic of 1930." *Journal of Economic History* 40: 571–83.

Wicker, E. 1996. *The Banking Panics of the Great Depression*. Cambridge: Cambridge University Press.

Wise, S. D. 1988. *Lifeline of the Confederacy: Blockade Running during the Civil War*. Columbia: University of South Carolina Press.

CHAPTER 32

THE CORPORATION AND THE STATE IN HISTORICAL POLITICAL ECONOMY

RON HARRIS

ALONGSIDE the nation state, the business corporation is a defining institution of the modern era. Over the last two centuries, corporations have become the cornerstone of the market economy, and the largest among them have capacities comparable to those of mid-size states. Moreover, the inability of states to regulate multinational corporations and (digital) information-based corporations is apparent. The complex history of the business corporation can be organized around various themes.[1] In the context of this handbook, in which the state features centrally, attention in this chapter is turned toward the interactions between the state and the business corporation. What were the historic relationships between states and corporations? How did we arrive at the current state of affairs, in which states are unable to control corporations? Answers to these questions are at the heart of this chapter.

According to the literature, we can think in terms of four distinct types of relationships between the corporation and the state. The first views the corporation as an independent organ that, from the outset, was not created by the state and was distinct from the state, existing in an intermediate sphere that is separate from the state, on the one hand, and individuals (and families), on the other. The second views the corporation as one of the arms of the state, which receives sovereign powers delegated by the state and performs functions on its behalf. The third relationship views the corporation as being able to develop only when and where the state can credibly commit not to expropriate the assets pooled together in the corporation. The fourth views the well-functioning state, offering enforcement of contracts, as a precondition for forming corporations. This relationship sees the state not only as a party to a contract with the corporation but also as an enforcer of the contract—or nexus of contracts—among the corporate stakeholders. While the third type emphasizes the state's negative role in the facilitation of corporate development, the fourth views it as playing a positive role. The third expects the state to have only limited capacity, so that it will not encroach on the corporation, while the fourth expects it to have strong capacity, so that it will serve the corporation.

In Britain, the paradigmatic country in terms of the history of the corporation, the four types appeared historically one after the other, but they did not instantaneously and universally replace each other. In other countries, different paths were followed. In some countries the second type prevails today, and the third type never materialized and (formally or informally) state-owned enterprises dominate the economy. The history of the corporation should not be viewed as always being an evolutionary process from one type to the next.

This chapter proceeds as follows. First we survey the manifestation of the four types of state-corporation relationships in the actual history of the West, with focus on the Dutch Republic, Britain, and the United States. While doing this we explain why other regions did not give rise to business corporations. Next we follow the transition to the modern corporate regime of free access, freedom of contract, and jurisdictional forum shopping. Finally we examine the new frontiers and challenges faced by corporations in their relationship with the state in the last century and speculate which type of relationship will prevail in the near future.

The Corporation—Independent from the State

Having outlined the four types of relationship, we now return to the eleventh century and the creation of the earliest type of relationship between states and the corporation. The Investiture Controversy was the conflict between the emperor of the Holy Roman Empire and the pope over the power to appoint bishops and other clergymen in the territories of the empire, and even the power to choose the pope himself, that unfolded in the eleventh and twelfth centuries. As Berman (1983), Tierney (1955), and others have shown, it led legal scholars connected to the Roman Catholic Church to develop the very earliest corporate conceptions. Issues arose that demanded practical answers: Who, if not the emperor, was to appoint the pope? Does the pope have to consult or seek the approval of those who appointed him for certain acts? Who owns the property of the Roman Catholic Church: individual religious officeholders or their seats, and what happens to that property upon the death of these religious office holders? In time, these matters were conceptualized in legal terms, and the organizing concept was termed the *corporation*.

Several of the features of the newly invented corporation related to internal governance. These included the election of officeholders by consent of the governed through majority decision-making, subject to set deliberation rules and voting procedure; the delegation of legal authority to act and make their decisions binding; and the jurisdiction of the collective body to issue bylaws for governing internal affairs. Based on these governance rules, the collective body became entitled to own property, convey property to third parties, and litigate disputes with those parties. The existence of these collective bodies was not confined to the life span of any single individual human being. Issues of cross-generational transfer of property were alleviated by the longevity of the collective entity—a major advantage in a church in which celibacy was required from monks and clergymen, and where the hereditary transmission of titles and property was therefore not an option. These governance and property rules for running collective bodies were used by a broad range of ecclesiastical offices and organizations, from the papacy and bishopry to the monastery, fraternity, and religious order. Jurists trained in Roman law and canon law conceptualized the corporation as a legal entity with various attributes. Corporate law ultimately served as the constitutional law of the church (Berman 1983; Grant 2001; Tierney 1955, 96–131).[2] The corporation was first developed as an institution separate from, and independent of, the state.

But why was the Roman Catholic Church, out of all the organized religions, the birthplace of the corporation? While several major religions, Confucianism and the early Eastern Orthodox Church, were an integral part of the apparatus of territorial states, the Catholic Church aspired to separate itself from the emperor and other secular rulers (Feldman 1997).[3] So the corporation at its Roman Catholic birth was separated from the state because that separation from the control of lay rulers was the rationale for its birth.

By the fifteenth century, the corporation was well established as an important organizational and constitutional platform in Europe, well beyond the church. It was increasingly used in the municipal context. Hundreds of cities were incorporated in Europe, particularly in Italy, England, the Low Countries, and German-speaking regions in central Europe. These municipal corporations assumed a level of independence and autonomy from popes and emperors and from the rural feudal system (Cantoni and Yuchtman 2014; Richardson 2004; Henrich 2020).[4] In the period up to 1500, more than fifty incorporated universities were formed throughout Europe, many composed of a larger number of incorporated colleges. Nowhere else in Eurasia outside Catholic Europe were municipalities and educational institutions based on the corporate form, and nowhere else did they enjoy such a high level of independence from territorial rulers by relying on other institutional frameworks, such as the waqf or the family clan (Kuran 2005; Roy 2010; Zelin 2009).

Gradually, the corporation was found to provide a valuable platform not only for organizing what we call today the public, political, or municipal aspects of towns, but also for organizing city-based economic activities. Guilds—the most significant late-medieval economically active corporations—had considerable social, fraternal, ritual, and even religious elements. They served as brotherhoods that controlled and ritualized entire aspects of their members' lives (Black 2003, 12–32; Epstein 1998; Ogilvie 2011). Guilds are usually categorized under two basic categories: craft guilds (composed of artisans, manufacturing and selling locally) and merchant guilds (composed of traders, buying and selling in distant markets). In the case of England, this terminology changed and became more formalized over the years, morphing into "livery companies" (akin to craft guilds) and "regulated companies" (a version of the merchant guild). Hundreds of guilds were established in various parts of Europe (Ogilvie 2019; Richardson 2004).[5]

Over time, the characteristics of the city-based corporation became quite stable, as a legal entity separate from that of its members. Its legal entity secured longevity: it did not terminate upon the death of any one individual but instead was potentially everlasting. A corporation could own and convey land. It did not have to litigate by listing all of its members' names but could sue and be sued, for better or worse, in its separate corporate personality. It could make bylaws to govern its internal affairs, and as a legal entity it could acquire additional franchises, liberties, and exemptions from the state, usually in the incorporating charter or act itself.[6]

The first four centuries in the history of the European corporation can be divided into two subperiods. In the first, the corporation was conceptualized exclusively in relation to the Roman Catholic Church: it was used for legitimizing and organizing many of its internal elements and served as the backbone of the church's constitution. In the second subperiod, the corporate concept spilled over from religious to secular contexts and was employed by municipalities and other urban organizational forms to address their governance needs and consolidate their autonomy vis-à-vis popes and emperors. Corporations of this first type formed organically: from below, via practices and self-proclamations. Some were created as subordinate corporations—the church could incorporate monasteries and religious orders, for instance; cities could form incorporated guilds; and universities could recognize colleges. All of this was achieved detached from, and independent of, any territorial political ruler.

The Corporation—Organ of the State

England, with its more centralized monarchy, was the first country to enter the second type of corporation-state relationship, which witnessed the subordination of the corporation to the state. In the fifteenth and sixteenth centuries, the English Crown gradually monopolized the privilege of creating corporations and used the corporate form in a manner akin to its agents of policy promotion and income generation. The Crown's jurists considered incorporation as an essential component of the monarch's exclusive and voluntary prerogative to create and grant dignities, jurisdictions, liberties, exemptions, and in this case, franchises (monopolies and corporations). This authorization was normally given in the form of charters or letters patent (Harris 2013a; Hale 1976; Maitland 1908). In the period up to 1500, the Crown issued thirty-two charters of incorporation; in the sixteenth century, a total of seventy-five new charters were granted; a further seventy-one were conceded in the seventeenth century (Harris 2020a).

Most charters incorporated universities, colleges, schools, hospitals, livery companies, and trade companies. Some of the charters were issued for the reincorporation of older craft and merchant guilds that were originally created de facto by practice and not by a formal charter, and others to companies formed by charters issued by municipalities rather than kings. The reincorporation of preexisting municipalities and ecclesiastical companies was politically sensitive due to the tensions between the Crown and the pre-Reformation church (and post-Reformation Stuart resurrection) and with the larger cities, notably London. Only a few of these preexisting municipalities and ecclesiastical companies were reincorporated by royal charters. An attempt to impose a royal charter on the city of London resulted in a constitutional crisis. The eventual way forward was to leave the old municipal and ecclesiastical corporation form aside and establish a clear rule for the future that corporations could only be established by the rulers. Similar processes occurred in other European countries, notably France, as the central governments consolidated their powers and assumed a monopoly over functions that came to be known as sovereign power—from the use of violence to border control. The rulers exercised their prerogative discretion to form corporations that served their aims. Corporations constructed common infrastructures, regulated and monitored members, advanced mercantilist foreign policy, and collected taxes collectively (in this latter function, serving as informal tax farmers).

The State—Negative Commitment to the Corporation

England also led the way in the transition to the third type of relationship. Merchant enterprises that engaged with the most distant trade destinations—the Levant, Russia, and the Indian Ocean—found it impossible to operate based on the traditional organizational model of guilds and regulated corporations. The solution, resorted to from the late sixteenth century, was to pool resources together. The older trading corporations were guildlike organizations in which each trader traded on his own account, investing his capital, bearing the trade risk, and drawing profits for himself. The corporation provided only the necessary collective infrastructure, such as warehouses, docks, and consuls. But this approach was insufficient for the long-distance trade that involved longer turnaround times, greater trade and maritime uncertainties, and significant information asymmetries—all of which translated into a large start-up capital requirement, regional specialization of employees, and longer investment horizons. The solution eventually designed was the joint-stock business corporation, in which hundreds of passive investors pooled together their resources into a common account. The trade was conducted in the name of the corporate capital account, and the payoffs or losses were divided among the investors according to their level of investment. This new model was designed wholly within the English East India Company, which was chartered in 1600, and was fully shaped over the next six decades.

This model could not have succeeded had it not satisfied one major precondition, which could only be met by the ruler—in the case of England, the Crown. The Crown had to commit *not* to expropriate in full or in large part, or to heavily and unilaterally tax, the assets that were about to be pooled. The pooling-together of large tangible capital created an almost irresistible temptation for the Crown. Investors' awareness of this risk and of the Crown's expropriation powers would cool off their desire to invest in a pool and render them likelier to keep their assets in less tangible and smaller hoards instead. The challenge, as North and Weingast (1989) show in the context of government borrowing from the public via bond issues, was to demand a credible commitment by the ruler not to expropriate. The challenge was that absolute rulers could *not* credibly commit not to do whatever they wanted at their unilateral discretion. Being an absolute ruler was not only a blessing but also a curse for these rulers.

North and Weingast (1989) demonstrated that the mechanisms for conveying credible commitment to repay the public debt through linked Parliamentary taxation were created after the 1688 Glorious Revolution. As I have shown elsewhere (Harris 2020a), charters issued by absolute rulers were not worth the parchment they were inked on. The concern here was not only the potential for expropriation of corporate assets but also the revocation, alteration, or bypassing of the corporate charter. Only with restrained government could the commitments made by rulers in charters of incorporation be credible. Without institutionalized and credible negative commitment, to refrain from acting against the corporation and the terms of its charter, the passive investors would have refrained from investing with the new, strange, and impersonal institution called the business corporation (Harris 2020a).

The ability to convey credible commitment to strangers through the corporate form was a breakthrough on the way to impersonal investment. Commitments toward corporations and their incorporators could credibly be conveyed by around 1600 but only in England and the Dutch Republic. Although in English doctrinal constitutional law, the granting of charters was formally still within the prerogative of the Crown, Parliament and the judiciary became highly influential institutions in the charter-granting arena in the 1558–1640 period. Parliament protested unilateral decisions by the Crown to grant charters (particularly ones that combined trade or manufacturing monopoly privileges with the incorporation) or to revoke them. Gradually, case by case, the common-law courts began to review the validity and scope of charters issued by the Crown. New constitutional ideas, developed in public discourse relating to the clashes between the Crown, Parliament, and the judiciary, constrained the Crown's prerogative. Shrewd jurists mixed these new ideas with old narratives and memories in a bid to lend them apparently ancient origins and thus render them entrenched and unalterable. The Crown had to take into account the vested interests of both the charter grantees and their competitors because these interest groups had access to Parliament and the courts of law, and had the option of refraining from doing business altogether or seeking alternatives overseas. In short, the Crown became constrained by reputational mechanisms, institutional devices, the consolidation of an independent judiciary, and new constitutional ideas. All of these factors culminated in a gradual shift from an absolute monarchy to a nascent rule-of-law model (North and Weingast 1989; Harris 2013a; Klerman and Mahoney 2005).

The Dutch Republic experienced a simultaneous process. It was able to credibly commit to paying back its loans by connecting loan repayment to specific taxes and making the loan bonds tradable on the Amsterdam stock market, in what came to be known as the financial revolution. It was able to credibly commit to respect the terms of the charter granted to the Dutch East India Company in 1602 and not to expropriate the unprecedentedly huge amount of capital raised by the company from investors. While the main commitment device in England was the separation of powers between the executive, legislative, and judicial branches, in the case of the Dutch Republic, the device was federalism—the separation of powers between the central, provincial, and municipal governments (Adams 2005; Gelderblom, de Jong, and Jonker 2013). In both England and the Dutch Republic, a few additional chartered joint-stock companies were formed during the seventeenth century for trade (including the slave trade) with Africa, the West Indies, and North America (Erikson 2014; Stern 2012; Pettigrew and Veevers 2018). As more corporations turned to for-profit business based on joint-stock finance, it became even more essential for them that the ruler's commitment not to expropriate would be credible.

Other European rulers—including the French king, the Habsburg kings of Portugal, and the Habsburg king of Austria—formed chartered joint-stock trade companies, but these were short-lived and ultimately failed. Elsewhere in Eurasia, the Ottoman sultans, India's Mughal rulers, and the Chinese emperors faced similar problems. The main reason was that these absolute monarchs could not credibly commit not to expropriate. This explains the absence of business corporations from the business organizational menu outside of Western Europe until the late nineteenth century (Kuran 2012; Rubin 2017; Greif and Tabellini 2017). Even when corporate law was introduced, through imperial imposition or voluntary reforms, it was not used in the establishment of large private corporations.[7]

THE STATE—POSITIVE LEGAL SERVICES TO THE CORPORATION

Did business corporations in the countries that provided this negative commitment—not to expropriate—also need positive services from the state, such as enforcement of contracts among corporate stakeholders? North, Wallis, and Weingast (2009) examine what they term the transition from an advanced limited-access social order to an open-access social order. According to these scholars, in the former, corporations could be formed by charters, whereas, once the transition to the open-access order was complete, corporations could be formed freely through general incorporation legislation. The three threshold conditions for the transition, as identified by the authors, were rule of law for elites, perpetually lived organizations in the public and the private spheres ("the two heads of the Crown" and corporations, respectively), and consolidated control of the military (North, Wallis, and Weingast 2009). These thresholds comprise more than just a negative credible commitment, namely the commitment not to expropriate.

In the advanced stage, the ruler also provides, via the court system, positive services under the umbrella of the rule of law, most importantly contract-enforcement services for transactions and disputes among the elites. Zhang and Morley argue that, for the development of the business corporation, the state was required not only to commit negatively, namely not to expropriate, but also to commit positively, namely to enforce contracts among the incorporators and investors and facilitate the mitigation of intracorporate agency problems (Zhang and Morley, 2023).

As I have argued previously (Harris 2013a; 2020a), to function effectively, business corporations had to solve a twofold commitment problem—on the part of the state, not to expropriate the corporation as a whole, and on the part of the corporate insiders (managers, directors), not to shirk or cheat at the expense of the outsiders (the passive shareholders). While, in my reading, the solution to the second commitment problem was organizational and informational and could be worked out by the charter and bylaws, Zhang and Morley (2023) make the case that a functioning legal and court system was required. The precondition for the birth of the business corporation was this: it was not enough for the state to be not *too* powerful and unrestrained; it also had to show itself to be not too weak and incapacitated. As Zhang and Morley (2023) argue, at an early stage China was too powerful to credibly commit not to expropriate corporations, and at a later stage it was too weak to enforce corporate contracts.[8]

The Transition to the Modern Corporate Regime

For 250 years following the establishment of the East India Company in 1600, joint-stock business corporations were formed through a grant by the state. In the case of England after the Glorious Revolution, Parliament also entered the business of incorporation. The Bank of England, established in 1694, was incorporated by both a Royal Charter and a Specific Act of Parliament. Gradually, charters became reserved primarily for corporations acting overseas in what was perceived as the prerogative of the Crown, while Acts became the only method for incorporation among domestic companies. The canal companies incorporated by the dozen in the second half of the eighteenth century were created by Acts of Parliament, as were the railway companies established after the marrying of the steam engine with the iron track in the 1820s. The water supply, gaslights, docks, bridges, and other utilities serving the growing urban population were also created by Acts (Harris 2000).

The reason that all these were established by Acts and not charters was primarily that they needed eminent domain powers in order to expropriate the lands on which projects were to be constructed. These Acts were not only enabling but concurrently also regulating—that is, each Act of Incorporation was also a targeted and individualized tool of regulation. It set the location or roadmap for the project, engineering specifications, service-level agreements, payment schedules, and governance. Initially, these aspects were negotiated individually for each Act. Then a copy-and-paste process began. In the third stage, the copying was formalized as Parliament enacted standard Companies Clauses Consolidation Acts that served as a template to be incorporated into future Acts of Incorporation in the same sector. Regulation was standardized: corporations could be regulated more easily than unincorporated businesses through the incorporating act. From being independent of the state, in its early days, the corporation in many respects became an organization that promoted and advanced state policies and increasingly came under state direction and even control.

The East India Company is a good example for demonstrating this point. Starting out as a Eurasian maritime trade enterprise, it turned into a colonial territorial ruler, a subcontractor of the British government in its efforts to subjugate the Indian subcontinent, having its own army, administration, and court system. In Great Britain in the mid-nineteenth century, the heyday of laissez-faire, what looked like minimal government was not exactly so. Activities that, in many Continental states, were handled by the government—such as transportation networks and utilities—were taking place in Great Britain's emerging corporate economy via Acts of Incorporation, subject to state regulation. The relationship between corporations and the state thus became reciprocal.

The mid-nineteenth century was also the time in which the relationship between corporations and the state began to change once again. General incorporation was first introduced in New York State in 1811 for some types of manufacturing companies, for a limited time. A few other Atlantic states copied the New York model in the following years. In Britain, state control over incorporation was loosened in a few steps in the first four decades of the nineteenth century. First, a few court cases from the beginning of the century ended the criminalization of the use of joint-stock investing without a charter or an Act of Incorporation. Then the Bubble Act was repealed in 1825, and incorporation by letters patent issued through the Board of Trade was established in 1834. Finally, in 1844, general incorporation was introduced in Britain. Over the next two decades, general incorporation acts were passed in France, Germany, and other European countries. Similar processes swept through the United States. Between the 1840s and the 1870s, state after state legislated General Acts of Incorporation, and many of them also passed constitutional amendments that prohibited the issuing of charters of incorporation. This amounted to a transformation from a limited-access economic order to an open-access order (North, Wallis, and Weingast 2009).

The Modern Business Corporation and the State

Once free and general incorporation was in place, a new set of issues presented itself. Incorporators were contractually free to draft their own constitutions (bylaws or articles of association). They could unilaterally select the objectives and purposes they pursued and change them from time to time. They could also choose where to incorporate or reincorporate, be it in different jurisdictions within the British Empire or different states within the United States. All of these freedoms, taken together, enabled business corporations to discharge themselves from the grip of the state. It is debatable how important it was for corporations at this stage that corporate law would positively provide mandatory rules, contract enforcement, and dispute resolution to stakeholders. In a sense, the relationship between corporations and states returned to where it had started five hundred years earlier, when corporations were created outside the realm of the state.

With the corporation now free, bringing it back under control was no trivial matter for any state. Railway companies, the largest business corporations of the mid-nineteenth century, were more easily controlled because they had a fixed location, and thus could not easily avoid or escape regulation, and needed the grant of privileges by the state. In the case of Britain, they still relied on specific Acts of Incorporation, which were also used for regulating them. In addition, the Railway Act of 1844 gave the British government the power to regulate for a duration of twenty-one years any new line that made high returns, with an option to nationalize such lines at the end of the period, in 1865 (Bailey 2004). Railway lines were not nationalized in 1865 but they were de facto nationalized for a period during World War I (until 1921) and World War II, and fully nationalized in 1947 (until 1994). In the United States, the introduction of regulation was slower. The expansion of railway lines, particularly over transcontinental routes, was combined in the 1850s to 1870s with massive land grants. State and federal governments granted land strips of twenty to fifty miles on both sides of the track to railroad corporations, to incentivize them to align their activities with their policies. In 1887, the US Congress enacted the Interstate Commerce Act, which was a major piece of regulation dealing with railway corporations' fares and services.

Regulating other business corporations proved to be more challenging. The American regulatory state developed slowly before the New Deal (Skowronek 1982; Novak 1996; Hughes 1991). In the United States, the effectiveness of antitrust law, notably the Sherman Antitrust Act (1890) and the Clayton Antitrust Act (1914), which aimed at the biggest corporations, was questionable. State supervision of business corporations through corporate law was confined by charter-mongering, the jurisdictional rivalry between US states over corporations. From the 1880s, this competition was led by New Jersey, and by the 1910s, Delaware. Most observers see this competition as a race to the bottom. Somewhat similar jurisdictional shopping existed within the British Empire because corporations could select between the metropole, colonies, and dominions and still benefit from the Imperial common market, the Sterling Zone, access to the highest Imperial Court in London (the Judicial Committee of the Privy Council), and the protection of the Royal Navy. Further into the twentieth century, forum shopping and jurisdictional competition also developed within the European Union, based on the *Centros* and *Inspire Art* decisions of the Court and Justice of the European Union. Concurrently, jurisdictional competition has developed on a global scale as the global availability of corporate personality and limited liability enabled incorporators to shop for tax havens, laxer company laws, and thinner regulation (Pistor 2019).

Once business corporations escaped the control of states, as these shifted from limited-access to open-access order, and as regulation failed to control and confine them, a new frontier opened. Over the course of the twentieth century, the purpose of business corporations became a contended issue. In their canonical book, *The Modern Corporation and Private Property*, Berle and Means (1932) identified this very process. The concentration of economic power in the hands of the largest corporations placed them on equal terms with states. Indeed, these authors predicted that business corporations might replace states as the dominant form of social organization. The solution Berle and Means suggested was to reshape the law of corporations and turn it into the constitutional law for the new economic state (just as corporation law served as the constitutional law of the Roman Catholic Church). Berle and Dodd subsequently debated the exact purpose of the business corporation and the extent to which it should serve the needs of society at large, and not only the interests of shareholders (Berle and Means 1932; Berle 1931; Berle 1932). Rather than trying to control the formation of corporations, as in the distant past, or to regulate them from the outside, as was tried more recently, the state should declare the raison d'être of all business corporations to be a public-spirited purpose. Some forty years later, Milton Friedman made a powerful statement to the contrary: that corporations have no responsibilities other than to maximize their profits for the benefit of their shareholders (Friedman 1970). These opposing views have been debated ever since.

Another frontier on the borderline between state and corporation was that of nationalization and privatization. In some countries, railways and airlines experienced more than one cycle of nationalization and privatization, while various utilities including electricity and water supply also went through similar cycles. On the other side of this frontier, some functions that were once considered to be at the heart of state sovereignty—from private police forces and armies to prisons—were privatized to be run by business corporations, yet such privatization is controversial and contested. In recent years missions that may affect the future of human civilization as a whole, such as interplanetary and intergalactic voyages, are being planned by business corporations just as governments are preparing them also. The shaping of freedom of speech and the marketplace for political ideas is also done by business corporations as well as governments. One may speculate that we are witnessing an era in which corporations are once again independent of states. One may also speculate that we are entering a new era in which a new type of relationship between states and corporations is emerging, one in which corporations manipulate states. These frontiers and speculations are very much alive, and their further exploration is beyond the scope of this historically focused chapter.

Conclusion

The relationship between corporations and states has not been constant throughout the history of the corporations, nor did it develop linearly or progressively. In Europe, early corporations were detached from states, and in a later period, some states took control over corporations and aspired to use them as state agents. By the seventeenth century, corporations were seeking to be protected from state expropriation, as they were in England and the Dutch Republic, while at the same time they hoped to benefit from state-supplied contract enforcement. Then, in the eighteenth and early nineteenth centuries, states used corporate charters to regulate corporate activities. By the middle of the nineteenth century, corporations took advantage of the open-access order offered by Britain, US states, and other countries to exercise contractual freedom, shop between jurisdictions and states, and avoid state control. In the twentieth century, states looked for new ways to gain a level of regulatory control over business corporations. Meanwhile, business corporations looked for new ways to avoid state control and bypass new forms of state regulation. Large business corporations wanted to enjoy state support without yielding to state control efforts and maneuvered constantly to enjoy both freedom and support. In this tango, corporations draw nearer to states and farther away from states in different times, places, and contexts. This renegotiation of the relationship between states and corporations is still ongoing, and it is not yet clear whether we will witness a new type of relationship emerging or the continued interplay of older types.

Acknowledgments

I would like to thank Omer Zuk for research assistance, Amada Dale for the editing, and Jeffery Jenkins and Jared Rubin for their valuable suggestions.

Notes

1. For the history (mostly modern) of other aspects of the business corporation, see, for example, Acheson et al. (2015); Cheffins (2019); Roe (1994); Harris (2020b); Hansmann, Kraakman, and Squire (2006); Dari-Mattiacci et al. (2017); Harris and Lamoreaux (2019); Guinnane, Harris, and Lamoreaux (2017); Harris (2013b); Gindis (2020); Ciepley (2020); Lamoreaux and Novak (2017).
2. Berman (1983) and Tierney (1955) base their analyses on earlier works such as Vauchez (1971) and Gillet (1927).
3. For the premodern periods I use the term "ruler" or "Crown" rather than "state" because modern, thicker, territorially based nation states did not yet exist at these periods.
4. Cantoni and Yuchtman (2014) mapped and dated 2,256 central European cities that were incorporated between 1100 and 1500; Richardson (2004) counted the British borough charters of 225 municipalities incorporated between 1042 and 1600.
5. Ogilvie (2019) found that London had 92 guilds in 1503; Paris had 100 guilds in 1270; Madrid had 113 guilds in 1659; Rome, 101 in 1708; Florence, 21 in 1300; Augsburg, 17 in 1548; Vienna, 150 in 1820; Amsterdam, 25 in 1551; and Fulda, 21 in 1784. According to Richardson (2004), a 1388 census in twelve English towns identified 49 guilds.

6. For the legal definition of the corporation in seventeenth-century England, see *The Case of Sutton's Hospital* (1612); Coke (1853); Sheppard (1659). For eighteenth-century definitions, see Blackstone (1890, 462–67); Kyd (1793, 69–70); Harris (2000, 14–36).
7. In addition to the ruler's inability to credibly commit not to expropriate, the absence of the corporate form outside Western Europe can be explained also by the ruler's concern over the political power of associations such as corporations and by the opposition of vested interests to new competitors.
8. The family clan was used in China as a substitute for the business corporation and was able to hold corporate assets and to be sufficiently flexible in its purposes and design. See Harris (2020a).

References

Acheson, Graeme G., Gareth Campbell, John D. Turner, and Nadia Vanteeva. 2015. "Corporate Ownership and Control in Victorian Britain." *Economic History Review* 68, no. 3: 911–36.

Adams, Julia. 2005. *The Familial State: Ruling Families and Merchant Capitalism in Early Modern Europe*. Ithaca, NY: Cornell University Press.

Bailey, Mark. 2004. "The 1844 Railway Act: A Violation of Laissez-Faire Political Economy?" *History of Economic Ideas* 12, no. 3: 7–24.

Berle, Adolf A. 1931. "Corporate Powers as Powers in Trust." *Harvard Law Review* 44, no. 7: 1049–74.

Berle, Adolf A. 1932. "For Whom Corporate Managers Are Trustees: A Note." *Harvard Law Review* 45, no. 8: 1365–72.

Berle, Adolf A., and Gardiner C Means. 1932. *The Modern Corporation and Private Property*. New York: Macmillan.

Berman, Harold J. 1983. *Law and Revolution: The Formation of the Western Legal Tradition*. Cambridge, MA: Harvard University Press.

Black, Antony. 2003. *Guild and State: European Political Thought from the Twelfth Century to the Present*. New Brunswick, NJ: Transaction.

Blackstone, William. 1890. *Commentaries on the Laws of England*, vol. 1. San Francisco: Bancroft-Whitney.

Cantoni, Davide, and Noam. Yuchtman. 2014. "Medieval Universities, Legal Institutions, and the Commercial Revolution. *Quarterly Journal of Economics* 129, no. 2: 823–87.

Case of Sutton's Hospital, The. 1612. 77 Eng Rep 960 (Court of Exchequer Chamber).

Cheffins, Brian R. 2019. *The Public Company Transformed*. New York: Oxford University Press.

Ciepley, David. 2020. "The Anglo-American Misconception of Stockholders as 'Owners' and 'Members': Its Origins and Consequences." *Journal of Institutional Economics* 16, no. 5: 623–42.

Coke, Edward. 1853. *The First Part of the Institutes of the Laws of England, or a Commentary upon Littleton: Not the Name of the Author Only, but of the Law Itself*, vol. 1. Philadelphia: Robert H. Small.

Dari-Mattiacci, Giuseppe, Oscar. Gelderblom, Joost. Jonker, and Enrico C. Perotti. 2017. "The Emergence of the Corporate Form." *Journal of Law, Economics, & Organization* 33, no. 2: 193–236.

Dodd, Edwin M. 1932. "For Whom Are Corporate Managers Trustees?" *Harvard Law Review* 45, no. 7: 1145–63.

Epstein, Stephan R. 1998. "Craft Guilds, Apprenticeship, and Technological Change in Preindustrial Europe." *Journal of Economic History* 58, no. 3: 684–713.

Erikson, Emily. 2014. *Between Monopoly and Free Trade: The English East India Company*. Princeton, NJ: Princeton University Press.

Feldman, Stephan M. 1997. *Please Don't Wish Me a Merry Christmas: A Critical History of the Separation of Church and State*. New York: New York University Press.

Friedman, Milton. 1970. "A Friedman Doctrine: The Social Responsibility of Business Is to Increase Its Profits." *New York Times Magazine* (Sept. 13, 1970).

Gelderblom, Oscar, Abe de. Jong, and Joost. Jonker. 2013. "The Formative Years of the Modern Corporation: The Dutch East India Company VOC, 1602–1623." *Journal of Economic History* 73, no. 4: 1050–76.

Gillet, Pierre. 1927. *La personnalité juridique en droit ecclésiastique: spécialement chez les décrétistes et les décrétalistes et dans le Code de droit canonique*. Malines: W. Godenne.

Gindis, David. 2020. "Conceptualizing the Business Corporation: Insights from History." *Journal of Institutional Economics* 16, no. 5: 569–77.

Grant, Edward. 2001. *God and Reason in the Middle Ages*. Cambridge: Cambridge University Press.

Greif, Avner, and Guido. Tabellini. 2017. "The Clan and the Corporation: Sustaining Cooperation in China and Europe." *Journal of Comparative Economics* 45, no. 1: 1–35.

Guinnane, Timothy, Ron. Harris, and Naomi R. Lamoreaux. 2017. "Contractual Freedom and the Evolution of Corporate Governance in Britain, 1862 to 1929." *Business History Review* 91, no. 2: 227–77.

Hale, Matthew. 1976. *The Prerogatives of the King*. Publications of the Selden Society 92, London: Selden Society.

Hansmann, Henry, Reinier. Kraakman, and Richard. Squire. 2006. "Law and the Rise of the Firm." *Harvard Law Review* 119, no. 5: 1333–403.

Harris, Ron. 2000. *Industrializing English Law Entrepreneurship and Business Organization, 1720–1844*. Cambridge: Cambridge University Press.

Harris, Ron. 2013a. "Could the Crown Credibly Commit to Respect Its Charters? England, 1558–1640." In *Questioning Credible Commitment*, ed. D'Maris. Coffman, Adrian. Leonard, and Larry. Neal, 21–47. Cambridge: Cambridge University Press.

Harris, Ron. 2013b. "The Private Origins of the Private Company: Britain 1862–1907." *Oxford Journal of Legal Studies* 33, no. 2: 339–78.

Harris, Ron. 2020a. *Going the Distance: Eurasian Trade and the Rise of the Business Corporation, 1400–1700*. Princeton, NJ: Princeton University Press.

Harris, Ron. 2020b. "A New Understanding of the History of Limited Liability: An Invitation for Theoretical Reframing." *Journal of Institutional Economics* 16, no. 5: 643–64.

Harris, Ron, and Naomi R. Lamoreaux. 2019. "Opening the Black Box of the Common-Law Legal Regime: Contrasts in the Development of Corporate Law in Britain and the United States in the Late Nineteenth and Early Twentieth Centuries." *Business History* 61, no. 7: 1199–221.

Henrich, Joseph. 2020. *The Weirdest People in the World: How the West Became Psychologically Peculiar and Particularly Prosperous*. New York: Picador (Farrar, Straus and Giroux).

Hughes, Jonathan R.T. 1991. *The Governmental Habit Redux: Economic Controls from Colonial Times to the Present*. Princeton, NJ: Princeton University Press.

Klerman, Daniel M., and Paul G. Mahoney. 2005. "The Value of Judicial Independence: Evidence from 18th Century England." *American Law and Economics Review* 7, no. 1: 1–27.

Kuran, Timur. 2005. "The Absence of the Corporation in Islamic Law: Origins and Persistence." *American Journal of Comparative Law* 53, no. 4: 784–834.

Kuran, Timur. 2012. *The Long Divergence: How Islamic Law Held Back the Middle East*. Princeton, NJ: Princeton University Press.

Kyd, Stewart. 1793. *A Treatise on the Law of Corporations*. London: J. Butterworth.

Lamoreaux, Naomi R., and William J. Novak, eds. 2017. *Corporations and American Democracy*. Cambridge, MA: Harvard University Press.

Maitland, Frederic W. 1908. *The Constitutional History of England: A Course of Lectures Delivered*. Cambridge: Cambridge University Press.

North, Douglass C., John J. Wallis, and Barry R. Weingast. 2009. *Violence and Social Orders: A Conceptual Framework for Interpreting Recorded Human History*. Cambridge: Cambridge University Press.

North, Douglass C., and Barry R. Weingast. 1989. "Constitutions and Commitment: The Evolution of Institutions Governing Public Choice in Seventeenth-Century England." *Journal of Economic History* 49, no. 4: 21–47.

Novak, William J. 1996. *The People's Welfare: Law and Regulation in Nineteenth-Century America*. Chapel Hill: University of North Carolina Press.

Ogilvie, Sheilagh C. 2011. *Institutions and European Trade: Merchant Guilds, 1000–1800*. New York: Cambridge University Press.

Ogilvie, Sheilagh C. 2019. *The European Guilds: An Economic Analysis*. Princeton, NJ: Princeton University Press.

Pettigrew, William A., and David. Veevers. 2018. *The Corporation as a Protagonist in Global History, c. 1550–1750*. Boston: Brill.

Pistor, Katharina. 2019. *The Code of Capital: How the Law Creates Wealth and Inequality*. Princeton, NJ: Princeton University Press.

Richardson, Gary. 2004. "Guilds, Laws, and Markets for Manufactured Merchandise in Late-Medieval England." *Explorations in Economic History* 41, no. 1: 1–25.

Roe, Mark J. 1994. *Strong Managers, Weak Owners: The Political Roots of American Corporate Finance*. Princeton, NJ: Princeton University Press.

Roy, Tirthankar. 2010. *Company of Kinsmen: Enterprise and Community in South Asian History 1700–1940*. Oxford: Oxford University Press.

Rubin, Jared. 2017. *Rulers, Religion, and Riches: Why the West Got Rich and the Middle East Did Not*. Cambridge: Cambridge University Press.

Sheppard, William. 1659. *Of Corporations, Fraternities, and Guilds*. London: H. Twyford, T. Dring, and J. Place.

Skowronek, Stephen. 1982. *Building a New American State: The Expansion of National Administrative Capacities, 1877–1920*. Cambridge: Cambridge University Press.

Stern, Philip. J. 2012. *The Company-State: Corporate Sovereignty and the Early Modern Foundations of the British Empire in India*. Oxford: Oxford University Press.

Tierney, Brian. 1955. *Foundations of the Conciliar Theory: The Contribution of the Medieval Canonists from Gratian to the Great Schism*. Cambridge: Cambridge University Press.

Vauchez, André. 1971. "Michaud-Quantin (Pierre) Universitas. Expressions du mouvement communautaire dans le Moyen Age latin." *Archives de sociologie des religions* 31, no. 1: 225–26.

Zelin, Madeleine H. 2009. "The Firm in Early Modern China." *Journal of Economic Behavior and Organization* 71, no. 3: 623–37.

Zhang, Taisu, and John D. Morley. 2023. "The Modern State and the Rise of the Business Corporation." *The Yale Law Journal* 132, no. 7: 1970–2359.

CHAPTER 33

ELECTORAL MALFEASANCE IN HISTORICAL POLITICAL ECONOMY

ISABELA MARES

Introduction

NINETEENTH-CENTURY elections—a period known also as the first wave of democratization (Huntington 1991)—were characterized by a variety of forms of malfeasance. During campaigns, candidates appealed to voters by deploying both private and public resources. One common campaign strategy used by candidates competing in British elections was offering food and drinks to voters, a practice known as "treating." Electoral reports from the time describe endless processions of voters from one public house to another, noting that "they spent the nights in public houses and the days in wandering about, begging from the assistant on either side or a few shillings to enable them to continue their debauch" (Hansard, P.P. 1867: 3777). In other countries, candidates did not compete by offering goods financed by private resources, but by politicizing resources of the state. In Third Republic France, prefects accompanied candidates during campaigns, "showering decorations" and "sprinkling kilometers of purple ribbon" (JORF Chamber Debates, June 24, 1906). Discussing their importance in French elections, Donald Frary and Charles Seymour remarked that prefects were viewed as "dispensers of an infinite number of favors. Their power and their credit with the central government were apparently limitless. Every village wanted its road, every city was seeking a spur of railway or a canal" (1918, 358). Contemporaries noted that voters "were promised paradise on earth, a paradise which was financed by contributions of taxpayers in exchange for a correct vote" (JORF Chamber Debates, March 17, 1910).

The study of electoral malfeasance in first-wave democracies has experienced a remarkable renaissance in recent years (Stokes et al. 2015; Kam 2017; Kasara and

Mares 2016; Kuo and Teorell 2017; Mares 2015; Mares 2022). This interest in the study of nonprogrammatic linkages between candidates and voters in historical settings goes hand in hand with efforts to study clientelistic practices in contemporary elections (Stokes et. al. 2015; Mares and Young 2016, 2020). As a result, we see interesting synergies between these two research agendas. In this chapter, I report on recent advances in the historical political economy (HPE) literature examining electoral malfeasance. One important development of the recent decade has been the broadening of the scope of nonprogrammatic strategies that are studied. While the early literature on nonprogrammatic strategies derived its theoretical intuitions exclusively from the British case and examined bribing and treating, we see growing attention to a variety of other vote-getting strategies. Using new parliamentary and archival sources, recent studies paint a rich picture of the variety of intermediaries mediating between candidates and brokers and of the strategies these brokers used to mobilize (or demobilize) voters on election day and efforts to pierce voting secrecy and influence voters' choices.

A second theme of the recent literature has been to understand the demand for reforms limiting various types of malfeasance. Why do legislators elected under rules that permit some form of malfeasance choose to modify the electoral rules that made their victory possible? To answer this question, numerous studies have turned to the established explanations in the literatures on democratization—the modernization or redistributivist approach—and examined how economic changes or considerations about redistribution and spending modified legislators' calculations about the attractiveness of the status quo. In this chapter, I present an alternative approach that reintroduces electoral calculations in explaining the demand for reforms and consider the joint importance of electoral considerations and economic changes in the formation of encompassing majorities to support reforms. I draw on comparative historical evidence from Third Republic France, Belgium, Germany, and Britain to explain the introduction of reforms limiting malfeasance.

Electoral Irregularities in First-Wave Democracies

The British case has occupied a central role in the literature on electoral malfeasance. Charles Seymour (1915) provides a detailed account of British electoral practices and efforts for electoral reform throughout the nineteenth century. In *The Efficient Secret* (1987), Gary Cox examines the rise of partisan voting in nineteenth-century British elections and the subsequent decline of backbenchers' influence in British elections. More recently, Susan Stokes and her coauthors have examined vote-buying practices in British elections, documenting the growing difficulties candidates experienced in monitoring the strategies of brokers (Stokes et al. 2015).

In British elections, candidates appealed to voters using both targeted and untargeted strategies. In targeted exchanges, candidates offered voters a highly heterogeneous mix of goods, including meat, coal, and groceries (Rogers 1880, 232). In addition to in-kind goods, candidates offered voters money in exchange for their vote. Some of these practices originated with ceremonial offers made by candidates in Elizabethan elections, which then "mutated into a system of head money in which candidates paid their supporters a fixed amount of money" (Kam 2017, 597). These amounts had different names. At Berwick-upon-Tweed, the customary payments made by candidates were called "gooseberries" and ranged from two to three pounds during the 1850s (597).

Candidates and their brokers developed several strategies to monitor voters' compliance. One strategy was to offer money right before the vote. In Macclesfield during the 1874 election, agents secured empty houses or sometimes pieces of land in the vicinity of the polling booth. Agents would sit in these spaces during election day, distributing money to voters. As the electoral report describes these transactions, "voters were being brought to the tent, bargained with and paid and then sent on straight into the polling booth" (H.C. Parliamentary Papers 1881, Nr. c2853). In Gloucester during the 1874 elections, brokers handed voters a ticket marking the amount of money they were to receive. After casting their ballot, voters were followed into an inner room where a seated person in disguise handed voters the amount of money promised on the ticket (H.C. Parliamentary Papers 1881, Nr. c2841).

The adoption of secret voting as part of the Ballot Act of 1872 significantly changed vote-buying practices. Using information from electoral petitions at the time, Christopher Kam developed a time series of the average price of bribes in Britain during the nineteenth century (Kam 2017). Kam's data reveal a significant decline in the price of bribes after the introduction of secret voting in 1872. He explains this trend by noting that after the introduction of the secret ballot, bribes became a much riskier political investment. The new price of bribes reflected politicians' estimate of the riskiness of this investment.

In addition to targeted vote-buying exchanges, candidates competing in British elections engaged in nontargeted treating of voters. Treating came in the form of free and open offers of food and drinks during campaigns. In Britain, most of the treating occurred in public houses, which served as parties' committee rooms. Describing these practices, Wilkinson noted that public houses "swarmed with fighting, cursing and drunken electors.... Electors were welcomed to drink as much as they chose at the expense of the candidate. This practice culminated on the day of election in a carnival of drunkenness and crime" (Wilkinson 1884, 130).

Several historians of British elections concluded that the importance of treating relative to bribing increased over time. Charles Seymour noted that "with the growth of the electorate, collective corruption becomes the economical means of influencing voters and under the ballot proved as productive of results as individual bribery. Treats, picnics and entertainment became the custom" (1915, 438). The literature has proposed two explanations for why candidates invested significant resources in exchanges that could not be monitored. One explanation was that such nontargeted exchanges were a strategy by which candidates signaled their private attributes. O'Malley and Hardcastle noted on this strategy, "By reason of treats and picnics you can produce a general feeling that the candidate is a good fellow and that he is willing to give a poor man a supper, or treat or entertainment of this kind, and if that idea gets generally spread over the division an enormous amount of polarity is produced" (O'Malley and Hardcastle 1893, 4:145). A second explanation suggests that nontargeted expenses were a form of turnout buying. Turnout buying is a clientelistic strategy premised on the indirect monitoring of turnout rather than the vote. Kam argues that the transition from open to secret voting in 1872 created incentives for candidates to invest more resources in turnout buying (2017, 628). He shows that when controlling for candidate expenditures, turnout increased by about 3 percent after the adoption of secret voting.

While the British case occupies an important place in the comparative canon describing nineteenth-century elections, British political developments were quite exceptional relative to political developments on the Continent. In its mix of clientelistic practices, Britain is an outlier rather than a modal case. Among the races investigated by the House of Commons between 1867 and 1883 for illicit practices, 80 percent of reports mention incidents of vote buying or treating (Kasara and Mares 2016). In contrast to Britain, vote buying has remained a residual campaign strategy in continental European countries. In both France and Germany, vote buying was used significantly less often as compared to other clientelistic strategies that politicized state resources. Using data from the electoral commissions in both France and Germany, I show that around 30 percent of election reports included complaints about vote buying. In Germany, around 15 percent of election reports voiced complaints about bribery (Mares 2022). Historians of the period offer a similar account of the limited use of vote buying in German elections:

> Cotters in the east Elbian Herrschaft Pnuwo were given a half bushel of dried peas for voting Conservative. Voters in the Rhenisch village of Rodenkirchen who accepted "loyal" ballots were handed a sausage from a large hamper at the door of the polls. A dram of schnapps at the beginning of our period and much larger quantities of "Freibier" at the end were common, although not always considered respectable features of German elections.... Whatever the incidence of these little reciprocities, it is clear that German voters were not considered venal even by parties hoping to overturn an election, nor did enough money change hands to give Reichstag deputies, unlike their British counterparts, any stake in regulating it. Bribery simply did not play a role in what Germans thought to be wrong with their political process.
>
> (Anderson 2000, 27)

One important factor explaining the lower incidence of bribing in continental European countries is the early penalization of vote buying in the Napoleonic Code. The Napoleonic Code, adopted in 1810, imposed very strong punishments for people who offered money in exchange for votes and for people who accepted such offers. Article 113 of the French penal code sanctioned any citizen who had bought or sold their vote with a loss of citizenship rights and a loss of employment for a period of five to ten years. Spurred by the Napoleonic invasion, the solution adopted in the French penal code spread across continental European countries (Mayer 1906). Civil codes adopted in Sweden, Finland, Denmark, and Austria introduced provisions that mirrored the French code closely. Such rules imposing strong sanctioning of bribing pioneered in the Napoleonic Code made it to the Prussian and German criminal code. Article 109 of the German criminal code sanctioned bribery with a prison term of one month to two years and possibly a loss of political rights (Mayer 1906).

This strong sanctioning of vote buying in Continental civil codes affected the mix of electoral irregularities one found in continental European countries as compared to Britain. It also created electoral incentives for candidates to use strategies that were less severely sanctioned. These additional electoral strategies included the politicization of state resources during elections as well as economic coercion used in conjunction with efforts to pierce voting secrecy. In France, about 70 percent of election reports contest an election because a candidate politicized state resources. For Germany, the average share of contested elections where candidates deployed state resources is around 60 percent.

In France, electoral practices that politicized state resources during campaigns were also known as the *candidature officielle* (official candidacy). The *candidature officielle* resurfaced as an electoral strategy during the first elections of the Third Republic, at a time of intense confrontation between Republic and Conservative or Monarchist candidates (Pierre 1893; Voilliot 2005; Pilenco 1930). The central pillar of the electoral machinery of the incumbent Republican Party was the prefect. In addition to announcing the immediate political advantages that voters who made the correct choice could enjoy, prefects played an important role in mobilizing brokers at lower levels of the administrative hierarchy (Pilenco 1930). These included deputy prefects, but most significantly, mayors. Mayors, in turn, coordinated the electoral activities of a variety of other local government employees. These local brokers included "teachers, postal employees, local policemen, road menders (*cantônniers*), secretaries and employees of the city halls" (JORF Chamber Debates, March 29, 1902).

Due to Germany's federal structure, the hierarchy of brokers was structured differently than in France. We do not find a clear command line connecting the central government, regional authorities, and candidates' campaigns. The most significant ministry that coordinated electoral operations was the Prussian Ministry of the Interior. The minister presided over a well-designed system of sanctions and rewards to incentivize electoral operations by members of the bureaucracy (Arsenscheck 2003, 194). The main brokers coordinating electoral campaigns of candidates in German elections were *Landräte*, heads of administrative districts, responsible for tax collection and military conscription. As in France, German mayors occupied an important role in mobilizing the network of election brokers. Mayors provided important logistical support to candidates during campaigns and facilitated candidates' access to the local administration's employees. Due to the asymmetric ability of some parties to access state resources, the electoral playing field among candidates was never level.

A final type of broker present in nineteenth-century elections was the economic broker. Such economic brokers included rural as well as industrial employers (see Robinson and Baland 2008; Ziblatt 2009; Mares and Zhu 2015). Candidates relied on employers to turn voters out to the polls. At the time of voting, candidates positioned employers—often foremen or other supervisors in the firm—in the vicinity of voting places. Taking advantage of imperfections in the design of ballots, employers used lists to monitor voting choices. In Alais (today's Alès), a district in Gard, were located near the urn during the duration of the vote, recording the votes of their employees in blue or red notebooks depending on the shape of the ballots they held in their hands (JORF Chamber Debates, June 16, 1902). We find similar practices in German elections. Consider the sophisticated system set in place by employers in Dortmund to keep track of voters' choices. "Supervisors from the mine stood at the entrance to the room, who distributed ballots for Möller. If a person that had received a ballot for Möller took another ballot from his pocket, then Schmidtmann pointed to his own back, which gave the supervisors from the mine a clear signal that the respective voter had not voted for Möller" (StBer DtRt 1893, Encl. Nr. 255).

Due to control of wages, employment, and benefits of their employees, employers could sanction voters who had voted "incorrectly." One finds ample evidence of such punishments in the election reports of the time. During the 1893 election in Bressuire, a constituency in Deux-Sèvres, local employers supporting a Monarchist candidate laid off all workers who were suspected to have supported the Republican candidates. Several days later, these workers were also evicted from their homes (JORF Chamber Debates, December 9, 1893). During the 1884 election in Arnsberg's Fifth District, workers who refused to take the ballot handed to them by the company's overseer who was stationed in the vicinity of the urn lost their company housing (StBer DtRt 1884, Encl. Nr. 57). In Ludwsigshafen during the 1881 election, employers laid off workers who refused to take the Social Democratic ballot (StBer DtRt 1881, Encl. Nr. 116).

As this discussion indicates, one significant accomplishment of the recent historical literature examining clientelistic practices is descriptive. To this end, political scientists and historians have dug up and evaluated a wealth of novel historical evidence primarily found in the reports of parliamentary commissions investigating electoral irregularities. By documenting a wide heterogeneity of brokers mediating between candidates and voters as well as variety in the strategies these brokers deployed, the historical literature moves away from the stylized British experience depicting campaigns where candidates used vote-buying offers alone. The mix of clientelistic brokers one encounters in continental European elections, such as France or Germany, is much more heterogeneous. Recent studies have also drawn on new evidence to examine additional questions pertaining to the relationship between brokers and voters, questions about conditions under which votes could be monitored as well the consequences of these shocks for the ability of brokers to monitor votes for electoral outcomes.

The new emphasis on the heterogeneity among brokers and their myriad resources to incentivize voters' choices has also opened up interesting avenues of research interrogating whether different forms of electoral malfeasance substituted or complemented each other. Kuo and Teorell (2017) document such substitution among different forms of malfeasance in the United States following the adoption of the secret ballot. The adoption of the secret ballot reduced the ability of brokers and candidates to observe votes. As such, these reforms limited the incidence of intimidation and vote buying. At the same time, these reformers created incentives for candidates to substitute other illicit strategies, such as ballot registration and ballot fraud (Kuo and Teorell 2017, 670). Using information on contested elections to the House of Representatives between 1860 and 1930, the authors document the existence of a pattern consistent with these hypotheses. Analyzing developments in Costa Rica, Lehoucq and Molina (2002) document a similar pattern in the aftermath of adoption of the secret ballot in 1925. While direct offers of money declined during the period, this electoral reforms "encouraged parties to expand their repertoire of illegal actions, by turning to more illicit forms of ballot stuffing" (Lehoucq and Molina 2002, 21).

Importantly, the historical literature on electoral malfeasance exercised feedback effects on the literature examining electoral clientelism in contemporary elections. The recent discovery of employers as brokers in the historical literature has been the catalyst of a new literature examining the presence of economic coercion in contemporary elections. A wave of recent studies has documented the presence of economic employers as brokers in contemporary elections in contexts as diverse as Bulgaria, Romania, Russia, and even the United States (Mares, Muntean, and Petrova 2018; Hertel Fernandez 2018). Similarly, in recent years, the literature examining clientelism in contemporary settings has paid increasing attention to state employees as brokers.

Finally, the recent literature examining nonprogrammatic strategies and electoral malfeasance generates new insights for understanding the origin of political parties. The findings of the last decade present a rich historical picture of ways that political parties in the early stages of democratization relied on different types of brokers. Economic changes and electoral reforms—such as adoption of the secret ballot—were important shocks that disrupted the network of brokers and created incentives to invest in centralized party organizations that took over some of the campaign responsibilities for individual candidates. Existing accounts of party developments in Europe have paid insufficient attention to the linkage mechanisms between candidates and voters and to questions about the identity of brokers (Caramani 2000; Kalyvas 1996). New recent studies on party development, such as Ziblatt's monograph on the development of conservative parties in Britain and Germany take up the challenge. Ziblatt (2017) develops an account of party developments that examines whether leaders of the centralized party organization (specifically in the case of the German Conservative Party) fail to respond to the economic changes that undermine their reliance on landlords as economic agents. While Ziblatt's study covers conservative parties, one avenue for future research is to examine similar processes of transformation for other political parties and to understand how economic changes and electoral reforms modified the development of political parties.

Impetus for Electoral Reforms

While the electoral landscape of European countries at the time of suffrage expansion resembled the landscape of many developing countries today, between 1860 and 1914, many first-wave democracies adopted a number of electoral reforms that improved voting technology, while also increasing sanctions on illicit campaign promises. These reforms were highly effective in reducing the incidence of electoral corruption.

For several decades, the literature on democratization has neglected the study of electoral reforms limiting malfeasance. The last comparative account of adoption of these electoral reforms is the study *How the World Votes* by Donald Frary and Charles Seymour, published in 1918. Recent scholarship has attempted to correct this gap. In recent years, a number of studies have examined adoption of reforms limiting electoral malpractice (Madrid 2019a; Madrid 2019b; Mares 2015; Mares 2022; Voilliot 2005; Ziblatt 2009). This has created the opportunity to test predictions of established theories of democratization, but also modify the excessively static frameworks.

Economic Modernization

The most influential theoretical perspective in the study of democratization is the modernization approach (Lipset 1959; Przeworski and Limongi 1997; Przeworski et al. 2000). In recent years, scholars have extended predictions from the modernization perspective to the study of reforms limiting electoral malfeasance. To unpack these relationships, these studies have spelled out the consequences of economic development on the costs of various strategies of electoral malfeasance (Cox 1987; Stokes et al. 2015). Cox (1987) examined several processes by which the growth in the size of constituencies reduced the attractiveness of electoral bribery. These developments stretched the budgets of politicians, "as a fixed amount of money would buy a smaller proportion of total votes in small towns," while it also increased "the costs of arranging bribes to many more electors" (Cox 1987, 57). Stokes and coauthors propose an additional mechanism linking economic development and the adoption of reforms limiting vote buying, suggesting that these developments exposed the monitoring difficulties endemic to vote-buying exchanges (Stokes et al. 2015, 216).

Extending the modernization perspective, a number of studies have turned to analysis of additional economic developments constraining electoral strategies involving economic coercion. Ardanaz and Mares (2014) discuss the importance of labor scarcity experienced during the process of economic development as a factor constraining the use of economic coercion in the Prussian countryside. Commenting on the political implications on the change in rural economic conditions, Martin Wulff, a historian writing at the beginning of the twentieth century, stated, "in recent periods, landowners had to use this means of power [*Machtmittel*] very carefully because of the labor shortage that existed in the countryside. One was happy if one could keep one's employees and one was careful to not antagonize the employees through electoral harassments and to not drive them to the cities" (Wulff 1922, 13). Such economic developments also had political consequences. Ardanaz and Mares (2014) document a split among Conservative legislators elected in the Prussian parliament on questions of electoral reforms. These authors show that Conservative legislators in districts that experienced labor scarcity supported electoral reforms, documenting that considerations about economic costs were high enough to bring about a change in legislators' positions.

Redistributivist Theories of Democratization

Other studies analyze reforms adopted in first-wave democracies to examine but also modify predictions of redistributivist accounts of democratization (Acemoglu and Robinson 2006; Boix 2003). In a number of publications, Daniel Ziblatt applies this approach to the study of democratic electoral reforms in Imperial Germany (Ziblatt 2009). Ziblatt documents the existence of a positive correlation between landholding inequality and the incidence of fraud in Imperial Germany, which he interprets as being in agreement with the claim that "landholding inequality depresses democratic reforms" (Ziblatt 2009, 2). Addressing episodes of electoral reforms, Ziblatt examines the relationship between the landholding inequality of a district and opposition to a reform to abolish the three-class voting system of Prussia's parliamentary elections. Using roll call votes, Ziblatt documents the existence of a negative relationship between landholding inequality and democratic reform, concluding that "economic development that nonetheless leaves immobile assets inequitably distributed poses a problem for democratization" (Ziblatt 2009, 640).

The relationship between landholding inequality and opposition to electoral reforms limiting malfeasance identified by Ziblatt does not hold up in other empirical contexts, such as Britain or France. In these situations, landholding inequality is not a predictor of opposition to electoral reforms (Kasara and Mares 2016; Mares 2022). A comparative study of electoral reforms limiting malfeasance in Belgium, Britain, France, and Germany also questions the theoretical mechanisms presupposed by redistributive explanations (Mares 2022). The most important limitation of these theories is the extremely long causal chain linking landholding inequality and support for democratic reforms. These theories assume that the opposition to democratic reforms of legislators elected in districts with high levels of landholding inequality can be explained by the fear of future taxes and spending following electoral reforms. This future redistributive threat that is the central mechanism in these explanations is never unpacked theoretically and empirically. Why should we assume that elites will have no role in the formulation of tax policy following the adoption of electoral reforms that increase the political voice of lower-income voters? Why should we assume that outgoing elites have no influence over the design of institutions implementing social policy? In particular, this study challenges the prediction that we need to include considerations about future levels of taxation to explain choices of electoral reforms (Mares 2022). Rather, it argues that in explaining demand for electoral reforms, we need to consider more immediate electoral considerations and examine how these considerations interact with elites' economic positions (Mares 2022).

Electoral Explanations of Reforms Limiting Malfeasance

A third theoretical perspective highlights the importance of electoral considerations following elite splits as the driver of demand for electoral reform. This perspective has a long intellectual tradition in political science, going back to the work of Schattschneider (1960). The literature on third-wave democratization anticipated the importance of elite splits. Scholars such as Guillermo O'Donnell and Philippe Schmitter (1986) and Adam Przeworski (1991) argued that an elite split sets in motion demand for incumbent elites to engage in democratic transition. In recent years, explanations emphasizing the importance of elite splits for demand for democratic reforms have experienced a comeback. In a number of articles analyzing the adoption of democratic reforms in Latin America, Raùl Madrid also focuses on the importance of elite splits but conceptualizes them in partisan terms (Madrid 2019a; 2019b). According to Madrid, splits within a ruling party weaken the control of insiders, while providing opportunities for the outside group to enact reforms (Madrid 2019b; 1540). Madrid shows how intra-elite splits within the ruling PAN party in Argentina contributed to the adoption of secret ballot reforms in 1912 (Madrid 2019b). Such reforms were supported by legislators who defected from the party in power in an effort to weaken the incumbent's political machine.

A recent contribution from Isabela Mares, Protecting the Ballot: How First-Wave Democracies Ended Electoral Corruption (2022) formulates an explanation that integrates electoral and economic motives in explaining legislative demand for these electoral reforms. In this study, Mares documents that the composition of electoral majorities supporting different reforms varied across reform dimensions. In Third Republic France, Monarchist legislators on the right favored reforms limiting the use of state resources during campaigns or reforms limiting fraud, but they opposed vote-buying reforms (Mares 2022). By contrast, Republicans opposed reforms limiting the use of state resources during campaigns, while favoring the adoption of ballot envelopes and isolating spaces and ballot envelopes. Redistributivist theories of democratization or modernization theories cannot account for the heterogeneity in the composition of electoral coalitions favoring these reforms and for the reform-specific positions held by legislators on the right on electoral reform questions.

This explanation posits that three factors can explain legislators' demand for electoral reforms: the resources available to engage in different forms of malfeasance and the economic and electoral costs associated with different illicit strategies. The initial cleavage over adoption of electoral reforms is one between legislators who have the resources to engage in different forms of electoral malfeasance and those lacking such resources. Such resources can be either public or private. Public resources come in the form of access to state employees who can act as brokers. Private resources come in the form of access to economic brokers (such as employers) or funds that can be used to offer money or goods to voters. While resource-constrained legislators support the adoption of reforms limiting malfeasance, resource-endowed legislators oppose their introduction. As long as a majority of legislators can access such resources and deploy them seamlessly during elections, the impetus for electoral change is low.

These initial electoral majorities are, however, not static. Both economic changes and political changes—in the form of elite splits—place constraints on the use of electoral malfeasance, modifying the calculations of resource-endowed legislators about the desirability of the status quo. Economic developments increase the costs associated with various forms of electoral malfeasance (Mares 2015; Stokes et al. 2015). At the same time, elite splits—such as between Republicans and Radicals in Third Republic France—create incentives for programmatic differentiation. For candidates competing based on programmatic promises, illicit strategies become an increasing liability, as voters can perceive them as undermining the credibility of their promises (Kitschelt 2000). In this explanation, the pivotal group of legislations are resource-endowed legislators facing economic or political constraints. These include the National Liberal politicians in Germany or Radicals or Republicans competing based on programmatic promises in France. If considerations about electoral or economic costs outweigh the relative resource advantage, we see a coalitional realignment in the formation of a political majority favoring reforms. Such realignments were decisive in explaining the creation of political majorities supporting electoral reforms in first-wave democracies. The advantage of this explanation over alternatives is that it can account for demand for electoral reforms without invoking considerations about future levels of spending and taxation. It also can explain why the composition of electoral coalitions supporting electoral reforms has varied across reform dimensions.

As this chapter has documented, HPE has made significant advances characterizing nonprogrammatic linkage strategies in first-wave democracies. By studying strategies by which candidates and their brokers target voters and attempt to modify their electoral choices, these studies have documented that the mix of different forms of electoral malfeasance differed significantly across countries and across constituencies. This research has provided novel insights into the origin and transformation of political parties during the decades after expansion of suffrage. At the same time, in studying the adoption of electoral reforms democratizing electoral practices, the recent literature has demonstrated that such changes cannot be understood by economic changes alone. Rather, a combination of political and economic changes can explain how political majorities emerged supporting reforms limiting various forms of malfeasance.

The study of reforms limiting malfeasance opens important avenues for the study of political development in first-wave democracies. One possible pursuit is study of these reforms' consequences for candidates' incentives to invest in alternative forms of campaigning. While some candidates and parties respond to the "resource shock" resulting from these electoral reforms by investing in party organizations, others fail to adapt electorally. Understanding the variation in political responses after these reforms can allow researchers to reassess the process of party development. By modifying political asymmetries, electoral reforms limiting malfeasance also change parties' incentives toward other electoral reforms, such as the adoption of proportional representation (Leemann and Mares 2014). Future comparative studies need to reassess the relationship between reforms limiting malfeasance and the adoption of proportional representation. Caramani (2023) discusses the state of the current literature examining the choice of electoral rules in first-wave democracies before World War I. Explanations inspired by Rokkan and those stressing economic considerations do not account for the significant shocks to the party systems that resulted from reforms limiting electoral malfeasance. In some countries, these shocks were a decisive factor contributing to the partisan realignment that led to the adoption of proportional representation. Future research needs to link these dots regarding these two episodes of electoral reform.

References

Acemoglu, Daron, and James Robinson. 2006. *Economic Origins of Dictatorship and Democracy.* New York: Cambridge University Press.

Ardanaz, Martin, and Isabela Mares. 2014. "Labor Shortages, Rural Inequality and Democratization." *Comparative Political Studies* 47, no. 12: 1637–69.

Arsenscheck, Robert. 2003. *Der Kampf um die Wahlfreiheit im Kaiserreich. Zur parlamentarischen Wahlprüfund und politischen Realität der Reichstagswahlen 1871–1914.* Düsseldorf: Droste.

Anderson, Lavinia. 2000. *Practicing Democracy: Elections and Political Culture in Imperial Germany.* Princeton: Princeton University Press.

Boix, Carles. 2003 *Democracy and Redistribution.* New York: Cambridge University Press.

Caramani, Daniele. 2000. *Elections in Western Europe since 1815: Electoral Results by Constituencies.* London: Macmillan.

Caramani, Daniele. 2023. "Electoral Systems in Historical Political Economy." In *The Oxford Handbook of Historical Politcal Economy*, ed. Jeffery A. Jenkins and Jared Rubin, 421–39. Oxford: Oxford University Press.

Cox, Gary. 1987. *The Efficient Secret.* New York: Cambridge University Press.

Frary, Donald, and Charles Seymour. 1918. *How the World Votes: The Story of Democratic Development in Elections.* Springfield: Nichols.

Hansard. 1867. Great Britain. *Parliamentary Debates House of Commons.* London: HMSO.

Hertel-Fernandez, Alexander. 2018. *Politics at Work: How Companies Turn their Workers into Lobbyists,* New York: Oxford University Press.

Huntington, Samuel. 1991. "Democracy's Third Wave." *Journal of Democracy* 26, no. 1: 141–55.

JORF Chamber Debates. [various years] *Journal Officiel de la République Française. Dèbats de la Chambre des Députés.* Paris: Imprimerie Nationale.

Kalyvas, Stathis. 1996. *The Rise of Christian Democracy in Europe.* Ithaca: Cornell University Press.

Kam, Christopher. 2017. "The Secret Ballot and the Market for Votes in Nineteenth-Century British Elections." *Comparative Political Studies* 50, no. 5: 594–635.

Kasara, Kimuli, and Mares, Isabela. 2016. "Unfinished Business: The Democratization of Electoral Practices in Britain and Germany." *Comparative Political Studies* 50, no. 3: 536–64.

Kitschelt, Herbert. 2000. "Linkages between Citizens and Politicians in Democratic Polities." *Comparative Political Studies* 33, no. 6: 845–79.

Kuo, Didi, and Jan Teorell. 2017. "Illicit Tactics as Substitutes: Election Fraud, Ballot Reform and Contested Congressional Elections in the United States, 1860–1930." *Comparative Political Studies* 50, no. 5: 665–96.

Leemann, Lucas, and Isabela Mares. 2014 "The Adoption of Proportional Representation." *Journal of Politics* 76, no. 2: 461–78.

Lehoucq, Fabrice, and Ivan Molina. 2002. *Stuffing the Ballot Box: Fraud, Electoral Reform, and Democratization in Costa Rica*. New York: Cambridge University Press.

Lipset, Seymour. 1959. Some Social Requisites of Democracy: Economic Development and Political Legitimacy. *American Political Science Review* 53, no. 5, 69–105.

Madrid, Raúl. 2019a. "Opposition Parties and the Origin of Democracy in Latin America." *Comparative Politics* 51, no. 2: 157–75.

Madrid, Raúl. 2019b. "The Partisan Path to Democracy: Argentina in Comparative Perspective." *Comparative Political Studies* 52, no. 10: 1535–69.

Mares, Isabela. 2015. *From Open Secret to Secret Voting*. New York: Cambridge University Press.

Mares, Isabela. 2022. *Protecting the Ballot: How First-Wave Democracies Ended Electoral Corruption*. Princeton, NJ: Princeton University Press.

Mares, Isabela, Muntean, Aurelian and Petrova, Tsveta. 2018. Economic intimidation in contemporary elections: Evidence from Romania and Bulgaria. *Government and Opposition* 53: 3, 2016–2039.

Mares, Isabela, and Lauren Young. 2020. *Conditionality and Coercion: Electoral Clientelism in Eastern Europe*. Oxford: Oxford University Press.

Mares, Isabela and Lauren, Young. 2016. Buying, expropriating and stealing votes. *Annual Review of Political Science* 19: 267–88.

Mares, Isabela, and Boliang Zhu. 2015. "Economic and Political Determinants of Electoral Intimidation." *Comparative Politics* 48, no. 1: 1–24.

Mayer, Max Ernst. 1906. "Verbrechen und Vergehen in Beziehung auf die Ausübung strafrechtlicher Rechte," in *Vergleichende Darstellung des deutschen und ausländischen Strafrechts: Vorarbeiten zur deutschen Strafrechtsreform*, Fritz von Calker ed., Berlin: Liebmann, 253–347.

O'Donnell, Guillermo, and Philipppe. Schmitter. 1986. *Transitions from Authoritarian Rule*. Baltimore: Johns Hopkins University Press.

O'Malley, Edward, and Hardcastle, Henry. 1893. *Reports of the Decisions of the Judges of the Trial of Election Petitions in Great Britain and Ireland, Pursuant to the Parliamentary Elections Act*, London: Stevens and Haynes.

Pierre, Eugène. 1893. *Traité de droit politique, electoral et parlementaire*. Paris: Imprimerie Réunis.

Pilenco, Alexandre. 1930. *Les mœurs du suffrage universel en France 1848–1928*. Paris: Editions du Monde Moderne.

Przeworski, Adam. 1991. *Democracy and the Market*. New York: Oxford.

Przeworski, Adam, and Fernando Limongi. 1997. "Modernization: Theories and Facts." *World Politics* 49, no. 2: 155–83.

Przeworski, Adam, Alvarez, Michael, Cheibub, Jose Antonio and Limongi, Fernando 2000. *Democracy and Development*. New York: Cambridge University Press.

Robinson, James, and Baland, Jean-Marie. 2008. Land and power: Theory and Evidence from Chile. *American Economic Review* 98, no. 5: 1737–65.

Rogers. Francis. 1880. *Rogers on Elections*. London: Steven and Sons.
Schattschneider, Elmer Eric. 1960. *The Semisovereign People*. Hinsdale: Dryden Press.
Seymour, Charles. 1915. *Electoral Reform in England and Wales: The Development and Operation of the Parliamentary Franchise, 1832–1885*. New Haven, CT: Yale University Press.
Stokes, Susan, Dunning, Thad, Nazareno, Marcelo and Brusco, Valeria. 2015. *Brokers, Voters and Clientelism: The Puzzle of Distributive Politics*. New York: Cambridge University Press.
StBer DtRt [Various years]. *Stenographische Berichte des Deutschen Reichstages*. Berlin: Verlag der Buchdruckerei der Norddeutschen Allgemeinen Zeitung.
Voilliot, Christophe. 2005. *La Candidature officielle*. Rennes: Presses Universitaires de Rennes.
Wilkinson, R. 1884. "New Bribery Act." *Nineteenth Century* 15: 129–31.
Wulff, Kurt. 1922. *Die Deutschkonservativen und die Preussische Wahlrechtsfrage*. PhD dissertation, University of Greisfwald.
Ziblatt, Daniel. 2009. "Shaping Democratic Practice and the Causes of Electoral Fraud: The Case of Nineteenth-Century Germany." *American Political Science Review* 103: 1–21.
Ziblatt, Daniel. 2017. *Conservative Parties and the Birth of Democracy in Europe*. New York: Cambridge University Press.

CHAPTER 34

ASSIMILATION IN HISTORICAL POLITICAL ECONOMY

VASILIKI FOUKA

"Assimilation" is the process through which members of one group, usually a numerical minority, become similar to and ultimately part of another group, usually a numerical majority that may also wield economic or political power. Assimilation entails two components: change on the part of the minority, for instance through adoption of the majority's religion or language, and acceptance on the part of the majority, which allows minority group members to become "credible claimant[s], ceteris paribus, in the labor and marriage markets" (Laitin 1995).

Understanding assimilation and its drivers is important. Lack of assimilation can be indicative of persistent minority disadvantages, discrimination, and social divisions. Yet elimination of all cultural distinction may also be undesirable, as individuals value their cultures and identities. Forced assimilation may even have unintended consequences in fueling segregation and conflict rather than increasing social cohesion.

Historical political economy (HPE) has much to contribute to our understanding of assimilation dynamics. Substantively, the study of historical cases is instructive for any social phenomenon, and more so for assimilation, a process that unfolds over the long run and in which decisions of one generation affect the outcomes of subsequent ones. Methodologically, history provides sources of causal identification in the form of policy changes or natural experiments, allowing researchers to credibly estimate drivers of assimilation. Digitization of censuses and other large data sets has made available novel empirical measures of assimilation choice, such as first names. Methodological advances in historical record linkage have improved measurement and made it possible to distinguish assimilation from migration and compositional changes in the minority population.

HPE researchers have studied assimilation in a variety of contexts, from Indigenous groups in the Americas to religious minorities in the Muslim world and ethnic groups in modern multiethnic states. A substantive part of the literature has focused on immigrants in the New World during the Age of Mass Migration, exploiting new historical census data and the large heterogeneity in characteristics and assimilation outcomes of immigrant groups. Across these disparate contexts, a few central questions have dominated the literature: Which groups are more likely to assimilate? Why do minorities persist even in the face of persecution? Which state interventions "succeed" in assimilating minorities, and when do we observe backlash to assimilationist policies?

This chapter summarizes this work, with an eye to drawing broader conceptual insights about the assimilation process. I sketch a simple framework in which minority and majority decisions are interdependent and driven by rational calculations that weigh both the material and psychological costs and benefits of different actions. I use this framework to make sense of findings in the existing literature, provide answers to commonly raised questions on assimilation dynamics, and highlight areas for future research.

A Two-Sided Conceptual Framework

I conceptualize assimilation as an equilibrium outcome, driven by actions of multiple rational actors.[1] In the simplest setup, assimilation is a two-sided process, resulting from the interdependent decisions of majority and minority members. The former choose whether to adopt markers of the dominant culture or to undertake other actions that might allow them to become part of the majority; the latter choose whether to accept minority members as part of their group.

In practice, researchers use the term "assimilation" to refer both to minority choices—such as the adoption of linguistic, religious, and other identity markers—and the joint outcome of those choices and the decisions of the majority. The latter equilibrium outcome is usually measured as the distance or rate of convergence of the minority group to some majority benchmark in dimensions such as education, labor market outcomes, or residential patterns. However, maintaining the conceptual distinction between assimilation choices and assimilation outcomes is useful for making sense of empirical patterns. For example, groups may display assimilation along choice dimensions (e.g., name changes) but not outcome dimensions (e.g., intermarriages with the dominant group).

Other actors and their choices may play a role in shaping equilibrium assimilation, such as, for instance, a state—usually representing the majority group—or minority group leaders. I start from sketching the simple two-sided problem and progressively introduce additional elements that the empirical literature in HPE has highlighted.

Decisions of Minority Members

Minority members decide whether to exert "assimilation effort," effort that corresponds to any action that may bring the minority member closer to the majority, such as adopting the majority religion, using the majority language, or embracing majority cultural norms.

Much empirical research in historical settings recognizes the choice component of assimilation and studies its determinants. The challenge in historical data is to identify measures that capture minority choices, uncontaminated by the behavior of the majority group. First names serve this purpose reasonably well and are systematically available in early censuses and other historical documents like naturalization records. For this reason, several studies have examined naming patterns as a proxy of assimilation effort, most frequently by focusing on name assimilation among the foreign-born (e.g., Biavaschi, Giulietti, and Siddique [2017]) and on names given to immigrant children (e.g., Abramitzky, Boustan, and Eriksson [2020]). Certain contexts provide even starker measures of assimilation effort, such as choice of racial identification ("passing"). Saperstein and Gullickson (2013) and Dahis, Nix, and Qian (2019) rely on linked census records between 1870 and 1940 to document changes in racial classification for a substantive proportion of African American men.

The choice of assimilation effort is guided by a cost-benefit calculation. Costs can be tangible, such as time spent learning a language, or psychological, such as the distress felt when abandoning a familiar behavior. Costs may differ across minority groups and within them. Groups that are culturally distant from the majority find it harder to learn the language or effectively adopt dominant group norms. Within groups, individuals may have varying capacities for adaptation to a different culture. Factors affecting the capacity to adjust to the standards of another society, like age at the time of immigration, are predictive of economic assimilation among immigrants in the United States (Alexander and Ward 2018).

Though costly, assimilation effort may yield benefits, if successful. In hierarchical societies, dominant majorities hold economic privileges and access to positions of power. Assimilation into the majority opens the door to these material and status benefits for lower-ranked groups. The benefits of assimilation may also come in the form of avoidance of penalties for nonassimilation, such as harassment of individuals with visible minority markers. All else equal, minority members are more likely to attempt assimilation the higher the material and status differentials between minority and majority and the higher the penalties to retaining minority identity.

Empirically, the response of effort to potential returns to assimilation is documented across a wide variety of historical contexts. Dippel and Frye (2020) study the policy of Native American allotment in the United States, which broke up communal lands and allotted them to individual households during the early twentieth century. Acquisition of full property rights on the land was conditioned on cultural assimilation, evaluated by federal agencies along dimensions such as education. Land allotment and the prospect of land ownership increased benefits from assimilation effort and led to higher educational attainment among Native American mothers and their children.

Outside the United States, Botticini and Eckstein (2007) document that around 200 CE, Judaism began requiring fathers to educate their male children. They show that the high cost of education for poor Jewish farmers greatly boosted conversions to Christianity, with the number of Jews shrinking from 4.5 million to 1.2 million over the course of seven centuries. Saleh and Tirole (2021) find that conversion rates among Christian Copts in Egypt were higher in *kuras* (administrative divisions) governed by Arab local authorities that levied higher tax rates on non-Muslim minorities. In Mexico, Díaz-Cayeros and Jha (2017) find higher rates of Hispanization among Indigenous communities that specialized in the production of cochineal dye, a highly prized good that was traded globally. Gains from trade increased the benefits to contact with the Spanish for settlements producing cochineal. At the same time, successful producers faced incentives to opt out of Indigenous institutions, which were highly redistributive. Both mechanisms served to increase the benefits of assimilation effort.

Similar effects have been documented for penalties to minority identity retention. Harassment and demands for expressions of loyalty increased returns to assimilation efforts for immigrant groups in US history. Studies have exploited exogenous shocks to anti-immigrant sentiment to examine minority assimilation choices using first names as proxies of assimilation effort. Using a regression discontinuity design, Saavedra (2021) finds that children of Japanese immigrants born right after the Pearl Harbor attack were more likely to be given American names. Fouka (2019) shows that anti-German sentiment during World War I led German immigrants not only to Americanize their own and their children's names but also to file more petitions for naturalization in an effort to signal assimilation and avoid ethnic targeting.

Assimilation effort does not guarantee acceptance. Attempts to pass for a member of the majority group by altering observable markers may be detected, and dominant group members may not appreciate signals of assimilation or loyalty. The likelihood that effort will translate into acceptance differs across groups. Most societies are characterized by group hierarchies based on race, ethnicity, or religion, which determine preferential access to resources. These hierarchies are defined by multiple attributes, some ascriptive and some malleable, which are sometimes collapsed into a single summary measure of distance, cultural or social (Bogardus 1925). For instance, skin color, national origin, religion, and class background all jointly determined the ethnoracial hierarchy of the United States during the late nineteenth and early twentieth centuries. African Americans were at the bottom of this hierarchy, White Anglo-Saxon Protestants at the top, and various immigrant groups occupied intermediate positions ordered by salient attributes such as skin color and religion (Bogardus 1928; Fox and Guglielmo 2012).

Cultural distance is a crucial determinant of successful assimilation, and culturally distant groups face a lower chance of acceptance by the dominant society. Yet racial passing among African Americans and name Americanization among non-White groups in the United States demonstrate that assimilation effort is exerted by minority members even when ascriptive characteristics make acceptance unlikely. All else equal, assimilation effort increases the likelihood of acceptance and thus the expected benefits to assimilation. For example, name Americanization among immigrants in the United States resulted in occupational upgrading, as Biavaschi, Giulietti, and Siddique (2017) show by tracking immigrants across the steps of the naturalization process in 1930s New York.

Assimilation effort increases expected benefits to assimilation precisely because cultural distance is partly malleable and can be reduced by minority actions. Changing one's name casts that individual as more familiar to majority members. It also indicates willingness to become part of the group rather than remain a foreign element and thus lowers perceptions of threat. Evidence suggests that this signaling pays off. Goldstein and Stecklov (2016) show that immigrants in the United States whose first names were less foreign-sounding had higher occupational attainment, even after accounting for the foreignness of last names. Majority members respond favorably to assimilation effort even conditional on an observable measure of "otherness."

Decisions of Majority Members

Assimilation depends as much on minority members' choices to adopt the dominant group's values and behavior as it does on majority members' choices to allow the former unfettered access to the society, economy, and polity. Majority decisions, then, center around discrimination against minority groups. The role of discrimination in constraining the assimilation outcomes of minorities is a dominant theme in HPE.

Discrimination as a choice—the decision of whether to engage in social interactions with minority members or to avoid and exclude them—is also guided by trade-offs. Segregation from the minority group is achieved through residential mobility, which is costly for the individual. Institutionalized discrimination requires collective action and resources to implement and maintain. Discrimination also implies forgone social interactions or economic transactions that could be beneficial for both sides. Ferrara and Fishback (2020) provide a quantification of the aggregate costs of discrimination by measuring the economic impact of anti-German sentiment in the United States during World War I. After the country's entry into the war, counties with higher anti-German sentiment, driven by exogenous variation in war casualties, experienced higher outflows of German immigrants. This, in turn, led to a reduction in manufacturing wages, hurting local economies. Huber, Lindenthal, and Waldinger (2021) quantify the costs of discrimination against individuals at the firm level by showing that expulsions of Jewish senior managers in Nazi Germany led to large reductions in the market value of firms.

On the benefit side, majorities maintain impermeable boundaries to retain their political and economic dominance and protect their social status. Benefits to discrimination may also be purely psychological, deriving from majorities' dislike of outgroups.[2] The benefit of avoiding interactions with others is increasing in the cultural or social distance from the minority group. Braun and Dwenger (2020) provide evidence for this in the context of post–World War II Germany. Expellees from the Reich's former Eastern Territories were resettled in West Germany. Despite the cultural proximity of (ethnic German) refugees and the local populations, religious differences at the county level predicted a higher incidence of hate crimes and more votes for anti-migrant parties.

Assimilation as an Equilibrium Outcome

Assimilation rates in a society are jointly determined by the interdependent decisions of minority and majority members. Minority members condition their assimilation efforts on their chances of acceptance by the majority, which in turn depend on minority members' efforts and their cultural distance.

Two important comparative statics results arise from this framework, both supported by empirical evidence in historical contexts. The first one relates assimilation—both as choice and as equilibrium outcome—to cultural distance; the second one to majority discrimination. In both cases, the distinction between assimilation effort and successful assimilation proves important. Assimilation choices of minorities—as measured by outcomes like naming, racial identification, or conversion rates—do not necessarily result in successful assimilation—as measured by intermarriages or parity in economic outcomes between minority and majority groups.

The Effect of Cultural Distance

Assimilation effort is non-monotonic in cultural distance. For relatively proximate groups, effort increases in distance, as minority members need to adopt more identity markers, behaviors, and values of the dominant group in order to achieve acceptance. Beyond a certain distance, however, further effort becomes too costly and increases in cultural distance lower assimilation efforts.

The non-monotonic relationship between cultural distance and returns to assimilation effort is illustrated in Catron (2020), which studies how citizenship affects the occupational standing of immigrants in the United States in the 1930s. Catron (2020) relies on fourteen studies of racial and ethnic attitudes conducted between 1925 and 1956 to rank immigrant groups in terms of social distance. These studies, pioneered by sociologist Robert Park and his student Emory Bogardus, elicited preferences of White Americans, primarily university students, for association and intimacy with different groups. Focusing on southwestern states, Catron (2020) finds that the effect of citizenship on occupational earnings—a proxy of economic assimilation—followed an inverted U shape in social distance. Citizenship acquisition conferred little economic benefit to socially very proximate and very distant groups. The former could become integrated in the labor market without effort; the latter faced barriers to acceptance even after naturalization. Intermediate groups reaped the highest returns.

Successful assimilation decreases with cultural distance. All else equal, higher cultural distance implies more discrimination by the majority and lower assimilation rates. Much evidence for this relationship comes from studies of immigrant assimilation during the Age of Mass Migration. Escamilla-Guerrero, Kosack, and Ward (2021) compare assimilation rates of Italian and Mexican immigrants in the United States during the first decades of the twentieth century using linked data. Mexicans assimilated at a slower rate than Italians, and the gap between the two groups cannot be explained by their observable characteristics. While the effect of cultural distance is not directly demonstrated, the findings are consistent with Mexicans ranking lower than Italians in the social distance scales computed by the studies of Bogardus (1925) and others.[3] Peréz (2017) provides an alternative indirect illustration of the effect of cultural distance by comparing the trajectories of Italian immigrants in Argentina and the United States. He shows that higher economic assimilation in Argentina, measured by rates of home ownership and work in skilled occupations, can be partly attributed to the low linguistic and cultural distance of Italians from Spanish-speaking Argentinians, which allowed them to enter a broader range of occupations.

A more direct demonstration of the role of social distance is provided in Boyd (2021). Relying on the social distance scale of Bogardus (1928) for European-origin immigrant groups in the United States, Boyd (2021) finds a strong correlation between social distance and residential segregation. Immigrants' literacy rates and socioeconomic background instead have little explanatory power for segregation patterns. Fouka, Mazumder, and Tabellini (2021) are able to verify that the effect of social distance on immigrant assimilation is causal. They exploit an exogenous shift in the perceived distance of immigrant groups from white Anglo-Saxons, which was triggered by inflows of African American migrants from the South during the first Great Migration (1910–1930). Inflows of Black migrants increased economic and social assimilation among white Europeans. This effect worked through a reduction in discrimination against European groups, as evidenced by lower anti-immigrant sentiment and less negative stereotyping of immigrants in the press.

The Effect of Majority Discrimination

The results of Fouka, Mazumder, and Tabellini (2021) also provide evidence for the role of majority discrimination on minority assimilation. All else equal, lower barriers to acceptance increase assimilation rates for minority groups, but assimilation effort responds non-monotonically to a reduction in discrimination depending on minority members' cultural distance. For groups close to the majority, a reduction in discrimination means that acceptance can be achieved with lower effort. Intermediate groups instead may ratchet up assimilation efforts. For those groups, lower discrimination implies that acceptance, formerly unattainable, now becomes a possibility. Signaling assimilation thus becomes a profitable strategy. Very distant groups will see their calculations unchanged and their effort remain low.

Fouka, Mazumder, and Tabellini (2021) estimate such an inverted U-shaped relationship between the effect of discrimination on assimilation efforts and distance of immigrant groups from the White majority in the early-twentieth-century United States. They measure distance using linguistic and genetic distance proxies and assimilation effort as citizenship acquisition. They find that inflows of Black migrants lowered naturalization rates among Western and Northern Europeans, increased them among Southern and Eastern Europeans, and had no effect on Mexican and Chinese immigrants. Southern and Eastern Europeans—mainly Italians and Russian or Eastern European Jews—correspond precisely to the intermediate ranks of the social distance scale of Bogardus (1928). These groups faced discrimination by the dominant society prior to the arrival of Black migrants, but were sufficiently similar in skin color and cultural background to be accepted by White Americans after the Great Migration.

Extensions

The simple two-sided static framework can easily be extended by additional important determinants of assimilation dynamics. I briefly discuss three such elements—group size, minority group leaders, and intergenerational transmission—which either have been studied in a historical context or represent fruitful avenues for research on assimilation in HPE.

Minority Group Size

Many empirical studies in historical contexts identify a relationship between group size and assimilation rates of minority groups. In most setups, group size acts as a parameter that affects either the costs of assimilation effort or the real or perceived benefits to assimilation.

On the one hand, a larger minority group faces lower benefits to assimilation, as the group offers network opportunities for employment, socialization, and intermarriage. This decreases assimilation effort and assimilation rates. Zucker (2021) finds that immigrant groups with a higher concentration in mining in the early-twentieth-century United States had lower naturalization rates, particularly during mining booms, when the group could provide insurance to its members. Carneiro, Lee, and Reis (2020) use census data from 1900 to 1930 and find that higher immigrant concentration at the county level predicts lower rates of name Americanization.

On the other hand, a larger group may also lower costs to assimilation effort by providing members with resources needed to interface with the majority society. Biavaschi, Giulietti, and Zenou (2021) use linked census records between/across 1930 and 1940 and find that a higher share of naturalized immigrants in a census block—a small neighborhood with approximately fifty residents—increased naturalization rates for immigrants of the same nationality. Information provided by the group lowered the costs of citizenship acquisition and also increased the perceived benefits of citizenship. Larger minority groups may also confer higher benefits to specific dimensions of assimilation, such as political incorporation. Shertzer (2016) finds higher naturalization rates in city wards where immigrants were numerous enough to affect the winning probability of the Democratic Party in 1900 and 1910. Importantly, Shertzer (2016) captures the trade-off of a larger group size by estimating a non-monotonic relationship between size and naturalization rates at the ward level. Large enough groups had incentives to mobilize politically, but these incentives dissipated once a minimum winning coalition was reached. Beyond that threshold, group size lowered benefits to assimilation through other channels like group-specific networks and resources.

Minority Leaders and Institutions

Minority group institutions or leaders can also affect minority members' calculations and assimilation decisions. While scholarship has emphasized the importance of these actors for assimilation, little evidence exists for their effects in historical studies. Seminal work like Gellner's (1964) posits that elites may have strategic reasons to promote or stall minority assimilation. Elites driven by their desire to retain high status within the minority, as opposed to becoming second-class citizens within the dominant group, may resist assimilation, even if assimilation increases payoffs for the minority group as a whole. Similarly, minority institutions may affect assimilation—for instance, by coordinating collective action among minority members for improving the position of the group, and lowering members' incentives to assimilate as individuals (Laitin 1995).

A rare study focusing on immigrant institutions comes from Gagliarducci and Tabellini (2021), who examine how Roman Catholic churches affected the assimilation of Italian immigrants in the United States. In this setup, churches acted as a focal point for group coordination. Similar to a larger group size, they simultaneously lowered the costs of assimilation effort and the benefits to assimilation, thus increasing assimilation in some dimensions and reducing it in others. This study treats the presence of churches as exogenous. More work is needed to examine the strategic incentives of institutions and group leaders and bridge the historical literature with existing theoretical hypotheses in comparative and ethnic politics.

Long-Run Dynamics

Assimilation is a process that unfolds over several generations. Studying assimilation in the long run necessitates extending the two-sided framework to introduce decisions of parents on their children's enculturation. The seminal framework of Bisin and Verdier (2000; 2001) models parents as "imperfect altruists," who care about their children's well-being—and thus the possible handicaps a particular cultural or religious trait may endow them with—but evaluate it under their own perceptions of what is appropriate and desirable. Children can be socialized vertically, by parents, and horizontally, by peers.

In such a setup, minorities are at a disadvantage and minority children face the "threat" of assimilation through horizontal socialization with the majority. Charnysh and Peisakhin (2022) exploit the quasi-random allocation of Galician refugees in Poland after World War II to show that communities in which Galicians settled as a minority were less likely to retain distinct Galician values. At the same time, minority parents can partly counteract this dynamic through increased socialization. This framework can thus also explain the persistence of minority identities and the lack of complete assimilation in the long run. The HPE literature has built on these insights to explain how assimilationist interventions of the state affect assimilation dynamics.

The Role of the State

Effects of State Interventions

A substantial portion of the literature focuses on the effects of state policies on minority assimilation. Some policies have assimilation as a goal, and others are explicitly exclusionary. Policies targeting minority identity span a wide range of interventions, such as schooling, conscription, taxation, and citizenship laws.

Most studies leverage natural experiments or other causal inference techniques to identify the effects of policy, and thus implicitly treat state policy as exogenous to characteristics and behaviors of minorities. Such empirical approaches neatly fit into the framework presented, because they help identify comparative statics. All else equal, how does policy alter the decision-making of minorities and change assimilation outcomes?

Types of State Interventions

Conditional rewards and penalties

One type of policy increases the benefits to assimilation by offering rewards conditional on assimilation effort or imposing penalties for minority members who do not adopt behaviors or markers of the majority. All else equal, such incentive-based policies increase assimilation effort and rates of successful assimilation if the incentives provided are strong enough. When such interventions bind, their effects are stronger for minority members facing higher effort costs, who exerted initially lower assimilation effort.

These predictions are confirmed by the literature. The land allotment policy that Dippel and Frye (2020) studied is a clear-cut case of incentive-based assimilation policy. The incentive of land ownership was sufficiently powerful to increase assimilation, in the form of educational attainment, among Native American households subject to the policy. Fouka (2020b) illustrates the role of incentives in the case of an assimilation policy adopted by a private company. The Five-Dollar Day plan introduced by the Ford Motor Company in 1914 was a profit-sharing scheme offered to workers conditional on attending English classes and embracing American lifestyle habits and behaviors. The plan was successful in increasing English proficiency and naturalization rates among immigrants in the auto industry in Detroit and Highland Park, Michigan, who were likely Ford employees. These effects were stronger for immigrant groups of higher linguistic distance from English, for whom the costs of assimilation effort were initially higher.

Exclusion

A second type of policy regards rights extended to minority groups. From citizenship policy to institutionalized discrimination, the state determines whether minority groups are granted access to societal resources and the conditions (assimilation effort) under which that happens. Policies of exclusion function in the same way as majority discrimination. Almost mechanically, exclusion lowers assimilation rates. As in the case of discrimination, the effects on assimilation effort depend on minority groups' characteristics.

Chen and Xie (2020) provide evidence for this in the context of the 1882 Chinese Exclusion Act, which prohibited immigration of Chinese laborers to the United States and barred those already present in the country from naturalizing. The Exclusion Era was characterized not only by state-led discrimination but also by higher anti-Asian sentiment among the broader population. Chen and Xie (2020) find that these higher institutional and social barriers to acceptance lowered the occupational progress of

Chinese immigrants. Yet they also led to more educational investment, higher English proficiency, and more name Americanization, as some Chinese immigrants perceived a possibility of integration in society and the labor market, contingent upon higher assimilation efforts.

State intervention in preferences

Instead of influencing minority decision-making through incentives and constraints, some assimilation policies directly target minority members' preferences. The goal of such interventions is to ensure that minority members place a higher value on majority behaviors and norms, and desire to embrace them.

There is some evidence for successful interventions of this type. Mazumder (2017) shows that mass conscription during World War I increased assimilation among immigrants in the United States, measured by naming patterns, rates of citizenship, and intermarriage. He hypothesizes that the effect on preferences worked through state propaganda and interaction with the majority group.

Socialization

Preference-based interventions often target the younger generation. In such cases, the state intervenes in minority members' socialization, with the goal of directly shaping the identity of minority children.

The historical literature offers evidence for two categories of assimilation policies that work through socialization. The first one is forced removal. In this radical intervention, the state breaks the link of vertical socialization by the family and changes horizontal socialization by altering the composition of peers and role models to whom minority children are exposed. Because of their sweeping nature, policies of forced removal lead to assimilation almost by default. Feir (2016) shows that Indigenous boarding schools operated by the Catholic Church led to both economic and cultural assimilation of Canadian Aboriginal children. Gregg (2018) finds similar effects in the United States for Native American reservations close to boarding schools. Though attendance in boarding schools in the US context was not forced, assimilation was ultimately achieved through a similar channel of vertical and horizontal socialization by majority role models.

The second type of state intervention in the socialization of minority children involves schooling and curriculum content. The effect of such policies is more ambiguous, as parents and the broader minority community may react to threats to their identity. Fouka (2020a) finds that German immigrants exposed to laws banning German in the school after World War I became more likely to marry other Germans and less likely to volunteer in the US Army during World War II. The backlash was driven by increased socialization efforts of German parents and a social multiplier at the group level, especially in counties where German identity was strong. Sakalli (2019) uncovers similar effects in response to a centralized secularizing educational reform in 1920s Turkey. The reform reduced educational attainment and increased the prevalence of religious naming in provinces with high levels of religiosity, as pious parents forwent the economic benefits of education to transmit their religious identity.

A Case Study: Education Policy

Schooling is the most well-researched assimilation policy in the HPE literature and as such deserves special attention. Education policy comes in various forms, from mass schooling in a national language to bans on minority identities in school curricula. Different types of education policies may have different effects on minority decision-making, and by extension on assimilation outcomes. But even the same policy type may differ in its effects depending on contextual factors, such as other policies enacted simultaneously or broader incentives for assimilation in the society under study.

One type of assimilation policy in education is forced monolingualism. Fouka (2020b) conceptualizes requirements to use the majority language in schools as imposing a threshold of minimum assimilation effort for minorities. Not meeting the effort threshold through exclusive use of the majority language implies exclusion from education. Prescriptions of this form can increase effort and assimilation for minority groups with relatively low effort costs—such as those whose language is similar to that of the majority—but instead decrease them for groups with high costs who find the required effort too high.[4] These heterogeneous responses can lead to monolingual education having mixed or null effects on assimilation. Both Lleras-Muney and Shertzer (2015) and Fouka (2020b) find no effects of English-only laws on English proficiency of immigrant children in the United States. Consistent with heterogeneity in the effects of such policies, Fouka (2020b) finds most positive (or least negative) effects on English proficiency and intermarriage rates for immigrants with English-speaking or US-born mothers, whose costs of assimilation effort were lower.

Unlike forced monolingualism, mass compulsory education with a nationalist character is shown to lead to assimilation of minorities and long-run homogenization. Blanc and Kubo (2021) use a regression discontinuity design to examine the effects of the 1833 Loi Guizot, which required French localities above a certain population threshold to construct public schools. Using a survey of local spoken dialects and a measure of distance to standard French, they show that the law led to language homogenization, confirming the conclusions of Weber (1976) on nation-building through education in France. In the case of Prussia, Cinnirella and Schueler (2018) find that public funds directed to primary education increased votes for nationalist parties, and more so among noncore minority groups.

The success of these policies is a combination of several factors. Perhaps most importantly, mass schooling was introduced simultaneously with a significant increase in the benefits of assimilation for noncore groups. This is well documented in the case of France, where knowledge of standard French became a vehicle of socioeconomic mobility through migration to urban centers and employment in the country's growing bureaucracy (Weber 1976). Additionally, mass schooling reforms were often accompanied by severe penalties for noncompliance. In the case of the French Loi Guizot, these penalties included corporal punishment and public humiliation. The end effect of mass national schooling should then be understood as a joint product of prescriptions and strong incentives for assimilation, in the form of high returns to majority language and penalties for noncompliance.

When one or multiple of these conditions fail, compulsory nationalist schooling has more mixed effects. Lleras-Muney and Shertzer (2015) and Mazumder (2019) find no noticeable effect of state compulsory schooling laws in the United States on assimilation outcomes of immigrants such as intermarriage or citizenship. As both studies emphasize, and in contrast to the strict penalties accompanying educational reforms in France, US states were lax in their enforcement of compulsory schooling laws and there was room for immigrants to avoid compliance by enrolling their children in private schools.

Taken together, the empirical evidence on education policies suggests two key takeaways. First, the effect of monolingual policies is ambiguous; whether the threshold of minimum effort imposed by such policies will be attained depends on minority members' costs of assimilation effort. Second, compulsory schooling with a nationalist character is more likely to assimilate minorities when combined with strong incentives, in the form of increased benefits to using the national language or adopting national identity, or in the form of penalties for noncompliance.

Backlash to State Policy

In many instances, state interventions aiming—at least nominally—at assimilation end up having the opposite effect. Not only do they result in lower assimilation rates, but they may even strengthen, instead of weakening, minority identification. While empirical work in HPE provides sufficient evidence for such dynamics, less research exists on theorizing and empirically disentangling possible drivers of backlash.

In classifying mechanisms leading to backlash, I broadly distinguish between individual and group-level processes. At the individual level, several studies in HPE consider backlash to be a psychological response of minority members to coercive policies. This "coercion resentment" (Schøyen 2021) is assumed to be an intrinsic feature of people and can, under certain conditions, limit the efficacy of assimilation policy. A broader literature has identified resentment and oppositional behavior as a response of groups not only to assimilationist policies, but to repression of any form (see, e.g., Rozenas, Schutte, and Zhukov [2017]). Resentment is most evident in the long run, when the immediate threat of repression is absent (Rozenas and Zhukov 2019). In line with this channel, Dehdari and Gehring (2022) show that odious homogenization policies imposed by both Germany and France during the twentieth century led to stronger regional identity in Alsace-Lorraine.

An alternative, possibly complementary, individual-level mechanism for backlash does not simply assume resentment, but microfounds it in a rational framework that incorporates identity considerations. Oppositional behavior may arise out of models of cultural transmission in which individuals can choose their identity (Bisin et al. 2011; Carvalho and Koyama 2016). Backlash is likely even within a single generation when individuals are guided by social identity concerns (Shayo 2009). Social identity theory posits that individuals derive positive self-image from group belonging, and that they desire to belong to groups of high status. When minority groups face unattainable assimilation prescriptions or exclusion, they may increase their identification with the minority group or engage in oppositional behavior as a means of increasing group status. Investment in minority identity emerges as a substitute strategy to assimilation effort, possibly with higher returns.

A second class of mechanisms that can drive minority backlash involves group-level processes. Assimilation policies that increase the cost of minority behaviors lead to negative externalities for all members of a minority community. Through the lens of a club goods model of groups (Iannaccone 1992), the community or its leaders may then increase the stringency of prescriptions or otherwise require stronger signals of commitment to the minority group, in order to screen out community free-riders.

Carvalho, Koyama, and Sacks (2017) show how both individual- and group-level channels drove backlash among European Jews in the nineteenth century. During this period, ultra-Orthodox communities emerged in countries like Hungary, which combined policies of Magyarization, compulsory state education, and relatively low returns to schooling. Low benefits to assimilation and high requirements in terms of assimilation effort increased the benefits to minority identity at the individual level, as well as incentives to maintain cohesion and commitment at the group level. Such backlash did not take place in countries like Germany, where both Reform and modern Orthodox Judaism embraced secular education in response to the increase in returns to schooling and the lifting of formal barriers to Jewish participation in society.

Additional evidence for the role of group-level mechanisms is provided by Fouka (2020a) in the case of backlash to language bans among German immigrants in the United States. In response to removal of German from school curricula, German communities substituted with higher enrollment in Sunday schools. The backlash of German identity was stronger in counties where the German group was smaller and in counties with stronger presence of the Lutheran Church, the institution that mostly contributed to the preservation of German culture. The heightened response of smaller and more committed groups is consistent with a role for communities in driving backlash to assimilation policy.

State Decisions

Most empirical studies in HPE identify the effects of state policy on assimilation, keeping other factors constant. Significantly less work endogenizes policy choices or assigns a strategic role to the state. Existing studies that have done so have emphasized two dimensions of the state's decision problem.

The first approach treats the state as a rational actor that conditions its choice of policy on the behavior of minorities. Greif and Tadelis (2010) formally study how cryptomorality—hidden socialization into a banned or persecuted trait—affects the trait's persistence in the long-run. They explicitly consider the problem from the point of view of a ruler who wishes to maximize the prevalence of their preferred trait in the population. Optimal policy may entail smaller penalties, as too-large penalties will reduce the public expression of an identity but also foster its perpetuation in private. Rich historical narratives provide support for the framework in the context of the Spanish Inquisition's persecution of Judaism. The inquisition did not succeed in eradicating Judaism, which persisted in secret for centuries. Counterintuitively, it was more successful in eliminating Protestantism and other minor heresies, because the lighter penalties accompanying these infractions did not encourage crypto-morality. Yet the empirical part of the study is more targeted at understanding the reactions of religious minorities than those of the moral authority.

The second approach focuses more directly on the decision problem of the state, by examining the trade-offs involved between assimilation and other valued objectives. Saleh and Tirole (2021) consider the trade-off between religious conversion and tax revenue. State authorities that place a higher weight on identity will impose inefficiently high taxes, a theoretical prediction confirmed by variation in tax rates and conversion rates across local authorities in Egypt during the early Arab Caliphate.

Much can be learned about the drivers of assimilation by examining state trade-offs in more detail. One question that remains unanswered concerns the conditions under which the state chooses to engage in assimilation policies as opposed to other strategies, such as demographic engineering (McNamee and Zhang 2019) or the construction of a new overarching identity that does not coincide with that of the majority (Kersting and Wolf 2019).

Conclusion

A coherent body of research in HPE supports an interpretation of assimilation as the joint outcome of interdependent decisions of minority members and members of the dominant group or the state. Currently, the bulk of the evidence on assimilation comes from studies of immigrants in the United States during the Age of Mass Migration. The availability of rich individual-level census data, which can be linked over time, has led to tremendous progress on measurement of assimilation, but has also imposed constraints on the field that future research should try to overcome.

First, most work on assimilation in HPE remains empirical. More engagement with theory would help bridge HPE studies with broader work on assimilation in political science and economics, offering more precise hypotheses for testing and a better way to evaluate empirical findings. Second, the relative abundance of individual-level historical data has placed the focus on individual decisions of minority members and their assimilation outcomes. Other important drivers of assimilation, such as the state, minority leaders, or group-level processes—that sustain group identity are understudied, theoretically and empirically. Finally, the focus on the United States has allowed researchers to leverage substantial variation across cultural groups and subnational units, but has also largely limited our empirical evidence to a single country. Expanding to a wider range of historical and geographic contexts has great potential to advance the study of assimilation in HPE.

Notes

1. This conceptualization is in line with work in economics (e.g., Lazear [1999]), political science (e.g., Laitin [1998; 1995]), and sociology (Waters 1990).
2. Homophily, or outgroup bias, may characterize minority members as well. To the extent that it is present, it increases the costs of assimilation effort.
3. Kosack and Ward (2020) confirm this "unexplained" lack of assimilation among Mexicans. They find persistent gaps from natives across three generations of Mexican immigrants, which do not disappear even after accounting for socioeconomic disadvantages of earlier generations or the neighborhoods in which second-generation immigrants grew up.
4. This is particularly true if failure to meet prescriptions negatively affects the likelihood of acceptance by the dominant group in other domains of life—a likely scenario in the case of education in a national language.

References

Abramitzky, Ran, Leah Boustan, and Katherine Eriksson. 2020. "Do Immigrants Assimilate More Slowly Today Than in the Past?" *American Economic Review: Insights* 2, no. 1: 125–41.

Alexander, Rohan, and Zachary Ward. 2018. "Age at Arrival and Assimilation during the Age of Mass Migration." *Journal of Economic History* 78, no. 3: 904–37.

Biavaschi, Costanza, Corrado Giulietti, and Zahra Siddique. 2017. "The Economic Payoff of Name Americanization." *Journal of Labor Economics* 35, no. 4: 1089–116.

Biavaschi, Costanza, Corrado Giulietti, and Yves Zenou. 2021. "Social Networks and (Political) Assimilation in the Age of Mass Migration." Unpublished manuscript.

Bisin, Alberto, Eleonora Patacchini, Thierry Verdier, and Yves Zenou. 2011. "Formation and Persistence of Oppositional Identities." *European Economic Review* 55, no. 8: 1046–71.

Bisin, Alberto, and Thierry Verdier. 2000. "'Beyond the Melting Pot': Cultural Transmission, Marriage, and the Evolution of Ethnic and Religious Traits." *Quarterly Journal of Economics* 115, no. 3: 955–88.

Bisin, Alberto, and Thierry Verdier. 2001. "The Economics of Cultural Transmission and the Dynamics of Preferences." *Journal of Economic Theory* 97, no. 2: 298–319.

Blanc, Guillaume, and Masahiro Kubo. 2021. "Schools, Language, and Nations: Evidence from a Natural Experiment in France." Unpublished manuscript.

Bogardus, Emory S. 1925. "Measuring Social Distance." *Journal of Applied Sociology* 9: 299–308.

Bogardus, Emory Stephen. 1928. *Immigration and Race Attitudes*. Washington, DC: Heath and Company.

Botticini, Maristella, and Zvi Eckstein. 2007. "From Farmers to Merchants, Conversions and Diaspora: Human Capital and Jewish History." *Journal of the European Economic Association* 5, no. 5: 885–926.

Boyd, Robert L. 2021. "The Residential Segregation of European Immigrant Groups in the Early Twentieth-Century United States: The Role of Natives' Social Distance Attitudes." *Journal of International Migration and Integration*: 1–18. https://link-springer-com.stanford.idm.oclc.org/article/10.1007/s12134-021-00885-3#citeas.

Braun, Sebastian T., and Nadja Dwenger. 2020. "Settlement Location Shapes the Integration of Forced Migrants: Evidence from Post-War Germany." *Explorations in Economic History* 77. https://doi.org/10.1016/j.eeh.2020.101330.

Carneiro, Pedro, Sokbae Lee, and Hugo Reis. 2020. "Please Call Me John: Name Choice and the Assimilation of Immigrants in the United States, 1900–1930." *Labour Economics* 62.https://doi.org/10.1016/j.labeco.2019.101778.

Carvalho, Jean-Paul, and Mark Koyama. 2016. "Resisting Education." GMU Working Paper in Economics.

Carvalho, Jean-Paul, Mark Koyama, and Michael Sacks. 2017. "Education, Identity, and Community: Lessons from Jewish Emancipation." *Public Choice* 171, no. 1: 119–43.

Catron, Peter. 2020. "The Alien Citizen: Social Distance and the Economic Returns to Naturalization in the Southwest." Unpublished manuscript.

Charnysh, Volha, and Leonid Peisakhin. 2022. "The Role of Communities in the Transmission of Political Values: Evidence from Forced Population Transfers." *British Journal of Political Science* 52, no. 1: 238–58.

Chen, Shuo, and Bin Xie. 2020. "Institutional Discrimination and Assimilation: Evidence from the Chinese Exclusion Act of 1882." IZA Discussion Paper No. 13647.

Cinnirella, Francesco, and Ruth Schueler. 2018. "Nation Building: The Role of Central Spending in Education." *Explorations in Economic History* 67: 18–39.

Dahis, Ricardo, Emily Nix, and Nancy Qian. 2019. "Choosing Racial Identity in the United States, 1880-1940." NBER Working Paper No. 26465.

Dehdari, Sirus H., and Kai Gehring. 2022. "The Origins of Common Identity: Evidence from Alsace-Lorraine." *American Economic Journal: Applied Economics* 14: 261–92.

Díaz-Cayeros, Alberto, and Saumitra Jha. 2017. "Conquered but Not Vanquished: Complementarities and Indigenous Entrepreneurs in the Shadow of Violence." Working Paper, Stanford University.

Dippel, Christian, and Dustin Frye. 2021. "The Effect of Land Allotment on Native American Households during the Assimilation Era." Unpublished manuscript. https://christiandippel.com/dawes_.pdf.

Escamilla-Guerrero, David, Edward Kosack, and Zachary Ward. 2021. "Life after Crossing the Border: Assimilation during the First Mexican Mass Migration." *Explorations in Economic History* 82. https://doi.org/10.1016/j.eeh.2021.101403.

Feir, Donna L. 2016. "The Long-Term Effects of Forcible Assimilation Policy: The Case of Indian Boarding Schools." *Canadian Journal of Economics/Revue Canadienne d'Economiqué* 49, no. 2: 433–80.

Ferrara, Andreas, and Price V. Fishback. 2020. "Discrimination, Migration, and Economic Outcomes: Evidence from World War I." NBER Working Paper No. 26936.

Fouka, Vasiliki. 2019. "How Do Immigrants Respond to Discrimination? The Case of Germans in the US during World War I." *American Political Science Review* 113, no. 2: 405–22.

Fouka, Vasiliki. 2020a. "Backlash: The Unintended Effects of Language Prohibition in US Schools after World War I." *Review of Economic Studies* 87, no. 1: 204–39.

Fouka, Vasiliki. 2020b. "What Works for Immigrant Integration? Lessons from the Americanization Movement." Unpublished manuscript.

Fouka, Vasiliki, Soumyajit Mazumder, and Marco Tabellini. 2021. "From Immigrants to Americans: Race and Assimilation during the Great Migration." *Review of Economic Studies* 89, no. 2: 811–42. https://doi-org.stanford.idm.oclc.org/10.1093/restud/rdab038.

Fox, Cybelle, and Thomas A. Guglielmo. 2012. "Defining America's Racial Boundaries: Blacks, Mexicans, and European Immigrants, 1890–1945." *American Journal of Sociology* 118, no. 2: 327–79.

Gagliarducci, Stefano, and Marco Tabellini. 2021. "Faith and Assimilation: Italian Immigrants in the US." CEPR Discussion Paper No. DP15794.

Gellner, Ernest. 1964. "Thought and Change." London: Weidenfeld and Nicolson.

Goldstein, Joshua R., and Guy Stecklov. 2016. "From Patrick to John F. Ethnic Names and Occupational Success in the Last Era of Mass Migration." *American Sociological Review* 81, no. 1: 85–106.

Gregg, Matthew T. 2018. "The Long-Term Effects of American Indian Boarding Schools." *Journal of Development Economics* 130: 17–32.

Greif, Avner, and Steven Tadelis. 2010. "A Theory of Moral Persistence: CryptoMorality and Political Legitimacy." *Journal of Comparative Economics* 38, no. 3: 229–44.

Huber, Kilian, Volker Lindenthal, and Fabian Waldinger. 2021. "Discrimination, Managers, and Firm Performance: Evidence from 'Aryanizations' in Nazi Germany." *Journal of Political Economy* 129, no. 9: 2455–503.

Iannaccone, Laurence R. 1992. "Sacrifice and Stigma: Reducing Free-Riding in Cults, Communes, and Other Collectives." *Journal of Political Economy* 100, no. 2: 271–91.

Kersting, Felix, and Nikolaus Wolf. 2019. "On the Origins of National Identity." LMU Discussion Paper No. 217.

Kosack, Edward, and Zachary Ward. 2020. "El Sueño Americano? The Generational Progress of Mexican Americans prior to World War II." *Journal of Economic History* 80, no. 4: 961–95.

Laitin, David. 1998. *Identity in Formation: The Russian-Speaking Populations in the Near Abroad*. Ithaca, NY: Cornell University Press.

Laitin, David D. 1995. "Marginality: A Microperspective." *Rationality and Society* 7, no. 1: 31–57.

Lazear, Edward P. 1999. "Culture and Language." *Journal of Political Economy* 107, no. S6: S95–S126.

Lleras-Muney, Adriana, and Allison Shertzer. 2015. "Did the Americanization Movement Succeed? An Evaluation of the Effect of English-Only and Compulsory Schooling Laws on Immigrants." *American Economic Journal: Economic Policy* 7, no. 3: 258–90.

Mazumder, Soumyajit. 2017. "Becoming White: How Mass Warfare Turned Immigrants into Americans." Unpublished manuscript.

Mazumder, Soumyajit. 2019. "No Nation Left Behind? Assessing the Impact of Compulsory Schooling Laws on Immigrant Assimilation." Unpublished manuscript.

McNamee, Lachlan, and Anna Zhang. 2019. "Demographic Engineering and International Conflict: Evidence from China and the Former USSR." *International Organization* 73, no. 2: 291–327.

Peréz, Santiago. 2017. "The (South) American Dream: Mobility and Economic Outcomes of First- and Second-Generation Immigrants in Nineteenth-Century Argentina." *Journal of Economic History* 77, no. 4: 971–1006.

Rozenas, Arturas, Sebastian Schutte, and Yuri Zhukov. 2017. "The Political Legacy of Violence: The Long-Term Impact of Stalin's Repression in Ukraine." *Journal of Politics* 79, no. 4: 1147–161.

Rozenas, Arturas, and Yuri M. Zhukov. 2019. "Mass Repression and Political Loyalty: Evidence from Stalin's 'Terror by Hunger.'" *American Political Science Review* 113, no. 2: 569–83.

Saavedra, Martin. 2021. "Kenji or Kenneth? Pearl Harbor and Japanese-American Assimilation." *Journal of Economic Behavior & Organization* 185: 602–24.

Sakalli, Seyhun Orcan. 2019. "Secularization and Religious Backlash: Evidence from Turkey." Unpublished manuscript.

Saleh, Mohamed, and Jean Tirole. 2021. "Taxing Identity: Theory and Evidence from Early Islam." *Econometrica* 89, no. 4: 1881–919.

Saperstein, Aliya, and Aaron Gullickson. 2013. "A Mulatto Escape Hatch in the United States? Examining Evidence of Racial and Social Mobility during the Jim Crow Era." *Demography* 50, no. 5: 1921–42.

Schøyen, Øivind. 2021. "What Limits the Efficacy of Coercion?" *Cliometrica* 15, no. 2: 267–318.

Shayo, Moses. 2009. "A Model of Social Identity with an Application to Political Economy: Nation, Class, and Redistribution." *American Political Science Review* 103, no. 2: 147–74.

Shertzer, Allison. 2016. "Immigrant Group Size and Political Mobilization: Evidence from European Migration to the United States." *Journal of Public Economics* 139: 1–12.

Waters, Mary C. 1990. *Ethnic Options: Choosing Identities in America*. Berkeley: University of California Press.

Weber, Eugen. 1976. *Peasants into Frenchmen: The Modernization of Rural France, 1870–1914*. Stanford University Press.

Zucker, Noah. 2021. "Group Ties amid Industrial Change: Historical Evidence from Fossil Fuel Industry." Unpublished manuscript.

PART V

THE STATE AND SOCIETY

CHAPTER 35

RACE AND HISTORICAL POLITICAL ECONOMY

DAVID BATEMAN, JACOB M. GRUMBACH, AND CHLOE THURSTON

In this chapter we discuss race and historical political economy, with a focus on the United States. This is no easy task. In the US case especially, the question of race permeates nearly all instances of political conflict. At the same time, political economy research has been less attentive to race than historical research in the fields of history, sociology, and American political development (APD). Accordingly, we advocate for a broad definition of HPE. Given the importance of structures and feedback in the development of racial categorization and hierarchy, we argue that it is critical to incorporate literature across disciplines, methodologies, and theoretical traditions into the study of race and HPE.

The chapter proceeds as follows. We begin by describing the development of research communities that contribute to questions of race and HPE. We then turn to specific research questions that animate much of the HPE literature on issues of race. First, how have race and racism shaped political institutions and public policies in the United States? Second, how have institutions and policies created and maintained racial disparities, inequalities, exploitation, and oppression? In reviewing literature on these two questions, we argue that an important deficiency in the HPE literature is insufficient attention to the instability of racial categorization and racial politics across geography and time. Accordingly, we turn to literature on a third question: the role of politics and political economy in "creating" race and shaping racial categories and identities.

Constitutive Questions and Debates

The HPE study of race is the study of the causes and consequences of racism and racist practices, attentive to how these shape or are shaped by broader economic processes.

This is a capacious definition, delineating as a field of study what in reality are multiple, and often only barely overlapping, research communities, strikingly heterogeneous in focus, methods, and analytical orientations. Multiple intellectual traditions—among them, radical political thought and critical history (e.g., Du Bois 1999 [1935]; Robinson 2000 [1983]); institutional and labor economics (e.g., Bonacich 1972; Naidu 2010; Boustan 2016); the new economic history of the 1970s (e.g., Fogel and Engerman 1974); labor history (e.g., Honey 1993); the new institutionalisms in economics, sociology, and political science; and recent work on the history of capitalism—have each made distinctive contributions. While these have never been entirely siloed, they are embedded within separate discursive communities, making it difficult to speak of a single field of study.

There are nonetheless some unifying characteristics across much of this work. For one, HPE approaches tend to be observational rather than experimental. They also tend to place a greater emphasis on the rational bases of racist practices, rather than the psychological bases that for decades were the dominant focus in the social scientific study of racism. Where psychological explanations are invoked, they are often cast in an important but subsidiary role: as an explanation for why a particular racist political project won adherence beyond the principal classes for whom it was most instrumentally useful, or as a potential mechanism connecting racist behavior to a changing political economic environment (e.g., Ransom and Sutch 2001 [1977]). Finally, HPE approaches often prioritize institutions, either as a focus of inquiry or as providing the context in which racist behavior or outcomes need to be understood (e.g., Frymer 2005; Frymer and Grumbach 2021; Schickler 2016; Trounstine 2018).

This work has also been characterized by questions and concerns that stretch across disciplinary divides. One that has loomed large is when racism should be considered a foundational and constitutive element of a given political economic regime or set of institutions, or as a factor "rationing" inequality (Harris 1972) within it. The distinction is obviously a blurry one, though of considerable significance. Other enduring questions include debates over how particular racial projects relate to different political economic classes or interests, and about the mechanisms by which these have been able to gain a wider adherence or operate beyond the specific periods and places of their emergence—and where racist attitudes or ideologies should be located in the causal chains connecting institutions and economic practices to unequal outcomes. Such questions provide points of connection across otherwise disparate fields, and have historically helped define a common set of concerns despite disciplinary differences.

Perhaps the most explicit claims that racism has been constitutive of a broader political economic order, rather than peripheral or an expression of its internal conflicts, have emerged from Marxist or other critical traditions, some of which have been categorized as part of a longer Black radical tradition (Robinson 2000 [1983]; Marable 1983). Many of these, however, have been picked up by other research traditions and broadly shaped debates across fields. Oliver C. Cox, for example, in his critique of "caste" theories of race, argued that racism emerged as an elite project for legitimizing colonial dispossession and slavery (Cox 1948). Racism continued to serve the function of legitimizing exploitation after emancipation in part through elites' recurring construction of competition that fostered racial identities and antagonisms on a wider scale, and that inhibited effective opposition to capitalist exploitation. To analyze capitalism without racism, or vice versa, was for Cox to miss something essential about both.

Scholarship in this tradition has emphasized the role of elites in creating and sustaining capitalism's "socioeconomic matrix of racial antagonism" (Cox 1948, 19; Reed 2002), or highlighted how elaborate articulations of race converged with managerial capitalism at the turn of the twentieth century, condensing racist caricatures of groups' capacities into a set of labor management techniques. Still others, building on W. E. B. Du Bois, argued that racism provided a mechanism through which favored classes of workers consented to capitalism in exchange for a "public and psychological wage" (Du Bois 1999 [1935], 700). In more material variations, Whites divide the surplus extracted from racialized persons among themselves or defend it as a form of property with real material value (Atal 2021). Even absent a material bargain, racially privileged workers are said to gain psychologically, providing a political economic basis for psycho-sociological accounts that stressed relative group position. Some have largely removed elites from the equation, assigning causal priority to the interests or psychology of working-class and "poor Whites," whether as a class interested in cartelizing labor markets for their own benefit (Bonacich 1972) or as most committed to social stratification with Blacks. Each of these attributes agency for the definition and practice of racism in a particular historical context.

Cox was not the first to provide racism with an origin story rooted in the political economic imperatives of slavery, coercive agriculture, and empire.[1] Eric Williams, for example, succinctly asserted, "No sugar, no negroes" (1944, 27), and this claim, while never uncontested, has similarly diffused well beyond critical approaches. The implications drawn from it, however, vary considerably. Oscar Handlin and Mary Handlin agreed that American racism had emerged as a result of slavery, but rejected the notion that it was a deliberate political project, stressing the relative ease of securing African over English servants and the cultural and psychological associations that emerged between what increasingly took the form of slavery and "the trace of color" (1950, 216–17). Edmund Morgan, by contrast, concluded that not only had racism emerged as a deliberate ploy by slaveholders but, more sweepingly, that it had provided the necessary ideological and political context for understanding the new country's republican egalitarianism (1975). Agreement about sequence did not imply agreement about agency or significance.

Williams offered a different account of the foundational significance of racial exploitation, arguing that the transatlantic slave trade and enslaved labor on the sugar plantations provided the economic foundation for the commercial and subsequent industrial revolutions. Variations on the Williams thesis have gained new traction in recent decades. That enslaved labor was profitable and productive (Fogel and Engerman 1974) is widely recognized, though there remains considerable debate about its vitality by the mid-nineteenth century. There is now some agreement, though not consensus, that slavery was not just embedded within capitalism but was itself capitalist (Clegg

2015), that it was a productive and innovative sector (e.g., Rosenthal 2018), and that it made lasting contributions to capital formation, labor techniques, the culture of the United States' political economy, and global capitalism.

Variations of these claims have gained prominence in the new history of capitalism research community (Baptist 2014; Beckert and Rockman 2016). Providing both local and global histories, this literature has found in racialized slavery a constitutive feature of the US and global economic order. This field has inspired considerable criticism and debate (e.g., Olmstead and Rhode 2018). But it can be understood as connected to a broader trend within HPE to discover the roots of contemporary institutions, economic patterns, or political attitudes or outcomes in long-run processes associated with slavery and colonialism. Historians have contributed to the quantification of historical data on slavery and the slave trade, but have sought to do so while retaining an attention to racism, the lived experiences of those living under slavery and colonialism, and their effect on broader cultural practices and understandings. Critical debate will hopefully encourage greater cross-pollination of ideas and findings.

Claims about the ideological and material significance of racism to political economy have in recent decades converged in the heterogeneous and interdisciplinary literature on racial capitalism. These accounts place an even greater emphasis on racism's foundational and constitutive significance to political economic life, and that "racial subjugation is not a special application of capitalist processes, but rather central to how capitalism operates" (Harris 2021, 4; see also Dawson and Francis 2016). In some variations, the origins of racism are pushed back to the medieval era and antiquity. Cedric Robinson has argued that capitalism emerged out of distinctly racialized processes of primitive accumulation in feudal Europe, whose racial patterning was then extended onto a global scale (2000 [1983]). Like earlier accounts, the racial capitalism literature emphasizes the instrumental value of racial hierarchies, the significance of historical acts of primitive accumulation, the global and imperial character of racist political economic projects, and the ways in which racialized subjects have resisted these projects. But as with an older literature that framed the "ghetto" as an "internal colony," this scholarship emphasizes racial hierarchies' intrinsic connection to *ongoing* processes of coercive expropriation and dispossession, ranging from gentrification to the carceral state (Gilmore 2007; Beckett and Francis 2020; Taylor 2019). Racist violence and dispossession, in these accounts, was not just generative for the emergence of capitalism, but is constitutive of it today.

THE EFFECT OF RACISM ON INSTITUTIONS AND POLICIES

Questions of constitutive significance, agency, and motive can lead to greater dialogue across different disciplines. This is perhaps most productively done through a focus on how racism, race, and racist inequalities have shaped historically specific institutions and regimes or have been reproduced and sustained by these institutions.

Collectively, research on the significance of racism to institutions and institutional change has profoundly enriched our understanding of political and economic history. This is perhaps most true for the United States.

The Revolution, the Constitution, and US State-Building

Morgan's claim that slavery and racism made it possible to envision republicanism has already been mentioned (Morgan 1975). Recent scholarship has identified additional ways in which slavery and settler colonialism pushed forward the revolutionary movement. British abolitionism was not likely a major motivation, but there is abundant evidence that slavery and desires for Indigenous lands deeply affected how different constituencies evaluated the conflict with Britain (e.g., Holton 1999).

Slavery and settler colonialism's contribution to the emergence of a revolutionary coalition is difficult to determine empirically. Their significance for the US Constitution, for which we have rich, if incomplete, records of debate and voting, allows for more grounded accounts. We know that many of the delegates to the Constitutional Convention believed slavery to be a critical axis of division, and that efforts to protect it informed numerous provisions, including some that might not initially appear to be related to slavery (Finkelman 1996).

HPE work has examined the underlying structure to the convention voting and mapped the personal and state characteristics of delegates to their preferred positions. While not one of the principal estimated dimensions of conflict,[2] bargains over slavery likely helped secure the "Great Compromise" (Pope and Treier 2011), which was essential to ratification.

The importance of racialized slavery for the US Constitution was profound, albeit complex and not unidirectional. The same can be said for the importance of racialized slavery and racial hierarchies in state-building more generally. For Robin Einhorn (2006), slavery's significance has been to deliberately weaken state capacity and constrain the degree to which states could raise taxes or apportion them fairly (see also Lieberman 2003). Pavithra Suryanarayan and Steven White (2021) agree about the direction of racism on state capacity, but treat bureaucratic weakening as an effect not of slavery but of elite efforts to undercut the redistributive threat posed by Black enfranchisement after the Civil War. David Ericson, by contrast, highlights how slavery often drove forward US state-building, strengthening its capacity to police its borders, its internal policing, and the military, and with it the power of the federal government relative to the states (2011).

US institutions were shaped by race and racism in other ways as well. Paul Frymer (2017) recovers strategic efforts of US state-builders to use land policy to contain the Indigenous nations and the limits it faced in Indian removal and the colonization of free persons of color. These different policies reflected a broadly shared desire to achieve a homogeneous White population, one which—once embraced by Whites in the postabolition South—limited the prospects for extracontinental imperial projects.

Racist institutions and commitments could both constrain and push forward state-building.[3] Conflicts over racial projects repeatedly led both opponents and supporters to mobilize the state in pursuit of their aims (King and Smith 2012). No matter how much antebellum state-builders might have preferred to keep slavery out of national politics, for instance, they repeatedly turned to the federal state and to political allies across the country to grapple with it; slavery and race were too important material and ideological concerns for it to have been otherwise. At the same time, federal administrators beyond the center were embedded within local milieus whose racial hierarchies were normatively valued and exerted a powerful effect on labor markets and economic activity (Ericson 2011). These became embedded in state practices, sometimes limiting its potential capacity or authority but just as often having the opposite effect.

By examining how slavery, dispossession, and racism affected specific contexts and institutional sites, we are able to recover the ways in which these left deep and lasting imprints on the structure of US institutions even when they might not otherwise appear as the primary axis of voting or debate.

Democratization, Authoritarianism, and Racial Violence

Almost immediately after the Constitution's ratification, Congress passed legislation imposing a racial boundary to naturalization, soon followed by a wave of racist state restrictions on Black mobility and voting rights (Bateman 2018). Various states held referenda on whether to reenfranchise Black male voters (Walton, Puckett, and Deskins 2012), an important goal of the antislavery movement and overlapping networks of Black activists. These efforts would converge with the partisan interests of the Republican Party, after a Civil War instigated to preserve slavery (e.g., Hall, Huff, and Kuriwaki 2019).

Reconstruction has become a central site for HPE research on race, with the period examined as a case study in democratization and de-democratization, for testing theories of state capacity, party-building, and elite endurance (Poulos 2021). HPE scholarship is especially attuned to the ways in which racist ideologies and practices were reshaped by the shock of emancipation, and how these informed the efforts of different classes to either reconstitute their economic or social position, to take advantage of the new opportunities created by abolition, or to keep from sinking further (e.g., Acharya, Blackwell, and Sen 2018; Suryanaryan and White 2021; Du Bois 1999 [1935]).

Richard Valelly, in his pathbreaking account of the "two reconstructions," argued that expansion of the right to vote was driven by partisan calculations about how to retain political power, but that its consolidation required the development of legal and political capacity to defend it (2004). The question of state capacity, especially coercive capacity, has loomed large in subsequent accounts. Chacón, Jensen, and Yntiso (2021) have examined the joint effect of Black enfranchisement and state capacity as measured by military base locations. They found that only in occupied counties was enfranchisement correlated with increased tax revenues, and that troop presence was positively correlated with the ability to elect Black candidates. Stewart and Kitchens similarly leverage army locations, finding that counties in which the military was able to protect Black rights and the opportunities of Reconstruction show both greater and more persistent reductions in inequality during Reconstruction, but also more pronounced and enduring violence (2021). The declining presence of the army had spillover consequences for party-building and federal state bureaucracy, including weakening the Freedmen's Bureau's capacity "to enforce locally unpopular rules and decisions" despite its early successes and their enduring importance (Lieberman 1994, 422). While greater federal state capacity might have been a prerequisite for durable democratization, subsequent state-building occurred under the control of the White supremacist redemption governments and their successors.

The literature on lynching highlights how racist commitments sustained alternative institutions of coercion and prompted new state-building efforts. Early research debated the causes of its occurrence, including economic and social factors (Beck and Tolnay 1990), as well as more bluntly political uses of lynching (Soule 1992). Recent work has examined the interactive effect of racial segregation on lynching (Cook, Logan, and Parman 2018); extended the analyses to cover targeted killings of Black politicians, which increased with the success of these politicians in producing more downwardly redistributive tax systems (Logan 2020); reevaluated the political and economic effects of lynching (Jones, Troesken, and Walsh 2017); and studied the role of lynching in activating and maintaining the racial identities upon which the White supremacist regimes rested (Smång 2016).

Scholars have also connected the occurrence of lynching to debates over state capacity and to states' efforts to secure investment. Southern states—supported in some cases by biracial, middle-class coalitions (Johnson 2010), anxious to attract industry, and often subjected to increased media exposure (Weaver 2019)—developed new resources and relationships to limit lynching's occurrence (Beck, Tolnay, and Bailey 2016). And yet at the national level southern lawmakers adamantly resisted federal antilynching bills, while civil rights organizations pressured Congress and the executive but also the courts (Francis 2014). As Megan Ming Francis highlights, one of the ways in which racism mattered for US state-building was through creating conditions against which racialized communities came to organize in opposition to racist institutions and violence, as well as the limits on problem definition imposed by White funders (Francis 2014; 2019).

Racist state-building could take forms as diverse as limiting lynching laws, strengthening state-controlled forms of coercion, expanding the carceral state (in its postbellum or late-twentieth-century variations), or changing the terms under which convicted persons were made to labor (Muller 2018). The growth of incarceration and convict leasing in the South after emancipation was not a reconstitution of slavery, but it was a rapid development of a coercive capacity that could be deployed to secure labor and social control over disproportionately racialized populations. The carceral state in the late twentieth and early twenty-first centuries has equally complex roots, and yet similarly requires an appreciation of the role of racism in sustaining support for highly punitive policies (Beckett and Francis 2020).

Valelly (2004) had connected prospects for enfranchisement's durability to the development of party organizations and of jurisprudence. Claims that the United States was a "White man's country" had become the mantra of the Democratic Party, reaching a fever pitch during the Civil War and Reconstruction (Kalmoe 2020). Black enfranchisement intensified and complicated this. Boris Heersink and Jeffery Jenkins have shown that Republican Party–building in the South continued from Reconstruction to the 1960s, but also that Republican efforts were conditioned by White racism and the extent of Black enfranchisement (2020). White racism limited but did not foreclose biracial coalitions or campaigns in which race was not the determining party cleavage or campaign issue (Jenkins and Peck 2021). But after disenfranchisement, Republican electoral prospects required attracting White voters, which many organizations did by reducing the visible presence of Black Republicans or excluding them outright. Reconstruction jurisprudence-building was similarly constrained.[4]

The political limits to Reconstruction, the changing orientation of the national parties, the rise and suppression of the Populist Party, and the defeat of additional voter protections in 1891 helped produce the context for the imposition of the Jim Crow regimes (Ali 2010; Ottinger and Winkler 2022). V. O. Key Jr. suggested that the disenfranchising constitutions of the turn of the century simply verified a fait accompli (1949). While voter suppression was important, the institutions of the 1890s–1910s effectively eradicated Blacks as a class from the electorate (Kousser 1974).[5] Disenfranchisement in turn facilitated the legal imposition of Jim Crow (Roback 1986). Kousser's analysis of disenfranchisement emphasized the central importance of Black Belt Democrats, although the specifics and timing varied with state circumstances: Black Belt Democrats simultaneously feared and relied on Black votes, using a combination of fraud, intimidation, and occasional bargaining to secure for themselves the representational weight of Black populations. White supremacy could be invoked in support of and opposition to disenfranchisement, and disenfranchisement's timing depended on local political threats, perceptions of external constraints, and the capacity of southern states to institute effective restrictions (Epperly et al. 2019).

The racist exclusions of the Jim Crow regimes fundamentally limited the quality and character of democratic representation and the outputs of government (more later). Racism's effect on democratic institutions was not least to deprive racially excluded populations the opportunity to elect representatives (e.g., Logan 2020) and to exert influence through the electoral connection.

Black Belt planters, however important, nonetheless relied on coalitions with other White interests, including new industrialists and non-elite Whites. This shaped the representation of White preferences, the efforts of regime elites to sustain power in the wake of a renewed federal threat and domestic organizing, and states' differing paths toward democracy (Mickey 2015). A central interpretative disagreement concerns the question of whether these regimes are better understood as polyarchies, in which its democratic features were real for Whites (Caughey 2018), or as subnational authoritarian regimes:

not democratic even for Whites, however much congruence might be observed between voting and opinion (Mickey 2015).

White supremacy had a presence and consequences well-beyond the governing institutions of the South. The region's post-disenfranchisement representatives were vital actors in the construction of the progressive regulatory state, the "agricultural welfare state," and the reorganization of US federalism (Johnson 2011; 2007; Bateman, Katznelson, and Lapinski 2018). A voluminous literature examines the ways in which southern representatives shaped New Deal programs to buttress, or at least not overly threaten, White supremacy and the unequal and low-wage labor regime with which it was entwined (Katznelson 2013; Lieberman 1998; Mazumder 2021; Alston and Ferrie 2007).

Collectively these works have explored the ways in which racism shaped the welfare state and, more broadly, the relation between capitalism, labor, and the state that emerged from the New Deal and Fair Deal. The incorporation of occupational exclusions or regional discriminations with clear racial patterns into New Deal programs, along with outright racial segregation or discrimination in some programs (e.g., Thurston 2018; Grant 1990; Turner and Bound 2003), have often been interpreted as a condition for the emergence of the welfare state, while reflecting and embedding into the new institutions ideological, psychological, and material commitments that would constrain its future development (Farhang and Katznelson 2005; Chen 2009). Even where the New Deal did address racial discrimination in a more egalitarian direction—as did the Fair Employment Practices Committee of the late war years—its impact was often not felt in the South, where a broad White consensus limited its effectiveness (Collins 2001).

The role of racism in shaping the New Deal, much like its role in shaping the Constitution or earlier moments of state-building, is hardly one-sided or unambivalent. In the short term, the New Deal's contribution to "modernizing" the South and integrating it into a national labor market often exacerbated racist inequalities and may even have helped fortify Jim Crow (Johnson 2010). Over the long term, however, the New Deal may have helped destabilize the political economic foundations of these regimes, while the organizations who would come to define post–New Deal liberalism threatened its political foundations through labor organizing, civil rights organizing, and litigation, perhaps most importantly that which abolished the White primary (Mickey 2015).

THE EFFECT OF INSTITUTIONS, POLICIES, AND BEHAVIOR ON RACIAL INEQUALITY

A second set of research questions concerns the effects of institutions and public policy on racial inequality and outcomes for racial minorities and across racial groups. A substantial descriptive literature has measured historical dynamics in income and wealth holding by race, especially in the United States (Higgs 1977; 1982; Hamilton and Darity

2010), including more specifically in terms of real estate capital (Kermani and Wong 2021). Recently, Derenoncourt et al. (2021) use historical US Census, state tax, and Survey of Consumer Finances data to systematically measure wealth inequality between Black and White Americans from 1860 to 2020.

A related scholarly debate involves the question of how much of current and historical racial inequality can be explained by institutional and behavioral discrimination, on the one hand, and human capital differences (which themselves can be the result of discrimination, such as via unequal access to schooling; see Margo 1990) on the other (Raphael 2002). Some studies find that a substantial proportion of racial inequality in economic outcomes can be explained by unequal human capital stemming from unequal schooling (e.g., Carruthers and Wanamaker 2017). A large number of other studies, however, suggest that a large proportion of racial inequality remains even when holding human capital constant (e.g., Sundstrom 2007). Correspondingly, many recent studies point to behavioral, policy, and institutional forms of discrimination—some of which arise from historical legacies of discrimination, but others of which persist today—that explain this "residual" inequality.

Research has focused on the economic effects of White supremacist terrorism and policies that disenfranchised Black Americans. Naidu (2012) finds that nineteenth-century southern "redemption" disenfranchisement policies had significant negative effects on Black labor income and investment in Black schools that expanded racial inequality. Research has also focused on Jim Crow–era racial labor practices and their political-economic effects. Studies examine, for instance, the significance of convict leasing of Black prisoners to the Jim Crow economy (Lichtenstein 1996; Muller 2018).

With data covering 1875 to 1930, Naidu (2010) finds that anti-enticement laws, which imposed criminal penalties on employers who offered higher wages to already employed Black workers, empowered White landowners and reduced the wages of newly emancipated Black sharecroppers. Aneja and Xu (2022) study the effect of the resegregation of the US federal government under President Woodrow Wilson, finding that it increased the racial wage gap due to its reallocation of black civil servants to lower-paid positions.

Turning from the post-Reconstruction and Jim Crow–era studies, another body of research investigates the effect of mid-twentieth-century economic policies and institutions on racial outcomes, often finding that the initiation or expansion of New Deal and Great Society economic policies benefited Black Americans' economic standing (notwithstanding the racially exclusionary aspects of the New Deal outlined earlier). Collins (2001) estimates the effect of fair employment laws during the New Deal and World War II on racial inequality and labor market outcomes for Black workers. Derenoncourt and Montialoux (2021) study the effects of expanded minimum wage coverage in the 1966 Fair Labor Standards Act on racial wage inequality. However, Derenoncourt (2022, 370) finds that the Great Migration of Black Americans to northern cities produced institutional changes that reduced the upward social mobility effects of living in northern cities, finding that "roughly 27 percent of the gap in upward mobility between Black and White families in the urban North can be attributed to changes induced by the Great Migration" (see also Boustan 2016). Jenkins (2021) further argues that racism interacted with municipal bond markets to produce racial inequality in city financing.

Research also looks into the economic impacts of the mid-century civil rights revolution in the US South, often with difference-in-differences and event study designs. Wright (2013) argues that the legal and regulatory ramifications of the Civil Rights Act (CRA) of 1964 and Voting Rights Act (VRA) of 1965 reduced Black poverty and racial inequality. Cascio and Washington (2014) find that the VRA's removal of Jim Crow literacy tests for voting increased the transfer of state funds to localities where Black residents lived. Investigating these mechanisms, Aneja and Avenancio-León (2019) find that the VRA rapidly increased Black wages and reduced racial inequality by opening up new opportunities for public sector employment of Black workers.

In contrast to arguments that highlight education and human capital development (e.g., Smith 1984; Carruthers and Wanamaker 2017), these studies on the effects of (dis) enfranchisement tend to emphasize the role of political power and distributive politics in economic equality, upward mobility, and expanded access to public goods. These findings are also somewhat in contrast with those of Kruse (2013) and other historical analyses that suggest that desegregation and Black in-migration provoked White flight from central cities with negative economic consequences for Black residents (Boustan 2016).

Mass incarceration in the United States since the 1970s has also had especially profound political-economic consequences for Black Americans and for racial inequality. Research has focused on mass incarceration's social (Pattillo, Western, and Weiman 2004) and economic effects (Zaw, Hamilton, and Darity 2016). Pettit (2012) shows that high rates of incarceration cause many Black men to "disappear" from national surveys, thereby biasing overall and racial group estimates of unemployment, health, and other socioeconomic outcomes in ways that overstate racial equality.

Finally, a literature on descriptive representation has investigated the effect of politicians' racial identities, often as a proxy for a racial group's political power, on policy and socioeconomic outcomes. A large number of these studies have focused on the effect of Black mayors during the period of increasing Black mayorships in the post–civil rights period (Eisinger 1982; Saltzstein 1989; Spence, McClerking, and Brown 2009).

Policies, Institutions, and Racial Formation: Some Future Directions

HPE continues to make significant inroads into our understanding of the effect of race and racism on institutional outcomes, and the effect of institutions on racial disparities. Several challenges remain that can structure future HPE research and put the field into better conversation with other academic disciplines working on these issues, while still leveraging HPE's core strengths. Here we describe two of these challenges and opportunities: (1) the fluidity of racial categories across multiple dimensions, and (2) the practical challenges associated with collecting historical data on political participation, particularly as it pertains to marginalized minority groups.

Race and Racial Categories as Variable

If situating race and racism in a scholarly understanding of political economy requires some sort of categorization, then taking an explicitly historical approach should draw our attention to the fluidity of racial categories. This fluidity takes multiple forms. As racial categories play a role in statecraft, government agencies regularly shift how they categorize populations in their official statistics. This occurs both in terms of the actual categories that are available, as well as with respect to who is responsible for making decisions about categories (e.g., whether this information is self-reported or decided by a survey enumerator) (Nobles 2000; Thompson 2016; Davenport 2020; Harris et al. 1993; Telles 2004). The sources of these changes are varied, emanating at different points from the top down, bottom up, and transnationally (for example, international communities of statisticians) (Thompson 2016). Individuals have also been found to change their racial self-identification over time or across different contexts (Doyle and Kao 2007; Saperstein and Penner 2012; Laird 2019; for an example outside of the United States, see Villarreal and Bailey 2020). Finally, and related, in-group and out-group racial boundaries can also change over time, as a vast scholarship examining the historically changing boundaries of Whiteness in the United States has shown (Jacobson 1999).

The fluidity of racial classification can also be seen in the shifting use of (and rationale for using) race in economic behavior and policymaking, issues of central concern to HPE. Economic actors and policymakers in their beliefs and actions can help to determine the extent to which race is a relevant factor in their decision-making. How race and racial difference come to be constructed, measured, and reported (for example, through redlining maps) can feed back into economic actors' ideas about profit and risk and for policymakers' actions.

For example, the commercial life insurance industry has historically relied on classifying individuals with similar risk profiles, relying on a small handful of classifiers for efficiency. Following the end of Reconstruction, some life insurance companies shifted from using region as a classifier for pricing to using race. Industry practices, scientific racism, and state-level regulatory decisions became deeply intertwined. While some industry statisticians said that the practice was necessary (and thus should not be outlawed, as six states had done by the early 1900s) in order to enable fair pricing and a functioning insurance market, others (as well as some social scientists) questioned whether race should be treated as an immutable characteristic, separate from the historical and social factors that had produced different mortality rates in the historical data used to make economic decisions (Bouk 2015; Wiggins 2020; Muhammad 2019). The practice fell out of favor by mid-century in the insurance industry with the international professional repudiation of scientific racism. Outside of insurance, Freund (2010), Hyman (2011), Thurston (2018), Taylor (2019), and Jenkins (2021) show how contingent racialized beliefs about real estate values were incorporated into public policies and then fed back into White cultural attitudes and behaviors, as well as real estate professionals' practices, ultimately helping to generate large racial disparities in wealth over the course of the twentieth century. In short, racial categories can shift in relevance to ideas about risk, value, and profit over time and across regulatory contexts. As many markets have become ever more algorithmic, the role of race in market outcomes has become more difficult to detect even as many have recovered substantial difficulties at the output level (Benjamin 2019; Fourcade and Healy 2017).

While the challenges associated with the empirical measurement of race and its utility as a "treatment" have long been recognized (see Sen and Wasow 2016), they pose challenges and opportunities for the field of HPE. The obvious challenge is that scholars cannot assume that racial categories themselves are constant over time, or that they are used for the same purposes by policymakers or economic actors over time. Some scholars have taken this logic further, arguing that race cannot be studied using positivist methods (Zuberi 2001). Scholars working in or near the HPE tradition have taken an opportunity to engage with these challenges head on by directing their attention to changing classifications as an outcome. Some early work on the intersection of politics, economics, and history explicitly engaged with these issues (Glaeser 2005; Darity, Mason, and Stewart 2006; Shayo 2009). Beginning with the premise that racial identity is a social norm rather than being exogenously assigned, Darity, Mason, and Stewart (2006), for example, used evolutionary game theory to model the formation of identity norms and how those might lead to societal-wide racial norms, with implications for material disparities over time. There has also been more recent engagement with the historical process of racial identity formation and its economic implications (Kranton 2016; Fouka, Mazumder, and Tabellini 2021). This builds productively on Omi and Winant's (2014 [1986]) argument that the selection of which human features will signify race "is always and necessarily a social and historical process" (55).

Agency and Participation from the Margins

A second challenge for HPE scholarship has to do with identifying and measuring historical forms of participation. To be sure, questions about conceptualization and measurement, as well as what to do about limited data availability, are core to the HPE enterprise. The collection and use of new evidence of historical participation is one of the core strengths of the field, as other chapters in this volume show.

These challenges are compounded in historical scholarship that centers the activities and agencies of racial minority groups. While contemporary scholarship has been able to respond to calls to center more marginalized views and activities through the intentional design of surveys and other data collection strategies (Prowse, Weaver, and Meares 2020; Rosenthal 2021; Michener 2019; for a discussion of these calls for centering marginalized voices in political science, see Soss and Weaver 2017; Rogers and Kim 2023; and Michener, SoRelle, and Thurston 2022), historical studies are far more limited, especially as one goes further back into time or into contexts where for various reasons participation may not be documented.

One major limitation has to do with what participants were and were not willing to allow into the record in the first place. For example, recent historical scholarship has uncovered robust Black populist organizing in the Reconstruction era that was distinctive from White populist organizing. Describing some of the activities of Black populism, Ali (2010, 9) writes, "In addition to launching independent and insurgent campaigns against the Democratic Party, Black Populists established farming exchanges, raised money for schools, published newspapers, led boycotts and strikes, and lobbied for political reforms." Yet even with this clear evidence of organizing, establishing exact membership numbers is impossible beyond the estimation that "several hundred thousand" may have participated. As Ali points out, "membership lists were almost never made for fear of reprisal from white authorities should they be discovered" (2010, 9). Lest this be just a nineteenth-century challenge, Thurston (2018, 183–220) also shows that advocacy groups have intentionally engaged in stealth organization in the twentieth century as well when they perceived their overt presence could undermine their goals or imperil their members' safety. In short, strategic concerns of marginalized actors may shape the availability of data and requires scholars to be careful about their conclusions.

Conclusion

In this chapter, we have investigated the study of race in HPE research. While the HPE study of race is generally focused on the causes and effects, as well as conceptualization and measurement, of racism and racist practices, our review has plumbed distinct intellectual traditions, including radical political thought, critical history and theory, institutional and labor economics, the new economic history of the 1970s, labor history, the history of capitalism, racial capitalism, and the new institutionalisms in economics, sociology, and political science. We argue that, by contrast, a more narrowly defined HPE as quantitative and game theoretic research from economics and political science gives insufficient attention to structural racism and hierarchy.

We have reviewed studies across these traditions that have investigated the questions of how racism shaped political institutions and public policies in the United States, how institutions and policies created and maintained racial inequality, and the role of politics and political economy in "creating" race and shaping racial categories and identities. In doing so, we hope to contribute to the bridging of the various disciplines, methods, and epistemological traditions engaged in the study of race in HPE.

Acknowledgments

We thank Jeffery A. Jenkins, Jared Rubin, Megan Ming Francis, Jared Clemons, and workshop participants at Northwestern for valuable feedback.

Notes

1. By contrast, most post–World War II economic studies of racial discrimination held that it could not "begin in the economic sphere or out of purely economic motives" (Arrow 1971, 26).
2. Slavery shaped positions and outcomes on a range of issues, and lower South delegates were often empowered by the multidimensionality of voting (Dougherty 2020; Pope and Treier 2011).
3. For a non-US analysis, see Lieberman (2003).
4. As with the twentieth-century civil rights laws (Cascio and Washington 2014), Reconstruction-era civil rights legislation very likely had real consequences (Harvey and West 2020; Logue and Blanck 2010; Costa 2010).
5. See also Keele, Cubbison, and White 2021.

References

Acharya, Avidit, Matthew Blackwell, and Maya Sen. 2018. *Deep Roots: How Slavery Still Shapes Southern Politics*. Princeton, NJ: Princeton University Press.

Ali, Omar H. 2010. *In the Lion's Mouth: Black Populism in the New South, 1886–1900*. Jackson: University Press of Mississippi.

Alston, Lee J., and Joseph P. Ferrie. 2007. *Southern Paternalism and the American Welfare State: Economics, Politics, and Institutions in the South, 1865–1965*. Cambridge: Cambridge University Press.

Aneja, Abhay P., and Carlos F. Avenancio-León. 2019. "Disenfranchisement and Economic Inequality: Downstream Effects of *Shelby County v. Holder*." *AEA Papers and Proceedings* 109: 161–65.

Aneja, Abhay, and Guo Xu. 2022. "The Costs of Employment Segregation: Evidence from the Federal Government under Woodrow Wilson." *Quarterly Journal of Economics* 137, no. 2: 911–58.

Arrow, Kenneth. 1971. *Some Models of Discrimination in the Labor Market*. Santa Monica, CA: RAND.

Atal, Maha Rafi. 2021. "Measuring the Wages of Whiteness: A Project for Political Economists." *Global Perspectives* 2, no. 1.

Baptist, Edward E. 2014. *The Half Has Never Been Told: Slavery and the Making of American Capitalism*. New York: Basic Books.

Bateman, David A. 2018. *Disenfranchising Democracy: Constructing the Electorate in the United States, United Kingdom, and France*. Cambridge: Cambridge University Press.

Bateman, David A., Ira Katznelson, and John S. Lapinski. 2018. *Southern Nation: Congress and White Supremacy after Reconstruction*. Princeton, NJ: Princeton University Press.

Beck, E. M., and Stewart Tolnay. 1990. "The Killing Fields of the Deep South: The Market for Cotton and the Lynching of Blacks, 1882–1930." *American Sociological Review* 55: 526–39.

Beck, E. M., Stewart E. Tolnay, and Amy Kate Bailey. 2016. "Contested Terrain: The State versus Threatened Lynch Mob Violence." *American Journal of Sociology* 121, no. 6: 1856–84.

Beckert, Sven, and Seth Rockman. 2016. *Slavery's Capitalism: A New History of American Economic Development*. Philadelphia: University of Pennsylvania Press.

Beckett, Katherine and Megan Ming Francis. 2020. "The Origins of Mass Incarceration: The Racial Politics of Crime and Punishment in the Post-Civil Rights Era." *Annual Reviews* 16: 433–52.

Benjamin, Ruha. 2019. *Race after Technology: Abolitionist Tools for the New Jim Code Era*. New York: Polity.

Bonacich, Edna. 1972. "A Theory of Ethnic Antagonism: The Split Labor Market." *American Sociological Review* 37, no. 5: 547–59.

Bouk, Dan. 2015. *How Our Days Became Numbered*. Chicago: University of Chicago Press.

Boustan, Leah. 2016. *Competition in the Promised Land: Black Migrants in Northern Cities and Labor Markets*. Princeton, NJ: Princeton University Press.

Carruthers, Celeste K., and Marianne H. Wanamaker. 2017. "Separate and Unequal in the Labor Market: Human Capital and the Jim Crow Wage Gap." *Journal of Labor Economics* 35, no. 3: 655–96.

Cascio, Elizabeth U., and Ebonya Washington. 2014. "Valuing the Vote: The Redistribution of Voting Rights and State Funds following the Voting Rights Act of 1965." *Quarterly Journal of Economics* 129, no. 1: 379–433.

Caughey, Devin. 2018. *The Unsolid South*. Princeton, NJ: Princeton University Press.

Chacón, Mario L., Jeffrey L. Jensen, and Sidak Yntiso. 2021. "Sustaining Democracy with Force: Black Representation during Reconstruction." *Journal of Historical Political Economy* 1, no. 3: 319–51.

Chen, Anthony. 2009. *The Fifth Freedom: Jobs, Politics, and Civil Rights in the United States, 1941–1972*. Princeton, NJ: Princeton University Press.

Clegg, John J. 2015. "Capitalism and slavery." *Critical Historical Studies* 2, no. 2: 281–304.

Collins, William J. 2001. "Race, Roosevelt, and Wartime Production: Fair Employment in World War II Labor Markets." *American Economic Review* 91, no. 1: 272–86.

Cook, Lisa D., Trevon D. Logan, and John M. Parman. 2018. "Racial Segregation and Southern Lynching." *Social Science History* 42, no. 4: 635–75.

Costa, Dora L. 2010. "Pensions and Retirement among Black Union Army Veterans." *Journal of Economic History* 70, no. 3: 567–92.

Cox, Oliver C. 1948. *Caste, Class, & Race*. New York: Monthly Review Press.

Darity, William A., Jr., Patrick L. Mason, and James B. Stewart. 2006. "The Economics of Identity: The Origin and Persistence of Racial Identity Norms." *Journal of Economic Behavior & Organization* 60, no. 3: 283–305.

Davenport, Lauren. 2020. "The Fluidity of Racial Classifications." *Annual Review of Political Science* 23: 221–40.

Dawson, Michael C., and Megan Ming Francis. 2016. "Black Politics and the Neoliberal Racial Order." *Public Culture* 28, no. 1: 23–62.

Derenoncourt, Ellora. 2022. "Can You Move to Opportunity? Evidence from the Great Migration." *American Economic Review* 112, no. 2: 369–408.

Derenoncourt, Ellora, and Claire Montialoux. 2021. "Minimum Wages and Racial Inequality." *Quarterly Journal of Economics* 136, no. 1: 169–228.

Derenoncourt, Ellora, Chi Hyun Kim, Moritz Kuhn, and Moritz Schularick. 2021. "The Racial Wealth Gap, 1860–2020." Manuscript, Princeton University and University of Bonn. Available at https://www.russellsage.org/sites/default/files/Derenoncourt.Proposal.pdf.

Dougherty, Keith L. 2020. "Slavery in the Constitution: Why the Lower South Occasionally Succeeded in the Constitutional Convention." *Political Research Quarterly* 73, no. 2: 638–50.

Doyle, Jamie Mihoko, and Grace Kao. 2007. "Are Racial Identities of Multiracials Stable? Changing Self-Identification among Single and Multiple Race Individuals." *Social Psychology Quarterly* 70, no. 4: 405–23.

Du Bois, W. E. B. 1999 [1935]. *Black Reconstruction in America, 1860–1880*. New York: Free Press.

Einhorn, Robin L. 2006. *American Taxation, American Slavery*. Chicago: University of Chicago Press.

Eisinger, Peter K. 1982. "Black Employment in Municipal Jobs: The Impact of Black Political Power." *American Political Science Review* 76, no. 2: 380–92.

Epperly, Brad, Christopher Witko, Ryan Strickler, and Paul White. 2019. "Rule by Violence, Rule by Law: Lynching, Jim Crow, and the Continuing Evolution of Voter Suppression in the U.S." *Perspectives on Politics* 18, no. 3: 756–59.

Ericson, David F. 2011. *Slavery in the American Republic: Developing the Federal Government, 1791–1861*. Lawrence: University of Kansas Press.

Farhang, Sean, and Ira Katznelson. 2005. "The Southern Imposition: Congress and Labor in the New Deal and Fair Deal." *Studies in American Political Development* 19, no. 1: 1–30.

Finkelman, Paul. 1996. *Slavery and the Founders: Race and Liberty in the Age of Jefferson*. Armonk, NY: M. E. Sharpe.

Fogel, Robert William, and Stanley L. Engerman. 1974. *Time on the Cross: The Economics of American Negro Slavery*. New York: W. W. Norton.

Fourcade, Marion, and Kieren Healy. 2017. "Seeing Like a Market." *Socio-Economic Review* 15, no. 1: 9–29.

Fouka, Vasiliki, Soumyajit Mazumder, and Marco Tabellini. 2021. "From Immigrants to Americans: Race and Assimilation during the Great Migration." Harvard Business School BGIE Unit Working Paper 19-018.

Francis, Megan Ming. 2014. *Civil Rights and the Making of the Modern American State*. Cambridge: Cambridge University Press.

Francis, Megan Ming. 2019. "The Price of Civil Rights: Black Lives, White Funding, and Movement Capture." *Law & Society Review* 53, no. 1: 275–309.

Freund, David M. P. 2010. *Colored Property: State Policy and White Racial Politics in Suburban America*. Chicago: University of Chicago Press.

Frymer, Paul. 2005. "Racism Revised: Courts, Labor Law, and the Institutional Construction of Racial Animus." *American Political Science Review* 99, no. 3: 373–87.

Frymer, Paul. 2017. *Building an American Empire: The Era of Territorial and Political Expansion*. Princeton, NJ: Princeton University Press.

Frymer, Paul, and Jake Grumbach. 2021. "Labor Unions and White Racial Politics." *American Journal of Political Science* 65, no. 1: 225–40.

Gilmore, Ruth Wilson. 2007. *Golden Gulag: Prisons, Surplus, Crisis, and Opposition in Globalizing California*. Berkeley: University of California Press.

Glaeser, Edward L. "The political economy of hatred." *The Quarterly Journal of Economics* 120, no. 1 (2005): 45–86.

Grant, Nancy L. 1990. *The TVA and Black Americans*. Philadelphia: Temple University Press.

Hall, Andrew B., Connor Huff, and Shiro Kuriwaki. 2019. "Wealth, Slaveownership, and Fighting for the Confederacy: An Empirical Study of the American Civil War." *American Political Science Review* 113, no. 3: 658–73.

Hamilton, Darrick, and William Darity Jr. 2010. "Can 'Baby Bonds' Eliminate the Racial Wealth Gap in Putative Post-Racial America?" *Review of Black Political Economy* 37, no. 3–4: 207–16.

Handlin, Oscar, and Mary F. Handlin. 1950. "Origins of the Southern Labor System." *William and Mary Quarterly* 7, no. 2: 199–222.

Harris, Angela. 2021. "Foreword." In *Histories of Racial Capitalism*, ed. Justin Leroy and Destin Jenkins, vii–xxii. New York: Columbia University Press.

Harris, Donald. 1972. "The Black Ghetto as Colony: A Theoretical Critique and Alternative Formulation." *Review of Black Political Economy* 2, no. 4: 3–33.

Harris, Marvin, Josildeth Gomes Consorte, Joseph Lang, and Bryan Byrne. 1993. "Who Are the Whites? Imposed Census Categories and the Racial Demography of Brazil." *Social Forces* 72, no. 2: 451–62.

Harvey, Anna, and Emily A. West. 2020. "Discrimination in Public Accommodations." *Political Science Research and Methods* 8, no. 4: 597–613.

Heersink, Boris, and Jeffery A. Jenkins. 2020. *Republican Party Politics and the American South, 1865–1968*. Cambridge: Cambridge University Press.

Higgs, Robert. 1977. "Firm-Specific Evidence on Racial Wage Differentials and Workforce Segregation." *American Economic Review* 67, no. 2: 236–45.

Higgs, Robert. 1982. "Accumulation of Property by Southern Blacks before World War I." *American Economic Review* 72, no. 4: 725–37.

Holton, Woody. 1999. *Forced Founders: Indians, Debtors, Slaves, and the Making of the American Revolution in Virginia*. Chapel Hill: University of North Carolina Press.

Honey, Michael K. 1993. *Southern Labor and Black Civil Rights: Organizing Memphis Workers*. Urbana: University of Illinois Press.

Hyman, Louis. 2011. *Debtor Nation*. Princeton, NJ: Princeton University Press.

Jacobson, Matthew Frye. 1999. *Whiteness of a Different Color*. Cambridge, MA: Harvard University Press.

Jenkins, Destin. 2021. *The Bonds of Inequality*. Chicago: University of Chicago Press.

Jenkins, Jeffery A., and Justin Peck. 2021. *Congress and the First Civil Rights Era, 1861–1918*. Chicago: University of Chicago Press.

Johnson, Kimberley S. 2007. *Governing the American State: Congress and the New Federalism, 1877–1929*. Princeton, NJ: Princeton University Press.

Johnson, Kimberley. 2010. *Reforming Jim Crow: Southern Politics and State in the Age before Brown*. New York: Oxford University Press.

Johnson, Kimberley S. 2011. "Racial Orders, Congress, and the Agricultural Welfare State, 1865–1940." *Studies in American Political Development* 25, no. 2: 143–61.

Jones, Daniel B., Werner Troesken, and Randall Walsh. 2017. "Political Participation in a Violent Society: The Impact of Lynching on Voter Turnout in the Post-Reconstruction South." *Journal of Development Economics* 129: 29–46.

Kalmoe, Nathan P. 2020. *With Ballots and Bullets: Partisanship and Violence in the American Civil War*. Cambridge: Cambridge University Press.

Katznelson, Ira. 2013. *Fear Itself: The New Deal and the Origins of Our Time*. New York: W. W. Norton.

Keele, Luke, William Cubbison, and Ismail White. 2021. "Suppressing Black Votes: A Historical Case Study of Voting Restrictions in Louisiana." *American Political Science Review* 115, no. 2: 694–700.

Kermani, Amir, and Francis Wong. 2021. *Racial Disparities in Housing Returns.* No. w29306. Cambridge, MA: National Bureau of Economic Research.

Key, Valdimer O. 1949. Southern politics in state and nation. New York: AA Knopf.

King, Desmond S., and Rogers M. Smith. 2012. *Still a House Divided: Race and Politics in Obama's America.* Princeton, NJ: Princeton University Press.

Kousser, J. Morgan. 1974. *The Shaping of Southern Politics: Suffrage Restrictions and the Establishment of the One-Party South, 1880–1910.* New Haven, CT: Yale University Press.

Kranton, Rachel E. 2016. "Identity Economics 2016: Where Do Social Distinctions and Norms Come From?" *American Economic Review* 106, no. 5: 405–9.

Kruse, Kevin M. 2013. *White Flight.* Princeton, NJ: Princeton University Press.

Laird, Chryl. 2019. "Black Like Me: How Political Communication Changes Racial Group Identification and Its Implications." *Politics, Groups, and Identities* 7, no. 2: 324–46.

Lichtenstein, Alex. 1996. *Twice the Work of Free Labor: The Political Economy of Convict Labor in the New South.* New York: Verso.

Lieberman, Evan S. 2003. *Race and Regionalism in the Politics of Taxation in Brazil and South Africa.* Cambridge: Cambridge University Press.

Lieberman, Robert C. 1994. "The Freedman's Bureau and the Politics of Institutional Structure." *Social Science History* 18, no. 3: 405–37.

Lieberman, Robert C. 1998. *Shifting the Color Line: Race and the American Welfare State.* Cambridge, MA: Harvard University Press.

Logan, Trevon D. 2020. "Do Black Politicians Matter? Evidence from Reconstruction." *Journal of Economic History* 80, no. 1: 1–37.

Logue, L. M., and P. D. Blanck. 2010. *Race, Ethnicity and Disability: Veterans and Benefits in Post–Civil War America.* New York: Cambridge University Press.

Marable, Manning. 1983. *How Capitalism Underdeveloped Black America: Problems in Race, Political Economy and Society.* Boston: South End Press.

Margo, Robert A. 1990. *Race and Schooling in the South, 1880–1950: An Economic History.* Chicago: University of Chicago Press.

Mazumder, Soumyajit. 2021. "Old South, New Deal: How the Legacy of Slavery Undermined the New Deal." *Journal of Historical Political Economy* 1, no. 3: 447–75.

Michener, Jamila. 2019. "Policy Feedback in a Racialized Polity." *Policy Studies Journal* 47, no. 2: 423–50.

Michener, Jamila, Mallory SoRelle, and Chloe Thurston. 2022. "From the Margins to the Center: A Bottom-Up Approach to Welfare State Scholarship." *Perspectives on Politics* 20, no. 1: 154–69.

Mickey, Robert. 2015. *Paths out of Dixie: The Democratization of Authoritarian Enclaves in America's Deep South, 1944–1972.* Princeton, NJ: Princeton University Press.

Morgan, Edmund S. 1975. *American Slavery, American Freedom: The Ordeal of Colonial Virginia.* New York: W. W. Norton.

Muhammad, Khalil Gibran. 2019. *The Condemnation of Blackness: Race, Crime, and the Making of Modern Urban America.* Cambridge, MA: Harvard University Press.

Muller, Christopher. 2018. "Freedom and Convict Leasing in the Postbellum South." *American Journal of Sociology* 124, no. 2: 367–405.

Naidu, Suresh. 2010. "Recruitment Restrictions and Labor Markets: Evidence from the Postbellum South." *Journal of Labor Economics* 28, no. 2: 413–45.

Naidu, Suresh. 2012. *Suffrage, Schooling, and Sorting in the Post-bellum US South.* No. w18129. Cambridge: National Bureau of Economic Research.

Nobles, Melissa. 2000. *Shades of Citizenship: Race and the Census in Modern Politics*. Redwood City, CA: Stanford University Press.

Olmstead, Alan L., and Paul W. Rhode. 2018. "Cotton, Slavery, and the New History of Capitalism." *Explorations in Economic History* 67, no. 1: 1–17.

Omi, M., and H. Winant. 2014 [1986]. *Racial Formation in the United States*. New York: Routledge.

Ottinger, Sebastian, and Max Winkler. 2022. *The Political Economy of Propaganda: Evidence from US Newspapers*. Working Paper. IZA DP No. 15078. Bonn: Institute of Labor Economics.

Pattillo, Mary, Bruce Western, and David Weiman, eds. 2004. *Imprisoning America: The Social Effects of Mass Incarceration*. New York: Russell Sage Foundation.

Pettit, Becky. 2012. *Invisible Men: Mass Incarceration and the Myth of Black Progress*. New York: Russell Sage Foundation.

Pope, Jeremy C., and Shawn Treier. 2011. "Reconsidering the Great Compromise at the Federal Convention of 1787: Deliberation and Agenda Effects on the Senate and Slavery." *American Journal of Political Science* 55, no. 2: 289–306.

Poulos, Jason., 2021. "Amnesty Policy and Elite Persistence in the Postbellum South: Evidence from a Regression Discontinuity Design." *Journal of Historical Political Economy* 1, no. 3: 353–75.

Prowse, Gwen, Vesla Weaver, and Tracey Meares. 2020. "The State from Below: Distorted Responsiveness in Policed Communities." *Urban Affairs Review* 56, no. 5: 1423–71.

Ransom, Roger L., and Richard Sutch. 2001 [1977]. *One Kind of Freedom: The Economic Consequences of Emancipation*. Cambridge: Cambridge University Press.

Raphael, Steven. 2002. "Anatomy of 'The Anatomy of Racial Inequality.'" *Journal of Economic Literature* 40, no. 4: 1202–14.

Reed, Adolph. 2002. "Unraveling the Relation of Race and Class in American Politics." *Political Power and Social Theory* 15: 265–74.

Roback, Jennifer. 1986. "The Political Economy of Segregation: The Case of Segregated Streetcars." *Journal of Economic History* 46, no. 4: 893–917.

Robinson, Cedric. 2000 [1983]. *Black Marxism: The Making of the Black Radical Tradition*. Chapel Hill: University of North Carolina Press.

Rogers, Reuel, and Jae Yeon Kim. 2023. "Rewiring Linked Fate: Bringing Back History, Agency, and Power." *Perspectives on Politics* 21, no. 1: 288–301.

Rosenthal, Aaron. 2021. "Submerged for Some? Government Visibility, Race, and American Political Trust." *Perspectives on Politics* 19, no. 4: 1098–114.

Rosenthal, Caitlin. 2018. *Accounting for Slavery: Masters and Management*. Cambridge, MA: Harvard University Press.

Saltzstein, Grace Hall. 1989. "Black Mayors and Police Policies." *Journal of Politics* 51, no. 3: 525–44.

Saperstein, Aliya, and Andrew M. Penner. 2012. "Racial Fluidity and Inequality in the United States." *American Journal of Sociology* 118, no. 3: 676–727.

Schickler, Eric. 2016. *Racial Realignment: The Transformation of American Liberalism, 1932–1965*. Princeton, NJ: Princeton University Press.

Sen, Maya, and Omar Wasow. 2016. "Race as a Bundle of Sticks: Designs That Estimate Effects of Seemingly Immutable Characteristics." *Annual Review of Political Science* 19, no. 1: 499–522.

Shayo, Moses. 2009. "A Model of Social Identity with an Application to Political Economy: Nation, Class, and Redistribution." *American Political Science Review* 103, no. 2: 147–74.

Småg, Mattias. 2016. "Doing Violence, Making Race: Southern Lynching and White Racial Group Formation." *American Journal of Sociology* 121, no. 5: 1329–74.

Smith, James P. 1984. "Race and Human Capital." *American Economic Review* 74, no. 4: 685–98.
Soss, Joe, and Vesla Weaver. 2017. "Police Are Our Government: Politics, Political Science, and the Policing of Race-Class Subjugated Communities." *Annual Review of Political Science* 20: 565–91.
Soule, Sarah A. 1992. "Populism and Black Lynching in Georgia, 1890–1900." *Social Forces* 71, no. 2: 431–49.
Spence, Lester K., Harwood K. McClerking, and Robert Brown. 2009. "Revisiting Black Incorporation and Local Political Participation." *Urban Affairs Review* 45, no. 2: 274–85.
Stewart, Megan, and Karin Kitchens. 2021. "Social Transformation and Violence: Evidence from US Reconstruction." *Comparative Political Studies* 54, no. 1: 1939–83.
Sundstrom, William A. 2007. "The Geography of Wage Discrimination in the Pre–Civil Rights South." *Journal of Economic History* 67, no. 2: 410–44.
Suryanarayan, Pavithra, and Steven White. 2021. "Slavery, Reconstruction, and Bureaucratic Capacity in the American South." *American Political Science Review* 115: 568–84.
Taylor, Keeanga-Yamattah. 2019. *Race for Profit*. Chapel Hill: University of North Carolina Press.
Telles, Edward E. 2004. *Race in Another America: The Significance of Skin Color in Brazil*. Princeton, NJ: Princeton University Press.
Thompson, Debra. 2016. *The Schematic State*. Cambridge: Cambridge University Press.
Thurston, Chloe. 2018. *At the Boundaries of Homeownership: Credit, Discrimination, and the American State*. New York: Cambridge University Press.
Trounstine, Jessica. 2018. *Segregation by Design: Local Politics and Inequality in American Cities*. Cambridge: Cambridge University Press.
Turner, Sarah, and John Bound. 2003. "Closing the Gap or Widening the Divide: The Effects of the G.I. Bill and World War II on the Educational Outcomes of Black Americans." *Journal of Economic History* 63: 145–77.
Valelly, Richard M. 2004. *The Two Reconstructions: The Struggle for Black Enfranchisement*. Chicago: University of Chicago Press.
Villarreal, Andrés, and Stanley R. Bailey. 2020. "The Endogeneity of Race: Black Racial Identification and Men's Earnings in Mexico." *Social Forces* 98, no. 4: 1744–72.
Walton, Hanes, Jr., Sherman C. Puckett, and Donald R. Deskins Jr. 2012. *The African-American Electorate: A Statistical History*. Thousand Oaks, CA: CQ Press.
Weaver, Michael. 2019. "'Judge Lynch' in the Court of Public Opinion: Publicity and the De-Legitimization of Lynching." *American Political Science Review* 113, no. 2: 293–310.
Wiggins, Benjamin. 2020. *Calculating Race: Racial Discrimination in Risk Assessment*. New York: Oxford University Press.
Williams, Eric. 1944. *Capitalism and Slavery*. Chapel Hill: University of North Carolina Press.
Wright, Gavin. 2013. *Sharing the Prize: The Economics of the Civil Rights Revolution in the American South*. Cambridge, MA: Belknap Press of Harvard University Press.
Zaw, Khaing, Darrick Hamilton, and William Darity. 2016. "Race, Wealth and Incarceration: Results from the National Longitudinal Survey of Youth." *Race and Social Problems* 8, no. 1: 103–15.
Zuberi, Tukufu. 2001. *Thicker Than Blood: How Racial Statistics Lie*. Minneapolis: University of Minnesota Press.

CHAPTER 36

IN SEARCH OF GENDER IN HISTORICAL POLITICAL ECONOMY

DAWN L. TEELE AND PAULINE A. GROSJEAN

THE historical turn that has, in recent years, galvanized much of political economy has also begun to percolate in the study of gender. Yet the issue of gender itself—of the social construction of value and meaning that echoes and distills centuries of inequality related to sex differentiation—presents a primary challenge for scholars in this field. The gender trouble is fundamental. It has influenced the process of record keeping, including whether the activities and desires of people from different sexes have been recorded throughout history; it has influenced the process of measurement, including how the formal and nonformal economic and political activities of men and women have been conceptualized and counted; it has influenced the scholarly record, including whether the promulgations and behavior of people other than men have been studied; it has influenced the primitives of formal models, informing the priorities and decision rules of supposedly representative agents; and it has influenced theoretical paradigms, including which types of argument draw the most attention and which ideas about human society resonate.

Scholars interested in the historical political economy of gender are tasked with two missions: fact-finding and theoretical innovation. Fact-finding is archaeological; in this step, scholars must dig into old sources and locate new repositories to uncover when, where, and why economic and political activities were mischaracterized due to gender bias. In fact-finding, we can discover how the very categories of men and women were constructed and reinforced by politics and economics, and how these categorizations reinforced the power of men over women in most societies. The second task is theoretical innovation; in this step, researchers must reveal to other scholars how the fact that most analyses and models of political economy took men as the basis for elaboration misses fundamental features of social and political life.[1] The study of gender in historical political economy (HPE) is therefore about much more than the study of what women or men did in the past; it is about how sex categorizations—and the way they are imbued in our data, our sources, our assumptions, our models, and our research questions—threaten to undermine the scholarly pursuit of truth.

The large and growing quantitative literature in the historical political economy of gender, which we review in this essay, has engaged vigorously with the fact-finding imperative. Scholars have combed through old records, considered standards of measurement and habits of assignment, and discovered creative new ways to expose the economic and political behavior of groups thought to be outside history (Branch 2011; Corder and Wolbrecht 2016; Morgan 2006; Ogilvie 2003; Sanday 1981). And some scholarship has made headway in the realm of theoretical innovation, revealing how canonical models of labor market choices, political power, and regime change and democratization have been stymied by theoretical frameworks that ignore gendered power and are based solely on the male experience (Adams 2005; Branch 2011; Goldin 1994; Iversen and Rosenbluth 2010; Teele 2018a). Yet the theoretical initiatives that have transformed the study of gender in cognate fields, such as sociology, anthropology, legal studies, and even international relations—which emphasize the position and roles of Brown and Black women (the study of intersectionality), and which focus more on analyses of masculinity and gender norms—have not yet become commonplace in the historical political economy of gender.[2] The literature is also much more developed in the context of historical Europe than other parts of the world.

The omissions hitherto are partly explained by the difficulty of uncovering facts. Though local parishes would keep records of births, marriages, and deaths, wide-scale aggregation of human data was a project of state formation and consolidation and was uncommon before the nineteenth century.[3] Not until the United Nations began its own efforts at measurement and data collection did most high-quality comparative data emerge. Today, new digitization efforts, combined with vast computing power and greater visibility of archival materials online, has opened new terrain for scholars of gender and power. Difficulties persist, however, and overcoming them requires new methods and new sources of data. For example, analyses of social and economic mobility in the long run are based on linking individuals across censuses, tax, and inheritance records based on names. Because they change names at marriage, women literally vanish from those records and hence can be impossible to trace in those studies. As scholars break into emerging sources of data and uncover new formations of political and economic activity in the past, we urge, and suspect, that the synthetic and creative exercise of theoretical revision will play a larger role in the study of gender in HPE. We conclude with a call for this paradigmatic shift.

Theoretical Paradigms

As scholars of political economy, we are interested in research that grounds political behavior and economic outcomes with reference to constraints, strategies, and incentives faced by individuals or groups of actors. As scholars of gender, we are interested in how power relations differ based on one's position relative to institutions, and access to the means of production in local, national, and global contexts. The theoretical paradigms that lurk in the background of scholarship on gender and power relations in the past are the Marxist and the human capital approach. Since the 1980s, the vigorous feminist responses to those theories have focused on how institutions and bargaining power influence gender equality, which we term the institutional approach to gender equality. We outline these three theoretical approaches before turning to the empirical literature.

The Marxist approach, articulated first by Friedrich Engels (2010 [1884]) in *The Origin of the Family, Private Property, and the State*, argued that women's inequality is a result of capitalist development. Pointing to the elevated position of women in certain noncapitalist communities, such as the Haudenosaunee (known to colonists as Iroquois) prior to colonization, Engels argued that the process of primitive accumulation that began first with herding, then with fiat money, and reached a pinnacle with the decline of the commons and land enclosures—and was always, as he points out in the case of ancient Greece, bolstered by slavery—allowed men to amass resources under their own names. A desire to build intergenerational wealth drove men to seek certainty in paternity, spurring the rise of monogamous marriage (which Engels noted wryly, and rightly, was really only monogamy for women). Capital accumulation, even prior to industrialization, precipitated the collapse of "mother right" and matrilineal family formations (where children were understood to belong to their mothers' clan and land passed on the female line) and ultimately led to the world historic overthrow of the female sex.*

The human capital approach, in contrast, sought to explain outcomes such as women's lower labor force participation and women's lower earnings as the result of a rational process of family and firm maximization.[4] In this approach, family units act like firms, so that, within the family, even small individual differences in productive endowments (i.e., women's ability to bear children) could lead "rational" (utility maximizing) family units to choose men's specialization in the market and women's specialization in the home. Within firms, the very fact of reproductive differences, which might cause women to take time out of the labor market during childbearing years, make women employees a riskier prospect, rendering them less worthy of investment (e.g., training opportunities), advancement, and remuneration than men. This approach, formalized by Gary Becker's (1981) *A Treatise on the Family*, finds that specialization of men in the market and women in the home is the equilibrium outcome chosen by rational, cooperative family units.

Grappling with two sets of facts—that women's status under state-directed socialism has also tended toward patriarchal arrangements, and that households in capitalist

---

* For other accounts of women's power in noncapitalist socieites and early democracies, see Brulé 2023 and Stasavage 2020.

societies are not necessarily cooperative organizations that maximize all members' utility—many feminist scholars pushed back against the Marxist and human capital approaches. Marxist feminists showed how Marxist scholarship missed the exploitation of women's labor in the home (Hartmann 1976; Folbre 1982). A host of scholarship considered gender egalitarianism in nonmarket societies (Leacock 1987; Sanday 1981 Brulé 2023) revealing how women's position, their social "adulthood," could vary with sex-based division of tasks and the nature of trade (Sacks 1974). And many sought to show how not only capitalist systems (MacKinnon 1982), but also state-directed socialist projects (Molyneux 1985), were based on male dominance.

The institutional approach forged a reproachment between the Marxist and the human capital accounts of gender inequality. Without jettisoning political economy models of the household, scholars working in the institutional tradition augmented models to think more seriously about bargaining power within the family (Iversen and Rosenbluth 2010; Goldstein and Udry 2008; Goldin 1994; Ogilvie 2003). Institutions—states, markets, firms, universities, churches, militaries, the police, and even the family—constrain and incentivize behavior in distinctive ways. Women and men will behave differently based on how their societies structure gender relations (Kandiyoti 1988). In this framework, institutions confer or capture the power of people with different sexed and gendered bodies, and in so doing, they influence bargaining power in the home and women's economic and political behavior thereafter. The goal of this new branch of research was often to show how different institutional configurations and "outside options" influence women's bargaining power, helping to explain variation in policies, participation, and welfare related to women and families.

If institutions and bargaining power are crucial for understanding economic and political power and gender inequality, the question naturally arises as to how they persist and how they change. Most political economists of gender orient themselves toward these questions of change, asking how major historical events have transformed gender relations, or tracing how institutional, technological, or cultural legacies inform the current state of gender relations.[5] In each area we describe prior research and point to open questions. We conclude the essay by outlining future directions for this dynamic area of scholarship.

Major Historical Events and Gendered Power Relations

Major historical events, sometimes called "critical junctures," are the focal point of a large body of political economy research on gender. This research can be further classified into work that looks at epochal shifts in the economy and how they influence women's power, and the causes and consequences of major institutional changes for women's social and economic position.

Epochal Shifts, Women in the Economy, and Women's Welfare

A primary macro-theoretical question driving research on epochal shifts in the economy asks whether economic development promotes women's empowerment or has an uneven effect on women's status. Epochal shifts such as the Neolithic Revolution—which scholars have suggested brought a transformation for some societies from hunting or gathering toward settled agricultural practice (but see Graeber and Wengrow 2021)—or the Industrial Revolution—which mechanized agriculture and ushered in new divisions of labor and modes of production, and new social class arrangements—are believed to have augmented the types of tasks performed by men and women and thereby shifted social and economic power among the sexes. For example, accounts of why the transition to sedentary agriculture might have empowered men vis-à-vis women suggest that early technological innovations, like the plow, required strength and became part of men's domain (Alesina, Giuliano, and Nunn 2011), and that this division reinforced men's power in the household.[6] Other research argues that gender-based comparative advantage might depend on ecology[7] and on earlier technological innovations (see e.g., BenYishay, Grosjean, and Vecci (2017) and Haas et al. (2020)).[8]

While much of this literature seeks to simplify the causes of women's inequality, anthropological and archaeological evidence suggests more diversity than we might have suspected (Graeber and Wengrow 2021). For example, drawing on the General Social Survey (GSS), Sanday (1981) shows that although hunting societies tended to oppress women more than gathering societies, the nature and degree of gender specialization in agriculture—whether related to who did the sowing, minded animals, or even used the plow—could vary substantially across locations. In a magisterial study of early-modern Germany, Sheilagh Ogilvie (2003) also shows considerable differences in the gender allocation of tasks, even among parishes in the same region. And Esther Boserup, the economist who first studied the interactions between agricultural intensification and socioeconomic transformation, argued that causality ran in the opposite direction: that agricultural intensification *followed* from "increasing population or ... the compulsion of a social hierarchy" (Boserup 1965, 54). Notwithstanding several compelling studies that argue for a causal relationship between the adoption or intensification of agriculture to the sexual division of labor (Alesina, Giuliano, and Nunn 2011; Hansen, Jensen, and Skovsgaard 2015), the relationship is highly complex, and systemic shifts may have been related to preexisting power dynamics.

The next epochal shift that has received extensive attention is the Industrial Revolution.[9] The late eighteenth and nineteenth centuries brings more opportunities for extensive econometric work because governmental data collection became more common.[10] Work on women's economic activity in the nineteenth century tries to understand the role of women's market and nonmarket economic activity in promoting changes in national income, the causes of the fertility transition in the late nineteenth century, and the ways that laws governing property within the family impacted women's economic productivity. Research argues that women's labor was much more important for the Industrial Revolution than has been acknowledged. Looking at the U.S. census of manufactures for the Northeast, Goldin and Sokoloff (1982) argue that women's labor was fundamental to the manufacturing labor force in the United States. Because of high relative wages for men in agricultural work (hay and dairy), manufacturing firms substituted women's (and children's) labor for men's. In 1840, women's labor was at its peak, representing about 32 percent of the industrial workforce.[11]

If women were highly active in the United States' labor force in the middle of the nineteenth century, when economic growth was lower than in the twentieth, and women were less active in the labor force immediately after World War II, even though growth was robust, this suggests a non-monotonic relationship between economic development and women's empowerment. Goldin (1995) argues that in intermediate stages of development, housewives become a status marker for the middle classes, which helps to explain a U shape in women's labor force participation over the last two hundred years. Yet Goldin's work, and that of Khan (1996) and Fernández (2014), acknowledge the legal barriers to women's participation into the twentieth century, including laws that limited women's ability to take out patents (Khan 1996), to be sole proprietors of businesses, to contract freely, to retain their wages in marriage (Skocpol 1992), to control their property, and, in some cases, to keep jobs upon becoming married or pregnant ("marriage bars") (see also Wikander, Kessler-Harris, and Lewis [1995] and Stewart 1989). Many of these restrictions, like that on married women's right to control property, were dismantled in the late nineteenth century, which again points to a positive correlation between women's rights and development (Fernández 2014). Yet the fact that many of these restrictions on women's political and economic activity were put into place during the eighteenth century—for example, by the diffusion of the French civil code to much of Europe and the Americas (Tudor 2022)—vitiates any simple story about the relationship between gender equality and development.[12]

Crucially, neither the macro theories nor the careful individual country or industry studies have adequately grappled with the interaction between wealth accumulation in industrializing countries, or accumulation within upwardly mobile segments of the working classes, and the welfare of women in primary goods–producing locales or in areas dominated by slavery. If the rise of women's relative wages in the global North was enabled through a constant supply of (coerced) cheap primary goods coming from the South, then the improvement of livelihoods, and even bargaining power in one region, was predicated on the subordination of women in another region. The example of slavery highlights the important role that institutions play in women's welfare (Roberts 1997) and underlines the argument that the Marxist or human capital approaches may miss key features of economic systems that are detrimental to the welfare of many, or even most, women. Though many historians, feminist theorists, and sociologists have pointed out the interlinkages between economic systems (and across nation states) during industrialization (e.g., Jones-Rogers 2019), no quantitative studies credibly demonstrate how the ascent of some groups of women depended on the immiseration of others. Clearly this is an important area for future inquiry.

Institutional Transformation, Women's Mobilization, and Political Power

Political scientists have taken up the question of the transformation in women's political power, asking how and when women exercise political agency (Corder and Wolbrecht 2016; Morgan 2006; Teele 2018a), and what impact women's agency in the past had on policies that support women's full participation in political and economic life (Lewis 1997; Sainsbury 1996). Some research examines women's contributions to early social movements, such as the fight to abolish slavery in the United States, showing how activism in another arena contributed to activism in the realm of women's suffrage (Carpenter and Moore 2014). Other research shows how some segments of American women were even more successful in attaining legislative reforms in the pre-suffrage era than they were thereafter. Writing about middle-class clubwomen, Skocpol argues that their unique nonpartisan, moralistic politics, which embraced the ideology of separate spheres, allowed them to leverage political connections and attract male allies in the service of legislation (like limiting women's working hours) that satisfied bourgeois sensibilities (Skocpol 1992, 319). After suffrage, politically active American women faced the same constraints and incentives as other U.S. citizens subject to party politics.

Considerable attention has been paid to understanding the causes and consequences of women's suffrage. The literature on franchise expansion in political economy has focused on the distributional consequences of suffrage expansion for the lower classes (implicitly, working-class men) and tended to see women's suffrage as a consequence of inevitable cultural change with rising income (see Hanlon XX, this volume). Political scientists have argued, instead, that legislative and partisan incentives are crucial for understanding the timing of women's suffrage reform, especially during the first wave of democratization from 1848 to 1920 (Teele 2018a; Przeworski 2009; Barnes 2020). Women's agency is crucial to the politics of suffrage, both because the strategies they pursue as activists inform the nature of women's voting behavior after suffrage (Skorge 2021; Morgan Collins 2021), and because politicians look to suffrage mobilization when deciding whether to extend the vote in the first place (Teele 2018b). While the suffrage movement is often thought of as an indication of women's demand for rights, Teele (2018a) argues that suffragists were strategic in a larger sense: sometimes they actively chose not to pursue broad movements because they feared the downstream consequences associated with *all* women having voting rights. To date there are few high-quality measures of women's political activism for suffrage, and more research is needed to understand the degree to which countries' movement sizes varied based on the strategic electoral incentives faced by women from specific socioeconomic groups.

Scholars disagree about the degree to which women's suffrage changed electoral politics writ large, that is, whether women as voters impacted the partisan distribution of legislatures after suffrage. Analyzing electoral politics in the US South after suffrage, Schuyler (2006) argues that southern white women were important lobbyists in the area of health, education, and moral reform, but notes that most supported the maintenance of Jim Crow policies. The impact of women voters on election outcomes is less obvious. A major recent work on the United States argues that women made more or less similar choices at the ballot box as men (albeit with lower inclinations to support fringe or third parties) (Corder and Wolbrecht 2016), findings that echo earlier research on the state of New York (Harvey 1996). Yet Morgan-Collins (2021) shows that politicians who were unfriendly to suffragist-supported progressive causes were more likely to lose their seats after suffrage was extended in the United States.

A key challenge for understanding women's post-suffrage vote choice stems from a problem known as "ecological inference"; because the ballot is secret, we have to estimate group-level behavior from aggregate electoral results. New scholarship seeks to probe these issues using fine-grained local data on women's turnout and electoral outcomes. For example, in the Scandinavian context, Teele (2022) shows that given the way that political geography correlates with partisan performance across space—and the fact that cities were more left-leaning—women in cities had to have been more liberal than women in the countryside. Future research should refine the techniques and levels of analysis employed in the study of women's vote choice.

Thanks to the fact that a host of countries recorded voter eligibility and participation separately across the sexes, the study of women's political participation is much more robust than that of vote choice. A growing body of evidence shows how women's post-suffrage participation hinged fundamentally on the electoral institutions in place when women attained voting rights. Focusing on municipal elections in Norway, Skorge (2021) shows that women's political mobilization—measured by women's petitioning activity—prior to suffrage is a good predictor of women's share of turnout after the vote was extended. He further demonstrates that this relationship is more robust in municipalities that adopted proportional electoral rules prior to a national Proportional Representation reform in 1919. Kim (2019) shows that women participated at higher rates in municipalities that used direct democratic procedures for local governance as opposed to those that utilized representative institutions. Future research should examine the degree to which the electoral rules in place at the time of suffrage impacted other variables besides turnout.

Unlike the literature on the electoral impact of women's suffrage, the cross-national literature on the impact of women's suffrage on human development and fiscal outcomes has been unequivocal: women's suffrage changed economic policies in a variety of ways.[13] Bromhead (2018) studies thirty countries from 1919 to 1939 (two-thirds are from Europe), showing that tariffs increased by around two percentage points on average after women secured voting rights.[14] He believes, and has some archival evidence showing, that this is due to women's preferences for higher tariffs, and to their mobilization by labor and various clubs in the interwar United States and United Kingdom. Bertocchi (2011), in a study of twenty-two countries, mostly from Europe, shows how women's suffrage had a positive effect on government pensions and health expenditures, as a share of GDP, even while the size of government spending remained unchanged. Similarly, Aidt and Dallal (2008) estimate that suffrage was immediately followed by an increase in spending on collective goods, with the long-run effect being more than 3 percent of GDP.[15] More research is needed to understand the micro-level processes that gave way to these macro-level correlations.

Finally, in the legislative realm, Moehling and Thomasson (2012) argue that the United States' Sheppard-Towner Act of 1921, which sought the promotion of welfare and hygiene for mothers and infants, was adopted right after the Nineteenth Amendment, when the threat of women's electoral backlash seemed greatest, yet ten years later it was dropped. The authors argue that upon learning that women did not vote as a bloc, politicians were able to vote with their wallets and shut down the program. Although the research on women's turnout is beginning to accumulate (Skorge 2021; Teele 2022), comparative knowledge of women's participation after suffrage, such as the effect of women's suffrage in the legislative realm, has been less well studied and is an area where more research is needed.

HISTORICAL LEGACIES AND GENDER EQUALITY IN THE PRESENT

A second common approach in the historical political economy of gender examines the historical roots of gender inequality. In some areas, such as education, women and girls have made unequivocal progress. Indeed, in most advanced democracies, and generally in most countries with high average levels of education, women have overtaken men in tertiary education, a phenomenon that occurred in the United States and Western Europe as early as 1980. Women's attachment to the labor force has also risen, spurred in part by the removal of bans on married women remaining in the labor force, the diffusion of contraception (Goldin and Katz 2002), and the introduction of maternity leave provisions and early childhood care (Morgan 2006; Olivetti and Petrongolo 2017). Nevertheless, these transformations sit side by side with gender inequality as a persistent reality today.[16] As a result, there has been growing interest in understanding why gender inequality persists, and why there is so much variation across countries, regions, and groups in the position of women. Two major strains of research deal with persistence. The first looks at historical shocks—for example, to prices, relative wages, or sex ratios in the population—tracking the relationship between these shocks and long-term development outcomes. The second looks to the realm of culture and the intergenerational transmission of values to understand the reproduction of inequality across social groups.

Technology, Demography, and Development Outcomes

The first set of studies focused on how shocks to commodity prices, and "sex-biased" technological changes—innovations that change the relative importance of men's and women's labor—can leave a long-lasting imprint on cultural norms and gender gaps. For example, the "cotton revolution" in China (1300–1840 CE) increased revenues in the textile industry and the demand for women's weaving. This led to a range of economic benefits for women and durably changed norms and attitudes toward women. After the cotton revolution, female breadwinning and industrial employment became more common; dowry use declined; and the sex ratio become more balanced, suggesting a weakening of historically male-biased parental preferences (Xue 2016). Following Mao's economic reforms in the twentieth century, and a boom in the tea industry, women's relative incomes rose in China's tea-producing regions because women's labor was essential for harvesting the export crop. This led to educational gains for all children, improvements in girls' survival, and less biased sex ratios (Qian 2008).

A series of papers show how the Neolithic Revolution, and particularly the use of the plow, continue to be correlated with present-day women's labor force participation, women's participation in politics, parental preference for boys, and norms guiding socially accepted behavior of women (Alesina, Giuliano, and Nunn 2011; Hansen, Jensen, and Skovsgaard 2015). The hypothesized mechanism of persistence relies on an internalization of sex-biased historical economic specialization as cultural norms of economic and social behavior, habits, and rules of thumb (similar to the sociological notion of *habitus* developed by, e.g., Bourdieu 1980). Given sex-based specialization in economic production, further sex-biased technological advances or relative commodity price fluctuations can alter or reinforce the dynamics of gendered economic specialization and gender norms.

Researchers have also examined the long-term legacy of sex-biased demographic shocks, that is, historical events that transform the ratio of men to women. Sex-biased demographic shocks can alter not only sex-specific economic specialization but also the conditions of household bargaining. For example, large-scale conflicts can create a deficit of men. This not only pushes women to substitute for men in the labor force, but also changes the conditions of the marriage market and household dynamics that should benefit the short side of the market. In France, the scarcity of men due to World War I and its 1.4 million military fatalities initially enabled men to "marry up" (Abramitzky, Delavande, and Vasconcelos 2011) and generated an upward shift in female labor force participation that has persisted until today (Gay 2019; Boehnke and Gay 2020). Teso (2019) documents similar long-term consequences on female labor force participation of a different historical shock that also created a deficit of men: the slave trade out of Africa. Grosjean and Khattar 2019 rely on the convict colonization of Australia in the beginning of the nineteenth century to study the long-term effects of a deficit of *women*. They find that historical male-biased sex ratios are associated with lower female labor force participation and a lower share of women in high-ranking economic occupations, and these effects have persisted until the present day. They also find evidence for persistence of a higher bargaining position for women, who still enjoy more hours of leisure in areas that were more male-biased in the past, despite balanced sex ratios today. In all these cases, long-term persistence is sustained by cultural transmission processes within families and local social interactions that "normalized" a given division of labor between men and women across market activities, household work, and leisure.

A final technological change that has influenced women's economic position is contraception. By enabling women to delay marriage age and childbirth (Bailey 2006), contraception revolutionized women's participation in, and attachment to, the labor force (Goldin and Katz 2002; Bailey and Lindo 2017). Greater control over the timing childbirth incentivized women to increase their educational achievement, which in turn enabled them to access highly skilled and previously exclusively male occupations, such as in law and medicine. It is estimated that about a third of women's professional advancement in the 1970s can be attributed to access to contraception and abortion (Goldin and Katz 2002)—and about 10 percent of the convergence in the gender gap in the 1980s and 1990s to the contraceptive pill alone (Bailey, Hershbein, and Miller 2012). Given medical evidence of a link between hormonal contraception and mental health and the negative consequences of depression on labor market outcomes, the economic gains of the pill might even be underestimated (Valder 2022).

Most existing work on the relationship between technology, demography, and development has focused on how these processes constrain the choices and opportunities of women, while the constraints that guide the behavior of men have received much less attention in the economics and political science literatures. One exception is Baranov et al. (2023), which establishes the enduring effects of male-biased sex ratios on masculinity norms in Australia. Historically, more male-biased areas saw higher levels of voluntary enlistment in World War I and are still characterized by heightened violence, less acceptance of homosexuality, higher levels of male (but not female) suicide, and riskier health behavior, including lower take-up of COVID-19 vaccination among men (but not women). The long-term impact of technological and demographic shocks on men, masculinity, and culture is a fruitful area of future research.

Kinship, Social and Political Institutions, and Gender Norms

A rapidly growing area of research examines the endurance and variation in gender gaps as a result of kinship structures, such as inheritance rules and marriage practices.[17] Not all of this work is historical in the sense of focusing on historical outcomes, but much of it does trace how the persistence of institutions related to lineage and inheritance impinge on women's equality and freedom (Brulé 2020). Lineage and inheritance structures sometimes go through the male line (patrilineal institutions), and sometimes through female group members (matrilineal institutions). Studies in economics and political science show that historically persistent practices of matrilineality are associated with better health and higher educational achievement among children, and greater autonomy for women (Lowes 2017; 2020), lower fertility (BenYishay, Grosjean, and Vecci 2017), and a lower, or even reversed, gender gap in engagement in politics and in political preferences over redistributive policy (Robinson and Gottlieb 2021; Brulé and Gaikwad 2021). Meanwhile, bride price payments are associated with higher opposition to domestic violence and higher self-reported happiness of the wife (Lowe and Nunn 2017).

This literature illustrates the need to take the broad social structure into account when designing public policy. Preexisting social structures condition behavioral responses to economic incentives. For example, while dowry payments have decreased with economic development in non-caste-based societies, such as Europe, the reverse has been true in caste-based societies. This is explained by the need for dowry payments to adjust for the rising income of the potential groom (Anderson 2003). Expansion of educational opportunities in Indonesia and Zambia only improved girls' educational outcomes in communities where husbands' families pay a bride price for the right to marry a daughter. The interpretation of these findings is that bridal payments enable parents to recoup part of their investment at the time of marriage and thus provide an additional monetary incentive for parents to invest in their daughters' education, improving the take-up of school construction programs (Ashraf et al. 2020). Religious practices can also condition responses to political reform. Inheritance rights granted to widows led to a *rise* in widows' immolation in colonial India, enabling families to recapture the wealth that would have been transferred to widows (Kulkarni 2017), while equal inheritance rights over agricultural land granted to women in the 1980s and 1990s led to an increase in female feticide and child mortality (Bhalotra, Brulé, and Roy 2020).

Political institutions also shape gender norms in a way that can outlive them (Tudor 2022). The gender-equalizing policies of the former Soviet Union and its satellite states, such as the German Democratic Republic, have shaped social norms durably. Twenty years after German reunification, women in East Germany contribute an equal fraction of total household income, when their Western counterparts only contribute 20 percent of total household income (Lippman, Georgieff, and Senik 2020). Women who migrated from the former Soviet Union to Israel as infants are much more likely to major in STEM subjects (science, technology, engineering, and math) to systematically avoid study fields leading to "pink collar" jobs, such as education and social work, compared to natives and other migrants. They also display a specific choice of work-life balance reflecting a greater commitment to paid work (Friedman-Sokuler and Senik 2020).

Searching for Gender in Historical Political Economy

As a field of inquiry, HPE finds itself in an exciting moment. Digitization efforts and computing power have made information about the past easier to access and analyze, and a renewed focus in the social sciences on long-term historical processes have created heightened interest in the field's discoveries. For decades, the mere fact of women's economic and political activity in history was not on the radar of most historians or social scientists (Scott 1986). What is actually a process of erasure—the systematic overlooking of women in historical archives, as well as the overlooking of women's economic activities—became a conclusion, namely, that women were simply not there in any meaningful way or did not engage in meaningful economic activity.[18] More troubling still, when scholars did turn their sights to the study of gender, they were happy to substitute myths for fact. For example, the prominence of "man-the-hunter" myths throughout the twentieth century (Cartmill 1993; Reyes-García et al. 2020) ignores the fact that gathered food has contributed more than three-quarters of the human diet's caloric intake. The focus on hunting, both a masculine and a masculinized activity, raises the question not so much of who hunted, but rather why so much of the focus of anthropological and ethnographic studies has been on the activity of hunting. As Goodman et al. (1985, 1200) put it, "Hunting is one of those activities which is susceptible through its symbolism to the projection of strongly marked gender roles."

In closing we suggest that the study of gender in historical political economy has reached the stage where higher-level theorizing and a synthetic integration of disparate literatures are urgently needed. The "add women and stir" approach, which may have taken root because it is less threatening to intellectual hierarchies, will no longer suffice. Instead, theoretical concepts that have already transformed other fields—from the concept of intersectionality, to theories of masculinity and femininity, to the conceptualization of gender as a social construct—need to be integrated into quantitative lines of inquiry. We therefore end with a call for a new theoretical paradigm to frame the historical political economy of gender. This new paradigm would move past the social scientific habit of conceptualizing the default economic agent as male (Lundberg 2022a; 2022b), would take seriously the origins of masculine cultural norms in social arrangements (Baranov et al. 2023), and would push more forcefully to show how the very categories of analysis that are imposed on the past are undermined by the gendered scaffolding on which they rest.

Acknowledgments

We thank Kate Baldwin, Alisha Holland, Carissa Tudor, Rachel Brulé, Sam Chambers, Solé Prillaman, and David Stasavage for their piquant criticisms and fruitful suggestions.

Notes

1. The theoretical mission echoes Joan Scott's (1986) famous article "Gender: A Useful Category of Historical Analysis," which argued that it is not enough to show that women were in the room when history happened (or that the stories of rooms women were in are also important), but instead to show what theories have *missed* by not treating gender as a category of analysis.
2. Some economists argue against the reflexive assumption of the default economic agent as male (Lundberg 2022a; 2022b) and consider the role and origins of masculine cultural norms (Baranov et al. 2023). As Towns (2021) describes it, critical IR, a subfield of political science, has already taken up the mantle of studying gender, but has yet to produce a large historical literature.

3. There are longer histories of systematic aggregation of human data in China and Prussia, and scholars can locate parish records into the Middle Ages in some places, but this has not yet become widespread or available for large geographic areas.
4. See Chambers (2016, 78ff.) for a discussion of human capital theory, which conceives of individuals as similar to firms, and wherein "the rationality of the firm in microeconomic theory simply is rationality *tout court*" (79). In this tradition, Gary Becker is a key figure.
5. This typology is adapted from Bateman and Teele (2019).
6. See, too, Giuliano (2018) on marital relations, and dowry versus bride price in cultures where women participate in farming or not.
7. BenYishay, Grosjean, and Vecci (2017) link the prevalence of matrilineal inheritance and male specialization in fishing to small-scale variation in the quality of the coral reef among communities of the Solomon Islands.
8. The introduction of the bow is thought to be associated with a reduction of women's involvement in hunting compared with spear-throwing, an easier-to-learn and less precise technology that required a larger number of less specialized hunters. Recent archaeological discoveries led to estimation of near-to-gender-equal participation in hunting among big-game hunting societies of the Late Pleistocene and Early Holocene Americas (Haas et al. 2020).
9. Historians have paved the way here. A classic text is Tilly and Scott (1987).
10. Though, as Goldin (1994) cautions, in the United States, nineteenth-century economic censuses often undercounted women's economic activity, labeling women "homemakers" even when they were assistants in household trades, producing materials consumed by the household, etc. Morgan (2006) makes a similar point about cross-national data on women's labor.
11. The economic history of women's employment has been more thoroughly studied in the United States than in Europe, though Tilly and Scott (1987), which compares France and England, and Horrell and Humphries (1995), which looks at women's economic activity in England. In the Scandinavian countries, the "takeoff" to industrialization was later. There is interesting work in this area, showing that relative increases in women's wages spurred the fertility transition in Sweden (Schultz 1985).
12. Eastin and Prakash (2013) argue that the relationship is S-shaped, in the sense of a takeoff, followed by a plateau as negative feedback and backlash mount against women.
13. The findings that suffrage improved educational attainment in the United States are also robust, particularly for children from disadvantaged backgrounds (Kose, Kuka, and Shenhav 2021).
14. With 1920 as the reference point, the extension of the franchise to women implies tariff rates would rise from 8.4 percent to 10.6 percent.
15. Immediately after a country introduced women's suffrage, spending on collective goods and transfers out of GDP increased by 0.6 to 0.8 percent relative to preexisting trends, with the long-run effect being 3.2 to 3.8 percent.
16. Educational achievement and attachment to the labor force have become more similar across genders, but gender wage gaps have persisted. Education and experience explained ten percentage points of the average gender wage gap in 1980, but less than three in 2010 (Blau and Kahn 2017), leaving a larger part of the wage gap unexplained.
17. See Dyson and Moore (1983) for an early contribution.
18. There are too many examples of erasure to list, but as an example, the outstanding efforts to categorize civic participation in temperance, unions, and the labor movement in

late-nineteenth through mid-twentieth-century Sweden by Andrae and Lundkvist (1998) does not have a single reference to women's activity despite the fact that women were key campaigners for temperance in Sweden, and that major organizations like the Labor Organization kept separate tallies of men's and women's membership on the same pages from which these data were collected.

References

Abramitzky, Ran, Adeline Delavande, and Luis Vasconcelos. 2011. "Marrying Up: The Role of Sex Ratio in Assortative Matching." *American Economic Journal: Applied Economics* 3, no. 3: 124–57.

Adams, Julia. 2005. *The Familial State: Ruling Families and Merchant Capitalism in Early Modern Europe.* Ithaca, NY: Cornell University Press.

Aidt, Toke S., and Bianca Dallal. 2008. "Female Voting Power: The Contribution of Women's Suffrage to the Growth of Social Spending in Western Europe (1869–1960)." *Public Choice* 134, no. 3–4: 391–417.

Alesina, Alberto, Paola Giuliano, and Nathan Nunn. 2011. "Fertility and the Plough." *American Economic Review* 101, no. 3: 499–503.

Anderson, Siwan. 2003. "Why Dowry Payments Declined with Modernization in Europe but Are Rising in India." *Journal of Political Economy* 111, no. 2: 269–310.

Andrae, C. G., and S. Lundkvist. 1998. "SND0209 Folkrörelsearkivet 1881–1950" [SND0209 population movement archive 1881–1950]. *Svensk Nationell Databastjänst.* https://snd.gu.se/en/catalogue/study/snd0209

Ashraf, Nava, Natalie Bau, Nathan Nunn, and Alessandra Voena. 2020. "Bride Price and Female Education." *Journal of Political Economy* 128, no. 2: 591–641.

Bailey, Martha J. 2006. "More Power to the Pill: The Impact of Contraceptive Freedom on Women's Life Cycle Labor Supply." *The Quarterly Journal of Economics* 121, no. 1: 289–320.

Bailey, Martha J., and Jason M. Lindo. 2017. "Access and Use of Contraception and Its Effects on Women's Outcomes in the United States." *The Oxford Handbook of Women and the Economy* 1, 219–57.

Bailey, Martha J., Brad Hershbein, and Amanda Miller. 2012. "The Opt-in Revolution? Contraception and the Gender Gap in Wages." *American Economic Journal: Applied Economics* 4, no. 3: 225–54.

Barnes, Mariel J. 2020. "Divining Disposition: The Role of Elite Beliefs and Gender Narratives in Women's Suffrage." *Comparative Politics* 52, no. 4: 581–601.

Baranov, Victoria, Ralph De Haas, and Pauline Grosjean. 2023. "Men. Male-Biased Sex Ratios and Masculitity Norms: Evidence from Australia's Colonial Past." *Journal of Economic Growth* 28, no. 3: 339–96.

Bateman, David A., and Dawn Langan Teele. 2019. "A Developmental Approach to Historical Causal Inference." *Public Choice* 185, no. 3–4: 253–79.

Becker, Gary Stanley. 1981. *A Treatise on the Family.* Cambridge, MA: Harvard University Press.

BenYishay, Ariel, Pauline Grosjean, and Joe Vecci. 2017. "The Fish Is the Friend of Matriliny: Reef Density and Matrilineal Inheritance." *Journal of Development Economics* 127: 234–49.

Bertocchi, Graziella. 2011. "The Enfranchisement of Women and the Welfare State." *European Economic Review* 55, no. 4: 535–53.

Bhalotra, Sonia, Rachel Brulé, and Sanchari Roy. 2020. "Women's Inheritance Rights Reform and the Preference for Sons in India." *Journal of Development Economics* 146, 102275.

Blau, Francine D., and Lawrence M. Kahn. 2017. "The Gender Wage Gap: Extent, Trends, and Explanations." *Journal of Economic Literature* 55, no. 3: 789–865.

Boehnke, Jörn, and Victor Gay. 2020. "The Missing Men: World War I and Female Labor Force Participation." *Journal of Human Resources* 57, no. 4: 1209–241.

Boserup, Esther. 1965. *The Conditions of Agricultural Growth: The Economics of Agrarian Change Under Population Pressure*; London: Allen & Unwin, 124 p.

Bourdieu, Pierre. 1980. *Le Sens Pratique*. Paris: Les Editions de Minuit.

Branch, Enobong. 2011. *Opportunity Denied: Limiting Black Women to Devalued Work*. New Brunswick, NJ: Rutgers University Press.

Bromhead, Alan de. 2018. "Women Voters and Trade Protectionism in the Interwar Years." *Oxford Economic Papers* 70, no. 1: 22–46.

Brulé, Rachel E. 2020. *Women, Power, and Property: The Paradox of Gender Equality Laws in India*. New York: Cambridge University Press.

Brulé, Rachel, and Nikhar Gaikwad. 2021. "Culture, Capital, and the Political Economy Gender Gap: Evidence from Meghalaya's Matrilineal Tribes." *Journal of Politics* 83, no. 3: 834–50.

Brulé, Rachel. 2023. "Women and Power in the Developing World." *Annual Review of Political Science* 26: 33–54.

Carpenter, Daniel, and Colin D. Moore. 2014. "When Canvassers Became Activists: Antislavery Petitioning and the Political Mobilization of American Women." *American Political Science Review* 108, no. 3: 479–98.

Cartmill, Matt. 1993. *A View to a Death in the Morning*. Cambridge, MA: Harvard University Press.

Chambers, Samuel A. 2016. "Learning How to Be a Capitalist: From Neoliberal Pedagogy to the Mystery of Learning." In *The Pedagogics of Unlearning*, ed. Éamonn Dunne and Aidan Seery, 73–110. Goleta, CA: Punctum Books.

Corder, J. Kevin, and Christina Wolbrecht. 2016. *Counting Women's Ballots*. New York: Cambridge University Press.

Dyson, Tim and Mick Moore. 1983. "On Kinship Structure, Female Autonomy, and Demographic Behavior in India." *Population and Development Review* 9, no. 1: 35–60.

Eastin, Joshua, and Aseem Prakash. 2013. "Economic Development and Gender Equality: Is There a Gender Kuznets Curve?" *World Politics* 65, no. 1: 156–86.

Engels, Friedrich. 2010 [1884]. *The Origin of the Family, Private Property, and the State*. New York: Penguin Group.

Fernández, Raquel. 2014. "Women's Rights and Development." *Journal of Economic Growth* 19, no. 1: 37–80.

Folbre, Nancy. 1982. "Exploitation Comes Home: A Critique of the Marxian Theory of Family Labour." *Cambridge Journal of Economics* 6, no. 4: 317–29.

Friedman-Sokuler, Naomi, and Claudia Senik. 2020. "From Pink-Collar to Lab Coat: Cultural Persistence and Diffusion of Socialist Gender Norms." Paris School of Economics Mimeo. https://papers.ssrn.com/sol3/papers.cfm?abstract_id=3631596.

Gay, Victor. 2019. "The Legacy of the Missing Men: The Long-Run Impact of World War I on Female Labor Force Participation." Toulouse School of Economics Mimeo. https://papers.ssrn.com/sol3/papers.cfm?abstract_id=3069582.

Giuliano, Paola. 2018. "Gender: A Historical Perspective." In *The Oxford Handbook of Women and the Economy*, ed. Susan L. Averett, Laura M. Argys, and Saul D. Hoffman, 645–72.

Oxford, UK: Oxford University Press. https://www.oxfordhandbooks.com/view/10.1093/oxfordhb/9780190628963.001.0001/oxfordhb-9780190628963-e-29.
Goldin, Claudia. 1994. "Understanding the Gender Gap: An Economic History of American Women." In *Equal Employment Opportunity: Labor Market Discrimination and Public Policy*, ed. Paul Burstein, 17–26. New York: Aldine de Gruyter.
Goldin, Claudia. 1995. "The U-Shaped Female Labor Force Function in Economic Development and Economic History." In *Investment in Women's Human Capital and Economic Development*, ed. T. Paul Schultz, 61–90. Chicago: University of Chicago Press.
Goldin, Claudia, and Lawrence F. Katz. 2002. "The Power of the Pill: Oral Contraceptives and Women's Career and Marriage Decisions." *Journal of Political Economy* 110, no. 4: 730–70.
Goldin, Claudia, and Kenneth L. Sokoloff. 1982. "Women, Children, and Industrialization in the Early Republic: Evidence from the Manufacturing Censuses." *Journal of Economic History* 42, no. 4: 741–74.
Goldstein, Markus, and Christopher Udry. 2008. "The Profits of Power: Land Rights and Agricultural Investment in Ghana." *Journal of Political Economy* 116, no. 6: 981–1022.
Goodman, Madeleine J., P. Griffin, Agnes A. Estioko-Griffin, and John S. Grove. 1985. "The Compatibility of Hunting and Mothering among the Agta Hunter-Gatherers of the Philippines." *Sex Roles* 12, no. 11: 1199–209.
Graeber, David, and David Wengrow. 2021. *The Dawn of Everything: A New History of Humanity*. London: Penguin.
Grosjean, Pauline, and Rose Khattar. 2019. "It's Raining Men! Hallelujah? The Long-Run Consequences of Male-Biased Sex Ratios." *Review of Economic Studies* 86, no. 2: 723–54.
Haas, Randall, James Watson, Tammy Buonasera, John Southon, Jennifer C. Chen, Sarah Noe, Kevin Smith, Carlos Viviano, Jelmer Eerkens, and Glendon Parker. 2020. "Female Hunters of the Early Americas." *Science Advances* 6, no. 45: eabd0310.
Hansen, Casper Worm, Peter Sandholt Jensen, and Christian Volmar Skovsgaard. 2015. "Modern Gender Roles and Agricultural History: The Neolithic Inheritance." *Journal of Economic Growth* 20, no. 4: 365–404.
Hartmann, Heidi. 1976. "Capitalism, Patriarchy, and Job Segregation by Sex." *Signs* 1, no. 3, Part 2, 137–69.
Harvey, Anna L. 1996. "The Political Consequences of Suffrage Exclusion: Organizations, Institutions, and the Electoral Mobilization of Women." *Social Science History* 20, no. 1: 97–132.
Horrell, Sara, and Jane Humphries. "Women's labour force participation and the transition to the male-breadwinner family, 1790–1865." *Economic History Review*, XLVIII, I(1995): 89–117.
Iversen, Torben, Frances McCall. Rosenbluth. 2010. *Women, Work, and Politics: The Political Economy of Gender Inequality*. New Haven, CT: Yale University Press.
Jones-Rogers, Stephanie E. 2019. "They Were Her Property White Women as Slave Owners in the American South." New Haven, CT: Yale University Press.
Kandiyoti, Deniz. 1988. "Bargaining with Patriarchy." *Gender & Society* 2, no. 3: 274–90.
Khan, B. Zorina. 1996. "Married Women's Property Laws and Female Commercial Activity: Evidence from United States Patent Records, 1790–1895." *Journal of Economic History* 56, no. 2: 356–88.
Kim, Jeong Hyun. 2019. "Direct Democracy and Women's Political Engagement." *American Journal of Political Science* 63, no. 3: 594–610.
Kose, Esra, Elira Kuka, and Na'ama Shenhav. 2021. "Women's Suffrage and Children's Education." *American Economic Journal: Economic Policy* 13, no. 3: 374–405.

Kulkarni, Parashar. 2017. "The British Academy Brian Barry Prize Essay: Can Religious Norms Undermine Effective Property Rights?: Evidence from Inheritance Rights of Widows in Colonial India." *British Journal of Political Science* 47, no. 3: 479–99.

Leacock, Eleanor. 1987. "Gender in Egalitarian Societies." In *Becoming Visible: Women in European History*, edited by Renate Bridenthal and Claudia Koonz. Boston: Houghton Mifflin.

Lewis, Jane. 1997. "Gender and Welfare Regimes: Further Thoughts." *Social Politics: International Studies in Gender, State & Society* 4, no. 2: 160–77.

Lippmann, Quentin, Alexandre Georgieff, and Claudia Senik. 2020. "Undoing Gender with Institutions: Lessons from the German Division and Reunification." *Economic Journal* 130, no. 629: 1445–70.

Lowes, Sara. 2017. "Matrilineal Kinship and Spousal Cooperation: Evidence from the Matrilineal Belt." Unpublished manuscript. https://scholar.harvard.edu/files/slowes/files/lowes_matrilineal.pdf.

Lowes, Sara. 2020. "Kinship Structure & Women: Evidence from Economics." *Daedalus*, 149 no. 1: 119–33.

Lowes, Sara, and Nathan Nunn. 2017. "Bride Price and the Well-Being of Women." In *Towards Gender Equity in Development*, vol. 117, ed. Siwan Anderson, Lori Beaman, and Jean-Philippe Platteau, 117–38. Oxford: Oxford University Press.

Lundberg, Shelly J. 2022a. "Gender Economics: Dead-Ends and New Opportunities." *SSRN Electronic Journal*. https://www.ssrn.com/abstract=4114792.

Lundberg, Shelly. 2022b. "Gender Economics and the Meaning of Discrimination." *AEA Papers and Proceedings* 112: 588–91.

MacKinnon, Catharine A. 1982. "Feminism, Marxism, Method, and the State: An Agenda for Theory." *Signs: Journal of Women in Culture and Society* 7, no. 3: 515–44.

Moehling, Carolyn M., and Melissa A. Thomasson. 2012. "The Political Economy of Saving Mothers and Babies: The Politics of State Participation in the Sheppard-Towner Program." *Journal of Economic History* 72, no. 1: 75–103.

Morgan, Kimberly J. 2006. *Working Mothers and the Welfare State: Religion and the Politics of Work-Family Policies in Western Europe and the United States*. Palo Alto: Stanford University Press.

Morgan-Collins, Mona. 2021. "The Electoral Impact of Newly Enfranchised Groups: The Case of Women's Suffrage in the United States." *Journal of Politics* 83, no. 1: 150–65.

Ogilvie, Sheilagh C. 2003. *A Bitter Living: Women, Markets, and Social Capital in Early Modern Germany*. Oxford: Oxford University Press.

Olivetti, Claudia, and Barbara Petrongolo. 2017. "The Economic Consequences of Family Policies: Lessons from a Century of Legislation in High-Income Countries." *Journal of Economic Perspectives* 31, no. 1: 205–30.

Przeworski, Adam. 2009. "Conquered or Granted? A History of Suffrage Extensions." *British Journal of Political Science* 39, no. 02: 291–321.

Qian, Nancy. 2008. "Missing Women and the Price of Tea in China: The Effect of Sex-Specific Earnings on Sex Imbalance." *Quarterly Journal of Economics* 123, no. 3: 1251–85.

Reyes-García, Victoria, Isabel Díaz-Reviriego, Romain Duda, Álvaro Fernández-Llamazares, and Sandrine Gallois. 2020. "Hunting Otherwise." *Human Nature* 31, no. 3: 203–21.

Roberts, Dorothy. 1997. *Killing the Black Body: Race, Reproduction, and the Meaning of Liberty*. New York: Pantheon Books.

Robinson, Amanda Lea, and Jessica Gottlieb. 2021. "How to Close the Gender Gap in Political Participation: Lessons from Matrilineal Societies in Africa." *British Journal of Political Science* 51, no. 1: 68–92.

Sacks, Karen. 1974. "Engels Revisited." In *Women, Culture and Society*, ed. Marie Rosaldo and Louise Lamphere, 207–22. Palo Alto: Stanford University Press.

Sainsbury, Diane. 1996. *Gender, Equality and Welfare States*. Cambridge: Cambridge University Press.

Sanday, Peggy Reeves. 1981. *Female Power and Male Dominance: On the Origins of Sexual Inequality*. Cambridge: Cambridge University Press.

Schuyler, Lorraine Gates. 2006. *The Weight of Their Votes: Southern Women and Political Leverage in the 1920s*. Chapel Hill: The University of North Carolina Press.

Schultz, T. Paul. 1985. "Changing World Prices, Women's Wages, and the Fertility Transition: Sweden, 1860–1910." *Journal of Political Economy* 93, no. 6: 1126–54.

Scott, John W. 1986. "Gender: A Useful Category of Historical Analysis." *American Historical Review* 91, no. 5: 1053–75.

Skocpol, Theda. 1992. *Protecting Soldiers and Mothers*. Cambridge, MA: Belknap Press of Harvard University Press.

Skorge, Øyvind Søraas. 2021. "Mobilizing the Underrepresented: Electoral Systems and Gender Inequality in Political Participation." *American Journal of Political Science*. Firstview Doi: 10.1111/ajps.12654.

Stasavage, David. 2020. *The Decline and Rise of Democracy*. Princeton: Princeton University Press.

Stewart, Mary Lynn. 1989. *Women, Work, and the French State: Labour Protection and Social Patriarchy, 1879–1919*. Montreal: McGill-Queen's Press-MQUP.

Teele, Dawn. 2018a. *Forging the Franchise: The Political Origins of the Women's Vote*. Princeton, NJ: Princeton University Press.

Teele, Dawn. 2018b. "How the West Was Won: Competition, Mobilization, and Women's Enfranchisement in the United States." *Journal of Politics* 80, no. 2: 442–61.

Teele, Dawn. 2022. "Gender and the Impact of Proportional Representation: A Comment on the Peripheral Voting Thesis." *American Political Science Review*, in press.

Teso, Edoardo. 2019. "The Long-Term Effect of Demographic Shocks on the Evolution of Gender Roles: Evidence from the Transatlantic Slave Trade." *Journal of the European Economic Association* 17, no. 2: 497–534.

Tilly, Louise, and Joan Wallach Scott. 1987. *Women, Work, and Family*. London, New York: Routledge, Taylor and Francis.

Towns, Ann E. 2021. "Gender in Historical International Relations." In *Routledge Handbook of Historical International Relations*, ed. B. De Carvalho, J. C. Lopez, and H. Leira, 153–61. London: Routledge.

Tudor, Carissa. 2022. *Whose Modernity? Revolution and the Rights of Woman*. PhD Thesis Princeton University.

Valder, Franziska. 2022. "Two Sides of the Same Pill? Fertility Control and Mental Health Effect of the Contraceptive Pill." University of Copenhagen Mimeo. https://papers.ssrn.com/sol3/papers.cfm?abstract_id=4089991.

Wikander, Ulla, Alice Kessler-Harris, and Jane E. Lewis. 1995. *Protecting Women: Labor Legislation in Europe, the United States, and Australia, 1880–1920*. Urbana and Chicago: University of Illinois Press.

Xue, Melanie Meng. 2016. "High-Value Work and the Rise of Women: The Cotton Revolution and Gender Equality in China." Mimeo LSE. https://www.dropbox.com/s/bcwypoogzcteg67/Textiles.pdf?dl=0.

CHAPTER 37

IDENTITY IN HISTORICAL POLITICAL ECONOMY

PAVITHRA SURYANARAYAN AND STEVEN WHITE

A vast literature in the social sciences focuses on the role of identity in politics. Scholars have sought to explain how identity shapes electoral behavior, political parties, government policies, social movements, and violence—and, in turn, how identity cleavages emerge and stabilize. Regardless of the specific type of identity in question, recent political developments in regions as different as North America, South Asia, and Western Europe have only further intensified the volume of scholarship on this topic.[1] In this chapter we focus on ways in which recent work in historical political economy (HPE) is advancing our understanding of the interplay between identity, institutional development, and political behavior.

Before we proceed, let us first deal with what we mean by identity in this chapter. While identity in political science generally focuses on ways in which a group can be distinguished by "rules deciding membership and (alleged) characteristic features or attributes" (Fearon 1999), our focus in this chapter is on one construct that has garnered increased attention in recent years: ethnic or racial identity. Our interrogation of new research in HPE research on ethnic identity allows us to engage in depth with the methodological and theoretical innovations being made in this burgeoning field, but the lessons from these studies likely hold valuable insights for understanding other types of identity politics as well.[2]

While definitions of ethnicity are themselves contentious (see Brubaker 2004; Chandra 2006), we follow broad convention in defining "ethnic identity" as membership into a descent-based group or more subjectively as "self-identification around a characteristic that is difficult or impossible to change, such as language, race, or location" (Birnir 2007, 66). Descent-based attributes have two intrinsic properties: constrained change and visibility (Chandra 2006). The range of ethnic identities we focus on in this chapter includes tribe, religion, caste, language, and race across a range of countries and cases.

Studies of identity politics grapple with several theoretical and empirical challenges. First, while we have considerable scholarship on how institutions shape the emergence of identity, and how identity in turn shapes state policies and public goods provision, we know less about how identity shapes institutional development, particularly the evolution of state capacity. This is in part because studying the interplay between institutions and identity is rife with challenges of causal inference. Second, studies of identity politics often assume that identities are relatively fixed and visible in the short run, making them a relevant category for political mobilization. However, explaining where and why some identities become activated, the role of political elites and propaganda in their emergence, and their subsequent impact on political outcomes has proven methodologically challenging. Third, some questions necessarily require a historical lens, such as where and why some identity categories have persisted and remained relevant to political outcomes while others have not.

In this chapter we focus on three ways in which HPE as a field has complemented existing work on identity. A growing body of HPE research has provided new tools, data, and theoretical perspectives. We show that focusing on historical episodes of exogenous change such as externally imposed franchise extension or moments of state development, notably during war, can help highlight the ways in which identity concerns of elites and groups shaped institutions—a task that is inherently more complicated in contemporary politics where identities are often seen as being "played" or "produced" by actors responding to institutional incentives (Laitin 1998). In doing so we showcase studies that can pinpoint the mechanisms through which identity-based decision-making can *shape* institutions. Second, we discuss recent empirical innovations that make it possible using historical episodes of media expansion to study when an identity becomes salient in politics. Finally, we discuss a growing body of literature on the mechanisms through which identities persist and stay relevant to contemporary politics.

Throughout this essay we also seek to find common ground between different types of ethnic categories at work in different social contexts historically. We discuss recent works in American political economy and comparative political economy to showcase how racialized institutional development in nineteenth-century America has parallels to caste-based developments in early twentieth-century India; how the tactics of anti-Semitic propaganda used by Father Charles Coughlin in the 1950s United States resonate with the tactics of anti-Muslim propaganda in early 1990s India; and how noneconomic considerations shaping Arab rulers' decision-making resonate with those of Chinese emperors and European city states. In this way, we put into dialogue disparate scholarship attempting to understand the preferences of actors motivated by a range of identity considerations such as social rank in regions characterized by caste and race, loyalty in regions where clan or tribal links proved to be strategically useful to rulers, or piety in times of religious wars and expansion. In each of these cases we discuss how focusing on identity leads to outcomes that canonical models do not predict.

IDENTITY AND INSTITUTIONS

Scholarship on the development of the state, particularly state capacity, has been largely silent on the role of identity in state-building. Take, for example, studies of fiscal capacity, which are in some ways core to the literature on state capacity. Much of this literature that focuses on the Western European cases tends to be macro-historical in orientation, focused on factors like wars, geography, and colonialism (Besley and Persson 2011; Centeno 2002; Engerman and Sokoloff 2002; Tilly 1992). One reason for this omission is that the extent to which group-based politics can shape extractive capacity is somewhat limited by the inability of rulers to ramp up capacity substantially in the short run (Soifer 2013).[3] To the extent that identity has been studied in historical development it is focused on the material concerns of groups and elites rather than on a noneconomic identity.[4]

Multiple recent works in HPE have challenged this thinking. Within the conventional war-focused literature on state-building in Europe, the work by Lisa Blaydes and Christopher Paik (2016) has shown that identity politics played a role in the development of the extractive state. As economic elites left cities across Europe to fight the religious Crusades, rulers were more easily able to build institutions of extraction. They also show that places with greater numbers of religious fighters experienced more political stability, and these places also experienced greater extraction through Crusade tithes—one of the first forms of "per head" taxation in Europe. Focusing on the religious motives of elites and how their exit reduced barriers to state-building offers insights into the mechanisms through which war can successfully lead to greater extractive capacity.

Scholarship in other contexts has found similar relationships between identity and state-building. In Turkey, for example, Yusuf Magiya (2020) uses local-level tax data from the late nineteenth century in the Ottoman Empire to show that during interstate wars administrative units with more ethnically homogeneous populations were able to collect more taxes and had more investments in fiscal capacity. This suggests that the conventional trope that "war makes the state" was mediated through the ethnic composition of the ruled. Similarly in China, Peng Peng (2022) finds that Chinese emperors during the Qing dynasty's reign between 1644 and 1722 were more likely to deploy co-ethnic bureaucrats to regions of the kingdom experiencing conflict. In contrast, they relied on meritocratically selected officials in areas where security concerns were less heightened. In this way, ethnic considerations shaped key state-building decisions during times of external and civil wars.

Historically oriented projects have some unique advantages in establishing how identity might matter to institutional development. Identity-based taxes, like a poll tax on minority ethnic/racial groups or crusade tithes, were explicit and observable, unlike implicit bias in contemporary outcomes such as the study of public goods or tax burdens. Second, in many instances, key institutional features—like per capita taxation, bureaucratic agencies, or state census undertakings—were introduced for the first time following franchise expansion, conquest, or war, allowing for causal claims-making on how identity mattered to politics. Third, recent HPE research deploys a wide range of quantitative and qualitative data to consider the specific mechanisms through which identity matters to the development of good-quality bureaucratic institutions.

For example, one strand of research seeks to understand how identity-based coalitions shaped institutions around extensions of the franchise that were somewhat exogenous to local politics. Suryanarayan (2016) shows that an episode of franchise extension to the taxpaying elite was associated with a weakening of tax institutions in colonial India. She argues that the expansion of the franchise threatened the social position of high-caste Brahmans who feared the rise of lower castes into politics. They sought to weaken taxation to limit future redistribution and the desegregation of institutions to lower castes. In the United States, Suryanarayan and White (2021) show that the end of the Civil War and the emancipation of African Americans was associated with a weakening of tax capacity at the county level in the post-Reconstruction era, as elites built cross-class coalitions of wealthy and poor whites against taxation. Both these studies use historical data to construct measures of group-based inequalities to study how emancipation shifted caste/race-based preferences.

A related strand focuses on the distinctive role of noneconomic identities that can lead to institutional outcomes not predicted by canonical models that focus on only economic interests. Identity can shape the quality of information the state can collect about its subjects. Research has shown that the ability to collect information is often contingent on sharing a language, eliciting the trust of subjects, or having reliable bureaucrats (Lee and Zhang 2017; Scott 1998). Rulers can more accurately collect information about their populations when ethnically homogeneous populations are more legible to bureaucrats. For example, Magiya finds that in the late Ottoman Empire, administrative units were more likely to complete a census when they were homogeneous. In imperial Russia, Volha Charnsyh (2022) argues that state officials faced greater barriers to collecting information from ethnic outgroups, particularly when they relied on intermediaries to give them information about their subjects instead of investing in bureaucratic capacity directly. As a result, Russian Orthodox officials delayed and withheld public assistance during famines in the late nineteenth century to districts with greater Muslim populations because they lacked information about Muslim communes. Similarly, Suryanarayan and White (2021) show that census collectors collected worse data from white populations in enumerator districts with greater proportions of African Americans after Reconstruction's demise. In each of these cases, ethnic identities shaped legibility and taxability, and ultimately the quality of public goods.

Identity can also explain who becomes a bureaucrat. Peng Peng's research on seventeenth-century China shows that rulers made trade-offs between ethnic loyalty and competence, and chose co-ethnics when loyalty was more prized as a way to secure information in perilous times. In Nigeria, Johnson-Kanu (2022) shows that ethnic groups that were more English-educated had a first-mover advantage within the colonial bureaucracy. These ethnic groups continued to be overrepresented in the bureaucracy a century later.

Rulers might seek to emphasize identity concerns even if they lose revenues in the process. Saleh and Tirole (2021) show that following the Arab conquest of Christian Egypt, the Arab caliphate levied both a nondiscriminatory tax and a poll tax on non-Muslims that would be eliminated upon conversion. When faced with declining revenues, as large numbers of Christians converted to Islam, pious rulers called for even more conversions, suggesting that identity motives dominated economic ones. In the United States, Nancy Qian and Marco Tabellini (2022) argue that identity-based discrimination can shape the military state because the lack of inclusiveness in institutions can discourage voluntary conscription, weaken the war effort, and intensify identity-based cleavages. They find that Black Americans enlisted in the military at lower rates after the attack on Pearl Harbor in counties with greater level of anti-Black discrimination.

Identity and Propaganda

A different challenge scholars face in the study of identity politics is how exactly cleavages come to be activated and the role of elite persuasion in shaping ethnic, religious, or racial identity formation. Studying the impact of elite appeals or persuasion can be tricky. First, we have to devise a way to measure people's exposure to an idea at a fine-grained geographic level. Second, we need to ensure that the exposure was not a consequence of picking places where people particularly susceptible to the idea could be found (i.e., the dreaded endogeneity problem). Third, given the explosion in communication, transportation, and media technology, it is hard to study the marginal effect of an idea on people's behavior given all the propaganda people have already consumed in their lifetimes. And finally, even if we were to solve these challenges, we have the ultimate one: how do we convincingly show a link between identity-based appeals and people's political behavior?

Several new HPE studies tackle these challenges explicitly. In the United States, Desmond Ang (2021) studies the effects of a cinematic blockbuster, *The Birth of a Nation*, that opened in 1915. The movie presented a sympathetic fictionalized depiction of the founding of the Ku Klux Klan (KKK) during the Reconstruction Era. Ang constructs a data set on the date and location of the film's roadshow-style release using local newspapers and trade reports. He shows that the release of the film led to sharp spikes in racial violence in the short run. Counties were five times more likely to experience a lynching during the month of the movie's arrival. To address endogeneity concerns, Ang uses the presence of a movie theater in 1914, the year prior to the movie's opening in 1915, as an instrument for whether the county received the movie. He finds that the screening of the film increased a county's likelihood of having a KKK chapter ("Klavern") in 1930 by sixty percentage points.

Moving forward two decades in American history, Tianyi Wang (2021) examines the consequences of America's first populist radio personality, Father Charles Coughlin. A Roman Catholic priest, he blended economic populism, anti-Semitism, and fascist sympathies. Known as the "Radio Messiah," Father Coughlin began his radio career in the 1920s and grew to amass a radio audience of thirty million by the mid-1930s. Wang studies the impact of exposure to Father Coughlin's radio program on voting outcomes in the 1936 presidential election. He uses unique data on the location and technical details of Coughlin's radio transmitters in 1936 in order to predict the strength of signals intercepted by radios in different counties—a measure of the intensity of listeners. He finds that a one-standard-deviation increase in exposure to Father Coughlin's radio program was associated with a reduction in FDR's vote share by about 3.8 percentage points.[5]

These studies of the US case have striking parallels with research on the effects of propaganda in India. Focusing on the rise of the right-wing Bharatiya Janata Party in the early 1990s, David Blakeslee (2018) studies the Ram Rath Yatra campaign of 1990 where the party leader, L. K. Advani, traveled close to ten thousand kilometers in a truck decorated to look like the chariot of the Hindu god Ram. The principal cause of the campaign was to demand the demolition of a mosque and the construction of a temple, and the campaign content was rich in religious symbolism, Hindu nationalist ideology, and anti-Muslim demagoguery. Blakeslee finds that electoral constituencies through which the yatra passed experienced a five-percentage-point increase in the BJP's vote share.

Taken together, these papers highlight key ways in which identity can intersect with propaganda to have major political consequences. They also collectively pay attention to the timing of the introduction of identity-based propaganda, the randomness in the spatial spread of the propaganda often due to technological or geographic oddities, and the mechanisms through which they come to shape political violence and electoral behavior. But to what extent does an identity, once activated in politics, persist over time and why?

Identity and Persistence

Another major area of interest for scholars of historical political economy has been persistence: how and under what conditions do events long ago still shape contemporary political outcomes? Some of the most interesting work in this tradition focuses on issues closely related to identity, including the origins and transmission of anti-Semitic attitudes and the legacies of slavery. Here we summarize some key findings from this literature and discuss future directions it might take.

One strand of research in this tradition has focused on the legacies of extractive institutions on development. One of the earliest examples of this kind of research, Acemoglu, Johnson, and Robinson (2001), demonstrated a relationship between historical European colonialism and settlement patterns and contemporary economic development. Another line of research examines the long-term consequences of the slave trade in Africa. Nunn (2008) shows that the African slave trade negatively affected economic development, and Nunn and Wantchekon (2011) find that having ancestors who were heavily raided during the slave trade is associated with lower levels of trust in Africa today. Together these papers set research agendas on how racialized institutions shaped long-run trajectories of growth, inequality, and politics, leading to a robust debate on the persistence of institutions.

More recent scholarship has extended this line of inquiry into a range of topics of interest to scholars of comparative politics. One important area of research has been on the long-term consequences of historical anti-Semitism and the Holocaust for contemporary politics. Charnysh (2015), for example, finds that latent anti-Semitism in Poland from earlier time periods was related to European Union (EU) accession in more recent times. In particular, she uses data measuring the size of the local Jewish population before the Holocaust, violence against Jews in 1941, and local opposition to EU accession in 2003, finding a relationship between the historical measures and more recent opposition to the EU. Far-right political actors used anti-Semitic arguments in making their case against the EU, and these arguments were more convincing to voters in areas where anti-Semitism was strongest in earlier periods and transmitted across generations even after the destruction of local Jewish populations.

Homola, Pereira, and Tavits (2020) similarly examine the relationship between the German Nazi regime and out-group intolerance in present-day Germany. Using data on historical proximity to concentration camps, they find that this predicts intolerance, xenophobia, and support for far-right parties among Germans today. Other work links older anti-Semitism with the initial rise of Nazism in the 1930s, finding that pogroms during the Black Death were predictive of anti-Semitic violence and support for the Nazi Party, among other outcomes, in the 1920s and 1930s (Voigtlander and Voth 2012).

In the US politics literature, a growing complementary body of scholarship has examined the long-run effects of slavery. Acharya, Blackwell, and Sen (2018) show a relationship between slavery in the pre–Civil War period and white political attitudes in southern states today, an effect that holds even accounting for contemporary population characteristics. Using data on the county-level prevalence of slavery from the 1860 census—the last census before the Civil War that led to slavery's abolition—they find that Whites in counties where slavery had been more prevalent before the Civil War are today less likely to identify as Democrats and more likely to hold a range of anti-Black attitudes on issues like affirmative action and rank higher on the racial resentment scale. They point to the decades following emancipation as a critical juncture where White elites, in trying to maintain a repressed class of Black workers, cultivated strong anti-Black attitudes in the larger White population. They also present evidence that the mechanisms for the persistence of such attitudes were generational transmission (using twentieth-century data on the attitudes of parents and their children) and institutional reinforcement (by showing that slavery's relationship with present-day attitudes is stronger in counties where the mechanization of agriculture was slower to arrive, where there were more lynchings, and where educational integration was slower to happen).

Scholars have also extended the study of slavery's political legacies to other realms and time periods. Mazumder (2021), for example, shows how the legacy of slavery weakened welfare state development during the New Deal period. Using the same metric of slavery as Acharya, Blackwell, and Sen (2018), Mazumder shows that higher county-level prevalence of slavery in 1860 is associated with receiving lower amounts of Works Progress Administration spending during the New Deal era (a program that would have been particularly beneficial to Black residents), but notably this relationship is more muted for programs that involved greater devolution to local authorities.

Not all persistence studies have findings with such negative implications for marginalized groups, however. Using a dataset on civil rights protests in the 1960s, Mazumder (2018) finds that White Americans who lived in places with such protests were more likely to be Democrats and support affirmative action, as well as exhibit lower racial resentment later. This provides some counterbalance to Acharya, Blackwell, and Sen (2018), who find that 1860 levels of slavery were associated with opposite outcomes. This article suggests that collective action can, in certain circumstances, help to weaken these historical legacies.

In an effort to generalize beyond the US case (and beyond the particulars of slavery), Acharya, Blackwell, and Sen (2018) describe their work as an example of behavioral path dependence. Drawing directly on historical institutionalist scholarship on institutional path dependence, they argue that attitudes and behaviors can also follow path-dependent processes stemming from events long ago. In this way, they directly relate their findings to research on other cases like those mentioned in previous paragraphs and suggest a generalizable theoretical framework for understanding work on identity and persistence.

Central Europe and the United States receive disproportionate attention in the persistence literature (Cirone and Pepinsky 2022), but some scholarship has examined the long-term consequences of identity in other cases. Suryanarayan (2019), for example, examines the historical underpinnings of poor voters supporting the political right in India. Using 1931 census data on upper-caste Brahmin dominance among caste groups as a measure of status inequality, she shows that areas with greater Brahmin dominance in 1931 shifted to the right in the aftermath of a 1990 policy change enacting quotas for government jobs to lower-status groups. She further finds that Brahmins in areas with higher historical social dominance were more likely than Brahmins elsewhere to shift to the right.

One of the key strengths of HPE work focused on identity and persistence has been to show the long-term consequences of the factors that were noted earlier in this chapter as shaping institutional development in the short run. Important challenges remain, however. Persistence studies related to identity politics raise complicated questions about how to theorize and understand identity across various contexts: across time within cases, as well as across cases. While identity in politics is often "sticky," it is not unchanging, which raises questions about how to interpret the relationship between measurements based on evidence that can sometimes be centuries apart. Such measurements themselves are also prone to error. Indeed, historical measurements of identity groups might even be especially likely to be prone to measurement problems. As Abad and Maurer (2021) show, some HPE work on persistence has relied on historical sources that have been critiqued not just by recent historians but even by experts at the time they were originally published. Their analysis of contemporaneous critiques of Murdock (1959), a common source for more recent quantitative studies of precolonial ethnicities in Africa, is particularly enlightening in this respect (Abad and Maurer 2021, 39–40). While this example might be extreme, it is likely the case that historians would call into question many standard sources for turning historical identities into data for regression analysis. As we note in the conclusion, greater engagement between HPE scholars interested in identity politics and scholars in more qualitative social science traditions, as well as historians, would be fruitful.

CONCLUSION

HPE scholarship on identity and politics has made several important contributions to our understanding of politics. In this chapter, we have pointed to three in particular. First, HPE scholars have demonstrated the relationship between identity and forms of institutional development and state capacity often thought to be solely related to larger macrohistorical forces. Second, scholars have made important contributions to studying the emergence of identity, with particular focus on how identity-based appeals by elites contribute to the substance and structure of identity politics in practice. Third, research on persistence has shown how some of these short-term outcomes can also have longer-term consequences that structure the politics of identity even up to the present day.

Research on identity politics has typically focused on either individual-level behavior and preference formation, or macro-level studies that seek to understand how the economic and cultural characteristics of groups shape aggregate political outcomes like violence, voting, or public goods. The studies discussed here suggest that we need to take seriously the role of identity at a meso-level in shaping institutions. From India to Turkey to the United States, identity prerogatives of elites and groups shape the ways in which actors interact in these contexts, and condition the ways in which institutions evolve. Local ethnic dynamics, ranging from the role of caste in India to race in the United States, can help us understand the evolution of tax instruments, census bureaucracies, or administrative agencies.

Future work on identity in HPE can also benefit from greater engagement with other approaches to historical social science research. One example is the literature in American political development (APD) that has developed largely separately. Novkov (2016) provides an overview of work on APD, law, and identity in a general sense. There is a particularly large body of work focusing on race and APD (Bateman et al. 2023; Frymer 2016; Johnson 2016), including attention to how the southern states democratized (Johnson 2010; Mickey 2015), how the intercurrence of shifts in the party system and social movement environment led to a major partisan realignment on racial issues (Schickler 2016; Grant 2020), and how major wars both compelled and constrained the inclusion of African Americans (Kryder 2000; White 2019), among other topics of interest to HPE scholars. APD scholarship on Native American politics also made several contributions to our understanding of both identity and institutional development. Bruyneel (2004), for example, highlights how top-down extensions of national citizenship to Native Americans was resisted by some, raising complicated questions about tensions between tribal and US national identities. Bloch Rubin (2020) describes the relationship between federal "Indian policy" and the growth of state capacity in the nineteenth century. Greater connections between HPE work focused on the United States and APD (and between HPE and historical institutionalist scholarship generally) could be fruitful, particularly in navigating disagreements between those who aspire to a single theoretical framework for understanding identity in politics and those who see race and caste, for example, as following distinct logics.

Notes

1. Within this scholarship, research has focused on the emergence of social cleavages and the ways in which those cleavages shaped and stabilized electoral politics and party-systems, often taking a historical institutionalist approach to the emergence of identity politics in the western world (Lipset and Rokkan 1967; Bartolini and Mair 1990; Birnir 2007). In the developing world instrumentalist approaches have sought to explain the rise of identity politics as being shaped by institutional incentives–identity groups emerge in order to give themselves the best chance at winning politics or placing their own into positions of power in order to redistribute goods from the state (Bates 1974, Posner 2005, Chandra 2007).
2. See other chapters in this volume for an extensive discussion on race (Bateman, Grumbach and Thurston 2023), ethnicity and conflict (Jha 2023), gender (Grosjean and Teele 2023), religion (Becker and Pfaff 2023), and culture (Lowes 2023).
3. Two notable exceptions are Lisa Blaydes (2018) writing about how sectarian identity shaped state-repression and everyday bureaucratic interactions in post-Saddam Iraq and Evan Lieberman (2003) on how racialized citizenship shaped intra-white coalitions in South Africa leading to better state capacity. A separate and robust literature on how ethnic diversity undermines public goods and policy-making in the developing world has focused on how identity weakens collective action, leads to taste based variation in public good preferences and how the overlap of economic and non-economic identities further exacerbate these trends. How identity matters to state-building is a burgeoning field (Habyarimanya et al 2009, Baldwin and Huber 2010, Lieberman and McClendon 2013).
4. Mares and Queralt (2015) study how the landed elites initiated the income tax in order to shift burden of taxation to capitalist classes and also deferred democratization. Hollenbach (2015) focuses on land inequality in the study of tax capacity in Prussia. Garfias (2018) and Garfias and Sellars (2022) focus on the role of economic shocks in state-building.
5. In a related paper, Wang (2022) shows how the proliferation of radio broadcasting mobilized Black political participation and activism in the South, even prior to the civil rights era.

References

Abad, Leticia Arroyo, and Noel Maurer. 2021. "History Never Really Says Goodbye: A Critical Review of the Persistence Literature." *Journal of Historical Political Economy* 1: 31–68.

Acemoglu, Daron, Simon Johnson, and James A. Robinson. 2001. "The Colonial Origins of Comparative Development: An Empirical Investigation." *American Economic Review* 91, no. 5: 1369–1401.

Acharya, Avidit, Matthew Blackwell, and Maya Sen. 2018. *Deep Roots: How Slavery Still Shapes Southern Politics*. Princeton, NJ: Princeton University Press.

Ang, Desmond. 2021. "The Birth of a Nation: Media and Racial Hate." Working paper.

Baldwin, Kate, and John D. Huber. 2010. "Economic versus Cultural Differences: Forms of Ethnic Diversity and Public Goods Provision." *American Political Science Review* 104, no. 4: 644–62.

Bartolini, Stefano, and Peter Mair. 1990. *Identity, Competition, and Electoral Availability: The Stabilization of European Electorates, 1885-1985*. New York: Cambridge University Press.

Bateman, David, Jacob M. Grumbach, and Chloe Thurston. 2023. "Race and Historical Political Economy." In *Oxford Handbook of Historical Political Economy*, ed. Jeffery A. Jenkins and Jared Rubin, 691–711. New York: Oxford University Press.

Bates, Robert H.. 1974. "Ethnic Competition and Modernization in Contemporary Africa." *Comparative Political Studies* 6, no. 4: 457–84.

Becker, Sascha O., and Steven Pfaff. 2023. "Church, State, and Historical Political Economy." *Oxford Handbook of Historical Political Economy*, ed. Jeffery A. Jenkins and Jared Rubin, 925–44. New York: Oxford University Press.

Besley, Timand, and Torsten Persson. 2011. *Pillars of Prosperity: The Political Economics of Developmental Clusters*. Princeton, NJ: Princeton University Press.

Birnir, Jóhanna Kristín. 2007. *Ethnicity and Electoral Politics*. New York: Cambridge University Press.

Blakeslee, David S. 2018. "The *Rath Yatra* Effect: Hindu Nationalist Propaganda and the Rise of the BJP." Working paper.

Blaydes, Lisa. 2018. *State of Repression: Iraq under Saddam Hussein*. Princeton, NJ: Princeton University Press.

Blaydes, Lisa, and Christopher Paik. 2016. "The Impact of Holy Land Crusades on State Formation: War Mobilization, Trade Integration and Political Development in Medieval Europe." *International Organization* 70, no. 3: 551–86.

Bloch Rubin, Ruth. 2020. "State Preventive Medicine: Public Health, Indian Removal, and the Growth of State Capacity, 1800-1840." *Studies in American Political Development* 34, no. 1: 24–43.

Brubaker, Rogers. 2004. *Ethnicity without Groups*. Cambridge, MA: Harvard University Press.

Bruyneel, Kevin. 2004. "Challenging American Boundaries: Indigenous People and the 'Gift' of U.S. Citizenship." *Studies in American Political Development* 18, no. 1: 30–43.

Centeno, Miguel Angel. 2002. *Blood and Debt: War and the Nation-State in Latin America*. University Park: Pennsylvania State University Press.

Chandra, Kanchan. 2006. "What Is Ethnic Identity and Does It Matter?" *Annual Review of Political Science* 9: 397–424.

Chandra, Kanchan. 2007. *Why Ethnic Parties Succeed: Patronage and Ethnic Head Counts in India*. New York: Cambridge University Press.

Charnysh, Volha. 2015. "Historical Legacies of Interethnic Competition: Anti-Semitism and the EU Referendum in Poland." *Comparative Political Studies* 48, no. 13: 1711–45.

Charnysh, Volha. 2022. "Explaining Outgroup Bias in Weak States: Religion and Legibility in the 1891-92 Russian Famine." *World Politics* 74, no. 2: 205–48.

Cirone, Alexandra, and Thomas B. Pepinsky. 2022. "Historical Persistence." *Annual Review of Political Science* 25: 241–59.

Engerman, Stanley L., and Kenneth L. Sokoloff. 2002. "Factor Endowments, Inequality, and Paths of Development among New World Economics." NBER Working Paper No. 9259.

Fearon, James D. 1999. "What is Identity (As We Now Use the Word)?" Working paper.

Frymer, Paul. 2016. "Citizenship and Race." *Oxford Handbook of Historical Institutionalism*, ed. Orfeo Fioretos, Tulia G. Falleti, and Adam Sheingate, 354–66. New York: Oxford University Press.

Garfias, Francisco. 2018. "Elite Competition and State Capacity Development: Theory and Evidence from Post-Revolutionary Mexico." *American Political Science Review* 112, no. 2: 339–57.

Garfias, Francisco, and Emily A. Sellars. 2022. "When State Building Backfires: Elite Coordination and Popular Grievance in Rebellion." *American Journal of Political Science* 66, no. 4: 977–92.

Grant, Keneshia N. 2020. *The Great Migration and the Democratic Party: Black Voters and the Realignment of American Politics in the 20th Century*. Philadelphia, PA: Temple University Press.

Habyarimana, James, Macartan Humphreys, Daniel N. Posner, and Jeremy M. Weinstein. 2009. *Coethnicity: Diversity and the Dilemmas of Collective Action*. New York: Russell Sage Foundation.

Hollenbach, Florian. 2015. "Elite Politics and Inequality: The Development of Fiscal Capacity in Authoritarian Regimes." PhD dissertation, Duke University.

Homola, Jonathan, Miguel M. Pereira, and Margit Tavits. 2020. "Legacies of the Third Reich: Concentration Camps and Out-Group Intolerance." *American Political Science Review* 114, no. 2: 573–90.

Jha, Saumitra. 2023. "Civil and Ethnic Conflict in Historical Political Economy." *Oxford Handbook of Historical Political Economy*, ed. Jeffery A. Jenkins and Jared Rubin, 597–622. New York: Oxford University Press.

Johnson, Kimberley S. 2010. *Reforming Jim Crow: Southern Politics and State in the Age Before Brown*. New York: Oxford University Press.

Johnson, Kimberley S. 2016. "The Color Line and the State: Race and American Political Development." *Oxford Handbook of American Political Development*, ed. Richard Valelly, Suzanne Mettler, and Robert Lieberman, 593–624. New York: Oxford University Press.

Johnson-Kanu, Ada. 2022. "Colonial Legacies in State Building: Ethnicity and Bureaucratic Representation in Nigeria."

Kryder, Daniel. 2000. *Divided Arsenal: Race and the American State during World War II*. New York: Cambridge University Press.

Laitin, David D. 1998. *Identity in Formation: The Russian-Speaking Population in the Near Abroad*. Ithaca: Cornell University Press.

Lee, Melissa M., and Nan Zhang. 2017. "Legibility and the Informational Foundations of State Capacity." *Journal of Politics* 79, no. 1: 118–32.

Lieberman, Evan S. 2003. *Race and Regionalism in the Politics of Taxation in Brazil and South Africa*. New York: Cambridge University Press.

Lieberman, Evan S., and Gwyneth H. McClendon. 2013. "The Ethnicity–Policy Preference Link in Sub-Saharan Africa." *Comparative Political Studies* 46, no. 5: 574–602.

Lowes, Sara. 2023. "Culture in Historical Political Economy." *Oxford Handbook of Historical Political Economy*, ed. Jeffery A. Jenkins and Jared Rubin, 887–924. New York: Oxford University Press.

Lipset, Seymour Martin, and Stein Rokkan. 1967. "Cleavage Structures, Party Systems, and Voter Alignments: An Introduction." *Party Systems and Voter Alignments: Cross-National Perspectives*, ed. Seymour M. Lipset and Stein Rokkan, 1–64. New York: Free Press.

Magiya, Yusuf. 2020. "Ethnic Composition, Legibility and the Conditional Effect of War on Fiscal Capacity." Working paper.

Mares, Isabela, and Didac Queralt. 2015. "The Non-Democratic Origins of Income Taxation." *Comparative Political Studies* 48, no. 14: 1974–2009.

Mazumder, Soumyajit. 2018. "The Persistent Effect of U.S. Civil Rights Protests on Political Attitudes." *American Journal of Political Science* 62, no. 4: 922–35.

Mazumder, Soumyajit. 2021. "Old South, New Deal: How the Legacy of Slavery Undermined the New Deal." *Journal of Historical Political Economy* 1, no. 3: 447–75.

Mickey, Robert. 2015. *Paths out of Dixie: The Democratization of Authoritarian Enclaves in America's Deep South, 1944–1972*. Princeton, NJ: Princeton University Press.

Murdock, George P. 1959. *Africa: Its Peoples and Their Culture History*. New York: McGraw Hill.

Novkov, Julie. 2016. "Identity and Law in American Political Development." *Oxford Handbook of American Political Development*, ed. Richard Valelly, Suzanne Mettler, and Robert Lieberman, 662–81. New York: Oxford University Press.

Nunn, Nathan. 2008. "The Long Term Effects of Africa's Slave Trades." *Quarterly Journal of Economics* 123, no. 1: 139–76.

Nunn, Nathan, and Leonard Wantchekon. 2011. "The Slave Trade and the Origins of Mistrust in Africa." *American Economic Review* 101, no. 7: 3221–52.

Peng, Peng. 2022. "Governing the Empire: Meritocracy and Patronage in Imperial China."

Posner, Daniel N. 2005. *Institutions and Ethnic Politics in Africa*. New York: Cambridge University Press.

Qian, Nancy, and Marco Tabellini. 2022. "Discrimination and State Capacity: Evidence from WWII U.S. Army Enlistment." Working paper.

Saleh, Mohamed, and Jean Tirole. 2021. "Taxing Identity: Theory and Evidence from Early Islam." *Econometrica* 89, no. 4: 1881–919.

Schickler, Eric. 2016. *Racial Realignment: The Transformation of American Liberalism, 1932–1965*. Princeton, NJ: Princeton University Press.

Scott, James C. 1998. *Seeing Like a State: How Certain Schemes to Improve the Human Condition Have Failed*. New Haven, CT: Yale University Press.

Soifer, Hillel David. 2013. "State Power and the Economic Origins of Democracy." *Studies in Comparative International Development* 48, no. 1: 1–22.

Suryanarayan, Pavithra. 2016. "Hollowing Out the State: Essays on Status Inequality, Fiscal Capacity, and Right-Wing Voting in India." PhD dissertation, Columbia University.

Suryanarayan, Pavithra. 2019. "When Do the Poor Vote for the Right Wing and Why: Status Hierarchy and Vote Choice in the Indian States." *Comparative Political Studies* 52, no. 2: 209–45.

Suryanarayan, Pavithra, and Steven White. 2021. "Slavery, Reconstruction, and Bureaucratic Capacity in the American South." *American Political Science Review* 115, no. 2: 568–84.

Teele, Dawn L., and Pauline A. Grosjean. 2023. "In Search of Gender in Historical Political Economy." *Oxford Handbook of Historical Political Economy*, ed. Jeffery A. Jenkins and Jared Rubin, 713–31. New York: Oxford University Press.

Tilly, Charles. 1992. *Coercion, Capital and European States, AD 990–1992*. Cambridge, MA: Blackwell.

Voigtländer, Nico, and Hans-Joachim Voth. 2012. "Persecution Perpetuated: The Medieval Origins of Anti-Semitic Violence in Nazi Germany." *Quarterly Journal of Economics* 127, no. 3: 1339–92.

Wang, Tianyi. 2021. "Media, Pulpit, and Populist Persuasion: Evidence from Father Coughlin." *American Economic Review* 111, no. 9: 3064–92.

Wang, Tianyi. 2022. "Waves of Empowerment: Black Radio and the Civil Rights Movement."

White, Steven. 2019. *World War II and American Racial Politics: Public Opinion, the Presidency, and Civil Rights Advocacy*. New York: Cambridge University Press.

CHAPTER 38

HISTORICAL POLITICAL ECONOMY OF MIGRATION

VOLHA CHARNYSH

THE history of humanity is a history of migration. The first humans migrated out of Africa some one hundred thousand to seventy thousand years ago, populating diverse environments and developing new cultures. In subsequent periods, migration became an important driver of social change. Encounters between people from different places accelerated innovation, trade, and institution-building, but also created competition and conflict. Migration continues unabated today, despite the growing number of restrictions on population mobility.

What are the consequences of migration for the receiving and sending societies? How does migration affect migrants themselves? Historical political economy (HPE) is well positioned to answer these questions. Because the effects of migration often unfold over generations rather than years and may change in magnitude or direction over time, looking deeper into the past allows for a more comprehensive understanding of migration phenomena. Moreover, from a methods standpoint, history can serve as a repository of cases and quasi-experimental designs for estimating causal effects of migration and studying specific causal channels through which migration operates.

This chapter highlights insights from recent HPE work on migration, understood as the movement of people, either across international borders or within countries.[1] The chapter is structured based on two broad distinctions that characterize this literature. The first concerns the subject of analysis: *receiving* societies, *sending* societies, or *migrants* themselves. The bulk of research examines the first—the effect of immigration on receiving societies—especially in relation to the Age of Mass Migration to the Americas. Within this large body of work, scholars have focused on economic as well as political and social effects—which I discuss in turn. I then consider the smaller bodies of HPE work on the consequences of emigration for the sending countries and on migrants and their children, respectively. International migration is reviewed most extensively, but I also reference some related studies on internal migration.

The second broad distinction is between the two types of migration: "Voluntary migration" is typically understood to result from economic considerations; "forced migration" is produced by conflict, natural or man-made disasters, or state policy, though the boundary is not so clear-cut in practice.[2] I discuss forced and voluntary migration side by side but emphasize important distinctions between their consequences, particularly for migrants themselves.

The chapter concludes with a brief discussion of the advantages of drawing on historical cases and HPE methods for studying migration and suggests directions for future research.

Effects of Migration on Receiving Societies

Economic Effects of Voluntary Migration

The economic effects of migration are a dominant theme in HPE research. This work typically concludes that immigration is beneficial for economic development and that its effects persist for a long time. Immigrants may benefit receiving economies through several distinct channels, including the introduction of new skills, knowledge, and human capital; the diversification of skills and occupations; the increase in the size of the labor force; and the diffusion of cultural traits that improve economic performance. Migrants can also reshape the trajectory of economic development by introducing new institutions and cultural norms, and here the effects are more ambiguous. Both the size and the composition of the immigrant population matter.

Much of the empirical evidence on the economic benefits of immigration comes from the Age of Mass Migration (1850–1920) (see review in Abramitzky and Boustan 2017). This is not surprising given the magnitude of the phenomenon and the availability of linked data at the county and individual levels, particularly for the United States. Some fifty-five million immigrants left Europe during this period, of whom nearly thirty million settled in the United States. The composition of immigration changed over time, as the arrivals from Southern and Eastern Europe increasingly outpaced those from Northern and Western Europe. Mass migration came to an end when the US Congress imposed a literacy test (1917) and national origin quotas (1921; 1924) (Hatton and Williamson 1998).

Empirical research suggests immigration had both immediate and long-term economic benefits. Sequeira, Nunn, and Qian (2020) offer one of the most comprehensive treatments of the economic effects of the size of immigrant population in the United States. Instrumenting for the share of immigrants at the county level with an interaction of railway access and aggregate immigration to the United States, they find that immigrants increased the supply of labor for industrialization and provided new skills and knowledge that raised innovation and agricultural productivity. These initial benefits persisted over time, as evidenced by higher income, educational attainment, and urbanization as well as lower poverty and unemployment rates today in counties with historically higher immigration.

Other studies find similar results using alternative identification strategies and outcome variables. Tabellini (2020a) shows that immigration increased natives' employment and industrial production in US cities in the short run. Focusing on the long-run impact, Rodríguez-Pose and von Berlepsch (2014) show that immigration predicts higher GDP per capita in 2005; they argue that immigration created a culture of entrepreneurship, ambition, and risk taking. Akcigit, Grigsby, and Nicholas (2017) demonstrate that immigrants were more likely to file patents in the 1880–1940 period, accounting for a higher share of inventors than their population share, and that areas where foreign-born expertise was more prevalent experienced faster growth from 1940 to 2000. Researchers also find that the imposition of immigration quotas in the 1920s lowered earnings of US-born workers (Abramitzky, Boustan, and Eriksson 2019) and reduced rates of innovation (Moser and San 2020).

One of the advantages of focusing on the United States during the Age of Mass Migration is the heterogeneity of immigrants' skills and countries of origin, which allows scholars to investigate whether the composition of immigrant population matters. Using a panel dataset from 1850 to 2010, Fulford, Petkov, and Schiantarelli (2020) find that migrants from countries with higher economic development, greater generalized trust and cooperation, and longer histories of stateness had a larger positive effect on GDP per worker.[3] Ager and Brückner (2013) demonstrate that the diversity of immigrants enhanced the variety of skills and occupations, which resulted in more diverse goods and services. They construct both fractionalization and polarization indices based on immigrants' countries of origin in the 1870–1920 period, showing that a within-county increase in the diversity of the migrant population increases output per capita, while a within-county increase in polarization decreases output per capita.[4]

Scholars also find that mass immigration from Europe spurred economic development in South America, where state governments often purposefully invited European settlers. Research on this region typically emphasizes immigrants' higher human capital as the primary causal channel. Droller (2018) shows that the arrival of European immigrants from 1869 to 1914 raised GDP per capita in Argentina; he argues that Europeans were on average more literate and brought knowledge and skills useful for industrial development. Focusing on Brazil, Rocha, Ferraz, and Soares (2017) find that the government-sponsored settlement of Europeans, who had higher human capital, shifted the occupational structure toward skill-intensive sectors such as manufacturing and increased the supply of educated labor, raising per capita income in the long run. De Carvalho Filho and Monasterio (2012) likewise find that Brazilian municipalities closer to nineteenth-century European settlements have higher per capita income, less poverty, and better health and education outcomes today. However, they argue that a more egalitarian distribution of land in European settlements was more important than human capital for explaining these beneficial effects.

Inviting high-skilled immigrants to benefit from their human capital has been common among governments throughout history.[5] One of the earliest examples analyzed in HPE is the 1685 Edict of Potsdam, which allowed the Huguenots, persecuted for their religion in France, to settle in Prussia. Hornung (2014) takes advantage of the fact that few alternative communication channels existed in this historical period to isolate the effect of immigration on the diffusion of knowledge. He finds that the Huguenots, who were more skilled than the local population, increased the productivity of textile manufacturing and that their economic impact was still visible a century later. In Russia, Catherine the Great invited European (predominantly German) immigrants in the late eighteenth century hoping to stimulate "development and growth of many kinds of manufacturing, plants, and various installations" (Deutsche Welle 2013). Natkhov and Vasilenok (2019) show that German settlements fulfilled her expectations; German presence increased labor productivity among Russian peasants by encouraging the adoption of new agricultural techniques, such as the use of heavy plows and fanning mills and the growth of wheat. Lankina (2012) further shows that European settlers raised literacy rates among other population groups. Russian tsars also encouraged settlement of the Russian Orthodox population in its frontier territories, to secure control over the regions populated by other ethnic groups. Natkhov (2015) finds that nineteenth-century Russian settlements in the North Caucasus increased literacy among the indigenous population, which led to higher incomes, educational attainment, and quality of governance in the long run.

Immigrants may also benefit receiving economies by creating stronger ties with their countries of origin and providing information about overseas markets. Their presence reduces transaction costs for cross-border trade and investment. Burchardi, Chaney, and Hassan (2019) argue that the ancestry of US population dating back to the Age of Mass Migration affects the information about specific overseas markets and thus shapes the direction of foreign direct investment (FDI) sent and received by local firms today. Relatedly, Burchardi and Hassan (2013) show that regions in West Germany that received more refugees from East Germany between 1949 and 1961 experienced faster growth of income per capita after the fall of the Berlin Wall in 1989, as these migrants benefitted from existing social ties to seize new economic opportunities in East Germany. The trade channel remains relatively understudied in HPE.

Finally, immigration may alter formal and informal institutions in the receiving societies, setting them on a different economic trajectory. First, immigration may change social relationships, resulting in the development of new governance mechanisms. Acemoglu, Johnson, and Robinson (2001) famously credit settler colonization with the creation of "development-minded" institutions that produced economic growth.[6] Using evidence from Indonesia, Pepinsky (2016) argues that migrant settlement may produce new subnational patterns of economic governance. He shows that Chinese migrants experienced greater social exclusion and thus relied on cooperation with local political elites for protection; the resulting informal relationships shaped the accommodativeness of economic governance to firm interests and persisted over time. Immigrants also bring norms and values from their places of origin, which have been shown to persist in a new environment for several generations and diffuse to the native population (see, e.g., Grosjean 2014; Bracco, De Paola, and Green 2015; Charnysh and Peisakhin 2022; Miho, Jarotschkin, and Zhuravskaya 2020). In principle, this "cultural baggage" may undermine the functioning of formal and informal institutions in the receiving societies, with implications for economic growth, although there is little evidence to support this channel for both historical and contemporary cases (Nowrasteh and Powell 2021).

Taken together, the empirical evidence reviewed above suggests that immigration benefits the receiving economies. The benefits are largest for high-skilled, better-educated immigrants from countries at higher levels of economic development. Human capital received more attention than other causal channels, possibly because it is easier to quantify.

Economic Effects of Forced Migration

Does it matter whether migrants are forced or voluntary? Forced migrants experience psychological trauma and property loss that may lower their economic productivity. They lose ties to their places of origin, which may reduce opportunities for economic exchange. Their legal status is often uncertain and impermanent, which may delay integration (Becker and Ferrara 2019). Forced migrants also have less control over their destinations, which may lead to occupational mismatch and delay economic integration (Braun and Dwenger 2020). Notwithstanding these features, studies have found that forced migration benefited receiving economies in the long run.[7] This was the case not only for smaller groups of refugees with superior education and skill levels, such as the French Huguenots in Prussia (Hornung 2014) and the German Jewish scientists in the United States (Moser, Voena, and Waldinger 2014), but also in cases of mass displacement of populations that were relatively similar to the natives or arrived from less developed regions.

In the aftermath of the Greco-Turkish War of 1919–1922, 1.2 million Orthodox Christians from Turkey were resettled to Greece, and 350,000 Muslims from Greece were resettled to Turkey. Murard and Sakalli (2018) find that Greek municipalities that had received more refugees in 1923 had higher average earnings, a larger manufacturing sector, and higher night light luminosity in 1991. Both high- and low-skilled refugees improved subnational economic outcomes, though the effects were larger for the former. The authors theorize that refugees brought complementary skills that fostered long-run growth by facilitating technology transfers and increasing agricultural know-how.

Population transfers on an even larger scale occurred after World War II. Some 12.5 million Germans and 5 million Poles were resettled following changes to the Polish and German borders in 1945. In Poland, Charnysh (2019) shows that localities populated by forced and voluntary migrants from more heterogeneous regions achieved higher entrepreneurship rates and incomes than localities populated by more homogeneous migrant populations after Poland's transition to a market economy, even though they were economically similar during state socialism. She argues that the benefits of diversity that come with immigration are conditional on the nature of state institutions. In West Germany, Braun and Kvasnicka (2014) demonstrate that expellees' arrival accelerated the transition away from agriculture and increased output per worker in the short term. They propose that, as a result, the expellees had lower costs of switching from one occupation to another and were more responsive to growing economic opportunities in the manufacturing sector than the native population. Focusing on Bavaria, Semrad (2015) shows that the inflow of German expellees from industrialized Sudetenland (Czechoslovakia) generated educational spillovers, increasing the human capital of the natives. Charnysh (2022) traces the effects of German expellees in West Germany on subnational economic outcomes over a longer time period, showing that places with a larger and more heterogeneous refugee population experienced a reversal of fortunes over time. Although expellee presence initially created economic challenges for receiving countries and municipalities, both the share and heterogeneity of expellee population increased education levels and entrepreneurship rates over time.

The partition of British India displaced nearly eighteen million people during the 1947–1951 period, changing the demographics of the population in affected districts (Bharadwaj, Khwaja, and Mian 2014). Bharadwaj and Mirza (2019) show that Indian districts that received more refugees increased their agricultural yields, took up more high-yielding varieties of seeds, and used more tractors and fertilizers in 2009. They attribute this long-run economic benefit to the composition of incoming refugees, who had higher literacy rates than both the native population and the refugees leaving for Pakistan, as well as to the land reforms in districts affected by the population exchange.

To summarize, forced migration created significant short-term challenges, but benefited receiving economies *in the long run*, through some of the same mechanisms as voluntary migration, such as human capital, skill complementarities, and an increase in the size of the labor force. Importantly, in the three cases of mass population transfers, the receiving governments—sometimes with the help of international organizations—responded to the arrival of refugees with redistributive reforms, financial aid, and other investments aimed at facilitating economic and political integration. Such active governmental support was less common in cases of voluntary immigration.

Political and Social Consequences of Immigration

HPE research on the political impact of immigration is considerably smaller. Studies typically find that the arrival of immigrants increases nativism and reduces public investment in the receiving communities in the short run. The effects are more ambiguous in the medium to long term, as immigrants may have an independent effect on policy by voting and engaging in political activism, on the one hand, and by transmitting their values to the local population, on the other.

Opposition to immigration appears to be a common response in all historical periods. Even though immigrant presence benefited local economies, US cities that received more immigrants during the Age of Mass Migration saw greater tax cuts and reduction in the provision of public goods and were more likely to elect conservative politicians and support restrictions on immigration (Tabellini 2020a). Backlash against newcomers also occurred during the Great Migration, which brought approximately six million African Americans from the US South to northern, midwestern, and western states (Boustan 2010; Shertzer and Walsh 2019; Tabellini 2020b). An increase in the share of Black residents induced "white flight" and lowered property values, which reduced public spending and tax revenues (Tabellini 2020b).

Intergroup tensions and nativism were common even in cases where migrants were ethnically and racially similar to the local population, such as West Germany and Poland after World War II. In the territories Poland acquired from Germany in 1945, migrants originating from different regions resented each other; the small indigenous population was perceived as German and treated poorly (Charnysh 2022; Charnysh 2019). Tensions were also high between German expellees and German natives in Germany. Braun and Dwenger (2020) show that the anti-immigrant Bavarian Party secured more votes in districts with a higher share of expellees as well as with the greatest religious distance between expellees and natives. Charnysh (2022) finds that tax rates on property and business, disproportionately owned by the native population, decreased with the share of expellees in municipalities where natives still dominated the local council. However, the relationship between the share of expellees and tax rates was positive in municipalities where expellees were in the majority, a sign of political polarization between two groups and the unwillingness of natives to contribute to local budgets following the arrival of refugees. Conversely, Chevalier et al. (2019) demonstrate a positive relationship between the share of expellees and tax rates for cities. Divergent findings between these two studies suggest that fiscal implications of immigration depend on context: backlash against refugees was likely higher in the countryside than in cities because cities received fewer expellees and were historically more diverse.

Counterintuitively, nativist concerns about immigrants can give rise to progressive reforms that increase public spending. Bandiera et al. (2019) show that US states that hosted European immigrants without exposure to compulsory schooling in their home countries passed compulsory schooling laws significantly earlier in order to teach civic values and discipline immigrants' children. Relatedly, Kevane and Sundstrom (2014) demonstrate that greater diversity of the immigrant population during the Age of Mass Migration contributed to the expansion of public libraries, perceived as a way to assimilate or control immigrant groups. In this way, the natives' apprehension about immigrant assimilation had incentivized nation-building and increased human capital in the long run.

Migrants often have different political preferences from the local population and may influence policy once they become eligible to vote. Giuliano and Tabellini (2020) find that European immigrants to the United States (1910–1930) brought greater support for the welfare state from their countries of origin and transmitted their values to the native population. They credit immigration with support for the Democratic Party and the New Deal. They also show that survey respondents in counties with higher historical immigration are today more likely to support welfare spending, the minimum wage, and higher taxes for financing fiscal deficits.

How do we square this conclusion with evidence from Tabellini (2020a) that immigration reduced public spending in cities? The short- and long-run effects of immigration may be different: opposition to redistribution and intolerance among the natives may decline as they become more accustomed to diversity and have more contact with outgroup members (Ramos et al. 2019; Christ et al. 2014), and as migrants' values diffuse to the native population over time. Calderón, Fouka, and Tabellini (2019) find some evidence for the diffusion of more tolerant values from immigrants to natives using data from the Great Migration of African Americans. They show that changes in racial composition of US counties during this period increased local political support for civil rights legislation and racial equality, not only among Black but also among White voters. At the same time, Black immigration increased polarization along party lines: Democratic legislators in Democratic districts became even more supportive of civil rights, while the Republican Congress members became even less supportive. Other studies emphasize the channel of intergroup contact and social learning. For example, Fielding (2018) argues that the positive effect of contact with medieval Jews in the United Kingdom had lasting effects on tolerance and predicts more positive attitudes toward immigrants today.

These findings are important because concerns that migrants may undermine social capital and increase social conflict in the receiving communities are prominent in contemporary debates about immigration. HPE scholars are well positioned to contribute to this debate by investigating how long anti-immigrant backlash persists and what policy interventions can mitigate it. Preliminary evidence from historical cases suggests that immigration leads to the adoption of more tolerant norms and progressive policies over time.

Another question for future research is how immigration affects state capacity. As societies become more diverse, transaction costs increase and more formal enforcement mechanisms are needed to support cooperation. Using data from post–World War II Poland, Charnysh (2019) argues that cultural heterogeneity that comes with migration increases the demand for formal enforcement and may lead to the strengthening of state capacity over time. Does immigration affect investment in governance mechanisms in other contexts?

How Emigration Affects Sending Societies

Migration also has important economic and political consequences for places migrants leave behind, and scholars have devoted more attention to this question in recent years (Kapur 2014). Emigration may advance economic growth through remittances, technological change, and the return of more skilled workers. It may also have negative economic consequences due to brain drain and the reduction in the labor force. On balance, studies found that voluntary emigration is more likely to benefit sending economies than forced emigration. Emigration may also affect political outcomes by creating an outside option for the domestic population, changing the distribution of economic resources, and diffusing new ideas and information.

The most straightforward immediate consequence of large-scale emigration is the reduction of labor supply, which may benefit those who stay by reducing competition. The effect may also vary depending on the characteristics of those who leave. Scholars have argued that emigration of low-skill labor from Europe during the Age of Mass Migration increased real wages in the sending countries and contributed to the convergence of income between the Old World and the New World (e.g., Ljungberg 1997; Hatton and Williamson 1998; Enflo, Lundh, and Prado 2014). By increasing the costs of labor, the decrease in labor supply may also encourage the adoption of labor-saving technologies. Andersson, Karadja, and Prawitz (2021) show that mass emigration from Sweden in the late nineteenth century increased the number of patents and accelerated the adoption of new technologies in labor-intensive industries. Relatedly, Coluccia and Spadavechia (2021) find that the 1921 immigration quotas in the United States increased labor supply in Italy, reducing incentives for the adoption of labor-saving technologies, such as the electrical engine.

The effects of the reduction in labor supply and population overall are likely to vary by historical period and institutional environment. Chaney and Hornbeck (2016) study the effects of the expulsion of Muslims (Moriscos) from Spain in 1609, during the Malthusian era, characterized by diminishing returns to labor. They find that the population levels in districts where Moriscos used to live did not recover for at least 177 years and that the reduction of population produced an enduring increase in per capita output. Such slow rates of convergence may be due to the persistence of extractive institutions established in Morisco-dominated districts after the expulsions. In post–World War II Europe, under a different set of political institutions, the consequences of mass expulsions were the opposite. Testa (2021) shows that the expulsion of three million Germans from Czechoslovakia at the end of World War II had persistent negative effects on population density, human capital, and sectoral composition of the economy using geographic regression discontinuity design to compare areas that experienced mass expulsions with areas just across the border that did not. Reasons for this pattern are complex, as migrants from other parts of the country replaced the German population of the affected districts. The expulsions were also accompanied by violence and destruction of physical capital. These features characterize most cases of forced emigration, making it more challenging to isolate a specific causal mechanism.

Emigration of the highly educated population may have negative consequences for the countries of origin, particularly when it is involuntary. Researchers have shown that the flight of Jewish teachers and professors from Germany and Austria during the 1930s reduced education levels (Akbulut-Yuksel and Yuksel 2015) and undermined economic success of university students (Waldinger 2010). The removal of Jewish managers in Nazi Germany lowered corporations' stock prices, dividends, and returns on assets (Huber, Lindenthal, and Waldinger 2021). However, voluntary emigration of the educated population can also increase the returns to education and encourage investment in human capital by those who stay behind. Fernández-Sánchez (2021) finds support for this mechanism in the case of emigration from Spanish Galicia to Latin America in the early twentieth century. He shows that although emigration reduced literacy rates in the short run, within ten years the effect turned positive. These gains in human capital in municipalities with higher emigration rates have persisted to this day.

Voluntary emigration may also influence sending economies through the channel of financial remittances. The flow of money across borders not only benefits emigrants' families, but also influences the development of financial institutions in countries of origin. Esteves and Khoudour-Castéras (2011) show that the demand for financial services and increased availability of capital in pre-1914 Europe contributed to the emergence of new domestic banks specializing in remittance activities, gave rise to reforms that encouraged channeling remittances through official financial institutions, and accelerated the expansion of the post office network in rural areas.

Large-scale emigration may affect the demand for political change directly, by providing outside options to potential emigrants, or indirectly, though financial or political remittances. Building on Hirschman's seminal framework of exit and voice, Sellars (2019) argues that the presence of exit options reduces political mobilization in contexts where collective action is risky and large-scale participation is necessary to effect change. She supports the predictions from a formal model using evidence from postrevolution Mexico and twentieth-century Japan. In a book manuscript, Sellars (2022) shows that Mexico's land reform initially lagged in areas with high emigration, but the trend reversed after the Great Depression, an exogenous shock that halted emigration to the United States. Conversely, Karadja and Prawitz (2019) argue that easier access to emigration increased the bargaining power of those who stayed behind vis-à-vis the local elites in Sweden during the Age of Mass Migration. They find that residents of municipalities with greater rates of emigration were more likely to join the labor movement, participate in strikes, turn out to vote, and cast ballots for the left. Through these mechanisms, emigration increased welfare spending and led to the introduction of representative democracy in local governments. Walter (2019) observes similar patterns for internal migration using a panel dataset of Swiss cantons in the 1930–1975 period.

A large literature suggests that financial remittances may bring about political change in autocracies, but it is based primarily on contemporary data (e.g., Escribà-Folch, Meseguer, and Wright 2019). The diffusion of norms, values, and resources from emigrants to their places of origin is another possible channel through which emigration can bring about political changes (Krawatzek and Müller-Funk 2020). Historical cases are particularly useful for estimating the impact of political remittances because there were fewer spillover effects between countries before the revolution of communications and information technology.

Migrants also influence politics in sending societies when they return. The rates of return are nontrivial. For instance, during the Age of Mass Migration, up to 60 to 75 percent of European migrants are estimated to have returned (Bandiera, Rasul, and Viarengo 2013), bringing new capital, knowledge, and transnational connections to their places of origin. The political effects of return migration can be significant even when migrants constitute a small proportion of the sending population. Aggarwal, Chaurey, and Suryanarayan (2022) demonstrate this by studying indentured migration from India to the British colony of Natal. They argue that migrants were exposed to new political ideas, which led them to challenge the status quo at home upon return. They show that sending districts experienced higher turnout and more competitive elections and that this effect was largely driven by migrants from intermediate castes, which were historically marginalized and were more likely to fight for political recognition.

Divergent findings on the economic and political impact of emigration on sending countries speak to the importance of institutional context and the nature of migration. HPE scholarship needs to devote more attention to understanding the role of contextual variables and specifying scope conditions under which a specific empirical pattern holds.

Effects on Migrants Themselves

There is also a growing literature on the effects of migration on migrants themselves. The distinction between forced and voluntary migration is particularly important here. Voluntary migrants have more agency regarding the decision to migrate, the choice of destination, and the possibility of return. Understanding how migration affects migrants requires addressing selection at multiple stages.[8] Selection is somewhat less problematic for cases of forced migration: forced migrants are forced to leave and cannot return freely; they have less control over their destination than voluntary migrants. The individual effects of forced migration are likely to differ significantly from the effects of voluntary migration because forced migrants experience violence and lose their possessions and political rights. Forced migration thus amounts to "a more life-changing experience" than voluntary migration (Becker and Ferrara 2019, 3).

Research on voluntary migration suggests that migrants gain in some domains but lose in others. Migration can improve economic opportunities for migrants and their children. For instance, Abramitzky, Boustan, and Eriksson (2012) find a large positive return to migration in the late nineteenth century by comparing Norwegian immigrants in the United States with their brothers in Norway. To overcome the selection bias, they match men from both countries by name and age and assign each individual mean earnings for their occupation in the relevant country. Similarly, Collins and Wanamaker (2014) identify large gains in earnings for Black Americans who moved to the North during the Great Migration in the United States, which reflects changes in occupations (a tendency to move into higher-paying jobs) and locations (within occupations, pay in the North was higher than in the South). To deal with selection, they compare men from the same county or household of origin and conduct within-person analyses. Using data linked from 1940 to 2000, Alexander et al. (2017) find gains in education, income, and economic status for the children of African Americans who moved, relative to the children of African American parents who remained in the South.

Economic benefits notwithstanding, the stresses of relocation to a new environment as well as a cold welcome from the local population may take a toll on migrants' health. Black et al. (2015) show that migration out of the South reduced longevity of African Americans, despite both positive selection of immigrants and economic and social improvements upon migration. They hypothesize that this negative outcome is due to discrimination in housing and employment as well as detrimental behaviors (smoking, drinking) after the relocation. Relatedly, Eriksson and Niemesh (2016) show that Black infant mortality rates increased following migration to the North. Additional disadvantages may come with migration in the presence of economic insecurity and discrimination in the labor market. Compared to brothers who stayed in the South, African American men who moved were more likely to be incarcerated (Eriksson 2019; Derenoncourt 2019).

It stands to reason that economic gains will be smaller and the detriment to health greater for forced migrants. The long-term economic implications depend, in part, on migrants' strategies following the loss of income, community, and economic status. Bauer, Braun, and Kvasnicka (2013) show that both first- and second-generation expellees in West Germany were economically worse off than the native population twenty-five years after the resettlement, even though they were economically similar just before the war. Displacement also reduced incomes, increased unemployment, and increased blue-collar employment. One exception is displaced agricultural workers, who left low-paid agriculture and experienced income gains. At the same time, the authors find that the children of expellees acquired more education, possibly as a strategy to compensate for the loss of wealth. Becker et al. (2020) find similar effects of displacement on human capital in Poland. They argue that refugees responded to the loss of physical assets by increasing investment in education. Using data from post–World War II displacement in Finland, Sarvimäki, Uusitalo, and Jäntti (2020) find that forced migration from the region annexed by the Soviet Union increased transitions to nonagricultural occupations, which in turn led to a large increase in long-term income among the displaced population. In one of the rare studies that focuses on displaced women, Lu, Siddiqui, and Bharadwaj (2021) show that uprooting during the Partition of India and Pakistan increased the rates of early marriage and the number of children women had and decreased their educational attainment.

Forced migrants also experience physical and psychological trauma, which can undermine their health and reduce longevity. Post–World War II German expellees in West Germany had a higher mortality risk in old age (Bauer, Giesecke, and Janisch 2017). Finns uprooted by the Soviet invasion had a higher risk of death due to heart disease (Haukka et al. 2017).

There is also some evidence that forced migration shapes the political attitudes of the affected individuals and their descendants. Menon (2021) argues that the violent process of expulsion and discrimination at the destination increased support for the far right among German expellees. He shows that the far right secured more votes in West German districts that received more expellees after World War II. Using a multigenerational survey, Lupu and Peisakhin (2017) show that the descendants of the Crimean Tatars who suffered more intensely during the deportation from Crimea by the Soviet Union had stronger in-group identity, more hostile attitudes toward the perpetrator nation (Russia), and greater rates of political participation. At the same time, there is some evidence that the experience of mass displacement makes refugees and their descendants more empathetic to the plight of others. In particular, Dinas, Fouka, and Schläpfer (2021) show that priming family history of forced migration increases sympathy toward refugees in contemporary Greece and Germany.

Separating different channels through which migration shapes attitudes and behavior can be challenging and requires considering not only the experience of migration, but also characteristics of the receiving communities. This is an important direction for future research.

The Advantages of Relying on Historical Cases

The studies reviewed here not only advance our understanding of the multifaceted effects of migration but also highlight distinct advantages of using historical cases and HPE methods. First, the effects of migration typically unfold over a long time horizon and may persist for more than a century (e.g., Sequeira, Nunn, and Qian 2020; Karadja and Prawitz 2019; Chaney and Hornbeck 2016; Hornung 2014). For individuals, the effects of migration unfold over generations rather than years (e.g., Abramitzky et al. 2021; Alexander et al. 2017; Lupu and Peisakhin 2017). Historical data can help understand the "life cycle" of migration and thus predict demographic pressures on receiving countries (Hatton and Williamson 2009). Extending the temporal lens also reveals that the impact of migration may change in magnitude and direction over time (e.g., Fernández-Sánchez 2021; Ramos et al. 2019), particularly when the institutional environment changes (e.g., Charnysh 2019; Burchardi and Hassan 2013). Adopting a longer perspective thus allows for a more comprehensive and accurate evaluation of the impact of migration.

Second, historical cases can be useful for addressing endogeneity issues. Selection bias, which can enter at different stages of migration, is one of the main concerns when estimating the economic and political consequences of migration. It is sometimes possible to address selection by drawing on historical cases and using quasi-experimental designs. Virtually all studies referenced in this chapter seek to identify the causal effects of migration. Some of the most common approaches are instrumental variables, including the variation on the shift-share instrument (e.g., Tabellini 2020b), and difference-in-differences estimation that compares locations before and after changes in the volume of migration (e.g., Coluccia and Spadavechia 2021).

Relatedly, focusing on historical periods when migration was relatively less regulated can illuminate the process of selection into migration itself. Whereas today the United States relies on a patchwork of legal restrictions that distinguish between migrants on the basis of skills, country of origin, and family background, it maintained relatively open borders until the 1920s. This has allowed researchers to study the decisions to emigrate and to estimate economic returns to immigration (e.g., Abramitzky, Boustan, and Eriksson 2012; Connor 2019). History can also serve as a repository of case studies for studying the effects of various types of restrictions on immigration on both sending and receiving communities (e.g., Moser and San 2020; Abramitzky, Boustan, and Eriksson 2019).

Finally, historical data are sometimes more fine-grained and detailed than contemporary data. This is the case, for example, for personal information that may be closed to research to protect individuals involved. In the United States, individual census records are released to the public seventy-two years after the day of the census. This means that the 1950 (earliest) census microdata became available only in April 2022. Microdata up to 1940, on the other hand, is freely available from IPUMS USA. Other countries have similar restrictions. Access to personal data is particularly important for research on migrant selection and assimilation and on the effects of migration on migrants and their children (e.g., Abramitzky, Boustan, and Eriksson 2012; Eriksson 2019; Escamilla-Guerrero, Kosack, and Ward 2021).

Conclusion: Directions for Further Research

HPE literature on migration is vast, but blind spots remain. Significantly more research exists on the receiving societies than on the sending societies and on migrants themselves. In addition, while the economic effects of migration are increasingly well understood, there is less work on its political and social consequences. It is important to ask how migration affects the quality of political and economic institutions, whether it facilitates or impedes nation- and state-building, and whether the effects of immigration on tolerance and social cohesion change over time. These relationships are harder to investigate, but arguably are more important because they mediate the effects of migration on economic outcomes. For example, discriminatory policies in the receiving countries affect the jobs immigrants take and how much they interact with the native population, which in turn mediates their contributions to local economies.

Much of what we know about the effects of immigration comes from the United States during the Age of Mass Migration—an important but atypical case given the nation's origins as a settler colony. Immigration will possibly have different social and political consequences in states where the population is more ethnically homogeneous and less geographically mobile. The economic benefits of immigration under extractive institutions or in weak states may also be smaller. Exploring the consequences of historic migration in other contexts, including China, Africa, and the Middle East, might provide new theoretical insights.

More broadly, the HPE of migration would benefit from integrating findings from different country cases into a more general theoretical framework. Much of the existing work addresses narrow empirical questions using subnational data from a specific historical period. This approach offers significant identification and measurement advantages, but the knowledge it generates does not necessarily aggregate to a general theory and may not apply to other settings. The biggest takeaway from studies reviewed here is that context matters: the political and economic effects of migration in one setting may be the exact opposite to its effects in another setting.

Few theories are likely to hold universally, but it is important to integrate information from these disparate projects into a broader framework and begin specifying the conditions under which a specific empirical pattern or causal channel applies. Understanding how the effects of migration vary with political institutions and the level of economic development at origin and destination, as well as with the nature of migration itself, is particularly important for extending the lessons from historic cases to contemporary immigration.

Notes

1. I also use the terms "immigration" (moving into, from the perspective of receiving countries or regions) and "emigration" (moving away, from the perspective of sending countries or regions).
2. Even in times of conflict and famine, only some people are able to emigrate; one may also debate whether leaving home to feed one's family is indeed a voluntary decision (Becker and Ferrara 2019).
3. This study builds on work by Putterman and Weil (2010), who construct a matrix of world migration between 1500 and 2000 for 165 countries that links the ancestry of each country's population groups to this group's history of stateness and the timing of agricultural transition. The authors also find that countries with a population whose ancestors have earlier histories of stateness and transitioned to agriculture earlier have higher GDP today and interpret this as evidence for the importance of human capital.
4. Increases in cultural polarization also predict the growth of the tax ratio and the share of public sector officials, which they interpret as evidence of distortionary taxation and excessively large government size due to conflict between immigrants of different origins (Ager and Brückner 2013).
5. State sponsorship often imparted significant economic advantages to the immigrant settlements, which can complicate the estimation of the contribution of immigrants' human capital.
6. Alternatively, scholars argued that European settlers' human capital explains higher levels of economic development in settler colonies (e.g., Glaeser et al. 2004).

7. In the short run, one study found that the arrival of expellees in West Germany after World War II reduced employment of the population in high-inflow regions (Braun and Mahmoud 2014). The expellees also increased the burdens on local budgets because they were disproportionately dependent on welfare in the immediate postwar period (Chevalier et al. 2019).
8. This is also an important concern for studying the effects of migration for sending and receiving countries.

References

Abramitzky, Ran, and Leah Boustan. 2017. "Immigration in American Economic History." *Journal of Economic Literature* 55, no. 4: 1311-45. https://doi.org/10.1257/jel.20151189.

Abramitzky, Ran, Leah Platt Boustan, and Katherine Eriksson. 2012. "Europe's Tired, Poor, Huddled Masses: Self-Selection and Economic Outcomes in the Age of Mass Migration." *American Economic Review* 102, no. 5: 1832-56. https://doi.org/10.1257/aer.102.5.1832.

Abramitzky, Ran, Leah Boustan, and Katherine Eriksson. 2019. "To the New World and Back Again: Return Migrants in the Age of Mass Migration." *ILR Review* 72, no. 2: 300-322. https://doi.org/10.1177/0019793917726981.

Abramitzky, Ran, Leah Boustan, Elisa Jácome, and Santiago Pérez. 2021. "Intergenerational Mobility of Immigrants in the United States over Two Centuries." *American Economic Review* 111, no. 2: 580-608.

Acemoglu, Daron, Simon Johnson, and James A. Robinson. 2001. "The Colonial Origins of Comparative Development: An Empirical Investigation." *American Economic Review* 91: 1369-401.

Ager, Philipp, and Markus Brückner. 2013. "Cultural Diversity and Economic Growth: Evidence from the US during the Age of Mass Migration." *European Economic Review* 64 (November): 76-97. https://doi.org/10.1016/j.euroecorev.2013.07.011.

Aggarwal, Ashish, Ritam Chaurey, and Pavithra Suryanarayan. 2022. "Indentured Migration, Caste and Electoral Competition in Colonial India." Working Paper. https://ssrn.com/abstract=4114673.

Akbulut-Yuksel, Mevlude, and Mutlu Yuksel. 2015. "The Long-Term Direct and External Effects of Jewish Expulsions in Nazi Germany." *American Economic Journal: Economic Policy* 7, no. 3: 58-85. https://doi.org/10.1257/pol.20130223.

Akcigit, Ufuk, John Grigsby, and Tom Nicholas. 2017. "Immigration and the Rise of American Ingenuity." *American Economic Review* 107, no. 5: 327-31. https://doi.org/10.1257/aer.p20171021.

Alexander, J. Trent, Christine Leibbrand, Catherine Massey, and Stewart Tolnay. 2017. "Second-Generation Outcomes of the Great Migration." *Demography* 54, no. 6: 2249-71. https://doi.org/10.1007/s13524-017-0625-8.

Andersson, David, Mounir Karadja, and Erik Prawitz. 2021. "Mass Migration and Technological Change." Working Paper. https://doi.org/10.31235/osf.io/74ub8.

Bandiera, Oriana, Myra Mohnen, Imran Rasul, and Martina Viarengo. 2019. "Nation-Building through Compulsory Schooling during the Age of Mass Migration." *Economic Journal* 129, no. 617: 62-109. https://doi.org/10.1111/ecoj.12624.

Bandiera, Oriana, Imran Rasul, and Martina Viarengo. 2013. "The Making of Modern America: Migratory Flows in the Age of Mass Migration." *Journal of Development Economics* 102 (May): 23-47. https://doi.org/10.1016/j.jdeveco.2012.11.005.

Bauer, Thomas K., Sebastian Braun, and Michael Kvasnicka. 2013. "The Economic Integration of Forced Migrants: Evidence for Post-War Germany." *Economic Journal* 123, no. 571: 998–1024. https://doi.org/10.1111/ecoj.12023.

Bauer, Thomas K., Matthias Giesecke, and Laura M. Janisch. 2017. "Forced Migration and Mortality." Ruhr Economic Papers no. 713. http://dx.doi.org/10.4419/86788832.

Becker, Sascha, and Andreas Ferrara. 2019. "Consequences of Forced Migration: A Survey of Recent Findings." *Labour Economics* 59 (August): 1–16. https://doi.org/10.1016/j.labeco.2019.02.007.

Becker, Sascha, Irena Grosfeld, Pauline Grosjean, Nico Voigtländer, and Ekaterina Zhuravskaya. 2020. "Forced Migration and Human Capital: Evidence from Post-WWII Population Transfers." *American Economic Review* 110, no. 5: 1430–63. https://doi.org/10.1257/aer.20181518.

Bharadwaj, Prashant, Asim I. Khwaja, and Atif Mian. 2014. "Population Exchange and Its Impact on Literacy, Occupation and Gender—Evidence from the Partition of India." *International Migration* 53, no. 4: 90–106. https://doi.org/10.1111/imig.12039.

Bharadwaj, Prashant, and Rinchan Ali Mirza. 2019. "Displacement and Development: Long-Term Impacts of Population Transfer in India." *Explorations in Economic History* 73 (July): 101273. https://doi.org/10.1016/j.eeh.2019.05.001.

Black, Dan A., Seth G. Sanders, Evan J. Taylor, and Lowell J. Taylor. 2015. "The Impact of the Great Migration on Mortality of African Americans: Evidence from the Deep South." *American Economic Review* 105, no. 2: 477–503.

Boustan, Leah Platt. 2010. "Was Postwar Suburbanization 'White Flight'? Evidence from the Black Migration." *Quarterly Journal of Economics* 125, no. 1: 417–43.

Bracco, Emanuele, Maria De Paola, and Colin P. Green. 2015. "Long-Lasting Differences in Civic Capital: Evidence from a Unique Immigration Event in Italy." *Journal of Economic Behavior & Organization* 120 (2015): 160–73. http://dx.doi.org/10.1016/j.jebo.2015.10.003.

Braun, Sebastian T., and Nadja Dwenger. 2020. "Settlement Location Shapes the Integration of Forced Migrants: Evidence from Post-War Germany." *Explorations in Economic History* 77 (July): 101330. https://doi.org/10.1016/j.eeh.2020.101330.

Braun, Sebastian, and Michael Kvasnicka. 2014. "Immigration and Structural Change: Evidence from Post-War Germany." *Journal of International Economics* 93: 253–69.

Braun, Sebastian T., and Tomar Oman Mahmoud. 2014. "The Employment Effects of Immigration: Evidence from the Mass Arrival of German Expellees in Postwar Germany." *Journal of Economic History* 74, no. 1: 69–108. https://www.jstor.org/stable/24550551.

Burchardi, Konrad B., Thomas Chaney, and Tarek A. Hassan. 2019. "Migrants, Ancestors, and Foreign Investments." *Review of Economic Studies* 86, no. 4: 1448–86. https://doi.org/10.1093/restud/rdy044.

Burchardi, Konrad B. and Tarek A. Hassan. 2013. "The Economic Impact of Social Ties: Evidence from German Reunification." *Quarterly Journal of Economics* 128, no. 3: 1219–71. https://doi.org/10.1093/qje/qjt009.

Calderón, Álvaro, Vasiliki Fouka, and Marco Tabellini. 2019. "Racial Diversity and Racial Policy Preferences: The Great Migration and Civil Rights." Harvard Business School BGIE Unit Working Paper No. 20-017. https://doi.org/10.2139/ssrn.3447469.

Chaney, Erik, and Richard Hornbeck. 2016. "Economic Dynamics in the Malthusian Era: Evidence from the 1609 Spanish Expulsion of the Moriscos." *Economic Journal* 126 (August): 1404–40. https://doi.org/10.1111/ecoj.12309.

Charnysh, Volha. 2019. "Diversity, Institutions, and Economic Outcomes: Post-WWII Displacement in Poland." *American Political Science Review* 113, no. 2: 423–41. https://doi.org/10.1017/S0003055419000042.

Charnysh, Volha. 2022. *Uprooted: How Post-WWII Population Transfers Remade Europe*. Book Manuscript.

Charnysh, Volha, and Leonid Peisakhin. 2022. "The Role of Communities in the Transmission of Political Values: Evidence from Forced Population Transfers." *British Journal of Political Science* 52, no. 1: 238–58. https://doi.org/10.1017/S0007123420000447.

Chevalier, Arnaud, Benjamin Elsner, Andreas Lichter, and Nico Pestel. 2019. "Immigrant Voters, Taxation and the Size of the Welfare State." *Proceedings. Annual Conference on Taxation and Minutes of the Annual Meeting of the National Tax Association* 112: 1–40.

Christ, Oliver, Katharina Schmid, Simon Lolliot, Hermann Swart, Dietling Stolle, Nicole Tausch, Ananthi Al Ramiah, Ulrich Wagner, Steven Vertovec, and Miles Hewstone. 2014. "Contextual Effect of Positive Intergroup Contact on Outgroup Prejudice." *PNAS* 111, no. 11: 3996–4000.

Collins, William J., and Marianne H. Wanamaker. 2014. "Selection and Economic Gains in the Great Migration of African Americans: New Evidence from Linked Census Data." *American Economic Journal: Applied Economics* 6, no. 1: 220–52.

Coluccia, Davide M., and Lorenzo Spadavecchia. 2021. "The Economic Effects of Immigration Restriction Policies—Evidence from the Italian Mass Migration to the US." CESifo Working Paper No. 9361. https://doi.org/10.2139/ssrn.3950096.

Connor, Dylan Shane. 2019. "The Cream of the Crop? Geography, Networks, and Irish Migrant Selection in the Age of Mass Migration." *Journal of Economic History* 79, no. 1: 139–75. https://doi.org/10.1017/S0022050718000682.

De Carvalho Filho, Irineu, and Leonardo Monasterio. 2012. "Immigration and the Origins of Regional Inequality: Government-Sponsored European Migration to Southern Brazil before World War I." *Regional Science and Urban Economics* 42, no. 5: 794–807. https://doi.org/10.1016/j.regsciurbeco.2011.08.002.

Derenoncourt, Ellora. 2022. "Can You Move to Opportunity? Evidence from the Great Migration." *American Economic Review* 112, no. 2: 369–408. https://doi.org/10.1257/aer.20200002.

Deutsche Welle. 2013. "Catherine the Great and the 'Russian-Germans.'" Accessed February 10, 2022. https://www.dw.com/en/catherine-the-great-and-the-russian-germans/a-16965100.

Dinas, Elias, Vasiliki Fouka, and Alain Schläpfer. 2021. "Family History and Attitudes toward Outgroups: Evidence from the European Refugee Crisis." *Journal of Politics* 83, no. 2: 647–61.

Droller, Federico. 2018. "Migration, Population Composition and Long-Run Economic Development: Evidence from Settlements in the Pampas." *Economic Journal* 128, no. 614: 2321–52. https://doi.org/10.1111/ecoj.12505.

Enflo, Kerstin, Christer Lundh, and Svante Prado. 2014. "The Role of Migration in Regional Wage Convergence: Evidence from Sweden 1860-1940." *Explorations in Economic History* 52: 93–110. https://doi.org/10.1016/j.eeh.2013.12.001.

Eriksson, Katherine. 2019. "Moving North and into Jail? The Great Migration and Black Incarceration." *Journal of Economic Behavior & Organization* 159 (March): 526–38. https://doi.org/10.1016/j.jebo.2018.04.024.

Eriksson, Katherine, and Niemesh, Gregory. 2016. "Death in the Promised Land: The Great Migration and Black Infant Mortality." Working Paper. http://dx.doi.org/10.2139/ssrn.3071053.

Escamilla-Guerrero, David, Edward Kosack, and Zachary Ward. 2021. "Life after Crossing the Border: Assimilation during the First Mexican Mass Migration." *Explorations in Economic History* 82: 101403. https://doi.org/10.1016/j.eeh.2021.101403.

Escribà-Folch, Abel, Covadonga Meseguer, and Joseph Wright. 2019. "Remittances and Protest in Dictatorships." *American Journal of Political Science* 62, no. 4: 889–904. https://doi.org/10.1111/ajps.12382.

Esteves, Rui, and David Khoudour-Castéras. 2011. "Remittances, Capital Flows and Financial Development during the Mass Migration Period, 1870–1913." *European Review of Economic History* 15, no. 3: 443–74. https://doi.org/10.1017/S1361491611000037.

Fernández-Sánchez, Martín. 2021. "Mass Emigration and Human Capital over a Century: Evidence from the Galician Diaspora." Working Paper.

Fielding, David. 2018. "Traditions of Tolerance: The Long-Run Persistence of Regional Variation in Attitudes towards English Immigrants." *British Journal of Political Science* 48, no. 1: 167–88. https://doi.org/10.1017/S0007123415000575.

Fulford, Scott L., Ivan Petkov, and Fabio Schiantarelli. 2020. "Does It Matter Where You Came From? Ancestry Composition and Economic Performance of US Counties, 1850–2010." *Journal of Economic Growth* 25: 341–80.

Giuliano, Paola, and Marco Tabellini. 2020. "The Seeds of Ideology: Historical Immigration and Political Preferences in the United States." NBER Working Paper No. 27238: 1–95. https://www.nber.org/papers/w27238.

Glaeser, Edward L., Rafael La Porta, Florencio Lopez-de-Silanes, and Andrei Shleifer. 2004. "Do Institutions Cause Growth?" *Journal of Economic Growth* 9: 271–303. https://doi.org/10.1023/B:JOEG.0000038933.16398.ed.

Grosjean, Pauline. 2014. "A History of Violence: The Culture of Honor and Homicide in the US South." *Journal of the European Economic Association* 12, no. 5: 1285–316. https://doi.org/10.1111/jeea.12096.

Hatton, Timothy J., and Jeffrey G. Williamson. 1998. *The Age of Mass Migration: Causes and Economic Impact*. New York: Oxford University Press.

Hatton, Timothy J., and Jeffrey G. Williamson. 2009. "Emigration in the Long Run: Evidence from Two Global Centuries." *Asian-Pacific Economic Literature* 23, no. 2: 17–28. https://doi.org/10.1111/j.1467-8411.2009.01238.x.

Haukka, Jari, Jaana Suvisaari, Matti Sarvimäki, and Pekka Martikainen. 2017. "The Impact of Forced Migration on Mortality: A Cohort Study of 242,075 Finns from 1939–2010." *Epidemiology* 28, no. 4: 587–93. https://doi.org/10.1097/EDE.0000000000000669.

Hornung, Erik. 2014. "Immigration and the Diffusion of Technology: The Huguenot Diaspora in Prussia." *American Economic Review* 104, no. 1: 84–122. https://doi.org/10.1257/aer.104.1.84.

Huber, Kilian, Volker Lindenthal, and Fabian Waldinger. 2021. "Discrimination, Managers, and Firm Performance: Evidence from 'Aryanizations' in Nazi Germany." *Journal of Political Economy* 129, no. 9: 2455–503.

Kapur, Devesh. 2014. "Political Effects of International Migration." *Annual Review of Political Science* 17, no. 1: 479–502. https://doi.org/10.1146/annurev-polisci-043010-095807.

Karadja, Mounir, and Erik Prawitz. 2019. "Exit, Voice, and Political Change: Evidence from Swedish Mass Migration to the United States." *Journal of Political Economy* 127, no. 4: 1864–925.

Kevane, Michael, and William A. Sundstrom. 2014. "The Development of Public Libraries in the United States, 1870–1930: A Quantitative Assessment." *Information & Culture: A Journal of History* 49, no. 2: 117–44. https://doi.org/10.1353/lac.2014.0009.

Krawatzek, Felix, and Lea Müller-Funk. 2020. "Two Centuries of Flows between 'Here' and 'There': Political Remittances and Their Transformative Potential." *Journal of Ethnic and Migration Studies* 46, no. 6: 1003–24. https://doi.org/10.1080/1369183X.2018.1554282.

Lankina, Tomila. 2012. "Religious Influences on Human Capital Variations in Imperial Russia." *Journal of Eurasian Studies* 3, no. 1: 10–19. https://doi.org/10.1016/j.euras.2011.10.002.

Ljungberg, Jonas. 1997. "The Impact of the Great Emigration on the Swedish Economy." *Scandinavian Economic History Review* 45, no. 2: 159–89. https://doi.org/10.1080/03585 522.1997.10414666.

Lu, Frances, Sameem Siddiqui, and Prashant Bharadwaj. 2021. "Marriage Outcomes of Displaced Women." *Journal of Development Economics* 152 (September): 102684. https://doi.org/10.1016/j.jdeveco.2021.102684.

Lupu, Noam, and Leonid Peisakhin. 2017. "The Legacy of Political Violence across Generations." *American Journal of Political Science* 61, no. 4: 836–51. https://doi.org/10.1111/ajps.12327.

Menon, Anil. 2021. "Refugees and the Radical Right: Evidence from Post-WWII Forced Migrations." Working Paper. https://dx.doi.org/10.2139/ssrn.3665689.

Miho, Antonela, Alexandra Jarotschkin, and Ekaterina Zhuravskaya. 2020. "Diffusion of Gender Norms: Evidence from Stalin's Ethnic Deportations." Working Paper. https://dx.doi.org/10.2139/ssrn.3417682.

Moser, Petra, and Shmuel San. 2020. "Immigration, Science, and Invention. Lessons from the Quota Acts." Available at *SSRN*. https://doi.org/10.2139/ssrn.3558718.

Moser, Petra, Alessandra Voena, and Fabian Waldinger. 2014. "German Jewish Émigrés and US Invention." *American Economic Review* 104, no. 10: 3222–55. https://doi.org/10.1257/aer.104.10.3222.

Murard, Elie, and Seyhun Orcan Sakalli. 2018. "Mass Refugee Inflow and Long-Run Prosperity: Lessons from the Greek Population Resettlement." Working Paper. https://doi.org/10.2139/ssrn.3209707.

Natkhov, Timur. 2015. "Colonization and Development: The Long-Term Effect of Russian Settlement in the North Caucasus, 1890s–2000s." *Journal of Comparative Economics* 43, no. 1: 76–97. https://doi.org/10.1016/j.jce.2014.09.003.

Natkhov, Timur, and Natalia Vasilenok. 2019. "Technology Adoption in Agrarian Societies: The Effect of Volga Germans in Imperial Russia." Higher School of Economics Research Paper No. WP BRP 220/EC/2019. https://doi.org/10.2139/ssrn.3451895.

Nowrasteh, Alex, and Benjamin Powell. 2021. *Wretched Refuse? The Political Economy of Immigration and Institutions*. New York: Cambridge University Press.

Pepinsky, Tom. 2016. "Colonial Migration and the Origins of Governance." *Comparative Political Studies* 49, no. 9: 1201–37.

Putterman, Louis, and David Weil. 2010. "Post-1500 Population Flows and the Long-Run Determinants of Economic Growth and Inequality." *Quarterly Journal of Economics* 125, no. 4: 1627–82.

Ramos, Miguel R., Matthew R. Bennett, Douglas S. Massey, and Miles Hewstone. 2019. "Humans Adapt to Social Diversity over Time." *PNAS* 116, no. 25: 12244–49. https://doi.org/10.1073/pnas.1818884116.

Rocha, Rudi, Claudio Ferraz, and Rodrigo R. Soares. 2017. "Human Capital Persistence and Development." *American Economic Journal: Applied Economics* 9, no. 4: 105–36. https://doi.org/10.1257/app.20150532.

Rodríguez-Pose, Andrés, and Viola von Berlepsch. 2014. "When Migrants Rule: The Legacy of Mass Migration on Economic Development in the United States." *Annals of the Association of American Geographers* 104, no. 3: 628–51. https://doi.org/10.1080/00045 608.2014.892381.

Sarvimäki, Matti, Roope Uusitalo, and Markus Jäntti. 2020. "Habit Formation and the Misallocation of Labor: Evidence from Forced Migrations." Working Paper. https://doi.org/10.2139/ssrn.3361356.

Sellars, Emily A. 2019. "Emigration, Collective Action, and Political Change." *Journal of Politics* 81, no. 4: 1210–22.

Sellars, Emily A. 2022. "Does Emigration Inhibit Political Reform? Evidence from the Mexican Agrarian Movement, 1916–1945." Unpublished book manuscript.

Semrad, Alexandra. 2015. "Immigration and Educational Spillovers: Evidence from Sudeten German Expellees in Post-War Bavaria." Munich Discussion Paper No. 2015-7. https://doi.org/10.5282/UBM/EPUB.24851.

Sequeira, Sandra, Nathan Nunn, and Nancy Qian. 2020. "Immigrants and the Making of America." *Review of Economic Studies* 87, no. 1: 382–419. https://doi.org/10.1093/restud/rdz003.

Shertzer, Allison, and Randall P. Walsh. 2019. "Racial Sorting and the Emergence of Segregation in American Cities." *Review of Economics and Statistics* 101, no. 3: 415–27. https://doi.org/10.1162/rest_a_00786.

Tabellini, Marco. 2020a. "Gifts of the Immigrants, Woes of the Natives: Lessons from the Age of Mass Migration." *Review of Economic Studies* 87: 454–86. https://doi:10.1093/restud/rdz027.

Tabellini, Marco. 2020b. "Racial Heterogeneity and Local Government Finances: Evidence from the Great Migration." CEPR Discussion Paper no. 14319. https://cepr.org/active/publications/discussion_papers/dp.php?dpno=14319.

Testa, Patrick A. 2021. "The Economic Legacy of Expulsion: Lessons from Post-War Czechoslovakia." *Economic Journal* 131, no. 637: 2233–71. https://doi.org/10.1093/ej/ueaa132.

Waldinger, Fabian. 2010. "Quality Matters: The Expulsion of Professors and the Consequences for PhD Student Outcomes in Nazi Germany." *Journal of Political Economy* 118, no. 4: 787–831. https://doi.org/10.1086/655976.

Walter, André. 2019. "A Race to the Middle: The Politics of Interstate Cost Distribution and Welfare State Expansion." *Journal of Politics* 81, no. 3: 952–67. https://doi.org/10.1086/703132.

CHAPTER 39

THE URBAN-RURAL DIVIDE IN HISTORICAL POLITICAL ECONOMY

JONATHAN A. RODDEN

From Hungary and France to the United States and Canada, one cannot help but notice the similarities of election-night maps in recent years: urban areas vote overwhelmingly for parties of the left, and rural areas for parties of the right. And in countries around the world, urban and rural survey respondents provide strikingly different answers when asked a wide range of questions about social values and politics. Inspired by these observations, a large literature has attempted to conceptualize and measure various aspects of the resurgent urban-rural divide. A central preoccupation in this literature is with contemporary political polarization and the rise of rural populism.

Much of this literature treats the urban-rural divide as a relatively new phenomenon. However, as Marx and Engels (1998) put it, "The antagonism between town and country begins with the transition from barbarism to civilization, from tribe to state, from locality to nation, and runs through the whole history of civilization to the present day" (27).

While this chapter stops well short of the "whole history of civilization," it sets out to broaden current discussions about the urban-rural divide by beginning in the late nineteenth century and asking some questions that harken back to the classic work of Lipset and Rokkan (1967): When and where is an urban-rural divide in political behavior most likely to emerge? Once established, why does it deepen in some countries and at some times, while dissipating in others?

The historical political economy (HPE) literature has not yet provided good answers to these questions. Some theoretical building blocks are in place, and the requisite data are beginning to come together, but the big picture is still blurry. This essay provides an overview of some of the things we already know and points toward a research agenda that might generate a clearer understanding of the causes and consequences of urban-rural political polarization. Rather than reviewing an established literature, I preview a nascent literature that will grow in the years ahead. I begin by assembling some stylized facts and point out the additional descriptive statistics that are still needed. Second, I consider a set of economic explanations for urban-rural political divisions, followed by a discussion of cultural and social explanations. Next I examine the role of political institutions and the nationalization of politics, and I consider the ways in which these might shape the transformation of latent economic or social divisions into cleavages as expressed in the party system.

What Are the Stylized Facts?

Marx and Engels wrote about an antagonism between "town" and "country." Today, much ink is spilled on the "urban-rural conflict" or the "density divide." It is useful to distinguish this concept from what might be called a "center-periphery" conflict, in which many of the places deemed "peripheral" are in fact relatively dense cities that have fallen on hard times. But how should we operationalize the notion of a density divide, especially in an era of suburban and exurban sprawl and polycentric cities? How should we define "rural" in an era when very few people are employed in agricultural or pastoral jobs? If we believe there is a clear concept running from the era of gradual franchise extension in the late nineteenth century to the present, how might it be defined and measured?

In Rodden (2019), I used data at the level of georeferenced polling places in order to examine changes in voting behavior as one moves from the urban core through the suburbs and into the rural periphery of a variety of cities in several countries. However, sufficiently granular geocoded electoral and demographic data are typically not available before the 1990s.

An alternative is to build on the broad insight running from Marx and Engels to recent studies like Gimpel et al. (2020) that population density is often correlated with voting behavior. Moreover, the relationship appears to be fractal, in that it persists as the unit of analysis moves from counties to municipalities to precincts. Thus, it might be possible to assess the nature of this relationship using data from slightly larger geographic units for which data are available going back to the nineteenth century or even earlier. As part of research on a broad range of topics, scholars are digitizing data at the level of electoral districts (Gregory and Southall 1998; Lewis et al. 2013), counties, or municipalities. In order to measure population density, it is important to calculate the land area of these units, which typically requires the creation of digitized boundaries.

To probe the potential of this approach, I have collected data from US and German counties and electoral districts. My goal is to gain some historical perspective on urban-rural conflict since the late nineteenth century, focusing primarily on the era during and after industrialization. Later in the chapter, I explore the possibility that institutions and party systems help explain cross-country variation in the urban-rural divide, so it is useful to contrast the United States—a two-party presidential democracy—and Germany, with its parliamentary, multiparty system.

This exercise is not as straightforward as it may seem. Germany switched from a system using single-member districts prior to World War I, to a system of proportional representation during the Weimar Republic, to a mixed-member plurality system in the postwar constitution. The Federal Republic of Germany lost much of its eastern territory after the world wars but then regained territory in 1990. The boundaries of electoral districts (*Wahlkreise*), counties (*Kreise*), and municipalities (*Gemeinden*) have changed over time, as have the levels at which electoral results and digitized boundaries are available. I have access to both digitized boundaries and election results for *Wahlkreise* during the German *Reich*, the *Kreise* during the Weimar Republic, and the *Wahlkreise* from World War II until the present.[1]

I calculate population density separately for each district or county in each year; then, weighting by population to deal with asymmetrically sized spatial units, I place these observations into density deciles. My simple technique is to contrast the voting behavior of the top two and bottom two density deciles. As an initial approach, I simply compare the combined average vote share of the parties of the left in the top two and bottom two deciles. I define the left as the Social Democratic Party (SPD), Independent Social Democrats (USPD), and Communists (KPD) until 1933. In the postwar period, I include the SPD, Greens, Party of Democratic Socialism (PDS), and the Left Party.

The difference in average left vote share between the top two and bottom two density deciles is plotted in Figure 39.1, in red for the years before World War I, and in orange for the Weimar Republic. From 1881 until the final prewar election in 1912, during a period of rapid industrialization and urbanization, the SPD steadily gained support, especially among working-class voters, but that support was highly concentrated in urban areas. As a result, Figure 39.1 demonstrates that urban-rural electoral polarization dramatically increased from 1881 to 1912. By 1912, the urban-rural difference in left support was 30 percentage points. This was a period during which, due to malapportionment and a highly inefficient distribution of support, the Social Democrats routinely won vote shares far greater than their seat shares.

Urban-rural electoral conflict was reduced in the first election of the Weimar Republic, but it quickly started to increase again, especially when the National Socialists gained support. As with contemporary far-right parties, the rise in Nazi support was disproportionately rural. By 1933, Nazi support was 14 percentage points higher in rural than urban counties. Support for the parties of the left was 24 percent higher in urban than in rural counties.

The urban-rural difference since 1949 is plotted in black. A substantial decrease in urban-rural polarization can be seen with the sudden inclusion of the five new *Bundesländer* in 1990. In the early postunification elections, parties of the left were somewhat more successful in rural areas in the East than in the West, and the Christian Democratic Union (CDU) was quite successful in cities like Leipzig. In gray, I also include the same measure for only the old *Länder*, demonstrating a smaller decrease.

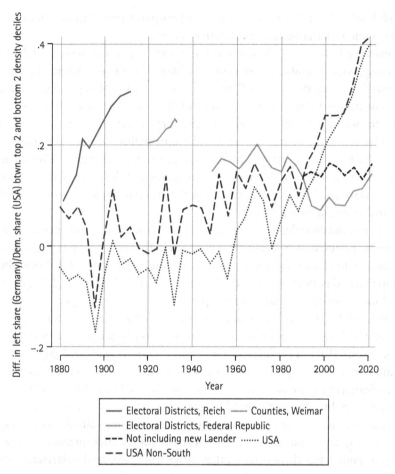

FIGURE 39.1. Difference between the bottom two and top two deciles of population density in average vote share for the left (Germany) or Democratic Party (United States), German *Reichstag/Bundestag* elections, US presidential elections, 1880–2021

Figure 39.1 tells an interesting long-run story about urban-rural polarization in Germany. Rapid urbanization and the mobilization of the working class in the era of industrialization led to quick growth of urban-rural polarization. Periods of intense social conflict in the runup to democratic breakdown and the outbreak of war corresponded with spikes in urban-rural conflict. However, recent decades have seen a process of geographic depolarization. They have been the least polarized since the 1800s, and the difference between the densest and sparsest counties of Germany is now around 14 percentage points.

The contrast with the United States is striking. Using county-level data, Figure 39.1 also includes the same measure for US presidential elections for the same period. I calculate the difference between the top two and bottom two density deciles in the average vote share of the Democratic Party.[2] In the United States, for much of the period since the Civil War, southern counties have voted overwhelmingly for the Democratic Party. Since the southern states are also relatively sparsely populated, the measure for the United States as a whole, portrayed with a dotted blue line in Figure 39.1, potentially conflates regional sectionalism with urban-rural conflict. Thus, it is useful to also calculate the difference for non-southern states separately (the blue dashed line in Figure 39.1).

In the United States as a whole, in the late 1800s and early 1900s, the Democratic Party had slightly higher support in sparser places. This was driven by Democratic dominance in less populated parts of the South. Outside the South, support for the Democrats was slightly higher in urban than rural areas. The correlation between population density and Democratic voting was already much higher in New York and Massachusetts than elsewhere in the early twentieth century, as ethnic and machine politics in cities spilled over into national elections. This relationship spread much more broadly in the North in 1928, when Al Smith—an urban Catholic—was the Democratic nominee. FDR was a dominant candidate in several elections in a wide swath of counties, leading to relatively small urban-rural differences, which then started a gradual increase in the 1950s.

In contrast with Germany, where the trends were linear and upward during both the Reich and Weimar periods, for the hundred-year period from the 1880s to the 1980s, the United States demonstrated considerable heterogeneity in the size of urban-rural differences from one election to another. The overall trend in the North was one of very gradual increase in urban-rural difference from World War II to the Reagan era, when the difference increased to around 12 percentage points. During this period, the urban-rural division that emerged first in the Northeast gradually spread to the Midwest, Great Plains, and West. In the 1980s, the non-South demonstrated slightly lower levels of urban-rural polarization than Germany, and the United States was considerably less divided than Germany along urban-rural lines.

However, the United States demonstrates a striking transformation after the 1980s—one that is reminiscent of Germany in the 1880s. The jagged pattern disappeared, and steady increases in urban-rural polarization occurred with every election. As the southern realignment unfolded, the polarization seen in the rest of the country finally spread to the South as well. From 1990 to 2020, the urban-rural divide more than doubled. By the 2020 presidential election, there was a truly remarkable 40-percentage-point difference in voting behavior between the top two and bottom two density deciles.

This difference is now well over three times the size of the difference in Germany. Applying the same technique to recent municipal data from the Netherlands, the difference is around 9.4 percentage points—less than a quarter of that in the United States. Using constituency-level data from the 2008 federal election in Canada, and classifying the Liberals, NDP, and Greens as left parties, the same approach reveals a substantial 17-percentage-point gap between urban and rural areas. By the 2017 election, this gap had expanded to 22 percentage points—something like the gap in the United States in the 1990s.

There is room for improvement over this simple comparison of density deciles using a binary left-right distinction. For instance, Armstrong, Lucas, and Taylor (2022) and

Taylor et al. (2022) use a long time-series of data at the level of legislative districts to explore the expected proportional reduction in error associated with empirical models of district-level election winners that include population density vis-à-vis models that include only regional fixed effects. They find evidence of an increasing urban-rural divide in the United States, Canada, and the United Kingdom. Their work, along with the analysis in Figure 39.1, can hopefully serve as a proof of concept for further systematic research on the density divide in a wide range of contexts, while also establishing some stylized facts that are of use in the remainder of this essay. Let us now take a closer look at explanations for some of these emergent cross-country and time-series differences.

Economic Geography

It is difficult to make sense of Figure 39.1 without reference to transformations of economic geography. Undoubtedly, the rapid increase in urban-rural voting differences in late-nineteenth-century Germany was associated with industrialization and the rapid rise of the urban working class and its mobilization by labor unions and parties of the left. Quick growth in the urban-rural divide was also associated with the entry of workers' parties elsewhere in Europe and in the United Kingdom early in the twentieth century. The timing of this process varied. In the United States, the Democratic Party did not begin to align with labor unions and urban industrial workers until the late 1920s.

The basic story of urban-rural polarization in the industrial era begins with an economic and spatial transformation rooted in technology—the rise of the factory and other forms of heavy industry that required many manual laborers. In an era when public transportation was in its infancy, this model led to the rapid construction of dense housing in proximity to factories. In many countries, the origins of leftist parties can be traced to the initial efforts of political entrepreneurs to mobilize wage laborers in these urban housing corridors. These parties often did not establish strong roots in sparser areas, although there are important exceptions, including forestry workers and landless laborers in agricultural areas in parts of Scandinavia, Andalusia, and Tuscany. Moreover, support for socialist and workers' parties also emerged in more far-flung areas with coal and other types of mines, and sometimes the towns surrounding these mines were not especially dense—for example, in Britain.

The density divide that emerged in the early twentieth century in many industrialized societies can be understood as a class divide with a particular spatial arrangement. Some version of this class-cum-density divide has persisted long after the era of heavy industry. The built environment from the industrial era—above all, the dense, affordable rental housing—continues to attract groups who are part of the core constituency of left parties: poor people, racial minorities, immigrants, and young voters.

Income and class are not the only economic building blocks for explanations of the density divide. Cities emerge in the first place because proximity is advantageous for carrying out certain types of economic activity, and interests form around these economic activities. A classic example is the early battle between Alexander Hamilton—an advocate for urban commercial and early manufacturing interests—and Thomas Jefferson—an advocate for planters. In the United States, Canada, and Australia, some of the earliest political battles emerged between urban manufacturers, who favored protection for their infant industries, and rural advocates of free trade. In Europe as well, Lipset and Rokkan (1967) document "increasing strains between the primary producers in the countryside and the merchants and the entrepreneurs in the towns and the cities" (19).

This type of sectoral politics has not gone away in the era of the mass franchise. In fact, it is a growing focus of the recent political economy literature. A large literature explores the political implications of the changing role of globalization and free trade in recent decades. A series of papers focuses on the "China shock." Import competition with Chinese manufacturers has led to geographically concentrated plant closures, declining employment and standards of living, and rising vote shares for the populist right (Autor et al. 2020; Colantone and Stanig 2018). In the United States, a burgeoning literature also focuses on the shock associated with the North American Free Trade Agreement (Choi et al. 2021), which created concentrated economic distress and a realignment of voting behavior in the affected areas.

In the United States, after an initial burst of manufacturing in city centers in the first half of the twentieth century, manufacturers relocated in the second half of the century from urban rail transit nodes to exurban and rural highway nodes. In addition to the rise of the interstate highway system and trucking, this was also a product of American-style competitive federalism, where it was possible for manufacturers to escape labor unions, wage demands, regulations, and taxes by moving. As a result, the shocks of NAFTA and Chinese entry into the World Trade Organization late in the twentieth century have been felt disproportionately in rural areas. This might be part of the explanation for the upward trajectory in the difference between urban and rural areas outlined in Figure 39.1. It is possible that some part of the rural electorate has migrated from the Democratic Party to the Republican Party as a form of retrospective voting in which blame for trade policy is thought to lie primarily with Democrats, or a more prospective policy-based form of voting in which local Republican candidates begin to articulate anti-trade or pro-manufacturing platforms.

In short, while industrialization may have given rise to the modern urban-rural divide, perhaps deindustrialization has given it a boost in recent decades. As I will discuss later, the political impact of the decline of manufacturing might also be wrapped up in a set of broader social and cultural grievances. It cannot be the case, however, that the large increase in urban-rural polarization in the United States and elsewhere since the 1980s is driven primarily by rural anger about the decline of manufacturing, for the simple reason that urban-rural polarization has increased even in areas that were relatively unaffected by the China shock or NAFTA, and indeed, in places that have never had large manufacturing sectors.

An alternative economic explanation for urban-rural polarization focuses on alliances between economic sectors and political parties. In an era of intense global competition, consider the interests of manufacturers in places that have managed to maintain or attract manufacturing clusters, like northern Indiana, South Carolina, or Alabama. Much of what local manufacturing elites need from government in order to be successful—from infrastructure to taxes to workforce development—involves state and local officials. Naturally, manufacturing leaders in such communities turn to locally dominant Republican officials for help, and Republican representatives from such communities have incentives to develop policy expertise related to manufacturing. Ties to manufacturers and campaign contributions can then be an important part of the development of a successful political career that moves from local government to the state legislature to perhaps the US Congress.

In this way, due to geographic concentration of an economic sector and the incentives of local politicians, a party can emerge as the champion of that sector. In an era of global competition and economic upheaval, when there is legitimate concern that the sector could simply disappear without the right type of government policy—destroying jobs and local economic prosperity along the way—the logic of sector-based politics can supplant class-based politics. That is to say, the factory owner, management, and hourly workers all support the party that has established itself as the champion of their economic sector.

This happens not only with manufacturing, but also with oil and gas, natural resources, and agriculture. Perhaps the most striking example of class politics giving way to sector-based politics is the partisan realignment of coal mining communities. In each of these instances, Republicans have emerged as "sectoral champions" of industries that are located outside of major cities.

Meanwhile, Democrats have emerged as sectoral champions of technology firms, which have emerged and flourished in places where agglomeration economies have taken hold in recent decades. For many of these hubs of innovation and knowledge employment, the origin story lies in heavy federal investment in sophisticated military technology, which eventually had externalities for universities and the private sector (Gross and Sampat 2020). Much of this happened in cities, like Boston, Seattle, and San Francisco, where Democratic officials had long been dominant, making them the obvious allies as the technology industry developed its own policy interests. As with manufacturing firms in the nonmetro South, capital owners, managers, and hourly employees in metropolitan technology hubs have come to vote largely for the same party.

If this narrative is correct, we might think of political parties as geographically constrained coalitions.[3] A party becomes dominant in a specific place because of some battle or cleavage from the distant past—the French Revolution, a confessional conflict, battles among elites over patronage, or class conflict during the industrial era—but once a new issue or cleavage emerges in a way that is spatially concentrated, existing patterns of local party dominance shape the options available to emergent interest groups, and likewise, the partisanship of the political entrepreneurs who face incentives to court them (Rodden 2019). Left parties became dominant in cities in the industrial era, and new urban interest groups—including tech firms and educated young professionals—eventually forged an alliance with the locally dominant party.

Since the pathbreaking work of Rogowski (1989), this type of sector-based story has received little attention in recent literature.[4] As a result, basic questions have not been answered. Clearly, business owners and managers have incentives to cultivate ties with party elites who can help them succeed. But do hourly workers think about parties as champions of the sector that employs them? And do people working in the service sector think about externalities produced by the industrial sector that drives the local economy? To be concrete, do restaurant workers in West Virginia (or Silicon Valley) vote to support the interests of coal (or technology)?

In the United States, the two parties have come to be closely associated with economic sectors that have a clear urban-rural orientation. The urban knowledge-based sector associated with the Democratic Party has created enormous wealth, fueling a long-term process of economic divergence (Gaubert et al. 2021), such that in recent years the small number of dense counties that return Democratic majorities in presidential elections are responsible for well over two-thirds of national gross domestic product and tax revenue.

By no means is this phenomenon unique to the United States. Through a similar process, mainstream parties of the left have come to be associated with the globalized urban knowledge economy in countries from Europe to Latin America to Australasia. Economic geographers have argued that voters in nonmetropolitan regions "left behind" by urban-centric growth in the era of globalization have demonstrated reduced trust in government (McKay, Jennings, and Stoker 2021; Mitsch, Lee, and Morrow 2021) and have turned to populist parties that advocate radical change (Rodríguez-Pose 2018; Colantone and Stanig 2018).

Comparative research on the political implications of growing knowledge-based cities and left-behind rural areas is only in its infancy. For one thing, it is not clear that urban-rural economic divergence is happening in the same way everywhere. Even within the United States, some rural areas have been thriving while others have suffered. In some countries of Western Europe, where manufacturing employment has been preserved, innovation is more geographically dispersed, and government policy prioritizes the creation of equivalent public services throughout the country, it is not entirely clear that urban-rural economic divergence is happening (Königs and Vindics 2021).

Moreover, we should not conflate studies of populism—which usually focus on the fate of a single party—like the Alternative für Deutschland or the Sweden Democrats—with the broader question of urban-rural conflict. Relatively small populist parties might gain new adherents, and do so disproportionately in declining rural areas, even in a context where the party system in the aggregate is not structured around an urban-rural divide.

Noneconomic Explanations

In the literature on the rise of right-wing populism in left-behind nonmetro areas, there is a growing realization that purely economic explanations can only go so far (Margalit 2019). For instance, it seems unlikely that the upward trend in urban-rural polarization in the United States in recent decades, and the downward trend in Germany, can be explained exclusively by economic geography.

A recent study finds sharp urban-rural attitudinal differences in a large group of European countries related to satisfaction with democracy, trust in government, globalization, and immigration, but no significant differences related to the scale of redistribution or the welfare state (Kenny and Luca 2021). Recent survey research demonstrates important differences between urban and rural respondents in levels of moral universalism, defined as the extent to which altruism and trust remain constant as social distance increases (Enke, Rodriguez-Padilla, and Zimmermann 2022).

Margalit, Raviv, and Solodoch (2022) review five noneconomic "storylines" about the electoral appeal of right-wing populism, several of which have some bearing on urban-rural differences in voting behavior. First, older voters, who reside disproportionately in rural areas, are thought to react against assaults by the young on cherished traditional values (Norris and Inglehart 2019). Second, natives with longstanding ties to their communities are said to become fearful of demographic and cultural changes brought about by immigration, even if immigrants settle mostly in urban areas (Eatwell and Goodwin 2018; Kaufmann 2018). Third, rural residents might feel increasingly disrespected and ignored by urban elites and policymakers (Cramer 2016; Rodríguez-Pose 2018; Wuthnow 2019). Fourth, white males are thought to experience anxiety about their declining social status (Gidron and Hall 2017; Mutz 2018; Hochschild 2018). A final argument is that populism is rooted in a feeling of isolation or alienation associated with the decline of civil society organizations (Bolet 2021; Giuliano and Wacziarg 2020).

Some of these social or cultural explanations are thought to be heightened by economic dislocation. An interesting claim by Bonomi, Gennaioli, and Tabellini (2021) is that when negative economic shocks are concentrated among socially conservative groups, voters switch from class to cultural identities as the basis for political conflict.

The general sense in this literature is that something new and disturbing is happening in the era of globalization. However, the advantage of historical political economy is that it often illuminates the ways in which social patterns repeat. According to Lipset and Rokkan (1967), "The initial result of a widening of the suffrage will often be an accentuation of the contrasts between the countryside and the urban centers and between the orthodox-fundamentalist beliefs of the peasantry and the small town citizens and the secularism fostered in the larger cities and the metropolis" (12). Their description of the antiurban mobilization of the Nordic peasantry in the late nineteenth and early twentieth centuries is reminiscent of Cathy Cramer's description of rural resentment in contemporary Wisconsin.

Lipset (1963) argued that the battles between the Jeffersonians and the Federalists, the Jacksonians and the Whigs, and the Democrats and the Republicans were largely about notions of public morality that pitted Protestants against Deists, Freemasons, and Jewish and Catholic immigrants. Urban-rural political differences were driven by an influx of poor immigrants into urban areas. It was probably the case that in parts of the United States, prior to the class-based party structure that emerged in the 1930s, emergent urban-rural differences in voting behavior were driven by ethnic politics and prohibition. In fact, the eventual association of the Democratic Party with the working class may have started with Irish machine politics in New York and Massachusetts, where local Democratic candidates started to adopt some of the policy positions of insurgent socialist candidates. These local ethnic and party affiliations eventually extended to national elections.

Even well before the industrial revolution, cities have been culturally and socially distinct from their surroundings. The economic activities available in cities have always attracted in-migrants—for example, merchants, artisans, clerics, and bureaucrats—with characteristics that distinguished them from the surrounding agricultural communities. During the era of industrialization, cities attracted migrant wage laborers from various ethnic, religious, and linguistic backgrounds. This type of mixing—and perhaps the self-selection of those drawn to cities versus those staying on the farm—created a cultural chasm. Even in the era of industrial decline, cities have continued to attract poor migrants from far away, while the surrounding areas are composed of families who have resided in the same area for generations.

As cities swelled with wage laborers from far away during the industrial era, ethnic divisions came to play an important role in politics. American urban political machines were often organized around a single ethnicity, but on many occasions they realized the need to broaden their coalition in order to capture city-wide offices. Democrats eventually discovered incentives to appeal to Black voters in northern cities; Irish machines had to integrate with Eastern European machines in Chicago. Likewise, the labor movement eventually found it necessary to build cross-ethnic and cross-race coalitions. This same phenomenon continues today in growing cities in countries like India or Kenya, where political entrepreneurs face incentives to attempt to build cross-ethnic coalitions in pursuit of electoral victory.

To the extent that urban political entrepreneurs build heterogeneous coalitions of in-migrants, if an "urban" political party or parties emerge in national politics, the building blocks are in place for political entrepreneurs to mobilize "nativists" outside cities in opposition to parties based in cities that are increasingly culturally distinctive. In many contexts, urban migrants have also been more likely than those staying in rural areas to leave behind traditional religious beliefs and practices, providing another divide that is ripe for political mobilization. A political division between diverse, immigrant-friendly, secular cities and more homogeneous, traditionalist exurbs and rural areas is visible in many settings around the world. Consider, for instance, the difference between cosmopolitan, polyglot cities and smaller towns in the former Austro-Hungarian Empire.

An important observation emerging in the literature is that the rise of sector-based political alliances and a cultural cleavage can push against class- or income-based voting patterns. By no means is this a new phenomenon. In the early twentieth century, peripheral religious and linguistic groups struggled against conformity with dominant areas in what Lipset and Rokkan (1967) called "the politics of cultural defense," which slowed the development of class-based politics (see also Ziblatt, Hilbig, and Bischof 2022). Lipset and Rokkan describe an alignment where "you vote with your community and its leaders irrespective of your economic position" (13). As urban-rural polarization unfolds, the "urban" parties often become a diverse, cross-class coalition of technology professionals, artists, intellectuals, minorities, and the working poor, whereas the "rural" parties obtain support from both capital owners and workers outside of urban areas. In the United States, for instance, the decline in income as a predictor of voting behavior has gone hand in hand with the increase in the correlation between population density and voting behavior.

A classic question in the study of political geography is whether observed urban-rural differences in attitudes and voting behavior are a function of sorting—whereby people with progressive or universalist views move into cities while conservatives or communalists move out—or whether urban (or rural) life might have a causal impact of its own. This has led to a lively empirical literature, including panel surveys (e.g., Maxwell 2019; Lueders 2022) and individual-level administrative data focusing on movers (Cantoni and Pons 2022). Recent research by Bazzi et al. (2022) examines the role of migration of conservative southern whites in the rightward drift of many nonurban areas in the West and Midwest of the United States.

It is worth noting that the period of rapid urban-rural polarization in the United States is occurring during a period of *declining* internal migration. Beyond sorting and contextual effects, a third possibility was introduced above: parties are geographically constrained coalitions that respond to newly emerging issues in a way that reinforces or expands existing geographic cleavages, such that urban and rural areas can pull apart over time even without residential migration. After a period during which parties' platforms are indistinguishable on some latent dimension of conflict, political entrepreneurs can face incentives to court geographically concentrated groups with strong preferences by taking a clearer stand in their favor.

For example, the Republican Party began to take conservative positions on social and religious issues like abortion in the 1980s. Social conservatives reside disproportionately in nonurban areas, and this growing distinctiveness of the two American parties led some nonurban voters with center-left economic views but highly salient conservative social views to realign to the Republican Party, which led to a gradual increase in the correlation between population density and voting. Another example of this logic comes from Schickler (2016), who explains how in efforts to court a growing population of Black voters in northern cities, Democratic legislative candidates started introducing civil rights legislation, setting in motion a long-term process whereby Black urban voters aligned with the Democratic Party.

No matter the nature of a party's origins as an "urban" party—early-twentieth-century ethnic patronage, the class politics of the industrial era, or confessional conflicts going back even further—it is more likely to take up positions favored by urban voters on other issue dimensions as they arise over time. In the United States, the politicization of civil rights, moral issues, women's rights, environmental protection, and immigration each involved the extension of partisan conflict to an issue on which preferences are correlated with population density, leading to a gradual increase in urban-rural polarization.

Political Institutions and the Nationalization of Politics

This introduces an interesting puzzle. A key insight in the literature on so-called postmaterial politics is that, from environmentalism to gender and sexuality or immigration, similar noneconomic issues have been politicized in the postwar period in other advanced industrial democracies, including Germany (Inglehart 1990). Yet American-style increases in urban-rural polarization have not always occurred.

This might have something to do with differences in political institutions. Above all, democracies with proportional representation and multiparty systems might absorb new dimensions of political conflict in a different way than in a strict two-party system like the United States. When the party of the left had gained an urban following in the early twentieth century era of heavy industry, and then a new noneconomic issue dimension correlated with population density is introduced, in a strict two-party system, cross-pressured voters are likely to realign in a way that brings additional urban voters into the party of the left, and additional rural voters into the party of the right.

The dynamic might play out differently, however, if multiple parties can take a wider range of positions throughout the multidimensional issue space, allowing for a constellation of parties in which some offer a mix of platforms that enable them to pull support from both urban and rural areas, or where urban- and rural-oriented parties might sometimes join the same coalition. The growth of two competing partisan bundles of issues—one predominantly urban and one exurban/rural—is likely shaped by majoritarian institutions that push toward a two-party system. In a two-party system, structured around a bundle of overlapping density-correlated issue dimensions, the rural-oriented party might rationally give up on winning in urban districts. In a proportional system with large multimember districts, it is still worthwhile for parties of the right to seek out urban supporters; in practice, parties of the center-right, including parties rooted in classical liberalism, are often able to craft packages that appeal to more affluent, educated urban voters with progressive social attitudes. As a result, while a government of the right in the United States, Canada, or Britain can come to power with virtually no urban support, governments of the right in most of Europe typically include significant urban representation.

Future research might examine these claims more carefully. Which parties most successfully straddle the urban-rural divide, and with what types of ideological packages? Under what conditions does the coalition-building process facilitate or undermine urban-rural bargains? As indicated by electoral data during the Weimar Republic in Figure 39.1, it is not the case that proportional representation always tempers urban-rural electoral conflict. In Sweden and Norway, there is an urban-rural divide, but it is parties of the right rather than the left that are over-represented in city centers. And perhaps contemporary Australia, with its system of ranked-choice voting and compulsory voting, indicates that there are ways to ameliorate urban-rural conflict even in a majoritarian democracy.

Additionally, what are the implications of urban-rural polarization for affective polarization? Data collected by Boxell, Gentzkow, and Shapiro (2022) suggest that the upward trend in urban-rural polarization in the United States displayed in Figure 39.1 corresponds closely to an increase in affective polarization, while the downward trend in urban-rural political conflict in Germany has gone hand in hand with a decrease in affective polarization.

Another important variable is the nationalization of the party system (Caramani 2004). If state, provincial, or local governments have significant power, urban or rural groups might focus on getting what they want at the state or local level, and burgeoning new partisan alliances might not spill over to national politics (Chhibber and Kollman 2004). In that case, the rise of new issue dimensions might not translate into urban-rural differences in national vote shares of parties.

Or even if the relevant policies are in the hands of the central government and a density-correlated dimension of conflict emerges, a party system can remain localized in that representatives from very different types of districts, with different preferences, can bargain over policies in a national legislature that is not marked by high levels of party discipline. Members of the same party can contain pro- and antiabortion representatives, for example. In an extreme case, the Democratic Party was able to exist for some time as the party of racial oppression in the rural South while its northern members of Congress started to push for civil rights in response to Black constituents in urban, industrial districts.

In this way, internally heterogeneous parties in a denationalized party system can reproduce some of the features of a multiparty system and prevent the emergence of an overarching urban-rural partisan conflict. This type of party system is most likely to emerge in a presidential system. In a parliamentary system, the no-confidence procedure and resulting party discipline can undermine the credibility of idiosyncratic district-specific promises of candidates that diverge from the party label. In a presidential system with weaker tools in the hands of party leaders, district-level candidates may be able to run insurgent campaigns against party leaders and their platforms, especially when candidates are selected via primaries.

The United States has changed significantly on the nationalization dimension (Hopkins 2018). In the early twentieth century, local ethnic and partisan affiliations sometimes spilled over to national elections, but Congressional candidates from urban and rural districts within the same party could credibly espouse very different platforms. Today, the spillovers are in the opposite direction. Attitudes toward national candidates spill over via party labels to Congressional and even local races, and it is difficult for candidates to adopt locally tailored platforms. The nationalization of party competition is likely an important part of the explanation for the increase in urban-rural polarization documented in Figure 39.1.

Conclusion

There is considerable heterogeneity over time and space in the strength of the urban-rural divide since the rise of the mass franchise. Economic geography provides one attractive but incomplete set of explanations. We still have much to learn about partisan implications of long-term variation in the geography of agriculture, manufacturing, innovation, and the knowledge economy. Even basic comparative stylized facts about urban-rural divergence in prosperity and the role of agglomeration economies vis-à-vis government policies remain contested. Another interesting but incomplete set of potential explanations has to do with the mobilization of ethnic, social, and cultural issues and grievances.

Consider the following statement from Lipset and Rokkan (1967): "In our Western democracies, the voters are only rarely called upon to express their stands on single issues. They are typically faced with choices among historically given 'packages' of programs, commitments, outlooks, and sometimes, *Weltanschauungen*, and their current behavior cannot be understood without some knowledge of the sequences of events and the combinations of forces that produced these 'packages'" (2–3).

A key theme in this chapter is that in order to understand the urban-rural divide, we must understand how parties assemble these packages in a way that is constrained by the geography of economic and social groups as well as political institutions, and the conditions under which this constrained "packaging" enhances or assuages urban-rural conflict. A worthwhile next step is to formalize the logic of parties as geographically constrained coalitions and establishing some comparative statics. For instance, when should we expect new spatially concentrated interest groups to form an alliance with the locally dominant party? When do such alliances lead cross-pressured voters to switch parties in a way that enhances urban-rural polarization? To what extent are officials in the locally dominant party constrained in what they can credibly offer to burgeoning local interests by the party's national leadership, brand, and preexisting commitments? How do electoral rules, executive-legislative relations, and federalism shape this process?

Above all, this chapter has attempted to build on some stylized facts to provide a road map for future refinements in both theoretical and empirical approaches to the historical political economy literature on the urban-rural divide. In an era of globalization, polarization, and populism, the questions posed by Lipset and Rokkan about geography and the origin and evolution of political cleavages are more pressing than ever.

Notes

1. Data for the *Reich* period are from Ziblatt (2009). Data for the Weimar Republic are from Falter and Hänisch (1989), linked to boundary files from Max Plank Institute for Demographic Research (2011). Postwar data are from the *Bundeswahlleiter*. I am thankful to Hans Lueders and Felix Hagemeister for help locating and wrangling the German data.

2. In the event of "fusion" Democratic candidacies, like William Jennings Bryan's, I include all the votes for the candidate, even if they were received in some counties under a different party label.
3. Thanks to Aditya Dasgupta for suggesting this term.
4. For exceptions, see Rickard (2018) and Short (2022).

References

Armstrong, David, Jack Lucas, and Zack Taylor. 2022. "The Urban-Rural Divide in Canadian Federal Elections, 1896–2019." *Canadian Journal of Political Science* 55, no. 1: 84–106.

Autor, David, David Dorn, Gordon Hanson, and Kaveh Majlesi. 2020. "Importing Political Polarization? The Electoral Consequences of Rising Trade Exposure." *American Economic Review* 110, no. 10: 3139–83.

Bazzi, Samuel, Andreas Ferrara, Martin Fiszbein, Thomas Pearson, and Patrick Testa. 2022. "The Other Great Migration: Southern Whites and the New Right." Working Paper, UCSD.

Bolet, Diane. 2021. "Drinking Alone: Local Socio-Cultural Degradation and Radical Right Support—The Case of British Pub Closures." *Comparative Political Studies* 54, no. 9: 1–40.

Bonomi, Giampaolo, Nicola Gennaioli, and Guido Tabellini. 2021. "Identity, Beliefs, and Political Conflict." *Quarterly Journal of Economics* 136, no. 4: 2371–411.

Boxell, Levi, Matthew Gentzkow, and Jesse Shapiro. 2022. "Cross-Country Trends in Affective Polarization." *The Review of Economics and Statistics*. https://doi.org/10.1162/rest_a_01160.

Cantoni, Enrico, and Vincent Pons. 2022. "Does Context Outweigh Individual Characteristics in Driving Voting Behavior? Evidence from Relocations within the United States." *American Economic Review* 112, no. 4: 1226–72.

Caramani, Daniele. 2004. *The Nationalization of Politics: The Formation of National Electorates and Party Systems in Western Europe*. Cambridge: Cambridge University Press.

Chhibber, Pradeep, and Ken Kollman. 2004. *The Formation of National Party Systems: Federalism and Party Competition in Canada, Great Britain, India, and the United States*. Princeton, NJ: Princeton University Press.

Choi, Jiwon, Ilyana Kuziemko, Ebonya Washington, and Gavin Wright. 2021. "Local Economic and Political Effects of Trade Deals: Evidence from NAFTA." NBER Working Paper 29525.

Colantone, Italo, and Piero Stanig. 2018. "The Trade Origins of Economic Nationalism: Import Competition and Voting Behavior in Western Europe." *American Journal of Political Science* 62: 936–53.

Cramer, Katherine J. 2016. *The Politics of Resentment: Rural Consciousness in Wisconsin and the Rise of Scott Walker*. Chicago: University of Chicago Press.

Eatwell, Roger, and Matthew Goodwin. 2018. *National Populism: The Revolt against Liberal Democracy*. London: Penguin UK.

Enke, Benjamin, Ricardo Rodriguez-Padilla, and Florian Zimmermann. 2022. "Moral Universalism: Measurement and Economic Relevance." *Management Science* 68, no. 5: 3175–973.

Falter, J. W., and D.H. Hänisch. 1989. *Wahl- und Sozialdaten der Kreise und Gemeinden des Deutschen Reiches von 1920 bis 1933*. Berlin: Zentralinstitut für Sozialwissenschaftliche Forschung.

Gaubert, Cecile, Patrick Kline, Damián Vergara, and Danny Yagan. 2021. "Trends in US Spatial Inequality: Concentrating Affluence and a Democratization of Poverty." *AEA Papers and Proceedings* 111: 520–25.

Gidron, Noam, and Peter A. Hall. 2017. "The Politics of Social Status: Economic and Cultural Roots of the Populist Right." *British Journal of Sociology* 68: S57–S84.

Gimpel, James, Nathan Lovin, Bryant Moy, and Andrew Reeves. 2020. "The Urban–Rural Gulf in American Political Behavior." *Political Behavior* 42: 1343–68.

Giuliano, Paola, and Romain Wacziarg. 2020. "Who Voted for Trump? Populism and Social Capital." NBER Working Paper 27651.

Gregory, Ian, and Humphrey Southall. 1998. "Putting the Past in Its Place: The Great Britain Historical GIS." In *Innovations in GIS 5*, ed. S. Carver, 210–21. London: Taylor and Francis.

Gross, Daniel, and Bhaven Sampat. 2020. "Inventing the Endless Frontier: The Effects of the World War II Research Effort on Post-War Innovation." Working Paper, Duke University.

Hochschild, Arlie Russell. 2018. *Strangers in Their Own Land: Anger and Mourning on the American Right*. New York: New Press.

Hopkins, Daniel. 2018. *The Increasingly United States: How and Why American Political Behavior Nationalized*. Chicago: University of Chicago Press.

Inglehart, Ronald. 1990. *Culture Shift in Advanced Industrial Society*. Princeton, NJ: Princeton University Press.

Kaufmann, Eric. 2018. *Whiteshift: Populism, Immigration and the Future of White Majorities*. London: Penguin UK.

Kenny, Michael, and Davide Luca. 2021. "The Urban-Rural Polarisation of Political Disenchantment: An Investigation of Social and Political Attitudes in 30 European Countries," *Cambridge Journal of Regions, Economy, and Society* 14, no. 3: 565–82.

Königs, Sabastian, and Anna Vindics. 2021. "The Geography of Income Inequalities in OECD Countries." Paper prepared for the 36th IARIW Virtual General Conference, August 23–27, 2021, Session 12: "Comparing Income and Price Levels and International Income Inequality."

Lewis, Jeffrey, Brandon DeVine, Lincoln Pitcher, and Kenneth C. Martis. 2013. *Digital Boundary Definitions of United States Congressional Districts, 1789–2012*. Retrieved from https://cdmaps.polisci.ucla.edu on November 10, 2022.

Lipset, Seymour Martin. 1963. *The First New Nation*. New York: Basic Books.

Lipset, Seymour Martin, and Stein Rokkan. 1967. "Cleavage Structures, Party Systems and Voter Alignments: An Introduction." In *Party Systems and Voter Alignments: Cross-National Perspectives*, ed. S. M. Lipset and S. Rokkan, 1–23. New York: Free Press.

Lueders, Hans. 2022. "Rooted at Home: How Domestic Migration Separates Voters into National and Local Electorates." Working Paper, Princeton University.

Margalit, Yotam. 2019. "Economic Insecurity and the Causes of Populism Reconsidered." *Journal of Economic Perspectives* 33, no. 4: 152–70.

Margalit, Yotam, Shir Raviv, and Omer Solodoch. 2022. "The Cultural Origins of Populism." Working Paper, Tel Aviv University.

Marx, Karl, and Friedrich Engels. 1998. *The German Ideology*. Amherst, NY: Prometheus Books.

Max Plank Institute for Demographic Research. 2011. MPIDR Population History GIS Collection (partly based on Hubatsch and Klein 1975), Rostock. Accessed from https://censusmosaic.demog.berkeley.edu/data/historical-gis-files

Maxwell, Rahsaan. 2019. "Cosmopolitan Immigration Attitudes in Large European Cities: Contextual or Compositional Effects?" *American Political Science Review* 113, no. 2: 456–74.

McKay, Lawrence, Will Jennings, and Gerry Stoker. 2021. "Political Trust in the Places That Don't Matter," *Frontiers in Political Science*, April 26. https://doi.org/10.3389/fpos.2021.642236

Mitsch, Frieder, Neil Lee, and Elizabeth Ralph Morrow. 2021. "Faith No More? The Divergence of Political Trust between Urban and Rural Europe." *Political Geography* 89: 102426.

Mutz, Diana. 2018. "Status Threat, Not Economic Hardship, Explains the 2016 Presidential Vote." *Proceedings of the National Academy of Science* 115, no. 19: 4330–39.

Norris, Pippa, and Ronald Inglehart. 2019. *Cultural Backlash: Trump, Brexit, and Authoritarian Populism*. Cambridge: Cambridge University Press.

Rickard, Stephanie. 2018. *Spending to Win: Political Institutions, Economic Geography, and Government Subsidies*. Cambridge: Cambridge University Press.

Rodden, Jonathan. 2019. *Why Cities Lose: The Deep Roots of the Urban-Rural Political Divide*. New York: Basic Books.

Rodríguez-Pose, Andrés. 2018. "The Revenge of Places That Don't Matter." *Cambridge Journal of Regions, Economy, and Society* 11, no. 1: 189–209.

Rogowski, Ronald. 1989. *Commerce and Coalitions: How Trade Affects Domestic Political Alignments*. Princeton, NJ: Princeton University Press.

Schickler, Eric. 2016. *Racial Realignment: The Transformation of American Liberalism, 1932–1965*. Princeton, NJ: Princeton University Press.

Short, Nicholas. 2022. "The Politics of the American Knowledge Economy." Working Paper, Harvard University.

Taylor, Zack, Jack Lucas, David Armstrong II, and Ryan Bakker. 2022. "The Development of the Urban-Rural Cleavage in Anglo-American Democracies." Paper presented at the Annual Meeting of the American Political Science Association, Montreal, Quebec, September 16, 2022.

Wuthnow, Robert. 2019. *The Left Behind*. Princeton, NJ: Princeton University Press.

Ziblatt, Daniel. 2009. "Shaping Democratic Practice and the Causes of Electoral Fraud: The Case of Nineteenth-Century Germany." *American Political Science Review* 103, no. 1: 1–21.

Ziblatt, Daniel, Hanno Hilbig, and Daniel Bischof. 2022. "Wealth of Tongues: Why Peripheral Regions Vote for the Far Right in Germany." *SocArXiv Papers*, 10.31235/osf.io/syr84.

CHAPTER 40

IMMIGRATION IN HISTORICAL POLITICAL ECONOMY

MARGARET E. PETERS

"Gobernar es poblar" (To govern is to populate)
—Juan Bautista Alberdi (1852)

"We asked for workers. We got people instead."
—Max Frisch (1974)

"Why do we want all these people from shithole countries coming here?"
—President Donald Trump, 2018[1]

The movement of people has always been an important issue for governments, but concerns over immigration—the movement of people by their own volition into a country and the policy governing who can enter a country—became an issue starting in the early-modern period as sovereigns gained more control over their borders.

The terms of the debate on immigration have shifted greatly over the last several centuries. The first epigraph, from Juan Bautista Alberdi, a mid-nineteenth-century Argentine philosopher and diplomat, shows that governments once encouraged immigration. Yet, today, as illustrated by the quote from former US president Donald Trump, many nations, especially the wealthy nations of the Global North, seek to discourage immigration.

In this chapter I discuss the reasons for this change and enduring issues in immigration. The first significant issue has been the need for manpower. Throughout much of history, the state has been synonymous with the ruler; the state's goals were the ruler's goals. The ruler wanted to stay in power, get rich, and gain status. The major threats to the ruler were external threats and other elites. To stave off these threats and get rich, the ruler needed people: people to serve in the army, work in agriculture, make things, and so on. The more people subject to the ruler, the more income he could extract, which he could use to fund an army, buy off other elites, and spend on castles, jewels, and other luxury goods that would aggrandize him.

The rise of democratic governance, industrialization, and globalization over the last two hundred years has changed this calculus. Democratic leaders must consider the effects of immigration on society. Industrialization and globalization mean that societies do not need as many people as they once did to produce the goods and services they desire.

In addition to the changing needs for manpower, there have been enduring concerns about immigrants. One of these concerns has been their loyalty; immigrants have often been perceived as "fifth columns." A second and related concern is the potential effect of immigrants on politics in the state. Especially in democracies, there has been a concern that immigrants simply do not understand the government, and their influence will undermine the state. A third concern has been the cost of supporting poor immigrants. Finally, a constant feature has been the fear of the other.

I begin this chapter by explaining immigration and immigration policy and tracing their history over the last few centuries. Much of the literature in the West has focused on immigration policy in Europe and its offshoots; thus, much of this discussion is based on policy in that region. This is not to say that immigration was not an issue elsewhere but simply that we have less scholarship about it. After setting the stage, I discuss the major factors that have affected immigration politics and policy.

What Are Immigration and Immigration Policy?

By "immigration," we mean the movement of people from one country into another (mostly) of their own volition; this article does not deal with individuals moved as enslaved people, though this movement has made up a large flow of people from ancient times to today. For much of history, people moved shorter distances primarily—such as from parish to parish—in part due to limits on their mobility, like serfdom (Peters 2022). Yet there were always individuals who traveled further as seasonal laborers, soldiers and sailors, and clergy, and cities were always a draw (Lucassen and Lucassen 2009). Nonetheless, the nineteenth century marked a turning point in mobility: with the rise of faster and safer transportation technology, large numbers of individuals could now make international and even intercontinental moves (Lucassen and Lucassen 2009).

Immigration policy consists of the policies governing this movement. States began codifying immigration during the long nineteenth century, which historians generally recognize as from 1789 to 1914. After World War I, most states adopted the requirement to have a passport and visas to enter the country, ending the legal permeability of borders (Torpey 2018). Immigration policy includes entry policies, the rights given to immigrants, and enforcement policies.

Entry Policies

States have governed the entry of immigrants in many ways. Throughout much of history, most states had a laissez-faire approach to immigration, placing no restrictions on who could enter. This approach was taken partly because most polities could not police their borders; the exceptions included city-states, which in medieval and early-modern Europe could control who entered the city[2]; some island nations, like Japan from 1639 to 1853; and a few highly developed states like China, which controlled entry from 1661 to 1727.

Starting in the nineteenth century, most states began regulating immigration. These regulations were more about controlling the kind of immigrants who entered rather than trying to decrease the flow. States sought the "right" kind of manpower. To do this, states or localities put restrictions on immigration of the poor, the infirm, and criminals (Neuman 1993). Yet at the same time, many states used inducements—from the 1862 Homestead Act in the United States, which provided free land (Zolberg 2006), to the Bounty System in Australia (1835–1841), which paid for transportation (Jupp 2002; Madgwick 1969)—to attract the "right" types of immigrants.

As the nineteenth century wore on, states, and the societies they represented, became concerned that these prohibitions were not enough. There were new, racialized groups that states sought to restrict. Most of the "settler" societies of the New World began by restricting immigration of individuals from Asia and Africa (although there was little free African migration)[3] and then from southern and eastern Europe, through prohibitions, national origin quotas, and literacy tests (Borrie 1994; Lepervanche 1975; Jupp 2002; Gibney, Hansen, and Credo 2005; Hawkins 1991; Henry 2008; Kelley and Trebilcock 1998; Smith 1981; Templeton 2008; Timmer and Williamson 1998; Tsuchida 1998; Zolberg 2006). World War I and the Great Depression intensified opposition to immigration and led to more restrictions (Peters 2015; 2017; Timmer and Williamson 1998).

After World War II, states largely continued their goals of allowing only the "right" immigrants. While the most racist aspects of the prewar policies were removed, they were replaced with family reunification policies in the United States and skills-based policies in Australia, Canada, and New Zealand meant to have the same effect (Jupp 2002; Tichenor 2016). Yet some states, especially those in Europe, needed workers and signed bilateral labor agreements to hire them (Castles 1986; Peters 2019). It was hoped that these agreements would allow states to bring in labor they needed but not bring long-term immigrants.

In most wealthy states, entry policy has continued along these lines since the 1970s. States increasingly restrict those they see as undesirable but provide additional carveouts for workers deemed essential. These essential workers typically are on the two ends of the wage spectrum: high-wage immigrants for the modern knowledge economy and low-wage immigrants for agriculture and the service sector. States further want to encourage the long-term settlement of high-wage immigrants while deterring low-wage immigrants from settling.

Refugees

Refugees have been something of an exception to this trend of increased exclusions. As a separate legal category, refugees did not exist in international law until after World War I. Before World War I, refugees as we know them today—individuals fleeing a well-founded fear of persecution based on reasons of race, religion, nationality, political opinion, or membership in a particular social group (Convention Relating to the Status of Refugees, 1951)—of course existed. The shifting boundaries of religions in the Eastern Hemisphere, especially fights between different Christian sects and along the Christian/Muslim borderlands, and pogroms against minority groups, including the Jews and Roma, led many to flee. Genocide and politicide were common events, from the destruction of Troy described by Homer to the destruction of indigenous groups during colonization. Individuals fled across borders to avoid advancing armies or criminal gangs (it was often hard to distinguish between the two).

However, these individuals were not recognized as refugees (Hamlin 2021). Societies have had notions of sanctuary from the ancient Greeks onward, but providing sanctuary was not the same as refugee status. In the case of the ancient Greeks, those seeking sanctuary were not given citizenship but were often confined to temple grounds (Rubinstein 2018). Later in history, some groups fleeing religious persecution, like the Huguenots, were invited to move to England and Prussia, but other groups, like the Palantines or Jews fleeing pogroms, were not (Hamlin 2021).[4]

Instead, most people whom we would now call refugees moved as migrants. They would be accepted, or not, according to the rules of a state. In the nineteenth century, most fled either to a neighboring state or to the New World if they could afford it. If the refugees were not deemed common criminals, disabled, or likely to become public charges, they could enter the state. States in the New World like the United States and Argentina even created carve-outs for those convicted of political crimes to enter the state, in what we might consider the first asylum laws (Hutchinson 1981; Iza 1994).

After World War I, the end of the Austro-Hungarian, Russian, and Ottoman Empires, combined with the creation of the passport and visa system, led to the creation of the refugee regime. The end of World War I resulted in a large-scale "unmixing" of populations, as many ethnic minorities no longer "belonged" in their state. These individuals, however, often would not have the papers—especially a passport—necessary to move elsewhere because they were effectively stateless (Loescher, Betts, and Milner 2008). Additionally, the Russian Civil War created millions of refugees.

This situation led to the creation of the League of Nations High Commission on Refugees. Under the league, a group-based definition of refugees was created (Loescher,

Betts, and Milner 2008), and the so-called Nansen passport, named after the first High Commissioner on Refugees, Fridtjof Nansen, was created to help the stateless move. The League succeeded in resettling Russian refugees and assisted in the Greek-Turkish population exchange, but it failed to help Jews fleeing the Nazi regime, Chinese escaping the Japanese invasion, and Ethiopians fleeing the Italian invasion (Loescher, Betts, and Milner 2008).

The plight of displaced persons in Europe after World War II led to the creation of the modern refugee regime. Even before the war's conclusion, Allied leaders realized they had to deal with many displaced persons in Europe, including Jews living in concentration camps and former slave laborers from Eastern Europe in Germany. With the Soviets' movement westward came migrants from the Baltic, many of whom were concerned about reprisals for their collaboration with the Nazis during the war (Nasaw 2021). At first, the Allies, including the Americans, planned to simply return the displaced to their country of origin (Nasaw 2021). When the displaced refused to return—either in the case of the Jews unwilling to return to the site of their persecution or those from Eastern Europe unwilling to live under Soviet rule—the Allies had to devise a new plan (Nasaw 2021).

After several institutional changes, the United States and its allies created the UN High Commission on Refugees (UNHCR)[5] and adopted the 1951 Convention on Refugees, creating the modern definition. This individual-based definition differed from the league's group-based definition, and it only covered those fleeing events in Europe before 1951.

Even before the 1951 Convention was formally adopted, this definition was challenged by states and events outside of Europe. The Indian and Pakistani governments wanted a more inclusive definition and assistance in dealing with the displacement crisis arising from the creation of the two states (Nasaw 2021), and there were no provisions for those fleeing the Chinese civil war or the Korean War or the displacement of Palestinians during the creation of the State of Israel. In this last case, the United Nations acted because it was argued that the organization itself was partly responsible for the crisis (Hamlin 2021). Nevertheless, instead of expanding the definition of a refugee to include Palestinians and giving the UNHCR authority over the situation, the United Nations created its Relief and Works Agency (UNRWA).

The creation of the UNHCR and the limited definition of a refugee were essentially products of US desires, which were for a limited regime. The sentiment in the United States was against immigration (Nasaw 2021), making support for a large agency difficult. In addition, the United States increasingly wanted to use refugees fleeing the Soviet Union and its satellites as evidence of the illegitimacy of communist rule (Loescher, Betts, and Milner 2008). The United States thus wanted nothing to do with international organizations that allowed the Soviet Union as a member and so created its own limited organization, the UNHCR (Karatani 2005; Loescher, Betts, and Milner 2008; Nasaw 2021).

Since 1951 the UNHCR has expanded its mission. It took on responsibility for other crises and pushed to remove the temporal and geographic restrictions on who is defined as a refugee. It also broadened its mission to include internally displaced persons (Hamlin 2021).

Another important aspect of the 1951 Convention was the creation of the principle of non-refoulment. As enshrined in the Convention Against Torture, this principle does not allow countries to return migrants to their home countries if the migrant faces torture or other harm to their physical integrity, yet increased fears that immigrants have been using asylum policy and non-refoulment as a back gate to enter the Global North has led to more draconian enforcement policies. For example, there is increased interdiction at sea, and the United States, the European Union, and Australia increasingly cooperate with transit countries to keep potential asylum seekers from reaching their shores (FitzGerald 2019).

Rights and Citizenship

While the idea of citizenship goes back to at least Ancient Greece, the modern concept of citizenship with its notions of shared governance of a nation-state—rather than subjecthood with its notion of subjugation to the rule of a higher-status individual—began with the French Revolution and its redefinition of state-society relations (Brubaker 1992). With the slow demise of monarchies in Europe and early decolonization movements, citizenship rather than subjecthood spread throughout Europe and the Western Hemisphere. Nonetheless, the British remained subjects, rather than citizens, until the 1948 British Nationality Act (Spencer 1997), even though people living in British dominions like Canada and Australia became citizens in 1867 (Kelley and Trebilcock 1998) and 1903 (Lynch and Simon 2003), respectively. Much of the world remained colonial subjects until their countries were granted independence in the twentieth century.

In addition to entry policy, governments have used citizenship and other rights to attract or repel immigrants. During the nineteenth century, most immigrants were bound to the United States; thus, other countries seeking immigrants had to compete with that nation (Timmer and Williamson 1998), offering to pay for transportation, land, and, for those settling in rural areas, tools and other supplies to get started (Browne 1972). Once states sought to decrease immigration, they limited rights in hopes of deterring entrants. For example, the 1996 IIRIRA Act in the United States limited access to welfare and other social programs specifically to deter immigration. Similar limitations have been passed on asylum seekers' access to the right to work and the social welfare system in the United States and Europe (Geddes 2003).

Research has shown that more fundamental rights can attract immigrants. For example, Fitzgerald, Leblang, and Teets (2014) and Leblang and Helms (forthcoming) find that fewer requirements for citizenship, and the rights that go with it, lead to increased immigration flows. Similarly, Ruhs (2013) finds that rights like permanent residence and family reunification help attract highly educated migrants. However, Zavodny (1997) finds that any relationship between welfare access and immigration is simply a correlation. Once she controlled for migrant networks and economic opportunities, the relationship between welfare access and migration disappeared (Zavodny 1997). These conflicting results may stem from the types of rights and populations studied. It is possible that all immigrants greatly care about fundamental rights but pay less attention to issues like welfare (likely because most migrants plan to work) and that highly skilled migrants care much more about rights because they are in higher demand than those who plan to work a low-wage job, who simply want a high-paying job somewhere.

Citizenship laws have largely tracked along the same lines as other rights: states made getting citizenship easier when seeking to attract immigrants and harder when trying to decrease their numbers. For example, in 1867, the new Canadian government enacted a citizenship law in which the only requirement was three years of residency in the country (Kelley and Trebilcock 1998). Australia in 1903 only required two years of residency (Department of Immigration 1988). In contrast, many European countries today required ten years of residency or longer (Wallace Goodman 2010).

Enforcement

The final component of immigration policy is enforcement. Most states had relatively little formal enforcement of immigration laws until the late nineteenth and early twentieth centuries.[6] For instance, early in the 1800s, US states essentially outsourced enforcement by requiring ship owners to return those inadmissible immigrants to the port of embarkment (Neuman 1993).

Immigration enforcement began in earnest in the early twentieth century as states regulated immigration to a much larger degree. Now immigrants had to pass through inspection points like Ellis Island to enter. There was also the widespread adoption of the passport during World War I. While passports had been used earlier by revolutionary France and by Prussia, they became almost ubiquitous in Europe during World War I to prevent the entry of "enemy aliens" (Torpey 2018). What was meant to be temporary became permanent as immigration restrictions were kept in place due to the economic recession in many countries after the war (Torpey 2018). The passport then spread to the rest of the world (Torpey 2018).

States have generally increased their enforcement measures since the early 1900s. The United States created the Border Patrol in 1924; other countries followed suit. States began to use carrier sanctions, transit agreements, and sea patrols to push the border back farther beginning in the 1980s (FitzGerald 2019).

In sum, states did not focus much attention on immigration prior to the long nineteenth century as most people could not move long distances. Once mass migration was possible, states were open to immigration in the first half of the long nineteenth century, began restricting immigration in the latter half of that period, most reopened some after World War II, and they have greatly restricted immigration since the 1970s (Peters 2015; 2017).

What Have Been the Primary Considerations on Immigration?

Manpower

A significant consideration for states on immigration has been their manpower needs. Immigrants have primarily been regarded as a source of labor for the state. Due to the relatively low level of productivity gains prior to the Industrial Revolution, the only way to increase the amount produced in the state was to increase the number of people. We see numerous examples of rulers seeking to increase their population through immigration. In the High Middle Ages, rulers in the relatively unpopulated lands of eastern Europe sought immigrants from western Europe to farm the land (Anderson 1979; Epstein 2009). Beginning in the seventeenth century, large-scale colonization efforts began in areas deemed to be "unpopulated," including North America, Australia, New Zealand, South Africa, and the Southern Cone. After World War I, France recruited additional workers from Algeria and its North African colonies to the Metropol (Ageron 1991), along with workers from other European countries (Cross 1983; Libet 1995), and after World War II, other European countries—West Germany, the Netherlands, and Switzerland, among others—followed suit signing bilateral labor agreements (Peters 2019).

States also sought manpower for fighting. Immigrants can be drafted into the military or can provide manpower at home, freeing up locals to fight (Mirilovic 2010). In the late nineteenth century, France encouraged immigration and the naturalization of young men to fight in its armies. Foreign residents of France at that time—even those who were second- or third-generation immigrants—were not required to serve in the military (Brubaker 1992). In 1889, France extended citizenship to those born in France in part to equalize immigrant and native-born French obligations to the military (Brubaker 1992, 106).

However, the need for manpower has declined with industrialization and globalization, leading to less support for immigration among elites and increased restrictions. While earlier inventions like the windmill, the heavy plow, horse collar, and the use of plow horses instead of oxen (Epstein 2009, 21, 35, 200), allowed farmers to grow much more food with less labor, which in turn allowed for increased population growth and urbanization (Barnebeck, Jensen, and Skovsgaard 2016, 3), there was still a great need for labor in most states prior to industrialization.

The Industrial Revolution, beginning around 1760, sparked a tremendous and continuing wave of automation and labor-saving. In agriculture, developments in the mid-nineteenth century like better plows, seed drills, and threshers led to dramatic declines in the need for labor (Atack, Passell, and Lee 1994); by the end of the century, the amount of labor needed to produce wheat reduced to less than a tenth of what was needed seventy years earlier (Atack, Passell, and Lee 1994, 269). The decline in manpower needs in agriculture led to a decrease in support for immigration as fewer new farmers or agricultural laborers were needed, and as former farmers and agricultural workers and their children moved to the cities to take jobs in the new industrial sector, fewer immigrant workers were needed in the industrial sector (Peters 2017). In turn, elites in these sectors reduced their support for immigration (Peters 2017).

As each country industrialized, it first increased support for immigration among elites. The first mechanizations of production in the 1760s through the 1890s changed production from using craft labor—in which one craftsman (and they were usually men) built the entire good—to factories and assembly lines in which unskilled labor made and assembled different parts of a good. This change necessitated much labor, relying upon the unskilled labor of immigrants, women, and even young children. Beginning in the 1890s, manufacturing switched again to continuous and batch-processing, which needed relatively fewer people overall but more skilled labor (Goldin and Katz 1998). Later industrializers (e.g., those industrializing after 1950) often began the process with the most labor-intensive industries, such as textiles or toys, which too necessitated much labor before moving on to more capital-intensive industries. Like the change in agriculture, this change from more labor-intensive to more capital-intensive industries led to less support for immigration as industry needed fewer workers, and with less support from industry, governments restricted immigration (Peters 2017).

Globalization in the nineteenth and twentieth centuries led to a decrease in support by elites for immigration as well. In both eras, technological changes—from canals to railroads and steamships to modern containerships—significantly reduced trade costs. Communication devices like the telegraph, telephone, and internet have allowed businesses to control production worldwide.

These changes allowed production to move where it was most efficient and profitable for firms. In the United States, for example, manufacturing of low-wage-intensive textiles and clothing moved from the Northeast, where labor costs were high, to the South, where labor costs were low (Wright 1981). These firms used to rely on immigrant labor but now use the cheaper, locally born labor of the South, taking their support for immigration with them (Peters 2017).

Similarly, manufacturing that relies on low-wage labor has moved from the Global North to the rest of the world, where labor costs are lower. In some cases, this movement has been caused by offshoring and foreign direct investment. Once firms moved abroad, they no longer cared about immigration at home, leading to less support for immigration and increased restrictions (Peters 2014; 2015; 2017; 2020). In other cases, new entrants arose in the Global South and traded their goods to the Global North. Global North firms could not compete with these new entrants and closed their doors (see Autor, Dorn, and Hanson 2016). These firms were also the firms that had employed much low-wage immigrant labor. When these firms closed, they took their support with them (Peters 2014; 2015; 2017; 2020).

Further, when these firms closed, they laid off their workers, lowering wages in the area. Businesses that remained in operation took advantage of the laid-off local labor instead of lobbying for more immigrant labor (Peters 2014; 2015; 2017; 2020).[7] Together, increased trade, increased ability to move production overseas, and increased automation and use of labor-saving technology have significantly changed the politics of immigration by reducing the need for labor. The decline in business support for immigration also explains the long-run increase in restrictions in the Global North discussed earlier (Peters 2015; 2017).

Competition with Domestic Labor

The flip side of the need for manpower is competition with local workers. The same demand for labor that attracts immigrants can potentially lead to higher wages in their absence, depending on whether immigrants are complements or substitutes for local labor.

Scholars disagree about whether immigrants lower wages for low-skilled locals (Borjas, Grogger, and Hanson 2008; Longhi, Nijkamp, and Poot 2005). There is some evidence that immigrants lower wages; for example, Hatton and Williamson argue that wages in the New World in 1910 would have been 2 percent higher in Brazil and 46 percent higher in Argentina if immigration had stopped after 1870 (Hatton and Williamson 1998, 224–25). Borjas has also found evidence using more recent data that higher levels of immigration lead to lower wages for similarly skilled natives (Borjas 2006; Borjas, Freeman, and Katz 1996). Other scholars have found that immigrant labor seems to complement local labor, leading to higher wages for natives (Card 2005; Clemens and Hunt 2019; Ottaviano and Peri 2012). In this case, low-wage immigrant labor can be used to perform the least-skilled tasks, and low-wage local labor can perform tasks demanding more skill. Then the local labor is used more productively, instead of being "wasted" on the very low-skill tasks. For example, in the 1860s, hiring Chinese laborers to work on the railroads allowed unskilled White laborers to advance their position to straw bosses, supervisors, teamsters, and skilled craftsmen (Saxton 1971, 63).

Regardless of immigration's actual economic effect on wages, local labor has often opposed immigration because it lowers wages. Opposition by labor has at times been channeled through more formal channels such as unions and at other times has been relatively unorganized and often more violent. For example, White miners attacked Chinese immigrant miners in California in the 1850s (Boswell 1986) and Australia in the late 1800s (Smith 1981) over the perceived competition. Around the same time, the budding labor unions in California pushed for the passage of the 1882 Chinese Exclusion Act (Saxton 1971). This anti-immigrant stance was echoed in labor unions later in the nineteenth and early twentieth centuries, especially by the American Federation of Labor (AFL) in the United States (Briggs 2001; Fine and Tichenor 2009).

Security

A third issue that often arises with immigration is the issue of security, and especially concerns over so-called fifth columns. A "fifth column" is a group that undermines the state from within. Immigrants, especially those from enemy countries, are often stereotyped as fifth columns due to their imagined or real loyalties to their home states.

The Alien and Sedition Acts of 1798 in the United States are early examples of how security concerns affect immigration policy. In particular, the Alien Enemy Act of 1798 allowed the president to imprison and deport noncitizens from an enemy nation, and the Alien Friends Act authorized the president to deport noncitizens deemed "dangerous." The fear of immigrant fifth columns is a through line in US immigration history: examples include the Enemy Alien Acts in World War I and World War II, the Red Scare after World War I and during the start of the Cold War, the internment of Japanese nationals and citizens of Japanese heritage in World War II, and the PATRIOT ACT today.

The United States is not the only country that has been concerned about fifth columnists. The German Empire in the late 1800s was greatly concerned that its Polish citizens and Polish immigrants were a likely fifth column. Prussia, the forebearer state of the German Empire, had only gained control over its section of Poland about a century before the unification of Germany, and many Polish noblemen and elites harbored dreams of a reunified Poland. At first, German leaders tried forced assimilation of Poles into German society, but when this failed, forced expulsions of Polish citizens and immigrants from the Austrian and Russian-controlled areas of Poland began (Lucassen 2005, 59).

Additional examples of concerns of immigrants and their descendants as fifth columnists abound. Australia followed the example of the United States and enacted restrictions on immigration from non-Allied countries during World War I (Jupp 2002). In 1942 New Zealand similarly placed restrictions on individuals from Axis countries who had naturalized (Beaglehole 2009). States have also expelled populations that they think are not loyal: China, for example, expelled ethnic Russians who lived in border regions with Russia after the Sino-Soviet split in 1959 (McNamee and Zhang 2019), and Vietnam expelled ethnic Chinese during the Sino-Vietnam War (Stern 1985).

Political Effects

Along with security concerns, there have been arguments that immigrants might irredeemably alter the politics of a country. Immigrants are not simply workers, but many can vote in local elections and/or eventually become citizens and vote. Immigrants, thus, can change the nature of politics.

This line of argument has a long history in the United States, partly driven by the fact that noncitizens could vote in many states in the Midwest, West, and South (Rusk 2001, 32). As with certain other rights, suffrage enticed settlers to new territories and states in the Midwest and West (Varsanyi 2005), and states in the South extended the franchise after the Civil War to attract more White settlers and have more White voters (Rusk 2001).

One reason for opposition has been the idea that those raised in autocracies cannot understand how to participate in a democracy. Benjamin Franklin complained in 1753 that Germans were "not used to liberty, they know not how to make a modest use of it" (Franklin 1753). Political theorists like Walzer (2008) have articulated this idea more recently.

The second version of this argument has focused on how the religious loyalties and practices of those of different religions, especially Catholics, might affect politics. There has long been a concern that Catholics would be loyal to the pope rather than the US government. In the colonial and early republic eras, these concerns led to provisions in the New York Constitution that stayed in place until 1806 that prohibited Catholics from naturalization or serving as elected officials unless they renounced their faith (Duncan 2005). These fears resurfaced as late as the 1950s and 1960s with the concern that presidential candidate John F. Kennedy would be loyal to the pope. While concerns about Catholics have subsided, we can see echoes of these fears in anti-Muslim sentiment in the United States and Europe. In this case, locals fear that immigrants will change and implement laws consistent with their religion instead of the local political traditions (Dancygier 2017).

A third strain, mainly present in the United States but also seen in Canada and Australia, has been concerns over the spread of radical economic ideas. In the wake of the French Revolution, the arrival of refugees from France and radical sympathizers from Great Britain and Ireland led to fears that immigrants would spread their radical ideas about the nature of society and ownership, leading to the passage of the Alien and Sedition Acts (Cogliano 1999, 662). These concerns resurfaced in the twentieth century around the spread of socialist, communist, and anarchist ideas (Higham 1963). In 1903, the Alien Exclusion Act banned anarchists, and a 1906 law denaturalized anarchists (Kraut 2020, 59). At the height of the 1920s Red Scare, approximately 3,000 immigrants were held as radicals at Ellis Island, and 556 were deported (Kraut 2020, 74). Concerns about the spread of leftist ideas also helped motivate the 1921 and 1924 Quota Acts (Kraut 2012; 2020). These fears were not just an American phenomenon; Australia passed a law banning anarchists in 1901, and Canada followed suit in 1926 (Mills 1930, 33–35, 83–86).

Similar concerns have even affected the reception of refugees. During debates over the admission of Jewish displaced persons after World War II, many US politicians claimed that Jews were likely communist sympathizers. For example, Congressman Ed Lee Gossett (D-TX) said in 1947 that "at least a good many of those [displaced persons] were more or less induced to come into our camps with the idea of being troublemakers . . . They were professional revolutionaries" (Nasaw 2021, 309). In the 1970 and early 1980s, Vietnamese refugees were often portrayed as communist enemies, even though most were fleeing their communist government's policies (Wooten 1975). The Thai government even described Vietnamese refugees as communist sympathizers and a potential "vanguard" for a communist invasion (Flood 1977, 39).

Fiscal Effects

Another factor that has long affected opinions on immigration and immigration policy is concern over the fiscal effects of immigrants. Although most immigrants move to places with economic opportunity (Zavodny 1997), there is fear that they may use the social welfare system more than locals or more than they provide in taxes (Hanson, Scheve, and Slaughter 2007).

While the rise of the large social welfare state is relatively recent, these fears go back, at least in Europe, to the early-modern period and the Reformation. Before the Reformation, social welfare services were the purview of the Catholic Church, which remained the case in Catholic countries (Kahl 2005). Newly Protestant countries, however, moved the provision of these services to the state. Reformed Protestant Church and Calvinist states adopted a low level of government-provided welfare due to their belief that poverty is a sign of sin. In contrast, Lutheran states created the most generous social welfare states, as they believed that poverty was simply bad luck (Kahl 2005). As early as the 1530s, Lutheran municipalities in Germany provided basic government-supported social insurance (Brubaker 1992).

The rise of social insurance and the welfare state meant that poor migrants were more costly to society. As these groups, almost by definition, had fewer social ties in the dominant society, they had less recourse if they lost a job or could no longer work. Because an immigrant, without naturalizing, was not necessarily eligible for full welfare benefits, there was an incentive in the nation to restrict citizenship and membership. A series of Prussian laws governing freedom of movement and internal migration was intended to "permit the state to exclude unwanted—that is, poor—foreigners" (Brubaker 1992, 71). The concern over poor immigrants later affected the German citizenship law of 1913. While Social Democrats offered a variety of paths to naturalization based on birth and residency, their proposals were soundly rejected in part based on the desire to maintain the ability to expel migrants "deemed 'burdensome'" (Brubaker 1992, 121).

Even with more limited relief for the poor, the American colonies, the later US states, and eventually the US federal government limited immigration to the United States based on concerns over the fiscal effects of immigrants. During the colonial period, colonies enacted laws to prevent the movement of the poor into their territories and then later codified this into state and federal laws (Neuman 1993). The laws against becoming a public charge remain in force today. European and British Commonwealth states, including Australia and Canada, have had similar provisions (Kelley and Trebilcock 1998; Lynch and Simon 2003).

The Other

Finally, the last major determinant of immigration policy has been the fear of the other, or what we might call nativism. "Nativism" is the dislike of immigrants for their very foreignness—in this view, their outsider status ensures that they can never fully assimilate into society. Of course, this fear of the other overlaps with labor market, security, political, and fiscal concerns but is more nebulous.

Nativism—fear of the other, has been a constant throughout history. Early American colonists were wary of immigrants from outside England; Benjamin Franklin famously called Germans "swarthy" and implied in the 1750s that they could not assimilate (Franklin 1753). The United States saw the rise of anti-immigrant sentiment against the Irish and Germans in the 1840s (leading to the rise of the virulently anti-immigrant party, the Know-Nothings), Chinese and other Asians in the mid-1800s, southern and eastern Europeans in the late nineteenth and early twentieth centuries, Japanese in the early twentieth century, Mexicans beginning in the 1920s, and currently Latinos/as, Muslims, and, with the COVID-19 pandemic, Asians. The British Dominions (Canada, Australia, South Africa, and New Zealand) have had similar waves of anti-immigrant sentiment (Jupp 2002; Kelley and Trebilcock 1998; Peberdy 2009; Tagupa 1994; Templeton 2008).

Nativist concerns helped lead to the rise of racist immigration legislation in the early twentieth century in most of the New World. The United States, followed by Brazil (La Cava 1999), enacted national origin quotas in 1921 and 1924, favoring people from northern and western Europe and prohibiting most others. In Australia, Canada, and New Zealand, there were "White-[country]" policies beginning in the early twentieth century, banning the migration of Asians and limiting European migration to those deemed acceptable (Jupp 2002; Kelley and Trebilcock 1998; Tagupa 1994; Templeton 2008). Similar laws were passed in South Africa, already on its road to apartheid (Peberdy 2009). Germany also prohibited immigration based on ethnicity (see, e.g., Berger 1997; Brubaker 1992; Confino 1997; Greenfeld 1992; Vick 2002).

After World War II, we see the continuation of concerns over race and ethnicity affecting immigration policy. While the United States, Australia, Canada, and New Zealand eliminated their explicitly racist policies in the 1960s and 1970s, they replaced them with race-neutral policies that were meant to have the same effect (Jupp 2002; Kelley and Trebilcock 1998; Tichenor 2016; Winkelmann 2000). At the same time, the United Kingdom limited migration from its former colonies to White, or at best, mixed-race individuals by creating patriality—the ability of only a White grandfather (but not grandmother) born in the United Kingdom to pass down citizenship (Booth 1992). In the rest of Europe, increased concerns over the immigration of former colonial subjects and people of color fleeing civil strife helped lead to increasingly restrictive immigration laws (Hammar 1985). Similarly, Japan limited migration from its former colonies, South Korea and Taiwan, even going so far as to make it extremely difficult for children of immigrants to gain citizenship (Chung 2010). This concern over the other continues to be high relevant today.

Conclusion

For most of human history, polities did not have immigration policies, largely because people couldn't move very far and polities' control over their borders was relatively weak. Of course, new groups moved into territories controlled by other polities. Yet these movements were often either the movement of conquering armies or the flight of those fleeing the conquering armies.

Large-scale immigration—the movement of individuals of their own volition—only started in the early-modern period and took off during the long nineteenth century due to changes in transportation technology that made it faster and safer to travel long distances (Lucassen and Lucassen 2009). With the rise of mass migration came the rise of political fights over immigration. On the one side have been the winners of more open immigration: (mostly) elites who want to increase the manpower of the state, including monarchs who gain more people and production to tax and soldiers to fight; agricultural barons and captains of industry who benefit from lower labor costs; and, in something of a Baptist-bootlegger coalition, the migrants themselves, who receive higher wages than at home, and the humanitarian groups who favor immigration for normative reasons (Freeman 1995). On the other side are the real or imagined losers: local labor, who fear job or wage loss; taxpayers, who are wary of increased fiscal demands; and nativists, who loathe the change in politics, their political power, or their culture.

The nineteenth century was a brief period in which many states welcomed immigrants on a large scale. Given the limited franchise in most states, it is not surprising that the elites won. Policymakers pushed aside the concern of laborers who feared competition and those who disliked immigrants because of their very foreignness to bring in labor to build their countries' new industries and agriculture.

This period did not last long. With the rising power of labor (Eichengreen 1996) came the social welfare state and concerns about immigrants' effects on the labor market (Timmer and Williamson 1998) and their effects on the fiscal system became more prominent (Kalm and Lindvall 2019). With productivity, open trade, and the increased ability to offshore production, business support for immigration waned (Peters 2014; 2015; 2017). This opened space for nativist concerns to gain more traction. Finally, security concerns have ebbed and flowed as states entered into conflicts. These forces have combined to make a much more restrictive immigration system than we saw 150 years ago.

Notes

1. Watkins and Phillip (2018).
2. European city-states often did not restrict entry but restricted citizenship (Van Zanden and Prak 2006). Ancient Athens was somewhat similar too (Fitzgerald 2017).
3. By the time slavery ended, it had decimated the population of Africa. This, in combination with increased activity in commodities production in Africa, led few Africans to migrate voluntarily outside of Africa. There was much migration within Africa though (Schuler 1986).
4. In the case of the Palatines, many were transported to Ireland or the North American colonies (Dickinson 1967).
5. See Nasaw (2021) for a detailed account of these institutions and the negotiations.

6. Japan and China during their periods of closure were outliers as they enforced their borders to a much greater extent.
7. They may still have lobbied but it was likely to be on another issue (Peters 2014; 2017).

References

Ageron, Charles Robert. 1991. *Modern Algeria: A History from 1830 to the Present.* Trenton, NJ: Africa Research and Publications.
Alberdi, Juan Bautista. 1852. *Bases y Puntos de Partida Para La Organizacion Politica de La Republica Argentina, Etc.* Buenos Aires: Imprenta Argentina.
Anderson, Perry. 1979. *Lineages of the Absolutist State.* London: Verso.
Atack, Jeremy, Peter Passell, and Susan Lee. 1994. *A New Economic View of American History: From Colonial Times to 1940.* New York: Norton.
Autor, David H., David Dorn, and Gordon H Hanson. 2016. "The China Shock: Learning from Labor-Market Adjustment to Large Changes in Trade." *Annual Review of Economics* 8: 205–40.
Barnebeck, Andersen Thomas, Peter Sandholt Jensen, and Christian Volmar Skovsgaard. 2016. "The Heavy Plough and the Agricultural Revolution in Medieval Europe." *Journal of Development Economics* 118: 133–49.
Beaglehole, A. 2009. "Looking Back and Glancing Sideways: Refugee Policy and Multicultural Nation-Building in New Zealand." In *Does History Matter? Making and Debating Citizenship, Immigration and Refugee Policy in Australia and New Zealand.*, ed. Klaus Neumann and Gwenda Tavan, 105–23. Canberra: ANU E Press.
Berger, Stefan. 1997. *The Search for Normality: National Identity and Historical Consciousness in Germany since 1800.* New York: Berghahn Books.
Booth, Heather. 1992. *The Migration Process in Britain and West Germany: Two Demographic Studies of Migrant Populations.* Research in Ethnic Relations Series. Aldershot, UK: Avebury.
Borjas, George J. 2006. "Native Internal Migration and the Labor Market Impact of Immigration." *Journal of Human Resources* 41, no. 2: 221–58.
Borjas, George J., Richard Freeman, and Lawrence Katz. 1996. "Searching for the Effect of Immigration on the Labor Market." *American Economic Review* 86, no. 2: 247–51.
Borjas, George J., Jeffrey Grogger, and Gordon H. Hanson. 2008. "Imperfect Substitution between Immigrants and Natives: A Reappraisal." *National Bureau of Economic Research.* Working Paper 13887.
Borrie, W. D. 1994. *The European Peopling of Australasia: A Demographic History, 1788–1988.* Canberra: Australian National University.
Boswell, Terry E. 1986. "A Split Labor Market Analysis of Discrimination against Chinese Immigrants, 1850–1882." *American Sociological Review* 51, no. 3: 352–71.
Briggs, Vernon M. 2001. *Immigration and American Unionism.* Cornell, NY: Cornell University Press.
Browne, George P. 1972. *Government Immigration Policy in Imperial Brazil, 1822–1870.* Thesis, Catholic University of America.
Brubaker, Rogers. 1992. *Citizenship and Nationhood in France and Germany.* Cambridge, MA: Harvard University Press.
Card, David. 2005. "Is the New Immigration Really So Bad?" *Economic Journal* 115 (507): F300–F323. https://doi.org/10.1111/j.1468-0297.2005.01037.x.

Castles, Stephen. 1986. "The Guest-Worker in Western Europe: An Obituary." *International Migration Review* 20, no. 4: 761–78.

Chung, Erin Aeran. 2010. *Immigration and Citizenship in Japan*. Cambridge, UK: Cambridge University Press.

Clemens, Michael A., and Jennifer Hunt. 2019. "The Labor Market Effects of Refugee Waves: Reconciling Conflicting Results." *ILR Review* 72, no. 4: 818–57.

Cogliano, Francis D. 1999. "America and the French Revolution." *History* 84, no. 276: 658–65.

Confino, Alon. 1997. *The Nation as a Local Metaphor: Württemberg, Imperial Germany, and National Memory, 1871–1918*. Chapel Hill: University of North Carolina Press.

Convention Relating to the Status of Refugees. Geneva, 28 July 1951. *United Nationas Treaty Series* vol. 189, No. 2545, p. 137, available from https://treaties.un.org/Pages/show Details.aspx?objid=080000028003002e&clang=_en

Cross, G. S. 1983. *Immigrant Workers in Industrial France: The Making of a New Laboring Class*. Philadelphia, PA: Temple University Press.

Dancygier, Rafaela M. 2017. *Dilemmas of Inclusion*. Princeton, NJ: Princeton University Press.

Department of Immigration, Local Government and Ethnic Affairs. 1988. *Australia and Immigration*. Canberra: Australian Government Publishing Service.

Dickinson, H. T. 1967. "The Poor Palatines and the Parties." *English Historical Review* 82, no. 324: 464–85.

Duncan, Jason K. 2005. *Citizens or Papists? The Politics of Anti-Catholicism in New York, 1685–1821*. New York: Fordham University Press.

Eichengreen, B. J. 1996. *Golden Fetters: The Gold Standard and the Great Depression, 1919–1939*. Oxford: Oxford University Press.

Epstein, Steven A. 2009. *An Economic and Social History of Later Medieval Europe, 1000–1500*. Cambridge: Cambridge University Press.

Fine, Janice, and Daniel J. Tichenor. 2009. "A Movement Wrestling: American Labor's Enduring Struggle with Immigration, 1866–2007." *Studies in American Political Development* 23: 84–113.

Fitzgerald, David. 2017. "The History of Racialized Citizenship." *Oxford Handbook of Citizenship* 103, no. 1: 129–52.

FitzGerald, David Scott. 2019. *Refuge beyond Reach: How Rich Democracies Repel Asylum Seekers*. New York: Oxford University Press.

Fitzgerald, Jennifer, David Leblang, and Jessica C. Teets. 2014. "Defying the Law of Gravity: The Political Economy of International Migration." *World Politics* 66, no. 3: 406–45. https://doi.org/10.1017/S0043887114000112.

Flood, E. Thadeus. 1977. "The Vietnamese Refugees in Thailand: Minority Manipulation in Counterinsurgency." *Bulletin of Concerned Asian Scholars* 9, no. 3: 31–47.

Franklin, Benjamin. 1753. "Letter to Peter Collison," May 9, 1753. https://founders.archives.gov/documents/Franklin/01-04-02-0173.

Freeman, Gary P. 1995. "Modes of Immigration Politics in Liberal Democratic States." *International Migration Review* 29, no. 4: 881–902.

Frisch, Max. 1974. "Uberfremdung I." In *Schweiz Als Heimat*, ed. Walter Obschlager, 219–21. Frankfurt a.M: Suhrkamp Verlang.

Geddes, Andrew. 2003. *The Politics of Migration and Immigration in Europe*. SAGE Politics Texts. London: SAGE.

Gibney, Matthew J., Randall Hansen, and Reference Credo. 2005. *Immigration and Asylum from 1900 to the Present*. Santa Barbara, CA: ABC-CLIO.

Goldin, Claudia, and L. F. Katz. 1998. "The Origins of Technology-Skill Complementarity." *Quarterly Journal of Economics* 113, no. 3: 693–732.

Greenfeld, Liah. 1992. *Nationalism: Five Roads to Modernity*. Cambridge, MA: Harvard University Press.

Hamlin, Rebecca. 2021. *Crossing: How We Label and React to People on the Move*. Stanford, CA: Stanford University Press.

Hammar, Tomas, ed. 1985. *European Immigration Policy: A Comparative Study*. Cambridge: Cambridge University Press.

Hanson, Gordon H., Kenneth Scheve, and Matthew J. Slaughter. 2007. "Public Finance and Individual Preferences over Globalization Strategies." *Economics & Politics* 19, no. 1: 1–33.

Hatton, Timothy J., and Jeffrey G. Williamson. 1998. *The Age of Mass Migration: Causes and Economic Impact*. New York: Oxford University Press.

Hawkins, Freda. 1991. *Critical Years in Immigration Canada and Australia Compared*. Kingston, ON: McGill-Queen's University Press.

Henry, M. 2008. "Border Geostrategies: Imagining and Administering New Zealand's Post-World War One Borders." *New Zealand Geographer* 64, no. 3: 194–204.

Higham, John. 1963. *Strangers in the Land: Patterns of American Nativism, 1860–1925*. New York: Atheneum.

Hutchinson, Edward P. 1981. *Legislative History of American Immigration Policy, 1798–1965*. Philadelphia: University of Pennsylvania Press.

Iza, A. O. 1994. "The Asylum and Refugee Procedure in the Argentine Legal System." *International Journal of Refugee Law* 6, no. 4: 643–48.

Jupp, James. 2002. *From White Australia to Woomera: The Story of Australian Immigration*. New York: Cambridge University Press.

Kahl, Sigrun. 2005. "The Religious Roots of Modern Poverty Policy: Catholic, Lutheran, and Reformed Protestant Traditions Compared." *Archives Européennes de Sociologie / European Journal of Sociology/Europäisches Archiv Für Soziologie* 46, no. 1: 91–126.

Kalm, Sara, and Johannes Lindvall. 2019. "Immigration Policy and the Modern Welfare State, 1880–1920." *Journal of European Social Policy* 29, no. 4: 463–77.

Karatani, R. 2005. "How History Separated Refugee and Migrant Regimes: In Search of Their Institutional Origins." *International Journal of Refugee Law* 17, no. 3: 517–41.

Kelley, Ninette, and M. J. Trebilcock. 1998. *The Making of the Mosaic: A History of Canadian Immigration Policy*. Toronto: University of Toronto Press.

Kraut, Julia Rose. 2012. "Global Anti-Anarchism: The Origins of Ideological Deportation and the Suppression of Expression." *Indiana Journal of Global Legal Studies* 19: 169–93.

Kraut, Julia Rose. 2020. *Threat of Dissent: A History of Ideological Exclusion and Deportation in the United States*. Cambridge, MA: Harvard University Press.

La Cava, Gloria. 1999. *Italians in Brazil*. New York: Peter Lang.

Leblang, David A., and Benjamin Helms. Forthcoming. *Migration in the Global Political Economy*. Cambridge: Cambridge University Press.

Lepervanche, Marie de. 1975. "Australian Immigrants, 1788–1940: Desired and Unwanted." In *Essays in the Political Economy of Australian Capitalism*, ed. E. L. Wheelwright and K. D. Buckley, 72–104. Sydney: Australia and New Zealand Book Company.

Libet, Ludwig Victor. 1995. "Building the Border: The Treatment of Immigrants in France, 1884–1914." PhD Dissertation, University of Illinois at Urbana-Champaign.

Loescher, Gil, Alexander Betts, and James Milner. 2008. *The United Nations High Commissioner for Refugees (UNHCR): The Politics and Practice of Refugee Protection into the 21st Century*. London: Routledge.

Longhi, Simonetta, Peter Nijkamp, and Jacques Poot. 2005. "A Meta-Analytic Assessment of the Effect of Immigration on Wages." *Journal of Economic Surveys* 19, no. 3: 451–77. https://doi.org/10.1111/j.0950-0804.2005.00255.x.

Lucassen, Jan, and Leo Lucassen. 2009. "The Mobility Transition Revisited, 1500–1900: What the Case of Europe Can Offer to Global History." *Journal of Global History* 4, no. 3: 347–77. https://doi.org/10.1017/S174002280999012X.

Lucassen, Leo. 2005. *The Immigrant Threat: The Integration of Old and New Migrants in Western Europe since 1850*. Urbana: University of Illinois Press.

Lynch, James P., and Rita J. Simon. 2003. *Immigration the World Over: Statutes, Policies, and Practices*. Lanham, MD: Rowman and Littlefield.

Madgwick, Robert Bowden. 1969. *Immigration into Eastern Australia, 1788–1851*. Sydney: Sydney University Press.

McNamee, Lachlan, and Anna Zhang. 2019. "Demographic engineering and international conflict: Evidence from China and the Former USSR." *International Organization* 73, no. 2: 291–327.

Mills, Albert Payne. 1930. "The Immigration Policies of the British Dominions, Canada, Australia, New Zealand, South Africa." Stanford University, Department of Economics.

Mirilovic, Nikola. 2010. "The Politics of Immigration: Dictatorship, Development, and Defense." *Comparative Politics* 42, no. 3: 273–92.

Nasaw, David. 2021. *The Last Million: Europe's Displaced Persons from World War to Cold War*. New York: Penguin.

Neuman, Gerald L. 1993. "The Lost Century of American Immigration Law (1776–1875)." *Columbia Law Review* 93, no. 8: 1833–901.

Ottaviano, Gianmarco I. P., and Giovanni Peri. 2012. "Rethinking the Effect of Immigration on Wages." *Journal of the European Economic Association* 10, no. 1: 152–97.

Peberdy, Sally. 2009. *Selecting Immigrants: National Identity and South Africa's Immigration Policies, 1910–2008*. Johannesburg: Wits University Press.

Peters, Margaret E. 2014. "Trade, Foreign Direct Investment and Immigration Policy Making in the US." *International Organization* 68, no. 4: 811–44.

Peters, Margaret E. 2015. "Open Trade, Closed Borders: Immigration in the Era of Globalization." *World Politics* 67, no. 1: 114–54.

Peters, Margaret E. 2017. *Trading Barriers: Immigration and the Remaking of Globalization*. Princeton, NJ: Princeton University Press.

Peters, Margaret E. 2019. "Immigration and International Law." *International Studies Quarterly* 63, no. 2: 281–95.

Peters, Margaret E. 2020. "Integration and Disintegration: Trade and Labor Market Integration." *Journal of International Economic Law* 23, no. 2: 391–412. https://doi.org/10.1093/jiel/jgaa007.

Peters, Margaret E. 2022. "Government Finance and the Re-Imposition of Serfdom after the Black Death." Working Paper. UCLA.

Rubinstein, Lene. 2018. "Immigration and Refugee Crises in Fourth-Century Greece: An Athenian Perspective." *European Legacy* 23, nos. 1–2: 5–24.

Ruhs, Martin. 2013. *The Price of Rights: Regulating International Labor Migration*. Princeton, NJ: Princeton University Press.

Rusk, Jerrold G. 2001. *Statistical History of the American Electorate*. Washington, D.C.: CQ Press.

Saxton, Alexander. 1971. *The Indispensable Enemy: Labor and the Anti-Chinese Movement in California*. Berkeley: University of California Press.

Schuler, Monica. 1986. "The Recruitment of African Indentured Labourers for European Colonies in the Nineteenth Century." In *Colonialism and Migration; Indentured Labour Before and After Slavery*, ed. P.C. Emmer, 125–61. Dordrecht: Springer Netherlands.

Smith, T. E. 1981. *Commonwealth Migration: Flows and Policies.* Cambridge Commonwealth Series. London: Macmillan.

Spencer, I. R. G. 1997. *British Immigration Policy since 1939: The Making of Multi-Racial Britain.* New York: Routledge.

Stern, Lewis M. 1985. "The Overseas Chinese in the Socialist Republic of Vietnam, 1979–82." *Asian Survey* 25, no. 5: 521–36.

Tagupa, W. 1994. "Law, Status and Citizenship: Conflict and Continuity in New Zealand and Western Samoa (1922–1982)." *Journal of Pacific History* 29, no. 1: 19–35.

Templeton, F. 2008. "Te Ara—The Encyclopedia of New Zealand." Ministry for Culture and Heritage. https://teara.govt.nz/en.

Tichenor, Daniel. 2016. "The Historical Presidency: Lyndon Johnson's Ambivalent Reform: The Immigration and Nationality Act of 1965." *Presidential Studies Quarterly* 46, no. 3: 691–705.

Timmer, Ashley S., and Jeffrey G. Williamson. 1998. "Immigration Policy Prior to the 1930s: Labor Markets, Policy Interactions, and Globalization Backlash." *Population and Development Review* 24, no. 4: 739–71.

Torpey, John C. 2018. *The Invention of the Passport: Surveillance, Citizenship, and the State.* New York: Cambridge University Press.

Tsuchida, Motoko. 1998. "A History of Japanese Emigration from the 1860s to the 1990s." In *Temporary Workers or Future Citizens? Japanese and U.S. Migration Policies*, ed. Tadashi Hanami and Myron Weiner, 77–119. London: Macmillan.

Van Zanden, Jan Luiten, and Maarten Prak. 2006. "Towards an Economic Interpretation of Citizenship: The Dutch Republic between Medieval Communes and Modern Nation-States." *European Review of Economic History* 10, no. 2: 111–45.

Varsanyi, Monica W. 2005. "The Rise and Fall (and Rise?) of Non-Citizen Voting: Immigration and the Shifting Scales of Citizenship and Suffrage in the United States." *Space and Polity* 9, no. 2: 113–34. https://doi.org/10.1080/13562570500304956.

Vick, Brian E. 2002. *Defining Germany.* Cambridge, MA: Harvard University Press.

Wallace Goodman, Sara. 2010. "Naturalisation Policies in Europe: Exploring Patterns of Inclusion and Exclusion." Comparative Report, RSCAS/EUDO-CIT-Comp. 2010/7. San Domenico di Fiesole (FI), Italy: EUDO Citizenship Observatory.

Walzer, Michael. 2008. *Spheres of Justice: A Defense of Pluralism and Equality.* New York: Basic Books.

Watkins, Eli, and Abby Phillip. 2018. "Trump Decries Immigrants from 'Shithole Countries' Coming to US." *CNNI*, January 12, 2018. https://www.cnn.com/2018/01/11/politics/immigrants-shithole-countries-trump/index.html.

Winkelmann, Rainer. 2000. "Immigration Policies and Their Impact: The Case of New Zealand and Australia." Institute for the Study of Labor. Bonn: IZA.

Wooten, James T. 1975. "The Vietnamese Are Corning and the Town of Niceville, Fla., Doesn't Like It." *New York Times*, May 1. https://www.nytimes.com/1975/05/01/archives/the-vietnamese-are-coming-and-the-town-of-niceville-fla-doesnt-like.html.

Wright, Gavin. 1981. "Cheap Labor and Southern Textiles, 1880–1930." *Quarterly Journal of Economics* 96, no. 4: 605–29.

Zavodny, M. 1997. "Welfare and the Locational Choices of New Immigrants." *Economic Review: Federal Reserve Bank of Dallas*: 2–10.

Zolberg, Aristide R. 2006. *A Nation by Design: Immigration Policy in the Fashioning of America.* Cambridge, MA: Harvard University Press.

CHAPTER 41

MARKET AND GOVERNMENT PROVISION OF SAFETY NETS AND SOCIAL WELFARE SPENDING IN HISTORICAL POLITICAL ECONOMY

PRICE FISHBACK

As nations experienced large increases in per capita income over the past two hundred years, they have increased the extent of their *safety nets*, defined as support during times of trouble. Before 1900, safety nets in most countries were provided by extended families, friends, and local communities. When problems developed, multiple generations in extended families provided care for the elderly, the infirm, or children. Friends, churches, and charities also helped, and local governments provided limited aid to the indigent. Some groups developed mutual societies in which members agreed to provide financial help to group members who became ill or were injured. Market insurance eventually grew out of the mutual societies, so that households could purchase life insurance, sickness insurance to replace lost earnings, and health insurance to pay for healthcare; invest in old-age pensions; and more recently parental leave upon the birth of a child. During the early 1900s in higher-income nations, employers increasingly provided these options to their workers.

Since then, governments have become more heavily involved. By far, the largest growth in safety net expenditures has occurred in government-funded social insurance programs, often financed by payroll taxes on employers and workers based on the worker's wage. Comparisons from Peter Lindert's study *Growing Public* (2004) in Table 41.1 show that Denmark and the Netherlands in 1900 had the highest level of government funding of the safety net at 1.4 percent relative to gross domestic product (GDP) in countries that later joined the Organisation of Economic Co-operation and Development (OECD). By 1930, Germany had taken over the lead at 5 percent relative

Table 41.1. Estimates of public social welfare expenditures as a percentage relative to GDP in OECD countries, 1900–2017

Country	1900	1930	1980	2000	2017
France	0.6	1.1	20.1	27.7	31.5
Finland	0.8	3.0	17.8	22.6	29.6
Denmark	1.4	3.4	20.3	23.8	29.2
Belgium	0.3	0.6	23.2	23.7	28.7
Italy	0.0	0.1	17.3	22.6	27.6
Austria	0.0	1.2	21.9	25.7	27.3
Sweden	0.9	2.6	24.5	26.5	26.0
Germany[a]	0.6	5.0	21.8	25.5	25.4
Norway	1.2	2.5	16.1	20.4	25.2
Greece	nv	nv	9.9	17.8	24.7
Spain	0.0	0.1	14.9	19.5	23.9
Portugal	0.0	0.0	9.5	18.5	22.7
Japan	0.2	0.2	10.0	15.4	22.3
Luxembourg	nv	nv	nv	18.7	21.5
Slovenia	nv	nv	nv	22.1	21.5
Poland	nv	nv	nv	20.2	20.8
United Kingdom	1.0	2.6	15.6	16.9	20.5
Hungary	nv	nv	nv	20.1	19.7
New Zealand	1.1	2.4	16.3	18.4	18.6
Czech Republic[b]	nv	0.5	nv	17.9	18.5
United States	0.6	0.6	12.9	14.1	18.4
Canada	0.0	0.3	13.2	15.7	18.0
Slovak Republic[b]	nv	0.5	nv	17.5	17.5
Estonia	nv	nv	nv	13.9	17.2
Switzerland	nv	nv	12.7	14.5	17.0
Australia	0.0	2.1	10.3	18.2	16.7
Netherlands	0.4	1.2	23.0	19.0	16.6
Israel	nv	nv	nv	16.2	16.2
Iceland	nv	nv	nv	14.5	16.0
Latvia	nv	nv	nv	15.4	15.9
Lithuania	nv	nv	nv	15.4	15.3
Ireland	nv	3.9	15.7	12.8	14.2
Colombia	nv	nv	nv	nv	13.3
Turkey	nv	nv	2.2	7.5	12.1
Costa Rica	nv	nv	nv	nv	11.9
Chile	nv	nv	nv	10.4	11.5

Table 41.1. Continued

Country	1900	1930	1980	2000	2017
South Korea	nv	nv	nv	4.4	10.1
Mexico	0.0	0.0	nv	4.4	7.5
Median	0.4	1.2	15.9	18.1	18.6
Maximum	1.4	5.0	24.5	27.7	31.5
Minimum	0.0	0.0	2.2	4.4	7.5

Bolded values are values above the median for reporting countries in that column.

[a] Calculated for German Empire in 1900 and 1930.

[b] Calculated for Czechoslovakia in 1900 and 1930.

nv = not available.

Note: The OECD measures of government social welfare expenditures include old-age pensions, survivor benefits (not from private life insurance), incapacity-related aid, health expenditures, aid to families, unemployment benefits, income maintenance, government job training, and housing subsidies. Gross public is the most widely reported figure.

Source: The data for 1900 and 1930 come from Lindert (1994, 10). For 1980, 2000, and 2017, the data come from the OECD.Stat database section on Social Expenditure–Aggregated Data, downloaded January 10, 2022.

to GDP, but most countries were still below 3 percent. By 2017, OECD statistics on gross public social welfare spending in Table 41.1 show that, among OECD countries, Mexico had the lowest share relative to GDP of 7.5 percent and the share reached as high as 31 percent in France.[1] Estimates in Table 41.2 for forty-five countries in the rest of the world in 2017 show a much broader range—from 22.2 percent in Ukraine to 0.2 in Pakistan. The two most populous countries, China and India, were at 6.3 and 2.7 percent, respectively.

The public social welfare expenditure shares of GDP show that countries around the world follow a wide range of practices with respect to social protection. The broad range of practices extends to how much different countries devote to the various categories of social protection expenditures, as well as the extent to which they rely on private and public provision of the support, how much they tax the benefits that are provided, and who pays for the benefits.

Markets, Governments, Adverse Events, and Poverty

Households have dealt with adverse events in a variety of ways for centuries. The adverse events include loss of income, loss of job, death, health problems, and disability. The

Table 41.2. Social protection expenditures, total and by category, as percentage relative to GDP in major non-OECD countries

Country	Total public including health 2000	Total public including health 2015 or latest year	Latest year	Older people without Health	Unemployment	Labor pro-gram	Sickness, maternal, work injury, disability	General social assi-stance	Children without health	Health All	Health Govt.
Ukraine	18.1	22.2	2015	13.7	0.4	nv	1.1	0.7	1.8	7.4	3.5
Brazil	14.2	18.3	2015	9.6	0.7	0.3	1.7	4.5	0.6	9.5	4.0
Cuba	11.9	18.0	2011	nv	nv	nv	nv	2.7	nv	11.7	10.5
Uruguay	17.8	17.0	2015	8.9	0.6	nv	0.3	3.1	0.4	8.8	6.1
Russian Fed.	9.4	15.6	2015	8.7	0.2	nv	2.7	1.8	0.6	5.4	3.1
Mongolia	8.6	14.4	2015	5.5	0.1	0.3	0.5	4.9	1.3	4.0	2.5
Colombia	7.3	14.1	2015	3.8	np	nv	3.9	0.8	0.4	7.7	5.5
Costa Rica	10.7	13.6	2015	5.7	np	nv	3.4	2.3	1.3	7.1	5.2
Iran	8.9	12.5	2010	5.9	0.3	nv	1.5	5.0	1.0	8.4	4.4
Kuwait	13.5	11.4	2011	3.5	np	nv	nv	nv	nv	4.7	4.0
Egypt	8.6	11.2	2015	3.0	nv	nv	nv	nv	nv	5.6	1.7
Georgia	5.1	10.6	2015	4.4	np	nv	0.8	1.4	2.3	7.1	2.6
South Africa	6.7	10.1	2015	3.4	0.2	nv	0.6	0.0	1.6	8.7	5.0
Taiwan	9.9	9.7	2010	4.7	0.3	0.2	0.6	0.5	0.4	nv	nv
Venezuela	6.1	8.8	2015	7.4	nv	nv	1.0	nv	nv	4.7	2.8
Guatemala	3.8	8.2	2010	0.5	np	nv	1.7	0.0	0.3	6.1	2.2
Algeria	6.3	7.4	2005	5.6	0.0	nv	0.3	0.9	0.1	6.3	4.1
Tanzania	2.1	6.8	2010	2.0	np	nv	0.0	0.4	0.0	4.1	1.6

Namibia	6.0	6.7	2015	2.4	0.1	nv	0.3	0.8	0.5	8.7	4.1
Morocco	3.9	6.6	2010	3.0	np	nv	1.5	0.1	0.1	5.2	2.3
China	4.7	6.3	2015	3.7	0.1	0.1	1.6	0.3	0.2	5.1	2.9
Vietnam	5.0	6.3	2015	5.5	0.0	0.1	0.3	0.3	0.0	4.7	2.2
Zimbabwe	5.6	5.6	2011	0.5	np	nv	0.1	0.1	0.2	7.5	1.8
Malaysia	2.4	3.8	2012	0.9	np	0.0	0.1	0.1	0.0	3.7	1.9
Thailand	2.6	3.7	2015	np	0.1	0.0	1.2	0.1	0.5	3.8	2.8
Saudi Arabia	nv	3.6	2011	0.3	nv	nv	nv	nv	nv	6.3	4.5
Papua New Guinea	3.8	3.6	2015	0.1	np	0.0	nv	0.0	0.1	2.2	1.7
Congo, DR	0.3	3.5	2012	1.0	0.0	nv	0.3	0.1	0.1	4.2	0.4
Ethiopia	6.0	3.2	2010	0.3	nv	nv	nv	nv	nv	3.5	0.9
Afghanistan	0.8	2.8	2013	nv	nv	nv	nv	nv	nv	nv	nv
Burkina Faso	3.5	2.7	2015	1.0	np	nv	0.2	1.4	0.0	6.0	2.6
India	1.6	2.7	2016	4.3	nv	0.4	0.1	0.4	0.1	2.9	1.0
Kenya	1.4	2.3	2012	1.6	np	nv	0.1	0.1	0.1	4.1	1.8
Cameroon	1.5	2.3	2010	0.5	np	nv	0.4	nv	0.0	3.5	0.2
Philippines	1.1	2.2	2015	0.6	0.0	0.0	0.2	0.5	0.1	4.0	1.5
Uganda	4.3	2.2	2015	0.4	np	nv	0.4	0.3	0.0	4.0	0.6
Cote d'Ivoire	1.7	2.0	2015	1.5	np	nv	0.2	nv	0.3	3.3	1.0
Sudan	1.4	2.0	2010	nv	nv	nv	nv	nv	nv	8.2	0.7
Bangladesh	1.1	1.7	2014	0.1	np	0.4	0.0	0.3	0.0	2.4	0.4
Indonesia	2.0	1.1	2015	1.0	np	0.0	0.0	0.8	0.7	2.9	1.4

(continued)

Table 41.2. Continued

	Total public including health			Public social protection expenditures by category							Health	
Country	2000	2015 or latest year	Latest year	Older people without Health	Unemployment	Labor pro-gram	Sickness, maternal, work injury, disability	General social assistance	Children without health		All	Govt.
Myanmar	0.5	1.0	2011	0.7	np	nv	0.1	0.0	0.0		5.1	0.8
Nigeria	0.7	0.7	2013	0.9	np	nv	0.3	0.2	0.0		3.8	0.5
Pakistan	0.3	0.2	2014	1.8	np	0.0	0.0	0.2	0.0		2.9	0.9
Argentina	nv	nv	2015	**9.0**	0.1	nv	**5.1**	**2.0**	**1.6**		**10.4**	**6.6**
Iraq	nv	nv	nv	nv	nv	nv	nv	nv	nv		4.2	1.8
Median	4.5	6.3		2.4	0.1	0.1	0.3	0.4	0.2		5.1	2.2
Minimum	0.3	0.2		0.1	0.0	0.0	0.0	0.0	0.0		2.2	0.2
Maximum	18.1	22.2		13.7	0.7	0.4	3.9	5	2.3		11.7	10.5

nv = not available; np = not applicable

Bolded values are values above the median for reporting countries in that column.

Sources: Social protection expenditures in first nine columns come from International Labor Organization (2017, 397–413). Health expenditures and government share of health expenditures in 2015 come from World Bank data downloaded April 9, 2022, from https://data.worldbank.org/indicator/SH.XPD.CHEX.GD.ZS?end=2019&most_recent_year_desc=true&start= and https://data.worldbank.org/indicator/SH.XPD.GHED.GD.ZS?most_recent_year_desc=true. Values in the Public Social Protection Expenditures by Category section come from a variety of years between 2009 and 2015.

causes can be innate problems from birth; new events like unemployment, injury, death of a breadwinner, or illness; or old age.

Consider a situation where the head of the household has a 2-in-100 chance of having an injury that disables him for a year, and his income is $1,000. This was not an uncommon situation around 1900 in mining or manufacturing. To protect against the possibility of an injury, the household might have saved in advance, yet savings often were inadequate because an injury could occur before a full year's earnings were saved. Some household heads joined mutual societies that pooled funds and provided limited benefits to injured members. As early as the fourteenth century there are records of German miners forming such a group (US Commissioner of Labor 1911, 38). Insurance companies often developed out of mutual societies and expanded their customer base.

If insurers knew the probability of the injury, their annual premium would likely equal the expected loss from the injury of $20—the injury probability of 2/100 times the $1,000 in earnings lost, plus the administrative costs associated with the insurance, say $10, for a total premium of $30. In competitive labor markets, competition among employers for workers for a dangerous job might have been enough to drive annual earnings high enough to cover much of this $30 cost. Insurance markets worked best when insurers knew the risk of injury, sold to workers who had the same risks, the risks were uncorrelated across workers, and insurers could sell to a large number of buyers to allow the actual risk of injury to hit the average through the law of large numbers. If the accident probability varied across workers, the insurance markets still could work well if insurers could identify the differences and charge higher premiums to the riskier purchasers.

The problem known as "adverse selection" developed when insurers could not identify the expected loss for each household. The risk in the example just presented was 2/100, and the expected loss was $20. Say, instead, that half of the workers had a 1/100 risk and half had a 3/100 risk. The expected risk for the group as a whole was still 2/100. If the insurer did not know who had which risk, charged a premium of the $20 expected value, and everybody was risk neutral, adverse selection arises because only the workers with the 3/100 risk would buy, and the insurer would soon be bankrupted.* This might not have happened if the workers with 1/100 risk were so averse to risk that they would have paid a $30 premium that was greater than their expected loss of $10. Alternatively, the insurer would have had to charge at least a $30 premium, leaving the people with 1/100 risk without insurance, or the insurer might not have sold insurance at all, and thus no workers could get insurance. Another way to solve this problem was for the government to mandate that all workers buy insurance. This avoided the adverse selection problem by including all workers in the insurance pool, so that the average risk is an accurate measure of the overall risk. Yet another way was for the government to require all employers to sign up for the government's own insurance system, which is essentially the path followed by many countries that have established universal health insurance.

---

*Risk neutral means that someone would value receiving $100 for sure the same way they would value a bet with a 50 percent chance of receiving 0 and a 50 percent chance of receiving $200.

Costly information can also lead to problems with "moral hazard," when someone who is insured against a specific risk takes more of that risk or reports more of that risk because they are protected against it. Most workplace risk insurers, whether government or private, have tried to protect against moral hazard by limiting the benefits to 50 to 75 percent of the lost earnings and requiring delays before payments start, thus forcing the worker to share some of the costs of the loss. Sweden's social insurance programs ran into serious budget problems after they raised replacement rates near 100 percent in the late 1970s. They responded by cutting the replacement rates closer to 80 percent in the 1990s (Lundberg and Amark 2001). Health insurers often required the buyer to pay a "deductible" and cover the costs of, say, the first $300 spent and/or pay a copay of, for example, 10 percent of the additional costs. The mutual societies, which often were smaller and knew a great deal about their fellow members, solved many of the adverse selection and moral hazard problems by carefully screening their recruits and cutting off members who were abusing the benefits.[2]

When workers and employers pay premiums to the government for workplace injury insurance, agencies like the OECD and various governments describe it as "public social insurance." If the employer operates the insurance with or without contributions from the worker, it is termed "private social insurance." A large majority of funds distributed for social welfare comes through governments, and many governments finance public social insurance through payroll taxes on workers and employers. In a subset of countries, the benefits paid could just be paid by general tax revenues that are not tied to contributions by the individual or employer. These are typically defined as "public assistance" or "safety net" programs and do not involve a contribution to the program from the recipient or their former employer. The programs are typically "means-tested" and designed for people in poverty who are unable to support themselves, particularly if they have children.

The issues of adverse selection and moral hazard have bedeviled private insurance markets, social insurance, and public assistance from their beginnings. Moral hazard in various forms has arguably been the issue that has led to the most administrative costs. Hardly anybody has had qualms about providing benefits to the "worthy" poor—that is, the people who are willing to work but have hit lean times through no fault of their own. The moral hazard issue arose when the benefits were being paid to people whose own choices greatly contributed to their demise. Charities, churches, and progressive reformers in the late 1800s and early 1900s interviewed recipients to determine their needs and the reason why they were in trouble, and to suggest ways for the recipients to reform their behavior, sometimes with threats to remove them from the relief rolls if the behavior continued. People on relief often felt a social stigma that limited moral hazard to some degree, but was painful for "worthy" recipients. Governments have resolved this issue by offering opportunities to work on government projects and thus "earn" their benefits, as in the New Deal in the 1930s and in rural work guarantees in modern India. Advocates for social insurance recognized that it reduced stigma because the person or their employer had paid the "premium" up-front for the benefits the worker received. Similarly, Gustav Moller, the Swedish minister of health and social affairs at various times in the early 1930s and from 1939 through 1951, also recognized this and advocated for a universal program so that all people would be eligible for the benefits and the stigma fully removed (Rothstein 2015).

Political Economy

The political economy of social welfare spending has depended heavily on the type of benefits discussed. The situation is quite different for pure means-tested transfers than for social insurance. Scholars often model pure transfer payments in median-voter models, and some add warm glows from charitable giving. Societies with higher incomes can afford the transfers, and the transfers are more likely when voice and voting power are spread throughout the population, particularly with the addition of political power for women. However, means-tested pure transfers to the poor have always been a small share of the economy. Peter Lindert's (2004, chapters 3 and 4) study of public poor relief in leading European countries between 1750 and 1880 showed that in most years the relief accounted for less than 1 percent of GDP, with a peak in the 1830s for England at around 2.5 percent. He argues that charity from churches for the poor was relatively low in the nineteenth century. Even in the modern era, these pure transfers account for less than 2 or 3 percent of GDP without health spending for the poor (World Bank 2018). Up to around 1900, healthcare spending for the poor was very low. Since then it has risen so that healthcare spending for the poor in OECD countries might add about 1–2 percent of GDP hidden in the universal spending and up to 6 percent in the United States, which has much higher overall health spending than any other country.

Why is this spending so low? In less developed nations with large numbers of people in poverty, the problem of poverty has been too large and the per capita resources available for distribution too few to do much. Even in more developed economies, where the vote is widely distributed, there have been mixed emotions about pure transfers. Many have been willing to provide aid to the "worthy" poor, which often tends to be a small share of the population in higher-income economies. Political battles have commonly been fought over why recipients end up in poverty, and these battles have been exacerbated in societies with greater religious, ethnic, racial, and cultural diversity. Were the economy and the environment at fault, or was the cause an individual's failure to take responsibility for one's actions? The latter issue focuses on the moral hazard problems in dealing with the "unworthy poor," fraud, disincentives to return to work, and the stimulus among poor mothers to have more children.

In the modern era, expansion of the contributory social insurance programs reduced the need for pure transfers through their provision of benefits in settings that would have led to pure transfers in the past. The growth in safety net and social welfare programs has mostly come through social insurance programs in which contributions from workers and employers largely fund the program (Fishback 2020). The political economy of these programs differed as a result. The social stigma was gone because the worker paid up front for the benefits or the benefits were part of an employment package covered by employer taxes. The political battles then became more of an interest group struggle between workers, employers, private insurers, and reformers. At first blush it might seem that employers would be opposed to making contributions. Their opposition would have been weakened if they believed that the new program would allow them to pay lower cash wages in compensating differences for their contributions. Fishback and Kantor (2000) found some evidence that this occurred for nonunion workers for injury insurance in the United States. A number of studies of US labor regulation have found that large employers joined reformers in compromise regulations that legislated programs matching what the employers had already been offering. The reformers gained broader coverage, and the employers stopped cost undercutting by competitors who now had to conform to the higher standards. Small firms, agricultural producers, and hirers of domestic servants often found ways to gain exceptions to being part of the program (Fishback 1998). Unions at times had mixed emotions because they had used sickness and injury funds and negotiations for better working conditions to attract members. Unions feared that government benefits would make it more difficult to attract workers. In Sweden and other Nordic countries, the unions resolved these issues by seeking subsidies from government for their funds, and unions today still play a significant role in the nation's social welfare systems (Van Rie, Marx, and Horemans 2011). These interest group struggles were also influenced by religious attitudes and political ideologies. For example, the US Commissioner of Labor (1893, 20) suggested that Bismarck and his followers partly chose the German path to employer mandates to "cure socialism 'by a hair from the dog that bit me.'"

It is generally accepted that social welfare expenditures as a share of GDP tend to be higher in countries where people have more political voice, GDP per capita is higher, and women have more economic clout. Higher social welfare expenditures are expected where there are larger ratios of the elderly to the economically active workforce, more children relative to the workforce, or both. Cross-sectional correlations between the social welfare measure around 2015 and these factors are all consistent with these views, as correlations were above 0.6 in absolute value. However, when they are included in a regression analysis in Table 41.3, the only statistically significant relationships are with the old-age dependency ratio, the gender inequality measure, and voice in the government. The strongest magnitudes are found for the old-age dependency ratio; a one-standard-deviation increase is associated with an increase of 0.62 standard deviations in the public spending measure. The one-standard deviation impacts of gender inequality and voice in the government are much smaller, at −0.16 and 0.15, respectively.

Activity before World War I

Households struck by adverse events historically relied on their own savings and aid from extended family and friends with some meager help from churches, local charities, and local governments. Family networks were stronger because many stayed near their

Table 41.3. Regression relationships between social protection expenditure as share relative to GDP in 2015 and key correlates circa 2010

	Coeff	t-statistic	Mean	Std. dev.	Min	Max
Per capita GDP (000) ppp$ 2010	0.03	1.06	16.6	16.4	0.6	85.8
Old-age Dependency ratio 2010	0.63	7.91	12.7	8.0	2.6	36.0
Youth dependency ratio 2010	0.01	0.48	46.8	23.8	19.8	105.1
Gender inequality index 2015	−7.00	−1.69	0.37	0.19	0.05	0.75
Voice and accountability	1.26	2.49	0.0	1.0	−2.1	1.6
Constant	4.28	1.76				
N	133					
Adj. R-squared	0.79					
Total Public Social Protection as Percentage Relative to GDP			10.9	8.2	0.17	31.7

Source: International Labor Organization (2017, 397–413) and Excel files downloaded from the ILO database on April 16, 2002, for all but the Voice and Accountability measure, which is from a data set developed by Daniel Kaufmann, Aart Kraay, and Massimo Mastruzzi (2010) and posted at the World Bank site www.govindicators.org. It was downloaded on April 16, 2022. Old-Age Dependency Ratio is population over 65 as a percentage relative to the working-age population. Youth Dependency Ratio is child population as a percentage relative to the working age population. Voice and Accountability is a measure of access to participation in the political process and ranges from −2.5 to 2.5. The gender inequality index ranges from 0 (fully equal) to 1 (fully unequal) and is based on the maternal mortality rate, fertility among women ages 15 to 19, female seats in national parliament, male and female population shares with at least a secondary education, and male and female labor force participation.

birthplaces. Poverty programs in countries like Great Britain and Germany were primarily run by local governments with tight residency requirements, orphanages for kids, almshouses, workhouses, and some outdoor relief (Boyer 1990; Boyer 2019; Hennock 2007). The current situation in the least developed countries in Africa looks similar. A survey of African households in the bottom 40 percent of the income distribution found that fewer than 3 percent of households in several African countries expected to rely most on aid from government and nongovernment organizations (NGOs). They were about 15 to 25 percent most likely to rely on their own savings and 5 to 20 percent most likely to rely on family and friends (Beegle and Christiaensen 2019, 218).

Past households also insured against risk by joining mutual societies. In the Germanic states, laws allowing the creation of voluntary mutual societies were enacted in the twelfth and thirteenth centuries (US Commissioner of Labor 1893, 38). Many mutual protection societies were associated with guilds. In the United Kingdom, some nonguild mutual societies around 1900 were organized in 1555 and 1687 (US Commissioner of Labor 1909, 1551). The German Empire under Bismarck was the first to set up compulsory mutual societies tied to employment. Before the empire was formed, several Germanic states passed laws to allow groups to form sickness, burial, and relief societies, and savings banks. Some made sickness associations mandatory for employers. By 1880, about half of workers in Prussian industry and mines were in a friendly society. The miners' societies were funded 50-50 by employers and workers, while providing insurance benefits for sickness, accidents, orphans, widows, and invalids. To expand coverage, Germany established compulsory programs for sickness insurance in 1883, accident insurance in 1884, and old-age pensions in 1889 (US Commissioner of Labor 1893, 1:30–42).

Hungary in 1891, Austria in 1898, Luxembourg in 1902, and Norway in 1909 followed Germany in making sickness insurance compulsory. Belgium, Denmark, and France provided subsidies, and Sweden followed suit in the early 1910s. Compulsion was far more common for workplace accidents. Until the 1890s most countries had handled workplace accidents by requiring negligent employers to compensate their injured workers. Between 1887 and 1909, eighteen European countries and parts of Australia and Canada adopted some form of workers' compensation that required employers to pay benefits for employment-related accidents. All but five US states adopted similar rules by 1929 (US Commissioner of Labor 1911, 3–27; Fishback and Kantor 2000).

Voluntary unemployment insurance funds arose in several countries. By 1909, local or national governments provided subsidies in Belgium, Denmark, France, Germany, and Norway. Old-age and invalidity insurance was provided in several ways. Among Austria, Belgium, France, Great Britain, Italy, and Spain, there were union funds in at least three of those countries, mutual societies in five of them, government subsidies in four, government-marketed annuities in four, and compulsory programs for at least one class of workers in six (US Commissioner of Labor 1911, 3–27).

Provisions were made for widows and orphans in miners' relief societies in five of the countries. In the United States, a large majority of states established specific "mothers' pension" laws between 1911 and 1920, often at the same time or soon after workers' compensation laws were adopted. By 1910, many social workers had decided that it was better to have children of widows live with their parent rather than in almshouses. The laws passed relatively quickly in part because widows and orphans accounted for a very small share of the population, it was often cheaper to pay direct benefits than house children in almshouses, and the states typically provided for the existence of the programs at the local level without funding them. The states added means-tested benefits for the elderly in the early 1930s, and the old-age and mothers' pension laws became fully funded in the 1935 Social Security Act, which required all counties to have funding and provided federal matching grants (Uguccioni 2022, 155–93).

Nearly all of the modern government and private social welfare programs developed out of these earlier programs. Old-age programs often started as means-tested programs designed to allow the elderly to live on their own. Central governments in the higher-income countries began to construct the modern old-age contributory pensions in the

1930s and soon after World War II with contributions from both workers and employers. Health insurance started to expand as medical technologies improved and the costs of obtaining care became increasingly expensive. These old-age pension and health insurance programs have accounted for a large portion of the rise in social welfare spending in high-income countries, while sickness insurance and unemployment insurance have remained a relatively small percentage of GDP. Accident insurance costs have also stayed low because workplaces have become dramatically safer, particularly in countries that have largely become service-based economies.

Categories of Social Welfare in the Modern Era

The focus of the rest of the paper is the modern era because social welfare programs have become much more complex in advanced countries. There is enormous worldwide variation in expenditures and institutional structures, even among countries long thought to be similar. The variation is documented in Tables 41.2 and 41.4 through 8, which show the different categories of spending across countries, differences in their reliance on private and public programs, the extent of taxation of benefits and consumption, and information on the shares of earnings going to payroll taxes.

Healthcare expenditures have contributed substantially to the rise in social welfare spending in the past eighty years. Many of the sickness insurance and accident insurance schemes in the early 1900s spent much less on medical care than on replacing lost earnings. As the range and effectiveness of healthcare have improved, expenditures as a share of GDP have risen markedly. For the eighteen countries with information for 1970 in Table 41.4, the median healthcare spending share of GDP rose from 4.8 percent in 1970 to 10.5 percent in 2017. Outside the OECD, the figures in Table 41.2 show that the median expenditures on health were about 5.1 percent of GDP.

To finance healthcare, countries have relied on a mix of government financing; government mandates that require the provision of health insurance, typically by employers; voluntary schemes through employers or mutual societies; and out-of-pocket expenditures by households. The OECD does not include the out-of-pocket expenditures in their calculations of social welfare spending. The OECD countries have relied heavily on government financing and mandates, with government shares of health spending funding above 50 percent in 2017, while the non-OECD countries in Tables 41.2 and 41.4 tend to be below 50 percent. A number of OECD countries in Table 41.4 have allowed more private activity after 1980, following the discovery that some groups were finding ways around the prior limitations.

Old-age and survivor benefits are the other category that accounts for large shares of the expenditures. The data in Table 41.5 for the OECD countries include pension programs, payments to the low-income elderly, and payments to the survivors of the

Table 41.4. Healthcare expenditures as share of GDP and share of health expenditures financed by government or compulsory requirements, OECD and major countries, 1970–2017

Country	All healthcare spending					Government and compulsory financed as share of total health			
	Level as percentage relative to GDP				Difference					
	1970	1980	2000	2017	2017–1970	2017–2000	1970	1980	2000	2017
Norway	4.0	5.4	7.7	10.3	6.3	2.6	0.90	0.98	0.82	0.85
Sweden	5.4	7.7	7.3	10.8	5.4	3.5	0.83	0.92	0.86	0.85
Germany	5.7	8.1	9.9	11.3	5.6	1.4	0.72	0.78	0.78	0.85
Japan	4.4	6.2	7.2	10.8	6.4	3.6	0.69	0.72	0.80	0.84
Denmark	nv	8.4	8.1	10.0	nv	1.9	nv	0.87	0.83	0.84
Luxembourg	nv	4.6	5.9	5.3	nv	-0.6	nv	0.93	0.82	0.84
France	5.2	6.8	9.6	11.3	6.1	1.7	0.75	0.80	0.79	0.83
United States	6.2	8.2	12.5	16.8	10.6	4.3	0.37	0.42	0.44	0.83
Czech Republic	nv	nv	5.7	7.1	nv	1.4	nv	nv	0.90	0.82
Iceland	4.7	5.9	8.9	8.3	3.6	-0.6	0.67	0.88	0.81	0.82
Netherlands	nv	6.5	7.7	10.1	nv	2.4	nv	0.74	0.69	0.82
Slovak Republic	nv	nv	5.3	6.8	nv	1.5	nv	nv	0.89	0.80
United Kingdom	4.0	5.1	7.2	9.8	5.8	2.6	0.86	0.89	0.76	0.79
New Zealand	5.1	5.7	7.5	9.0	3.9	1.5	0.81	0.89	0.78	0.79
Turkey	nv	2.4	4.6	4.2	nv	-0.4	nv	0.30	0.62	0.78
Belgium	3.9	6.2	8.0	10.8	6.9	2.8	0.00	0.00	0.75	0.77
Colombia	nv	nv	5.6	7.7	nv	2.0	nv	nv	0.77	0.77
Finland	5.0	5.9	7.1	9.1	4.1	2.0	0.72	0.78	0.74	0.76
Costa Rica	nv	nv	6.6	7.0	nv	0.5	nv	nv	0.66	0.75
Austria	4.8	7.0	9.2	10.4	5.5	1.2	0.60	0.67	0.76	0.74
Italy	nv	nv	7.6	8.7	nv	1.1	nv	nv	0.73	0.74

Estonia	nv	5.2	6.6	nv	1.4	nv	nv	**0.77**	**0.74**
Ireland	**7.5**	5.9	7.1	2.2	1.2	0.00	0.00	**0.78**	0.73
Slovenia	nv	**7.8**	8.2	nv	0.4	nv	nv	**0.73**	0.72
Spain	5.0	6.8	9.0	5.8	2.2	0.64	**0.81**	**0.71**	0.71
Canada	**6.6**	**8.2**	**10.8**	4.5	**2.6**	0.00	0.00	0.70	0.70
Poland	nv	5.3	6.6	nv	1.3	nv	nv	0.69	0.69
Hungary	nv	6.8	6.8	nv	-0.0	nv	nv	0.70	0.69
Australia	5.8	**7.6**	**9.3**		**1.7**	nv	0.63	0.68	0.66
Lithuania	nv	6.2	6.5	nv	0.3	nv	nv	0.69	0.66
Switzerland	**6.4**	**9.1**	**11.5**	**6.7**	**2.4**	0.00	0.00	0.58	0.66
Israel	**6.9**	6.8	7.3	nv	0.5	nv	nv	0.63	0.64
Portugal	4.8	**8.6**	**9.3**	**7.0**	0.7	0.57	0.63	0.70	0.61
Greece	nv	**7.2**	8.1	nv	0.9	nv	nv	0.62	0.60
Chile	nv	7.0	**9.1**	nv	**2.0**	nv	nv	0.53	0.60
South Korea, South	3.4	3.9	7.1	4.5	**3.2**	0.00	0.00	0.54	0.60
Latvia	nv	5.4	6.0	nv	0.5	nv	nv	0.51	0.57
Russia	nv	5.0	5.4	nv	0.3	nv	nv	0.59	0.57
China (PRC)	nv	4.5	5.0	nv	0.6	nv	nv	0.22	0.57
Mexico	nv	4.4	5.5	nv	1.0	nv	nv	0.45	0.51
Indonesia	nv	1.9	2.9	nv	1.0	nv	nv	0.31	0.47
South Africa	nv	**7.4**	8.1	nv	0.7	nv	nv	0.37	0.43
Brazil	nv	**8.3**	**9.5**	nv	1.1	nv	nv	0.42	0.42
India	nv	4.2	3.6	nv	-0.6	nv	nv	0.23	0.27
Median	4.8	7.1	8.2	5.7	1.4	0.65	0.73	0.70	0.73
Minimum	2.3	1.9	2.9	2.2	-0.6	0.00	0.00	0.22	0.27
Maximum	8.4	12.5	16.8	10.6	4.3	0.90	0.98	0.90	0.85

Bolded values are values above the median for reporting countries in that column. nv = not available.

Source: Calculated from OECD.Stat dataset on Health Expenditure and Financing, downloaded March 29, 2022.

Table 41.5. Public old-age and survivor, incapacity-related, and family benefits as percentage relative to GDP in OECD countries, 1980, 2000, 2017

Country	Old-age and survivors' cash benefits 1980	2000	2017	Incapacity-related 1980	2000	2017	Family cash and in-kind benefits 1980	2000	2017
Italy	8.5	13.5	15.6	1.7	1.3	1.7	1.0	1.2	2.0
Greece	5.2	10.2	15.5	1.0	1.4	1.7	0.3	0.8	1.6
France	9.3	11.5	13.6	2.3	1.5	1.6	2.2	3.0	2.9
Austria	10.4	11.9	13.0	2.6	2.4	1.5	3.2	2.9	2.6
Portugal	3.7	7.8	12.7	1.9	2.2	1.7	0.6	1.0	1.2
Finland	5.4	7.4	11.8	3.0	2.9	2.1	2.0	2.9	2.9
Spain	6.0	8.4	10.9	2.3	2.2	2.2	0.5	0.9	1.2
Poland	nv	10.5	10.6	nv	3.4	2.1	nv	1.2	2.6
Belgium	8.8	8.8	10.5	3.5	1.7	2.4	3.0	2.5	2.7
Slovenia	nv	10.4	10.4	nv	2.4	1.5	nv	2.1	1.8
Germany	10.4	10.9	10.2	1.9	1.4	1.3	2.0	2.1	2.3
Japan	3.7	7.0	9.4	0.5	0.5	0.6	0.5	0.5	1.6
Hungary	nv	7.4	8.5	nv	2.4	1.4	nv	3.0	2.7
Luxembourg	8.7	7.1	8.5	3.8	2.4	1.4	1.6	3.0	3.3
Denmark	5.7	6.3	8.0	3.8	2.8	2.8	2.7	3.4	3.4
Czech Rep.	nv	6.8	7.7	nv	2.2	1.6	nv	1.8	2.0
Turkey	0.3	3.9	7.4	0.1	0.2	0.3	0.6	0.2	0.5
Slovak Rep.	nv	6.2	7.3	nv	2.0	1.7	nv	2.0	1.7
Sweden	6.6	6.8	7.2	4.0	3.4	1.8	3.5	2.8	3.4
United States	6.0	5.7	7.1	1.1	0.9	1.1	0.8	0.8	0.6
Norway	4.5	4.7	6.9	3.3	3.7	3.8	1.8	3.0	3.2
Latvia	nv	8.7	6.8	nv	1.2	1.8	nv	1.5	2.2
Estonia	nv	6.0	6.5	nv	1.4	2.0	nv	1.7	2.8
Lithuania	nv	7.1	6.2	nv	1.5	1.8	nv	1.3	1.8
Colombia	nv	nv	5.9	nv	nv	0.1	nv	nv	1.7
United Kingdom	5.3	4.8	5.6	0.8	2.0	1.6	2.2	2.4	3.2
Netherlands	5.9	4.6	5.2	6.0	3.1	2.1	2.3	1.4	1.5
New Zealand	7.0	4.9	4.9	1.2	2.6	2.3	2.1	2.7	2.5
Canada	3.1	4.2	4.8	0.7	0.9	0.7	0.7	0.9	1.7
Israel	nv	4.5	4.7	nv	1.7	2.1	nv	2.4	2.3
Australia	3.6	4.7	4.0	0.9	2.1	1.9	0.9	2.9	2.1
Ireland	5.0	2.9	3.7	2.3	1.3	1.6	1.1	1.7	1.6
Costa Rica	nv	nv	3.4	nv	nv	0.1	nv	nv	0.7
South Korea	nv	1.3	2.8	nv	0.2	0.3	nv	0.1	1.1

Table 41.5. Continued

Country	Old-age and survivors' cash benefits 1980	2000	2017	Incapacity-related 1980	2000	2017	Family cash and in-kind benefits 1980	2000	2017
Chile	nv	5.0	2.8	nv	0.8	0.7	nv	1.1	1.8
Mexico	nv	0.8	2.7	nv	0.1	0.0	nv	0.6	0.9
Iceland	nv	2.1	2.6	nv	1.3	2.2	nv	2.1	3.3
Median	5.8	6.8	7.2	2.1	1.7	1.7	1.7	1.8	2.0
Minimum	0.3	0.8	2.6	0.1	0.1	0.0	0.3	0.1	0.5
Maximum	10.4	13.5	15.6	6.0	3.7	3.8	3.5	3.4	3.4

Source: OECD.Stat dataset on Social Expenditures–Aggregate Data downloaded March 29, 2022.
nv = available.

deceased. Comparisons of the medians at the bottom of Table 41.1 and Table 41.5 for OECD countries suggest that old-age expenditures have accounted for one-third or more of public social welfare expenditures since 1980. In many countries in the rest of the world in Table 41.2, public elderly nonhealth spending is an even higher share of public social spending. Some elderly expenditures in the table are larger than the total public social welfare expenditures because of differences in reporting years for the specific categories.

Many of the countries face long-term challenges in the financing of old-age pensions because they have been operating pay-as-you-go systems. The benefits are being paid out to current retirees based on trust funds containing bonds that are commitments to collect enough taxes in the future to pay promised benefits. The countries facing problems often have rising elderly population shares relative to the working share of the population who pay taxes into the program. Some countries, like Sweden, have begun to address these problems by moving away from promising a defined benefit amount to basing future payouts on the payroll contributions made by the workers and their employers. Sweden and other countries, like Chile, have also set up private accounts (Scheiber and Shoven 1999; Weaver 2003/2004).

Sickness programs provide payments for lost earnings during times of illness, while **disability and injury programs** replace potential earnings and offer medical care related to a disability or injury. These cash payments as a percentage of GDP are much lower than in the health and old-age programs. For twenty-two OECD countries in Table 41.5, the median percentage fell from 2.1 percentage points of GDP in 1980 to 1.7 percentage points by 2017.

The path of cash benefit payments in these categories has been influenced by multiple changes. In general, injury rates for occupations have fallen markedly over the past 120 years, pushing the shares down while improving workers' lives. On the other hand, there are increasing pressures on health costs associated with expansions of the types of injuries and diseases covered by the programs.

Public family benefits in Table 41.5 include means-tested payments to poor households with children, cash allowances for all children, parental leave, schooling and care for children under age five, and nutritional programs. Much of the growth in spending in this area has taken the form of increased parental leave and public education and care for children under age five. In most countries with high public child spending, the large majority of the spending goes to families that are not poor because the benefits are universal.

PRIVATE EXPENDITURES, TAXATION, AND NET TOTAL SOCIAL WELFARE EXPENDITURES

Although observers and analysts emphasize gross public spending in discussions of social welfare, gross public spending offers an incomplete portrayal of social welfare spending. In the late 1800s and early 1900s the countries that began expanding access to safety nets often followed two paths: (1) setting up laws that allowed for the creation of voluntary mutual societies among groups and workers, and (2) mandating that employers provide funds for sickness, accidents, pensions, or all three. A number of countries in the modern era still rely on voluntary private social welfare expenditures, which are primarily provided in programs through employers. In 2017 the leaders shown in Table 41.6 are Canada at 7.1 percent of GDP followed by the Netherlands, the United States, and the United Kingdom above 5.5 percent. The countries relying the most on mandatory private benefits were Switzerland at 10.8 percent of GDP and the Netherlands, Iceland, and the United States above 6.2.

The value of the social welfare spending for recipients is strongly influenced by the taxes that recipients are required to pay on their benefits and the sales taxes and value-added taxes they pay when purchasing items. Meanwhile, some countries provide social welfare benefits through the tax code by allowing tax deductions for each child and cutting taxes or providing subsidies to the working poor with children. The countries where taxes reduced the ability of recipients to consume most typically taxed the benefits to recipients more heavily and had high value-added taxes on consumption. Among the OECD countries in Table 41.7, Denmark and Finland had the largest gaps between gross public and net public spending of more than 6 percentage points of GDP. Only the United States in 2005 and 2017 and South Korea and Mexico in 2005 had tax structures in which net public spending was higher than gross public spending. Adding net private benefits leads to dramatic changes in the rankings when comparing net public to net total spending of GDP. For example, the Netherlands moves from thirty-first to eighth, Switzerland moves from twenty-sixth to sixth, and the United States moves from eleventh to second.

Table 41.6. Private social welfare expenditures as percentage relative to GDP

Source	Private (mandatory and voluntary) 1980	2000	2017	Mandatory private 1980	2000	2017	Voluntary private 1980	2000	2017
Netherlands	3.8	7.5	13.5	0.4	0.9	6.6	3.4	6.6	6.9
United States	4.8	9.2	12.5	0.4	0.4	6.3	4.4	8.8	6.1
Switzerland	1.7	9.2	11.8	1.7	8.0	10.8	0.0	1.1	1.0
Canada	1.5	5.0	7.1	ne	ne	ne	1.5	5.0	7.1
Australia	1.2	3.7	6.6	ne	2.9	5.1	1.2	0.8	1.4
Iceland	nv	4.1	6.5	ne	4.1	6.3	nv	0.0	0.1
United Kingdom	3.4	7.1	6.4	0.2	0.6	0.9	3.2	6.5	5.6
Denmark	5.0	3.9	3.8	ne	ne	2.1	5.0	3.9	1.7
Sweden	1.1	2.4	3.8	ne	0.5	0.4	1.1	1.9	3.4
Chile	nv	2.7	3.7	nv	2.4	3.1	nv	0.3	0.6
Germany	3.4	3.1	3.6	1.9	1.3	2.4	1.5	1.8	1.2
France	0.7	2.7	3.6	ne	ne	0.7	0.7	2.7	2.8
Japan	0.1	3.5	2.9	0.1	0.4	0.4	0.0	3.1	2.5
South Korea	nv	2.5	2.7	na	0.7	0.8	nv	1.8	1.9
Norway	0.8	2.0	2.6	0.2	1.2	1.3	0.6	0.8	1.3
Portugal	0.6	1.6	2.5	0.2	0.4	0.2	0.4	1.2	2.3
Israel	nv	2.3	2.5	ne	1.1	0.2	nv	1.2	2.3
Colombia	nv	nv	2.4	na	na	1.7	nv	nv	0.7
Austria	2.5	2.1	2.2	1.4	0.9	0.8	1.1	1.2	1.4
* Ireland	1.2	3.4	2.0	ne	ne	ne	1.2	3.4	2.0
Italy	0.8	1.6	1.9	0.8	1.1	1.0	0.0	0.5	0.9
Belgium	1.0	1.7	1.9	0.1	0.0	0.0	0.9	1.7	1.9
Finland	0.9	1.3	1.3	ne	0.1	0.1	0.9	1.2	1.2
Spain	0.2	0.3	1.3	ne	ne	ne	0.2	0.3	1.3
Slovenia	nv	0.0	1.3	nv	ne	ne	nv	0.0	1.3
Luxembourg	0.0	0.2	1.1	ne	ne	0.9	0.0	0.2	0.2
Slovak Republic	nv	0.8	1.0	nv	0.2	0.1	nv	0.6	0.9
Greece	nv	0.0	1.0	nv	ne	0.5	nv	nv	0.5
Czech Republic	nv	0.3	0.9	nv	0.2	0.4	nv	0.1	0.4
New Zealand	0.1	0.5	0.7	ne	ne	ne	0.1	0.5	0.7
Poland	nv	nv	0.5	nv	ne	0.0	nv	nv	0.5
Lithuania	nv	0.3	0.5	nv	0.0	0.2	nv	0.3	0.2
Costa Rica	nv	nv	0.5	nv	na	nv	nv	nv	0.5
Mexico	nv	0.1	0.4	ne	ne	ne	nv	0.1	0.4

(continued)

Table 41.6. Continued

Source	Private (mandatory and voluntary)			Mandatory private			Voluntary private		
Year	1980	2000	2017	1980	2000	2017	1980	2000	2017
Hungary	nv	0.2	0.3	nv	ne	ne	nv	0.2	0.3
Turkey	nv	0.4	0.2	ne	ne	ne	nv	0.4	0.3
Estonia	nv	0.1	0.1	nv	ne	ne	nv	0.1	0.1
Latvia	nv	0.1	0.1	nv	ne	ne	nv	0.1	0.1
Median	1.1	2.0	2.1	0.4	0.7	0.8	0.9	1.0	1.2
Minimum	0.0	0.0	0.1	0.1	0.0	0.0	0.0	0.0	0.1
Maximum	5.0	9.2	13.5	1.9	8.0	10.8	5.0	8.8	7.1

ne = information not collected; nv = not available
Bolded values are above the median in the column.
Source: OECD.Stat database on Social Expenditure–Aggregated Data. Downloaded March 29, 2022.

In most countries, a large share of public social welfare expenditures is financed through payroll taxes on workers' earnings paid by employers and workers. Table 41.8 shows estimates of the tax rates paid by a production worker who was single with no children and was paid average earnings (including overtime) in that country. The Organisation of Economic Co-operation and Development (2002) descriptions of these payroll taxes for workers and employers in nearly all of the countries explicitly tie them to specific programs. The combined social welfare tax bite for workers and employers ranged from a high of 49.5 percent in France to a low of zero in New Zealand and Denmark, with a median of 30.6 percent. The employers' contributions exceeded the workers' contributions in twenty-five of the 34 countries in the table. Outside the tax system, employers also finance most of the private voluntary and mandated expenditures for their workers, and a sense of their payments can be seen in Table 41.5.

The Large Variation in Spending, Institutions, and Financing across Countries in the Modern Era

The fascinating feature about the modern safety nets and social protection programs is the extensive variation in how countries structure their institutions and financing of the benefits. Most of the focus here is on the OECD countries because the OECD provides the extensive detail shown in Tables 41.4.

Table 41.7. Public, net public, and net total (including private) social welfare spending as percentage relative to GDP in 2017 in OECD countries and change between 2005 and 2017

Country	Public	Net public	Net public minus public	Net total	Net total minus net public	Public	Net public	Net total
France	31.5	27.8	−3.7	31.2	3.3	2.7	1.9	2.5
United States	18.4	20.3	1.8	29.6	9.4	2.9	3.6	4.7
Belgium	28.7	25.0	−3.7	26.6	1.5	3.4	4.0	3.6
Germany	25.4	23.8	−1.6	25.2	1.5	−1.0	−0.9	−1.2
Denmark	29.2	22.9	−6.3	25.2	2.3	4.0	3.4	3.4
Switzerland	17.0	14.8	−2.3	24.9	10.1	0.9	nv	nv
Italy	27.6	23.1	−4.6	24.7	1.6	3.5	2.5	2.8
Netherlands	16.6	13.5	−3.1	24.7	11.1	−3.3	−3.6	1.7
Finland	29.6	23.5	−6.2	24.5	1.0	5.7	4.8	4.9
Sweden	26.0	21.8	−4.3	24.4	2.6	−1.1	0.4	1.2
Austria	27.3	22.5	−4.7	24.3	1.7	1.3	1.5	1.7
Japan	22.3	21.2	−1.2	23.8	2.6	5.2	4.6	4.6
United Kingdom	20.5	18.6	−1.9	23.3	4.7	1.2	0.3	−0.1
Canada	18.0	17.5	−0.5	23.1	5.6	1.9	2.1	3.5
Norway	25.2	21.0	−4.2	22.6	1.6	4.5	4.0	4.4
Australia	16.7	16.6	−0.1	22.5	5.9	0.0	0.3	3.8
Spain	23.9	21.3	−2.7	22.5	1.2	3.5	3.5	4.2
Portugal	22.7	20.0	−2.6	22.3	2.3	0.4	−0.2	0.3
Greece	24.7	20.3	−4.4	21.1	0.9	5.1	nv	nv
Slovenia	21.5	18.5	−3.0	19.6	1.2	0.0	nv	nv
Iceland	16.0	13.7	−2.3	19.0	5.3	0.2	−0.9	1.4
Czech Rep.	18.5	17.2	−1.4	17.9	0.7	0.6	0.6	1.0
Luxembourg	21.5	16.7	−4.9	17.4	0.7	−1.3	−1.4	−1.1
Hungary	19.7	17.4	−2.3	17.4	−0.0	−2.2	nv	nv
Israel	16.2	15.2	−1.1	17.3	2.2	0.9	nv	nv
Poland	20.8	16.7	−4.1	17.2	0.5	−0.1	−0.3	0.0
Slovak Rep.	17.5	16.2	−1.2	17.1	0.8	2.1	2.4	2.3
New Zealand	18.6	16.3	−2.3	16.9	0.6	0.5	0.7	0.9
Ireland	14.2	13.0	−1.2	14.7	1.6	−1.2	−0.6	−0.7

(continued)

Table 41.7. Continued

	Percentage relative to GDP in 2017					Change in pct. GDP from 2005 to 2017		
Country	Public	Net public	Net public minus public	Net total	Net total minus net public	Public	Net public	Net total
Estonia	17.2	14.5	−2.8	14.5	0.0	**4.4**	nv	nv
Lithuania	15.3	14.0	−1.3	14.4	0.4	**1.7**	nv	nv
Chile	11.5	11.1	−0.3	14.0	**2.9**	**2.6**	nv	nv
Latvia	15.9	13.6	−2.3	13.7	0.1	**3.6**	nv	nv
South Korea	10.1	10.1	**0.0**	12.6	**2.6**	**4.2**	**4.1**	**4.7**
Turkey	12.1	11.7	−0.4	11.9	0.2	**2.0**	**2.6**	**2.4**
Mexico	7.5	7.2	−0.3	7.6	0.3	1.4	0.3	0.6
Median	18.6	17.2	−2.3	21.1	1.6	1.4	1.1	2.0
Minimum	7.5	7.2	−6.3	7.6	−0.0	−3.3	−3.6	−1.2
Maximum	29.6	25.0	1.8	29.6	11.1	5.7	4.8	4.9

Bolded values are values above the median for reporting countries in that column. nv = not available.

Note: The OECD measures of government social welfare expenditures include old-age pensions, survivor benefits (not from private life insurance), incapacity-related aid, health expenditures, aid to families, unemployment benefits, income maintenance, government job training, and housing subsidies. Gross public is the most widely reported figure. Net public adjusts for taxes paid on benefits, consumption taxes, and tax breaks related to the social welfare categories. Net public and private adds in net private expenditures (mandatory and voluntary). The OECD did not report full information for Switzerland in 2003.

Source: OECD.Stat database on Social Expenditure–Aggregated Data downloaded January 6, 2022.

In 2017 France was the leader in public (31.5 percent), net public (27.8 percent), and net total spending (31.2 percent) of GDP in Table 41.6. France is the classic European social democratic model. It ranks third in old-age spending (13.6 percent in Table 41.5) and health spending (11.3 percent in Table 41.4), and seventh in family spending (2.9 percent in Table 41.5) as shares of GDP. France had a high combination of income taxes on recipients' benefits and consumption taxes that caused the net public percentage to be 3.7 percent lower than the public percentage of GDP in Table 41.6. France also followed a strong social insurance model because they ranked first among countries in the total payroll tax rate on production workers' earnings at 49.5 percent overall and 35.1 percent for employers in Table 41.7. The workers' payroll tax rate was 14.4 percent, which ranked ninth among the OECD countries. France's government financed 83 percent of its healthcare in Table 41.4, which ranked seventh. France also offered opportunities for private voluntary social spending in Table 41.5 and ranked sixth at 2.8 percent of GDP.

Table 41.8. Average earnings and estimated average income and social welfare payroll tax rates for single production workers with no children in OECD countries in 2017

Country	1 Worker earnings ($PPP)	Percentage of workers' earnings paid by 2 Worker for income tax	3 Worker for social welfare payroll taxes	4 Employer for social welfare payroll taxes	5 Total social welfare payroll taxes (4+5)	6 Worker and employer for taxes (3+4+5)	7 Workers' after-tax earnings ($PPP)
France	50,328	14.8	14.4	35.1	49.5	64.3	35,638
Austria	59,714	14.5	18.0	28.5	46.5	60.9	40,347
Czech Republic	28,873	13.1	11.0	34.0	45.0	58.1	21,901
Slovak Republic	23,360	10.3	13.4	31.0	44.4	54.7	17,824
Belgium	61,493	26.6	14.0	28.5	42.5	69.1	36,536
Hungary	27,765	15.0	18.5	23.5	42.0	57.0	18,464
Italy	44,711	21.6	9.5	31.6	41.1	62.7	30,790
Greece	36,317	9.7	16.0	25.1	41.1	50.8	26,981
Germany	66,301	19.0	20.8	19.4	40.2	59.2	39,916
Sweden	49,983	18.0	7.0	31.4	38.4	56.4	37,485
Slovenia	33,191	11.6	22.1	16.1	38.2	49.8	22,000
Spain	42,136	14.7	6.4	29.9	36.3	51.0	33,246
Estonia	28,094	16.8	1.6	33.8	35.4	52.2	22,925
Portugal	31,272	16.5	11.0	23.8	34.8	51.2	22,681
Poland	29,048	7.3	17.8	16.4	34.2	41.5	21,759
Turkey	30,159	13.2	15.0	17.5	32.5	45.7	21,652
Finland	51,147	20.9	9.3	22.3	31.6	52.6	35,676
Japan	48,827	7.9	14.4	15.2	29.6	37.5	37,956
Luxembourg	68,966	16.7	12.3	14.1	26.4	43.1	48,956

(continued)

Table 41.8. Continued

Country	Worker earnings ($PPP)	Worker for income tax	Worker for social welfare payroll taxes	Employer for social welfare payroll taxes	Total social welfare payroll taxes (4+5)	Worker and employer for taxes (3+4+5)	Workers' after-tax earnings ($PPP)
	1	2	3	4	5	6	7
Netherlands	65,319	17.2	13.1	11.3	24.4	41.6	45,508
Norway	58,360	19.4	8.2	13.0	21.2	40.6	42,237
United Kingdom	56,471	14.0	9.5	10.9	20.3	34.4	43,206
South Korea	48,872	5.5	8.4	10.4	18.8	24.3	42,064
Canada	42,852	15.4	7.4	11.2	18.6	34.0	33,068
United States	53,376	18.4	7.7	8.3	16.0	34.4	39,444
Ireland	57,520	21.3	4.0	10.8	14.8	36.1	42,949
Israel	39,502	9.7	8.0	5.6	13.6	23.3	32,505
Mexico	13,194	9.8	1.4	11.6	13.0	22.8	11,726
Switzerland	75,910	11.0	6.2	6.2	12.5	23.5	62,834
Iceland	61,872	28.0	0.3	6.8	7.1	35.1	44,354
Chile	22,731	0.0	7.0	0.0	7.0	7.0	21,140
Australia	56,853	24.4	0.0	6.0	6.0	30.3	43,004
Denmark	60,136	36.0	0.0	0.0	0.0	36.0	38,467
New Zealand	40,473	18.1	0.0	0.0	0.0	18.1	33,134
Median	48,850	15.2	9.4	15.6	30.6	42.4	35,657
Minimum	13,194	0.0	0.0	0.0	0.0	7.0	11,726
Maximum	75,910	36.0	22.1	35.1	49.5	69.1	62,834

Bolded values are above the median in that column.

Source: Calculated from data in the OECD.Stat data on Taxing Wages downloaded April 1, 2022.

The country that seems the closest to France was Sweden, which also had high private voluntary spending of 3.4 percent of GDP along with high rankings in the same categories as France. Japan resembles a lower-spending version of France, with top-eight rankings in health and government health spending, worker payroll taxes, and voluntary private expenditures but rankings of twelfth and thirteenth in public and net total social welfare spending. The other countries that were most similar were Austria, Belgium, and Germany.

Sweden is often described as a primary example of the Nordic model of social welfare spending, joined by Denmark, Finland, and Norway. All four countries are ranked in the top nine in public spending of GDP. They all rank highly in family benefits and in the eighth to twelfth range for health spending. All four also rank in the top eight in terms of taxing benefits and consumption with reductions from gross public to net public spending ranging from 4.2 to 6.3 percentage points of GDP.

They diverge, however, in the way they finance the spending. Sweden largely follows a government social insurance model in which employers pay most of the freight, ranking fifth in the payroll tax rate for employers at 31.4 percent. Denmark is at the other extreme. They have no payroll taxes for workers or for employers, although they do have mandatory private expenditures for old-age pensions and disability that add 2.1 percent of GDP in private spending. Instead, Denmark has relied most heavily on general taxation, including income taxes, where it ranks first in Table 41.8, with an average income tax rate of 36 percent.

The southern European countries—Greece, Spain, Italy, and Portugal—also have high public spending at 23 to 27 percent of GDP, which ranked them between fifth and twelfth. The high expenditures are driven largely by old-age pensions. Italy and Greece rank first and second, with expenditures greater than 15 percent of GDP, while Portugal was fifth with 12.7 percent and Spain seventh at 10.9 percent. The countries followed the French social insurance model in relying heavily on employer payroll taxes to finance benefits; they rank fourth through eleventh with employer tax rates ranging from 31.6 percent in Italy to 23.8 percent in Portugal. Portugal is similar to France in ranking eighth in voluntary private spending at 2.3 percent of GDP.

The United States, Switzerland, and the Netherlands offer a sharp contrast with the continental Western European countries. They rank twenty-first, twenty-fifth, and twenty-seventh, respectively, among the countries in public spending at less than 18.5 percent of GDP. All three spend heavily on healthcare, as the United States and Switzerland are ranked first and second and the Netherlands eleventh in Table 41.5. Switzerland and the Netherlands collect enough in taxes on benefits and consumption taxes to drive their net public spending rankings down to twenty-sixth and thirty-first, while the United States actually moves up in the rankings to eleventh because it taxes benefits lightly, has low sales taxes, offers substantial tax breaks for children, and uses the tax system to pay subsidies to low-income working families.

The spending picture changes dramatically when the private spending is added. The grouping accounts for the top three countries in total private spending, which puts all three in the top eight in net total social welfare spending in Table 41.7 with percentages of GDP of 29.6, 24.7, and 24.9, respectively. Switzerland began relying on mandatory private spending for most of its healthcare and part of its old-age pensions in the early 1990s and ranked first in 2017 in mandatory private spending at 10.8 percent. Both the United States and the Netherlands relied heavily on voluntary private spending into the 2000s, ranking first and second in both 1980 and 2000. The Netherlands then passed a reform measure that shifted a substantial share of health spending from government funds to mandatory private programs and now leads in 2017 in total private spending and mandatory private spending, while ranking second in voluntary private spending. The United States also relied heavily on voluntary private spending, typically funded by employers, until the 2010s. The Affordable Care Act of 2010 required employers with more than fifty full-time workers to provide health insurance. The shift from voluntary to mandatory moved the United States up in the rankings to second in private mandatory spending with 6.6 percent of GDP in 2017, while the country continued to spend 6.1 percent of GDP in the voluntary private sector, which left them ranked third.

A relatively high share of private spending also characterizes the United Kingdom and its former colonies of Canada and Australia. All three are ranked in the top seven of OECD countries. As a result, they move up from rankings of seventeenth to twenty-fifth in public spending to thirteenth to sixteenth in net total spending in Table 41.7. Even though Canada is known for its government health system, Canada leads among OECD countries in 2017 in private voluntary social welfare expenditures with 7.1 percent of GDP, after ranking third in 2000 and fifth in 1980. The voluntary expenditures accounted for over half of Canada's old-age pension benefits and roughly 20 percent of social welfare health expenditures in 2017. The United Kingdom has also relied on private voluntary expenditures more than most countries, ranking fourth or higher in Table 41.5 since 1980. Australia has instead focused on mandatory private programs with rankings of third in 2000 and fifth in 2017.

The European countries that left the Soviet bloc after the Berlin Wall fell ranked between fifteenth for Slovenia and thirty-first for Lithuania in public spending of GDP. Nearly all had higher expenditures in 2015 than the 15.6 percent for the Russian Federation in Table 41.2. Since these countries relied very little on private spending, they rank in Table 41.7 between twentieth in Slovenia and thirty-third in Latvia for net total spending. These countries rely the most on workers paying high social welfare payroll taxes, as Slovenia ranks first, Hungary third, and Poland fifth in Table 41.8. Slovakia at eleventh and the Czech Republic at fourteenth also rank highly in worker payroll tax rates but also rely heavily on employer payroll taxes, ranking sixth and second, respectively, and they are joined by Estonia, which ranked third.

With the exceptions of Ireland and Iceland, the OECD countries that spent the least were generally the countries with GDP per capita below the median. Several countries in this group ranked highly on one or more dimensions. Iceland ranked fourth in family spending. Iceland, Ireland, Chile, and Colombia all ranked in the top ten in mandatory private spending, and Turkey ranked seventh in the payroll tax rate paid by workers. South Korea's per capita income has risen more than fourfold since 1990, and its rise in net public and private spending of 4.7 percentage points of GDP between 2005 and 2017 is tied for second with the United States—behind Finland at 4.9 percentage points. Like

Denmark, New Zealand has no payroll taxes, but its income tax and net spending are much lower.

The OECD countries all rank in the top half of the world's distribution. To get a sense of what was happening in the bottom half of the distribution, consider the situations in China and India, which account for more than one-third of the world's population. China's public social protection expenditures as a share of GDP have risen from 4.7 percent in 2000 to 6.3 percent in 2015, which ranks them 100th out of 168 countries reporting information in the International Labour Organization's database. In the early 1980s under central planning, China's employees in government and the urban state sectors received social insurance benefits under pay-as-you-go systems at the enterprise level but left out nonstate and rural workers did not receive these benefits. During China's economic transition toward markets, the government in the 1990s provided reemployment centers to provide job aid and basic social insurance for displaced workers. In the late 1990s, basic medical insurance provided health insurance for all urban formal-sector workers but not their dependents. In the early 2000s China started the process of funding social protection through contributions to individual accounts by individuals, enterprises, and local and central governments. Around 2013 the urban enterprise workers' programs were funded by employer contributions of 29 to 31 percent and worker contributions of 11 percent of the worker's wage. By 2009, new rules for employer-based social insurance and new voluntary programs were aimed at insuring migrants, the self-employed, and family members. Coverage of urban workers for pensions rose from 43.9 percent in 1993 to 55.9 percent by 2010, medical from 1.5 percent to 51.3 percent, work injury from 6 percent to 46.6 percent, and maternity from 3.1 percent to 35.6 percent. In 2010, the coverage for migrating workers ranged from 13 percent for unemployment to 41.1 percent for work injury (Giles, Wang, and Park 2013). The central government has announced a strong push toward providing benefits to the rural population in the last decade, so the social spending share likely has risen.

India's GDP per capita was higher than China's in 1990 but has grown much more slowly since then. The slower growth and a much younger population has contributed to smaller changes in India's public social welfare expenditures of GDP from 1.6 percent in 2000 to only 2.7 percent in 2015. As a result, India ranks 143rd in the ILO rankings. Most of India's public expenditures are on poverty programs. The social insurance programs for formal-sector workers and civil servants had employers and workers paying 10 to 12 percent each for pensions and disability while employers pay more for health insurance. Coverage in these programs has been thin, rising from 1 percent of the total workforce (including formal and informal) in the 1950s to only 5 percent around 2009 (World Bank 2011, 111).

Conclusion

The safety nets before 1900 typically came from savings and aid from extended family, friends, charities, and churches, and a limited amount of aid from local governments.

Mutual societies composed of similar individuals developed to help households guard against lost earnings from sickness, injury, death, and old age. Governments often established the rules for the societies, and in the late nineteenth century employers and unions were often involved. A handful of countries led by Germany required employers to provide some forms of social insurance, while other countries began to provide subsidies to the societies. Insurance companies developed and allowed many people to purchase insurance directly. The societies and government programs all designed access to coverage and the percentage of earnings replaced by benefits to reduce problems with moral hazard and adverse selection. The social welfare systems in the poorer nations in the modern era seem to be roughly similar to the situations in the higher-income countries circa 1900.

Over the past one hundred years, higher-income nations have sharply increased public and private social welfare expenditures. A large share of this rise has come in increases in aid to the elderly and programs to cover healthcare expenses. The pure transfer programs that redistribute general tax dollars have risen relatively little as a share of GDP. A large majority of the rise has come through contributory social insurance programs in which workers and employers contribute payroll taxes into government-run programs. In most countries, the employer's share of payroll taxes is higher than the worker's share. Some major countries have followed a path of reliance on private programs, which are largely financed by employers. Probably the most striking feature of social welfare programs worldwide is the very large variation in expenditures and in the categories of spending, and in the mix of taxation, private programs, and government programs.

Acknowledgments

I received very helpful comments on the issues in this chapter from Shari Eli, Susanna Fellman, Reino Hjerppe, Riitta Hjerppe, Taylor Jaworski, Jeffery A. Jenkins, Shawn Kantor, Edward Kubu, Naomi Lamoreaux, Peter Lindert, Adriana Lleras Muney, Christopher Lloyd, Paul Rhode, Jared Rubin, Pamela Slaten, Han Sjogren, Melissa Thomasson, Jeroen Touwen, James Uguccioni, Mark Walker, and John Wallis.

Notes

1. The phrase "relative to GDP" is used because many social welfare expenditures are transfer payments, which are not included as expenditures in GDP calculations. To promote brevity, we use "of GDP" in the rest of the paper but mean "relative to GDP" unless otherwise specified.
2. For economic history papers on adverse selection and moral hazard in various settings, see Andersson, Eriksson, and Nystedt (2022), Fishback and Kantor (2000), Guinnane and Streb (2011), Murray (2005; 2007), and US Commissioner of Labor (1893).

REFERENCES

Andersson, Lars Fredrik, Liselotte Eriksson, and Paul Nystedt. 2022. "Workplace Accidents and Workers' Solidarity: Mutual Health Insurance in Early Twentieth-Century Sweden." *Economic History Review* 75, no. 1: 1–30.

Beegle, Kathleen, and Luc Christiaensen, eds. 2019. *Accelerating Poverty Reduction in Africa*. Washington, DC: World Bank.

Boyer, George. 1990. *An Economic History of the English Poor Law, 1750–1850*. New York: Cambridge University Press.

Boyer, George. 2019. *The Winding Road to the Welfare State: Economic Insecurity and Social Welfare Policy in Britain*. Princeton, NJ: Princeton University Press.

Fishback, Price. 1998. "Operations of 'Unfettered' Labor Markets: Exit and Voice in American Labor Markets at the Turn of the Century." *Journal of Economic Literature* 36 (June): 722–65.

Fishback, Price. 2020. "Social Insurance and Public Assistance in the Twentieth-Century United States." *Journal of Economic History* 80, no. 2: 311–50.

Fishback, Price, and Shawn Kantor. 2000. *Prelude to the Welfare State: The Origins of Workers' Compensation*. Chicago: University of Chicago Press.

Giles, John, Dewen Wang, and Albert Park. 2013. "Expanding Social Insurance Coverage in Urban China." World Bank Development Research Group Policy Research Paper 6497.

Guinnane, Timothy, and Joachim Streb. 2011. "Moral Hazard in a Mutual Insurance System: German Knappschaften, 1867–1914." *Journal of Economic History* 71 (March): 70–103.

Hennock, E.P. 2007. *The Origin of the Welfare State in England and Germany, 1850–1914: Social Policies Compared*. New York: Cambridge University Press.

International Labor Organization. 2017. *World Social Protection Report, 2017–19: Universal Social Protection to Achieve the Sustainable Development Goals*. Geneva: International Labor Organization.

Kaufmann, Daniel, Aart Kraay and Massimo Mastruzzi. 2010. "The Worldwide Governance Indicators: A Summary of Methodology, Data and Analytical Issues." World Bank Policy Research Working Paper No. 5430. http://papers.ssrn.com/sol3/papers.cfm?abstract_id=1682130.

Lindert, Peter. 1994. "The Rise of Social Spending, 1880–1930." *Explorations in Economic History* 31: 1–37.

Lindert, Peter. 2004. *Growing Public: Social Spending and Economic Growth since the Eighteenth Century*, Volume 1: *The Story*. New York: Cambridge University Press.

Lundberg, Urban, and Kas Amark. 2001. "Social Rights and Social Security: The Swedish Welfare State, 1900–2000." *Scandinavian Journal of History* 26, no. 3: 157–76.

Murray, John. 2005. "Worker Absenteeism under Voluntary and Compulsory Sickness Insurance: Continental Europe, 1885–1908." *Research in Economic History* 23: 177–207.

Murray, John. 2007. *Origins of American Health Insurance: A History of Industrial Sickness Funds*. New Haven, CT: Yale University Press.

Organisation for Economic Co-operation and Development (OECD). 2022. OECD.Stat. Internet database https://stats.oecd.org/Index.aspx?ThemeTreeId=9 (accessed April 28, 2022).

Rothstein, Bo. 2015. "The Moral, Economic, and Political Logic of the Swedish Welfare State." In *The Oxford Handbook of Swedish Politics*, ed. Jon Pierre, 69–83. Oxford: Oxford University Press.

Schieber, Sylvester, and John Shoven. 1999. *The Real Deal: The History and Future of Social Security*. New Haven, CT: Yale University Press.

Uguccioni, James. 2002. *Essays on Intergenerational Inequality*. PhD dissertation, University of Toronto.

US Commissioner of Labor. 1893. *Compulsory Insurance in Germany: Fourth Special Report of the Commissioner of Labor*. Washington, DC: Government Printing Office.

US Commissioner of Labor. 1911. *Workmen's Insurance and Compensation Systems in Europe in Two Volumes: Twenty-Fourth Annual Report of the Commissioner of Labor, 1909*. Washington, DC: Government Printing Office.

Van Rie, Tim, Ive Marx, and Jeroen Horemans. 2011. "Ghent Revisited: Unemployment Insurance and Union Membership in Belgium and the Nordic Countries." *European Journal of Industrial Relations* 17, no. 2: 125–39.

Weaver, R. Kent. 2003/2004. "Design and Implementation Issues in Swedish Individual Pension Accounts." *Social Security Bulletin* 65, no. 4: 1–25.

World Bank. 2011. *Social Protection for a Changing India, Volume II*. Washington, DC: World Bank.

World Bank. 2018. *The State of Social Safety Nets, 2018*. Washington, DC: World Bank.

CHAPTER 42

THE HISTORICAL POLITICAL ECONOMY OF EDUCATION

AGUSTINA S. PAGLAYAN

EDUCATION systems today are charged with many responsibilities. Parents expect schools to equip their children with useful knowledge and skills to live empowered, autonomous lives—or, at the very least, to find good jobs. Businesses want education systems to support economic growth and technological progress. Governments also care about the role that schools play in forming good citizens, promoting political legitimacy and social cohesion, and maintaining peace. No other area of state intervention is charged with as many important responsibilities as those we assign to education systems today.

The provision of education is a state matter, but this wasn't always so. Before the nineteenth century, children's education was typically left to families and religious organizations; the notion that a centralized political authority could be a legitimate actor in regulating and providing education for young children was inconceivable for most people. Today, by contrast, states regulate, fund, manage, and monitor schools; set curriculum guidelines and teacher certification requirements; dictate the duration of compulsory schooling; determine whether education is free; and make other policy decisions that affect both the quantity and quality of schooling, most often throughout the national territory.

While centralized state intervention, particularly at the primary school level, helps explain the remarkable expansion of access to basic schooling over the last two centuries, when it comes to the quality of education, the picture is less encouraging. Yes, children have access to education at unprecedented levels: in the early nineteenth century only 5 percent of children were enrolled in school, whereas today every region in the world has reached universal or near-universal primary education. But many students who attend school regularly are not acquiring the kinds of knowledge and skills that enhance productivity, expand career choices, and enable social mobility. Across countries, the correlation between average years of schooling and reading and math skills is close to zero (Paglayan 2021). The disjoint between access to schooling and student learning, or between educational quantity and quality, is indeed the most important challenge facing education systems today (World Bank 2018). Why should this be?

Looking at history can teach us a lot about the characteristics, accomplishments, and challenges of present-day education systems. One common perspective locates the roots of modern systems' failure to promote reading and math skills in recent education policies. From this perspective, politicians *want* to promote skills but, because of limited technical knowledge about the consequences of different education policies, adopt policies that are not conducive to student learning, giving way to a recent "learning crisis" (World Bank 2018). An alternative perspective I have proposed elsewhere is that the low quality of present-day education systems has deep historical roots (Paglayan 2017; 2022). From this perspective, failure to teach basic reading and math skills is not a recent phenomenon but reflects the fact that promoting these goals was *not* a major driver of the emergence, design, and historical expansion of state-regulated education systems. Recent evidence provides some support for this perspective, showing that educational quality remained stable in most countries since at least the mid-twentieth century (Le Nestour, Moscovitz, and Sandefur 2021). Schools today teach knowledge and skills (only) as well as they did seven decades ago.

While in principle it is possible that education systems emerged in response to societal pressure to promote skills and social mobility, it is also possible that central governments took control of education systems to legitimate the existing social order and, with that, perpetuate the existing distribution of political and economic power. By the end of the chapter, it will become clearer that there is relatively more empirical support for the latter view. In particular, mass education systems were conceived as crucial policy tools for accomplishing both nation- and state-building goals. By contrast, governments historically gave much less importance to mass education's potential to improve individual earnings and promote economic growth than they do today.

I reach these conclusions based on a review of the historical political economy (HPE) literature on the origins, centralization, and expansion of state-regulated primary education systems. I do not examine the HPE of educational quality or educational equity because the literature on these topics is currently too sparse. I focus on primary education systems because they provide the foundation for all subsequent learning and represent the type of schooling available to most people. For this reason, and in line with much research, I use the terms "primary," "basic," and "mass" education interchangeably. While the general conclusions I extract are based on my interpretation of HPE studies that use quantitative data and econometric methods to study the history of education systems, it is important to acknowledge that a vast literature exists on the history of education. Reviewing this broader literature exceeds the scope of this chapter and volume, but a deep understanding of the origins and evolution of education systems undoubtedly requires considering both HPE studies and the work of historians.

The chapter is organized as follows. I begin by presenting a conceptual framework to help readers organize and integrate the literature. The framework highlights that different political and economic actors will want schools to pursue different goals; whose interests prevail will shape the character of education systems. I then use this framework to identify and classify four common HPE theories of education: democratization, industrialization, nation-building, and state-building theories. Next, I review what recent HPE research has to say about the plausibility of each theory. I conclude by outlining important questions for future research and discuss how a knowledge of history can inform current debates about education reform.

THE WHY AND THE WHO OF EDUCATION REFORM: A CONCEPTUAL FRAMEWORK

To organize and synthesize the large body of HPE studies, I use a conceptual framework that proposes that existing political economy theories of education differ from each other along two crucial dimensions: what they argue is the main goal of education, and who they argue is the main actor behind education reform. Different political and economic actors will want schools to pursue different goals in different circumstances; what circumstances obtain and whose interests prevail will shape education policy decisions, including the decision to centralize, fund, and expand education systems as well as the characteristics of these systems.

With respect to the question "What is the main goal of education systems?," I classify existing theories into two groups: those that argue or assume that the main goal of education systems is to teach skills, and those that argue or assume that their main goal is to mold individual values. By "skills" I mean the knowledge, practical or abstract, that enhances individual and economic productivity. Political economy theories that propose that education systems promote economic growth, poverty reduction, social mobility, income equality, and technological progress are indeed united by the assumption that education systems are designed to teach skills. The term "values" encompasses the beliefs, attitudes, ideologies, and behaviors that constitute an individual's character. Theories that propose that education systems promote good citizenship, a strong national identity, obedience to authority, or adherence to a particular political ideology, to name just some examples, all emphasize the transmission of values as the main goal of education systems. In practice, education systems seek to teach both skills and values, but because school time is limited, there is a trade-off between how much time can be devoted to each. Existing theories make varied claims about which of these goals was prioritized when states decided to centralize and expand access to primary education.

The second dimension along which theories of education differ is in their answer to "Who was the main actor behind the expansion of primary education?". Here again I group theories into two categories: those that argue that education policies are responsive to pressure from below—what many theories call "the masses"—and those that argue that the emergence and expansion of state-regulated education systems was an elite-driven process. Within this second group, theories differ in terms

Table 42.1. Goals and actors behind education reform: A conceptual framework

		Main actor pushing for public education provision	
		The masses	Elites
Main goal of public education is to teach	Skills	Democratization theory	Industrialization theory
	values		Nation-building theory
			State-building theory

of whether they emphasize the role of economic elites such as industrialists, or of political elites such as national politicians. We will examine these distinctions later in the chapter.

Table 42.1 summarizes how this simple framework can clarify the main differences between four common theories of what drove states to centralize and expand access to primary education. First, the **democratization theory** argues that states expanded access to schooling in response to widespread pressure from newly enfranchised citizens, particularly those from less affluent backgrounds, who demanded education so that their children could gain the knowledge and skills needed to get good jobs and climb the social ladder. Second, the **industrialization theory** also argues that the centralization and expansion of education systems sought to teach skills to the population, but instead of locating the source of this expansion in pressure from below, it contends that governments invested in education in response to pressure from economic elites who demanded a skilled workforce to support industrialization. Third, the **nation-building theory** and the **state-building theory** refer to a class of value-centered theories that maintain that national governments centralized and expanded primary education systems out of self-interest in order to inculcate a national identity (nation-building), or to teach obedience and respect for the state and its laws (state-building). Like the industrialization theory, these theories propose an elite-driven process of educational expansion, but while industrialization theory highlights the role of education systems in teaching skills, both the nation- and state-building theories stress schools' role in molding political values and behaviors.

What do HPE studies tell us about the plausibility of these theories? The answer depends on what time period we examine. To preview an important conclusion from the next section, theories that conceptualize the expansion of primary education as an effort to equip people with useful skills find some support in recent decades, but find relatively little support when we consider the origins and expansion of primary education systems from the 1800s to the 1960s. For this earlier and longer period, the existing evidence suggests that value-based theories better explain the rise and expansion of primary education systems. This conclusion has important implications for our understanding of the challenges facing current education systems, an issue I return to at the end of the chapter.

What We Know about the Historical Political Economy of Education

To extract conclusions about what we have learned so far from HPE research about primary education systems, I first consider skills-based theories that assume that the expansion of mass education sought to teach knowledge and skills that enhance economic productivity, and then turn to value-based theories that propose that the main goal of primary education systems was to mold political values and behaviors. I consider not only the claims made by different studies but also the quality of the data and methods underlying those claims. As will become evident, some claims are more rigorously supported than others. This is to be expected; methods evolve and improve over time, which helps us reach progressively more reliable conclusions. For that same reason, readers should view this section as a synthesis of what we know so far, keeping in mind that future studies may lead us to revise some of these conclusions.

"Governments Provide Education in Response to Mass Demand for Skills and Social Mobility"

Democratization theory has been the most influential political economy theory of education provision of the last thirty years. However, recent research casts doubt on its ability to explain the rise and expansion of mass education systems. The theory's core theoretical prediction is that democratization—especially the extension of the franchise to the lower classes, who presumably were historically more excluded from and more interested in education—leads to an increase in both the quantity and quality of primary education. Underlying this prediction are four assumptions: one, educational quantity and quality go hand in hand, or, put differently, attending school leads to the acquisition of useful knowledge and skills; two, for this reason, schooling is universally demanded by parents; three, at the time when countries transitioned from nondemocracy to democracy, a majority of the population lacked access to, and demanded, primary schooling; and four, democratic regimes are more responsive to citizens' demands than nondemocratic ones.

The first assumption—that the quantity and quality of education move together—does not find much empirical support today. For over a decade, the World Bank has been arguing that developing countries face a "learning crisis" in which schooling does not lead to learning (World Bank 2011), and we know from Paglayan (2021) that a country's average years of schooling, a common measure of the quantity of education, is a poor predictor of the level of math skills among students (the correlation is almost zero).

Despite this disjunction between quantity and quality, it is still possible that democratic governments expanded education systems in an effort to address the demand for skills from the population, even if those efforts ultimately failed to accomplish that goal. (After all, there are countless examples of education reforms that have failed to meet their stated goal.) If this were true, we should observe that democratization led to an expansion of access to, and investment in, primary education systems, as measured by school enrollment rates and education expenditures, regardless of whether this was accompanied by an improvement in skills. This is precisely the question on which empirical tests of democratization theory have focused.

The conclusion that democratization and the extension of suffrage rights to the lower classes was a leading driver of the expansion of primary education around the world stems from studies produced before the causal inference revolution in the social sciences. In the late 1990s, as social scientists grappled with the puzzling absence of solid evidence that democracies are better at promoting economic growth than autocracies, a new pro-democracy argument emerged that held that democracies *are* better at promoting education and human capital (Baum and Lake 2003). In economics, Stanley Engerman, Elisa Mariscal, and Kenneth Sokoloff were among the first to document a correlation between suffrage and school enrollment rates in the Americas during the nineteenth century, a finding they interpreted as evidence that a more equal distribution of political power *leads to* greater incentives to provide public services (Engerman and Sokoloff 2002; Mariscal and Sokoloff 2000). Peter Lindert provided additional support for the democratization thesis based on an analysis of the relationship between democracy and primary school enrollment rates in twenty-one developed countries from 1880 to 1930. In his book *Growing Public*, Lindert (2004, 105) concludes that "the spread of democratic voting rights played a leading role in explaining ... the rise of primary schooling." This conclusion was further popularized by Acemoglu and Robinson's (2006) book *Economic Origins of Dictatorship and Democracy*, which cites Lindert's findings as evidence that democratization leads to pro-poor redistributive policies, including primary education. Political science also contributed to this consensus. For example, focusing on cross-national data from the 1960s onward, early studies interpreted the cross-sectional pattern that primary school enrollment rates are higher in democratic than nondemocratic regimes as evidence that democratic institutions "have an important effect on primary school enrollment" (Brown 1999, 681). Other studies analyzed temporal changes in education spending among countries that transitioned to democracy after the 1960s; noticing an uptick in spending after democratization, they also concluded that democracy leads to increased spending on primary education (e.g., Brown and Hunter 2004; Stasavage 2005; Ansell 2010). The consensus around these conclusions was such that several surveys of the literature characterize as an established truth the argument that democracies provide higher quantities of education (Busemeyer and Trampusch 2011; Gift and Wibbels 2014; Hoffman 2015).

A more recent wave of studies, however, suggests a very different story—one in which mass demand for education and the enfranchisement of the lower classes played, at best, a minor role in explaining the expansion of primary education systems. In my own work, I reexamined the relationship between democratization and school enrollment rates using modern causal inference tools and analyzing data for 109 countries from 1830 to 2010, thus covering more countries and a longer time period than previous research (Paglayan 2021). After netting out (a) the fact that countries that historically had higher primary school enrollment rates were more likely to eventually become democratic and (b) the fact that countries that remained nondemocratic experienced the same uptick in primary school enrollment rates and education spending seen in those that democratized, I no longer find evidence to support the claim that democratization was an important driver of the global expansion of primary education. Aghion et al. (2019) arrive at a similar conclusion about the spurious nature of the positive relationship between democracy and primary school enrollment rates. Their study highlights that democratization often coincided with interstate wars, which can provide incentives to expand mass education to train loyal and skilled soldiers. After netting out the effect of these wars on primary school enrollment rates, they find, democratization no longer plays a role in explaining the expansion of primary schooling.

Why didn't democratization lead to the expansion of primary schooling? Is it because a majority of voters did not actually demand this, or is it because democracies are not in fact more responsive to voters' demands than nondemocracies? Paglayan (2021) explores both possibilities and finds more support for the first interpretation than for the second. That is, although much research suggests that many policy decisions in democratic settings are captured by the rich, when it comes to the quantity of primary education, democracies do seem to be responsive to what a majority of voters want. In particular, when a majority of voters lack access to primary education, democratization does lead to the expansion of primary schooling. However, historically, this condition has rarely been met. On average, 70 percent of the school-age population was already enrolled in primary school *before* countries transitioned to democracy. In these cases, a majority of voters most likely did not demand increased access to primary schooling because they already had access to it before democracy emerged.

These findings shift the conversation from a focus on the effect of democratization on access to primary schooling to the question of why nondemocracies have historically provided high quantities of it. One possibility is that nondemocratic regimes expanded primary schooling because they wanted to cater to the needs of lower-class citizens. This could be the case among nondemocracies that embrace a left-wing ideology or need the lower class to survive. This argument has some support during the second half of the twentieth century (Manzano 2017). However, left-wing autocracies cannot explain the rise and rapid expansion of state-regulated primary education systems in nineteenth-century Europe and Latin America, simply because there were no left-wing autocracies at that time (Paglayan 2021; 2022).

In principle, it could still be the case that nonprogressive rulers engaged in progressive redistributive policies in order to keep the population content and avoid rebellion against the regime. That is, perhaps the expansion of education in nondemocracies, even ones that were not left-wing, responded to pressure from below. However, what most studies suggest is that nondemocracies expanded primary education systems during the nineteenth and early twentieth century despite the fact that the masses were largely uninterested in sending their children to school. Several studies document that parental demand for education was particularly low in rural areas and agrarian economies, where families relied on child labor for agricultural productivity (Cinnirella and Hornung 2016; Baker 2015; Baker, Blanchette, and Eriksson 2020). This did not stop countries—particularly in Europe—from expanding primary education while they were still primarily rural. Nineteenth-century Sweden provides an example of rapid expansion of primary education under a primarily rural economy. Andersson and Berger (2019) use municipal data on suffrage rights and educational expenditures to show that during the 1870s, when enrollment in primary education was near universal but the level of expenditure in primary schools differed considerably across municipalities, investments in schooling were greater not in those municipalities with a more extensive franchise but in those where voting rights were restricted to a small and wealthy elite. Nineteenth-century Swedish elites, they argue, supported mass schooling because of its promise as a mechanism of enlightenment and social control, whereas most parents, by contrast, were uninterested in schooling because it competed with their children's work responsibilities. Evidence from Italy between 1870 and 1911, a period when access to voting rights expanded at different rates across provinces, also suggests that the extension of the franchise played no role in explaining which provinces invested more in primary education (Cappelli 2016). In France, too, the national government under the July Monarchy (1830–1848) promoted an unprecedented expansion of primary schooling even though, as Squicciarini and Voigtländer (2016) document, demand for education from the lower classes was low.

In sum, recent studies challenge three assumptions of the democratization theory of mass education provision: first, the idea that schooling results in human capital accumulation; second, the belief that education is universally demanded by parents; and third, the assumption that at the time when countries transitioned from nondemocracy to democracy, a majority of the population lacked access to primary education. What these studies suggest is that nondemocracies often provided high access to primary education even in contexts where parental demand for primary education was low.

"Governments Provide Education in Response to Economic Elites' Pressure for a Skilled Workforce"

Even if democratization was not a major driver of the expansion of mass education systems in most parts of the world, it is still possible that the main goal behind these systems' expansion was to provide skills to the population—not because of demand from below but because of elites' demands for a skilled workforce. This is what the industrialization theory argues. The basic idea is that technology has become increasingly dependent on skilled workers over time (Galor and Moav 2000; Goldin and Katz

2009), creating an increasing complementarity between physical capital and skills. As a result of this process of technological change, capitalists have increasingly pressured governments to provide mass education to the working class so that workers have the skills that capitalists need to maximize their profits (Galor and Moav 2000; 2002; 2006). In particular, the theory predicts that industrialization will create a new economic elite that both needs skilled workers and has the power to pressure governments to supply these workers through investments in mass education. Moreover, according to this theory, capitalists' demand for education provision will increase over time as technology becomes more complex and more dependent on the availability of human capital.

Existing studies provide mixed support for the view that the economic needs of the industrial and capital-owning class were an important driver of the expansion of primary education systems. On one hand, there is considerable evidence from England (Mitch 1998; Clark 2005), France (Squicciarini and Voigtländer 2015), and Europe generally (Allen 2003; Mokyr 1990; 2005) suggesting that the First Industrial Revolution did not require a large skilled workforce, but instead relied on a few "knowledge elites" who could contribute scientific discoveries and technological innovation. On the contrary, several studies find that the wage premium for skilled workers declined during the First Industrial Revolution, suggesting that industrial elites demanded more *unskilled* labor—a phenomenon that has led economic historians to refer to the first phase of industrialization as "deskilling."

Of course, it could still be that governments expanded primary education during this period if they mistakenly believed that it would support the industrialization process. However, existing studies suggest that this was not the case. England, for example, was a laggard in primary education provision with respect to the rest of Europe throughout most of the nineteenth century. In a study of literacy rates, enrollment rates, and number of schools in England from 1300 to 1900, de Pleijt (2018) finds evidence of a strong decline in schooling from the 1720s to the 1880s. It was only with Forster's Elementary Education Act of 1870 that the central government began to make considerable efforts to catch up with the rest of the region in education—a full century after the introduction of steam power (Green 1990). In France, on the other hand, central government intervention in primary education began much earlier, in 1833, when parliament passed the country's first national law of primary education, the Guizot Law, which established a national school curriculum and required municipalities to establish primary schools for boys. The result of this law was the most rapid expansion in the number of primary schools and in enrollment rates seen in French history (Grew and Harrigan 1991). Because this expansion also coincided with France's first industrialization, an important question is whether the two phenomena were causally related. The answer appears to be no: In a study of the differential rates of expansion of primary schooling across municipalities during the July Monarchy, Squicciarini and Voigtländer (2016) find that primary schooling expanded because of the pressure exerted by intellectual, not industrial, elites. Also focusing on early nineteenth-century France, Montalbo (2020) finds that although more industrialized municipalities had more resources to support the creation of public primary schools, industrial activities led to a reduction in school enrollment rates because industrialists during this period relied heavily on unskilled workers.

On the other hand, economic needs do appear to have played a role in triggering educational expansion during the Second Industrial Revolution and in more recent time periods. For example, Ansell (2008), Avelino, Brown, and Hunter (2005), and Kaufman and Segura-Ubiergo (2001) find cross-national evidence consistent with the argument that educational expansion from the 1960s onward increased because firms exposed to globalization required an increasingly skilled workforce to remain competitive. The Prussian case provides a good illustration of how the relationship between industrialization and mass education provision changed over time, from the absence of a relationship during early periods of industrialization that did not require a skilled workforce, to a positive relationship during later periods when industrialization *has* relied on skilled workers. During the early history of educational expansion in Prussia in the late 1700s, most of the state's effort to promote primary schooling was focused on rural, not industrializing, areas (Melton 2002). However, by the beginning of the twentieth century, cities with a larger industrial economy were likely to invest more in education than less industrialized areas (Hollenbach 2021).

To recap, the discussion so far points to two important questions that neither democratization nor industrialization theory can answer. First, why did nondemocratic regimes provide widespread access to primary education even in the absence of mass demand for it? Second, why did many nineteenth-century governments promote primary education even though their economies remained largely agrarian or were undergoing early industrialization processes that did not require a skilled workforce?

One possibility is that the expansion of primary education systems was an elite-driven process that responded not to economic elites' demand for skills but to the interests of political elites who believed that their permanence in power required shaping the values and behaviors of future citizens. From this perspective, mass education is used as a social control tool more than anything else, a conceptualization that is adopted by two main theories: theories of education as *nation-building* and theories of education as *state-building*. Both theories share an emphasis on elites' interest in molding values and behaviors, but, as I discuss next, advance different arguments about the types of values and behaviors that education systems prioritized, make different predictions about the conditions under which governments invested in mass education, and rely on different pieces of evidence to back them up.

"Governments Provide Education out of Their Own Interest in Nation-Building"

Growing awareness about the limitations of the democratization and industrialization theories of education provision has been accompanied by a shift in scholars' attention to a set of explanations that stress not the role of education systems in promoting human capital accumulation but their nation-building role. Nation-building theories propose that the main goal of education systems is—or at least was—to teach a common language (Gellner 1983), inculcate emotional attachment to an imagined national community (Anderson 1983), and promote a national identity. There is growing evidence from HPE studies that states became increasingly interested in regulating and expanding primary education systems because of these systems' nation-building potential (Darden and Grzymala-Busse 2006; Ansell and Lindvall 2013; Darden and Mylonas 2015), albeit with varying levels of success in accomplishing that goal (Cinnirella and Schueler 2018; cf. Fouka 2020; Bazzi, Himly, and Marx 2021).

What is less clear is what conditions or factors prompted states to become interested in the nation-building role of primary education systems. Based on common beliefs about the economic and political benefits of nation-building, social scientists have proposed two main factors that incentivized states to turn to mass schooling to accomplish their nation-building goals: industrialization and interstate military rivalry. The argument that industrialization and economic modernization provides incentives for nation-building has received considerable attention owing to the influential work of Ernest Gellner (1983), who argues that industrialization required everyone to speak the same language, the nation's language, in order for workers to communicate efficiently with one another and with their supervisors. Much research has focused on the relationship between economic modernization and nation-building in France, with Eugene Weber (1976) being a key proponent of the relationship between these variables. However, recent HPE studies challenge Gellner's argument and Weber's interpretation of the history of French schooling. While there is little doubt that one of the goals of the primary education law of 1833, or Guizot Law, was to ensure that French was spoken by everyone across the territory, and there is evidence that the resulting expansion of schooling indeed helped reach this goal (Blanc and Kubo 2021), industrialization does not appear to explain the impetus for educational expansion during this foundational period in the history of education in France (Squicciarini and Voigtländer 2016; Montalbo 2020).

Another condition that may provide states with incentives to nation-build through mass schooling is the presence of interstate military rivalry. According to proponents of this argument, interstate wars, especially those involving territorial threats from neighbor states, were crucial drivers of the centralization and expansion of primary education (Ramirez and Boli 1987). Such wars not only increased the state's need for skilled and loyal soldiers—which, in principle, education systems could help train—but also its need to teach patriotism and instill nationalist sentiment from a young age to inoculate the population from rival states' claims. This, the argument goes, helped prevent defection to foreign countries, of particular interest to states under foreign threat. While arguments about the role of interstate military rivalry have been part of the vast literature on the history of education systems for a long time, only recently have they gained attention in HPE. In a recent study, Aghion et al. (2019) find support for the interstate military rivalry theory among European countries from 1830 to 2010, and among a larger set of 166 countries from 1945 to 2010.[1]

An open question is why some countries engaged in considerable expansion of primary education even in the absence of interstate wars. France again is a useful example. While many have argued that France's defeat in the Franco-Prussian War of 1870 helped propel the education reforms of the 1880s, most of its primary school expansion took place during the 1830s as a result of the Guizot Law of 1833, approved in a context of relative peace with neighbors. Similarly, Latin America during the nineteenth century led the expansion of primary education within the developing world, even though interstate wars in the region were relatively uncommon. As I argue in the next section, *state-building* theories of education can help explain a variety of landmark education laws and periods of mass education expansion, including the French education reforms of the 1830s, the expansion of primary schooling in nineteenth-century Latin America, and the introduction of compulsory schooling laws across the United States.

"Governments Provide Education out of Their Own Interest in State-Building"

State-building theories of education propose that states regulate and expand mass schooling first and foremost to consolidate the power of a centralized political authority, that is, the state. Such theories have a long tradition among historians but have attracted the attention of the HPE community only very recently. There are many ways in which education systems could in principle help consolidate the power of a central political authority. First, by targeting children at an age when their minds are more susceptible, schools can inculcate in future citizens moral and civic values and behaviors of discipline, obedience, and respect for the state's authority, thus helping to prevent future political instability, rebellion, violence, crime, and dissident behavior (Paglayan 2022). Second, central governments seeking to consolidate their control in the periphery can hire teachers and school inspectors and deploy them as agents of the state to monitor remote communities and regions (Cermeño, Enflo, and Lindvall 2022). Third, teaching everyone to speak the language preferred by national elites can help the state communicate and enforce laws and collect taxes, two central features of strong states (Scott 1998; Lee and Zhang 2017; Zhang and Lee 2020).

While both nation- and state-building theories of education propose an elite-driven process of educational expansion to mold values and behaviors, key differences exist. First, nation-building theories stress the role that schools play in instilling patriotism or support for one's country as opposed to other countries. By contrast, state-building theories stress schools' role in teaching loyalty to the state as opposed to other competing domestic authorities such as local governments or churches. Second, nation-building theories focus primarily on the role that schools play in teaching a common language. By contrast, state-building theories focus on schools' role in teaching civic duties and moral values and behaviors of discipline, obedience, and respect for the state and its laws. Sometimes, as in nineteenth-century France, state-building goals can encompass nation-building tools; that is, teaching a common language can help accomplish the broader political goal of consolidating the state's authority. However, not all efforts to promote state-building through mass education will include a nation-building component. In several cases, such as Prussia and Argentina, mass education was used as a state-building tool well before central governments turned to schooling as a means to forge a national identity and promote nationalist sentiments (Paglayan 2022).

What prompted central governments' interest in the state-building potential of primary education systems? Elsewhere (Paglayan 2017; 2022) I have proposed that states became increasingly interested in the potential of mass education systems to promote long-term political stability when faced with internal conflict concerns and the inability to ensure social order through traditional policy tools such as repression and redistribution. Fearing the breakdown of social order in the absence of innovative policy tools, states turned to primary education systems, regulating and expanding them to promote long-term social order by indoctrinating young children to accept the status quo, behave as "good citizens," and respect the state and its laws.

This political economy argument highlighting the role of internal conflict and social disorder in driving the centralization and expansion of mass education systems offers a unifying theoretical framework for seemingly disconnected findings about the role of civil wars, social revolutions, ethnic mobilization, and immigration waves in driving educational expansion. In my own work, I find evidence that nondemocratic rulers in Europe and Latin America responded to civil wars—an extreme form of internal conflict—by expanding primary education for the masses, an effort that is not explained by liberals coming to power as a result of these wars, nor by war-induced improvements in state capacity or attempts to appease discontented sectors of society through redistribution (Paglayan 2017; 2022). In a similar spirit and building on this work, Alesina, Giuliano, and Reich (2021) argue that nondemocratic elites facing the threat of social revolution and democratization are likely to turn to mass education to teach people that the status quo is not as bad as they might think. Moving away from class conflict to consider instead ethnic and religious conflict, Bozcaga and Cansunar (2021) find that in Turkey the central government expanded primary education in Kurdish villages after Kurds began to mobilize against the state, a finding that the authors interpret as evidence of the social control purpose of education in contexts of political instability. Another example comes from the United States during the Age of Mass Migration, when the arrival of Catholic immigrants from Europe provoked fear among traditional White, Anglo-Saxon, Protestant elites (Tyack 1974). In particular, beliefs about the "moral deficiency" of these newly arrived immigrants and their presumed greater tendency to commit crimes and disrupt public life triggered a wave of state compulsory schooling laws designed to ensure that everyone learned civic values and behaviors of discipline conducive to political stability (Bandiera et al. 2019). Revealingly, and against a nation-building interpretation of these laws, states that received immigrants from parts of Europe that already had compulsory schooling were slower in introducing their own compulsory schooling laws, suggesting that elites were not interested so much in inculcating an "American" identity as they were in molding general moral and civic values.[2]

The HPE literature has devoted remarkably little attention to the role that education systems played in state-building efforts. Understanding the types of internal conflict that prompted state-building through mass schooling (e.g., center vs. periphery, elites vs. the masses, church vs. state, intra-elite conflict, etc.), how education systems were designed in order to accomplish their state-building goal, and whether they actually succeeded in promoting long-term social order also remain crucial questions for future research. Refining the conditions under which elites are likely to turn to education for state-building purposes would also be useful.

Open Questions

The HPE literature to date has focused primarily on explaining the centralization and expansion of mass schooling. We know much less, for example, about why some countries are more successful than others at promoting skills, or what explains the varying levels of socioeconomic, gender, and ethnic disparities in educational access and quality across countries. For example, it could be that even though the spread of democracy played a minor role in explaining the expansion of access to primary schooling, it did lead to improvements in educational quality or equity. Research on the political economy of educational quality and educational equity should undoubtedly constitute the next generation of studies on education systems.

Another question that has received relatively scant attention in quantitative HPE studies—but has received much attention from historians—is how religious conflict has shaped education systems. It is well known that, historically, religious actors (churches, missionaries, etc.) were the main providers of education. Indeed, the history of public education systems over the last two hundred years in most parts of the world is one in which states gradually took over many if not all of the educational functions previously carried out by religious actors, and reshaped education systems to meet the state's need. This process predictably entailed considerable political conflict (Ansell and Lindvall 2013). How this conflict played out and shaped school curricula, teacher training, education funding, the supervision of schools, and the relative size of public versus private school options are important questions for future research.

Finally, we know considerably more about the political factors that shaped the expansion of education systems than we do about the political consequences of this expansion. While many primary education systems were designed to accomplish nation- and state-building goals, the extent to which they succeeded, and the conditions under which they did, remain less understood. In some cases, education systems appear to have successfully established a common national identity (Blanc and Kubo 2021), whereas in other cases, they failed to do so (Fouka 2020). Understanding these varied outcomes will require scholars to abandon a monolithic understanding of "education systems" to consider instead the differences in the content of education; the varying ways in which teachers are recruited, trained, and monitored; and the consequences of these education policies.

Conclusion

The history of education systems is relevant not only to social scientists interested in understanding how the world works but also to anyone interested in improving modern education systems. Across countries today, considerable access to schooling coexists with glaring failures on the part of schools to promote skills. Some social scientists have recommended to rectify this situation by conducting experimental studies that identify cost-effective education interventions to promote skills. This chapter provides an alternative perspective based on the findings of HPE studies. These studies suggest that the historical emergence and expansion of mass education systems was primarily an elite-driven process that sought to shape the political values and behaviors of the population to create loyal and well-behaved future citizens. The characteristics of education systems reflected those goals, from regimented school curricula to the teacher-centered design of classrooms. In recent decades, the goals of education have shifted, and educational reforms have been introduced to reduce income inequality, promote economic growth, and empower citizens. However, the success of these reforms largely rests on institutional foundations inherited from over a century ago that never intended for citizens to be empowered or for schools to promote social mobility. Coming to terms with this incongruency is essential to understand and improve modern education systems.

Notes

1. Darden and Mylonas (2015) argue that the extent to which new independent states worry about enforcing their borders and, therefore, invest in nation-building and language homogenization will depend on how they became independent. Countries that fought independence wars, they argue, will invest more in nation-building than newly independent states whose borders were fixed by international agreements.
2. In all these cases, elites believed that mass schooling would promote obedience and social order. An important question is how racism and xenophobia shape elites' beliefs about who could be "civilized" or not. In the United States during the nineteenth century, for example, politicians who viewed the arrival of Catholic European immigrants as a threat to social order turned to compulsory schooling because they indeed believed that these immigrants could be "civilized" through public schools. However, White plantation owners did not turn to education as a means of promoting orderly behavior among enslaved Black people, both because they feared that teaching slaves how to read would empower them to rebel and because they viewed individuals of African descent as inferior and ineducable.

Bibliography

Acemoglu, Daron, and James A. Robinson. 2006. *Economic Origins of Dictatorship and Democracy.* Cambridge: Cambridge University Press.

Aghion, Philippe, Xavier Jaravel, Torsten Persson, and Dorothee Rouzet. 2019. "Education and Military Rivalry." *Journal of the European Economic Association* 17, no. 2: 376–412.

Alesina, Alberto, Paola Giuliano, and Bryoni Reich. 2021. "Nation-Building and Education." *Economic Journal* 131, no. 638: 2273–303.

Allen, R. C. 2003. "Progress and Poverty in Early Modern Europe." *Economic History Review* 56, no. 3: 403–43.

Anderson, Benedict. 1983. *Imagined Communities: Reflections on the Origin and Spread of Nationalism.* London: Verso.

Andersson, Jens, and Thor Berger. 2019. "Elites and the Expansion of Education in Nineteenth-Century Sweden." *Economic History Review* 72, no. 3: 897–924.

Ansell, Ben. 2008. "Traders, Teachers, and Tyrants: Democracy, Globalization, and Public Investment in Education." *International Organization* 62, no. 2: 289–322.

Ansell, Ben W. 2010. *From the Ballot to the Blackboard: The Redistributive Political Economy of Education.* Cambridge: Cambridge University Press.

Ansell, Ben, and Johannes Lindvall. 2013. "The Political Origins of Primary Education Systems: Ideology, Institutions, and Interdenominational Conflict in an Age of Nation-Building." *American Political Science Review* 107, no. 3: 505–22.

Avelino, George, David S. Brown, and Wendy Hunter. 2005. "The Effects of Capital Mobility, Trade Openness, and Democracy on Social Spending in Latin America, 1980–1999." *American Journal of Political Science* 49, no. 3: 625–41.

Baker, Richard. 2015. "From the Field to the Classroom: The Boll Weevil's Impact on Education in Rural Georgia." *Journal of Economic History* 75, no. 4: 1128–60.

Baker, Richard, John Blanchette, and Katherine Eriksson. 2020. "Long-Run Impacts of Agricultural Shocks on Educational Attainment: Evidence from the Boll Weevil." *Journal of Economic History* 80, no. 1: 136–74.

Bandiera, Oriana, Myra Mohnen, Imran Rasul, and Martina Viarengo. 2019. "Nation-Building through Compulsory Schooling during the Age of Mass Migration." *Economic Journal* 129, no. 617: 62–109.

Baum, Matthew A., and David A. Lake. 2003. "The Political Economy of Growth: Democracy and Human Capital." *American Journal of Political Science* 47, no. 2: 333–47.

Bazzi, Samuel, Masyhur Hilmy, and Benjamin Marx. 2021. "Islam and the State: Religious Education in the Age of Mass Schooling." NBER Working Paper No. 27073.

Blanc, Guillaume, and Masahiro Kubo. 2021. "Schools, Language, and Nations: Evidence from a Natural Experiment in France." Working Paper.

Bozcaga, Tugba, and Asli Cansunar. 2021. "The Education Dilemma: Favoring the In-Group or Assimilating the Out-Group." Working Paper.

Brown, David S. 1999. "Reading, Writing and Regime Type: Democracy's Impact on Primary School Enrollment." *Political Research Quarterly* 52, no. 4: 681–707.

Brown, David S., and Wendy Hunter. 2004. "Democracy and Human Capital Formation: Education Spending in Latin America, 1980 to 1997." *Comparative Political Studies* 37: 842–64.

Busemeyer, Marius R., and Christine Trampusch. 2011. "Comparative Political Science and the Study of Education." *British Journal of Political Science* 41, no. 2: 413–43.

Cappelli, Gabriele. 2016. "One Size That Didn't Fit All? Electoral Franchise, Fiscal Capacity and the Rise of Mass Schooling across Italy's Provinces, 1870–1911." *Cliometrica* 10, no. 1: 311–43.

Cermeño, Alexandra L., Kerstin Enflo, and Johannes Lindvall. 2022. "Railroads and Reform: How Trains Strengthened the Nation State." *British Journal of Political Science* 52, no. 2: 715–35.

Cinnirella, Francesco, and Erik Hornung. 2016. "Landownership Concentration and the Expansion of Education." *Journal of Development Economics* 121, no. 1: 135–52.

Cinnirella, Francesco, and Ruth Schueler. 2018. "Nation Building: The Role of Central Spending in Education." *Explorations in Economic History* 67, no. 1: 18–39.

Clark, G. 2005. "The Condition of the Working Class in England, 1209-2004." *Journal of Political Economy* 113, no. 6: 1307–340.

Darden, Keith, and Anna Grzymala-Busse. 2006. "The Great Divide: Literacy, Nationalism, and the Communist Collapse." *World Politics* 59, no. 1: 83–115.

Darden, Keith, and Harris Mylonas. 2015. "Threats to Territorial Integrity, National Mass Schooling, Linguistic Commonality." *Comparative Political Studies* 49, no. 11: 1446–79.

De Pleijt, Alexandra. 2018. "Human Capital Formation in the Long Run: Evidence from Average Years of Schooling in England, 1300–1900." *Cliometrica* 12, no. 1: 99–126.

Engerman, Stanley, and Kenneth Sokoloff. 2002. "Factor Endowments, Inequality, and Paths of Development Among New World Economics." NBER Working Paper No. 9259.

Fouka, Vasiliki. 2020. "Backlash: The Unintended Effects of Language Prohibition in US Schools after World War I." *Review of Economic Studies* 87, no. 1: 204–39.

Galor, Oded, and Omer Moav. 2000. "Ability-Biased Technological Transition, Wage Inequality, and Economic Growth." *Quarterly Journal of Economics* 115, no. 2: 469–97.

Galor, Oded, and Omer Moav. 2002. "Natural Selection and the Origin of Economic Growth." *Quarterly Journal of Economics* 117, no. 4: 1133–91.

Galor, Oded, and Omer Moav. 2006. "Das Human-Kapital: A Theory of the Demise of the Class Structure." *The Review of Economic Studies* 73, no. 1: 85–117.

Gellner, Ernest. 1983. *Nations and Nationalism*. Ithaca, NY: Cornell University Press.

Gift, Thomas, and Erik Wibbels. 2014. "Reading, Writing, and the Regrettable Status of Education Research in Comparative Politics." *Annual Review of Political Science* 17: 291–312.

Goldin, Claudia, and Lawrence F. Katz. 2009. *The Race between Education and Technology*. Cambridge, MA: Belknap Press of the Harvard University Press.

Green, Andy. 1990. *Education and State Formation: The Rise of Education Systems in England, France, and the USA*. New York: St. Martin's Press.

Grew, Raymond, and Patrick J. Harrigan. 1991. *School, State, and Society: The Growth of Elementary Schooling in Nineteenth-Century France: A Quantitative Analysis*. Ann Arbor: University of Michigan Press.

Hoffman, Philip. 2015. "What Do States Do? Politics and Economic History." *Journal of Economic History* 75, no. 2: 303–32.

Hollenbach, Florian M. 2021. "Elite Interests and Public Spending: Evidence from Prussian Cities." *Review of International Organizations* 16, no. 1: 189–211.

Kaufman, Robert R., and Alex Segura-Ubiergo. 2001. "Globalization, Domestic Politics, and Social Spending in Latin America: A Time-Series Cross-Section Analysis, 1973-97." *World Politics* 53, no. 4: 553–87.

Lee, Melissa, and Nan Zhang. 2017. "Legibility and the Informational Foundations of State Capacity." *Journal of Politics* 79, no. 1: 118–32.

Le Nestour, Alexis, Laura Moscoviz, and Justin Sandefur. 2021. "The Long-Term Decline of School Quality in the Developing World." Center for Global Development Working Paper.

Lindert, Peter. 2004. *Growing Public: Social Spending and Economic Growth since the Eighteenth Century*. Cambridge: Cambridge University Press.

Manzano, Dulce. 2017. *Bringing down the Educational Wall: Political Regimes, Ideology and the Expansion of Education*. Cambridge: Cambridge University Press.

Mariscal, Elisa, and Kenneth L. Sokoloff. 2000. "Schooling, Suffrage, and the Persistence of Inequality in the Americas, 1800–1945." In *Political Institutions and Economic Growth in Latin America: Essays in Policy, History, and Political Economy*, ed. Stephen Haber, 159–218. Stanford, CA: Hoover Institutions Press.

Melton, James. 2002. *Absolutism and the Eighteenth-Century Origins of Compulsory Schooling in Prussia and Austria*. Cambridge: Cambridge University Press.

Mitch, David. 1998. "The Role of Education and Skill in the British Industrial Revolution." In *The British Industrial Revolution: An Economic Perspective*, ed. Joel Mokyr, 241–79. Boulder, CO: Westview Press.

Mokyr, Joel. 1990. *The Lever of Riches: Technological Creativity and Economic Progress*. New York: Oxford University Press.

Mokyr, Joel. 2005. "Long-Term Economic Growth and the History of Technology." In *Handbook of Economic Growth*, Volume 1B, ed. Philippe Aghion and Steven N. Durlauf, 1114–80. Elsevier B.V.

Montalbo, Adrien. 2020. "Industrial Activities and Primary Schooling in Early Nineteenth-Century France." *Cliometrica* 14, no. 2: 325–65.

Paglayan, Agustina S. 2017. "Political Origins of Public Education Systems." PhD dissertation, Stanford University.

Paglayan, Agustina. 2021. "The Non-Democratic Roots of Mass Education: Evidence from 200 Years." *American Political Science Review* 115, no. 1: 179–98.

Paglayan, Agustina S. 2022. "Education or Indoctrination? The Violent Origins of Public School Systems in an Era of State-Building." *American Political Science Review*. DOI: https://doi.org/10.1017/S0003055422000247.

Ramirez, Francisco, and John Boli. 1987. "The Political Construction of Mass Schooling: European Origins and Worldwide Institutionalization." *Sociology of Education* 60, no. 1: 2–17.

Scott, James. 1998. *Seeing Like a State. How Certain Schemes to Improve the Human Condition Have Failed*. New Haven, CT: Yale University Press.

Squicciarini, Mara, and Nico Voigtländer. 2015. "Human Capital and Industrialization: Evidence from the Age of Enlightenment." *Quarterly Journal of Economics* 30, no. 4: 1825–83.

Squicciarini, Mara P., and Nico Voigtländer. 2016. "Knowledge Elites and Modernization: Evidence from Revolutionary France." NBER Working Paper No. 22779.

Stasavage, David. 2005. "Democracy and Education Spending in Africa." *American Journal of Political Science* 49, no. 2: 343–58.

Tyack, David B. 1974. *The One Best System: A History of American Urban Education*. Cambridge, MA: Harvard University Press.

Weber, Eugen. 1976. *Peasants into Frenchmen: The Modernization of Rural France, 1870–1914*. Stanford, CA: Stanford University Press.

World Bank. 2011. *Learning for All: Investing in People's Knowledge and Skills to Promote Development*. Washington, DC: World Bank.

World Bank. 2018. *World Development Report 2018: Learning to Realize Education's Promise*. Washington, DC: World Bank.

Zhang, Nan, and Melissa Lee. 2020. "Literacy and State-Society Interactions in Nineteenth-Century France." *American Journal of Political Science* 64, no. 4: 1001–16.

CHAPTER 43

HEALTH IN HISTORICAL POLITICAL ECONOMY

JAMES J. FEIGENBAUM

In his epic The Rise and Fall of American Growth, Gordon (2017) decries the America of 1870 for its poor-quality consumer goods and boring food, its lackluster communication and entertainment options, and its lousy working conditions. But while vast improvements in all of these categories contributed to the growth in the US standard of living from the nineteenth century to today, just as important were the "set of developments that made possible increasing life expectancy, thus raising the number of years over which new products and uses of time could be enjoyed" (Gordon 2017, 206). Health—both how long we live and how healthy we are during that time—is, as Sen (1999) emphasizes, an essential part of well-being. As Cutler, Deaton, and Lleras-Muney (2006, 97) write, "The pleasures of life are worth nothing if one is not alive to experience them." Deaton (2013, 33) continues, "You need a life to have a good life, and poor health and disability among the living can severely limit the capability to enjoy an otherwise good life."

And the improvements in health over the last two centuries or so, as outlined by Gordon (2017), Deaton (2013), Fogel (2004), Costa (2015), Steckel (2006), Preston and Haines (1991), and many others, both in the United States and around the world, are staggering. Oeppen and Vaupel (2002) find that from 1840 to 2000, life expectancy at the frontier—the country in any given year with the longest life expectancy—has grown steadily by three months per calendar year. Gains in the United States, though not the leader in most of this period, have been stunningly large (see Figure 43.1), though racial health disparities remain stubbornly persistent (Boustan and Margo 2015).[1] Though it is more difficult to measure improving quality of life, the near-elimination of many childhood diseases that disabled and scarred their victims suggests gains beyond years lived.

Today, we live long, healthy lives unimaginable just a few generations ago. Other than appreciating our fortunate place in history—an ongoing pandemic notwithstanding—what does the scholar of historical political economy (HPE) take

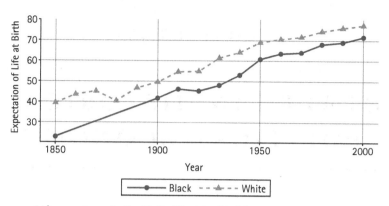

FIGURE 43.1. Life expectancy in the United States at birth by race, 1850–2000

Source: Carter et al. (2006), Series Ab7–Ab8

from the sustained decline in mortality over the last two centuries? This chapter argues that few of the major factors that drove health improvements would have been possible without the state. And where there is the state, there are political economy questions to interrogate.

Health and income are nearly always correlated,[2] whether we look over time, across countries, or within countries across people. Is there a causal relationship? Though in some cases improvements in health might be driven by improvements in economic resources (nutrition is one key example), and in others improvements in economic conditions might be driven by better health,[3] overall the case for causality in either direction is not strong (Deaton 2013; Weil 2015) and requires nuance (Troesken 2015). The classic Preston curves, first traced by the demographer Sam Preston (1975), show a positive correlation between national income and life expectancy across countries. But, over time, countries grow and do not simply move along the Preston curve. Instead the whole curve shifts up: the same level of national income today "buys" even better health outcomes than it did historically.

The state, Deaton (2013) argues, is the omitted factor that correlates with both health and wealth and that explains the shift in the Preston curve. Institutions that encourage economic growth also tend to promote advances in health. This includes the production of medical knowledge but also the implementation of that knowledge through public health efforts, regulation, and more.[4]

In this chapter, I ask two related questions about health in the United States: What was the political economy behind the transition, and what were the political economic effects of the epidemiological transition? I focus on the era of the epidemiological transition, the period from the late nineteenth to the early twentieth centuries when infectious disease death rates fell sharply (Armstrong, Conn, and Pinner 1999). My temporal and geographic constraints—the United States during the transition—reflect both the limits of a single chapter and the narrow focus of my own research. But neither geography nor time period should limit future work in this area.

The growth of the American state—in size, complexity, and ambition—played a large role, and many scholars have studied the institutional features (and quirks) that helped spur the dramatic improvements in health seen over the last two hundred years. Many more scholars have studied the plethora of policies, regulations, and investments that affect health outcomes without an explicit focus on political economy—but the political story behind the scene that generated variation in which cities filtered or chlorinated their water supplies earlier or later or which counties built local health centers or how the federal government taxed and regulated health insurance is ever-present.[5] These public health interventions prompt important HPE questions, such as: Who is included or excluded from public health investments and programs? What level of government should provide public health? How do changes in political power or institutions affect public health?

Less attention has been paid to the second question: what are the political economic effects of the mortality transition? The changes in mortality were so dramatic that they must have made some impact on politics or culture or society. While this chapter outlines some excellent work in this area, one conclusion is that more scholars should ask these questions.[6] Many of the gains in life expectancy shown in Figure 43.1 were driven by reduced death at an early age, both in infancy and childhood. Considering cumulative mortality, Murphy and Topel (2006) calculate that while, in 1900, 18 percent of males born in the United States died before age one, around the year 2000, only 18 percent died before age sixty-two.[7] (See Figures 43.2 and 43.3.) The central role of the state in the epidemiological transition should also prompt scholars to ask about the effects of seeing government successfully save lives.

Cutler, Deaton, and Lleras-Muney (2006) trace in three phases the history of mortality reduction from the 1700s to today. First, rising incomes bought improved nutrition; humans grew larger and stronger, as Fogel (2004) and Floud et al. (2011) show. Second, from the late nineteenth century to the mid-twentieth century, the germ theory of disease and its application to public health measures countered infectious disease, brought down infant and child mortality, and reduced the frequency of epidemics. Finally, from the 1930s onward, the "era of big medicine" took the lead, first with vaccinations and antibiotics and then in improving the quality of life and extending lives at older ages (Cutler, Deaton, and Lleras-Muney 2006, 106).

The first section of this chapter focuses on the public health measures and investments in the era of the epidemiological transition.[8] All of these "treatments" have a political economy behind them. The second section of this chapter considers the political economy of epidemics and pandemics and the political economy left in their wake.[9] The third section of this chapter traces the development of American healthcare as both a profession and an industry.[10]

Interwoven through the three main sections are leitmotifs that sit at the intersection of health with race and ethnicity: who belongs, whose lives could or should be saved, and whose deaths count? Racial disparities in health outcomes in the United

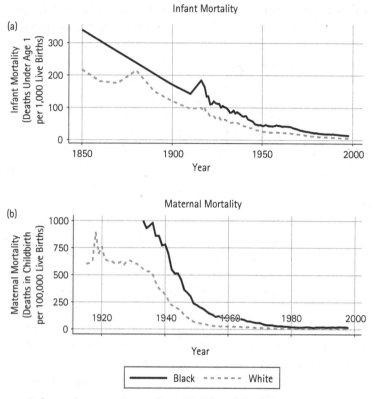

FIGURE 43.2. Infant and maternal mortality in the United States by race, 1850–2000
(a) Infant Mortality (b) Maternal Mortality

Source: Carter et al. (2006), Series Ab921, Ab923, Ab925, and Ab927

States are large today and they were large historically (Boustan and Margo 2015; Margo 2016; Alsan and Wanamaker 2018; Du Bois 1906). For urban dwellers, the infectious mortality rates faced by African Americans were higher in any given year (1906 to 1920) than the White mortality rates during the 1918 influenza pandemic (Feigenbaum, Muller, and Wrigley-Field 2019). Even as mortality improved overall, racial inequality often got worse (Zelner, Muller, and Feigenbaum 2017; Feigenbaum et al. 2022). As Bailey, Feldman, and Bassett (2021) argue, these racial health disparities today are often rooted in racist policies. Some are driven by mistrust seeded by historical wrongs (Alsan and Wanamaker 2018). Structural factors are likely root causes of historical disparities as well. Health disparities between the US-born and the foreign-born were also large during the epidemiological transition (Ager et al. 2020b). Nativists exploited health differences, especially during epidemics and pandemics, for political purposes, promoting immigration restriction, segregation, and unequal access to public health measures. Understanding the ugly political economy of how health disparities are used (and likely compounded) to further racist and nativist agendas is an important task for HPE scholars.

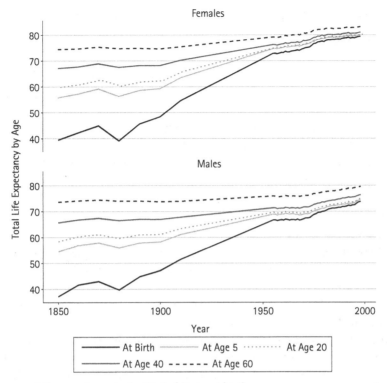

FIGURE 43.3. Life expectancy in the United States at birth, age 5, age 20, age 40, age 60, and age 70 by race and sex, 1850–2000

Source: Carter et al. (2006), Series Ab656–Ab667

Public Health Investments

Governments, primarily cities, spent vast amounts of money and effort on public health in the late nineteenth and early twentieth centuries (Melosi 1999). Cities built water systems, cleaned that water with filtration and chlorination, and removed and treated sewage.[11] Cities and states inspected milk, while states, and eventually the federal government, inspected food. City and rural health departments were formed and staffed, providing primary care, public health education, and vaccination campaigns.

These actions saved lives and changed life.[12] Naturally, much of the literature in the social sciences on the epidemiological transition parses the factors that drove down mortality so dramatically. In this section, I highlight the HPE angles. Some of these questions are addressed directly in the literature, while others are present but not centered. Others still—most notably the political economy consequences of both the rapid changes in the mortality and disease environment and the political economy effect of seeing government (for the most part) successfully work to save lives—are important avenues for future research.

Who Is Included and Excluded? Race, Segregation, and Provision

Mortality fell when cities cleaned their water.[13] While most research on clean water historically has considered cities as treated or untreated—owing largely to aggregate mortality and infrastructure data—the reality is more complex. As Beach, Parman, and Saavedra (2022) remind us, "Infrastructure rarely arrives all at once." Within that reality, an odious HPE angle emerges: there was a willingness to ignore the health of poor, minority, or immigrant groups, a choice that often undermined the health of the groups that politicians prioritized.

The income bias of public health infrastructure is clear. Costa and Kahn (2015) and Kesztenbaum and Rosenthal (2017) both show mortality reductions in richer neighborhoods as they are connected first.

Racial inequality in access to clean water and treated sewage may be more complicated. Segregation, especially in southern cities, often took the form of Whites on main streets and African Americans living nearby in alleys (Grigoryeva and Ruef 2015; Logan and Parman 2017). Troesken (2004) argued that because there was a low marginal cost of connecting additional households and because planners had some understanding of contagion, access to piped water would be more equitable. Focusing on the cases of Memphis, Tennessee, and Savannah, Georgia, Troesken (2004) shows that the more segregated Savannah had a larger racial disparity in sewer system connections.

Beach, Parman, and Saavedra (2022) investigate the Troesken theory across many more cities and build a theoretical model of a racist city planner. They show that more segregated cities built municipal water systems earlier but struggled more to suppress waterborne death rates. They reconcile this puzzle by emphasizing the last-mile problem. It appears that racist city planners did exclude Black neighborhoods from water service, either ignoring or not appreciating the risk of contagion across the color line. As Beach, Parman, and Saavedra (2022) concludes, "[Racial] exclusion appears to have come at a cost: more segregated cities were much slower to eliminate waterborne diseases." More public health measures of this era would benefit from the focus that Troesken (2004) and Beach, Parman, and Saavedra (2022) bring to water.

In addition to race, immigration status has had large impacts on inclusion and exclusion from public health. From the earliest days of American history, nativists had accused immigrants of spreading poor health and infecting the "native" population with foreign diseases. In the eighteenth century, Germans were associated with yellow fever ("Palatine fever"). In the nineteenth century, the Irish were linked to cholera, the Chinese to typhoid and smallpox, and Jews to tuberculosis (a "tailors' disease") (Kraut 1995). In the early twentieth century, the foreign-born mortality penalty was used as justification for draconian immigration quotas enacted in 1921 and 1924. Debate over changes to immigration policy at mid-century often devolved into the association between germs and foreigners (Markel and Stern 2002). In the 1980s, Haitian migrants were tagged as high-risk for HIV infection (Kraut 1995). Today, ugly nativist rhetoric has emerged in COVID-19's wake.

Ager et al. (2020b) study the effects of immigration on health, untangling the nativist myth from the empirical reality. They use variation across cities in the number of "missing" immigrants after the 1920s Quota Acts to estimate the effect of immigration on mortality. Immigrants, like other poor and newly arrived urban dwellers, were more likely to live in multifamily households, live with (or be) boarders or lodgers, and generally live in more "internally" dense conditions.[14] After the quota acts, proxies for crowded living conditions fell, both overall and for the foreign-born in particular. In addition, cities that were more crowded before the quotas saw larger relative declines in mortality afterwards. Eriksson, Lin, and Niemesh (2020) echo these results in a study of Massachusetts from 1860 to 1915, looking specifically at infant mortality. Their results are also driven by communicable diseases and over-crowded living arrangements.

These studies point to the importance of crowding and living conditions—like those vividly documented by Riis (1890)—in affecting mortality. They argue that such living conditions arose in large part because policymakers were swayed by nativist arguments about the inherent ill-health of immigrants and did little to address root causes like dilapidated living conditions without ventilation that were breeding grounds for diseases of the crowd.

The most pressing HPE question to ask is how did the terrible living conditions that characterize urban slums and tenements arise in the first place and why were cities doing so little to address public health crises in immigrant wards? Eriksson, Lin, and Niemesh (2020) suggest that public health interventions mitigated some of the negative mortality effects of crowding. But most zoning in the early twentieth century, a natural policy response, was more often a tool of racial and ethnic segregation than of public health policy (Shertzer, Twinam, and Walsh 2016).

Who Provides Public Health?

This subsection considers two axes of provision of public health: public versus private and local versus federal government. Scholars studying the interplay of public health and private actors or intragovernmental provision would do well to consider more historical examples.

Urban waterworks were incredibly expensive to build but also costly and complicated to maintain. Who is best positioned to run these systems, private or public entities? Optimal ownership structure is a classic political economy question that scholars are still debating today (Galiani, Gertler, and Schargrodsky 2005), complicated by the reality that regime changes are not random and pre-trends could generate spurious correlations in these settings (Beach, Troesken, and Tynan 2016b). Troesken (1999) suggests that ownership, at least in the United States, did not affect typhoid rates in either direction. However, "municipalization" in England and Wales in the nineteenth century appears to have had positive effects, reducing death rates from typhoid by about

20 percent (Beach, Troesken, and Tynan 2016b). Public ownership also intersects with race in a surprising way. Troesken (2001) finds that water service to African Americans was better when water companies were public rather than private. Why did better public provision come in a context where African Americans were effectively disenfranchised and discriminated against in most other dimensions?

Beyond waterworks, nongovernment entities also played huge roles in public health campaigns when local government would not. Bleakley (2007) documents the work of the Rockefeller Sanitary Commission (RSC) in eradicating hookworm in the southern United States. The RSC funded an initial survey of six hundred counties (40 percent of schoolchildren suffered from hookworm), treatment dispensaries, and anti-hookworm education programs. Only after the RSC wound down did state governments increase their own spending on anti-hookworm campaigns, and many of the public health efforts were modeled on what the RSC had done (Bleakley 2007).

Provision is not just a question of public versus private, but of the level of government. For much of American history, the more local the government, the more active it was in providing public health. In the nineteenth and early twentieth centuries, county and city governments were better able to collect taxes than state or national governments (Wallis 2000). But the vast heterogeneity in local governments meant vast differences in public health provision. Anderson et al. (2019) trace the success of the public health campaign against tuberculosis, an effort propelled by "hundreds of state and local TB associations" in the early twentieth century.[15] Hoehn-Velasco (2020) studies the creation of local health departments and emphasizes state capacity drove when and how public health departments were created, more than local health conditions or need. The institutional form of health departments is one possible explanation for why city health departments had minimal effects (Hoehn-Velasco and Wrigley-Field 2021), while Hoehn-Velasco (2018) shows that their rural counterparts had long-lasting effects on health and downstream outcomes.

The federal government took on an expanded role in public health during the Great Depression, mirroring growth in most other aspects of American life during that crisis (Wallis 2010; Wallis, Fishback, and Kantor 2005). Fishback, Haines, and Kantor (2007) show that New Deal relief spending during the Great Depression was effective at reducing mortality rates. The effects of the New Deal on infant mortality, both overall and in racial disparities, was more complex and varied program by program (Fishback, Haines, and Kantor 2001). As the era of public health became the era of big medicine, the central government's role would grow more and more. Understanding more of both the causes and effects of this shift is a field ripe for future HPE study.

Political Institutions, Political Power, and Health

If institutions explain much of the link between health and economic outcomes (Deaton 2013), then the structure of those institutions must shape health. Some evidence for this connection exists, but it remains an open area for research.

In one seminal paper, Miller (2008) studies the effects of women's suffrage on health outcomes. Exploiting variation in the timing of enfranchisement across states—before the Nineteenth Amendment, some states had allowed (White) women to vote—Miller shows that when women get the vote, spending on local public health increases. This extra spending had downstream effects, reducing child mortality.[16] Miller's findings suggest that women and men, on average, had different preferences over public health spending and that politicians were responsive to the newly enfranchised voters.[17] However, the history of the Sheppard-Towner program complicates the picture. Sheppard-Towner was passed in 1922 and funded matching grants to states for public health education for mothers. Moehling and Thomasson (2012) find that women's suffrage pushed participation in the program, but the effects were short-lived as suffrage did not prevent its repeal just seven years later.

Less is known about the public health effects of the two other great changes in access to voting rights in American history. Though the political empowerment of African Americans in the South during Reconstruction increased public spending overall, that spending appears to have been mostly dedicated to schooling and land reform (Logan 2020). While there is a long literature on the effects of the Voting Rights Act on economic and political outcomes (see Cascio and Washington [2014]; Ang [2019]; Aneja and Avenancio-Leon [2019]), the public health effects are less clear.[18]

But, as all scholars of HPE know, voting rights are not the only political institution that could shape policy. Here, there is much more work to be done. One recent paper comes from Gamm and Kousser (2021). The authors find that party competition since 1880 is associated with more state spending, particularly on human capital investments like health. This spending had positive downstream health effects in the form of longer life expectancies and reduced rates of infant mortality.

Who Pays for Externalities: Environmental Toxins

The history of environmental toxins and their regulation is an important question for scholars working at the intersection of HPE and health. In this subsection, I cover research on lead and air pollution, but this survey is brief and incomplete.

Many of the urban water systems that helped eliminate typhoid and other waterborne illnesses were built using lead pipes. The effects of lead historically are now understood. Lead exposure via piped water increased violent crime rates, lowered cognitive abilities, and increased infant mortality (Feigenbaum and Muller 2016; Ferrie, Rolf, and Troesken 2012; Clay, Troesken, and Haines 2014), results that hold in a variety of settings and with different identification strategies (Aizer and Currie 2019; Billings and Schnepel 2018; Reyes 2007).

Burning coal powered economic progress from the Industrial Revolution on, but it also polluted the air. Scholars have documented the clear costs to health of air pollution, both in the United States (Barreca, Clay, and Tarr 2014; Clay, Lewis, and Severnini 2016) and elsewhere (Beach and Hanlon 2018; Bailey, Hatton, and Inwood

2018). Pollution also has the power to shape cities in the very long run (Heblich, Trew, and Zylerberg 2021).

The HPE questions are natural. First, why are some places and the people who live there subjected to a vast amount of pollution with health and other consequences? Answers vary across toxins and time periods. For lead, many of the long-run harms from low levels of lead exposure were not well understood historically, while other concerned voices were drowned out (Nielsen 2021).[19] With air pollution, poorer communities and neighborhoods with more immigrants or racial minorities were subjected to it while those who could afford to move away did, and those with political power to preserve clean environments did. For more on inequalities in environmental exposure, see Currie (2011) and Muller, Sampson, and Winter (2018).

Second, how does regulation emerge and at what levels? In a review of urban economic history research, Hanlon and Heblich (2021) contrast the regulation of the air with water and note that cities were generally unable to clean their air, possibly fearing mobile firms and competition with other more pollution-friendly cities. Air pollution required national regulation: the London Fog in 1954 was followed by the 1956 Clean Air Act in England, and other countries began regulating air pollution in short order (Hanlon and Heblich 2021).[20]

Third, what are the political economy effects of historical exposure to environmental dangers? This area is much less studied. We know there are large cognitive effects from lead exposure that can reduce impulse control and increase aggressiveness. Are there political effects to whole generations being dosed with lead? What about the political preferences or choices of individuals exposed to more lead as children? The political economy effects could be massive if, for example, observed neighborhood effects of poverty on outcomes are in reality driven by lead exposure, as in Wodtke, Ramaj, and Schachner (2020).

Health and Politics of Urbanization

The share of Americans living in urban areas has grown every decade except one since 1790.[21] But while economic forces pushed for more agglomeration, cities were dangerous places to live, with significantly higher death rates than in rural areas, especially for infants (Preston and Haines 1991). Though there is some debate over when exactly the urban mortality penalty disappeared (Haines 2001; Feigenbaum, Hoehn-Velasco, and Wrigley-Field 2020), there is no doubt that cities became healthier and safer during the era of public health. Curing one of the "demons of density" (Glaeser and Cutler 2021)—higher mortality due to the deadly mix of crowded living conditions and contagious diseases—played some role in enabling the rise of the city (Glaeser 2011). The urban-rural divide is a key political question today (Gimpel et al. 2020; Rodden 2019). If the benefits of agglomeration were still checked so ruthlessly by density-caused ill-health, the density-politics gradient might not loom so large or be so steep.

The effect of density on political economy is not a new question. In the nineteenth century, de Tocqueville (2000) emphasized the important effects of America's small towns. Troesken (2015) takes that argument to health, suggesting that one reason American cities struggled with controlling epidemic diseases historically was not directly because of the dangers of density; instead, the anonymity of larger towns and cities eroded the public spirit of the township that de Tocqueville had identified.

Public Health Research

Public health was also improved through ambitious public research projects. To give one example, the public health laboratory in New York City created a diphtheria antitoxin in 1892. Over the next twenty years, the city ran a vaccination campaign during which death rates from diphtheria shrank dramatically (Gordon 2017).[22]

But research in the first half of the twentieth century had a nefarious side. Alsan and Wanamaker (2018) document the Tuskegee Study, where the US Public Health Service followed six hundred Black men in Alabama for forty years. Many of the men had syphilis initially, and others contracted it during the course of the study. The men were denied treatment for syphilis, including penicillin after its discovery; subjected to spinal taps and other procedures; and told they had "bad blood." The exposure of the study in 1972 seeded mistrust among African Americans about the medical community.[23] Alsan and Wanamaker (2018) show that African American men, after 1972, were much less likely to go to the doctor and had worse mortality outcomes.[24]

PANDEMICS AND EPIDEMICS

Pandemics and epidemics are shocks to nearly every aspect of life. They are also important case studies at the intersection of health and HPE that illustrate many of the key questions and patterns that animate this chapter. In this section, I ask two questions. First, what are the effects of political economy on pandemics and epidemics? In particular, what are the political economy forces that shape the public response? Second, what are the political economy effects of pandemics and epidemics?[25]

The Political Economy of Pandemic and Epidemic Response

How does a government respond to a public health crisis? In part, responses are shaped by medical and technological constraints.[26] But the responses are also shaped by important HPE factors.

Nonpharmaceutical interventions (NPIs) are an important locus of study in HPE. NPIs range from lockdowns to closing schools and other public venues to requiring masking. NPIs were used during many pandemics, including the 1918 influenza, to halt the spread of various pathogens.[27] As a matter of public policy, NPIs may require trade-offs and thus raise several political economy questions: Do they work? Who wins and who loses from them? Are they always politicized?

While the epidemiological literature suggests that NPIs reduce mortality (Markel et al. 2007; Hatchett, Mecher, and Lispitch 2007; Bootsma and Ferguson 2007), recent work is less confident. Barro (2020) finds that NPIs flatten the curve but do not lower overall mortality, while Chapelle (2021) argues that NPIs, at least in 1918, increased mortality by reducing herd immunity after lowering mortality initially.[28]

The costs to the economy are even more debated. While Correia, Luck, and Verner (2020) sketch a picture of NPIs revving up the economy in the medium run, neither Velde (2020) nor Lilley, Lilley, and Rinaldi (2020) find any negative (or positive) effects of NPIs on economic activity.[29]

NPIs have included school closures both during the 1918 influenza and during earlier polio outbreaks. Ager et al. (2020a) find precise null effects of school closures during 1918 on the treated students in terms of educational attainment and adult earnings while Meyers and Thomasson (2021), studying polio, find negligible effects on education. Of course, economic outcomes like earnings and years of education are not the only margin through which school closures might matter in the long run. Though challenging, connecting exposure to NPIs to political preferences later in life could be informative, especially as we imagine what the effects of the COVID-19 NPIs could be in the coming decades.

Was there resistance to the NPIs like we have seen during COVID? Beach, Clay, and Saavedra (2020) argue that social distancing and other NPIs were neither politicized nor polarized during 1918. Why not? As Beach, Clay, and Saavedra (2020) note, there are many differences between 1918 and today that could explain this, including the number of past epidemics people had endured and the expectations (or lack thereof) about what the government could reasonably do to control the epidemic. But extrapolating from only two data points is challenging. NPIs have been applied at other times during local epidemics, and a study could look at variations in the levels of resistance to NPIs and other anti-pandemic measures across time and location.

Scholars might also look at the many nineteenth-century epidemics and NPIs. Troesken (2015) and Shah (2001) describe the deplorable treatment of Chinese immigrants in San Francisco during epidemic outbreaks. More scapegoating of immigrants and foreigners during pandemics is detailed in Kraut (1995), historical evidence of the implementation of policy in an era when nativists viewed immigrants as pathogenically dangerous.

The very existence or frequency of pandemics historically is a puzzle of its own. In the nineteenth century, the United States was quite rich but it was also susceptible to epidemics (Troesken 2015). The explanation, Troesken (2015) argues, is that the imagined causality (from wealth to health) is not the whole story. Instead, the same factors—in Troesken's telling, commitments to individual liberty and strong property rights—led to high levels of American economic development and uneven levels of American health. Just as Beach, Parman, and Saavedra (2022) take the Troesken (2004) theory to the data, scholars pushing research on pandemic responses would do well to measure variation in the institutions Troesken (2015) emphasizes, either across cities or states or even nations, and compare public health or epidemic outcomes.

Pandemics are challenging crises that can be revelatory about the state and its bureaucrats. Evidence from outside the United States could be illuminating, and the best is a recent study by Guo Xu (2021) on bureaucrats in India during 1918. More people died in India during the pandemic than in any other place on earth, a staggering ten million to twenty million deaths. When the pandemic hit, India was under British dominion but towns could have been headed by either Indian or British district officers. Xu finds that the towns with Indian heads had mortality rates that were fifteen percentage points lower and were driven by more and faster provision of public works employment and other relief measures. Xu's results tell us that the mechanics of the state—even simply the identity of the state bureaucrat—matter to mortality during a pandemic.

Effects of Pandemics and Epidemics

Effects in the Short Run

Are political leaders punished for pandemics? Such punishment could be rational if those who mismanaged a crisis are ejected from office having revealed their inability to keep constituents safe. Voters could also engage in "blind retrospective voting" (Achen and Bartels 2017). In this case, politicians are punished just for holding office at a time when something bad (and outside their control) occurred.

Two studies have focused on the effects of the 1918 pandemic on voting in the US. Achen and Bartels (2004) look in the cross-section at sixteen states and then twenty-nine cities and find no evidence that the 1918 pandemic swayed voters in the gubernatorial elections in 1918. Arroyo Abad and Maurer (2021) revisit this question with substantially more data and find more nuanced results. Voters moved away from incumbent governors and away from Democratic members of Congress (Democrats were the party in power during the flu). But the estimated effects in Arroyo Abad and Maurer (2021) are small: none of the gubernatorial winners would have lost but for the pandemic. By the 1920 presidential election, Arroyo Abad and Maurer (2021) find that the effects of the flu had faded and the Democratic candidate (James Cox) was not blamed for Wilson's handling or mishandling of the flu.

In related work, Hilt and Rahn (2020) use influenza severity as an instrument for Liberty Bond purchases. As Hilt and Rahn (2020) document, many cities and counties cancelled public events that were planned to drum up sales of Liberty Bonds. To the extent that pandemics disrupt the patterns of normal life—and between school closures, bans on public gathering, and more, they surely do—there could be reverberation. In Hilt and Rahn (2020), the reverberation eventually comes back to voting: people holding more Liberty Bonds (because the pandemic hit their county weaker or later) punish Democratic candidates for president in 1920 and 1924 for their role in movements in the value of their Liberty Bond assets.

But 1918 was not the only pandemic in American history.[30] Future scholars would do well to study the political effects of other pandemics.[31] One theory to investigate is proposed by Beach, Clay, and Saavedra (2020): the political effects of pandemics—incumbents blamed for deaths generally or for their failed mitigation attempts—are likely to be small in the past, given the high rates of infectious death mortality prevailing. While the 1918 influenza pandemic was exceptional, voters circa 1918 faced a high risk of infectious mortality in all years. The same would be the case for voters threatened by previous epidemics. But this argument is testable: as the "normal" infectious mortality rates fell over time, we should expect to see pandemics mattering more and more. If the ability of the government to protect its citizens (or voters' expectations or beliefs about that ability) grows over time, that makes it even more likely that pandemics should have political consequences. So, when (if ever) does the short-run political effect of a pandemic turn on?

Two studies of a recent epidemic and a recent feared epidemic present some evidence in that direction. Mansour, Rees, and Reeves (2020) study the HIV/AIDS epidemic and find that, at least after 1994, congressional districts with higher death rates from HIV/AIDS voted more for Democrats, spurred by higher Democratic turnout. Meanwhile, Campante, Depetris-Chauvin, and Durante (2020) trace the link between the news coverage of Ebola in 2014 and vote shares and turnout in that November's election. In our era of low mortality rates from infectious disease, these two events seemed to move voters in ways that the 1918 pandemic did not.

What about the people who are personally or directly affected? Even if the punishment of inept politicians presiding over the 1918 flu was minimal (Arroyo Abad and Maurer 2021), did the families of people who died feel the same way? Here, individual-level data could point the way. Saavedra (2017) studied yellow fever by linking census data to death records, and Cook, Logan, and Parman (2016) linked death records to uniquely Black names. Could linking death records with data on individual political outcomes unlock more nuanced stories about the short-run political economy effects of pandemics?

Effects in the Long Run

As we look out from our COVID-19 present, HPE's ability to help us understand the long-run political economy effects of a pandemic may be especially valuable.

One long-lasting, even multigenerational effect could be on trust, as Aassve et al. (2021) and Aksoy, Eichengreen, and Saka (2020) document. Looking in the General Social Survey, Aassve et al. (2021) find that the descendants of immigrants' levels of trust are shaped by their ancestors' experience of the 1918 pandemic in their countries of origin. A similar finding emerges in Aksoy, Eichengreen, and Saka (2020), which studies pandemics post-1970, exploiting variation across 142 countries and cohorts (born from 1970 to 2012). For people exposed to a pandemic during their impressionable years (ages eighteen to twenty-five), the authors find reduced confidence in political institutions and leaders, effects that seem driven by lower confidence in public health systems. The negative long-run effects of pandemic exposure during one's impressionable years are especially acute for people coming of age in states with weak governments, possibly because those governments were noticeably ineffective at fighting the pandemics.

Pandemics and epidemics can also shape places rather than people. Ambrus, Field, and Gonzalez (2020) show the long-run effects of a cholera epidemic on the spatial distribution of poverty in London. Lower housing prices arise in the neighborhood of the pandemic within 10 years and then persist for more than 160.

Beyond people and places, future scholars should ask whether pandemics can also fundamentally reorder government and institutions. Higgs (1987) argues that throughout American history, crises—especially wars and economic downturns—have spurred the growth of the American state. In some ways, these crises served as demonstration projects, making clear to the American people what an active and engaged state could accomplish (and what it could not). Did the pandemics of the past have similar effects? One cannot help but wonder what effects the failures and successes of the COVID-19 response will have on future public policy and support or opposition to those policies. Looking to the past, with all of the usual caveats, may be illuminating. When the state grew to combat past pandemics, did it then retreat or, as Higgs criticizes, did a ratcheting take hold? From the voters' side, we might ask how voters felt about such changes in the nature and scope of government. Cultural ideas about the role of government can be deeply rooted in history (Bazzi, Fizbein, and Gebresilasse 2020), but could they also be shocked by extreme events like pandemics?

Short versus Long Run

Why are there large (even transformative) effects of pandemics in the long run, but small political costs in the short run? Clearly, more work is needed to put the pieces of the previous two sections together. One unifying theory could be, as Beach, Clay, and Saavedra (2020) suggest, that historical pandemics occurred against a background of very high mortality and weak states. But in the long run, the children of the 1918 pandemic were making political choices in a period several decades forward in eras with lower mortality rates.

HEALTHCARE

Why does the American healthcare system look the way it does? While a serious answer to this question is well beyond the scope of a single chapter,[32] let alone this short section, some of the seeds were planted during the early twentieth century and many of the questions this era prompts should be of interest to HPE scholars.

While I consider the medical profession and health insurance in more detail later, there are other important actors in the HPE of health. Consider hospitals. In just the few decades after 1900, American hospitals were transformed, in the memorable phrasing of Thomasson and Treber (2008), "from almshouses to centers of medical science." While scholars who have studied hospitals in this era have focused on the health and mortality effects, there are HPE questions about hospital regulation. Anderson, Charles, and Rees (2020b) study one episode: the Lyndon Johnson administration tied Medicaid funding to hospital desegregation. Anderson, Charles, and Rees (2020b) exploit this change to study the effects of hospital access on Black-White infant mortality gaps. Though they find no effects on mortality disparity, HPE scholars might look to federally mandated desegregation in hospitals as a political and social shock with unexpected downstream outcomes. How did patients, doctors, and others react to these changes?

Regulation and regulators could be another area of HPE interest. The world of patent medicine and medicinal narcotics like opium, cocaine, and heroin eventually morphed into the world of prescriptions today; Carpenter (2014) traces much of this transition through his study of the US Food and Drug Administration. But there are regulators of not just pharmaceuticals, but of doctors and nurses, of hospitals, and more. Understanding how regulators and other public health agencies make choices during times of a pandemic would benefit from rich HPE analysis.

Medical Education and Healthcare Workers

American medical education in the nineteenth century was an embarrassment.[33] As the supply of medical schools rose, competition pushed down quality: students were admitted with little to no screening and graduated with little to no experience. Two key developments changed medical education and then American medicine. First, the 1893 opening of the Johns Hopkins Medical School gave America its first first-rate medical education. Second, in 1910, Abraham Flexner completed a report that made clear just how second rate most medical education in the United States was. Hopkins, modeled on leading European medical schools, was an example to other schools; Flexner's report put those other schools, and their potential students and those students' future patients, on notice. Negative reviews, either by the American Medical Association or Flexner, drove schools out of business (Treber 2005), and American medicine eventually became a world leader. Scholars of HPE might consider how and why medical school reforms succeeded as lessons for other reform movements in all eras or areas.

The changes wrought by the Johns Hopkins Medical School and the Flexner Report had some unintended consequences. Physicians trained in more challenging schools were pulled more strongly to settle in urban areas (often with more hospitals), creating a rural-urban disparity in access to quality healthcare (Moehling et al. 2020). Such rural-urban healthcare disparities persist today, but do they play some role in the larger urban-rural political divide (Rodden 2019)? This era also saw the closure of the majority of Black medical schools; whether driven by Flexner, the AMA, or state boards, the reduction in the supply of Black physicians in an era of segregated medical care—and limited pathways for upward mobility for African Americans—complicates the history of medical "progress" (Savitt 2006; Miller and Weiss 2012).

Medical education was not the only institution that changed in the early twentieth century. Law and Kim (2005) study occupational licensing in the Progressive Era. Their findings suggest that asymmetric information drove the adoption of occupational licensing for physicians, nurses, and other "new" professions. Licensing for physicians (but not nurses) was also more likely in urban settings. Licensing could also have had important mortality effects. Anderson et al. (2020a) study the occupational licensing of midwives in the Progressive Era and find reductions in maternal mortality.

Health Insurance (Public and Private)

It is impossible to understand the unique structure of health insurance, both public and private, in the United States today without understanding its history. Scholars of the contemporary American healthcare system, especially those interested in policy and political economy questions, would be wise to include history and HPE in their research agendas.

Thomasson (2000; 2002) traces the history of the American system from 1900 to 1960. In the early decades of the twentieth century, demand for health insurance was low mostly because limited medical technology kept down the monetary costs of illness. The true costs of getting sick weren't medical treatment but lost income and wages. In the 1930s, as medical technology improved, costs grew; coupled with rising incomes, demand for health insurance emerged. However, Thomasson (2002) argues, the supply side was just as important. Hospitals innovated insurance as a way to smooth demand during the Great Depression and reduce competition; the plans were later combined into Blue Cross. Physicians, opposed generally to insurance but especially wary of the nationalized compulsory health insurance plans that had emerged in sixteen European countries by 1920, created their own insurance offering, Blue Shield. To scholars of HPE, the complex dynamics of hospitals, doctors, and state regulations that led to the Blues rather than nationalized health insurance is a rich area to study that will inform both HPE and contemporary health economics.

But American health insurance does not end with the Blues. The vast majority of Americans under age sixty-five who have private health insurance receive it through employers in group plans. Thomasson (2003) argues that this is the result of three historical factors. First, in 1942, the Stabilization Act to fight World War II–era inflation allowed employers to use fringe benefits like health insurance to draw workers. Second, while the Blues were nonprofits and had to community rate policies without differential pricing based on underlying health, employee groups allowed insurance companies to avoid adverse selection. Third, and as Thomasson (2003) suggests most importantly, as of 1943, tax policy made employer contributions to employee health plans tax-free.

Not until the Great Society did the large government-funded health insurance programs, Medicaid and Medicare, emerge. Recent work has traced the mortality effects of Great Society health programs like Medicaid and community health centers (Goodman-Bacon 2018; Bailey and Goodman-Bacon 2015). Extending this work toward political economy questions—what are the effects of the expansion of state health insurance on political attitudes, voting, and voters?—would be natural and illuminating.

Though federal, Medicaid, Medicare, and other public health insurance programs, both historically and today, have a vast amount of state-level variation in implementation. A different literature has tried to understand the political economy of the differences across states, starting with Barrilleaux and Miller (1988). Combining these political economy questions with a deeper focus on the history of these programs and their antecedents as in Thomasson's work could be quite productive.

Conclusion

From the late nineteenth century to the early twentieth century, death rates, especially from infectious diseases, declined and did so rapidly. The role of the American government—especially local but other levels as well—cannot be understated. What was the political economy behind the transition, and what were the political economic effects of the transition? This chapter posed this pair of questions about the history of health in the United States and provided some answers. But, as I hope I made clear, there are many avenues open for important future research in the HPE of health.

This future scholarship can inform our understanding of both political economy and health and mortality, historically and today. Future work should also push the HPE of health beyond the temporal and geographic limits of this chapter. What lessons are there beyond the borders of the United States and further back in time? Surely, some HPE findings are universal—every public policy, intervention, and investment has a political economy behind it—while others are likely US-specific. Understanding the political economy effects, in the short and the long run, of changes in health and mortality may require cross-country analysis. And questions about the inequality of health—about who is and is not included in public health efforts and whose lives are or are not saved—though they may take different forms in other places or periods, are, unfortunately, likely to reoccur.

Acknowledgments

I thank Mark Anderson, Philipp Ager, Brian Beach, Jacob Brown, Randy Ellis, Grant Goehring, Casper Worm Hansen, Lauren Hoehn-Velasco, Apoorva Lal, Bob Margo, Ross Mattheis, Soumyajit Mazumder, Christopher Muller, John Parman, Dan Rees, Gianluca Russo, Martin Saavedra, Orkun Saka, Hanna Schwank, Mark Shepard, Cory Smith, Marco Tabellini, Huiren Tan, Daniel Thompson, Tianyi Wang, Danielle Williamson, and Elizabeth Wrigley-Field for helpful comments and suggestions.

Notes

1. Costa (2015) traces parallel increases in adults' heights in at least the late nineteenth century. Height is a "measure of net nutritional status during growing years" that "depends on both nutritional intake and on nutritional demands, including those from disease, climate, and work."
2. Periods of rapid urbanization can complicate this correlation (Glaeser and Cutler 2021; Preston and Haines 1991).
3. At the individual level, many studies show the positive and negative long-run effects of good and bad health shocks. Almond (2006) and Bleakley (2007) are notable examples. Lleras-Muney (2005) goes the other direction, showing the large causal effect of education on mortality. At a more macro or aggregate level, scholars have studied the effects of health on the wealth of nations (Acemoglu and Johnson 2007; Well 2007; Ashraf, Lester, and Weil 2008; Alsan 2015).
4. This institutional argument is related to the ideas traced in Troesken (2015). However, Troesken suggests the institutional story is not quite so simple; he argues that the institutional forces that made American rich and economically dynamic in the nineteenth and early twentieth centuries also served, in some circumstances, to retard its ability to fight infectious diseases (including vaccination efforts and public goods problems).
5. The political economy story is even evident in the collection of health data itself. Haines (2006) documents the uneven, political order in which cities and states joined the unified national Death Registration Area to report their mortality data.
6. This is an area where social scientists could look more to historians. One recent important monograph is Golden (2018), which shows how babies shaped twentieth-century American society and culture, in part by connecting parents to new medical knowledge and technology in an era of plummeting infant mortality.
7. As shown in Figure 43.2a, in 1850, more than 2 white infants died for every 10 born (216.8 per 1,000 born), a rate that fell nearly in half by 1900 and then shrank to a quarter of the size by 1950. Life expectancy at older ages grew as well, as Figure 43.3 shows. The gains for women were larger than for men, driven in part by a rapid decrease in maternal mortality (Figure 43.2b).
8. I start with public health investments, the second era of mortality reduction that Cutler, Deaton, and Lleras-Muney (2006) trace rather than the first (nutrition and rising incomes). My reason is that the research that might intersect nutrition with HPE is more sparse, or—to put it more optimistically—primed for future important work.
9. Writing during the COVID-19 pandemic, we might also be tempted to draw lessons from the past, though without a deep understanding of the differences in context, these exercises can be fraught (Beach, Clay, and Saavedra 2020; Arthi and Parman 2021). Still, understanding both the political economic dimensions of a pandemic—how did (or did not) government respond and why—as well as the short- and long-run political consequences could be illuminating, as moments of crisis can reveal fundamental truths about people, society, and the state.
10. This is the dawn of the era, as Cutler, Deaton, and Lleras-Muney (2006) put it, of "big medicine." This is a very complex topic, so I focus on only two key aspects, mostly in the first half of the twentieth century: the medical profession (physicians and others) and health insurance (a short history of the political economy rationale for why the American healthcare system looks in most respects so vastly different from those in other countries).

11. While my focus in this chapter is on American public health interventions in the United States, the mortality consequences of bad water are global. For example, Antman (2022) exploits the rise of British tea drinking—and of boiling water—to estimate the effects of water quality on mortality in eighteenth-century England.
12. These interventions arose contemporaneously with a darker set of Progressive-Era public health measures, including eugenics, child separation, poorhouse reforms, slum clearance, and forced sterilizations. More work on where these policies came from and their short- and long-run effects is needed from HPE scholars.
13. Alsan and Goldin (2019) show significant declines in infant mortality from access to clean water and sewerage in nineteenth-century Massachusetts. Ferrie and Troesken (2008) study Chicago over the period from 1850 to 1925 and find 30 to 50 percent of the mortality reduction was caused by water purification. Cutler and Miller (2005) show large effects of cleaner water—via filtration and chlorination—on typhoid death rates in the first half of the twentieth century, the top waterborne killer of that era. Anderson, Charles, and Rees (2022) question the magnitudes of the Cutler and Miller (2005) results on total and infant mortality. See also Beach (2022) on the empirical challenge of estimating the effects of public health infrastructure that arrives in different cities in different orders and might have cumulative effects. Cleaning city water supplies had long-run effects, increasing adult earnings and educational attainment of treated children (Beach et al. 2016a).
14. Density is commonly reported as people per square mile or per square acre but this is "external" density. Internal density, likely more important for measuring crowding, relates the number of people per dwelling or per household.
15. For HPE scholars interested in the design and implementation of community-wide programs, Clay et al. (2020) study the Framingham Health and Tuberculosis Demonstration from 1917 to 1923, a community-wide health experiment that had limited effects on tuberculosis mortality.
16. Women gaining the vote increased the size and scope of government (Lott and Kenny 1999) and had effects on racial inequality (Carruthers and Wanamaker 2015)); women's suffrage also had effects in the long run (Kose, Kuka, and Shenhav 2021). See also the chapter on suffrage and HPE from Hanlon (2022) in this handbook.
17. The findings also deepen the puzzle in Troesken (2001), where, despite disenfranchisement, African Americans in southern cities do receive some access to water infrastructure.
18. I discuss Anderson, Charles, and Rees (2020b), which studies changes to racial inequality in infant mortality driven by the Civil Rights Act and Medicaid, in the next section. See also Bateman, Grumbach, and Thuston (2022) in this handbook on the intersection of race and HPE, especially their discussion of the effects of political institutions on racial inequality. Though their focus is more on economic inequality, health inequality is large, important, and potentially distinct.
19. Nelson (2011) documents the Black Panthers' public health efforts, which included raising awareness of the damaging effects of lead exposure.
20. Work by Karen Clay and coauthors (Clay and Troesken 2011; Clay, Lewis, and Severnini 2018) trace the interactions of pollution and pandemics.
21. The urbanization rate fell from 7.3 percent in 1810 to 7.2 percent in 1820. While only 15 percent of Americans were in urban areas in 1850, by 1900 it was 39.6 percent. In 1920, the urbanization rate broke 50 percent for the first time and today stands at 80.7 percent.
22. From 785 per 100,000 in 1894 to 1.1 per 100,000 in 1950 (Gordon 2017).
23. The Tuskegee Study, while striking, is sadly not unique. Markowitz and Rosner (2013) document a study conducted by researchers at Johns Hopkins on lead exposure in 108 Black

children. Skloot (2017) traced the use, without consent, of Henrietta Lacks's cell line in decades of medical research.
24. This is a growing literature on the importance of trust to health outcomes that exploits other medical mistreatment around the world (Lowes and Montero 2021; Martinez-Bravo and Stegmann 2021).
25. See Jedwab, Johnson, and Koyama (2022) and the references therein for a review of the social science literature on the Black Death, including its HPE. However, to keep this section focused, I primarily look at the literature on the 1918 influenza pandemic. The 1918 pandemic killed 50 million to 100 million people worldwide and between 550,000 and 850,000 in the United States. Though the origins are still not precisely understood, the flu was caused by a novel and highly contagious virus now known as H1N1. Unique to the 1918 pandemic, mortality was in a W shape: prime age adults who rarely die of influenza were at elevated risk, as were the very young and very old. For more detailed discussion of the 1918 pandemic and comparisons with the COVID-19 pandemic, see Beach, Clay, and Saavedra (2020). For more on the long-run human capital effects of pandemics (including 1918), see Arthi and Parman (2021).
26. The rapid development and deployment of mRNA vaccines within a year of the onset of the COVID-19 pandemic would have been impossible a decade ago, let alone a century ago.
27. Glaeser and Cutler (2021) trace the histories of quarantines to stop infectious disease at the borders of cities, countries, and communities from Athens in 430 BCE to today.
28. In light of the segregated residential patterns, and disparities in both medical access and baseline population health, interestingly NPIs seem no differentially effective for Whites and Blacks (Eiermann et al. 2021).
29. NPIs can have long-run consequences but in unexpected directions. Berkes et al. (2020) study the effects of NPIs during the 1918 pandemic on innovative activity and find no short-run effects on patenting. However, in the long run, cities with stricter NPIs actually patent more, perhaps because these cities used the NPIs to preserve local inventive factors in the face of the pandemic.
30. And the United States was not the only country hit by 1918. For example, Blickle (2020) studies the effects of 1918 influenza deaths on Nazi vote share in Weimar Germany.
31. Arroyo Abad and Maurer (2021) recount the story of the politicization of the 1793 yellow fever epidemic in Philadelphia with Republicans and Federalists squabbling over blame for the epidemic's origin and treatment.
32. As a starting point, see Starr (1982). One could also trace backward from differences today; for example, Ellis et al. (2014) compare health insurance across wealthy countries.
33. This brief history of medical education in the United States and its transformation in the late nineteenth and early twentieth centuries draws on Treber (2005); see Treber's dissertation, especially ch. 2, for more details. Gordon (2017) also describes the history of medical education.

References

Aassve, Arnstein, Guido Alfani, Francesco Gandolfi, and Marco Le Moglie. 2021. "Epidemics and Trust: The Case of the Spanish Flu." *Health Economics* 30: 840–57.
Acemoglu, Daron, and Simon Johnson. 2007. "Disease and Development: The Effect of Life Expectancy on Economic Growth." *Journal of Political Economy* 115: 925–85.

Achen, Christopher H., and Larry M. Bartels. 2004. "Blind Retrospection: Electoral Responses to Drought, Flu, and Shark Attacks." Technical report, Estudio Working Paper 199.

Achen, Christopher, and Larry Bartels. 2017. *Democracy for Realists*. Princeton, NJ: Princeton University Press.

Ager, Philipp, Katherine Eriksson, Ezra Karger, Peter Nencka, and Melissa A Thomasson. 2020a. "School Closures during the 1918 Flu Pandemic." Technical report, National Bureau of Economic Research.

Ager, Philipp, James J. Feigenbaum, Casper Worm Hansen, and Hui Ren Tan. 2020b. "How the Other Half Died: Immigration and Mortality in US Cities." Technical report, National Bureau of Economic Research.

Aizer, Anna, and Janet Currie. 2019. "Lead and Juvenile Delinquency: New Evidence from Linked Birth, School, and Juvenile Detention Records." *Review of Economics and Statistics* 101: 575–87.

Aksoy, Cevat Giray, Barry Eichengreen, and Orkun Saka. 2020. "The Political Scar of Epidemics." NBER Working Paper Version. https://www.nber.org/papers/w27401.

Almond, Douglas. 2006. " Is the 1918 Influenza Pandemic Over? Long-Term Effects of In Utero Influenza Exposure in the Post-1940 US Population." *Journal of Political Economy* 114: 672–712.

Alsan, Marcella. 2015. "The Effect of the Tsetse Fly on African Development." *American Economic Review* 105: 382–410.

Alsan, Marcella, and Claudia Goldin. 2019. "Watersheds in Child Mortality: The Role of Effective Water and Sewerage Infrastructure, 1880–1920." *Journal of Political Economy* 127: 586–638.

Alsan, Marcella, and Marianne Wanamaker. 2018. "Tuskegee and the Health of Black Men." *Quarterly Journal of Economics* 133: 407–55.

Ambrus, Attila, Erica Field, and Robert Gonzalez. 2020. "Loss in the Time of Cholera: Long-Run Impact of a Disease Epidemic on the Urban Landscape." *American Economic Review* 110: 475–525.

Anderson, D. Mark, Ryan Brown, Kerwin Kofi Charles, and Daniel I. Rees. 2020a. "Occupational Licensing and Maternal Health: Evidence from Early Midwifery Laws." *Journal of Political Economy* 128: 4337–83.

Anderson, D. Mark, Kerwin Kofi Charles, Claudio Las Heras Olivares, and Daniel I. Rees. 2019. "Was the First Public Health Campaign Successful?" *American Economic Journal: Applied Economics* 11: 143–75.

Anderson, D. Mark, Kerwin Kofi Charles, and Daniel I. Rees. 2020b. "The Federal Effort to Desegregate Southern Hospitals and the Black-White Infant Mortality Gap." Technical report, National Bureau of Economic Research.

Anderson, D. Mark, Kerwin Kofi Charles, and Daniel I. Rees. 2022. "Re-Examining the Contribution of Public Health Efforts to the Decline in Urban Mortality." *American Economic Journal: Applied Economics* 14, no. 2: 126–57.

Aneja, Abhay, and Carlos F. Avenancio-Leon. 2019. "The Effect of Political Power on Labor Market Inequality: Evidence from the 1965 Voting Rights Act." Unpublished Working Paper. https://equitablegrowth.org/working-papers/the-effect-of-political-power-on-labor-market-inequality-evidence-from-the-1965-voting-rights-act/.

Ang, Desmond. 2019. "Do 40-Year-Old Facts Still Matter? Long-Run Effects of Federal Oversight under the Voting Rights Act." *American Economic Journal: Applied Economics* 11: 1–53.

Antman, Francisca M. 2022. "For Want of a Cup: The Rise of Tea in England and the Impact of Water Quality on Mortality." *Review of Economics and Statistics* : 1–45. https://doi.org/10.1162/rest_a_01158.

Armstrong, Gregory L., Laura A. Conn, and Robert W. Pinner. 1999. "Trends in Infectious Disease Mortality in the United States during the 20th Century." *JAMA* 281: 61–66.

Arroyo Abad, Leticia, and Noel Maurer. 2021. "Do Pandemics Shape Elections? Retrospective Voting in the 1918 Spanish Flu Pandemic in the United States." Technical report, CEPR Discussion Paper No. DP15678.

Arthi, Vellore, and John Parman. 2021. "Disease, Downturns, and Well-Being: Economic History and the Long-Run Impacts of COVID-19." *Explorations in Economic History* 79: 101381.

Ashraf, Quamrul H., Ashley Lester, and David N. Weil. 2008. "When Does Improving Health Raise GDP?" *NBER Macroeconomics Annual* 23: 157–204.

Bailey, Martha J., and Andrew Goodman-Bacon. 2015. "The War on Poverty's Experiment in Public Medicine: Community Health Centers and the Mortality of Older Americans." *American Economic Review* 105: 1067–104.

Bailey, Roy E., Timothy J. Hatton, and Kris Inwood. 2018. "Atmospheric Pollution, Health, and Height in Late-Nineteenth-Century Britain." *Journal of Economic History* 78: 1210–47.

Bailey, Zinzi D., Justin M. Feldman, and Mary T. Bassett. 2021. "How Structural Racism Works—Racist Policies as a Root Cause of US Racial Health Inequities." *New England Journal of Medicine* 384: 768–73.

Barreca, Alan, Karen Clay, and Joel Tarr. 2014. "Coal, Smoke, and Death: Bituminous Coal and American HomeH." Technical report, National Bureau of Economic Research.

Barrilleaux, Charles J., and Mark E. Miller. 1988. "The Political Economy of State Medicaid Policy." *American Political Science Review* 82: 1089–107.

Barro, Robert J. 2020. "Non-Pharmaceutical Interventions and Mortality in US Cities during the Great Influenza Pandemic, 1918–1919." Technical report, National Bureau of Economic Research.

Bazzi, Samuel, Martin Fiszbein, and Mesay Gebresilasse. 2020. "Frontier Culture: The Roots and Persistence of Rugged Individualism in the United States." *Econometrica* 88: 2329–68.

Beach, Brian. 2022. "Water Infrastructure and Health in U.S. Cities." *Regional Science and Urban Economics* 94: 1–9.

Beach, Brian, Karen Clay, and Martin H Saavedra. 2020. "The 1918 Influenza Pandemic and Its lessons for COVID-19." Technical report, National Bureau of Economic Research.

Beach, Brian, Joseph Ferrie, Martin Saavedra, and Werner Troesken. 2016a. "Typhoid Fever, Water Quality, and Human Capital Formation." *Journal of Economic History* 76: 41–75.

Beach, Brian, and W. Walker Hanlon. 2018. "Coal Smoke and Mortality in an Early Industrial Economy." *Economic Journal* 128: 2652–75.

Beach, Brian, John Parman, and Martin Saavedra. 2022. "Segregation and the Initial Provision of Water in the United States." AEA Papers and Proceedings 112.

Beach, Brian, Werner Troesken, and Nicola Tynan. 2016b. "Who Should Own and Control Urban Water Systems? Historical Evidence from England and Wales." Technical report, National Bureau of Economic Research.

Berkes, Enrico, Olivier Deschenes, Ruben Gaetani, Jeffrey Lin, and Christopher Severen. 2020. "Lockdowns and Innovation: Evidence from the 1918 Flu Pandemic." Technical report, National Bureau of Economic Research.

Billings, Stephen B., and Kevin T. Schnepel. 2018. "Life after Lead: Effects of Early Interventions for Children Exposed to Lead." *American Economic Journal: Applied Economics* 10: 315–44.

Bleakley, Hoyt. 2007. "Disease and Development: Evidence from Hookworm Eradication in the American South." *Quarterly Journal of Economics* 122: 73–117.

Blickle, Kristian. 2020. "Pandemics Change Cities: Municipal Spending and Voter Extremism in Germany, 1918–1933." Technical report, Federal Reserve Bank of New York Staff Report No. 921.

Bootsma, Martin C. J., and Neil M. Ferguson. 2007. "The Effect of Public Health Measures on the 1918 Influenza Pandemic in US Cities." *Proceedings of the National Academy of Sciences* 104: 7588–93.

Boustan, Leah Platt, and Robert A. Margo. 2015. "Racial Differences in Health in the United States: A Long-Run Perspective." *The Oxford Handbook of Economics and Human Biology*, ed. John Komlos and Inas Kelly, 730–50. Oxford, UK: Oxford University Press.

Campante, Filipe R., Emilio Depetris-Chauvin, and Ruben Durante. 2020. "The Virus of Fear: The Political Impact of Ebola in the US." Technical report, National Bureau of Economic Research.

Carpenter, Daniel. 2014. *Reputation and Power*. Princeton, NJ: Princeton University Press.

Carruthers, Celeste K., and Marianne H. Wanamaker. 2015. "Municipal Housekeeping: The Impact of Women's Suffrage on Public Education." *Journal of Human Resources* 50: 837–72.

Carter, Susan B., Scott S. Gartner, Michael R. Haines, Alan L. Olmstead, Richard Sutch, and Gavin Wright. 2006. *Historical Statistics of the United States: Millennial Edition*, Volume 3. Cambridge: Cambridge University Press.

Cascio, Elizabeth U., and Ebonya Washington. 2014. "Valuing the Vote: The Redistribution of Voting Rights and State Funds following the Voting Rights Act of 1965." *Quarterly Journal of Economics* 129: 379–433.

Chapelle, Guillaume. 2021. "The Medium-Run Impact of Non-Pharmaceutical Interventions: Evidence from the 1918 Flu in US Cities." https://cepr.org/content/covid-economics-vetted-and-real-time-papers-0.

Clay, Karen, Peter Juul Egedesø, Casper Worm Hansen, Peter Sandholt Jensen, and Avery Calkins. 2020. "Controlling Tuberculosis? Evidence from the First Community-Wide Health Experiment." *Journal of Development Economics* 146: 102510.

Clay, Karen, Joshua Lewis, and Edson Severnini. 2016. "Canary in a Coal Mine: Infant Mortality, Property Values, and Tradeoffs Associated with Mid-20th-Century Air Pollution." Technical report, National Bureau of Economic Research.

Clay, Karen, Joshua Lewis, and Edson Severnini. 2018. "Pollution, Infectious Disease, and Mortality: Evidence from the 1918 Spanish Influenza Pandemic." *Journal of Economic History* 78: 1179–209.

Clay, Karen, and Werner Troesken. 2011. "Did Frederick Brodie Discover the World's First Environmental Kuznets Curve?" *The Econmoics of Climate Change: Adaptations Past and Present*, ed. Gary D. Libecap and Richard H. Steckel, 281–309. Chicago, IL: University of Chicago Press.

Clay, Karen, Werner Troesken, and Michael Haines. 2014. "Lead and Mortality." *Review of Economics and Statistics* 96: 458–70.

Cook, Lisa D., Trevon D. Logan, and John M. Parman. 2016. "The Mortality Consequences of Distinctively Black Names." *Explorations in Economic History* 59: 114–25.

Correia, Sergio, Stephan Luck, and Emil Verner. 2020. "Pandemics Depress the Economy, Public Health Interventions Do Not: Evidence from the 1918 Flu." SSRN Working Paper. Available at: https://papers.ssrn.com/sol3/papers.cfm?abstract_id=3561560.

Costa, Dora L. 2015. "Health and the Economy in the United States from 1750 to the Present." *Journal of Economic Literature* 53: 503–70.

Costa, Dora L., and Matthew E. Kahn. 2015. "Declining Mortality Inequality within Cities during the Health Transition." *American Economic Review* 105: 564–69.

Currie, Janet. 2011. "Inequality at Birth: Some Causes and Consequences." *American Economic Review* 101: 1–22.

Cutler, David, Angus Deaton, and Adriana Lleras-Muney. 2006. "The Determinants of Mortality." *Journal of Economic Perspectives* 20: 97–120.

Cutler, David, and Grant Miller. 2005. "The Role of Public Health Improvements in Health Advances: The Twentieth-Century United States." *Demography* 42: 1–22.

Deaton, Angus. 2013. *The Great Escape: Health, Wealth, and the Origins of Inequality*. Princeton, NJ: Princeton University Press.

de Tocqueville, Alexis. 2000. *Democracy in America*, edited and translated by Harvey C. Mansfield and Delba Winthrop. Chicago: University of Chicago Press.

Du Bois, William Edward Burghardt. 1906. *The Health and Physique of the Negro American: Report of a Social Study Made under the Direction of Atlanta University, Together with the Proceedings of the Eleventh Conference for the Study of the Negro Problems, Held at Atlanta University, on May the 29th, 1906*. Atlanta: Atlanta University Press.

Eiermann, Martin, Elizabeth Wrigley-Field, James J. Feigenbaum, Jonas Helgertz, Elaine Hernandez, and Courtney E. Boen. 2021. "Racial Disparities in Mortality during the 1918 Influenza Pandemic in United States Cities." Technical report, SocArXiv.

Ellis, Randall P., Tianxu Chen, and Calvin E. Luscombe. 2014. "Comparisons of Health Insurance Systems in Developed Countries." *Encyclopedia of Health Economics*, ed. Anthony Culyer, 396–406. Amsterdam: Elsevier Science.

Eriksson, Katherine, Peter Z. Lin, and Gregory Niemesh. 2020. "Immigration and Infant Mortality in Massachusetts: Evidence from the Age of Mass Migration." Technical report. Available at: http://kaeriksson.ucdavis.edu/uploads/6/0/6/7/60676749/ma_mortality_paper.pdf.

Feigenbaum, James, Lauren Hoehn-Velasco, and Elizabeth Wrigley-Field. 2020. "Did the Urban Mortality Penalty Disappear? Revisiting the Early Twentieth Century's Urban-Rural Mortality Convergence." MPC Series, Working Paper No. 2020-09. https://doi.org/10.18128/MPC2020-09.

Feigenbaum, James J., Lauren Hoehn-Velasco, Christopher Muller, and Elizabeth Wrigley-Field. 2022. "1918 Every Year: Racial Inequality in Infectious Mortality, 1900–1942." *AEA Papers and Proceedings* 112: 199–204.

Feigenbaum, James J., and Christopher Muller. 2016. "Lead Exposure and Violent Crime in the Early Twentieth Century." *Explorations in Economic History* 62: 51–86.

Feigenbaum, James J., Christopher Muller, and Elizabeth Wrigley-Field. 2019. "Regional and Racial Inequality in Infectious Disease Mortality in U.S. Cities, 1900–1948." *Demography* 56: 1371–88.

Ferrie, Joseph P., Karen Rolf, and Werner Troesken. 2012. "Cognitive Disparities, Lead Plumbing, and Water Chemistry: Prior Exposure to Water-Borne Lead and Intelligence Test Scores among World War Two US Army Enlistees." *Economics & Human Biology* 10: 98–111.

Ferrie, Joseph P., and Werner Troesken. 2008. "Water and Chicago's Mortality Transition, 1850–1925." *Explorations in Economic History* 45: 1–16.

Fishback, Price V., Michael R. Haines, and Shawn Kantor. 2001. "The Impact of the New Deal on Black and White Infant Mortality in the South." *Explorations in Economic History* 38: 93–122.

Fishback, Price V., Michael R. Haines, and Shawn Kantor. 2007. "Births, Deaths, and New Deal Relief during the Great Depression." *Review of Economics and Statistics* 89: 1–14.

Floud, Roderick, Robert W. Fogel, Bernard Harris, and Sok Chul Hong. 2011. *The Changing Body: Health, Nutrition, and Human Development in the Western World since 1700*. Cambridge, UK: Cambridge University Press.

Fogel, Robert W. 2004. *The Escape from Hunger and Premature Death, 1700–2100: Europe, America, and the Third World*. Cambridge: Cambridge University Press.

Galiani, Sebastian, Paul Gertler, and Ernesto Schargrodsky. 2005. "Water for Life: The Impact of the Privatization of Water Services on Child Mortality." *Journal of Political Economy* 113: 83–120.

Gamm, Gerald, and Thad Kousser. 2021. "Life, Literacy, and the Pursuit of Prosperity: Party Competition and Policy Outcomes in 50 States." *American Political Science Review* 115: 1442–63.

Gimpel, James G., Nathan Lovin, Bryant Moy, and Andrew Reeves. 2020. "The Urban-Rural Gulf in American Political Behavior." *Political Behavior* 42: 1343–68.

Glaeser, Edward. 2011. *Triumph of the City: How Urban Spaces Make Us Human*. London: Pan Macmillan.

Glaeser, Edward, and David Cutler. 2021. *Survival of the City: Living and Thriving in an Age of Isolation*. New York: Penguin.

Golden, Janet. 2018. *Babies Made Us Modern: How Infants Brought America into the Twentieth Century*. Cambridge, England: Cambridge University Press.

Goodman-Bacon, Andrew. 2018. "Public Insurance and Mortality: Evidence from Medicaid Implementation." *Journal of Political Economy* 126: 216–62.

Gordon, Robert J. 2017. *The Rise and Fall of American Growth*. Princeton, NJ: Princeton University Press.

Grigoryeva, Angelina, and Martin Ruef. 2015. "The Historical Demography of Racial Segregation." *American Sociological Review* 80: 814–42.

Haines, Michael R. 2001. "The Urban Mortality Transition in the United States, 1800–1940." *Annales de Demographie Historiqué* 101: 33–64.

Haines, Michael R. 2006. "Vital Statistics." In *Historical Statistics of the United States, Volume 1: Population*, ed. Susan B. Carter, Scott Sigmund Gartner, Michael R. Haines, Alan L. Olmstead, Richard Sutch, and Gavin Wright, 1-381 to 1-390. Cambridge, UK: Cambridge University Press.

Hanlon, W. Walker, and Stephan Heblich. 2021. "History and Urban Economics." *Regional Science and Urban Economics* 94: 1–18.

Hatchett, Richard J., Carter E. Mecher, and Marc Lipsitch. 2007. "Public Health Interventions and Epidemic Intensity during the 1918 Influenza Pandemic." *Proceedings of the National Academy of Sciences* 104: 7582–87.

Heblich, Stephan, Alex Trew, and Yanos Zylberberg. 2021. "East-Side Story: Historical Pollution and Persistent Neighborhood Sorting." *Journal of Political Economy* 129: 1508–52.

Higgs, Robert. 1987. *Crisis and Leviathan*. New York: Oxford University Press.

Hilt, Eric, and Wendy Rahn. 2020. "Financial Asset Ownership and Political Partisanship: Liberty Bonds and Republican Electoral Success in the 1920s." *Journal of Economic History* 80: 746–81.

Hoehn-Velasco, Lauren. 2018. "Explaining Declines in US Rural Mortality, 1910–1933: The Role of County Health Departments." *Explorations in Economic History* 70: 42–72.

Hoehn-Velasco, Lauren. 2020. "The Historical Roots of Local Public Finance and the Provision of Public Health, 1900–1930." Working Paper. Available at: https://drive.google.com/file/d/1JZIjRIQ8fQzJcMOVyE-75JMcxOJLocvN/view.

Hoehn-Velasco, Lauren, and Elizabeth Wrigley-Field. 2021. "City Health Departments, Public Health Expenditures, and Urban Mortality over 1910–1940." *Economic Inquiry* 60, no. 2: 929–953.

Jedwab, Remi, Noel D. Johnson, and Mark Koyama. 2022. "The Economic Impact of the Black Death." *Journal of Economic Literature* 60: 132–78.

Kesztenbaum, Lionel, and Jean-Laurent Rosenthal. 2017. "Sewers' Diffusion and the Decline of Mortality: The Case of Paris, 1880–1914." *Journal of Urban Economics* 98: 174–86.

Kose, Esra, Elira Kuka, and Na'ama Shenhav. 2021. "Women's Suffrage and Children's Education." *American Economic Journal: Economic Policy* 13: 374–405.

Kraut, Alan M. 1995. *Silent Travelers: Germs, Genes, and the Immigrant Menace*. Baltimore, MD: Johns Hopkins University Press.

Law, Marc T., and Sukkoo Kim. 2005. "Specialization and Regulation: The Rise of Professionals and the Emergence of Occupational Licensing Regulation." *Journal of Economic History* 65: 723–56.

Lilley, Andrew, Matthew Lilley, and Gianluca Rinaldi. 2020. "Public Health Interventions and Economic Growth: Revisiting the Spanish Flu Evidence." Available at SSRN: https://papers.ssrn.com/sol3/papers.cfm?abstract_id=3590008.

Lleras-Muney, Adriana. 2005. "The Relationship between Education and Adult Mortality in the United States." *Review of Economic Studies* 72: 189–221.

Logan, Trevon D. 2020. "Do Black Politicians Matter? Evidence from Reconstruction." *Journal of Economic History* 80: 1–37.

Logan, Trevon D., and John M. Parman. 2017. "The National Rise in Residential Segregation." *Journal of Economic History* 77: 127–70.

Lott, John R., Jr., and Lawrence W. Kenny. 1999. "Did Women's Suffrage Change the Size and Scope of Government?" *Journal of Political Economy* 107: 1163–98.

Lowes, Sara, and Eduardo Montero. 2021. "The Legacy of Colonial Medicine in Central Africa." *American Economic Review* 111: 1284–314.

Mansour, Hani, Daniel I. Rees, and James M. Reeves. 2020. "Voting and Political Participation in the Aftermath of the HIV/AIDS Epidemic." Technical report, National Bureau of Economic Research.

Margo, Robert A. 2016. "Obama, Katrina, and the Persistence of Racial Inequality." *Journal of Economic History* 76: 301–41.

Markel, Howard, Harvey B. Lipman, J. Alexander Navarro, Alexandra Sloan, Joseph R. Michalsen, Alexandra Minna Stern, and Martin S. Cetron. 2007. "Nonpharmaceutical Interventions Implemented by US Cities during the 1918–1919 Influenza Pandemic." *JAMA* 298: 644–54.

Markel, Howard, and Alexandra Minna Stern. 2002. "The Foreignness of Germs: The Persistent Association of Immigrants and Disease in American Society." *Milbank Quarterly* 80: 757–88.

Markowitz, Gerald, and David Rosner. 2013. *Lead Wars*. Oakland, CA: University of California Press.

Martinez-Bravo, Monica, and Andreas Stegmann. 2021. "In Vaccines We Trust? The Effects of the CIA's Vaccine Ruse on Immunization in Pakistan." *Journal of the European Economic Association* 20, no. 1: 150–86.

Melosi, Martin V. 1999. *The Sanitary City: Urban Infrastructure in America from Colonial Times to the Present*. Baltimore, MD: Johns Hopkins University Press.

Meyers, Keith, and Melissa A. Thomasson. 2021. "Can Pandemics Affect Educational Attainment? Evidence from the Polio Epidemic of 1916." *Cliometrica* 15: 231–65.

Miller, Grant. 2008. "Women's Suffrage, Political Responsiveness, and Child Survival in American History." *Quarterly Journal of Economics* 123: 1287–327.

Miller, Lynn E., and Richard M. Weiss. 2012. "Revisiting Black Medical School Extinctions in the Flexner Era." *Journal of the History of Medicine and Allied Sciences* 67: 217–43.

Moehling, Carolyn M., Gregory T. Niemesh, Melissa A. Thomasson, and Jaret Treber. 2020. "Medical Education Reforms and the Origins of the Rural Physician Shortage." *Cliometrica* 14: 181–225.

Moehling, Carolyn M., and Melissa A. Thomasson. 2012. "The Political Economy of Saving Mothers and Babies: The Politics of State Participation in the Sheppard-Towner Program." *Journal of Economic History* 72: 75–103.

Muller, Christopher, Robert J. Sampson, and Alix S. Winter. 2018. "Environmental Inequality: The Social Causes and Consequences of Lead Exposure." *Annual Review of Sociology* 44: 263–82.

Murphy, Kevin M., and Robert H. Topel. 2006. "The Value of Health and Longevity." *Journal of Political Economy* 114: 871–904.

Nelson, Alondra. 2011. *Body and Soul: The Black Panther Party and the Fight against Medical Discrimination*. Minneapolis: University of Minnesota Press.

Nielsen, Carrie. 2021. *Unleaded: How Changing Our Gasoline Changed Everything*. New Brunswick, NJ: Rutgers University Press.

Oeppen, Jim, and James W. Vaupel. 2002. "Broken Limits to Life Expectancy." *Science* 296, no. 5570: 1029–31.

Preston, Samuel H. 1975. "The Changing Relation between Mortality and Level of Economic Development." *Population Studies* 29: 231–48.

Preston, Samuel H., and Michael R. Haines. 1991. *Fatal Years: Child Mortality in Late Nineteenth-Century America*. Princeton, NJ: Princeton University Press.

Reyes, Jessica Wolpaw. 2007. "Environmental Policy as Social Policy? The Impact of Childhood Lead Exposure on Crime." *BE Journal of Economic Analysis & Policy* 7, no. 1: 1–41.

Riis, Jacob A. 1890. *How the Other Half Lives: Studies among the Tenements of New York*. New York: Scribner's Books.

Rodden, Jonathan A. 2019. *Why Cities Lose: The Deep Roots of the Urban-Rural Political Divide*. New York: Basic Books.

Saavedra, Martin. 2017. "Early-Life Disease Exposure and Occupational Status: The Impact of Yellow Fever during the 19th Century." *Explorations in Economic History* 64: 62–81.

Savitt, Todd. 2006. "Abraham Flexner and the Black Medical Schools. 1992." *Journal of the National Medical Association* 98: 1415–24.

Sen, Amartya. 1999. *Development as Freedom*. New York: Alfred A. Knopf.

Shah, Nayan. 2001. *Contagious Divides: Epidemics and Race in San Francisco's Chinatown*. Oakland, CA: University of California Press.

Shertzer, Allison, Tate Twinam, and Randall P. Walsh. 2016. "Race, Ethnicity, and Discriminatory Zoning." *American Economic Journal: Applied Economics* 8: 217–46.

Skloot, Rebecca. 2017. *The Immortal Life of Henrietta Lacks*. New York: Broadway Paperbacks.

Starr, Paul. 1982. *The Social Transformation of American Medicine*. New York: Basic Books.

Steckel, Richard. 2006. "Health, Nutrition and Physical Well-Being." In *Historical Statistics of the United States, Volume 1: Population*, ed. Susan B. Carter, Scott Sigmund Gartner, Michael R. Haines, Alan L. Olmstead, Richard Sutch, and Gavin Wright, 499–620. Cambridge University Press.

Thomasson, Melissa A. 2000. "From Sickness to Health. The Twentieth-Century Development of the Demand for Health Insurance." *Journal of Economic History* 60: 504–8.

Thomasson, Melissa A. 2002. "From Sickness to Health: The Twentieth-Century Development of US Health Insurance." *Explorations in Economic History* 39: 233–53.

Thomasson, Melissa A. 2003. "The Importance of Group Coverage: How Tax Policy Shaped US Health Insurance." *American Economic Review* 93: 1373–84.

Thomasson, Melissa A., and Jaret Treber. 2008. "From Home to Hospital: The Evolution of Childbirth in the United States, 1928–1940." *Explorations in Economic History* 45: 76–99.

Treber, Jaret Scott. 2005. *From Lancets to Laboratories: Medical Schools, Physicians, and Healthcare in the United States from 1870 to 1940*. Dissertation, The University of Arizona. https://repository.arizona.edu/handle/10150/194977.

Troesken, Werner. 1999. "Typhoid Rates and the Public Acquisition of Private Waterwork, 1880–1920." *Journal of Economic History* 59: 927–48.

Troesken, Werner. 2001. "Race, Disease, and the Provision of Water in American Cities, 1889–1921." *Journal of Economic History* 61: 750–76.

Troesken, Werner. 2004. *Water, Race, and Disease*. Cambridge, MA: MIT Press.

Troesken, Werner. 2015. *The Pox of Liberty*. Chicago: University of Chicago Press.

Velde, Francois R. 2020. "What Happened to the US Economy during the 1918 Influenza Pandemic? A View through High-Frequency Data." Technical report, Federal Reserve Bank of Chicago Working Paper.

Wallis, John Joseph. 2000. "American Government Finance in the Long Run: 1790 to 1990." *Journal of Economic Perspectives* 14: 61–82.

Wallis, John Joseph. 2010. "Lessons from the Political Economy of the New Deal." *Oxford Review of Economic Policy* 26: 442–62.

Wallis, John Joseph, Price V. Fishback, and Shawn E. Kantor. 2005. "Politics, Relief, and Reform: The Transformation of America's Social Welfare System during the New Deal." NBER Working Paper. Available at: https://www.nber.org/papers/w11080.

Weil, David N. 2015. "A Review of Angus Deaton's The Great Escape: Health, Wealth, and the Origins of Inequality." *Journal of Economic Literature* 53: 102–14.

Well, David N. 2007. "Accounting for the Effect of Health on Economic Growth." *Quarterly Journal of Economics* 122: 1265–306.

Wodtke, Geoffrey, Sagi Ramaj, and Jared Schachner. 2020. "Toxic Neighborhoods: The Joint Effects of Concentrated Poverty and Environmental Lead Contamination on Cognitive Development during Early Childhood." SocArXiv. doi:10.31235/osf.io/mv9d7.

Xu, Guo. 2021. "Bureaucratic Representation and State Responsiveness during Times of Crisis: The 1918 Pandemic in India." *Review of Economics and Statistics*: 1–29. https://doi.org/10.1162/rest_a_01060.

Zelner, Jonathan L., Christopher Muller, and James J. Feigenbaum. 2017. "Racial Inequality in the Annual Risk of Tuberculosis Infection in the United States, 1910–1933." *Epidemiology & Infection* 145: 1797–804.

CHAPTER 44

CULTURE IN HISTORICAL POLITICAL ECONOMY

SARA LOWES

Introduction

SOCIETIES differ greatly in their economic outcomes; they also vary in the types of values and beliefs people hold. A large literature has established that cultural beliefs—that is, those beliefs that are socially learned and transmitted—have important implications for a wide variety of economic outcomes, such as preferences over policy, trust, economic development, institutional development, cooperation, and conflict.

There is substantial variation within and across countries in cultural values and beliefs (Desmet, Ortuño-Ortín, and Wacziarg 2017; Falk et al. 2018). Understanding culture and what drives variation in culture is important. Culture shapes key development outcomes such as growth and conflict. It also helps us understand why individuals hold different values and how this is linked to their economic behavior. Finally, an understanding of culture may help improve the efficacy of policymaking.

As interest in the role of culture for shaping economic outcomes has grown, so has work exploring the origins and consequences of various cultural traits. Much of this work falls in the realm of historical political economy (HPE)—understanding from a historical perspective what shapes culture and how it changes over time, as well as linking historical cultural traits to present-day outcomes.

HPE has much to contribute to our understanding of cultural dynamics. This is for two reasons. First, processes involving culture—including cultural change and persistence—necessarily unfold over time. Thus, a historical perspective allows us to observe these processes across a variety of settings. Second, history also provides opportunities to gain traction on the difficult problem of the identification of causal effects of culture. Given that culture is determined by a wide variety of factors, including ecology, institutions, and historical events, a historical perspective generates natural experiments to help address causality.

The work on culture in HPE can be organized into two overarching questions: First, what explains variation in culture? Second, what are the economic consequences of differences in culture? Research in HPE has studied many cultural traits, such as religiosity, gender norms, trust, rule following, and norms of cooperation. The work on the origins of cultural traits has focused on how cultural traits have been shaped by factors such as the ecological environment, institutions, conflict, and colonial rule. Likewise, work on the effects of culture covers many important economic consequences of culture, such as economic growth, investments in education, political preferences, and income. The work varies in its scope and its approach to identifying the causal effects of culture. The extent to which culture is an important subject of study in HPE is evidenced by the number of chapters in this handbook that explore various facets of culture—for example, historical persistence (Acharya, Blackwell, and Sen 2023), assimilation (Fouka 2023), gender (Teele and Grosjean 2023), identity (Suryanarayan and White 2023), and religion (Becker and Pfaff 2023).

This chapter is organized as follows. First, I introduce various definitions of culture that have been used in the related literature. Second, I discuss influential models that highlight the role of culture, how culture is transmitted, and the dynamics of cultural persistence and change. Finally, I discuss some of the rich empirical literature from HPE examining the origins of cultural variation and the effects of culture.

Definition of Culture

There are various ways of conceptualizing culture. Guiso, Sapienza, and Zingales (2006) define culture "as those customary beliefs and values that ethnic, religious, and social groups transmit fairly unchanged from generation to generation." A related definition from Huntington (2000, xv) describes culture "as the values, attitudes, beliefs, orientations, and underlying assumptions prevalent among people in a society." These conceptualizations emphasize the sticky and slow-moving nature of culture.

Greif (1994), in his work on Genoese and Maghribi traders, defines culture as determinate social equilibria. He focuses on rational cultural beliefs that capture individuals' expectations with respect to actions that others will take in various situations. In distinguishing culture from strategies, he writes, "Past cultural beliefs provide focal points and coordinate expectations, thereby influencing equilibrium selection and society's enforcement institutions" (Greif 1994, 914). Thus, culture serves as a type of coordination device and has important implications for institutional development.

Acemoglu and Robinson (2021, 2) define culture as "historically transmitted patterns of beliefs, relationships, rituals, attitudes and obligations that furnish meaning to human interactions and provide a framework for interpreting the world, coordinating expectations and enabling or constraining behaviors." The authors contrast their definition with previous definitions, such as Guiso, Sapienza, and Zingales's (2006), by emphasizing that culture can be fluid, is not necessarily coherent, and is adaptable. They cite work in sociology, which defines culture as "a 'toolkit' or repertoire from which actors select differing pieces for constructing lines of action. Both individuals and groups know how to do different kinds of things in different circumstances" (Swidler 1986, 277). Acemoglu and Robinson (2021) highlight the definition of sociologist DiMaggio (1997, 265): "once we acknowledge that people behave as if they use culture strategically, it follows that the cultures into which people are socialized leave much opportunity for choice and variation." These definitions emphasize the adaptable nature of culture.

Much of the work on culture in economics has been influenced by the definition of culture operationalized in evolutionary anthropology. Works by Boyd and Richerson (1985) and Richerson and Boyd (2005) define culture as "information capable of affecting individuals' behavior that they acquire from other members of their species through teaching, imitation, and other forms of social transmission." This definition emphasizes the social learning aspect of culture. In this conceptualization, culture is information that is learned from elders or peers. One way to think about this conceptualization of culture is that culture provides a heuristic, or a mental shortcut, for choosing the optimal action in a particular situation. Previous generations share that information with subsequent generations, thus allowing individuals to engage in other productive tasks, rather than having to experiment to figure out the right choice (Nunn 2022).

Theories of Culture, Cultural Transmission, and Cultural Change

Cultural Transmission

Evolutionary approaches to culture (e.g., Boyd and Richerson 1985; Richerson and Boyd 2005) are useful and tractable frameworks that help clarify how culture may be efficient and highlight the cumulative nature of human knowledge (Muthukrishna and Henrich 2016; Nunn 2021). The evolutionary approach emphasizes that culture contains knowledge that is transmitted to subsequent generations, and thus differs from the definition from Guiso, Sapienza, and Zingales (2006), which emphasizes values. Nunn (2021) discusses the relationship between human capital formation and culture; he argues that conceptually economists' perception of human capital formation is quite similar to the notion of culture as understood in evolutionary anthropology.

There have been various efforts to formalize how culture is formed and how it is transmitted. Early theoretical contributions from Cavalli-Sforza and Feldman (1981) and Boyd and Richerson (1985) use models from evolutionary biology but apply them to the transmission of cultural traits. In a series of papers, Bisin and Verdier (2000; 2001) build on these previous models by allowing for parental socialization, so that children's preferences depend on their parents' socialization actions. Their insight is that parents have preferences over the cultural traits acquired by their children. They model parental socialization choice with imperfect empathy: "a form of altruism biased towards the parents' own cultural traits: parents care about their children's choices, but they evaluate them using their own preferences" (Bisin and Verdier 2011, 343). Bisin and Verdier (2001) predict that cultural heterogeneity exists when direct vertical socialization is a substitute for horizontal socialization. Moreover, when family- and society-level traits are substitutes and the parents' preferred trait is in the minority, parents will exert more effort in socializing their children.

Identity

While the previous literature discusses how parents shape the preferences of their children, a related literature focuses on identity formation. Akerlof and Kranton (2000, 715) model how identity shapes economic outcomes. They define identity as "a person's sense of self." In their model, the payoffs associated with different actions are affected by various forms of identity (e.g., gender identity). Akerlof and Kranton's (2000) model produces several insights. First, identity can help explain choices that appear detrimental if these choices help bolster a sense of identity. Expression of identity may also generate externalities. Third, identity can be manipulated. Finally, choice of identity can be considered an "economic" choice. In Akerlof and Kranton (2011), the authors explore how identity and norms have important implications for economic choices, such as work, education, and gender roles.

Culture and Institutions

Important theoretical work considers the relationship between culture and institutions. Tabellini (2008) examines the transmission of a norm of cooperation. In the model, there is a psychological cost of not cooperating with another player, but that cost decreases as the other person becomes more culturally distant. There are two types of players. First, there are those whose preference for cooperation decreases slowly with cultural distance, and therefore they will cooperate with other players who are culturally proximate and culturally distant. In other words, these types of players exhibit moral universalism, in which close and distant individuals are treated similarly. There are also types for whom this psychological cost of not cooperating decreases quickly, and therefore they are less likely to cooperate with people who are more distant. These types are considered parochial—that is, they demonstrate limited morality.

Tabellini also models the interplay between the scope of cooperation and institutions. He distinguishes between institutions that enforce behavior locally versus those that enforce behavior with more distant transactions. He finds that generalized morality is hurt if institutions only enforce cooperation locally. In that case, local enforcement may crowd out norms of cooperation because there is less incentive for parents to invest in values that sustain cooperation. In contrast, institutions that enforce more distant transactions may crowd in generalized morality.

Bisin and Verdier (2017) also model the interplay between culture and institutions. They emphasize that important feedback exists between institutions and culture, and thus they build a model where culture and institutions jointly evolve. They conceptualize culture—as in their prior work (Bisin and Verdier 2000; 2001)—as preference traits, norms, and attitudes that can be transmitted across generations by means of various socialization practices or interactions between peers. They define institutions as "Pareto weights assigned to different groups in a social choice problem" (Bisin and Verdier 2017, 5). The authors highlight under what circumstances cultural and institutional dynamics reinforce one another, and the implications under different institutional and cultural regimes—for example, extractive institutions, formation of civic capital, and protection of property rights.

Acemoglu and Robinson (2021) propose an alternative framework for the interplay between culture and institutions. In their conceptual framework, they define culture as a "culture set": a set of cultural attributes and the feasible connections between these attributes. The authors argue that the attributes form various cultural configurations. In contrast to the culture set, which is persistent, cultural configurations change in response to circumstances—for example, to changes in institutions. Their definition emphasizes that culture is adaptable and that it can be employed "strategically." They then examine how changes in institutions lead to changes in cultural configurations; similarly, they explore how cultural configurations can support different institutional arrangements.

Cultural Persistence and Change

While previous models have focused on explaining heterogeneity in beliefs and how values are transmitted, work by Giuliano and Nunn (2021) is motivated by trying to understand under what conditions culture persists and changes. The authors highlight instances of remarkable cultural persistence (e.g., Fernandez and Fogli 2009; Voigtländer and Voth 2012), but also instances of rapid cultural change (Becker and Woessmann 2009). Giuliano and Nunn (2021) focus on how the stability of the environment affects cultural change. They build on work by Rogers (1988) and present a model in which the variability of the environment affects the value individuals place on tradition. In the model, there are "traditionalists"—those who adopt the action of a randomly chosen person from the previous generation—and "non-traditionalists"—those who experiment at a cost to determine the correct action for the environment. The model predicts that in equilibrium, there will be both traditionalists and non-traditionalists, since there is a cost to determining the correct action as a non-traditionalist. The key insight of the model is that when the environment is stable, the evolved tradition is more likely to contain valuable information for the current generation. When the environment is less stable, it is relatively less beneficial to rely on the traditions of the previous generation.

The model presented in Giuliano and Nunn (2021) also has several other predictions that are useful for thinking about the effects of culture. For example, the model generates persistence in culture, particularly when the share of "traditionalists"—those who use culture to determine the right action relative to those who individually verify the correct action—in society is large. As the environment changes, there is scope for "mismatch," as the evolved cultural trait may not match the new environment. Mismatch has important implications for policy. In cases where mismatch exists, relatively light-touch interventions may actually be quite effective in changing behavior. Mismatch is more likely with greater environmental instability and with a greater cost of verifying the right action for the environment. The predictions of the model and their implications are discussed in detail in Nunn (2022).

Methods

There are multiple approaches to measuring culture. However, measuring culture faces the challenge of disentangling the effects of culture from other factors that also shape behavior, such as the institutional or ecological environment. In the next sections I describe several common strategies for measuring culture that aim to isolate the effects of culture from other factors.

Survey Questions

A common approach to measuring culture is through survey questions. For example, survey questions may be used to ask people how much they trust various other individuals or what they view as the appropriate role of women. However, there are two shortcomings of survey measures. First, because survey measures are rarely incentivized, the answers respondents give may not reflect their actual views or preferences. To address this concern, Falk et al. (2023) collected survey and experimental data from 409 individuals measuring risk aversion, time discounting, trust, altruism, and positive and negative reciprocity. They use these data to examine the correlation between the survey measures and the incentivized experimental measures. Reassuringly, they find a strong correlation between them. However, an additional concern with survey questions is that it can be difficult to disentangle the effects of culture from other factors.

Epidemiological Approach

One strategy for isolating the effects of culture from other factors that vary alongside culture is the epidemiological approach (Fernández 2011). The epidemiological approach studies migrants from varying cultural backgrounds who are in a common institutional setting. The benefit of this strategy is that it allows researchers to disentangle the effects of culture from the effects of the original institutional and economic environment. However, a potential limitation of this strategy is that migrants are a selected sample, and they may not be representative of their home country's or region's culture. Additionally, the effect of home-country culture may be weakened in a new environment. Fernández (2008) proposes addressing the issue of selection by focusing on second-generation immigrants, since they themselves did not select into migration. However, this may weaken any measurable effects of culture if the effects of culture diminish over time and across generations.

Many papers have employed the epidemiological approach in research in HPE. Alesina, Giuliano, and Nunn (2013) examine how reliance on plow agriculture relative to hoe agriculture has shaped gender norms using an analysis with second-generation immigrants in the United States and Europe. They find that women whose parents are from countries with greater historical reliance on the plow have lower rates of female labor force participation. They attribute this to plow agriculture being less amenable to women's participation in agriculture, and thus leading to a gendered division of labor. Giuliano and Nunn (2021) employ a similar strategy, looking at children of immigrants in the United States to examine how environmental stability affects cultural persistence. Children of immigrants from countries with more unstable environments are less likely to rely on tradition, as proxied by speaking their traditional language at home and marrying someone from the same ancestry.

Other examples of papers in HPE that employ versions of the epidemiological approach include Lowes et al. (2017), Lowes (2018), Lowes and Montero (2021a), and Bergeron (2020). In these studies, participants are recruited from a major urban area, but vary in their exposure to some historical or cultural treatment. For example, Lowes and Montero (2021a) examine how exploitative rubber concessions granted to companies in the Congo Free State era affect present-day outcomes in the Democratic Republic of the Congo (DRC). They work in a major urban area, but survey individuals whose ancestors come from in and outside of the former concessions. Lowes and Montero (2021a) find that individuals from outside the former concessions have worse development outcomes but exhibit more prosocial behavior. When they examine the effects by first- and second-generation migrants, they find that development outcomes—such as wealth and education—actually converge for second generation migrants, but that the cultural outcomes—such as trust and sharing norms—tend to persist.

Lab Experiments

Another strategy to isolate the effect of culture is to use lab experiments. In lab experiments, the rules of the game are fixed across settings. The payoffs associated with any particular action are set by the experiment. Differences in game play can thus be attributed to differences in culture.

An early example of this type of work is from Henrich et al. (2001), who conducted ultimatum game experiments with individuals from fifteen small-scale societies around the globe. In the ultimatum game, Player 1 is given an endowment to split between themselves and Player 2. Player 2 is told what the proposed allocation is and is given the opportunity to accept or reject this offer. If Player 2 accepts the offer, then each player receives the proposed allocation. If Player 2 rejects the offer, both players get 0. The subgame perfect Nash Equilibrium of this game is for Player 1 to offer just a little above 0, and for Player 2 to accept this offer. In practice, this is rarely observed: Player 1 generally offers positive amounts, and Player 2 rejects low offers. In fact, in many university student samples or samples with individuals from Europe or the United States, the most common allocation was to offer about half of the endowment and for offers that deviate from an even split to be rejected. However, the evidence suggesting little variation in game play was from mostly "W.E.I.R.D." societies—Western Educated Industrialized Rich Democratic (Henrich 2020). The works by Henrich et al. (2001) and Henrich et al. (2005), which represent a broader sample of societies, demonstrate that there is indeed quite a lot of variation in game play across societies.

Lab-in-the-field methods have become increasingly popular in HPE, particularly in contexts with limited data availability. Common lab-in-the-field experiments include the dictator game, ultimatum game, public goods game, random allocation game, and measures of time and risk preferences. Examples of papers that employ lab-in-the-field methods to answer questions related to historical political economy include Blouin (2022), Chaudhary et al. 2020), Heldring (2021), Karaja and Rubin (2017), Lowes (2018), Lowes et al. (2017), Ramos-Toro (2019), Rustagi (2020), Schulz et al. (2019), Valencia Caicedo and Voth (2018), and Walker (2020). For example, Blouin (2022) asks how historical exposure to labor coercion and indirect rule shape interethnic relations in the context of Rwanda and Burundi. Using survey and experimental data, he finds that in areas where Hutu were exposed to more labor coercion from Tutsi during the colonial era, Hutu exhibit lower levels of interethnic trust in a trust game today. (For more information on lab-in-the-field methods in historical economics, see Lowes [2021a].)

These lab-in-the-field methods can also be combined with the epidemiological approach. For example, Lowes et al. (2017) are interested in how institutions shape cultural outcomes. They study the case of the Kuba Kingdom in what is today the DRC. The Kuba Kingdom, which was formed by an innovating outsider, had highly developed state institutions, but its boundaries were constrained by rivers. It thus provides a natural experiment to ask how institutions affect culture. The authors collected data from individuals who are located in one major city today, but some of whom have ancestors who were from the historical Kuba Kingdom, to examine how historical institutions shape norms of rule following. Similar strategies of implementing lab experiments with residents of one city but who have different cultural backgrounds or historical treatments are pursued in Lowes (2018), Lowes and Montero (2021a), and Bergeron (2020).

Data Sources

Many rich data sources are available to study culture in a historical perspective. Much of this data comes from work in anthropology and is based off of historical ethnographies of groups. A commonly used data source is the Ethnographic Atlas (EA) (Murdock 1967), which has data on preindustrial cultural characteristics for 1,265 ethnic groups globally. A related data set, the Standard Cross Cultural Survey (SCCS), is a sample of 186 ethnic groups from the EA, but with a much richer set of variables (Murdock and White 1969).

Giuliano and Nunn (2018) extend the EA data by supplementing it with additional data sources for Europe and by merging it with the Ethnologue (Gordon 2009), which provides geographic information on the current distribution of language groups at the grid cell level. Another rich source of ethnographic data is the Human Relations Area Files (HRAF), a collection of ethnographies that have been subject indexed (Ember 2012).

Other interesting data sources include work indexing motifs in folklore (Michalopoulos and Xue 2021). The authors define *folklore* as the "collection of traditional beliefs, customs, and stories of a community." Their data catalogs oral traditions of approximately 1,000 societies. The authors also demonstrate that the motifs present in folklore correlate with various cultural features, such as gender norms or trust. The Global Preferences Survey (GPS) is a survey with a sample of eighty thousand respondents across seventy-six countries measuring a wide variety of preferences such as time and risk preferences, altruism, and trust (Falk et al. 2018). (For a detailed overview of these and other data sources, as well as a description of recent research that has used these data sources, refer to Lowes [2021a].)

What Historical Factors Shape Culture?

A large literature in HPE examines the factors that shape cultural outcomes. This work highlights the role of the environment and historical experiences such as the slave trades, colonialism, and conflict in shaping cultural outcomes. Here I discuss examples of empirical work that focuses on the historical determinants of different cultural values or beliefs.

Economic Preferences

Economic preferences encompass a wide variety of outcomes, such as time preferences, risk preferences, willingness to compete, and work ethic. Literature within HPE has asked what historical and environmental factors may generate variation in these key economic preferences. Table 44.1 presents papers on the historical determinants of economic preferences.

Time preferences, or the extent to which an individual values future consumption relative to present-day consumption, vary widely across societies. The ability to delay

Table 44.1. Historical determinants of culture: Economic preferences

Authors	Cultural trait	Historical determinant	Unit of observation	Geographic scope	Cultural data source	Research design
Alesina and Fuchs-Schündeln (2007)	Preference for redistribution	Communism	Household	East and West Germany	GSP	OLS, NE
Andersen et al. (2017)	Work ethic	Catholic Order of Cistercians	County	England	EVS	OLS, IV
Booth et al. (2019)	Competitiveness	Communism	Women	Beijing, Taipei	Original lab	DD
Becker, Enke, and Falk (2020)	Risk and time preferences	Ancient migration patterns	Individual, country	Global	GPS	OLS
Fouka and Schläpfer (2020)	Work ethic	Marginal return to labor of crop mix	Individual, district, country	Europe	ESS	OLS
Galor and Özak (2016)	Patience	Agricultural suitability	Individual, country	Global	Hofstede	OLS, NE, DD
Galor and Savitskiy (2018)	Loss aversion	Climatic volatility	Individual, ethnic group, country	Global	WVS	OLS
Giuliano and Tabellini (2020)	Preference for redistribution	European immigration	Individual	US	CCES	OLS, IV
Gneezy, Leonard and List (2009)	Competition	Matrilineal kinship	Individual	Tanzania, India	Original lab	OLS
Lowes (2021b)	Competition	Matrilineal kinship	Individual	DRC	Original lab	OLS

Note: DD is difference-in-differences. IV is instrumental variable. NE is natural experiment. OLS is Ordinary Least Squares. CCES is Cooperative Congressional Election Study. ESS is European Social Survey. EVS is European Values Survey. GSP is German Socioeconomic Panel. GPS is Global Preferences Survey. Hofstede is Hofstede, Hofstede, and Minkov (2010). WVS is World Values Survey.

gratification in the present for rewards in the future is correlated with a wide variety of economic benefits. Galor and Özak (2016) test the hypothesis that agro-climatic conditions affect the long-term orientation of a society. They find that populations exposed to higher crop yields historically are more likely to exhibit long-term orientation. Related work by Galor and Savitskiy (2018) suggests that another important economic preference—loss aversion—may also be shaped by agro-climatic conditions. Loss aversion is the tendency for individuals to value losses and gains asymmetrically (Tversky and Kahneman 1991; Kahneman, Knetsch, and Thale 1991). They find that in places where climatic shocks were spatially correlated and thus more aggregate in nature, people exhibit greater loss aversion. Becker, Enke, and Falk (2020) ask how ancestral distance—or the approximate amount of time since two populations shared a common ancestor—affects the difference in preferences between populations. They find that greater ancestral distance is associated with greater average differences in preferences, such as risk taking, prosociality, and patience. Thus, the more time since populations diverged, the less cultural similarity they share. These papers all suggest deep-rooted determinants of time and risk preferences.

Another key economic preference is willingness to compete, which has been associated with a wide variety of economic outcomes, such as educational attainment and labor market outcomes (Niederle and Vesterlund 2007; Niederle 2017). Generally, women are less likely to compete than men. However, there is evidence that cultural practices and institutions may shape willingness to compete. For example, Gneezy, Leonard, and List (2009) ask how willingness to compete differs between a patrilineal society, in which lineage and inheritance are traced through men, and a matrilineal society, in which lineage and inheritance are traced through women. Contrary to results with W.E.I.R.D. samples, the authors do not find that women are less willing to compete than men in the matrilineal society. Booth et al. (2019) find that institutions can also shape willingness to compete by comparing individuals in Beijing relative to Taipei. Women exposed to the communist regime during their formative years are more likely to compete than women from Taipei and their male counterparts in Beijing. These papers suggest that preference for competition responds to the cultural and institutional environment.

Attitudes toward work and leisure vary widely across societies. This may then translate into differences in economic output. Andersen et al. (2017) examine the origins of the so-called Protestant work ethic—or appreciation of hard work and thrift. They find that the cultural values generally associated with Protestantism may actually have had their origin in the Order of Cistercians, a Catholic order that spread across Europe in the eleventh century. Fouka and Schläpfer (2020) explore whether preference for work has been shaped by the historical role of labor in production. They test the hypothesis that in places with a greater marginal return to labor in agricultural production, individuals develop a preference for hard work. Fouka and Schläpfer (2020) constructed an index of estimated marginal returns to labor, finding it is correlated with present-day work hours and attitudes toward work in Europe.

Social Preferences

The ability to cooperate is crucial for a wide variety of outcomes, including economic development. Prosocial preferences and behavior are key to facilitating this cooperation. However, prosocial preferences vary widely across and within countries (Desmet, Ortuño-Ortn, and Wacziarg 2017; Falk et al. 2018; Desmet and Wacziarg 2018). Much of the work in HPE on culture focuses on what shapes various preferences for cooperation and prosocial behavior. Many papers related to the historical factors that shape social preferences appear in Tables 44.2 and 44.3.

Social and Institutional Trust

Historical circumstances—particularly those characterized by violence and coercion—have been shown to be an important determinant of social trust (Bauer et al. 2016). Nunn and Wantchekon (2011) test the hypothesis that exposure to the slave trades diminished trust in sub-Saharan Africa. The slave trades resulted in millions of individuals being forcibly removed from the continent. Nunn and Wantchekon (2011) highlight how many people were enslaved through trickery by their neighbors, family, or friends. The authors find that greater exposure to the slave trades leads to lower levels of trust in a wide variety of other individuals, such as neighbors, relatives, and local government councils. Colonial experiences have also been shown to be important in shaping trust. For example, Blouin (2022) tests the legacy of indirect rule policies implemented by the Belgians in Rwanda and Burundi. He finds that the Belgian policy of labor coercion, in which Tutsi forced Hutu to produce coffee, is associated with lower Hutu trust of Tutsi presently. Additionally, Hutu are less likely to engage in insurance contracts with Tutsi.

In contrast to the work by Blouin (2022) and Nunn and Wantchekon (2011), Lowes and Montero (2021a) find that exposure to violent and extractive concession companies during the Congo Free State era led to worse development outcomes, but may have led to greater trust as groups had to cooperate to survive. Bauer et al. (2016) summarize much of the work on how exposure to conflict affects prosociality. Their results suggest that conflict may actually incentivize greater cooperation, particularly among in-group members. However, this may come at the expense of out-group cooperation.

Environmental risk may also shape incentives for trust. Buggle and Durante (2021) examine how variability in climatic conditions may incentivize greater trust, as subsistence farmers rely on each other to mitigate risk. Using climate data from Europe and present-day survey data on trust, the authors find that greater climatic variability is associated with higher levels of trust, particularly in regions that relied primarily on agriculture.

Another driver of trust may be the quality of institutions. For example, high-quality institutions that can effectively deliver public goods may increase trust in the state. Becker et al. (2016) examine the legacy of the Habsburg Empire, which was known for its well-functioning bureaucracy. The authors find that places that were historically part of the Habsburg Empire exhibit greater trust in the state and in the police, as well as

Table 44.2. Historical determinants of culture: Social preferences

Authors	Cultural trait	Historical determinant	Unit of observation	Geographic scope	Cultural data source	Research design
Panel A: Social and Institutional Trust						
Alsan and Wanamaker (2018)	Trust in medicine	Tuskegee experiment	Individual	United States	GSS	DD
Blouin (2022)	Trust	Colonial-era forced labor	Individual	Rwanda, Burundi	Original survey and lab	OLS, NE
Becker et al. (2016)	Trust in state	Habsburg Empire	Individual	Eastern Europe	LITS	RD
Buggle and Durante (2021)	Trust	Climatic variability	Region (subnational)	Europe	ESS	OLS
Buggle (2016)	Trust	The Napoleonic Civil Code	Household	Germany	GSP	OLS, RD
D'Acunto, Prokopczuk and Weber (2019)	Trust in financial sector	Historical anti-Semitism	County	Germany	Original survey	OLS, IV
Grosjean (2011)	Trust	Shared imperial rule	Village	Europe	LITS	OLS
Karaja and Rubin (2017)	Trust	Habsburg versus Ottoman state	Individual, village	Region of Romania	Original survey	NE, OLS
Lowes and Montero (2021b)	Trust in medicine	French colonial medical campaigns	Individual	Cameroon, Central African Republic, Chad, Congo, Gabon	DHS	OLS, IV
Lowes and Montero (2021a)	Trust	Concession system	Individual, village	Democratic Republic of Congo	Original survey	OLS, RD
Nunn and Wantchekon (2011)	Trust	Slave trades	Individual	Sub-Saharan Africa	Afrobarometer	IV

(continued)

Table 44.2. Continued

Authors	Cultural trait	Historical determinant	Unit of observation	Geographic scope	Cultural data source	Research design
Okoye (2021)	Trust	18th-century Christian missions	Individual, ethnic group	Nigeria	Afrobarometer	OLS
Ramos-Toro (2019)	Parochialism, trust in medicine	Social exclusion in leper colony	Individual	Colombia	Original survey and lab	OLS
Prats and Valencia (2020)	Trust	Spanish civil war	Individual	Spain	CIS	OLS, RD, IV
Panel B: Cooperation						
Chaudhary et al. (2020)	Cooperation	Colonial rule	Individual, village	Rajasthan, India	Original survey	NE, OLS
Dell, Lane, and Querubin (2018)	Cooperation	Dai Viet Kingdom	Individual, village	Vietnam	HES	RD
Guiso, Sapienza, and Zingales (2016)	Civic engagement, social capital	Medieval independent city states	Individual, village	Italy	NSI PRVO	OLS, IV
Rustagi (2020)	Cooperation	Medieval democracy	Individual, municipality	Switzerland	WVS, original lab	OLS, IV

Note: DD is difference-in-differences. IV is instrumental variable. NE is natural experiment. OLS is Ordinary Least Squares. RD is regression discontinuity. CIS is Centro de Investigaciones Sociológicas. DHS is Demographic and Health Surveys. ESS is European Social Survey. EVS is European Values Survey. GPS is Global Preferences Survey (Falk et al., 2018). GSP is German Socioeconomic Panel. GSS is the General Social Survey. HES is Hamlet Evaluation System. LITS is Life in Transition Survey. NSI PRVO is the National Statistical Institute Provincial Register of Voluntary Organizations. WVS is World Values Survey.

Table 44.3. Historical determinants of culture: Social preferences (continued)

Authors	Cultural trait	Historical determinant	Unit of observation	Geographic scope	Cultural data source	Research design
Panel C: Scope of Morality, Individualism, and Collectivism						
Ang (2019)	Individualism versus collectivism	Labor intensive agriculture	Individual, ethnic group, country	Global	WVS	OLS
Bazzi, Fiszbein, and Gebresilasse (2020)	Individualism versus collectivism	Frontier experience	County	United States	US Census	OLS, DD, IV
Bergeron (2020)	Universal morality	Colonial-era Christian missions	Individual	Province of Democratic Republic of Congo	Original survey and lab	OLS
Buggle (2020)	Individualism versus collectivism	Irrigation	Individual, country	Global	Hofstede	OLS, IV
Enke (2019)	Moral systems	Kinship tightness	Individual, ethnic group, country	Global	WVS	OLS, IV
Le Rossignol and Lowes (2022)	Universal morality	Transhumant pastoralism	Individual, country	Global	IVS	OLS, IV
Moscona, Nunn, and Robinson (2017)	Universal morality	Segmentary lineage organization	Individual, ethnic group	Africa	Afrobarometer	OLS
Schulz et al. (2019)	Consanguineous marriage rates	Catholic Church's medieval policies, individualism, prosociality	Individual, region, country	Europe, global	EA	OLS
Talhelm et al. (2014)	Individualism versus collectivism	Rice versus wheat agriculture	Individual	China	Original survey	OLS

(continued)

Table 44.3. Continued

Authors	Cultural trait	Historical determinant	Unit of observation	Geographic scope	Cultural data source	Research design
Panel D: Obedience, Violence, and a Culture of Honor						
Cao et al. (2021)	Culture of honor, violence	Herding	Individual, ethnic group	Global	GPS	OLS
Couttenier, Grosjean, and Sangnier (2017)	Homicides	Mineral discoveries	County	United States	UCRP	NE, OLS
Grosjean (2014)	Culture of honor, violence	Scots-Irish immigration	County	United States	GSS	OLS, IV
Heldring (2021)	Rule following and violence	State formation	Individual	Rwanda	WVS, Original lab and survey	NE, OLS, IV
Lowes et al. (2017)	Rule following	State formation	Individual	Province in Democratic Republic of Congo	Original lab and survey	NE, OLS

Note: DD is difference-in-differences. IV is instrumental variable. NE is natural experiment. OLS is Ordinary Least Squares. RD is regression discontinuity. CIS is Centro de Investigaciones Sociológicas. DHS is Demographic and Health Surveys. ESS is European Social Survey. EVS is European Values Survey. GPS is Global Preferences Survey. GSP is German Socioeconomic Panel. GSS is the General Social Survey. Hofstede is Hofstede, Hofstede, and Minkov (2010). IVS is Integrated Values Survey. UCRP is Uniform Crime Reporting Program. WVS is World Values Survey.

less corruption. Karaja and Rubin (2017) combine lab-in-the-field data with a similar historical natural experiment, comparing individuals who live along a historical border between the Habsburg Empire and the Ottoman Empire in present-day Romania. They find experimental evidence of greater out-group trust among those with historical exposure to the Habsburg Empire.

Historical events may also drive trust in the medical sector, which may have important implications for health policies. For example, Black men at Tuskegee, Alabama, in the United States were the subjects of a study on the effects of syphilis. Doctors knew the men had syphilis, but withheld treatment so that they could study the course of the disease, which is lethal when untreated. Alsan and Wanamaker (2018) find that the revelation in 1972 of the medical experimentation that happened at Tuskegee is associated with lower levels of trust in medicine as well as worse health outcomes for Black men. Related work examines the legacy of French colonial medical campaigns aimed at preventing the spread of sleeping sickness during the colonial era. The medical campaigns were characterized by the use of medications of dubious efficacy and with serious side effects and the forced immunization of millions of individuals across former French Equatorial Africa (present-day Chad, Gabon, Republic of Congo, the Central African Republic, and Cameroon). Lowes and Montero (2021b) find that historical exposure to these campaigns is associated with lower childhood immunization rates and higher refusal rates of free and noninvasive blood tests for either HIV or anemia. These results highlight that historical medical malpractice can have long-run effects on the efficacy of health interventions.

A question that naturally arises is why these effects of medical mistrust persist. Ramos-Toro (2019) examines this question in the context of Colombia. He combines survey and experimental data to examine how having ancestors who were forcibly interned in a leper colony in Colombia affects trust in medicine. The forcible exclusion of lepers and their placement into leper colonies was common practice historically. He finds that those whose ancestors were in the former leper colony are less likely to trust the HPV vaccine and to take up an antiparasite medication. Using a survey experiment that primes individuals with information on the leper colony and the inefficacy of doctors' treatments, he finds that those with excluded ancestors are also more likely to believe doctors are uninformed. This exercise helps highlight how historical narratives may explain the persistence of mistrust in medicine well after the historical event.

Scope of Morality, Individualism, and Collectivism

While much of the work on trust has focused on generalized trust levels, the scope of trust is also important. To what extent do individuals exhibit greater trust of in-group members, such as family or friends, relative to out-group members, such as those from another religion or country? Understanding what determines the scope of trust is important; moral universalism has been shown to affect a wide variety of outcomes, such as policy preferences, willingness to redistribute, and altruism (Cappelen, Enke, and Tungodden 2022).

Exposure to the church may have played an important role in increasing the scope of morality. For example, the Catholic Church implemented laws barring cousin marriage, which undermined kin networks (Schulz et al. 2019; 2022. This led to changes in psychology: individuals are more individualistic and independent and more trusting of and cooperative with strangers. Related work by Bergeron (2020) tests how exposure to Christian missions leads to greater moral universalism. Within the DRC, he finds that greater missionary exposure improves views of the out-group, with no effect on in-group preference, thus reducing in-group favoritism.

Other work asks how underlying social structures, such as kinship systems, affect the scope of trust. Moscona, Nunn, and Robinson (2017) find that individuals from segmentary lineage societies, which are organized around well-structured clans, are less trusting of outsiders. Enke (2019) explores how "looser" kinship structures may enable more universal moral values. He contrasts "tight kinship," in which individuals cooperate mainly with in-group members, with "loose" systems in which individuals interact with strangers and do not favor in-group members. He finds that kinship tightness is associated with: greater acceptability of violence toward the out-group, less likelihood of a moralizing god, greater importance of loyalty to the community, and lower levels of centralization.

Le Rossignol and Lowes (2022) build on this work to examine how historical forms of economic production affect the scope of trust. They test the hypothesis from anthropology that transhumant pastoralism, a form of economic production in which societies undergo seasonal migration and herd animals, leads to more parochial trust. Transhumant pastoralism is characterized by a need for in-group cohesion to survive the environmental and human threats these groups faced. They find that groups that relied historically on transhumant pastoralism are more trusting of in-group members and less trusting of out-group members. They find evidence that this greater parochialism may actually constrain firm growth.

A common cultural distinction is made between "collectivist" societies, which place the group above the individual and value conformity, relative to "individualist" societies, which value autonomy, freedom, and personal achievement (Hofstede 1980; Gorodnichenko and Roland 2011). Talhelm et al. (2014) ask how a history of farming rice relative to wheat affects level of interdependence. They hypothesize that farming rice makes cultures more interdependent, while farming wheat makes them more independent, because rice production requires more cooperation relative to wheat production. They find evidence in favor of this hypothesis in China where there is historical variation in agricultural traditions. Buggle (2020) also explores how agricultural traditions affect collectivism. He finds that those societies that practiced irrigation historically have more collectivist norms today. This is because the construction and maintenance of irrigation requires coordination among individuals. He also finds that historical reliance on irrigation is associated with lower levels of innovation presently.

Bazzi, Fiszbein, and Gebresilasse (2020) test the hypothesis that frontiers foster a culture of "rugged individualism." They find that the American frontier gave rise to a culture of individualism in the United States; those places with a greater amount of time on the frontier are more individualistic and more likely to oppose redistribution and regulation. The authors suggest these effects are driven by the returns to individualism in a frontier setting.

Obedience, Violence, and a Culture of Honor

Another set of research explores the determinants of traits like obedience, propensity for violence, and a culture of honor. Lowes et al. (2017) ask how institutions affect the propensity to follow the rules. They examine the effects of the Kuba Kingdom, which existed in the DRC and was characterized by its highly developed institutions. Consistent with Tabellini (2008), the authors find that exposure to high-quality institutions crowds out norms of rule following. Kuba participants are less likely to follow the rules in an incentivized lab experiment.

In contrast, Heldring (2021) tests whether historical exposure to a centralized state in Rwanda may have led to increased participation in the Rwandan genocide and greater obedience to the state. He finds that more years under the historical state's control are associated with more violence during the genocide as well as greater rule following an incentivized lab experiment. He interprets this as evidence that the historical state inculcated norms of obedience, which then can be leveraged by the state.

Grosjean (2014) explores the effects of a culture of honor, which encourages male aggression and defense of honor (Nisbett and Cohen 1996; 1993). This may serve an important function in a setting with limited state presence, as aggression and willingness to engage in violence may deter threats. She finds that part of the variation in homicide rates in the US South can be explained by the historical presence of Scots-Irish, who migrated to the United States and held these culture of honor beliefs. Cao et al. (2021) look globally at pastoralism and values associated with a culture of honor, such as violence, punishment, and revenge-taking. They find that reliance on pastoralism is associated with greater violence and with folklore motifs related to violence and punishment.

Diversity and Assimilation

Many papers in HPE have tried to understand the origins of diversity (see Table 44.4 for an overview). Why do some places have many ethnic or linguistic groups? Why are other places more homogeneous? For example, Michalopoulos (2012) examines how geographic variability shapes ethno-linguistic diversity. He finds that countries with more diverse land attributes have higher levels of linguistic diversity. He suggests that different land attributes incentivize the creation of location-specific human capital, and thus greater diversity. Cervellati, Chiovelli, and Esposito (2019) propose that diversity may also be driven by the epidemiological environment. They test the hypothesis that greater suitability for malaria may lead to greater incentives to isolate to prevent disease transmission, leading to higher levels of endogamy. They find that greater suitability for malaria is associated with more ethnic diversity.

Table 44.4. Historical determinants of culture: Diversity, kinship, and gender norms

Authors	Cultural trait	Historical determinant	Unit of observation	Geographic scope	Cultural data	Research design
Panel A: Diversity, Fractionalization, and Polarization						
Bazzi et al. (2019)	Ethnic fractionalization and polarization	Population resettlement program	Individual	Indonesia	2010 Census	NE, OLS
Cervellati, Chiovelli, and Esposito (2019)	Ethnic endogamy	Malaria prevalence	Individual	Africa	DHS	OLS
Dickens (2022)	Linguistic diversity	Geographic variability	Ethnic boundary	Global	Ethnologue	OLS
Michalopoulos (2012)	Ethnolinguistic diversity	Geographic variability	Grid cell, country	Global	Ethnologue	OLS
Panel B: Assimilation and Discrimination						
Calderon, Fouka and Tabellini (2022)	Support for civil rights	The Second Great Migration	County	United States	Gregory and Hermida (2019)	IV
Fouka (2020)	Cultural assimilation	Language restrictions	Individual	United States	Census	DD
Fouka, Mazmunder and Tabellini (2022)	Cultural assimilation	The First Great Migration	Individual	United States	Census	IV
Voigtländer and Voth (2012)	Anti-Semitism	Medieval anti-Semitism	City	Germany	Hänisch (1988)	OLS
Panel C: Family, Kinship, and Marriage						
Akbari, Bahrami-Rad and Kimbrough (2019)	Consanguineous marriage rates	Catholic Church's medieval policies, corruption	Province, country	Italy, global	EA	OLS, IV
Ang and Fredriksson (2017)	Strength of family ties	Wheat agriculture	Individual, state, country	United States, global	WVS	OLS
BenYishay, Grosjean, and Vecci (2017)	Matrilineal inheritance	Presence of coral reefs	Island, ethnic group	The Solomon Islands, global	SCCS	OLS

Dalton and Leung (2014)	Polygyny	Slave trades	Ethnic group, country	Africa	DHS	OLS, IV
Fenske (2015)	Polygyny	Historical mission stations and education	Individual	Africa	DHS	OLS, IV
Lowes and Nunn (2022)	Matrilineal kinship	Slave trades	Ethnic group	Africa	EA	OLS, IV
Schulz (2022)	Consanguineous marriage rates	Catholic Church's medieval policies, political institutions	Individual, region, country	Europe, global	EA	DD, OLS
Schulz et al. (2019)	Consanguineous marriage rates	Catholic Church's medieval policies, individualism, prosociality	Individual, region, country	Europe, global	EA	OLS
Panel D: Gender Norms and Sexuality						
Alesina et al. (2013)	Gender norms	Plow agriculture	Individual, country	Global	WVS	OLS, IV
Baranov, De Haas and Grosjean (2021)	Masculinity norms	18th-century sex ratios	Individual	Australia	HILD	OLS, IV
Becker (2019)	Restrictions on women's sexuality	Pastoralism	Individual, ethnic group	Africa, global	EA, DHS	OLS, IV
Brodeur and Haddad (2021)	Attitudes towards homosexuality	19th-century gold rush	County	United States	GSS	OLS, DD
Campa and Serafinelli (2019)	Gender norms	Communism	Individual	Germany, Europe	GSP	IV, RD, DD
Fernández, Fogli, and Olivetti (2004)	Gender norms	Female employment during World War II	Individual	United States	GSS	OLS, DD
Grosjean and Khattar (2019)	Gender norms	18th-century male-biased sex ratios	County	Australia	HILD	IV
Teso (2019)	Gender norms	Slave trades	Individual, ethnic group	Sub-Saharan Africa	DHS	OLS, IV
Xue (2016)	Gender norms	The cotton revolution	County	China	CGSS	IV

Note: DD is difference-in-differences. IV is instrumental variable. NE is natural experiment. OLS is Ordinary Least Squares. RD is regression discontinuity. CGSS is Chinese General Social Surveys. DHS is Demographic and Health Surveys. EA is Ethnographic Atlas. Ethnologue is Gordon (2009). GSP is German Socioeconomic Panel. GSS is the General Social Survey. HILD is Household Income and Labour Dynamic in Australia Survey. SCCS is Standard Cross Cultural Survey. WVS is World Values Survey.

Assimilation is related to ethnic diversity: how do migrants to a region integrate into the new cultural environment? Much of the work on assimilation has focused on the United States, and tried to understand under what circumstances immigrants assimilate and how policies affect assimilation. Fouka (2020) examines the effects of attempts at forced assimilation. She studies the context of the United States after World War I, in which the German language was banned in some US schools. She finds that the policy seems to have backfired; those affected by the language laws were more likely to marry a German partner and more likely to name their children German names. See Fouka (2023) for an overview of the literature on assimilation in HPE.

Family, Kinship, and Marriage

Across cultures, there is a lot of variation in family structure and customs around marriage. For example, societies vary in the extent to which individuals may have multiple partners and how kinship systems are organized.

Polygyny is the marriage practice where men can marry multiple women. This is relative to monogamy, where men have a single formal parter. Dalton and Leung (2014) examine how the slave trades may have affected marriage institutions. The trans-Atlantic slave trade exported a higher percentage of men than women, creating sex-ratio imbalances in the affected areas where there were fewer men than women. This may have increased the incentive to adopt polygyny. The authors find that exposure to the trans-Atlantic slave trade is associated with greater polygyny historically and presently. Fenske (2015) examines how education affects polygyny rates. He differentiates between colonial education and modern education. He finds that areas of West Africa that received greater exposure to colonial education have lower polygyny rates. However, he finds no effect of modern-day expansion of schooling on polygyny.

A limited literature explores the origins of variation in kinship structure. Kinship structure describes how families are organized. Many Western societies practice cognatic descent, in which lineage and inheritance are traced through both mothers and fathers. However, unilineal decent, in which lineage is traced through either men or women, is quite common. BenYishay, Grosjean, and Vecci (2017) examine how natural resource endowments—in particular, reef density—affect the prevalence of matrilineal kinship relative to patrilineal kinship in the Solomon Islands. The authors test the hypothesis that reliance on fishing may be associated with matrilineal kinship. Reliance on fishing may encourage adoption of matrilineal kinship because if men specialize in fishing, a system in which women own and inherit land may increase agricultural productivity. They find that greater reef density is associated with more matrilineal kinship, even within ethno-linguistic groups. Lowes and Nunn (2022) explore another hypothesis to explain the prevalence of matrilineal kinship: exposure to the slave trades. The vast majority of matrilineal groups are located along the "matrilineal belt" in sub-Saharan Africa, which also experienced high levels of exposure to the slave trades. They find that greater exposure to the trans-Atlantic and Indian Ocean slave trades is significantly associated with matrilineal kinship.

Gender Norms

A rich subfield of HPE studies the historical origins of gender norms: norms that dictate the role of women within a society. A key outcome of interest is the extent to which women participate in the labor market. Fernández, Fogli, and Olivetti (2004) explore how exposure to a working mother affects a man's wife's labor force participation. Using World War II as a shock to women's labor force participation, they find that men with working mothers are more likely to have a wife who works. Their work suggests the important effect of a different family model for these men.

Alesina, Giuliano, and Nunn (2013) test the hypothesis that historical reliance on the plow—which favors men's participation in agriculture—affected gendered division of labor and hence gender norms. Historical reliance on plow agriculture relative to hoe agriculture is associated with less women's labor force participation today. Using data on immigrants, they find evidence of transmission of these norms: women whose parents are from a country with greater historical reliance on the plow are less likely to participate in the labor force. Xue (2016) asks how women's historical labor contributions may shape their perceived value by using variation in exposure to the cotton revolution, which increased the value of women's participation in cotton production. She finds that exposure to the cotton revolution is associated with less male-biased gender ratios today.

Historical factors also affect efforts to control women's sexuality. Becker (2019) examines how pastoralism, a traditional form of economic production in which groups rely on herding animals, shapes incentives to control women's sexuality. Pastoralist groups may face greater incentive to control women's sexuality, since men are gone from home for periods of time, and thus may face lower paternal certainty. She finds that greater traditional reliance on pastoralism is associated with norms restricting women's movement and sexuality.

Other work examines how changes to the sex ratio—that is, the ratio of men to women—affect gender norms. Grosjean and Khattar (2019) leverage variation in the historical sex-ratio in Australia generated by the transportation of convicts to the colony. Historically male-biased sex ratios are associated with more conservative gender norms: women are more likely to be married and less likely to work outside the home. Related work by Baranov, De Haas, and Grosjean (2022) finds that historically male-biased sex ratios are associated with more violence and more male-stereotypical occupation segregation. Teso (2019) examines the effects of changes in sex ratios induced by the slave trades in sub-Saharan Africa. In the trans-Atlantic slave trade, men were removed as slaves at a much higher rate than women; thus, women had to take on roles and responsibilities previously held by men. In contrast, the Indian Ocean slave trade did not favor male as slaves. He finds that the trans-Atlantic slave trade is associated with more labor force participation by women presently, but he finds no analogous effect for the Indian Ocean trade.

Religiosity

Religion and strength of belief in God are important components of individuals' identities. A natural question is what helps explain variation in the extent of and types of religious beliefs. Table 44.5 provides an overview of papers related to the historical origins of variation in religiosity. Work in HPE has focused on how environmental shocks and political shocks, such as war, affect religiosity (Ager and Ciccone 2018; Bentzen 2019; Henrich et al. 2019). Bentzen (2019) tests the hypothesis that some societies are more religious than others as a form of coping with difficult life events. She uses data on natural disasters paired with survey data on religiosity. She finds that individuals are more religious if recently exposed to an earthquake.

While much of the work on religion focuses on organized religions, such as Christianity, Islam, and Judaism, many individuals around the world adhere to more traditional religions, characterized by belief in witchcraft, the supernatural, and the importance of the role of ancestors. Belief in witchcraft is widespread and has been associated with lower levels of trust (Gershman 2016). Gershman (2020) explores the origins of belief in witchcraft, defined as the belief in the ability of certain people to use supernatural means to cause harm. He finds that ethnic groups in sub-Saharan Africa with greater exposure to the trans-Atlantic slave trade are more likely to believe in witchcraft. Similarly, areas in Latin America that historically received more slave labor during the slave trades are also more likely to believe in witchcraft.

WHAT ARE THE CONSEQUENCES OF CULTURE?

A large literature has documented that culture affects a wide variety of outcomes (Fernández 2008; Guiso, Sapienza, and Zingales 2006; Henrich 2015; Nunn 2021). Here I highlight some examples of empirical work on the effects of historically determined cultural values or practices on present-day outcomes. An overview of papers related to the effects of culture is presented in Table 44.6.

Economic Preferences

The ability to delay gratification may have important economic implications. Sunde et al. (2022) ask how patience is associated with comparative development. Using data from

Table 44.5. Historical determinants of culture: Religiosity

Authors	Cultural trait	Historical determinant	Unit of observation	Geographic scope	Cultural data	Research design
Ager and Ciccone (2018)	Religiosity	Rainfall risk	County	United States	1890 Census	OLS
Bentzen (2019)	Religiosity	Earthquakes	Individual	Global	WVS	NE, DD
Henrich et al. (2019)	Religiosity	War	Individual	Uganda, Sierra Leone, Tajikistan	Original survey data	NE, OLS
Barro and McCleary (2003)	Religiosity	State regulation of religion	Country	Global	WVS	OLS, IV
Nunn (2010)	Adherence to Christianity	Colonial mission stations	Individual, ethnic group, village	Africa	2005 Afro-barometer	OLS
Cantoni (2012)	Protestantism	Distance to Wittenberg	City, territory	The Holy Roman Empire	Bairoch (1988)	OLS
Rubin (2014)	Protestantism	Early access to printing press	City	Europe	Bairoch (1988)	OLS, IV
Michalopoulos, Naghavi, and Prarolo (2018)	Adherence to Islam	Trade routes, land suitability	Ethnic group, country	Global	WRD	OLS
Gershman (2020)	Belief in witchcraft	Trans-Atlantic slave trade	Individual, ethnic group, region	Africa, Latin America	PEW RPLS	OLS, IV

Note: DD is difference-in-differences. IV is instrumental variable. NE is natural experiment. OLS is Ordinary Least Squares. PEW RPL is Pew Forum on Religion and Public Life Surveys. WRD is World Religion Database. WVS is World Values Survey.

Table 44.6. Consequences of culture

Authors	Outcome	Cultural determinant	Unit of observation	Geographic scope	Cultural data	Research design
Panel A: Economic Preferences						
Figlio et al. (2019)	Educational performance	Time preferences	Individual	Florida	Hofstede	OLS
Sunde et al. (2022)	Capital accumulation, economic growth	Time preferences	Individual, country	Global	GPS	OLS
Panel B: Social and Institutional Trust						
Aghion et al. (2010)	Preference for government regulation	Trust	Individual, country	Global	WVS	OLS
Algan and Cahuc (2010)	Economic growth	Trust	Individual, country	Global	GSS	NE, IV
Butler, Giuliano and Guiso (2016)	Income	Trust	Individual	Europe	ESS	OLS
Panel C: Scope of Morality, Individualism, and Collectivism						
Enke (2020)	Voting in US presidential elections	Universal versus limited morality	County	United States	MFQ	OLS
Enke et al. (2021)	Charitable giving, social capital	Universal versus limited morality	Individual	United States	Original survey	OLS
Gorodnichenko and Roland (2011)	Economic growth	Individualism versus collectivism	Country	Global	Hofstede	OLS, IV
Gorodnichenko and Roland (2017)	Economic growth	Individualism versus collectivism	Country	Global	Hofstede	OLS, IV
Gorodnichenko and Roland (2021)	Autocracy versus democracy	Individualism versus collectivism	Country	Global	Hofstede	OLS, IV

Panel D: Family, Kinship, and Marriage					
Alesina et al. (2015)	Strength of family ties	Labor market regulation	Individual	Global	WVS	OLS
Alesina and Giuliano (2010)	Strength of family ties	Economic activity	Individual	Global	WVS	OLS
Alesina and Giuliano (2011)	Strength of family ties	Civic engagement, social capital	Individual	Global	WVS	OLS
Ashraf et al. (2020)	Bride price	Children's education	Individual	Indonesia, Zambia	EA	OLS, DD
Bau (2021)	Matrilocal versus patrilocality	Child investment	Individuals	Indonesia, Ghana	EA	DD
Corno, Hildebrandt, and Voenn (2020)	Marriage transfers	Child marriage	Individual	Sub-Saharan Africa, India	EA	OLS
Ermisch and Gambetta (2010)	Strength of family ties	Trust in strangers	Individual	United Kingdom	BHPS	OLS, IV
Lowes (2018)	Matrilineal versus patrilineal	Cooperation, child investment	Individual, ethnic group	Democratic Republic of the Congo; Sub-Saharan Africa	EA	OLS, RD
Moscona, Nunn, and Robinson (2020)	Segmentary lineage	Conflict	Ethnic group, grid cell	Africa	ESA	OLS, RD
Panel E: Religiosity					
Becker and Woessmann (2008)	Protestantism	Education gender gap	County	Prussia	1816 Prussian Census	OLS, IV
Becker and Woessmann (2009)	Protestantism	Education, economic growth	County	Prussia	1871 Prussian Census	OLS, IV
Cantoni (2014)	Protestantism	Economic growth	City	German–speaking Holy Roman Empire	Bairoch (1988)	OLS, IV
Cantoni, Dittmar and Yuchtman (2018)	Secularization	Education, occupational choice, public construction	Individual, territory	German–speaking Holy Roman Empire	Bairoch (1988)	DD
Le Rossignol, Lowes, and Nunn (2022)	Traditional supernatural beliefs	Prosocial preferences	Individual	Province of Democratic Republic of the Congo	Original survey and lab	OLS

Note: DD is difference-in-differences. IV is instrumental variable. NE is natural experiment. OLS is Ordinary Least Squares. RD is regression discontinuity. BHPS is British Household Panel Survey. EA is Ethnographic Atlas. ESA is Ethnographic Survey of Africa. ESS is European Social Survey. GPS is Global Preferences Survey. GSS is the General Social Survey. Hofstede is Hofstede, Hofstede, and Minkov (2010). MFQ is Moral Foundations Questionnaire. WVS is World Values Survey.

the GPS, they find that patience is correlated with per capita income, as well as the accumulation of human and physical capital. Patience may also be culturally transmitted. Figlio et al. (2019) find related evidence from Florida that students from cultures with more long-term orientation and values perform better on tests and have better school performance.

Social Preferences

Individualist cultures emphasize personal accomplishments, individual freedom, and status. In contrast, collectivist societies encourage conformity, which may make collective action easier. Gorodnichenko and Roland (2011; 2017) find evidence of higher levels of innovation and growth in individualist cultures.

Early work has established that trust is beneficial for economic growth (Tabellini 2010; Algan and Cahuc 2010). One important aspect of trust is the scope of trust, or how much you trust in-group members relative to out-group members. Enke, Rodríguez-Padilla, and Zimmermann (2021) find that moral universalism—that is, the tendency to trust in-group and out-group members equally—is associated with different policy preferences and altruism.

Family, Kinship, and Marriage

Kinship structure and marriage are fundamental institutions for most societies. They also have important implications for a wide variety of outcomes, such as the scope of trust, dynamics within the family, investment in children, and gender norms (Alesina and Giuliano 2011).

A key dimension on which kinship structures can vary is whether group membership and inheritance are traced through women, as in matrilineal systems, or through men, as in patrilineal systems. Lowes (2018) tests how matrilineal relative to patrilineal kinship systems affect outcomes within the family, including domestic violence, cooperation, and investment in children. Anthropologists had hypothesized that matrilineal systems relatively empower women, but may reduce cooperation in the household. Using experimental and survey data, she finds that women in matrilineal groups experience less domestic violence and greater autonomy in decision making. Matrilineal kinship closes the gender gap in educational attainment between male and female children and improves child health outcomes. However, in a lab experiment with their spouses, matrilineal individuals cooperate less.

Another dimension on which kinship structures vary is the extent to which there are structures organizing the extended family. Moscona, Nunn, and Robinson (2020) examine how segmentary lineage systems, in which extended family groups are organized in clans and have specific obligations to defend each other, affect incidence of conflict in sub-Saharan Africa. Using a geographic regression discontinuity design, they find that segmentary lineage groups experience greater conflict intensity. Moscona, Nunn, and Robinson (2017) also find that segmentary lineage decreases trust in outsiders.

Bau (2021) tests how variation in traditional kinship practices interacts with government policies. She examines residence after marriage, comparing matrilocal systems in which daughters reside with their parents after marriage, with patrilocal systems, in which sons reside with their parents after marriage. A key insight of the paper is that parents have an incentive to invest in the children who provide old-age support. However, she finds that the introduction of pension systems crowd out the residence practice, since parents no longer need to rely on their children for old-age support. Additionally, it also reduces educational investment.

In some societies, marriage is marked with an exchange of goods and money between the bride's family and the groom's family. For example, in bride price societies, the groom's family typically transfers money and items to the bride's family. These payments can amount to fairly substantial sums; in some cases, the bride price can be valued at over a year's income (Lowes and Nunn 2018). Ashraf et al. (2020) find that bride price practices may affect the incentive to invest in a girl's education. Using variation in education expansion and in the custom of bride price payments, the authors find that schooling expansions benefit girls in bride price societies but do not benefit girls in non–bride price societies in Indonesia and Zambia. The authors interpret this as evidence that in bride price societies, parents get additional benefits from investing in their daughters' educations. Corno, Hildebrandt, and Voena (2020) find that age of marriage responds to aggregate economic conditions. In societies that practice bride price, a negative shock increases the chance of child marriage. In contrast, in India where dowry is practiced, negative economic shocks lead to delay in marriage.

Religiosity

Henrich (2020) suggests that one of the benefits of religion may be to create collective identity. This will also have important implications for the scope of cooperation. Important work explores the effects of exposure to various religious denominations. Schulz et al. (2019) examine how the Catholic Church's policy that prevented cousin marriages changed family orientation and kin networks. Becker and Woessmann (2009) provide evidence that Protestantism led to greater economic prosperity because it encouraged the accumulation of human capital. Relatedly, Becker and Woessmann (2008) find that Protestantism decreased the gender gap in basic education. They highlight the Protestant emphasis on accumulation on the ability of girls being able to read the Bible.

Le Rossignol, Lowes, and Nunn (2022) focus on indigenous spiritual belief systems, such as belief in witchcraft and the role of ancestors, in the Democratic Republic of the Congo. They find that contrary to the effects of moralizing God religions, indigenous spiritual beliefs do not seem to promote prosocial behavior. Being paired with an individual with a stronger traditional supernatural belief leads to less prosocial behavior in a series of lab experiments.

Conclusion

This chapter has provided an overview of the work on culture in HPE. I've offered various definitions of culture that have been used in the literature, as well as an overview of theoretical work on the role of and transmission of culture. I then provided an overview of empirical literature exploring the origins of variation in culture and the economic consequences of culture.

The literature in HPE has contributed to our understanding of culture in several ways. First, it has highlighted how culture has deep roots. Variation in culture can be linked to a wide variety of historical factors, such as historical events, institutions, and the ecological environment. Second, culture tends to persist. Individuals retain their cultural values, even when they move to new locations and institutional environments, and they tend to transmit those values to subsequent generations. Finally, historically determined cultural values and practices have been shown to affect a wide variety of key economic outcomes.

Given how deeply rooted cultural beliefs and traits can be and how much they vary across societies, an exciting avenue for future research is to understand how culture affects and interacts with economic policies. This is an important next step for improving the efficacy of economic policy. A related promising avenue for future research is to explore how and when culture changes. Research in HPE is important for furthering both of these research agendas.

References

Acemoglu, Daron, and James A. Robinson. 2021. "Culture, Institutions and Social Equilibria: A Framework." May. NBER Working Paper 28832.

Acharya, Avidit, Matthew Blackwell, and Maya Sen. 2023. "Historical Persistence." Oxford Handbook of Historical Political Economy. Oxford: Oxford University Press, 117–41.

Ager, Philipp, and Antonio Ciccone. 2018. "Agricultural Risk and the Spread of Religious Communities." *Journal of the European Economic Association* 16, no. 4: 1021–68.

Aghion, Philippe, Yann Algan, Pierre Cahuc, and Andrei Shleifer. 2010. "Regulation and Distrust." *Quarterly Journal of Economics* 125, no. 3: 1015–49.

Akbari, Mahsa, Duman Bahrami-Rad, and Erik O. Kimbrough. 2019. "Kinship, Fractionalization and Corruption." *Journal of Economic Behavior and Organization* 166: 493–528.

Akerlof, George A., and Rachel E. Kranton. 2000. "Economics and Identity." *Quarterly Journal of Economics* 115, no. 3 (August): 715–53.

Akerlof, George A. and Rachel E. Kranton. 2011. *Identity Economics: How Our Identities Shape Our Work, Wages, and Well-Being.* Princeton, NJ: Princeton University Press.

Alesina, Alberto, Yann Algan, Pierre Cahuc, and Paola Giuliano. 2015. "Family Values and the Regulation of Labor." *Journal of the European Economic Association* 13, no. 4: 599–630.

Alesina, Alberto, and Nicola Fuchs-Schündeln. 2007. "Good-Bye Lenin (or Not?): The Effect of Communism on People's Preferences." *American Economic Review*, September 97, no. 4 (September): 1507–28.

Alesina, Alberto, and Paola Giuliano. 2010. "The Power of the Family." *Journal of Economic Growth* 15, no. 2 (June): 93–125.

Alesina, Alberto, and Paola Giuliano. 2011. "Family Ties and Political Participation." *Journal of the European Economic Association* 9, no. 5 (October): 817–39.

Alesina, Alberto, Paola Giuliano, and Nathan Nunn. 2013. "On the Origins of Gender Roles: Women and the Plough." *Quarterly Journal of Economics* 128, no. 2: 469–530.

Algan, Yann, and Pierre Cahuc. 2010. "Inherited Trust and Growth." *American Economic Review* 100, no. 5: 2060–92.

Alsan, Marcella, and Marianne Wanamaker. 2018. "Tuskegee and the Health of Black Men." *Quarterly Journal of Economics* 133, no. 1 (February): 407–55.

Andersen, Thomas Barnebeck, Jeanet Bentzen, Carl-Johan Dalgaard, and Paul Sharp. 2017. "Pre-Reformation Roots of the Protestant Ethic." *Economic Journal* 127, no. 604: 1756–93.

Ang, James B. 2019. "Agricultural Legacy and Individualistic Culture." *Journal of Economic Growth* 24, no. 4 (December): 397–425.

Ang, James B., and Per G. Fredriksson. 2017. "Wheat Agriculture and Family Ties." *European Economic Review* 100 (November): 236–56.

Ashraf, Nava, Natalie Bau, Nathan Nunn, and Alessandra Voena. 2020. "Bride Price and Female Education." *Journal of Political Economy* 128, no. 2: 591–641.

Bairoch, Paul. 1988. *Cities and Economic Development: From the Dawn of History to the Present.* Chicago: University of Chicago Press.

Baranov, Victoria, Ralph De Haas, and Pauline A. Grosjean. 2022. "Male-biased Sex Ratios and Masculinity Norms: Evidence from Australia's Colonial Past." *Journal of Economic Growth.*

Barro, Robert J., and Rachel M. McCleary. 2003. "Religion and Economic Growth across Countries." *American Sociological Review* 68, no. 5: 760–81.

Bau, Natalie. 2021. "Can Policy Change Culture? Government Pension Plans and Traditional Kinship Practices." *American Economic Review* 111, no. 6 (June): 1880–917.

Bauer, Michal, Christopher Blattman, Julie Chytilová, Joseph Henrich, Edward Miguel, and Tamar Mitts. 2016. "Can War Foster Cooperation?" *Journal of Economic Perspectives* 30, no. 3: 249–74.

Bazzi, Samuel, Martin Fiszbein, and Mesay Gebresilasse. 2020. "Frontier Culture: The Roots and Persistence of "Rugged Individualism" in the United States." *Econometrica* 88, no. 6: 2329–68.

Bazzi, Samuel, Arya Gaduh, Alexander D. Rothenberg, and Maisy Wong. 2019. "Unity in Diversity? How Intergroup Contact Can Foster Nation Building." *American Economic Review* 109, no. 11 (November): 3979–4025.

Becker, Anke. 2019. "On the Economic Origins of Restrictions on Women's Sexuality." June. CESifo Working Paper No. 7770.

Becker, Anke, Benjamin Enke, and Armin Falk. 2020. "Ancient Origins of the Global Variation in Economic Preferences." *AEA Papers and Proceedings* 110 (May): 319–23.

Becker, Sascha O., and Steven Pfaff. 2023. "Church, State, and Historical Political Economy." *The Oxford Handbook of Historical Political Economy.* ed. Jeffery A. Jenkins and Jared Rubin, 925–44. New York: Oxford University Press.

Becker, Sascha O., and Ludger Woessmann. 2008. "Luther and the Girls: Religious Denomination and the Female Education Gap in Nineteenth-Century Prussia." *Scandinavian Journal of Economics* 110, no. 4: 777–805.

Becker, Sascha O., and Ludger Woessmann. 2009. "Was Weber Wrong? A Human Capital Theory of Protestant Economic History." *Quarterly Journal of Economics* 124, no. 2: 531–96.

Becker, Sascha O., Katrin Boeckh, Christa Hainz, and Ludger Woessmann. 2016. "The Empire Is Dead, Long Live the Empire! Long-Run Persistence of Trust and Corruption in the Bureaucracy." *Economic Journal* 126, no. 590: 40–74.

Bentzen, Jeanet. 2019. "Acts of God? Religiosity and Natural Disasters across Subnational World Districts." *Economic Journal* 129, no. 622 (August): 2295–321.

BenYishay, Ariel, Pauline Grosjean, and Joe Vecci. 2017. "The Fish Is the Friend of Matriliny: Reef Density and Matrilineal Inheritance." *Journal of Development Economics* 127 (July): 234–49.

Bergeron, Augustin. 2020. "Religion and the Scope of Morality: Evidence from Exposure to Missions in the D.R. Congo." May. Working Paper.

Bisin, Alberto and Thierry Verdier. 2000. "Beyond the Melting Pot: Cultural Transmission, Marriage and the Evolution of Ethnic and Religious Traits." *Quarterly Journal of Economics* 115: 955–88.

Bisin, Alberto, and Thierry Verdier. 2001. "The Economics of Cultural Transmission and the Dynamics of Preferences." *Journal of Economic Theory* 97: 298–319.

Bisin, Alberto, and Thierry Verdier. 2011. "The Economics of Cultural Transmission and Socialization." In *Handbooks in Economics: Social Economics.* ed. Jess Benhabib, Alberto Bisin, and Matthew O. Jackson, 340–99. North Holland: Elsevier.

Bisin, Alberto, and Thierry Verdier. 2017. "On the Joint Evolution of Culture and Institutions." NBER Working Paper 23375.

Blouin, Arthur. 2022. "Culture and Contracts: The Historical Legacy of Forced Labour." *Economic Journal* 132, no. 641 (January): 89–105.

Booth, Alison, Elliott Fan, Xin Meng, and Dandan Zhang. 2019. "Gender Differences in Willingness to Compete: The Role of Culture and Institutions." *Economic Journal* 129, no. 618 (February): 734–64.

Boyd, Robert, and Peter J. Richerson. 1985. *Culture and the Evolutionary Process.* London: University of Chicago Press.

Brodeur, Abel, and Joanne Haddad. 2021. "Institutions, Attitudes and LGBT: Evidence from the Gold Rush." *Journal of Economic Behavior & Organization* 187 (July): 92–110.

Buggle, Johannes 2016. "Law and Social Capital: Evidence from the Code Napoleon." *European Economic Review* 87: 148–75.

Buggle, Johannes. 2020. "Growing Collectivism: Irrigation, Group Conformity and Technological Divergence." *Journal of Economic Growth* 25, no. 2: 147–93.

Buggle, Johannes C., and Ruben Durante. 2021. "Climate Risk, Cooperation and the Co-Evolution of Culture and Institutions." *Economic Journal* 131, no. 637 (July): 1947–87.

Butler, Jeffrey V., Paola Giuliano, and Luigi Guiso. 2016. "The Right Amount of Trust." *Journal of the European Economic Association* 14, no. 5 (October): 1155–80.

Calderon, Alvaro, Vasiliki Fouka, and Marco Tabellini. 2022. "Racial Diversity and Racial Policy Preferences: The Great Migration and Civil Rights." *Review of Economic Studies.*

Campa, Pamela and Michel Serafinelli. 2019. "Politico-Economic Regimes and Attitudes: Female Workers under State Socialism." *Review of Economics and Statistics* 101, no. 2 (May): 233–48.

Cantoni, Davide. 2012. "Adopting a New Religion: The Case of Protestantism in 16th Century Germany." *Economic Journal* 122, no. 560 (May): 502–31.

Cantoni, Davide. 2014. "The Economic Effects of the Protestant Reformation: Testing the Weber Hypothesis in the German Lands." *Journal of the European Economic Association* 13, no. 4 (August): 561–98.

Cantoni, Davide, Jeremiah Dittmar, and Noam Yuchtman. 2018. "Religious Competition and Reallocation: The Political Economy of Secularization in the Protestant Reformation." *Quarterly Journal of Economics* 133, no. 4 (November): 2037–96.

Cao, Yiming, Benjamin Enke, Armin Falk, Paola Giuliano. and Nathan Nunn. 2021. "Herding, Warfare, and a Culture of Honor: Global Evidence." September. Technical Report. NBER Working Paper 29250.

Cappelen, Alexander W., Benjamin Enke, and Bertil Tungodden. 2022. "Universalism: Global Evidence." June. NBER Working Paper 30157.

Cavalli-Sforza, L. L., and M. W. Feldman. 1981. *Cultural Transmission and Evolution: A Quantitative Approach*. Princeton, NJ: Princeton University Press.

Cervellati, Matteo, Giorgio Chiovelli, and Elena Esposito. 2019. "Bite and Divide: Malaria and Ethnolinguistic Diversity." January. SSRN Working Paper 3315364.

Chaudhary, Latika, Jared Rubin, Sriya Iyer, and Anand Shrivastava. 2020. "Culture and Colonial Legacy: Evidence from Public Goods Games." *Journal of Economic Behavior and Organization* 173: 107–29.

Corno, Lucia, Nicole Hildebrandt, and Alessandra Voena. 2020. "Age of Marriage, Weather Shocks and the Direction of Marriage Payments." *Econometrica* 88, no. 3 (May): 879–915.

Couttenier, Mathieu, Pauline Grosjean, and Marc Sangnier. 2017. "The Wild West IS Wild: The Homicide Resource Curse." *Journal of the European Economic Association* 15, no. 3 (July): 558–85.

D'Acunto, Francesco, Marcel Prokopczuk, and Michael Weber. 2019. "Historical Antisemitism, Ethnic Specialization, and Financial Development." *Review of Economic Studies* 86, no. 3 (May): 1170–206.

Dalton, John T., and Tin Cheuk Leung. 2014. "Why Is Polygyny More Prevalent in Western Africa? An African Slave Trade Perspective." *Economic Development and Cultural Change* 62, no. 4 (July): 599–632.

Dell, Melissa, Nathan Lane, and Pablo Querubin. 2018. "The Historical State, Local Collective Action, and Economic Development in Vietnam." *Econometrica* 86, no. 6: 2083–121.

Desmet, Klaus, Ignacio Ortuño-Ortn, and Romain Wacziarg. 2017. "Culture, Ethnicity, and Diversity." *American Economic Review* 107, no. 9 (September): 2479–513.

Desmet, Klaus, and Romain Wacziarg. 2018. "The Cultural Divide." NBER Working Paper 24630.

Dickens, Andrew. 2022. "Understanding Ethnolinguistic Differences: The Roles of Geography and Trade." *Economic Journal* 132, no. 642: 953–80.

DiMaggio, Paul. 1997. "Culture and Cognition." *Annual Review of Sociology* 23: 263–87.

Ember, C. 2012. "Human Relations Area Files." In: *Leadership in Science and Technology: A Reference Handbook*, ed. William Sims Bainbridge, 619–27. Thousand Oaks, CA: SAGE.

Enke, Benjamin. 2019. "Kinship, Cooperation, and the Evolution of Moral Systems." *Quarterly Journal of Economics* 134, no. 2: 953–1019.

Enke, Benjamin. 2020. "Moral Values and Voting." *Journal of Political Economy* 128, no. 10: 3679–729.

Enke, Benjamin, Ricardo Rodrguez-Padilla, and Florian Zimmermann. 2022. "Moral Universalism: Measurement and Economic Relevance." *Management Science* 68, no. 5: 3175–973.

Ermisch, John and Diego Gambetta. 2010. "Do Strong Family Ties Inhibit Trust?" *Journal of Economic Behavior and Organization* 75, no. 3 (September): 365–76.

Falk, Armin, Anke Becker, Thomas Dohmen, Benjamin Enke, David Huffman, and Uwe Sunde. 2018. "Global Evidence on Economic Preferences." *Quarterly Journal of Economics* 133, no. 4: 1645–92.

Falk, Armin, Anke Becker, Thomas Dohmen, David B. Huffman, and Uwe Sunde. 2023. "The Preference Survey Module: A Validated Instrument for Measuring Risk, Time and Social Preferences." *Management Science* 69, no. 4 (April): 1935–50.

Fenske, James. 2015. "African Polygamy: Past and Present." *Journal of Development Economics* 117: 58–73.

Fernández, Raquel. 2008. "Culture and Economics." In *New Palgrave Dictionary of Economics*, ed. Steven N. Durlauf and E. Lawrence, 1–10. London: Palgrave Macmillan.

Fernández, Raquel. 2011. "Does Culture Matter?" in *Handbook of Social Economics*, Vol. 1A, ed. Matthew O. Jackson, Jess Benhabib, and Alberto Bisin, 481–510. Elsevier.

Fernández, Raquel, Alessandra Fogli, and Claudia Olivetti. 2004. "Mothers and Sons: Preference Formation and Female Labor Force Dynamics." *Quarterly Journal of Economics* 119, no. 4 (November): 1249–99.

Fernandez, Raquel and Alessandra Fogli. 2009. "Culture: An Empirical Investigation of Beliefs, Work, and Fertility." *American Economic Journal: Macroeconomics* 1, no. 1: 146–77.

Figlio, David, Paola Giuliano, Umut Özek, and Paola Sapienza. 2019. "Long-Term Orientation and Educational Performance." *American Economic Journal: Economic Policy* 11, no. 4: 272–309.

Fouka, Vasiliki. 2020. "Backlash: The Unintended Effects of Language Prohibition in U.S. Schools after World War I." *Review of Economic Studies* 87, no. 1 (January): 204–39.

Fouka, Vasiliki. 2023. "Assimilation in Historical Political Economy." *The Oxford Handbook of Historical Political Economy*. ed. Jeffery A. Jenkins and Jared Rubin, 669–89. New York: Oxford University Press.

Fouka, Vasiliki, Soumyajit Mazmunder, and Marco Tabellini. 2022. "From Immigrants to Americans: Race and Assimilation during the Great Migration." *Review of Economic Studies* 89, no. 2: 811–42.

Fouka, Vasiliki and Alain Schläpfer. 2020. "Agricultural Returns to Labour and the Origins of Work Ethics." *Economic Journal* 130, no. 628 (May): 1081–13.

Galor, Oded, and Ömer Özak. 2016. "The Agricultural Origins of Time Preference." *American Economic Review* 106, no. 10 (October): 3064–103.

Galor, Oded, and Viacheslav Savitskiy. 2018. "Climatic Roots of Loss Aversion." November. NBER Working Paper 25273.

Gershman, Boris. 2016. "Witchcraft Beliefs and the Erosion of Social Capital: Evidence from Sub-Saharan." *Journal of Development Economics* 120: 182–208.

Gershman, Boris. 2020. "Witchcraft Beliefs as a Cultural Legacy of the Atlantic Slave Trade: Evidence from Two Continents." *European Economic Review* 122: 103362.

Giuliano, Paola, and Nathan Nunn. 2018. "Ancestral Characteristics of Modern Populations." *Economic History of Developing Regions* 33, no. 1: 1–17.

Giuliano, Paola, and Nathan Nunn. 2021. "Understanding Cultural Persistence and Change." *Review of Economic Studies* 88, no. 4: 1541–81.

Giuliano, Paola, and Marco Tabellini. 2020. "The Seeds of Ideology: Historical Immigration and Political Preferences in the United States." Harvard Business School Working Paper, No. 20-118.

Gneezy, Uri, Kenneth L. Leonard, and John A. List. 2009. "Gender Differences in Competition: Evidence from a Matrilineal and a Patriarchal Society." *Econometrica* 77, no. 5: 1637–1664.

Gordon, Raymond G. 2009. *Ethnologue: Languages of the World*, 16th ed. Dallas, Texas: SIL International.

Gorodnichenko, Yuriy, and Gerard Roland. 2011. "Individualism, Innovation, and Long-Run Growth." *PNAS* 108, no. 4: 21316–19.

Gorodnichenko, Yuriy, and Gerard Roland. 2017. "Culture, Institutions, and the Wealth of Nations." *Review of Economics and Statistics* 99: 402–16.

Gorodnichenko, Yuriy, and Gerard Roland. 2021. "Culture, Institutions and Democratization." *Public Choice* 187, no. 1 (April): 165–95.

Gregory, James, and A. Hermida. 2019. "Congress of Racial Equality (CORE) Actions, 1942–1972. Mapping American Social Movement."

Greif, Avner. 1994. "Cultural Beliefs and the Organization of Society: A Historical and Theoretical Reflection on Collectivist and Individualist Societies." *Journal of Political Economy* 102, no. 5: 912–50.

Grosjean, Pauline. 2011. "The Weight of History on European Cultural Integration: A Gravity Approach." *American Economic Review Papers and Proceedings* 101, no. 3: 504–8.

Grosjean, Pauline. 2014. "A History of Violence: The Culture of Honor as a Determinant of Homicide in the US South." *Journal of the European Economic Association* 12, no. 5: 1285–316.

Grosjean, Pauline, and Rose Khattar. 2019. "It's Raining Men! Hallelujah? The Long-Run Consequences of Male-Biased Sex Ratios." *Review of Economic Studies* 86, no. 2: 723–54.

Guiso, Luigi, Paola Sapienza, and Luigi Zingales. 2006. "Does Culture Affect Economic Outcomes?" *Journal of Economic Perspectives* 20, no. 2: 23–48.

Guiso, Luigi, Paola Sapienza, and Luigi Zingales. 2016. "Long-Term Persistence." *Journal of the European Economic Association* 14, no. 6 (December): 1401–36.

Hänisch, Dieter. 1988. *Wahl- und Sozialdaten der Kreise und Gemeinden des Deutschen Reiches 1920–1933, Database ZA8013*. Berlin: Leibniz-Institut für Sozialwissenschaften-GESIS.

Heldring, Leander. 2021. "The Origins of Violence in Rwanda." *Review of Economic Studies* 88, no. 2: 730–63.

Henrich, Joseph. 2015. *The Secret of Our Success: How Culture Is Driving Human Evolution*. Princeton, New York: Princeton University Press.

Henrich, Joseph. 2020. *The WEIRDest People in the World: How the West Became Psychologically Peculiar and Particularly Prosperous*. New York: Farrar, Straus and Giroux.

Henrich, Joseph, Michal Bauer, Alessandra Cassar, Julie Chytilová, and Benjamin Grant Purzycki. 2019. "War Increases Religiosity." *Nature Human Behaviour* 3 (February): 129–35.

Henrich, Joseph, Robert Boyd, Sam Bowles, Colin Camerer, Herbert Gintis, Richard McElreath, and Ernst Fehr. 2001. "In Search of Homo Economicus: Experiments in 15 Small-Scale Societies." *American Economic Review* 91, no. 2: 73–79.

Henrich, Joseph, R. Boyd, S. Bowles, H. Gintis, E. Fehr, C. Camerer, R. McElreath, M. Gurven, K. Hill, A. Barr, J. Ensminger, D. Tracer, F. Marlow, J. Patton, M. Alvard, F. Gil-White, and N. Henrich. 2005. "'Economic Man' in Cross-Cultural Perspective: Ethnography and Experiments from 15 Small-Scale Societies." *Behavioral and Brain Sciences* 28: 795–855.

Hofstede, Geert. 1980. *Culture's Consequences: International Differences in Work-Related Values*. Beverly Hills, CA: SAGE.

Hofstede, Geert, Gert Jan Hofstede, and Michael Minkov. 2010. *Culture and Organizations: Software of the Mind*, 3rd ed. New York: McGraw-Hill.

Huntington, Samuel P. 2000. "Culture Makes Almost All the Difference." In *Culture Matters: How Values Shape Human Progress*, ed. Lawrence E. Harrison and Samuel P. Huntington, xiii–xvi. New York: Basic Books.

Kahneman, Daniel, Jack L. Knetsch, and Richard H. Thale. 1991. "Anomalies: The Endowment Effect, Loss Aversion, and Status Quo Bias." *Journal of Economic Perspectives* 5, no. 1: 193–206.

Karaja, Elira, and Jared Rubin. 2017. "The Cultural Transmission of Trust: Evidence from a Lab in the Field on a Natural Experiment." June. SSRN Working Paper 2954336.

Le Rossignol, Etienne, and Sara Lowes. 2022. "Ancestral Livelihoods and Moral Universalism: Evidence from Transhumant Pastoralist Societies." NBER Working Paper 30259.

Le Rossignol, Etienne, Sara Lowes, and Nathan Nunn. 2022. "Traditional Supernatural Beliefs and Prosocial Behavior." January. NBER Working Paper 29695.

Lowes, Sara. 2018. "Matrilineal Kinship and Spousal Cooperation: Evidence from the Matrilineal Belt." Mimeo.

Lowes, Sara. 2021a. "Ethnographic and Field Data in Historical Economics." In *The Handbook of Historical Economics*, ed. Alberto Bisin and Giovanni Federico, 147–77. Elsevier.

Lowes, Sara. 2021b. "Kinship Structure, Stress, and the Gender Gap in Competition." *Journal of Economic Behavior and Organization* 192 (December): 36–57.

Lowes, Sara, and Eduardo Montero. 2021a. "Concessions, Violence, and Indirect Rule: Evidence from the Congo Free State." *Quarterly Journal of Economics* 136, no. 4: 2047–91.

Lowes, Sara, and Eduardo Montero. 2021b. "The Legacy of Colonial Medicine Campaigns in Central Africa." *American Economic Review* 111, no. 4 (April): 1284–314.

Lowes, Sara, and Nathan Nunn. 2018. "Does Bride Price Promote or Hinder Women's Well-Being?" In *Gender and Development*, ed. Siwan Siwan Anderson, Lori Beaman, and Jean-Philippe Platteau, 117–38. Oxford: Oxford University Press.

Lowes, Sara, and Nathan Nunn. 2022. "The Slave Trade and Matrilineal Kinship." Working paper.

Lowes, Sara, Nathan Nunn, James A. Robinson, and Jonathan L. Weigel. 2017. "The Evolution of Culture and Institutions: Evidence from the Kuba Kingdom." *Econometrica* 85, no. 4: 1065–91.

Michalopoulos, Stelios. 2012. "The Origins of Ethnolinguistic Diversity." *American Economic Review* 102, no. 4: 1508–39.

Michalopoulos, Stelios, Alireza Naghavi, and Giovanni Prarolo. 2018. "Trade and Geography in the Spread of Islam." *Economic Journal* 128, no. 616: 3210–41.

Michalopoulos, Stelios, and Melanie Xue. 2021. "Folklore." *Quarterly Journal of Economic* 136, no. 4 (November): 1993–2046.

Moscona, Jacob, Nathan Nunn, and James A. Robinson. 2017. "Keeping It in the Family: Lineage Organization and the Scope of Trust in Sub-Saharan Africa." *American Economic Review: Papers and Proceedings* 107, no. 5: 565–71.

Moscona, Jacob, Nathan Nunn, and James A. Robinson. 2020. "Social Structure and Conflict: Evidence from Sub-Saharan Africa." *Econometrica* 88, no. 5: 1999–2036.

Murdock, George Peter. 1967. *Ethnographic Atlas*. Pittsburgh: University of Pittsburgh Press.

Murdock, George Peter, and Douglas R. White. 1969. "Standard Cross-Cultural Sample." *Ethnology* 8, no. 4: 329–69.

Muthukrishna, Michael, and Joseph Henrich. 2016. "Innovation and the Collective Brain." *Philosophical Transactions B* 371, no. 1690: 20150192.

Niederle, Muriel. 2017. "A Gender Agenda: A Progress Report on Competitiveness." *American Economic Review Papers and Proceedings* 107, no. 5: 115–19.

Niederle, Muriel, and Lise Vesterlund. 2007. "Do Women Shy Away from Competition? Do Men Compete Too Much?" *Quarterly Journal of Economics* 122, no. 3 (August): 1067–101.

Nisbett, Richard E., and Dov Cohen. 1993. "Self-Protection and the Culture of Honor: Explaining Southern Homicide." *Personality and Social Psychology Bulletin* 20: 551–67.

Nisbett, Richard E., and Dov Cohen. 1996. *Culture of Honor: The Psychology of Violence in the South*, Boulder, CO: Westview Press.

Nunn, Nathan. 2010. "Religious Conversion in Colonial Africa." *American Economic Review* 100, no. 2 (May): 147–52.

Nunn, Nathan. 2021. "History as Evolution." In *The Handbook of Historical Economics*, ed. Alberto Bisin and Giovanni Federico, 41–91. Elsevier.

Nunn, Nathan. 2022. "On the Dynamics of Human Behavior: The Past, Present, and Future of Culture, Conflict, and Cooperation." *American Economic Association Papers and Proceedings* 112 (May): 15–37.

Nunn, Nathan, and Leonard Wantchekon. 2011. "The Slave Trade and the Origins of Mistrust in Africa." *American Economic Review* 101, no. 7: 3221–52.

Okoye, Dozie. 2021. "Things Fall Apart? Missions, Institutions, and Interpersonal Trust." *Journal of Development Economics* 148 (January): 102568.

Prats, Ana Tur, and Felipe Valencia. 2020. "The Long Shadow of the Spanish Civil War." July. CEPR Working Paper DP15091.

Ramos-Toro, Diego. 2019. "Social Exclusion and Social Preferences: Evidence from Colombia's Leper Colony." October.

Richerson, Peter J., and Robert Boyd. 2005. *Not by Genes Alone: How Culture Transformed Human Evolution*. Chicago: University of Chicago Press.

Rogers, Alan R. 1988. "Does Biology Constrain Culture?" *American Anthropologist* 90, no. 4: 819–31.

Rubin, Jared. 2014. "Printing and Protestants: An Empirical Test of the Role of Printing in the Reformation." *Review of Economics and Statistics* 96, no. 2 (May): 270–86.

Rustagi, Devesh. 2020. "Historical Self-Governance and Norms of Cooperation." Working Paper.

Schulz, Jonathan. 2022. "The Churches' Bans on Consanguineous Marriages, Kin Networks and Democracy." *Economic Journal* 132, no. 647: 1578–2613.

Schulz, Jonathan F., Duman Bahrami-Rad, Jonathan P. Beauchamp, and Joseph Henrich. 2019. "The Church, Intensive Kinship, and Global Psychological Variation." *Science* 366, no. 6466: eaau5141.

Sunde, Uwe, Thomas Dohmen, Benjamin Enke, Armin Falk, David Huffman, and Gerrit Meyerheim. 2022. "Patience and Comparative Development." *Review of Economic Studies* 89, no. 10 (December): 2806–840.

Suryanarayan, Pavithra, and Steven White. 2023. "Identity Politics in Historical Political Economy." *The Oxford Handbook of Historical Political Economy*. ed. Jeffery A. Jenkins and Jared Rubin, 733–46. New York: Oxford University Press.

Swidler, Ann. 1986. "Culture in Action: Symbols and Strategies." *American Sociological Review* 51, no. 2: 273–86.

Tabellini, Guido. 2008. "The Scope of Cooperation: Values and Incentives." *Quarterly Journal of Economics* 123, no. 3: 905–50.

Tabellini, Guido. 2010. "Culture and Institutions: Economic Development in the Regions of Europe." *Journal of the European Economic Association* 8, no. 4: 677–716.

Talhelm, Thomas, X. Zhang, S. Oishi, C. Shimin, D. Duan, X. Lan, and S. Kitayama. 2014. "Large-Scale Psychological Differences within China Explained by Rice Versus Wheat Agriculture." *Science* 344, no. 6184: 603–8.

Teele, Dawn L., and Pauline A. Grosjean. 2023. "Gender in Historical Political Economy." *The Oxford Handbook of Historical Political Economy*. ed. Jeffery A. Jenkins and Jared Rubin, 713–37. New York: Oxford University Press.

Teso, Edoardo. 2019. "The Long-Term Effect of Demographic Shocks on the Evolution of Gender Roles: Evidence from the Transatlantic Slave Trade." *Journal of the European Economic Association* 17, no. 2: 497–534.

Tversky, Amos, and Daniel Kahneman. 1991. "Loss Aversion in Riskless Choice: A Reference-Dependent Model." *Quarterly Journal of Economics* 106, no. 4: 1039–61.

Valencia Caicedo, Felipe, and Hans-Joachim Voth. 2018. "Christ's Shadow: Non-Cognitive Skills and Prosocial Behavior amongst the Guarani." October. UBC Working Paper.

Voigtländer, Nico, and Hans-Joachim Voth. 2012. "Persecution Perpetuated: The Medieval Origins of Anti-Semitic Violence in Nazi Germany." *Quarterly Journal of Economics* 127, no. 3: 1339–92.

Walker, Sarah. 2020. "Historical Legacies in Savings: Evidence from Romania." *Journal of Comparative Economics* 48, no. 1: 76–99.

Xue, Melanie Meng. 2016. "High-Value Work and the Rise of Women: The Cotton Revolution and Gender Equality in China." November. SSRN Working Paper 2389218.

CHAPTER 45

CHURCH, STATE, AND HISTORICAL POLITICAL ECONOMY

SASCHA O. BECKER AND STEVEN PFAFF

But if politicks had never called in the aid of religion, had the conquering party never adopted the tenets of one sect more than those of another, when it had gained victory . . . There would in this case, no doubt, have been a great multitude of religious sects, [the state] would have probably dealt impartially with all the different sects, and have allowed each man to chuse his own priest and his own religion as he thought proper. . . . In a country where the law favoured the teachers of no one religion more than those of another, it would not be necessary that any of them should have any particular influence or immediate dependency upon the sovereign or executive power; or that he should have anything to do, either in appointing, or in dismissing them from their offices.
Adam Smith, *An Inquiry into the Nature and Causes of the Wealth of Nations*, Volume 2 (1976 [1776], 792–93)

The starting point in any analysis of church and state is that religious and political powers in society are organizationally distinct. Of course, this is a profound departure from many conventional ideas about the organization of society in which the polity is defined, in great part, by membership in a religious community (Durkheim 1964 [1912]; Henrich 2020). For much of human history, neither the institutional nor the intellectual separation of religion and state obtain; to be subject to sovereign authority is to be subject to the authority of a shared god or gods.

The particular notion that, no matter how intertwined in practice, political and religious institutions can be thought of as different and separate is an idea that owes much to the Christian doctrine of two powers (temporal and spiritual) that together constitute social order. The doctrine had an enormous influence on the development of secular law and delimited sovereignty in Western Europe (Berman 1983; Bueno de Mesquita

2000; Grzymala-Busse 2020). However, the extensive literature in theology and comparative religious studies on these issues is not the focus of this essay. In this review we use the conventional terms "church and state" or "church-state relations" because they are standard in the literature, not because we endorse a Western or Christian-centric perspective on the relationship between religious organizations and states. Without denying that doctrinal and institutional differences matter across religions, our perspective is informed by political economy. Since the beginning of complex agrarian civilizations, social differentiation has produced specialization in religion as distinct from political specialization (Lenski 1984; Mann 1986). Once such specialization is present, the relationship between political and religious organization has major importance for understanding the evolution of societies (Weber 1963 [1922]). A historical and comparative political economy of religion seeks to understand the dynamic relationship between polities and religious groups and its manifold consequences across time, place, and cultural traditions (Becker, Rubin, and Woessmann 2021; Coşgel, Histen, Miceli, and Yıldırım 2018; Iyer 2016). Contemporary work examining diverse cases continues to show that church-state relations are important for understanding economics, politics and society. This essay discusses the major themes in the literature on church and state and some of the findings in the political economy of religion, and evaluates emerging directions in research on church-state relations.

The Church-State Bargain

The most important idea in the literature on church and state in the social sciences is that the relationship between governments and religions is predicated on a bargain between rulers and religious authorities. Max Weber (1978 [1921–1922], 908) suggested that, in exchange for fiscal and political support from rulers, religious authorities can offer ideological support that legitimates the political order. Although Weber recognized that secular ideologies can perform this function, at least until modern times religions provided the most complete ideological systems. Consequently, the historical linkage between religion, rule, and economic institutions has been tight, and religious ideologies have been implicated in the evolution of economic and political institutions (Weber 1978 [1921–1922]; 1981).

The Logic of Church-State Alliances

The parties implicated in church-state relations contend with the potential costs and benefits of cooperation.[1] From the perspective of a ruler, an established religion can be a valuable partner because it lends ideological legitimation through teachings that lower the cost of rule. It does this by justifying the role of the ruling class and convincing at least some subjects that they must obey because of divine will and, perhaps, divine sanctions like blessings and punishments. Although this is potentially a very attractive partnership for rulers, it also depends on the incentives that they can offer religious authorities in exchange for supporting the regime. Religious organizations are social enterprises that supply religion to potential adherents and regulate their exchanges with god/gods. They operate in a religious economy in which they may compete with other religious firms for adherents and revenues (Ekelund, Hébert, and Tollison 2006; Hull and Bold 1989; Iannaccone 1995; 1998; Iyer 2016; Stark and Finke 2000). One strategy for increasing adherents and revenues is to attain a monopoly position as the sole supplier of religious goods. Outside of natural monopoly conditions (such as those that obtain in small-scale and tribal societies; see Durkheim 1964 [1912]; Henrich 2020), this usually means eliminating the competition. A religious organization can become the only (licit) source of spiritual goods when it is established through regulation or through state-sponsored violence. Ideally, from the incumbent monopolist's perspective, it will enjoy an incontestable position that guarantees a predictable revenue stream and shields it from market rivals, such as foreign imports or upstart sects offering superior products or lower prices (Iannaccone 2005). Historically and comparatively, this means that such monopolies depend on a bargain struck between a ruler or ruling class and religious leaders.

Religion may help to constitute nascent polities by involving people in group rituals that create collective identity and communally integrative emotions (Henrich 2020). However, it is debatable whether such polities can scale up to the level of kingdoms and empires. Recent work suggests that some religious organizations are more attractive partners to rulers than others because of the kinds of religious ideas they supply. For instance, moralizing gods seem more important than other gods for attaining large-scale social order and exchange networks (Beheim et al. 2021; Lang et al. 2019; Roes and Raymond 2003). Moralizing gods provide divine incentives, particularly punishments, for noncooperators and those who defy the political community. The character of religious doctrines seems to matter. Gods who are indifferent to human fates, who are morally inconsistent, who lack omnipotence and omniscience, and whose authority is limited to certain regions, tribes, or holy places may be much less useful for backing claims to broad political authority. In particular, religious organizations that have offered the notion of "One True God"—universal, moralizing, omnipotent, and omniscient—seem to have conveyed a political advantage on the states that adopted them (Stark 2001; Stark and Finke 2000). In many instances, a state and a religious group become very closely associated with each other such that religion effectively determines the state's nationality, as was historically the case in examples such as the Orthodox churches in Eastern Europe, the state Lutheran churches in the Nordic countries, or Theravada Buddhism in the Thai kingdoms.

The role of the Catholic Church in medieval Europe is a much-studied case of church-state bargaining in which the religious organization, at least initially, held the upper hand (Grzymala-Busse 2020). Ekelund, Hébert, and Tollison (2006) show that the medieval Catholic Church made an exclusive claim on products and services focusing on sanctification and redemption from sin. Over time, it evolved into a multidivisional economic firm with substantial political power as it expanded first within the boundaries of the late Roman Empire and later throughout Europe, North Africa, and the Middle East through its missions to the barbarians. Achieving a transnational monopoly, it generally had a superior bargaining position relative to local princes because of its organization, scale of operation, wealth, and human capital resources. Nevertheless, the Church needed secular rulers. In order to defend its monopoly, the Church had two tasks: maintain its exclusive claim to the promise of salvation and prevent rivals from entering the religious marketplace (Ekelund et al. 1996). In the wake of the collapse of the Western Roman Empire, both imperatives required cooperation with the local feudal nobility and nascent kingdoms to provide armed force to battle infidels, "heretics," and schismatics (Rubin 2017; Stark 2001). The medieval arrangement was thus one in which the Roman Church conferred legitimacy on a warrior caste and gradually attained an effective and practically incontestable monopoly in return. Because the Roman Church was (usually) organizationally unified and resourceful, it tended to bargain favorably with secular princes until the early-modern era, particularly once the sixteenth-century Reformation overturned its monopoly in Western Europe.

Why Do Church-State Bargains Fall Apart?

Religious organizations are generally cost-effective legitimating agents that can produce semivoluntary compliance among believers (Greif and Rubin 2022). However, these costs can rise because of both exogenous and endogenous institutional reasons. The well-documented case of the Roman Catholic Church forces us to consider the robustness of church-state institutions once established. North (1981) proposes that rulers invest in ideological legitimation in order to deter free riding on the political order and lower the costs of enforcing the dominant property rights regime. However, legitimating ideologies must be both persuasive and flexible, effective to the extent that they make sense of property rights, exchange relations, and labor market positions. A church-state equilibrium can be disturbed by endogenous or exogenous factors that alter beliefs about the fairness and inevitability of the institutions, whether through empowering new groups, threatening the welfare of others, or by providing new sources of information that suggest most favorable terms of exchange (North 1981, 48–52). In Europe, urbanization, economic growth, legal rationalization, administrative consolidation—each abetted in various ways by the growing sophistication of the medieval Church—gradually undermined its bargaining power vis-à-vis the rising secular princes (Grzymala-Busse 2020).

Economic development can also put dominant religious explanations into doubt and increase the costs of restrictions on the economic behavior beyond the point elites are willing to bear. For example, growth that improves material welfare and existential security can make religious explanations stressing divine immanence and supernatural assistance in everyday subsistence unsatisfactory, at least to the privileged classes (Weber 1963 [1922]: 140–411; see also Norris and Inglehart 2004). The Protestant Reformation, for instance, appears to have exploited demand-side dissatisfaction with Roman Catholicism among burghers that resulted from urbanization and commercial expansion (Becker, Pfaff, and Rubin 2016).

Building on North's model, Gill (1998) argues that a prevailing church-state arrangement reflects the relative power of the two institutions. He proposes that episodes of church-state conflict occur "when the opportunity costs of cooperation for any one party exceed the present or future benefits of cooperation" (Gill 1998, 83). Where rulers are weak and insecure, they will exchange much in return for legitimacy. Weak states may not only establish and protect a religious monopolist, but also grant it extensive privileges in the secular political and economic domains. These concessions can prove very costly over time. However, where rulers are stronger, the monopoly firm may be compelled to allow rulers to become the de facto head of the religion (e.g., caesaropapism, as in the Eastern Church), grant them the right to appoint senior clerics and fill clerical vacancies (e.g., investiture in the Western Church), exempt ruling classes from tithes, and share religious revenues with the state.

Gill (1998) finds that shifting calculations as to whether the state would protect them from competition from Protestant sects explain why some Latin American churches backed authoritarian regimes while others switched their support to opposition forces. Clearly, church-state conflicts are not always resolved in favor of the state. The papacy successfully worked to keep the medieval Holy Roman Empire politically divided, and papal intrigue helped to weaken the Italian city states, major factors helping to explain why Europe remained politically fragmented into the modern era (Grzymala-Busse 2020). Part of the reason for the subsequent divergence between the economic fates of Western Europe and the Middle East appears to have been that the Islamic clerical establishment consolidated its advantages vis-à-vis Ottoman rulers (Kuran 2012; Rubin 2017). If alternative ideologies to legitimate the state become available at a lower cost, or when the religious monopoly holds coveted financial assets that can only be had by the state through expropriation, rulers may seek to depose the incumbent monopoly, as many European rulers did during the Reformation (Cantoni 2012; Pfaff and Corcoran 2012). At the extreme ends of the continuum of the church-state rivalry, conflict between rulers and incumbent monopolists can result in theocracies in which the religious elite captures the state (e.g., Iran after the 1979 revolution), or one in which the state fully captures the church, perhaps abolishing religion outright (as communist regimes attempted to do; see Froese 2008; Pfaff 2011; Yang 2011).

In the long run, a cooperation with rulers can be quite costly to a religion. Monopolism may harm the vitality of an established religion, as first discussed by Adam Smith (1976 [1776]). Establishment reduces clerical incentives to act with energy and religious zeal in attracting and retaining adherents. A state-established religion is probably most secure and cost-efficient when its customers have brand loyalty and its institutions are self-enforcing. Self-enforcement depends on the credibility of religious goods such as sanctification and salvation that the established religion produces exclusively. For instance, the Catholic Church long maintained that it controlled the only route to eternal salvation. However, inherent tensions created by its monopoly status undercut performance and created incentives to exploit religious consumers through rent-seeking (Ekelund et al. 1996). Religious ideologies are credence goods whose value can be spoiled by behaviors and organizational practices that diminish faith (Ekelund, Hébert, and Tollison 2006; Iannaccone 1998; Hungerman 2013). Rent-seeking, clerical neglect, and corruption are thus endogenous features of monopoly religious institutions that can undercut their self-enforcing properties. Moreover, because of their closeness to power and identification with the state, established religions are often obliged to make doctrinal or theological compromises that damage their reputation and violate their original foundations in scripture and revelation (Bénabou, Ticchi, and Vindigni 2022).

As the historian Ernst Troeltsch (1960 [1912]) observed, sectarian rebellions tend to erupt from the perception that a church has grown too worldly, betraying its original message and surrendering its religious legitimacy. Once worldliness, greed, and indolence combine to undermine an incumbent monopolist, the demand for its services typically weakens, which reduces the legitimation benefits it can credibly offer a ruler. Once this point is reached, existing church-state institutions are in jeopardy. Rulers will either depose the established church and replace it with another (as many Protestant princes such as England's Henry VIII did in the wake of the Reformation); pluralize the religious economy, allowing a variety of approved religious groups to operate under state license (effectively, a religious oligopoly of the kind established in Russia under Vladimir Putin or as in the People's Republic of China after Mao; see e.g., Yang 2011); or thoroughly deregulate the religious economy as part of the secularization of the state.

Secularization depends, in part, on the remaining clout of religious leaders generally and, in part, on the level of education in society (Becker, Nagler, and Woessmann 2017). Secularization of church-state relations implies that rulers have calculated that they no longer rely on religious legitimation to propagate their rule and can rely on ideologies such as liberalism, nationalism, or socialism to win popular assent (Greif and Rubin 2015; Pfaff 2008; Rubin 2017). It then becomes appealing to secularize religious organizations and assets, either to reward regime loyalists (Heldring, Robinson, and Vollmer 2021) or to reallocate resources toward other political and economic purposes (Cantoni, Dittmar, and Yuchtman 2018). Despite the apparent benefits of disestablishing religion, in the contemporary world truly secular states in which no religious firm is officially privileged or dis-privileged by government regulation and all firms rely entirely on voluntary financial donations remain unusual (Barro and McCleary 2005; Finke 1990; Fox 2008; Grim and Finke 2010).

On the other side of the bargain, a close church-state arrangement can become politically costly to rulers. This is because legitimacy bargains between an established religion and the state constrain the future actions of both parties (Greif and Rubin 2022). Rulers who act in ways that obviously contradict their religious commitments risk the loss of their legitimacy. Moreover, a regime closely associated with a discredited or failing religious establishment can become tarnished, weakening the reputation of its ruling elite. In the fourteenth century, Ibn Khaldun described a dynamic in the Islamic Mahgreb in which urbanized rulers are gradually corrupted by prosperity and luxury, their civilized worldliness contradicting the austere religion of the desert. Reliance on increasingly scholarly and urbane clerics further undermines the ruler's popular legitimacy. Religious unrest in the towns and encroaching barbarians in the wastes weaken the regime that, in short order, is overthrown and replaced by a more militant elite (Khaldun 2005 [1377]; see also Gellner 1981). In modern times, close relationships between rulers and established clerics mean that religious unrest can also mushroom into political rebellion, as has been witnessed in the rise of Islamism across the Muslim world (Berman 2009; Brooke and Ketchley 2018). In fact, sectarian rebellions against established religions are a reoccurring source of conflict in the contemporary era (Fox 2008; Grim and Finke 2010).

The Institutional Legacies of Church-State Bargains

Conservative religious institutions have long been understood as brakes on the modern economy. Weber (1963 [1922]: 207–208) observed, "The dominance of law that has been stereotyped by religion constitutes one of the most significant limitations on the rationalization of the legal order and hence also on the rationalization of the economy." Weak states have often relied on the clergy to staff courts, make laws, and educate the public. Economically, studies by Kuran (2012) and Rubin (2017), among others, show that when states rely heavily on established religions to propagate their rule, clerical interests may have a large say in setting economic policies or shaping legal institutions. This influence can persist long after institutions are formally secularized by imprinting dominant attitudes and practices on a society. Religious influence over economic and educational policy has been shown to affect economic growth through a number of mechanisms: first, inefficient property rights regimes, such as Islamic waqfs that tied wealth to be spent on religious services and diverted it from commercial activities (Adiguzel and Kuran 2021; Michalopoulos, Naghavi, and Prarolo 2016). Second, the duty to pay *zakat* (often translated as "alms") once a year, gave preference to religious purposes and equated limited fiscal capacity for broader purposes (Kuran 2020). Third, religious conservativism puts limitations on innovations by constraining scientific discoveries that raise productivity but sometimes erode religious beliefs (Bénabou, Ticchi, and Vindigni 2015; 2022). Fourth, and related, the Catholic Church issued an Index of Forbidden Books and thereby constrained the freedom of the printing press, holding back the spread of new ideas (Becker, Pino, and Vidal-Robert 2021). Fifth, religious influence affects the allocation of public spending: Cantoni, Dittmar, and Yuchtman (2018) show that after the Protestant Reformation, Protestant rulers redirected spending toward secular purposes., Sixth, human capital acquisition is strongly influenced by religious institutions that either see education as a threat to their rule, or as a force for good (Bazzi, Hilmy, and Marx 2020; Becker and Woessmann 2008; 2009; Dittmar and Meisenzahl 2020; Chaudhary and Rubin 2011; Meyersson 2014; Squicciarini 2020; West and Woessmann 2010). Seventh, religious groups that are more educated also invest more in new technology, which explains the positive influence of (Protestant) Huguenot refugees in Prussia's nascent textiles industry (Hornung 2014) and the constraining influence of Muslim rulers on introducing the printing press (Coşgel, Miceli, and Rubin 2012). Finally, where the clergy control courts or schools, they can use those institutions to undermine reforms they oppose through direct resistance or biased exercise of their offices (Kuran and Lustig 2012). Sectarianism of this kind promotes insurrection and religious persecution of minorities (Kulkarni and Pfaff 2022a; 2022b).

Even in advanced capitalist democracies where the social importance of churches has declined and established religious organizations no longer play the central legitimating role they once did, religion still affects political economy. For example, the imprint of church-state arrangements is evident in welfare-state institutions and beliefs about the appropriate relationship between citizens and the state. Anna Grzymala-Busse's (2015) work shows that the "political theology" underlying historical church-state bargains continues to influence attitudes about legitimacy and what leaders and citizens can properly ask of each other. In modern democracies, these ideas become salient when political competition compels religious organizations to become interest groups that mobilize adherents, make alliances with parties, and try to influence voting all with the aim of influencing policy. The legacy of church-state institutions can also raise hurdles that make it difficult for new religious movements and immigrant faiths to gain official recognition and exercise civil liberties (Pfaff and Gill 2006). In many countries, historically established religions remain strongly associated with nationalism and political belonging, a serious obstacle to social acceptance and political integration in newly diverse societies (Grzymala-Busse 2019).

Research on Religion and State-Making

Whereas religion informed the art of politics in the medieval Christian and Islamic worlds, by the Renaissance era European political discourse was becoming progressively secularized in ways that are not mirrored in the Middle East (Blaydes, Grimmer, and McQueen 2018). This seems like further evidence of a "long divergence" that marked the trajectories of the Middle East and the Western world up through the present. Important research has shown that, because of eroding political-military standing and the proliferation of independent religious endowments, Muslim rulers in the late medieval and early modern eras needed the legitimation bestowed by Islamic schools and courts more than clerics, who controlled substantial trusts (waqfs), needed the state (Kuran 2012; Rubin 2017). Religion, which had fostered early Islamic state-building, became a hindrance in the modern era. Other religions seem to have enhanced state efficiency in the early-modern era. This seems especially true of European states that adopted Protestantism. Cooperation between politically dependent churches and ambitious rulers helped many states to improve administration and impose social discipline (Becker, Pfaff and Rubin 2016). Gorski (2003) argues that Calvinism, in particular, made societies more orderly and tractable because of bottom-up religious governance and its ability to impose moral surveillance at the congregational level.

The role of religion may have been more general and less tied to Protestantism particularly. In the "confessional" age in the sixteenth and seventeenth centuries, the newly established Protestant churches and their antagonist, the Counter-Reformation Catholic Church, played substantial roles across European countries and their colonies by shaping government and administrative practices (Gorski 2000; Schilling 1986). Scholars have argued that the Counter-Reformation in the sixteenth and seventeenth centuries was a key development that helped the Habsburg Monarchy unite its empire, and that the Jesuits played a crucial role in fostering education and human capital and the cultivation of a literate elite dedicated to state service (e.g., Evans 1979; Grendler 2019). The confessional era of state-making and administrative centralization did much to pacify countries internally, even as states devoted ever-greater resources to making war abroad. As hand-in-glove cooperation between centralizing states and religious authorities expanded, distinctive differences in the provision of welfare and the management of the poor became apparent. Distinctively Catholic, Lutheran, and Calvinist doctrines concerning the interpretation of poverty and the proper delivery of assistance imprinted policy, with enduring consequences for welfare-state development and stratification today (Kahl 2005; Pullan 2005; van Kersbergen and Manow 2009). By contrast, the waqf system in the early-modern Ottoman Middle East was the main mechanism through which welfare benefits were distributed, but inefficiently and in ways that hampered state formation (Kuran 2001; 2016).

Missionaries, Colonial States, and Human Capital

Church-state interactions in Christianity are not limited to Europe, but also extend into other continents. Pioneered by Woodberry (2004), researchers have looked at whether the presence of missionaries (Protestant or Catholic) had long-term effects on modern-day outcomes.[2] Interestingly, a lot of the literature looks at missionaries in isolation, abstracting from the role of the (secular) colonial forces. But some work explicitly looks at the constraints imposed on missionaries by the colonial powers. Gallego and Woodberry (2010) provide evidence that regions in former colonial Africa in which Protestant missionaries dominated have higher literacy rates than those where Catholic missionaries dominated. This is largely the result of the different degree of regulation in British colonies where missionaries from different denominations had to compete for students, and in Belgian, Portuguese, and Spanish colonies, which had a bias toward Catholic missionaries, giving them a quasi-monopolistic position. While the French initially favored Catholic missionaries, they later took a more neutral stance. Woodberry (2012) highlights the role Protestant missionaries played in influencing the rise and spread of stable democracy around the world. Statistically, the historic prevalence of Protestant missionaries explains about half the variation in democracy in Africa, Asia, Latin America, and Oceania. The key mechanism behind this finding is that Protestants supported religious liberty, mass education, mass printing, newspapers, voluntary organizations, and colonial reforms, thereby creating the conditions that made stable democracy more likely. Valencia Caicedo (2019b) studies the long-term effects on human capital investment of Jesuit presence in South America that lasted to this day despite the expulsion of the Jesuit order by the Spanish Crown (an example of conflict between the Church and also in colonial areas).

While these examples illustrate how church and state mutually influence each other in colonial countries, rarely do researchers try to quantify the relative contributions of missionaries and colonizers. Wietzke (2015) exploits historical differences in the timing and organization of historical school investments and colonial legal-institutional reforms in Madagascar. Christian missionaries introduced formal schooling several decades before the imposition of French colonial rule and were thus unrelated to the economic or military objectives of the colonizers. Results indicate that colonial institutions had comparatively stronger effects on local economic outcomes than missionary school investments.

The growing literature on the role of missions in development should not limit our appreciation of their often destructive legacy (e.g., Cagé and Rueda 2020). Just focusing on their legacy on state-making, missionaries and colonial churches often sowed seeds of division among native populations and helped create oppressive institutions. One of the most notorious cases is Belgian-ruled Rwanda-Burundi (1916–1962) where Catholic missions became de facto education and welfare agencies of the colonial state; "nowhere was the marriage of convenience between church and state more evident than in Belgian Africa" (Carney 2015, 366). Missions ran primary and secondary schooling and sent selected candidates to Belgium for university study, mostly on religious scholarships (Duarte 1995), which allowed them to promote a race policy favoring the putatively superior Tutsi "race" (Mamdani 2001). After World War II, lower-class mobilization against colonial rule changed the Church's calculations. Prelates distanced themselves from the Tutsi and supported the Hutu majority's nationalist awakening. When Rwanda became independent in 1962, the ruling elite in both state and Church comprised ethnic Hutus. Leading prelates backed an increasingly virulent and exclusive Hutu nationalism, which repeatedly triggered violence and civil war. Many of the politicians who incited the genocide against the Tutsi in 1994 had close ties to the Church leadership, and some priests abetted it at the local level (Des Forges 1999, 39; Longman 2010).

Secularization and the Deregulation of Religion

All early-modern states, to varying extents, imposed religious monopolies and restricted religious minorities. The United States is probably the country that first and most thoroughly deregulated the religious sphere. Earlier instances of toleration, such as the Peace of Augsburg in 1555, effectively split territories of the Holy Roman Empire along denominational lines, so that those who did not follow the ruler's religion had to convert or migrate. Historically, most instances of institutional toleration have been "conditional"; that is, the religious outsider was tolerated based on the goodwill of the ruler, secured through payments, services, or political support (Johnson and Koyama 2019).

The US Constitution prohibits the federal government from the establishment of religion (in the First Amendment) and forbids the imposition of religious tests on officeholding (Article VI). The new republic instituted national religious freedom after having had established churches in the original colonies and the postindependence states. The new federal government rejected an established church, and the various states abandoned theirs by the early nineteenth century. Besides normative commitments to religious freedom among the founders, the economics of church and state in a frontier society seem to have demanded disestablishment. Politicians found that there were simply too many upstart sects to suppress, that established churches were unpopular and relied on expensive subsidies, and that the ability to exit beyond the frontier or to operate across state boundaries made the costs of enforcing a monopoly church prohibitive (Finke 1990; Finke and Stark 1992). Having effectively deregulated the religious economy, America experienced an unprecedented supply-side expansion of churches and sects that Finke and Stark (1992) have aptly called the "churching" of America. For the next two centuries, a competitive religious marketplace thrived both in terms of its diversity and levels of American religiosity achieved.

The situation tended to be quite different in a heavily regulated European market, where waning religious establishments based on historical throne-and-altar alliances gradually lost their grip on the population while still imposing regulatory burdens on firms entering the market and restricting public religious activities (Iannaccone, Finke, and Stark 1997; Pfaff 2008). By contrast, America's early disestablishment made religion a feature of voluntary associational life that enabled religious leaders to compete unhindered for influence in the public sphere. The legacy of American civil religion is evident in comparative perspective in that the contemporary United States is unusual among advanced democracies not only for its religiosity but also for the influence of religious interest groups on politics and the surprisingly high share of the population (somewhat less than half) that believes that religious leaders *should* influence public life (Grzymala-Busse 2015).

What Drives Secularization and the Expansion of Religious Freedom?

The state remains a major player in religious markets around the world, either through religious establishment or through active regulation of religious groups (Barro and McCleary 2005; Fox 2008; Grim and Finke 2010). Nevertheless, secularization has advanced in many polities, and declining popular religiosity can diminish the political benefits that churches can offer parties or regimes in an alliance. Comparatively speaking, there are many pathways to secularism (Gorski and Altinordu 2008; Grzymala-Busse 2020), but the changing incentives of rulers to maintain established religions is one of the most important. For example, Greif and Rubin (2015) regard the "Glorious" Revolution of 1688 in England as a watershed moment in the history of secularization. The revolution overthrew Stuart absolutism, completing the transition from governments making sacred claims to legitimacy to ones relying on the rule of law and parliamentary consent to propagate rule. Johnson and Koyama (2019) show that regimes with established state-church institutions favor religious identity-based inclusion rules that, over the long run, foster instability and undermine effective governance. They too see the year 1688 as a decisive moment in the secularization of political authority because it meant the stepwise reduction of religious influence in government and, as secular elites gained strength, the rise of general citizenship rules over older sectarian "identity-rules" (Johnson and Koyama 2019, 174–79). Finally, Gill (2008) argues that what really matters is a ruler's adopting a pragmatic approach to religious diversity. Commercially valuable religious minorities are more likely to enjoy toleration in a state with a religious establishment. Political liberty is the gradual result of rulers perceiving economic benefits to religious toleration.

Education has been highlighted as another factor driving secularization. At the turn of the 19th to the 20th century, cities in Germany where secondary education expanded more quickly saw a faster decline in church attendance (Becker, Nagler, and Woessmann 2017). The shift in the sectoral composition of the economy from agriculture to manufacturing and services made taxation easier. Concomitantly the rise of income taxes as a source of government revenue made governments less dependent on institutional support by nonstate actors like the church. Seemingly innocuous policy changes may also drive down the influence of the church, such as in the case of the liberation of shop opening hours on Sundays (Gruber and Hungerman 2008). Finally, as the share of those seeing religion as central to their lives increases, the state relies less and less on religious legitimacy and can afford to offer more religious freedom. Over time, the support for separation between church and state grows, with support even from rural constituencies that one would expect to be less favorable to secularization, as in the French case (Franck 2010).

Frontiers and Future Research

Historical scholarship has much to offer as we seek to understand the origins of church-state institutions and the consequences of doctrines for the organization of state and society. So far, the vast majority of the research in the social sciences on church-state interactions that we are aware of—and we freely admit our own shortsightedness—is concerned with the Islamic world and Western Christianity. There seems to be less research in the social sciences on Orthodox Christianity in Eastern and southeastern

Europe, where churches tend to be organized along national lines (e.g., Greek-Orthodox, Russian-Orthodox, Serbian-Orthodox). This contrasts quite starkly with the Roman Catholic Church as a supranational entity. The Islamic world is often treated as a monolithic bloc without regard to differences between Sunni and Shia Islam. More research into the historical roots of these differences and their persistence to the present day would be welcome.

The political economy of religion would also benefit from sustained attention to Asia, where different models of religious organization and church-state interaction may be at work. For example, recent research on China suggests that perspectives drawn from political economy can be useful in a comparative context. However, different models for supplying religion and regulating it in Asian societies can also challenge existing understandings of church and state. Some important research suggests that commercial involvement and an interest in economic development among rulers may be fostering an attitude of pragmatic accommodation toward competitive religious pluralism, albeit within strongly defined limits (Chan and Long 2014; Lang, Chan, and Ragvald 2005; Yang 2011; Yang and Tamney 2005).

Text analysis has entered many areas of the social sciences. It would be fruitful to see more work analyzing the church-state nexus, over time, through the lens of newspapers, contracts, organizational charters, speeches, and diaries. Church-state separation during the nineteenth and twentieth centuries can be traced, to some extent, through roll call votes and election results (see, e.g., Franck 2010), but a more systematic analysis could yield deeper insights.

More provocative questions still seem understudied. For example, why does the state still support churches in many countries, through tax breaks, subsidies, or charitable status (e.g., Bentzen and Sperling 2020)? Religious loyalties were among the most important social cleavages that shaped the emergence of party systems in many democracies (Kalyvas 1996; Kalyvas and van Kersbergen 2010; Warner 2000). However, in many advanced industrial democracies, the share of religiously involved people in the population has been decreasing for decades. Do favored religious organizations continue to provide legitimation benefits to rulers, or do they hang on as entrenched interest groups protecting their interests through political alliances?

The privatization of religion in many wealthy democracies seems to limit the public role that churches can play. However, the causal arrow could operate in the opposite direction. In other words, is it the spontaneous decline of religion that diminished the political role of churches or rather politics that intentionally displaced the churches? Did elite-led secularization of public institutions such as education and the substitution of public welfare systems for religious charity undercut religion's standing, as some provocative studies suggest (Gill and Lundsgaarde 2004; Smith 2003)?

What of newly democratizing societies? There is good reason to think that, paradoxically, as societies become more secular, religious parties become more salient as a means by which to assert the interests of confessional groups and renegotiate their bargains with the state (Grzymala-Busse 2012). What new church-state arrangements are taking shape around the world, and how will they influence political economy? How have migration and religious pluralism affected church-state institutions that are often the legacy of intolerant religious establishments?

Clearly, despite widespread secularization in many countries, church-state interactions will continue to be a central feature of our political economy—and, as such, a research area for decades to come.

Acknowledgments

Detailed comments by the editors, Jeffery A. Jenkins and Jared Rubin, are gratefully acknowledged.

Notes

1. For an elaboration of a bargaining model of political legitimation, see Greif and Rubin 2022, this volume.
2. See Woodberry (2011) for an early survey on the literature on missionaries, and recent surveys for Africa by Meier zu Selhausen 2019 and for Latin America and Asia by Valencia Caicedo 2019a.

References

Adiguzel, Fatih Serkant, and Timur Kuran. 2021. "The Islamic Waqf: Instrument of Unequal Security, Worldly and Otherworldly." Economic Research Initiatives at Duke (ERID) Working Paper No. 305.

Barro, Robert J., and Rachel M. McCleary. 2005. "Which Countries Have State Religions?" *Quarterly Journal of Economics* 120, no. 4: 1331–70.

Bazzi, Samuel, Masyhur Hilmy, and Benjamin Marx. 2020. "Islam and the State: Religious Education in the Age of Mass Schooling." NBER Working Paper 27073.

Becker, Sascha O., Markus Nagler, and Ludger Woessmann. 2017. "Education and Religious Participation: City-Level Evidence from Germany's Secularization Period, 1890-1930." *Journal of Economic Growth* 22, no. 3: 273–311.

Becker, Sascha O., Steven Pfaff, and Jared Rubin. 2016. "Causes and Consequences of the Protestant Reformation." *Explorations in Economic History* 62: 1–25.

Becker, Sascha O., Francisco Pino, and Jordi Vidal-Robert. 2021. "Freedom of the Press? Catholic Censorship during the Counter-Reformation." CEPR Discussion Paper 16092.

Becker, Sascha O., Jared Rubin, and Ludger Woessmann. 2021. "Religion in Economic History: A Survey." In *Handbook of Historical Economics*, ed. Alberto Bisin and Giovanni Federico, 585–639. Amsterdam: North Holland.

Becker, Sascha O., and Ludger Woessmann. 2008. "Luther and the Girls: Religious Denomination and the Female Education Gap in 19th-Century Prussia." *Scandinavian Journal of Economics* 110, no. 4: 777–805.

Becker, Sascha O., and Ludger Woessmann. 2009. "Was Weber Wrong? A Human Capital Theory of Protestant Economic History." *Quarterly Journal of Economics* 124, no. 2: 531–96.

Beheim, Bret, Quentin D. Atkinson, Joseph Bulbulia, Will Gervais, Russell D. Gray, Joseph Henrich, Martin Lang, M. Willis Monroe, Michael Muthukrishna, Ara Norenzayan, Benjamin Grant Purzycki, Azim Shariff, Edward Slingerland, Rachel Spicer, and Aiyana K. Willard. 2021. "Treatment of Missing Data Determined Conclusions regarding Moralizing Gods." *Nature* 595: E29–E34.

Bénabou, Roland, Davide Ticchi, and Andrea Vindigni. 2015. "Religion and Innovation." *American Economic Review Papers and Proceedings* 105, no. 5: 346–51.

Bénabou, Roland, Davide Ticchi, and Andrea Vindigni. 2022. "Forbidden Fruits: The Political Economy of Science, Religion, and Growth." *Review of Economic Studies* 89, no. 4: 1785–832.

Bentzen, Jeanet, and Lena Sperling. 2020. "God Politics: Religion, Attitudes, and Outcomes." CEPR Discussion Paper 37664.

Berman, Eli. 2009. *Radical, Religious and Violent: The New Economics of Terrorism*. Cambridge, MA: MIT Press.

Berman, Harold J. 1983. *Law and Revolution: The Formation of the Western Legal Tradition*. Cambridge, MA: Harvard University Press.

Blaydes, Lisa, Justin Grimmer, and Alison McQueen. 2018. "Mirrors for Princes and Sultans: Advice on the Art of Governance in the Medieval Christian and Islamic Worlds." *Journal of Politics* 80, no. 4: 1150–167.

Brooke, Steven, and Neil Ketchley. 2018. "Social and Institutional Origins of Political Islam." *American Political Science Review* 112, no. 2: 376–94.

Bueno de Mesquita, Bruce. 2000. "Popes, Kings, and Endogenous Institutions: The Concordat of Worms and the Origins of Sovereignty." *International Studies Review* 2, no. 2: 93–118.

Cagé, Julia, and Valeria Rueda. 2020. "Sex and the Mission: The Conflicting Effects of Early Christian Missions on HIV in Sub-Saharan Africa." *Journal of Demographic Economics* 86, no. 3: 213–57.

Cantoni, Davide. 2012. "Adopting a New Religion: The Case of Protestantism in 16th-Century Germany." *Economic Journal* 122, no. 560: 502–31.

Cantoni, Davide, Jeremiah Dittmar, and Noam Yuchtman. 2018. "Religious Competition and Reallocation: The Political Economy of Secularization in the Protestant Reformation." *Quarterly Journal of Economics* 133, no. 4: 2037–96.

Carney, James Jay. 2015. "Christendom in Crisis: The Catholic Church and Postcolonial Politics in Central Africa." In *Routledge Companion to Christianity in Africa*, ed. Elias Kifon Bongmba, 365–84. New York: Routledge.

Chan, Selena Ching, and Graeme Long. 2014. *Building Temples in China: Memories, Tourism, and Identities*. London: Routledge.

Chaudhary, Latika, and Jared Rubin. 2011. "Reading, Writing, and Religion: Institutions and Human Capital Formation." *Journal of Comparative Economics* 39, no. 1: 17–33.

Coşgel, Metin M., Thomas J. Miceli, and Jared Rubin. 2012. "The Political Economy of Mass Printing: Legitimacy, Revolt, and Technology Change in the Ottoman Empire." *Journal of Comparative Economics* 40, no. 3: 357–71.

Coşgel, Metin M., Matthew Histen, Thomas J. Miceli, and Sadullah Yıldırım. 2018. "State and Religion over Time." *Journal of Comparative Economics* 46, no. 1: 20–34.

Des Forges, Alison. 1999. *Leave None to Tell the Story: Genocide in Rwanda*. New York: Human Rights Watch.

Dittmar, Jeremiah, and Ralf Meisenzahl. 2020. "Public Goods Institutions, Human Capital, and Growth: Evidence from German History." *Review of Economic Studies* 87, no. 2: 959–96.

Duarte, Mary T. 1995. "Education in Ruanda-Urundi, 1946–61." *The Historian* 57, no. 2: 275–84.

Durkheim, Émile. 1964 [1912]. *The Elementary Forms of the Religious Life.* [*Les formes élémentaires de la vie religieuse.*] Translated by Joseph Ward Swain. 5th edition. London: George Allen & Unwin. https://www.gutenberg.org/files/41360/41360-h/41360-h.htm.

Ekelund, Robert B., Robert F. Hébert, and Robert D. Tollison. 2006. *The Marketplace of Christianity.* Cambridge, MA: MIT Press.

Ekelund, Robert B., Robert F. Hébert, Robert D. Tollison, Gary M. Anderson, and Audrey B. Davidson. 1996. *Sacred Trust: The Medieval Church as an Economic Firm.* New York: Oxford University Press.

Evans, Robert John Weston. 1979. *The Making of the Habsburg Monarchy, 1550–1700.* New York: Oxford University Press.

Finke, Roger. 1990. "Religious Deregulation: Origins and Consequences." *Journal of Church and State* 32, no. 3: 609–26.

Finke, Roger, and Rodney Stark. 1992. *The Churching of America, 1776–1990: Winners and Losers in Our Religious Economy*; New Brunswick, NJ: Rutgers University Press.

Fox, Jonathan. 2008. *A World Survey of Religion and the State.* Cambridge: Cambridge University Press.

Franck, Raphael. 2010. "Economic Growth and the Separation of Church and State: The French Case." *Economic Inquiry* 48, no. 4: 841–59.

Froese, Paul. 2008. *The Plot to Kill God: Findings from the Soviet Experiment in Secularization.* Berkeley: University of California Press.

Gallego, Francisco A., and Robert Woodberry. 2010. "Christian Missionaries and Education in Former African Colonies: How Competition Mattered." *Journal of African Economics* 19, no. 3: 294–329.

Gellner, Ernest. 1981. *Muslim Society.* Cambridge: Cambridge University Press.

Gill, Anthony. 1998. *Rendering unto Caesar: The Catholic Church and the State in Latin America.* Chicago: University of Chicago Press.

Gill, Anthony. 2008. *The Political Origins of Religious Liberty.* Cambridge: Cambridge University Press.

Gill, Anthony, and Erik Lundsgaarde. 2004. "State Welfare Spending and Religiosity: A Cross-National Analysis." *Rationality and Society* 16, no. 4: 399–436.

Gorski, Philip S. 2000. "Historicizing the Secularization Debate: Church, State, and Society in the Late Medieval and Early Modern Europe, ca. 1300 to 1700." *American Sociological Review* 65, no. 1: 138–67.

Gorski, Philip S. 2003. *The Disciplinary Revolution: Calvinism and the Rise of the State in Early Modern Europe.* Chicago: University of Chicago Press.

Gorski, Philip S., and Ateş Altınordu. 2008. "After Secularization?" *Annual Review of Sociology* 34: 55–85.

Greif, Avner, and Jared Rubin. 2015. "Endogenous Political Legitimacy: The England Reformation and the Institutional Foundations of Limited Government." Chapman University Working Paper.

Greif, Avner, and Jared Rubin. 2022. "Political Legitimacy in Historical Political Economy." In *The Oxford Handbook of Historical Political Economy.* Oxford: Oxford University Press. 293–310.

Grendler, Paul F. 2019. *Jesuit Schools and Universities in Europe, 1548–1773.* Leiden: Brill.

Grim, Brian J., and Roger Finke. 2010. *The Price of Freedom Denied: Religious Persecution and Conflict in the Twenty-First Century.* Cambridge: Cambridge University Press.

Gruber, Jonathan, and Daniel M. Hungerman. 2008. "The Church versus the Mall: What Happens When Religion Faces Increased Secular Competition?" *Quarterly Journal of Economics* 123, no. 2: 831–862.

Grzymala-Busse, Anna. 2012. "Why Comparative Politics Should Take Religion, no. More) Seriously." *Annual Review of Political Science* 15: 221–42.

Grzymala-Busse, Anna. 2015. *Nations under God: How Churches Use Moral Authority to Influence Policy*. Princeton, NJ: Princeton University Press.

Grzymala-Busse, Anna. 2019. "Religious Nationalism and Religious Influence." *Oxford Research Encyclopedia of Politics*. https://doi.org/10.1093/acrefore/9780190228637.013.813.

Grzymala-Busse, Anna. 2020. "Beyond War and Contracts: The Medieval and Religious Roots of the European State." *Annual Review of Political Science* 23: 2.1–2.18.

Heldring, Leander, James A. Robinson, and Sebastian Vollmer. 2021. "The Long-Run Impact of the Dissolution of the English Monasteries." *Quarterly Journal of Economics* 136, no. 4: 2093–145.

Henrich, Joseph. 2020. *The WEIRDest People in the World: How the West Became Psychologically Peculiar and Particularly Prosperous*. 1st edition. New York: Farrar, Straus and Giroux.

Hornung, Erik. 2014. "Immigration and the Diffusion of Technology: The Huguenot Diaspora in Prussia." *The American Economic Review* 104, no. 1: 84–122.

Hull, Brooks B. and Frederick Bold. 1989. "Towards an Economic Theory of the Church." *International Journal of Social Economics* 16, no. 7: 5–15.

Hungerman, Dan. 2013. "Substitution and Stigma: Evidence on Religious Competition from the Catholic Sex-Abuse Scandal." *American Economic Journal: Economic Policy* 5, no. 3: 227–53.

Iannaccone, Laurence R. 1995. "Risk, Rationality, and Religious Portfolios." *Economic Inquiry* 33, no. 2: 285–95.

Iannaccone, Laurence R. 1998. "Introduction to the Economics of Religion." *Journal of Economic Literature* 36, no. 3: 1465–95.

Iannaccone, Laurence R. 2005. "Economy." In *Handbook of Religion and Social Institutions*, ed. Helen Rose Ebaugh, 21–39. New York: Springer.

Iannaccone, Laurence R., Roger Finke, and Rodney Stark. 1997. "Deregulating Religion: The Economics of Church and State." *Economic Inquiry* 35, no. 2: 350–64.

Iyer, Sriya. 2016. "The New Economics of Religion." *Journal of Economic Literature* 54, no. 2: 395–441.

Johnson, Noel D., and Mark Koyama. 2019. *Persecution and Toleration: The Long Road to Religious Freedom*. New York: Cambridge University Press.

Kahl, Sigrun. 2005. "The Religious Roots of Modern Poverty Policy: Catholic, Lutheran, and Reformed Protestant Traditions Compared." *European Journal of Sociology* 46, no. 1: 91–126.

Kalyvas, Stathis N. 1996. *The Rise of Christian Democracy in Europe*. Ithaca, NY: Cornell University Press.

Kalyvas, Stathis N., and Kees van Kersbergen. 2010. "Christian Democracy." *Annual Review of Political Science* 13: 183–209.

van Kersbergen, Kees, and Philip Manow. eds. 2009. *Religion, Class Coalitions, and Welfare States. Cambridge Studies in Social Theory, Religion and Politics*. New York: Cambridge University Press.

Khaldun, Ibn. 2005 [1377]. *The Muqaddimah: An Introduction to History*. Princeton, NJ: Princeton University Press.

Kulkarni, Parashar, and Steven Pfaff. 2022a. "Church Politics, Sectarianism, and Judicial Terror: The Scottish Witch-Hunt, 1563–1736." *Explorations in Economic History* 84: 101447.

Kulkarni, Parashar, and Steven Pfaff. 2022b. "The 'Glorious' Revolution's Inglorious Religious Commitment: Why Parliamentary Rule Failed to Secure Religious Liberty." *Social Science History* 46, no. 4: 693–718.

Kuran, Timur. 2001. "The Provision of Public Goods under Islamic Law: Origins, Impact, and Limitations of the Waqf System." *Law & Society Review* 35, no. 4: 841–98.

Kuran, Timur. 2012. *The Long Divergence: How Islamic Law Held Back the Middle East*. Princeton, NJ: Princeton University Press.

Kuran, Timur. 2016. "Legal Roots of Authoritarian Rule in the Middle East: Civic Legacies of the Islamic Waqf." *The American Journal of Comparative Law* 64, no. 2: 419–54.

Kuran, Timur. 2020. "Zakat: Islam's Missed Opportunity to Limit Predatory Taxation." *Public Choice* 182: 395–416.

Kuran, Timur, and Scott Lustig. 2012. "Judicial Biases in Ottoman Istanbul: Islamic Justice and Its Compatibility with Modern Economic Life." *Journal of Law and Economics* 55, no. 3: 631–66.

Lang, Graeme, Selena Ching Chan, and Lars Ragvald. 2005. "Folk Temples and the Chinese Religious Economy." *Interdisciplinary Journal of Research on Religion* 1, no. 4: 1–29.

Lang, Martin, Benjamin G. Purzycki, Coren L. Apicella, Quentin D. Atkinson, Alexander Bolyanatz, Emma Cohen, Carla Handley, Eva Kundtová Klocová, Carolyn Lesorogol, Sarah Mathew, Rita A. McNamara, Cristina Moya, Caitlyn D. Placek, Montserrat Soler, Thomas Vardy, Jonathan L. Weigel, Aiyana K. Willard, Dimitris Xygalatas, Ara Norenzayan, and Joseph Henrich. 2019. "Moralizing Gods, Impartiality and Religious Parochialism across 15 Societies." *Proceedings of the Royal Society B: Biological Sciences* 286: 20190202.

Lenski, Gerhard E. 1984. *Power and Privilege. A Theory of Social Stratification*. Chapel Hill: University of North Carolina Press.

Longman, Timothy. 2010. *Christianity and Genocide in Rwanda*. Cambridge: Cambridge University Press.

Mamdani, Mahmood. 2001. *Genocide in Rwanda*. Princeton, NJ: Princeton University Press.

Mann, Michael. 1986. *The Sources of Social Power*, Volume 1: *A History of Power from the Beginning to AD 1760*. New York: Cambridge University Press.

Meier zu Selhausen, Felix. 2019. "Missions, Education and Conversion in Colonial Africa." In *Globalization and Mass Education*, ed. David Mitch and Gabriele Cappelli, 25–59. London: Palgrave Macmillan.

Meyersson, Erik. 2014. "Islamic Rule and the Empowerment of the Poor and Pious." *Econometrica* 82, no. 1: 229–69.

Michalopoulos, Stelios, Alireza Naghavi, and Giovanni Prarolo. 2016. "Islam, Inequality and Pre-Industrial Comparative Development." *Journal of Development Economics* 120: 86–98.

Norris, Pippa, and Ronald Inglehart. 2004. *Sacred and Secular: Religion and Politics Worldwide*. New York: Cambridge University Press.

North, Douglass C. 1981. *Structure and Change in Economic History*. New York: W. W. Norton & Co.

Pfaff, Steven. 2008. "The Religious Divide: Why Religion Seems to Be Thriving in the United States and Waning in Europe." In *Growing Apart: America and Europe in the Twenty-First Century*, ed. Jeffrey Kopstein and Sven Steinmo, 24–52. New York: Cambridge University Press.

Pfaff, Steven. 2011. "Religion under Communism: State Regulation, Atheist Competition, and the Dynamics of Supply and Demand." In *Oxford Handbook of the Economics of Religion*, ed. Rachel McCleary, 235–56. New York: Oxford University Press.

Pfaff, Steven, and Katie E. Corcoran. 2012. "Piety, Power, and the Purse: Religious Economies Theory and Urban Reform in the Holy Roman Empire." *Journal for the Scientific Study of Religion* 51, no. 4: 757–76.

Pfaff, Steven, and Anthony Gill. 2006. "Will a Million Muslims March? Muslim Interest Organizations and Political Integration in Europe." *Comparative Political Studies* 39, no. 7: 803–28.

Pullan, Brian S. 2005. "Catholics, Protestants and the Poor in Early Modern Europe." *Journal of Interdisciplinary History* 35, no. 3: 441–56.

Roes, Frans L., and Michel Raymond. 2003. "Belief in Moralizing Gods." *Evolution and Human Behavior* 24, no. 2: 126–35.

Rubin, Jared. 2017. *Rulers, Religion, and Riches: Why the West Got Rich and the Middle East Did Not*. Cambridge: Cambridge University Press.

Schilling, Heinz. 1986. *The Reformation and the Rise of the Early Modern State*. Kirkwood, MO: Sixteenth Century Journal Publishers.

Smith, Adam. 1776. *An Inquiry into the Nature and Causes of the Wealth of Nations*. London: W. Strahan.

Smith, Christian, ed. 2003. *The Secular Revolution: Power, Interests, and Conflict in the Secularization of American Life*. Berkeley: University of California Press.

Squicciarini, Mara. 2020. "Devotion and Development: Religiosity, Education, and Economic Progress in 19th-Century France." *American Economic Review* 110, no. 11: 3454–91.

Stark, Rodney. 2001. *One True God: Historical Consequences of Monotheism*. Princeton, NJ: Princeton University Press.

Stark, Rodney, and Roger Finke. 2000. *Acts of Faith: Explaining the Human Side of Religion*. Berkeley: University of California Press.

Troeltsch, Ernst. 1960 [1912]. *The Social Teaching of the Christian Churches*. [*Die Soziallehren der christlichen Kirchen und Gruppen.*] Volume 1. New York: Harper.

Valencia Caicedo, Felipe. 2019a. "Missionaries in Latin America and Asia: A First Global Mass Education Wave." In *Globalization and Mass Education*, ed. David Mitch and Gabriele Cappelli, 61–97. London: Palgrave Macmillan.

Valencia Caicedo, Felipe. 2019b. "The Mission: Human Capital Transmission, Economic Persistence, and Culture in South America." *Quarterly Journal of Economics* 134, no. 1: 507–56.

Warner, Carolyn. 2000. *Confessions of an Interest Group: The Catholic Church and Political Parties in Europe*. Princeton, NJ: Princeton University Press.

Weber, Max. 1963 [1922]. *The Sociology of Religion*. Boston: Beacon.

Weber, Max. 1978 [1921–1922]. *Economy and Society*. 2 volumes. Edited by Guenther Roth and Claus Wittich. Berkeley: University of California Press.

Weber, Max. 1981. *General Economic History*. London: Routledge.

West, Martin R., and Ludger Woessmann. 2010. "'Every Catholic Child in a Catholic School': Historical Resistance to State Schooling, Contemporary Private Competition and Student Achievement across Countries." *Economic Journal* 120, no. 546: F229–F255.

Wietzke, Frank-Borge. 2015. "Long-Term Consequences of Colonial Institutions and Human Capital Investments: Subnational Evidence from Madagascar." *World Development* 66: 293–307.

Woodberry, Robert D. 2004. "The Shadow of Empire: Christian Missions, Colonial Policy, and Democracy in Postcolonial Societies." PhD dissertation, University of North Carolina at Chapel Hill.

Woodberry, Robert D. 2011. "Religion and the Spread of Human Capital and Political Institutions: Christian Missions as a Quasi-Natural Experiment." In *The Oxford Handbook of the Economics of Religion*, ed. Rachel McCleary, 111–31. Oxford: Oxford University Press.

Woodberry, Robert D. 2012. "The Missionary Roots of Liberal Democracy." *American Political Science Review* 106, no. 2: 244–74.

Yang, Fenggang. 2011. *Religion in China: Survival and Revival under Communist Rule*. New York: Oxford University Press.

Yang, Fenggang, and Joseph B. Tamney. 2005. *State, Market, and Religions in Chinese Societies*. Leiden: Brill.

Index

Note: Tables and figures are indicated by *t* and *f* following the page number

A
abolitionism, 451, 695–696, 719, 739
absolute monarchies, 161–163, 186–189, 188*f*, 329, 332, 337–338. *See also* monarchies
absolute persistence, 130–131
absolutism/absolutists, 103, 168, 176 n.2, 244, 424, 450, 504–505, 511 n.9, 523–524, 550, 936
Acemoglu-Robinson model, 107
active cooperation, 336
Act of Settlement, 363
Adams, John, 403
adaptive efficiency, 443
adjacency matrix, 76, 78
administrative traditions, 378–379
Advani, L. K., 738
adverse selection, 813–814, 834, 834 n.2, 873
Affordable Care Act (ACA), 832
African conflicts, 599–600
African slave trade
   barbarians by design, 261
   culture and, 895
   cumulative learning about, 57, 67–68, 70 n.18
   family structure customs, 908–909
   gender norms and, 722, 909–910
   historical persistence and, 122
   historical shipping data, 39
   identity and, 738–740
   network analysis, 80
   racial exploitation of, 693–694
   religiosity and, 910
   social trust and, 895, 899
age-based suffrage, 461
Age of Mass Migration, 32–33, 670, 674, 683, 747–750, 753–757, 760–761, 849

agreed upon rules, 314, 326
Alberdi, Juan Bautista, 787
Alexander II, Tsar, 23, 36
Alexander the Great, 238
Alien and Sedition Acts, 797
alienation, 210, 217, 223, 345 n.2, 601, 778
Alien Exclusion Act, 798
altruism, 677, 778, 890, 892, 895, 903, 914
American Economic Review, 6, 20
American Journal of Political Science, 6
American Medical Association, 872
American political development (APD), 741–742
American Political Science Review, 6, 20
American Revolution, 80, 107, 190, 549
analytic narrative (AN), 110, 533
Analytic Narratives project, 21
Ancestral Characteristics Database, 39
Ancien Régime, 548, 551
Anderson, Benedict, 541, 545–546
Ang, Desmond, 737
Anglo-Saxon legal system, 281–284
anti-German sentiment, 672, 673
anti-Muslim sentiment, 733, 738, 798
anti-Semitism, 31, 121–122, 130, 135 n.9, 165, 174, 611, 734, 737–739
Aristotle, 153–154, 237–238
Armed Conflict Location and Event Data (ACLED), 598–599
Asian conflicts, 599–600
as-if random assignment, 55, 63
assimilation/assimilation effort
   conceptual framework, 670–677
   cultural distance effect, 674–675
   defined, 669–670
   education policy case study, 680–681

assimilation/assimilation effort (*cont.*)
    equilibrium outcome, 674–677
    long-run dynamics, 677
    majority discrimination impact, 675
    majority members and, 673
    minority group size, 676
    minority leaders and institutions, 676–677
    minority members and, 670–673
    overview, 669–670
    role of state, 677–683
    socialization efforts, 679
    state decision-making, 682–683
    state interventions, 677–682
assimilation culture, 905–908, 906t–907t
Association for Slavic, East European, and Eurasian Studies (ASEEES), 26–27
asynchronous collaboration, 21
autarky, 477–478, 490 n.3
authoritarianism
    bureaucracies and, 386–387
    democracy and, 135 n.7, 165–168
    executive leaders in, 199, 262–263
    historical influence of bureaucracies, 386–388
    institutions and, 481
    Latin American churches and, 929
    long-term impacts of, 173–174
    overview, 11, 161
    racism and, 696–699
    scholarship on, 175
    subnational authoritarianism, 171
    transition to, 153
autocracy. *See also* dynasties; monarchies
    death of, 169–172
    democracy and, 166
    dynasties and, 186–189, 188*f*
    emergence of, 161–165
    future research contributions, 175–176
    legacies of, 172–175
    overview, 161, 175–176
    personalist autocracies and, 186–189, 188*f*
    primogeniture and, 166, 170, 187
    survival of, 165–169
    taxation and, 507, 509–510
Axial Age, 239

B

Ballot Act, 657
Banking Act, 635
Bank of England, 631
Bank of Tennessee, 633
barbarians by design, 261
Barro, Robert, 243
Beramendi, Pablo, 5
Berlin Wall, 750
Bharatiya Janata Party (BJP), 738
Bilateral Trade Historical Series (1827-2014), 38
The Birth of a Nation (1915), 737
Black Death, 34, 122, 135 n.8, 147, 520–521, 591, 611, 739, 877 n.25
Black migrants, 675
Black voters, 151, 469
Blakeslee, David, 738
bottom-up state formation, 333, 334–335
bourgeois revolution, 551
British East India Company, 33, 609, 643, 646–647
British Industrial Revolution, 589–590
broad scale rules, 320
Bronze Age, 584
Bunting, David, 78
bureaucracies. *See* modern public bureaucracies
Burr, Aaron, 409
business corporations. *See* corporation-state relations

C

Calico Acts, 531
Calvinism, 385, 799, 932–933
candidate explanations, 111, 145
candidature officielle (official candidacy), 659
capitalism
    church and state relations, 932
    democratization and, 465
    education and, 845
    franchise extension and, 106
    gender inequality and, 715–716
    interdisciplinary collaboration, 27–28
    market economies and, 430–431
    path to absolutism, 168
    print capitalism, 546

racism and, 692–694, 699, 704
radicalism and, 435 n.22
taxation and, 742 n.4
Capitalism: A Journal of History and Economics, 27
Catherine the Great, 750
Catholic Church, 148, 155 n.8, 164, 304, 403, 571, 611, 640–642, 649, 677–679, 799, 904, 915, 927–933, 937
causal arguments, 3–4, 96
causal effects in historical persistence, 131–133, 132f
causal identification, 8–12, 112 n.12, 145, 669
causal inference in knowledge accumulation
　as-if random assignment, 55, 63
　design-based strategies for, 55–63, 65–69
　empirical strategies for, 60–63
　European expansion and, 63–68
　generalizability of causal claims, 56–60, 69
　implicit mediation analysis, 61, 65–66, 68
　overview, 55–57, 63–69
　selection-on-observables assumptions, 55–56, 59–60, 132
center-periphery conflict, 408, 770
Central American Free Trade Agreement (CAFTA), 486
central authority, 209–212, 215–224, 218f, 223t, 330
central banks/banking, 530, 623–624, 631–635
Central State Archive of the October Revolution (TsGAOR), 23
central-state lawmaking, 329–330, 333–336
Charles V, Emperor, 338–339
Charnsyh, Volha, 736
Chicago Federal Reserve District, 633
child mortality, 468, 724, 859, 865
China
　autocracies in, 168
　cotton revolution in, 722, 909
　Cultural Revolution in, 123, 532
　early globalization and trade, 583–584
　economic development, 531–533
　Great Leap Forward, 532
　Han Chinese, 302
　polities in, 240–245, 241f, 242f
　Qing dynasty, 104, 242, 254, 274, 735
　representative assemblies and, 147
　social protection funding, 833

China shock, 775
Christian Democratic Union (CDU), 771
church and state relations
　conflict among, 928–931
　future research on, 936–938
　human capital and, 933–934
　institutions and, 931–932
　logic of, 926–928
　missionaries and, 933–934
　overview, 925–926
　religious freedom, 935–936
　religious organizations, 609, 837, 926–928, 930, 932, 937
　research on, 932–934
　secularization and, 934–936
　urbanization and, 66, 342, 928–930
Cirone, Alexandra, 10
citizenship rights, 792–793
civil codes, 658–659
civil conflict
　Cold War and, 597–599
　drivers of, 604–609
　effect of research study, 613–615
　ethnic conflict/divisions, 600–601, 616 n.7, 779, 6161 n.9
　historical elements, 602–604
　in India, 604–611, 605f, 606f, 607f, 608f, 617 n.14
　interethnic complementarities, 611–613
　organizational, 612–613
　organizing violence and, 609–611
　overview, 597
　patterns of, 597–600, 598f
Civil Rights Act (CRA), 701
civil rights movement, 37
civil society, 10, 31, 36, 40–42, 146, 153, 163, 200, 412, 505, 523, 554 n.8, 778
classic HPE, 5–6
Clayton Antitrust Act, 648
Cleveland Federal Reserve District, 633
clientelism, 285, 414, 434 n.17, 466, 661
climate change, 612
closed bureaucracies, 377–378
co-administration, 332–333, 338–340, 344–345, 345 n.6
Coase theorem, 442, 447
Cold War, 360, 488, 502–506, 597–599, 797

co-legislation, 331–332, 335, 340, 345
collective action
  civil rights movement and, 37
  creation of, 430
  culture and, 914
  human capital and, 257
  identity and, 742 n.3
  Industrial Revolution and, 406
  institutionalized discrimination and, 673, 677
  legislative power, 344, 345 n.5
  library of mechanisms, 110
  migration and, 756
  network analysis in HPE, 88
  property rights and, 447, 452
  rules for, 314, 344
  slavery and, 740
  Tanzania and, 123–124
  taxation, 493
  tax development as, 493, 498, 503
  working class identity and, 88
collectivism, 122, 124, 164, 452–453, 532, 901t, 903–904, 914
collectivist culture, 452–453
colonialism/colonization
  counterfactual analyses, 568–570
  decolonization, 105, 120, 566–567, 792
  direct colonial rule, 64–65
  economic effects of, 566–570
  economic growth and, 570–572
  European, 119, 260, 559–560, 560f, 574, 738–739
  formal models in HPE, 102–105
  historical institutions and practices, 119–120
  historical persistence and, 117–120
  human capital and, 571–572
  identity in, 564–566, 565f, 735
  impact on talent, 573
  imperial governance and, 102–105
  indirect colonial rule, 64–65
  Japanese, 560f
  length of, 563–564, 563f
  long-run legacies of, 572–574
  overview, 559–560
  physical capital and, 570–571
  precolonial trends vs., 567–568
  research findings, 560–566
  role of missionaries, 933–934
  spatial distribution of, 573
  taxation and, 504–505
  timing of independence, 566–570
  varieties of, 561–563, 562f
commenda partnerships, 83
commercial revolution, 83, 147, 281, 302, 342, 452, 526
commoners, 221–225
common law, 119, 278–279, 279f, 281–284, 313, 359, 363, 524, 644
Commons, John, 313
Communists (KPD), 771
community responsibility systems, 355
Companies Clauses Consolidation Acts, 647
comparative politics, 20–21
competitive elections, 152, 323–324, 727
compulsory adjudication, 358
Confederate cotton bonds. See Southern Confederacy cotton bonds
Congress of Vienna, 123
Constituency-Level Elections Archive (CLEA), 36
constitutional arrangements, 324, 449
constitutional monarchy, 303, 403
contemporary HPE, 5–6, 188
contentious politics, 86–88
continental axis hypothesis, 522
controlled direct effect, 133
Conventions (Lewis), 314
convergence in HPE, 129–130
coordinating organization, 316–317, 326
Corn Laws, 407, 481–482
corporation-state relations
  corporate independence from state, 640–642
  corporate subordination to state, 642–643
  credible commitment and, 643–645
  modern business corporation, 647–650
  overview, 639–640
  positive legal services, 645–646
  transition to modern regime, 646–647
Corrupt and Illegal Practices Act, 411
cotton bonds. See Southern Confederacy cotton bonds
cotton revolution in China, 722, 909
Coughlin, Charles, 734, 737–738

Counter-Reformation, 933
courts/judicial institutions. *See also* individual courts
  activation of, 360–361
  compulsory adjudication, 358
  constraint through political capacity, 364
  credible commitments, 366–367
  high-stakes conflict among, 361–362
  origins of, 358–362
  overview, 353
  political costs with, 365–366
  power and independence through, 362–368
  private dispute resolutions by, 354–358
  quasi-judicial institutions, 356–358
  third-party adjudication, 354, 356
  trade and, 355–356
  value of, 366–368
COVID pandemic, 153, 509, 800, 863, 870–871, 875 n.9, 877 nn.25–26
Cox, Gary, 656
Cox, Oliver C., 692–693
credibility revolution, 8, 12, 55–56, 57–63, 69, 96
credible commitments, 366–367, 643–645
credit sanctions, 626–627
critical junctures, 9, 26, 62–63, 70 n.11, 118, 385, 447, 716, 739
Croce, Benedetto, 585
cross-disciplinary collaboration, 25
cross-party coordination, 428
cultural distance effect, 674–675
cultural outcomes, 121–124
cultural revivals, 102
Cultural Revolution in China, 123, 532
cultural transmission, 889–890
culture/cultural beliefs
  altruism and, 890, 892, 895, 903, 914
  consequences of, 910–916, 912t–913t
  cultural transmission, 889–890
  data sources, 894–895
  defined, 888–889
  determinants of traits, 905
  diversity and assimilation, 905–908, 906t–907t
  economic preferences, 895, 897, 910, 914
  epidemiological approach, 892–893
  family structure and customs, 908–909, 914–915
  gender norms, 909–910
  historical factors shaping, 895–910, 896t
  identity and, 890
  institutions and, 890–891
  kinship structure, 914–915
  lab experimentation, 893–894
  marriage cultures, 914–915
  overview, 887–888
  persistence and change, 891–892
  religiosity, 910, 911t, 915–916
  research methodology, 892–895
  scope of trust, 903–905
  social preferences, 898–905, 899t–900t, 901t–902t, 914
  theories of, 889–892
cumulative learning, 9–11, 56–57, 60–69. *See also* causal inference in knowledge accumulation
curia regis, 288 n.14

D

data/data gathering
  on African slave trade, 39
  civil society data, 40–42
  culture/cultural beliefs, 894–895
  economic data, 38–39
  ethnographic data, 39–40
  geographic and spatial data, 34–35
  global trade data, 38, 343
  government or institutional records, 33–34
  historical data in HPE, 10–13, 31–32, 76–80, 77f, 79f
  on organized religion, 41–42
  overview, 10–13, 31–32
  political data, 35–37
  sociodemographic and population data, 32–33
  spatial data, 34–35
Davis, Jefferson, 624–625
decision-theoretic model, 210–212
decolonization, 105, 120, 566–567, 792
default rules, 317–319, 326
deglobalization, 586
delegation of power (DOP), 329–331, 332–333, 336–337
democracy
  authoritarianism and, 135 n.7, 165–168

democracy (cont.)
  autocracy and, 166, 171
  candidate explanations and, 111, 145
  defined, 145–146, 155 n.2
  elections with alternation, 152–154
  electoral malfeasance in, 655, 656–661
  first-wave democracies, 414, 655–666
  impact on urbanization, 171
  industrial democracies, 364, 781, 937
  pluralistic definition of, 200
  representative assemblies, 146–148
  size of polities and, 246–247
  in small-scale settings, 161
  taxation and, 507–510, 508f
  transitions to, 171
  universal suffrage and, 145–146, 149–152, 154, 403, 424, 432
democratic dynasties, 189–193, 191f
democratic governance, 154, 295, 359, 788
democratization
  capitalism and, 465
  dynasties and, 189–193, 191f, 200
  education systems and, 840, 840t, 841–842, 844, 849
  electoral systems and, 424–425
  models, 105–107, 168, 171
  path dependence and, 107
  redistributivist accounts of, 663–664
  suffrage and, 461–462
  theory, 840, 840t, 841–842, 844
  third-wave, 664
demographic transition, 521
Demokratische Partei (DDP), 412–413
Demsetz, Harold, 443–445, 444f, 447, 454
design-based empirical research, 55, 68
design-based strategies, 55–63, 65–69
Deutsche Volkspartei (DVP), 412–413
Deutschkonservative Partei (DKP), 412–413
developmental outcomes
  economic activity of, 121
  effects of war and conquest, 120
  historical institutions and practices, 119–120
  in historical persistence, 119–121
Diamond, Jared, 522
Dickinson, Marshe, 407
dictatorships, 174, 186, 189, 330, 481, 533, 548
digital humanities, 35

direct colonial rule, 64–65
direct primaries, 410–411
direct tax system, 155 n.10, 167, 211, 241, 494–496, 495f, 497f, 501, 506–508
disability and injury programs, 823
displaced persons, 791–792, 798
distal effects in historical persistence, 131–133, 132f
diversity culture, 905–908, 906t–907t
divine will, 926–927
Doctrine of Lapse, 64
Doing Business Survey, 275
Domar hypothesis, 176 n.4
domestic labor, 796
dual veto, 405–406
Dutch East India Company, 645
dynasties. *See also* autocracy; monarchies
  advantages at the top, 195–198, 197t
  defined, 201 n.2
  democratization and, 189–193, 191f, 200
  future research on, 199–201
  gender representation and, 193–195, 194f
  personalist autocracies and, 186–189, 188f
  political power and, 185–186
  succession rule, 186–187

E

East Asian administrative systems, 376
East Asian tributary system, 246
Eastern Orthodox Church, 641
economic development and growth
  developmental outcomes, 121
  geographic impact on, 521–523
  Great Acceleration and, 520–521
  Great Divergence and, 520–521
  historical explanations for, 520–527
  human capital and, 519–522, 525–533
  incentives of, 523–525
  institutional constraints, 523–525, 528
  overview, 38–39, 519–520
  public policies and, 528–533
  state-led policies, 528–531
  technological innovation and, 519, 525–527
economic effects of impersonal rules, 320–321
Economic Freedom of the World Report, 275
economic geography, 774–777, 783
economic modernization, 662–663

Economic Origins of Dictatorship and Democracy (Acemoglu, Robinson), 842
economic property rights
  comparative cases, 452–454
  cultural evolution of, 454–455
  defined, 455 n.1
  emergence of, 445–447
  overview, 441–442
  persisting wedges, 447–449
  transaction costs of, 442–445, 444*f*
  withering wedges, 449–452
The Economist, 630
Edict of Potsdam, 750
Education Act, 469
education systems
  demand for, 841–844
  democratization theory, 840, 840*t*, 841–842, 844, 849
  framework and goals of, 839–840, 840*t*
  industrialization theory, 840, 840*t*, 844–846
  learning crisis, 838, 841
  mass schooling, 41, 680–681, 844, 847–851, 851 n.2
  medical education, 872–873
  nation-building theory, 840, 840*t*, 847–848
  open questions about, 850–851
  overview, 40–42, 837–839, 841
  skilled workforce pressures, 844–846
  state-building theory, 840, 840*t*, 848–850
The Efficient Secret (Cox), 656
Egerton, Francis, 407
elections. *See also* voters/votes
  with alternation, 152–154
  aristocracy and, 190
  competitive elections, 152, 323–324, 727
  cost of, 423
  dynasties and, 190–191
  research agenda, 414–415
electoral malfeasance
  economic modernization, 662–663
  in first-wave democracies, 655, 656–661
  impetus for reforms, 662–666
  overview, 655–656
  redistributivist accounts of democratization, 663–664
electoral revolution, 408–413
electoral systems. *See also* voters/votes

competitive-electoral explanation, 426–428
democratization and, 424–425
historical political economy, 425–431
literature assessment, 431–433
majoritarian systems, 421–430, 433 n.10, 434 n.20
political economy argument, 422–424
politics of, 421–422
protocorporatists and, 429–432
reforms, 192, 424–425
socioeconomic approach, 428–431
Elementary Education Act, 845
elites
  historical political economy, 232–235
  interdependence of, 224
  judicial institutions and, 359
  limited government and, 220–221
  national elites, 541, 542–545, 552, 554 n.7
  political power of, 220, 223
  state-building and, 216–225
  undemocratic elite, 466
Emancipation Proclamation, 627
emigration, defined, 761 n.1
Enemy Alien Acts, 797
Engels, Friedrich, 715
English Civil War, 85–86, 549
English East India Company (EIC), 81, 83
English imperialism, 104
English Swing riots, 37, 169, 462
Enlightenment thinkers, 238–239
environmental toxins, 865–866
epidemics and pandemics, 867–871. *See also* *see* COVID pandemic
equivalence class, 96
ethnic conflict/divisions, 600–601, 616 n.7, 779, 616l n.9
ethnic identity, 602–603, 733–734, 736
Ethnic Power Relations Dataset family, 39
Ethnographic Atlas, 39
ethnographic data, 39–40
ethno-linguistic fractionalization (ELF), 600–601
Ethnologue database, 40
European colonialism/colonization, 119, 260, 559–560, 560*f*, 574, 738–739
European Court of Justice, 360, 648
European East India Companies, 39

INDEX

European Economic Community (EEC), 480, 506
European expansion
   cumulative learning and, 63–68
   direct *vs.* indirect colonial rule, 64–65
   forced labor, 66–67
   missionary activity, 65–66
   slave trade, 67–68
European immigrants, 675, 749, 753, 851 n.2
European legislative power, 343–-344
European Union (EU) accession, 739
executive constraint, 162–166, 187, 329–332, 340–345, 524
Explorations in Economic History, 6
external conflict in state-building, 213–214
external rules, 315–317, 326

F

falsifiable argument, 3
family structure and customs, 908–909, 914–915
Faulkner, William, 117
Federal Deposit Insurance Corporation (FDIC), 634
Federalist No. 10 (Madison), 246–247, 263
Federal Reserve, 628–632
Federal Reserve Act, 624
Felton, Rebecca Latimer, 193
feudalism, 83, 120, 216, 245, 282–283, 334, 338, 362, 548, 641, 694, 928
financial crises
   founding of Federal Reserve, 628–632
   Great Depression, 488–489, 624, 632–634
   lessons from, 634–635
   overview, 623–624
   panic of 1907 and, 628–632, 634
   Southern Confederacy cotton bonds, 624–628
Finland, 322, 425, 531, 659, 758, 824, 831, 832
First Reform Act, 462, 471
first-wave democracies, 414, 655–666
Flexner, Abraham, 872
Florentine banking, 83
Food and Agriculture Organization (FAO), 38
forced labor, 57, 66–67, 119, 122, 525, 561, 566, 573, 603
forced migration, 751–752, 757–759

Ford Motor Company, 678
foreign direct investment (FDI), 750
formal models
   colonialism and imperial governance, 102–105
   democratization, franchise, and representation, 105–107, 168, 171
   incomplete survey of, 97–108
   institutional persistence, 101–102
   political reform in party systems, 108
   research on, 109–112
   role of, 95–97
   states and state-like organizations, 97–101
formal theory, 5, 12, 21
Fourth Reform Act, 470, 471
franchise models, 105–107
Frary, Donald, 662
French Revolution, 33, 148, 286, 547–550, 776, 792, 798
French Second Empire, 403–404
Frisch, Max, 787

G

gender-based suffrage, 460
gender studies
   cultural beliefs, 909–910
   dynasties and representation, 193–195, 194*f*
   historical events and relations, 716–721
   historical studies on, 721–724
   homosexuality, 723
   kinship structures, 723–724
   overview, 713–714, 724–725
   technological changes and, 721–723
   theoretical paradigms, 714–716
   transformation in women's political power, 719–721
   women's economic status, 717–718
General Agreement on Tariffs and Trade (GATT), 480, 486
generalizability of causal claims, 56–60, 69, 95–96
General Social Survey, 870
General Social Survey (GSS), 717
genocide, 790, 905, 934
geographic data, 34–35
geographic information systems (GIS), 35
geographic sorting, 126–127

geography-based suffrage, 461
Germanic legal systems, 280
German immigrants, 33, 672–673, 679, 682, 750
German migration, 750, 752–753
Germany
   female labor force, 724
   Imperial Germany, 36, 171, 663
   Nazi Germany, 164–165, 174, 673, 739, 755–756
   political parties in, 412–413
   urban-rural divide, 771–773
   Weimar Republic, 164, 423, 771, 781
Gladstone, William, 627
Glass-Steagall Act, 634–635
Global Agro-Ecological Zones dataset (GAEZ), 38
globalization
   beginning of, 582–586
   deglobalization, 586
   historical development, 588–591
   immigrants/immigration, 795
   immigration and, 788
   irreversibility of, 586–587
   overview, 581
   trade and, 582–586
Global Preferences Survey (GPS), 895
global trade data, 38, 343
Glorious Revolution, 26, 57, 216, 303, 359, 363, 403, 449–450, 500, 531, 644, 646, 936
Gossett, Ed Lee, 798
government records, 33–34
government regulation, 623, 632, 930
Great Acceleration, 520–521
Great Depression, 488–489, 624, 632–634
Great Divergence, 520–521
Great Leap Forward, 532
Great Migration, 675, 700–701, 753–754, 757
Great Powers, 380, 598
Great Reforms, 20, 22
Great Society, 700, 873–874
Greco-Turkish War, 751
Greens party, 771, 773
group-based suffrage, 460–461
Growing Public (Lindert), 807, 842
Guizot Law, 847–848
Guns, Germs, and Steel (Diamond), 522

H

Hamilton, Alexander, 403, 451, 529, 775
Han Chinese, 302
Handbook of Historical Economics (Bisin, Federico), 38
hard constructivism, 542–545
Hart, H. L. A., 314, 315
Harvard Dataverse, 36
Haussmann, Georges-Eugene, 88
healthcare, 871–874
health improvements
   bias around, 862–863
   child mortality and, 468, 724, 859, 865
   environmental toxins and, 865–866
   epidemics and pandemics, 867–871
   healthcare and, 871–874
   health insurance, 873–874
   historical factors shaping, 903
   infant mortality and, 758, 859, 860f, 863–865, 872, 875 n.6, 876 n.13, 876 n.18
   institutions and, 864–865
   medical education, 872–873
   overview, 857–860, 858f, 860f, 861f
   public health investments, 861–867
   public health providers, 863–864
   public health research, 867
   urbanization and, 866–867
health insurance, 873–874
Heckscher-Ohlin chain of causation, 585
Henry II, King, 282–283
Henry III, King, 283
Henry VI, King, 303–304
Henry VIII, King, 930
heterogeneous behavior, 320–321
Himmelfarb, Gertrude, 464
Hindu-Muslim conflict, 604–611, 605f, 606f, 607f, 608f, 617 n.14, 617 n.21
Hintze, Otto, 213
historical institutions and practices, 119–120, 121–122
historical persistence
   absolute *vs.* relative, 130–131
   conditions of brokenness, 128–130
   cultural outcomes, 121–124
   decay of, 129–130
   defined, 9–10, 17, 117–118
   developmental outcomes, 119–121

historical persistence (cont.)
  explanations of, 124–127, 125f
  future of, 134–135
  geographic sorting, 126–127
  institutional returns and costs, 125–126
  intergenerational socialization, 127
  methodological issues in, 131–133
  past politics and state policy, 123–124
  political and social equilibrium, 126
  political outcomes, 121–124
  post-treatment bias, 133
  proximate vs. distal effects, 131–133, 132f
  research findings, 118–124
  reversals to, 128–129
  societal disruptions, 122–123
  theories of, 124–131
historical political economy (HPE)
  causal identification, 8–12, 112 n.12, 145, 669
  classic HPE, 5–6
  contemporary HPE, 5–6, 188
  cumulative learning, 9–11, 56–57, 60–69
  data on, 10–13, 31–32, 76–80, 77f, 79f
  defined, 1–7, 6f
  in electoral systems, 422–424
  formal theory and, 5, 12, 21
  future of, 11–13
  major themes, 7–11
  modern HPE, 5
  safety nets and, 815–816
Historical Public Debt database, 38
HIV/AIDS epidemic, 870
Hobbes, Thomas, 162, 255, 293, 315
Holocaust, 120, 122, 174, 739
homophily, 90, 126, 684 n.2
homosexuality, 723
How the World Votes (Frary, Seymour), 662
Huck, Winifred S., 193
human capital
  church and state relations, 933–934
  collective action and, 257
  colonialism/colonization and, 571–572
  economic development and, 519–522, 525–533
  in gender studies, 715, 718
  migration impact on, 755
  racism and, 700–701

Human Relations Area Files (HRAF), 895
Hume, David, 244, 293, 355, 357

I
Ibn Khaldun, 930
identity-based taxation, 735–736
identity/identity politics
  collective action and, 742 n.3
  in colonialism/colonization, 564–566, 565f, 735
  cultural beliefs, 890
  ethnic identity, 602–603
  institutions and, 735–737
  Native American politics and, 741–742
  noneconomic identities, 735–736
  overview, 733–734
  path dependence in politics of, 740
  persistence and, 738–741
  propaganda and, 737–738
  rules in HPE, 319–320, 322–324, 326, 327 n.2
  self-identification, 702, 733–734
identity rules, 319–320, 322–324, 326, 327 n.2
IIRIRA Act, 792
Imagined Communities (Anderson), 545–546
immigrants/immigration. *See also* migrants/migration
  citizenship rights, 792–793
  defined, 761 n.1, 788
  displaced persons, 791–792, 798
  domestic labor and, 796
  enforcement policies, 793
  entry policies, 789–790, 792
  European immigrants, 675, 749, 753, 851 n.2
  fear of others/othering, 799–800
  fiscal effects of, 799
  German immigrants, 33, 672–673, 679, 682, 750
  groups, 100, 602–603, 670–678, 753, 862
  manpower needs, 794–796
  Mexican immigrants, 674–675, 684 n.3
  Norwegian immigrants, 757
  policies governing, 788–793
  political effects of, 797–798
  primary considerations, 794–800
  refugees, 790–792
  security concerns, 796–797
Imperial Chamber Court, 362, 363, 365
Imperial Court in London, 648

Imperial Germany, 36, 171, 663
imperial governance
  bureaucracies and, 380–381
  colonialism and, 102–105
  English imperialism, 104
  Imperial Germany, 36, 171, 663
  Ottoman Empire, 4, 42, 88, 214, 260, 302, 344, 357, 387, 496, 502, 504–505, 552, 554 n.15, 735–736, 790, 903
  Qing dynasty, 104, 242, 254, 735
  Russian Empire, 23–24, 170–173
  Spanish Empire, 104, 387
Imperial Russia, 12, 18, 20, 22, 36, 84, 107, 736
impersonal rules, 319–324, 326
implicit mediation analysis, 61, 65–66, 68
income taxes, 167, 257, 258f, 468, 494, 500–506, 742 n.4, 828, 831–833, 936
Independent Social Democrats (USPD), 771
India, 604–611, 605f, 606f, 607f, 608f, 617 n.14, 740
Indira Gandhi National Open University, 244
indirect colonial rule, 64–65
inductive approach, 58
industrialization
  democracies of, 364, 781, 937
  modern public bureaucracies, 529–530
  socioeconomic complexity, 380
  theory in education systems, 840, 840t, 844–846
Industrial Revolution
  British Industrial Revolution, 589–590
  collective action and, 406
  economic development and, 520–521, 525–527
  globalization and, 588–590
  immigrants/immigration, 794–795
  political parties, 406–408
  property rights, 449–450
  Second Industrial Revolution, 846
  taxation and, 499–502
infant mortality, 758, 859, 860f, 863–865, 872, 875 n.6, 876 n.13, 876 n.18
informal constraints, 313
information capacity, 255, 257, 259f
institutional collaboration, 21, 26–28
institutionalisms, 27, 118, 131, 136 n.12, 692, 704
institutionalized discrimination, 673, 677–678

institutionalized riot systems, 609
institutional persistence, 101–102
institutional records, 33–34
institutions. *See also* courts/judicial institutions
  assimilation effort, 676–677
  authoritarianism and, 481
  church and state relations, 931–932
  colonialism/colonization and, 119–120
  cultural beliefs and, 890–891
  data gathering, 33–34
  defined, 313
  developmental outcomes, 119–120
  economic development and growth, 523–525, 528
  formal models of persistence, 101–102
  health improvements and, 864–865
  historical institutions and practices, 119–120, 121–122
  historical persistence, 125–126
  identity politics and, 735–737
  institutionalized riot systems, 609
  interdisciplinary collaboration, 21, 26–28
  legal capacity in, 280–281
  political institutions, 781–782
  quasi-judicial institutions, 356–358
  racism and, 694–701
Institutions, Institutional Change, and Economic Performance (North), 313–314
insurance theory, 368
integrated career tracks, 377–378
intellectual revolution, 402–404
interdisciplinary co-authorship, 21, 24–26
interdisciplinary collaboration
  asynchronous, 21
  comparative politics and, 20–21
  institutional, 21, 26–28
  interdisciplinary co-authorship, 21, 24–26
  intergenerational, 21–24, 22f
  Methodenstreit and, 18–21
  overview of, 7, 17–18
interest-group perspective, 382–383
interethnic complementarities, 611–613
intergenerational collaboration, 21–24, 22f
intergenerational socialization, 127
internal migration, 747, 756, 780, 799
internal rules, 315–317, 326

International Country Risk Guide, 275
International Historical Geographic Information System (IHGIS), 35
International Monetary Fund, 38
Interstate Commerce Act, 648
Inter-university Consortium for Political and Social Research (ICSPR), 36
Investiture Controversy, 640
Israel, 150, 486, 531, 533, 724, 791

J

J. P. Morgan, 631–632
Jacobinism, 547–548, 555 n.19
Japanese colonialism/colonization, 560f
Japanese conflicts, 600
Japanese Liberal Democratic Party (LDP), 364
Jefferson, Thomas, 775
Jim Crow racism, 102, 698–701, 720
Johns Hopkins Medical School, 872
Johnson, Lyndon, 872
Journal of Economic History, 6
Journal of Historical Political Economy (JHPE), 7, 10, 13, 27
Journal of Legal Studies, 443
Judaism
  anti-Semitism, 31, 121–122, 130, 135 n.9, 611, 737–739
  assimilation effort, 671–672
  Holocaust, 120, 122, 174, 739
  Nazi Germany and, 164–165, 174, 673, 739, 755–756

K

Kahn, Florence, 193
Katznelson, Ira, 27
Kelsen, Hans, 360
Khrushchev Thaw, 21, 23
knowledge accumulation. *See* causal inference in knowledge accumulation
Korean War, 597–598, 791
Kragh, Martin, 26
Krest'ianskoe Dvizhenie v Rossii (The Peasant Movement in Russia), 22
Ku Klux Klan (KKK), 737

L

labor activism, 88
labor force
  education and, 519, 526
  migrants in, 748, 752, 755
  women in, 715, 718, 721–723, 726 n.16, 893, 909–910
Laird, John, 627
Langley, Kathleen, 193
Latin American conflicts, 599, 612
League of Nations High Commission on Refugees, 790–791
learning crisis, 838, 841. *See also* education systems
Left Party, 771
legal capacity
  common law and, 281–284
  defined, 271–272
  in early modern France, 284–286
  legal origins and, 277–279, 279f
  measuring of, 275–277, 276f, 277f
  in Medieval England, 280
  in private and public institutions, 280–281
  research on, 286–287
  rule of law and, 272–275
  transaction costs and, 272, 274, 281, 286
leges barbarorum, 280
legislative cartels, 404–406
legislative power
  bottom-up state formation, 333, 334–335
  central-state lawmaking, 329–330, 333–336
  co-administration, 332–333, 338–340, 344–345, 345 n.6
  co-legislation, 331–332, 335, 340, 345
  decision making, 4
  delegation of power, 329–331, 332–333, 336–337
  executive constraint and, 329–332, 340–345
  local-state lawmaking, 333–336
  outside Europe, 343–-344
  overview in, 329
  rent extraction and, 339
  ruler survival and, 338
  self-government rights and, 341–342
  separation of power, 329–332, 336–337
  sovereign debt and, 338–339
  state-building and, 339–3340
  suppression of parliaments, 336–337
  top-down administrative origin, 335–336
  trade potential, 341–343
legislative research agenda, 413–414
legislative revolution, 404–408

legitimacy principles, 296–298, 304–306. *See also* political legitimacy
legitimate opposition, 403
legitimating agent, 296–305, 928. *See also* political legitimacy
legitimation principle, 547–549
Lerner Price Index, 625
levée en masse, 548
Lewis, David, 314
library of mechanisms, 110
limited government, 220–221
Lindert, Peter, 807
Lindsay, William, 627
linguistic discontinuity, 546–547
Linking Ethnic Data from Africa (LEDA) Project, 40
Lipset, Seymour Martin, 294
liquidity crisis, 631, 634
local-state lawmaking, 333–336
long-run impacts, 62–63
Louis XIV, King, 285–286
Lowe, Robert, 470
Lu shi chunqiu collection, 239

M

macroeconomic studies, 4
Madison, James, 246–247, 263
Mafia, 162
Magiya, Yusuf, 735
Magna Carta, 283
Magyarization policies, 682
majoritarian systems, 421–430, 433 n.10, 434 n.20
Malouin economy, 83
"man-the-hunter" myths, 725
Mao Zedong, 240, 304–305
market building in modern economy, 81–84
marriage cultures, 914–915
Marx, Karl, 5
Marxism, 22, 692, 715–716, 718
mass mobilization/protest, 85–88, 169–170, 424, 434 n.19, 465, 610
mass political parties, 411–412
mass schooling, 41, 680–681, 844, 847–851, 851 n.2
Maximilian I, King, 362, 365
McFadden Act, 632
Medicaid, 872, 873–874
medical education, 872–873
Medicare, 873–874

Medici, Cosimo de', 85
Mencius, 237
meritocracies, 378
Methodenstreit, 18–21
Mexican immigrants, 674–675, 684 n.3
Mexico's War of Independence, 221
Michels, Robert, 162
migrants/migration. *See also* immigrants/immigration
  Age of Mass Migration, 32–33, 670, 674, 683, 747–750, 753–757, 760–761, 849
  Black migrants, 675, 754
  effects of, 757–759
  forced migration, 751–752, 757–759
  future research, 760–761
  Great Migration, 675, 700–701, 753–754, 757
  internal migration, 747, 756, 780, 799
  in labor force, 748, 752, 755
  nativism/nativists, 752–753, 779, 799–801, 860, 862–863, 868
  overview, 747–748
  political and social consequences of, 752–754
  receiving societies, 748–754
  research on historical cases, 759–760
  sending societies, 754–757
  transaction costs and, 750, 754
  voluntary migration, 748–751, 757–759
military pressures, 380, 384
military technology and state-building, 214
missionaries, 65–66, 933–934
The Modern Corporation and Private Property (Berle, Means), 360, 649
modernization theory, 442, 461, 526, 529
modern public bureaucracies
  administrative traditions, 378–379
  defined, 374–375, 389 n.1
  distinctions among, 375
  domestic factors and, 381–382
  East Asian administrative systems, 376
  external factors and, 383–385
  factors shaping, 381–385
  historical emergence of bureaucracies, 379–381
  historical influence of bureaucracies, 386–388
  industrial policy bureaucracy, 529–530
  integrated vs. separated career tracks, 377–378
  interest-group perspective, 382–383

958   INDEX

modern public bureaucracies (*cont.*)
   organizational differentiation, 379
   organizational *vs.* professional, 377
   path dependence in, 385
   political control and meritocracies, 378
   relevance of, 373–374
   role of, 388
   types of, 376–379
   Weber, Max on, 375–376, 381, 389 n.8
Moller, Gustav, 814–815
monarchies. *See also* autocracy; dynasties
   absolute monarchies, 161–163, 186–189, 188*f*, 329, 332, 337–338
   constitutional, 303, 403
   emergence of, 161, 166–167
   sovereign debt, 338–339
   succession rule, 186–187
monolingualism, 680–681
Montesquieu, 238–239, 244
moral hazard model, 103, 814–815, 834
Morgan, Edmund, 693
Murdock ethnic group boundary map, 39
Muslims. *See* Hindu-Muslim conflict

N

Nansen, Fridtjof, 791
Napoleonic Code, 278, 286, 658–659
Napoleonic Wars, 566, 586, 598, 599*f*
Nash Equilibrium, 894
national elites, 541, 542–545, 552, 554 n.7
National Historical Geographic Information System (NHGIS), 35
nationalism
   congruency in nation states, 549–552
   cultural modernization, 545–547
   economic modernization and, 542–545
   emergence of concept, 552–553
   ethnic nationalism, 600–601
   hard constructivism, 542–545
   legitimation principle, 547–549
   overview, 541–542
   political fragmentation, 551–552
   self-determinism, 547–549
   soft constructivism, 545–547
   sovereign states, 547–551
nationalization of politics, 412, 430–431, 434 n.14, 504, 649, 770, 781–782

National Monetary Commission, 630, 632
National Socialists (NSDAP), 164–165
nation-building theory, 840, 840*t*, 847–848
nation states, 549–552
Native American politics, 741–742
nativism/nativists, 752–753, 779, 799–801, 860, 862–863, 868
Nazism/Nazi Germany, 164–165, 174, 673, 739, 755–756
NBER Macrohistory database, 38
network analysis
   collective action, 88
   contentious politics, 86–88
   emergence of modern firm, 82–84
   historical data on, 76–80, 77*f*, 79*f*
   market building in modern economy, 81–84
   overview of, 75–76, 88–90
   states, parties, and movements, 84–88
New Deal, 431, 648, 700, 739–740, 753, 814, 864
New York City Charity Directory, 80
New York Stock Exchange (NYSE), 633
New York Times, 629–630
Nigerian Federal Civil Service, 34
Nolan, Mae Ella, 193
noneconomic identities, 735–736
nonelectoral costs, 423
nongovernment organizations (NGOs), 817
non-tax revenue, 214–215
Norman Conquest, 107, 282, 358, 363
North American Free Trade Agreement (NAFTA), 480, 486, 488, 775
North Korea, 128, 189, 448, 523, 524*f*, 529, 531
Norwegian immigrants, 757
not agreed upon rules, 314, 326

O

Obergefell v. Hodges, 361
Oldfield, Pearl Peden, 193
Olson, Macur, 162
One True God, 927
open bureaucracies, 377–378
oppositional behavior, 681–682
Organisation of Economic Co-operation and Development (OECD), 807–809, 819, 822, 824, 826, 832–833
organizational bureaucracies, 377
organizational differentiation, 379

organizational knowledge, 81
organizational legitimacy, 306 n.1
Organization of Petroleum Exporting Countries (OPEC), 479
organizations of organizations, 316
organized religion data, 41–42
The Origin of the Family, Private Property, and the State (Engels), 715
Ostrom, Elinor, 451–452
others/othering, 799–800
Ottoman Empire, 4, 42, 88, 214, 260, 302, 344, 357, 387, 496, 502, 504–505, 552, 554 n.15, 735–736, 790, 903
Owen, Ruth Bryan, 193

P

Pale of Settlement, 173, 611
pandemics. *See* COVID pandemic; epidemics and pandemics
panic of 1907 crisis, 628–632, 634
Party of Democratic Socialism (PDS), 771
party systems, 324–325
path dependence
  in bureaucratic organization, 385
  democratization and, 107
  economic activity and, 121, 534 n.3
  in identity politics, 740
  intergenerational socialization and, 127
  overview, 9, 118
  in property rights, 446
Patriot Act, 797
Pax Tokugawa, 246
payoffs, 110, 217, 222, 233–235, 422–423, 643, 677, 890, 893
peace arbitrators, 23
peaceful coexistence equilibrium, 603
peacemakers/peacemaking, 354
Pelosi, Nancy, 194
Peng Peng, 735
physical capital, 570–571
place-based discourses, 80
Plato, 238
Pliny the Elder, 583
Polish-Lithuanian Commonwealth, 85
Polish migration, 751–752
political agency, 544, 719
political data, 35–37

political equilibrium, 126
political institutions, 781–782
political legitimacy
  analysis of, 297–301
  defined, 293–297
  future research, 305–306
  implications of, 301–305
  legitimacy principles, 296–298, 304–306
  legitimating agent, 296–305, 928
political liberalization, 424–426, 434 n.19
political outcomes, 121–124
political parties
  in Britain, 411–412
  defined, 402–403
  direct primaries and, 410–411
  electoral research agenda, 414–415
  electoral revolution, 408–413
  in Germany, 412–413
  impersonal rules and, 322–324
  Industrial Revolution, 406–408
  intellectual revolution, 402–404
  legislative cartels, 404–406
  legislative research agenda, 413–414
  legislative revolution, 404–408
  legitimate opposition, 403
  mass parties, 411–412
  overview, 401
  reform systems in, 108
  in United States, 409–411
  Van Buren, Martin and, 409–411
politicide, 790
politics/political power
  data gathering, 35–37
  effects of impersonal rules, 322–324
  electoral systems, 421–422
  of elites, 220, 223
  modern public bureaucracies, 378
polities. *See* size of polities
Poole, Keith T., 36
population data, 32–33
positive legal services, 645–646
post-treatment bias, 133
preference alignment, 219
prescriptive rules, 317–319, 326, 327 n.1
primary rules, 315, 326
primogeniture, 166, 170, 187

960 INDEX

principal-agent problem, 102–104, 110, 241–242, 448–449
print capitalism, 546
private dispute resolutions, 354–358
professional bureaucracies, 377
property rights. *See* economic property rights
Protestantism, 799, 897
Protestant Reformation, 611, 928–929, 931
protocorporatists, 429–432
proximate effects in historical persistence, 131–133, 132*f*
Przeworski, Adam, 170
public family benefits, 824
Puritan citizens' movement, 86

Q

Qing dynasty, 104, 242, 254, 274, 735
Qin Shi Huang, 239
qualitative evidence, 10, 13, 26, 58
Quarterly Journal of Economics, 6
quasi-judicial institutions, 356–358

R

race/racism
    agency concerns, 703–704
    capitalism and, 692–694, 699, 704
    categorization of, 702–703
    effects on institutions and policies, 694–699
    future research directions, 701–704
    health improvements and, 859–860, 860*f*
    institutions and policies effect on, 699–701
    Jim Crow racism, 102, 698–701, 720
    overview, 691
    questions and debates over, 691–694
racial identity, 733–734
Railway Act, 648
Ram Rath Yatra campaign, 738
Rankin, Jeannette, 193
Reciprocal Trade Agreements Act, 481
Reciprocal Trade Agreements Act (RTAA), 488
redistributivist accounts of democratization, 663–664
Reed, Thomas B., 405–406
Reform Act, 411
refugees, 790–792
regulated companies, 642

relative persistence, 130–131
religiosity, 910, 911*t*, 915–916
religious data, 41–42
religious freedom, 935–936
religious legitimacy, 302–304, 930, 936
religious organizations, 609, 837, 926–928, 930, 932, 937
Renaissance Florence, 85
rent extraction, 339
rent-seeking, 220, 285, 287, 447, 523, 930
representation models, 105–107
representative assemblies, 146–148
representative government, 4–5, 154, 424, 449
revenue collection, 20, 103, 255, 262, 336, 499–507
riots
    English Swing riots, 37, 169, 462
    Hindu-Muslim conflict, 604–611, 605*f*, 606*f*, 607*f*, 608*f*, 617 n.14, 617 n.21
    institutionalized riot systems, 609
Rockefeller Sanitary Commission (RSC), 864
Rogers, Edith Nourse, 193
Roman Empire, 42, 166, 168, 240, 248 n.5, 275, 280, 302, 330, 340, 362, 583, 586, 640, 928–929, 935
Roman law, 278, 280–281, 641
Rosenthal, Howard, 36
Rousseau, Jacques, 238–239
rule-of-law, 272–275, 643
ruler survival, 338
rules in HPE
    agreed and not agreed upon, 314, 326
    broad scale, 320
    coordinating organization, 316–317, 326
    creating and enforcing, 313–314
    economic effects of impersonal rules, 320–321
    identity and, 319–320, 322–324, 326, 327 n.2
    impersonal rules, 319–324
    implications of, 324–326
    internal and external, 315–317, 326
    organizations of organizations, 316
    political effects of impersonal rules, 322–324
    prescriptive and default, 317–319, 326, 327 n.1
    primary rules, 315, 326
    secondary rules, 314–316, 322, 324–326
Russian Civil War, 790
Russian Empire, 23–24, 170–173

S

safety nets and welfare spending
  adverse events and, 809–815, 810t–811t, 811t–812t
  categories in modern era, 819–824, 820t–821t, 822t
  overview, 807–809, 808t–809t
  political economy and, 815–816
  spending on, 824–833, 825t–826t, 828t, 829t, 829t–830t
  before WWI, 816–819, 817t
Sanborn Fire Insurance Maps, 35
San Francisco earthquake, 629, 634
Schattschneider, E. E., 325
Schumpeter, Joseph, 162
scope of trust, 903–905
secondary rules, 314–316, 322, 324–326
Second Continental Congress, 450
Second Industrial Revolution, 846
Second Reform Act, 469–470
secret ballots, 108, 382, 405, 459, 657, 661, 664
secularization, 934–936
selection-on-observables assumptions, 55–56, 59–60, 132
self-determinism, 547–549
self-government, 20, 124, 335, 340, 341–343
self-government rights, 341–342
self-identification, 702, 733–734
self-selection, 18, 20–21, 164, 779
separated career tracks, 377–378
separation of power (SOP), 329–332, 336–337
Seshat Global History Databank, 39
Seymour, Charles, 657, 662
Shaw, George Bernard, 602
Shaw, Leslie M., 630
Sherman Antitrust Act, 648
sickness programs, 823
Siege of Osaka, 246
size of polities
  democracy and, 246–247
  determinants of, 243–246
  historical thinkers on, 238–239
  overview of, 237–238
skilled workforce, 844–846
slavery, 451, 693, 695–699, 719, 739, 898. *See also* African slave trade
Slavic Review, 26

Smith, Adam, 584, 925, 929
Smith, Anthony, 551
Smoot-Hawley tariff, 483
Social Democratic Party (SPD), 771
social democrats, 150, 425–426, 435 n.23, 435 n.26, 660, 771, 799, 828
social equilibrium, 126
social facts, 314
social insurance, 380, 497, 799, 807, 814–815, 828, 831–834
social movements, 85–88, 200, 470, 719, 733, 741
social networks, 25, 80, 83, 86, 100, 260, 376, 409
social norms, 121, 354, 466, 613, 724
social preferences in culture, 898–905, 899t–900t, 901t–902t
social revolutions, 849
social science, 23–25
social welfare spending. *See* safety nets and welfare spending
societal disruptions, 122–123
societal wealth, 215
sociodemographic data, 32–33
socioeconomic complexity, 380
socioeconomic electoral systems, 428–431
soft constructivism, 545–547
Sombart, Werner, 5
source criticism, 19
Southern Confederacy cotton bonds, 624–628
South Korea, 128, 441, 494, 523, 528–533, 800, 824, 832
sovereign debt, 338–339, 623, 634
sovereign states, 547–551
Sozialdemokratische Partei Deutschlands (SPD), 412–413
Spanish Crown, 33
Spanish Empire, 104, 387
spatial data, 34–35
Spatially Interpolated Data on Ethnicity (SIDE) dataset, 40
St. Louis Federal Reserve District, 633
Stabilization Act, 873
Stable Unit Treatment Variance Assumption (SUTVA), 136 n.13
Standard Cross Cultural Survey (SCCS), 39, 895

state-building, 211, 339–3340, 840t, 848–850
state-building through taxation
 basic model, 212
 central authority, 209–212, 215–224, 218f, 223t, 330
 commoners and, 221–225, 223t
 elites and, 216–225
 external conflict and, 213–214
 future research directions, 225–226
 military technology and, 214
 non-tax revenue and, 214–215
 overview, 232–235
 political bargaining and, 217–219
 preference alignment, 219
 recent research on HPE, 209–210
 societal wealth and, 215
 state, defined, 210–211
 taxation and, 211–216, 222–225
 theory of, 211–216
state capacity
 dark side of, 261
 definitions and measurements, 253–255
 development and, 256–259, 258f, 259f
 how to constraint, 261–263
 information capacity, 255, 257, 259f
 problems with, 259–261
"state of the field" project, 24, 28
states and state-like organizations, 97–101
stationary bandits, 162, 187, 262, 531
Sterling Zone, 648
Stolper-Samuelson Theorem, 585
Stuart England, 85
Studies in American Political Development, 6
stylized facts, 20, 101, 519–520, 770–774, 783
subnational authoritarianism, 171
subsidies, 479
succession rule, 186–187
suffrage. *See also* voters/votes
 age-based, 461
 democratization and, 461–462
 gender-based, 460
 geography-based, 461
 group-based, 460–461
 overview, 459–460
 policy consequences, 466–471
 reform theory, 461–466
 taxonomy of, 460–461

 universal suffrage, 145–146, 149–152, 154, 403, 408, 424, 432
 woman's suffrage, 465–466, 468, 471, 472 n.6
Supreme Court of the Holy Roman Empire, 362
synthetic control, 614

T
Taiwan, 441, 528–532, 800
tariffs, 479
Tawney, R. H., 5
taxation. *See also* state-building through taxation
 capitalism and, 742 n.4
 dependency and, 502–504
 direct tax system, 155 n.10, 167, 211, 241, 494–496, 495f, 497f, 501, 506–508
 early path to, 499–502
 fiscal performance, 507–510, 508f
 fiscal trajectories, 505–507
 identity-based, 735–736
 income taxes, 167, 257, 258f, 468, 494, 500–506, 742 n.4, 828, 831–833, 936
 inequalities and, 496
 legacy of colonialism, 504–505
 limits to, 502–505
 overview, 493–496, 495f
 returns and, 496–498, 497f
 varieties of, 498–507
tax collection, 33, 102, 119, 149, 254, 335, 337–339, 387, 390 n.24, 500, 659
technological innovation, 33, 68, 171, 186, 216, 256–257, 503, 519, 525–527, 717, 845
Teele, Dawn Langan, 464
third-party adjudication, 354, 356
third-wave democratization, 664
Tilly, Charles, 213
Time Counts: Quantitative Analysis for Historical Social Science (Katznelson, Wawro), 27
Tocqueville, Alexis de, 5, 169
top-down administrative origin, 335–336
trade
 credit sanctions, 626–627
 dispute resolution, 355–356
 globalization and, 582–586
 in market-building, 81–82
 potential of, 341–343

trade policy
  autarky and, 477–478, 490 n.3
  conceptual framework, 478–482
  drivers of, 480–482
  goals of, 479–480
  overview, 477
  tariffs and subsidies, 479
  US trade policy applications, 482–489, 484f, 486t, 487f, 489f
transaction costs
  bureaucracies and, 387
  of economic property rights, 442–445, 444f
  increasing returns and, 125
  judicial institutions and, 357, 374
  lack of trust and, 574
  legal capacity and, 272, 274, 281, 286
  migration and, 750, 754
  polities and, 240
  property rights and, 441–445, 447, 455
transparency, 13, 97–98, 342, 385, 477
Troeltsch, Ernst, 930
Trump, Donald, 480, 787
Tuskegee syphilis study, 903

U
undemocratic elite, 466
unemployment insurance, 818–819
UN General Assembly, 37
UN High Commission on Refugees (UNHCR), 791–792
United Nations, 467
United Nations Relief and Works Agency (UNRWA), 791
universal suffrage, 145–146, 149–152, 154, 403, 408, 424, 432
urbanization
  church and state relations, 66, 120, 342, 928–930
  cross-regional research on, 147
  democracy impact on, 171
  economic development and, 521, 526
  electoral systems and, 425
  health politics and, 866–867, 876 n.21
  migration and, 749
  socioeconomic developments and, 381, 383
  taxation and, 501

urban-rural divide
  defining and measuring, 770–774, 772f
  economic geography, 774–777, 783
  noneconomic explanations of, 777–780
  overview, 769–770
  political institutions and, 781–782
US Articles of Confederation, 403, 450, 451
US Bill of Rights, 451
US-China trade war, 480
US Constitution, 148, 319, 359, 450, 455 n.10, 695, 935
US Constitutional Convention, 451, 483
US Food and Drug Administration, 872
US-Mexico-Canada Agreement (USMCA), 480
US Supreme Court, 36–37, 365
US trade policy applications, 482–489, 484f, 486t, 487f, 489f

V
Van Buren, Martin, 409–411
Varieties of Democracy (V-Dem) dataset, 36
violent repression, 170
voluntary migration, 748–751, 757–759
voter suppression, 151
voters/votes. *See also* elections; electoral systems; suffrage
  age-based suffrage, 461
  Black voters, 151, 469
  buying of, 657
  political parties and, 415 n.3
VoteView, 36
voting rights, 424, 481–482
Voting Rights Act (VRA), 701
vulnerable groups, 602–603

W
Wall Street Journal, 243
Walpole, Robert, 531
Tianyi Wang, 737
war debt, 451, 626–627
Waro, Gregory, 27
Washington Consensus, 530
Weber, Max, 5, 293, 375–376, 381, 389 n.8, 926
Weimar Republic, 164, 423, 771, 781
WEIRD (Western, educated, individualistic, rich, and developed) societies, 453–454, 894, 897

welfare spending. *See* safety nets and welfare spending
Whiskey Rebellion, 86, 153
White, Harrison, 75, 87
William the Conqueror, 282–283
Wilson, Woodrow, 700
woman's suffrage, 465–466, 468, 471, 472 n.6, 719–721
women. *See also* gender studies
   cotton revolution in China, 722, 909
   gender representation dynasties, 193–195, 194*f*
   in labor force, 715, 718, 721–723, 726 n.16, 893, 909–910
   political power transformations, 719–721
Works Progress Administration, 740
World Bank, 467
World Trade Organization (WTO), 480, 486, 775
World War I, 501
World War II, 123, 154, 501, 505, 532, 598
Wright, Gavin, 589–590

Z

zemstvo assembly, 22, 36